CHILDREN'S RIGHTS AND HUMAN DEVELOPMENT

CHILDREN'S RIGHTS AND HUMAN DEVELOPMENT

A Multidisciplinary Reader

Edited by
Jan CM Willems

intersentia
Antwerp – Oxford – Portland

Distribution for the UK:
Hart Publishing Ltd.
16C Worcester Place
Oxford OX1 2JW
UK
Tel.: +44 1865 51 75 30
Email: mail@hartpub.co.uk

Distribution for the USA and Canada:
International Specialized Book Services
920 NE 58th Ave. Suite 300
Portland, OR 97213
USA
Tel.: +1 800 944 6190 (toll free)
Tel.: +1 503 287 3093
Email: info@isbs.com

Distribution for Austria:
Neuer Wissenschaftlicher Verlag
Argentinierstraße 42/6
1040 Wien
Austria
Tel.: +43 1 535 61 03 24
Email: office@nwv.at

Distribution for other countries:
Intersentia Publishers
Groenstraat 31
2640 Mortsel
Belgium
Tel.: +32 3 680 15 50
Email: mail@intersentia.be

Children's Rights and Human Development. A Multidisciplinary Reader
Jan CM Willems (ed.)

Cover photograph: © Phovoir

ISBN 978-94-000-0032-2
D/2010/7849/28
NUR 828

TABLE OF CONTENTS

INTRODUCTION

CHILDREN'S RIGHTS AND HUMAN DEVELOPMENT

Children's rights and Human development is a new and uncharted domain in human rights and psychology research. This multidisciplinary Child Rights Reader is a first attempt to introduce this domain to students and researchers of children's rights, child development, child maltreatment, family and child studies and related fields.

For many lawyers, children's rights are limited to their legal dimension: the norms and institutions of international human rights law, often with an exclusive focus on the Convention on the Rights of the Child and its monitoring treaty body, the Committee on the Rights of the Child. However, there are three more dimensions to children's rights. Children's rights share a moral and a political dimension with all human rights, which most non-international lawyers – and many international lawyers as well – all too often overlook. And children's rights have a fourth dimension: the time dimension of child and human development. This time dimension is multidisciplinary in itself.

What is human development?

According to Wikipedia (<http://en.wikipedia.org/wiki/Human_development>, visited 21 December 2009), "[h]uman development may refer to:
- Human development (biology) – the process of a human becoming biologically mature [from prenatal development into senescence; especially brain development in the first years of life, JW].
- Human development in psychology – developmental psychology [from pre- and perinatal psychology into the psychology of old age; especially attachment development in the first year(s) of life, JW].
- Human development can refer to anthropological, sociological, and psychological approaches to examining human development in context.
- Human development (humanity) as it relates to economics and standards of living [see <http://hdr.undp.org/en>]."

Also see task/text 0.1 below: The Human Development Concept.

Personality, health and resilience

Human development begins – at least – nine months before child birth. When we are four years of age, our brain is ninety percent adult size. The infrastructure of our personality, health and resilience is formed in our first years of life – determined by the quality and sheer quantity of parent-child interaction and based on the successful outcome of our first developmental task in life: secure attachment formation. Yet, more than one third of our children are not securily attached. According to research published in *The Lancet* in 2009, one in ten children in high income countries is maltreated. Violence against children is a worldwide plague. Socio-economic and socio-emotional deprivation are still transmitted from generation to generation in both rich and poor states.

Transism

The nature, scale and seriousness of worldwide transgenerational transmission of trauma, insecure attachment, violence, and socio-emotional and (related) socio-economic deprivation justify the term transgenerational discrimination, or "transism," on which see Jan CM Willems, *Developmental and Autonomy Rights of Children; Empowering Children, Caregivers and Communities*, second edition (Intersentia 2007), which may serve as a companion text to this Reader.

Children's rights, especially when seen in their human development dimension, are the very opposite of transism. Transism refers to systemic harm and injustice, caused by ignorance and indifference, as deeply rooted in tradition and superstition as racism and sexism have been in the past – a past still not overcome. Children's rights, in their holistic – moral, political, legal and human development – conceptualization, refer to the emancipation from harm and injustice, to true change through interdisciplinary knowledge, moral passion, political activism – and the active use of the law.

Investing in early childhood

Human development refers to building human capabilities from conception onwards. This implies, *inter alia*, eliminating transgenerational deprivation, and especially child abuse, neglect and exploitation; and promoting mental health, secure infant attachment and "positive" (effective and non-violent) parenting. Investing in early childhood, positive parenting and child rights education makes sense – from both a human, a human development, a human rights, a child rights and an economic perspective.

This Child Rights Reader brings together substantial and fascinating texts from many fields and disciplines which illustrate and elaborate this point. Arranged in ten chapters titled according to pertinent child rights principles and concepts, these texts offer a state-of-the-art view of the enormous progress made in the past decades and years in several fields of human knowledge. In between these texts several news and factual items inform the reader on the huge gap that still exists between what we know and what we do to make this world a better place for children, and thus to promote human development and better protect human rights. Child rights violations are still met with more rhetoric than leadership. But change is on its way.

How to use this book?

This book may be seen as a multidisciplinary "sourcebook" or Reader on Children's rights and Human development, to be used by itself or in combination with the "corebook" *Developmental and Autonomy Rights of Children* (second edition, Intersentia 2007) by the same editor. This Reader consists of 284 smaller and some somewhat larger texts, including the text of the Convention on the Rights of the Child (CRC) in the Appendix. The texts in this book may be used both as background readings and as tasks for group discussion in problem based learning or other educational settings in child rights law and psychology courses. Therefore, all the texts, items and excerpts in this book are labeled as "task/text" and grouped as much as possible in a (sub)categorical and chronological order. But this book also aims at a broader academic and public audience interested in the many aspects and ramifications of Children's rights and Human development. The interested reader can start with any "task/text" he or she prefers, either upon skimming through the chapters or going by the table of contents. Although this Reader is arranged according to themes which occasionally overlap, and contains multidisciplinary information on recurring topics, several tasks/texts are of an analytical and critical nature and may require closer reading. To assist the reader, keywords and key sentences in more complex or especially relevant texts have been put in bold.

Ten chapters

1. Violence against Children – UN Study and related issues
2. Violence against Children – Child abuse and neglect / child maltreatment
3. Violence against Children – Sexual exploitation
4. Violence against Children – Child marriage, corporal punishment and other traditional practices
5. Safety and development – Affection, secure attachment, brain development, early childhood
6. Best interests of the child – Positive parenting, public policy
7. Direction and guidance – Positive discipline, parent education
8. Evolving capacities – Participation, identity, youth violence, youth rights
9. Aims of education – Psychological, human rights/citizenship and child rights education
10. Various items and issues – Legal, other

Attachment security as a human right

If one looks at the work of child rights organisations and institutions, one often wonders: Where are the youngest children? And where are the maltreated children? This Reader attempts to contribute to remedying these perceived deficiencies by putting early childhood and the prevention of child maltreatment at the very heart of children's rights. Central to both early childhood and the prevention of child maltreatment is infant attachment security. As several texts in this Reader illustrate, attachment security – secure attachment of infants and young children to their primary caregivers – is the first and foremost element of the best interests of the child. The best interests of the child is not only the basic concern of parents or legal guardians (Article 18 para 1 CRC), but also a primary consideration for public or private authorities and institutions, courts and legislatures (Article 3 para 1 CRC). The best interests of the child may therefore be seen as a prioritized principle in international human rights law. Attachment security, being a core element of this prioritized principle, it is submitted should be considered a basic human right in itself.

Money in the Bank: Secure attachment

> "'[N]othing is more important in children's development than how they are treated by parents, beginning in the early years of life. One may look at early secure relationships between parents and children not as a permanent protective coating, but as a foundation for later positive relationships with parents, peers and others. As Eleanor Maccoby (1992) describes it, it is "money in the bank" for parents and children.' (...) Without a doubt, when parents have access to information and support on healthy parenting, everyone benefits."

Barbara Nicholson and Lysa Parker, Attachment Parenting International, e-list 18 December 2009.

Respect, protect, fulfill

As with all human rights, attachment security implies state obligations to respect, protect and fulfill. *Respect* means: do not unnecessarily interfere in the private and family life of expecting parents, infants, young children and their carers (Article 5 CRC, Article 16 CRC).

Protect means: do intervene in the private and family life of expecting parents, infants, young children and their carers when attachment security is at serious risk, that is, when no prospect exists for (the development of) parental responsiveness (Article 19 para 2 CRC).

Fulfill means, *inter alia:*

- provide attachment education as part of primary and secondary school Personal, Social, Health and Economics (PSHE) education, and of primary and secondary school Human Rights and Citizenship education, which should include, it is submitted, Children's Rights and Parenthood education (Article 29 para 1 CRC);
- provide attachment education as part of parenting education to expecting parents (Article 18 para 2, and Article 24 para 2 sub e and f CRC);
- facilitate parenthood through parental leave for parenting education purposes, and through all other appropriate means (Article 18 para 2, and Article 27 para 3 CRC);
- provide parenting assistance and support services, including therapy (counseling and psychotherapy) whenever needed (Article 18 para 2, and Article 19 para 2 CRC).

ERF-A-TAC care continuum

Respect, protect and fulfill, taken together, means: create a high quality care continuum according to the "ERF-A-TAC formula": (provide or organize) Education, Responsibilisation, Facilitation, Assistance, Therapy, Alternative family (adoption and foster) care, and Child protection measures. In this formula, ERF is the basis for A, and A is linked to TAC. In other words, Education, Responsibilisation and Facilitation precede Assistance for families and parents, as forms of universal prevention; and all four are linked to Therapy, Alternative care and Child protection, as forms of selective prevention. Universal and selective prevention programmes and policies should be closely linked together in any comprehensive care continuum. "Universal" refers to all parents-to-be, parents and children. "Selective" refers to specific groups or individual parents-to-be, parents and children. For further explanation, and especially on Responsibilisation, see task/text 0.4 below: The Convention on the Rights of the Child as a source of parental duties and responsibilities.

Serious and systemic human rights violation

Several texts in this Reader illustrate that industrialized states have the knowledge and means to create this ERF-A-TAC care continuum. Other texts present research on the opposite of attachment security: child abuse, neglect and exploitation. An astonishing ten percent of children is maltreated (abused, neglected, exploited) in welfare states. An equally astonishing one third of children is not securily attached, not only in poor but also in rich states. This may and should be seen as a serious and systemic human rights violation in western states, where this structural violation of human and children's rights can be prevented. The cost in human suffering as well as the economic cost of not doing so is enormous. Several other texts in this Reader document these costs. Of the many child rights violations in the world, in both rich and poor states, the serious and systemic violation of attachment security as a (as submitted above) basic human right of all of us, as citizens and parents, as children and adults, is truly appalling. This Reader, it is hoped, may contribute to the opening of our minds to this gross and systemic preventable injustice.

Child maltreatment

Child maltreatment by a parent may be defined as a parent's failing or not being able to meet his or her parental responsibilities to such an extent that a child's physical and/or emotional security, health, wellbeing or dignity is put at serious risk. The state's responsibility lies primarily in not preparing parents for parenthood and supporting parenting through systematic ERF-A-TAC laws and policies. In his inaugural address, on January 20, 2009, President Obama stated: "It is (…) a parent's willingness to nurture a child that finally decides our fate." It is a state's responsibility, however, to eliminate transism, and especially to stop "parent discrimination" – on which see task/text 0.3 below: Stop parent discrimination.

Our collective future

> "[N]o issue is more important to our collective future than the health and well-being of our nation's children. The abuse or neglect of a child not only prevents the normal development of the child, it scars families and degrades society as a whole. From the national financial costs of over $103 billion per year, to the lost educational potential of the child, to increased community violent crime and families affected by lost work potential, our country is substantially impacted by the abuse and neglect which is not prevented."

Chris Greeley, Chair, Prevent Child Abuse America Board of Directors, e-list 17 December 2009.

Children's rights as human rights

Children's rights are (prioritized) human rights. Human rights are international legal norms. Since 1945, the United Nations (UN) have been working to create these norms and make them binding upon states. This is done in a treaty making process. Today, we have nine UN human rights treaties. That is, nine treaties with monitoring bodies: one treaty body in and for each treaty. These treaties are binding on the states that have become parties to those treaties. States become parties by signing-and-ratifying treaties, or by acceding to treaties. They are then obliged to send state reports on the progress they make to the monitoring body of the treaty. Human rights organizations (NGOs, CSOs: non-governmental organizations, civil society organizations) may send alternative reports, allowing the treaty bodies to critically, yet diplomatically, examine governments' policies. In democratic states, this may, at times, be an effective process. In not so democratic states, additional international scrutiny, through other mechanisms or procedures, or ultimately through shaming and blaming (in exceptional cases leading to Security Council intervention), may be warranted. Apart from occasional individual complaint procedures, the whole process is political and psychological rather than (strictly) legal.

Education, emancipation and empowerment

Human rights are more than just law. Human rights are about much more than legal proceedings. Human rights are about education, emancipation and empowerment. This is certainly the case with children's rights – also in democratic states, also in rich states. Children's rights violations, especially in families and in relation to families, are structural in all states. One out of three children in rich states are not securely attached to their caregivers. One out of ten are abused and neglected. All too often, trauma is transmitted from generation to generation. Most (violent) criminals will tell you they were abused as a child (<www.freewebs.com/projectincite/videocallforaction.htm>). Children's rights are about breaking this cycle of trauma, insecure attachment, violence, crime, abuse and neglect. Children's rights are about human development.

Convention on the Rights of the Child

On November 20, 1989 the General Assembly of the UN adopted the Convention on the Rights of the Child (CRC). The CRC is unique for two reasons. In the first place, it is the only UN human rights treaty that has been signed or acceded to by all states (192 UN member states and 3 other state-like entities). Only two states – Somalia and the US – still have to ratify (making the total number of states parties 193). In the US, several myths about children's rights persist (see task/text 0.2 below: Myths about children's rights).

In the second place, the CRC is an interdisciplinary instrument. This means that it cannot be studied from a legal perspective only. Several concepts, old and new, give meaning and content to the CRC. These concepts are interdisciplinary: they combine the state of the art of several disciplines which are related to the field of human rights and to the field of psychology. Such as: history of human rights, theory of human rights, human rights law, human rights education, women's rights … Developmental psychology, (developmental) psychopathology, psychology of relationships, parenthood and parenting, as well as aspects of neuropsychology, evolutionary psychology, social psychology … Overlapping disciplines which may also be of interest are pedagogics, family studies, sociology, social work, child/human development, political science, economics, public health, education, criminal justice, social/public policy …

CRC and interdisciplinary concepts

The CRC is a (near-)universal international pledge to love, care for and educate all our children. Children's rights in the CRC may be defined as state obligations regarding the healthy holistic development of children, based on the participation of all actors, first of all parents and children themselves. Holistic development means "interdependent and interrelated" physical-emotional-social-moral-intellectual development. Key concepts regarding holistic development are: secure attachment, early childhood (early child development, early brain development), the best interests of the child, evolving capacities, parental direction and guidance; and, in a negative sense, child maltreatment (child abuse, neglect and exploitation), and adverse childhood experiences (ACEs, on which see <www.acestudy.org>). Related parenting ("parental direction and guidance") concepts are: positive parenting, positive (versus violent and/or humiliating) discipline, attachment parenting (versus non-responsive parenting), authoritative or effective (vs. ineffective, e.g., permissive or authoritarian) parenting. In this Reader, texts are included on all these concepts and terms. Further interdisciplinary study on these concepts may be found in Willems, *Developmental and Autonomy Rights of Children* (second edition, Intersentia 2007).

In the paragraphs that follow, the themes touched upon above will be briefly discussed from an international law and human rights perspective.

International law

Human rights as a legal subject is a relatively new branch of international law. If we want to fix a date for the birth of international law, 1625 might be a good candidate. Hugo Grotius (Hugo de Groot, 1583–1645) published in that year his treatise on the Law of War and Peace (*De Jure Belli ac Pacis*, Paris 1625). For human rights, the birth year may be 1945, when the Charter of the United Nations entered into force, creating, *inter alia*, the Security Council with its supreme powers in relation to peace and human rights. For children's rights, the birth year may be 1990, when the CRC entered into force and the Committee on the Rights of the Child could become functional.

Whereas some branches of national law are millennia old, international law has a much shorter history. And, judging by the dates above, human rights and children's rights are basically a "baby" subject. International law is by and large conventional law, based on contracts between states (treaties or international conventions) or custom (unwritten convention). Custom is becoming more and more codified, that is, translated into treaty law. Treaties are negotiated by states. States operate on a horizontal level. Only the Security Council can legally impose its will on states (if none of its permanent members uses its veto power).

Some of the Latin terminology in international law goes back to Roman law. Hugo Grotius wrote in Latin, the "English" of his age. Even his name is a Latinization of his Dutch name Hugo de Groot. Later, French became the international diplomatic language. A French term as "travaux préparatoires" ("legislative" history of a treaty) still reminds us of this.

Human rights are more than international law

However, human rights are more than international law. Human rights are:

- ethics: values and virtues, general principles, common standards of achievement – in Nowak's words: "the only universally recognized system of values" (Manfred Nowak, *Introduction to the International Human Rights Regime*, Leiden 2003, p. 1);
- politics: the national and international policies and politics of states and several other actors (CSOs, IGOs, NGOs, MNCs, NHRIs);
- diplomacy: the "constructive dialogue" between monitoring human rights bodies and states parties to human rights treaties;
- psychology: naming, blaming and shaming …

As a "baby" subject of international law, human rights have all the weaknesses of international law – and many others. Human rights (monitoring or treaty) bodies are as diverse and limited in powers as national tribunals and courts once were, many centuries ago. Much of its law is soft law, and often more soft than law. Its main aspiration is its translation into national law. National law is hard law. And so is European law, that is, the law of the European Union and some of the law of the Council of Europe (mainly the case law of the European Court of Human Rights in Strasbourg).

Collective experience of mankind

Although a "baby" subject for lawyers, human rights have philosophical and religious roots as old as mankind. In legal terms, human rights are the positivation (incorporation into positive law, that is, treaty law) of the lessons learnt from mankind's collective experience. As such, they are a means to an end: the end of "nunca mas" (never again) to evil and cruelty, and, in a positive sense, of "human dignity."

Human rights: a means to an end

According to David Forsythe, "human rights are a means to an end, namely human dignity, and not the end itself." The main methodological question for human rights students and researchers, therefore, should be: "Does [our] legal human rights discourse lead to a positive impact on human dignity?" Forsythe criticises continental European human rights lawyers for being "too uncritical, too legalistic, and not aware of other possible approaches, except [their legal, or even legalistic] human rights discourse, to ensure human dignity." (Quoted in *Newsletter School of Human Rights Research*, December 2007, p. 11; <www.uu.nl/uupublish/content/OZS_newsl.pdf>.)

Human dignity is not only the "object and purpose" of human rights, it is also its universal foundation. Moreover, although Forsythe does not say so, his words imply something else. One might conclude from his words the principle, or notion, that if my liberty violates your human dignity, it cannot be my human right (e.g., freedom of speech versus hate speech or insulting people). This would mean that human rights are dignitarian (rights as responsibilities), not libertarian (rights as claims); to which we will return below.

Human dignity: respect and self-respect

[Willems, *Developmental and Autonomy Rights of Children*, pp. 114–117:]

The fundament – the universal philosophical (moral) and legal fundament – of human rights is human dignity. Human dignity can, it is submitted, best be described as the inherent *right* of every individual to be respected as a person, and to be treated as such, and the inherent *duty* of every individual to both respect others (treat others as human beings and not as objects or means), and not to "deny oneself," that is, to develop his or her own self-respect. In brief: human dignity is, or is about, the combination of respect for others and self-respect.

This combination refers to both personal (physical and mental) health and personal (physical and mental) integrity as basic human rights, and implies, among other things, that one should never discriminate between groups (in-and-out groups, "we" and "they": we the superior, they the inferior, we the good, they the bad), but only between individuals, and, obviously, not between individuals on the basis of group characteristics, but only on the basis of their moral (basically, their prosocial versus antisocial) qualities and potential.

Human dignity: a double message

[Willems, *Developmental and Autonomy Rights of Children*, pp. 149–150:]

Human dignity is a concept that refers to the equal rights and to the inherent dignity of all human beings. Human dignity as a concept contains a double message:

(1) no person is superior or inferior because of sex, colour, religion, property, social origin, birth or other status;
(2) every person is entitled to respect for his or her personal integrity.

The first message can be seen as the essence of democracy, the second message as the essence of the rule of law ("nomocracy").

In the modern world, believing that you are superior because of your sex, religion, etc., is seen not only as a lack of respect but somehow also as a lack of self-respect. Psychological frustration or overcompensation is suspected. Child-rearing styles or practices, either culturally embedded or in a particular family, may be the root causes of such frustration or overcompensation. The same is probably true for those who violate the personal integrity of others.

Self-respect (or rather "positive core self-evaluations: self-esteem, generalized self-efficacy, locus of control, and emotional stability") is linked to personal development and thus to mental health. Mental health is a broad concept that includes or is related to such concepts as personal growth, empathy and emotional (intra-personal) and social (inter-personal) intelligence.

WHO definition of mental health

> "Mental health is not just the absence of mental disorder. It is defined as a state of well-being in which every individual realizes his or her own potential, can cope with the normal stresses of life, can work productively and fruitfully, and is able to make a contribution to her or his community."

See <www.who.int/features/qa/62/en/index.html>, accessed 20 December 2009.

The twin messages of inherent dignity and equal rights overlap, just as democracy and the rule of law ("nomocracy") do. The inherent dignity of the other is a message to me to respect his or her personal integrity, but the degree to which I am able to do so, depends on my self-respect, and hence on my mental health. The same goes for my respect or disrespect for the equal rights of others. Although a lack of psychological education or of human rights education may also play a role.

Secure attachment and inclusion

In simple terms: human dignity means no one is the property or "instrument" of others. This is the main message of both human rights and children's rights. This implies respect for others, but from within, therefore on the basis of self-respect. The basis of self-respect (self-esteem) is secure attachment of infants, which leads to mental health and resilience.

A second basis are messages of inclusion, belonging and participation to children, adolescents and (young) adults, which contributes to empathy and social cohesion (prosocial development). Inclusion should be a central theme in human rights education; secure attachment should be a central theme in child rights education.

Discrimination and emancipation

Human rights – which, it is submitted, should be seen as, first of all, fully including the concepts and ideals of democracy and the rule of law ("nomocracy") – are, at the same time, mainly about two things: non-discrimination and emancipation. Non-discrimination refers, *inter alia,* to overcoming prejudice, xenophobia, misogyny and transgenerational and other forms of exclusion (which directly violate human dignity, *dignitas hominis:* "the dignity of man"). Emancipation refers, in a collective sense, to overcoming human suffering (*miseria humanae conditionis*: "the misery of the human condition"), and especially three forms of poverty:

- (socio-)economic poverty: poor standard of living;
- mental poverty: ignorance, superstition, lack of school education;
- (socio-)emotional poverty: poor mental health, transgenerational traumatization.

Universal and relative

No one wants to be humiliated, excluded and exploited. Human beings want to be respected, included and treated fairly. In that sense human rights are universal. But you cannot have emancipation – nor democracy – at gunpoint. Human rights require individual and social courage, struggle and sacrifice. In that sense they are relative, that is, depending on the moral heroes who and the generations which have suffered, struggled and sacrificed before us. Or are doing so today, on behalf of their group, society and humankind, with our sympathy, solidarity and support – and every aid possible, short of force. Only in extreme cases may force be justified. In the words of Paolo Carozza: "The core of freedom that the idea of human rights seeks to recognize and protect (…) requires that they be advanced principally through reason, persuasion, education and example." (Paolo Carozza in A Communitarian Letter 15, <www.gwu.edu/~ccps/documents/CommunitarianLetter15.doc>.)

No room for relativism

Human rights are universal ideals that have been translated into legal principles and legal obligations for states, either as treaty obligations (for states parties to specific treaties) or as general international law (of a customary or even peremptory nature). All states (states parties) and cultures (of or within states parties) have to meet the minimum standards and requirements of human rights, including the requirement not to humiliate others or to act as if their culture is superior and other states' or peoples' cultures are inferior, and to protect their inhabitants against such humiliation. But also including requirements to educate, emancipate and enlighten both children and adults, with a view to abolishing cultural practices which may harm children (Article 24 para 3 CRC), achieving the elimination of cultural practices which constitute gender discrimination (Article 5 of the Women's Convention), and combating prejudices which lead to racial discrimination, intolerance and xenophobia (Article 7 of the Racial Discrimination Convention). Human rights leave no room for relativism in relation to barbaric and cruel practices, cultural, traditional or otherwise. On the other hand, calculated humiliation of other peoples' religion, culture or tradition violates human rights and constitutes an abuse of freedoms.

Declaration of *Inter*dependence

Four freedoms lay at the heart of human rights: freedom from want, freedom from fear, freedom of belief, freedom of speech (see the preamble of the Universal Declaration of Human Rights). In human rights law, however, a libertarian and a dignitarian stand or tradition may be discerned in relation to these four freedoms. Whereas the former (libertarianism) emphasizes individual freedoms, especially against state intervention, and formal individual autonomy (formal or superficial "self-determination" as opposed to substantive or psychological autonomy), the latter (dignitarianism) tries to clarify the aspect of duties and responsibilities in relation to rights, and to integrate freedom, equal opportunities and solidarity into its concept of human dignity. Not so much "respect" as a claim against others, but the combination of self-respect and respect for others, as a core value or virtue, underlies this concept. Not only human rights but also human beings are interdependent. However, as Bruce Perry remarks, a Declaration of *Inter*dependence still has to be written – and needs to be written by our generation if cultural evolution is not to turn into cultural devolution. (Bruce D. Perry, *Early Childhood and Brain Development; How Experience Shapes Child, Community and Culture*, Child Trauma Academy DVD lecture [2007], available at <http://store.ctaproducts.org/eachandbrde.html>.)

Libertarian, communitarian, dignitarian

To say that human rights are not social *(quid-pro-quo)* contracts between states and their citizens may be true from a strictly legal perspective. However, one only needs to read Articles 1 and 29–30 of the Universal Declaration of Human Rights (spirit of brotherhood; duties to the community, respect for the rights of others and for the purposes and principles of the UN; no abuse of rights), and, e.g., Articles 5 (direction and guidance to children) and 29 (aims of education) of the Convention on the Rights of the Child, to understand that human rights not only have a social context but also a prosocial (and even pedagogical and educational) dimension. It is submitted that human rights are not libertarian – nor, to some other extreme, communitarian – but that they are dignitarian. *Dignitarian* refers to the ideal that all human beings should be treated and should act as persons endowed with both rights and responsibilities. Therefore, a strictly legal perspective is not enough, for it may easily lead to an egocentric or "a-social" (and "a-pedagogical") view of human rights. It is submitted that, in interpreting human rights, lawyers may be well advised to not limit themselves to a strictly legal perspective.

New struggles and investments

Once established in law, human rights require continuous investments by society and the state, especially but certainly not only from a dignitarian perspective. In addition, new groups may be discovered which have thus far been overlooked, left out, excluded. Conditions that have been taken for granted, maybe for centuries, may no longer be acceptable. New knowledge or a new understanding of society may expose a new form of discrimination. New struggles for recognition – and new investments – may then prove necessary. Even in industrialized states not all groups are included yet. A huge gap still exists between what we know and what we do in relation to, especially:

- early child development: the human brain develops for ninety percent in the first years of life but we put most of our money in attempts to treat developmental damage rather than preventing it;
- mental health care: e.g., counseling and psychotherapy, therapeutic parenting support, childhood trauma treatment;
- psychological education: e.g., on controlling anger, healthy relationships, effective communication, healthy child development, non-violent child-rearing;
- democratic citizenship education: including, *inter alia*, human rights education, child rights education and parenthood education;
- community building: social integration and reintegration, reweaving the social fabric of communities and societies, overcoming compartmentalization of government.

This lack of investments which directly address root causes of violence in both developing and developed states, violates – as we are beginning to understand – the human rights of large minorities of children and caregivers, but many more are victimized (to a certain degree, we all are). In industrialized states, serious and large-scale (as opposed to more or less incidental) human rights violations occur mainly – if not only – in relation to these still excluded groups.

Large-scale violations

Large-scale violations of the human rights of children occur all over the world. Apart from food, shelter, health care and education, children also need affection-based direction and guidance, or, as one author puts it: rights, room and respect (M.H. van IJzendoorn, *Opvoeding over de* grens, 2008, p. 35). Their parents should be empowered to provide these, as the CRC stipulates in its Articles 24 (health care), 27 para 3 (material support for parents), 28 (education), and 18 para 2 (psychological and pedagogical support for parents). Especially the latter Article implies state obligations which are not fully met in even the most affluent states.

One third of children are not securely attached

Even in rich states, one third of children are not securely attached. Although all kinds of child rights violations are well documented, few people have any knowledge of the grave violations connected with insecure attachment. Since insecure attachment is exacerbated by toxic social influences on children's healthy development in modern society (Sue Palmer, *Toxic Childhood*, 2006), as well as by rampant child abuse, one of the greatest challenges for human dignity today is to be found here.

What is attachment?

> "Children are attached if they tend to seek proximity to and contact with a specific caregiver in times of distress, illness and tiredness (Bowlby, 1969). Attachment to a protective caregiver helps the child to regulate his or her negative emotions in times of stress and distress. It enables the child to explore the environment even if this environment contains somewhat frightening stimuli. Attachment is a *major developmental milestone in a child's life with immediate and long-term consequences* for the child's neurobiological functioning, cognitive development, emotional well-being, and social relationships. It will remain an important issue *throughout the life span*. In adolescence and adulthood, cognitive representations of past attachment experiences shape the way adolescents and adults feel about the stresses and strains of intimate relationships, *including parent-child relationships,* and the way in which the self is perceived."

See<www.socialsciences.leidenuniv.nl/educationandchildstudies/childandfamilystudies/research/attachment.jsp>, visited 20 December 2009; emphasis added.

A little bit of resistance

As was said above: human rights are the positivation (incorporation into positive law) of the lessons learnt from the collective experience of mankind. That is why the universality of human rights is fundamental – fundamental in two respects. Human rights are universal *(de lege lata)*. And human rights should be universal *(de lege ferenda)*. *Lex lata* refers to international law. *Lex ferenda* to national law (implementation of international law into national legal systems). Implementation seldom occurs without struggle and sacrifice. In the West, we seem to have forgotten that human rights do not, in fact, exist without struggle and sacrifice. We had to learn it again in relation to women's rights. We will have to learn it all over again in relation to children's rights, and especially in relation to transgenerational discrimination. In democracies, however, a little bit of resistance and a little bit of sacrifice can do miracles … Maybe animal protectionists once again lead the way (see task/text 0.5 below: L'histoire se répète?) and inspire women's rights, child rights and other human rights activists?

Children's rights and human development

> "One good thing about the Convention on the Rights of the Child is that it is the only convention which is based on the idea that human beings need love and care, and that this is something fundamental in the development of human beings. If the Convention was respected, the world would be a much happier place."
>
> "If I had to sum up children's rights in one word, it is the foundation of a better society, basically it's a better world."

Shirin Aumeeruddy-Cziffra, Ombudsperson for Children for the Republic of Mauritius, interview, Crinmail 28 November 2008 – Update: The Secretary-General's Study on Violence against Children 40; <www.crin.org>.

TASK/TEXT 0.1: THE HUMAN DEVELOPMENT CONCEPT

United Nations Development Programme (<www.undp.org>); Human Development Reports (<www.hdr.undp.org>); The Human Development concept: <http://hdr.undp.org/en/humandev>, Origins of the Human Development Approach: <http://hdr.undp.org/en/humandev/origins> (accessed 19 July 2009)

The Human Development concept

Human Development is a development paradigm that is about much more than the rise or fall of national incomes. It is about creating an environment in which people can develop their full potential and lead productive, creative lives in accord with their needs and interests. People are the real wealth of nations. Development is thus about expanding the choices people have to lead lives that they value. And it is thus about much more than economic growth, which is only a means – if a very important one – of enlarging people's choices.

Fundamental to enlarging these choices is building human capabilities – the range of things that people can do or be in life. The most basic capabilities for human development are to lead long and healthy lives, to be knowledgeable, to have access to the resources needed for a decent standard of living and to be able to participate in the life of the community. Without these, many choices are simply not available, and many opportunities in life remain inaccessible.

> "The basic purpose of development is to enlarge people's choices. In principle, these choices can be infinite and can change over time. People often value achievements that do not show up at all, or not immediately, in income or growth figures: greater access to knowledge, better nutrition and health services, more secure livelihoods, security against crime and physical violence, satisfying leisure hours, political and cultural freedoms and sense of participation in community activities. The objective of development is to create an enabling environment for people to enjoy long, healthy and creative lives." – Mahbub ul Haq (Founder of the Human Development Report)

This way of looking at development, often forgotten in the immediate concern with accumulating commodities and financial wealth, is not new. Philosophers, economists and political leaders have long emphasized human wellbeing as the purpose, the end, of development. As Aristotle said in ancient Greece, "Wealth is evidently not the good we are seeking, for it is merely useful for the sake of something else."

In seeking that something else, human development shares a common vision with human rights. The goal is human freedom. And in pursuing capabilities and realizing rights, this freedom is vital. People must be free to exercise their choices and to participate in decision-making that affects their lives. Human development and human rights are mutually reinforcing, helping to secure the well-being and dignity of all people, building self-respect and the respect of others.

Origins of the Human Development Approach

The Human Development approach arose in part as a result of growing criticism to the leading development approach of the 1980s, which presumed a close link between national economic growth and the expansion of individual human choices. Many, such as Dr. Mahbub ul Haq, the Pakistani economist who played a key role in formulating the human development paradigm, came to recognize the need for an alternative development model due to many factors, including:

- Growing evidence that did not support the then prevailing belief in the "trickle down" power of market forces to spread economic benefits and end poverty;
- The human costs of Structural Adjustment Programmes became more apparent;
- Social ills (crime, weakening of social fabric, HIV/AIDS, pollution, etc.) were still spreading even in cases of strong and consistent economic growth;
- A wave of democratization in the early 90's raised hopes for people-centred models.

Many of its key principles, however, can be found in the writings of scholars and philosophers from past eras and across many societies.

As of 1990, the human development concept was applied to a systematic study of global themes, as published in the yearly global Human Development Reports under the auspice of the UNDP. The work of Amartya Sen and others provided the conceptual foundation for an alternative and broader human development approach defined as a process of **enlarging people's choices and enhancing human capabilities** (the range of things people can be and do) **and freedoms**, enabling them to: live a long and healthy life, have access to knowledge and a decent standard of living, and participate in the life of their community and decisions affecting their lives.

> "Human development, as an approach, is concerned with what I take to be the basic development idea: namely, advancing the richness of human life, rather than the richness of the economy in which human beings live, which is only a part of it." – Amartya Sen (Professor of Economics, Harvard University, Nobel Laureate in Economics, 1998)

Human development has always been flexible and "open-ended" with respect to more specific definitions. There can be as many human development dimensions as there are ways of enlarging people's choices. The key or priority parameters of human development can **evolve over time and vary both across and within countries.**

Some of the issues and themes currently considered most central to human development include:

- **Social progress** – greater access to knowledge, better nutrition and health services.
- **Economics** – the importance of economic growth as a means to reduce inequality and improve levels of human development.
- **Efficiency** – in terms of resource use and availability; human development is pro-growth and productivity as long as such growth directly benefits the poor, women and other marginalized groups.
- **Equity** – in terms of economic growth and other human development parameters.
- **Participation and freedom** – particularly empowerment, democratic governance, gender equality, civil and political rights, and cultural liberty, particularly for marginalized groups defined by urban-rural, sex, age, religion, ethnicity, physical/mental parameters, etc.
- **Sustainability** – for future generations in ecological, economic and social terms.
- **Human security** – security in daily life against such chronic threats as hunger and abrupt disruptions including joblessness, famine, conflict, etc.

TASK/TEXT 0.2: MYTHS ABOUT CHILDREN'S RIGHTS

Child rights fact sheet, CRIN 2009, <www.crin.org/docs/factsheet.pdf>, accessed 27 November 2009

[- **Children's rights and Culture or Tradition**]
Human rights [and thus children's rights] are governed by three core principles:

1. [Human rights] are **universal** – they apply to every human being everywhere in the world, at all times. No political leader can say that human rights are not applicable in their country because it has a different culture or tradition. They are really saying they do not believe in them.
2. [Human rights] **cannot be given up or taken away** (they are *inalienable*).
3. [Human rights] **cannot be divided up** – they are like different parts of the same body. You cannot pick and choose which rights to respect. Denying some rights undermines others, for example, failing to provide protection from violence also violates the right to health. (...)
   States must **respect**, **protect** and **fulfil** [human] rights. (...)

- *"The CRC [Convention on the Rights of the Child] takes rights away from parents"*

Rights are not pieces of property which can be exchanged. If a child has a right, a right is not automatically removed from someone else. The CRC places parents centre-stage in children's development. It recognises the family "as the fundamental group of society and the natural environment for the growth and well-being of all its members and particularly children," and acknowledges "that the child, for the full and harmonious development of his or her personality, should grow up in a family environment, in an atmosphere of happiness, love, and understanding" (Preamble). The Convention repeatedly reinforces the integral role of parents. For example:

- Article 3 says: States Parties undertake to ensure the child such protection and care as is necessary for his or her well-being, taking into account the rights and duties of his or her parents, legal guardians, or other individuals legally responsible for him or her.
- Article 5 says: States Parties shall respect the responsibilities, rights and duties of parents or, where applicable, the members of the extended family or community as provided for by local custom.
- Article 18 says: Parents or, as the case may be, legal guardians, have the primary responsibility for the upbringing and development of the child.
- Article 29 requires respect for parents to be integrated into the education of the child.

However, as Yakin Ertürk, former UN Special Rapporteur on Violence Against Women, argued: "We think that children are our property. They come from us, but they do not belong to us. They are in our trust temporarily." Parental rights do not mean we can beat our children, exploit them, take decisions without reference to their views, or deny them rights to which they are entitled.

- *"Child rights erode the family unit"*

A related argument is that the concept of rights is 'individualistic' and 'self-interested,' and therefore opposes family and social units. However, child rights and a close, sharing family are not different things – you do not have *either* rights *or* a strong family/community. Indeed, respecting and fulfilling a child's rights means *more* loving and close relationships, because the well being of that child is being nurtured, enabling him/her to form positive, loving communal ties. Just because a child possesses rights, it does not mean that every dispute between children and parents/guardians will end up in a court of law. Nonetheless, the recognition of such rights, and the availability of legal remedies, is essential when relationships break down, especially in circumstances of violence or exploitation.

Relying on love alone for a child's wellbeing does not ensure protection when family units erode.

– ***"Child rights are a Western concept and cannot apply to other cultures"***
While it has been argued that human rights are a 'Western' concept, based on a Western notion of law and legislature, representatives of many States in all regions assisted with its drafting. It was adopted unanimously by Member States of the UN in 1989, while all but two States – the US and Somalia – (…) are (…) bound by its provisions (indeed, both the US and Somalia have signed the Convention, signifying an intention to ratify). Those arguing that a particular State's law, culture or tradition disallows the full implementation of the CRC are ignoring the legal obligations undertaken when the Convention was ratified. Furthermore, Article 27 of the Vienna Convention on the Law of Treaties, considered binding on all States because it restates customary international law (i.e. law that is unwritten, but exists because most or all countries agree to abide by it), states: "A party [State] may not invoke the provisions of its internal law as justification for its failure to perform a treaty." This means that domestic law cannot be used as an excuse for the breach of a State's obligations under international law.

– ***"Children have enough rights already. What about responsibilities?"***
[Human r]ights are unconditional, not earned or matched by responsibilities. Just because a child has a [human] right, it does not mean they forgo a responsibility. It is not for us to decide how many rights a person can have. We cannot pick and choose the rights we feel children most *deserve*. Either a child's rights, as listed in the Convention on the Rights of the Child, are respected, fulfilled and protected, or they are not. The rights of hundreds of millions of children are violated. They die early, or have their right to survival and development permanently warped by poverty, lack of food and clean water, and the denial of/discriminatory access to basic health services. They are recruited into armed forces, as well as physically, sexually and emotionally abused [by their parents and other carers, JW]. Why do some children have plentiful access to the most nutritious food, the best education and free healthcare, while others die before their first birthday? While such extreme violations may find their way to the front pages, subtler forms of discrimination may be less evident. Why, for the vast majority of the world's children, is their right not to be assaulted ignored? In reality, children rarely grow up without responsibility and indeed, many are burdened with a level of responsibility that is not in accordance with their maturity, such as child soldiers [or children in marital conflict situations, JW]. However, we do all have responsibilities to respect each others' rights, and the respect of children's rights encourages children themselves to be more aware of the rights of others.

– "We don't need 'extra' rights for children"

Some argue that if human rights apply to all human beings, then we do not need 'special' rights for children. While human rights do indeed apply to all, as mentioned above, children's developmental status and the particular exclusions and discrimination they face demand special provision. Children traditionally have been regarded as possessions of their parents, not individual people or rights holders. Children may be exposed to unfair, discriminatory treatment as a result of such societal views. This is why there are a number of rights in the Convention on the Rights of the Child (CRC) which apply especially to children and are not provided for in human rights law generally. These include specific rights to maximum survival and development, to [pedagogical aims of] education, to protection from sexual exploitation and abuse including child pornography, the right not only to express their views, but to have them given due weight in all matters concerning them, and the right to be detained only as a last resort. (...)

[– *"The CRC is a flimsy tool anyway"*]

A note on enforcement

There is as yet no international court to investigate breaches of children's rights only. Some say that this makes the CRC a flimsy tool, but this is a defeatist argument. States are required to incorporate the CRC within their own domestic law, and to ensure that all domestic law fully reflects and upholds the rights in the Convention, but it is very hard to force governments to do something. This is why we must all work hard to ensure governments are held accountable for their obligations. For example, most governments do not want to be embarrassed in public, such as before the Committee on the Rights of the Child, or at the Human Rights Council, because they have failed children. Civil society and others can submit reports, and sometimes make oral statements, both to the Committee and the Council. On a national level, given the traditional place of children in societies, it is hard to assert children's right to remedies when their rights are breached, including the right to go to court. But children's rights advocacy, while still in its infancy, is growing. There is a range of other ways that children's rights can be enforced internationally. Other UN mechanisms, such as the 'Special Procedures' (human rights experts), investigate and report on child rights violations. Regional mechanisms, such as the Inter-American Commission and Court of Human Rights and the African Committee on the Rights and Welfare of the Child, also hold governments to account, while regional courts such as the European Court of Human Rights adjudicate on individual complaints of breaches of rights. And all these mechanisms now quote and use the CRC as the standard for the treatment of children.

Note: A group of agencies are campaigning for the United Nations to establish a communications (complaints) mechanism to the Convention on the Rights of the Child (CRC). Such a procedure would provide a mechanism that would ensure the availability of legal remedies for children at the international level. Read more here: <www.crin.org/law/CRC_complaints>.

'Non-State actors'

Although the enjoyment of human rights has historically been about the compliance of State governments with internationally-agreed instruments (indeed, only States can ratify the CRC), there is growing consideration of the role of other groups, such as global companies, civil society groups, armed opposition groups and international organisations. A General Comment adopted by the Human Rights Committee (which monitors implementation of the Covenant on Civil and Political Rights) in 2004 (<www1.umn.edu/humanrts/gencomm/hrcom31.html>), spoke of the obligations on States to "address the activities of private persons or entities." It continues: "States Parties have to take positive measures to ensure that private persons or entities do not inflict torture or cruel, inhuman or degrading treatment or punishment on others within their power. In fields affecting basic aspects of ordinary life such as work or housing, individuals are to be protected from discrimination."

Codes of conduct have been adopted by thousands of transnational corporations, but they vary hugely in their content and effect. Indeed, many have been criticised by NGOs for either their limited scope or inadequate implementation. The UN has appointed a Special Representative on the issue of human rights and transnational corporations. Read more about his work here: <www2.ohchr.org/english/issues/trans_corporations/index.htm>.

In addition to corporations, some have argued that there is a shortage of international law in dealing with human rights abuses by armed opposition groups, although article four of the Optional Protocol to the CRC on the involvement of children in armed conflict states that, among other provisions, "[a]rmed groups that are distinct from the armed forces of a State should not, under any circumstances, recruit or use in hostilities persons under the age of 18 years." Many humanitarian law experts agree that human rights law does not just apply to governments. Of course, implementation is another challenge entirely.

TASK/TEXT 0.3: STOP PARENT DISCRIMINATION

Attachment Parenting International, e-list 3 December 2009

Billions of dollars are spent annually on "family" and "healthy child" programs. That's a warm fuzzy thought until a closer look reveals **the startling truth: funding discriminates against parents**. Consider:

1. **Only a tiny fraction** of those billions are spent **for parent support and education** which are shown to be highly productive, effective and promising programs;
2. **Parents and family are a child's first and most profoundly influential "village."** Because parents help their babies establish neural pathways that can persist for life, it seems obvious that we'd want to help them set the most healthy ones instead of waiting until corrections are needed at a greater cost to all.
3. **Parent education and support is a more cost effective investment** in every context. Parents cannot be effectively replaced or substituted by institutions or organizations. If we can help parents set their children up for success from the start, the work and the cost of the "village" is exponentially reduced.

Billions of dollars fund a deficit view of parents and parenting. **We've witnessed the consequences of this system and insist on taking a fresh approach.** We choose to support and educate parents in raising healthy, confident and compassionate children. Help us raise the image of parenting and broadcast the message: **informed and supported families provide the most cost effective and fertile environment for children to thrive and become capable of reaching their fullest potential.**

TASK/TEXT 0.4: THE CONVENTION ON THE RIGHTS OF THE CHILD AS A SOURCE OF PARENTAL DUTIES AND RESPONSIBILITIES

Excerpted from: Jan CM Willems, What may parents be asked to pledge? The Convention on the Rights of the Child as a source of parental duties and responsibilities, in: Hans Van Crombrugge, Wouter Vandenhole, Jan C.M. Willems (eds.), *Shared pedagogical responsibility*, Antwerp–Oxford–Portland: Intersentia, 2008, pp. 17–36

INTRODUCTION

[A] child rights based approach to parenting (...) combines two elements: empowerment of (future) parents, and their so-called responsibilisation. Empowerment means: facilitating, uniting (bringing young parents together, facilitating organisations of parents), educating, supporting, assisting, listening to and guiding parents, providing leadership to parents, and holding them accountable. Responsibilisation means: legislating child rights based parental responsibilities – basically legislating what is in the Convention on the Rights of the Child (CRC).[1] In other words, making CRC parental responsibilities part and parcel of national family law, turning international children's rights into crystal clear national parental duties – and holding parents accountable in relation to these duties.[2] In this, but also in other respects, empowerment and responsibilisation overlap. Both may be seen as elements of psychological emancipation – emancipation through law and education. Both are crucial. One needs the law to educate people on the law: to educate children and adults on child rights and on the parental responsibilities and duties based on those rights and translated into national law. But not only legislation is needed. Investments are needed in all kinds of parent and child facilities and services. And parents need to be educated as well on the availability of programmes and services, on what may and what must be asked from all kinds of professionals – doctors, teachers, social workers, therapists, youth care professionals, and so forth. Empowerment begins with education, but it includes many other things, such as child care and early childhood services, counselling, psychotherapy, mediation, and many other forms of both material and immaterial support and assistance.[3]

Transism

(...) Transism, or transgenerational discrimination, refers to a state's not adequately addressing socio-economic and, more specifically, socio-emotional differences between (young) parents. Socio-economic differences refer to extreme inequalities between (young) parents in relation to income and income-related time – time parents can devote to their children and to child rearing. Socio-emotional differences refer to extreme inequalities between (young) parents in relation to parenting knowledge ("child rearing literacy") and parental awareness, which includes qualities and conditions such as parents' sense of responsibility, parents' responsiveness and sensitivity to their child's needs, parents' reparation of own childhood trauma, parents' mental health, emotional stability and maturity, social network, social integration, and so forth. By not or not adequately addressing these inequalities states contribute to widespread transgenerational

1 UN General Assembly 20 November 1989. Text available at <www2.ohchr.org/english/law/crc.htm>.

2 In this contribution, "duties" refer to legal obligations, either explicitly formulated in national law, or generally accepted to be implied in comprehensive legal obligations such as parental authority, c.q. parental responsibility, being the duty and the right of the parent to care for and raise his or her minor child (*cf.* Dutch Civil Code Article 1:247 para 1). "Responsibilities" refer to pre-legal or quasi-legal ("moral") duties, which may be justiciable under specific or exceptional circumstances only. In other words, duties may be seen as hard law, responsibilities as soft law. It is not always possible, however, to clearly distinguish between the two. (...)

3 For further elaboration, and several proposals in relation to empowerment and responsibilisation, as well as constitutionalisation, see my four chapters in Jan C.M. Willems (ed.), *Developmental and Autonomy Rights of Children; Empowering Children, Caregivers and Communities*, Antwerp-Oxford, Intersentia, 2007 (second edition), pp. 65–210.

transmission of poor mental health or other forms of emotional poverty, of poor parenting and of social – socio-emotional and related socio-economic – exclusion.[4]

Announcing Report Card No. 8 on Early Childhood Development, UNICEF Innocenti Research Centre states:[5]

> "A considerable body of evidence points to the importance of the early years as a window of opportunity to make a difference in the lives of children and to break the [trans]generational cycle of poverty [of both socio-economic and socio-emotional poverty, that is, to eliminate transism, JW]. Recognizing this evidence, many countries of the Organisation for Economic Co-operation and Development (OECD) have national strategies for enhancing the experiences of young children. Report Card No. 8 will analyse these countries' response to families and young children, notably in the area of early childhood care and education. OECD governments invest public resources in early childhood services. However, from the point of view of the best interests of the child, the situation in many OECD countries leaves room for improvement and requires a doubling of resources."

UNICEF Innocenti Research Centre thus points at the need of a "doubling" of resources. Independent experts who operate within the UN framework also stress the importance of early childhood care and education and, more specifically, of preparation for parenthood and parent (that is, parenthood and parenting) education, in order to contribute to the world-wide elimination of transism. The independent monitoring body of the CRC, the Committee on the Rights of the Child, observes in its General Comment No. 5:[6]

> "(...) The Convention [on the Rights of the Child] highlights the importance of the family in its preamble and in many articles. It is particularly important that the promotion of children's rights should be integrated into preparation for parenthood and parenting education."

---

4 On the concept of transism, see Willems (ed.), *Developmental and Autonomy Rights of Children* (note 3). On state responsibility and accountability in relation to transism (transgenerational state responsibility), see Jan C.M. Willems, *Wie zal de Opvoeders Opvoeden? Kindermishandeling en het Recht van het Kind op Persoonswording [Who will Educate the Educators? Child Abuse and the Right of the Child to Become a Person]* (with a summary in English), The Hague, T.M.C. Asser Press, 1999, pp. 629–991.

5 UNICEF Innocenti Research Centre, at <www.unicef-irc.org>, visited 17 March 2008.

6 Committee on the Rights of the Child, General Comment No. 5 (2003), *General measures of implementation for the Convention on the Rights of the Child*, para 54. Text available at <www.unhchr.ch/tbs/doc.nsf/(symbol)/CRC.GC.2003.5.En?OpenDocument>.

And in the UN Secretary-General's Study on Violence Against Children it is stated by the Study's independent expert Paulo Sérgio Pinheiro:[7]

> "Bearing in mind that the family has the primary responsibility for the upbringing and development of the child and that the State should support parents and caregivers to care for children, I recommend that States: (a) Develop or enhance programmes to support parents and other carers in their child-rearing role. Investments in health care, education and social welfare services should include quality early childhood development programmes, home visitation, pre- and post-natal services and income-generation programmes for disadvantaged groups; (...) (c) Develop gender-sensitive parent education programmes focusing on non-violent forms of discipline. Such programmes should promote healthy parent-child relationships and orient parents towards constructive and positive forms of discipline and child development approaches, taking into account children's evolving capacities and the importance of respecting their views."

Against this broad background of investment and empowerment, the child rights' basis of responsibilisation may be further investigated.

A list of responsibilities

(...) [W]hat does the CRC say about parental responsibilities? Or, to put it more concretely, which child rights in the CRC may be seen, or construed, as explicit or rather implied parental responsibilities? In this contribution, I will submit such a list, which is neither meant to be exhaustive, nor meant to be fully incorporated (...) in national family law (...). (...) Some of the responsibilities in the list are already duties in the national law of some or many states. Some may never be legislated, nor need be. Some should be legislated as a matter of urgency, such as non-violent discipline – as a much needed framework for education on positive parenting[8] and positive discipline.[9] The list may also be seen as a starting point for creating a tool for child rights education on parental duties and responsibilities in schools and elsewhere. Before the list is submitted (...), we will have a closer look at state obligations in the CRC in the child-parent-state relationship (...).

---

7 UN Secretary-General's Study on Violence Against Children (2006), para 110. Text available at <www.violencestudy.org/IMG/pdf/English-2-2.pdf>.

8 On which see Recommendation (2006)19 of the Committee of Ministers to [Council of Europe] member states on policy to support positive parenting (Adopted by the Committee of Ministers on 13 December 2006), <www.coe.int>, Institutions/Committee of Ministers, Documents/Adopted texts, Recommendations of the Committee of Ministers to member states, All Recommendations.

9 On which see Joan E. Durrant, *Positive Discipline: What it is and how to do it*, 2007, online <http://seap.savethechildren.se/South_East_Asia/Misc/Puffs/Positive-Discipline-What-it-is-and-how-to-do-it>.

STATE EMPOWERMENT AND RESPONSIBILISATION OBLIGATIONS

Article 3 para 2 of the Convention on the Rights of the Child (CRC) establishes a *Trias pedagogica* of children, parents and the state.[10] It reads as follows:

Article 3 para 2 – States Parties undertake to ensure the child such protection and care as is necessary for his or her well-being, taking into account the rights and duties of his or her parents, legal guardians, or other individuals legally responsible for him or her, and, to this end, shall take all appropriate legislative and administrative measures.

This paragraph is preceded by the articulation, in Article 3 para 1, of the best interests of the child as a prioritised principle in international (child rights) law. This paragraph reads as follows:

Article 3 para 1 – In all actions concerning children, whether undertaken by public or private social welfare institutions, courts of law, administrative authorities or legislative bodies, the best interests of the child shall be a primary consideration.

In Article 18 para 1, where the best interests of the child is linked to parental responsibility, the wording appears to be even stronger. This paragraph reads as follows:

Article 18 para 1 – States Parties shall use their best efforts to ensure recognition of the principle that both parents have common responsibilities for the upbringing and development of the child. Parents or, as the case may be, legal guardians, have the primary responsibility for the upbringing and development of the child. The best interests of the child will be their basic concern.

The best interests of the child, therefore, are concerns of both the state (Article 3 para 1) and parents (Article 18 para 1). According to the whole concept of childrens' rights, and especially according to Article 12: child participation as a general principle, the child is also an actor in his or her own best interests, that is, in his or her own healthy holistic (that is, physical-emotional-social-moral-intellectual) development, including the pursuit of the other pedagogical aims of the Convention, mentioned – strictly speaking in relation to school education only – in Article 29 para 1. This paragraph reads as follows:

---

10 On the concept of the Trias pedagogica, see Willems (ed.), *Developmental and Autonomy Rights of Children* (note 3).

Article 29 para 1 – States Parties agree that the education of the child shall be directed to:

(a) The development of the child's personality, talents and mental and physical abilities to their fullest potential;
(b) The development of respect for human rights and fundamental freedoms, and for the principles enshrined in the Charter of the United Nations;
(c) The development of respect for the child's parents, his or her own cultural identity, language and values, for the national values of the country in which the child is living, the country from which he or she may originate, and for civilisations different from his or her own;
(d) The preparation of the child for responsible life in a free society, in the spirit of understanding, peace, tolerance, equality of sexes, and friendship among all peoples, ethnic, national and religious groups and persons of indigenous origin;
(e) The development of respect for the natural environment.

Taken together, the aims enumerated sub (a) and sub (b)-(e), respectively, may be summarised as holistic development and preparation for democratic citizenship, or rather democratic and cosmopolitan citizenship. And the latter may be construed – on the basis, *inter alia*, of Article 18 para 1 (primary responsibility of parents for the development of the child), and Article 29 para 1 sub (d) (preparation of the child for responsible life) – as including preparation for responsible parenthood. Thus, three actors are involved in child development: the state (through its agents and through its responsibilities towards institutions and professionals[11]), parents, and the child him- or herself. All these actors have rights, duties and responsibilities, which, according to their fundamental character, should be constitutionalised, but at any rate should be specified – and clarified – in the national legal system.

State obligations

Two of the most outstanding state obligations, in my opinion, in the CRC are to be found in Article 27 para 3, and Article 18 para 2, which require the state to empower, that is to facilitate, educate, assist and support parents, in socio-economic and socio-emotional ways, respectively. Article 27 reads as follows:

---

11 On which see Article 3 para 3 CRC: States Parties shall ensure that the institutions, services and facilities responsible for the care or protection of children shall conform with the standards established by competent authorities, particularly in the areas of safety, health, in the number and suitability of their staff, as well as competent supervision.

Article 27 para 1 – States Parties recognise the right of every child to a standard of living adequate for the child's physical, mental, spiritual, moral and social development.

2. The parent(s) or others responsible for the child have the primary responsibility to secure, within their abilities and financial capacities, the conditions of living necessary for the child's development.

3. States Parties, in accordance with national conditions and within their means, shall take appropriate measures to assist parents and others responsible for the child to implement this right and shall in case of need provide material assistance and support programmes, particularly with regard to nutrition, clothing and housing.

And Article 18 para 2 states:

Article 18 para 2 – For the purpose of guaranteeing and promoting the rights set forth in the present Convention, States Parties shall render appropriate assistance to parents and legal guardians in the performance of their child-rearing responsibilities and shall ensure the development of institutions, facilities and services for the care of children.

Specifying and clarifying parental duties and responsibilities, as they appear in the CRC, is also a very important state responsibility, however. Such a specification and clarification provide us with an essential yardstick for parenthood education in schools and parenting education for parents and parents-to-be. As such, they are an integral part of preparation for parenthood and empowerment of children, parents and other carers and the community (neighbours, relatives, professionals, volunteers, bystanders, etc.). Therefore, specification and clarification of parental duties and responsibilities should be considered as an implied state obligation. Furthermore, it may be argued that specifying and clarifying parental duties falls within the scope of the "appropriate legislative and administrative measures" called for by Article 3 para 2, to ensure the child's care and protection with positive regard to parental duties. Responsibilisation is the term I use to denote, *inter alia*, the state's obligation to specify and clarify parental duties and responsibilities in the national legal system. The combination of CRC provisions and state obligations mentioned above enables us to present the following definition of (a child rights based) *Trias pedagogica*.

Trias pedagogica

Trias pedagogica means the national or constitutional relationship between the state, parents and children, based on children's rights and other human rights and, therefore, implying state obligations in relation to the healthy holistic development of children, including the participation of the child and his or her preparation for democratic citizenship and responsible parenthood, and, more specifically, to the responsibilisation and empowerment of parents and other caregivers, professional and otherwise.

Even though the CRC may not make it possible to exactly define the concept of responsible parenthood, it does stipulate the core conditions that have to be met by parents and the state. Apart from CRC Article 18 para 2, and Article 27 para 3 (and a few other provisions), however, it does so in a rather implicit way. Most implicit, of course, are the conditions that have to be distilled out of the principle of the best interests of the child. Let us first have a look at empowerment obligations of states, and then return to parental duties and responsibilities.

Empowerment obligations

The following empowerment Articles, divided into two sections (A and B, relating to parents and to children as parents-to-be, respectively), may be discerned in the CRC. This "empowerment list" should not be seen as exhaustive. Also, it should be kept in mind that the state has several obligations which indirectly empower parents, for instance in relation to health care (Article 24), education (Articles 28 and 29), quality of institutions and supervision of professionals (Article 3 para 3), the mass media (Article 17), children's play, sport and cultural acitivities (Article 31), disabled children (Article 23), foster care (Article 20), and so forth and so on.

Empowerment Articles (A): the state's positive obligations to facilitate, educate, assist and support parents.

- Article 18 para 2 contains the obligation of the state to provide parenting assistance (assistance in the performance of child-rearing responsibilities) and support (institutions, facilities and services for the care of children).
- Article 18 para 3, in conjunction with Article 3 para 3, contains the obligation of the state to provide sufficient and high-quality child-care services and facilities.
- Article 24 para 2 sub (d)-(f) contains the obligation of the state to provide pre- and postnatal care; to provide information, education and support for parents, children and all others on child health and nutrition, breastfeeding, hygiene etc.; and to develop preventive health care, guidance for parents and family planning education and services.
- Article 27 para 3 (in conjunction with para 1) contains the obligation of the state to provide material (financial, fiscal and other) assistance and support

for parents so that families may have a standard of living adequate for the child's holistic development.
- Article 27 para 3, in conjunction with Article 18 para 1 (both parents are responsible) and para 2 (parenting assistance), imply a state obligation to (at least) facilitate paid parental leave.

Empowerment Articles (B): the state's positive obligations to empower children as citizens and parents-to-be.

- Article 29 para 1 contains the obligation of the state to see to it that school education be directed to the holistic development of the child and his or her preparation for democratic citizenship (including, as indicated above, responsible parenthood).
- Article 31 para 2 contains the obligation of the state to promote child participation in cultural, recreational and leisure activities.
- Article 39 contains the obligation of the state to promote child trauma reparation (and thus prevent transgenerational transmission of trauma and end cycles of violence, insecure attachment, poor mental health, child abuse and neglect, delinquency,[12] etc.).

In relation to the empowerment list above, it is important to highlight three CRC Articles, namely Article 3 para 3, containing the obligation of the state to empower, that is, to ensure the quantity and quality of, and to supervise institutions and professionals working with parents and/or children; and Article 4 and Article 6 para 2, containing the obligation of the state to invest in children's rights and child development to the maximum extent of its resources. We will now turn to the "responsibilisation list": a list of fifty-plus parental duties and responsibilities.

FIFTY-PLUS-ONE PARENTAL DUTIES AND RESPONSIBILITIES

The following responsibilisation Articles, and ("fifty-plus-one") parental duties and responsibilities to be legislated and/or made known – through information campaigns and education – by the state on the basis of these Articles, may be

12 According to Tekin and Currie (Erdal Tekin & Janet Currie, Does child abuse cause crime?; Abstract, April 2006, available at <papers.ssrn.com/sol3/papers.cfm?abstract_id=895178>), child maltreatment "approximately doubles the probability of engaging in many types of crime. Low SES [socio-economic status, JW] children are both more likely to be mistreated and suffer more damaging effects. Boys are at greater risk than girls, at least in terms of increased propensity to commit crime. Sexual abuse appears to have the largest negative effects (…). Finally, the probability of engaging in crime increases with the experience of multiple forms of maltreatment (…)."

discerned in the CRC. This list, rather long as it may appear to be, should not be seen as exhaustive, however. It should also be kept in mind that the degree of specification and the details of clarification in national legislation is subject to national democratic process and discretion. (...)

Article 18 para 1 CRC contains three closely related parental duties[13]:

- 1. *both* parents (c.q. caregivers, whatever their gender and marital status) have *common* responsibilities for the upbringing and development of the child;
- 2. parents have the *primary* responsibility for the upbringing and development of the child;
- 3. the best interests of the child will be their *basic concern*. – The "best interests" principle consists of fourteen conditions, one of which consists of six subconditions (pedagogical model of Margrite Kalverboer & Elianne Zijlstra, 2006).[14] Based on this model, parents have the duty:
  - 3.1 to provide physical security;
  - 3.2 to provide physical care;
  - 3.3 to provide loving care and emotional security;
  - 3.4 to provide a supportive and flexible pedagogical structure (in CRC terminology: "direction and guidance consistent with the child's evolving capacities"), for which six sub-conditions have to be met:
    - 3.4.1 regularity (so-called routines, rituals and rules);
    - 3.4.2 realistic demands (stimulating and instructing the child based on realistic demands);
    - 3.4.3 room (to experience, experiment, negotiate);
    - 3.4.4 responsibilities (participation in family and community responsibilities);
    - 3.4.5 rules (boundaries or limits, which are explained to the child); and

13 In this list, "duty" or "duties" is used as shorthand for duty (duties) and/or responsibility (responsibilities) as defined earlier (note 2).

14 On this model, see Willems (ed.), *Developmental and Autonomy Rights of Children* (note 3), Chapter 7, at pp. 199–201. The original model is described in Dutch (Margrite Kalverboer & Elianne Zijlstra, *Het belang van het kind in het Nederlands recht; Voorwaarden voor ontwikkeling vanuit een pedagogisch perspectief*, Amsterdam, SWP, 2006). However, several elements of the best interests of the child concept are enumerated and elaborated in the Council of Europe recommendation mentioned in note 8 above, as well as in the Explanatory Report to the recommendation (<www.coe.int>, CM(2006)194 add 27 November 2006). Both are included in Mary Daly (ed.), *Parenting in contemporary Europe: A positive approach*, Strasbourg, Council of Europe Publishing, 2007, pp. 141–175. In May 2008, the UN High Commissioner for Refugees released guidelines on determining the best interests of the child (*UNHCR Guidelines on Determining the Best Interests of the Child*, available at <www.unhcr.org>). These guidelines specifically aim at refugee children, and are predominantly of a legal and procedural nature. They do not contain universal pedagogical criteria, let alone a pedagogical model.

  - **3.4.6** supervision;
- **3.5** to provide continuity in child-rearing;
- **3.6** to give personal attention to each individual child;
- **3.7** to set good examples;
- **3.8** to see to their child's education (school, vocational training; including sports, music, etc.);
- **3.9** to see to their child's physical and emotional security in school and community;
- **3.10** to stimulate their child's interaction with peers;
- **3.11** to stimulate their child's access to a social support network;
- **3.12** to devote themselves to active respect for (the human dignity, personal integrity and equal developmental opportunities of) children in school, community and society;
- **3.13** to contribute to good adult examples in community and society;
- **3.14** to contribute to stable living conditions in community and society.

Taken together (and in conjunction with the ninth – "before as well as after birth" – preambular paragraph), these duties imply a fourth duty:

- **4.** both parents have to prepare themselves and actively seek information and support from family, community, and the state before their child is born. – Pre- and perinatal (preparation, c.q. preparation and reparation) responsibilities include:
  - **4.1** a physically and mentally healthy lifestyle (*cf.* ninth preambular paragraph and Article 24);
  - **4.2** a healthy, stable relationship (*cf.* ninth preambular paragraph and Article 18 para 1);
  - **4.3** a stable family income (*cf.* ninth preambular paragraph and Article 27 para 2);
  - **4.4** parenting education (*cf.* ninth preambular paragraph and Article 18 para 1, and Article 24);
  - **4.5** mental health counselling (own childhood trauma reparation, psychotherapy; *cf.* ninth preambular paragraph and Article 18 para 1, Article 19 para 1, and Article 24).

Article 5, in conjunction with the sixth – "love and understanding" – preambular paragraph, contains the duty of parents:

- **5.** to provide affection-based direction and guidance, consistent with the child's evolving capacities (*cf.* 3.4 above).
  This duty implies the duty:
- **6.** to acquire knowledge on child rearing and child development in general, and

- **7.** to seek specific information, advice, feedback and counselling on the rearing and development of their child.
  It may even imply the duty:
- **8.** to seek psychotherapy in case of relational or psychological problems, or unresolved childhood trauma of parents themselves.

Article 27 para 2 (in conjunction with para 1) contains the duty of parents:
- **9.** to provide a standard of living adequate for the holistic development of their child.
  If this is not "within their abilities and financial capacities" (Article 27 para 2), another duty is implied, namely:
- **10.** to actively seek family, community and state assistance (*cf.* Article 27 para 3).
  It may also imply the (civic) duty:
- **11.** to mobilise parents' organisations, trade unions, child rights NGOs, political parties and the media with a view to improving parenting allowances, benefits and credits.

Taken together, Article 18 para 1 (*both* parents; child's best interests basic concern) and Article 27 para 2 contain the duty of parents:
- **12.** to prudently combine work and care, and seek high-quality child-care services.
  This duty implies the (civic) duty:
- **13.** to mobilise parents' organisations, trade unions, child rights NGOs, political parties and the media if national policies are lacking or inadequate in this regard.

Article 19 para 1, in conjunction with General Comment No. 8,[15] contains the duty of parents:
- **14.** not to use any form of violence, including humiliation, in child rearing.
  This duty implies the duty:
- **15.** to acquire knowledge on positive parenting[16] and non-violent child rearing (positive discipline[17]), and
- **16.** to seek advice, feedback and counselling if this causes any problems or difficulties.

---

15 Committee on the Rights of the Child, General Comment No. 8 (2006), *The right of the child to protection from corporal punishment and other cruel or degrading forms of punishment.* Text available at <www.unhchr.ch/tbs/doc.nsf/(Symbol)/CRC.C.GC.8.En?OpenDocument>.

16 See note 8.

17 See note 9.

Article 24 para 1, in conjunction with Article 39, contains the duty of parents:
- **17.** to seek the best available physical and mental health care for their child.
  This duty implies the (civic) duty:
- **18.** to mobilise parents' organisations, trade unions, child rights NGOs, political parties and the media, or to go to court, if health care is lacking or inadequate.

Article 24 para 3 contains the duty of parents:
- **19.** not to resort to and to abandon any harmful child-rearing practices and traditions.
  This duty implies the (civic) duty:
- **20.** to mobilise parents' organisations, trade unions, child rights NGOs, political parties and the media if the state is not doing enough to ban such practices and to support parents in child rights based parenting and positive discipline.

Article 28 para 1 contains the duty of parents:
- **21.** to send their child to school and see to their child's education and vocational training.
  This duty implies the (civic) duty:
- **22.** to mobilise parents' organisations, trade unions, child rights NGOs, political parties and the media, or to go to court, if schools are lacking or school education is inadequate.

Article 29 para 1, in conjunction with the seventh – "fully prepared and brought up" – preambular paragraph, as well as in conjunction with Article 18 para 1, and Article 19 para 1, contains the duty of parents:
- **23.** not to harm and confuse their child, and compromise his or her loyalty, by raising him or her contrary to the CRC's holistic development and democratic and cosmopolitan citizenship aims of education.

Article 17 contains the two-sided duty of parents:
- **24.** to stimulate the child's use of media that contribute to his or her holistic development and physical and mental health, including his or her democratic and cosmopolitan citizenship education; and
- **25.** to protect the child from harmful material.
  These duties implies the (civic) duty:
- **26.** to mobilise parents' organisations, trade unions, child rights NGOs, political parties and the media themselves if the state and/or the media are not meeting the standards of Article 17.

Article 30 in conjunction with Article 29 contains the duty of parents who belong to an ethnic, religious or linguistic minority:
- **27.** to promote their child's and their family's integration in society on the basis of their own cultural identity.

Article 31 para 1, in conjunction with Article 18 para 1, and Article 24, contains the duty of parents:
- **28.** to provide age-appropriate play and recreational and cultural activities for their child.
  This duty implies the (civic) duty:
- **29.** to mobilise parents' organisations, trade unions, child rights NGOs, political parties and the media if national policies or community facilities in this respect are lacking or inadequate.

Article 7 para 1 contains two duties of parents:
- **30.** to register their child at birth, and
- **31.** to inform their child about his or her biological origins.

Article 8 para 1 contains the duty of parents:
- **32.** not to deprive their child of his or her personal identity (the knowledge of his or her origins).

Article 9 para 3 contains the two-sided duty of divorced or separated parents:
- **33.** to enable their child to maintain personal relations and direct contact with both parents on a regular basis, and
- **34.** to prevent contact if it is contrary to the child's best interests.

Article 2 in conjunction with Article 18 para 1 contains the duty of parents:
- **35.** not to discriminate between boy and girl children, and
- **36.** not to favour one child above the other.

Article 12, in conjunction with Article 18 para 1, and Articles 5 and 29, contains the duty of parents:
- **37.** to stimulate their child to form his or her own views and to freely express him- or herself, and
- **38.** to stimulate their child, and to provide direction and guidance in this respect, to bear his or her own responsibilities in family, school, community and country.

Article 13, in conjunction with Article 18 para 1, and Articles 5, 17 and 36, contains the duty of parents:

- **39.** to respect and promote their child's freedom of expression and freedom to seek, receive and impart information and ideas, and to provide direction, guidance and protection in this respect.

Article 14 para 1, in conjunction with Article 18 para 1, and Articles 5, 14 para 2, 17 and 36, contains the duty of parents:

- **40.** to respect and promote their child's freedom of thought, conscience and religion, and to provide direction, guidance and protection in this respect.

Article 15, in conjunction with Article 18 para 1, and Articles 5, 17 and 36, contains the duty of parents:

- **41.** to respect and promote their child's freedom of association and peaceful assembly, and to provide direction, guidance and protection in this respect.

Article 16 in conjunction with Article 18 para 1 contains the duty of parents:

- **42.** to respect their child's privacy and personal integrity.

Article 20 para 3, in conjunction with Article 18 para 1, and Article 24, contains the duty of parents:

- **43.** to seek foster care or adoption if they are unable to raise the child themselves.

Article 23, in conjunction with Article 18 para 1, and Article 24, contains the duty of parents:

- **44.** to seek special care and opportunities for their physically, mentally and/or emotionally disabled child.
  This duty implies the (civic) duty:
- **45.** to mobilise parents' organisations, trade unions, child rights NGOs, political parties and the media if national policies or community facilities in this respect are lacking or inadequate.

Article 32, in conjunction with Article 18 para 1, and Article 24, contains the duty of parents:

- **46.** to stimulate their child to work for as many hours as – and to prevent their child from working for more hours than – are beneficial for his or her holistic development.

Article 33, in conjunction with Article 18 para 1, and Article 24, contains the duty of parents:

- **47.** to prevent their child (in cooperation and coordination with other parents and social partners) from smoking, using illegal drugs and abusing alcohol.

Article 34, in conjunction with Articles 17, 18 para 1, 24 and 29, contains the duty of parents:

- **48.** to see to their child's sexual education and to prevent their child (in cooperation and coordination with other parents and social partners) from falling victim to sexual exploitation and sexual abuse by peers, predators and pedophiles.

Article 36, in conjunction with Articles 17, 18 para 1, 24 and 29, contains the duty of parents:

- **49.** to see to their child's financial, consumer and "screen" or "electronic" (TV, PC, MSN, computer games, internet, video, mobile phones, etc.) education and to prevent their child from falling victim to commercial, "electronic" and any other exploitation.
  This duty implies the (civic) duty:
- **50.** to mobilise parents' organisations, trade unions, child rights NGOs, political parties and the media if national policies are lacking or inadequate in this regard.

Article 42 in conjunction with Article 18 para 1, and Article 29 contains the duty of parents:

- **51.** to educate their child on his or her rights and to see to their child's child rights education in school (and community).
  (...)

TASK/TEXT 0.5: L'HISTOIRE SE RÉPÈTE?

TASK/TEXT 0.5.1: CRUELTY TO CHILDREN – THE MARY ELLEN CASE

New York Society for the Prevention of Cruelty to Children (founded in 1875), <www.nyspcc.org/nyspcc/history/the_catalyst>, visited 10 January 2010

The first anti-cruelty laws were enacted on behalf of animals, not children, but the founding of the American Society for the Prevention of Cruelty to Animals [ASPCA] in New York by Henry Bergh in 1866 proved fortuitous, for its applicability to human needs was recognized almost immediately.

"The children of New York are sadly in need of a champion …" (*The New York Evening Telegram*, 1866)

"It is not alone the lower animals that are subject to ill-treatment and cruelty." (*The Northern Budget*, Troy, NY, 1867)

Within four years, Bergh enlisted Elbridge Gerry as ASPCA counsel. The sensitivity imbuing these men with concern for animals also filled them with distress over the maltreatment of children. In the winter of 1873, in a New York neighborhood called "Hell's Kitchen," a rooming-house janitress told a church worker about a case of child cruelty. Dedicated and compassionate, Etta Wheeler made discrete inquiries and determined to rescue the abused child, a little girl named Mary Ellen. When others declined to intervene, Wheeler approached Henry Bergh and Bergh appealed to Gerry: "No time is to be lost – instruct me how to proceed."

Gerry made clever use of an obscure section of *habeas corpus* to secure their legal standing. The "Mary Ellen case" was a classic child protective intervention. Within forty-eight hours of Wheeler's initial report, an investigation was conducted, a petition filed, a protective removal effected, a hearing commenced, a temporary placement arranged and a criminal prosecution in preparation.

"I was in a courtroom full of men with pale, stern looks. I saw a child brought in … at the sight of which men wept aloud. And as I looked, I knew I was where the first chapter of children's rights was written … For from that dingy courtroom … came forth The New York Society for the Prevention of Cruelty to Children with all it has meant to the world's life." (Jacob Riis)

Mary Ellen's court statement

"My name is Mary Ellen ____. I don't know how old I am; my mother and father are both dead; I call Mrs. C____ momma; I have never had but one pair of shoes, but can't recollect when that was; I have no shoes or stockings this winter; I have never been allowed to go out … except in the night time, and only in the yard [to use the outdoor privy]; my bed at night is only a piece of carpet stretched on the floor underneath a window and I sleep in my little undergarment with a quilt over me; I am never allowed to play with other children; momma has been in the habit of whipping me almost everyday; she used to whip me with a twisted whip – a rawhide; the whip always left black and blue marks on my body; I have now on my head two black and blue marks which were made by momma with the whip, and a cut on the left side of my forehead which was made by a pair of scissors in momma's hand; she struck me with the scissors and cut me; I have no recollection of ever having been kissed and I have never been kissed by momma:

I have never been taken on momma's lap or caressed or petted; I never dared speak to anybody, because if I did I would get whipped; I have never had ... any more clothing than I have on at present ...; I have seen stockings and other clothes in our room, but I am not allowed to put them on; whenever momma went out, I was locked up in the bedroom; ... I don't know for what I was whipped; momma never said anything when she whipped me; I do not want to go back to live with momma because she beats me so."

Mary Ellen was placed in a loving home, married, raised a family of her own, and died at the age of 92 in 1956.

TASK/TEXT 0.5.2: SWITZERLAND – AN ADVOCATE FOR ANIMALS? WHAT ABOUT CHILDREN?

Editorial by Clara Balestra, Foundation Sarah Oberson, Institut international des Droits de l'Enfant (IDE), <www.childsrights.org/html/site_en/index.php?c>, 8 January 2010 (references omitted)

On March 7th, 2010, the Swiss populace is to pronounce itself on the "Initiative for the establishment of an advocate in charge of animal protection." If the answer is a YES, cantons will be pledged to set up a position of advocate to fend for abused animals, within criminal procedures. The advocate will be independent both from Education Ministries, and from the animal's owner. It will defend only the interests of the animal itself (...).

The Swiss Animal Protection organisation (SPA) has launched the initiative to fight the impunity of such abuse on animals. It claims that "criminal prosecution authorities are showing flawed commitment to start criminal procedures, and lack of care in elaborating evidence, since they can base themselves only on the convict's statement. This situation is owed to the fact that in the majority of cantons, wronged animals have no advocate, while the animal's owner is allowed to enjoy all the rights conferred by his/her statute of party to the trial (...)."

When maltreated, children experience a similar legal situation. Statistics show that violence happens predominantly in the family circle, which makes it difficult to detect. Numerous situations falling under automatic prosecution accordingly remain unknown. Children themselves are entitled to lodge a complaint only through their legal representative – most of the time parents, i.e. the probable perpetrator of these acts – or if their discerning capabilities are assessed sufficient. This indeed excludes a high number of children (...).

So, if the initiative referendum is accepted, animals in Switzerland would enjoy better legal protection than children, in case of abuse. Quite a paradox indeed!

International human rights bodies, including the Committee on the Rights of the Child, have been requesting for years that Switzerland "establish a federal independent human rights institution in accordance with the Paris Principles (…) to monitor and evaluate progress in the implementation of the Convention. It should be accessible to children, empowered to receive and investigate complaints of violations of child rights in a child-sensitive manner, and address them effectively." (Concluding Observations, 2002, para 16.)

As for the Swiss Government, in response to international and Parliament pressure (…), it expressed in July 2009 its view that it was premature to establish such an institution, and launched "a five-year pilot project aimed at providing cantons, municipalities and the private sector with extra support and services in the field of human rights." One of the numerous gaps of this pilor project (…) is the absence of the issue of receiving or addressing complaints from children.

The functioning of democracy accounts for this paradoxical situation: the groups enjoy the best advocacy of their rights are the ones with most influence on decision-makers. So, we face a strange case where animal rights advocates seem to be stronger (better organized? better funded? better represented?) than child advocates? Furthermore, the view of animals as full-fledged beings seems to be acquired, in a time when children, still, are often considered exclusively as part of the family, and accordingly an intimate concern.

Is it not a duty of the Federal Governement's to re-balance priorities, keeping politics at bay?

TASK/TEXT 0.5.3: THE NETHERLANDS – A PARTY FOR THE ANIMALS (WHAT ABOUT A PARTY FOR CHILDREN'S RIGHTS …? (1))

International website of the Party for the Animals (Partij voor de Dieren, <www.partijvoordedieren.nl>), <www.partyfortheanimals.nl>, visited 10 January 2010

We are a Dutch political party whose highest priority is animal welfare and the respectful treatment of animals. In the Netherlands, we are represented in the House of Representatives, the Senate and the Provincial States. That is unique: never before has a political party devoted to animal welfare been elected to a national parliament anywhere else in the world.

The Party for the Animals is the fastest growing political party in the Netherlands. We act as a "pacemaker" in the parliament; in other words, we encourage the other political parties to move faster when it comes to animal welfare.

Ever since the establishment of the Party for the Animals, there has been a great deal of interest in the party abroad. That is why we have created this international website, which provides a lot of useful information. Each week Marianne Thieme, the leader of the Party for the Animals, will write a new worldlog about her experiences in politics. This worldlog will not only be available in English, but also in French, German, Italian, Spanish, Portuguese. Turkish and Russian.

The Party for the Animals believes that animals should be given the rights that they deserve. Animal interests should no longer continually be subordinated to economic interests. Not just in the Netherlands, but also beyond. We would therefore like to join forces with kindred spirits in other countries. The more animal welfare parties that are set up across the globe, the better.

TASK/TEXT 0.5.4: DUTCH COURT APPROVES PEDOPHILE POLITICAL PARTY (WHAT ABOUT A PARTY FOR CHILDREN'S RIGHTS ...? (2))

<www.lifesitenews.com/ldn/2006/jul/06071705.html>, visited 10 January 2010

AMSTERDAM, July 17, 2006 (LifeSiteNews.com, Hilary White) – A court at The Hague has refused to outlaw the proposed political party that supports legalized pedophilia and child pornography. The BBC reports that the Brotherly Love, Freedom and Diversity Party (PNVD) has received the nod from Judge HFM Hofhuis who said the group has the same right to exist as any other political party.

In late May, observers around the world were stunned by the announcement that a group of self-professed pedophiles in the Netherlands was seeking to form a political party. The announcement spurred outrage with a poll showing that 82 per cent wanted the government to do something to stop the new party, while 67 per cent said promoting pedophilia should be illegal.

The party, which has only three known members, seeks to lower the age of sexual consent from 16 to 12. They want to legalize child pornography and sex with animals. They argue that prohibitions only make children "curious" and seek to overturn all sexual taboos that are left in Dutch society.

The Associated Press news agency reports that Judge Hofhuis wrote in the ruling, "Freedom of expression ... including the freedom to set up a political party can be seen as the basis for a democratic society." "It is the right of the voter to judge the appeal of political parties," he said.

The Netherlands has pioneered the legalization of abortion and euthanasia for adults and infants, prostitution, 'soft' recreational drugs and was the first country to institute homosexual "marriage."

1. VIOLENCE AGAINST CHILDREN – UN STUDY AND RELATED ISSUES

TASK/TEXT 1.1: SUMMARY OF THE REPORT OF THE INDEPENDENT EXPERT FOR THE UNITED NATIONS STUDY ON VIOLENCE AGAINST CHILDREN, A/61/299

The key message of the report of the UNSG's Study on violence against children, submitted to the General Assembly in October 2006, is that no violence against children is justifiable; all violence against children is preventable. The report begins: 'In every region, in contradiction to human rights obligations and children's developmental needs, violence against children is socially approved, and is frequently legal and State-authorised. The Study should mark a turning point – an end to adult justification of violence against children, whether accepted as "tradition" or disguised as "discipline." There can be no compromise in challenging violence against children. Children's uniqueness – their potential and vulnerability, their dependence on adults – makes it imperative that they have more, not less, protection from violence. Protection of children from violence is a matter of urgency. Children have suffered adult violence unseen and unheard for centuries. Now that the scale and impact of all forms of violence against children is becoming better known, children must be provided with the effective prevention and protection to which they have an unqualified right. Children are tired of being called the future. They want to enjoy their childhood, free of violence, now!' (Paulo Sérgio Pinheiro, introducing the report of the UN Secretary General's Study on Violence against Children to the General Assembly, October 2006.)

THE STUDY BACKGROUND

In 2000 and 2001, the Committee on the Rights of the Child, the internationally-elected monitoring treaty body for the Convention on the Rights of the Child, organised two days of general discussion on violence against children. Following them, the Committee proposed that the General Assembly should initiate an in-depth, comprehensive global study on violence against children. The General Assembly agreed and in February 2003, Professor Paulo Sérgio Pinheiro was appointed as Independent Expert to lead the Study, on behalf of the Secretary

General. The aim of the study was to report on the scale of violence against children in five settings: home and family, schools, care and justice systems, the workplace and the community and to make recommendations. Pinheiro presented his report including recommendations to the General Assembly 61st session in October 2006 (A/61/299). The concise 34-page report is complemented by the detailed *World Report on Violence against Children*.

THE STUDY PROCESS

In March 2004, a detailed questionnaire was sent to all governments by the Independent Expert, seeking information on their approaches to violence against children; over 130 responses were received. About 300 individuals and organisations from all parts of the world responded to the Study's call for submissions. The Study involved regional, sub-regional and national consultations, expert thematic meetings and field visits by the Independent Expert. Nine major regional consultations were held between March and July 2005, for the Caribbean, South Asia, West and Central Africa, Latin America, North America, East Asia and the Pacific, the Middle East and North Africa, Europe and Central Asia, and Eastern and Southern Africa. A key feature of the regional consultations was the direct involvement of children, who in each case met in advance with adult facilitators to plan their input and were then involved in working groups and plenary sessions, often presenting their own declarations. In each region, the children met informally and privately with Paulo Pinheiro. The Independent Expert and the Study Secretariat were supported by three key agencies: the Office of the United Nations High Commissioner for Human Rights, UNICEF and the World Health Organisation (WHO). Professor Pinheiro appointed a multi-disciplinary Editorial Board of experts to advise him and was also supported by an Advisory Panel of non-governmental organisations, including children and young people.

KEY FINDINGS OF THE STUDY

Violence against children takes a variety of forms and is influenced by a wide range of factors, from the personal characteristics of the victim and perpetrator to their cultural and physical environments. There are a number of reasons why violence is widespread and has often not been dealt with:

Much violence remains hidden

Children are often afraid of reporting incidents of violence against them, and parents who should protect their children may remain silent if violence is perpetrated by a spouse or other close relative. There are many places where stigma may be the reason why violence is not reported, for instance where family 'honour' is placed above the safety and wellbeing of children, particularly in cases of rape or other forms of sexual violence. Violence can also remain hidden because there are no safe or trusted ways for children or adults to report it. In some parts of the world, people do not trust police, social services or others in authority; or in rural areas, often there are no places to go to report incidences of violence.

Violence is accepted in society

Both children and perpetrators may accept physical, sexual and psychological violence as inevitable and normal. Discipline through physical, bullying and sexual harassment are frequently perceived as normal, particularly when no 'visible' or lasting physical injury results. The lack of an explicit legal prohibition of corporal punishment reflects this. Furthermore, even though some acts of violence are unexpected and isolated, the majority of acts experienced by children are perpetrated by people who are part of their lives, such as parents, teachers, schoolmates, employers, boyfriends or girlfriends, spouses and partners.

The following examples show the range of violence against children:

- Almost 53,000 children are estimated to have died worldwide in 2002 as a result of homicide. In some industrialised countries, infants under one year faced three times the risk of homicide, almost invariably at the hands of parents, than children aged 1 to 4, and twice the risk of those aged 5 to 14.
- Of these child homicide victims, 22,000 (or nearly 42 per cent) were 15 to 17 years old and nearly 75 per cent were boys.
- As many as 80 to 90 per cent of children suffer physical punishment in their homes, with a third or more experiencing severe physical punishment resulting from the use of implements, according to studies from countries in all regions of the world.
- In over 100 countries, children still suffer the threat or reality of corporal punishment with canes, belts or other implements in schools.
- In at least 30 countries, sentences of whipping or caning are still being imposed on children in penal systems.
- Only 2.4 per cent of the world's children are legally protected from corporal punishment in all settings.
- Each year, between 133 and 275 million children witness frequent violence between their parents.
- Between 20 and 65 per cent of school-aged children in developing countries reported having been verbally or physically bullied in the previous 30 days.
- In Central and Eastern Europe, 35 per cent of schoolchildren responding to a survey said they had been bullied within the last two months, with the percentage ranging from 15 to 64 per cent.

- An estimated 150 million girls and 73 million boys under 18 experience forced sexual intercourse or other forms of sexual violence during 2002.
- In surveys of 21 countries, at least 7 per cent of females (ranging up to 36 per cent) and 3 per cent of males (ranging up to 29 per cent) report sexual victimisation during their childhood.
- Of women who reported first sex prior to the age of 15, between 11 and 45 per cent reported it was forced.
- At least 82 million girls now between 10 and 17 years old will marry before they turn 18, including significant numbers of girls married at much younger ages.
- Between 100 million and 140 million girls and women in the world have undergone some form of female genital mutilation/cutting (FGM/C).
- Rates of FGM/C are as high as 71 to 99 per cent in some countries of some regions; some girls are cut before the age of four.
- In sub-Saharan Africa, Egypt and Sudan, an estimated 3 million girls and women are subjected to genital mutilation/cutting every year.
- In 2004, 218 million children were involved in child labour, of which 126 million were in hazardous work.
- Estimates from 2000 suggest that 5.7 million children participated in forced or bonded labour, 1.8 million were exploited in prostitution and pornography, and 1.2 million were victims of trafficking.

GUIDING PRINCIPLES ADOPTED BY THE INDEPENDENT EXPERT

Professor Pinheiro states in the reports that he has been guided by the following principles, which are reflected in the recommendations:

- No violence against children is justifiable. Children should never receive less protection than adults;
- All violence against children is preventable. States must invest in evidence-based policies and programmes to address factors that give rise to violence against children;
- States have the primary responsibility to uphold children's rights to protection and access to services, and to support families' capacity to provide children with care in a safe environment;
- States have the obligation to ensure accountability in every case of violence;
- The vulnerability of children to violence is linked to their age and evolving capacity. Some children, because of gender, race, ethnic origin, disability or social status, are particularly vulnerable;
- Children have the right to express their views, and to have these views taken into account in the implementation of policies and programmes.
  (Paulo Sérgio Pinheiro, UNSG's Study Report, para. 93.)

WHAT THE STUDY RECOMMENDS

The UN Secretary General's Report to the General Assembly includes a set of 12 'overarching' recommendations. There are also more detailed recommendations, applying to the five settings of childhood in which violence occurs – home and family, schools, care and justice systems, the workplace and the community. These are the overarching recommendations (see full text below):

1. **Strengthen national and local commitment and action.**
2. **Prohibit all violence against children.**
3. **Prioritise prevention.**
4. **Promote non-violent values and awareness-raising.**
5. **Enhance the capacity of all who work with and for children.**
6. **Provide recovery and social reintegration services.**
7. **Ensure participation of children.**
8. **Create accessible and child-friendly reporting systems and services.**
9. **Ensure accountability and end impunity.**
10. **Address the gender dimension of violence against children.**
11. **Develop and implement systematic national data collection and research.**
12. **Strengthen international commitment.**

Other recommendations cover regional and international follow-up, including the proposal that a Special Representative to the UN Secretary General on Violence against Children should be appointed – see below. The urgency of acting on the Study's recommendations is underlined throughout Professor Pinheiro's reports. Three recommendations are singled out and **time-bound goals** set for them:

- **By 2007: integrating into national planning process measures to prevent and respond to violence against children, including the identification of a focal point, preferably at ministerial level;**
- **By 2009: prohibiting all violence against children by law;**
- **By 2009: initiating a process to develop reliable national data collection systems.** (...)

OVERARCHING RECOMMENDATIONS

1. Strengthen national and local commitment and action

States should develop a varied and detailed plan to respond to violence against children which is made part of national planning processes. This strategy, policy or plan of action must set realistic targets and deadlines. It should be coordinated by an agency which is able to involve different parts of Government and society, whilst a range of people and organisations should be involved in putting it into action. National laws, policies, plans and programmes should fully comply with international human rights and current scientific knowledge. The implementation of the national strategy, policy or plan should be systematically evaluated according to established targets and timetables. Enough human and financial resources should be provided to help put the plan into action.

2. Prohibit all violence against children

States must ensure that no person below 18 years of age is given the death penalty or a sentence of life imprisonment without possibility of release. States are recommended to take all necessary measures to immediately suspend the execution of all death penalties imposed on persons for crimes committed before reaching the age of 18. They should take the appropriate legal measures to convert them into penalties that are in keeping with international human rights standards. Abolishing the death penalty for those who committed crimes before reaching the age of 18 should be of the highest priority. States must prohibit all forms of violence against children, in all settings. This includes: corporal punishment; harmful traditional practices, such as early and forced marriages; female genital mutilation and so-called honour crimes; sexual violence and torture and other cruel, inhuman or degrading treatment or punishment, (which is required by international treaties, including the Convention against Torture and Other Cruel, Inhuman or Degrading Treatment or Punishment and the Convention on the Rights of the Child, further reaffirmed in the General Comment No. 8).

3. Prioritise prevention

States must prioritise preventing violence against children by addressing its underlying causes. It is essential to devote resources towards helping children after violence has occurred, while States should set aside adequate resources to address **risk factors** and prevent violence before it occurs. Policies and programmes should address **immediate risk factors, such as a lack of a parent-child bond, family breakdown, abuse of alcohol or drugs**, and access to guns and other weapons. In line with the Millennium Development Goals, attention should be focused on economic and social policies that address **poverty, gender and other forms of inequality, income gaps, unemployment, urban overcrowding, and other factors which undermine society.**

4. Promote non-violent values and awareness-raising

States and civil society must strive to change attitudes that condone or normalise violence against children. This includes stereotypical gender roles and discrimination, acceptance of corporal punishment, and harmful traditional practices. States should ensure that information about children's rights is publicised and understood, including by children. Public information campaigns should be used to sensitise the public about the harmful effects that violence has on children. States should encourage the media to promote non-violent values and ensure full respect for the rights of the child in all media coverage through guidelines.

5. Enhance the capacity of all who work with and for children

States should invest in systematic education and training programmes for all those who work with and for children and families to prevent, detect and respond to violence against children, by promoting knowledge and respect for children's rights. Codes of conduct and clear standards of practice which ban all forms of violence, should be created and put into action.

6. Provide recovery and social reintegration services

States should provide accessible, child-sensitive and universal health and social services. This should include pre-hospital and emergency care, legal assistance to children and, where appropriate, their families, when violence is discovered. Health, criminal justice and social service systems should be designed to meet the special needs of children.

7. Ensure participation of children

As stated in Article 12 of the Convention on the Rights of the Child, States must actively listen to children and respect their views in all aspects of prevention, response and monitoring of violence against them. Children's organisations and child-led initiatives to address violence guided by the best interests of the child should be supported and encouraged.

8. Create accessible and child-friendly reporting systems and services

States should establish safe, well-publicised, confidential and accessible mechanisms for children, their representatives and others to report violence against children. All children, including those in care and justice institutions, should be aware of the existence of mechanisms of complaint. Mechanisms such as telephone helplines, through which children can report abuse, speak to a trained counsellor in confidence and ask for support and advice, should be established. The creation of other ways of reporting violence through new technologies should be considered.

9. Ensure accountability and end impunity

States should build community confidence in the justice system by, among other things, bringing all perpetrators of violence against children to justice. They must ensure that they are held accountable through appropriate criminal, civil, administrative and professional proceedings and punishments. Persons convicted of violent offences and sexual abuse of children should be prevented from working with children.

10. Address the gender dimension of violence against children
States should ensure that anti-violence policies and programmes are designed and implemented from a gender perspective, taking into account the different risks facing girls and boys in respect of violence. States should promote and protect the human rights of women and girls and address all forms of gender discrimination as part of a comprehensive violence-prevention plan.

11. Develop and implement systematic national data collection and research
States should improve data collection and information systems in order to identify vulnerable subgroups, inform policy and programming at all levels, and track progress towards the goal of preventing violence against children. States should use national indicators based on internationally agreed standards, and ensure that data are compiled, analysed and distributed to monitor progress over time. Where not currently in place, birth, death and marriage data registries with full national coverage should be created and maintained. States should also create and maintain data on children without parental care and children in the criminal justice system. Data should be separated according to sex, age, urban/rural, household and family characteristics, education and ethnicity. States should also conduct research on violence against children across settings where violence occurs. This should include interview studies with children and parents, with particular attention to vulnerable groups of girls and boys.

12. Strengthen international commitment
All States must ratify and implement the Convention on the Rights of the Child and its two Optional Protocols on the involvement of children in armed conflict and on the sale of children, child prostitution and child pornography. All reservations that are incompatible with the object and purpose of the Convention and the Optional Protocols should be withdrawn in accordance with the Vienna Declaration and Plan of Action of the World Conference on Human Rights of 1993.

States should ratify all relevant international and regional human rights instruments that provide protection for children including: the Convention against Torture and Other Cruel, Inhuman or Degrading Treatment or Punishment and its Optional Protocol; the Rome Statute of the International Criminal Court; the Convention on the Elimination of All Forms of Discrimination against Women and its Optional Protocol; ILO Conventions No. 138 on the Minimum Age for Admission to Employment and No. 182 on the

Worst Forms of Child Labour; and the United Nations Convention against Transnational Organised Crime and the Protocol to Prevent, Suppress and Punish Trafficking in Persons, Especially Women and Children, supplementing the United Nations Convention against Transnational Organised Crime.

States should implement all their international legal obligations and strengthen their cooperation with the treaty bodies.

States should fulfil their commitments on the prevention of violence made at the Special Session of the General Assembly on children, and in the context of the WHO Health Assembly resolution 76 on implementing the recommendations of the *World Report on Violence and Health*. A number of regional public health resolutions further reinforce these commitments.

Measures to prevent and respond to violence against children should be made part of national planning processes by 2007. This should include the appointment of a focal point, preferably at ministerial level. Violence against children should be made illegal, and a plan to develop reliable national data-collection systems should be created, by 2009.

States should provide information on the implementation of these recommendations in their reports to the Committee on the Rights of the Child. A progress report on the implementation of the recommendations should be submitted to the General Assembly at its sixty-fifth session.

PROPOSAL FOR A SPECIAL REPRESENTATIVE TO THE UN SECRETARY GENERAL

In view of the importance of coordination in addressing violence against children, the Independent Expert recommends that the General Assembly request the Secretary-General to appoint a special representative on violence against children. This person should act as a high-profile global advocate to promote prevention and elimination of all violence against children, encourage international and regional cooperation and ensure follow-up to the present recommendations. The special representative should distribute and promote the recommendations of the Study in different international, regional and national forums. He or she should periodically report to the Human Rights Council and the General Assembly, and should coordinate the preparation of a report on implementation of the recommendations, to be presented to the General Assembly at its sixty-fifth session. The special representative will work closely with, but not duplicate the work of, the Committee on the Rights of the Child, the Special Representative of the Secretary-General for Children and Armed Conflict, the Special Rapporteur on the sale of children, child prostitution and child pornography and the Special Rapporteur on violence against women, its causes and consequences and the Special Rapporteur on trafficking in persons, especially women and children. He or she should work with regional human rights protection systems and all other regional and national follow-up plans. The special representative should have an initial mandate of four years. Building on the successful United Nations partnerships that marked the Study, he or she should be supported by OHCHR, UNICEF and WHO. A United Nations inter-agency group on violence against children with representation from NGOs and children should support follow-up (see full report in documents section).

OTHER RECOMMENDATIONS, INCLUDING ON INTERNATIONAL AND REGIONAL FOLLOW-UP

International organisations should encourage and support Governments in the implementation of these recommendations. International financial institutions are recommended to review their policies and activities to take account of the impact they may have on children. United Nations country teams should include measures to address violence against children within poverty reduction plans, country assessments and development frameworks. Governments should consider establishing an ombudsperson or commissioner for children's rights in keeping with the Principles relating to the status of national human right institutions (The Paris Principles). Working closely with other agencies dealing with public health and child protection issues, this institution should have a clear mandate to monitor children' s rights at regional, national and local levels. Where appropriate, they should have the authority to receive and investigate complaints of violations of children's rights from the public, including children. In light of the contribution of regional organisations in the development of the Study, these should be involved in implementing and following-up the recommendations. The development of regional mechanisms should be encouraged as an important part of the overall framework for follow-up as well monitoring implementation.

THE STUDY DOCUMENTS: WHERE TO FIND THEM

Report of the independent expert for the United Nations study on violence against children, 61st Session UN General Assembly, 2006, A/61/299; available at <www.violencestudy.org/IMG/pdf/English.pdf>. This is the short, 34-page formal report transmitted to the General Assembly by the UN Secretary-General in October 2006, available in the six UN languages: English, French, Spanish, Arabic, Chinese and Russian (…).

World Report on Violence against Children, Paulo Sérgio Pinheiro, published by the United Nations Secretary-General's Study on Violence against Children, Geneva, 2006; can be downloaded in English in PDF format at <www.violencestudy.org> (…).

This is the complementary 364-page report, which includes prefaces from the UN Secretary-General and a foreword from the High Commissioner for Human Rights, directors of UNICEF and WHO and a message from the NGO Advisory Panel. There is an introductory chapter and a commentary on relevant international human rights law and standards. Five major chapters cover violence against children in the home and family, schools, care and justice systems, workplaces and the community.

Follow-up to the UN Secretary-General's Study on Violence against Children: Establishment of a Special Representative of the Secretary-General, NGO Advisory Council for follow up to the UN Study on Violence Against Children, <www.crin.org/docs/SRSG_May2007.pdf>.

Child-friendly materials
A child-friendly version of the report and educational materials are also available: *United Nations Secretary-General's Study on Violence against Children. Adapted for Children and young people.*

Our right to be protected from violence: activities for learning and taking action for children and young people. These can also be downloaded in English in PDF format at <www.violencestudy.org> (...). *Safe you and Safe Me*, for younger children: <www.violencestudy.org/IMG/pdf/safeyoufinal.pdf>.

Reports of the nine regional consultations held in connection with the Study are available at: <www.violencestudy.org>, as well as an overview of the public submissions received by the Independent Expert: see <www.violencestudy.org/r95>. The reports of the expert thematic consultations are also available; see: <www.violencestudy.org/r180>. Responses to the detailed questionnaire circulated by the Independent Expert in 2004 were received from 137 Member States; available at <www.ohchr.org/english/bodies/crc/study.htm>.

The Child Rights Information Network (CRIN) acts as a civil society gateway to the Study and its follow-up and many materials connected with the Study and the Regional Consultations are available at <www.crin.org/violence/index.asp>.

This summary of the Secretary General's Study on Violence Against Children by Paulo Sergio Pinheiro was published by the NGO Advisory Council for Follow up to the UN Study on Violence Against Children. The Council includes nine regional representatives and nine representing international NGOs: CRIN, Defense for Children International, ECPAT, Global Initiative to End All Corporal Punishment of Children, Human Rights Watch, OMCT/World Organization Against Torture, Plan International, Save the Children Alliance, and World Vision.

"If they [kids] are beaten at home, they are going to beat, that is, if parents ill treat them or don't talk to them, kids will beat others because they are beaten. They are going to drag with them what they see at home. This is the basis of violence." – Adolescent girls, Latin America, 2005.

"I used to think that being a girl I don't have the right to protest when boys and men misbehave with me. But after joining the child club I came to know that I have all the right to feel safe all the time. I can protect and protest whenever someone tries to harass or abuse me. My body is mine and I have the right to protect it." – Girl, 12, South Asia, 2005.

"You were not here to protect me as a child and I'll live with that damage for the rest of my life. But I vow, as a young person in this society, to put an end to this violence for the next generation. You can stand by me, or you can turn your back." – Youth leader, survivor and street involved youth, North America, 2005.

DEFINITIONS

UN Study on violence against children (A/61/299), para 8:

The Study adopts the **definition of the child** as contained in article 1 of the Convention on the Rights of the Child: "[e]very human being below the age of eighteen years unless, under the law applicable to the child, majority is attained earlier."

The **definition of violence** is that of article 19 of the Convention: "all forms of physical or mental violence, injury and abuse, neglect or negligent treatment, maltreatment or exploitation, including sexual abuse." It also draws on the definition in the *World Report on Violence and Health* (2002): the intentional use of physical force or power, threatened or actual, against a child, by an individual or group, that either results in or has a high likelihood of resulting in actual or potential harm to the child's health, survival, development or dignity.

TASK/TEXT 1.2:

TASK/TEXT 1.2.1: UN – NEW POST TO COMBAT VIOLENCE AGAINST CHILDREN

Crinmail Violence against Children 34 – 27 November 2007 (<www.crin.org>)

NEW YORK, 27 November 2007 – The UN General Assembly's decision today to establish a Special Representative to the Secretary-General on violence against children is a welcome step toward combating this worldwide problem, said a broad coalition of human rights groups and child rights advocates. The decision to create the new position was made under the General Assembly's annual resolution on the Rights of the Child, adopted today in the Third Committee [by a vote of 176 to 1]. The only country voting against was the United States.

The appointment follows the release last year of the UN Secretary-General's Study on Violence Against Children. This study exposed the shocking scope of violence against children worldwide and its devastating effects on children, their families, their communities and broader society.

"Violence is a daily reality for millions of children around the world," said Jo Becker of Human Rights Watch, co-chair of the NGO Advisory Council for follow-up to the UN Study. "The Special Representative to the Secretary-General will provide high-level international leadership to confront this global scourge."

More than 1,000 non-governmental organisations from 134 countries around the world signed a petition launched by the NGO Advisory Council calling for the appointment of the Special Representative.

The mandate for the new Special Representative includes enhancing the visibility of all forms of violence against children, advocating for the elimination of this violence, and supporting the implementation of the Violence Study's recommendations. Other aspects of the mandate include identifying and sharing good practices and enhancing coordination and communication among key actors (including the UN system, member states, NGOs, children and youth).

"It is vital to maintain the momentum created by the Violence Study and maximise its potential for achieving the necessary urgent action," said Roberta Cecchetti of the International Save the Children Alliance and a Council co-chair. "NGOs look forward to working with the Special Representative to protect all children's right to live free from violence."

The NGO Advisory Council also welcomed the resolution's call to change attitudes that condone or normalise violence, including violent forms of child discipline. However, the NGO Advisory Council expressed deep regret that the General Assembly's annual resolution had once again failed to explicitly identify corporal punishment among the many forms of violence that states are urged to prohibit and eliminate. This is a key recommendation made both by UN Secretary-General's Study on Violence Against Children and the Committee on the Rights of the Child.

The NGO Advisory Council was established in 2006 to enhance follow-up to the UN Study on Violence against Children. It includes nine regional representatives, and nine representatives from international NGOs. The international NGO representatives include Human Rights Watch, Save the Children, the Global Initiative to End all Corporal Punishment of Children, the Child Rights Information Network, Defence for Children International, ECPAT (End Child Prostitution, Child Pornography and Trafficking of Children for

Sexual Purposes), World Organization against Torture, Plan International, and World Vision.

TASK/TEXT 1.2.2: MISSION IMPOSSIBLE? IN SEARCH OF AN SRSG

Crinmail Violence against Children 37 – 21 November 2008, <www.crin.org>

Two years after the UN Study on Violence Against Children revealed widespread violence faced by millions of children worldwide, we are still waiting for the UN to act by appointing a Special Representative on Violence Against Children. In 2006, the Secretary-General's Study on Violence against Children found that the short and long-term repercussions of the violence faced by millions of children are devastating – including injuries, disabilities, life-long emotional and psychological effects, sometimes death, as well as significant economic and other costs to society. The Study presented a comprehensive set of recommendations detailing necessary steps to prevent and respond to violence against children. The study further recommended that "governments act to establish a Special Representative to the Secretary General on Violence against Children (SRSG)." The role of the SRSG would be to "act as a high-profile global advocate to promote prevention and elimination of all violence against children."

As the process stalls, children wait

The UN General Assembly did not act on this recommendation in 2006, but requested the Secretary-General's independent expert, Paulo Sergio Pinheiro, to submit to the 62nd session of the General Assembly a report on progress made and "to anticipate the necessary strategy for the implementation of the study."

In May 2007, the NGO Advisory Council for follow up to the UN Study on Violence Against Children invited NGOs from around the world to sign a petition calling on UN member states to fully implement the Study's important recommendations, and calling on the UN to establish a Special Representative to the UN Secretary-General on Violence against Children. The petition gathered over 1,000 signatures from around the world and was presented at the 62nd session of the UN General Assembly (GA) in October 2007.

The 2007 GA Resolution on the rights of the child reaffirmed the NGO request, affirming the need for "the Secretary-General to appoint for a period of three years a Special Representative on violence against children, at the highest possible level" (...). The resolution was adopted on 18 December 2007 by a vote of 183 to 1.

A loud silence

Despite NGO pressure and the full force of a GA resolution, such a crucial appointment remains elusive. Children must wait.

Throughout the process, the NGO Advisory Council and other NGOs made direct representation to the Secretary-General's office on matters relating to the appointment of the SRSG, including on the terms of reference, the location of the office of the SRSG and the level at which such a post was to be established. In May 2008, CRIN invited all signatories to the 2007 petition to write to the Secretary-General's office calling on him once again to establish the SRSG. Still no word.

As the 63rd session of the UN GA gets underway, sources suggest that a number of candidates have been interviewed by a panel which included representatives of the SG's office, the Special Representative on children and armed conflict and UNICEF, who then proposed a short list of three for interview by the Secretary General. An announcement is said to be imminent.

Meanwhile, the GA is currently debating this year's resolution on the rights of the child. A Draft resolution of the Third Committee includes strong language in relation to the SRSG's apointment – or lack thereof – expressing "deep concern about the delay in the appointment of a new Special Representative on violence against children, as requested by the General Assembly in its resolution 62/141, and requests the Secretary-General to fully comply with the request and to take urgent action to appoint, in accordance with the resolution, at the highest possible level and without delay, a Special Representative."

No more excuses

It is time for the Secretary-General to act. As Prof Pinheiro, once said: "We should stop excusing ourselves and respond to the children's call for a world free from violence ... there are no excuses for inaction. We should treat this as a matter of urgency. We must prove to our children that we fulfill our commitments if we expect them to do the same. And they should not have to wait until they are adults to confirm our commitment. The reality can and must change now."

TASK/TEXT 1.2.3: VIOLENCE AGAINST CHILDREN – SECRETARY-GENERAL NAMES SPECIAL REPRESENTATIVE

Crinmail Violence against Children 43 – 1 May 2009, <www.crin.org>

NEW YORK, 1 May 2009 – It has been a long time coming, and some lost heart altogether, but the UN has finally answered the calls of child rights advocates across the world and appointed a top-level official on violence against children.

Secretary-General Ban Ki Moon today announced the appointment of **Marta Santos Pais** as his Special Representative on Violence Against Children (SRSG).

Human Rights Watch's Jo Becker, co-Chair of the NGO Advisory Council for the follow-up to the UN Study on Violence Against Children, told CRIN: "We've waited a long time for this appointment, and are delighted that Marta Santos Pais will be taking on this critical new mandate. The SRSG will be a powerful voice for children, and a force to challenge the entrenched laws, attitudes and practices that still cause children to suffer intolerable violence. We are incredibly eager to work with her to make sure that the important recommendations that came out of the UN Study are fully implemented."

The establishment of the post was one of 12 recommendations of the UN Study on Violence Against Children, concluded in 2006. The Study, by **Paulo Sergio Pinheiro**, found that millions of children throughout the world live with the devastating effects of violence, including injuries, disabilities, life-long emotional and psychological effects, sometimes death, as well as significant economic and other costs to society. The study recommended that "governments act to establish a Special Representative to the Secretary General on Violence against Children (SRSG)." The role of the SRSG would be to "act as a high-profile global advocate to promote prevention and elimination of all violence against children."

The new role

Marta Santos Pais is currently Executive Director of UNICEF Innocenti Research Centre, based in Florence, Italy. She also served on the [CRC] Committee on the Rights of the Child.

Peter Newell, Co-Chair of the NGO Advisory Council and Coordinator of the Global Initiative to End All Corporal Punishment of Children, said the new position was crucial. He said: "Making a success of this long-awaited appointment is of huge importance to children in all States. Marta's demonstrated deep commitment to children's status as rights holders, her fearless advocacy of difficult issues and her very broad international experience should enable her and her office to quickly build on the momentum established by Paulo Pinheiro's Study. The task, as the Study set out, is enormous and urgent. As Paulo reported to the UN in 2007: 'Children are sick of being called "the future": they want to enjoy their childhood, free of violence, now!'."

Delay

In October 2007, the NGO Advisory Council launched a petition, signed by over 1,000 NGOs from across the world, calling on Member States to implement the Study's recommendations, including the appointment of the SRSG. The 2007 General Assembly resolution on the rights of the child endorsed the NGO request, demanding that the "the Secretary-General (...) appoint for a period of three years a Special Representative on violence against children, at the highest possible level" (...). The resolution was adopted on 18 December 2007 by a vote of 183 to 1. The GA's resolution on the rights of the child in November 2008 went on to express "deep concern about the delay in the appointment of a new Special Representative on violence against children (...) and requests the Secretary-General to fully comply with the request and to take urgent action to appoint, in accordance with the resolution, at the highest possible level and without delay, a Special Representative." During the debate on the rights of the child at the Human Rights Council session in March, a number of experts from the UN, representatives from Europe and Latin America, as well as a number of States, expressed their concern regarding the delay in the appointment and called, once again, on the SG to appoint the SRSG without further delay.

TASK/TEXT 1.3: VIOLENCE AGAINST CHILDREN (OHCHR)

<www.ohchr.org/EN/NewsEvents/Pages/ViolenceAgainstChildren.aspx>

The United Nations General Assembly in November 2007 established the post of Special Representative of the Secretary-General on violence against children. The resolution encourages the Office of the High Commissioner for Human Rights (OHCHR), the United Nations Children's Fund (UNICEF), the World Health Organization (WHO) and the International Labour Organization (ILO) to cooperate with and support the Special Representative.

Much of the violence against children, including physical violence, psychological violence, discrimination, neglect and maltreatment, remains hidden and is often socially approved. Although the consequences may vary according to the nature and severity of the violence inflicted, the short- and long-term repercussions for children are very often grave and damaging. The physical, emotional and psychological scars of violence can have severe implications for a child's development, health and ability to learn.

These are some of the conclusions of the United Nations Secretary-General's Study on Violence against Children presented to the General Assembly in 2006. The study provided for the first time a comprehensive global view of the range and scale of violence against children. Independent Expert Professor Paulo Sérgio Pinheiro led the Study, in collaboration with OHCHR, UNICEF, and WHO. Since 2001, when the Secretary-General was requested by the General Assembly to conduct an in-depth study on the question of violence against children, OHCHR, along with other UN agencies, has made an advocacy effort to bring this issue to the general public's attention.

The Study, which combines human rights, public health and child protection perspectives, focuses on five 'settings' where violence occurs: the home and family, schools and educational settings, institutions (care and judicial), the workplace, and the community.

Extreme violence against children may hit the headlines but the Study concludes that for many children violence is routine, a part of their daily reality.

"Violence against children is a violation of their human rights, a disturbing reality of our societies," says Louise Arbour, United Nations High Commissioner for Human Rights. "It can never be justified whether for disciplinary reasons or cultural tradition. No such thing as a 'reasonable' level of violence is acceptable. Legalized violence against children in one context risks tolerance of violence against children generally."

TASK/TEXT 1.4: VIOLENCE AGAINST WOMEN (OHCHR)

<www.ohchr.org/EN/NewsEvents/Pages/ViolenceAgainstWomen.aspx>

To combat the rising phenomenon of violence against women and girls, those committing the crimes must be prosecuted. On the occasion of the International Day for the Elimination of Violence against Women (25 November), United Nations High Commissioner for Human Rights Louise Arbour said most perpetrators of these crimes enjoyed impunity.

"This impunity is built on a foundation of discrimination and inequality. States have largely accepted the international human rights framework in place to prevent, condemn and punish discrimination against women. But unless these inequalities are addressed, including in the economic and social spheres, the violence will persist."

Countless women and girls are killed, mutilated, beaten, raped, sold into sexual slavery or tortured every day in the world. Violence against women and girls, including domestic violence and sexual violence, is increasing. Domestic gender-based violence is still, in some parts of the world, an issue that is confined to the private domain, and a symptom of how women are generally considered as objects. Men often use domestic violence to diminish women's autonomy and self-worth.

"A woman is more likely to remain in a relationship in which she is the victim of domestic violence when the alternative is homelessness for herself and her children. A woman will not report rape if we continue to stigmatize the victims of violence rather than the perpetrators," said the High Commissioner.

Violence against women is one of the most pervasive human rights violations. It devastates lives, fractures communities, and stalls development. At least one out of every three women around the world has been beaten, coerced into sex, or otherwise abused in her lifetime – with the abuser usually someone known to her, according to the *In-Depth Study on All Forms of Violence against Women: Report of the Secretary General*, 2006.

Most of the survivors have little hope of seeing their perpetrators pay for their crimes, and so the violence perpetuates. States must ensure, under international law, that crimes of violence against women and girls are prosecuted and that the economic and social rights of the victims are protected. Putting such a system in place will bring perpetrators to justice, encourage victims and witnesses to testify, and put an end to impunity for crimes of sexual violence against women and girls, including rape.

The International Day for the Elimination of Violence against Women, began the "16 Days of Activism against Gender-based Violence." This campaign, originating from the first Women's Global Leadership Institute, runs until Human Rights Day on 10 December.

TASK/TEXT 1.5: UN CONSULTATION ON VIOLENCE AGAINST CHILDREN IN EUROPE AND CENTRAL ASIA (5–7 JULY 2005, LJUBLJANA, SLOVENIA)

<www.violencestudy.org/europe-ca/Word/KIT/overview.doc>
<www.violencestudy.org/europe-ca/Word/KIT/HOME.doc>

Over the next twelve months, around 3,500 children under the age of 15 will die as a result of physical assault and neglect in the world's richest nations. In Germany and the United Kingdom, two children die every week – three in France [one in The Netherlands]. More than 1 million children are trafficked across international borders every year. Over 300 million children in the world work – some of them in hazardous conditions, some of them forced. Street children fight for survival daily on the streets of Europe and Central Asia, exploited by criminals, dodging the police. One out of every ten schoolchildren faces violence at school – some of it so traumatic that suicide seems the only way out.

These figures from UNICEF, the World Health Organization (WHO), the International Labour Organization and the United Nations show that the children of our region are as vulnerable to violence as any in the world. We can't assume that we are more developed or more civilized – the figures show we are not. Behind every case that hits the headlines and shocks people's hearts there are thousands of children who simply become statistics. Violence against children is hidden and corrosive. It destroys lives and potential and breeds societies that accept the unacceptable – that children can be punched, kicked, beaten, starved, taunted and tortured.

Violence has so many different faces, and can take place anywhere children spend their time – in the family, in the street, in schools, in State care and custody. Anyone who comes into direct contact with children is a potential perpetrator – parent, caregiver, relative, community member, an other child, school teacher, police officer. But no matter what the abuse and where it takes place, the root causes are often the same. The causes of violence include:

Discrimination – Whether it is for reasons of gender, ethnic origin, religion, disability, disease or sexual orientation, discrimination legitimizes violent behaviour. Discrimination in social, education or health services can result in ethnic groups, such as Roma, being socially excluded, increasing the vulnerability of children to violence.

Social acceptance – Countries across Europe and Central Asia have different thresholds of acceptance to violence. For instance, almost all countries accept corporal punishment as a means of disciplining children. These attitudes reflect the way that people react, both in their own behaviour and in the low incidence of reports of violence.

Poverty and social stress – Studies on child maltreatment deaths within the family in rich nations have found that poverty and stress, along with drug and alcohol abuse seem to be closely linked with child abuse and neglect. At its worst, poverty has proved an underlying factor in various world conflicts that have set communities against each other.

Yet the UN Convention on the Rights of the Child guarantees the physical integrity, safety and dignity of children, and countries have laws to stop violence … don't they?

Somewhere between theory and practice something is missing. And it's time to find out and to act. (…)

The UN Convention on the Rights of the Child calls the family "the natural environment for growth and well-being," but studies throughout Europe and Central Asia paint a darker picture. Quite simply, for many children home is not a haven but a hell – the place where they face the most violence, yet the place where it is the least visible.

Society still hesitates to act against violence within families. Children are often considered the "property" of parents, rather than people with their own rights to protection. Violent and humiliating punishment by parents and close carers remains lawful and very common in the majority of Europe and Central

Asia countries. Harmful traditional practices such as female genital circumcision and honour killings are left unchallenged because of ignorance or a fear of offending.

Every day, many children across Europe are hit, kicked, threatened, ridiculed or isolated. If an adult were subject to any of these actions it would be a criminal assault in any European country. (…)

What is being done?

Reports show that Europe is ahead of other regions in taking measures to stop violence against children. All countries in Europe are quickly changing from a past in which violent and humiliating punishment of children was common and accepted. Sweden started the process of law reform half a century ago and became the first State in the world to explicitly ban corporal punishment in 1979. It is now also illegal in Austria, Bulgaria, Croatia, Cyprus, Denmark, Finland, Germany, Hungary, Iceland, Italy, Latvia, Norway, Portugal, Romania and Ukraine. Other countries, which have said they intend to bring in a law against corporal punishment, include the Netherlands [2007], Slovakia and Slovenia.

Law reform is accelerating. The European Court of Human Rights has issued a number of judgements that require laws against child violence to be toughened up in Europe and stressed that Governments have an obligation to criminalize non-consensual sex.

Programmes to promote good parenting are a growing trend in Europe. For example, in Moldova, parent education is being mainstreamed through the health-care system. In Serbia and Montenegro, mobile outreach teams and multidisciplinary groups for child protection have been set up in towns and cities using different professional skills and mobilizing the communities.

How do we go forward?

- States should be made accountable for failures to protect children from all forms of violence;
- Europe must become a corporal punishment free zone;
- The best interests of affected children should be the primary consideration in all policies and individual decisions on action to prevent and respond to violence against children;
- Governments must listen to children and take their views into account when they decide on anti-violence action;
- Schools, the health service and social services need to be mobilized to teach adults that violence against children is wrong;
- Children should learn how to solve conflicts non-violently. They should learn about sexual responsibility and consent at school;

- All deaths and serious injury to children in the home should be routinely and rigorously investigated;
- Anyone working in child protection should be properly paid, trained and subject to ethical codes;
- Courts should set up child-friendly ways of taking evidence;
- Regional and international human rights mechanisms should be open to children. For instance, they should be able to bring cases to the Court of Human Rights;
- Child victims/survivors of violence must have ready access to free treatment focused on rehabilitation and reintegration;
- Journalists should play their part in showing the extent of the problem, not just sensationalizing individual cases;
- European countries need to be made more aware of harmful traditional practices.

TASK/TEXT 1.6: IRAN – GIRL, 16, HANGED

Crinmail 921 – 4 October 2007, <www.crin.org> [Source: Sunday Mirror (UK), Associated Press]

3 October 2007 – It was exactly 6 a.m. and the start of another blisteringly hot summer day [in 2004; *see* Crinmail 922] when 16-year-old Atefeh Rajabi was dragged from her prison cell and taken to be executed.

Every step of the way the troubled teenager plagued by mental problems shouted 'repentance, repentance' as the militiamen marched her to the town's Railway Square.

The Iranian judge who had sentenced Atefeh to death was left unmoved as he personally put the noose around her neck and signalled to the crane driver.

Kicking and screaming, Atefeh was left dangling for 45 minutes from the arm of the crane as the crowd sobbed and – under their breath – damned the mullahs.

Atefeh's crime? Offending public morality. She was found guilty of 'acts incompatible with chastity' by having sex with an unmarried man, even though friends say Atefeh was in such a fragile mental state that she wasn't in a position to say no.

But Judge Haji Rezaii was determined she should hang, regardless of the rules of international law which say only adults over 18 can be executed, and that the courts have a duty to children and the mentally ill.

The brutal end to Atefeh's short life has shone a new light on Iran's Shariah law, where adultery, theft and rape all carry the same punishment – death.

Officially around 100 people – some just children like Atefeh – are executed each year. But human rights groups say the true figure could be much higher in a country where only half of the women can read, only one in 10 have a job and two-thirds are beaten in their homes.

Difficult life led to mental health problems

Life was never easy for Atefeh, who was brought up in the industrial town of Neka, 250 miles from Tehran and close to the Caspian Sea. Her mother died when she was a child and her father Ghasseem, a heroin addict, left her grandparents to bring her up. She suffered from bi-polar disorder, which led to severe mood swings from hyperactivity to depression.

Mina, a childhood friend, said Atefeh was abused by a close relative. 'She never dared talk about it with an adult,' said Mina. 'If she had told her teacher they'd have called her a whore. Tell the police? They lock you up and rape you.' Atefeh first appeared in court, accused of having sex with an unmarried man at 14. Over the next two years she was accused of the same crime with different men.

They denied it and were sentenced to the lash and then released. But Atefeh pleaded guilty and each time received 100 lashes and a prison term. Mina said: 'Atefeh sometimes talked about what these "moral" Islamic policemen did to her while she was in jail. She still had nightmares about that. Atefeh said her mood swings made it easy for men to take advantage of her, and that most of her lovers were in the security force.'

Two of them were members of the anti-vice militia. They encouraged other men to sign statements saying Atefeh had engaged in vice, and even claimed she had AIDS.

It was when Atefeh appeared before Judge Rezaii for a fourth time that she lost her temper – and also her life. In a rage she tore off her hi jab – a headscarf – and told the judge she had been raped and it was his duty to punish her tormentors, not their victim.

Rezaii told her she would hang for her 'sharp tongue' and that he would put the noose around her neck himself. It became a personal crusade as he travelled to Tehran and convinced the Supreme Court to uphold his verdict.

Two petitions by her friends, saying she was mentally unwell, were ignored. Her father produced her birth certificate proving she was 16. Yet the judges 'decreed' she was 22.

The day before she died she wrote again, saying: 'Repentance, repentance, repentance.' In Iranian law anyone who shows remorse has an automatic stay of execution and a right to appeal, but she was ignored.

Amnesty International UK director Kate Allen said: 'The killing of Atefeh is a catalogue of the most appalling human rights violations. The public hanging of a child, believed to be mentally incompetent, totally beggars belief. To hang a child flies in the face of all that is humane.'

Response from the UN

Louise Arbour, the UN High Commissioner for Human Rights, said she met with Iranian officials during a visit to Tehran earlier this month and urged them to impose a moratorium on the execution of minors.

'Even if the legislation in the books appears to permit the imposition of the death penalty on minors … it would be imperative that they not be executed,' she told journalists in Geneva.

Iran is one of the few countries in the world that executes minors, in violation of the Convention on the Rights of the Child (Article 37).

On Sunday Iranian media reported that a 16 year old was among two teenagers sentenced to death for raping and killing two young boys earlier this year.

Arbour said she opposed the death penalty in principle, but that countries who continue to apply it should at least abide by international law, which prohibits the execution of children.

TASK/TEXT 1.7:

TASK/TEXT 1.7.1: STATEMENT BY UN HIGH COMMISSIONER FOR HUMAN RIGHTS ON THE ENTRY INTO FORCE OF THE ARAB CHARTER ON HUMAN RIGHTS

<www.unhchr.ch/huricane/huricane.nsf/view01/6C211162E43235FAC12573E00056E19D?opendocument>

UN High Commissioner for Human Rights, Louise Arbour, issued the following statement today:

Geneva, 30 January 2008 – On 24 January 2008 (incorrectly issued as 24 March statement), I welcomed the 7th ratification required to bring the Arab Charter on Human Rights into force. While emphasizing universal human rights, I noted that regional systems of protection and promotion can help further strengthen the enjoyment of human rights. As the 1993 Vienna Declaration and Programme of Action affirmed "regional arrangements play a fundamental role in promoting and protecting human rights. They should reinforce universal human rights standards, as contained in international human rights instruments, and their protection."

Throughout the development of the Arab Charter, my office shared concerns with the drafters about the incompatibility of some of its provisions with international norms and standards. These concerns included the approach to death penalty for children and the rights of women and non-citizens. Moreover, to the extent that it equates Zionism with racism, we reiterated that the Arab Charter is not in conformity with General Assembly Resolution 46/86, which rejects that Zionism is a form of racism and racial discrimination. OHCHR does not endorse these inconsistencies. We continue to work with all stakeholders in the region to ensure the implementation of universal human rights norms.

TASK/TEXT 1.7.2: DEATH PENALTY – NEW ARAB CHARTER DEVIATES FROM THE CONVENTION ON THE RIGHTS OF THE CHILD

Crinmail 953 – 31 January 2008, <www.crin.org>

31 January 2008 – The Arab Charter on Human Rights contains provisions that do not meet international norms and standards, including the application of the death penalty for children, and the treatment of women and non-citizens, the United Nations human rights chief said.

UN High Commissioner for Human Rights Louise Arbour issued a statement saying that her office "does not endorse these inconsistencies [and] we continue to work with all stakeholders in the region to ensure the implementation of universal human rights norms."

Conflict with the CRC?

Under the Arab Charter, the death penalty can be applied to children in certain circumstances, in contradiction with its prohibition in the UN Convention on the Rights of the Child.

Article 37 of the Convention on the Rights of the Child forbids the death penalty for children under the age of 18 years. However, Article 7 of the Charter states:

> "Sentence of death shall not be imposed on persons under 18 years of age, unless otherwise stipulated in the laws in force at the time of the commission of the crime."

But, another provision in the Charter suggests that the Convention may override it. Article 43 of the Charter says:

> "Nothing in this Charter may be construed or interpreted as impairing the rights and freedoms protected by the domestic laws of the States parties or those set forth in the

> international and regional human rights instruments which the States parties have adopted or ratified, including the rights of women, the rights of the child and the rights of persons belonging to minorities."

Human rights law expert Professor Bill Bowring, of the University of London, said: "It would seem to me that if a country has ratified both the Charter and the Convention, it is going to run into problems."

The Arab Charter entered into force earlier this month after seven countries ratified the text, prompting Ms. Arbour to release a statement last Thursday in which she noted that while human rights are universal, "regional systems of promotion and protection can further help strengthen the enjoyment of human rights."

Ms. Arbour said that throughout the development of the Charter, her office shared concerns with the drafters about the incompatibility of some provisions with international norms and standards. "These concerns included the approach to death penalty for children and the rights of women and non-citizens."

The global campaign against the death penalty for all people secured a landmark victory last month when the United Nations General Assembly endorsed the call for a worldwide moratorium (suspension) on executions.

The story of the Charter

The Arab Charter on Human Rights (ACHR) was adopted by the Council of the League of Arab States by its resolution 5437 (102nd regular session) on 15 September 1994. The ACHR will enter into force on 15 March 2008, 60 days after ratification by the seventh state, the United Arab Emirates. This followed ratification by Jordan, Bahrain, Algeria, Syria, Palestine and Libya. The revised version was adopted by the 16th Arab Summit, hosted in Tunis in May 2004.

In April 2002, the office of the High Commissioner for Human Rights officially approached the Arab League Secretary General to form a working group of Arab independent experts working in the UN human rights bodies, with the aim of revising the ACHR in order to be consistent with international human rights standards. The experts included members of the Committee on the Rights of the Child.

It is unclear why the Charter was amended, although NGOs working in Lebanon have suggested the revision may in part be due to anti-terror initiatives and the number of children currently in detention on terror charges.

TASK/TEXT 1.8:

TASK/TEXT 1.8.1: SOMALIA – GIRL OF 13 STONED FOR BEING RAPED

Crinmail 1032 – 11 November 2008, <www.crin.org>

Contrary to many initial news reports, the girl stoned to death in Somalia last week was 13, not 23, Amnesty International has revealed.

Aisha Ibrahim Duhulow was killed on Monday, 27 October, by a group of 50 men who stoned her to death in a stadium in the southern port of Kismayu, in front of around 1,000 spectators.

Some of the Somali journalists who had reported she was 23 have told Amnesty International that this age was based upon a judgement of her age from her physical appearance.

She was accused of adultery in breach of Islamic law but, her father and other sources told said that she had in fact been raped by three men, and had attempted to report this rape to the al-Shabab militia who control Kismayo, and it was this act that resulted in her being accused of adultery and detained. None of the men she accused of rape were arrested.

"This was not justice, nor was it an execution. This child suffered a horrendous death at the behest of the armed opposition groups who currently control Kismayo," said David Copeman, Amnesty International's Somalia Campaigner.

> "This killing is yet another human rights abuse committed by the combatants to the conflict in Somalia, and again demonstrates the importance of international action to investigate and document such abuses, through an International Commission of Inquiry."

Amnesty International has learnt that:

- Aisha Ibrahim Duhulow was reported as being 23, based upon a judgement on her physical appearance, according to one of the journalists who had reported the stoning. Her actual age was confirmed to Amnesty International by other sources, including her father.
- Her father said she had only travelled to Kismayo from Hagardeer refugee camp in north eastern Kenya three months earlier.
- She was detained by militia of the Kismayo authorities, a coalition of Al-shabab and clan militias. During this time, she was reportedly extremely distressed, with some individuals stating she had become mentally unstable.
- A truckload of stones was brought into the stadium to be used in the stoning.

- At one point during the stoning, nurses were instructed to check whether Aisha Ibrahim Duhulow was still alive when buried in the ground. They removed her from the ground, declared that she was, and she was replaced in the hole where she had been buried for the stoning to continue.
- An individual calling himself Sheik Hayakalah, was quoted on Radio Shabelle saying: "The evidence came from her side and she officially confirmed her guilt, while she told us that she is happy with the punishment under Islamic law." In contradiction to this claim, a number of eye witnesses said she struggled with her captors and had to be forcibly carried into the stadium.
- Inside the stadium, militia members opened fire when some of the witnesses to the killing attempted to save her life, and shot dead a boy who was a bystander. An al-Shabab spokeperson was later reported to have apologized for the death of the child, and said the milita member would be punished.

Background

This killing of Aisha Ibrahim Duhulow demonstrates the cruelty and the inherent discrimination against women of this punishment.

The reports on this killing should be understood within the climate of fear that armed insurgent groups such as al-Shabab have created within the areas they control in Somalia. Government officials, journalists and human rights defenders face death threats and killing if they are perceived to have spoken against al-Shabab, who have waged a campaign of intimidation against the Somali people through such killings.

Since the death, a number of individuals said they have fled from Kismayo out of fear of suffering a similar fate to Aisha Ibrahim Duhulow.

TASK/TEXT 1.8.2: AFGHANISTAN – GIRLS ATTACKED WITH ACID FOR GOING TO SCHOOL

Crinmail 1033 – 13 November 2008, <www.crin.org>

Five Afghan schoolgirls have been attacked with battery acid by suspected Taliban fighters in the southern city of Kandahar. The attack on Wednesday occurred when two men on motorbikes confronted the students outside the Mirwais Nika Girls High School. Two girls were seriously injured by what was discovered to be battery acid. School girls in Kandahar are easily identifiable by their uniform – black trousers, a white shirt, black coat and a headscarf.

"We were on the way to school when two men on motorbikes stopped next to us. One of them threw acid on my sister's face. I tried to help her and then they threw acid on me too," said Latefa, a 16-year-old student.

"We were shouting and people came to see what was going on, then the two men escaped," she said.

Latefa, who did not give her family name, was hurt and Shamsia, her 18-year-old sister, remains in a serious condition with acid burns across her face.

Girls were banned from attending schools under the Taliban government, which ruled Afghanistan from 1996 to 2001. Women were also not allowed to leave the house without a male family member escorting them.

'In shock'

Al Jazeera's David Chater, reporting from Kandahar, said that Shamsia was in shock. "She is shaking, and in extreme pain, and was not able to describe the event," he said. "But Latefa, her sister, said that she is determined to continue her education, and she will not let this attack stop her from learning. Chater also said that the school was empty, as students were afraid to attend classes. The Afghan government condemned the attack, saying it was "unIslamic" and perpetrated by the "country's enemies," a usual reference to Taliban fighters.

"By such actions, they cannot prevent six million children going to school," the government said in a statement. No one immediately claimed responsibility for the acid attack, and Qari Yousef Ahmadi, a Taliban spokesman, denied any involvement.

Bibi Meryam, Latefa and Shamsia's aunt, said that the family had not received any threats not to send their girls to school, but now they would consider keeping the girls at home until security stabilised.

TASK/TEXT 1.9:

TASK/TEXT 1.9.1: SECURITY COUNCIL AND CHILD RIGHTS

<www.crin.org/resources/infoDetail.asp?ID=17990&flag=news>, accessed 30 July 2008

What is the Security Council?

The Security Council has primary responsibility, under the UN Charter, for maintaining international peace and security.

When a complaint concerning a threat to peace is brought before it, the Council's first action is usually to recommend that the parties try to reach agreement by peaceful means.

In some cases, the Council itself undertakes investigation and mediation. It may appoint Special Representatives or request the Secretary-General to do so.

Members of the Security Council

The Council has five permanent members: China, *France*, Russian Federation, *the United Kingdom* and the United States. It has another ten non-permament members who are elected by the General Assembly for a term of two years.

How does the Security Council make decisions?

Each Council member has one vote. Decisions on procedural matters are made by an affirmative vote of at least nine of the 15 members. Decisions on substantive matters require nine votes, including agreement by all five permanent members. This is the rule of "great Power unanimity," often referred to as the "veto" power.

Child rights and the Security Council

The Council began to pay attention to the issue of children and armed conflict when it realised that the use of children in armed conflict had serious consequences for peace and stability. Internal conflicts give rise to displaced families and communities, refugee flows across borders and the use of child soldiers creating the conditions for long-term regional and international instability.

Since 1999, the Council has become more active on the issue. While its early resolutions contained mainly generic statements about how children should be treated in conflict situations, from 2001 the resolutions began to contain more concrete requests that addressed the practical reality of children involved in situations of armed conflict.

The **Resolutions** of the Security Council on this issue are:

1261 (1999), 1314 (2000), *1379 (2001)*, 1460 (2003), *1539 (2004)* and 1612 (2005).

What are 'Annex I' and 'Annex II' that are often mentioned in relation to the Security Council's work on children and armed conflict?

Annex I and Annex II are "naming and shaming" lists of parties which violate international standards on children and armed conflict. These are included in the UN Secretary General's annual report.

Annex I lists parties on the agenda of the Council and Annex II lists the parties that are not on the Council agenda. States listed in Annex II are concerned that their listing will lead the Council to look at situations of armed conflict in their countries.

How does the Security Council monitor violations of the rights of children who are affected by armed conflict?

The Security Council passed *Resolution 1612* in 2005, which called for the creation of a monitoring and reporting mechanism on six grave violations of children's rights, as well as for the creation of the Working Group on Children and Armed Conflict. The Working Group is piloting its work in seven countries: Burundi, Côte d'Ivoire, Democratic Republic of Congo, Somalia, Sudan, Sri Lanka and Nepal.

The first reports to come out of these mechanisms, which were on Somalia and *Uganda*, were published in May 2007.

Does the Security Council have anyone working specifically on the issue of children and armed conflict?

The Working Group on Children and Armed Conflict works with the Council to:

- review the reports of the Council's monitoring and reporting mechanism.
- look at progress made in developing and implementing action plans by groups named in the Secretary General's lists to stop recruitment and use of children in armed conflict.
- make recommendations on measures to promote the protection of children affected by armed conflict.
- consider country reports. It has begun its work with seven pilot countries: Burundi, Côte d'Ivoire, Democratic Republic of Congo, Somalia, Sudan, Sri Lanka and Nepal.

What are some of the internal challenges which the Security Council faces in protecting children in situations of armed conflict?

France has led on the protection of children and armed conflict within the Security Council, but the other four permanent members have sometimes shown reluctance in acting on this issue. Below are some of the political concerns of different countries and regions.

China and Russia: Both countries have expressed concern that thematic issues such as children and armed conflict provide a possibility for issues which are not on the Council's agenda to be pushed onto the Council's formal agenda.

China: The policy concern about the number of situations that the Security Council is dealing with on its formal agenda.

UK and Russia: The UK expressed concern about the mention of Northern Ireland and Russia about the reference to Chechnya in the Secretary-General's 2003 report. They were included because there were groups involved in recruiting and using children in armed conflict. However, the UK and Russia argued that these were not situations of armed conflict. As a result of these protests, corrections were issued and references to Northern Ireland and Chechnya were dropped.

US: The US argues that the Security Council should be a place for action and must react to specific situations. The US is reluctant for the Council's mandate on this issue to be expanded until it shows clear results.

South America: Some countries in South America, for example, Argentina and Brazil, have been strongly lobbied by Colombia, which often appears in Annex II. They have therefore not always been supportive of initiatives involving armed conflicts listed in Annex II.

Africa: Some African members countries, for example, Tanzania and Benin, have expressed unhappiness that most of the countries listed in Annex 1 are African countries.

Other issues that divide Security Council members on the issue of children and armed conflict include whether there should be one or two annexes and whether to use targeted sanctions or just send warning letters to groups involved in recruiting and using children in armed conflict.

TASK/TEXT 1.9.2: SECURITY COUNCIL – CALL TO END IMPUNITY OF CHILD RIGHTS VIOLATORS

Crinmail Children and Armed Conflict 121 – 30 July 2008, <www.crin.org>

NEW YORK, 17 July 2008 – On the tenth anniversary of the statute classifying child recruitment as a war crime, members of the United Nations Security Council were urged this month to take measures offering greater protection for children in conflict zones and ending impunity for violators of children's rights.

Speaking at the conference, Special Representative of the Secretary-General for Children and Armed Conflict, Radhika Coomaraswamy, said: "The Security Council is the UN body of action on issues of peace and security." She urged that the Security Council consider "imposing targeted measures" against persistent violators on the so-called 'shame list,' an annex compiled by the Working Group on Children in Armed Conflict in the latest Secretary-General's reports.

Conflict and child mortality

In addition to physical crimes and family losses imposed upon children by violence and warfare, armed conflict takes a grave toll on children's health. In conflict and post-conflict areas said Ms Veneman, Executive Director of UNICEF, there is often a resurgence of preventable diseases such as malaria, measles and diarrhoea.

In the 33 countries most affected by armed conflict from 2002 to 2006, 20 have made little or no progress in reducing mortality among children under the age of five.

Sexual violence as 'trigger for action'
Speakers also urged that the rampant use of sexual violence in conflict situations be addressed by the Security Council, recalling the recent adoption of Resolution 1820, which classifies rape as a war crime.

During the meeting, Kathleen Hunt of Watchlist, a coalition of non-governmental organisations, called for expanding the scope of the UN monitoring and reporting arm to include sexual violence as a "trigger for action" by the Special Representative.

Such an expansion of the current annex, which is limited only to parties who use and recruit child soldiers, was supported by representatives of member states Belgium, France, the United States and Italy.

Furthering Resolution 1612
The debate was called by the Government of Viet Nam, whose Minister of Foreign Affairs is the current President of the Security Council. Past debates on the topic of children in armed conflict have resulted in statements, but no new Security Council resolution since the 2005 resolution enabling the monitoring and reporting of child recruitment.

TASK/TEXT 1.10:

TASK/TEXT 1.10.1: EUROPEAN [EU] PARLIAMENT – EU STRATEGY

<www.europarl.europa.eu/oeil/FindByProcnum.do?lang=2&procnum=INI/2007/2093>

[A.] 18/12/2007 – EP [European Union Parliament]: decision of the committee responsible, 1st reading/single reading

The Committee on Civil Liberties, Justice and Home Affairs adopted the own-initiative report by Roberta ANGELILLI (UEN, IT) in response to the Commission's communication on the implementation of an EU strategy on the rights of the child. It calls for children's rights to be mainstreamed in all external policies and actions of the EU and reaffirms its denunciation of all forms of violence against children. MEPs [members of EU Parliament] have called for a wide range of measures aimed at strengthening and completing the strategy proposed by the Commission. In particular, they call on the Commission to create a specific budget line for children's rights, in order to finance work to implement the strategy or projects such as a European early warning system to combat "child abductions."

A strategy based on 4 pillars: the strategy should be rooted in the 4 basic principles enshrined in the UN Convention on the Rights of the Child, which should be better adhered to: 1) protection against all forms of discrimination, 2) the best interests of the child as a primary consideration, 3) the right to life and development, 4) the right to express an opinion and to have that opinion taken into account, in any matter or procedure affecting the child. The MEPs point out, in particular, that the strategy should "recognise the important role of family as a basic institution of society for the survival, protection and development of the child."

However, the strategy proposed by the Commission has proved insufficient for the full protection of the rights of the child. That is why MEPs have proposed a series of measures that can be summarised as follows:

- **Fight strongly against violence towards children**: MEPs call for the pure and simple prohibition of all forms of violence against children; they therefore call for Community legislation that prohibits all forms of violence, sexual abuse, degrading punishment and harmful traditional practices (such as genital mutilations and forced marriages). MEPs condemn all forms of physical, psychological and sexual violence, torture, child abuse and exploitation, child abduction, trafficking in or sale of children and their organs, domestic violence, child pornography, child prostitution, paedophilia, and forced marriages. In addition to strengthening the legislative process, MEPs call for the strategy to include preventive measures against violence. While they applaud the Commission's plan to introduce an EU-wide child helpline telephone number, MEPs point to the need for this service to be free of charge and available 24 hours a day. In addition, Member States must inform children of their rights through informational measures;

- **Fight against sexual exploitation of children**: MEPs reaffirm that this should be considered equivalent to the crime of rape insofar as concerns penal sanctions. All the institutions and the Member States should take a more active part in combating child sexual exploitation, child trafficking and paedophilia by taking all the necessary measures to complete the approximation of national legislation based on common minimum principles. MEPs also call for the buying of sex from a minor to be criminalised. In this respect, they welcome the initiative taken by the Commission aimed at excluding websites involved in online sales of child pornography material from the online payment system (or introducing other restrictions);

– **"Children at risk"**: MEPs propose that the EU define as 'children at risk' **all children who are victims of a social situation that threatens their mental or physical health and/or exposes them to the risks of delinquency.** They call for the adoption of several measures (information campaigns, exchanges of best practice, and so on) to prevent children from being put 'at risk,' including the prevention of juvenile delinquency, such as, for example, measures to prevent the sale of drugs and alcohol. They also call on all Member States to regard a child who has witnessed domestic violence as a victim of crime;

– **Fight against harmful contents**: MEPs call for the creation of an adequate, effective and proportionate regulation system in dialogue with the media (public and private TV companies, advertisers the press, video games, mobile telephones and the Internet) aimed at prohibiting the broadcasting of harmful images and contents (including cyberbullying) and the marketing of violent video games. In this respect, they highlight the growing problem of MMS exchanges of pornographic or child-abuse related images. They also call for the systematic blocking of all illegal websites related to the sexual services of children. In terms of television, MEPs suggest the tightening of controls over the content of television programmes shown at a time when the number of child viewers is at its highest;

– **Juvenile delinquency: towards a global strategy?**: For MEPs, juvenile delinquency, which is increasing at an alarming rate, requires an integrated response, not only at national, but also at Community level. They believe it necessary to draw up a framework programme integrated at Community level, grouping together measures around 1) prevention, 2) social integration of juvenile perpetrators and 3) judicial and extrajudicial intervention. They also call on the Commission to draw up a comprehensive prevention plan against youth crime and bullying in schools and the specific problem of youth gangs. In judicial terms, MEPs call for Member States to favour, where possible, alternatives to imprisonment;

– **Fight against child poverty and social exclusion**: recalling that 19% of children in the European Union live below the poverty line, MEPs call for the implementation of a real strategy to fight against poverty of families. The measures should go from the fight against malnutrition to the prevention of disease but should also focus on the fight against ill treatment, which is often linked to the social situation or legal status of the parents. The EU should, in particular, set itself the objective of ensuring that there are "no homeless children or street children in the EU";

– **Fight against child labour**: MEPs stress that it is essential to ensure that those children who are legally old enough to be in employment are remunerated on the basis of equal work for equal pay. They strongly condemn all forms of child labour, slavery and bonded labour and other forms of work which adversely affect children's health and safety;

– **Towards a Community instrument on adoptions**: Among the most innovative measures, MEPs call for the creation of a Community instrument on adoptions, aimed at improving the quality of care with regard to information services, the preparation of international adoptions, the processing of international adoption applications and post-adoption services. For the MEPs, adoption should take place either within the national country of the child, or by finding a family through international adoption so that placement in institutions is only used as a temporary solution;

– **Better protect migrant children and unaccompanied minors**: MEPs point out that particular attention should be paid to the situation of refugee and migrant children and those seeking asylum so that they can enjoy the same rights as any other child, irrespective of the legal status of their parents. In particular, special attention should be paid to unaccompanied minors as they are often victims of exploitation through organised crime (they represent some 5% of asylum seekers in Europe).

In addition, MEPs call for measures aimed at improving the training and education of children, especially for girls, as well as measures to ensure better childcare facilities in the Member States. They also call for measures to protect child soldiers and victims of war.

Moreover, MEPs call for the possibility to introduce **in all international agreements between the EU and third parties, a specific legally binding clause on the respect of the rights of the child as defined by international law.**

Finally, MEPs call for very specific measures to ensure that all children are registered at birth, making it, according to them, a basic legal right such as obtaining a nationality or an identity at birth.

[B.] 16/01/2008 – EP: non-legislative resolution

The European Parliament adopted a resolution based on the own-initiative report drawn up by Roberta ANGELILLI (UEN, IT) in response to the Commission's communication on an EU strategy on the rights of the child. The resolution was adopted by 630 votes for, 26 against and 62 abstentions.

Overview of the strategy: Parliament calls on the Commission to put forward a proposal to create a **specific budget line** for children's rights, in order to finance work to implement the Commission Communication, and child-specific projects, such as a European early warning system on child abductions. The budget line should also include subsidies for NGO networks working in this field and ensure children's participation in the work to implement that Communication and those projects. It also calls for an **effective monitoring system backed with financial means and annual reports** to ensure the implementation of the commitments set out in the Commission Communication and the future strategy on the rights of the child. Furthermore, the Commission should draw up a comprehensive EU **Child and Youth Report every two years**, beginning in 2008. Parliament applauds the Commission's plan to introduce an EU-wide child helpline telephone number. It calls for the following, inter alia:

- the protection of children's rights to be included among the priorities Multiannual Framework of the European Union Agency for Fundamental Rights (the Agency), and for the Agency to set up a network for cooperation with international institutions, particularly ombudspeople for children and NGOs;
- children's rights to be mainstreamed in the external policies of the EU. The Commission should submit a report on the possible inclusion in all international agreements between the EC and third countries of a specific and legally binding clause on respect for children's rights, as defined at international level.

Parliament feels it is regrettable that not all Member States have yet established an ombudsperson for children's rights, as called for by the Committee on the Rights of the Child. The EU should make financial support available to the European Network of Ombudspeople for Children (ENOC).

Violence: Parliament affirms that no forms of violence against children in any setting can be justified and that all violence must be condemned. It calls for Community legislation that prohibits all forms of violence, sexual abuse, degrading punishment and harmful traditional practices. Member States must either implement specific legal provisions on female genital mutilation or adopt laws under which any person who carries out genital mutilation may be prosecuted. Member States must also act against honour crimes, and raise medical practitioners' awareness of harmful traditional practices. A legal framework should be established on sexual exploitation and child abuse and judicial cooperation should be strengthened between Member States, Europol, Eurojust and all competent international bodies. Parliament affirms that the sexual exploitation of children should be considered equivalent to the crime of rape insofar as concerns penal sanctions.

It goes on to state its support for the commitment shown by the Commission which, in conjunction with the main credit card issuing companies, is assessing the technical feasibility of excluding websites involved in online sales of child pornography material to be excluded from the online payment system. Parliament calls on other economic players such as banks, bureaux de change, Internet service providers and search engine operators to take an active part in efforts to combat child pornography and other forms of commercial exploitation of children. One of the Commission's basic priorities should be to strengthen cross-border operations against child pornography internet sites with a view to making a commitment to closing down illegal websites.

Members call for the creation of an adequate regulation system in dialogue with providers, the media and industry, aimed at prohibiting the broadcasting of harmful images and content (including cyber bullying) and the marketing of violent video games. Parliament points with concern, moreover, to the growing problem of MMS exchanges of pornographic images, calling on Member States and Internet service providers, in collaboration with search engine companies and the police, to implement blocking technology to stop Internet users from accessing illegal sites related to child sexual abuse.

Sex tourism involving children should be considered a crime in all Member States and subject to extraterritorial criminal laws. Any citizen of the Union committing a crime in a third country should be dealt with under a single set of extraterritorial criminal laws applicable throughout the EU.

Poverty/Discrimination: 19% of children in the EU live below the poverty line and assistance measures must therefore be taken, including measures to support their families. Member States must adopt ambitious targets for reducing – and eventually eradicating – child poverty, and perform their duty to assist all children against the risks of malnutrition, disease, ill-treatment and abuse, whatever their social and/or legal status or that of their parents. Roma children and children belonging to other national minorities in particular should be covered by targeted measures, in particular with a view to ending the discrimination, segregation, social and educational exclusion of which they are often victims. Parliament takes the view that the EU should set itself the objective of ensuring that there are no homeless children or street children in the EU, calling for appropriate measures to be taken to assist homeless children, since most of them are badly traumatised and socially excluded. It asks for consideration to be given to the possibility of devising a Community instrument on adoptions, that improves the quality of care with regard to information services, the preparation of international adoptions, the processing of international adoption applications and post-adoption services.

Child labour: it is essential to ensure that those children who are legally old enough to be in employment are remunerated on the basis of equal work for equal pay. The Commission must ensure that deliberations by human rights committees set up under trade and cooperation agreements focus on the problem of child labour. Products being sold in the EU may be produced by child labour. The Commission is asked to implement a mechanism by which victims of child labour can seek redress against EU companies in the national courts of the Member States. It is also asked to enforce supply-chain compliance and especially to come forward with mechanisms that make the main contractor liable in the EU in cases of violation of UN conventions on child labour in the supply chain.

Children in armed conflicts: MEPs call for measures to protect child soldiers and victims of war.

Lastly, MEPs call for very specific measures to ensure that all children are **registered at birth**, making it, a basic legal right such as obtaining a nationality or an identity at birth.

TASK/TEXT 1.10.2: EU AGENCY FOR FUNDAMENTAL RIGHTS – DEVELOPING INDICATORS

European Union, Agency for Fundamental Rights (FRA), *Developing indicators for the protection, respect and promotion of the rights of the child in the European Union*, March 2009, <www.fra.europa.eu/fraWebsite/attachments/RightsofChild_summary-report_en.pdf>, p. 37

Indicators on positive parenting education [one only, JW]: Evidence of designated public funding for positive parenting education **campaigns** (addressing non-violent forms of discipline, and aimed at **reducing spanking of infants, shaking of babies** etc.), which have been implemented with active participation of children.

TASK/TEXT 1.11:

TASK/TEXT 1.11.1: 25,000 YOUNG CHILDREN WILL DIE TODAY FOR LACK OF BASIC SURVIVAL NEEDS

UNICEF USA appeals for public involvement, Presidential Initiative to save 9.2 million children annually (US Fund for UNICEF Press release, HREA e-list 20 November 2008)

New York, 20 November 2008 – Calling the daily preventable deaths of 25,000 children worldwide "profoundly shameful and unnecessary," the US Fund for UNICEF today marked Universal Children's Day[18] by launching "Believe in Zero," a campaign that encourages policy makers and the general public to reduce daily child deaths from 25,000 to zero.

"These children are not dying from incurable diseases or causes. These children are dying from diarrhea, pneumonia, measles and malaria – things that cost pennies to treat or prevent," said Caryl Stern, President and CEO, US Fund for UNICEF. "It is unacceptable and inexcusable that defenseless children continue to die when the technology, expertise and solutions to save them exist right now."

In 1980, the annual rate of under-five child deaths hovered at 14.6 million, which totaled 40,000 children a day. By 1990 that number was reduced to 12.7 million children annually. Last year annual child deaths declined to about 9.2 million, in spite of rapid population growth, many prolonged civil conflicts and the HIV/AIDS pandemic.

UNICEF health experts cite basic health interventions, such as the immunization of children, the use of insecticide-treated bed nets to prevent malaria, and the provision of vitamin A supplementation as leading factors in the reduction of child deaths. The basic cost of a lifetime vaccination package, which includes, vaccinations against measles/mumps/rubella, polio, tetanus and meningitis, as well as the tools to administer the vaccines, totals $17.

The US Fund led initiative will be rolled-out over multiple platforms and comprises a series of Believe in Zero PSAs [public service announcements] scheduled to run on cable television networks and network affiliates as well as radio. The PSAs feature an ensemble cast of UNICEF supporters and ambassadors

[18] Universal Children's Day – Established in 1954 by the United Nations General Assembly, Universal Children's Day [after November 20, 1959 (adoption by General Assembly of Declaration of the Rights of the Child): International Day of the Rights of the Child, JW] is observed worldwide to promote the welfare of the world's children. The landmark UN Convention on the Rights of the Child was adopted on November 20th in 1989, and that is also the date when most countries formally recognize the international community's obligation to help children who are struggling for survival.

including: Lucy Liu, Laurence Fishburne, Al Roker, Nicole Richie, Joel Madden, Rachael Ray, Regis Philbin and Kelly Ripa. The PSA spots will be complemented by a campaign creative appearing in national print publications and select online spaces with a particular focus on social media sites like Facebook.

The Believe in Zero campaign includes an effort to create a Presidential Initiative to Accelerate Child Survival. Riding the wave of unprecedented political enthusiasm that characterized this presidential campaign season and underscoring a deep sense of urgency, the Believe in Zero campaign encourages Americans to sign a petition addressed to President-elect Barack Obama, urging his administration to provide immediate leadership on the issue.

The petition, which is posted on the Believe in Zero micro-site ibelieveinzero.org, specifically calls for a dramatic scale-up of the coordinated, high-impact interventions that are proven to save children's lives in even the poorest communities around the world. The initiative would provide $1 billion a year for the next five years to implement accelerated child survival strategies in the countries with the highest child mortality rates. UNICEF calculates that an investment of this amount from the US Government could save 3 million children's lives by 2012.

"Since joining UNICEF two years ago, I have met mothers around the world who've shared with me the anguish of losing their children to preventable causes," said Stern. "As a mother of three, I am deeply grateful that my children are healthy and safe. As an American, I am extremely proud of our legacy for standing up to injustice and suffering, and I know that my fellow citizens care as deeply as I do about innocent children dying because they are not visible or vocal enough to register the outrage of the world. Let's get this done – we need everyone to donate and advocate until we reach zero preventable deaths."

TASK/TEXT 1.11.2: TODDLER BEATEN AND UNCONSCIOUS. INFANT FOUND STARVED. CHILD SHAKEN TO DEATH. BABY DISCOVERED DEAD IN SWELTERING CAR …

<www.ndaa.org/pdf/childFatalities09_SantaFe_final.pdf>, accessed 25 November 2009

These are all too familiar headlines about child homicides and the tragic consequences of child physical abuse and neglect. In 2007, some 1,760 American children died at the hands of their caretakers and in 2005, approximately 899,000 children were found to be victims of child abuse or neglect. These staggering statistics underestimate the true extent of the problem. The actual number of child abuse homicides is far higher, since many deaths are mistakenly labeled as "accidental", "natural causes", "sudden infant death syndrome" or "unexplained." Successful investigations and prosecutions are possible when professionals thoroughly understand the complex issues involved in child homicide and physical abuse cases. The implementation of an effective protocol and multidisciplinary team approach is the basis for an effective investigation. Professionals need to understand the biomechanics of inflicted injuries in order to recognize a false caretaker history, collect pertinent evidence, document suspicious injuries and identify potential perpetrators. Professionals must understand the mechanism, amount of force, and timing of the infliction of injury to confront conflicting medical opinions and overcome untrue defenses at trial. Professionals must recognize the dynamics and meet the challenge of convincing jurors and judges that "loving" caretakers are capable of abusing their children in vicious and horrific ways.

TASK/TEXT 1.11.3: UK CHILD MIGRANTS APOLOGY PLANNED

BBC news, <http://news.bbc.co.uk/go/pr/fr/-/2/hi/uk_news/8361025.stm>, 15 November 2009

Gordon Brown is to apologise for the UK's role in sending thousands of its children to former colonies in the 20th century, the BBC has learned. Under the Child Migrants Programme – which ended just 40 years ago – poor children were sent to a "better life" in Australia, Canada and elsewhere. But many were abused and ended up in institutions or as labourers on farms. Officials are consulting survivors of the programme so that a statement can be made in the new year.

On Monday, Australia's prime minister will apologise to the 7,000 UK migrants living there for the mistreatment. He will deliver a national apology to the "Forgotten Australians" and recognise the mistreatment and ongoing suffering of some 500,000 people held in orphanages or children's homes between 1930 and 1970.

As they were compulsorily shipped out of Britain, many of the children were told – wrongly – their parents were dead, and that a more abundant life awaited them. Many parents did not know their children, aged as young as three, had been sent to Australia. Care agencies worked with the government to send disadvantaged children to a rosy future and supply what was deemed "good white stock" to a former colony.

In many cases they were educated only for farm work, and suffered cruelty and hardship including physical, psychological and sexual abuse.

In a letter to the chairman of the health select committee this weekend, Mr Brown said "the time is now right" for the UK to apologise for the actions of previous governments. "It is important that we take the time to listen to the voices of the survivors and victims of these misguided policies," he wrote. Kevin Barron, chairman of the select committee which looked into what happened, said he was "very pleased" to have received a written commitment from Mr Brown. "After consultation with organisations directly involved with child migrants we are going to make an apology early in the new year," he said.

Baroness Amos, Britain's high commissioner in Canberra, said an apology was an important part of addressing the damage. She told the BBC: "We've always said that this was an absolutely shocking period in our history and it's important that there is an apology. "The next stage will be consultation with the Child Migrants Trust and others on the actual form and wording of that apology."

Trust founder Margaret Humphreys has travelled from the UK to Canberra for Mr Rudd's apology.

She said: "The trust has campaigned for over 20 years for this kind and degree of recognition. For child migrants, of course, it has been all their lives and for their families. "This is a moment – a significant moment – in the history of child migration. The recognition is vital if people are to recover."

History of UK child migrants *(Source: Child Migrants Trust)*

- UK the only country with a sustained history of child migration – over four centuries.
- In 1618, 100 sent from London to Richmond, Virginia.
- In total 130,000 sent from the UK to Canada, New Zealand, South Africa, Zimbabwe (formerly Rhodesia) and Australia.
- Post-war, 7,000 shipped to Australia and 1,300 to New Zealand, Rhodesia and Canada.

TASK/TEXT 1.12: NEW WEBSITE HIGHLIGHTS WHAT WORKS TO PREVENT VIOLENCE

<www.nwph.net/preventviolence/default.aspx>, December 1, 2008 (ISPCAN-list)

WHO and Liverpool John Moores University's Centre for Public Health have launched today an important new website highlighting what works to prevent violence. Geared towards policy-makers and violence prevention researchers, practitioners and advocates, the website marks the first time that information on effective violence prevention programmes is available in a searchable web-based data base.

Violence is responsible for 1.6 million deaths every year of which half are suicides, a third homicides, and a tenth due to war and other forms of collective violence. Millions more people are injured and psychologically scarred by violence each year, often with life-long consequences. Violence costs economies billions of dollars annually in direct health, legal, and welfare costs and indirect costs due to lost productivity. This seriously impedes the development of low-income and middle-income countries.

Violence can be prevented and its impact reduced by adopting an evidence-based public health approach. Such an approach seeks to prevent violence before it occurs, by reducing the factors that place people at risk and reinforcing those which protect them. The new website includes:

- A searchable data base of abstracts from published studies that measure the effectiveness of interventions to prevent violence. The abstracts can be searched by violence type (child abuse, elder abuse, intimate partner violence, youth violence, sexual violence), keywords, and geographical area of implementation.
- Resources including key publications on violence and its prevention.
- Information and links to relevant organizations, including the Violence Prevention Alliance (VPA), a WHO-led network of agencies dedicated to preventing violence using the public health approach.
- News, including updates on new violence prevention events and publications.
- An opportunity for organizations to contribute to the website by submitting resources.

The Violence Prevention website can be accessed at: <www.nwph.net/preventviolence/default.aspx>.

Related links:

- WHO violence prevention: <www.who.int/violence_injury_prevention/violence/en>
- Violence Prevention Alliance: <www.who.int/violenceprevention/en/index.html>
- Global Campaign for Violence Prevention: <www.who.int/violence_injury_prevention/violence/global_campaign/en/index.html>.

TASK/TEXT 1.13: PROMOTION AND PROTECTION OF THE RIGHTS OF CHILDREN

General Assembly, Third Committee, 20 November 2008, draft resolution <www.crin.org/docs/FileManager/ga63_third_committee_res2008.pdf>

The General Assembly,

Recalling its previous resolutions on the rights of the child (...),

Emphasizing that the Convention on the Rights of the Child must constitute the standard in the promotion and protection of the rights of the child (...),

Reaffirming the Vienna Declaration and Programme of Action, the United Nations Millennium Declaration and the outcome document of the twenty-seventh special session of the General Assembly on children, entitled "A world fit for children" (...),

Recognizing the link between an improved situation for children and achieving the internationally agreed development goals, including the Millennium Development Goals, in particular those related to education, poverty eradication, gender equality, reduction of child mortality and global partnership for development (...),

Recognizing also the importance of the integration of child rights issues into the follow-up of the outcome documents of all major United Nations conferences, special sessions and summits, (...)

Profoundly concerned that the situation of children in many parts of the world remains critical, in an increasingly globalized environment, as a result of the persistence of poverty, social inequality, inadequate social and economic conditions, pandemics, in particular HIV/AIDS, malaria and tuberculosis, environmental damage, natural disasters, armed conflict, foreign occupation, displacement, violence, terrorism, abuse, trafficking in children and their organs, all forms of exploitation, commercial sexual exploitation of children, child prostitution, child pornography and child sex tourism, neglect, illiteracy, hunger, intolerance, discrimination, racism, xenophobia, gender inequality, disability and inadequate legal protection, and convinced that urgent and effective national and international action is called for,

Reiterating that eradicating poverty is the greatest global challenge facing the world today and an indispensable requirement for sustainable development, in particular for developing countries, and recognizing that chronic poverty remains the single biggest obstacle to meeting the needs of and promoting and protecting the rights of children, and that urgent national and international action is therefore required to eliminate it,

Reaffirming that democracy, development, peace and security, and the full and effective enjoyment of all human rights and fundamental freedoms are interdependent and mutually reinforcing and contribute to the eradication of extreme poverty,

Reaffirming also the need for mainstreaming a gender perspective in all policies and programmes relating to children, and recognizing the child as a rights holder in all policies and programmes relating to children,

Bearing in mind that the year 2009 marks the twentieth anniversary of the adoption of the Convention on the Rights of the Child and the fiftieth anniversary of the Declaration of the Rights of the Child, which provided a foundation for the Convention, and considering that these anniversaries are suitable occasions for strengthening the efforts of Member States to promote the rights of the child,

Implementation of the Convention on the Rights of the Child and the Optional Protocols thereto

1. *Reaffirms* that the general principles of, inter alia, the best interests of the child, non-discrimination, participation and survival and development provide the framework for all actions concerning children, including adolescents;

2. *Urges* States that have not yet done so to become parties to the Convention on the Rights of the Child and the Optional Protocols thereto as a matter of priority and to implement them fully by, inter alia, putting in place effective national legislation, policies and action plans, strengthening relevant governmental structures for children and ensuring adequate and systematic training in the rights of the child for all those working with and for children, as well as ensuring child rights education for children themselves;

3. *Urges* States parties to withdraw reservations that are incompatible with the object and purpose of the Convention or the Optional Protocols thereto and to consider reviewing regularly other reservations with a view to withdrawing them in accordance with the Vienna Declaration and Programme of Action;

4. *Calls upon* States to designate, establish or strengthen governmental structures for children, including, where appropriate, **ministers in charge of child and youth issues** and independent **ombudspersons for children** or other institutions for the promotion and protection of the rights of the child;

5. *Welcomes* the work of the Committee on the Rights of the Child, and calls upon all States to strengthen their cooperation with the Committee, to comply in a timely manner with their reporting obligations under the Convention and the Optional Protocols thereto, in accordance with the guidelines elaborated by the Committee, and to take into account its recommendations on the implementation of the Convention;

6. *Takes note with appreciation* of the initiatives undertaken by the Committee aimed at promoting a better understanding of and fuller compliance with the rights enshrined in the Convention, namely, through the organization of days of general discussion and the adoption of general comments;

7. *Requests* all relevant organs and mechanisms of the United Nations system regularly and systematically to incorporate a strong child rights perspective throughout all activities in the fulfilment of their mandates, as well as to ensure that their staff are trained in child rights matters, and calls upon States to continue to cooperate closely with all those organs and mechanisms, in particular the special rapporteurs and special representatives of the United Nations system;

8. *Encourages* States to strengthen their national statistical capacities and to use statistics disaggregated, inter alia, by age, gender and other relevant factors that may lead to disparities and other statistical indicators at the national, subregional, regional and international levels to develop and assess social policies and programmes so that economic and social resources are used efficiently and effectively for the full realization of the rights of the child;

Promotion and protection of the rights of the child and non-discrimination against children

Non-discrimination

9. *Calls upon* all States:

(a) To ensure the enjoyment by children of all their civil, cultural, economic, political and social rights without discrimination of any kind;

(b) To provide special support and ensure equal access to services for all children, noting with concern the large number of children who are among the victims of racism, racial discrimination, xenophobia and related intolerance, stressing the need to incorporate special measures, in accordance with the principles of the best interests of the child and respect for his or her views and the child's gender-specific needs, in education programmes and programmes to combat such practices;

(c) To take all necessary and effective measures, including legal reforms where appropriate, to eliminate all forms of discrimination against girls and all forms of violence, including female infanticide and prenatal sex selection, rape, sexual abuse and harmful traditional or customary practices, including female genital mutilation, early marriage, marriage without the free and full consent of the intending spouses and forced sterilization, by enacting and enforcing legislation and, where appropriate, by formulating comprehensive, multidisciplinary and coordinated national plans, programmes or strategies to protect girls;

(d) To ensure the full and equal enjoyment of all human rights and fundamental freedoms by children with disabilities, in both the public and private spheres, including by ensuring that the principle of the best interests of the child and the rights of children with disabilities are integrated into policies and programmes for children, including their rights to education, to the highest attainable standard of physical and mental health and to protection from violence, abuse and neglect, and to develop and, where it already exists, enforce legislation to prohibit discrimination against them in order to ensure their inherent dignity, to promote their self-reliance and to facilitate their full and active participation and inclusion in their communities, taking into account the particular situation of children with disabilities who may be subject to multiple or aggravated forms of discrimination, including girls with disabilities and children with disabilities living in poverty;

10. *Urges* all States to respect and promote the right of girls and boys to express themselves freely, to ensure that their views are given due weight, in accordance with their age and maturity, in all matters affecting them and to involve children, including children with special needs, in decision-making processes, taking into account the evolving capacities of children and the importance of involving children's organizations and child-led initiatives;

11. *Also urges* all States in particular to strengthen the participation of children and adolescents in planning and implementation relating to matters that affect them, such as health, environment, education, social and economic welfare and protection against violence, abuse and exploitation;

Registration, family relations and adoption or other forms of alternative care

12. *Once again urges* all States parties to intensify their efforts to comply with their obligations under the Convention on the Rights of the Child to preserve the child's identity, including nationality, name and family relations, as recognized by law, to allow for the registration of the child immediately after birth, to ensure that registration procedures are simple, expeditious and effective and provided at minimal or no cost and to raise awareness of the importance of birth registration at the national, regional and local levels;

13. *Encourages* States to adopt and enforce laws and improve the implementation of policies and programmes to protect children growing up without parents or caregivers, recognizing that, where alternative care is necessary, family and community-based care should be promoted over placement in institutions, and in this context invites States to dedicate all their efforts, in a transparent process, with a view to taking possible action on the draft United Nations guidelines for the appropriate use and conditions of alternative care for children at the tenth session of the Human Rights Council;

14. *Calls upon* States to guarantee, to the extent consistent with the obligations of each State, the right of a child whose parents reside in different States to maintain, on a regular basis, save in exceptional circumstances, personal relations and direct contact with both parents by providing enforceable means of

access and visitation in both States and by respecting the principle that both parents have common responsibilities for the upbringing and development of their children;

15. *Also calls upon* States to address and pay particular attention to cases of international parental or familial child abduction, and encourages States to engage in multilateral and bilateral cooperation to resolve those cases, preferably by accession to or ratification of the Hague Convention on the Civil Aspects of International Child Abduction, and to comply fully with the Convention, and to facilitate, inter alia, the return of the child to the country in which he or she resided immediately before the removal or retention;

16. *Further calls upon* States to take all necessary measures to prevent and combat illegal adoptions and all adoptions that are not in the best interests of the child;

Economic and social well-being of children

17. *Calls upon* States and the international community to create an environment in which the well-being of the child is ensured, including by strengthening international cooperation in this field;

Eradication of poverty

18. *Calls upon* States to cooperate, support and participate in the global efforts for poverty eradication at the global, regional and country levels, recognizing that strengthened availability and effective allocation of resources are required at all these levels, in order to ensure that all the internationally agreed development and poverty eradication goals, including those set out in the United Nations Millennium Declaration, are realized within their time framework, and reaffirms that investments in children and the realization of their rights are among the most effective ways to eradicate poverty;

19. *Reaffirms* that the primary responsibility for ensuring an enabling environment for securing the well-being of children, in which the rights of each and every child are promoted and respected, rests with each individual State;

20. *Calls upon* all States and the international community to mobilize all necessary resources, support and efforts to eradicate poverty, according to national plans and strategies and in consultation with national Governments, including through an integrated and multifaceted approach based on the rights and well-being of children, and to continue their efforts to realize the internationally agreed development and poverty eradication goals, including the Millennium Development Goals;

Right to education

21. *Recognizes* the right to education on the basis of equal opportunity and non-discrimination by making primary education compulsory and available free to all children, ensuring that all children have access to education of good quality, as well as making secondary education generally available and accessible to all, in particular through the progressive introduction of free education, bearing in mind that special measures to ensure equal access, including affirmative action, contribute to achieving equal opportunity and combating exclusion, and ensuring school attendance, in particular for girls and children from low-income families in order to achieve the objectives of Education for All, with the aim of realizing the millennium development goal aimed at achieving universal primary education; (...)

Right to the enjoyment of the highest attainable standard of health

24. *Calls upon* States:

(a) To take all necessary measures to ensure the right of the child to the enjoyment of the highest attainable standard of health and to develop sustainable health systems and social services, ensuring access to such systems and services without discrimination, paying special attention to adequate food and nutrition and combating disease and malnutrition, to access to safe drinking water and sanitation, to the special needs of male and female adolescents and to reproductive and sexual health, and securing appropriate prenatal and post-natal care for mothers, including measures to prevent mother-to-child transmission of HIV, and in this context to realize the millennium development goals aimed at reducing child mortality, improving maternal health and combating HIV/AIDS, malaria and other diseases;

(b) To assign priority to developing and implementing activities and programmes aimed at treating and preventing addictions, in particular **addiction to alcohol and tobacco**, and the abuse of narcotic drugs, psychotropic substances and inhalants;

(c) To support adolescents to be able to deal positively and responsibly with their sexuality in order to protect themselves from HIV/AIDS infection and to implement measures to increase their capacity to protect themselves from HIV/AIDS through, inter alia, the provision of health care, including for sexual and reproductive health, and through preventive education that promotes gender equality;

(d) To develop and implement strategies, policies and programmes that identify and address those factors that make individuals particularly vulnerable to HIV infection in order to complement prevention programmes that address activities that place individuals at risk for HIV infection, such as risky and unsafe behaviour and injecting drug use; (...)

(f) To design and implement programmes to provide social services and support to pregnant adolescents and adolescent mothers, in particular by enabling them and also the adolescent fathers to continue and complete their education;

Right to food

25. *Expresses grave concern* at the worsening of the world food crisis, which seriously undermines the realization of the right to food for all, including mothers and children, and also expresses grave concern that this crisis threatens to further undermine the achievement of the Millennium Development Goals, and stresses that solutions need a comprehensive and multifaceted approach requiring short-, medium- and long-term and sustained actions;

26. *Calls upon* all States to take immediate steps to eliminate child hunger, including through the adoption or strengthening of national programmes to address food security and adequate livelihoods, as well as nutritional security, especially regarding vitamin A, iron and iodine deficiencies, the **promotion of breastfeeding**, as well as programmes, for example, school meal programmes, that should ensure adequate nutrition for all children;

Elimination of violence against children

27. *Condemns* all forms of violence against children, and urges all States:

(a) To take effective and appropriate legislative and other measures or, where it exists, to strengthen legislation to prohibit and eliminate **all forms of violence against children in all settings**;

(b) To respect fully the rights, human dignity and physical integrity of children and to **prohibit and eliminate any emotional or physical violence or any other humiliating or degrading treatment**;

(c) To give priority attention to the prevention of all forms of violence against children and to addressing its underlying causes and its gender dimension through a systematic, comprehensive and multifaceted approach, recognizing that witnessing violence, including domestic violence, also causes harm to children;

(d) To protect children from all forms of violence or abuse by all those who work with and for children, including in educational settings, as well as by Government officials, such as the police, law enforcement authorities and employees and officials in detention centres or welfare institutions;

(e) To establish complaint mechanisms that are confidential, age-appropriate, gender-sensitive and accessible to all children and to undertake thorough and prompt investigations of all acts of violence and discrimination;
(f) To take measures to ensure that all those who work with and for children protect children from bullying and implement preventive and anti-bullying policies in order to ensure a safe and supportive environment free from harassment and violence;
(g) To strive to change attitudes that condone or normalize any form of violence against children, including cruel, inhuman or degrading forms of discipline, harmful traditional practices and all forms of sexual violence;
(h) To take measures to **promote constructive and positive forms of discipline** and child development approaches in all settings, **including the home**, schools and other educational settings, and throughout care and justice systems;
(i) To **end impunity** for perpetrators of crimes against children and to investigate and prosecute such acts of violence and impose appropriate penalties, recognizing that persons convicted of violent offences against children, including sexual abuse, who continue to pose a risk of harm to children should be **prevented from working with children**;
(j) To establish and develop safe, well-publicized, confidential and accessible mechanisms to enable children, their representatives and others to report violence against children as well as to file complaints in cases of violence against children, and to ensure that all victims of violence have access to appropriate confidential, child-sensitive health and social services, paying special attention to the gender-specific needs of girls and boys who are victims of violence;
(k) To address the gender dimension of all forms of violence against children and incorporate a gender perspective in all policies adopted and actions taken to protect children against all forms of violence, acknowledging that girls and boys face varying risks from different forms of violence at different ages and in different situations, and in this context recalls the agreed conclusions on the elimination of all forms of discrimination and violence against the girl child adopted by the Commission on the Status of Women at its fifty-first session;

28. *Expresses* deep concern about the impact of all forms of sexual violence in situations of armed conflict and about the harm caused by witnessing sexual violence, reaffirms in this regard relevant General Assembly, Economic and Social Council and Human Rights Council resolutions, and notes with appreciation the attention paid to this issue in Security Council resolution 1820 (2008) of 19 June 2008;

29. *Condemns* all kinds of abduction of children, in particular extortive abduction and abduction of children in situations of armed conflict, including for their recruitment and use in armed conflict, and urges States to take all appropriate measures to secure their unconditional release, rehabilitation and reintegration and their reunification with their families;

30. *Urges* all States to strengthen international cooperation and mutual assistance to prevent and protect children from all forms of violence and to end impunity for crimes against children;

31. *Recognizes* the contribution of the International Criminal Court in ending impunity for the most serious crimes against children, including genocide, crimes against humanity and war crimes, and calls upon States not to grant amnesties for such crimes;

32. *Encourages* all States and requests United Nations entities, regional organizations and civil society, including non-governmental organizations, to continue to widely disseminate and follow up on the study on violence against children by the independent expert appointed by the Secretary-General and to cooperate with the Special Representative of the Secretary-General on violence against children, once appointed, in promoting the implementation of the recommendations of the study, while promoting and ensuring country ownership and national plans and programmes in this regard;

33. *Expresses deep concern* about the delay in the appointment of the new mandate holder requested by the General Assembly in its resolution 62/141, requests the Secretary-General to comply fully with the request and to take urgent action to appoint, in accordance with the above-mentioned resolution, at the highest possible level and without delay, a Special Representative on violence against children;

Promoting and protecting the rights of children, including children in particularly difficult situations

34. *Calls upon* all States to prevent violations of the rights of children working and/or living on the street, including discrimination, arbitrary detention and extrajudicial, arbitrary or summary executions, torture and all kinds of violence and exploitation, and to bring the perpetrators to justice, to adopt and implement policies for the protection, social and psychosocial rehabilitation and reintegration of those children and to adopt economic, social and educational strategies to address the problems of children working and/or living on the street;

35. *Also calls upon* all States to protect refugee, asylum-seeking and internally displaced children, taking into account their gender-specific needs, in particular those who are unaccompanied, who are particularly exposed to violence and risks in connection with armed conflict, such as recruitment, killing, maiming,

sexual violence and exploitation, as well as trafficking, stressing the need for States as well as the international community to continue to pay more systematic and indepth attention to the special assistance, protection and development needs of those children through, inter alia, programmes aimed at rehabilitation and physical and psychological recovery, and to programmes for voluntary repatriation and, where appropriate and feasible, local integration and resettlement, to give priority to family tracing and family reunification and, where appropriate, to cooperate with international humanitarian and refugee organizations, including by facilitating their work;

36. *Further calls upon* all States to ensure, for children belonging to minorities and vulnerable groups, including migrant children and indigenous children, the enjoyment of all human rights as well as access to health care, social services and education on an equal basis with others and to ensure that all such children, in particular victims of violence and exploitation, receive special protection and assistance;

37. *Calls upon* all States to ensure that any migration policies, including repatriation mechanisms, **be in accordance with the best interests of the child** and to take all necessary actions to ensure that unaccompanied migrant children and those who are victims of violence and exploitation receive special protection and assistance in accordance international law; (...)

40. *Encourages* States to promote actions, including through bilateral and multilateral technical cooperation and financial assistance, for the social reintegration of children in difficult situations, considering, inter alia, views, skills and capacities that those children have developed in the conditions in which they lived and, where appropriate, with their meaningful participation;

41. *Calls upon* States to protect all human rights of these children in particularly difficult situations and to ensure that the best interests of the child are accorded primary consideration, and encourages the Committee on the Rights of the Child, the United Nations Children's Fund, other relevant United Nations bodies and mandate holders, within their respective mandates, to pay particular attention to the conditions of these children **in all States** and, as appropriate, to make recommendations to strengthen their protection;

42. *Recognizes* that the mass media and their organizations have a key role to play in raising awareness about the situation of children and the challenges facing them and that they should also play a more active role in informing children, parents, families and the general public about initiatives that protect and promote the rights of children and should also contribute to educational programmes for children;

Children alleged to have infringed or recognized as having infringed penal law (...)
Prevention and eradication of the sale of children, child prostitution and child pornography (...)
Children affected by armed conflict (...)
Child labour (...)
Follow-up
80. *Decides*:

(a) To request the Secretary-General to submit to the General Assembly at its sixty-fourth session a report on the rights of the child containing information on the status of the Convention on the Rights of the Child and the issues addressed in the present resolution, with a focus on international efforts and national progress in tackling child labour and progress towards meeting the target of eliminating the worst forms of child labour by the year 2016, as agreed in the context of the International Labour Organization;
(b) To request the Special Representative of the Secretary-General for Children and Armed Conflict to continue to submit reports to the General Assembly and the Human Rights Council on the activities undertaken in discharging her mandate, including information on her field visits, and on the progress achieved and the challenges remaining on the children and armed conflict agenda;
(c) To invite the Chairperson of the Committee on the Rights of the Child to present an oral report on the work of the Committee to the General Assembly at its sixty-fourth session as a way to enhance communication between the Assembly and the Committee;
(d) To invite all Member States, organizations of the United Nations system, non-governmental organizations and individuals to observe the twentieth anniversary of the Convention on the Rights of the Child and to request the Secretary-General to take necessary measures, within existing resources, for the observance by the United Nations of those anniversaries;
(e) To continue its consideration of the question at its sixty-fourth session under the item entitled "Promotion and protection of the rights of children," focusing section III of the resolution on the rights of the child on "The right of the child to express his or her views freely in all matters affecting him or her."

TASK/TEXT 1.14: NATIONAL STRATEGIES FOR THE PROTECTION OF CHILDREN FROM VIOLENCE

Recommendation CM/Rec(2009)10 of the Committee of Ministers to member states on integrated national strategies for the protection of children from violence *(Adopted by the Committee of Ministers on 18 November 2009 ...)* [references omitted]

The Committee of Ministers, under the terms of Article 15.*b* of the Statute of the Council of Europe;

- Recalling the Third Summit of Heads of State and Government (Warsaw, 16–17 May 2005) and the commitment made therein to take specific action to eradicate all forms of violence against children;
- Recalling "Building a Europe for and with Children – 2009–2011 Strategy," giving the Council of Europe the role of regional initiator and co-ordinator of national and regional initiatives to combat violence against children and of the European forum for follow-up to the recommendations included in the United Nations Secretary General's Study on Violence against Children;
- Recalling the pan-European awareness-raising campaign against corporal punishment of children "Raise your hand against smacking," launched by the Council of Europe on 15 June 2008 in Zagreb, Croatia;
- Considering that the well-being and best interests of children are fundamental values shared by all member states and must be promoted without any discrimination;
- Recognising that violence against children constitutes a violation of the rights of the child, compromises children's development and affects the enjoyment of their other fundamental rights;
- Observing that violence against children exists in every state and cuts across boundaries of sex, race, colour, language, religion, political or other opinion, national or social origin, association with a national minority, property, birth, sexual orientation, state of health, disability or other status;
- Considering that children's fragility and vulnerability and their dependence on adults for the growth and development call for greater investment in the prevention of violence and protection of children on the part of families, society and the state;
- Having regard to the European Convention on Human Rights (...), securing to everyone within the member states' jurisdiction, including children, the right to be protected from torture and inhuman or degrading treatment or punishment, the right to liberty and security, and the right to a fair trial;

- Having regard to the revised European Social Charter (...), in particular its provisions on the right of children to be protected from negligence, violence and exploitation;
- Bearing in mind the European Convention on the Exercise of Children's Rights (...), the Convention on Action against Trafficking in Human Beings (...), the Convention on the Protection of Children against Sexual Exploitation and Sexual Abuse (...) and other relevant Council of Europe legal instruments;
- Having regard to the following recommendations of the Committee of Ministers to member states: CM/Rec(2009)5 on measures to protect children against harmful content and behaviour and to promote their active participation in the new information and communications environment; CM/Rec(2008)11 on the European Rules for juvenile offenders subject to sanctions or measures; Rec(2006)19 on policy to support positive parenting; Rec(2006)12 on empowering children in the new information and communication environment; Rec(2006)5 on the Council of Europe Action Plan to promote the rights and full participation of people with disabilities in society: improving the quality of life for people with disabilities in Europe 2006–2015; Rec(2005)5 on the rights of children living in residential institutions; Rec(2002)5 on the protection of women against violence; and Rec(2001)16 on the protection of children against sexual exploitation;
- Having regard to the following recommendations of the Council of Europe Parliamentary Assembly: Recommendation 1854 (2009) on "Access to rights for people with disabilities and their full and active participation in society"; Recommendation 1828 (2008) on the "Disappearance of newborn babies for illegal adoption in Europe"; Recommendation 1815 (2007) on "Prostitution – which stance to take?"; Recommendation 1778 (2007) on "Child victims: stamping out all forms of violence, exploitation and abuse"; and Recommendation 1666 (2004) on "A Europe-wide ban on corporal punishment of children";
- Also bearing in mind the United Nations Convention on the Rights of the Child, especially Article 19 thereof, providing for the clear obligation that states protect children from all forms of violence at all times and in all settings;
- Taking due account of other relevant international instruments and commitments in this field, including the Rio de Janeiro Declaration and Action Plan to Prevent and Stop Sexual Exploitation of Children and Adolescents (2008);
- Recalling the recommendations of the United Nations Secretary General's Study on Violence against Children in particular to develop a multifaceted and systematic framework to respond to violence against children, integrated

into the national planning process through a national strategy, policy or plan, and to identify a focal point, preferably at ministerial level, to oversee the implementation of measures to prevent and respond to violence;

- Committed to the promotion of integrated national strategies aimed at safeguarding the rights of the child and protecting children from all forms of violence, rooted in the United Nations Convention on the Rights of the Child, Council of Europe standards, and developed with children's participation,
- Recommends that the member states' governments, honouring their international obligations and having due regard to their specific national, regional and local structures and respective responsibilities:
  a. integrate, as appropriate, in their legislation, policy and practice the principles, and implement, as appropriate, the actions set out in the Council of Europe Policy guidelines on integrated national strategies for the protection of children from violence, as they appear in Appendix 1 to this recommendation;
  b. promote the implementation and application of the guidelines in areas which are not the direct responsibility or competence of public authorities, but where they nonetheless have a certain power or may play a certain role;
  c. ensure the widest possible dissemination of this recommendation through awareness-raising campaigns and co-operation with civil society, independent children's rights institutions, the media, the private sector, children and families;
  d. through their focal points on the rights of the child and elimination of violence against children, co-operate with the Council of Europe in developing, implementing and monitoring the national strategies;
  e. co-operate with and support the United Nations Special Representative to the Secretary General on Violence against Children. (…)

Appendix 1 – Council of Europe Policy guidelines on integrated national strategies for the protection of children from violence

1. Executive summary

In line with the recommendations of the [CRC's] Committee on the Rights of the Child and of the United Nations Secretary General's Study on Violence against Children, these guidelines promote the development and implementation of a holistic national framework to safeguard the rights of the child and to eradicate violence against children. The guidelines refer to the definitions of "children" and "violence" as contained in Articles 1 and 19, respectively, of the United Nations Convention on the Rights of the Child (hereinafter referred to as CRC).

The guidelines are based on eight general principles (protection against violence, the right to life and maximum survival and development, non-discrimination, gender equality, child participation, a state's obligations, other actors' obligations and participation, best interests of the child) and four operative principles (multidimensional nature of violence, integrated approach, cross-sectoral co-operation, multi-stakeholder approach). These have been mainstreamed throughout, including into sections on integrated national, regional and local action; education and awareness-raising measures; legal, policy and institutional frameworks; research and data collection.

The guidelines support the promotion of a culture of respect for the rights of the child, based on an in-depth knowledge of the rights of the child and an understanding of children's vulnerabilities and capacities. The primary target group includes all relevant professionals in contact with children.

The guidelines' core recommendations call for the development of an integrated national strategy for the protection of children from violence. The strategy is understood as a multi-faceted and systematic framework fully integrated into a national policy for the promotion and protection of the rights of the child, with a specific timeframe, with realistic targets, co-ordinated and monitored by a single agency (where possible, and in conformity with national regulations), supported by adequate human and financial resources and based on current scientific knowledge.

The guidelines encourage the setting up of child-friendly services and mechanisms. These are understood as safeguarding the rights of the child and pursuing children's best interests. An important recommendation calls for the mandatory reporting by all relevant professionals of incidents of violence against children.

The guidelines recommend strengthening international co-operation to prevent violence against children Europe-wide.

2. Aims, scope, definitions and principles

2.1. Aims

The aims of these guidelines are to:

a. protect the rights of children, in particular those who are victims of violence;
b. prevent and combat all forms of violence against children;
c. promote the adoption, implementation and monitoring of integrated national strategies for the protection of children from violence;
d. reinforce international co-operation to safeguard the rights of the child and to protect children from violence.

2.2. Scope and definitions

1. "Child" shall mean any person under the age of 18 years, including child victims, witnesses and perpetrators of violence.

2. In line with Article 19 of the CRC, "violence" is defined as including all forms of physical or mental violence, injury and abuse, neglect and negligent treatment, maltreatment or exploitation, including sexual abuse. This definition covers the exposure of children to violence in the home and elsewhere. Violence is understood to occur not only between adults and children but also between children.

2.3. Principles

General principles

Protection against violence – All children have the right to protection from all forms of physical or mental violence, injury or abuse, neglect or negligent treatment, maltreatment or exploitation, including sexual abuse, while in the care of parent(s), legal guardian(s) or any other person who has the care of the child.

The right to life and maximum survival and development – Every child has the inherent right to life and to survival and development to the maximum extent possible.

Non-discrimination – All children regardless of their sex, race, colour, language, religion, political or other opinion, national or social origin, association with a national minority, property, birth, sexual orientation, state of health, disability or other status, should be protected from all forms of violence and be provided with such care and assistance as to ensure to the maximum extent possible their survival and development.

Gender equality – Gender aspects of violence should be addressed as part of the integrated approach to violence, and due account should be taken of the different risks girls and boys face in respect of violence and of the different consequences of violence for boys and girls.

Child participation – 1. Children have the right to express themselves freely on all matters affecting their lives, and their views should be given due weight depending on the child's age and maturity. Child participation entails in particular:

a. supporting children's expression of their views and respecting and taking into consideration the views of the child in all situations affecting her or him;

b. providing the child with the opportunity to be heard in any judicial, administrative or extra-judicial proceedings.

2. Children should be actively engaged in and empowered, according to their evolving capacity and with their informed consent, to participate meaningfully in the planning, implementation and evaluation of policies and programmes to

prevent violence. The state and other appropriate actors should listen carefully to children's views in the light of the contribution that the child's perspective can bring to the quality of solutions under examination.

A state's obligations – 1. The state has the paramount responsibility to uphold the rights of the child and to protect all children within its jurisdiction from all forms of violence, however mild, at all times and in all settings. States should invest in evidence-based policies and programmes, guided by the child's best interests, to address factors that give rise to violence and to respond effectively when violence occurs.

2. Recognising the central role that families play in children's development and well-being and in the safeguarding of their rights, including the right to protection from all forms of violence, the state should support families in their child-rearing role by:

a. providing for a network of accessible, flexible and quality childcare services;

b. facilitating positive reconciliation of family and working life;

c. drawing up programmes to improve parental skills and to foster a healthy and positive family environment;

d. incorporating a child rights perspective at all levels of the budgetary process.

Other actors' obligations and participation – The responsibility to prevent violence against children also extends to all services, institutions and professionals working for and with children, parents and the extended family, the media, private sector, religious communities and civil society.

Best interests of the child – In all actions affecting children, including those to protect them from all forms of violence, the best interests of the child should be the primary consideration.

Operative principles

1. Violence against children is multidimensional. This approach presupposes that a combination of factors needs to come into play in order for violence to occur, recur, or cease. It calls for holistic treatment of the circumstances of the violent incident, on the basis of their interdependence, not dealing with a single cause and effect relationship.

2. Prevention of violence requires cross-sectoral co-operation and co-ordination. This involves, in particular, co-ordination across central government departments, across provinces and regions, and between government and civil society.

3. Violence against children demands an integrated (systemic, holistic) approach. This approach allows factors of different orders (cultural, psychological, pedagogical, behavioural, physical, political, socio-economic, etc.) to be treated

on the basis of common ground. It implies that all programmes and actions aimed at preventing and protecting children from violence, in the broad context of the promotion of the rights of the child, should operate across a range of disciplines and sectors. In the same spirit, the guidelines' sections are interrelated and should be read in conjunction with each other.

4. A multi-stakeholder approach is indispensable for the eradication of violence against children, as this is a responsibility that extends beyond state-controlled bodies and services to include all members of society, such as state institutions, local authorities, non-governmental organisations, professionals, the media, families and children. In the planning, implementation and evaluation of programmes and actions to protect children from violence priority should be attached to:

a. building partnerships between families and the state, based on trust and respect for different cultures and traditions;

b. engaging in true dialogue with children and progressively building a culture of respect for children's views, including by informing them of the outcome of the processes and explaining how their views were taken into account.

3. Integrated national, regional and local action

3.1. Integrated national strategies for the protection of children from violence

1. A multidisciplinary and systematic framework (hereinafter referred to as "the strategy") integrated into the national planning process, rooted in the CRC and bringing together all stakeholders, represents the most effective response to violence against children that is sustainable over time. The strategy's core element should be a complex of effective and comprehensive primary, secondary and tertiary prevention measures that are child-centred, families-focused, multidisciplinary and oriented towards fulfilling children's and families' needs. [Note: Preventive work directed at society at large is known as primary prevention. It prevents violence by addressing broad issues, such as health or education, and reduces risk factors, such as unemployment and social exclusion. Children who run a high risk of being subjected to violence or inflicting violence upon others are targets of secondary prevention. Its examples include measures for children of drug or alcohol abusers, etc. Tertiary prevention attempts to prevent, reverse or limit the consequences of violence that has already occurred. It focuses on victims' and perpetrators' rehabilitation and re-integration.] The strategy should contain realistic and time-bound targets, be supported by adequate human and financial resources, be based on current scientific knowledge (with regard to what works) and be systematically evaluated.

2. The strategy should rely on cross-sectoral co-operation and co-ordination involving health, education and social sectors, agencies responsible for planning and budgetary appropriations, law enforcement authorities, and the justice system. At national level, an agency with primary responsibility for the protection of children against violence should assume (where possible and in conformity with national regulations) a key co-ordinating and monitoring role. Its capacity to involve multiple sectors in a broad-based action is crucial for the strategy's long-term success.

3. All actors concerned with the promotion and protection of the rights of the child, such as national, regional and local authorities, families, independent human rights institutions, professionals working for and with children, researchers, civil society and the media should be involved in the strategy's design, implementation and evaluation. Children should not only be heard but be empowered to contribute, with their informed consent and according to their evolving capacity, to this multi-stakeholder action. Adequate resources should be made available to ensure children's meaningful participation.

4. Methodologies should be developed to assess progress and evaluate actions foreseen by the strategy at all levels, including the cross-sectoral level. Evaluations should be conducted on a regular basis with a view to identifying policies and measures that are appropriate and effective in preventing and addressing violence.

5. Information on the strategy's implementation should be widely disseminated. The visibility of actions taken to prevent and to address violence should be increased, *inter alia*, through their discussion in elected fora at national, regional and local levels.

3.2. Regional and local action

1. Local action to prevent violence is particularly important in view of its proximity to children and families as end recipients of services. It is at this level that the persons concerned will receive assistance, in line with their needs and characteristics.

2. Whereas national authorities set forth common standards for service provision, it is the regions' and municipalities' obligation to adhere to these standards and to provide for a network of child-friendly services and mechanisms. Responsibilities of regional and local authorities also include the collection of data on violence against children; the development, implementation and monitoring of preventive measures; funding and allocation of premises; etc.

3. National and regional authorities should provide adequate support to local violence prevention programmes in terms of financing, training, evaluation and follow-up. Co-operation and co-ordination among these levels are indispensable for constant improvements in service delivery and resource optimisation.

4. Community interventions to prevent violence against children, involving all sectors and stakeholders, should be supported. Such interventions could be effected via open platforms, councils or networks bringing together, for instance, municipal authorities, social and health care services, schools, local judiciary, police, migrants' or community associations, faith-based organisations and children and families.

5. Co-operation and co-ordination between municipalities (and regions) should be reinforced, including through the exchange of experiences and good practices.

6. The appropriately regulated and monitored involvement of the private sector and of non-governmental organisations should be promoted.

7. As large-scale decentralisation and privatisation of social services are now common in European states, the capacity of regional and local authorities to contribute to the strategy's implementation should be carefully assessed.

4. Building a culture of respect for the rights of the child

The strategy should have as its main objective the qualitative change in the perception of children and childhood, and of violence against children. This objective can only be achieved when all segments of society have become sufficiently aware of the rights of the child and of the harmful impact of violence on children; when organisational cultures and practices have been strengthened in this regard, and bridges built across professions to afford more and better protection to children; when mindsets have been transformed, including through the means of information and communication technologies; when the underlying economic and social conditions associated with violence have been addressed – in other words it is only possible when a genuine culture of respect for the rights of the child has permeated the fabric of society.

4.1. Education and awareness raising

1. It is the state's obligation to make information on the rights of the child widely known, by appropriate and active means, to children and adults alike. This entails in particular:

a. incorporating the rights of the child into school curricula and promoting a child rights approach in education at all levels;

b. regular and ongoing training on the rights of the child for all those who work with and for children;

c. raising awareness, by means of public information and media campaigns, on the rights of the child, including the right to be protected from all forms of violence, the right to respect for human dignity and physical integrity and the right to be heard and taken seriously.

2. A clear and unequivocal intolerance of all forms of violence against children, however mild, should be promoted throughout society. Public attitudes rooted in social and cultural norms and traditions which accept, condone or support violence, including stereotypical gender roles, racial or ethnic discrimination, acceptance of corporal punishment and other harmful traditional practices should be publicly condemned and eliminated. The harmful effects that all forms of violence have on children should be made widely known. An understanding of the state's obligations and the individual's responsibility to condemn and prevent violence and to assist child victims should be reinforced.

3. Parents' and carers' knowledge of the rights of the child and of positive parenting practices should be strengthened by all means, including encouraging their enrolment in positive parenting programmes.

4.2. Professional training

1. The training of professionals working for and with children represents an important long-term investment in children's development and well-being. Therefore, the state and society should value these professions by attributing to them the requisite moral, financial and other forms of public and private support.

2. It is the state's obligation to instil the culture of the rights of the child and responsibility for children into all professionals who come into contact with children through their work (for example, social workers, foster carers, police officers, judges, teachers, school principals, youth workers, people employed by detention facilities and child-care institutions, immigration and humanitarian workers, sports coaches, etc.). To promote knowledge of the rights of the child, relevant courses should be integrated into university and other training curricula.

3. All relevant professionals who in their work come in contact with children should be familiar with the CRC and methodologies and approaches, including those required for listening effectively to children, and be trained to work in a diverse ethnic, cultural, religious and linguistic environment.

4. All relevant professionals should have skills to prevent, detect and respond effectively to violence against children. To this end, national curriculum regulations should include compulsory, ongoing training on the prevention, identification, assessment and reporting of violence against children, and the protection and continuity of care of children. The training should pursue a comprehensive approach and prioritise early identification of potential risks to a child's well-being.

5. Specialised training should be offered to professionals working for and with vulnerable groups of children, such as children with disabilities.

6. Bearing in mind the often difficult physical and psychological environment surrounding services assisting children affected by violence, adequate support should be rendered to their staff in terms of supervision, counselling, complementary training and the possibility of setting up professional interest groups.

4.3. Media and the information society

1. Free and independent media, with due respect for their self-regulation, can play a powerful role in building a culture of respect for the rights of the child and act as a natural partner in the strategy's implementation. The media should be encouraged to educate both children and adults in the rights of the child, promote child participation, foster positive parenting practices, strengthen intercultural and interfaith dialogue, and foster non-violent values in society.

2. The state bears the primary responsibility for the protection of children against harmful media content and for the promotion of children's active participation in the information and communications environment.

3. With regard to the portrayal of violence and the distribution of content potentially harmful to children, those responsible for the media should fully assume their duties and responsibilities which the exercise of their freedom of expression entails. This could be done through the removal of or blocking access to inappropriate material, or through the development of automated content rating systems, the adoption of codes of conduct and standards for content evaluation, the setting up of control mechanisms, the establishment of content complaints systems, etc.

4. In order to meet children's and families' expectations for accessible, secure and reliable internet services, internet service providers should be encouraged to supply information on potential risks to their customers' rights, security and privacy online. Co-operation with law enforcement authorities in the investigation of crimes committed through the use of telecommunication technologies should be strengthened.

5. Given the potential impact of online games on the rights and sensibilities of children, game designers and publishers should be encouraged to regularly evaluate policies and practices regarding child safety.

6. The media should be encouraged to build partnerships with all relevant actors in order to:

a. develop children's media literacy skills;

b. work with child safety experts, policy makers, social services and law enforcement authorities to develop, incorporate and monitor the application of new technologies to protect children from harm online;

c. raise media professionals' awareness of the rights of the child and of violence against children.

7. Parents and teachers have a special responsibility as far as children's access to and the use of the media at home and in school is concerned. They may assume this responsibility in various ways, including by conscious and selective use of the media, stimulation of children's critical attitudes, restriction of access to content that may adversely affect children's physical, emotional or psychological well-being, etc.

8. The establishment of the media by children and with children, for purposes including the elimination of violence, should be strongly encouraged and supported.

5. Frameworks

5.1. Legal framework

Compliance with CRC and other international standards – 1. All member states of the Council of Europe are parties to the CRC and are bound to implement its provisions and to act in accordance with its principles. All reservations incompatible with the CRC's object and purpose should be withdrawn.

2. At global and regional levels numerous instruments have been adopted to safeguard the rights of the child and to protect children from various forms of violence. Accession to these treaties should be strongly encouraged. Once ratified, they should be effectively implemented and monitored, and national laws, bylaws, policies, regulations, plans and programmes should be brought in line with them.

Prevention – The national legal framework should prioritise the prevention of violence and safeguard the rights of the child by taking action, such as:

a. registering children immediately after birth, subject to national regulations and state obligations under the relevant international treaties in this field;

b. setting a minimum age of marriage that is not too low and that is applicable to both boys and girls;

c. setting a minimum age for sexual consent;

d. prohibiting employment into positions involving child supervision of persons convicted of violent, including sexual, offences against children;

e. developing intervention programmes and measures to evaluate and prevent the risk of violence against children from being committed;

f. devising a system to vet fully those working with children, in any capacity, that ensures an appropriate balance between the child's right to protection from violence and the individual's right to a good name;

g. integrating in national laws an obligation to respect the right of the child to be heard and to attribute due weight to children's views.

Prohibition of violence – The state has an explicit obligation to secure children's right to protection from all forms of violence, however mild.

Appropriate legislative, administrative, social and educational measures should be taken to prohibit all violence against children at all times and in all settings and to render protection to all children within the state's jurisdiction. Legal defences and authorisations for any form of violence, including for the purposes of correction, discipline or punishment, within or outside families, should be repealed. Prohibition should imperatively cover:

a. all forms of sexual violence and abuse, corruption of children and solicitation of children for sexual purposes;

b. all forms of exploitation of children, including child prostitution, child pornography, sexual exploitation in travel and tourism, trafficking, sale of children, illegal adoption, forced labour or services, slavery and practices similar to it, removal of organs, for any purpose or in any form;

c. all forms of exploitation of children through the use of new technologies;

d. all harmful traditional or customary practices, such as early or forced marriage, honour killing and female genital mutilation;

e. exposure of children to violent or harmful content, irrespective of its origin and through any medium;

f. all forms of violence in residential institutions;

g. all forms of violence in school;

h. all corporal punishment and all other cruel, inhuman or degrading treatment or punishment of children, both physical and psychological;

i. exposure of children to violence within the families and home.

The role of corporate actors – Necessary legislative or other measures should be taken to ensure that legal persons can be held liable for offences established pursuant to Article 26 of the Council of Europe Convention on the Protection of Children against Sexual Exploitation and Sexual Abuse (...).

Sanctions and measures – 1. Violent, including sexual, offences against children should be punishable by effective, proportionate and dissuasive sanctions and measures, taking into account the seriousness of the offence.

2. Those convicted of violent, including sexual, offences against children, as well as those subject to criminal proceedings should be provided with access to effective intervention programmes and measures with a view to preventing and minimising the risks of repeated offences.

3. In accordance with the principles of social integration and education and of the prevention of re-offending, any justice system dealing with child perpetrators of violence should be integrated with wider social initiatives aimed at ensuring a holistic approach to and continuity of care of such children (principle of community involvement and continuous care).

4. In accordance with its basic principles, the national legal system should provide for a possibility of not imposing penalties on child victims of violence

for their involvement in unlawful activities, to the extent that they have been compelled to do so.

Aggravating circumstances – Resorting to violence against children should be taken into consideration as an aggravating circumstance in the determination of a sanction. Other circumstances to be taken into account, in so far as they do not already form part of the constituent elements of the offence, should include the abuse of a recognised position of trust, authority or influence over the child, of a relationship based on economic or any other form of dependence, and the involvement in a criminal organisation.

Jurisdiction – 1. Necessary legislative or other measures should be taken to establish jurisdiction over violent, including sexual, offences against children who are the state's nationals or have their habitual residence on the state's territory.

2. Subject to international treaties' requirements, necessary legislative or other measures should be taken to establish national jurisdiction over violent, including sexual, offences against children committed abroad by the state's nationals and persons who have their habitual residence on the state's territory. To ensure effective extraterritorial legislation, prosecution of perpetrators and imposition of sanctions, the requirement of double criminality should be abolished and mutual legal assistance facilitated.

Statute of limitation – With regard to offences identified by Article 33 of the Council of Europe Convention on the Protection of Children against Sexual Exploitation and Sexual Abuse, the statute of limitation should continue for a period of time which is sufficient to allow the efficient starting of proceedings after the child victim has reached the age of majority and which is commensurate with the gravity of the crime in question.

Enforcement – Legislation safeguarding the rights of the child and protecting children from all forms of violence should be fully and appropriately enforced. To that effect, it should be supported by relevant institutions, including independent national institutions for the rights of the child and independent monitoring mechanisms, human and financial resources, and be accompanied by guidance to all relevant sectors and professionals.

5.2. Policy framework

National child rights policy – 1. The existence of a national child rights policy is crucial for the realisation of the child's right to be protected from all forms of violence. Such a policy initiates, promotes and co-ordinates processes aimed at ensuring that the provisions and principles of the CRC permeate all aspects of government policy and all public actions affecting children.

2. All national policies relevant to children's well-being (social policy, health care policy, educational policy, housing policy, etc.) should contribute to the

promotion and protection of the rights of the child. Priority should be attached to policies aimed at reducing inequality, poverty and marginalisation; supporting families; addressing unemployment and income gaps; addressing social tolerance, beliefs and values that condone and sustain violence; improving social networks; facilitating social inclusion of migrants and their families. Policies and measures developed in related areas should be properly co-ordinated, and their outputs should be mutually reinforcing.

3. Policies, based on research, evidence, and children's own experiences, should be developed to prevent, detect and respond to violence against children. Particular attention should be paid to the protection of vulnerable groups, such as children with disabilities, children in or having experienced state care, children in foster care, abandoned children, unaccompanied and separated children, refugee and asylum seeking children, children belonging to minorities, children working and/or living on the street, children living in extreme poverty and disadvantaged or segregated areas, children in armed conflicts and emergency situations, children in detention or in conflict with the law, etc.

Children and families policies – 1. The overall goal of children and families policies should be:

a. to support families in their child-rearing responsibilities;

b. to prevent, as far as possible, the separation of children from their families;

c. to provide for family-like and community-based alternatives to placement of children in institutions that are in the children's best interests; and

d. in cases of separation (...), when appropriate, to ensure ongoing contact between children and their parents and to support family reunification where that is in the best interests of the child.

2. The promotion of positive and non-violent forms of child-rearing should be central to children and families policies. Positive parenting refers to parental behaviour that respects the rights of the child and children's best interests, nurtures, empowers, guides and recognises children as individuals in their own right. Positive parenting is not permissive but sets the boundaries that children need to help them develop their potential to the full.

3. Institutionalised care should be used only in a child's best interests, as a matter of last resort, for the shortest possible period of time, and have as the primary objective the child's successful integration and/or re-integration in society. Children can be placed in institutions only to meet needs that have been established as imperative on the basis of a multidisciplinary assessment.

5.3. Institutional framework

1. The sustainable institutional framework required for the strategy's realisation should comprise the following key elements:

a. an agency at national level (where possible and in accordance with national regulations) entrusted with the primary responsibility for the protection of children from violence. This authority should play a key co-ordinating and monitoring function as far as the strategy's implementation is concerned and assume overall responsibility in cases of violence against children;

b. each public institution contributing to child protection should have a clearly defined role consistent with the strategy's broader goals. Institutions' mandates should have a clear obligation to collaborate with the co-ordinating agency and all other institutions and actors, including civil society. The different institutions' mandates and the job descriptions of their staff should be linked;

c. an independent human rights institution should be established in line with the Paris principles to promote and protect the rights of the child (for example, an ombudsperson/commissioner specifically for the rights of the child, established through legislation, either independently or as a focal point within an existing human rights institution). This institution should be accorded such powers as are necessary to enable it to discharge its mandate effectively and independently, including the power to hear any person; obtain any information and/or document necessary for assessing situations falling within its competence; access facilities providing care for children at all times; propose initiatives and measures, including legislative measures; conduct awareness-raising campaigns; disseminate information on the rights of the child, to children in particular; and monitor governments' actions. The institution should be provided with an adequate infrastructure, funding (including specifically for the rights of the child, within broad-based institutions), staff and premises. It should be associated with the strategy's design, evaluation and follow-up;

d. a body, such as an observatory on the rights of the child, a national statistical office or a research institute dealing with children should co-ordinate the collection, analysis, management and dissemination of data on violence and promote research to inform the strategy's design and implementation;

e. all institutions providing care and services for children should be accredited and registered with competent public authorities on the basis of relevant legislation and national minimum standards of care. Internal control and independent monitoring mechanisms should be put in place to ensure compliance with the standards;

f. all institutions, services and facilities responsible for the care and protection of children should be encouraged to adopt codes of good conduct, incorporating the prohibition, prevention and rejection of all forms of violence against children, and be expected to adhere fully to these codes. Model job descriptions should be established for each professional category. They should contain an obligation to respect the rights of the child and to report violence to competent authorities;

g. the necessary links should be established between institutions at national, regional and local levels, and effective partnerships should be built, based on the clear division of competencies fixed in respective partnership agreements;

h. civil society should become an integral part of the institutional framework, and actors, such as human rights institutions, professional networks, children and children's organisations, should be invited to contribute to the strategy's design, implementation, evaluation and follow-up.

6. Child-friendly services and mechanisms

6.1. General principles

1. The prime objective of institutions, services and facilities responsible for the care, education and protection of children should be to ensure, to the maximum extent possible, children's survival, development and well-being.

2. All children should have access to quality services adapted to their needs. The use of multidisciplinary models of services, comprising welfare, health, educational and psychological assistance and family guidance should be widely promoted. Such models should rely on strong intersectoral co-operation, appropriately qualified staff, an integrated curriculum, and a centralised implementation framework.

3. Services for the prevention of violence, the protection of children and the treatment of victims should be made available particularly at local level. Reliable procedures and mechanisms, including for the exchange of relevant information and best practice, should be put in place through inter-agency agreements and protocols.

6.2. Child care standards

1. Regulations should be established for all institutions, services and facilities responsible for the care, education and protection of children, setting standards aimed at the best interests and full development of the child. Respect for these standards should be ensured through training of staff, internal control and regular independent monitoring. Any infringements of the rights of the child in such establishments should be sanctioned in conformity with appropriate and effective procedures.

2. Specific requirements should apply to the juvenile justice system and facilities providing institutionalised care to ensure that the rights of the child are fully protected, children enjoy a good quality of life and there are opportunities for them to participate in all activities normally enjoyed by their peers.

3. A system should be put in place to vet fully those working in contact with children, in any capacity, that ensures an appropriate balance between the child's right to protection from violence and the individual's right to a good name.

6.3. Independent monitoring

1. All institutions, services and facilities responsible for the care, education and protection of children should be subject to regular independent monitoring with a view to:

a. providing legal safeguards for both children and staff that are fully observed;

b. verifying the appropriateness and correctness of public expenditure;

c. supplying guidance on the execution of child welfare laws and regulations.

2. Monitoring should be performed by an independent body determined by law and staffed with specially trained personnel.

6.4. Reporting of violence

1. Education on the rights of the child and the knowledge and understanding of authorities to whom violence can be reported are two essential conditions enabling wider reporting of violence by both children and adults. To be truly effective, the reporting mechanism should be child-friendly and part of a broader system comprising reporting, referral and support services. Such a system should respect the rights of the child and offer children (and, where appropriate, their families) the necessary protection, including the protection of their privacy, without undue delay.

2. Reporting of violence should be mandatory for all professionals working for and with children, including those in organisations and private entities performing tasks on behalf of the state. Where mandatory reporting already exists, the extent to which various agencies fulfil their reporting obligations should be examined and kept under regular review.

3. To encourage wider reporting by professionals, legislative changes can be introduced in order to:

a. protect those who report or initiate complaints from liability in cases of reasonable mistakes in the assessment of the risk of violence;

b. remove a requirement to obtain parents' or carers' permission to file a complaint;

c. ensure that confidentiality norms do not hamper the reporting where the child consents, or is judged not to have the capacity to understand, and where professionals believe reporting or referring is in the child's best interests.

4. Children and their families should have access to information, including in a child-friendly format, on what acts and practices constitute violence, for instance bullying and mobbing in schools, and to whom and how these cases could be reported. A child should be able to file a report without the consent of her or his parent or guardian.

5. Every service, institution or facility responsible for the care, education and protection of children should have a well-publicised and easily accessible service, respectful of the child's privacy and be required to investigate allegations of violence promptly and fully. All children, including those in care in a legal establishment, as well as children with disabilities, their parents and carers should be informed of such complaint mechanisms. The procedure should allow for effective access to support services while avoiding any stigmatisation of the child victim.

6. An independent, confidential, well-advertised, easy to memorise, toll-free telephone help line should be made available for children to seek confidential and professional counselling and to report violence.

7. Emergency response services should be established in every locality for child victims of violence, including victims of sexual exploitation, sexual abuse, harmful traditional practices and all forms of violence in the home and family. The services' contact details should be made known to children, families and others in contact with children.

6.5. Referral mechanisms

1. Procedures for the referral of child victims of violence and the modalities for inter-agency co-operation should be clearly defined (that is, between social services, education, health, police, prosecution authorities, voluntary and private agencies). Such procedures should be adopted following an assessment of the specific circumstances of each particular victim, giving due weight to her or his views and, when it is in the child's best interests, also to her or his parents' or guardian's views.

2. Children should be encouraged, including through the provision of independent advocacy and support services, to speak to the relevant authority about their experience of violence.

3. Child victims should be assessed without delay, and for victims of violence within the home and family, the protective capacity of the non-violent caregiver and the situation of other children living in the home should be established.

6.6. Recovery, rehabilitation and social reintegration

1. The state should take all appropriate measures to promote physical and psychological recovery and rehabilitation of child victims and witnesses of violence and, if need be, of their families. Such services should be provided without delay and in an environment which fosters the child's health, self-respect and dignity.

2. The implementation of recovery and reintegration measures for child perpetrators of violence should be based on the child's best interests, limited by the gravity of the offence committed (principle of proportionality) and take

account of the age, physical and mental well-being, development, capacities and personal circumstances (principle of individualisation), as ascertained when necessary by psychological, psychiatric or social inquiry reports.

3. The services responsible for the recovery, rehabilitation and social reintegration of child victims, witnesses or perpetrators of violence should follow a multidisciplinary and multi-agency approach, seeing the child in the wider context of family, community and her or his cultural background. A proper balance should be sought between mainstream and specialised services, as well as programmes addressing individual and relationship factors and those focusing on community and societal aspects.

6.7. The justice system

1. Judicial and extra-judicial proceedings should be pursued in the best interests and in full respect of the rights of the child, including the right to be protected from all forms of violence.

2. To protect the rights of the child and children's legitimate interests throughout the process, children should be granted access to mediation, free and independent legal services, and advocacy and support services. Efforts should be made to ensure that the remedies available are effective and that there is effective enforcement of judicial decisions and judgments.

3. Judicial and extra-judicial proceedings involving children should be expedited, treated as a priority and be completed without unjustified delay. To this end, stronger co-operation and co-ordination among all parties to the judicial process should be encouraged.

4. Judicial and extra-judicial proceedings should respect the child's right to be heard and to have her or his views given due weight. To allow their meaningful participation, children should be informed about their procedural rights in a manner which takes full account of their age and level of maturity and supported by an independent representative.

5. Special protection, procedures and facilities should be provided to ensure child victims and witnesses of violence are fully supported. In particular:

a. judicial proceedings should not aggravate the trauma experienced by the child. Where appropriate, the justice response should be followed swiftly by adequate support services;

b. the privacy of children and of their families should be protected throughout the process. Where necessary, appropriate security measures should be taken to avoid intimidation, subjection to retaliation or repeat victimisation of child victims and witnesses of violence and of their families.

6. The age of criminal responsibility should be determined by law and be set suitably high, bearing in mind factors related to the child's development. For child perpetrators of violence, concepts of retribution and repression should give

way to rehabilitation and restorative justice objectives, with due attention to effective public safety and appropriate human rights and legal safeguards for the child victims.

7. Alternatives to institutionalised care for child perpetrators of violence should be established, such as help, guidance and supervision orders; counselling; probation; foster care; and educational and vocational training programmes. The overall objective of such measures should be to facilitate children's successful socialisation and reintegration in the family, the community and society.

8. Child perpetrators of violence should not be deprived of their liberty other than where it is necessary as a measure of last resort, used for the shortest period of time and takes place in specially designed premises. The conditions of the detention should be in conformity with the CRC and other relevant standards and take into account children's specific needs. Children undergoing any form of detention should be detained separately from adults, unless this is considered to be contrary to their best interests.

7. Research and data

1. Identification of an effective strategy for the protection of children from violence depends on the availability and proper analysis of data at national, regional and local levels. The adoption of a national research agenda represents the most appropriate way of promoting an integrated and systematic approach to data collection, analysis, dissemination and research. This approach, *inter alia*, implies the following:

Research –

a. baseline study on violence against children as a prerequisite to any strategic planning process;

b. ethical and regular research involving interviews with children and separately with their parents or carers, in conditions of confidentiality and trust, to establish as accurately as possible the actual experience of violence by children;

c. longitudinal large-scale research on the root causes of violence and the inter-dependence of its various forms;

d. development of a harmonised methodology with a common set of indicators, allowing for the identification of groups of children vulnerable to violence;

e. ongoing research into the precise nature of risks to children via the internet, and how these risks shift over time and are mitigated by interventions;

f. research into protective factors, notably children's resilience mechanisms;

g. surveys on adult and child perpetrators of violence to develop criteria and parameters for their assessment and treatment;

h. research into what works to protect children from violence and to evaluate existing responses, including methodologies for the evaluation and assessment of violence prevention services and programmes and the development of quality criteria;

i. surveys to quantify the social costs of violence against children.

Statistical monitoring –

a. regular statistical monitoring, on the basis of established methodology, of violence against children at national, regional and local levels in all settings. The data should be broken down by gender, age, form of violence, urban or rural household, families' characteristics, level of education and national, social and ethnic origin;

b. collection of quantitative and qualitative data on the length and outcomes of judicial proceedings involving children, including protective measures provided for child victims of violence.

Establishment of national databases –

a. on children's births and deaths, including the establishment of a child death (and serious injury) review mechanism;

b. on children entering, leaving, or changing institutions, and all forms of alternative care and detention facilities, including the recording of all cases of violence against children in such institutions;

c. on persons convicted of violent offences against children, including their genetic profile (DNA).

Co-ordination –

a. the designation (where possible and in conformity with national circumstances) of a single authority, preferably an observatory on the rights of the child, a national statistical office or a research institute, to co-ordinate and disseminate children-related data nationwide and exchange information internationally;

b. active contribution by all agencies with a child protection role to data collection.

2. All institutions, services and facilities recruiting personnel to work for and with children should be afforded easy but appropriately controlled access to data on persons convicted of violent offences against children.

3. Personal data processing at national, regional and local levels should comply with internationally accepted standards and ethical safeguards.

4. Internationally agreed uniform standards should be established to facilitate international comparability of data.

8. International co-operation

1. Member states of the Council of Europe should co-operate with each other, in accordance with these guidelines and through application of relevant

international and regional instruments and arrangements agreed on the basis of uniform or reciprocal legislation and internal laws, to the widest extent possible, for the purpose of:

a. preventing and combating all forms of violence against children;

b. protecting and assisting child victims and witnesses;

c. investigating or prosecuting criminal offences involving violence against children.

2. Member states should afford each other the widest measure of mutual assistance in proceedings on offences involving violence against children, such as child abductions, trafficking in children, sexual exploitation and sexual abuse of children.

3. To facilitate implementation of the guidelines, member states should strengthen, as appropriate, co-operation within relevant intergovernmental bodies, transnational networks and other international organisations.

4. Each member state should endeavour to integrate, where appropriate, prevention and eradication of all forms of violence against children into development assistance programmes provided for the benefit of third countries.

Appendix 2 – Glossary of terms

Best interests of the child: That the best interests of the child shall be a primary consideration in all actions concerning children is a concept contained in Article 3 of the CRC. It stands out as one of the CRC general principles, alongside Articles 2, 6 and 12, and acquires particular significance in situations where other more specific provisions of the convention do not apply. Article 3(1) emphasises that governments and public and private bodies must ascertain the impact on children of their actions, in order to ensure that the best interests of the child are a primary consideration, giving proper priority to children and building child-friendly societies. Article 3(2) outlines an active overall obligation for states to provide the necessary protection and care for the child's well-being in all circumstances, while respecting the rights and duties of parents. Article 3(3) requires that standards be established by "competent bodies" for all institutions, services and facilities for children, and that the state ensures that the standards are complied with (...).

Bullying is an act of repeated aggressive behavior in order to intentionally hurt another person, physically or mentally. Bullying is characterised by an individual behaving in a certain way to gain power over another person (...). Behaviour may include name calling, verbal or written abuse, exclusion from activities, exclusion from social situations, physical abuse, or coercion (...). Bullies may behave in this way to be perceived as popular or tough or to get attention. They may bully out of jealousy or because they themselves are bullied (...).

Child exploitation: The term exploitation includes, at a minimum, the exploitation of the prostitution of others or other forms of sexual exploitation, forced labour or services, slavery or practices similar to slavery, servitude or the removal of organs (Article 3 of the Protocol to Prevent, Suppress and Punish Trafficking in Persons, especially Women and Children, Supplementing the United Nations Convention against Transnational Organised Crime).

Child pornography means any material that visually depicts a child engaged in real or simulated sexually explicit conduct or any depiction of a child's sexual organs for primarily sexual purposes. Offences related to child pornography include the following intentional conduct, when committed without right: a) producing child pornography; b) offering or making available child pornography; c) distributing or transmitting child pornography; d) procuring child pornography for oneself or for another person; e) possessing child pornography; and f) knowingly obtaining access, through information and communication technologies, to child pornography (Article 20 Council of Europe Convention on the Protection of Children against Sexual Exploitation and Sexual Abuse).

Child prostitution means the fact of using a child for sexual activities where money or any other form of remuneration or consideration is given or promised as payment, regardless of whether this payment, promise or consideration is made to the child or to a third person. Offences related to child prostitution include the following intentional conduct: a) recruiting a child into prostitution or causing a child to participate in prostitution; b) coercing a child into prostitution or profiting from or otherwise exploiting a child for such purposes; c) having recourse to child prostitution (Article 19 Council of Europe Convention on the Protection of Children against Sexual Exploitation and Sexual Abuse).

Child trafficking means the recruitment, transportation, transfer, harbouring or receipt of a child for the purpose of exploitation even if this does not involve (...) the threat or use of force or other forms of coercion, of abduction, of fraud, of deception, of the abuse of power or of a position of vulnerability or of the giving or receiving of payments or benefits to achieve the consent of a person having control over another person (Article 3 of the Protocol to Prevent, Suppress and Punish Trafficking in Persons, especially Women and Children, Supplementing the United Nations Convention against Transnational Organised Crime). See also the definition of trafficking below.

Corporal punishment is a form of violence, defined as any punishment in which physical force is used and intended to cause some degree of pain or discomfort, however light, to a child (for detailed definition, see Committee on the Rights of the Child, General Comment No. 8, paragraph 11).

Corruption of children means the intentional causing, for sexual purposes, of a child who has not reached the nationally prescribed legal age for sexual consent to witness sexual abuse or sexual activities, even without having to participate (Article 22 Council of Europe Convention on the Protection of Children against Sexual Exploitation and Sexual Abuse).

Harmful traditional practices: Every social grouping in the world has specific traditional cultural practices and beliefs, some of which are beneficial to all members, while others are harmful to a specific group, such as women. Harmful traditional practices include female genital mutilation; early marriage; female infanticide; honour killings; early pregnancy, etc. (Factsheet 23, Harmful Traditional Practices Affecting the Health of Women and Children, <www.ohchr.org/Documents/Publications/FactSheet23en.pdf>).

Mobbing: Mobbying is a group bullying. It is ganging up on someone using the tactics of rumor, innuendo, discrediting, isolating, intimidating, and above all, making it look as of the targeted person is responsible. As is typical of many abusive situations, the perpetrators maintain that the victim "deserved it" (School Mobbying and Emotional Abuse, <www.selfgrowth.com/articles/Elliott9.html>).

Monitoring is the authorities' activities to ensure that child welfare legislation is maintained. It consists of the following three distinct elements: a) the central authorities passing laws and regulations; b) the municipal level and childcare institutions delivering services; and c) an independent body monitoring performance at local level. Monitoring can be conducted as either announced or unannounced inspections or management system audits. The establishment of a standardised national monitoring regime facilitates the gathering of statistics on child welfare in a country and contributes to governmental decision making.

Neglect means the failure of parents or carers to meet a child's physical and emotional needs when they have the means, knowledge and access to necessary services; or failure to protect her or him from exposure to danger (World Report on Violence against Children, World Health Oranisation, Geneva, 2002).

Participation of a child in a pornographic performance: Offences related to the participation of a child in pornographic performance include the following intentional conduct: a) recruiting a child to participate in pornographic performances or causing a child to participate in such performances; b) coercing a child to participate in pornographic performances or profiting from or otherwise exploiting a child for such purposes; c) knowingly attending pornographic performances involving the participation of children (Article 21 Council of Europe Convention on the Protection of Children against Sexual Exploitation and Sexual Abuse).

Psychological violence refers to insults, name-calling, ignoring, isolation, rejection, threats, manipulation, emotional indifference, and belittlement, witnessing domestic violence, and other behaviour that can be detrimental to a child's psychological development and well-being (UN Secretary General's World Report on Violence against Children).

Sex tourism means trips organised from within the tourist sector, or from outside this sector but using its structures and networks, with the primary purpose of effecting a commercial sexual relationship between the tourist and residents at the destination (World Tourism Organisation (WTO), Statement on the Prevention of Organised Sex Tourism, 1995).

Sexual abuse: Offences related to sexual abuse of children include the following intentional conduct: a) engaging in sexual activities with a child who, according to the relevant provisions of national law, has not reached the legal age for sexual activities (this does not apply to consensual sexual activities between minors), and b) engaging in sexual activities with a child where use is made of coercion, force or threats; or abuse is made of a recognised position of trust, authority or influence over the child, including within the family; or abuse is made of a particularly vulnerable situation of the child, notably because of a mental or physical disability or a situation of dependence (Article 18 Council of Europe Convention on the Protection of Children against Sexual Exploitation and Sexual Abuse).

Sale of children means any act or transaction whereby a child is transferred by any person or group of persons to another for remuneration or any other consideration (Article 2 of the Optional Protocol to the Convention on the Rights of the Child on the sale of children, child prostitution and child pornography).

Solicitation of children for sexual purposes: Offences related to solicitation of children for sexual purposes include the intentional proposal, through information and communication technologies, of an adult to meet a child who has not reached the nationally prescribed legal age for sexual activities for the purpose of engaging in sexual activities with the child or producing child pornography and where this proposal has been followed by material acts leading to such a meeting (Article 23 of the Council of Europe Convention on the Protection of Children against Sexual Exploitation and Sexual Abuse).

Trafficking in human beings means the recruitment, transportation, transfer, harbouring or receipt of persons, by means of the threat or use of force or other forms of coercion, of abduction, of fraud, of deception, of the abuse of power or of a position of vulnerability or the giving or receiving of payments or benefits to achieve the consent of a person having control over another person, for the purpose of exploitation. "Exploitation" shall include, at a minimum, the exploitation of the prostitution of others or other forms of sexual exploitation, forced labour or services, slavery or practices similar to slavery, servitude or removal or organs. The consent of a victim of "trafficking in human beings" to the intended exploitation is irrelevant where any of the means cited above have been used. The recruitment, transportation, transfer, harbouring or receipt of a child for the purpose of exploitation shall be considered "trafficking in human beings" even if this does not involve any of the means set forth above (Article 4, Council of Europe Convention on Action against Trafficking in Human Beings).

(…)

2. VIOLENCE AGAINST CHILDREN – CHILD ABUSE AND NEGLECT / CHILD MALTREATMENT

TASK/TEXT 2.1:

TASK/TEXT 2.1.1: CHILD ABUSE AND NEGLECT – THE NEED FOR COURAGE

By Karen Polonko (professor in the Department of Sociology and Criminal Justice at Old Dominion University, Norfork, Virginia), <www.odu.edu/ao/instadv/quest/ChildAbuse.html>, accessed 12 November 2008 (*Old Dominion University's Quest* 2005/2)

True stories

In India, a 3-year-old is exposed to hazardous substances while working in an unventilated room in a small village factory. Her fingers are wrapped so that the blood from her cuts will not interfere with her work. At the same moment, in Thailand, a child, age 8, is sold into sexual slavery. Forced to have sex with an average of 15 customers a day, she is likely to be infected with HIV within six months.

Closer to home, a 4-year-old boy labors in the grape fields in upstate New York alongside other migrant workers. He suffers chronic respiratory infections; his hands are in constant pain.

Meanwhile, in the Midwest, a desperate girl tells her mother that her father is molesting her. The father says that she is making this up to get even with him for something else. After the mom (who was sexually abused as a child herself) leaves, the father ties his daughter to a tree and partially buries her cat next to her. He then runs the lawn mower over the animal, as the child screams that she will be good and take everything back if he will let her cat live.

Elsewhere, a little boy, age 4, has his hands amputated after they were tied tightly behind his back as punishment for using his father's paint. His father, an alcoholic, fell asleep and forgot to untie his son. When they finally return from the hospital, the son asks his father if he is really good, can he have his hands back. Later that day, the father kills himself.

These are the stories that we do not want to hear. We want to believe that all children are safe. We argue that these cases are the rare exception. It is too painful to believe otherwise.

Prevalence

Unfortunately, child maltreatment is not rare. According to the latest UNICEF reports, literally hundreds of millions of children throughout the world are victims of abuse, neglect and exploitation. At the extremes, children are killed, abandoned, sold or given in "debt" bondage. Close to 6 million children work under conditions of virtual slavery. Every year, millions of girls are trafficked, exploited in the sex industry and/or genitally mutilated. Millions more at home and abroad are beaten, emotionally abused, molested and/or neglected by their parents.

In the United States alone, more than 3 million children are reported to official agencies for severe maltreatment in any given year. Surveys indicate that this figure grossly underestimates the true extent of the problem as **more than one-third of adults in the United States** report having experienced physical abuse, sexual abuse, emotional abuse and/or neglect as a child.

Definitions

Like our need to believe that child maltreatment is rare, many people believe that only the most egregious forms of maltreatment could harm a child. The rest just "toughens them up," "keeps them under control" and is "for their own good." Unfortunately, the reality is that both extreme and less severe levels of maltreatment can harm children in profound ways.

Reflecting the myths, child abuse and neglect are typically distinguished from other levels of child maltreatment by severity and evidence of intentionally inflicted, observable injury or impairment, under the mistaken assumption that only such extremes indicate that a child has been harmed. So, for example, in a study that Old Dominion University colleague Lucien Lombardo, professor of sociology, and I conducted, titled "A Comparative Analysis of Human Rights' and United States' Law on Corporal Punishment: Implications for Understanding Human Rights and Colonial Models of Child-Adult Relationships," we found that most US statutes relating to corporal punishment are concerned with explicitly safeguarding the rights of parents to use violence against children. The exceptions are specified as excessive violence or "physical abuse" – i.e., violence that intentionally caused substantial injury such as the child's death, disfigurement, or brain or spinal cord damage.

Similarly, other forms of child maltreatment are defined in terms of granting parents permission to inflict maximal harm on children, finding abuse only in the extremes that result in demonstrable injury. Child emotional abuse is an extreme or habitual pattern of hostile and aggressive parenting that results in mental or emotional injury. Emotional neglect is extreme lack of emotional responsiveness and involvement that causes mental or developmental harm. Child sexual abuse is extreme oral, genital or anal contact (or defined legally in terms of age difference, minor status and/or relationship to perpetrator). Child neglect is restricted to the extremes of parental lack of involvement and supervision, and failure to meet the child's needs, which place the child's life in serious danger.

Consequences

Given the above, it is surprising that many people do not believe that child maltreatment has profoundly negative consequences that go beyond the specific childhood injury to impact the rest of the child's life. Instead, people often mistakenly attribute the long-term consequences of child abuse to irrelevant factors. However, the reality is that the consequences of child maltreatment are enormous, not only for the survivor, but also for society.

Some consequences of maltreatment differ according to the child's vulnerability. For instance, infants and toddlers are at greatest risk of fatal abuse, with a blow to the baby's head as the most common cause of death. Some consequences for the child are greater for one type of maltreatment than another. For example, child neglect is most strongly associated with the child having a lower IQ and lower educational achievement; child physical abuse with the child engaging in violent crime as a teen and adult; and child emotional abuse with subsequent psychopathology. However, all forms of maltreatment are associated with adverse effects for children and the adults they become. As discussed in my paper "Causes and Consequences of Child Abuse: Shedding More Light on the Cycle of Violence and Neglect," prior research points to the following:

Child physical and emotional abuse and neglect all increase the likelihood that the child will subsequently:

- Be cognitively impaired (including having a lower IQ and cognitive development; lower grades and educational achievement);
- Have impaired moral reasoning (including having less empathy, less compliance and less developed conscience);
- Engage in violence and crime (including higher rates of juvenile delinquency, teen and adult violent and nonviolent crime);
- Be violent in relationships (including being more likely to assault their siblings and other children as a child, and later to abuse their own children, spouse and elderly parents).

In addition, all types of child maltreatment – physical and emotional abuse and neglect and sexual abuse – increase the likelihood that the child will subsequently:

- Have mental health problems (including higher rates of depression, anxiety, dissociation, etc.);
- Become a substance abuser of both legal and illegal substances as a teenager and adult;
- Become pregnant as a teenager and engage in risky sexual behavior (including earlier first intercourse, exposure to sexually transmitted diseases and greater number of partners).

Aside from the obvious, part of the reason these effects are so profound is that much child maltreatment occurs before age 6, during "critical windows" of development. Being neglected early in life, for example, is linked to the underdevelopment of those parts of the brain responsible for cognitive development and empathy. Being the target of or witnessing physical violence early in life is more likely to result in the overdevelopment of parts of the brain that ultimately affect impulsivity, reactivity, anxiety and aggression. As research by Bruce D. Perry, M.D., Ph.D., senior fellow of the Child Trauma Academy, shows, both abuse and neglect physiologically predispose a child to a series of neurobiological problems and violent behavior. These physiological changes are compounded by the modeling effect of seriously inadequate parenting; the adoption of a belief system about self, others and the world as malevolent; and the defense mechanisms abused children must develop to cope with their terror, despair and hopelessness. For example, the child blames himself for the abuse or denies that the parent is maltreating him.

Causes

The general belief is that parents who maltreat their children are rare, pathological and certainly not like us. The reality is that most parents engage in culturally permissible or low levels of child abuse and neglect. Inflicting these permissible levels of maltreatment not only harms children, but also often escalates to the more severe forms of maltreatment.

Many of the parents who abuse and neglect their children were themselves maltreated as children. They are the little ones we failed to protect a generation ago. Also, many of the harmful consequences that resulted from their abuse and neglect, such as mental health problems, substance abuse and teen pregnancy, caused them to maltreat their children, laying the foundation for a cycle of abuse and neglect across generations. As reviewed in "Causes and Consequences of Child Abuse," research indicates the following.

First, parents who abuse or neglect their children are more likely to:

- Have been maltreated as a child;
- Have mental health problems, including parent depression;
- Have a violent marriage;
- Be a substance abuser;
- Be a teenage mother;
- Have lower levels of education and income.

Second, parents who abuse or neglect their children are also more likely to:

- Have serious parenting deficits (e.g., have unrealistic expectations for their children);
- Use harsh and aggressive parenting with their children (i.e., low levels of emotional abuse);
- Have low levels of parental involvement and supervision, and give their children very little positive attention and affection (i.e., low levels of physical and emotional neglect);
- Frequently use corporal punishment on their children (i.e., low levels of physical abuse);
- Have few cognitively stimulating materials in the home for their children (i.e., low levels of neglect).

The first group of factors provides insights into the cycle of abuse and neglect. Being maltreated as a child models parenting behaviors and leads to the adoption of beliefs and defenses that increase the survivor's chances of harming his own children. In addition, being maltreated as a child increases the likelihood that one will suffer other outcomes such as lower IQ and educational attainment, more mental health problems, substance abuse and teen pregnancy – each of which, in turn, independently increases the risk of maltreating one's own child.

The second set of factors shows that parents who severely maltreat their children are more likely than other parents to more frequently subject their children to low levels of abuse and neglect. In other words, when parents engage in "culturally acceptable" levels of harsh parenting, corporal punishment, verbal aggression, and minimal involvement and supervision, they are significantly more likely to proceed to more severe abuse and neglect of their children. Thus, in contrast to what is typically assumed, low levels of maltreatment are dangerous for children. Moreover, at least in the area of physical violence, more frequent corporal punishment has the same adverse consequences as physical abuse, from lower IQ to more violent behavior and mental problems, except to lesser degrees. (This includes a finding from a master's-level study in Old Dominion's

Department of Sociology and Criminal Justice that the more frequently a girl is subjected to corporal punishment when young, the more likely she is to become pregnant as a teenager.)

As discussed in "Causes and Consequences of Child Abuse," these findings help us to understand another important reason why children of teenage mothers and socioeconomically disadvantaged parents are more likely to be abused and neglected. These parents are also significantly more likely to use "low levels of abuse and neglect," such as more hostile and aggressive parenting, more frequent corporal punishment, and less responsiveness and involvement. They also are less likely to get care and more likely to use both legal and illegal drugs while pregnant, which is related to premature birth and neurological and cognitive problems in the baby. In turn, substance-abusing mothers are also more likely to be young and impoverished. All of this is related to having been abused and neglected themselves as children.

Intervention

Some people believe that intervention on behalf of maltreated children is so effective that even adequate parents now have to worry about outside interference. The reality is that intervention and prevention programs have not been effective in reducing the prevalence of child abuse and neglect.

As many researchers and practitioners acknowledge, few resources are committed; agencies have little power to intervene; and treatment is often low cost, short term and focused on keeping the family together, rather than ensuring that the child is safe from abuse and neglect. We refuse to acknowledge that both child abuse and neglect, as well as low levels of child maltreatment, have serious consequences for the child and society. Instead, we blame child maltreatment and its consequences (for example, delinquency and drug abuse), on people and conditions that fit preconceived stereotypes and political agendas, such as a common belief that maternal employment causes delinquency, even though there is no evidence to support this. In this country, we continue to spend hundreds of millions of dollars on programs like Abstinence Only or Just Say No that just don't work because they don't address the underlying problems.

The need to unite

Discussions of child maltreatment are often polarized around issues of religion, class, race, ethnicity and culture, both within and across countries. Often, parents may believe that group status justifies how they treat their children. However, the reality that emerges from a multicultural look at child abuse and neglect is that while children of certain groups may experience different types of abuse, children of all religions, income levels, races, ethnic groups and countries suffer from maltreatment.

A review of research on rates in the United States indicates that incidences of child sexual abuse and emotional abuse do not differ significantly for African American, Caucasian and Hispanic girls. On the other hand, African American children have higher rates of physical abuse and neglect than Caucasians, although a significant portion of this difference is due to variations in education, income and poverty – i.e., factors that increase the child's risk of maltreatment. However, with rare exception, research shows that children of all races and ethnic groups suffer adverse consequences when abused or neglected.

Lighting the way to concerted action on behalf of children, African American leaders like Dr. Alvin Poussaint and the Rev. Jesse Jackson have joined other leaders in the fight to end not only severe child abuse, but also lower levels of abuse and neglect, including corporal punishment.

Internationally, we are urged to look for ways that we have inadvertently supported child maltreatment, such as buying products made by young children, refusing to confront travel agencies that covertly advertise sex tours to Thailand for young virgins, and simply remaining silent.

Standing in the way of preventing child maltreatment is the power differential between parents and children. Parents are for the most part lawfully free to engage in child abuse and neglect, short of serious injury, as part of their parental prerogative. As discussed in several papers that I have written with Professor Lombardo, including "Cycles of Trauma and Cycles of Nurturing: The UN Convention on the Rights of the Child and the Path from Childhood to Adulthood" and "The Enlightened Witness: Reasserting Humanity in the Face of Violence at the Beginning of the 21st Century," the key is to extend to children the rights of human beings.

As many scholars have stressed, the most logical way for the United States to begin this process of reducing child maltreatment is to join every other country (except for Somalia) in the United Nations that has adopted the UN Convention on the Rights of the Child. This will take courage, for in granting children human rights, we must challenge not only the beliefs and laws which support the power parents have to hit, harm, ignore and exploit their children, but also the beliefs, defenses and behaviors that parents developed to survive their own childhood maltreatment.

As Dr. Perry concludes in his paper *Incubated in Terror: Neurodevelopmental Factors in the 'Cycle of Violence'*: "In order to solve the problems of violence, we need to transform our culture. We need to change our child rearing practices, we need to change the malignant and destructive view that children are the property of their biological parents. … Children belong to the community, they are entrusted to parents."

As researchers and practitioners emphasize, we, as a society, must do everything in our power to prevent and treat child maltreatment, not only because of the suffering of the victims, or even because of the benefits that society stands to gain, but because it is the right thing to do. It is an ethical imperative. It is our moral responsibility.

For more information about child abuse and how you can help prevent it, visit UNICEF at <www.unicef.org>; Child Trauma Institute at <www.childtrauma.com>; In Support of Children, an ODU student organization devoted to ending child abuse, at <http://groups.hamptonroads.com/SupportChildren>; the Post Institute for Family Centered Therapy at <www.postinstitute.com>; and Child Abuse Prevention Network at <http://child-abuse.com>.

Dr. Perry's paper *Incubated in Terror: Neurodevelopmental Factors in the 'Cycle of Violence'* is available at <www.childtrauma.org/CTAMATERIALS/incubated.asp>.

An excellent sourcebook, *The APSAC Handbook on Child Maltreatment*, written in 2002, can be found at <www.APSAC.org>.

TASK/TEXT 2.1.2: NEGLECT THE CHILD, DAMAGE THE ADULT

By Tapu Misa, *The New Zealand Herald*, 24 November 2008, <www.nzherald.co.nz>

In the wake of last week's convictions for Nia Glassie's brutal abuse and murder, I can't really argue with those who say some people shouldn't be allowed to have children – though I have trouble working out exactly how we'd stop people breeding. Forced sterilisation on the grounds of low IQ and low income, perhaps?

I once worked with a woman who came from a well-to-do South Island family. Her mother was mentally ill, but her family kept that shameful fact hidden, so that she never received any psychiatric help. She married and had children, whom she basically terrorised behind a wall of respectability.

Her mother should never have had children. Given the science on child brain development, my colleague was lucky to emerge relatively sane and functional.

I remember talking once to a social worker about another child. He'd suffered such awful abuse in his short life that if he had lived, she said, he would have been a severely damaged individual and in all likelihood an abuser.

It's frighteningly easy to create a sociopath. Just deprive a baby of love, of nurturing touch and smiles, of enriching experiences, and let it experience only violence, fear and anger in its first few years, and then watch the damage.

The result might look a lot like Michael and Wiremu Curtis, who were convicted last week of Nia's murder. And had Nia lived, had she survived the brutal injuries to her head, she might have grown up to find herself in much the same situation as her mother – publicly vilified for abusing her own children.

Neglect and violence affect brain chemistry and architecture, often irreversibly.

According to Dr Bruce Perry, an expert on child trauma and developing brains, children who suffer early and chronic neglect have brains that are smaller than those of the average child. Their brains have fewer cells and fewer connections between these cells. These differences can be dramatic; children who endured severe, pervasive and early neglect can have brains that are smaller than the brains of 90 per cent of children their age.

Neuroscientists tell us that the neural wiring that takes place in the early years of life sets a child's course for life.

In the first three years, the human brain develops to 90 per cent of adult size and puts in place most of the systems responsible for all future emotional, behavioural, social and physiological functioning.

Our brain architecture is the result of genetics interacting with the environment. We need specific sensory experiences, the right signals from our environment at the right time, to complete our brains.

But neglect and abuse can disrupt the process, Perry has written, resulting in "malorganisation and compromised function," and affecting our capacity for humour, empathy and attachment.

"Just as the brain allows us to see, smell, taste, think, talk and move, it is the organ that allows us to love or not," Perry writes.

"The systems in the human brain that allow us to form and maintain emotional relationships develop during infancy and the first years of life. Empathy, caring, sharing, inhibition of aggression, capacity to love and a host of other characteristics of a healthy, happy and productive person are related to the core attachment capabilities which are formed in infancy and early childhood."

Perry writes it may take many years of hard work to repair the damage from only a few months of neglect in infancy – if repair is possible at all. "Most neglect is not due to evil caregivers. It is due to isolated, overwhelmed, ignorant or distressed caregivers. In addition, there is a wide range of caregiving beliefs and practices tolerated in our society. Unfortunately, some of these are developmentally ignorant and insensitive to the needs of developing children."

Actually, most of us are ignorant of how children's brains develop. If we knew as much as the authors of a 2007 Canadian report (*The Early Years Study 2: Putting Science into Action*), we would be outraged at how little is being done for our youngest citizens.

The report's authors say the most serious brain drain in our societies is happening before children get to school, and that science and logic provide compelling evidence that investment in early childhood development would provide greater returns for society than any other type of human capital investment.

Nobel economics laureate James Heckman agrees. Society underinvests in the early years, yet such investment would not only save money in later interventions, it would boost economic productivity, too, he believes.

"Many major economic and social problems can be traced to low levels of skill and ability in the population," he wrote in *Science* magazine (June 2006), citing a rising highschool dropout rate, the 20 per cent of the US workforce that's functionally illiterate, rising levels of violent crime and property-crime levels.

TASK/TEXT 2.1.3: BRAIN DOC IN TRENTON [SAYS] EARLY CHILDHOOD CRUCIAL

By L.A. Parker, *The Trentonian* (serving Trenton, NJ), 8 April 2009, <www.trentonian.com>

TRENTON – A world-renowned authority on early childhood brain development confirmed the mission of several New Jersey-based nonprofit organizations created to improve healthy development outcomes for children. Dr. Bruce Perry, a neuroscientist, child psychiatrist and senior fellow at Houston's ChildTrauma Institute, said what happens to children between birth and age 3 sets the stage for future educational successes or failure and frustration. Perry addressed a well-attended conference at the Trenton War Memorial building, delivering a message that called for a change of direction in education and child development programs. Perry's determinations dovetailed with efforts being made by Children's Futures, The Children's Home Society of New Jersey and the Association for Children of New Jersey, all agencies who advocate for infants and children.

Production of well-adjusted and educated children starts with an understanding of the brain, Perry said. "We are in a unique position as a species," Perry said. "Human beings have the capacity to reinvent ourselves in many, many ways. Every generation we have an opportunity to change the way that we raise our children." Perry said an understanding of how the brain develops and works should impact programs and policies that focus on early childhood development. However, Perry described a disconnect between policy makers and the child population they serve. "People who make policy about children don't understand children," Perry said. He predicted social disaster without implementation of programs that coincide with what we know about brain development.

"Currently, about 10 percent of (US) families have been identified as high risk. If we continue along this path, a century from now that number could be as high as 25 percent," Perry predicted. While government programs attempt to identify at-risk children, Perry said many kids are off the radar. According to Perry, millions of babies and toddlers are being raised in families where neglect may be significant, but they are not known to state agencies. Perry said the US suffers from an arrogance that proclaims ours is a great culture. "But how advanced can we be when we require a governmental agency to protect children from parents?" Perry asked.

Children who experience child abuse or significant neglect are 59 percent more likely to be arrested as juveniles, 28 percent more likely to be arrested as adults, and 30 percent more likely to commit a violent crime. Adding to a potential for future unsuccessful outcomes is what Perry termed "relational poverty," an absence of nurturing early childhood relationships. "Children are starving for relationships, for human touch and positive interaction," Perry said.

TASK/TEXT 2.2:

TASK/TEXT 2.2.1: WORLD HEALTH ORGANIZATION'S DEFINITION OF CHILD ABUSE

Child maltreatment, sometimes referred to as **child abuse and neglect**, includes all forms of physical and emotional ill-treatment, sexual abuse, neglect, and exploitation that result in actual or potential harm to the child's health, development or dignity. – Within this broad definition, five subtypes can be distinguished: physical abuse; sexual abuse; neglect and negligent treatment; emotional abuse; and exploitation. – <www.who.int/topics/child_abuse/en>.

Five subtypes – or ten? Or eleven? (LONGSCAN classification)

"(...) five subtypes can be distinguished: physical abuse; sexual abuse; neglect and negligent treatment [etc.]." – However, neglect (and negligent treatment) may be subdivided into:

(a) emotional neglect (lack of affection & parental sensitivity/responsiveness);
(b) physical neglect (lack of care & lack of supervision);
(c) pedagogical neglect (lack of direction & guidance according to the child's evolving capacities);
(d) educational neglect (not 'insuring the child's adequate [school] education').

Moreover, lack of care and lack of supervision are sometimes seen as two distinct subtypes.

Increasingly, witnessing inter-parental ("domestic") violence is also included into the concept of child abuse. This would bring the total number of subtypes of child maltreatment to ten.

Involving the child in criminal activity is sometimes coded as moral-legal maltreatment, which would be an eleventh subtype. (However, the moral corruption of a child may also be seen as a form of emotional abuse or a form of exploitation.)

See Modified Maltreatment Classification System (MMCS): Injury Prevention Research Center, University of North Carolina, Longitudinal Studies of Child Abuse and Neglect (LONGSCAN): <www.iprc.unc.edu/longscan>, Maltreatment Coding, MMCS Coding Scheme (English, D.J. *et al.*, 1997).

TASK/TEXT 2.2.2: INTERNATIONAL SOCIETY FOR PREVENTION OF CHILD ABUSE AND NEGLECT (ISPCAN) – DEFINITION OF CAN [CHILD ABUSE AND NEGLECT]

<www.ispcan.org/CAN-facts/definition.html>, accessed 3 May 2009

General Definition
Child abuse or maltreatment constitutes all forms of physical and/or emotional ill-treatment, sexual abuse, neglect or negligent treatment or commercial or other exploitation, resulting in actual or potential harm to the child's health, survival, development or dignity in the context of a relationship of responsibility, trust or power.

Proposed Clarifications
– ***Physical abuse***
Physical abuse of a child is that which results in actual or potential physical harm from an interaction or lack of an interaction, which is reasonably within the control of a parent or person in a position of responsibility, power or trust. There may be a single or repeated incidents.
– ***Emotional abuse***
Emotional abuse includes the failure to provide a developmentally appropriate, supportive environment, including the availability of a primary attachment figure, so that the child can develop a stable and full range of emotional and social competencies commensurate with her or his personal potentials and in the context of the society in which the child dwells. There may also be acts towards the child that cause or have a high probability of causing harm to the child's health or physical, mental, spiritual, moral or social development. These acts must be reasonably within the control of the parent or person in a relationship of responsibility, trust or power. Acts include restriction of movement, patterns of belittling, denigrating, scapegoating, threatening, scaring, discriminating, ridiculing or other non-physical forms of hostile or rejecting treatment.

– ***Neglect and negligent treatment***
Neglect is the failure to provide for the development of the child in all spheres: health, education, emotional development, nutrition, shelter, and safe living conditions, in the context of resources reasonably available to the family or caretakers and causes or has a high probability of causing harm to the child's health or physical, mental, spiritual, moral or social development. This includes the failure to properly supervise and protect children from harm as much as is feasible.
– ***Sexual Abuse***
Child sexual abuse is the involvement of a child in sexual activity that he or she does not fully comprehend, is unable to give informed consent to, or for which the child is not developmentally prepared and cannot give consent, or that violate the laws or social taboos of society. Child sexual abuse is evidenced by this activity between a child and an adult or another child who by age or development is in a relationship of responsibility, trust or power, the activity being intended to gratify or satisfy the needs of the other person. This may include but is not limited to:

- The inducement or coercion of a child to engage in any unlawful sexual activity.
- The exploitative use of child in prostitution or other unlawful sexual practices.
- The exploitative use of children in pornographic performances and materials.

– ***Exploitation***
Commercial or other exploitation of a child refers to use of the child in work or other activities for the benefit of others. This includes, but is not limited to, child labour and child prostitution. These activities are to the detriment of the child's physical or mental health, education, or spiritual, moral or social-emotional development.

TASK/TEXT 2.2.3: THE INTERVIEW FOR TRAUMATIC EVENTS IN CHILDHOOD (ITEC)

Jill Lobbestael *et al.* (Maastricht University), *Child Abuse & Neglect* 2009, pp. 506, 516 and 510–511 (Table 2), <www.sciencedirect.com>

The ITEC [Interview for Traumatic Events in Childhood] is a retrospective trauma interview (…).

[It] is a promising new instrument for brief yet comprehensive assessment of childhood maltreatment.

Abusive events in the ITEC

Sexual abuse

1. Forced into sexually sadistic acts (...)
2. Forced into anal intercourse
3. Forced into vaginal intercourse
4. Sexual acts [with] spectators (...)
5. Sexual acts in which objects were used
6. Sexually satisfying someone by mouth
7. Being sexually satisfied (by hand or mouth)
8. Blackmailed to remain silent about the sexual acts
9. Sexually satisfying someone by hand
10. Sexually palpitated
11. Forced to observe sexual acts
12. Sexually approached

Physical abuse

1. Being cut with knife or other sharp object
2. Taken by the throat
3. Caused burns by someone
4. Hit with a stick or other object
5. Tied with a rope or locked up
6. Being punched
7. Being kicked
8. Dragged along the ground
9. Clothes ripped of the body
10. Being hit
11. Pulled by hair
12. Threatened with a physical abusive act
13. Something thrown at [you]

Emotional abuse

1. Forced to protect yourself from family members
2. Wrongfully or cruelly punished
3. Nagged, belittled or called names
4. Not being allowed to express feeling or needs, or being punished if you did
5. An object you liked was destroyed
6. Hurtful or insulting things were said
7. Threatened with words
8. Many arguments between family members
9. Many problems with the police in the family

Emotional neglect

1. Received no warmth or love
2. Left to your own device
3. No one in the family who took your defense
4. Parents addicted to alcohol or drugs
5. Take care of parents or other family members
6. Left alone a lot
7. No clear agreements or responsibilities

Physical neglect

1. Having too little to eat
2. Having to wear dirty or torn clothes.

TASK/TEXT 2.3: PARENTS WHO KILL THEIR CHILDREN

Summary – Anton Jan Verheugt, *Moordouders – Kinderdoding in Nederland; Een klinisch en forensisch psychologische studie naar de persoon van de kinderdoder* (PhD Tilburg University 2007)

This clinical and forensic psychological study is about the person of the child murderer in the Netherlands. (...) [A] profile is sketched of the persons who commit neonaticide, infanticide and filicide (...):

[C]hild murderers have often lost one or more (young) loved ones at an early age;

they generally have an [**insecure**] **attachment** relationship with their parents, who were emotionally unavailable; and in the course of their life – whether due to this loss, to the [**insecure**] **attachment** relationship or to some other factor – they have developed a mental disorder, often with depressive characteristics.

On the basis of their [**insecure**] **attachment** and perhaps reinforced by the mental disorder, they have difficulties in making compromises between distance and closeness, in delineating themselves from others, both in the relationship with their parents and in that with their children. If in real life their self-esteem is highly impaired by a new loss, such as abandonment or imminent abandonment due to divorce or death, and/or if the child does not satisfy the parent's expectations (which are often overly high), which gives the parent the feeling that he or she has failed as a parent, this combination of factors can cause the basic explosive mixture in the parent to ignite in the form of killing his or her own child.

TASK/TEXT 2.4:

TASK/TEXT 2.4.1: UK – PREVALENCE OF CHILD ABUSE

According to a major UK study (NSPCC, *Child Maltreatment in the United Kingdom*, 2000; <www.nspcc.org.uk>) on the prevalence of child abuse, "significant minorities" of young people (18–24 years old) "suffered serious abuse or neglect at home:

seven per cent suffered serious physical abuse as children at the hands of parents and carers, including being hit with a fist or implement, beaten up, burned and scalded;

six per cent suffered serious physical neglect at home, including being left regularly without food as a young child, not being looked after or taken to the doctor when ill, or being left to fend for themselves because parents were absent or had drug or alcohol problems; **five per cent** had been placed at risk by being left alone at home overnight or out overnight – whereabouts unknown – at young ages;

six per cent had suffered multiple attacks on their emotional well being and self-confidence, including living with frequent violence between parents, being 'really afraid' of parents, being regularly humiliated, being threatened with being sent away or thrown out, or told that their parents wished them dead or never born;

one per cent had been sexually abused by a parent and **three per cent** suffered sexual abuse by another relative, ranging from penetrative or oral sex to taking pornographic photographs of them.

In all, **one in four** young people said that there were things that had happened to them during their childhood which they found difficult to talk about. (…) [H] ardly any of the young people had told police, social services, teachers or other professionals."

TASK/TEXT 2.4.2: PUPILS ON ABUSE

PUPILS ON ABUSE – Summary (VU Amsterdam 2007), <www.wodc.nl> – 25 April 2007

Background to the study

To date, there are no figures available in the Netherlands on the scale of child abuse. Such figures are sorely needed; in order to effectively tackle this problem, and monitor the effects of the countermeasures, detailed knowledge of the nature and scale of child abuse in our country is an absolute prerequisite. The *Pupils on abuse* study aims to contribute to this vital knowledge. On the one hand, the study focuses on the prevalence of child abuse, that is to say, the number of individuals who have been abused at one point in their lives. On the other hand, it focuses on the incidence of child abuse, that is to say, the number of young people who have experienced some form of child abuse during the past twelve months [2005].

In *Pupils on abuse*, child abuse is understood to mean: behavioural acts towards children which may be regarded as serious forms of physical/ psychological violence, neglect or sexual abuse. The exposure of children to serious violence between parents is also considered to be a serious threat to their safety and, as such, a form of child abuse. In addition, the study focuses on other forms of victimization, such as bullying, theft and discrimination.

Study objective and question

This study aims to provide information which can be used in the (further) development, direction and evaluation of the approach to child abuse in the Netherlands.

In deciding how to obtain this information, a choice was made for a direct approach to the adolescents themselves. They are, after all, the ones who know best what has happened to them and, thus, an important source of information.

The following questions should be answered in the course of the study:

1. To what extent have adolescents in the first four forms of secondary school experienced child abuse?
2. Is there a relationship between the incidence of the discernable categories of child abuse?
3. What is the connection between the incidence of child abuse and other forms of victimization?
4. Which characteristics distinguish adolescents who have not experienced child abuse from those who have frequently been subjected to child abuse? (...)

Findings – Child abuse as experienced by the young people

Over one third of the adolescents indicated that they had experienced an incident at one point in their lives which may be regarded as a form of child abuse. Nearly twenty per cent of the adolescents appear to have experienced one form or another of child abuse during the past twelve months (see table).

Prevalence and incidence of child abuse per category (# per 1000 young people)

Category	Prevalence*	Incidence*
Neglect**	52	–
Psychological aggression by parents	221	120
Domestic violence	157	83
Sexual abuse	79	44
Outside their (extended) family	*70*	*40*
Within their (extended) family	*23*	*9*
Exposure to parental conflict: physical confrontation and/or threatened with a weapon	117	41
Total across all categories	373	195

* Number of adolescents per 1000. Prevalence: experienced at one point in their lives. Incidence: experienced during the past twelve months [2005].

** With regard to "Neglect," the adolescents were exclusively questioned about early childhood experiences; no data offering insight into the incidence of this form of child abuse was collected.

Both the prevalence and incidence figures revealed that *Psychological aggression by parents* and *Domestic violence* (physical abuse) are the most prevalent categories of child abuse. The incidences of *Sexual Abuse* and *Exposure to parental conflict* are roughly the same; the prevalence figures are not, however. A larger number of adolescents reported having witnessed violent confrontations between their parents at one point in their lives. Most of the sexual acts or activities took place with or by persons outside the (extended) family environment. Only prevalence data was collected on the different forms of *Neglect*. This revealed that these forms of child abuse were reported least often. On the whole, the study revealed that there were no great differences between boys and girls. *Sexual abuse* occurs three to four times as often amongst girls, however. Conversely, boys reported a greater number of serious forms of *Neglect*.

It appears that the experiences of the majority (209 per 1000) of the adolescents who had to deal with child abuse at one point in their lives (373 per 1000 adolescents) are limited to one of the discernable categories (thus: either neglect, psychological aggression between parents, domestic violence, sexual abuse or exposure to parental conflict). The remainder (164 per 1000) experienced incidents which can be grouped into two or more categories. Of these, a total of 17 adolescents (per 1000) had experiences of four or five different categories. The incidence figures revealed a similar pattern. Of all the adolescents who experienced a form of child abuse during the past year (195/1000), most had to deal with incidents of a single category (127/1000). The remaining 68 adolescents (per 1000) indicated having had to deal with forms of child abuse which can be placed in two or more categories. The incidence of all four categories of child abuse comprises 5 per 1000 adolescents.

The relationship between different categories of child abuse

Adolescents who have experienced several forms of child abuse within one category (for example, neglect, psychological aggression by parents, domestic violence, sexual abuse or exposure to parental conflict) often turned out to have various experiences within one of the other categories as well. The relationships are statistically not very strong. The strongest relationships were found between *Domestic violence* on the one hand and *Psychological aggression by parents* and *Exposure to parental conflict* on the other hand, i.e. adolescents who have experienced many different forms of physical violence (by their parents) often experience verbally aggressive behaviour by their parents as well.

The relationship between incidence of child abuse and other forms of victimization

The *Psychological aggression by parents*, *Domestic violence* and *Exposure to parental conflict* categories of child abuse are systematically related to the incidence of forms of victimization with a low impact, such as theft, bullying and other conflicts. Adolescents who had many different experiences with serious forms of abuse during the past twelve months were – coincidentally – often subjected to other forms of victimization as well.

The characteristics of young people who have been frequently subjected to child abuse

There appears to be a relationship between the variable *Sex* and, to a slightly lesser extent, the variables *Ethno-cultural background* and *Age* and the risk of child abuse. In comparison with boys, girls appear to run more than twice the risk of becoming a victim of child abuse. Adolescents who count themselves as belonging to a non-Dutch social group appear to run almost twice the risk of experiencing child abuse when compared with adolescents who consider themselves native Dutch. The age of adolescents also appears to enhance the risk of abuse. The older the adolescent, the higher the likelihood that he or she was the victim of child abuse during the past twelve months.

Of the variables which characterized aspects of the living conditions and family situations of the adolescents, the *Number of parents* in the family appears to be relevant. Compared with families headed by two parents, adolescents who are being raised in other family configurations or forms of cohabitation run a greater risk of child abuse.

Experiences with other forms of victimization (such as arguments with parents, bullying in school, theft, discrimination or conflicts with teachers) appear to be demonstrably related to the prevalence of child abuse. The probability of child abuse becomes more substantial in case where there is an accumulation of incidents and experiences in which a adolescent is the victim.

There also appears to be a demonstrable, albeit small, connection between the antisocial behaviour of adolescents (such as theft, fighting and substance abuse) and the incidence of child abuse. When adolescents report a lot of antisocial behaviour, the odds that they have been subjected to child abuse are greater than in the case of children who do not report such behaviour.

Adolescents who have witnessed a lot of arguments between their parents appear to have a slightly higher probability of experiencing child abuse. A non-violent style of disciplining or child-rearing also appears to contribute to this risk, which is rather strange.

Conclusions

Over a third of the adolescents appear to have experienced child abuse in the form of serious psychological aggression by parents, domestic violence, perceived physical conflicts between parents, sexual abuse and/or severe neglect at one point in their lives. One out of five adolescents was the victim of (a form of) child abuse during the past year [2005]. One out of fifteen adolescents was the victim of a combination of different forms of child abuse during the past year.

In comparison with other studies, one may conclude that the adolescents who took part in *Pupils on abuse* are more likely to have understated than overstated facts. As a result, it may not be ruled out that the estimate made of the degree of child abuse is somewhat conservative.

The results of *Pupils on abuse* are important and meaningful, but leave many questions unanswered. Follow-up research should concern a normal sample and be longitudinal in nature so that more will become known about the cause-and-effect relationships, about possible developmental trajectories and about the developmental outcomes in the long term.

TASK/TEXT 2.4.3: ABUSE OF INDIAN CHILDREN 'COMMON'

Story from BBC NEWS: <news.bbc.co.uk/go/pr/fr/-/2/hi/south_asia/6539027.stm>; published: 2007/04/09; By Geeta Pandey, BBC News, Delhi

(On the India National Study on Child Abuse see: <www.prayasonline.org/ActivitiesAdvocacyChildAbuseStudy.html?id=12214>)

Two out of every three children in India are physically abused, according to a landmark government study

Commissioned by the Ministry of Women and Child Development, the study says 53% of the surveyed children reported one or more forms of sexual abuse. This is the first time the government has done such an exhaustive survey on the controversial issue of child abuse. Abuse of children, particularly sexual abuse, is rarely admitted in India and activists have welcomed the study.

Releasing the report at a press conference in the capital, Delhi, Minister for Women and Child Development Renuka Chowdhury said: "In India there's a tradition of denying child abuse. It doesn't happen here is what we normally say. But by remaining silent, we have aided and abetted the abuse of children."

Thousands quizzed

Describing the findings of the study as "disturbing," Ms Chowdhury called for an end to the "conspiracy of silence." The issue of child abuse has been raised in the past by non-governmental organisations, but this is the first time an attempt has been made by the government to document the scale of the problem. The study took two years to complete, and covered 13 states where 12,247 children (between five and 12) and 2,324 young adults (over the age of 12) were quizzed.

Dr Loveleen Kacker, the official in charge of child welfare in the ministry, compiled the report. She said the study had revealed that contrary to the general belief that only girls were abused, boys were equally at risk, if not more. She said a substantial number of the abusers were "persons in trust and care-givers" who included parents, relatives and school teachers. Dr Kacker said a disturbing finding of the study had been that 70% had not reported the abuse to anyone.

Besides surveying physical and sexual abuse, the study also collected statistics on emotional abuse and neglect of girls. The study called for efforts to make society aware of the rights of children and officials say the data will help them formulate better policies to protect children.

'One too many'

The report has been welcomed by child rights activists who say such a study was sorely needed in India. Roland Angerer, country director of Plan International, told BBC News it was "very important that the government has finally taken up the issue."

"It doesn't matter what statistics say. Whether the percentage of abused children is 75 or whether it is 58 is unimportant. Each child that is abused is one too many," he said. "It's important that parents and adults must learn that children are not property, that they have rights too."

In India, parents are often reluctant to admit child abuse and sexual abuse of children involving family members is almost always hushed up. Perhaps that is why – as the study shows – more than 50% of the young adults surveyed wanted the matter of abuse to remain within the family. Only 17% of the abused young adults wanted harsh punishment for the abusers. Officials and activists say the biggest challenge for the authorities and society is to ensure that children are encouraged to report abuse.

India is home to almost 19% of the world's children. More than one-third of the country's population – 440m people – is made up of children below 18 years of age. According to one study, at least 40% of these children are in need of care and protection.

The country has millions of child workers. Many are employed in hazardous industries and also in homes and small restaurants, which makes them vulnerable to violence and exploitation. Last year the government banned children under 14 from being employed in homes and at restaurants to avoid their exploitation and abuse, but millions of children continue to work in these sectors. India is a signatory to various international laws on the protection of children, but implementation of these laws is often lax.

TASK/TEXT 2.5: PARENTS MAIN PERPETRATORS OF RAMPANT CHILD ABUSE

Crinmail 915 – 13 September 2007, <www.crin.org>; <www.jamaica-gleaner.com/gleaner/20070911/carib/carib3.html>

GEORGETOWN, 11 September 2007 – Government officials in Jamaica say they are troubled by a survey which has revealed that parents are the main perpetrators of physical and sexual violence in Guyanese homes. The government/United Nations Children's Fund (UNICEF) survey found that fathers and stepfathers were the most common perpetrators of sexual violence in homes, while mothers and other females were largely behind physical abuse cases.

The survey said girls were twice as likely to be raped at home than boys, with 10 per cent girls and five per cent boys suffering sexual abuse. A senior Human Services and Social Security Ministry official said the revelations were troubling. "We are very concerned about the apparent child abuse and we seriously want to tackle it," Ann Green, chief probation officer, said.

National consensus

Green called for national backing to help root out the scourge afflicting the nation's vulnerable population. "We want to get the public at large aware that they have a responsibility to protect a child," Green noted.

As well as sexual exploitation, the survey also revealed that physical abuse is a major problem in the country; 33 per cent of Guyanese children have been mistreated by adults. The study concluded that the majority of physical abuse perpetuated against children in homes actually occurred as a result of beatings or other physical punishments administered as discipline, especially by mothers. It blamed the violence on alcoholism, financial pressure, and infidelity by a parent. Of the [33 per cent] children who reported being physically hurt, 16 per cent had been hurt by their mothers; seven per cent by their fathers; two per cent by both parents; five per cent by related caregivers (aunts, uncles, grandparents); and three per cent by stepparents [in toto 33 per cent, JW].

Officials said with sexual and physical violence increasingly characterising Guyanese homes, more children were seeking refuge on the streets, with the number of male street children rising by 50 per cent, according to the most recent figures.

TASK/TEXT 2.6: CRUDE/SKETCHY ESTIMATE OF CHILD ABUSE

Jan CM Willems, Children's rights and the prevention of child abuse and neglect: The quest for a Trias Pedagogica of children, parents and society, in: Ingrid Westendorp & Ria Wolleswinkel (eds.), *Violence in the domestic sphere*, Intersentia, Antwerp–Oxford, 2005, pp. 165–167

Transgenerational discrimination, or transism, does not have so much to do, at least on the outside, with ideas, or doctrines, of inferiority or superiority. But it certainly has a lot to do with subtle, or not so subtle, forms of social exclusion. Let us, therefore, look at some (and face some) Western realities before having a closer look at how the CRC tries to fight transism (as CERD tries to fight racism and CEDAW tries to fight sexism). In order to give an impression of these realities, I propose the following semi- or quasi-hypothetical estimate:

Two out of three children (approximately 67%) in industrialized countries benefit more or less from family life: their parents are 'good enough' (that is not too poorly, too ill-equipped) in terms of their being prepared for parenthood *c.q.* their parental awareness: their emotional maturity, mental health, intelligence, marriage stability, alcohol use, income and employment, neighbourhood situation, etcetera.

One out of five children (approximately 20%) in industrialized countries both benefit and suffer from family life, and are at risk of some form or degree of developmental damage, *c.q.* of developing psychosocial problems; parental behavior may at times fall in some child abuse and neglect scale or chronically in the lower scales of child abuse and neglect classifications.

One out of ten children (approximately 10%) in industrialized countries see their fundamental rights to physical and psychological security, integrity, dignity and healthy holistic development seriously threatened and violated, they may suffer chronic degrading treatment (for instance chronic negativism and non-communication within the family), and fall within classifications of child abuse and neglect into the upper scales.

One to three out of one hundred children (1 to 3%) in industrialized countries suffer forms of child abuse and neglect to degrees, well in the upper scales, amounting to torture, that is treatment which would be labeled torture if it were not parents or other carers but official or semi-official figures who would be responsible for the cruelty, abuse or neglect in question.

So, in a hypothetical group of 30 children, 20 are by and large fine and safe, six have been or will be at risk at some time or are all the time, three are or have been or will be victims of child abuse and neglect, one is or has been or will be victim of one or more very serious forms of child abuse and neglect. In human rights terms: in any group of 30 children, there is one torture victim, three victims of degrading treatment, and six potential or semi-victims. Imagine that in any industrialized country the same were true for any group of 30 more or less vulnerable adults, let us say prison inmates, physically or mentally handicapped or elderly persons or psychiatric patients in understaffed institutions ... Imagine the public outrage, and outcry, if such numbers were broadcasted and made public ...

The parents of the 20 relatively happy children have prepared themselves in one way or other for parenthood or have learned very fast along the way. The 10 other children are likely to have parents with all kinds of problems, from relatively mild to very serious, regardless whether they have prepared or tried to prepare themselves for parenthood.

TASK/TEXT 2.7:

TASK/TEXT 2.7.1: TOTAL ESTIMATED COST OF CHILD ABUSE AND NEGLECT IN THE US

Economic Impact Study (September 2007; January 2008) – Prevent Child Abuse America, Chicago, Illinois – Ching-Tung Wang, Ph.D. and John Holton, Ph.D. (Source: <http://kidsarewaiting.org>, Estimated Economic Impact of Child Abuse and Neglect)

Child abuse and neglect are preventable, yet each year in the United States, close to one million children are confirmed victims of child maltreatment. An extensive body of research provides promising and best practices on what works to improve child safety and well-being outcomes and reduce the occurrence of child abuse and neglect. These efforts are essential as child abuse and neglect have pervasive and long-lasting effects on children, their families, and the society. Adverse consequences for children's development often are evident immediately, encompassing multiple domains including physical, emotional, social, and cognitive. For many children, these effects extend far beyond childhood into adolescence and adulthood, potentially compromising the lifetime productivity of maltreatment victims (...).

It is well documented that children who have been abused or neglected are more likely to experience adverse outcomes throughout their life span in a number of areas:

- Poor physical health (e.g., chronic fatigue, altered immune function, hypertension, sexually transmitted diseases, obesity);

- Poor emotional and mental health (e.g., depression, anxiety, eating disorders, suicidal thoughts and attempts, post-traumatic stress disorder);
- Social difficulties (e.g., insecure attachments with caregivers, which may lead to difficulties in developing trusting relationships with peers and adults later in life);
- Cognitive dysfunction (e.g., deficits in attention, abstract reasoning, language development, and problem-solving skills, which ultimately affect academic achievement and school performance);
- High-risk health behaviors (e.g., a higher number of lifetime sexual partners, younger age at first voluntary intercourse, teen pregnancy, alcohol and substance abuse); and:
- Behavioral problems (e.g., aggression, juvenile delinquency, adult criminality, abusive or violent behavior) (…).

The costs of responding to the impact of child abuse and neglect are borne by the victims and their families but also by society.

This brief updates an earlier publication documenting the nationwide costs as a result of child abuse and neglect (S. Fromm, 2001). Similar to the earlier document, this brief places costs in two categories: direct costs, that is, those costs associated with the immediate needs of children who are abused or neglected; and indirect costs, that is, those costs associated with the long-term and/or secondary effects of child abuse and neglect. All estimated costs are presented in 2007 dollars. Adjustments for inflation have been conducted using the price indexes for gross domestic product published by the Bureau of Economic Analysis (<www.bea.gov>).

Based on data drawn from a variety of sources, the estimated annual cost of child abuse and neglect is **$103.8 billion** in 2007 value. [This would amount to several billion euro each year for a country like The Netherlands, JW.] This figure represents a conservative estimate as a result of the methods used for the calculation. First, only children who could be classified as being abused or neglected according to the Harm Standard in the Third National Incidence Study of Child Abuse and Neglect *(NIS-3)* are included in the analysis. The Harm Standard requirements, compared to the Endangerment Standard requirements used in *NIS-3*, are more stringent (…). Second, only those costs related to victims are included. We have not attempted to quantify other costs associated with abuse and neglect, such as the costs of intervention or treatment services for the perpetrators or other members of the victim's family. Third, the categories of costs included in this analysis are by no means exhaustive. As examples, a large number of child victims require medical examinations or outpatient treatment for injuries not serious enough to require hospitalization; maltreated children are at greater risk of engaging in substance abuse and require alcohol and drug treatment services; and youth with histories of child abuse and neglect may be at greater risk of engaging in risky behaviors such as unprotected sexual activities as well as greater risk of teen pregnancy. We were not able to estimate these types of costs as data are not readily available.

Although the economic costs associated with child abuse and neglect are substantial, it is essential to recognize that it is impossible to calculate the impact of the pain, suffering, and reduced quality of life that victims of child abuse and neglect experience. These "intangible losses," though difficult to quantify in monetary terms, are real and should not be overlooked. Intangible losses, in fact, may represent the largest cost component of violence against children and should be taken into account when allocating resources (...).

Direct Costs		*Indirect Costs*	
Hospitalization ...	6.626 m$	Special Education ...	2.410 m$
Mental Health Care System ...	1.081 m$	Juvenile Delinquency ...	7.175 m$
Child Welfare Services System ...	25.361 m$	Mental Health & Health Care ...	68 m$
Law Enforcement ...	33 m$		
	33.101 m$	Adult Criminal Justice System ...	27.980 m$
		Lost Productivity to Society ...	33.020 m$
Total Direct Costs →		Total Indirect Costs	70.653 m$
		Total Direct Costs	33.101 m$
		Total Cost	103.754 m$

TASK/TEXT 2.7.2: [APRIL IS] CHILD ABUSE PREVENTION MONTH

Prevent Child Abuse America – We can prevent child abuse – Child Abuse Prevention Month, Vol. 3, No. 4 [email 24 April 2008]

During Child Abuse Prevention Month, there is no better time for us to recognize that all parents experience stress. It's the toughest job there is. So why don't we provide them with the tools they need to be the best parents they can be? When resources like **home visiting** and **in-depth parenting education** are sufficient, the risks to families decrease and unhealthy experiences are less likely to occur. When these resources are insufficient, the resulting effects can lead to a host of lifelong challenges for the child that may also affect the world around them.

We can choose to believe that abuse happens to someone else and that we're not personally affected by it or we can respond to study after study that show us that the lasting affects of child abuse and neglect manifest themselves into social concerns like drug abuse, violent crime and chronic health problems such as depression.

It's time we re-think our public policies on prevention and child development both because it makes good common sense and because it makes 'cents' for our country and economy.

TASK/TEXT 2.8: THE STORY OF MIKEY

ISPCAN list – Trauma counselling information; April 21, 2008 – Michael Durfee MD, USA

One of the ignored topics with abused children is traumatic grief following loss to death. Children may enter foster care and not know that their parent is dead. One toddler was in therapy and foster care for three months while the therapist was waiting for the child to "bring it up." These are not bad people, they don't want to tell a child, "your mother is dead." Professions in turn are damaged by the failure of agencies to support them. If a child dies under jurisdiction the social worker will be investigated to make sure that papers are up to date. Support for the worker is limited to personal contacts. But, we are learning. We have an annual conference on "Child Grief and Traumatic Loss – Returning Joy to Children and Families." Our speakers include national experts. Some of them worked with children and families after the misery of 9/11. We have the beginning of work with military families who have child survivors of a parents death.

We see this as possible violence prevention. Children who grow up with violence and death may **temper some of their fear and frustration with distain for the lives of others.** This seems to fit with histories we are beginning to collect on violent youth. The program is available at: <http://ican-ncfr.org/documents/Grief.REGISTRATION.Booklet.pdf>. With ancient rituals like funerals, grave visitation, much of the response is known. It may be that nations with less affluence than the US may serve children much better with issues of loss to death.

[Attached:] **The story of Mikey**
Five year old Jennifer saw her infant brother Mikey beaten by her mothers boyfriend the previous night. The children shared a bedroom and it was quiet until late morning when their mother entered and began to scream. Jennifer was left with her grandmother after the police and ambulance arrived. No one asked her what happened.

Several weeks later the body had been released and buried with three adults as the only witnesses. No one spoke to Jennifer about the death except to reassure her that "it will be O.K." The exception was a uniformed police officer that tried to ask her what she had seen. A half sibling in another state is never told of the death.

Jennifer's school teacher now knows about the death but doesn't know how to find the case worker or the grave and doesn't know if she should talk to the mother that used to visit Jennifer at school. All of the school staff talks about the case but only the teacher talks to Jennifer who was generally withdrawn except for episodes of hitting others or kicking dolls.

No one speaks to the 12 year old babysitter who held Mikey, and is now wondering what she should have done. Her parents note that "it is good that she never has to go there again."

No one speaks to the paramedic and medical staff who tried to keep the battered infant alive. The ambulance hurried away from the hospital minutes after leaving their small victim. The cold blue infant body was eventually described as dead on anival although hospital staff had continued Intervention until a new resident had arrived to pronounce the baby officially dead.

Jennifer's mother and grandmother speak occasionally, mostly to argue about the mother's parenting and choice of men and the failure of the grandmother or other family members to help when Jennifer's mother had been beaten by her boyfriend.

Law enforcement and jail staff had conversed as necessary, mostly to seek a confession. The boyfriend told law enforcement how the baby made him mad and that he didn't mean to kill Mikey. His family later told him to stay away. He moved in with an old girlfriend who had children. She loved him, and told herself that this time it would be different for her.

The homicide detective had no training in child abuse. The pictures of the dead baby were seen by many of his fellow officers and some of the clerical staff. One officer went home during the day to check on his new infant son. High levels of energy the day of the arrest were followed by a strange quiet the following day.

The medical examiner who did the autopsy was a professional and "an autopsy was an autopsy." He did find himself sleeping poorly, drank a little more than usual, and seemed to have trouble getting his report done.

Preparation of the body at the funeral home had been problematic. It was hard to cover all of the bruises and the technician found herself crying for the first time-in her career. The minister did well at the services, but seemed irritable for some months after. He repeatedly assured his wife, who hadn't asked, "that of course there is a God."

The Deputy District Attomey did not prosecute the case for technical reasons. At home she talked about the pictures and her anger with her work until her husband physically avoided her.

A reporter who covered the death, got angry with her editor, who finally put the story in a single paragraph. The paper had just covered a notorious child homicide in another county and the editor was concerned about two similar stories. An old man who read the story wondered again, what had happened to his baby sister who had suddenly died when he was seven.

A mental health worker, had two interviews with Jennifer, as part of the six months of court ordered intervention before the case was closed. The mother finished most of the court ordered parenting. The class on adolescence confused her. The session on diapers and babies had made her sad. She hoped that no one had noticed her tears or the fact that she was pregnant again.

A mental health counselor missed several comments Jennifer made about "the worms come eat you." The mother stated that she had the right to keep Jennifer away from the funeral although she was not sure if she had made the right decision.

Several hundred people felt the loss of this generally unnamed baby. Jennifer became known as the girl who had the murdered baby brother. Case records were closed. The major follow-up was a departmental investigation of another protective service worker who had seen the mother and Jennifer at a shelter before Mikey was bom. Questions about that contact were generally handled by senior staff and an attorney to make sure that there was no liability. Two workers knew the family but never spoke to each other about the case.

The grave became noticed by an elderly woman. The new stone sat on a small wedge of grass next to her deceased husband's grave. She kept the grave clean for a while and even brought flowers. Jennifer, her mother, the boyfriend and those close to them will be affected by the death for all of their lives. Some will pass anger and fear on to new generations.

Most people damaged by this death will generally repair themselves with time. Soon no one will visit the grave or otherwise face the death of that murdered child.

It seems that most cases of fatal child abuse/neglect receive little intervention for the problems that follow such a death. Many are ignored, even undetected. Others are glibly labeled as Post Traumatic Stress Disorder as if their reaction is a disease and not a reasonable response to an unreasonable act.

Families are left alone with baby furniture, clothes, smells, and daily rituals now empty. Friends, family and neighbors may withdraw not knowing what to do and wishing to avoid their own pain.

Almost no intervention is given to friends, extended family, neighbors, and the large number of professionals and volunteer service providers that are effected by such a death. An occasional exception is a Critical Incident Debriefing, or a supervisor who can balance the need for empathy and support with the need to be seen as competent and continue at work.

Few departments have protocols for staff support or necessary evaluations of previous contacts much less both. Professionals that share the same pain are seldom linked with each other and almost never attend to the funeral, wake, visit the grave, or attend to the social gatherings that have been the response of social people for tens of thousands of years.

But, we are learning.

TASK/TEXT 2.9: UNITED KINGDOM – OVER-CAUTIOUS PARENTS STOP PLAY (NEW FORM OF CHILD ABUSE?)

Crinmail 1004 – 5 August 2008, <www.crin.org>

Children in the UK are being denied adventurous play because their parents are nervous about exposing them to risk, a new survey suggests. The UK-wide poll, commissioned by Play England, found half of 7–12 year olds have been stopped from climbing trees. It also showed 21 per cent of those surveyed had been banned from playing conkers, and 17 per cent were not allowed to play chase.

The ICM poll interviewed 1,030 children and young people aged 7–16, and 1,031 adults during July 2007. Play England, which says it promotes free play opportunities, insists that parents "constantly wrapping children in cotton wool" can harm the children's development. The poll found showed 51 per cent of children aged 7–12 were not allowed to climb a tree without adult supervision, with 49 per cent stopped from climbing trees altogether because it was considered too dangerous.

'Life skills'

According to the research, 70 per cent of adults had their biggest childhood adventures outdoors among trees, rivers and woods, compared with only 29 per cent of children today.

It found children's experiences of adventure are confined to designated areas such as playgrounds (56 per cent), their homes (48 per cent) or theme parks (44 per cent).

Adrian Voce, director of Play England, which is part of the charity National Children's Bureau, said playing was "an essential part of growing up."

"Adventurous play both challenges and excites children and helps instil critical life skills," he said. "Constantly wrapping children in cotton wool can leave them ill equipped to deal with stressful or challenging situations they might encounter later in life. Children both need and want to push their boundaries in order to explore their limits and develop their abilities."

The survey was carried out to mark Playday, the annual celebration of children's right to play, which is co-ordinated by Play England. Hundreds of events will be taking place across the UK on Wednesday 6 August to celebrate Playday.

TASK/TEXT 2.10: RECOGNIZING CHILD ABUSE – WHAT YOU SHOULD KNOW

Prevent Child Abuse America, <www.preventchildabuse.org>, Publications, Prevention Tips for All of Us (retrieved 11 August 2008)

The first step in helping abused children is learning to recognize the symptoms of child abuse. Although child abuse is divided into four types – physical abuse, neglect, sexual abuse, and emotional maltreatment – the types are more typically found in combination than alone.

A physically abused child for example is often emotionally maltreated as well, and a sexually abused child may be also neglected. Any child at any age may experience any of the types of child abuse. Children over age five are more likely to be physically abused and to suffer moderate injury than are children under age five.

RECOGNIZING CHILD ABUSE

Experienced educators likely have seen all forms of child abuse at one time or another. They are alert to signs like these that may signal the presence of child abuse.

The Child:

- Shows sudden changes in behavior or school performance;
- Has not received help for physical or medical problems brought to the parents' attention;
- Has learning problems that cannot be attributed to specific physical or psychological causes;
- Is always watchful, as though preparing for something bad to happen;
- Lacks adult supervision;
- Is overly compliant, an overachiever, or too responsible; or
- Comes to school early, stays late, and does not want to go home.

The Parent:

- Shows little concern for the child, rarely responding to the school's requests for information, for conferences, or for home visits;
- Denies the existence of – or blames the child for – the child's problems in school or at home;
- Asks the classroom teacher to use harsh physical discipline if the child misbehaves;
- Sees the child entirely bad, worthless, or burdensome;
- Demands perfection or a level of physical or academic performance the child cannot achieve;
- Looks primarily to the child for care, attention, and satisfaction of emotional needs.

The Parent and Child:

- Rarely touch or look at each other;
- Consider their relationship entirely negative; or
- State that they do not like each other.

None of these signs proves that child abuse is present in a family. Any of them may be found in any parent or child at one time or another. But when these signs appear repeatedly or in combination, they should cause the educator to take closer look at the situation and to consider the possibility of child abuse. That second look may reveal further signs of abuse or signs of a particular kind of child abuse.

SIGNS OF PHYSICAL ABUSE

Consider the possibility of physical abuse when the child:

- Has unexplained burns, bites, bruises, broken bones, or black eyes;
- Has fading bruises or other marks noticeable after an absence from school;
- Seems frightened of the parents and protests or cries when it is time to go home from school;
- Shrinks at the approach of adults; or
- Reports injury by a parent or another adult caregiver.

Consider the possibility of physical abuse when the parent or other adult caregiver:

- Offers conflicting, unconvincing, or no explanation for the child's injury;
- Describes the child as "evil," or in some other very negative way;

- Uses harsh physical discipline with the child; or
- Has a history of abuse as a child.

SIGNS OF NEGLECT

Consider the possibility of neglect when the child:

- Is frequently absent from school;
- Begs or steals food or money from classmates;
- Lacks needed medical or dental care, immunizations, or glasses;
- Is consistently dirty and has severe body odor;
- Lacks sufficient clothing for the weather;
- Abuses alcohol or other drugs; or
- States there is no one at home to provide care.

Consider the possibility of neglect when the parent or other adult caregiver:

- Appears to be indifferent to the child;
- Seems apathetic or depressed;
- Behaves irrationally or in a bizarre manner; or
- Is abusing alcohol or other drugs.

SIGNS OF SEXUAL ABUSE

Consider the possibility of sexual abuse when the child:

- Has difficulty walking or sitting;
- Suddenly refuses to change for gym or to participate in physical activities;
- Demonstrates bizarre, sophisticated, or unusual sexual knowledge or behavior;
- Becomes pregnant or contracts a venereal disease, particularly if under age fourteen;
- Runs away; or
- Reports sexual abuse by a parent or another adult caregiver.

Consider the possibility of sexual abuse when the parent or other adult caregiver:

- Is unduly protective of the child, severely limits the child's contact with other children, especially of the opposite sex;
- Is secretive and isolated; or

- Describes marital difficulties involving family power struggles or sexual relations.

SIGNS OF EMOTIONAL MALTREATMENT

Consider the possibility of emotional maltreatment when the child:

- Shows extremes in behavior, such as overly compliant or demanding behavior, extreme passivity or aggression;
- Is either inappropriately adult (parenting other children, for example) or inappropriately infantile (frequently rocking or head-banging, for example);
- Is delayed in physical or emotional development;
- Has attempted suicide; or
- Reports a lack of attachment to the parent.

Consider the possibility of emotional maltreatment when the parent or other adult caregiver:

- Constantly blames, belittles, or berates the child;
- Is unconcerned about the child and refuses to consider offers of help for the child's school problems; or
- Overtly rejects the child.

TASK/TEXT 2.11: EMOTIONAL CHILD ABUSE

Prevent Child Abuse America, <www.preventchildabuse.org>, Publications, Prevention Tips for All of Us, Fact Sheets about Child Abuse and Neglect (retrieved 11 August 2008; references omitted)

FACT SHEET: EMOTIONAL CHILD ABUSE

What is it?

Emotional child abuse is maltreatment which results in impaired psychological growth and development. It involves words, actions, and indifference. Abusers constantly reject, ignore, belittle, dominate, and criticize the victims. This form of abuse may occur with or without physical abuse, but there is often an overlap. Examples of emotional child abuse are verbal abuse; excessive demands on a child's performance; penalizing a child for positive, normal behavior (smiling, mobility, exploration, vocalization, manipulation of objects); discouraging caregiver and infant attachment; penalizing a child for demonstrating signs of positive self-esteem; and penalizing a child for using interpersonal skills needed for adequate performance in school and peer groups. In addition, frequently exposing children to family violence and unwillingness or inability to provide affection or stimulation for the child in the course of daily care may also result in emotional abuse.

How is it identified?

Although emotional abuse can hurt as much as physical abuse, it can be harder to identify because the marks are left on the inside instead of the outside. Not surprising, there exist few well-validated measures of childhood emotional abuse. Clinicians can use a revised version of the Child Abuse and Trauma Scale (CATS) which targets measures for emotional abuse.

Caregivers can also closely observe children's behaviors and personalities. Children suffering from emotional abuse are often extremely loyal to the parent, afraid of being punished if they report abuse, or think that this type of abuse is a normal way of life.

Behavioral indicators of an emotionally abused child include inappropriate behavior that is immature or more mature for the child's age, dramatic behavioral changes (disruption of activities, clinging or compulsively seeking affection and attention), aggressiveness, uncooperativeness, bedwetting or loss of bowel control (after a child has been trained), and destructive or antisocial behavior (being constantly withdrawn and sad). Furthermore, poor relationships with peers, lack of self confidence, unusual fears for the child's age (fear of going home, being left alone, specific objects), or inability to react with emotion or develop an emotional bond with others are also indicators. Realistically, any of the above behaviors may also be seen in normal children, but a change in pattern of these behaviors is a strong indicator of emotional abuse.

Who are the perpetrators?

Almost any adult involved in a relationship with a child is a potential perpetrator. Parents, teachers, pastors, social workers, neighbors, lawyers, or judges may all be capable of emotional maltreatment. Common characteristics of the abusing adult include blaming or belittling the child in public, describing the child negatively, always assuming the child is at fault, having unrealistic expectations of the child, openly admitting to disliking or hating the child, threatening the child with severe punishment, withdrawing comfort as a means of discipline, being emotionally cold and un-supportive, suffering from alcohol and drug abuse, and possessing a violent nature.

Why does this happen?

Most emotional abuse occurs for many of the same reasons that physical abuse occurs. Parents are vulnerable to becoming involved in maltreatment if stresses in their lives build up or if they are unable to manage these stresses. They may also have diminished capacity for understanding and dealing with children (mental retardation, psychopathology, alcoholism, drug abuse), false ideas about children's needs, or sadistic psychosis. Also, the abuser's goal may be to control. Nevertheless, a single factor may not lead to abuse, but in combination they can create the social and emotional pressures that lead to emotional abuse. Specific types of problems that can contribute to emotional abuse are social problems that can contribute to family stress (unemployment, poverty, isolation from relatives and friends, divorce, death, immature parents), health crises (illness of a family member, disability of a family member, drug and alcohol abuse within the family), and mental health problems (mental disability, depression).

What are the effects?

The consequences of emotional child abuse can be serious and long-term. Many research studies conclude that psychopathologic symptoms are more likely to develop in emotionally abused children. These children may experience a lifelong pattern of depression, estrangement, anxiety, low self-esteem, inappropriate or troubled relationships, or a lack of empathy. During their childhood, victims may fail to thrive or their developmental progress may be halted. Some may also become poorly adjusted emotionally and psychologically. As teenagers, they find it difficult to trust, participate in and achieve happiness in interpersonal relationships, and resolve the complex feelings left over from their childhoods. As adults, they may have trouble recognizing and appreciating the needs and feelings of their own children and emotionally abuse them as well.

What can be done for the victims?

To effectively identify and confirm emotional abuse, it is necessary to observe the abuser-child interaction on varied and repeated occasions. If emotional abuse is suspected, action can be taken regardless of whether the suspected offender is within the child's home, child care setting, or elsewhere in the community. It is the caregiver's responsibility to report and not investigate suspicions of child abuse. It is the child protection agency's responsibility to investigate reports of any type of abuse. A careful evaluation of those involved and the sources of stress should be completed by appropriate and skilled professionals. Usually, a team consisting of a child protection worker, a physician, a psychiatrist or psychologist, a public health nurse, a childcare staff, and a teacher will become involved.

What can be done to prevent it?

Health care professionals and concerned individuals need to increase awareness for and education in emotional child abuse in the community and among parents. Secondly, parents and guardians need to be encouraged to develop strong attachments with their children and learn to express warmth and positive regard for them. Finally, families have to be encouraged to form relationships with support systems available to them. In addition, more research in topics related to emotional child abuse and parent-child relationships must be undertaken.

TASK/TEXT 2.12: A CONTINUUM OF EDUCATIONAL, SUPPORTIVE AND THERAPEUTIC SERVICES

Prevent Child Abuse America, <www.preventchildabuse.org>, Publications, Prevention Tips for All of Us, An Approach to Preventing Child Abuse (retrieved 11 August 2008)

FACT SHEET: AN APPROACH TO PREVENTING CHILD ABUSE

Prevent Child Abuse America is committed to preventing child abuse before it occurs. Since child maltreatment is a complex problem with a multitude of causes, an approach to prevention must respond to a range of needs. Therefore, Prevent Child Abuse America has designed a comprehensive strategy comprised of a variety of community-based programs to prevent child abuse. Reflective of the phases of the family life cycle, this approach provides parents and children with the education and support necessary for healthy family functioning. Based on what is known or believed to enhance an individual's ability to function within the family unit, several program areas contributing to the strategy can be identified. Beginning with the prenatal period, these programs offer a **continuum of educational, supportive and therapeutic services** for parents and children enduring throughout the school years. Although a community may not choose to offer services in all program areas, as a group they respond to the needs of all family members.

THE PREVENTION PROGRAMS

Support programs for new parents

The purpose of support programs for new parents, such as prenatal support programs, is to prepare individuals for the job of parenting. Such programs should include supports during both the pre- and postnatal periods to ease the difficulties associated with having a new infant at home. Prenatal and postnatal medical care is clearly important, particularly since low birth weight babies, drug exposed babies and babies otherwise sick in infancy are at risk for being abused. Many prospective parents now participate in prenatal care programs that go beyond the medical needs of the pregnant mother and the growing fetus to include attention to the demands of parenting. Prenatal programs can build on existing medical programs and educate about-to-be parents in child development, parent-child relationships, and adult relationships.

Currently, home visitation is the most innovative and holistic prevention program used in approaching the difficulties of educating and supporting the at-risk family, while at the same time making a wide range of community and professional services available to the family. This strategy is a comprehensive program in which services vary widely in both scope and content. An array of services may be offered, including nurse visitation to monitor the health of an infant and mother, in-home parenting education, and the intervention of a social worker for the purpose of preventing the placement of an infant in foster care. Most importantly, home visitation programs strive to create social networks for new parents by connecting them with other center-, community-, and hospital-based prevention programs. This helps break down the social isolation experienced by many new parents, especially those in poverty stricken communities. **Social isolation is a proven risk factor** for child abuse.

Education for parents

Since 1989, the family support movement has pointed to an increasing need among all-American families for support, advice, and role models. Consequently, many parent education and support programs have encouraged the participation of all families, without regard to specified risk. By targeting all families, rather than low-income or otherwise at-risk groups, parent education and family support programs have achieved the broad-based backing necessary to underwrite statewide programs.

Nationally known programs that target at-risk families such as Parent Effectiveness Training (PET), the Parent Nurturing Program, and Systematic Training for Effective Parenting (STEP) have various approaches toward parenting education and are distinct in their use of such teaching tools as reward and punishment, praise, and specific encouragement. Such parent focused interventions with well-specified training components aimed at improving child-rearing competence and stress management have been supported by empirical findings as effective measures for **reducing risk factors** associated with physical child abuse.

Many groups that provide parenting education, such as natural childbirth groups, community-based prevention programs, and mental health services also can provide social support systems for families either at risk for or in treatment for abuse. Mutual support or self-help groups also provide a network of support to members in adjusting to new roles, problems, or changes in family circumstances. These groups can help members expand their social contacts, improve their feelings of self-esteem, and increase their knowledge of child development.

Early and regular child and family screening and treatment

Because abusive behavior is often cyclic, many health and developmental problems in early childhood can lead to behavioral, educational, and psycho-emotional problems in later adolescence and adulthood, which could lead to the recurrence of abusive behavior. Also, many abused children at first appear acquiescent, cooperative, shy, affectionate, and abnormal, but this apparent serenity may mask multiple psychological problems. For this reason, detecting and treating health and developmental problems early in life is important. Early childhood screening and treatment programs should be seen as a continuation of the preschool screening services, such as those offered by a home visitor. The purpose of such programs is to detect problems children may be having, including abuse and neglect, and to ensure that these children receive the necessary health, mental health, and other services that will best protect them from becoming abusive parents. Programs also remain sensitive to the possibility that a child may be inappropriately labeled, with long-term negative consequences.

Child care opportunities

The purpose of child care or day care programs is to furnish parents with regular or occasional out-of-home care for their children. While child care is a necessity in households in which all adults are employed, such services also are beneficial for parents who do not work outside the home but who find continuous child care responsibilities very stressful. Child care programs also provide opportunities for children to learn basic social skills. Head Start programs in particular provide a rich mix of child care and child development services.

Programs for abused children

It has been argued that prevention of abuse is in part tied to providing therapeutic treatment to children or young people who have been abused or neglected. To minimize the long-term effects of abuse, age-appropriate treatment services should be available to all maltreated children.

Treatment programs for abused children include therapeutic day school programs as well as day hospital programs, residential programs, and home and clinic setting treatment. These programs most often concentrate on improving the cognitive and developmental skills of younger children and psychodynamic treatment for children in older age groups.

Life skills training for children and young adults

The purposes of life skills training are first to equip children, adolescents, and young adults with interpersonal skills and knowledge that are valuable in adulthood, especially in the parenting role; and second, to provide children with skills to help them protect themselves from abuse. Knowledge and skills can be imparted in a variety of ways; irrespective of the specific techniques, educational classes or supports would be provided through the school systems and through adult education centers.

Skill and knowledge building should be stressed in the areas of child development, family and life management, self-development, self-actualization, and methods of seeking help. For adolescents in particular, education in sexuality, pregnancy prevention, and issues related to parenting should be provided.

Family support services

Lacking a support network in times of crisis puts families at significantly greater risk for abuse or neglect. To provide immediate assistance to parents in times of stress, crisis care programs should be available on a 24-hour basis and should include the following services: telephone hot line, crisis caretakers, crisis babysitters, crisis nurseries, and crisis counseling. Through these programs, parents facing immediate problems could receive immediate support to alleviate the stresses of a particular situation. Help should be available over the phone or through in-person counseling.

The program also should offer parents the options of having someone come into their homes on a temporary basis to assist with child and home care or of taking the child to a crisis nursery. Because crisis care is temporary and short-term, such programs should be equipped to refer parents to long-term services as needed.

PUBLIC INFORMATION AND EDUCATION

While hospitals, schools, and community agencies have a critical role to play in implementing this child abuse prevention strategy, they cannot fully shoulder the responsibility. **Educational campaigns** are necessary to make the public aware of the seriousness of the problem and its implications as well how individuals can make a difference. The effectiveness of the preceding prevention strategy will only be realized when there is a fully aware public, committed to preventing child abuse.

TASK/TEXT 2.13:

TASK/TEXT 2.13.1: CHILD ABUSE PREVENTION MONTH PROCLAMATION

Prevent Child Abuse America, <www.preventchildabuse.org>, Tools for Child Abuse Prevention Month, 2005 Child Abuse Prevention Month Proclamation (retrieved 11 August 2008)

SAMPLE CAP [CHILD ABUSE PREVENTION] MONTH PROCLAMATION

Whereas, preventing child abuse and neglect is a community problem that depends on involvement among people throughout the community;

Whereas, child maltreatment occurs when people find themselves in stressful situations, without community resources, and don't know how to cope;

Whereas, the majority of child abuse cases stem from situations and conditions that are preventable in an engaged and supportive community;

Whereas, child abuse and neglect can be reduced by making sure each family has the support they need to raise their children in a healthy environment;

Whereas, child abuse and neglect not only directly harm children, but also increase the likelihood of criminal behavior, substance abuse, health problems such as heart disease and obesity, and risky behavior such as smoking;

Whereas, all citizens should become involved in supporting families in raising their children in a safe, nurturing environment;

Whereas, effective child abuse prevention programs succeed because of partnerships created among social service agencies, schools, faith communities, civic organizations, law enforcement agencies, and the business community;

Therefore, I do hereby proclaim April as Child Abuse Prevention Month …

and call upon all citizens, community agencies, faith groups, medical facilities, and businesses to increase their participation in our efforts to support families, thereby preventing child abuse and strengthening the communities in which we live.

TASK/TEXT 2.13.2: PREVENT CHILD ABUSE AMERICA – OBAMA TRANSITION TEAM LETTER

<www.preventchildabuse.org/about_us/media_releases/
ObamaTransitionTeam_Letter.pdf>

The Honorable Barack Obama, Office of Presidential Transitions, Washington DC
November 25, 2008

Dear President-elect Obama:

Prevent Child Abuse America and our national network of 47 state chapters and over than 400 Healthy Families America home visitation programs, congratulate you on your election to the office of President of the United States of America. Like you, our organization believes that the early years are a critical time for a developing child. Please count on this organization's knowledge, extensive communications network and support for public policies that address the problems that arise when a child is denied healthy childhood experiences.

Research is clear that there is a relationship between child abuse and neglect and often life long consequences in many other areas, including chronic health problems, academic achievement, juvenile delinquency, criminal behavior, drug abuse and mental health issues. Our organization is committed to working with your Administration to help ensure that every child has the opportunity to grow up in a nurturing, stimulating and stable environment. Below for your consideration are policy recommendations to promote healthy child development based in proven prevention strategies.

1. Develop a National Strategy for Prevention

Sustainable change cannot occur until there is a national policy and commitment to prevent child abuse and neglect. Implementing a national strategy will require the coordination of federal agencies, and the assurance that all federal funding, policies, and regulations related to child well-being are coordinated and working towards complimentary goals. The attached paper, *A New Way of Thinking About Prevention*, outlines specific steps that our nation must take to embrace child abuse and neglect prevention in a more effective, meaningful, and comprehensive manner.

2. Invest in Evidence-Based Early Childhood Home Visitation

Prevent Child Abuse America is grateful for your support of early childhood home visitation, and for your commitment to making a range of quality home visiting programs more widely available, as evidenced by your support as Senator of the *Education Begins at Home Act (EBAH).* Introduced by Senators Hillary Clinton and Chris Bond and Representatives Danny Davis and Todd Platts, EBAH enjoys broad bipartisan support and has been endorsed by over 700 national, state and local organizations. (...)

3. Increase Investments in Prevention
For far too long, prevention has been undervalued and underfunded. We urge you to support increasing investments in prevention through both discretionary and mandatory funding mechanisms. (...)

Conclusion
Prevent Child Abuse America believes that there is no issue more important to the future of our society than how we raise our youth. Yet, a recent UNICEF report found the United Sates was ranked 20th in child well-being out of the world's 21 wealthiest nations. The measures used by UNICEF represent educational, health and safety, material, and family and peer well being; measures that can reduce the potential for child maltreatment. The UNICEF study reinforces countless reports and government data showing that child neglect and maltreatment is a significant but preventable public health problem in our country today.

Research, such as the *Adverse Childhood Experiences* study, has shown that child abuse and neglect have life-long impacts, not only for child but for the nation. These studies show a strong correlation between child abuse and neglect and debilitating and chronic health consequences, delinquency, criminal behavior, mental health illness, drug dependency and lower academic performance.

Getting prevention right early is less costly to the nation, and to individuals, than trying to fix things later. Prevent Child Abuse America estimates that implementing effective policies and strategies to prevent child abuse and neglect can save taxpayers $104 billion per year. The cost of not doing so includes more than $33 billion in direct costs for foster care services, hospitalization, mental health treatment, and law enforcement. Indirect costs of over $70 billion include loss of productivity, as well as expenditures related to chronic health problems, special education, and the criminal justice system.

With your leadership, together we will finally be able to shift our federal policies *from* addressing the issues that arise because of child abuse and neglect *towards* making sure that abuse and neglect does not occur in the first place. Please consider Prevent Child Abuse America and our national network a resource to you as you consider opportunities to address this pressing issue.

TASK/TEXT 2.13.3: PREVENT CHILD ABUSE AMERICA – PINWHEELS FOR PREVENTION

<www.pinwheelsforprevention.org>, <www.preventchildabuse.org>, 31 March 2009

Prevent Child Abuse America is proud to unveil its new campaign, **Pinwheels for Prevention**, introducing the pinwheel as a symbol for child abuse and neglect prevention nationwide.

The pinwheel represents PCA America's efforts to change the way our nation thinks about prevention, focusing on community activities and public policies that prioritize prevention right from the start to make sure child abuse and neglect never occur. It represents our efforts to ensure the healthy development of children nationwide, while recognizing that child development is a building block for community development and economic development.

The campaign is taking root as more than 400,000 blue and silver pinwheels were displayed in communities across the US in 2008. Shining in the sun, the pinwheel is reflective of the bright future all children deserve and our belief that getting it right early is less costly than trying to fix it later.

About Pinwheels for Prevention

For over a decade, market research consistently has shown that the public views child abuse and neglect as a serious problem. As a national organization whose mission is ***"to prevent the abuse and neglect of our nation's children,"*** we must apply that research to engage all people in our society to act to prevent abuse and neglect from ever happening in the first place. Therefore, **Prevent Child Abuse America** is proud to unveil its new campaign, **Pinwheels for Prevention**, introducing the pinwheel as a symbol for child abuse and neglect prevention nationwide.

Through this campaign, we will create a national effort to effect measurable change in the public's beliefs and behaviors regarding the prevention of child abuse and neglect. This goes beyond making Americans aware of our issue to motivating them to take an active role in prevention and in their community.

The pinwheel represents PCA America's efforts to change the way our nation thinks about prevention, focusing on community activities and public policies that prioritize prevention right from the start to make sure child abuse and neglect never occur.

Prevent Child Abuse America

Founded in Chicago in 1972, **Prevent Child Abuse America** is the nation's leading organization working solely to prevent the abuse and neglect or our nation's children. Through its chapters in 47 states and its voluntary home visitation services provided by **Healthy Families America** in more than 400 communities nationwide, Prevent Child Abuse America helps provide healthy, stable and nurturing experiences for more than 100,000 families every year. For more information, please visit **<www.preventchildabuse.org>** and **<www.healthyfamiliesamerica.org>**.

TASK/TEXT 2.14:

TASK/TEXT 2.14.1: AWARENESS OF CHILD ABUSE

Chris Goddard & Joe Tucci, Foreword in: Max Liddell *et al.*, *The State of Child Protection: Australian Child Welfare and Child Protection Developments 2005*, Caulfield East: National Research Centre for the Prevention of Child Abuse, Monash University, September 2006; <www.nrcpca.monash.org/assets/files/childprotection.pdf>

The simple phrase "child abuse" is an "umbrella" term that covers a wide range of activities that harm children (…) …The early focus of research in the field was on severe child abuse and neglect, in largely hospital based studies. This meant that child deaths and disabilities featured prominently in discussion of the consequences of child abuse. While it is essential to stress that many children who are abused grow up to lead [more or less] healthy and fulfilling lives, many others will be less fortunate. Some children, particularly babies and infants, will be permanently physically and/or intellectually handicapped as a result of abuse or neglect. Some children die. …[I]t is infants up to the age of 12 months who are at the greatest risk of violent death. The consequences of child abuse and neglect for some children are devastating. We are learning a great deal about the effects of abuse and neglect. For many children, the effects of abuse continue into adulthood. The downstream costs for the individual and for society are catastrophic.

The World Report on Violence and Health describes child abuse as a "serious global health problem" (World Health Organisation 2002: 80). The report points out that:

> "… Lack of good data on the extent and consequences of abuse and neglect has held back the development of appropriate responses in most parts of the world. Without good local data, it is also difficult to develop a proper awareness of child abuse and neglect …" (World Health Organisation 2002: 78).

The World Health Organisation makes a number of recommendations. The first two, better data and better research, are urgently required in this country. As we have repeatedly pointed out:

> "... We have national debates about industrial relations, education, water, nuclear power. But we have no national debates about our most valuable asset, our children and their protection ... We still have no national standards for child protection, no federal children's minister, no national policies or legislation, no national definitions, no federal system of children's commissioners, no independent scrutiny of child protection, and no reliable national data ..." (...).

It is not surprising therefore that as a community, we continue to place child abuse as a peripheral social problem that is too uncomfortable and challenging to confront (...). It is also not surprising that we fail to hold those who hurt children accountable for their actions.

TASK/TEXT 2.14.2: CHILD ABUSE AS CAUSE OF CRIME

Erdal Tekin, Janet Currie, *Does child abuse cause crime?* Abstract, April 2006, <http://papers.ssrn.com/sol3/papers.cfm?abstract_id=895178>

Child maltreatment, which includes both child abuse and child neglect, is a major social problem. (...) [C]rime (...) is one of the most socially costly potential outcomes of maltreatment (...). We find that maltreatment approximately doubles the probability of engaging in many types of crime. Low SES [socio-economic status] children are both more likely to be mistreated and suffer more damaging effects. Boys are at greater risk than girls, at least in terms of increased propensity to commit crime.

Sexual abuse appears to have the largest negative effects, perhaps justifying the emphasis on this type of abuse in the literature. Finally, the probability of engaging in crime increases with the experience of multiple forms of maltreatment (...).

TASK/TEXT 2.14.3: CHILD MALTREATMENT CAN BE PREVENTED

World Health Organization says violence against children can and must be prevented, Geneva, 16 October 2006, <www.who.int/mediacentre/news/releases/2006/pr57/en/print.html>

Research shows that child maltreatment can be prevented. The need to increase investment in prevention is urgent and global. Promising strategies include reducing unintended pregnancies; improving access to high-quality pre- and post-natal care; reducing harmful levels of alcohol and illicit drug use during pregnancy and by new parents; providing home visitation services by nurses and social workers to families at risk of maltreatment, and training parents on child development, non-violent discipline and problem-solving skills. (…)

> "For too long now the response to child maltreatment has been dominated by systems for reacting to cases once maltreatment has already started. The scientific evidence for preventing physical, sexual and psychological abuse from occurring in the first place is already quite strong, and the time is ripe for a paradigm shift from reaction to prevention" (…).

TASK/TEXT 2.14.4: BROAD ACCESS TO PARENTING SUPPORT REDUCES RISK OF CHILD MALTREATMENT

Centers for Disease Control and Prevention (CDC), International violence prevention efforts, <www.cdc.gov/ncipc/dvp/ppp.htm>, 26 January 2009

When parents have access to **parenting information and support** that address problems families face – from tantrums to encouraging good behavior – key measures of child maltreatment fall, according to a study released in the January 26th online edition of the journal *Prevention Science* [<www.springerlink.com/content/a73718k76218j7k2/fulltext.pdf>]. The US Triple P System Trial, funded by the Centers for Disease Control and Prevention (CDC), found lower rates of substantiated abuse cases, child out-of-home placements, and reductions in hospitalizations and emergency room visits for child injuries in nine study counties in South Carolina where parenting interventions were implemented. The Triple P – Positive Parenting Program, utilized a wide range of support mechanisms for parents including local media, brief public seminars, and parent consultation with specially trained child service providers. Researchers estimate that in an area containing 100,000 children less than eight years of age, the results found in the study could translate annually into 688 fewer cases of child maltreatment, 240 fewer out-of-home placements, and 60 fewer children with injuries requiring hospitalization or emergency room treatment.

TASK/TEXT 2.14.5: WHY A WORLD DAY FOR PREVENTION OF CHILD ABUSE?

Women's World Summit Foundation WWSF, <www.woman.ch>, accessed 17 April 2009

Together, let us create a culture of prevention

Child abuse, especially sexual abuse, is a universal and alarming problem and increased attention and efficient protection skills and prevention measures are necessary at family, local, national and international level. After a long tradition of silence, sexual child abuse is being more and more denounced and becoming a public and political topic.

Alerting Governments and civil society organizations to play a more active role in the promotion of and respect for the rights of the child (article 19 and 34 of the Convention on the Rights of the Child), and contribute to the prevention of child abuse, WWSF launched in 2000 the **World Day for Prevention of Child Abuse**, a Day to be commemorated every **19 November** in synergy with the anniversary of the International Day for the rights of the child (20 November) which has as its objective to be a rallying point around the issue of child abuse and the need for urgent **effective prevention programs.**

To make the Day a global call for action, WWSF launched in 2001 an **international NGO coalition that marks the World Day** with appropriate events and activities to focus on and increase **prevention education.**

Women's World Summit Foundation WWSF

WWSF, a humanitarian, non-governmental and international, non-confessional and non-profit organization with United Nations consultative status (ECOSOC, UNFPA and DPI), works for a new development paradigm with and for women and children.

Created in Geneva on 8 March 1991 (International Women's Day), its principle objective is to empower women, children and NGOs. WWSF programs serve to help implement women's and children's rights, to generate increased commitment and support for the realization of agreed development goals, and to hold world leaders accountable to their promises made at numerous UN summits and international conferences.

Why was WWSF created?

Recognizing that women and children (girls and boys under the age of 18) represent the world's largest constituency who have almost nothing to say in shaping the economic and political space in which they live, it is imperative that their thoughts and visions, intuitive skills, concrete and effective participation in development, and their deep aspiration for a more peaceful world be considered to help catalyze the necessary political will for the transformation of systems and structures into pathways of equality, development and peace.

YouthEngage-international.ch: A pledge to prevent child abuse and violence (<www.woman.ch/children/files/Registration_Form_Intro_E.pdf>)

Launched in 2009, the YouthEngage campaign aims to involve young people **never to commit, condone or remain silent about abuse and violence against children and to learn about the Convention on the Rights of the Child** (20th anniversary in 2009).

TASK/TEXT 2.14.6: NEGLECT [BY PARENTS] IS VIOLENCE TO BE PREVENTED – AND NEGLECT BY NGOs

Editorial by Clara Balestra, Foundation Sarah Oberson, Institut international des Droits de l'Enfant (IDE), <www.childsrights.org/html/site_en/index.php?c=>, 10 August 2009

On July 17th, 2009, a six-month baby and an 11-year old girl were swallowed by the waters of the Engelberger River in the Nidwald canton, due to parental neglect. Jessica, the 11-year old, was walking home with baby Nils and Rahel, his four-year old sister. The latter escaped drowning. At the Luzern railway station, Jessica's mother had entrusted her to bring home Rahel and Nils, daughter and son of Michela, a newly-made friend. The journey from Luzern to Grafenort took them about 60 minutes, and then there was a two-kilometer walk to take. They apparently made an unsuccessful attempt at crossing a stream swelled by recent rainfall. The two bodies have not been found yet.

Such horrifying news reminds us and shows once more that **child neglect (1) is an expression of violence**, of maltreatment (2), bearing serious consequences on the life and health, as well as physical, intellectual, psychological and social development, of the child. Consequences include personality trouble, addictive behaviour, stunted development …

The Convention on the Rights of the Child (CRC) requires from State parties to "take all adequate measures to protect the child from all forms of (…) violence or negligent treatment" (art. 19 al. 1), which implies **first and foremost the adoption of preventive measures.**

A high number of scientific studies assert that violence against children can be prevented. Research also stresses the possibility to implement a similar prevention model for all types of child abuse, provided the chosen model encompasses the complexity of the issue. Moreover, the programmes that have given scientific proof of their efficiency in curbing child abuse (of all kind), are based on **home visits** and **parent education**: such programmes already exist in several Swiss cantons.

In Switzerland, there is a large deficit in data on violence against children (...). The Committee on the Rights of the Child has requested already in 2002, to improve and systematize data collection and analysis on this issue (...). Moreover, a national child abuse prevention strategy must be adopted and implemented (...).

Setting up those two processes is made difficult by the various competences held by municipalities, cantons, and the federal government in the field of child protection and prevention. It also collides with the **dominant liberal ideology, reluctant to invest the private sphere, and with a focus on intervention rather than prevention.**

It is also to be deplored that the second **NGO report to the Committee on the Rights of the Child does not insist on setting up a global child abuse prevention strategy**, but evokes rather timidly to "develop specific prevention notions against family violence, in schools (...)," which seems **grossly insufficient**. (...).

TASK/TEXT 2.15:

TASK/TEXT 2.15.1: ADVERSE CHILDHOOD EXPERIENCES AND SMOKING – LIVES GONE UP IN SMOKE

Carol A. Redding, *ACE Reporter* Summer 2007, <www.acestudy.org/files/AR-Summer2007.pdf> (footnotes and figures not included)

I. All categories of adverse childhood experiences (ACEs) found to be significantly associated with smoking

Every life is touched – to greater or lesser extent – by tragedy. Such is the human condition. When that tragedy begins as trauma in early life, it is not uncommon for people to seek comfort in behaviors that make them feel better. Smoking is one such behavior. "Nicotine has demonstrable psychoactive benefits in the regulation of affect; therefore, persons exposed to adverse childhood experiences may benefit from using nicotine to regulate their mood." What is puzzling, however, is why we sometimes chose to continue such behaviors even after they are proven to cause more direct harm than comfort.

The ACE Study sought to gain insight into the reasons why, when faced with medical conditions that clearly indicate a smoker should stop smoking, smokers continue to smoke anyway. Such medical conditions include heart disease, chronic lung disease, and diabetes, and symptoms of these illnesses (chronic bronchitis, chronic cough, and shortness of breath). Investigators from the Centers of Disease Control and Prevention, and Kaiser Permanente, analyzed the medical, emotional, psychological, and exposure-to-childhood-trauma data of more than 17,000 Kaiser patients. What they learned is alarming. Quit rates among those with cardiovascular disease do not exceed quit rates for the general population, and about a third of those people who are diagnosed with cancer do not quit smoking. Many patients simply never quit, regardless of the nature or severity of their medical status. The following attributes were found to apply to those hard-core smokers who are disinclined to quit, regardless of their health status. They tend to be: • Younger; • Less well educated; • Less socio-economically advantaged; • Living with other smokers in the household. They also tend to have less belief in their ability to quit.

Smoking is also seen to be much more prevalent among people with poor mental health. Depression was found to be a significant independent predictor of smoking persistence, and depressed smokers were found to be more likely to relapse after quitting. In addition, they experience greater discomfort and more withdrawal-related symptoms than non-depressed smokers who quit.

ACE Study research suggests that ACEs may play a role in the *maintenance* of smoking behavior in the presence of illness and poor health. These results extend our understanding of the impact of child maltreatment on adult health behavior. Furthermore, the association of ACEs with smoking persistence was sustained even after accounting for the presence of past or current depression. It is easy to see how inextricably interwoven ACEs are to not just one, but many aspects of our past, current, and prospective health.

Because "heredity" is often blamed for health-related issues such as obesity and smoking, researchers considered whether or not a history of parental smoking and/or substance abuse influenced the smoker's behavior. They found that the outcome was similar, regardless of familial history, and that smoking was therefore not likely linked to genetics or behavior modeling.

Smoking was, however, strongly associated with adverse childhood experiences. It is therefore likely that primary prevention of adverse childhood experiences and improved treatment of exposed children could reduce smoking among both adolescents and adults.

Regardless of our plight as humans, we can perhaps be more courageous, more willing to strive toward life rather than death, when we know that we have the support of those around us. The sooner all modern health care practitioners include childhood trauma as part of their patients' medical records – and take action to help their patients recover from such trauma – the sooner we are likely to see a healthier global population. To that end, we owe our health care communities the education and training that will help them achieve such goals.

Is it enough for the health care community to embrace these concepts? It is not. Individual family members must be prepared to break down the secrecy and shame that allow trauma to thrive. We must be strong enough, we must find the courage, to do what is even harder than dying: Embracing and improving lives that are flawed but not irretrievably broken; breaking the cycle of trauma by supporting one another in healing those still-open wounds of the past. To that end, we owe families the resources that will support this difficult introspection and outreach for help.

Is it enough for families to work toward healing? It is not. Whole communities must work together as a united front dedicated toward protecting today's children, and salving the wounds of today's adults who still harbor their traumatized childhoods inside their bodies. To that end, our governing agencies owe us the policies and resources that it takes to build stronger, healthier nations.

All of this takes uncommon courage.

II. In loving memory of Joseph J. Reich (August 23, 1919-April 6, 1987)

A victim of child abuse, Joe finally smoked himself to death at the age of 67. He was first diagnosed with throat and lung cancer when he was in his mid-late 50's. This diagnosis came from a dentist, and then only when the pain of Joe's rotting teeth was so bad that he could no longer tolerate it. Joe would never otherwise have sought medical attention. He didn't trust doctors; he didn't trust people in general. There were good reasons for that.

Joe was a first-generation American. His parents migrated from Europe at the turn of the 20th century, in the hope of a better life. They didn't find it. What they did find was the South Side of Chicago, the legacy of Upton Sinclair's *The Jungle* – big labor and small wages, and mounting hopelessness that manifested in his father's alcoholic rage. Joe's father was a weekend beer drunk.

One of six living siblings, Joe saw his father repeatedly kick his pregnant wife down the stairs. Joe's mother took in laundry to help make ends meet. He felt the blow of his father's mis-directed anger and frustration.

By the age of 10, Joe found comfort in cigarettes. He bummed them off other kids; he smoked unspent butts he found on the street; he rolled his own. He learned his parenting skills from his father.

Joe was a good student. He was especially good with numbers. How many days did he miss school because he was too injured to attend? People didn't speak of such things in the 1920s and 30s. A father's "discipline" – regardless how absent the reason for it – was never questioned.

Joe graduated high school and went to work, like his father, at the Stock Yards. Soon after, he was drafted into the Army. WWII raged. So did Joe's silent fear.

He watched his friends die around him. He drank. He smoked. He survived. But he would never be the same. He returned from war with shrapnel buried in his leg, and an agony of the soul that would never leave him. The US Army had taken a traumatized child and multiplied his trauma many times over.

Not surprisingly, Joe suffered from what we now call Post-Traumatic Stress Disorder (PTSD). He would sometimes drift off onto the battle field while sitting on his living room couch, surrounded by his children.

Joe had worked his way out of the Stock Yards and become a machinist in a local factory. He seemed to like his work. He had found respect from others, and himself.

Joe had also found comfort in the love of Anne, a beautiful woman with a strong sense of familial duty.

They had a passionate love, and they fought with passion, too. Cast iron pans, fists through the kitchen plaster – injuries, sorrow, regret, make-up; and the cycle would start all over again. They made a life together, and they were hopeful, saving money to buy a home. Their family grew.

Joe was a generous man. When he had money, he shared it. He loved his family, and when he was feeling well, he would come home from work singing. He bounced his little ones on his knee and recited the lyrics to modern songs slowly, so his kids could learn them. He made sad and smiley faces. He made puns and laughed a smoker's laugh that usually resulted in a cough.

And then Anne died – suddenly, from a brain hemorrhage. And Joe seeped into a darkness from which he never fully returned.

Joe drank very heavily. Like his father, he was a mean drunk, and his children took the brunt of it.

Within a year, he lost everything: The woman who loved him, his livelihood, his home, his children, the respect of his siblings and the community.

Joe hit skid row. He lived there on and off, drinking and chain-smoking his way into oblivion. Occasionally, when he was so sick that he couldn't even panhandle his way into another drunken stupor, he would call and ask for help. His voice would come across the wires, weak, weary, "I don't know where I am, but come get me." These are the words that fell on the ears of his ten-year-old daughter who wanted desperately to help him but was powerless to do so.

Imagine how small his self-esteem shrank every time he saw the pity in the eyes of the people who finally did came to his rescue.

It would be more than a decade before he'd be "back on his feet" again. What many other agencies had failed to accomplish, time, self-will and the Salvation Army finally achieved. Joe was sober. He was a middle-aged, chain-smoking, caffeine-addicted survivor of child abuse and the trauma of war. He struggled to make a living as a painter, carrying his gallons of paint and supplies with him on the buses and rails.

Although he was terrified of heights, he hung out the windows of tall buildings to paint the tuition for his kids' Catholic School education. He bought his clothes at the thrift shop. In the fall and winter, he stored his groceries on the outside windowsill of his one-room apartment. He taped off the baseboards and electrical outlets with boric-acid-coated duct tape to keep the cockroaches down to manageable numbers.

Joe loved to play with his grandchild and the child's dog. He gave most of his meager earnings to one of his sisters, who raised some of his younger children. He saw all of his kids as often as he could, showing up freshly scrubbed, walking deliberately, with a hitch in his step, with open arms and a pained smile.

He once said that if he had known that smoking would be such a slow death, he would have chosen a different way to die. He didn't quit when he got the first diagnosis from his dentist. He didn't quit when the diagnosis was confirmed by a physician treating him for injuries sustained by him as a pedestrian hit-and-run victim. He never quit smoking.

Joe was my dad. As his life went up in smoke, so did mine. I missed him every moment that he was absent from my life. I miss him still. I am sometimes asked, "How can you forgive him for what he did to you?" I respond, "How can I not forgive him? Inside, he was just a confused child."

His most lasting legacy to me is that agony of the soul that is sometimes softer, but never really leaves.

Mine is most deeply felt when I realize just how much better things could have been for all of us, if we had known then what we know now about the connection between our pasts as child victims, and our presents as adult survivors. Dad didn't stand a chance, but – while we live – there is still hope for the rest of us.

III. Coffin nails: an historic view of smoking

- 1604, Great Britain's King James I wrote "Counterblaste to Tobacco," citing smoking as "dangerous to the lungs."
- 1867, George William Curtis, Editor of *Harper's Weekly*, began a series of health warnings regarding the hazards of smoking, including statements such as "the very prevalent use of tobacco is among the prominent causes of ill-health."
- 1870, a Dr. Sigmund reported smokers suffered "affections" of the nose, mouth and throat that were more frequent and severe than those of non-smokers.

- 1897, Dr. Mendelssohn reported such "affections" 60% greater in smokers than non-smokers.

These historic perspectives are culled from Harper's Weekly, 1857–1912 (<http://tobacco.harpweek.com>; Copyright Internet Scout Project, 1994–2003, <http://scout.cs.wisc.edu>).

TASK/TEXT 2.15.2: TEN ACE'S & RELATED HEALTH AND SOCIAL PROBLEMS

Robert Anda, The Health and Social Impact of Growing up with Adverse Childhood Experiences [ACEs]; The Human and Economic Costs of the Status Quo [2006/2007?; 20 pp.], available at <www.acestudy.org>, About us (or directly: <www.acestudy.org/files/Review_of_ACE_Study_with_references_summary_table_2_.pdf>), p. 6, p. 14, and Appendix, p. 20, respectively.

1. The 10 ACEs studied are as follows (p. 6):

- *Childhood abuse:*
  1. Emotional
  2. Physical
  3. Sexual
- *Neglect:*
  4. Emotional
  5. Physical
- *Growing up in a seriously dysfunctional household as evidenced by:*
  6. Witnessing domestic violence
  7. Alcohol or other substance abuse in the home
  8. Mentally ill or suicidal household members
  9. Parental marital discord (as evidenced by separation or divorce)
  10. Crime in the home (as evidenced by having a household member imprisoned).

2. Implications (p. 14):

(...) Stressful and traumatic childhood and adolescent experiences literally become "biology" affecting brain structure and function (as well as endocrine, immune, and other biologic functions) thus leading to persistent effects. Until now, these persistent effects were "hidden" from the view of both neuroscientists and public health researchers. **This is no longer the case. In fact, with this information comes *the responsibility to use it.*** (...)

Children experiencing alcohol abuse in the home should be screened for other types of maltreatment and traumatic stressors – and vice versa! This information, if routinely gathered will likely contribute to more meaningful diagnoses, earlier and improved treatment of exposed *children and their caretakers*, and better integration of prevention, social services, and legal venues.

3. Detailed Listing of Health and Social Problems Shown to Have a Graded Relationship to the ACE Score (p. 20):

A. Prevalent Diseases:

- ischemic heart disease
- cancer
- chronic lung disease
- skeletal fractures
- sexually transmitted diseases
- liver disease

B. Risk Factors for Common Diseases/Poor Health:

- smoking
- alcohol abuse
- promiscuity
- obesity
- illicit drug use
- injected drug use
- multiple somatic symptoms
- poor self-rated health
- high perceived risk of AIDS

C. Poor Mental Health:

- depressive disorders
- anxiety
- hallucinations
- panic reactions
- sleep disturbances
- memory disturbances
- poor anger control
- risk of perpetrating or being a victim of domestic violence

D. Sexual and Reproductive Health:

- early age at first intercourse
- sexual dissatisfaction
- teen pregnancy
- unintended pregnancy
- teen paternity
- fetal death

E. General Health and Social Problems:

- high perceived stress
- difficulty with job performance
- relationship problems
- marriage to an alcoholic.

Also see: Vincent J. Felitti, The Relationship of Adverse Childhood Experiences to Adult Health: Turning Gold into Lead (2002); Vincent J. Felitti, The Origins of Addiction: Evidence from the Adverse Childhood Experiences Study (2004), available at: <www.acestudy.org>, About us.

TASK/TEXT 2.15.3: ACE STUDY FINDINGS

The following excerpts are taken from the ACE study websites mentioned (accessed 21 April 2009):

1. <www.acestudy.org/index.html>:

What is the ACE Study?
The ACE Study is an ongoing collaboration between the Centers for Disease Control and Prevention and Kaiser Permanente. Led by Co-principal Investigators Robert F. Anda, MD, MS, and Vincent J. Felitti, MD, the ACE Study is perhaps the largest scientific research study of its kind, analyzing the relationship between multiple categories of childhood trauma (ACEs), and health and behavioral outcomes later in life.

What's an ACE?
Growing up experiencing any of the following conditions in the household prior to age 18:

- Recurrent physical abuse;
- Recurrent emotional abuse;
- Contact sexual abuse;
- An alcohol and/or drug abuser in the household;
- An incarcerated household member;
- Someone who is chronically depressed, mentally ill, institutionalized, or suicidal;
- Mother is treated violently;
- One or no parents;
- Emotional or physical neglect.

The ACE Score

The ACE Study used a simple scoring method to determine the extent of each study participant's exposure to childhood trauma. Exposure to one category (not incident) of ACE, qualifies as one point. When the points are added up, the ACE Score is achieved. An ACE Score of 0 (zero) would mean that the person reported no exposure to any of the categories of trauma listed as ACEs above. An ACE Score of 9 would mean that the person reported exposure to all of the categories of trauma listed above. The ACE Score is referred to throughout all of the peer-reviewed publications about the ACE Study findings.

What's YOUR ACE Score? Go to: <www.acestudy.org/files/ACE_Score_Calculator.pdf>.

2. <www.cdc.gov/nccdphp/ace>:

Welcome

The Adverse Childhood Experiences (ACE) Study is one of the largest investigations ever conducted on the links between childhood maltreatment and later-life health and well-being. As a collaboration between the Centers for Disease Control and Prevention and Kaiser Permanente's Health Appraisal Clinic in San Diego, Health Maintenance Organization (HMO) members undergoing a comprehensive physical examination provided detailed information about their childhood experience of abuse, neglect, and family dysfunction. Over 17,000 members chose to participate. To date, over 50 scientific articles have been published and over 100 conference and workshop presentations have been made.

The ACE Study findings suggest that these experiences are major risk factors for the leading causes of illness and death as well as poor quality of life in the United States. Progress in preventing and recovering from the nation's worst health and social problems is likely to benefit from the understanding that many of these problems arise as a consequence of adverse childhood experiences.

3. <www.cdc.gov/nccdphp/ace/about.htm>:

About the Study

The ACE Study was initiated at Kaiser Permanente from 1995 to 1997, and its participants are over 17,000 members who were undergoing a standardized physical examination. No further participants will be enrolled, but we are tracking the medical status of the baseline participants.

Each study participant completed a confidential survey that contained questions about childhood maltreatment and family dysfunction, as well as items detailing their current health status and behaviors. This information was combined with the results of their physical examination to form the baseline data for the study.

The prospective phase of the ACE Study is currently underway, and will assess the relationship between adverse childhood experiences, health care use, and causes of death.

4. <www.cdc.gov/nccdphp/ace/findings.htm>:

Major Findings

Childhood abuse, neglect, and exposure to other traumatic stressors which we term *adverse childhood experiences* (ACE) are common. Almost two-thirds of our study participants reported at least one ACE, and more than one in five reported three or more ACE. The short- and long-term outcomes of these childhood exposures include a multitude of health and social problems. The ACE Study uses the ACE Score, which is a count of the total number of ACE respondents reported. The ACE Score is used to assess the total amount of stress during childhood and has demonstrated that as the number of ACE increase, the risk for the following health problems increases in a strong and graded fashion:

- alcoholism and alcohol abuse
- chronic obstructive pulmonary disease (COPD)
- depression
- fetal death
- health-related quality of life
- illicit drug use
- ischemic heart disease (IHD)
- liver disease
- risk for intimate partner violence
- multiple sexual partners
- sexually transmitted diseases (STDs)
- smoking
- suicide attempts
- unintended pregnancies

In addition, the ACE Study has also demonstrated that the ACE Score has a strong and graded relationship to health-related behaviors and outcomes during childhood and adolescence including early initiation of smoking, sexual activity, and illicit drug use, adolescent pregnancies, and suicide attempts. Finally, as the number of ACE increases the number of co-occurring or "co-morbid" conditions increases.

5. <www.cdc.gov/nccdphp/ace/pyramid.htm>:

Pyramid

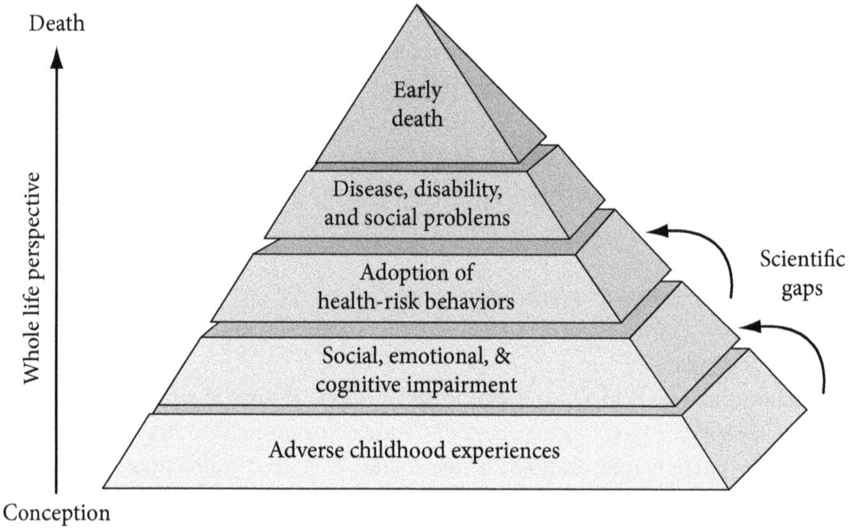

The ACE Pyramid represents the conceptual framework for the Study. During the time period of the 1980s and early 1990s information about risk factors for disease had been widely researched and merged into public education and prevention programs. However, it was also clear that risk factors, such as smoking, alcohol abuse, and sexual behaviors for many common diseases were not randomly distributed in the population. In fact, it was known that risk factors for many chronic diseases tended to cluster, that is, persons who had one risk factor tended to have one or more others.

Because of this knowledge, the ACE Study was designed to assess what we considered to be "scientific gaps" about the origins of risk factors. These gaps are depicted as the two arrows linking Adverse Childhood Experiences to risk factors that lead to the health and social consequences higher up the pyramid. Specifically, the study was designed to provide data that would help answer the question: "If risk factors for disease, disability, and early mortality are not randomly distributed, what influences precede the adoption or development of them?" By providing information to answer this question, we hoped to provide scientific information that would be useful for the development of new and more effective prevention programs.

The ACE Study takes a whole life perspective, as indicated on the orange arrow leading from conception to death. By working within this framework, the ACE Study began to progressively uncover how childhood stressors (ACE) are strongly related to development and prevalence of risk factors for disease and health and social well-being throughout the lifespan.

2*BIS*. THE LANCET'S SERIES ON CHILD MALTREATMENT

TASK/TEXT 2.16:

TASK/TEXT 2.16.1: STAFF 'TOO TIMID' ON CHILD ABUSE

Crinmail 1039 – 4 December 2008, <www.crin.org>; <http://news.bbc.co.uk/2/hi/health/7760806.stm>

3 December 2008 – Professionals must not be too reluctant to remove children from abusive parents, a group of experts has said. The call comes in a series of articles on child abuse published in the Lancet medical journal. The studies also claim that **10% of children in wealthy countries** suffer ill-treatment every year, but that neglect and abuse are under-reported. The findings come as child protection services in the UK are stepped up in the wake of the Baby P case. One study in the Lancet's Series on Child Maltreatment, says that one in 10 children in high income countries is maltreated – but that **only a tenth of these are investigated and even fewer removed from danger**.

Maltreatment includes hitting, punching, burning and serious emotional abuse as well as sexual abuse [as well as all kinds of neglect, JW]. In the UK it is estimated that one million children are affected each year. The author says "it is estimated" that at least 15% of girls and 5% of boys have been exposed to sexual abuse of some kind by the age of 18, and that 5–10% of girls and 1–5% of boys are exposed to penetrative sexual abuse.

Child abuse is **grossly under-reported** – even by the schools and community health services that have continuous contact with children – another study says. There is a reluctance by professionals to intervene when they suspect abuse for fear of doing more harm than good and being accused of breaking up families, according to the experts. Professor Ruth Gilbert, a child health expert from University College London, said: "Scarce reporting to child-protection agencies is a cause for concern, and we need to find out whether maltreatment is being recognised and dealt with in other ways."

Dangerous environment

Professor Jane Barlow, professor of public health at Warwick University, says there is a strong argument for removing children from dangerous homes. There is evidence that removing the child from the dangerous environment and placing them in care can be beneficial, she adds.

Professor Barlow insists: "We have to ensure we are taking children away from dangerous situations. **Removing a child is likely to have better outcomes.** We currently attempt to reunite 50–75% of children that have been removed. Up to half end up back in foster care."

But she warns that social services would be overwhelmed by demand. "If you lower the threshold, the number of children being removed is going to increase considerably and social services will be overrun." She also said the onus should be on teachers, GPs [general practitioners] and community health workers to raise the alarm if they saw signs suggesting abuse.

Another of the studies' authors, Professor Cathy Spatz Widom, of the City University of New York, says: "There's a perception by the public and by some professionals and policy makers that placing children in foster care is a bad thing. By looking at the empirical evidence, it's a more complicated story. We should not just dismiss foster care."

More from Today programme

Professor Gilbert said there would have to be certainty that a child was being maltreated before taking them out of their home.

John Simmonds, of the British Association for Adoption & Fostering, said there was a danger of going too far. "Most certainly some children are better off separated from their parents, and this probably isn't happening as much as it needs to be. Baby P was one example of that. But foster care is not a perfect solution. There is such an atmosphere of blame and recrimination at the moment, with social workers and parents watching their backs. I do worry about the consequences and things swinging too far the other way."

Dr Patricia Hamilton, president of the Royal College of Paediatrics and Child Health, said: "It is sometimes extremely hard to make judgements in child abuse cases. Our society has to accept that child abuse happens and that paediatricians and social workers have a duty to act when they suspect any forms of maltreatment."

Baby P died with multiple injuries, despite receiving 60 visits from welfare professionals. Last month, the 17-month-old's mother, her boyfriend and a lodger were found guilty of causing the child's death.

TASK/TEXT 2.16.2: CHILD ABUSE MUCH MORE COMMON THAN OFFICIAL STATISTICS INDICATE

Caroline Cassels, Medscape Medical News 2008 (Cornell child-maltreatment-research e-list 6 December 2008), New Lancet Report on Incidence of Child Maltreatment

December 5, 2008 – Child abuse in high-income countries is far more common than official statistics show, with just 10% of suspected cases investigated and substantiated annually, new research suggests.

Published online December 4 in the Lancet, the study, led by Ruth Gilbert, MD, from University College London Institute of Child Health, United Kingdom, is 1 of a series of 4 papers in this issue of the Lancet that highlight the issue of childhood maltreatment.

According to the study, 4% to 16% of children are physically abused and 1 in 10 is neglected or psychologically abused every year. In addition, between 5% and 10% of girls and up to 5% of boys are exposed to penetrative sexual abuse, and up to 3 times this number are exposed to any type of sexual abuse. However, the investigators note that official rates for substantiated child maltreatment indicate less than a tenth of this burden.

The impact of child maltreatment can have devastating and long-lasting consequences that persist into adulthood. For instance, the authors note that maltreated children are at increased risk for criminal behavior, are more likely to engage in risky sexual behavior, and are at significantly higher risk for drug and alcohol abuse.

"The most tragic manifestation of the burden of child maltreatment is the thousands of child deaths every year due to murder or neglect," the authors write.

According to the World Health Organization, worldwide, 155,000 children younger than 15 years die annually as a result of abuse or neglect. Biological parents are responsible for 80% of cases and stepparents for 15%.

In the United Kingdom, 35% of child murder victims are younger than 1 year. It is estimated that in the European Union, 4 in every 1 million children die from homicide or manslaughter every year. In central and eastern Europe and the Newly Independent States, the rate is 3 times greater, the authors report.

Abuse Significantly Underreported

A second study, also conducted by Dr. Gilbert and colleagues, shows that in most settings child abuse is significantly underreported – even by schools and community-health services that have continuous contact with children. However, this phenomenon also extends to professionals in primary care, mental health, and law enforcement.

Reasons for underreporting, say the authors, include lack of awareness about the signs of maltreatment and the processes for reporting to child-protection agencies, and the perception that reporting might do more harm than good. However, even when maltreatment is suspected, the authors note, professionals often do not report the case unless they have a high level of certainty that maltreatment has occurred.

To illustrate the extent of uncertainty about maltreatment, the researchers highlight a prospective study from the United States that showed that doctors suspected about 10% of 15,000 child-injury visits were due to maltreatment. However, only 6% of cases were reported (Pediatrics 2008;122:611–619).

"Professionals who have continuous contact with children, such as people working in schools and community health services, can have a leading role in recognizing, responding to, and supporting maltreated children. Their scarce reporting to child-protection agencies is a cause for concern, and we need to find out whether maltreatment is being recognized and dealt with in other ways. Doubts are widespread that the benefits of reporting suspected cases of maltreatment to child-protection services outweigh the harms," the authors conclude.

In an accompanying editorial, Richard Horton, MB, editor of the Lancet, and senior editor Richard Turner, MD, express hope that this series of articles will raise awareness about child abuse and will help guide clinicians and other professionals who come in contact with children who might be abuse victims.

"It is to clinicians and other professionals responsible for caring for children that the Lancet's Child Maltreatment Series is aimed, with the intention of providing them with a rigorous and up-to-date summary of scientific evidence and conceptual work on this complex and demanding topic," they write.

TASK/TEXT 2.16.3: WHEN CHILDHOOD DIES

Richard Turner, Richard Horton, *The Lancet*, London; <www.thelancet.com>, 3 December 2008 (references not included)

Few topics are more emotive than child maltreatment. Human societies place a high value on the richness and diversity that parents contribute to their children's upbringing, and bystanders and professionals alike will hesitate to intervene in or undermine the parent-child relationship unless there is definitive evidence that serious harm is being done. Yet the grating litany of child abuse by parents and other carers is familiar to all. The forced child labour endured by children in

Victorian England more than a century ago remains common in developing countries today, and in the developed world formal child-protection systems document a depressing range of maltreatment, from deliberate neglect to the vilest sexual abuse. This cruel treatment can lead to serious physical and mental-health consequences, and risks creating a damaging intergenerational cycle of maltreatment, disadvantage, and ill health. Children, the most precious and vulnerable members of our societies, deserve closer attention to their care and education and better protection against abuse.

Child maltreatment can be especially difficult to ascertain – after all, the victim might be unwilling or unable to provide an accurate account of abuse, the perpetrator bent on concealment, witnesses silent, clinical signs equivocal, and professionals reluctant to act owing to uncertainty about the existence or severity of abuse, or concern that the treatment of abuse will itself lead to undue disruption or damage to a child's upbringing. When severe child abuse culminates in death, however, as in the tragic recent cases of Victoria Climbié and Baby P in the UK, the law, news media, and public can be expected to cast a harsh and unforgiving spotlight on social workers and doctors who might be perceived or portrayed as having missed opportunities to help the victims.

It is to clinicians and other professionals responsible for caring for children that The Lancet's Child Maltreatment Series is aimed, with the intention of providing them with a rigorous and up-to-date summary of scientific evidence and conceptual work on this complex and demanding topic. Ruth Gilbert and colleagues begin by reviewing the literature on the classification and worldwide burden of child maltreatment, and in a second paper discuss the methodology and challenges involved in identifying abuse. Harriet MacMillan and coauthors summarise the evidence base on interventions that are available to prevent child maltreatment and mitigate its effects; and finally Richard Reading and colleagues acknowledge the complexity of social influences and policy involving children, and argue in favour of a human-rights approach to child maltreatment.

Too often, the safety of children is debated in the polarising light of litigation or political division. Whilst this outcome is inevitable because of the public outrage child maltreatment engenders, a damaging consequence is that the evidence surrounding child neglect and abuse often fails to influence serious policy discussion. It is this marginalisation of the science of child maltreatment that we are seeking to reverse.

We would like to extend warm thanks to Patricia Hamilton of the Royal College of Paediatrics and Child Health for supporting this Series, and to the authors and peer reviewers of the accompanying papers and Comments for their unstinting work. This Lancet Series will unfortunately not halt the blight of child abuse, because the phenomenon is too common, too surreptitious, and too deeply rooted in deprivation and other social ills – but we nonetheless hope to raise awareness of the scientific evidence that is available, and indeed essential, to guide paediatricians and other professionals in their practice with children who might have been abused; and to help bring a new logic and clarity to public debate about this contentious area.

TASK/TEXT 2.16.4: THE LANDSCAPE OF CHILD MALTREATMENT

Dorothy A Scott, Australian Centre for Child Protection, University of South Australia, Magill, Australia; <www.thelancet.com>, 3 December 2008 (references not included)

In the face of the persistent and pervasive problem of child maltreatment, history can be a harbinger of hope while teaching us painful lessons about the legacy of the so-called rescue of children from their families.

In the 19th century, the first wave of the child-rescue movement gave the state and non-government organisations power to protect children from maltreatment. In the mid-20th century the second wave of the movement emerged, resulting in the identification of previously undetected bone fractures in very young children, which was followed in the 1980s by wider recognition of child sexual abuse.

The modern child protection movement in developed countries stems from the acceptance of two inspiring ideas – that children possess human rights and that children are psychological beings. The first notion has led to governments increasing their role in upholding a child's right to protection, but not necessarily their rights to provision of and participation in care. The second idea has substantially broadened how child maltreatment is defined, and now includes situations such as children witnessing intimate-partner violence. However, in many developing countries the right of children to protection, provision, and participation has yet to be tackled, while poverty remains a dominant cause of children's suffering.

In recent decades there has been a massive change in statutory child-protection services, particularly in English-speaking countries, which have introduced very extensive mandatory reporting laws, and invested more in detection, investigation, and legal intervention than western European systems. Consequently, these statutory child-protection systems have become overwhelmed and unsustainable, with more than one in five children reported as suspected victims of child maltreatment by the age of 18 years.

One of the factors contributing to an increase in child neglect is parental substance dependence – most notably parental alcohol abuse, which is especially frequent in eastern Europe. Parental substance dependence is a common factor in substantiated child-protection cases, and intimate-partner violence and parental mental illness are further important and interrelated problems.

Although child physical and sexual abuse has a high public profile, child neglect and emotional abuse are the most common reasons that children are placed in child-protection systems, and the serious cumulative harm they cause is only beginning to receive the attention it deserves.

The development of a knowledge base to help inform our responses to child maltreatment is still in its infancy. The Lancet's Series on child maltreatment provides disturbing evidence of the prevalence of child abuse and neglect, and its serious and long-term effects. Further, the Series discusses the difficulties in recognising and reporting child maltreatment and the limited evidence of effective interventions for preventing and responding to maltreatment. Results from US research highlighting poor outcomes associated with the widespread problem of multiple foster placements suggest that removing children "on the margins of placement" from their families can result in worse outcomes. This research stresses that child-rescue impulses must be first tempered by a commitment to do no further harm.

The shift in some jurisdictions towards approaches that attempt to integrate child health, education, and social services to promote early intervention and holistic care are encouraging signs. Moreover, adult-focused sectors – such as services for drug and alcohol rehabilitation, mental health, domestic violence, homelessness, and refugee resettlement – have, by building capacity to be child and parent sensitive, untapped potential to reduce risk and increase protection against child maltreatment.

However, the problem of child maltreatment will not be solved solely by services when social inequality is the underlying social determinant. A public-health approach will add to the existing responses that cannot cope with such a complex, large-scale problem. Further opportunities that need to be explored include social marketing campaigns and national measures to reduce parental alcohol abuse, such as banning alcohol advertising and increasing taxes on beverages with a high content of alcohol.

In the 21st century, will a public-health approach be the third wave of the child-protection movement? To achieve this goal we need a collective commitment to make children central to our culture. We have come a long way in a century, but we have a very long way to go.

TASK/TEXT 2.16.5: SUPPORTING PAEDIATRICIANS WHO WORK IN CHILD MALTREATMENT

Carole Jenny, Warren Alpert Medical School of Brown University, Providence, USA; <www.thelancet.com>, 3 December 2008 (references not included)

The Lancet's Series on child maltreatment distils the ample evidence that child abuse and neglect is common, both in developed and developing countries. We know that such maltreatment is harmful to children and society. And we all agree that child maltreatment is unfair and that we should be doing something to stop it. This Series is one indication of how far society has come in recognising an obligation to its young and vulnerable members. However, as a society we still might not want to acknowledge that individual children are being harmed. How else can we explain how easy it has been to vilify paediatricians who venture to say that an individual child might need protection from his or her carers?

The identification of child maltreatment is difficult under the best of conditions, as shown in the paper by Ruth Gilbert and colleagues in this Series. It is rare for parents who mistreat their children to come forward and say "I'm sorry, I need help," or "I lost my temper and did a bad thing." Instead, child maltreatment presents as an accident ("he rolled off the sofa"), an illness ("she bruises easily"), or perhaps a failure to grow and gain weight ("he eats constantly, I don't know why he's so thin"). Paediatricians who take care of abused and neglected children are asked to practise rational medicine while many of their patients' parents are lying to them. Imagine trying to make a diagnosis when the history presented is not only wrong but also presented in a way that will mislead the doctor away from the true diagnosis.

Let me offer a few suggestions about how paediatricians could be supported as they go about helping society protect children from maltreatment. First, recognise that the nature of "evidence" that paediatricians have available to them when diagnosing child abuse is often different from the evidence they use to solve other clinical dilemmas. For example, when prescribing the right antibiotic for a certain type of infection, paediatricians will rely on evidence gathered in prospective clinical trials. When diagnosing child abuse, paediatricians rely on observational studies based on clinical experience. There will never be "prospective controlled clinical experiments" in which children are purposefully abused and then observed to see how they are affected. Some have suggested that there is no evidence base to child-abuse diagnoses, such as shaken baby syndrome. However, years of carefully collected and analysed clinical series have been retrospectively collected (including confession cases). From this vast collection of observational data, we can make measured clinical decisions.

Second, regulate professionals. Rogue expert witnesses for the defence or prosecution should be required to present sound science before their pet theories are presented in court. What is the evidence that coughing, immunisations, and vitamin C deficiency cause severe head injuries in children? How can children's bones be brittle on the day they sustain five fractures and normal the next day? A recent example of this misuse of science was testimony based on the totally discredited theory that hypoxia causes subdural haemorrhages.

Third, we need to look again at the current policy that experts should limit their testimony to their specific area of expertise. Currently in the UK, a radiologist can testify about radiological evidence and ignore obvious physical injuries on the skin by saying he or she only looks at bones. It is reasonable that people should be experts before they give an opinion, but they should not be allowed to use the policy to mislead a court.

We should encourage paediatricians to become experts in child abuse. In the USA, child-abuse paediatrics is a recognised subspecialty certified by the American Board of Pediatrics. By 2012, all new child-abuse paediatricians will have to complete 3 years of postresidency fellowship in a credentialled programme and pass board examinations. The National Association of Children's Hospitals also recommends that every children's hospital has paediatricians on staff who are experts in child abuse and neglect.

Finally, do something about the mass media. We all know that "man bites dog" is a more sensational news story than "dog bites man." Similarly, the press are more likely to highlight stories about parents who are "wrongly accused" by paediatricians, and paediatricians have no means to protect themselves from press attacks in view of the rules on patients' confidentiality. Trying cases in the press before they get to court is inappropriate and unfair. Paediatricians play an important part in protecting children – such doctors should be valued, encouraged, and supported as part of the safety net that safeguards vulnerable citizens.

TASK/TEXT 2.16.6: SAFEGUARDING CHILDREN – A CALL TO ACTION

Albert Aynsley-Green, The Children's Commissioner for England [<www.11million.org.uk>], 11 MILLION, London, UK; David Hall, School of Child and Adolescent Health, University of Cape Town, Western Cape, South Africa; <www.thelancet.com>, 3 December 2008 (references not included)

Since Kempe's description, almost 50 years ago, of the "battered baby," we have become all too familiar with sexual and emotional abuse of children, neglect, fabricated illness, bullying, and exposure to domestic violence. In many countries the catalogue of abuse and exploitation also includes female genital mutilation, child trafficking and prostitution, sweatshop labour, and coercive enrolment into military service. The Lancet's Series on child maltreatment describes the progress that has been made in recognising maltreatment and its effects in the short and long term, and in evaluating interventions once abuse has occurred. However, mental-health professionals and social services too often lack the resources to apply this knowledge.

Sadly, we are far from understanding why maltreatment is so common and how to stop it. Child maltreatment occurs in all societies and all socioeconomic groups but poverty, unemployment, and overcrowding – which might lead to, or be associated with, parental mental-health problems and drug or alcohol abuse – all predispose to abuse. Often parents' life circumstances help to explain why children are neglected or abused, but there are also many people who cynically exploit children for self-gratification or personal gain.

Prevention of child maltreatment can be approached at the level of the individual child or family, the local area or school, or the community as a whole. In the Series, Harriet MacMillan and colleagues explore the immense difficulties in researching these approaches. Some interventions focus on one issue – e.g., those designed to reduce the risk of sexual abuse. Others seek to address problems of early parent–infant attachment and parenting skills. Involving fathers is important – yet in the Series fathers seem to be perceived as perpetrators of abuse rather than key figures in a child's life.

Many of the children at high risk of maltreatment grow up with multiple disadvantages: lack of vital preschool learning opportunities, behavioural problems, harsh inconsistent parenting, poor schools, food insecurity, unhealthy diet causing undernutrition or obesity and dental disease, and an increased risk of illness and death from sudden infant death syndrome, infections, substance abuse, suicide, and violent crime. The apparent success of the Nurse Family Partnership (currently undergoing a replication trial in the UK) suggests that for many families **a focus only on preventing maltreatment is less effective than a positive approach of building child-care skills, self-esteem, and financial independence**. However, such programmes are expensive, need scarce human resources, and must be targeted to those most likely to benefit.

The ecological approach to child maltreatment emphasises neighbourhood risk: inadequate or decaying infrastructure, endemic community violence, and social impoverishment. This approach applies equally to the decrepit featureless estates and ghettos of the industrialised nations and the slums and shanty towns of the developing world, all of which present overwhelming challenges to governments. Reducing neighbourhood risk by developing and strengthening local communities is an attractive option, although such programmes are complex to plan and expensive to implement.

Child maltreatment, like many other manifestations of violence, is the end result of interaction between genetic and temperamental factors (e.g., escalating aggressive behaviour in childhood or the callous–unemotional personality type), the socioeconomic environment, and societal attitudes. A UN report reviewed violence against children in the light of the Convention on the Rights of the Child and, in the Series, a human-rights approach is proposed by Richard Reading and coauthors. This approach involves listening to children's concerns and helping them to understand that they have rights – but that other people have rights as well and that these rights go hand in hand with respect and responsibilities. UNICEF [<www.unicef.org.uk>, Talking rights; taking responsibility] and the Roots of Empathy programme [<www.rootsofempathy.org>] have developed guidance to help teachers working with these themes in school. Mass entertainment or edutainment programmes could help young people to modify their attitudes and behaviour – e.g., in southern Africa the programme Soul City tackles the problems of coercive sex, teenage rape, and domestic violence, which young people too readily accept as just part of life.

Population pressures are likely to increase the risks of child maltreatment, particularly in developing countries. Climate experts question whether the world can sustain current levels of consumption and the projected population increase. To improve quality of life and reduce maltreatment in all its manifestations, child-health professionals should advocate not only for the Millennium Development Goal of child survival but also for family planning services, which currently are inaccessible to millions of couples. **Children who are wanted and planned according to parental and environmental resources must surely have a better chance of enjoying their childhood free of maltreatment or neglect.**

TASK/TEXT 2.16.7: BURDEN AND CONSEQUENCES OF CHILD MALTREATMENT IN HIGH-INCOME COUNTRIES

<www.thelancet.com>, Series Child Maltreatment no. 1, Published online December 3, 2008 (references, tables and panels not included)

Ruth Gilbert, Cathy Spatz Widom, Kevin Browne, David Fergusson, Elspeth Webb, Staffan Janson

Child maltreatment remains a major public-health and social-welfare problem in high-income countries. Every year, about 4–16% of children are physically abused and one in ten is neglected or psychologically abused. During childhood, between

5% and 10% of girls and up to 5% of boys are exposed to penetrative sexual abuse, and up to three times this number are exposed to any type of sexual abuse. However, official rates for substantiated child maltreatment indicate less than a tenth of this burden. Exposure to multiple types and repeated episodes of maltreatment is associated with increased risks of severe maltreatment and psychological consequences. Child maltreatment substantially contributes to child mortality and morbidity and has longlasting effects on mental health, drug and alcohol misuse (especially in girls), risky sexual behaviour, obesity, and criminal behaviour, which persist into adulthood. Neglect is at least as damaging as physical or sexual abuse in the long term but has received the least scientific and public attention. The high burden and serious and long-term consequences of child maltreatment warrant increased investment in preventive and therapeutic strategies from early childhood.

Key messages

- A substantial minority of children in high-income countries are maltreated by their caregivers.
- Repeated abuse and high levels of neglect mean that for many children maltreatment is a chronic condition.
- Parental poverty [material poverty, JW], low educational achievement [mental poverty, JW], and mental illness [emotional poverty, JW] are often associated with child maltreatment.
- Child maltreatment has longlasting effects on mental health, drug and alcohol problems, risky sexual behaviour, obesity, and criminal behaviour, from childhood to adulthood.
- Neglect is at least as damaging as physical or sexual abuse in the long term, but has received the least scientific and public attention.
- The high burden and serious, longlasting consequences of child maltreatment warrant increased investment in preventive and therapeutic strategies from early childhood.

Introduction

Maltreatment of children by their parents or other caregivers is a major public-health and social-welfare problem in high-income countries. It is common and can cause death, serious injury, and long-term consequences that affect the child's life into adulthood, their family, and society in general. The 2006 WHO report on prevention of child maltreatment [*Preventing child maltreatment: A guide to taking action and generating evidence*, Geneva: WHO and International Society for the Prevention of Child Abuse and Neglect, 2006] drew attention to the need for this topic to achieve the prominence and investment in prevention and epidemiological monitoring that is given to other serious public-health concerns with lifelong consequences affecting children – such as HIV/AIDS, smoking, and obesity – and it recommended expansion of the scientific evidence base for the magnitude, effects, and preventability of the problem. This Series of four papers critically assesses this expanding evidence base with the aim of informing policy and practice relating to child maltreatment. We focus mainly on high-income countries and eastern European countries that are in economic transition, since the problem and systems for response differ in low-income and many middle-income countries. In this first paper of the Series, we aim to quantify the magnitude of the problem, its determinants, and consequences. The second charts the evidence underpinning recognition and response by professional agencies dealing with children. The third assesses what works for prevention of child maltreatment and associated impairment, and the final paper discusses how consideration of children's rights could enable a more coherent and effective approach to child maltreatment.

Burden of child maltreatment and definitions

Child maltreatment encompasses any acts of commission or omission by a parent or other caregiver that result in harm, potential for harm, or threat of harm to a child (usually interpreted as up to 18 years of age), even if harm is not the intended result. Four forms of maltreatment are widely recognised: physical abuse; sexual abuse; psychological abuse, sometimes referred to as emotional abuse; and neglect. Increasingly, witnessing intimate-partner violence is also regarded as a form of child maltreatment. Consensus definitions place responsibility for safeguarding children from maltreatment on all caregivers, including teachers, trainers, or child minders (...). In practice, however, 80% or more of maltreatment is perpetrated by parents or parental guardians, apart from sexual abuse, which is mostly perpetrated by acquaintances or other relatives (...).

Reliable measurement of the frequency and severity of child maltreatment is not straightforward. We review three types of studies that measure the frequency of maltreatment. The first two types are community studies based on self-reports from victims who are old enough to comply with surveys, or studies based on parents reporting severe physical punishment or patterns of care. The third type involves official statistics from agencies investigating victims (e.g., child-protection services) or police (investigating victims and offenders). All these measures have biases and inconsistencies: thus the prevalence figures in panel 1 are presented as **a range of estimates**. Despite the uncertainty of these estimates, the gap between the low rates of maltreatment substantiated by child-protection agencies and the **ten-fold higher rates reported by victims or parents** underlines the fact that only a few children who are maltreated receive official attention.

Studies that have linked self-reports to official statistics for child protection provide direct evidence of under-reporting to agencies. One study reported evidence of contact with child-protection services in only 5% of children who were physically abused and 8% of those sexually abused. Another showed that even children who were being monitored by agencies reported four to six times more episodes of abuse than did official records.

The discrepancies between official statistics and community studies are even more substantial when examined by age at maltreatment. National statistics from child-protection agencies in the UK and USA show an inverse relation between rate of reports and age for all categories of maltreatment apart from sexual abuse, which is stable across the age range. Opposite trends have been noted for self-report or parent-report studies in the UK and USA for physical, sexual, or psychological abuse, whereas the prevalence of neglect seems to remain relatively constant. Explanations for these diverging trends include increased risks of under-reporting by parents of younger children, and underdetection of maltreatment by child-protection agencies in older children.

Although self-reports or parent reports are probably closer to the true, unobserved rate of maltreatment than are official reports to agencies, they might still be underestimates. Biases in self-reports of sexual abuse have been investigated, although problems such as forgetting, denial, misunderstanding, and embarrassment also apply to other forms of maltreatment. All these problems are likely to lead to the under-reporting rather than over-reporting of sexual abuse of children. Test-retest studies have shown modest to moderate agreement between successive self-reports by young adults of sexual or physical abuse several years later (κ coefficient 0.4–0.6) and good agreement is shown for all types of victimisation several weeks later. One study using latent class methods estimated that reported rates of child sexual abuse were roughly half the true but non-observed rate.

Studies measuring physical abuse in young children use parent reports of physical violence, whereas parent or adolescent self-reports can be used in older children to yield similar estimates. Comparison between official statistics and parent-report studies within a country suggest that only a small proportion of these cases are investigated by child-protection services (panel 1). For example, a systematic review in the UK estimated that around one in 30 children who were physically abused by parents (yearly prevalence 9%) were investigated by social-welfare services responsible for child protection, and only one in 250 children who were physically abused were monitored in accordance with a child-protection plan.

Measurement of sexual abuse relies on retrospective self-report studies of episodes that are recalled years later by adolescents or adults. Between 5% and 10% of girls and 1% to 5% of boys are exposed to penetrative sexual abuse during childhood, although figures that include any form of sexual abuse are much higher (panel 1). These estimates are supported by results of a meta-analysis of worldwide studies of variable quality and methodologies, but they probably give a lower limit of the true rate of sexual abuse because of under-reporting.

Few studies have examined the prevalence of psychological abuse. Results from large population-based, self-report studies in the UK and USA showed that 8–9% of women and about 4% of men reported exposure to severe psychological abuse during childhood. Similar figures have been recorded for psychological abuse in the past year in boys and girls (10.3%). Higher rates have been reported in eastern Europe by similar measures (panel 1). Measurement of neglect in the community is difficult, partly because there are many aspects of omission or lack of provision of care that are harmful or could place a child at risk of harm. UK and US studies noted that between 1.4% and 10.1% of children or their mothers reported persistent absence of care or instances in which a child was hurt because of insufficient supervision (panel 1). Neglect has received little attention from self-report and parent-report studies despite being the most frequent category of child maltreatment recorded by child-protection agencies (panel 1).

Children who witness intimate-partner violence can be harmed psychologically by witnessing the experience or by being caught up in the violence. The reported prevalence of witnessing intimate-partner violence during childhood ranges from 8–10% in Swedish children aged 15–16 years, who were surveyed in 2000 and 2006, to 24% reported in a survey of 8600 adult members of a US health maintenance organisation. The risk of other forms of child maltreatment for witnesses of intimate-partner violence is 30–60%.

Children who are exposed to one type of maltreatment are often exposed to other types on several occasions or continuously. How frequently this abuse occurs is underestimated by official reports because recording of more than one type of maltreatment is often discouraged by child-protection agencies and official reports often do not capture the chronology of exposure over time. However, retrospective self-report studies consistently show that some children are exposed to more than one type of maltreatment. This pattern is emphasised by detailed examination of narratives in US child-protection reports of 519 cases of maltreatment, in which high rates of multiple types of maltreatment were reported (36–91% depending on the classification used) with emotional abuse rarely occurring alone (1.2%). Exposure to multiple types of abuse contributes to high rates of repeated referrals to child-protection services – e.g., 22% of children with substantiated maltreatment in the US were re-reported within 24 months, 39 with similar rates in the UK (24% within 27 months) and in eight European countries (7–33%). Factors that consistently affect re-reporting to agencies are primarily ongoing risk factors in the child (such as disability or chronic medical disorders), in the parent (such as alcohol misuse), indices of social adversity (such as low income, contact with services), and multiple or chronic maltreatment, particularly neglect. Re-report can also indicate increased surveillance.

Much less is known from self-report studies about patterns of maltreatment for more than one child in a family. However, an analysis of child-protection referrals in the UK showed that maltreatment was restricted to one specific child, who was more likely to be abused physically or sexually, in 44% of 310 index cases. Referrals of multiple siblings (56% of cases) were linked to neglect or psychological abuse. Parental difficulties and family stressors – such as family conflict and separation, drug or alcohol misuse, or family criminality – were associated with maltreatment of all children in the family (37%).

Throughout childhood, maltreatment by parents or other caregivers merges with other forms of victimisation. In a nationally representative study, Finkelhor and colleagues noted that the 22% of children aged 2–17 years who had four or more types of victimisation in the previous year – including physical, sexual, or psychological abuse; neglect; or exposure to crime, assault, witnessing intimate-partner violence; or peer or sibling victimisation – were much more likely to be victimised the following year than were those who had fewer types of victimisation, and to have the most serious victimisations and most serious psychological symptomology. Evidence from several studies suggests that children who are exposed to one type of maltreatment are at high risk of other types and of repeated exposure over time, and that the frequency of exposure is correlated with the severity of maltreatment. For a few children, maltreatment is a chronic condition, not an event.

DETERMINANTS OF MALTREATMENT

Characteristics of the victim

Understanding what characteristics of parent–child relationships place children at increased risk of maltreatment within a family is complex and beyond the scope of this review. Girls have a higher risk of being sexually abused than do boys, although rates of other types of maltreatment are similar for both sexes in high-income countries. In low-income countries, girls are at higher risk for infanticide, sexual abuse, and neglect, whereas boys seem to be at greater risk of harsh physical punishment.

Disabled children are at increased risk of maltreatment, although whether their disability is a cause or consequence is uncertain. A record-linkage study in the USA showed a cumulative prevalence of any maltreatment in 9% of non-disabled children and in 31% of disabled children. The overall prevalence of any recorded disability was 8%, but a quarter of all maltreated children had a disability.

Characteristics of the parents and community

Identification of the separate effects of parental characeristics on the risk of child maltreatment is challenging since many factors are inextricably clustered. Poverty, mental-health problems, low educational achievement, alcohol and drug misuse, and exposure to maltreatment as a child are strongly associated with parents maltreating their children. The extent to which each of these risk factors is causally related to the occurrence of maltreatment is hard to establish. Risk factors might affect the child differently depending on the type of maltreatment and might also be linked to the adverse consequences of maltreatment. The ecological model conceptualises maltreatment as multiply determined by forces at work in the individual, in the family, and in the community and culture, and suggests that these determinants modify each other. Thus, parental risk factors can be modified by the environment and community. Nevertheless, some relationships can be generalised. First, **income and parental education are risk factors for child maltreatment**, although their importance varies with the type of maltreatment. Second, socioeconomic inequalities are especially steep for deaths from child abuse. Third, in the USA, there is controversy about the extent to which ethnic differences in allegations and substantiation of maltreatment, and in deaths from injury due to maltreatment, are explained by sociodemographic characteristics. However, ethnic differences in the overall risk of maltreatment are largely explained by sociodemographic characteristics, apart from for children of mixed or multiracial heritage who have an increased risk. Fourth, although a clear pathway exists by which parental drug and alcohol problems can cause child maltreatment in individual families, evidence for a causal link within populations is less certain. However, substance misuse is undoubtedly a common factor in incidents involving both spouse and child maltreatment.

Last, the **community environment seems to have a small to moderate effect in addition to family and individual characteristics**. A UK cohort study reported that individual strengths distinguished resilient from non-resilient children who were exposed to physical abuse under conditions of low but not high family and neighbourhood stress, which was manifested by high crime and low social cohesion, and informal social control. Similarly, a systematic review reported that 10% of the variation in child health and adolescent outcomes, including maltreatment, was explained by neighbourhood socioeconomic status and social climate.

Changes over time

Evidence suggests that physical and sexual abuse are decreasing in some settings. In the USA, substantiated reports of sexual and physical abuse have fallen by around 50% from the mid-1990s to 2005 (...), with a similar trend in England

(...). These decreases are probably accurate estimates since they are present across both types of abuse with no preponderance of equivocal cases. No analysis of trends in Europe has been done, despite clear evidence, at least **in Sweden, of a reduction in acceptance and occurrence of parental violence towards children** since the 1960s (...). Further research is needed to confirm these trends that emphasise the predominance and continuing problem of neglect and the rise in recognition of psychological abuse, which is often associated with other forms of family violence (...).

Differences between countries

Comparisons of the prevalence or incidence of maltreatment between different countries need parent-report or self-report studies using similar survey methods. Few such studies have been published. 30 years ago, Gelles and Edfeldt reported a 5% higher prevalence of physical abuse in the past year in the USA than in Sweden when the same instrument was used. A meta-regression of self-report studies indicates higher rates of sexual abuse in the USA than in Europe (22% vs 15%), although differences might be partly due to less sensitive survey methods in the European studies. The agency reports for different countries in panel 1 are difficult to compare since they reflect different systems and thresholds.

Child maltreatment is a particular concern in the newly independent eastern and central European states, where the economic transition in the past 15 years has been associated with substantial rises in premature adult mortality (panel 1). Although data are scarce, a questionnaire survey of children aged 10–14 years (n=1145) in Macedonia, Latvia, Lithuania, and Moldova recorded the lowest yearly prevalence rates of severe and moderate psychological abuse and physical abuse in Macedonia (18% and 12%, respectively) and the highest in Moldova (43% and 29%, respectively). Abuse was higher in rural areas than in urban areas, and was associated with parental overuse of alcohol. Other studies report similar rates of child sexual abuse to those in western Europe. As in western Europe, by far the greatest problem is neglect. The WHO national prevalence study of child maltreatment in Romanian families showed that physical neglect was reported by 46% of adolescents surveyed, emotional neglect by 44%, and educational neglect by 34%. These rates are much higher than are those in western Europe. A WHO study in Samara, Russia, reported that the identification of neglect by health and social services is seven times more common than is identification of physical abuse. In two-thirds of all cases of maltreatment, the parents were recorded as alcoholic. The usual response to such cases in 2002 was to place the child into residential or foster care. However, the chances of physical and sexual abuse in residential care are even higher than in family-based care (...).

DEATH FROM CHILD MALTREATMENT

The most tragic manifestation of the burden of child maltreatment is the thousands of child deaths every year due to deliberate killing (homicide) or neglect (manslaughter). WHO estimated that 155.000 deaths in children younger than 15 years occur worldwide every year as a result of abuse or neglect, which is 0.6% of all deaths and 12.7% of deaths due to any injury. Only a third of these deaths are classified as homicide. Furthermore, substantial under-reporting occurs because of insufficient routine investigations and post-mortem examinations of child deaths in most countries. The biological parents are responsible for four-fifths of cases, and step-parents are to blame for most of the remaining cases (15% of the total).

Child homicide occurs most frequently during infancy – in the UK, 35% of child homicide victims (<16 years) are younger than 1 year. In infancy, homicide is equally likely to be perpetrated by the mother and the father; however, for older children, the perpetrator is usually a man. Large differences in infant homicide rates exist between high-income countries, with the highest rates recorded in the USA and lowest in Scandinavia and southern Europe. An analysis of infant homicide rates between 1945 and 1998 in 39 countries confirmed previously reported associations between infant homicide and higher rates of female participation in the workforce and income inequalities.

According to WHO estimates, rates of death in children younger than 15 years due to homicide or manslaughter in central and eastern Europe and the newly independent states of the former Soviet Union are consistently higher than in the western European countries of the EU (...). The peak incidence from 1993 to 2003 coincided with the period of economic and political transition when community services were severely disrupted. Despite improvement over the past 30 years in child protection in western European countries and the USA, there has been very little decrease in the rate of child homicides.

LONG-TERM CONSEQUENCES OF CHILD MALTREATMENT

Since groundbreaking work in the early 1970s drew attention to the battered child syndrome, research designed to quantify the long-term consequences of child maltreatment has grown. Here we summarise the evidence for associations between different types of maltreatment and outcomes related to education, mental health, physical health, and violence or criminal behaviour. Findings from cohort studies that prospectively ascertained whether children were maltreated or not, and which followed up these children over time to identify later outcomes, are contrasted with more diverse work of cohort and cross-sectional studies that measure maltreatment retrospectively, usually on the basis of self-reporting in adolescence or adulthood. Since we are interested in the consequences of child maltreatment, we want to assess causality. Thus, the strengths of prospective studies include the temporal ordering of maltreatment and subsequent outcomes, objective measurement of maltreatment, avoidance of recall bias, minimisation of selective inclusion of participants on the basis of the outcome, and the opportunity to adjust for social and individual confounding factors as they occur.

All these factors are weaknesses of studies using retrospective measurement of maltreatment, especially since the temporal ordering of maltreatment and outcomes cannot be reliably established. Recall bias is also a concern, with ambiguity about whether consequences are due to the actual abuse experience, aftermath of the abuse experience, or a person's cognitive appraisal of the experience. However, studies that use only official cases of child maltreatment might detect only the few maltreated children who come to professional attention, who might differ in some ways from other maltreated children and whose outcomes could also be different. The problem of representativeness, which can distort the prevalence and effect size, is reduced for population-based longitudinal cohort studies. The validity of various methods of assessing and studying maltreatment is a source of ongoing debate. Our analysis endeavours to draw on the strengths of prospective and retrospective studies and, when available, on findings from systematic reviews (…).

Education and employment

Child maltreatment is associated with long-term deficits in educational achievement. Prospective longitudinal studies have consistently shown that maltreated children have lower educational achievement than do their peers, and are more likely to receive special education (Jonson-Reid and colleagues found that 24% of maltreated children received special education at a mean age of 8 years, compared with 14% of children with no maltreatment record). The differences are substantial – e.g., only 42% of the maltreated children completed high school compared with two-thirds of community-matched controls. Another prospective study showed that decreases in school attendance and school performance were related to the timing of maltreatment, and were cumulative. Most of these associations persisted after adjustment for family and social characteristics (e.g., ethnic origin, age, sex, and socioeconomic status), as seen in some but not all studies. A longitudinal population-based cohort study in New Zealand, with retrospective ascertainment of child maltreatment, confirmed these reduced levels of educational achievement in adults who had been physically or sexually abused (e.g., 6–10% of abused children attained a university degree compared with 28% of those not abused) but such differences were largely explained by social, parental, and individual characteristics. Exposure of children to intimate-partner violence also seems to be linked to low educational achievement, but the extent to which this factor is independent of other forms of child maltreatment is unclear.

Although the risk of underachievement in education is clearly high in children who are maltreated, evidence for a causal link is mixed. Studies are needed from outside the USA to help quantify the extent of this burden in different educational settings.

Maltreatment has longlasting economic consequences for affected individuals. In a prospective study of court documented cases of childhood maltreatment and community-matched controls, significantly more of the abused and neglected individuals were in menial and semi-skilled occupations than were controls (62% vs 45%) at 29 years of age, and fewer had remained in employment during the past 5 years (41% vs 58%). Further research is needed to examine the effect of child maltreatment on economic productivity throughout life and in different settings.

Mental-health outcomes

Child maltreatment increases the risk of behaviour problems, including internalising (anxiety, depression) and externalising (aggression, acting out) behaviour.

Children who witness intimate-partner violence are at increased risk of behaviour problems, but whether this factor is independent of other forms of maltreatment is contentious. Behaviour problems in childhood seem to be strongly determined by early timing of maltreatment, although whether early physical or psychological abuse, or neglect, is most damaging at this age is unclear. Behaviour problems that arise later in adolescence might be related most strongly to maltreatment during adolescence. Consistent evidence suggests a cumulative effect of different types of maltreatment on later behaviour problems, with one group concluding "there is no point beyond which services for children are hopeless…every risk factor we can reduce matters."

Maltreated children have a moderately increased risk of depression in adolescence and adulthood (adjusted odds ratios ranging from 1.3 to 2.4), which only partly reflects the family context in which maltreatment occurs. Because depression is common and serious – around a quarter to a third of maltreated children meet criteria for major depression by their late 20s (with use of criteria from the Diagnostic and Statistical Manual of Mental Disorders [DSM]) – this association represents a substantial burden. For many affected individuals, the onset of depression begins in childhood, reinforcing the need for early intervention in the lives of these abused and neglected children, before symptoms of depression cascade into other spheres of functioning. Depression is associated with neglect and physical and sexual abuse, with no clear evidence for a specific effect of any particular type of maltreatment. Some investigators have shown a dose response, with depression more likely with harsh or severe physical abuse than with less severe forms of maltreatment.

Evidence suggests that child maltreatment increases the risk of post-traumatic stress disorder, which, by definition, develops after a terrifying event or ordeal. Symptoms include recurrent intrusion of frightening thoughts and memories, sleep difficulties, and detached or numb feelings, which can substantially affect a person's ability to function. Prospective and retrospective studies consistently show associations between physical or sexual abuse or neglect and post-traumatic stress disorder in adolescents and adults, which persist after controlling for family and child characteristics that are correlated with maltreatment. These effects can be longlasting. One prospective study of children who were maltreated before 12 years of age and assessed at 29 years reported that 23% of people who were sexually abused, 19% of those physically abused, and 17% of those neglected, had a present diagnosis of post-traumatic stress disorder (with use of DSM-III criteria) compared with 10% of controls, and lifetime risks of this disorder were much higher in cases than in controls. However, family, individual, and lifestyle variables, such as having a parent who is an alcoholic or has been arrested, also increased the risk of post-traumatic stress disorder. A meta-analysis of studies of children who have been sexually abused suggests a dose-response effect, with higher risks associated with penetrative sexual abuse than with contact or non-contact abuse.

Evidence for an association between childhood maltreatment and adult psychosis is inconclusive. No clear link between personality disorder and maltreatment has been noted, although one prospective study showed an increased risk of personality disorder in maltreated children including those exposed to verbal abuse, which was independent of physical or sexual abuse or neglect. These findings emphasise the need for further research into the effects of psychological abuse.

Consistent evidence suggests that both physical abuse and sexual abuse are associated with a **doubling of the risk of attempted suicide** for young people who are followed up into their late 20s. For physical and sexual abuse, these effects persist after adjustment for confounding family and individual variables, but for neglect, these effects are mainly explained by family context. According to cross-sectional studies, the risk of attempted suicide increases with the accumulation of multiple adversities, including repeated maltreatment and witnessing intimate-partner violence. The risk of attempted suicide can be very high in young people. Widom and colleagues reported lifetime rates of 19% in 29-year-old adults who were abused or neglected as children compared with 8% of community-matched controls, whereas a population-based cohort in New Zealand reported suicide attempts by 11–21% of young adults or adolescents who were exposed to severe physical abuse or penetrative sexual abuse compared with

1–3% of controls. Similar rates have been reported in a systematic review of ten studies and one prospective study in New York, which showed that 6% of adolescents who were abused made multiple suicide attempts.

The hypothesis that children who have been sexually abused use self-injurious behaviour (such as cutting) as a maladaptive coping mechanism is only weakly supported by a systematic review of 45 retrospective studies. By contrast, a prospective study reported a strong association with sexual abuse but no association with physical abuse or neglect.

Converging evidence from prospective and retrospective studies suggests that child maltreatment increases the risk of alcohol problems in adolescence and adulthood. These effects are moderate and persist in some but not all studies after adjustment for family characteristics and parental alcohol use. On the basis of results from a prospective study with follow up at 29 and 39 years of age, and from a systematic review of 224 studies, the association with alcohol problems, at least in adulthood, is confined to girls. These findings emphasise the need for interventions for girls and young women to prevent the development of alcohol problems and the associated health, safety, and social problems that excessive drinking in women can cause. For example, problem drinking in women increases the risk of fetal alcohol syndrome and might affect their ability to look after a child.

The link between child maltreatment and drug dependency is not straightforward. One prospective study reported that individuals who were maltreated in childhood were no more likely to have a diagnosis of drug dependency by the age of 29 years than were community controls. However, when a different measure of drug use is used, individuals who were abused and neglected were at increased risk for present illicit drug use at roughly 40 years of age. Investigators of this study speculated that although individuals who had experienced neglect or abuse would mature out of drug use, **abused and neglected individuals might continue in a problematic drug-use trajectory.** Cross-sectional studies indicate that exposure to multiple forms of abuse and other childhood adversities, including witnessing intimate-partner violence, leads to a cumulative increase in the risk of self-reported alcohol or drug misuse in adulthood.

Overall, the burden of mental ill health resulting from child maltreatment is substantial. A New Zealand cohort study estimated that physical abuse accounted for 5% of mental disorders and sexual abuse for 13%, after taking account of the family context in which maltreatment occurs.

How exposure to maltreatment of different types, at different developmental stages, leads to adverse mental-health outcomes is complex, although **early and cumulative maltreatment** seem to be **particularly harmful to the development of the brain.**

The webappendix summarises the evidence for biological mechanisms that link child maltreatment and later outcomes.

Physical-health outcomes

Four very different prospective longitudinal studies have reported strong associations between physical abuse, neglect, and sexual abuse and **obesity**, which persist after accounting for family characteristics and individual risk factors, such as childhood obesity. Large differences in the magnitude of this association between studies (adjusted odds ratios range from 1.3 to 9.8) probably indicate differences in exposure and outcome measures and analyses. Retrospective studies also suggest an association between child sexual abuse and **eating disorders** (e.g., bulimia and anorexia), but there is less information about other forms of maltreatment. Several large cross-sectional studies have reported relations between multiple child adversities, including child maltreatment, and a range of health outcomes in adulthood (e.g., ischaemic heart disease, cancer, chronic lung disease, skeletal fractures, and liver disease), albeit with little adjustment for lifetime confounders.

Abnormally overt or intrusive sexualised behaviour is a common problem in preteen children who are exposed to sexual abuse. However, sexualised behaviour is not specific to child sexual abuse and has been associated with physical abuse, characteristics of family adversity, coercive parenting, child behaviour, and modelling of sexual behaviour.

Most studies that have examined the relation between child maltreatment and sexual behaviour in adolescence and adulthood have focused on outcomes for sexual abuse. An exception is a prospective study with follow-up at 29 years of age, which reported a significant association between physical or sexual abuse or neglect and arrest for **prostitution** or being paid for sex (13% of cases vs 4% of controls for girls, $p=0.001$; 15% vs 8% for boys, $p=0.17$), but no significant associations with promiscuity or teenage pregnancy. In two prospective studies, child maltreatment was associated with teenage pregnancy. In one study, HIV was twice as common in abused and neglected individuals as in controls, although the difference did not reach conventional levels of significance most likely because of weak statistical power. A systematic review and meta-analysis of various types of study, most with retrospective ascertainment of abuse status, similarly reported the strongest associations between child sexual abuse and sex trading in adolescence or adulthood, and showed greater effects for women than for men. Small to moderate effects of child sexual abuse on increased rates of teenage pregnancy have been noted, as well as earlier onset of sexual activity, greater numbers of sexual partners, increased rates of **abortion**, and increased risks of sexually transmitted disease. These effects are stronger with more severe or repeated sexual abuse or exposure to multiple childhood adversities. Emerging evidence also suggests that exposure to child sexual abuse might be related to later sexual orientation. Overall, these findings suggest associations between exposure to child sexual abuse and subsequent sexual adjustment.

Controversy about a possible link between childhood maltreatment and chronic pain in adulthood emphasises the differences between prospective and retrospective measures of child maltreatment and the advantages of considering both types of study design. A prospective study based on children with maltreatment documented by courts and community-matched controls showed no association with chronic pain reported in adulthood at 29 years of age. However, when groups were compared on the basis of retrospective self-reports of child maltreatment, the association with chronic pain was significant ($p<0.0001$). Similar evidence of a modest association between child sexual or physical abuse (but not neglect), and pain in adulthood has been reported.

These findings draw attention to the distinction between how people remember and interpret abusive childhood experiences and exposure to child abuse. They establish an association between memories of childhood abuse and chronic pain in adulthood and further suggest that abused individuals with chronic pain are more likely to seek health care than are non-abused individuals with chronic pain. However, we cannot conclude that child abuse or neglect causes chronic pain in adulthood. Despite the evidence for diverse and serious consequences of child maltreatment, a systematic review found no studies measuring quality of life during childhood after maltreatment, and only four studies in adults. Further research, based on modification of existing methods and development of measures that can be used for younger children, is needed for economic assessments of the burden of child maltreatment and cost-effectiveness of intervention strategies. Studies in North America and Australia have shown increased service use and costs associated with child maltreatment, but research is lacking elsewhere in the world and in other public sectors.

Aggression, crime, and violence

In addition to feeling considerable pain and suffering themselves, abused and neglected children are at increased risk of becoming aggressive and **inflicting pain and suffering on others**, often **perpetrating crime and violence**. One paper on the cycle of violence reported that being physically abused or neglected as a child increased the likelihood of arrest as a juvenile (31% arrested vs 19% of community-matched controls) and as an adult (48% vs 36%). Since that time, similar effects on criminal behaviour have been reported in the USA despite differences in geographical region, time period, age of adolescent, definition of maltreatment, and assessment technique. These findings are supported by systematic reviews of retrospective studies, showing that physical and sexual abuse predict delinquency or violence in boys and girls, although physical abuse might be most strongly related to youth violence in girls. A direct comparison of different types of maltreatment found that children who were physically or sexually abused were more likely to **carry a weapon** in adolescence than were neglected children, because of a perceived need for self protection. Evidence that risks of youth violence cumulate when child abuse persists into adolescence suggests a need for interventions to prevent ongoing abuse.

FUTURE RESEARCH

Child maltreatment is common, and for many it is a chronic condition, with repeated and ongoing maltreatment merging into adverse outcomes throughout childhood and into adulthood. The burden on the children themselves and on society is substantial. At the same time, variation in rates of maltreatment between countries, particularly for infant homicides, and a possible decrease in recent years in sexual and physical abuse in some high-income countries, shows that the present high burden of child maltreatment is not inevitable. International comparative studies are needed, especially in countries outside North America and northern Europe, to help learn lessons from different settings about how to prevent child maltreatment and its consequences. The high burden and serious and longlasting consequences of child maltreatment warrant increased investment in preventive and therapeutic strategies from early childhood. Research into what works at an individual and policy level is a priority.

More research is needed into characteristics of responses by communities, families, and services that help with healthy development rather than exacerbate the child's problems. This research includes improved understanding of the many ways in which children are victimised at different stages of development.

More attention needs to be given to neglected children. There is mounting evidence that the consequences of childhood neglect can be as damaging – or perhaps even more damaging – to a child than physical or sexual abuse. More attention also needs to be paid to the potentially different needs of boys and girls who are maltreated. Although classrooms and neighbourhoods are disrupted more by deviant behaviour of boys than of girls, research shows that maltreatment doubles a girl's risk of being arrested for a violent crime and increases risk for subsequent alcohol and drug problems, with implications for her children.

TASK/TEXT 2.16.8: PROMOTION OF CHILDREN'S RIGHTS AND PREVENTION OF CHILD MALTREATMENT

<www.thelancet.com>, Series Child Maltreatment no. 4, Published online December 3, 2008 (references not included)

Richard Reading, Susan Bissell, Jeffrey Goldhagen, Judith Harwin, Judith Masson, Sian Moynihan, Nigel Parton, Marta Santos Pais, June Thoburn, Elspeth Webb

In medical literature, child maltreatment is considered as a public-health problem or an issue of harm to individuals, but less frequently as a violation of children's human rights. Public-health approaches emphasise monitoring, prevention, cost-effectiveness, and population strategies; protective approaches concentrate on the legal and professional response to cases of maltreatment. Both approaches have been associated with improvement in outcomes for children, yet maltreatment remains a major global problem. We describe how children's rights provide a different perspective on child maltreatment, and contribute to both public-health and protective responses. Children's rights as laid out in the UN Convention on the Rights of the Child (CRC) provide a framework for understanding child maltreatment as part of a range of violence, harm, and exploitation of children at the individual, institutional, and societal levels. Rights of participation and provision are as important as rights of protection. The principles embodied in the CRC are concordant with those of medical ethics. The greatest strength of an approach based on the CRC is that it provides a legal instrument for implementing policy, accountability, and social justice, all of which enhance public-health responses. Incorporation of the principles of the CRC into laws, research, public-health policy, and professional training and practice will result in further progress in the area of child maltreatment.

Key messages

- Child maltreatment is both a human-rights violation and a global public-health problem, and incurs huge costs for both individuals and society.
- Ambivalence in the public and professional responses to child maltreatment indicates the status of children in society.
- An appropriate framework for consideration of child maltreatment is the UN Convention on the Rights of the Child (CRC).
- A child-rights-based approach to maltreatment requires implementation of rights for provision and participation in society and the right of protection.
- A rights-based approach is concordant with the core principles of medical ethics.
- A rights-based approach enhances epidemiological and public-health responses and does not detract from consideration of the social determinants and population-based interventions for maltreatment.
- The strength of a rights-based approach is that human rights are legal obligations that underpin mechanisms to hold governments accountable. Use of the CRC in this way would result in a more effective public-health response to child maltreatment.

Introduction

Over the past half century since Kempe described the battered child syndrome, the response of child-protection systems has been on the basis of identification, assessment, and intervention to treat and prevent further harm, similar to the conventional medical model of diagnosis and treatment. This approach has achieved considerable progress but inevitably does not prevent the occurrence of child maltreatment in the first place. The previous three papers in this Series, describing the burden, recognition, and effect of interventions on child maltreatment, have argued that further progress requires increased emphasis on prevention and the underlying causes, in other words a public-health approach. This paper describes how a consideration of children's rights strengthens both public-health and child-protective approaches.

Children's rights are delineated in the principles and articles of the UN Convention on the Rights of the Child (CRC). Crucially, these include rights of provision of services and of participation in society, besides rights of protection and care. The articles of the CRC and the distinction between these different types of right are described in panel 1. The Committee on the Rights of the Child argues that all three types of right are inseparable and should be implemented as a package rather than selectively. The CRC obtains its power to influence policy and enforce accountability by being a legal instrument rather than a moral code, even though it is based on ethical and moral foundations. These are important principles that a rights-based approach brings to public-health and protective strategies to reduce the prevalence and consequences of child maltreatment.

In common with the other papers in this Series, much of the evidence and literature we rely on relates to high-income countries, although maltreatment of children takes place in all societies and most evidence suggests that it is more common in low-income and middle-income countries. We have restricted most of our discussion to high-income countries, which we recognise is a limitation both of this paper and the Series. Concentration on high-income countries tends to focus attention on the types of maltreatment that are more prevalent in these countries and might not help poorer countries when they come to assess evidence for their own prevention and intervention programmes. However, consideration of the obligations that the CRC imposes is necessary for the child-maltreatment policy of any country.

In this paper we begin by describing the social and legal contexts in which society responds to child maltreatment. We then describe what a rights-based approach to child maltreatment entails, and discuss its strengths and weaknesses. We explain how the CRC offers a framework for effective legislation and policy, and provides new insights for professional responsibilities, ethical codes, and training. The objectives and approach of rights-based and public-health approaches complement each other and, when combined, offer a legal and moral force to a coherent scientifically based strategy.

SOCIAL AND LEGAL CONTEXT

Definitions of maltreatment

How child maltreatment is defined is central to how it is recognised, managed, and prevented. Definitions range from those that focus on the acts and harm caused to children by parents or carers, such as the definitions of the US Centers for Disease Control and Prevention, to those that define abuse relative to the social and cultural environment, such as Kempe's: "parents unable to cope at a level assumed to be reasonable by the society in which they reside." In both these definitions, maltreatment is defined mainly in terms of physical, emotional, and sexual violence, or neglect perpetrated by individual adults, usually parents or those close to the child. Professional and societal responses have been framed in terms of protection of the child from adult perpetrators. These approaches do not permit collective harm and exploitation, for instance that caused by institutions, harmful policies and laws, and avoidable war, conflict, failure of governance, or social disruption.

An attempt at a more comprehensive definition was made by Gil more than 30 years ago: "the inflicted gaps or deficits between circumstances of living which would facilitate the optimum development of children, to which they should be entitled, and to their actual circumstances, irrespective of the sources or agents of the deficit." Thus any act of commission or omission by individuals, institutions, government, or society, together with their resultant conditions, which "deprive children of equal rights and liberties, and/or interfere with their optimal development constitute, by definition, abusive or neglectful acts or conditions." This type of definition would be the foundation for an approach that subsumed maltreatment as an aspect of overall child wellbeing. Its disadvantage is that it becomes too broad and encompassing, making epidemiological measurement impossible, blurring the focus of possible targets, and hence risking the success of any intervention based on the definition.

The definition chosen for the UN's Study on Violence Against Children follows article 19 of the CRC that includes "all forms of physical or mental violence, injury and abuse, neglect or negligent treatment, maltreatment or exploitation, including sexual abuse." It bases the understanding of physical violence on the definition in the World Report on Violence and Health: "the intentional use of physical force or power, threatened or actual, against a child, by an individual or group, that either results in or has a high likelihood of resulting in actual or potential harm to the child's health, survival, development or dignity." WHO pointed out that the inclusion of the abuse of power broadened the definition to include acts of commission or omission that resulted in emotional harm and allowed social, political, and economic violence to be incorporated; the use of the term exploitation in the CRC broadens the scope of maltreatment from simply violence and yet still offers the possibility of operationalising the definition to enable epidemiological measurement and monitoring.

All such definitions include a compromise. On the one hand, a precise and limited definition, which focuses on intentional harm, is necessary for epidemiological and public-health monitoring and to engage constructively with governments and legislators over specific policy responses to maltreatment. On the other hand, a children's-rights-based definition will always push these boundaries to encompass social and environmental harm because from a child's perspective these can be indistinguishable. Kydd has described maltreatment in terms of abandonment and argues that this definition includes societal, economic, and professional abandonment, besides the abandonment of nurture, protection, and care within families.

Attitudes to children's rights and maltreatment

Each country and region has tensions between children's rights and other competing values, all of which will have implications for the wellbeing of children. For example, the African Charter on the Rights and Welfare of the Child states in article 31 that "children have a responsibility to work for the cohesion of the family, to respect parents and elders at all times, and to assist them in cases of need," indicating the survival needs of communities living in environmentally harsh conditions with scarce resources. This cultural relativism has relevance for attitudes towards child maltreatment. Some countries might still be trying to understand what it means to value a child as an individual no matter what the sex is; others see aspects of physical discipline, such as shaking, to be acceptable.

There are cogent arguments for any definition and response to child maltreatment to respect cultural values and attitudes, yet these could classify female genital mutilation as non-abusive since, in the context of those cultures in which it is traditional, it is perceived as a responsible act by parents. This example in which a relativistic approach is easily challenged is quite clear. In less overt cases, such as the neglect of a profoundly disabled child in a culture perceived as having a less accepting attitude towards disability, the balance between respect for cultural values and protection of the child might be more equivocal. The tension between absolute and relative values underlies one of the main ethical dilemmas in the specialty of child maltreatment. A relativistic approach is justified on the basis that what constitutes child abuse is socially and culturally determined. However, children have an absolute need for protection against harm. Put another way, a relativistic approach to child protection across cultural divides runs the risk of not protecting children, whereas an absolutist approach, which ignores the context in which abuse has occurred, might lead to inappropriate interventions that compound the harm a child has already suffered.

Clashes between absolute and relative responses to child maltreatment go well beyond issues of cultural difference. They throw up barriers between professionals for management of individual cases of maltreatment, underlie differences in approach between professional groups, lead to disagreement between countries about what to define as maltreatment and how to implement international goals into national policy, and result in clear failures of child-protection systems that have been identified in many countries. Thus the tricky balance between absolute and relative standpoints operates at all levels.

Consideration of children's rights within the social, cultural, and historical contexts in different countries is an important aspect of resolving these dilemmas.

Poverty, discrimination, and child maltreatment

Since the CRC was ratified by most countries in the early 1990s, the status of children has improved in many ways, yet policy is still being implemented that is not in the best interests of children. In the UK until recently, laws to discourage asylum seeking and force those denied asylum to leave included withholding basic benefits and services from their children. Meanwhile in the USA, the marginalisation of Latino families and the disproportionate effect of welfare policy has resulted in their children being more likely to live in poverty, being over-represented in the child-protection system, and receiving fewer services. So in the UK and the USA at least, the situation for some children seems to have worsened. As an aside, the failure to ratify the CRC should not be taken to indicate that the USA disregards children's rights, as it has been a perverse incentive to policy makers and academics to pay greater attention than in many other high-income countries that take their obligations less seriously.

Published work provides strong evidence for the harm to children associated with poverty, including high overall mortality, teenage pregnancy, disorganised parenting, risk of offending, drug and alcohol abuse, and sexually transmitted diseases; besides the increased risk of neglect and physical and emotional maltreatment discussed in the first paper of this Series. In most countries, at whatever stage of development, child poverty and inequalities (i.e., the gap between rich and poor) disproportionately affect families with children. During the 1980s, much of the west moved towards increased free-market economies; some countries, most notably the Scandinavian nations, took steps to protect children from these developments whereas others did not. Thus a more radical interpretation is that child poverty is a policy choice harmful to children. The UK has been consistently criticised by the CRC Committee for the magnitude of health and education inequalities among children, and the failure to commit an adequate share of its resources to children despite the government commitment to end child poverty.

Legal response and children's rights

Legislation to protect children was first introduced in most societies in the developed world in the final quarter of the nineteenth century, long predating any consideration of children's rights. Since its inception, such legislation has had many substantial challenges; for any child-protection system operating in a liberal democracy in which adults' votes count, there is a fine balance between protection of children without intrusion on the privacy of the family. These are important issues for the legitimacy of the state itself. Although the state has a duty to protect the vulnerable, it cannot afford to undermine the freedom of parents to bring up their children in the ways they see as most appropriate. Three inter-related issues have therefore always provided key contexts for child-protection services and legislation: the role of parents in relation to the state in cases of disagreement about a child's need for protection; the scope of the government's intervention; and the nature of government's intervention. Legislation might be restricted to proscription and punishment of maltreatment, but the state can have a far wider role in prevention. The provision of universal services and financial support can go a considerable way to ensure that parents have adequate resources to bring up their children and is an important part of showing that compulsory intervention, should it be necessary, is justified within the terms of the European Convention on Human Rights and other constitutional protections for the family.

Children's welfare legislation in high-income countries is gradually incorporating children's rights principles. For example, in the UK, the successive Children acts since 1989 and related public policy have given the requirements of the CRC, such as giving children a voice in assessment and court proceedings and considering their welfare to be paramount, greater and greater prominence. Some of the Nordic countries have taken a low-key approach to written legislation and yet they have a long tradition of promotion of children's welfare, and have high rates of indicators of children's wellbeing.

In addition to laws and policy taking account of children's rights in high-income countries, academic analysis of the operation and effect of such policy has increasingly looked at outcomes in terms of children's rights. For example, a study of court processes in civil custody cases described decisions affecting children in terms of whether they upheld their rights, and many in fact were oppressive and classed as violations. Similarly studies of young children in institutional care in Europe have shown wide variation between different countries despite evidence of emotional harm and institutional maltreatment. These studies take as their starting point the right of children to family life, either their own or a culturally appropriate alternative (articles 9 and 20 in the CRC).

By contrast with high-income countries, many low-income and middle-income countries are developing a legal response to child maltreatment in the context of already having ratified the CRC. Many of the new states in central and eastern Europe, for instance, have written the articles of the CRC into their constitution, yet prevalence of various forms of child maltreatment remains high. Incorporation of the wording of the CRC into legislation might be less important than a public embrace of the principles and spirit of the Convention.

One of the far-reaching consequences of the CRC is that it makes the child an individual with rights and not just a passive recipient, and hence the child has the right to actively participate at all levels of decision making. The traditional association between the state, the family, and the child could be conceptualised as a series of concentric circles with the child at the centre. The CRC implies that this association should now be understood to be triangular in which the state has a direct responsibility to the child to promote her or his rights [Trias pedagogica, JW]. The child has the right to make a direct call on the state and to be heard in the development of legislation and policy, besides receiving protection.

CHILDREN'S RIGHTS AND PROFESSIONALS' DUTIES

The contribution of a rights-based approach to both the protective and public-health responses to child maltreatment rests on the CRC, both in its principles and specific articles. The CRC is first and foremost a legal instrument. However, the individual articles can also be translated into specific interventions and policy objectives, and can act as an ethical guide for professionals.

Children's rights are not abstract and idealistic aspirations, but are grounded firmly and pragmatically in the basic human needs for life, growth, and development. Several articles specifically grant children the right to protection against maltreatment – e.g., the right to life (article 6); right to protection from physical, sexual, or mental abuse, neglect, or exploitation (article 19), and protection against exposure to drugs (article 33), sexual exploitation (article 34), abduction (article 35), exploitation (article 36), torture or illegal detention (article 37), and armed conflict (article 38).

However, the CRC goes beyond protection to include rights of provision and participation. The inseparability of these rights, which has been endorsed by the Committee on the Rights of the Child, is crucially important to the discipline of child maltreatment for practical rather than idealistic reasons. Protection alone is insufficient to allow optimum growth and development of children; equally protection, though necessary, is not sufficient to ensure children are not maltreated. A direct example why children need to be able to contribute to their own protection is the death of Victoria Climbié in the UK, which might have been prevented had she had access to an interpreter. The rights of participation and provision in the CRC are required to ensure a comprehensive approach to child maltreatment and its consequences. For instance, in panel 2, we describe the association between parental substance misuse and maltreatment of children. From a public-health perspective, the problem is one of neglect and exposure to harm, with parental substance misuse being seen as a potent risk factor. From a rights perspective this problem can be reformulated as an infringement of children's rights of participation, provision, and protection. This example illustrates how both approaches complement each other, and can help decision making in a notoriously difficult specialty.

Although rights attributable to children are indivisible, to adequately deal with all forms of child maltreatment, five rights delineated in the CRC are fundamental, and underpin the specific rights of protection. First, all the rights in the Convention apply to all children without discrimination on any grounds (article 2). Second, in all actions affecting children, their best interests must be the main consideration (article 3). Third, all children have the right to life, optimum survival, and development (article 6). Fourth, all children capable of expressing a view have the right to express that view freely and to have it taken seriously in accordance with their age and maturity (article 12). Last, to have an informed voice, children have the right to access information from various diverse sources (article 17).

These rights are directly comparable with the principles of medical ethics. Panel 3 describes this link and the table shows one example of how consideration of children's rights can guide medical and health-care professionals' response to child maltreatment. However, this approach requires new knowledge, skills, and resources, and places the promotion of children's rights as central in the delivery of health care to children and young people as the implementation of biomedical and scientific evidence. Working knowledge of the CRC is increasingly a core part of training for all child-health professionals, particularly those working in the specialty of child maltreatment. The skills of advocacy can be used at the clinical, community, and public-policy levels. Although political lobbying can be best done by well organised groups, there are many examples of clinicians advocating at all these levels and of how these activities are integrated into standard clinical practice. Indeed, some child-abuse assessment services in the USA are described as child-advocacy centres. Resources include the CRC itself, legislation that implements the articles of the CRC, guidance for professionals on the CRC, and a commitment by health commissioners and policy makers to incorporate children's rights into their brief.

CHILDREN'S RIGHTS AND PUBLIC-HEALTH APPROACHES

The public-health approach to child maltreatment incorporates research into monitoring, recognition, and diagnosis; investment in early preventative interventions; prioritisation based on cost-effectiveness; and improvements in access to support and treatment services. In view of the comprehensive nature of the public-health agenda on violence and maltreatment, what extra does a children's-rights approach add? There are several components to the answer, but all of them lead back to the principle that the definition of child maltreatment as a violation of rights implies that the responsibility and accountability of policy makers to intervene is an international legal obligation based on standards upheld universally, and that nearly every government in the world has ratified.

Rights-based and public-health approaches to child maltreatment have the same goals and frequently have a common justification for the same or similar interventions. However, tensions and discrepancies between the approaches should be discussed because a creative engagement with these differences can enhance rather than detract from the synergy of both approaches.

Measuring and monitoring maltreatment

In a strongly argued plea for better epidemiological data, Butchart has suggested that too much emphasis on the human-rights aspects of child maltreatment might undermine a public-health approach to prevention because of the emphasis on individuals. The counter argument is that a public-health perspective reduces the priority of the right to be safe from violence. Conversely, public health itself has been claimed to be dominated by an emphasis on individual behaviour and biomedical mechanisms to the neglect of societal and social pathways to ill health. None of these positions takes account of the spirit and wording of the CRC that is concerned not only with the child but also children as a body. Thus the CRC offers an equally valid framework for advocacy for interventions at the population and national-policy levels. For instance, high-quality epidemiological monitoring data are instrumental to ensure, according to article 19, the right to protection from violence: "State parties shall take all appropriate measures...for identification...of child maltreatment." Furthermore, articles 42–45, which describe the states' obligations for reporting to the Committee on the Rights of the Child require systems for data gathering to be in place or to be established. The need for improved and pragmatic definitions can be made equally from an epidemiological and a rights-based standpoint.

Further support for a mix of legislative and public-health measures based strongly on the principles of the CRC is found in an analysis by UNICEF of child sexual exploitation. Their evidence, reasoning, and recommendations are similar to our conclusions. They argue for better systems for gathering data and epidemiological research that is informed by children's interests and views. The obligation to have reliable systems for gathering data in place, mandated by the CRC, is a persuasive argument that could be articulated by children's-rights practitioners. The contribution of public health to children's rights in this respect is to provide guidance on the most robust, reliable, and valid epidemiological data that states ought to be gathering.

Identification of risk factors

Public health has led the way in researching, publicising, and tackling health inequalities over the past 30 years. In the specialty of child maltreatment, the risks associated with poverty and inequalities, socially vulnerable families, and the intergenerational cycle of deprivation and violence are well recognised. Strategies for prevention of maltreatment are recommended to target these high-risk groups, and intervention programmes are advised to be sensitive to social inequalities and not to inadvertently widen them. However, poverty itself can be represented as a violation of children's rights. The Universal Declaration of Human Rights grants the freedom from want; article 27 of the CRC recognises the right to "a standard of living adequate for the child's physical, mental, spiritual, moral and social development," and the concept of rights as capabilities for living (e.g., the capability to be alive, healthy, and have self-respect) justify the argument that poverty infringes on children's rights by prevention of their optimum development.

Phinney and De Hovre have argued that violence is both an infringement of human rights and arises from inadequate fulfilment of rights. What public health would describe as risk factors are here argued to be partly responsibilities of the state. This approach avoids blaming individuals, who are often the most powerless politically and economically, although it does not absolve them from responsibility. The approach also makes the state accountable for improving social justice as a direct intervention to prevent maltreatment.

A rights-based perspective allows risk factors to be reformulated as instances of discrimination, exclusion, and victimisation. For example, there are sex differences in types and rates of maltreatment, ethnic discrepancies in both occurrence and notification, associations with unemployment, social isolation and absence of family support, and risks linked to families that have caregivers with mental illness, drug misuse, and intimate-partner violence. These are all violations of children's rights of protection, provision, or participation either explicitly as mandated under the articles of the CRC or less directly. Reinforcement of non-discrimination by law is claimed to be a more powerful means of affecting policy than public-health arguments based on equity.

Preventive interventions

Few assessments of prevention programmes based on children's rights have been done. A systematic review of population-based interventions that addresses issues, such as public perceptions of acceptable punishment, income and poverty relief, exposure to parental violence, and reduction in young parenthood, has suggested that these are well supported theoretically, but have not been robustly assessed.

The policy of criminalising physical punishment in Sweden and campaigns to change public attitudes to violence against children have had positive effects on reported child maltreatment and in public acceptance of physical punishment even though the figures on deaths have changed little. These changes, besides being attributed to the legal ban, have been linked to greater economic equity, a welfare system that transfers money to families with young children, improved child health care, equity between the sexes, recognition of family violence, and widespread public awareness of the CRC such that it is regularly talked about by children.

In the USA, welfare reform has had complex effects on maltreatment rates because it has tended to increase income among families at the expense of increasing stresses on unsupported families of having to cope with employment (predominantly lone-parent worker families). The evidence suggests that maltreatment rates have fallen among families with increased income, but risen among those in which the predominant effect has been increased stress.

Whether rights-based approaches to prevention might deflect attention from the need to implement interventions of proven effectiveness has been extensively debated with respect to HIV/AIDS. The recognition of the contribution human rights can make to public health began with the work of Jonathan Mann, the first director of the WHO global programme against AIDS. However, De Cock and colleagues have argued that too great an emphasis on individual rights has diverted attention from the disastrous proportion of the epidemic, and that the benchmarks for the effectiveness of an approach should be conventional public-health measures, such as reductions in incidence, morbidity, and mortality, and the social cost of these interventions. The case is easier to argue for child maltreatment because both public-health and rights-based approaches assert the right of children to effective preventive interventions. The Convention mandates these interventions according to articles 3 (the best-interests principle), 6 (right to life and development, and the obligation of states to ensure this right to the maximum extent possible), 9 and 18 (support for family life), 19 (protection from violence and maltreatment), 24 (right to the highest attainable standard of health and preventive health care), 32–38 (specific rights of protection), and 39 (the right to rehabilitation and social reintegration from maltreatment: "in an environment which fosters the health, self-respect and dignity of the child"). For HIV/AIDS, the Committee on the Rights of the Child has made a similar case that the articles of the CRC explicitly endorse all the components of a public-health response to childhood HIV/AIDS, illustrating how obligations based on children's rights give political and legal power to public-health recommendations.

Policy and legislative changes

Both rights-based and public-health approaches seek to change policy and laws as an essential part of their strategy. Public-health approaches argue the case on the basis of scientific evidence of effectiveness and economic evidence of value and cost. The basis for advocating policy change from a rights perspective is that countries are obliged to meet internationally accepted standards. An example of how both approaches can support each other relates to the prohibition of physical punishment of children. Many countries still allow the legal defence of parental discipline, and some also permit institutional corporal punishment. The UN has argued that specific laws relating to violence against children should not sanction any mitigation for reasonable punishment, chastisement, or parental or institutional authority. Besides a rights-based argument, public-health evidence supports laws prohibiting physical punishment of children. Physical chastisement is ineffective in eliciting behaviour change, and a punitive approach to parenting fosters long-term emotional and behavioural problems in children.

Rights-based arguments can be made for introduction of antipoverty measures as a means of prevention of maltreatment. One of the recommendations of the UN Study of Violence against Children, which addresses prevention includes the statement "attention should be focused on economic and social policies that address poverty, gender, and other forms of inequality, income gaps, unemployment, urban overcrowding, and other factors which undermine society." The evidence on which this recommendation is based derives from public-health research; the justification derives from a broader consideration of the rights of children than those purely of protection.

Prioritisation and cost-effectiveness

Human-rights approaches to child maltreatment and health more generally have been criticised for ignoring the economic realities in different countries. Important questions about prioritisation are not addressed in the CRC, which is not just a problem for low-income countries but for any state in which health-care and social-care services are paid for from the public purse. Child maltreatment incurs huge costs to society and appropriate interventions can result in net savings. Resource allocation and cost-effectiveness analyses are core elements of the public-health response to child maltreatment, but human rights are a necessary consideration in these types of decisions. They offer the means to attribute human values to different outcomes over and above cost and maximum benefits to most people. The CRC recognises resource constraints in its wording. Thus article 6, after affirming the right to life, obliges states to "ensure to the maximum extent possible the survival and development of the child." In the context of the right to the highest attainable standard of health, states are expected to implement measures subject to progressive realisation and resource availability.

Progressive realisation is UN terminology for a planned programme that moves steadily towards achievement of a goal (in this case adequate health care, but the argument equally applies to maltreatment prevention). The corollary to not expecting immediate full implementation is that states implement the most effective measures first.

Participation of children

Rights of participation are an essential aspect of the CRC, as they are of all human-rights approaches. They include the right of the child to information, to express views without hindrance, and the expectation that his or her views will be listened to and taken account of in any decision affecting the child. The rights include the right of disabled children to participate fully in society, and for all children to family life, play, and leisure. The Committee [on] the Rights of the Child has stated that rights embodied in the CRC are indivisible, thus the coherence of any rights-based approach to child maltreatment will depend on how well it shows that implementation of participatory rights is essential to both prevention and response. Children's involvement in responding to maltreatment is already part of legislation, policy, and practice in many countries, for instance in the development of family group conferences in New Zealand, involvement of children in case conferences set up to decide whether maltreatment has occurred in the UK, and in legislation to ensure children have a voice in court proceedings affecting them.

Children's participation in the public-health approach to prevention is insufficiently articulated or practised. However, child maltreatment rates are generally lower in countries that promote children's wellbeing and participation. Kydd has argued that prevention policies are more likely to be successful if they address child-centric perspectives of participation and promotion of best interests rather than focusing on acts most offensive to adults. Doek, while chair of the Committee on the Rights of the Child, described how attitudes towards child protection have moved from compassion and charity, to entitlement of children to their rights. Santos Pais and Pinheiro have commented that measures to combat violence must address the general circumstances in which children live, and that these will not work if they do not involve children in the design of prevention and recovery programmes. The UN Study on Violence against

Children states "I recommend that States actively engage with children and respect their views in all aspects of prevention, response and monitoring of violence against them, taking into account article 12 of the Convention on the Rights of the Child."

Opportunities and challenges to rights-based approaches

Despite the inspiration offered by the UN Study on Violence against Children, there is still a long way to go to integrate children's rights and public-health approaches to child maltreatment. Phinney and De Hovre argue that although neither is sufficient by itself, together they can compel states to change policy and institute preventive measures. Addressing the human-rights aspects of public-health problems has enabled more effective action to take place in other specialties. For example, reconciliation of both approaches has resulted in substantial advances in maternal and neonatal health in the past 10 years, when previously there had been slow progress. Rights-based legislation has been used in other situations to enforce implementation of public-health interventions. However, few examples of such a combined approach in child maltreatment exist.

The ability to enforce compliance with human-rights legislation is limited. In the case of the CRC, governments must report to the Committee on the Rights of the Child every 5 years, and there are other opportunities for pressure and persuasion, but realistically many governments do not take their responsibilities seriously and others are slow to implement change. For example, the Concluding Observations of the Committee on the Rights of the Child criticised performance of the UK Government on children in the penal system, irregular migrants, and health and educational inequalities. Non-governmental submissions in the next phase of the cycle have described problems in the same areas and the report of the Committee in October, 2008, again criticises progress in these areas. However, this process of scrutiny and accountability might have been the reason for the decision of the UK Government to grant full rights to all migrant children and to those in custody. Elsewhere, progress on implementation is happening but there is still much to do.

Maltreatment from an adult's point of view needs both an act and an intention but from the child's perspective the consequence is of most importance. The challenge is to broaden the definition of maltreatment to encompass preventable societal, environmental, corporate, and political harm without the loss of clarity in present definitions that lend themselves to epidemiological monitoring, and allow governments and society to engage with the issue. There is considerable resistance at present to widening the scope of child maltreatment, but over the past 50 years concepts about what constitutes maltreatment have changed in line with scientific knowledge, and public understanding and values.

As society comes to accept the spirit of the CRC, views about harm to children will probably change.

Conclusions

Rights-based and public-health approaches to child maltreatment are complementary, and when harnessed in concert they can act as a highly effective instrument of change in policy, professional activity, and public values. The unique strength of a rights-based approach is the legal status of rights conventions, and thus the accountability and transparency this facilitates. The strength of a public-health approach is the scientific rigour behind monitoring, identification of risks, and assessment of preventive interventions and prioritisation. Promotion and upholding the principles of the CRC are highly effective strategies for committed child public-health workers, whereas being conversant with scientific evidence is essential in making decisions about appropriate interventions in health and social care, and advocates of children's rights should make greater use of it in arguing for policy and practice changes. Paul Hunt, the UN Special Rapporteur on the right to the highest attainable standard of health, has made a similar point with respect to health. He describes how use of this right can help health workers achieve their objectives, and urges them to grasp the opportunity to use this resource to fulfil their professional responsibilities. Exactly the same argument applies to child maltreatment. Adoption of the framework of the CRC is the basis for making further progress against child maltreatment in the 21st century.

Panel 1: Convention on the Rights of the Child

The Convention on the Rights of the Child was adopted by the UN in 1989 and was rapidly ratified by most countries in the world. Ratification requires countries to report every 5 years to the Committee on the Rights of the Child, which monitors implementation of the Convention.

The Convention sets out rights for the survival, development, wellbeing, and participation of children up to the age of 18 years. The Committee has divided the provisions of the Convention into clusters as follows:

- General principles such as non-discrimination, the best interests of the child being the main consideration, and respect for the views of the child;
- Civil rights and freedoms, such as a right to an identity, freedom of expression, and protection of privacy;
- Family environment and alternative care such as the right to be cared for by parents, and to an alternative secure form of care such as adoption if deprived of a family environment;

- Basic health and welfare such as the right to health care and to an adequate standard of living;
- Education, leisure, and cultural activities, such as the right to leisure and play;
- Special protection measures, such as for refugee children, those in the juvenile justice system, and those belonging to a minority group.

Rights can more conveniently be divided into those of protection, participation, and provision:

- Rights of protection include the right to be protected from any form of maltreatment or exploitation;
- Rights of participation enable children to be involved in decisions and actions that affect them and allow them to participate actively in society. They include the right for children to express and have due weight given to views about decisions affecting them;
- Rights of provision include the right to education, and the obligation of the state to support parents and families.

The UN Convention places the interests of the child first. However, in prioritisation of the rights of children, the UN does not truncate the rights of parents. The Convention obliges states to provide parents with the capacity to fulfil their children's rights, and three of its articles (5, 9, and 18) deal explicitly with the rights [and responsibilities, JW] of parents.

Panel 2: Harm to children arising from parental substance misuse
Parental substance misuse is a major risk factor for child maltreatment. It is estimated to be a factor in 80% of child maltreatment cases in the USA, whereas alcohol alone accounts for between 10–50% of cases in individual countries of the European Union. Parental substance misuse is over-represented in child fatalities and abandonment, and is a major cause of family separation, often involving compulsory removal. In London, UK, 54% of children have been removed 2 years after referral, in the USA, substance misusing parents are least likely to be reunited successfully with their children, and in countries of the former Soviet Union, long-term child institutionalisation is associated with parental alcohol misuse.

The harms arise from the financial, social, behavioural, and biological consequences of parental substance misuse that can affect every domain of wellbeing – i.e., education, health, self-esteem, family life, and social relationships. Furthermore, because parental substance misuse can result in severe social exclusion, children's participatory rights are undermined. The harm associated with parental substance misuse is a major child-rights issue that has been neglected and hidden for too long.

The central challenge is to find ways of ensuring that children can be helped to remain at home safely or be removed in a timely way to a stable alternative family life. To achieve this, a continuum of services is needed, but rarely present. Although several components associated with successful programmes have been identified, partnership with parents is often difficult to achieve. In consequence, child safety and wellbeing can be neglected. These long-standing challenges require innovative solutions, such as specialist family drug and alcohol courts. In the US national assessment, these showed such promising results that a similar court is being trialled in London, UK. However, in general there is uncertainty about the role of courts, whether criminal law has any part to play, and on the timing of proceedings. Cases that are brought to court early are associated with better outcomes, but often proceedings last a long time, with more rapid and proactive intervention when illegal drugs are implicated than when alcohol is implicated.

The problem of parental substance misuse cannot be separated from its wider public-policy context. Yet few countries gather relevant data, which is a prerequisite to monitoring the problem. There is often an unhelpful fragmentation of policy and service delivery between illegal and legal drugs, despite the fact that frequently parents misuse both. In view of this overlap, the time has come for policy and service development to focus on the extent of harm to the child, not on the arbitrary legal status and pharmacological properties of the drug in question.

Panel 3: Integration of medical ethics and the principles of children's rights

Medical ethics has evolved as a set of four principles – beneficence, justice, non-malfeasance, and autonomy – that serve as a foundation for medical decision making. Four equivalent core principles – promotion of the child's best interest, non-discrimination, survival and optimum development, and to be listened to and taken seriously – among the articles of the UN Convention on the Rights of the Child provide context for the implementation of the rights defined in the Convention. These principles are comparable and have particular relevance to the discipline of child maltreatment. When combined, they provide strategies and methods for advancing the practice of paediatrics, child advocacy, and health-services research.

TASK/TEXT 2.16.9: PAULO SÉRGIO PINHEIRO'S PRESENTATION FROM THE SERIES LAUNCH

<http://multimedia.thelancet.com/pdf/child-maltreatment-launch.pdf>, accessed 7 March 2009

The Lancet and Royal College of Paediatricians and Child Health – Seminar to Launch the "Child Maltreatment" Series London, 2 December 2008

Paulo Sérgio Pinheiro, Independent Expert appointed to lead the UN Secretary-General's Study on Violence against Children; Commissioner and Rapporteur on Children, Inter-American Commission on Human Rights, IACHR, Organization of American States, OAS

Ladies and Gentlemen,

First, my congratulations to the Lancet and the Royal College for developing this series on "Child Maltreatment" and holding this seminar. I hope it will help to create the necessary sense of urgency and passion which challenging child maltreatment deserves. I would also like to thank my friend Peter Newell, from End of Corporal Punishment, for his remarkable contribution for the *World Report on Violence against Children.*

The adult world is taking far too long to come to terms with the scale and extent of violence against children and the imperative to end it. As I told States' representatives in the UN General Assembly when I delivered a progress report last year: "Children are sick of being called 'the future'; they want to enjoy their childhood, free of violence, now."

I was appointed by the then UN Secretary-General Kofi Annan to lead the UN Study in 2003, and submitted my report to the UN General Assembly in October 2006. This was the first comprehensive global study to address violence against children. It was also the first UN exercise of this kind to attempt to involve children themselves in the process.

Governments and UN agencies combined to organise nine regional consultations and at each, children and young people who had been involved in their own countries in combating violence, many of them victims themselves, came together, developing their own declarations and recommendations.

Their involvement and their presence was of vital importance; it made it impossible for the adults present – politicians and professionals – to remain in denial about the extent and scale of adult violence against children. In particular, it led to a focus not only on the severe violence that leads to death or serious injury, the trafficking and rape and sexual exploitation of children; there is already a clear consensus of adult condemnation of all this.

But children required us also to take account of the daily, routine violence that so many of them, certainly a majority, face in their homes, and in many countries also in schools, institutions, workplaces and penal systems. I spoke in private to groups of children at all these consultations and at many other meetings around the world and felt humbled by their vision and their quiet passion, but also by their astonishing patience with an adult world which has for so long abused and belittled them. Childhood, as one American historian describes it, is a nightmare from which we are only now beginning to emerge.

It is good that the series of articles being launched today includes one written from the perspective of children's human rights. It was the Committee on the Rights of the Child which proposed the UN Study. The Committee is the internationally-elected (...) Treaty Body which monitors states' compliance with the UN Convention on the Rights of the Child. My Study was human rights-based. It was valuable that the Study brought together, as do the Lancet papers, various perspectives, including very prominently that of public health – with the active involvement of the World Health Organization. But the Study's foundation was children's human rights. This is not simply another "approach" to, or perspective on child maltreatment: when States sign and then ratify – fully accept – international human rights instruments like the Convention on the Rights of the Child, they take on legal obligations to fully respect the rights guaranteed by the Convention. This is not simply advice for governments, and governments cannot pick and choose which rights they will take seriously. Governments are not doing children favours by considering how to protect them from deliberate adult violence against them. They are – or should be – fulfilling legal obligations.

It is almost 50 years since researchers first began to seriously "discover" and document the extent of deliberate adult violence against children; of course children have known about it intimately for centuries. Now that the scale and extent of the violence is becoming increasingly visible, now that children are beginning to speak out about it themselves, what can we do to accelerate the process of eliminating it? You will not be surprised to hear that I believe we have to pursue ending violence against children as a human rights imperative. This is not in any sense to downgrade the importance of the public health perspective and many other perspectives. But it does provide a foundation, an imperative for effective action, and it should also inject a real urgency. In gaining public, and political support for giving prevention of violence against children a high priority, we need to make the true extent of violence against children more widely known. Governments, I am afraid, even in rich countries like this one, tend to hide behind the fact that so little, even of the extreme violence against children, is reported and recorded as it happens, as the first two Lancet Papers confirm.

I have been asked to talk about the way forward. I am convinced that if we are to make real progress, in any country, we need to develop a child protection system which is explicitly human rights-based and child-centred, and we need to engage with children with relevant experiences in the design and evaluation of it. Politicians, and community and faith leaders, must unequivocally reject all violence against children. Governments must reveal through research, as honestly as they can, the true level of all forms of violence against children.

We all need to work with, as well as for children, to challenge and end this violence – now.

While things are undoubtedly changing, there is still an ambivalent attitude to violence against children, in so-called developed as well as developing countries – and that attitude is still reflected in the law tolerating violence against children in this and many other countries. During the process of the UN Study, I came to London in 2005 and addressed a meeting in your Parliament.

I noted then how surprised I was that my statement that the Study would certainly be recommending prohibition of all corporal punishment of children was causing controversy.

If I was conducting a study on violence against animals, would I be expected to defend smacking puppies and kittens? The fact is, I could not look those many children I had met around the world in the eyes and say that I had decided they were worthy of less legal protection from assault than myself or other adults. Really, it is absurd and offensive that adults and governments continue to defend the concept of "reasonable" punishment, of some arbitrary level of violence when disguised as "discipline."

Too many people, including some of those working in child protection, try and keep completely separate consideration of physical "abuse" and consideration of corporal punishment. But of course the vast majority of physical abuse of children is administered as punishment or control; there can be no separation.

Children have exactly the same right to respect for their human dignity and physical integrity as the rest of us, and that respect must be fully reflected in the law. My friend Maud De Boer Buquicchio, the Deputy Secretary General of the Council of Europe, likes to emphasize that – I quote: "For the Council of Europe, children are not mini-persons with mini-rights, mini-feelings and mini-human dignity. They are vulnerable human beings with full rights which require more, not less protection. It is therefore absolutely unacceptable that when it comes to the protection of their physical and psychological integrity, they should be worse off than adults."

The Council of Europe launched its campaign for universal prohibition and elimination of corporal punishment across its 47 member states in June this year in Zagreb, with the slogan "Raise your hand against smacking," and quoting my Study's recommendation that all States should prohibit all violence against children, including all corporal punishment, by the end of 2009. Since my Study reported, several more European states have prohibited all smacking and many more have committed to doing so soon: in fact the Council is half way towards its target – denoting a cultural change across the region of vast significance to children's well-being.

I make no apology for dwelling on this issue of "smacking," or "spanking" children. Most languages have soft words like these, whose purpose is to make adults feel more comfortable about defending hitting – assaulting – children. Too often, politicians and professionals trivialise the issue. But in doing so, they insult children and miss the point.

While we deny children equal protection of their human dignity, we are denying them their status as individual human beings and holders of human rights alongside the rest of us. We are treating them as possessions not people. In women's long struggle for equality, challenging routine violence against them in their homes has been a vital part of the struggle. Now, nobody would get away with defending "loving slaps" of wives or partners.

While the rule of thumb was at one time the legal measure of the thickness of the stick with which a husband could lawfully beat his wife, such concepts are now confined to the history books – except for children. I am confident that we will all soon look back with embarrassment at the fact that in 2008, governments were still defending "reasonable" violence against children.

My dear friend Thomas Hammarberg, the Council of Europe's Commissioner for Human Rights, says in the memorandum on corporal punishment which he submitted to the UK Government in October, following several visits and meetings with your Secretary of State for Children and others. In the memorandum he emphasises – I quote – "that laws allowing the definition of 'justifiable assaults' and 'reasonable punishments' on children are not compliant with international human rights standards. That children, uniquely, should have *less* protection under the criminal law from assault is additionally discriminatory and unimaginable, given children's obvious special vulnerability." I am aware and commend the fact that the UK has moved to limit the application of the "reasonable punishment" defence. I know that Government Ministers now state clearly that they do not "condone" smacking. But, as Mr. Hammarberg makes clear, that is not enough: without the complete removal of the concept of "reasonable" violence against children, "this position of not condoning smacking lacks credibility." I believe that the law perpetuates a dangerous and disrespectful confusion, a confusion that is the permissive context for very high levels of violence, not just so-called "loving smacking." If we are to deter parents from traditionally acceptable violence, we have to send the clearest possible message into the "privacy" of the home: that it is no more legal or acceptable to smack a child than to smack anyone else.

As you may know, the "reasonable chastisement" common law defense which has its origins in Roman and then English law, has been adopted by more than 70 states worldwide. In June last year, New Zealand became the first English-speaking state to discard the defense completely and prohibit all corporal punishment. If the UK were to follow, I know this would be highly influential, in Europe and for all the world.

The Committee on the Rights of the Child issued a General Comment in 2006, on the right of the child to protection from corporal punishment. General Comments are authoritative interpretations of the Convention. In it, the Committee states that eliminating violent and humiliating punishment of children, through law reform and other necessary measures, is "an immediate and unqualified obligation" of states parties. Referring to article 19 of the Convention on the Rights of the Child, it notes: "There is no ambiguity: 'all forms of physical or mental violence' does not leave room for any level of legalised violence against children ..."

I understand that one of the judges of your highest court, the House of Lords, recently described the Committee on the Rights of the Child as "the authoritative international view of what the UN Convention requires." I know that the Committee has three times recommended a full ban on corporal punishment to the UK, in 1995, 2002 and most recently in October this year, and two other UN treaty bodies have echoed it – the Committee on Economic, Social and Cultural Rights and the Committee on the Elimination of Discrimination against Women.

Of course, removing the "reasonable punishment" defense is not going to end violence against children. It is a necessary, but not of course sufficient, step. **Law reform has to be accompanied by widespread awareness-raising, of the law and children's right to protection and also to promote positive, non-violent relationships with children**: this needs to be build into all the state's contacts with future parents and parents, as my Study advocated, and we know from the example of Sweden and other countries that instituted a ban decades ago, that education will need to be sustained over a long period. There is no shortage of materials and programmes, for adaptation for use in every country. But it is impossible to send a clear message while the law undermines it.

A key right upheld in the Convention on the Rights of the Child is the article 12 right of children to express their views "freely in all matters affecting them" and to have those views given due weight. This has implications for all aspects and stages of child protection.

I was glad to hear that your Children Act introduced in 2004 included a specific article 12 duty on those involved in child protection. The recent tragic "Baby P" case in London, which I have read a little about, is just one of far too many in the UK and other well-developed countries where, despite a highly developed interdisciplinary child protection system, somehow the necessary focus on the child is missing.

We also know that it is not only babies and very young children who suffer unheard. We know from the retrospective studies referred to in the Lancet series, interviewing young adults about their childhood experiences, that a majority of children do not report even severe physical or sexual abuse during their childhood. We have to accept that this means that our existing child protection services are not acceptable to many of the children who need them. I sometimes ask audiences what they would do if they discovered, for example, that one of their young children was being sexually abused by an uncle. Would you feel confident in going straight to the police or social services, confident that they would act with sufficient sensitivity and in the best interests of your child? If we are to devise effective and sensitive services that are acceptable to children, we have to seek advice from those children who have been the recent subjects of the services: did the process work for them? Did it serve their best interests? Were there unintended negative consequences? How could things have been better? We need to regard children with relevant experiences as the experts. We need their advice on reporting systems and procedures, on investigation and on every aspect of prevention and response.

During the Study process, I came to realize that the debate about mandatory reporting of violence against children is not at all a simple one. If we require all those services which children have access to, to refer on any information which the child gives them, we may well be deterring many children from confiding in adults at all and thus condemning them to continue to suffer even extreme forms of abuse and exploitation. I believe children – children with the capacity to understand – must be offered access to advice and advocacy with a guarantee of a very high standard of confidentiality, a guarantee to the child that referring the case on or other action will not be taken without the child's consent unless the child, or another person, is judged to be at risk of death or serious injury. These confidential services need to exist alongside conventional services which have an obligation to investigate if they believe a child to be at risk of significant harm (to quote what I understand to be the English law threshold for formal investigation). Some people see offering children confidentiality as colluding with abusers. I see it as another aspect of respect for children as people, challenging their traditional status as possessions or simply objects of concern.

Confidential telephone helplines, like your pioneering ChildLine, are important but not enough: they need to be able to refer children in appropriate cases to local advocates operating with the same confidentiality policy.

It is well known that the process of investigation of maltreatment, and child victims' involvement in criminal justice processes can add further trauma for them. I believe that the UN Guidelines on Justice in Matters Involving Child

Victims and Witnesses of Crime, adopted by the Economic and Social Council in 2005 provide very valuable standards and guidance. The preamble emphasizes that children who are victims and witnesses "are particularly vulnerable and need special protection, assistance and support appropriate to their age, level of maturity and unique needs in order to prevent further hardship and trauma that may result from their participation in the criminal justice process ..." The guidelines call for a child-sensitive approach throughout, defining "child-sensitive" as an approach that balances the child's right to protection and that takes into account the child's individual needs and views."

While there should be no impunity for those who perpetrate violence against children, we have to be wary of systems of protection that become in practice servants of the criminal justice system. In relation to responding to sexual abuse, I am impressed by the detailed new standards set in the Council of Europe's Convention on the Protection of Children against Sexual Exploitation and Sexual Abuse. It recognises that a crudely punitive approach to perpetrators is most unlikely to reduce the assault on children; that States are required to take detailed measures to prevent offending and to prevent re-offending. They must ensure through widespread awareness-raising that adults who may pose a threat to children know that programmes of counselling and treatment are available to them; they must ensure treatment for offenders in and outside prison, and offender management schemes. And there must be systems of records and checks to ensure that those who do pose a risk cannot gain employment which gives them significant access to children.

The Committee on the Rights of the Child recommended, after holding two major days of discussion on violence against children in 2000 and 2001 that – I quote – "In conceptualising violence ... the critical starting point and frame of reference must be the experience of children themselves ..."

Analysis of the calls children make to helplines gives some indication of the scale of children's suffering. But if we are to get near to revealing the true extent of all forms of violence against children, we have to carry out interview research with them, in conditions of trust and confidentiality. We also have to interview their parents, to determine what is happening to babies and very young children. Retrospective studies interviewing young adults cannot recall early childhood experiences and it is well known that adults tend to take a rosy view of their childhoods.

Every state needs to carry out these interview studies with children and with parents and other carers, at regular intervals to determine the baseline and measure progress towards eliminating violence.

We know, particularly from research in this country and in the US and more recently in Eastern Europe, that children in all forms of care are at particular risk of violence. They need to be given opportunities to talk in private to adults they can trust. All children leaving placements in foster-care or in institutions should in my view be given the formal opportunity of a confidential interview in which they can disclose anything negative (and indeed positive) in their experiences.

We need research, and the UK and the US have been the leaders in research into child maltreatment. But we need research which takes as its starting point that all violence against children is a violation of their human rights. Research into the impact of violence against children is in a sense irrelevant and even disrespectful of children. The violence must stop; that is children's right. We do not research the impact of domestic violence on women. We recognise their right to freedom from violence and adopt zero tolerance policies.

During the UN Study process, some children expressed their cynicism to me concerning adults' ability to stop their violence against children. For example, at the Middle East and North Africa consultation in Cairo, a young girl said to me: "I feel that all recommendations are only words and nothing will be done with them." Another said: "There are a lot of conferences around the world but when it comes to results, not much happens, it is only talking."

I believe that my Study did create some expectations, and also some momentum for action, in many countries. My report recommended the appointment of a Special Representative to the UN Secretary-General, on violence against children, to act as a high-level global advocate. In 2007, the General Assembly took up that recommendation and asked the Secretary-General to make the appointment. I am concerned that a year has passed and we – and children – are still waiting.

I very much hope that the debate started by these papers and this seminar will be a lively and well-disseminated one. But above all I hope that the debate will focus on building a child-sensitive child protection system, founded on respect for the human rights of children and illuminated by children's own experiences and views.

Thank you.

TASK/TEXT 2.17: PROGRESS FOR CHILDREN

A Report Card on Child Protection, Unicef, September 2009 (pp. 1 and 36–38), <www.unicef.org/media/files/Progress_for_Children-No.8_HiRes_EN_USLetter_08132009.pdf>, accessed 7 October 2009 (references omitted)

FOREWORD (Ann M. Veneman Executive Director, Unicef)

Around the world, far too many children are subject to violence, exploitation and abuse. Some are forced to work under harmful conditions. Others face violence or abuse in their homes, their schools, their communities or in institutional care. In some places children are targets for illegal recruitment by armed groups and armed forces or are forced to flee their homes due to conflict or natural disaster. And millions, especially girls, are subject to sexual violence and abuse as well as harmful traditional practices.

This edition of *Progress for Children*, the eighth in the series that monitors progress towards the Millennium Development Goals (MDGs), is a compendium of data that serves as a report card on global and national efforts to protect the rights of children.

Data on many child protection issues are more readily available today than ever before. However on some issues – notably sexual exploitation and abuse of children, trafficking and migration – data remain difficult to obtain. More must be done to fill these gaps, and with more available data the prospects for concrete results for children will improve.

But the data reveal some progress. For example, in some countries where child marriage has been commonplace, girls are now getting married at a later age.

Data also show that female genital mutilation/cutting has declined in recent decades. While progress is being made on these issues, the challenge is to accelerate the pace.

Effective child protection systems help ensure that vulnerable children and families have access to school, health care, social welfare, social protection, justice and other essential services. These systems can contribute to breaking the cycle of [trans]generational poverty and exploitation, thus contributing to achieving the MDGs.

The collective aim must be to create protective environments in which girls and boys are safe from all forms of violence and exploitation. There must be a concerted effort to protect the rights of children and to expand the opportunities they have to reach their full potential.

It is now two decades since the landmark Convention on the Rights of the Child was adopted. As we mark its 20th anniversary this year, this edition of *Progress for Children* provides key information on child protection.

While progress has been made, each child still suffering must inspire us to greater urgency until the Convention's protections extend to every child, everywhere.

INDUSTRIALIZED COUNTRIES

A recent review of studies [*The Lancet* 2009] measuring child maltreatment found that at least 4 per cent of children in industrialized countries are physically abused each year, and 1 in 10 is neglected or psychologically abused – by their parents or guardians in at least 80 per cent of these cases. In many industrialized countries, large majorities of parents still consider corporal punishment of children to be acceptable. It is estimated that throughout the course of their childhood, 5–10 per cent of girls and up to 5 per cent of boys suffer penetrative sexual abuse, and up to three times this percentage experience some type of sexual abuse. Evidence suggests, however, that physical and sexual abuse may be decreasing in some settings.

During recent years, physical and especially sexual abuse of children have been high-profile issues in industrialized countries. But the harm done by neglect and emotional abuse has garnered insufficient attention. Among the risk factors associated with parents who abuse their children are poverty, mental health problems, low education achievement, alcohol and drug misuse – as well as parents' own experience of maltreatment during childhood. Children of migrants to industrialized countries are vulnerable to exploitation, particularly if their families have migrated illegally and therefore have no access to basic support services. They suffer a higher risk of being trafficked into sexual exploitation, forced labour or domestic servitude.

Not all trafficking is across borders, however – in Germany and the Netherlands, for example, around one quarter of victims have been trafficked within the country. Birth registration is almost universal in industrialized countries, but the children of immigrants or other marginalized groups are least likely to be registered. Child marriage is less common in industrialized than in developing countries, but at least 10 per cent of adolescents marry before age 18 in Britain, France and the United States. Many teenagers who become pregnant do so outside marriage or other types of formal union. FGM/C is practised in certain immigrant communities, although scant data are available with respect to its prevalence.

As of February 2009, 12 industrialized countries had passed laws criminalizing female genital mutilation or cutting: Australia, Belgium, Canada, Cyprus, Denmark, Italy, New Zealand, Norway, Spain, Sweden, the United Kingdom and the United States. The number of children exposed to violence, exploitation and abuse all over the world is profoundly disturbing.

The sheer scale of the problem makes it clear that the Millennium Development Goals cannot be achieved unless faster and more resolute progress is made to protect children.

Preventing and responding to violence, exploitation and abuse are essential if children's rights as set out in the Convention on the Rights of the Child are to be guaranteed.

Abusive practices against children aggravate poverty, social exclusion and the transmission of HIV, and create an unwelcome legacy for succeeding generations. By contrast, where children are protected, their health, education and wellbeing are improved as well as their ability to contribute to society as future parents and citizens.

This report card shows that there has been progress in some areas, but that it has been altogether too little and too slow.

The multiple factors that contribute to the violation of children's right to protection – including poverty and gender inequality, harmful traditional practices, inadequate legislation and policies, and unresponsive government services – are evidence that child protection cannot be pursued single issue by single issue but must be embraced systematically and holistically.

The lack of good data on many of the topics covered in this report card is acutely problematic, particularly for the purposes of mobilization and action. There is a clear need for standardized measurement instruments and for consistent data that are disaggregated at the sub-national level and by gender and other socio-economic variables. And there is a clear need to better interpret and understand such data and apply them in the context of policymaking and programming.

But rather than starting from scratch, this effort should draw on the relevant resources of experience, knowledge and evidence of results.

Today, there is a much greater understanding of the myriad factors that combine to enhance children's protection.

The understanding now needs to be translated into urgent action – because every year that passes without that action is another year in which children are subjected to intolerable violence, exploitation and abuse.

BUILDING A PROTECTIVE ENVIRONMENT: A CALL TO ACTION

1. Commit governments to ensuring holistic protection for all children

Governments must provide adequate budgetary resources for child protection and build up sectors that have a role in child protection, particularly social welfare and justice. Services need to be responsive and preventive, and need to coordinate with each other.

The protection roles of all professionals must be strengthened, from planning and policy right through to codes of conduct, training and management systems.

Governments should also secure greater access to social protection for vulnerable families.

2. Pass and enforce laws that comprehensively address child protection concerns

The starting point must be the ratification by governments of international child protection standards and, beyond that, a commitment to meeting them. Legislative frameworks that are in line with international norms and standards need to be effectively enforced and consistently implemented.

Accountability and the end of impunity for crimes against children are essential.

3. Provide correct information from credible sources on viable alternatives to existing attitudes, behaviours and practices that violate children's rights

Communities must be enabled to identify and adopt better ways to pursue the well-being of their children and protect them from violence, abuse and exploitation. In addition to activities at the community level, public awareness campaigns, including active and responsible media engagement, can play a role in changing attitudes, beliefs and practices that threaten child protection.

4. Promote open discussion of child protection issues

Where harmful practices are the result of social attitudes and norms, open discussion is essential to reach the coordinated, collective consensus necessary for large-scale abandonment. All forms of violence, abuse and exploitation should be recognized, documented and reported in the media, as should positive changes in attitudes and behaviours, because knowledge about these can contribute to further positive change.

Protection failures should be acknowledged, and an enabling environment should be established to allow young people to discuss their concerns at home, at school and with each other. Survivors should not be threatened or ostracized, and non-governmental organizations and media should be able to work with minimal interference.

5. Promote meaningful child participation and empowerment

Engaging children in the issues that affect them is critical for their empowerment as actors in their own protection and that of their peers. This includes child participation through life skills education, peer communication, and activities to prevent stigma and discrimination, as well as participation in legal processes and in finding solutions to issues that concern them.

6. Strengthen the protective role of families and communities

Parents and caregivers can benefit from programmes that address gender stereotypes, increase their understanding of child development and promote non-violent forms of discipline. Governments can foster the protective environment through making social services available, supporting community-based child protection networks and dialogue, and promoting the elimination of all forms of violence against women and children.

7. Improve monitoring and oversight through better data collection, analysis and use

Countries need to improve data collection and information systems in order to identify vulnerable groups, inform policy and track progress. National data collection on child protection must become routine and include disaggregation by sex, age and other vulnerability factors. In alignment with a 'systems approach' to child protection, indicators need to be identified to measure progress and trends on the capacities of child protection systems. Additional support for the capacity of governments, aid organizations and communities to collect data and apply information tools in child protection is essential. Research and diagnosis of child protection challenges, as well as systematic evaluation of child protection initiatives, also need to be strengthened.

8. Ensure a protective environment for children in emergencies

This involves a multi-sectoral approach encompassing social welfare, education, health, law enforcement and justice components. Parties to conflict must ensure that children are protected from death, injury, harm, arbitrary arrest and detention, recruitment by armed groups, gender-based violence, torture, and other cruel, inhuman and degrading treatment. To this end, conflict-affected countries must actively monitor and report grave child rights violations under UN Security Council Resolution 1612, end impunity for such violations and adhere to agreed-upon plans of action.

2*TER*. US SURVEY OF CHILDREN'S EXPOSURE TO VIOLENCE

TASK/TEXT 2.18: CHILDREN'S EXPOSURE TO VIOLENCE: A COMPREHENSIVE NATIONAL SURVEY (NATSCEV)

David Finkelhor, Heather Turner, Richard Ormrod, Sherry Hamby, and Kristen Kracke, *Juvenile Justice Bulletin* (Office of Juvenile Justice and Delinquency Prevention, OJJDP, US Department of Justice), October 2009, <www.unh.edu/ccrc/pdf/DOJ-NatSCEV-bulletin.pdf> (methodology, endnotes and references omitted)

A message from OJJDP

Children are exposed to violence every day in their homes, schools, and communities. They may be struck by a boyfriend, bullied by a classmate, or abused by an adult. They may witness an assault on a parent or a shooting on the street. Such exposure can cause significant physical, mental, and emotional harm with long-term effects that can last well into adulthood. In 1999, OJJDP created the Safe Start Initiative to prevent and reduce the impact of children's exposure to violence through enhanced practice, research, evaluation, training and technical assistance, resources, and outreach. The initiative has improved the delivery of developmentally appropriate services for children exposed to violence and their families. Understanding the nature and extent of children's exposure to violence is essential to combating its effects. Partnering with the Centers for Disease Control and Prevention, OJJDP has sponsored the most comprehensive effort to date to measure children's exposure to violence. The National Survey of Children's Exposure to Violence [NatSCEV] is the first survey to ask children and caregivers about exposure to a range of violent incidents and maltreatment. As amply evidenced in this Bulletin, children's exposure to violence is pervasive and crosses all ages. The research findings reported here are critical to informing our efforts to protect children from its damaging effects.

National Survey of Children's Exposure to Violence (NatSCEV)

This Bulletin discusses the National Survey of Children's Exposure to Violence (NatSCEV), the most comprehensive nationwide survey of the incidence and prevalence of children's exposure to violence to date, sponsored by the Office of

Juvenile Justice and Delinquency Prevention (OJJDP) and supported by the Centers for Disease Control and Prevention (CDC). Conducted between January and May 2008, it measured the **past-year** and **lifetime** exposure to violence for children **age 17 and younger** across several major categories: **conventional crime, child maltreatment, victimization by peers and siblings, sexual victimization, witnessing and indirect victimization (including exposure to community violence and family violence), school violence and threats, and internet victimization.** (For more detailed information on the types of violence that children were questioned about, see "Screening Questions.") This survey is the first comprehensive attempt to measure children's exposure to violence in the home, school, and community across all age groups from birth to age 17, and the first attempt to measure the cumulative exposure to violence over the child's lifetime.

The survey confirms that most of our society's children are exposed to violence in their daily lives. More than 60 percent of the children surveyed were exposed to violence within the past year, either directly or indirectly (i.e., as a witness to a violent act; by learning of a violent act against a family member, neighbor, or close friend; or from a threat against their home or school) (…). Nearly one-half of the children and adolescents surveyed (46.3 percent) were assaulted at least once in the past year, and more than 1 in 10 (10.2 percent) were injured in an assault; 1 in 4 (24.6 percent) were victims of robbery, vandalism, or theft; **1 in 10 (10.2 percent) suffered from child maltreatment (including physical and emotional abuse, neglect, or a family abduction)**; and **1 in 16 (6.1 percent) were victimized sexually**. More than 1 in 4 (25.3 percent) witnessed a violent act and **nearly 1 in 10 (9.8 percent) saw one family member assault another**. Multiple victimizations were common: more than one-third (38.7 percent) experienced 2 or more direct victimizations in the previous year; more than 1 in 10 (10.9 percent) experienced 5 or more direct victimizations in the previous year; and more than 1 in 75 (1.4 percent) experienced 10 or more direct victimizations in the previous year.

Reports of lifetime exposure to violence were generally about one-third to one-half higher than reports of past-year exposure, although the difference tended to be greater for less frequent and more severe types of victimization. (For example, more than three times as many respondents reported being victims of a kidnapping over their lifetimes as did in the past year.) Nearly seven in eight children (86.6 percent) who reported being exposed to violence during their lifetimes also reported being exposed to violence within the past year, which indicated that these children were at ongoing risk of violent victimization. The reports of lifetime exposure also indicate how certain types of exposure change and accumulate as a child grows up; nearly one in five girls ages 14 to 17

(18.7 percent) had been victims of a sexual assault or attempted sexual assault, and more than one-third of all 14- to 17-year-olds had seen a parent assaulted.

Screening Questions

The survey asked screening questions about 48 types of victimization in the following categories:

- **Conventional crime.** Nine types of victimization, including robbery, theft, destruction of property, attack with an object or weapon, attack without an object or weapon, attempted attack, threatened attack, kidnapping or attempted kidnapping, and hate crime or bias attack (an attack on a child because of the child's or parent's skin color, religion, physical problem, or perceived sexual orientation).
- **Child maltreatment.** Four types of victimization, including being hit, kicked, or beaten by an adult (other than spanking on the bottom); psychological or emotional abuse; neglect; and abduction by a parent or caregiver, also known as custodial interference.
- **Peer and sibling victimization.** Six types of victimization, including being attacked by a group of children; being hit or beaten by another child, including a brother or sister; being hit or kicked in the private parts; being chased, grabbed, or forced to do something; being teased or emotionally bullied; and being a victim of dating violence.
- **Sexual victimization.** Seven types of victimization, including sexual contact or fondling by an adult the child knew, sexual contact or fondling by an adult stranger, sexual contact or fondling by another child or teenager, attempted or completed intercourse, exposure or "flashing," sexual harassment, and consensual sexual conduct with an adult.
- **Witnessing and indirect victimization.** These fall into two general categories, exposure to community violence and exposure to family violence. For exposure to ***community violence***, the survey included 10 types of victimization, including seeing someone attacked with an object or weapon; seeing someone attacked without an object or weapon; having something stolen from the household; having a friend, neighbor, or family member murdered; witnessing a murder; witnessing or hearing a shooting, bombing, or riot; being in a war zone; knowing a family member or close friend who was fondled or forced to have sex; knowing a family member or close friend who was robbed or mugged; and knowing a family member or close friend who was threatened with a gun or knife.

  For exposure to ***family violence***, eight types of victimization were assessed: seeing a parent assaulted by a spouse, domestic partner, or boyfriend or girlfriend; seeing a brother or sister assaulted by a parent; threat by one parent to assault the other; threat by a parent to damage the other parent's property; one parent pushing the other; one parent hitting or slapping the other; one parent kicking, choking, or beating up the other; and assault by another adult household member against a child or adult in the household.

- **School violence and threat.** Two types of victimization, including a credible bomb threat against the child's school and fire or other property damage to the school.
- **Internet violence and victimization.** Two types of victimization, including internet threats or harassment and unwanted online sexual solicitation.

The Problem of Violence Against Children

Children in the United States are more likely to be exposed to violence and crime than are adults (...). In 2005, juveniles and young adults ages 12 to 19 were more than twice as likely to be victims of violent crimes as the population as a whole (...). Each year, millions of children and adolescents in the United States are exposed to violence in their homes, schools, and communities as both victims and witnesses. Even if they are not physically present, children may be affected by intentional harm done by another (for example, by the murder of or an assault on a family member or close neighbor). Children react to exposure to violence in different ways, and many children show remarkable resilience. All too often, however, children who are exposed to violence undergo lasting physical, mental, and emotional harm. They suffer from **difficulties with attachment, regressive behavior, anxiety and depression, and aggression and conduct problems**. They may be more prone to dating violence, delinquency, further victimization, and involvement with the child welfare and juvenile justice systems. Moreover, being exposed to violence **may impair a child's capacity for partnering and parenting later in life, continuing the cycle of violence into the next generation**. Research has found that early identification, intervention, and continued followup are valuable strategies to prevent or decrease the impact of exposure to violence. **Families, teachers, police, judges, pediatricians, mental health providers, child protection workers, domestic violence advocates, and others who interact with children have a responsibility to create interventions, both physical and psychological, that decrease or prevent the harms associated with exposure to violence. These include ways of interacting sensitively and expeditiously with children, ensuring protective environments and caregivers, and helping children use positive coping skills.** Much more research is warranted about what works to mitigate the effects of exposure to violence.

Too little is known about the numbers of children exposed to violence. Although several studies have attempted to measure children's exposure to violence, these estimates have varied greatly and have often measured only a subset of that exposure. Not only does this partial measurement fail to reveal the full extent of violence against children, it also fails to account fully for the multiple victimizations that many children experience; the co-occurrence of certain types of violence (for example, intimate partner violence and child maltreatment or neglect within a household); the extent to which exposure to one type of violence may make a child more vulnerable to other types of violence and victimization; and the cumulative effects of repeated exposure to violence as both a direct victim and a witness. Basic epidemiological data are important to determine the extent of the public health problem, the need for services, and a baseline for evaluating progress.

Prior Attempts at Comprehensive Measurements

There have been many studies on the health and behavioral consequences of child maltreatment and, to a lesser extent, on other forms of violence against children. However, most of these studies focused on only one type of violence or on a few types within a single category such as child abuse. Two notable earlier studies attempted to measure children's exposure to violence and its adverse effects in a more comprehensive fashion. The **Adverse Childhood Experiences (ACE) Study**, cosponsored by CDC and Kaiser Permanente, looked at the consequences for future health and well-being of exposure to seven types of adverse childhood experiences under the categories of abuse, neglect, and household dysfunction. **Almost two-thirds of those surveyed had suffered at least one adverse childhood experience, and more than one in five respondents reported three or more such experiences. The survey found increased rates of a number of long-term harms to physical, mental, and emotional health associated with those experiences, including alcoholism, drug abuse, depression, severe obesity, and several chronic adult diseases.** The survey further found that multiple adverse experiences compounded those harms. Although the ACE Study was one of the first to document the long-term consequences of multiple childhood victimizations, it had a different focus than NatSCEV. For one, the study questioned adults on their memories of adverse childhood experiences rather than surveying children directly, and the set of adverse experiences was more limited than those included in NatSCEV.

The other major attempt to examine the prevalence and incidence of children's exposure to violence was the Developmental Victimization Survey (DVS), a precursor to NatSCEV. DVS asked a nationally representative sample of 2,030 children ages 10 to 17 and caregivers of children ages 2 to 9 about their past-year exposure to crime and violence in five categories: conventional crime, child maltreatment, peer and sibling victimization, sexual assault, and witnessing and indirect victimization (…). DVS was the first survey to simultaneously examine these various forms of victimization to obtain a comprehensive picture of children's exposure to violence. It was also the first national survey to estimate the incidence of many specific forms of victimization such as bias attacks and witnessing physical abuse (...). DVS generally found a higher rate of specific types of victimization than earlier studies such as the National Crime Victimization Survey.

Nearly three-quarters of the respondents (71 percent) reported a direct or indirect victimization within the past year, and the average young victim reported three separate types of victimizations in separate incidents. More than one-third of those surveyed reported that they witnessed violence or were otherwise indirect victims of violence. DVS, however, provided only a limited assessment of lifetime incidence of exposure to violence; did not look specifically at such items as threats and internet victimization; and had limited measurement of exposure to family violence, exposure to community violence, and school violence and threats. DVS also did not include children younger than age 2. NatSCEV expands on DVS by comprehensively assessing lifetime exposure, considering additional forms of violence, and including infants in the sample. With its much larger sample size, NatSCEV also allows for much more reliable estimates of rarer forms of victimization and more accurate rates within different subgroups of the population (...).

History of the Current Study

Under the leadership of then Deputy Attorney General Eric Holder in June 1999, OJJDP created the Safe Start initiative to prevent and reduce the impact of children's exposure to violence. As a part of this initiative and with a growing need to document the full extent of children's exposure to violence, OJJDP launched the National Survey of Children's Exposure to Violence. Safe Start's NatSCEV is the first national incidence and prevalence study to examine comprehensively the extent and nature of children's exposure to violence across all ages, settings, and timeframes (...). It measures their experience of violence in the home, school, and community. It asked children and their adult caregivers about not only the incidents of violence that children suffered and witnessed themselves but also other related crime and threat exposures, such as theft or burglary from a child's household, being in a school that was the target of a credible bomb threat, and being in a war zone or an area where ethnic violence occurred. It includes both the past-year and lifetime exposure to violence of children of all ages up to age 17. The study was developed under the direction of OJJDP, and was designed and conducted by the Crimes against Children Research Center of the University of New Hampshire. It provides comprehensive data on the full extent of violence in the daily lives of children. The primary purpose of NatSCEV is to document the incidence and prevalence of children's exposure to a broad array of violent experiences across a wide developmental spectrum. The research team asked follow-up questions about specific events, including where the exposure to violence occurred, whether injury resulted, how often the child was exposed to a specific type of violence, and the child's relationship to the perpetrator and (when the child witnessed violence) the victim. In addition, the study documents differences in exposure to violence across gender, race, socioeconomic status, family structure, region, urban/rural residence, and developmental stage of the child; specifies how different forms of violent victimization "cluster" or co-occur; identifies individual, family, and community-level predictors of violence exposure among children; examines associations between levels/types of violence exposure and child mental and emotional health; and assesses the extent to which children disclose incidents of violence to various individuals and the nature and source of assistance or treatment provided (if any).

This study began in 2007 with funding from OJJDP's Safe Start Initiative. OJJDP then partnered with CDC to collect additional data on safe, stable and nurturing relationships – a key focus for CDC's child maltreatment prevention activities. The combined approach by OJJDP and CDC is providing critical national data on levels of violence as well as data on key indicators of protective factors.

Highlights of the Survey Results

NatSCEV estimates both past-year and lifetime exposure to violence across a number of categories, including physical assault, bullying, sexual victimization, child maltreatment, dating violence, and witnessed and indirect victimization (See "Methodology" for more detailed definitions of these terms [omitted]). (...)

As noted earlier, the NatSCEV survey found that children's exposure to violence is common; more than 60 percent of the children surveyed had been exposed to violence in the past year and more than 1 in 10 reported 5 or more exposures. This exposure occurs across all age ranges of childhood and both genders. In general, however, the types of exposure that were most prevalent among younger children were less serious, such as assaults without a weapon or without injury, assaults by a juvenile sibling, or bullying and teasing, all of which were most common among 6- to 9-year-olds and declined thereafter. Older adolescents ages 14 to 17 were the most likely to experience more serious forms of violence, including assaults with injury, gang assaults, sexual victimizations, and physical and emotional abuse (...) and to witness violence in the community. This is not a hard and fast distinction; some serious forms of victimization, including kidnapping and assaults with a weapon, were most common among 10- to 13-year-olds. This age group was also the most likely to witness violence within the home, including domestic violence involving their parents and assaults by other family members.

The following sections provide more details about the findings of the study as regards children's exposure to major categories of violence, including assaults, bullying, sexual victimization, child maltreatment, and witnessing and indirect victimization. This Bulletin then discusses the study's findings about multiple and cumulative exposures to violence, including documentation that children who are exposed to one form of violence are at greatly increased risk for being exposed to violence in other forms.

Physical Assault

Nearly one-half (46.3 percent) of all the children surveyed were physically assaulted within the previous year, and more than one-half (56.7 percent) had been assaulted during their lifetime. Physical assaults are extremely common across the entire span of childhood and peak during middle childhood. Assaults by siblings especially show a marked developmental trend, peaking during the middle childhood years (ages 6 to 9) and then declining. Incidence for the most severe assaults, however, rises steadily with age. Among 14- to 17-year-olds, nearly 1 in 5 (18.8 percent) had been injured in the past year in a physical assault. New forms of violence, such as dating violence, also emerge during adolescence, reaching a 5.6 percent past-year incidence rate and an 8.8 percent lifetime rate for the oldest adolescents. The lifetime incidence of assault victimization generally rose steadily as children grew older, with more than 7 in 10 14- to 17-year-olds (71.1 percent) reporting that they had been assaulted during their lifetimes (…).

In general, boys are somewhat more likely than girls to be victims of assault. The past-year incidence of assault is 50.2 percent for boys and 42.1 percent for girls, and the lifetime incidence of assault is 60.3 percent for boys and 52.9 percent for girls. These patterns are consistent with other data on criminal victimization, which typically show that males are the most common targets of physical assault (…).

Bullying

The survey looked at bullying separately from assault and asked about multiple types of bullying: physical bullying, emotional bullying, and internet harassment. Overall, 13.2 percent of those surveyed reported having been physically bullied within the past year, and more than one in five (21.6 percent) reported having been physically bullied during their lifetimes. The risk of bullying peaks during middle childhood in a pattern similar to that for sibling assault. The highest incidence occurs among 6- to 9-year-olds, who had rates of 21.5 percent past-year incidence and 28.0 percent lifetime incidence.

About 1 in 5 children (19.7 percent) reported having been teased or emotionally bullied in the previous year and nearly 3 in 10 reported having been teased or emotionally bullied in their lifetimes. Teasing or emotional bullying followed a similar pattern to physical bullying among age groups, rising to reach a peak among 6- to 9-year-olds, nearly one-third of whom (30.4 percent) reported having been teased in the past year and then falling steadily thereafter.

Internet harassment was less common than other forms of bullying. Questions about internet harassment were asked only of youth aged 10 and older, who might be most likely to independently use a computer. Unlike other forms of bullying, the peak risk period for internet harassment was ages 14 to 17. In this group, 5.6 percent reported internet harassment within the past year and 7.9 percent during their lifetimes.

Boys were more likely than girls to be physically bullied or threatened, but girls were more likely to be victims of internet harassment. For past-year rates, there were no significant gender differences in emotional bullying, but for lifetime rates, girls reported more cumulative exposure to emotional bullying than boys (…).

Sexual Victimization

Overall, 6.1 percent of all children surveyed had been sexually victimized in the past year and nearly 1 in 10 (9.8 percent) over their lifetimes. Sexual victimizations included attempted and completed rape (1.1 percent past year, 2.4 percent lifetime); sexual assault by a known adult (0.3 percent past year, 1.2 percent lifetime), an adult stranger (0.3 percent past year, 0.5 percent lifetime), or a peer (1.3 percent past year, 2.7 percent lifetime); flashing or sexual exposure by an adult (0.4 percent past year, 0.6 percent lifetime) or peer (2.2 percent past year, 3.7 percent lifetime); sexual harassment (2.6 percent past year, 4.2 percent lifetime); and statutory sexual offenses (0.1 percent past year, 0.4 percent lifetime). Adolescents ages 14 to 17 were by far the most likely to be sexually victimized; nearly one in six (16.3 percent) was sexually victimized in the past year, and more than one in four (27.3 percent) had been sexually victimized during their lifetimes. The most common forms of sexual victimization were flashing or exposure by a peer, sexual harassment, and sexual assault.

Girls were more likely to be sexually victimized than boys: 7.4 percent of girls reported a sexual victimization within the past year, and nearly one in eight (12.2 percent) reported being sexually victimized during their lifetimes. Girls ages 14 to 17 had the highest rates of sexual victimization: 7.9 percent were victims of sexual assault in the past year and 18.7 percent during their lifetimes (…).

Child Maltreatment

Overall, **more than 1 in 10 children** surveyed (10.2 percent) suffered some form of maltreatment (including physical abuse other than sexual assault, psychological or emotional abuse, child neglect, and custodial interference) **during the past year** and **nearly 1 in 5** (18.6 percent) **during their lifetimes**. Both the past-year and lifetime rates of exposure to maltreatment rose as children grew older, particularly for children 10 and older: one in six 14- to 17-year-olds (16.6 percent) suffered maltreatment during the past year and nearly one in three (32.1 percent) during their lifetimes.

Patterns of child maltreatment were similar for girls and boys with the exception of psychological or emotional abuse, the incidence of which was somewhat higher for girls than for boys. Rates of sexual assault by a known adult (not limited to caregivers) were also higher for girls than for boys, in a pattern that was similar to other forms of sexual victimization.

Witnessing and Indirect Exposure to Violence

The NatSCEV survey found that witnessing violence was a common occurrence for children, particularly as they grew older. Overall, more than one-quarter of children surveyed (25.3 percent) had witnessed violence in their homes, schools, and communities during the past year; and more than one-third (37.8 percent) had witnessed violence against another person during their lifetimes. The proportion of children who witnessed violence both within the past year and during their lifetimes rose from one age group to the next. Of all forms of victimization measured in NatSCEV, witnessing community violence showed the strongest age trends. There was more than a sevenfold increase in rates from toddlers (2- to 5-year-olds) to older adolescents (14- to 17-year-olds). More than 7 in 10 14- to 17-year-olds had witnessed violence against another person during their lives.

These age trends were due mostly to witnessing violence in the community. The past-year incidence of witnessing assaults in the community rose from 5.8 percent among 2- to 5-year-olds to 42.2 percent among 14- to 17-year-olds; lifetime incidence rose even more dramatically, from 9.0 percent of 2- to 5-year-olds to nearly two-thirds (64.2 percent) of 14- to 17-year-olds. Witnessing of shootings also rose sharply in both past-year and lifetime incidence from one age group to the next. Among children younger than 2 years old, 1.1 percent were exposed to shootings in the past year, whereas more than 1 in 10 14- to 17-year-olds (10.2 percent) witnessed a shooting in the past year. Similarly, 3.5 percent of 2- to 5-year-olds had witnessed a shooting during their lifetimes, whereas more than one in five 14- to 17-year-olds (22.2 percent) had. As striking as these age trends are, even the lower numbers among children so young are cause for great concern.

In contrast to the patterns for witnessing community violence, few age trends in exposure can be seen for witnessing violence within the family. Witnessing family violence rates were fairly constant across the span of childhood, with all age groups falling in a fairly narrow range of approximately 6 to 11 percent.

Over the course of their lifetimes, boys overall were slightly more likely than girls to witness violence (40.1 percent of boys and 35.4 percent of girls). Boys were more likely to witness violence in the community, murder, and shootings both in the past year and during their lifetimes. There were no gender differences in witnessing family violence (...).

Multiple and Cumulative Victimizations

A large proportion of children surveyed (38.7 percent) reported more than one direct victimization (a victimization directed toward the child, as opposed to an incident that the child witnessed, heard, or was otherwise exposed to) within the previous year. Of those who reported any direct victimization, nearly two-thirds (64.5 percent) reported more than one. A significant number of children reported high levels of exposure to violence in the past year: more than 1 in 10 (10.9 percent) reported 5 or more direct exposures to violence, and 1.4 percent reported 10 or more direct victimizations. (Victimizations that could be counted in more than one category, such as physical abuse by a parent or caregiver that could also be considered an assault, were not included in the counting of multiple victimizations. See "Methodology" for a discussion of this point [omitted].)

Children who were exposed to one type of violence, both within the past year and over their lifetimes, were at far greater risk of experiencing other types of violence. For example, a child who was physically assaulted in the past year would be five times as likely to also have been sexually victimized and more than four times as likely also to have been maltreated during that period. Similarly, a child who was physically assaulted during his or her lifetime would be more than six times as likely to have been sexually victimized and more than five times as likely to have been maltreated during his or her lifetime.

Implications for Policymakers, Researchers, and Practitioners

The findings of the NatSCEV study confirm that for many children in the United States, violence is a frequent occurrence. Of the nationally representative sample of US youth who participated in the study, more than 60 percent reported that they were victims of direct or indirect violence in the past year. Furthermore, nearly two-thirds of those participants were victimized more than once. Nearly one-half of the children surveyed reported that they were assaulted during the previous year, and more than 10 percent of them were injured as a result. More than one-fourth of the children witnessed another person being violently attacked. More than 10 percent of the children surveyed reported that they were indirectly exposed to violence.

More needs to be understood about how exposure to individual episodes of violence, repeated exposure to violence, and multiple types of exposure affect children and families, providing many avenues for research and policy development. As in this study, future research and policy development efforts must incorporate a broader perspective in documenting the full scope of children's exposure to violence.

Understanding the Progression of Violence

NatSCEV detailed the extent to which children in this country are exposed to serious violence. The study found that in the year prior to being interviewed, 1 in 20 children witnessed someone being shot, 1 in 200 witnessed a murder, and 1 in 50 was sexually assaulted. The survey showed that as children grow older the incidences of victimization increase. Among 14- to 17-year-old participants, 1 in 10 witnessed a shooting in the past year, 1 in 75 witnessed a murder, and 1 in 20 was sexually assaulted. NatSCEV differs from earlier studies in that it looks across the full spectrum of violence, examining and comparing the incidence of different types of violence within broad categories and determining which types are more or less frequent. The study looks not only at when and how children become more vulnerable to increasingly serious types of violence as they grow older, it also tracks the cumulative effects of exposure to violence over time. For example, although all age groups are vulnerable to simple assault, older children and adolescents are several times more likely to be sexually assaulted or to witness a shooting than are younger children.

The NatSCEV study clearly illustrates the cumulative effects on children exposed to multiple incidents of violence and how exposure to one form of violence may make a child more vulnerable to other forms. Nearly two in five children surveyed were exposed to two or more types of violence in the previous year. More than 1 in 10 was exposed to 5 or more different types of violence during that year. These children are the most likely to suffer serious long-term physical, emotional, and mental harm (…). Many previous studies have shown how the exposure to violence has damaging consequences for the physical and mental health of youth (…) and their long-term functioning and well-being as adults (…).

Expanding the Inquiry

Researchers and practitioners need to ask children more specific questions about a broader range of victimizations, including dating violence, emotional abuse, and exposure to violence within the family. It is also critical to ask children who are suffering from one form of victimization about additional forms of victimizations they may have experienced to fully address their mental and emotional health needs. Practitioners also need to investigate victimization across all age ranges with the help of instruments geared to younger children and (as was done in the NatSCEV study) the use of proxies, such as parents and caretakers.

NatSCEV differs from earlier studies in that it examines and compares the incidence of different types of violence within broad categories and determines which types of violence occur more or less frequently. For example, the research team broke assaults down into peer and sibling assaults and assaults without weapon or injury and more serious types of assaults. Peer and sibling assaults were common across all age ranges and across both genders. More serious types of assaults included assaults with a weapon, assaults with injury, gang assaults, attempted assaults, genital assaults, dating violence, and bias attacks, which were less common.

Monitoring Exposure Over Time

More research is also needed that follows children into adulthood to assess the effects of violence on their long-term health and well-being. Such research would complement those studies, such as the ACE study discussed earlier, that have taken a retrospective look at the effects of adverse childhood experiences. NatSCEV's findings affirm that more needs to be done to measure children's exposure to violence on an ongoing and systematic basis using public surveillance mechanisms, including follow-up surveys and long-term monitoring (...).

The estimates of specific exposures in this study are roughly equivalent to or somewhat higher than the estimates in previous community survey studies of child physical abuse (...), sexual victimization (...), sexual assault (...), physical assault with a weapon (...), witnessing violence (...), dating violence (...), and bullying (...). Differences in age range and definition account for some variations between the findings of this and other studies. Because this is the first national study to ask children and their caregivers directly about exposure to certain types of family violence, such as assaults by one parent on another, **the exposure rate of 6.2 percent is several times greater than estimates obtained from cases disclosed to child protection agencies** (Administration on Children, Youth, and Families ...) and law enforcement (Federal Bureau of Investigation ...).

Reaching Across Disciplines

This study's findings confirm that more needs to be done at all levels of policy and practice to reach across disciplines to identify children at risk from exposure to violence and to coordinate the delivery of services to these children. For example, first responders and providers who are involved in incidents of domestic violence and deal with victims in their aftermath (e.g., police, emergency room physicians and nurses, social workers, domestic violence advocates, and judges) should be aware not only of the adult victims but also of the children who may have witnessed the incident. They may also need to work with childcare providers, teachers, and school counselors and psychologists to assess the effects on a child's interaction with his or her classmates and to provide needed help.

Expanding Identification Capabilities

Researchers, practitioners, and policymakers need to collaborate to develop and expand effective screening and assessment tools that are developmentally appropriate for children across all age ranges and types of violence. These instruments and tools can identify children who are suffering emotionally, socially, physically, and developmentally. More importantly, these instruments can aid practitioners, advocates, frontline service providers, and responders across all service sectors to reach and help those children. Understanding the full extent of children's exposure to violence and the interactions among multiple types of violence more comprehensively can further practitioners' ability to respond to those families who need support and to alleviate the harmful effects of exposure to violence (…).

Coordinating Across Sectors

Finally, just as the NatSCEV study by its comprehensive nature addresses the fragmentation that, until now, characterized many attempts to look at child victimization and exposure to violence, greater coordination of the efforts to combat the effects of that victimization are needed. For example, recent initiatives have formed to separately address bullying, dating violence, and sexual harassment. At the Federal, State, tribal, and local levels, responsibility for dealing with children's exposure to violence is distributed across all service and response sectors (e.g., health departments, hospitals, child welfare and protection agencies, early childhood educators and childcare providers, schools and educational institutions, domestic violence service providers and advocates, law enforcement agencies, and the justice system). The Safe Start initiative has worked toward a comprehensive approach across the **continuum of prevention, intervention, treatment, and response** for 10 years and has made significant progress in increasing knowledge, skills, and awareness of children's exposure to violence. More work is needed.

The next step in addressing children's exposure to violence and efforts to ameliorate or eliminate the harm it causes is to foster and sustain a comprehensive approach in both practice and research that builds on the groundwork established under Safe Start and this study. It is important to develop, implement, and evaluate programs and policies designed to prevent children's exposure to violence; to craft and implement strategies and interventions to help children who have been exposed to violence and their families; and to replicate those programs, policies, and interventions that prove to be effective in preventing and lessening violence against children in communities across the Nation.

The NatSCEV study represents the best attempt to date to quantify children's exposure to violence. Understanding categories and forms of violence is critical to creating appropriate interventions to prevent and suppress violence and to treat its victims. This study's greatest contribution, however, is that it highlights the degree to which children in this country live with violence in their daily lives. **Violence takes a toll on children whether as victims or witnesses. Seemingly minor incidents may have long-lasting and far-reaching consequences. If policymakers, practitioners, advocates, and the general public are to respond effectively to curb the negative effects of children's exposure to violence, everyone must look at the problem in its totality and make a coordinated effort to help the children and their families who suffer these effects.**

For Further Information

To learn more about the Safe Start Initiative, visit <www.safestartcenter.org>.

For more information about the National Survey of Children's Exposure to Violence, visit the Crimes against Children Research Center website at <www.unh.edu/ccrc>.

Access OJJDP publications online at <www.ojjdp.ncjrs.gov>.

3. VIOLENCE AGAINST CHILDREN – SEXUAL EXPLOITATION

TASK/TEXT 3.1: COUNCIL OF EUROPE CONVENTION ON THE PROTECTION OF CHILDREN AGAINST SEXUAL EXPLOITATION AND SEXUAL ABUSE

(Adopted by the Committee of Ministers on 12 July 2007 at the 1002nd meeting of the Ministers' Deputies); signed 25 October 2007, Lanzarote

[**Convention (CETS 201) and Explanatory Report**: Council of Europe Publishing May 2008, <http://book.coe.int>; **internet**: <http://conventions.coe.int/Treaty/Commun/QueVoulezVous.asp?NT=201&CL=ENG>; **Dutch translation**: *Tractatenblad* 2008, 58 (C. Vertaling); <www.overheid.nl>, Officiële publicaties]

The member states of the Council of Europe and the other signatories hereto;

[1] Considering that the aim of the Council of Europe is to achieve a greater unity between its members;

[2] Considering that every child has the right to such measures of protection as are required by his or her status as a minor, on the part of his or her family, society and the state;

[3] Observing that the sexual exploitation of children, in particular child pornography and prostitution, and all forms of sexual abuse of children, including acts which are committed abroad, are **destructive to children's health and psycho-social development**;

[4] Observing that the sexual exploitation and sexual abuse of children have grown to worrying proportions at both national and international level, in particular as regards the increased use by both children and perpetrators of information and communication technologies (ICTs), and that preventing and combating such sexual exploitation and sexual abuse of children require international co-operation;

[5] **Considering that the well-being and best interests of children are fundamental values shared by all member states and must be promoted without any discrimination;**

[6] Recalling the Action Plan adopted at the Third Summit of Heads of State and Governments of the Council of Europe (Warsaw, 16–17 May 2005), calling for the elaboration of measures to stop sexual exploitation of children;

[7] Recalling in particular Committee of Ministers' Recommendation No. R (91) 11 concerning sexual exploitation, pornography and prostitution of, and trafficking in, children and young adults, Recommendation Rec(2001)16 on the protection of children against sexual exploitation, and the Convention on Cybercrime (ETS No. 185), especially Article 9 thereof, as well as the Council of Europe Convention on Action against Trafficking in Human Beings (ETS No. 197);

[8] Bearing in mind the Convention for the Protection of Human Rights and Fundamental Freedoms (1950, ETS No. 5), the revised European Social Charter (1996, ETS No. 163), and the European Convention on the Exercise of Children's Rights (1996, ETS No. 160);

[9] Also bearing in mind the United Nations Convention on the Rights of the Child, especially Article 34 thereof, the Optional Protocol on the sale of children, child prostitution and child pornography, the Protocol to Prevent, Suppress and Punish Trafficking in Persons, Especially Women and Children, supplementing the United Nations Convention against Transnational Organised Crime, as well as the International Labour Organisation Convention concerning the Prohibition and Immediate Action for the Elimination of the Worst Forms of Child Labour;

[10] Bearing in mind the Council of the European Union Framework Decision on combating the sexual exploitation of children and child pornography (2004/68/JHA), the Council of the European Union Framework Decision on the standing of victims in criminal proceedings (2001/220/JHA), and the Council of the European Union Framework Decision on combating trafficking in human beings (2002/629/JHA);

[11] Taking due account of other relevant international instruments and programmes in this field, in particular the Stockholm Declaration and Agenda for Action, adopted at the 1st World Congress against Commercial Sexual Exploitation of Children (27–31 August 1996), the Yokohama Global Commitment adopted at the 2nd World Congress against Commercial Sexual Exploitation of Children (17–20 December 2001), the Budapest Commitment and Plan of Action, adopted at the preparatory Conference for the 2nd World Congress against Commercial Sexual Exploitation of Children (20–21 November 2001), the United Nations General Assembly Resolution S-27/2 "A world fit for children" and the three-year programme "Building a Europe for and with children," adopted following the Third Summit and launched by the Monaco Conference (4–5 April 2006);

[12] Determined to contribute effectively to the common goal of protecting children against sexual exploitation and sexual abuse, whoever the perpetrator may be, and of providing assistance to victims;
[13] Taking into account the need to prepare a comprehensive international instrument focusing on the preventive, protective and criminal law aspects of the fight against all forms of sexual exploitation and sexual abuse of children and setting up a specific monitoring mechanism,

Have agreed as follows: (...)

Chapter I – Purposes, non-discrimination principle and definitions

Article 1 – Purposes

1. The purposes of this Convention are to:

a. prevent and combat sexual exploitation and sexual abuse of children;
b. protect the rights of child victims of sexual exploitation and sexual abuse;
c. promote national and international co-operation against sexual exploitation and sexual abuse of children.

2. (...)

Article 2 – Non-discrimination principle

The implementation of the provisions of this Convention by the Parties, in particular the enjoyment of measures to protect the rights of victims, shall be secured without discrimination on any ground such as sex, race, colour, language, religion, political or other opinion, national or social origin, association with a national minority, property, birth, sexual orientation, state of health, disability or other status.

Article 3 – Definitions

For the purposes of this Convention:

a. "child" shall mean any person under the age of 18 years;
b. "sexual exploitation and sexual abuse of children" shall include the behaviour as referred to in Articles 18 to 23 of this Convention;
c. "victim" shall mean any child subject to sexual exploitation or sexual abuse.

Chapter II – Preventive measures

Article 4 – Principles

Each Party shall take the necessary legislative or other measures to prevent all forms of sexual exploitation and sexual abuse of children and to protect children.

Article 5 – Recruitment, training and awareness raising of persons working in contact with children

1. Each Party shall take the necessary legislative or other measures to encourage **awareness of the protection and rights of children** among persons who have regular contacts with children in the education, health, social protection, judicial and law-enforcement sectors and in areas relating to sport, culture and leisure activities.

2. Each Party shall take the necessary legislative or other measures to ensure that the persons referred to in paragraph 1 have an **adequate knowledge** of sexual exploitation and sexual abuse of children, of the means to identify them and of the possibility mentioned in Article 12, paragraph 1.

3. Each Party shall take the necessary legislative or other measures, in conformity with its internal law, to ensure that the conditions to accede those professions whose exercise implies regular contacts with children ensure that the candidates to these professions **have not been convicted** of acts of sexual exploitation or sexual abuse of children.

Article 6 – Education for children

Each Party shall take the necessary legislative or other measures to ensure that children, during **primary and secondary education**, receive information on the risks of sexual exploitation and sexual abuse, as well as on the means to protect themselves, adapted to their evolving capacity. This information, provided **in collaboration with parents**, where appropriate, shall be given within a more general context of information on sexuality and shall pay special attention to situations of risk, especially those involving the use of new information and communication technologies.

Article 7 – Preventive intervention programmes or measures

Each Party shall ensure that persons who fear that they might commit any of the offences established in accordance with this Convention may have access, where appropriate, to effective intervention programmes or measures designed to evaluate and prevent the risk of offences being committed.

Article 8 – Measures for the general public

1. Each Party shall promote or conduct **awareness raising campaigns** addressed to the general public providing information on the phenomenon of sexual exploitation and sexual abuse of children and on the preventive measures which can be taken.

2. Each Party shall take the necessary legislative or other measures **to prevent or prohibit the dissemination of materials advertising the offences established in accordance with this Convention.**

Article 9 – Participation of children, the private sector, the media and civil society

1. Each Party shall encourage the participation of children, according to their evolving capacity, in the development and the implementation of state policies, programmes or others initiatives concerning the fight against sexual exploitation and sexual abuse of children.

2. Each Party shall encourage the private sector, in particular the information and communication technology sector, the tourism and travel industry and the banking and finance sectors, as well as civil society, to participate in the elaboration and implementation of policies to prevent sexual exploitation and sexual abuse of children and to implement internal norms through self-regulation or co-regulation.

3. Each Party shall encourage the media to provide appropriate information concerning all aspects of sexual exploitation and sexual abuse of children, with due respect for the independence of the media and freedom of the press.

4. Each Party shall encourage the financing, including, where appropriate, by the creation of funds, of the projects and programmes carried out by civil society aiming at preventing and protecting children from sexual exploitation and sexual abuse.

Chapter III – Specialised authorities and co-ordinating bodies

Article 10 – National measures of co-ordination and collaboration

1. Each Party shall take the necessary measures to ensure the co-ordination on a national or local level between the different agencies in charge of the protection from, the prevention of and the fight against sexual exploitation and sexual abuse of children, notably the education sector, the health sector, the social services and the law-enforcement and judicial authorities.

2. Each Party shall take the necessary legislative or other measures to set up or designate:

a. **independent competent national or local institutions for the promotion and protection of the rights of the child, ensuring that they are provided with specific resources and responsibilities;**
b. mechanisms for data collection or focal points, at the national or local levels and in collaboration with civil society, for the purpose of observing and evaluating the phenomenon of sexual exploitation and sexual abuse of children, with due respect for the requirements of personal data protection.

3. Each Party shall encourage co-operation between the competent state authorities, civil society and the private sector, in order to better prevent and combat sexual exploitation and sexual abuse of children.

Chapter IV – Protective measures and assistance to victims

Article 11 – Principles

1. Each Party shall establish effective social programmes and set up **multidisciplinary structures to provide the necessary support for victims, their close relatives and for any person who is responsible for their care.**

2. Each Party shall take the necessary legislative or other measures to ensure that when the age of the victim is uncertain and there are reasons to believe that the victim is a child, the protection and assistance measures provided for children shall be accorded to him or her pending verification of his or her age.

Article 12 – Reporting suspicion of sexual exploitation or sexual abuse

1. Each Party shall take the necessary legislative or other measures to ensure that the **confidentiality rules** imposed by internal law on certain professionals called upon to work in contact with children **do not constitute an obstacle** to the possibility, for those professionals, of their reporting to the services responsible for child protection any situation where they have reasonable grounds for believing that a child is the victim of sexual exploitation or sexual abuse.

2. Each Party shall take the necessary legislative or other measures to encourage any person who knows about or suspects, in good faith, sexual exploitation or sexual abuse of children to **report** these facts to the competent services.

Article 13 – Helplines

Each Party shall take the necessary legislative or other measures to encourage and support the setting up of information services, such as telephone or Internet helplines, to provide advice to callers, even confidentially or with due regard for their anonymity.

Article 14 – Assistance to victims

1. Each Party shall take the necessary legislative or other measures to assist victims, in the short and long term, in their **physical and psycho-social recovery**. Measures taken pursuant to this paragraph shall take due account of the child's views, needs and concerns.

2. Each Party shall take measures, under the conditions provided for by its internal law, to co-operate with non-governmental organisations, other relevant organisations or other elements of civil society engaged in assistance to victims.

3. When the **parents** or persons who have care of the child are involved in his or her sexual exploitation or sexual abuse, the intervention procedures taken in application of Article 11, paragraph 1, shall include:

- the possibility of **removing the alleged perpetrator**;
- the possibility of **removing the victim from his or her family environment**. The conditions and duration of such removal shall be determined in accordance with the **best interests of the child**.

4. Each Party shall take the necessary legislative or other measures to ensure that the persons who are close to the victim may benefit, where appropriate, from **therapeutic assistance**, notably emergency psychological care.

Chapter V – Intervention programmes or measures

Article 15 – General principles

1. Each Party shall ensure or promote, in accordance with its internal law, effective intervention programmes or measures for the persons referred to in Article 16, paragraphs 1 and 2, with a view to preventing and minimising the risks of repeated offences of a sexual nature against children. Such programmes or measures shall be accessible at any time during the proceedings, inside and outside prison, according to the conditions laid down in internal law.

2. Each Party shall ensure or promote, in accordance with its internal law, the development of partnerships or other forms of co-operation between the competent authorities, in particular health-care services and the social services, and the judicial authorities and other bodies responsible for the follow-up of the persons referred to in Article 16, paragraphs 1 and 2.

3. Each Party shall provide, in accordance with its internal law, for an assessment of the dangerousness and possible risks of repetition of the offences established in accordance with this Convention, by the persons referred to in Article 16, paragraphs 1 and 2, with the aim of identifying appropriate programmes or measures.

4. Each Party shall, in accordance with its internal law, provide for assessing the effectiveness of the programmes and measures implemented.

Article 16 – Recipients of intervention programmes and measures

1. Each Party shall ensure, in accordance with its internal law, that persons subject to criminal proceedings for any of the offences established in accordance with this Convention may have access to the programmes or measures mentioned in Article 15, paragraph 1, under conditions which are neither detrimental nor contrary to the rights of the defence and to the requirements of a fair and impartial trial, and particularly with due respect for the rules governing the principle of the presumption of innocence.

2. Each Party shall ensure, in accordance with its internal law, that persons convicted of any of the offences established in accordance with this Convention

may have access to the programmes or measures mentioned in Article 15, paragraph 1.

3. Each Party shall ensure, in accordance with its internal law, that intervention programmes or measures are developed or adapted to meet the **developmental needs of children who sexually offend**, including those who are below the age of criminal responsibility, with the aim of addressing their sexual behavioural problems.

Article 17 – Information and consent

1. Each Party shall ensure, in accordance with its internal law, that the persons referred to in Article 16 to whom intervention programmes or measures have been proposed are fully informed of the reasons for the proposal and consent to the programme or measure with full knowledge of the facts.

2. Each Party shall ensure, in accordance with its internal law, that persons to whom intervention programmes or measures have been proposed may refuse them and, in the case of convicted persons, that they are made aware of the possible consequences a refusal might have.

Chapter VI – Substantive criminal law

Article 18 – Sexual abuse

1. Each Party shall take the necessary legislative or other measures to ensure that the following intentional conduct is criminalised:

a. engaging in sexual activities with a child who, according to the relevant provisions of national law, has not reached the legal age for sexual activities;
b. engaging in sexual activities with a child where:
   - use is made of coercion, force or threats; or
   - abuse is made of a recognised position of trust, authority or influence over the child, including within the family; or
   - abuse is made of a particularly vulnerable situation of the child, notably because of a mental or physical disability or a situation of dependence.

2. For the purpose of paragraph 1 above, each Party shall decide the age below which it is prohibited to engage in sexual activities with a child.

3. The provisions of Article 18, paragraph 1*a* do not intend to govern consensual sexual activities between minors.

Article 19 – Offences concerning child prostitution

1. Each Party shall take the necessary legislative or other measures to ensure that the following intentional conduct is criminalised:

a. recruiting a child into prostitution or causing a child to participate in prostitution;
b. coercing a child into prostitution or profiting from or otherwise exploiting a child for such purposes;
c. having recourse to child prostitution.

2. For the purpose of the present article, the term "child prostitution" shall mean the fact of using a child for sexual activities where money or any other form of remuneration or consideration is given or promised as payment, regardless if this payment, promise or consideration is made to the child or to a third person.

Article 20 – Offences concerning child pornography
1. Each Party shall take the necessary legislative or other measures to ensure that the following intentional conduct, when committed without right, is criminalised:

a. producing child pornography;
b. offering or making available child pornography;
c. distributing or transmitting child pornography;
d. procuring child pornography for oneself or for another person;
e. possessing child pornography;
f. knowingly obtaining access, through information and communication technologies, to child pornography.

2. For the purpose of the present article, the term "child pornography" shall mean any material that visually depicts a child engaged in real or simulated sexually explicit conduct or any depiction of a child's sexual organs for primarily sexual purposes.

3. Each Party may reserve the right not to apply, in whole or in part, paragraph 1*a* and *e* to the production and possession of pornographic material:

- consisting exclusively of simulated representations or realistic images of a non-existent child;
- involving children who have reached the age set in application of Article 18, paragraph 2, where these images are produced and possessed by them with their consent and solely for their own private use.

4. Each Party may reserve the right not to apply, in whole or in part, paragraph 1*f*.

Article 21 – Offences concerning the participation of a child in pornographic performances

1. Each Party shall take the necessary legislative or other measures to ensure that the following intentional conduct is criminalised:

a. recruiting a child into participating in pornographic performances or causing a hild to participate in such performances;
b. coercing a child into participating in pornographic performances or profiting from or otherwise exploiting a child for such purposes;
c. knowingly attending pornographic performances involving the participation of children.

2. Each Party may reserve the right to limit the application of paragraph 1*c* to cases where children have been recruited or coerced in conformity with paragraph 1*a* or *b*.

Article 22 – Corruption of children

Each Party shall take the necessary legislative or other measures to criminalise the intentional causing, for sexual purposes, of a child who has not reached the age set in application of Article 18, paragraph 2, to witness sexual abuse or sexual activities, even without having to participate.

Article 23 – Solicitation of children for sexual purposes

Each Party shall take the necessary legislative or other measures to criminalise the intentional proposal, through information and communication technologies, of an adult to meet a child who has not reached the age set in application of Article 18, paragraph 2, for the purpose of committing any of the offences established in accordance with Article 18, paragraph 1*a*, or Article 20, paragraph 1*a*, against him or her, where this proposal has been followed by material acts leading to such a meeting.

Article 24 – Aiding or abetting and attempt

1. Each Party shall take the necessary legislative or other measures to establish as criminal offences when committed intentionally, aiding or abetting the commission of any of the offences established in accordance with this Convention.

2. Each Party shall take the necessary legislative or other measures to establish as criminal offences, when committed intentionally, an attempt to commit the offences established in accordance with this Convention.

3. Each Party may reserve the right not to apply, in whole or in part, paragraph 2 to offences established in accordance with Article 20, paragraph 1*b*, *d*, *e* and *f*, Article 21, paragraph 1*c*, Article 22 and Article 23.

Article 25 – Jurisdiction
1. Each Party shall take the necessary legislative or other measures to establish jurisdiction over any offence established in accordance with this Convention, when the offence is committed: (…)

Article 27 – Sanctions and measures
1. Each Party shall take the necessary legislative or other measures to ensure that the offences established in accordance with this Convention are punishable by effective, proportionate and dissuasive sanctions, taking into account their seriousness. These sanctions shall include penalties involving deprivation of liberty which can give rise to extradition.

(…)

4. Each Party may adopt other measures in relation to perpetrators, such as withdrawal of parental rights or monitoring or supervision of convicted persons.

(…)

Article 28 – Aggravating circumstances
Each Party shall take the necessary legislative or other measures to ensure that the following circumstances, in so far as they do not already form part of the constituent elements of the offence, may, in conformity with the relevant provisions of internal law, be taken into consideration as aggravating circumstances in the determination of the sanctions in relation to the offences established in accordance with this Convention:

a. the offence seriously damaged the physical or mental health of the victim;
b. the offence was preceded or accompanied by acts of torture or serious violence;
c. the offence was committed against a particularly vulnerable victim;
d. the offence was committed by a member of the family, a person cohabiting with the child or a person having abused his or her authority;
e. the offence was committed by several people acting together;
f. the offence was committed within the framework of a criminal organisation;
g. the perpetrator has previously been convicted of offences of the same nature.

Chapter VII – Investigation, prosecution and procedural law

Article 30 – Principles

1. Each Party shall take the necessary legislative or other measures to ensure that investigations and criminal proceedings are carried out in the **best interests and respecting the rights of the child.**

2. Each Party shall adopt a protective approach towards victims, ensuring that the investigations and criminal proceedings **do not aggravate the trauma** experienced by the child and that the criminal justice response is followed by assistance, where appropriate.

3. Each Party shall ensure that the investigations and criminal proceedings are treated as priority and carried out without any unjustified delay.

4. Each Party shall ensure that the measures applicable under the current chapter are not prejudicial to the rights of the defence and the requirements of a fair and impartial trial, in conformity with Article 6 of the Convention for the Protection of Human Rights and Fundamental Freedoms.

5. Each Party shall take the necessary legislative or other measures, in conformity with the fundamental principles of its internal law:

- to ensure an effective investigation and prosecution of offences established in accordance with this Convention, allowing, where appropriate, for the **possibility of covert operations**;
- to enable units or investigative services to identify the victims of the offences established in accordance with Article 20, in particular by analysing child pornography material, such as photographs and audiovisual recordings transmitted or made available through the use of information and communication technologies.

Article 31 – General measures of protection

1. Each Party shall take the necessary legislative or other measures to protect the rights and interests of victims, including their special needs as witnesses, at all stages of investigations and criminal proceedings, in particular by:

a. informing them of their rights and the services at their disposal and, unless they do not wish to receive such information, the follow-up given to their complaint, the charges, the general progress of the investigation or proceedings, and their role as well as the outcome of their cases;
b. ensuring, at least in cases where the victims and their families might be in danger, that they may be informed, if necessary, when the person prosecuted or convicted is released temporarily or definitively;

c. enabling them, in a manner consistent with the procedural rules of internal law, to be heard, to supply evidence and to chose the means of having their views, needs and concerns presented, directly or through an intermediary, and considered;
d. providing them with appropriate support services so that their rights and interests are duly presented and taken into account;
e. protecting their privacy, their identity and their image and by taking measures in accordance with internal law to prevent the public dissemination of any information that could lead to their identification;
f. providing for their safety, as well as that of their families and witnesses on their behalf, from intimidation, retaliation and repeat victimisation;
g. ensuring that contact between victims and perpetrators within court and law enforcement agency premises is avoided, unless the competent authorities establish otherwise in the best interests of the child or when the investigations or proceedings require such contact.

2. Each Party shall ensure that victims have access, as from their first contact with the competent authorities, to information on relevant judicial and administrative proceedings.

3. Each Party shall ensure that victims have access, provided free of charge where warranted, to legal aid when it is possible for them to have the status of parties to criminal proceedings.

4. Each Party shall provide for the possibility for the judicial authorities to appoint a special representative for the victim when, by internal law, he or she may have the status of a party to the criminal proceedings and where the holders of parental responsibility are precluded from representing the child in such proceedings as a result of a conflict of interest between them and the victim.

5. Each Party shall provide, by means of legislative or other measures, in accordance with the conditions provided for by its internal law, the possibility for groups, foundations, associations or governmental or non-governmental organisations, to assist and/or support the victims with their consent during criminal proceedings concerning the offences established in accordance with this Convention.

6. Each Party shall ensure that the information given to victims in conformity with the provisions of this article is done so in a manner adapted to their age and maturity and in a language that they can understand.

Article 32 – Initiation of proceedings

Each Party shall take the necessary legislative or other measures to ensure that investigations or prosecution of offences established in accordance with this Convention shall not be dependent upon the report or accusation made by a victim, and that the proceedings may continue even if the victim has withdrawn his or her statements.

Article 33 – Statute of limitation
Each Party shall take the necessary legislative or other measures to ensure that the statute of limitation for initiating proceedings with regard to the offences established in accordance with Articles 18, 19, paragraph 1*a* and *b*, and 21, paragraph 1*a* and *b* shall continue for a period of time sufficient to allow the efficient starting of proceedings after the victim has reached the age of majority and which is commensurate with the gravity of the crime in question.

Article 34 – Investigations
1. Each Party shall adopt such measures as may be necessary to ensure that persons, units or services in charge of investigations are specialised in the field of combating sexual exploitation and sexual abuse of children or that persons are trained for this purpose. Such units or services shall have adequate financial resources.

2. Each Party shall take the necessary legislative or other measures to ensure that uncertainty as to the actual age of the victim shall not prevent the initiation of criminal investigations.

Article 35 – Interviews with the child
1. Each Party shall take the necessary legislative or other measures to ensure that:

a. interviews with the child take place without unjustified delay after the facts have been reported to the competent authorities;
b. interviews with the child take place, where necessary, in premises designed or adapted for this purpose;
c. interviews with the child are carried out by professionals trained for this purpose;
d. the same persons, if possible and where appropriate, conduct all interviews with the child;
e. the number of interviews are as limited as possible and in so far as necessary for the purpose of criminal proceedings;
f. the child may be accompanied by his or her legal representative or, where appropriate, an adult of his or her choice, unless a reasoned decision has been made to the contrary in respect of that person.

2. Each Party shall take the necessary legislative or other measures to ensure that all interviews with the victim or, where appropriate, those with a child witness,

may be videotaped and that these videotaped interviews may be accepted as evidence during the court proceedings, according to the rules provided by its internal law.

3. When the age of the victim is uncertain and there are reasons to believe that the victim is a child, the measures established in paragraphs 1 and 2 shall be applied pending verification of his or her age.

Article 36 – Criminal court proceedings

1. Each Party shall take the necessary legislative or other measures, with due respect for the rules governing the autonomy of legal professions, to ensure that training on children's rights and sexual exploitation and sexual abuse of children is available for the benefit of all persons involved in the proceedings, in particular judges, prosecutors and lawyers.

2. Each Party shall take the necessary legislative or other measures to ensure, according to the rules provided by its internal law, that:

a. the judge may order the hearing to take place without the presence of the public;
b. the victim may be heard in the courtroom without being present, notably through the use of appropriate communication technologies.

Chapter VIII – Recording and storing of data

Article 37 – Recording and storing of national data on convicted sexual offenders

1. For the purposes of prevention and prosecution of the offences established in accordance with this Convention, each Party shall take the necessary legislative or other measures to collect and store, in accordance with the relevant provisions on the protection of personal data and other appropriate rules and guarantees as prescribed by domestic law, data relating to the identity and to the genetic profile (DNA) of persons convicted of the offences established in accordance with this Convention.

(…)

Chapter XI – Relationship with other international instruments

Article 42 – Relation to the United Nations Convention on the Rights of the Child and its Optional Protocol on the sale of children, child prostitution and child pornography

This Convention shall not affect the rights and obligations arising from the provisions of the United Nations Convention on the Rights of the Child and its Optional Protocol on the sale of children, child prostitution and child pornography, and is intended to enhance the protection afforded by them and develop and complement the standards contained therein.

(...)

TASK/TEXT 3.2: CHILD PORNOGRAPHY AND CHILD MOLESTING

Crinmail 900 – 24 July 2007, <www.crin.org>

USA: Debate on child pornography's link to molesting (20 July 2007)

NEW YORK, 19 July 2007 – Experts have often wondered what proportion of men who download explicit sexual images of children also molest them. A new government study of convicted internet offenders suggests that the number may be startlingly high: 85 per cent of the offenders said they had committed acts of sexual abuse against minors, from inappropriate touching to rape.

The study, which has not yet been published, is stirring a vehement debate among psychologists, law enforcement officers and prison officials, who cannot agree on how the findings should be presented or interpreted.

The research, carried out by psychologists at the Federal Bureau of Prisons, is the first in-depth survey of such online offenders' sexual behavior done by prison therapists who were actively performing treatment. Its findings have circulated privately among experts, who say they could have enormous implications for public safety and law enforcement.

Traffic in online child pornography has exploded in recent years, and the new study, some experts say, should be made public as soon as possible, to identify men who claim to be "just looking at pictures" but could, in fact, be predators.

Yet others say that the results, while significant, risk tarring some men unfairly. The findings, based on offenders serving prison time who volunteered for the study, do not necessarily apply to the large and diverse group of adults who have at some point downloaded child pornography, and whose behavior is far too variable to be captured by a single survey.

Adding to the controversy, the prison bureau in April ordered the paper withdrawn from a peer-reviewed academic journal where it had been accepted for publication, apparently concerned that the results might be misinterpreted. A spokeswoman for the bureau said the agency was reviewing a study of child pornography offenders but declined to comment further.

Ernie Allen, who leads the National Center for Missing and Exploited Children [<www.missingkids.com>], which is mandated to coordinate the nation's efforts to combat child pornography, said he was surprised that the full study had not been released. "This is the kind of research the public needs to know about," Mr Allen said. Others agreed that the report should be published but were more cautious about the findings. "The results could have tremendous implications for community safety and for individual liberties," said Dr. Fred Berlin, founder of the Johns Hopkins Sexual Disorders Clinic. "If people we thought were not dangerous are more so, then we need to know that and we should treat them that way. But if we're wrong, then their liberties aren't going to be fairly addressed."

Everyone agrees that researchers need to learn more about online consumers of illegal child images. The volume of material seized from computers appears to be doubling each year – the National Center collected more than eight million images of explicit child pornography in the last five years – and Attorney General Alberto R. Gonzales made child protection a national priority in 2006.

Those who are arrested on charges of possession or distribution of child pornography generally receive lighter sentences and shorter parole periods than sexual abusers. They do not fit any criminal stereotype; recent arrests have included politicians, police officers, teachers and businessmen.

"It's crucial to understand the sexual history of all these offenders, because sometimes the crime they were arrested for is the tip of the iceberg, and does not reflect their real patterns and interests," said Jill S. Levenson, an assistant professor of human services at Lynn University in Boca Raton, [Florida], and head of the ethics committee of the Association for the Treatment of Sexual Abusers.

Previous studies, based on surveys of criminal records, estimated that 30 per cent to 40 per cent of those arrested for possessing child pornography also had molested children.

The psychologists who conducted the new study, Andres E. Hernandez and Michael L. Bourke, focused on 155 male inmates who had volunteered to be treated at the Federal Correctional Institution in Butner, [North Carolina], according to a draft of the paper obtained by *The New York Times* from outside experts who want the study published.

The Butner clinic is the only residential program devoted to the treatment of sexual offenders in the federal prison system. The inmates in the study were all serving sentences for possession or distribution of child pornography.

About every six months as part of an 18-month treatment programme, they filled out a record of their sexual history, including a "victims list" tallying their previous victims of abuse. Therapists encouraged the men to be honest as part of their treatment, and the sexual histories were anonymous, according to the paper.

The psychologists compared these confessions with the men's criminal sexual histories at the time of sentencing. More than 85 per cent admitted to abusing at least one child, they found, compared with 26 per cent who were known to have committed any "hands on" offenses at sentencing. The researchers also counted many more total victims: 1,777, a more than 20-fold increase from the 75 identified when the men were sentenced.

Dr. Hernandez and Dr. Bourke concluded in the paper that "many Internet child pornography offenders may be undetected child molesters." But they also cautioned that offenders who volunteer for treatment may differ in their behaviour from those who do not seek treatment.

They submitted the paper to *The Journal of Family Violence*, a widely read peer-reviewed publication in the field, and it was accepted.

But in a letter obtained by *The Times*, dated April 3, Judi Garrett, an official of the Bureau of Prisons, requested that the editors of the journal withdraw the study, because it did not meet "agency approval."

Editors at *The Journal of Family Violence* did not respond to phone or email messages asking about the withdrawal.

Dr. Hernandez mentioned the research briefly during testimony before a Senate committee last year. But the bureau blocked Dr. Hernandez and Dr. Bourke from attending some law enforcement conferences to speak about the findings, said two prosecutors who did not want to be identified because they have a continuing work relationship with the bureau.

"We believe it unwise to generalize from limited observations gained in treatment or in records review to the broader population of persons who engage in such behaviour," a bureau official wrote to the organisers of a recent law enforcement conference, in a letter dated May 2 and given to *The Times* by an expert who is hoping the study will be published.

Some prosecutors say they could use the study to argue for stiffer sentences. While some outside researchers agreed that the risk of over-generalising the study's results was real, almost all the experts interviewed also said that the study should still be made public.

Dr. Peter Collins, who leads the Forensic Psychiatry Unit of the Ontario Provincial Police, called the findings "cutting-edge stuff."

"We're really on the cusp of learning more about these individuals and studies should be encouraged, not quashed," Dr. Collins said.

Understanding the relationship between looking at child pornography and sexually assaulting children is central to developing effective treatment, psychologists say.

It is not at all clear when, or in whom, the viewing spurs action or activates a latent, unconscious desire; or whether such images have little or no effect on the offender's subsequent behaviour. But the relationship probably varies widely.

"My concern is about sensationalism, about the way something like this is handled in the media," said Michael Miner, an associate professor in the department of family medicine at the University of Minnesota who treats sex offenders. "The public perception is that all of these guys will re-offend, and we know that just isn't true."

At least some men convicted of sexual abuse say that child pornography from the Internet fueled their urges. In a recent interview, one convicted pedophile serving a 14-year sentence in a Canadian federal prison said that looking at images online certainly gave him no release from his desires – exactly the opposite.

"Because there is no way I can look at a picture of a child on a video screen and not get turned on by that and want to do something about it," he said. "I knew that in my mind. I knew that in my heart. I didn't want it to happen, but it was going to happen."

How many offenders does he speak for? The study may help answer that question, some say.

"The penalties we seek, the vigour with which we prosecute – the very importance we give to child pornography cases – all of these things are affected by what we know about the offenders," said Leura G. Canary, the United States attorney for Middle Alabama who also leads the Attorney General's Working Group on Child Exploitation and Obscenity. "And right now we know very little."

See Optional Protocol to the Convention on the Rights of the Child on the sale of children, child prostitution and child pornography.

TASK/TEXT 3.3: CANADA – FIRST MANDATORY REPORTING LAW FOR CHILD PORNOGRAPHY

Crinmail 937 – 29 November 2007, <www.crin.org>

28 November 2007 – The Canadian province of Manitoba will bring forward the first legislation of its kind in Canada to compel all citizens, including computer

technicians and Internet service providers, to report any images or examples of child pornography.

The initiative is being introduced as an amendment to the province's Child and Family Services legislation by minister Gord MacIntosh and will expand the definition of child abuse, which already has a mandatory reporting law, to include child pornography.

"Under the new law, if someone comes across something they believe to be child pornography they have a duty to report it to Cybertip.ca," said Lianna McDonald, director of the Canadian Centre for Child Protection, the registered charity that runs the Cybertip website.

The penalty for failing to report will be up to two years in jail and a $50,000 fine, Ms. McDonald said. It's the same penalty for those who don't report child abuse, although Ms. McDonald said she doesn't know of any instances where that provision has led to a prosecution.

"What it means is that under the proposed legislation, [citizens] have a legal responsibility," she said. "The idea is to facilitate reporting."

Ms. McDonald said that making it a legal requirement might remove some of the moral qualms that exist for those who find images of abuse on a computer, for example, and might be concerned about violating someone's privacy.

"It certainly will facilitate things for people thinking, 'Should I or shouldn't I report?' It makes it clear. For companies that repair computers, it's clear they have a duty to report," she said.

The proposed law could have significant implications for Internet service providers, according to Roz Prober of Beyond Borders, an organization that advocates for the protection of children.

It's already mandatory in the United States for Internet service providers to report instances of child pornography, but the issue has not been tackled in Canada until now.

"The foot-draggers in this scenario are the Internet service providers," Ms. Prober said. "In the US they can be heavily fined [for not reporting child porn] and I think that's the way to go here."

Ms. Prober said she hasn't seen the proposed legislation but expects it to be comprehensive. Citizens will be directed to report their suspicions to the Cybertip.ca website. The site receives funding from the federal Department of Public Safety and from Manitoba Justice, Ms. McDonald said, and since 2005 it has acted as a national clearinghouse for all Internet child sexual-abuse reporting. In that time, it has received more than 25,000 reports from the public.

Ms. Prober said the site is very sophisticated and secure and would be able to resist attempts to infiltrate its database. She said it's important the public pass on as many tips as possible because each new image allows police to narrow in on the victims and perpetrators of sexual abuse.

TASK/TEXT 3.4: UK HAS 5,000 CHILD PROSTITUTES

Crinmail 910 – 28 August 2007, <www.crin.org> [Source: The Guardian; <www.guardian.co.uk>]

22 August 2007 – The UK has 5,000 child prostitutes, a report into slavery claims. And Save The Children's Small Hands Of Slavery claims millions of youngsters are regularly attacked and raped in their lives as child slaves. The shocking figures were released to coincide with Slavery Remembrance Day, the bicentenary of the trade's abolition.

Bill Bell, Save the Children's head of protection, said: "Child slavery is not a thing of the past. There are still millions of children in both rich and poor countries who are being forced to lead slave-like lives under horrific conditions of humiliation and abuse. Currently across the world there are, for example, 1.8 million children trapped in the sex trade, over a million children risking their lives working in mines, and millions more, some as young as six, forced to work up to 15 hour days as domestic workers. These children are treated as commodities, liable to be lent or sold to other owners without warning. World leaders and international donors must act with urgency to address child slavery and put in place the laws and resources needed to eradicate these terrible practices."

The report states that 1.2 million children and babies are trafficked every year, including into Western Europe, the Americas and the Caribbean, and the number is increasing. Gangs involved in child and people trafficking make an estimated profit of 32 billion dollars (£16 billion) per year, the charity said.

Approximately 1.8 million children are being abused through prostitution, child pornography and sex tourism – and 75% of the UK's child prostitutes are girls.

The report states that youngsters often lose their childhood by being sold into adult relationships. The report states: "Child marriage, which often includes mail order and internet brides, is one of the most widespread – yet hidden – forms of slavery. Girls as young as four are forced to live and have sex with their husband, and are often kept trapped indoors. Girls under 15 are five times more likely to die during pregnancy and childbirth than women over 20. In Afghanistan more than half of all girls are married before they are 16."

TASK/TEXT 3.5: THIRD WORLD CONGRESS ON COMMERCIAL SEXUAL EXPLOITATION (BRAZIL)

Crinmail 944 – 27 December 2007, <www.crin.org>; <www.ecpat.net/World_Congress/en/background.html>

The fight against CSEC

Global efforts to combat the commercial sexual exploitation of children (CSEC) began more than a decade ago with a campaign that focused the world's attention on the problem. NGOs around the world were galvanized to document the problem, propose action needed and call on governments to address the issue. Through close collaboration that enabled them to mobilize the necessary support, UNICEF, the NGO Group for the Convention on the Rights of the Child (CRC), ECPAT International and the Government of Sweden successfully organized the First World Congress against Commercial Sexual Exploitation of Children, held in Stockholm, Sweden in 1996.

1996 Stockholm (1st) World Congress against CSEC

The Congress attracted world attention to CSEC, which was largely unrecognized at the time. It mobilized support from a broad range of stakeholders, involving governments, NGOs, children, civil society groups, academics, police and many others. This event had several unique elements including the joint presence and participation of NGOs with government representatives which broke away from the structure of NGO parallel or side meetings. Most importantly it also included the participation of children and young people which added to the ground breaking nature of the Stockholm Congress. Since the First World Congress, the **Declaration** and **Agenda** have become essential tools for mobilizing action to protect children from sexual exploitation.

2001 Yokohama (2nd) World Congress

In 2001, a Second World Congress was held in Yokohama, Japan to review progress in protecting children against sexual exploitation. This Congress strengthened and consolidated worldwide partnerships made since the First World Congress, and reinforced global commitment to protect children from sexual exploitation and sexual abuse. It also provided growing and more in-depth knowledge and experience on different aspects of CSEC. Among the agreed outcomes were the necessity to tackle both supply taken together as a means of combating CSEC effectively and the importance of increased child and youth participation.

2004–5 Mid-term Review

Following the Second World Congress, Mid-Term Review meetings were organized for the first time in all the regions of the world over the period 2004–2005. These assessments demonstrated some consistent trends across regions, for example, a positive movement to amend or enact new laws to protect children from different forms of sexual exploitation. However, these developments were still not matched by improvement in application of the law or providing care for child survivors. Recognizing that governments and other actors have many competing agendas that can draw their attention away from the more complex social problems which require long term engagement, resources and support, those actively working to combat CSEC have underscored the importance of maintaining government attention and action on the issue.

2008 World Congress

In preparation for the Third World Congress, the **NGO Group for the Convention on the Rights of the Child** and **ECPAT International** agreed to conduct a broad consultation with their members and with other concerned groups and individuals. This is to ensure that the structure, content and outcomes of the Congress reflect the aims of all those who strive to reinforce the rights of children to live free from all forms of sexual exploitation.

In preparation for the Congress we have formulated some questions based on recommendations that emerged from the Mid-Term Reviews (MTR) and those that have been highlighted by groups working directly to combat sexual exploitation and abuse. Your feedback is essential to ensure a truly representative approach in building the agendas for the next Congress.

A recent study conducted by the Focal Point Programme of the NGO Group shows that reports to the Committee for the Convention on the Rights of the Child, contain more references to violations related to CSEC than to the violation of any other right.

Although global awareness of sexual abuse and violence against children is ever increasing, the MTRs highlighted that this awareness is not always followed by action. More follow up is still required to ensure that government commitments are implemented.

TASK/TEXT 3.6: CHILD ON CHILD ABUSE

ISPCAN-list – Child Internet Exploitation – January 16, 2008

Colleagues, – Although I do not doubt the importance of addressing the risk of online predation via the internet there is the "elephant in the room" for which little attention is given. "The elephant" is the huge increase in child on child sexual victimization that I believe is the direct result of exposure to pornography by young, immature and at times socially isolated adolescent males on the internet either through random exposure and/or curiosity. As a result of this exposure to pornography these males usually between 10 & 14 then act out what they have seen with those who they have easy access and control over. The victims are generally younger siblings & cousins.

At our Institute approximately 1/3 of the cases we see now are child on child (…). I think this problem eclipses the risk of sexual victimization on the internet. (…) As many children have expressed in one manner or another: "He made me watch that disgusting stuff and he then did the same to me."

– Martin A. Finkel, D.O., FACOP, FAAP, Professor of Pediatrics – Medical Director CARES [Child Abuse Research Education & Service] Institute University of Medicine and Dentistry of New Jersey School of Osteopathic Medicine, Stratford, New Jersey

January 17, 2008

I concur with Dr. Finkel. As a career Juvenile Detective and Child Abuse Investigator the issue is the child on child abuse. I am seeing a rise in offenses as well as a rise in the severity of sexual abuse cases committed by juveniles, as well as a new evolving etiology for perpetration. Access and exposure to Internet Porn is serving both to create as well as condition the problematic behavior. Although there are "exceptions to every rule" I feel comfortable in stating that the vast majority of Juvenile Sex Offenders are "Heavy Internet Pornography Abusers." As well, this viewing in and of itself is, (not singularly) a significant contributor to the onset of predation of the stated, younger siblings, cousins, classmates etc.

– Detective Mike Johnson, Criminal Investigation Division, Plano Police Department, USA

January 17, 2008

I totally agree with this "elephant in the room" threat, i.e. exposure of children to pornography via internet. Some studies conducted by the Pakistan Pediatric Association have clearly demonstrated an alarmingly higher ratio of children (almost 70%) being exposed to web-based pornographic stuff on a daily

basis. It is a process of grooming that has the potential to turn the child into a child abuser and at the same time becomes more vulnerable to be abused him/herself.
– Dr. Tufail Muhammad, Pakistan Pediatric Association

February 7, 2008

While we agree that exposing children to pornography is exploitative and abusive, your point beckons a point that was raised in research by Mark Chaffin and Bill Friedrich. **Family dysfunction** has the highest correlation to sexual acting out behavior in pre-pubescent children. Boundary violations are exemplified in these families, conveying the message that it is OK to do to others as one wishes. Also, children in these families often feel powerless and angry, and the sexual contact – often with siblings but also often with younger neighbors – provides a way to feel powerful and in control. Again, this is modeled behavior, as the children experience their parents and/or older siblings exerting power and control over them. We often saw this in our outpatient programs. Against this backdrop, the experience of being sexualized, whether through contact by others or exposure to explicit sexuality, provides an outlet for the sexual expression or sexual aggression. I have seen this in cases where there are no televisions or internet in the homes.

Also, in reference to Mike Johnson's observations, yes, Internet porn is a serious factor in the backgrounds of juvenile sex offenders, but we should be careful in looking at different etiologies in Juvenile Sex Offenders (JSO's), who are pubescent, versus children with sexual behavior problems. Family dysfunction is common to both populations, but the adolescents are able to act more independently of the family. Children with sexual behavior problems are still children.
– Doug Martinez, Ph.D., Clinical Psychologist, Montclair, New Jersey, USA

TASK/TEXT 3.7: 18,000 WOMEN AND CHILDREN TRAFFICKED INTO UK SEX TRADE

Crinmail 996 – 3 July 2008, <www.crin.org>

LONDON, 3 July 2008 – Up to 18,000 females, including girls as young as 14, are working in brothels across Britain after being smuggled into the country to meet the booming demand for prostitutes. Police, unveiling the results of the largest ever crackdown on people smuggling yesterday, revealed that nearly five times more women than previously thought are working under duress in massage parlours and suburban homes.

Operation Pentameter 2, a six-month campaign by police forces across the country, resulted in the release of 154 women and 13 girls put to work as part of a lucrative trade dominated by organised crime gangs, which increasingly co-operate via the internet to maximise earnings from their victims.

The campaign, which saw the arrest of 528 suspected traffickers and the closure of 822 brothels and premises being used to sell sexual services, also revealed an increasing use of young British women, who are trafficked within the UK after being groomed by older men who lure them to towns away from their homes. The Home Office highlighted one recent case in Sheffield where 33 victims had been recruited by men in public places and taken away for sexual exploitation.

Most victims are foreign, with least 85 per cent of the women working as prostitutes coming from countries including Brazil, China, Lithuania and Thailand. Many victims are lured to Britain with false promises of work in bars or nightclubs only to be sold for up to £5,000, often at airports or service stations, to pimps and brothel-keepers. The women are then set quotas of the number of men they must have sex with each week, working for little or nothing under threat of violence against their families.

Tim Brain, the Chief Constable of Gloucestershire, whose force co-ordinated Pentameter 2, said that police forces were becoming more effective in tracing prostitution networks and seizing their assets, but admitted that they remained a significant problem. The first phase of Pentameter in 2006 rescued 88 victims and made 232 arrests.

The Government insisted that the success of the campaign, which has resulted in 24 convictions, was evidence of its determination to hinder the work of the gangs behind sex trafficking. Of the 167 women and teenagers released, all but five were being used as prostitutes. The rest, of whom three were children, had been sold as domestic slaves.

Mr Brain also revealed that a large number of residential properties were being used to sell sex (of the 822 premises raided, nearly 600 were private homes). "In some of the cases, neighbours have not suspected any kind of unusual activity," he said.

Prostitution and people-trafficking is now the third most lucrative black-market trade in the world after gun-running and drugs-smuggling. It is being driven by growing demand for prostitutes in the UK, with websites promoting sex flourishing and local newspapers carrying advertisements for prostitutes. Gangs often share the income from internet "bookings."

Ministers also said children were being trafficked into Britain to grow cannabis or to join street crime gangs. There are plans for a further crackdown on fraudsters who smuggle children to make bogus welfare claims.

Olena's story

Olena, 23, escaped last year from a brothel in Sheffield:

> "I come from a very poor area of Ukraine. I went to Moldova with a friend who said he could help me get work, but he sold me to some Albanians. They locked me in their house, raped me and beat me regularly. I was taken to the UK, to a massage parlour in Sheffield, where I was forced to see up to 15 clients a day but could not keep any of the money. The men visited my mother and told her that if I returned home they would kill me."

Sex trafficking in numbers

- 6,000–18,000 Trafficked women are thought to work as prostitutes in Britain
- 167 Victims identified in a police operation to free them
- 13 Victims aged between 14 and 17
- £500,000 Amount seized in brothel raids
- 500,000 Number of women trafficked into the EU each year.

TASK/TEXT 3.8: NEW PROPOSALS WILL MAKE ALL OBSCENE IMAGES OF CHILDREN ILLEGAL

News Distribution Service, <http://nds.coi.gov.uk>, Advanced search, Ministry of Justice, 28 May 2008

All images of child sexual abuse, including drawings and computer-generated images of child abuse will be illegal and offenders holding such images will face criminal charges and up to three years in prison under new proposals announced by Justice Minister Maria Eagle today.

The proposals were announced as part of the Government's response to a public consultation on the possession of non-photographic visual depictions of under-aged children engaged in sexual activity. It acknowledges the view that paedophiles could be circumventing the law by using computer technology to manipulate real photographs or videos of abuse into drawings or cartoons.

Commenting, Maria Eagle, Parliamentary under Secretary of State for Justice, said:

"These new proposals will help close a loophole that we believe paedophiles are using to create images of child sexual abuse.

"This is not about criminalising art or pornographic cartoons more generally, but about targeting obscene, and often very realistic, images of child sexual abuse which have no place in our society."

The distribution or sale of material is currently illegal under the Obscene Publications Act, and possession of photos of child pornography is unlawful, but it is not yet a criminal offence to possess drawings and computer generated images of child abuse. The proposals announced today will create a new criminal offence to possess drawings and computer-generated images of under-aged children in sexual activity.

The Consultation on the Possession of Non-Photographic Visual Depictions of Child Sexual Abuse was launched by the Home Office on 2nd April 2007 and closed on 22nd June 2007. Government, <www.justice.gov.uk/publications/non-photographic-depictions.htm>.

TASK/TEXT 3.9: ENDING LAWFUL ASSAULT OF CHILDREN – A FOUNDATION FOR ELIMINATING SEXUAL EXPLOITATION AND ABUSE

Global Initiative to End All Corporal Punishment of Children, <www.endcorporalpunishment.org>, 31 July 2008

Briefing in preparation for the World Congress III against Sexual Exploitation of Children, 25–28 November 2008, Rio de Janeiro, Brazil

There can be no more potent symbol of the low status of children than the continuing legality of corporal punishment. Prohibiting corporal punishment is a huge step towards the recognition of children as human beings and rights-holders. Sexual and other exploitation of children depends on viewing them as objects, as possessions that adults can do what they want with. Prohibiting corporal punishment – putting children on an equal footing with adults when it comes to attacks on their physical integrity – finally removes the legal basis for this view.

Prohibiting and eliminating corporal punishment is important in the fight against sexual exploitation. Giving children equal protection from assault under the law will end the legal reinforcement of the idea that children deserve less protection from violence than adults – a situation which underpins the commodification of children who are sexually exploited.

Prohibiting corporal punishment will ensure that the legal frameworks put in place to address sexual exploitation extend to contributing factors.

Replacing corporal punishment in families with positive parenting and non-violent relationships between adults and children will strengthen and protect families, reducing children's vulnerability to sexual exploitation.

The widespread legality and social approval of corporal punishment markedly increases children's vulnerability to exploitation. The fact that corporal punishment of children is lawful, when laws in all states criminalise even the most minor assaults on adults, reflects and reinforces the low status of children as less than human, as objects and possessions – the very status that allows them to become economic commodities in the sex trade.

Prohibiting corporal punishment of children gives them equal protection under the criminal law from assault, wherever they are and whoever the perpetrator is. This provides fundamental protection from all forms of assault, and asserts children's right to full respect for their physical integrity and human dignity. Prohibition is an essential element of the strategy to eliminate sexual abuse and exploitation of children.

We urge you to support the inclusion in the Outcome Document of the World Congress III on Sexual Exploitation of Children of an explicit recommendation for full prohibition of all violence against children – including all corporal punishment and other cruel and degrading forms of punishment of boys and girls (echoing key recommendation 2 of the UNSG's Study on Violence Against Children).

Violent punishment contributes to sexual exploitation

Corporal punishment – and its legality – contributes to children's vulnerability to sexual exploitation and abuse in a number of ways:

- The widespread practice of physically hurting children in the name of punishment or "discipline" violates their physical integrity and human dignity, and makes other physical and sexual invasion "easier" and more likely. The legality of violent punishment undermines the rights-based challenge to all violence against children – including sexual abuse and exploitation.
- The lack of zero tolerance of violence against children, in the law and in social attitudes, impedes the prevention of all forms of violence and exploitation.
- Children often experience both corporal punishment and sexual abuse in the family. A home environment where a certain degree or kind of violence against children is condoned is an environment where boundaries are blurred and children are vulnerable.
- Some corporal punishment is sexual (e.g. spanking on bare buttocks), and much child pornography depicts scenes of physical punishment of children.
- Corporal punishment, and the threat of it, may be used to coerce children into sexual relationships within or outside the family and into other forms of sexual exploitation.

- Corporal punishment by parents is often the reason why children run away from home, making them more vulnerable to exploitation on the street.
- Corporal punishment is a common means of control over child labourers (including those in the sex trade) and over girls in conflict areas (who often become slave-wives).
- Experiencing corporal punishment has a negative impact on a child's emotional and interpersonal development and is associated, in adulthood, with aggression, poor mental health and risky sexual behaviour.

The CRC and its Optional Protocol

Implementation of the UN Convention on the Rights of the Child – and other regional and international human rights treaties – requires prohibition of all corporal punishment of children, including in the home. The Committee on the Rights of the Child has long recommended this to States parties, and in June 2006 consolidated its approach in General Comment No. 8 on "The right of the child to protection from corporal punishment." The Committee affirms that prohibiting and eliminating corporal punishment is "a key strategy for reducing and preventing all forms of violence in societies" (para. 3).

The preamble to the Optional Protocol on the sale of children, child prostitution and child pornography emphasises the importance of "a holistic approach," including "addressing the contributing factors." The legality and social approval of violent punishment is a contributing factor.

The emphasis on prevention in the Optional Protocol (article 9) supports the call for prohibition of corporal punishment to be included in strategies to address sexual exploitation. This is also stressed in the report of the UNSG's Study on Violence Against Children, which recommended prohibition of all violence against children, including corporal punishment, and set a target date of 2009.

> "*The Study should mark a turning point – an end to adult justification of violence against children, whether accepted as 'tradition' or disguised as 'discipline.' There can be no compromise in challenging violence against children. Children's uniqueness – their potential and vulnerability, their dependence on adults – makes it imperative that they have more, not less, protection from violence.*" (Professor Paulo Sérgio Pinheiro, Report to the General Assembly on the UN Study on Violence Against Children)

> "*Addressing the widespread acceptance or tolerance of corporal punishment of children and eliminating it, in the family, schools and other settings, is not only an obligation of States parties under the Convention. It is also a key strategy for reducing and preventing all forms of violence in societies.*" (Committee on the Rights of the Child, General Comment No. 8, para. 3)

"The UN Convention on the Rights of the Child must be used as a guiding tool for all legislation, plans of action, and services related to the fight against commercial and sexual exploitation of children. We believe that, if children's rights to survival, development, protection and participation are not ensured, we can NEVER eliminate commercial and sexual exploitation of children." (Children's Final Appeal, Second World Congress in Yokohoma, 2001)

TASK/TEXT 3.10: JAPAN – CHILD PORN CASES HIT RECORD HIGH

Crinmail 1006 – 12 August 2008, <www.crin.org>

TOKYO, 8 August 2008 – The number of child pornography cases uncovered in Japan soared 17.2 per cent from a year earlier to a record high in the first half of this year, police said this week. Police made arrests in 307 cases of production and distribution of pornography involving children aged below 18, the most for the first half of a year since comparable records began in 2000. The number of child victims identified by the police reached 165, also a record and up 36.4 per cent from a year earlier.

The report did not give a reason for the surge although local media quoted police as saying that it was linked to the spread of digital media, which allow easy copying.

The incidents identified by police are believed to be a fraction of the total in Japan, considered a major provider of child pornography. The United States and other developed countries have accused Japan of laxity in allowing child pornography. Lawmakers are reviewing the nation's 1999 child porn law to close a loophole allowing individual possession. The law bans production and sale of sexually arousing photos, videos and other materials involving children and their possession for commercial purposes or other distribution. But it does not cover individual possession.

The police report also said 166 children fell victim to abuse in the first half, also a record and up 5.7 per cent from a year earlier. Twenty-nine children died after being abused, including a 16-year-old boy whose mother and step father had beaten him, tied up his hands and legs and poured cold water over him in January, police said.

TASK/TEXT 3.11: LAUNCH OF THE 'STOPX' ONLINE COMMUNITY TO FIGHT CHILD SEXUAL EXPLOITATION

By Yvonne Lester, <www.unicef.org/protection/index_46639.html>

NEW YORK, USA, 28 November 2008 – To coincide with the opening of World Congress III on the Sexual Exploitation of Children and Adolescents in Brazil, UNICEF and partners launched <StopX.org>, an online community of young activists fighting sexual exploitation of children and adolescents.

StopX.org offers extensive resources on this issue, including links to other websites and national help lines for young people to call in an emergency. One of the site's main features is a private community where users are invited to collaborate with each other and showcase their work on fighting sexual exploitation.

"The site provides a powerful tool for young people, helping them become a positive force for change in their communities," said head of UNICEF's Division of Communication Youth Section Gerrit Beger.

Every child's right

Sexual exploitation happens everywhere – at school, at home or at work, in communities and online. UNICEF and partners are advocating for every child's right to freedom from sexual exploitation and abuse. Children and young people are demanding their right to protection and every one of us has a role to play in making this right a reality.

Please visit <StopX.org> to:

- Learn important facts about sexual exploitation of children and adolescents.
- Find information to help young people become leaders in the fight against sexual exploitation.
- Connect with other young activist groups from around the world, discuss ideas and experiences and propose solutions.
- Share videos, audio reports, pictures and articles produced by young people.
- Showcase projects to media outlets such as newspapers, television and radio stations.

TASK/TEXT 3.12: EXPLOITATION – VATICAN TO BE SUED OVER SEX ABUSE CLAIMS

Crinmail 1042 – 16 December 2008, <www.crin.org>

Three men who claim they were abused by Catholic clergy in America have succeeded in naming the Vatican as sole defendant in a lawsuit and are hoping to force Pope Benedict XVI to give evidence in the case.

The 6th US circuit court of appeal recently ruled that although the Holy See, as a sovereign state, was immune from most lawsuits, the plaintiffs could proceed with their argument that its officials were involved in a deliberate effort to cover up evidence of sexual abuse by American priests.

Their case centres on a 1962 directive from the Vatican telling church officials to hide sex abuse complaints against clergy.

William F. McMurray, a lawyer representing the men, who claim they were abused in Louisville, Kentucky, says the document, which became public in 2003, makes the Vatican liable for the acts of clergy whose crimes were kept secret because of the directive. He says the pope, at 81, is the only living witness to the establishment of the 1962 policy. Before his election to the papacy, Joseph Ratzinger spent 24 years heading the Vatican department charged with investigating and disciplining abusive priests, a role that would have led him to brief his predecessor, John Paul II, on the situation.

McMurray, who has spent four years working on the case, told the Guardian that the pope was the best-placed individual to reveal what was reported to the Congregation for the Doctrine of Faith, when and by whom.

"The fact he is pope does not change anything. He knew what nobody else knew and what the Vatican knew is crucial. They were supposed to be disciplining priests: how were they doing it? We would call him as a witness so I could find out what he did for two and a half decades."

The three men, who allege they were abused between the 1920s and 1970s, are seeking class action status on behalf of all US abuse victims. The US Catholic church has already paid out more than $2bn (£1.3bn; [€1.500.000.000]) since 1950.

Jeffrey Lena, the Vatican's attorney, has said the plaintiffs would find it difficult to establish the Vatican's liability for the sexual misconduct of US clergy.

TASK/TEXT 3.13: IRELAND – CHURCH 'ROUTINELY COVERED UP' CHILD SEXUAL ABUSE FOR 30 YEARS

Crinmail 1130 – 1 December 2009, <www.crin.org>

Four successive archbishops of Dublin responded to clerical child sexual abuse over a 30-year period in their diocese with "denial, arrogance and cover-up." This is one of the main conclusions of the report of the Commission of Investigation into the Catholic Archdiocese of Dublin.

The three-year inquiry, led by Judge Yvonne Murphy, found the "structures and rules" of the Catholic Church facilitated the cover-up. "The State authorities facilitated the cover up by not fulfilling their responsibilities to ensure that the law was applied equally to all and allowing the Church institutions to be beyond the reach of the normal law enforcement processes," the report also found. Minister for Justice Dermot Ahern, who published the report yesterday, said it documented "a scandal on an astonishing scale."

"Obsessive concern with secrecy"

The report also found current child protection laws did not provide adequate powers to health authorities to protect the welfare of children who are abused, or in danger of abuse, by people with privileged access to children. The report, which took three years to complete, said the archdiocese had an "obsessive concern with secrecy and the avoidance of scandal" and had "little or no concern for the welfare of the abused child." The commission investigated the handling of allegations made against a sample out of 46 priests out of 102 against whom complaints were made between 1975 and 2004.

Among its other main findings were:

- All archbishops and many of the auxiliary bishops in Dublin handled child sexual abuse complaints badly. None of the four archbishops reported their knowledge of abuse to gardaí [Irish police] "throughout the 1960s, 1970s or 1980s."
- Church authorities used the concept of "mental reservation," which allows senior clergy to mislead people without being guilty, in the church's eyes, of lying.
- Senior members of the gardaí regarded priests as outside their remit, with some members reporting complaints to the archdiocese instead of investigating them.
- It said there were some courageous priests who brought complaints to the attention of their superiors. But in general there was a "don't ask, don't tell" policy.

The report concluded that it is the responsibility of the State to ensure that no similar institutional immunity was ever allowed to occur again. Speaking at a press conference, Mr Ahern warned: "A collar will protect no criminal."

"Sorrow and shame"

Responding to the report yesterday, Archbishop of Dublin Diarmuid Martin said "no words of apology would ever be sufficient" and offered "to each and every survivor, my apology, my sorrow and my shame for what happened to them." Catholic Primate Cardinal Seán Brady also said he was deeply ashamed and saddened by the findings.

The report is likely to place pressure on a number of senior clergy. Asked if individuals named in the report should step down, Dr Martin said: "I have always expressed the position that every bishop should evaluate their ministry in terms of commitments they make in reality to the protection of children." Last night Cardinal Desmond Connell, who is criticised in the report for not promptly handing over information to gardaí, expressed "bitter regret that failures on my part contributed to the suffering of victims in any form." Bishop of Limerick Donal Murray, a former auxiliary bishop in the Dublin diocese and who is strongly criticised in the report, said he regretted his actions but did not intend to resign.

Responding to the report's severe criticism of gardaí, Garda Commissioner Fachtna Murphy said the report made for "difficult and disturbing reading", in particular the failure of State authorities to protect victims. The Government said it apologised "without reservation or equivocation" for failures by State agencies in dealing with the issue of clerical child abuse in the Dublin archdiocese.

Abuse victims said they felt vindicated by the report but expressed dismay that it took so long to expose wrongdoing, while campaign group One in Four called for the prosecution of those who covered up abuse. "This report is a shocking indictment on the Catholic Church in Dublin. Its publication, if not acted upon, will have been a wasted opportunity to raise standards of child protection in this country," said Andrew Madden, a victim of Fr Ivan Payne.

4. VIOLENCE AGAINST CHILDREN – CHILD MARRIAGE, CORPORAL PUNISHMENT AND OTHER TRADITIONAL PRACTICES

TASK/TEXT 4.1: CHILD MARRIAGE

Crinmail 899 – 19 July 2007, <www.crin.org>, Special edition on child marriage

"A girl came to our area after she got married to her husband. When she refused to have sex with him, he beat her up. Then my parents and some other people intervened. After that, she ran away in the middle of the night to her parents and said to them that she wants to go to school. But, since they refused to send her to school, they married her again. Then she hanged herself ... She didn't want that [marriage], but we don't have a choice." – Amhara girl (Ethiopia), age 15, married at age 4.

What is child marriage?
Child marriage involves the marriage of anyone below the age of 18. It is the marriage of a child to an adult or another child, and may be legally condoned by national laws. These marriages are often given legal sanction because of legislative loopholes that in fact camouflage the sexual exploitation of children. And while a child cannot be expected to appreciate all the implications of marriage and give full and informed consent to it, their wishes are generally overlooked in the arrangement of such a marriage.

Are both boys and girls involved?
Child marriages are arranged in various ways and involve both boys and girls. It is more usual for girls to be married to boys and men who are older than them while boys are more commonly married to girls of a similar age. Such marriages may be arranged between two very young children as a means of maintaining or ensuring social, economic or political ties between families. In other cases, girls may be married to much older men who are more able to pay the dowries expected or demanded by a family. As such, girls are often the vulnerable party in child marriages. Many children may know their marriage partner and have been raised with him or her. Others may be married to strangers.

Does marriage have to be 'forced' to violate children's rights?

Forced marriage is a marriage that is performed under duress and without the full and informed consent or free will of both parties. Being under duress includes feeling both physical and emotional pressure. Some victims of forced marriage are tricked into going to another country by their families. Victims fall prey to forced marriage through deception, abduction, coercion, fear, and inducements.

It is sometimes difficult to define what 'forced' means, and whether a child 'consented.' It may be easy to claim a person under the age of 18 said they agreed to marriage. However, if a person is under the age of eighteen, many believe they cannot have given their full and informed consent if their wishes were not taken into consideration throughout the marriage process. Clearly, the younger the child, the less able they are to give free and informed consent.

Why is it a problem?

Child marriage is a violation of human rights. It forces children to assume responsibilities and handle situations for which they are often physically and psychologically unprepared. In places where child marriage is practiced, girls rarely have any say in when and whom they marry. Once married, these young girls have little power and limited autonomy. Girls are frequently much younger than their spouses, and the younger a girl's age at marriage, the greater the age difference between her and her husband.

In its overarching recommendations, the UN study on Violence Against Children states the prohibition of violence "refers to legal reforms including implementation of laws to stop all forms of violence against children, in all settings, including all corporal punishment, harmful traditional practices, such as early and forced marriages, female genital mutilation and so-called honour crimes, sexual violence, and torture and other cruel, inhuman or degrading treatment or punishment, as required by international treaties."

Early marriage can have serious harmful consequences for children, including:

- Denial of girls' **education**. Once married, girls tend not to go to school, and so they lose out on the benefits of education: better health, lower fertility, and increased economic productivity. They also lose out on any form of sexuality education, which is rarely taught before secondary school.
- **Health** problems. These include premature pregnancies that cause higher rates of maternal and infant mortality. Most girls enter marriage with little or no information about their reproductive health, including contraception, safe motherhood, and sexually transmitted diseases. Because they cannot abstain from sex or insist on condom use, child brides are often exposed to such

serious health risks as premature pregnancy, sexually transmitted infections and, increasingly, HIV and AIDS.

- Child brides typically become sexually active as soon as they are married, and they face enormous pressure to bear children as soon as possible. Because their bodies are not fully developed, they are at greater risk of complications in pregnancy and childbirth. These complications can result in death – in many developing countries, pregnancy is the leading cause of death for adolescent girls – or ongoing health problems, such as obstetric fistula. Fistula is a debilitating condition that causes chronic incontinence and discomfort, and often results in extreme social isolation.
- **Abuse** – including **physical, emotional and sexual.** This is common in child marriages. In addition, children who refuse to marry or who choose a marriage partner against the wishes of their parents are often punished or even killed by their families in so-called 'honour killings.'
- **Separation** from families and friends.
- Lack of **freedom** to interact with peers and participate in community activities.
- Involvement in **bonded labour** such as domestic slavery.

Where does it happen?

The practice of girls marrying at a young age is most common in sub-Saharan Africa and South Asia. However, in the Middle East, North Africa and other parts of Asia, marriage at, or shortly after, puberty is common among some groups. There are also parts of West and Eastern Africa and South Asia where marriages much earlier than puberty are not unusual. The marriage of girls between the ages of 16 and 18 is common in parts of Latin America and Eastern Europe. It is hard to know the number of early marriages as so many are unregistered and unofficial.

Why does it happen?

As mentioned earlier, such marriages may be arranged between two children as a means of maintaining or ensuring social, economic or political ties between families.

Parents may consent to child marriages out of economic necessity. Marriage may be seen as a way to provide male guardianship for their daughters, protect them from sexual assault, avoid pregnancy outside marriage, extend their childbearing years or ensure obedience to the husband's household.

What about the Convention on the Rights of the Child?
Different societies have different perceptions of childhood, but most governments have committed through the Convention on the Rights of the Child (CRC) to ensure the overall protection of children and young people aged under 18.

In particular, governments have committed to safeguarding children from all forms of abuse and exploitation, as well as upholding their rights to health and protection from harmful traditional practices, which include child marriages.

Any rationalisation of child marriage as the practice of tradition overlooks the fact that such marriages are often arranged within social milieux where the rights of children to protection as embodied in the CRC are absent.

As such, these marriages may cater to a demand for children as sexual partners in ways that are not identified by society as abuse. Overall, the argument for tradition or common law practices lends legitimacy to this sexual abuse and exploitation of children.

Nevertheless, child marriages can be seen to contravene the rights of all children to protection, development and survival as defined throughout the CRC, as well as in other instruments that include articles reinforcing the right to marry based on full and informed consent.

Where the marriage of children aged under 18 is permitted by a national legal code, without regard for whether young people have the opportunity and means to give full and informed consent, that country is violating its commitment to the Convention.

Statistics and country information on child marriage: IWHC Factsheet: Child Marriage

Sources: Ecpat International (definition: child marriages); International Women's Health Coalition Factsheet on child marriage; UNICEF factsheet: Early marriage; UNICEF: Early Marriage: A Harmful Traditional Practice.

INDIA: Child wife suicide
(Source: The Telegraph India: <www.telegraphindia.com>)

A man in his mid-40s has been arrested in Calcutta on charges of abetting the suicide of his second wife, a minor aged 15. The arrest followed a complaint lodged by the victim's family, who also alleged that she had often been tortured by her husband and in-laws for dowry. Police said Jyoti, a school dropout, consumed poison at her in-laws' house in Chitpur on Friday night. She was taken to RG Kar Medical College and Hospital, where she died this week.

"The girl had an affair with next-door neighbour Premlal Khatik, a daily-wager. Premlal is married and has a 19-year-old daughter," said Gyanwant Singh, the deputy commissioner of police (headquarters).

The Khatiks and Jyoti's family went to a wedding in the locality from where the duo fled. "Premlal and Jyoti returned home after a couple of weeks, claiming that they had married," said an officer of Chitpur police station. Jyoti's parents said "poverty and concerns about the girl's future" had forced them to accept the marriage.

"But Premlal soon pressed the girl's parents for money. He started torturing her after her parents turned down his demand for Rs 50,000. They did not have the means to pay the money," said an officer. Failing to bear the torture, Jyoti had fled her in-laws' house several times, but Premlal would woo her back on each occasion.

"The complaint says that Jyoti was beaten up for the past two weeks. They hardly gave her anything to eat and locked her in a room," the officer said. "On Friday night, Jyoti could lay her hands on a packet of pesticide and consumed it."

The police raided Premlal's house after receiving the complaint and arrested him, his wife and brother. "The names of all three were mentioned in the complaint," said deputy commissioner Singh.

The police claimed that Jyoti's family had not earlier complained about the torture.

ZIMBABWE: Daughters Fetch High Prices as Brides
(Source: IRIN News: <www.irinnews.org>)

HARARE, 17 July 2007 – Daughters have become a high-priced commodity in Zimbabwe, where a dowry has become a means of escaping poverty in a rapidly declining economy.

"When people are mired in such hunger as we have been seeing in this country for over seven years, they will do anything to survive," Innocent Makwiramiti, a Harare-based economist, told IRIN.

Parents have taken to demanding "absurd" amounts of money and other commodities from their in-laws. "It is not surprising that many parents are looking to the bride-price as one way to make ends meet," he said.

The dowry, a cultural practice, "has ceased to be a social problem and now needs to be seen from an economic point of view, with girl children being used to generate income," Makwiramiti said. "Unless the economic meltdown is addressed, we will continue to see parents commodifying their daughters."

Most Zimbabweans are struggling to survive: unemployment is out of control, inflation has topped 4,000 per cent, and 80 per cent of the population is living below the poverty datum line.

Daughters as a pension fund

Moses Jaison, 54, from the populous suburb of Mabvuku in southeastern Harare, the capital, last year betrothed his daughter Miriam, 15, still a minor in Zimbabwean law, to a polygamous businessman thirty years older than she was.

"The pain of seeing my family go without food and other basic necessities drove me into such a decision," Jaison said. "At that age, Miriam should have been in school and, being as intelligent as she is, might have ended up as a doctor or pilot, but poverty has rendered that only a pipedream."

Miriam stopped going to school at the age of eleven, after her father was laid off when the company that had employed him for thirty years closed down. Miriam's husband paid Jaison Z$15 million [US$115] and settled the mortgage on the family home, which had almost been repossessed when they fell behind with the monthly instalments.

Jaison barely scrapes a living by selling sculptures along the road linking Harare with Mutare, a city about 280km southeast of the capital, but because tourism has plummeted as a result of Zimbabwe's poor image, sales are slow and he does not earn nearly enough to take care of his wife and five children.

However, Miriam found living with three other wives too demanding and recently sought refuge at a local non-governmental organisation that promotes the welfare of girl children.

"That has worsened my plight, because the businessman who had married her has told me that I should give him back what he paid me as a [dowry]," said Jaison.

"That money has run out, and the police have indicated that they want to arrest me for ill-treating my daughter by marrying her off before she attained the legal age for marriage, and her husband could also be taken in for making a minor his wife."

Rich men, who have often generated their wealth illegally by trading in foreign currency or fuel on the informal market, do not have a problem in meeting the demands of in-laws, but those who do not earn much find the wooing tough.

USA: Plan to stem global child marriage scourge

(Source: USA Today: <www.usatoday.com>)

WASHINGTON, 17 July 2007 – Hundreds of millions of dollars in US aid goes to countries where girls as young as 12 are forced to marry, a rights abuse that is the focus of legislation to be introduced in Congress this month. In 2006, $623 million in US funds went to 16 of 20 countries with the highest child-marriage rates, including Bangladesh, Mali and Mozambique, according to the International Center for Research on Women (ICRW), a Washington non-profit group that works with governments on development and women's issues. The new legislation would authorise $100 million over four years to try to stop the practice, most prevalent in West Africa and South Asia. Bills by Rep. Betty McCollum, D-Minn., and Sens. Dick Durbin, D-Ill., and Chuck Hagel, R-Neb., also would require the State Department to include child-marriage statistics in annual human rights reports on other countries.

"Every year in poor countries, millions of girls – preteens and teens – become the wives of older men," McCollum says. "This custom is not marriage, but rather sanctioned sexual abuse and a human rights violation that destroys girls' lives."

Child marriage deprives girls of education, threatens their health and the health of their children, and thwarts efforts to combat HIV/AIDS, says Anju Malhorta, ICRW vice president.

About 51 million women worldwide now ages 20–24 were married before age 18, and 100 million more girls will become child brides over the next decade, according to figures compiled for the *US Agency for International Development* (USAID). One in three girls in developing countries marries before age 18. In Niger, a poor West African nation, more than three-quarters of girls are married before 18, most at age 15, USAID says.

Poverty and culture factors

Parents in poor countries often marry off young daughters to ensure that they will be cared for and because traditional cultures prefer that brides be virgins.

The ICRW says young brides are more likely to die in childbirth and contract HIV than women in their 20s and older. The group also says children born to teen mothers are more likely to die in infancy. "They (child brides) cannot negotiate the terms of sex" with husbands, who are usually older and have had previous sexual partners, says Kathleen Selvaggio, author of an ICRW report. They "can't insist on fidelity or condom use." Researchers have focused on keeping girls in school as a way to discourage child marriages. Half of girls in India are married before age 18 even though underage marriages violate national law, the ICRW says.

Rahul Chhabra, spokesman for the Indian Embassy in Washington, says his government "is aware of the problem and trying to do its best," imposing jail terms and fines, even for those attending weddings of underage brides.

'Battle'
An official at the Niger Embassy, Amadou Sounna, says his government is "in the battle against child marriage, recognising the terrible consequences it can have, especially for the health of girls." Sounna says Niger works against the practice through information campaigns and tries to keep girls in school. About a third of girls in Niger are enrolled in school, he notes.

Katherine Blakeslee, director of USAID's Office of Women in Development, says the Bush administration tries to deal with the issue by integrating it into other programs. Says Rep. McCollum: "USAID and the State Department know this is a major problem and have started taking positive steps, but it's simply not enough."

THE LAW: **Instruments and Mechanisms**

Instruments

– What the Convention on the Rights of the Child says about harmful traditional practices:

Article 24.3 States Parties shall take all effective and appropriate measures with a view to abolishing traditional practices prejudicial to the health of children.

– What the *African Charter on the Rights and Welfare of the Child* says about harmful traditional practices:

Article 21 Protection against Harmful Social and Cultural Practices

1. States Parties to the present Charter shall take all appropriate measures to eliminate harmful social and cultural practices affecting the welfare, dignity, normal growth and development of the child and in particular:

(a) those customs and practices prejudicial to the health or life of the child; and

(b) those customs and practices discriminatory to the child on the grounds of sex or other status.

2. Child marriage and the betrothal of girls and boys shall be prohibited and effective action, including legislation, shall be taken to specify the minimum age of marriage to be 18 years and make registration of all marriages in an official registry compulsory.

- Convention on Consent to Marriage, Minimum Age for Marriage and Registration of Marriages (1964).
- Recommendation on Consent to Marriage, Minimum Age for Marriage and Registration of Marriages (1965).

- Convention on the Elimination of All Forms of Discrimination Against Women (1979), particularly article 16 on marriage and family life.
- Declaration on the Elimination of Violence against Women (1993).
- Protocol to the African Charter on Human and People's Rights on the Rights of Women in Africa [Maputo, 11 July 2003], particularly articles 5 and 6 (2003).
- "The Legal Status and Human Rights of the Child," Advisory Opinion of the Inter-American Court of Human Rights (2002).

Mechanisms

- Committee on the Elimination of Discrimination against Women
- Committee on the Rights of the Child
- Human Rights Council
- Special Rapporteur on trafficking in persons, especially in women and children
- Special Rapporteur on violence against women, its causes and consequences
- Special Rapporteur on the sale of children, child prostitution and child pornography
- Special Rapporteur of the Commission on Human Rights on the right of everyone to the enjoyment of the highest attainable standard of physical and mental health.

MORE RESOURCES and INFORMATION

Reports

- Report of the Special Rapporteur on the human rights aspects of the victims of trafficking in persons, especially women and children – with a focus on child marriage (January 2007)
- Because I am a Girl: The State of the World's Girls 2007 (May 2007)
- International Monetary Fund: Getting All Girls into School (July 2007)
- Hope for the Girl Child: A Briefing Paper to the UN Commission on the Status of Women at its 51st session (February 2007)
- The Dynamics of Honour Killings in Turkey: Propects for action (February 2007)
- UNICEF: Early Marriage – extract from State of the World's Children 2006
- State of the World's Children 2007: Women and Children – the double dividend of gender equality (December 2006)
- Centers for Disease Control and Protection: Health Consequences of Child Marriage in Africa (November 2006)

- Ideal Marriage Programme 2006: A proactive step to counter child marriages (August 2006)
- Early Marriage – Sexual Exploitation and the Human Rights of Girls (February 2002).

Factsheets

- International Women's Health Coalition Factsheet: Child Marriage
- Office of the High Commissioner for Human Rights: Fact Sheet No. 23, Harmful Traditional Practices Affecting the Health of Women and Children
- UNICEF: Early Marriage: A Harmful Traditional Practice
- Child and Woman Abuse Study Unit (CWASU): Basic Statistics on Child Marriage
- Culture of Discrimination: A Fact Sheet on "Honor" Killings.

Organisations

- International Women's Health Coalition
- Child and Woman Abuse Study Unit
- African Commission on Human and People's Rights
- Defence for Children International
- International Council of Women
- Women's World Summit Foundation.

TASK/TEXT 4.2: MARRIAGE WITHOUT CONSENT – "BE WARY OF CULTURE"

Child Rights at the Human Rights Council 39 – 12 March 2008, <www.crin.org>

12 March 2008 – During an NGO side event on the spectre of forced marriage, Prof. Yakin Ertürk, Special Rapporteur on Violence Against Women, said she was "wary of cultural discussions."

"We are culture. Culture is ours. We shouldn't be so ready to attribute everything we are critical of to the sphere of culture, and we should not allow the holders of power to represent culture in oppressive ways," she said.

By uncritically accepting cultural arguments, we do not look at the issues behind it, she continued.

"Cultural diversity is our strength, not our weakness," she added. Her 2007 report dealt with the issue of culture and violence against women.

Boys also vulnerable

Prof. Erturk, speaking at the event Women and Girls Human Rights: Marriage without Consent, organised by WURN, also warned against neglecting the experiences of boys.

"Forced marriage does not necessarily mean a forced marriage of the woman – it is also an imposition on the men. You have a hostile and unhappy man too. His target is then often his bride. Violence becomes a component of this," she said.

Concluding, Prof. Ertürk emphasised the transnational dimension of forced marriages, noting that it was often used for migration purposes.

TASK/TEXT 4.3: SAUDI ARABIA – GIRL, EIGHT, MARRIED OFF TO 58-YEAR-OLD IS DENIED ANNULMENT

Crinmail 1045 – 23 December 2008, <www.crin.org>

An eight-year old Saudi Arabian girl who was married off by her father to a 58-year-old man has been told she will have to wait until she reaches puberty to seek an annulment.

Lawyer Abdu Jtili said a petition was filed by the unnamed girl's mother in August after the marriage contract was signed by her father and the groom. "The judge has dismissed the plea because she [the mother] does not have the right to file, and ordered that the plea should be filed by the girl herself when she reaches puberty," lawyer Abdullah Jtili told the AFP news agency.

The case was handled by a court in Qasim province, north of the Saudi capital Riyadh. The girl does not know she is married, said Jtili, adding that he will appeal.

In many child marriages, girls are given away to older men in return for dowries or following the custom by which a father promises his daughters and sons to marriage while still children. But the issue is complicated by different interpretations of sharia law and a lack of legal certainty.

"There is confusion in Saudi Arabia over the fundamental question of what constitutes adulthood," said Clarisa Bencomo of Human Rights Watch. "There is also vast judicial discretion." The case appears to fit a pattern of divorced fathers using their children to take revenge against their ex-wives. Mothers usually only have custody while the children are young.

Relatives said the marriage had not been consummated and that the girl was still living with her mother. They said that the father had set a verbal condition by which the marriage was not to be consummated until the girl turns 18 –

although it was unclear how this could be enforced. The father agreed to marry off his daughter for a dowry of 30,000 riyals (£5,400) as he was facing financial problems.

Bencomo dismissed the idea that the girl would be able to file for an annulment once she reached puberty since there was no standard definition of this. In addition, Saudi judges often insist that even adult women speak to them through a male guardian or lawyer.

No figures are available for the number of arranged marriages involving pre-adolescents in Saudi Arabia, where the strictly conservative Wahhabi version of Sunni Islam holds sway and polygamy is common. But human rights groups say they are aware of many such cases.

Senior clerics, including Sheikh Abdul-Aziz Al-Sheikh, the kingdom's grand mufti, have denounced child marriage. But it is still prevalent in conservative areas. The Shura council recently defined adulthood as starting at age 18 but objections prevented it from being ratified as required by the council of ministers.

TASK/TEXT 4.4: INDIA – CHILD MARRIAGE IS MAJOR PERIL

Crinmail 1065 – 10 March 2009, <www.crin.org>

PARIS, 10 March 2009 – Child marriage is a crippling medical and social burden to women in India and poses a demographic threat to the entire world, health experts warned in The Lancet on Tuesday.

Specialists in public health from India and the United States looked at data for 22,807 women aged 20–24, selected from a geographical and social cross-section of Indian society, who took part in a survey in 2005 and 2006.

A total of 44.5 per cent of the women had been wed by the time they were 18, set as the legal age for marriage since 1978. Of these, 22.6 per cent had been married before the age of 16 and 2.6 per cent before the age of 13.

Women who had been child brides were 37 per cent likelier not to have used contraception before their first child was born; seven times likelier to have three or more births; and three times likelier to have a repeat childbirth in less than 24 months. They were also more than twice as likely to have multiple unwanted pregnancies, nearly 50 percent likelier to have an abortion and more than six times likelier to seek sterilisation compared with counterparts who had married after the age of 18.

Child brides were also at greater risk of a fistula – a tear in the genital tract – as well as pregnancy complications and death and sickness as a result of childbirth.

"Child marriage has serious consequences for national development, stunting education and vocational opportunities for a large sector of the population," says the paper, led by Anita Raj, a doctor at Boston University School of Public Health in Massachusetts. "Furthermore, marriage at a very young age has grave health consequences for both the young women and their children."

The paper gives the lie to those who claim that the practice would shrivel as a result of India's rising prosperity and national policies aimed at preventing early marriage and encouraging access to contraception, education and economic opportunities for women.

A survey conducted in 1998–1999 estimated that 50 per cent of Indian women aged 20–24 were married as children, which means that the phenomenon has retreated by just a fraction.

The paper calls for efforts against child marriage to be beefed up, especially in rural areas.

"These results suggest that neither recent progress in economic and women's development, nor existing policy or programmatic efforts to prevent child marriage and promote maternal and child health have been sufficient to reduce the prevalence of child marriage in India to that of most other developing nations," it says.

The legal age of marriage in India is 18 for women and 21 for men. In a commentary also published by The Lancet, fertility expert Vinita Salvi of the King Edward Memorial Hospital in Mumbai said legislation against child marriage in India "exists largely on paper."

The country has 1.15 billion people, a phenomenon that was detrimental "not only for India but also for the entire world," and child marriage played an important role in the demographic surge, said Salvi. "Marriage at such ages has enormous adverse implications, not just for women's health and empowerment in general, but also for humankind in the long term."

TASK/TEXT 4.5:

TASK/TEXT 4.5.1: FIGHTING FEMALE GENITAL MUTILATION – MOBILIZATION IN SWITZERLAND

The International Institute for the Rights of the Child – IDE – L'Institut International des Droits de l'Enfant, <www.childsrights.org/html/site_en/index.php?c=>, 13 June 2008

The issue of genital mutilation and the need to protect young girls of migrant communities from this practice are making headlines in Switzerland, with several high-profile law cases.

On June 11th, 2008, a Judge of the *Fribourg cantonal Court* has given a suspended sentence of six months imprisonment, against a Somali citizen settled in the canton, on the charge of exposing her stepsister to genital cutting in Somalia. Since female genital mutilation (FGM) is not punished under Somalian law, Swiss Justice has based its condemnation on violation of the duty to assist and educate.

"*Justice has sent out a clear message: be it in Switzerland or abroad, female genital mutilation is not tolerable and must be punished,*" commented Paola Riva Gapany, Assistant-Director of IDE, during the Swiss French-speaking Television evening news.

Another much waited-for sentence will be the one concerning a mother and father, also of Somali origin, who had their daughter mutilated in Switzerland when she was two years. The Public Prosecutor has charged them with serious body damage. They face a sentence up to ten years imprisonment.

Another complaint has been filed in the canton of Geneva: it concerns two young girls.

Moreover, media denounce the case of a Nigerian women, arrived to Switzerland with her baby-daughter threatened to undergo mutilation. The asylum claim she has lodged was rejected by the two competent instances, leading to imminent deportation back to Nigeria. Federal authorities were summoned on this case, and *explained* that Nigeria has passed a law against female genital mutilation. According to them, protection accordingly falls under the responsibility of the country of origin.

The Swiss Parliament must also tackle a postulate investigating the relation between acceptance of asylum claims and threat of female genital mutilation.

Estimates set the number of mutilated women and girls living in Switzerland at 7,000, and thousands of young girls are the potential victims of the practice. Several cantons have set up prevention policies, notably by training intercultural mediators.

In 2007, IDE participated in making *Mutilated Women, Never More*! a documentary film breaking the silence on the legal, medical, and psychosocial aspects of FGM. A public success as awareness-raising tool, this film is available *from the IDE* (French – English – German).

TASK/TEXT 4.5.2: BURKINA FASO – CUTTERS TURN RAZORS ON BABIES TO EVADE FGM/C LAW

Crinmail 1054 – 29 January 2009, <www.crin.org>

OUAGADOUGOU, 27 January 2009 – Women performing excisions in Burkina Faso are cutting babies instead of young girls to escape increased scrutiny, according to the government and organisations fighting female genital mutilation/cutting (FGM/C).

FGM/C has been outlawed in Burkina Faso since 1996 and is punishable by up to 10 years in prison and US$1500 in fines. In the years following the law the number of FGM/C victims younger than five years old increased from 20 percent in 1998 to 31 percent in 2003, according to the government.

At least 70 newborns nationwide were admitted for hospital emergency care after botched cuttings in the first three months of 2008, according to the government.

Drowned-out cries

Babies' screams are often hidden from unsuspecting neighbours during noisy cutting ceremonies, according to the government's National Committee Against FGM/C, known as CNLPE.

FGM/C is defined by the World Health Organisation (WHO) as any injury to female genital organs for cultural, religious or other non-therapeutic reasons.

WHO has stated that consequences can include lifelong debilitating psychological and physical trauma – such as extreme pain during childbirth, sexual relations and urination. Some three million girls, the majority under 15 years old, are cut every year.

"It is a perverse effect of our denunciation and awareness campaign that to avoid being caught they [circumcisers] turn to babies who can undergo FGM/C unnoticed," said CNLPE's permanent secretary Marie Rose Sawadogo.

Baby cuttings

The fact that people have "developed strategies to violate the [1996] law" means some communities still do not understand why they need to abandon FGM/C, said Brigitte Yameogo with the non-profit Mwangaza Action. (Mwangaza means "light" in Swahili.)

In a 2008 survey the NGO conducted in the capital Ouagadougou, a majority of the 140 residents surveyed reported returning to their villages or finding remote areas to have their babies cut.

Pascaline Sebgo, an adviser in charge of FGM/C control for the German aid agency GTZ, told IRIN [IRIN News, <www.irinnews.org>] newborn victims are even more vulnerable at the hands of aging cutters.

"Most of the circumcisers are old, cannot see well and just cut what they feel in their hands," Sebgo told IRIN. She added that the average age of cutters has not changed much since a 1996 government survey reported 58 as the average age, with some cutters working into their 80s.

The new fight

Prevalence of FGM/C in Burkina Faso had dropped from 77 percent in the 1990s to less than 50 per cent among women 15 to 49 years old in 2005, according to CNLPE.

But some leaders are still resisting pressure to wipe out FGM/C, said Mwangaza Action's Yameogo.

"FGM/C is still a reality in Burkina Faso and populations strongly believe that the practice is rooted in their traditional values," she told IRIN. "Though some traditional chiefs publicly denounce FGM/C, they still favour the practice in private." Yameogo said anti-FGM/C messages can get lost in nationwide "massive campaigns" and that FGM/C supporters may better "understand the heart of the [cutting] problem" if they are approached in smaller settings.

The government's Sawadogo said the increase in newborn FGM/C victims [since adoption of 1996 law] does not cancel out previous gains made in the fight against FGM/C, but that new strategies are needed to stop those who "thwart the law" by cutting younger and younger girls.

But she said that since 2004 the government has not had funds to run anti-FGM/C campaigns.

GTZ's technical adviser Sebgo said CNLPE has lacked "clear objectives" and is working from an outdated action plan. Sebgo said GTZ will work with partners to increase funding as soon as the government adopts a new anti-FGM/C action plan, which is being finalised.

TASK/TEXT 4.5.3: BERLIN – KAMPAGNE 'SCHUTZ VON PATENMÄDCHEN VOR GENITALVERSTÜMMELUNG'

Giordano Bruno Stiftung [presse@giordano-bruno-stiftung.de], e-list 2 September 2009

Recherchen und Berechnungen zufolge werden bis zu 400.000 Patenmädchen in 18 Ländern schutzlos der Genitalverstümmelung ausgeliefert. Die Organisationen dulden diese schwere Kinderrechtsverletzung an den Patenmädchen und unterlassen es, den Verzicht auf diese Gewalt aktiv zu vereinbaren und in ihren Förderkriterien zu verankern. Diesen unerträglichen Zustand zu ändern, ist das Ziel der Kampagne 'Schutz von Patenmädchen vor Genitalverstümmelung,' die u.a. von der Giordano Bruno Stiftung unterstützt wird.

Vorstandssprecher Michael Schmidt-Salomon erklärte das Engagement der Stiftung wie folgt: "Genitalverstümmelung ist keine kulturell legitimierte Praxis, sondern ein Verbrechen! Man muss dies so deutlich hervorheben, da der **kulturelle Relativismus, der absurderweise Traditionen statt Menschen schützt,** in unseren Breitengraden allzu häufig als ein Zeichen 'echter Toleranz' gewertet wird. In Wahrheit jedoch ist er ein Zeichen von Ignoranz, von Abstumpfung gegenüber dem realen Leid, das durch 'altehrwürdige' kulturelle Praktiken oftmals erzeugt wird."

Im Fall der Genitalverstümmelung sei dieses Leid besonders offensichtlich, so der [Giordano Bruno Stiftung]-Sprecher. "Deshalb ist es ein Skandal, dass deutsche Hilfsorganisationen so wenig unternehmen, um die von ihnen betreuten Patenkinder zu schützen! Wir dürfen die Gewalt, die den Mädchen angetan wird, nicht weiter verdrängen, sondern müssen alles daran setzen, um sie effektiv zu bekämpfen. Rücksichtsnahme auf kulturelle Traditionen wäre hier völlig unangebracht: Schließlich müssen die Menschenrechte für alle gelten – unabhängig von Geschlecht, Alter oder Herkunft."

Am Donnerstag, dem 17. September [2009] (...) wird (...) die Kampagnen-Website <www.patenmaedchen.de> freigeschaltet werden.

TASK/TEXT 4.5.4: UGANDA – FEMALE CIRCUMCISION STILL A VOTE WINNER

Crinmail Violence against Children 46 – 21 October 2009, <www.crin.org>

KAMPALA, 19 October – Over three decades ago a 14-year-old girl, her sister and a group of young teenagers from Bukwo headed to the River Amana for a ceremony that would change their lives forever. Since her childhood, Gertrude Chebet had been told of the day she would become a woman. She was led to believe it would be a great moment of change and it was something to look forward to with much joy. As she and her sister began that early morning trek, from their village in eastern Uganda, in the cold and through the bushes to the place of initiation, she expected it to be the best day of her life. But she was wrong. It turned out to be the most harrowing.

"One of the elder women overseeing the circumcision took a sample of our saliva, urine and pubic hair and buried it. She then ordered us to lie on the ground and after the first cut, I lost consciousness and cannot remember what happened next," she remembers now. Even after passing out she and the other girls were not allowed to use modern medicine to treat their wounds. Instead she was forced to use cow urine, prescribed by her elders.

Today Chebet is a primary school teacher and campaigns against female circumcision, otherwise known as female genital mutilation. Chebet condemns it as unnecessarily cruel and inhuman. She is the chairperson of the Kapchorwa/ Bukwo Women in Peace Initiative, a lobby group advocating for the enactment of laws to abolish female genital mutilation. But it has turned out to be a long, hard battle to change an age-old tradition that involves the total removal of the clitoris and scraping of the female private parts. In fact, even those in positions of power are finding it difficult to change the culture of mutilation against young girls. While earlier this year President Yoweri Museveni condemned the practice, his government has been slow to pass a total ban on female circumcision, partly because his party needs the votes of those who largely support the practice.

The strength of the voters is especially evident in communities where female circumcision is a wide-spread practice. Here, women who have not been mutilated have difficulty being elected and some have lost elections because of their anti-female-genital-mutilation campaign. Jane Frances Kuka, the former Gender Minister and former woman Member of Parliament (MP) for Kapchorwa district, an area that has laws banning female circumcision, lost her parliamentary seat partly for having campaigned against female genital mutilation. "My opponents used my stand against female genital mutilation as a weapon against me. Elders were saying who is this (she) to interfere with our culture?" she says.

Female circumcision is practiced among the Sabiny, Sebei and Pokot in eastern Uganda. It is conducted in various ways around the world, but in Uganda it involves the total removal of the clitoris and scraping of the female private parts. "It is common for girls to bleed to death after circumcision. Others are infected with disease, some dying of tetanus. Many girls develop problems that affect them during child birth," Chebet says. In 2007 the district councils of Kapchorwa and Bukwo passed by-laws prohibiting female circumcision. However these laws are largely ignored and in December 2008 close to 40 girls in Kapchorwa and more than 100 in Bukwo were subjected to the ritual.

Chebet says the road to elimination of female genital mutilation is long and hard. However a few strides are being made through the enactment of by-laws against practice by sub-counties in Kapchorwa and Bukwo. She says the key lies in a national law against female genital mutilation. Chebet admits that there is great resistance to the abolition of the practice, because it is risky especially for those with political ambitions.

Although Uganda is a signatory to the Maputo Protocol, a charter adopted by the African Union that guarantees the rights of women including the right to end female genital mutilation, it has not passed a law outlawing the practice. Museveni's government has been hailed at international female activist conferences for advancing the emancipation of women but has been slow to pass a total ban to female genital mutilation. Museveni and his party members have had the wider support of voters from Kapchorwa and Bukwo districts partly because he has not interfered with their culture – especially the practice of female circumcision.

In April 2007 women activists under their umbrella boy known as Law and Advocacy for Women in Uganda petitioned the constitutional court in an effort to ban female circumcision. They argue female genital mutilation is a violation of women's constitutional rights and that it is a form of torture that constitutes cruel and inhuman treatment. The Attorney General's Chambers headed by Attorney General also Ministry of Justice asked the court to dismiss the petition. The constitutional court heard the matter [but h]as yet to pass a ruling.

Rukia Nakadama, a culture minister in Uganda says the government was now resolved to work with communities where female genital mutilation was practiced in order to ban it. She says government will also back the anti-female genital mutilation bill presented to Parliament by a back bench MP, who is a member of the ruling National Resistance Movement party. Kinkizi East MP, Chris Baryomunsi, a medical doctor from an area where female genital mutilation is not performed has tabled a private member's bill in the Ugandan Parliament to ban the practice. Ugandan MPs, under article 94 of the Constitution, can initiate a law (under the private member's bill) if they feel the executive arm of government has not initiated one. Baryomunsi tells IPS [news] that he feels obliged as a medical practitioner and a legislator to do something for girls and women in that part of Uganda. "I feel pain and sadness that this is going on in Uganda. That women, willing or unwilling, are subjected to crude methods of having part of their bodies cut when there is no medical benefit. I had to take the lead to fight this injustice," he says.

Baryomunsi is backed by some female activists including Uganda's Parliament Deputy Speaker, Rebecca Kadaga, and he wants the law to criminalise female genital mutilation. The bill proposes harsh penalties for traditional surgeons and parents who promote female genital mutilation; it suggests that they face up to 15 years in jail once implicated. Baryomunsi also wants the law to provide that the consent of a girl or woman will not be valid defence, given the health risks associated with female genital mutilation.

The World Health Organisation in June 2006 released a first study to give evidence of the harmful effects of female genital mutilation. The study indicated that women who have had female circumcision were likely to experience difficulties during child birth and their babies were more likely to die as a result of the traditional yet gruesome practice.

Even male contestants in elections agree that the female genital mutilation has always come up as an issue among the elders concerned about preserving their culture. Dr John Yeko, a MP representing Kween county, says the stand against female genital mutilation was not the only issue of concern during elections. It was the way people spoke about the issue that also made a difference. "I agree some people have lost (elections) because of the language they use against female genital mutilation. I have personally spoken against it by emphasising its negative aspects." Yeko has three daughters and they have not undergone the practice. "I totally support the ban against (it) because it is a useless part of our culture which should not be tolerated at this point in time," he says.

The situation is no different in neighbouring Kenya. Linah Jebbi a MP from Marakwet in northern Kenya says the issue of anti-female genital mutilation has always come up during the (...) elections. She says she may have lost the elections if she was not involved in other campaigns, like the campaign for peace among the pastoralist tribes. Even at the age of 46, many elderly persons view her as a child who should not be entrusted with leadership responsibility. "Today I accept that I am a child according to their perceptions. But I tell them that to be a leader – to be a member of parliament – is to be a servant. And whom do you send to be a servant? You don't send a grown up, you send a child," she says. (She was referring to that fact that in most African cultures it is believed that it is easy to send a child to perform a task rather than an adult because a child is presumed submissive and easy to send.)

Kuka agrees and told IPS most times male politicians used the female genital mutilation and male patriarchal culture to undermine female politicians. If a female politician is not circumcised it would be used against her as a campaign issue. "This may explain why women who have all the qualifications to contest for parliament find it easier to contest for a 'woman seat' in parliament even when they can compete for the main constituencies dominated by men in Kapchorwa and Bukwo districts," Kuka says. In Uganda because of affirmative action, each district has to have a district women MP elected to Parliament. This is called the 'woman seat'. For this seat, women compete with only fellow women. But a woman can compete for a constituency on the county level where she will compete with men as well. But in areas were female genital mutilation is widespread, like the districts of Kapchorwa and Bukwo, women prefer to contest for the 'woman seat' rather than competing for constituencies to tussle it out with men.

Gertrude Kulany, also a former MP, says banning the practice through the law alone may not be the answer. She tells IPS [news] that there should be affirmative action aimed at increasing girl-child education so that young girls themselves were educated enough to refuse to undergo the practice. "I'm one of the lucky ones who escaped the practice because I had support from my parents. Most of my contemporaries went through it because every girl in the village who attained puberty had to be initiated into womanhood through circumcision." She explains that the issue of female genital mutilation used to come up at every campaign and she had to tell people the facts about it. She adds that even women were prejudiced against women who had not undergone female circumcision. "Even some women have been discouraged from voting for women who have not gone through female genital mutilation. (It is) because they have been made to accept the (belief) that a woman who has not been circumcised is not yet mature," Kulany says.

Baryomunsi expects the bill to win the two-thirds support needed for its passage and for it to become law. Public hearings are yet to be held in Parliament but several MPs have already committed themselves to support its enactment into law.

TASK/TEXT 4.6: STRENGTHENING THE PROTECTION OF WOMEN FROM TORTURE

Child Rights at the Human Rights Council 39 – 12 March 2008, <www.crin.org>

Three Special Procedures gathered to discuss protecting women and girls from torture.

Prof. Manfred Nowak, Special Rapporteur (...) on Torture and other cruel, inhuman or degrading treatment or punishment, Ms. Yakin Ertürk, Special Rapporteur on Violence against Women, and Ms. Hina Jilani, Special Representative of the Secretary-General on the situation of Human Rights Defenders, spoke about **female genital mutilation** and trafficking, among other issues.

Prof. Nowak noted that the Convention Against Torture (CAT) defines torture under article 1 as (1) an infliction of severe physical or mental pain or suffering; (2) an infliction which is deliberate (with an intention to discriminate, intimidate etc.); (3) An act related to the government. He suggests introducing "powerlessness" as an added element to this definition. He explained that torture is the most serious form of ill treatment; not because of its intensity, but because of its purpose, with one person exercising full and effective control over another. With the addition of "powerlessness," the scope of torture extends beyond detention and into the private sphere. "Domestic violence for example is such a situation of powerlessness because one person exercises total control over another," he said.

FGM link

In Prof. Nowak's report, he notes that powerlessness in respect of FGM is pertinent since "the cutting is usually carried out before a girl's tenth birthday."

In such circumstances, girls are clearly under the complete control of their parents and communities and are unable to resist. On the other hand, adolescent girls and women very often agree to undergo FGM because they fear the non-acceptance of their communities, families and peers, he said.

Prof. Nowak also pointed out that rape is always torture, and spoke of the nature of "due diligence" which means a state may be liable for the actions of, for example, a private individual.

With FGM, he said, due diligence obliges the State to take all necessary legislative action to prevent torture. However, he said, "this is not enough." He said that in Togo, for example, there are very good laws prohibiting FGM but in practice no one is incriminated; only one case reached the courts during the first year following the adoption of the law. Failure to implement laws is also considered a State responsibility concluded Prof. Nowak.

One way to strengthen implementation, Prof. Nowak said, would be "naming particular forms of violence as torture." He added that: "the creation and support to rehabilitation centres for girls is another way."

Ertürk: Disempowerment, not powerlessness

Ms Ertürk disagreed to some extent with the term "powerlessness" that Prof. Nowak wants to add to the torture definition, as for her, when it comes to women, it stresses the disability and victimisation of women. She would suggest the use of the word "disempowerment," because it goes beyond the victim and relates also to the question of who is causing the suffering.

The Special Rapporteur has used her report to make proposals, guided by human rights standards, for indicators to measure violence against women and girls.

Ms Ertürk proposed a new sub-category of grave violence against women, which would include any incident of rape/serious sexual assault/sexual coercion in childhood or adulthood, female genital mutilation, child/forced marriage, trafficking and sexual exploitation.

[Jilani]

Ms. Hina Jilani, spoke of rape case[s] against married girls, and said that it was not considered a crime by the court, but was classified as a "misuse of wife." This illustrates how women and child's rights are subordinate to the actual status of marriage, she said. She said that in her country, married children are considered adults. "This is totally unacceptable," she said.

TASK/TEXT 4.7:

TASK/TEXT 4.7.1: DENMARK – PLAN TO BAN ALL CIRCUMCISION [STOP MESSING WITH CHILDREN'S GENITALS]

Crinmail 1035 – 20 November 2008, <www.crin.org>

Denmark's National Council for Children has recommended the legislation of a law banning circumcision of boys under the age of 15. "Circumcision is the irreversible damage to a child's body before he is given the chance to object," the National Council for Children argued. The proposal may be on its way to parliament after intense discussions by MPs over the past week, reports Kristeligt Dagblad newspaper.

Although circumcision of girls was outlawed in response to the practice being common among immigrants from some Muslim countries, boys may still be circumcised if a certified physician is present. Jewish traditions calls for the circumcision of newborn boys, and many Muslims and Christians support the practice as well. But both the Ethics Council and the National Council for Children have recently criticised the practice, stating that a boy should be able to decide for himself if he wants the procedure performed when he reaches the age of 15 – the legal age in Denmark for a child to have sole jurisdiction over his own body.

While the Social Democrats, Red-Green Alliance and Liberal Alliance have come out in support of a ban, the Danish People's Party called it "tyranny." "It's completely ridiculous to compare the circumcision of girls – which is a barbaric mutilation – with that of boys, where it's just the removal of a skin flap," said the party's Jesper Langballe. But the party's own health spokeswoman, Liselott Brixt, said she supports a ban. "A lot of parents want it done to their children because they themselves had it done. But we're living in the present and it isn't fair to expose healthy children to religious circumcision."

TASK/TEXT 4.7.2: AUSTRALIA – CONCERNS OVER MALE CIRCUMCISION

Crinmail 1101 – 20 August 2009, <www.crin.org>

Laws protect girls from genital surgery but parents wanting to circumcise boys can "go around willy-nilly chopping up bits of their sons," an Australian state children's commissioner says. Tasmania's commissioner for children Paul Mason and the Tasmanian Law Reform Institute have embarked on what they say is the largest review into the legalities of male circumcision in Australia's history.

Mr Mason said a critical issue for any non-therapeutic circumcision is whether parental consent is sufficient to protect a surgeon from legal action if the child's genital autonomy is thought to have been infringed. "The only thing that protects a doctor from an action for assault or a civil prosecution is the valid consent of the patient," he said. "The law is getting pretty hazy about whether a parent can give a valid consent for a child's non-medical procedure." Mr Mason said about 90 per cent of Australian male babies were circumcised in the 1970s, dropping to about two per cent these days. Its infrequency nowadays only heightens the chance of a circumcised boy feeling aggrieved as an adult that his rights were ignored as a child, he said. But High Court rulings and United Nations conventions and legal consent in terms of bodily integrity argue against parental-consent circumcision, he said. "To me they suggest parents are not entitled to cut or wound their children unless it is for a medical purpose," he said.

Mr Mason said another grey legal area was that many jurisdiction outlaw female genital alteration, not just the most severe form, because it infringed on girls' rights. "But we have a situation where girls have legal protection from any surgery on their genitals but parents can go around willy-nilly chopping up bits of their boys. "That is a discrimination any way you look at it," he said.

University of Tasmania circumcision-law researcher Warwick Marshall is working closely with Mr Mason and the Tasmanian Law Reform Institute review. Mr Marshall says criminal and civil laws fail to provide adequate certainty for parents and doctors. "The crux of the uncertainty is whether the consent of the parent of the child being circumcised provides the circumciser with protection from criminal and civil actions which may be brought against them for performing a circumcision," Mr Marshall said. Public submissions to law reform review close on August 28.

4*BIS*. CORPORAL PUNISHMENT

TASK/TEXT 4.8: COUNCIL OF EUROPE CAMPAIGN FOR THE ABOLITION OF CORPORAL PUNISHMENT, AUTUMN 2007

<www.coe.int/t/transversalprojects/children/violence/corporalPunishment_en.asp> (visited 13 August 2007)

The Council of Europe is campaigning for a global ban on all forms of corporal punishment of children in all settings. In many European countries, society tolerates and even approves some recurrent forms of violence against children, in particular those inflicted in the family setting.

However, no religion, belief, economic situation or 'educational' method can ever justify hitting, smacking, spanking, mutilating, abusing, humiliating, or any other practice that violates a child's dignity.

It is internationally recognised in human rights law that children have a right to protection from all forms of violence, including corporal punishment in all settings. Europe must become a continent where practices such as corporal punishment, whether at home, at school or in institutions no longer exist.

One third of our member states have abolished corporal punishment and others are committed to legal reform. Despite these positive developments, corporal punishment remains lawful in most countries and is still perceived as an acceptable form of 'discipline.'

Banning corporal punishment in the home is not about prosecuting parents: it is about changing attitudes by advising parents on non-violent methods of bringing up their children and adopting a more positive form of parenting.

TASK/TEXT 4.9: NETHERLANDS BECOMES 17TH EUROPEAN STATE TO BAN CORPORAL PUNISHMENT BY PARENTS

Crinmail 862 – 8 March 2007, <www.crin.org>

On 6 March 2007, a new law prohibiting all corporal punishment by parents and carers was passed in the Senate. The law amends the provisions in the Civil Code on parental authority so that article 1:247 now states (unofficial translation):

'(1) Parental authority includes the duty and the right of the parent to care for and raise his or her minor child.

(2) Caring for and raising one's child includes the care and the responsibility for the emotional and physical wellbeing of the child and for his or her safety as well as for the promotion of the development of his or her personality. **In the care and upbringing of the child the parents will not use emotional or physical violence or any other humiliating treatment.**'

Article 1:248 of the Code applies article 1:247 to all other persons acting in loco parentis.

The Cabinet agreed to proceed with prohibition in February 2005, following a government-commissioned study on the experiences of abolition in other European countries. Department of Justice press releases at the time the *Bill to contribute to the prevention of emotional and physical abuse of children or any other humiliating treatment of children in care and upbringing* was introduced to the Cabinet stressed that the primary purpose of the new law is 'to set a standard.'

It emphasised that the law would bring the Netherlands into compliance with the UN Convention on the Rights of the Child and article 17 of the European Social Charter, and address the recommendations made to the Netherlands government by the Committee on the Rights of the Child and the European Committee of Social Rights.

Now that the law has been passed, a government Communication Plan to inform parents and the general public about the ban is being prepared.

The law is expected to come into force by [25 April 2007: Law of 8 March 2007 (...), *Staatsblad* 24 April 2007, No. 145, JW].

At least 16 countries in Europe have enacted bans on corporal punishment by parents and all other carers: Sweden (1979); Finland (1983); Norway (1987); Austria (1989); Cyprus (1994); Denmark (1997); Latvia (1998); Croatia (1999); Germany (2000); Bulgaria (2000), Iceland (2003); Romania (2004); Ukraine (2004), Hungary (2004), Greece (2006); Netherlands (2007). In addition, a Supreme Court judgment in Italy (1996) declared all corporal punishment to be unlawful, but this has not yet been confirmed in legislation. At least six more states have committed themselves to full law reform in the near future: Lithuania, Luxembourg, Portugal, Slovakia, Slovenia, Spain.

The pace of reform is gathering momentum in light of the UN Secretary General's Study on Violence against Children, which recommended in its final report prohibition in law of all corporal punishment of children by 2009. Many more governments across the world have committed themselves to full prohibition, including at least a further six in Europe.

TASK/TEXT 4.10:

TASK/TEXT 4.10.1: NEW ZEALAND – FATHER CONVICTED FOR SMACKING SON UNDER NEW LAW

Crinmail 936 – 27 November 2007, <www.crin.org>

WELLINGTON, 23 November 2007 – A New Zealand father has been convicted of assault for smacking his eight-year-old son on the bottom in what is believed to be the first case under a controversial new law. "One time, maybe you could have got away with this, but you can't do that now," Judge Anthony Walsh told the 33-year-old man on Wednesday. You must understand that what you did amounted to an assault. Our law has been amended so that children are protected," the Wairarapa Times-Age newspaper reported him saying. A new law was passed in May, removing a provision allowing parents to use "reasonable force" in disciplining their children.

The court was told the boy received a bruised shoulder when his father roughly grabbed him before smacking his bottom three times with his open hand after he had misbehaved at school. The boy's mother took a photograph of the bruise and showed it to a relative, who later reported it to police.

Child advocacy group Barnardo's New Zealand welcomed the court's decision.

"I believe this is the first reported case in which the new law relating to child discipline in the home has been tested in court and the law has worked well," acting chief executive Peter Gerrie said.

It showed that parents had to accept non-violent ways of disciplining their children, he said.

Bob McCoskrie, director of the conservative lobby group Family First New Zealand said the new law had created a "paranoid parenting environment. This case has confirmed Kiwi parents' worst nightmare." Child advocates argue that children should be protected from assault in the same way that adults are, and that smacking teaches children violence.

Read the Commitee on the Rights of the Child's General Comment No. 8: The right of the child to protection from corporal punishment and other cruel or degrading forms of punishment.

TASK/TEXT 4.10.2: NEW ZEALAND – BATTLE OVER CORPORAL PUNISHMENT COMES TO A HEAD

Crinmail 1096 – 29 July 2009, <www.crin.org>

A raging battle over the ban on all corporal punishment of children in New Zealand is about to spill over from the news reels to the ballot boxes, as voters turn out for a referendum on the issue.

Voters will be asked to say yes or no to the question "Should a smack as part of good parental correction be a criminal offence in New Zealand?" Yet the referendum, which has cost the country more than $7 million, is non-binding, and the government has already indicated that it is unlikely to change the law. Moreover, the phrasing of the question has itself been criticised. Prime Minister John Key called it "weird," and said he does not intend to vote. Opposition leader Phil Goff says the same.

On the question of smacking itself, organisations including Barnardos, Plunket, Save the Children and UNICEF, have joined forces to call on New Zealanders to vote 'yes.'

Legitimacy

Spokesperson Deborah Morris-Travers said that the Yes Vote Coalition stands apart from the 'pro-smackers' because of their long-standing reputations in New Zealand communities, giving their campaign greater legitimacy, particularly in the eyes of politicians and the media.

"One of the things that was really important in the debate last time around, particularly for members of parliament, was an appreciation of the fact that we are offering services to families and communities up and down the country," Morris-Travers says. "I think that's the single biggest difference between us and the pro-smackers...they're not in the business of service delivery, they're conservative advocates. They're not people who are working in communities to build stronger families."

She added that human rights are not just for adults. "It is a human rights issue, and when we uphold the rights of children, we uphold the rights of all of us," she said.

The Convention on the Rights of the Child, which New Zealand has ratified, asserts the right of children to their own physical integrity and protection from physical assault. "It's all wrong for us to have a law that discriminates against children and makes them the only group of people in our country where if they're assaulted, there's a defence for doing so," Morris-Travers says. "I think it's really important for us to grant our most vulnerable citizens the same protection as every other group of citizens. "It is a massive social and cultural change for us to view children in a different way, but it's really important that we do understand...that children are people now, that they are citizens with their own rights, and that...when we nurture them appropriately, we all benefit."

Background

A ban on smacking in the country was introduced in 2007, but a determined clutch of 'pro smackers' have since waged a campaign against the State for tabling the legislation. Last year, the group gathered the necessary number of signatures to launch a referendum seeking to repeal the law. The postal ballot is scheduled to go ahead from 30 July to 21 August.

The passing of the S59 Amendment Act in 2007 by Parliament-with a majority of 113 votes to 8-saw the demise of a parent's defence of "reasonable force." The old section 59 of the Crimes Act 1961 stated that "every parent or person in place of a parent of a child is justified in using force by way of correction towards a child if that force is reasonable in the circumstance."

The new law clearly states that the use of force for the purpose of correction is unjustified, giving New Zealand children the same legal status as adults and animals against the use of force and physical assault.

The controversial change to smacking legislation has had little impact on day-to-day policing, a police review of crimes shows. New evidence that parents are increasingly shunning physical punishment as an effective method of parenting was also recently published by the New Zealand Herald. It shows a steep drop in the numbers of both mothers and fathers using smacking frequently or at all.

The vast majority of people in New Zealand say an upcoming referendum on the so-called Anti-Smacking Bill will be a waste of tax dollars, according to a poll by Research New Zealand. 77 per cent of respondents think the vote on a piece of legislation dealing with domestic violence against children is not worth the money.

TASK/TEXT 4.10.3: THE CAMPAIGN [PRO-/]AGAINST SMACKING IN NEW ZEALAND

Crinmail 1097 – 6 August 2009, <www.crin.org>

Deborah Morris-Travers, 39, is leading the Yes Vote campaign on corporal punishment in New Zealand. In a referendum on a 2005 law that banned smacking, forced by a coalition of pro-smacking groups, voters will be asked to say yes or no to the question "Should a smack as part of good parental correction be a criminal offence in New Zealand?" Formerly a Member of Parliament, Ms Morris-Travers is now Advocacy Manager at Barnardos.

With advocacy, for an issue such as this anyway, you have to be prepared for a long battle. A priority is always gaining sufficient political support. Even now, that's where we concentrate our efforts – getting the right legal framework is important, as public opinion will take years to change. Over the years, the government has invested a lot in positive parenting practices, so it only makes sense that this would be reflected in the law on corporal punishment.

People are being misled about the extent of police involvement in families. The opposition campaign has been fought quite aggressively, so for example they have taken out large adverts in national newspapers citing supposed cases of parents being criminalised. But when they have been asked by us, or others, to provide evidence about the cases, they have not been able to produce it, so we can't counter it.

Apparently, a lot of the money for their campaign comes from US conservative groups, but we cannot justify spending millions on advertising campaigns or newspaper pages because we have a duty to service delivery. We can't use core funding for this campaign, and the money comes from private donors.

Having a background as a politician and minister has definitely helped with understanding parliamentary and political processes. I used to be a minister, but I left parliament to work in public affairs in the private sector, where I came into contact with NGOs working on law change. I then went overseas to South East Asia, and when I came back in 2004, I decided I wanted to work on community projects.

It is important that advocacy is based on research and evidence. It is also important to build a network of people and organisations working together on the issue, and it has been vital for us to have the major children's organisations, working in the delivery of children's services, working in partnership.

Building allies in the community and parliament, and in the news media, who understand the issue and can act as champions has made a real difference. Celebrities are also good to get on board, where possible, and of course it is crucial to the campaign that children's voices are incorporated. So, for example, the opposition campaign and some parents argue that a light smack is OK, and doesn't hurt or harm children. However, children respond that smacking does actually hurt, and they say they are harmed by it.

Most people will probably vote 'no' in the referendum. Even though a lot of people would condone positive parenting practices, it shows that a lot of them still don't understand the law. The way the referendum question is phrased suggests that, firstly, smacking is part of good parenting practices, and secondly that parents are, or will be, criminalised for smacking.

In fact, research has found that parents are not being criminalised for smacking, and there has hardly been any increase in police reporting of the issue. There has, however, been an increase in the reporting of serious assaults.

A lot of people are talking about it. The debate has been going on for a while. The first call to change the law came in 1979, and there was calls made right through the 1990s especially. There was a really intense public debate when the law was introduced in 2005, and the referendum has reignited the debate. But we are seeing a much more mature attitude in the media and elsewhere towards the issue, which is a positive sign of progress. There is also more interest in the views of children.

The biggest challenge remains public opinion – you are talking about generations of beliefs and attitudes, and in particular the perceived rights of parents to treat children in a particular way. I always tell people that we are in the middle of a 20 to 30 year campaign.

The key is getting people through the emotion, and the belief that it is all about the 'nanny state' interfering in the private lives of families. Getting people to believe that children are human beings and therefore rights holders is therefore crucial.

The opposition campaign tries to pit adults against children, but when you uphold the rights of one section of the population, you uphold the rights of all of us.

TASK/TEXT 4.10.4: SMACKING POLL 'NO' LANDSLIDE CONFIRMED

<www.stuff.co.nz/national/politics/2787019/Smacking-poll-no-landslide-confirmed>, 25 August 2009

The final results of the smacking referendum have been released, showing that more than 1.68 million ballots were cast – with 87 per cent voting 'no.' The poll question asked: "Should a smack as part of good parental correction be a criminal offence in New Zealand?" Preliminary results released on Friday indicated 1,622,150 valid votes were cast, but with the release of the official results today that was bumped up to 1,682,717 – a voter turnout of 56 per cent. More than 1.47 million 'no' votes were cast – 87.4 per cent. Around 201,000 'yes' votes were cast – 11.98 per cent. (...)

TASK/TEXT 4.11:

TASK/TEXT 4.11.1: URUGUAY – FIRST LATIN AMERICAN COUNTRY TO BAN CORPORAL PUNISHMENT

Crinmail 935 – 22 November 2007, <www.crin.org>

On 20 November 2007, the 18th anniversary of the UN Convention on the Rights of the Child, Uruguay became the first Latin American country to ban all physical and humiliating punishment of children.

The ban was approved in a bill voted for by 56 of the 99 parliamentarians who make up the House of Representatives. The bill had already been agreed unanimously by the Senate in August this year.

This signals a new landmark in the defence of child rights in Latin America. An important element of this precedent was the creation in October this year of the Parliamentary Group for Children and Young People's Rights, which was responsible for pushing this and other child rights bills forward.

One of the organisations to play a key role in the process was Organización Servicios y Acciones por la Infancia (SAI) – Programa ARCOIRIS.

Ending violence against children

Physical and humiliating punishment is a form of violence against children, it is a violation of their right to physical integrity and dignity. In many countries, it remains the only form of aggression against a human being which is condoned by the law.

In consultations around the world, children have said that physical and humiliating punishment is the most common and widespread form of violence against them. Save the Children Sweden, which works in partnership with local organisations, believes it is essential not only to listen to children, but also to take action to change this reality.

TASK/TEXT 4.11.2: VENEZUELA – SECOND LATIN AMERICAN COUNTRY TO BAN CORPORAL PUNISHMENT

Crinmail 943 – 20 December 2007, <www.crin.org>

CARACAS, 10 December 2007 – On 10 December 2007, a new law was passed in Venezuela which bans all forms of physical and humiliating punishment of children. The law makes Venezuela the second Latin American country to pass such a law; Uruguay last month became the first.

The reform of the law which protects children and young people includes a provision for children's right to be well treated and bans all forms of physical and humiliating punishment.

Carlos Trapani from child rights NGO Cecodap, who led the advocacy campaign, said: "Corporal punishment is a violent phenomenon. It is a violation of human rights."

The new law:

Article 32a. The right to good treatment.

All children and young people have a right to be treated well. This right includes a non-violent education and upbringing, based on love, affection, mutual understanding and respect, and solidarity.

Parents, representatives, guardians, relatives, and teachers should use non-violent methods of education and discipline to raise and educate their children. Consequently, all forms of physical and humiliating punishment are prohibited. The State, with the active participation of society, must ensure policies, programmes and protection measures [which] are in place to abolish all forms of physical and humiliating punishment of children and young people.

Corporal punishment is defined as the use of force, in raising or educating children, with the intention of causing any degree of physical pain or discomfort to correct, control or change the behaviour of children and young people.

Humiliating punishment can be understood as any form of offensive, denigrating, devaluing, stigmatising or mocking, treatment, carried out to raise or educate children and young people, with the aim of disciplining, controlling or changing their behaviour.

Article 56. The right to be respected by teachers.

All children and young people have the right to be respected by their teachers, and receive an education based on love, affection, mutual understanding, national identity, mutual respect for ideas and beliefs, and solidarity. Consequently, all forms of physical and humiliating punishment are prohibited.

Article 358. Content of the responsibility for raising children.

The responsibility for raising children includes the shared duty and right, which is equal and non-derogable, of the father and mother to love, raise, train, educate, and look after their children, sustain and assist them financially, morally and emotionally, using appropriate corrective measures that do not violate their dignity, rights, guarantees or overall development. Consequently, all forms of physical punishment, psychological violence and humiliating treatment, which harm children and young people, are prohibited.

Stated purpose: A new human right – the right to be treated well – has been introduced to reinforce children and young people's status as rights-holders, and to ensure the full recognition of their dignity and personal integrity. This right includes a non-violent upbringing and education, based on love, affection, mutual understanding and respect, and solidarity. In addition to an express ban on all forms of physical and humiliating punishment, fathers, mothers, representatives, guardians, relatives and teachers have an obligation to use non-violent methods to raise, train, educate and discipline children and young people, to ensure the implementation of this right. This new regulation is a step towards achieving abolition of all forms of abuse of children and young people, and building the legal foundations for a new and peaceful society.

TASK/TEXT 4.11.3: SPAIN – PARENTS BANNED FROM SMACKING CHILDREN

<http://crin.org/resources/infoDetail.asp?ID=15892&flag=news>

MADRID, 20 December 2007 – Spanish parents will be banned from smacking their children, congress voted on Thursday.

Until now parents have been allowed to "reasonably and moderately correct" their children, but deputies deleted that clause and rewrote Spain's civil code to make clear a child's physical and psychological integrity should be respected.

Spain's Socialist government, which pushed through the change, has often been accused by the conservative Popular Party opposition of undermining traditional values and the family with policies such as legalising gay marriage.

Popular Party deputies, who voted against the change, said the measure would leave parents powerless, but Socialists said the law shut the door to any chance of misunderstanding.

Around 16 European countries have already banned smacking at school and in the home. In October the British government rejected the banning of corporal punishment at home as long as parents did not leave bruises, grazes or swelling.

TASK/TEXT 4.11.4: CHILE – CORPORAL PUNISHMENT BANNED

Crinmail 945 – 3 January 2008, <www.crin.org>

18 December 2007 – In December 2007, an amendment to the Civil Code in Chile was passed which effectively prohibited corporal punishment of children by parents. Previously, the Code had recognised that "parents shall have the

power to punish their children" (article 234), although it also stated that this should not endanger the child's health or include abuse (articles 234, 235, 238 and 239). With the new legislation, article 234 has been amended to make it clear that the power to correct children excludes all forms of physical punishment.

The prohibition of all corporal punishment was passed unanimously by the Commission of the Constitution of the Senate, and is part of a broad campaign to promote good treatment of children.

The press release published at the time the law was passed stated that important modifications had been made to article 234 of the Civil Code "establishing clearly that the [provision permitting correction of children] excludes all types of physical punishment." It also noted that the next step is to ensure that everyone is aware of the new law – "eradicating violence and physical punishment in the family is a task for us all."

[On <www.endcorporalpunishment.org>, visited 19 December 2009, no confirmation can be found, JW.]

TASK/TEXT 4.11.5: COSTA RICA – BAN ON CORPORAL PUNISHMENT APPROVED

Crinmail 995 – 1 July 2008, <www.crin.org>

SAN JOSE, 25 June 2008 – Costa Rica will become the first country in Central America to pass a law banning all corporal punishment of children, assuming the President signs the bill – usually a mere formality.

Parlimentarian for the Partido Unidad (Unity Party), Ana Elena Chacón, who put forward the law, expressed satisfaction with the move: "Sweden was the first country in the world to abolish physical punishment of children in 1979. This decision has resulted in a reduction in violence in Swedish society. It has taken us five years to take this important step which was advanced by the ombudsperson for human rights and children."

The law includes the fundamental right of children to receive training, education, care and discipline from their mother, father or guardian, teaching and healthcare staff, as well as those working in the justice system, without the use of physical or humiliating treatment. According to statistics from the Patronato Nacional de la Infancia, there were 4,469 cases of abuse during 2006: 697 more than in 2005. "This move is not denying parents the power to discipline their children, but just saying they must do this without violence. It is not a case of not using discipline, but of re-educating ourselves in establishing boundaries. These boundaries must be set without humiliation, without smacking and without anger if we want to raise respectful, responsible and confident young people," said the parliamentarian.

The UN Study on Violence Against Children set 2009 as the deadline for all Member States to have banned all corporal punishment of children. In the last year, Spain, Chile, Portugal, Croatia, Venezuela, Uruguay are among those to have banned the practice.

TASK/TEXT 4.11.6: COSTA RICA ACHIEVES FULL PROHIBITION; MORE EUROPEAN STATES COMMIT THEMSELVES TO ABOLITION

Global Initiative Newsletter 4 – September 2008, <www.endcorporalpunishment.org>

Costa Rica has joined the list of countries explicitly prohibiting all corporal punishment of children, in the family home and all other settings. Following a long and sustained campaign involving government ministries and non-government organisations and with the support of the Office of the Ombudsperson, two major amendments were made to the law. A new article (24 bis) was added to the Code of Children and Adolescents, which states:

Children and adolescents have a right to receive counselling, education, care and discipline from their mother, father or tutor, as well as from their caretakers or the personnel from educational and health centres, shelters, youth detention or any other type of centres, that in no way represents an authorisation of any sort to these parties for the use of corporal punishment or degrading treatment.

The Patronato Nacional de la Infancia shall coordinate with the institutions conforming to the National Integral Protection System and NGOs, for the implementation of educational campaigns and programmes directed to parents and other adults in custodial or caring roles.

Article 143, which had previously allowed "moderate correction" of children, was amended to state:

Parental authority confers the rights and imposes the duties to orient, educate, care, supervise and discipline the children, which in no case authorises the use of corporal punishment or any other form of degrading treatment against the minors.

Under the Swedish presidency of the Committee of Ministers of the **Council of Europe** (May – November 2008), a conference on "Building a Europe for and with Children: Towards a Strategy from 2009–2011" was organised in Stockholm in September, during which 15 states committed themselves to abolition by signing the Council of Europe's petition supporting the abolition of corporal punishment of children in all settings. Many of those are already committed to or have achieved full prohibition, but six others have expressed their commitment – Albania, Azerbaijan, France, Georgia, Montenegro and Turkey.

In her opening speech to the conference, Her Majesty Queen Silvia of Sweden stated: "Our efforts here are all about making the Convention on the Rights of the Child a reality. The Convention recognises that children have special human rights. These rights are to guarantee that every child enjoys an everyday life that offers opportunities for development, regardless of personal circumstances. No child may be discriminated against – the Convention makes this clear. Society must ensure that this principle becomes a reality. The Convention places demands on decision-makers, but it also provides us adults with some guidance. It's not enough to love our own children. We must treat all children – our own and others' – with care and respect."

TASK/TEXT 4.11.7: MOLDOVA – CORPORAL PUNISHMENT BANNED IN ALL SETTINGS

Crinmail 1072 – 2 April 2009, <www.crin.org>

Moldova has prohibited corporal punishment of children in all settings, including the family home. They have amended their Family Code to explicitly prohibit corporal punishment by parents and others with parental authority.

The new Article 53 of the code covers "the right of the child to be protected" and states in paragraph 4 that the child "has the right to be protected against abuses, including corporal punishment by parents or persons who replace them." Article 62 concerns parents' rights [responsibilities? – JW] and states in paragraph 2 that "**methods to educate children, chosen by parents, will exclude abusive behaviour, insults and ill-treatments of all types, discrimination, psychological and physical violence, corporal punishment ...**"

Moldova now joins the 18 other Council of Europe member states with a total ban on corporal punishment to make a total of nineteen [out of 47 total states].

Corporal punishment of children is prohibited in all settings (home, schools, penal systems, alternative care) in: Austria, Bulgaria, Croatia, Cyprus, Denmark, Finland, Germany, Greece, Hungary, Iceland, Latvia, Moldova Netherlands, Norway, Portugal, Romania, Spain, Sweden, Ukraine.

TASK/TEXT 4.11.8: INTER-AMERICAN COURT CONFIRMS OBLIGATION TO PROHIBIT ALL CORPORAL PUNISHMENT

Crinmail 1073 – 7 April 2009, <www.crin.org>

30 March 2009 – The Inter-American Court of Human Rights has confirmed the human rights obligations of Member States of the Organization of American States (OAS) to prohibit and eliminate all corporal punishment of children.

In December 2008 the Inter-American Commission on Human Rights formally asked the Inter-American Court of Human Rights to issue an advisory opinion on whether corporal punishment of children is compatible with various articles in the American Convention on Human Rights and the American Declaration of Human Rights and Duties.

Referring to articles 1 (non-discrimination), 2 (obligation to adapt domestic law to the American Convention), 5 (right to humane treatment) and 19 (rights of the child) of the American Convention and article VII (right to protection for mothers and children) of the American Declaration, the Commission asked the Court whether these provisions, in light of the best interests of the child, oblige OAS Member States (1) to "regulate paternal [parental, JW] authority and protection in such a way as to protect children against all forms of corporal punishment"; and (2) to "adopt legislative and other measures for the purpose of ensuring that children are not subjected to corporal punishment as a method of discipline within the family, at school or in institutions."

The basis for the Commission's petition was, firstly, that there is no standard in the Inter-American context which clearly states that corporal punishment should be prohibited because it is incompatible with respect for human rights and, secondly, that corporal punishment is widely practised and in most states is lawful, and although nearly all states [all but the US, JW] have ratified the Convention on the Rights of the Child, very few have adapted their national laws in line with the Convention. The Commission argued that a statement by the Court on the issue would have a positive influence on elimination and prohibition of corporal punishment through legislative and other reforms in the states concerned.

In its response to the request, the Court makes it clear that there is no need to issue an advisory opinion on this matter because the questions can be answered with reference to the existing jurisprudence of the Court, "as well as from the obligations issued by other international instruments ratified by the States in the region."

The Court refers to the Convention on the Rights of the Child, and notes that the obligation of states to respect the responsibilities, rights and duties of parents is subject to "the duty to establish the best interests of the child as the fundamental elements of his or her upbringing and development, whether this be in the hands of the child's parents or legal guardians." The Court also refers to the rights of the child to respect for their human dignity with regard to school discipline (article 28 of the Convention) and to protection from all forms of violence (article 19) and from torture or other cruel, inhuman or degrading treatment or punishment (article 37).

With reference to General Comment No. 8 adopted by the Committee on the Rights of the Child, the Court draws particular attention to the definitions of "corporal punishment" and "other cruel or degrading forms of punishment," their incompatibility with the Convention on the Rights of the Child in the home and family as in any other environment, and the standards set by the Committee for protecting children against corporal punishment which include legislative, educational, monitoring and evaluation measures. The Court stresses the Committee's view that "eliminating the violence and humiliating punishment of children is an immediate and unqualified obligation of the States Parties."

The Court also highlights its own jurisprudence which has emphasised, for example, that children "have rights and are not just an object of protection," that they have the same rights as all human beings, that the State must protect these rights in the private as well as the public sphere, and that this requires legislative as well as other measures.

The protection of children against corporal punishment begins with the adoption of a legal provision banning the use of corporal punishment, but its effective implementation compels the state to ensure appropriate mechanisms, programs and policies to support families in learning and using positive discipline to upbringing their children. Only in this manner can a state ensure less violent societies that respect human rights.

TASK/TEXT 4.12: EUROPE IS MOVING TOWARDS A TOTAL BAN OF DOMESTIC VIOLENCE AGAINST CHILDREN

Viewpoint 21 January 2008, Commissioner for Human Rights, Council of Europe, Thomas Hammarberg, <www.commissioner.coe.int>, Viewpoints; <www.coe.int/t/commissioner/Viewpoints/080121_en.asp>

A majority of the 47 Council of Europe member states have now committed themselves to put an end to all corporal punishment of children. Full prohibition in law has so far been adopted by 18 member states and at least seven others have publicly pledged to do the same within the near future. If these governments fulfil their commitment, Europe will be more than halfway to universal prohibition. This is welcome progress. Some positive steps have also been taken in other parts of the world. Last year, New Zealand became the first English-speaking country to prohibit all corporal punishment, including in the family. And so did three Latin American countries: Uruguay, Venezuela and Chile.

They had responded to recommendations in the report of the UN Secretary General's Study on violence against children, submitted to the General Assembly in October 2006. Its main message was that *"no violence against children is justifiable; all violence against children is preventable."* It recommended all states to move quickly to prohibit all forms of violence against children, including all corporal punishment, before the end of 2009.

This was another strong challenge to the still fairly widespread opinion that relations inside the family are no matter for outsiders. Already, the 1989 UN Convention on the Rights of the Child, adopted and ratified by almost every member state of the United Nations, had made clear that there are situations in which authorities have to protect a child from all forms of violence behind the family door. This is not a zero-sum-game between children and parents. The Convention is very family-friendly, it stresses the absolute importance of a good family environment and the need, in some cases, for community support to parents in crisis. Violence against children is a reflection of family breakdown and calls for the protection of the life, well-being and dignity of the child. This is a major reason why the prevention of domestic violence against children is nowadays recognised as a human rights concern.

The purpose of prohibiting corporal punishment of children is precisely *prevention*. The idea is to encourage a change of attitudes and practice and to promote non-violent methods of child-rearing. An unambiguous message of what is unacceptable is very important. Adults responsible for children are sometimes confused about how to handle difficult situations. The line should simply be drawn between physical or psychological violence on the one hand and non-violence on the other.

The problem is deep and serious. As part of their daily lives, children across Europe and the world continue to be spanked, slapped, hit, smacked, shaken, kicked, pinched, punched, caned, flogged, belted, beaten and battered in the name of "discipline," mainly by adults whom they depend upon.

This violence may be a deliberate act of punishment or just the impulsive reaction of an irritated parent or teacher. Both cases constitute a breach of human rights. Respect for human dignity and the right to physical integrity are universal principles. But despite this, social and legal acceptance of adults hitting children and inflicting other humiliating treatment on them persists.

Corporal punishment of children is often inhuman or degrading, and it invariably violates their physical integrity, demonstrates disrespect for their human dignity and undermines their self-esteem. This sense of deeper damage was described by the Polish doctor, writer and educationalist Janusz Korczak who once said: "There are many terrible things in the world, but the worst is when a child is afraid of his father, mother or teacher."

Special exceptions allowing for some level of violence against children in otherwise universally applicable laws against assault are therefore particularly unfortunate. They also breach the basic human rights principle of equal protection under the law.

The invention of concepts such as "reasonable punishment" and "lawful correction" arises from the perception of children as the property of their parents. Such "rights" are based on the power of the stronger over the weaker and are upheld by means of violence and humiliation.

The Parliamentary Assembly of the Council of Europe called in 2004 for a Europe-wide ban of corporal punishment. It stated that "any corporal punishment of children is in breach of their fundamental right to human dignity and physical integrity. The fact that such corporal punishment is still lawful in certain member states violates their equally fundamental right to the same legal protection as adults. Striking a human being is prohibited in European society and children are human beings. The social and legal acceptance of corporal punishment of children must be ended."

Progress has been made since then, but some member states have not acted upon this suggestion or those from the UN study. In order to encourage further discussion, I have been in correspondence with the government heads of those member states which have yet to reform their laws adequately.

Their responses give a hint that further progress is possible. In fact, no one defended the use of corporal punishment. Seven indicated that reforms to prohibit all corporal punishment were in progress. Some of the others replied that their existing law was sufficient, but demonstrated an open attitude towards further progress and considering explicit reform.

Of course, eliminating corporal punishment requires more than legal reform. Sustained public education and awareness-raising of the law and of children's right to protection is required, together with promotion of positive, non-violent relationships with children. The Council of Europe programme "Building a Europe for and with children" is promoting the abolition of corporal punishment through law reform, the promotion of positive parenting and awareness-raising efforts likely to change public attitudes and behaviours.

Children have had to wait the longest to be given equal legal protection from deliberate assaults – a protection the rest of us take for granted. It is extraordinary that children, whose developmental state and small size is acknowledged to make them particularly vulnerable to physical and psychological harm, have been singled out for less protection from assaults on their fragile bodies, minds and dignity.

Challenging legal and social acceptance of violence has been a fundamental part of women's struggle for equal status. The same applies to children: there could not be a more symbolic reflection of children's persisting low status as property than adults' assumption of their "right" and even "duty," to hit children.

TASK/TEXT 4.13: CORPORAL PUNISHMENT – MAKE ME A CRIMINAL; PREVENTING YOUTH CRIME

Crinmail 956 – 12 February 2008, <www.crin.org>

Smacking children, however lightly, should be outlawed because it increases the chances of aggression and anti-social and criminal behaviour in later life, a new report concludes.

An outright ban would 'reduce criminality in the long run but also send out a message about the kind of society we want to be, according to the study by the UK's Institute for Public Policy Research.

The think-tank, which is close to the UK government, also calls for children to be given cognitive behavioural therapy from the age of five, in an attempt to stop them turning into teenage criminals.

"The evidence shows that the most prolific criminals start offending between the ages of 10 and 13," said Julia Margo, associate director at IPPR and author of *Make Me A Criminal, Preventing Youth Crime.* "You need to deal with the problem before it manifests. **The biggest risk factor is not their behaviour, but their parents.**" Instead of punishing young children with anti-social behaviour orders, specialists should look into whether their parents were condoning delinquent behaviour, Margo argued. She called for 'sure start plus' centres for children aged five to 12, through which parenting classes, one-to-one reading sessions and counselling could be carried out. But Margo said a total ban on smacking would also reduce the number of children turning to crime. 'There is a lot of evidence that children who are smacked regularly – once a week – are more likely to develop aggressive personality disorder,' said Margo. "Hitting a child teaches them to act out on emotional impulses. We need to give out the message that children should be nurtured and taught to manage their behaviour. We should ban corporal punishment properly."

In the UK, it is currently not lawful for a parent to smack a child if it leaves a bruise but a lighter smack or 'reasonable chastisement' is allowed. It is a policy that many doctors oppose. 'This is an extremely important report,' said Rosalyn Proops, the child protection officer at the Royal College of Paediatrics and Child Health. "Like all people, paediatricians have a variety of opinions. However, the majority believe that all forms of smacking are an assault of a child and should not take place."

But others argued that making smacking illegal would need to be accompanied with **guidelines for positive discipline**.

Alex Griffiths, an educational psychologist, said any ban would have to be met with an educational programme: "My worry is that **before it can be made illegal parents need realistic alternatives** as to how they should handle their children. Otherwise, a large group of people, whose children are out of control, will be left with no sanctions whatsoever."

A spokeswoman for the Department for Schools and Families said they were not prepared to change the laws on smacking, arguing that violence against a child was illegal but decent parents should not be criminalised.

TASK/TEXT 4.14: CHILD DISCIPLINE

<www.unicef.org/progressforchildren/2007n6/index_41849.htm>

World Fit for Children goal: Protect children from all forms of abuse, neglect, exploitation and violence [...]

Violent methods of child discipline are widespread. In 29 countries and territories surveyed, an average of 86 per cent of children aged 2–14 experienced violent discipline at home; in almost every one of these countries more than half of the children have been violently disciplined and one in five children has experienced severe physical punishment.

Violent discipline is used in all socio-economic settings. In most countries, children from the poorest households are as likely to experience violent punishment as children from the richest households; children living in rural areas are as likely to experience violent punishment as children living in cities.

The proportion of mothers or caregivers who say they believe corporal punishment of children is necessary varies across countries but is consistently lower than the proportion indicating their children have experienced minor physical punishment in the month before the survey – 28 per cent and 62 per cent, respectively. The relationship between such attitudes and behaviours is deeply influenced by the social and cultural environment.

The United Nations Secretary-General's Study on Violence Against Children (2006) calls for an end to the justification of violence against children, whether accepted as tradition or disguised as discipline, and asks States to prohibit all forms of violent practice, including corporal punishment.

Definitions
Violent discipline is defined as actions taken by a parent or caregiver that are intended to cause a child physical pain or emotional distress as a way to correct behaviour and act as a deterrent. Violent discipline can take two forms: psychological aggression and physical, or corporal, punishment. The former includes shouting, yelling and screaming at the child, and addressing her or him with offensive names. Physical or corporal punishment comprises actions intended to cause the child physical pain or discomfort but not injuries. Minor physical punishment includes shaking the child and slapping or hitting him or her on the hand, arm, leg or bottom. Severe physical punishment includes hitting the child on the face, head or ears, or hitting the child hard or repeatedly. In surveys, mothers and caregivers are asked whether their children experienced any such violent discipline in the household during the past month.

See also <www.endcorporalpunishment.org>:

Global Initiative Newsletter 1 (February 2008) – [March 3, 2008; email]

Last year (2007) saw seven states added to the list of states achieving **full prohibition** of corporal punishment, including within the family home, including the first English speaking state (New Zealand) and the first Latin American states (Chile, Uruguay and Venezuela).

There are now 23 states worldwide where all corporal punishment of children is prohibited in legislation: Austria, Bulgaria, Chile, Croatia, Cyprus, Denmark, Finland, Germany, Greece, Hungary, Iceland, Israel, Latvia, Netherlands, New Zealand, Norway, Portugal, Romania, Spain, Sweden, Ukraine, Uruguay and Venezuela.

Prohibition in **schools** has been achieved by 103 states. In **penal systems**, 146 states have prohibited corporal punishment of children as a sentence of the courts and 106 as a disciplinary measure in penal institutions. Only 35 have prohibited corporal punishment in all alternative **care settings**.

Explicit prohibition, including in the home, is **under consideration** by the parliaments or parliamentary bodies in Brazil, Canada, Costa Rica, Nicaragua, Peru, the Philippines, South Africa and Switzerland.

Many other governments have made a **public commitment** to full prohibition, including Afghanistan, Bangladesh, Bhutan, Czech Republic, Estonia, Ireland, Lithuania, Luxembourg, Maldives, Pakistan, Serbia, Slovakia, Slovenia, Sri Lanka and Taiwan.

TASK/TEXT 4.15: THE RIGHT NOT TO BE HIT, ALSO A CHILDREN'S RIGHT

Commissioner for Human Rights of the Council of Europe (Thomas Hammarberg), *Children and corporal punishment: "The right not to be hit, also a children's right,"* Issue paper 2006/1, Updated version January 2008, CommDH/IssuePaper(2006)1REV

Introduction

A majority of the Council of Europe member states have now committed themselves to put an end to all corporal punishment of children. Full prohibition in law has so far been adopted by 18 member states and at least seven others have publicly pledged to do the same within the near future.

The Commissioner for Human Rights has welcomed this development and urged other countries as well to consider moving towards prohibition and elimination of all corporal punishment against children. This Issue Paper explains why and gives background information on steps already taken by the European Court of Human Rights and other international and European human rights mechanisms.

The problem is deep and serious. As part of their daily lives, children all over Europe are spanked, slapped, hit, smacked, shaken, kicked, pinched, punched, caned, flogged, belted, beaten and battered by adults – mainly by those whom they trust the most.

This violence may be a deliberate act of punishment or just the impulsive reaction of an irritated parent or teacher. In every case, it is a breach of fundamental human rights. Respect for human dignity and the right to physical integrity are universal principles. Yet social and legal acceptance of the hitting and other humiliating treatment of children by adults persists in most countries across the world.

Corporal punishment of children often becomes inhuman or degrading, and it always violates their physical integrity, demonstrates disrespect for human dignity and undermines self-esteem. Furthermore, the existence of special exceptions for violence against *children* in otherwise universally applicable laws against assault breaches the principle of equal protection under the law.

The invention of concepts such as 'reasonable chastisement' and 'lawful correction' in the law arises from the perception of children as **the property of their parents**. This is the modern equivalent of laws in force a century or two ago allowing masters to beat their slaves or servants, and husbands to beat their wives. Such 'rights' are based on the power of the stronger over the weaker and are upheld by means of violence and humiliation.

Children have had to wait until last to be given equal legal protection from deliberate assaults – a protection the rest of us take for granted. It is extraordinary that children, whose developmental state and small size is acknowledged to make them particularly vulnerable to physical and psychological injury, should be singled out for less protection from assaults on their fragile bodies, minds and dignity.

For women, challenging legal and social acceptance of violence, in particular the daily experience of routine violence in their homes, has been a fundamental part of the struggle for equal status. So it is with children: there is no more telling symbol of their downgrading than adults' assumption that they have a 'right,' even a duty, to hit children.

Definition of corporal punishment

The United Nations Committee on the Rights of the Child[19] has defined corporal punishment in these words:

> *"any punishment in which physical force is used and intended to cause some degree of pain or discomfort, however light. Most involves hitting ('smacking'; 'slapping'; 'spanking') children, with the hand or with an implement – whip, stick, belt, shoe, wooden spoon, etc. But it can also involve, for example, kicking, shaking or throwing children, scratching, pinching, biting, pulling hair or boxing ears, forcing children to stay in uncomfortable positions, burning, scalding or forced ingestion (for example, washing children's mouths out with soap or forcing them to swallow hot spices). In the view of the Committee, corporal punishment is invariably degrading. In addition, there are other non physical forms of punishment which are also cruel and degrading and thus incompatible with the Convention. These include, for example, punishment which belittles, humiliates, denigrates, scapegoats, threatens, scares or ridicules the child."*

Protection against corporal punishment is a human rights issue

We do nowadays talk about human rights also for children. Children are not any more "half" persons with a limited number of rights. This reflects an important change of attitude which made possible international treaties such as the United Nations Convention on the Rights of the Child.

The United Nations Convention on the Rights of the Child (CRC) is the most ratified human rights treaty. It has been ratified by all Member States of the Council of Europe. It is the first international human rights binding instrument to expressly address the protection of children from violence.

Article 19 of the Convention on the Rights of the Child requires states to take:

---

19 CRC Committee, General Comment No. 8 on the right of the child to protection from corporal punishment and other cruel or degrading forms of punishment, CRC/C/GC/8, 2 June 2006, <www.ohchr.org/english/bodies/crc/docs/co/CRC.C.GC.8.pdf>.

> *"all appropriate legislative, administrative, social and educational measures to protect the child from all forms of physical or mental violence, injury or abuse, neglect or negligent treatment, maltreatment or exploitation, including sexual abuse, while in the care of parent(s), legal guardian(s) or any other person who has the care of the child."*

Various other articles reinforce the child's right to physical integrity and protection of his or her human dignity. The Preamble affirms that precisely because of their "physical and mental immaturity" children need "special safeguards and care, including appropriate legal protection." Article 37 requires protection from "torture or other cruel, inhuman or degrading treatment or punishment."

The Council of Europe's human rights mechanisms first challenged corporal punishment of children 30 years ago. In 1978, the European Court of Human Rights (ECtHR) found the judicial birching of a 15-year-old boy breached his right to protection from degrading punishment.[20] Subsequent decisions during the 1980s and early 1990s condemned school corporal punishment, first in state schools and later in private schools in the UK.[21]

Other significant European Commission on Human Rights and European Court decisions have emphasised that rights to private or family life or to freedom of religious belief cannot be used as relevant arguments to reject banning all corporal punishment.[22]

The European Court issued its landmark *A v UK* judgment in 1998, its first ruling concerned with parental corporal punishment, and one of the relatively few cases brought before the Court by a child applicant.[23] "A," a young English boy, had been beaten by his stepfather with a cane, causing bruising. The stepfather was prosecuted but was acquitted, using the common law defence of "reasonable chastisement."

The European Court found that the boy's right to protection from degrading punishment had been breached, and that the UK was responsible because its law, allowing "reasonable chastisement," failed to provide adequate protection including effective deterrence. It ordered the UK to pay the boy £10,000.

The execution of this judgment by the United Kingdom authorities is still being supervised, nearly 10 years later, by the Committee of Ministers.[24] The

---

20 European Court of Human Rights, *Tyrer v. UK*, 1978; all judgments of the Court are available at <hudoc.echr.coe.int/hudoc>.

21 European Court of Human Rights; see in particular *Campbell and Cosans v. UK*, 1982; *Y v. UK*, 1992; *Costello-Roberts v. UK*, 1993.

22 European Commission on Human Rights, admissibility decision, *Seven Individuals v. Sweden*, 1982; application no. 8811/79; European Court of Human Rights, decision on admissibility, *Philip Williamson and Others v. UK*, 2000; application no. 55211/00.

23 European Court of Human Rights, *A v. UK*, 1998.

24 Committee of Ministers, supervision of execution of judgments of the European Court of Human Rights; annotated agendas are available at <www.coe.int/t/cm/humanRights_en.asp>.

UK's response to date has been to revise the "reasonable chastisement" defence, but not to remove it completely. As asserted by the UK's Children's Commissioners and a very large alliance of NGOs,[25] this approach leaves children with less protection than adults under the criminal law on assault.

The European Committee of Social Rights (ECSR) has stated that corporal punishment was not in accordance with human rights standards as defined by the Social Charter. It considers that:

> *"Article 17 [of the Social Charter] requires a prohibition in legislation against any form of violence against children, whether at school, in other institutions, in their home or elsewhere. It furthermore considers that any other form of degrading punishment or treatment of children must be prohibited in legislation and combined with adequate sanctions in penal or civil law."*[26]

This prohibition includes forms of punishing which do not necessarily involve the use of physical force, such as isolating or humiliating children.

In examining Member States reports under Article 17, the Committee asks questions about the legality of corporal punishment, in the home, schools and other institutions and day-care. In its Conclusions concerning many countries, the ECSR has found, since 2003, a breach of the Social Charter because corporal punishment of children is not prohibited.[27]

In 2005, the Committee issued its decisions on a series of collective complaints, brought under the Additional Protocol to the Social Charter by the World Organisation against Torture; in three cases, States were found to be not in compliance because of the lack of effective legislation prohibiting corporal punishment. In two other decisions, on complaints against Italy and Portugal, the Committee found that Supreme Court decisions in those countries which had declared corporal punishment to be unlawful were sufficient to comply with article 17.[28]

---

25 Submissions from Children's Commissioners for England, Northern Ireland, Scotland and Wales (May 2007); also from Dame Mary Marsh, Director and Chief Executive, National Society for the Prevention of Cruelty to Children and "Children are unbeatable!" Alliance, May, October and November 2007.

26 Conclusions XV-2, Vol. 1, General Introduction.

27 For details of the reporting process under the European Social Charter and Revised Social Charter, see <www.coe.int/t/e/human_rights/esc/3_Reporting_procedure/default.asp#TopOfPage>.

28 European Committee of Social Rights, decision on collective complaints No. 17/2003 OMCT vs. Greece, No. 18/2003 OMCT vs. Ireland, and No. 21/2003 OMCT vs. Belgium. In two other decisions, the Committee found that Supreme Court decisions in Italy and Portugal were adequate to comply: No. 19/2003, OMCT vs. Italy, and No. 20/2003, OMCT vs. Portugal; a further complaint was made against Portugal in 2006 – see note 11. For details see <www.coe.int/t/e/human_rights/esc/4_collective_complaints/List_of_collective_complaints/default.asp#TopOfPage>.

But in 2006, Portugal's Supreme Court issued a decision which condoned corporal punishment, thus effectively reversing previous decisions of the Court. A further collective complaint was submitted and in a unanimous and detailed decision issued in December 2006, the ECSR concluded: "To comply with Article 17, **states' domestic law must prohibit and penalize** all forms of violence against children, that is acts or behaviour likely to affect the physical integrity, dignity, development or psychological well being of children.

"The relevant provisions must be sufficiently clear, binding and precise, so as to preclude the courts from refusing to apply them to violence against children. Moreover, states must act with **due diligence to ensure** that such violence is eliminated in practice.[29]

Thus, the ECSR has emphasised the inadequacy of achieving prohibition simply through high-level court decisions; **explicit legislation is needed, together with other necessary educational** measures. During 2007, Portugal adopted legislation confirming explicit prohibition.

Progress towards ending corporal punishment of children at global level

There is a global context for making quick progress: the key message of the United Nations Secretary General's Study on Violence against Children, reported to the General Assembly in October 2006, is that no violence against children is justifiable; all violence against children is preventable. The Study urges all States to move quickly to prohibit all forms of violence against children – including all corporal punishment – setting a target of 2009.

> *"The Study should mark a turning point – an end to adult justification of violence against children, whether accepted as 'tradition' or disguised as 'discipline.' There can be no compromise in challenging violence against children. Children's uniqueness – their potential and vulnerability, their dependence on adults – makes it imperative that they have more, not less, protection from violence."*

At present, globally, some 23 states have prohibited all corporal punishment, including in the family.

The Committee on the Rights of the Child has consistently recommended the prohibition of all corporal punishment, including in the family, and suggested that **campaigns be carried out** to raise awareness of its negative effects and to encourage the development of **positive, non-violent child-rearing** and educational practices.[30] Human rights are universal, and Committees monitoring

---

29 Collective complaint No. 34/2006, OMCT vs. Portugal, decision on the merits, December 2006, paras. 19–22.

30 All of the CRC Committee documents are at <www.ohchr.org/english/bodies/crc/index.htm>. For an analysis of the Committee's comments related to corporal punishment, see <www.endcorporalpunishment.org>.

the implementation of other international instruments, including the two International Covenants, on Civil and Political Rights and on Economic, Social and Cultural Rights, have also condemned corporal punishment of children.

Vocal opposition to banning all corporal punishment comes in some countries from minority religious groups, quoting texts which, they believe, give them a right or even a duty to discipline their children with violence. While **freedom of religious belief** should be respected, such beliefs cannot justify practices which breach the rights of others, including children's rights to respect for their physical integrity and human dignity.

Mainstream faith communities and respected leaders are now supporting moves to prohibit and eliminate all violence against children. For example, the World Conference of Religions for Peace, comprising over 800 faith leaders, adopted "A Multi-Religious Commitment to Confront Violence against Children" in 2006. It called on governments "to adopt legislation to prohibit all forms of violence against children, including corporal punishment, and to ensure

the full rights of children consistent with the Convention on the Rights of the Child and other international and regional agreements. We urge them to establish appropriate mechanisms to ensure the effective implementation of these laws and to ensure that religious communities participate formally in these mechanisms."[31]

Progress towards ending corporal punishment of children in Europe

Though some progress has been made in efforts against corporal punishment, it is clear that this form of abuse has an alarming frequency and prevalence all over the world. Statistics show that it is a world-wide phenomenon which affects children irrespective of their country or social origin. The prevalence of corporal punishment has been substantiated by interview surveys conducted in a number of countries with parents, other carers and increasingly with children to determine more about why and how often corporal punishment occurs.

In its Recommendation 1666(2004) calling for a Europe-wide ban on corporal punishment of children, the Parliamentary Assembly of the Council of Europe considered that:

> *"any corporal punishment of children is in breach of their fundamental right to human dignity and physical integrity. The fact that such corporal punishment is still lawful in certain member states violates their equally fundamental right to the same legal protection as adults. The social and legal acceptance of corporal punishment of children must be ended."*

31 Declaration on Violence against Children, endorsed at the 8th World Assembly of the World Conference of Religions for Peace, Kyoto, August 2006.

Therefore the Recommendation called for a coordinated and concerted campaign for the total abolition of corporal punishment of children. Noticing the success of the Council of Europe in abolishing the death penalty, it called for Europe to become, as soon as possible, "*a corporal punishment-free zone for children*."

The Committee of Ministers of the Council of Europe has for more than 20 years encouraged Member States to prohibit corporal punishment. It started in 1985 with a Recommendation of which the preamble notes that "the defence of the family involves the protection of all its members against any form of violence, which all too often occurs among them." The **explanatory memorandum** describes corporal punishment as "an evil which must at least be discouraged as a first step towards outright prohibition. It is the very assumption that corporal punishment of children is legitimate that opens the way to all kinds of excesses and makes the traces and symptoms of such punishment acceptable to third parties." This condemnation was echoed in further recommendations in 1990 and 1993.[32]

The Committee of Ministers has insisted on the need to begin, in all Member States, a coordinated and concerted campaign for the abolition of all violence against children. Therefore, in order to pursue that objective, it announced a comprehensive three-year programme of action on "Children and Violence" with the following objectives:

- assist member states in implementing international standards at national and local levels, in particular the United Nations Convention on the Rights of the Child, the European Social Charter and the European Convention on the Exercise of Children's Rights;
- by 2008, to propose a coherent and comprehensive set of instruments and methodological guidelines covering all aspects of the question;
- improve the visibility and the impact of Council of Europe's work in the field.[33]

Banning corporal punishment at national level

There is encouraging and accelerating progress across the Council of Europe's 47 Member States towards achieving the goal of eliminating all corporal punishment of children. By January 2008, 18 Member States had adopted full prohibition and at least another seven had publicly committed themselves to achieving this goal in the near future. In addition, the Supreme Court of Italy has outlawed it, but

[32] Council of Europe Committee of Ministers, Recommendations on: "Violence in the family" (R(85)4), "Social measures concerning violence within the family" (R(90)2), and "The medico-social aspects of child abuse" (R(93)2). All recommendations are available at <www.coe.int/t/E/Committee_of_Ministers/Home/Documents>.

[33] Reply adopted by the Committee of Ministers to Parliamentary Assembly Recommendation 1666(2004), 20 April 2005, *CM/AS(2005)Rec1666 final.*

this judgment is not yet reflected in specific law. If these States fulfil their commitment, Europe will be more than halfway to universal prohibition.

European countries which have banned corporal punishment in legislation are:

Austria (1989), Bulgaria (2000), Croatia (1999), Cyprus (1994), Denmark (1997), Finland (1983), Germany (2000), Greece (2006), Hungary (2004), Iceland (2003), Latvia (1998), Netherlands (2007), Norway (1987), Portugal (2007), Romania (2004), Spain (2007), Sweden (1979) and Ukraine (2001). European countries that have committed themselves to banning it in the near future [are:] Czech Republic, Estonia, Ireland, Lithuania, Luxembourg, Slovakia and Slovenia.

During 2007, the Commissioner wrote to the Heads of Government in those Member States which have yet to reform their laws adequately. In their responses, no state defended the use of corporal punishment. Seven indicated that reforms to prohibit all corporal punishment were in progress. Some of the others replied that their existing law was sufficient, but demonstrated an open attitude towards further progress and considering explicit reform.

The purpose of criminalizing all corporal punishment is not, of course, to prosecute and punish more parents. It satisfies human rights by giving children equal protection of their physical integrity and human dignity. It gives a clear message that hitting children is wrong – at least as wrong as hitting anyone else. Thus it provides a consistent basis for child protection and for **public education promoting positive forms of discipline**. As attitudes change, so the need for prosecution and for formal interventions into families to protect children will diminish.

The goals of the ban in Sweden were to alter public attitudes towards corporal punishment, establish a clear **framework for parent education and support**, and facilitate **earlier and less intrusive intervention** in child-protection cases. Public support for corporal punishment has declined markedly. Whereas in 1965 a majority of Swedes were supportive of corporal punishment, a recent survey found only six per cent of under-35-year-olds supporting the use of even the mildest forms. Practice has also changed; of those whose childhood occurred shortly after the ban, only three per cent report harsh slaps from their parents, and only one per cent report being hit with an implement. **Child abuse mortality rates are extremely low in Sweden.**

Increased sensitivity to violence against children in Sweden has led to an increase in reporting of assaults, but there has been a declining trend in prosecutions of parents, and a substantial **reduction in compulsory social work interventions and in numbers of children taken into care**. Public attitudes towards hitting children have changed, which has facilitated early supportive intervention in individual cases.

Of course, eliminating corporal punishment requires more than legislation prohibiting it. Sustained public education and awareness-raising of the law and of children's right to protection is required, together with promotion of positive, non-violent relationships with children. A Committee of Ministers' recommendation adopted in 2006 defines **positive parenting** as "parental behaviour based on the best interests of the child that is nurturing, empowering, non-violent and provides recognition and guidance which involves setting of boundaries to enable the full development of the child."[34]

In 2008, the programme "Building a Europe for and with children" will launch a Europe-wide initiative, promoting **law reform, positive parenting and public education** through the production of user-friendly information and communication material developed to be used as campaign resources within its 47 Member States.

In states which have not yet achieved full prohibition, the public needs to be reassured that the first purpose of prohibition of corporal punishment in the family is educational, not punitive. The existence of the law emphasises that it is no more acceptable or lawful to hit a child than to hit anyone else and the law is there when necessary to protect children from significant harm.

Prosecution of parents and other **formal, as opposed to supportive, interventions should be reserved for serious cases**. As the Committee on the Rights of the Child advises:

> *"The first purpose of law reform to prohibit corporal punishment of children within the family is prevention: to prevent violence against children by changing attitudes and practice, underlining children's right to equal protection and providing an unambiguous foundation for child protection and for the promotion of* ***positive, non-violent and participatory forms of child-rearing*** *[...]*
> *The principle of equal protection of children and adults from assault, including within the family, does not mean that all cases of corporal punishment of children by their parents that come to light should lead to prosecution of parents. The* de minimis *principle – that the law does not concern itself with trivial matters – ensures that minor assaults between adults only come to court in very exceptional circumstances; the same will be true of minor assaults on children. States need to develop effective reporting and referral mechanisms. While all reports of violence against children should be appropriately investigated and their protection from significant harm assured, the aim should be to stop parents from using violent or other cruel or degrading punishments through* ***supportive and educational, not punitive, interventions.****"*[35]

---

34 Committee of Ministers Recommendation (2006)19, on policy to support positive parenting, 13 December 2006.

35 CRC Committee, General Comment No. 8, paras. 38 and 40.

Implementation of prohibition requires guidance to all those working with children and families and sustained, long-term public education to challenge the deeply ingrained tradition of violent and humiliating discipline.

Conclusions

The imperative for removing adults' assumed rights to hit children is that of human rights principles. It should therefore not be necessary to prove that alternative and positive means of socializing children are more effective. However, research into the **harmful physical and psychological effects of corporal punishment in childhood and later life** and into the links with other forms of violence do indeed add further compelling arguments for banning the practice and thereby **breaking the [transgenerational] cycle of violence.**

The Commissioner hopes that those Council of Europe Member States – a minority now – which have not reformed their legislation or committed themselves to doing so will recognise this as a priority. Among this minority, a very small number have explicit defences in their criminal or civil law, or common law, confirming parents' freedom to use some degree of violent discipline. These must of course be removed completely. In the other states, the law is silent, but nevertheless parents' "right" to use corporal punishment is assumed. Advice from the Committee on the Rights of the Child, echoed by the European Committee of Social Rights, suggests that explicit prohibition is required to put beyond doubt that the criminal law on assault does apply equally to assaults on children, whether or not disguised as discipline.

A Europe without corporal punishment does not only require amendment to national laws, banning such practices. Any national strategy for the elimination of corporal punishment has to include a combination of short-term measures including legal reform to prohibit clearly all forms of corporal punishment and longer-term measures to influence social attitudes and promote positive alternative methods of relating and communicating. Any strategy should include the following steps:

- review of existing legislation to ensure effective prohibition of all corporal punishment;
- awareness-raising among parents and professionals working with children about the rationale for abandoning corporal punishment as a form of discipline in the home and in institutions; this could include information on legal reform against corporal punishment in other countries and its positive effects;
- information to children about their rights, including the right to be treated with respect. This should be part of the **school curriculum** but also be disseminated through the mass media;

- clear guidance to teachers and pre-school staff, health personnel, social workers and other key professionals on their role in preventing such violations and how to respond in concrete situations when there are indications that a child may suffer violence and need help;
- research in order to develop a better understanding of the magnitude and nature of the practice and to identify groups of children at particular risk, and
- **parenting education courses and discussions** – involving children – on child-rearing practices and positive, non-violent forms of discipline in homes, schools and institutions.

All these steps will require awareness-raising among politicians and other decision-makers, and for this NGOs, professional groups and media are of strategic importance.

Sadly, the issue of corporal punishment has tended to fall off political and other adult agendas, even the agendas of strong human rights advocates. Its low priority is probably because of the very personal nature of the problem – **most adults, all over the world, were hit as children and may have hit their own children**. Politicians find it an unpopular issue; it is easier to focus only on extreme forms of violence to children and on violence by children, against which there is already a popular consensus. Also, many politicians are particularly wary of interference in the **traditionally 'private' arena of the family**.

All of this may be understandable but does not provide good excuses. Non-violent conflict resolution, tolerance and respect for others should be taught through setting good examples. How can we expect children to take human rights seriously and to help build a culture of human rights, while we adults not only persist in slapping, spanking, smacking and beating them, but actually defend doing so as being 'for their own good'? Smacking children is not just a lesson in bad behaviour; it is a potent demonstration of contempt for the human rights of smaller, weaker people.

TASK/TEXT 4.16: RAISE YOUR HAND AGAINST SMACKING!

Crinmail 982 – 13 May 2008, <www.crin.org>; Strasbourg, 29 April 2008, <www.coe.int/t/transversalprojects/children/Source/zagreg/AnnouceZagreb_en.doc>

A Council of Europe initiative against corporal punishment of children
International launch in Zagreb, 15 June 2008

Why this initiative?

The Third Summit of Heads of State and Government of the Council of Europe decided to launch a programme of action to eliminate all forms of violence against children. Corporal punishment is the most widespread form of violence against children, and it is in response to this that the Council of Europe is now launching a Europe-wide initiative calling for its abolition in all settings – schools, penal systems, alternative care structures and the home. This is also concrete follow-up to the recommendations contained in the *United Nations Secretary-General's Study on Violence against Children,* which has set 2009 as the target date for achieving universal abolition of corporal punishment.

How do we intend to achieve abolition?

We are basing our actions on three pillars – legal reform, positive parenting and awareness raising – none of which can be neglected if abolition is to be achieved in both law and practice.

1. **Legal reform**: Netherlands, Greece, Portugal and Spain recently introduced a full ban on corporal punishment in all settings, raising to 18 [Austria, Bulgaria, Croatia, Cyprus, Denmark, Finland, Germany, Greece, Hungary, Iceland, Latvia, Netherlands, Norway, Portugal, Romania, Spain, Sweden, Ukraine] the number of Council of Europe member states to do so. Our objective is to promote a ban in the remaining member states.

2. **Promotion of positive parenting policies**: Positive parenting refers to parental behaviour based on the best interests of the child: it provides nurturing, empowering, recognition and guidance to enable the child's full development. Positive parenting is rooted in respect for children's rights and thus a non-violent environment. Our objective is to promote the implementation of the Council of Europe recommendation on "policies to support positive parenting" by encouraging governments to set up policies and services promoting positive parenting and offering alternatives to violent methods of discipline.

3. **Awareness raising.** Most European societies still tolerate or even encourage corporal punishment as a means of disciplining children. There is a strong need to send out a clear message that children have the right to protection from all kinds of violence and to equal protection under the law. The information and media packs produced by the Council of Europe can greatly facilitate the dissemination of this message at national level, with a view to changing attitudes and behaviours. (...)

Who to contact at the Council of Europe?
Comprehensive information, in both English and French, on this Council of Europe initiative can be found at <www.coe.int/children>. (…)

Building a Europe for and with children
Directorate General of Social Cohesion, Council of Europe, F-67075 Strasbourg Cedex, France

TASK/TEXT 4.17: SPEECH BY MAUD DE BOER-BUQUICCHIO, DEPUTY SECRETARY GENERAL OF THE COUNCIL OF EUROPE

Zagreb, 15 June 2008, <www.coe.int/t/dc/press/News/20080615_disc_dsg_corppun_en.asp>

Many years ago, corporal punishment was very much in fashion, in all parts of the world and in many different settings – from prison to home, military units, mental hospitals, even places of work – people were physically hurt for all sort of offences, or none at all.

Times have fortunately changed. Today we live in civilised and humane societies which no longer allow human beings to inflict physical pain and humiliate other human beings. Except when it comes to children. Somehow, they were left out in this great humanistic evolution, and in many places it is still perfectly normal to smack them and do all other things that would most likely land you in prison if you tried them on someone your own size.

We have therefore decided at the Council of Europe to launch this awareness-raising campaign *[Raise your hand against smacking!]* to protect children from corporal punishment AND to challenge society's perception of the child as a mini human being with mini human rights.

There are many good reasons why corporal punishment of children should be abolished:

- Corporal punishment is a violation of children's rights to physical integrity, human dignity and equal protection under the law.
- Corporal punishment teaches children that violence is an acceptable and appropriate strategy for resolving conflict or getting people to do what they want.
- Corporal punishment is ineffective as a means of discipline.

The Council of Europe initiative aims to abolish corporal punishment in all settings – schools, penal systems, alternative care structures, and in particular, in the home. This is also our response to the recommendations contained in the United Nations Secretary General's *Study on violence against children*, which has set 2009 as the target date for achieving universal abolition of corporal punishment.

The legal and political basis for our action against corporal punishment are as clear as our motives to act: the United Nations Convention on the Rights of the Child, the European Convention on Human Rights, the European Social Charter and the case-law of the Social Rights Committee, decisions of the Committee of Ministers of the Council of Europe, recommendations by the Parliamentary Assembly, judgments of the European Court of Human Rights.

Now that we know why, we should look into "how." What needs to be done to eliminate corporal punishment?

– Abolishing corporal punishment requires intensive work in at least three areas. The first one is **legal reform**. Abolishing corporal punishment calls for a legal framework which clearly prohibits corporal punishment and protects children from all kinds of assaults including in the family setting.

Eighteen countries in Europe have abolished corporal punishment. Sweden was the first one to do it and the Swedish example is remarkable as it clearly shows – through a whole generation – how society has evolved following legal reform, positive parenting policies and awareness-raising. Contrary to what many believe, legal prohibition is however not restricted to Scandinavian countries. Countries from the south of Europe, such as Cyprus, Spain, Greece and Portugal, but also Germany, the Netherlands, Latvia, Hungary, Croatia, Austria, Bulgaria, Romania and Ukraine have joined Denmark, Finland, Iceland and Norway in banning the corporal punishment of children.

– The second facet of our action is the **promotion of positive parenting.**

Positive parenting refers to parental behaviour that is based on the best interest of the child: it is nurturing, empowering, and provides recognition and guidance to enable the child's full development.

– Finally, we will work on awareness-raising. Most European societies still tolerate corporal punishment as a means of disciplining children. There is a compelling need to send out a clear message that children have the right to protection from all kinds of violence and to equal protection under the law.

But we will not be able to accomplish this task by working alone. Even with the best will and the best of luck, the Council of Europe will not be able to reach the 800 million people living in [Council of] Europe [member states]. We are most grateful to all the partners who are joining us in our efforts to challenge violence against children. We are particularly grateful to the governments supporting our initiative, in particular to our host Croatia, to Sweden as the

Chair of the Committee of Ministers and to Finland, who has provided considerable financial support.

We are also encouraged by the co-operation with other international organisations such as UNICEF, the Office of the High Commissioner for Human Rights and others.

We particularly appreciate the assistance, advice and support from civil society. The help of the National Society for the prevention of Cruelty to Children, a UK charity and Saatchi & Saatchi, has been decisive in the realisation of the TV spot. At the Council of Europe, we like saying "children's rights concern us all."

I now invite you to view the TV spot prepared in co-operation with the National Society for the prevention of Cruelty to Children, and Saatchi and Saatchi. It carries a wonderful and powerful message "Hands should nurture, not punish."

I think this says it all. Thank you very much.

TASK/TEXT 4.18: UAE – NON-VIOLENT DISCIPLINE IS KEY

Crinmail 989 – 10 June 2008, <www.crin.org> [Source: Al-Bawaba]

9 June 2008 – Hitting is not the answer to child discipline, said Dr Hala Hammad, a child and teenagers psychiatrist addressing a Bepanthen Women Only seminar for mothers held at the Cultural Palace (Qasr Al-Thaqafah) in Sharjah. The seminar, sponsored by the Supreme Council for Family Affairs and General Administration of Children and Girls Center and Bayer HealthCare, aimed to educate mothers on understanding their child's behaviour and cognitive development, particularly during the crucial first five years of life. Dr Hammad, who specialises in early childhood development and hosts the television programme Beit Sgheer (Little Home) stressed that understanding a child's behaviour was the key to moulding all aspects of their development and socialisation.

She said: "Families frequently hurt and abuse their children in the misguided belief that they are guiding and disciplining them."

Dr Hammad said that **the lack of information and education on proper child-rearing practices was found to be a major inducer of child abuse and neglect**. To overcome this **ignorance** it was important to raise awareness about the ineffectiveness of corporal punishment, since many parents justify using violence by saying it is the only effective way, and teaching parents positive non-violent discipline techniques instead.

She said it was also important **to provide parenting education** on children's sexual, cognitive and emotional development **before becoming parents**, and in some cases to provide anger management counselling.

Over the coming weeks Dr Hammad will be giving similar lectures to mothers across the Middle East in the Bepanthen Women Only road-show, which has been organised and sponsored by Bayer Healthcare.

According to a World Health Organisation study about violence against children, 80 to 90 per cent of all children suffer varying degrees of physical punishment in their homes, of which a third or more is inflicted with instruments. The worldwide study said that over 50,000 child a year die from such abuse.

The latest scientific research confirms that 90 per cent of the growth of the human brain occurs in the first five years of life. Newborn babies have approximately 200 billion brain cells but have very few connections between these cells in their forebrain. How these connections are formed will determine the emotional and social intelligence of the child, and it is over these connections that mothers and other carers have a great deal of influence.

TASK/TEXT 4.19: CORPORAL PUNISHMENT – GUIDE TO LEGAL REFORM FOR EUROPE'S PARLIAMENTS

Crinmail 996 – 3 July 2008, <www.crin.org>

In every nation in Europe it is illegal to hit people. Children are people too, yet in two thirds of Council of Europe Member States, the criminal assault laws that protect adults from violence fall far short of protecting children. Everyday children are hit in the name of "educative" discipline and "reasonable chastisement."

"Off the books!" aims to brief parliamentarians and other lawmakers on the legal and support measures needed to achieve effective prohibition of all corporal punishment of children.

The first part provides guidance on analysing and improving national legislation. This may involve removing legal defences that allow corporal punishment to slip through the net. Or it may entail adding explicit provisions in child protection acts, civil and family codes, and so forth, clearly stating that neither parents nor other adults are allowed to use corporal punishment and other forms of humiliating treatment on children. The second part focuses on understanding and implementation.

Once full prohibition is achieved in law, governments must raise awareness at all levels on children's human rights and implement policy measures to support prohibition, applying to both families and child professionals.

TASK/TEXT 4.20: AFRICA – SPEAK OUT AGAINST ALL CORPORAL PUNISHMENT, COMMITTEE URGED

Crinmail 1030 – 4 November 2008, <www.crin.org>

A wide range of child rights organisations from across Africa supported by Save the Children Sweden have presented a submission to the **African Committee of Experts on the Rights and Welfare of the Child** [see chapter 10] in Addis Ababa requesting the Committee to issue a written statement urging States in Africa to prohibit corporal and other forms of humiliating punishment of children in all settings and to promote measures to implement and promote this prohibition.

An All Africa Special Report (2007) indicates that corporal and other forms of humiliating punishment are widely practiced in Africa. In many African countries corporal punishment is still legally sanctioned as a sentence in the penal system, as a disciplinary measure in alternative care settings and also in schools. Corporal punishment of children by their parents is still permitted in all African countries provided it is reasonable and moderate.

Children are physically, emotionally and socially the most vulnerable members of our society. Despite this children are given the least protection against physical violence than anyone else. In addition to slapping and smacking children are subjected to being kicked and to beatings with fists, sjambocks, whips, sticks, hosepipes and belts.

Children are burnt, tied up, locked up, required to kneel on hard and uneven surfaces, pinched, forced to undertake excessive labour and to stand in the hot sun for long periods of time. All in this is done in the name of discipline. This result in a range of injuries to children including fractures, loss of consciousness, burns and permanent disabilities.

"This state of affairs continues to exist despite various calls made by the [CRC] Committee on the Rights of the Child as well as the recent United Nations Study on Violence Against Children calling for an outright ban of all forms of corporal and other forms of humiliating punishment of children as this amounts to a violation of children's human rights to physical integrity, human dignity, equality and their right to be protected from all forms of violence," says Mr Assefa Bequele, Director of the African Child Policy Forum.

"We are approaching the African Committee of Experts as it is our view that support from this Committee in relation to the provisions of the African Charter on the Rights and Welfare of the Child on the issue, is critical to strengthen efforts to protect African children from these forms of violence," he added.

Members of this group of child rights organisations also highlighted that disciplining children through violent means may contribute to future societal violence. "Corporal and other forms of humiliating punishment have serious psychological effects as children feel humiliated and degraded and they become angry and resentful towards those who punish them this way. This leads to repressed anger which can be manifested in hatred towards themselves and others," says Judith Mulenga, Director of the Zambian Civic Education Association.

DITSHWANELO, the Botswana Centre for Human Rights, called for the development and adoption of positive discipline measure as a way of building trust in the child-parent relationship. "We know that children must be disciplined, but this can be achieved through a range of other positive discipline measures which do not cause pain and violence against a child. Children learn from their environment and by the behaviour of their parents and immediate relatives and friends," Ms Emily Ruhukwa said.

The African child rights organisations are calling on the African Committee of Experts on the Rights and Welfare of the Child, which is a group of experts overseeing the implementation of the African Charter on the Rights and Welfare of the Child, to take a clear public stance against all forms of corporal and other forms of humiliating punishment and to actively engage with the member States to ensure that Africans states outlaw corporal punishment without delay. The Committee should also support the recommendation in the Africa Declaration on Violence Against Girls for the African Union to establish a Special Envoy on Violence against Children to support the efforts of the Committee towards preventing, reporting and monitoring violence against children on the Continent.

The group of African child rights organisations will be represented at the hearing by the African Committee of Experts on the Right and Welfare of the Child by the African Child Policy Forum and representatives of the Southern African Network to End Corporal and Humiliating Punishment of Children.

TASK/TEXT 4.21: BEING HIT BY PARENTS MOST IGNORED CHILD TRAUMA

Murray A. Straus (<http://pubpages.unh.edu/~mas2>) (email to Child Maltreatment Researchers, 16 January 2009)

The most pervasive, and also the most ignored child trauma, is being hit by parents in the name of "discipline." Our national surveys and other studies have found that at least a third of parents hit infants – typically a slap on the hand for touching something forbidden or dangerous or for repeatedly pushing food off a high chair tray. The percentage increases to over 90% for spanking or slapping toddlers. American culture (and most others) define this as harmless if done "in moderation" by loving parents. However, the empirical evidence indicates the harmlessness is a cultural myth.

Below is a list of some of the studies providing the evidence indicating that being hit by parents is a traumatic experience for children, and that it has the typical effects of being a victim of a traumatic experience. All of the studies are available in the Corporal Punishment Papers section of my website <http://pubpages.unh.edu/~mas2>.

These studies, which can be downloaded from my website, have found that more corporal punishment, the greater the probability of:

- Post traumatic stress symptoms (…).
- Slower than average growth in cognitive ability (…).
- Antisocial behavior (…).
- Depressive symptoms (…).
- Physical violence to dating and marital partners later in life (…).
- A summary of longitudinal studies which help establish the causal direction (…).

The "effect sizes" for the above are low, but because corporal punishment is experienced by over 90% of American children, the cumulative adverse effect on American children and American society is very large (…).

Also of interest may be the following on my website:

- National survey showing that 94% of parents hit toddlers, at least occasionally (…).
- Article documenting the neglect in the scholarly literature of research showing harmful effects of corporal punishment (…).

I also recommend the following excellent meta analysis:

Gershoff, E. T. (2002). Corporal punishment by parents and associated child behaviors and experiences: A meta-analytic and theoretical review. *Psychological Bulletin, 128*, 539–579.

TASK/TEXT 4.22: SPARE THE ROD – WHY YOU SHOULDN'T HIT YOUR KIDS

<www.slate.com/id/2200450>, posted September 24, 2008

By Alan E. Kazdin[36]

The typical parent, when whacking a misbehaving child, doesn't pause to wonder: "What does science have to say about the efficacy of corporal punishment?" If they are thinking anything at all, it's: "Here comes justice!" And while the typical parent may not know or care, the science on corporal punishment of kids is pretty clear. Despite the rise of the timeout and other nonphysical forms of punishment, most American parents hit, pinch, shake, or otherwise lay violent hands on their youngsters: 63 percent of parents physically discipline their 1- to 2-year-olds, and 85 percent of adolescents have been physically punished by their parents. Parents cite children's aggression and failure to comply with a request as the most common reasons for hitting them.

The science also shows that corporal punishment is like smoking: It's a rare human being who can refrain from stepping up from a mild, relatively harmless dose to an excessive and harmful one. Three cigarettes a month won't hurt you much, and a little smack on the behind once a month won't harm your child. But who smokes three cigarettes a month? To call corporal punishment addictive would be imprecise, but there's a strong natural tendency to escalate the frequency and severity of punishment. More than one-third of all parents who start out with relatively mild punishments end up crossing the line drawn by the state to define child abuse: hitting with an object, harsh and cruel hitting, and so on. Children, endowed with wonderful flexibility and ability to learn, typically adapt to punishment faster than parents can escalate it, which helps encourage a little hitting to lead to a lot of hitting. And, like frequent smoking, frequent corporal punishment has serious, well-proven bad effects.

---

36 Alan E. Kazdin is John M. Musser professor of psychology and child psychiatry at Yale University and director of Yale's Parenting Center and Child Conduct Clinic. He is also president of the American Psychological Association and author, most recently, of *The Kazdin Method for Parenting the Defiant Child.*

The negative effects on children include increased aggression and noncompliance – the very misbehaviors that most often inspire parents to hit in the first place – as well as poor academic achievement, poor quality of parent-child relationships, and increased risk of a mental-health problem (depression or anxiety, for instance). High levels of corporal punishment are also associated with problems that crop up later in life, including diminished ability to control one's impulses and poor physical-health outcomes (cancer, heart disease, chronic respiratory disease). Plus, there's the effect of increasing *parents'* aggression, and don't forget the consistent finding that physical punishment is a weak strategy for permanently changing behavior.

But parents keep on hitting. Why? The key is corporal punishment's temporary effectiveness in stopping a behavior. It does work – for a moment, anyway. The direct experience of that momentary pause in misbehavior has a powerful effect, conditioning the parent to hit again next time to achieve that jolt of fleeting success and blinding the parent to the long-term failure of hitting to improve behavior. The research consistently shows that the unwanted behavior will return at the same rate as before. But parents believe that corporal punishment works, and they are further encouraged in that belief by feeling that they have a right and even a duty to punish as harshly as necessary.

Part of the problem is that most of us pay, at best, selective attention to science – and scientists, for their part, have not done a good job of publicizing what they know about corporal punishment. Studies of parents have demonstrated that if they are predisposed not to see a problem in the way they rear their children, then they tend to dismiss any scientific finding suggesting that this presumed nonproblem is, in fact, a problem. In other words, if parents believe that hitting is an effective way to control children's behavior, and especially if that conviction is backed up by a strong moral, religious, or other cultural rationale for corporal punishment, they will confidently throw out any scientific findings that don't comport with their sense of their own experience.

The catch is that we frequently misperceive our own experience. Studies of parents' perceptions of child rearing, in particular, show that memory is an extremely unreliable guide in judging the efficacy of punishment. Those who believe in corporal punishment tend to remember that hitting a child worked: She talked back to me, I slapped her face, she shut her mouth. But they tend to forget that, after the brief pause brought on by having her face slapped, the child talked back again, and the talking back grew nastier and more frequent over time as the slaps grew harder.

So what's the case for *not* hitting? It can be argued from the science: Physical discipline doesn't work over the long run, it has bad side effects, and mild punishment often becomes more severe over time. Opponents of corporal punishment also advance moral and legal arguments. If you hit another adult you can be arrested and sued, after all, so shouldn't our smallest, weakest citizens have a right to equal or even more-than-equal protection under the law? In this country, if you do the same thing to your dog that you do to your child, you're more likely to get in trouble for mistreating the dog.

The combination of scientific and moral/legal arguments has been effective in debates about discipline in public schools. Twenty-eight states and the District of Columbia have banned corporal punishment in the schools. But so far, we have shown ourselves unwilling to extend that debate beyond the schools and into the ideologically sacred circle of the family. Where the argument against corporal punishment in the schools has prevailed, in fact, it has often cited parents' individual right to punish their own children as they, and not educators acting for the state, see fit. The situation is different in other countries. You may not be surprised to hear that 91 countries have banned corporal punishment in the schools, but you may be surprised to hear that 23 countries have banned corporal punishment everywhere within their borders, including in the home.

I know what you're thinking: *Are there really 23 Scandinavian countries?* Sweden was, indeed, the first to pass a comprehensive ban, but the list also includes Hungary, Bulgaria, Spain, Israel, Portugal, Greece, Uruguay, Chile, Venezuela, and New Zealand. According to advocates of the ban, another 20 or so countries are committed to full prohibition and/or are debating prohibitionist bills in parliament. The Council of Europe was the first intergovernmental body to launch a campaign for universal prohibition across its 47 member countries.

Practically nobody in America knows or cares that the United Nations has set a target date of 2009 for a universal prohibition of violence against children that would include a ban on corporal punishment in the home. Americans no doubt have many reasons – some of them quite good – to ignore or laugh off instructions from the United Nations on how to raise their kids. And it's naive to think that comprehensive bans are comprehensively effective. Kids still get hit in every country on earth. But especially because such bans are usually promoted with large public campaigns of education and opinion-shaping (similar to successful efforts in this country to change attitudes toward littering and smoking), they do have measurable good effects. So far, the results suggest that after the ban is passed, parents hit less and are less favorably inclined toward physical discipline, and the country is not overwhelmed by a wave of brattiness and delinquency. The opposite, in fact. If anything, the results tell us that there's *less* deviant child behavior.

There could conceivably be good reasons for Americans to decide, after careful consideration, that our commitment to the privacy and individual rights of parents is too strong to allow for an enforceable comprehensive ban on corporal punishment. But we don't seem to be ready to join much of the rest of the world in even having a serious discussion about such a ban. In the overheated climate of nondebate encouraged by those who would have us believe that we are embroiled in an ongoing high-stakes culture war, we mostly just declaim our fixed opinions at one another.

One result of this standoff is that the United States, despite being one of the primary authors of the UN's Convention on the Rights of Children, which specifies that governments must take appropriate measures to protect children from "all forms of physical or mental violence, injury or abuse, neglect or negligent treatment, maltreatment or exploitation," is one of only two nations that have not ratified it. The other is Somalia; 192 [193] nations have ratified [or acceded to] it. According to my colleague Liz Gershoff of the University of Michigan, a leading expert on corporal punishment of children, the main arguments that have so far prevented us from ratifying it include the ones you would expect – it would undermine American parents' authority as well as US sovereignty – plus a couple of others that you might not have expected: It would not allow 17-year-olds to enlist in the armed forces, and (although the Supreme Court's decision in *Roper v. Simmons* has made this one moot, at least for now) it would not allow executions of people who committed capital crimes when they were under 18. We have so far limited our national debate on corporal punishment by focusing it on the schools and conducting it at the local and state level. We have shied away from even theoretically questioning the primacy of rights that parents exercise in the home, where most of the hitting takes place. Whatever one's position on corporal punishment, we ought to be able to at least discuss it with each other like grownups.

TASK/TEXT 4.23: RESPECT WORKS OUT – SZACUNEK-TO DZIAŁA – MIT RESPEKT GEHT'S BESSER!

<www.respectworks.eu>, accessed 28 February 2009

Respect works out is a tri-national European partnership project implemented in the UK, Poland and Germany with the aim of strengthening the right of the child to a non-violent upbringing. Our focus lies on the prevention of all forms of physical punishment in the home through supporting parents' positive parenting skills and the promotion of law reform – there are countries in Europe, including the UK and Poland, in which physical punishment is not yet legally banned.

Our vision is a Europe in which children are fully protected against violence by the law and by a public that condemns violence outright.

Why Reinvent the Wheel?! Sharing Experience throughout Europe
This website (<www.respectworks.eu>) seeks to share our project experience and to serve as a platform for the exchange with and amongst different organisations, initiatives and interested people working towards similar goals. This way we would like to contribute to the building of new synergies and to foster cooperation across Europe.

For many children in Europe, physical punishment is still a reality. This must stop!

Set on this goal, the German organisation *Association for a New Education* (ANE), the *National Society for the Prevention of Cruelty to Children* (NSPCC) in the UK and the *Nobody–Children Foundation* (FDN) in Poland are together working in the project *Respect Works Out!* (April 2007 – April 2009).

We consider non-violence as the basis for a child-friendly, democratic Europe. Non-violence we define as the absence of all forms of physical punishment against children, including a light smack.

In Germany, the introduction of a new law on the right of the child to a non-violent upbringing in 2000 in connection with a broad awareness raising campaign has lead to a significant decline in physical punishment against children.

The project builds on this positive experience in order to advance the EU-wide implementation of a legal ban and to promote non-violent parenting across Europe.

Family as a Team – Supporting Positive Parenting
We see the family as a team that takes diverging interests seriously and negotiates solutions that are suitable for all team members. There is no place for physical punishment of any kind here. Highlighting the benefits of non-violent parenting is a central aim of a letter for parents developed by the German project partner. It helps parents to understand children's behaviour better and provides useful advice on how to avoid situations getting out of control.

Exchange of Good Practice – The Positive Parenting Booklet
The project partners FDN and NSPCC have translated and adapted this positive parenting booklet to the country-specific context for parents in Poland and the UK. Around 50.000 copies have been disseminated to parents in Poland, the UK and in Germany. We evaluated parents' responses in each country and made a transnational comparison of the results. (...)

The adaption process itself provided us with new and interesting insights into the cultural differences of each of the three partner countries, starting with the format chosen through to the means of disseminating the booklet. (...)

Awareness Raising – Equal Protection for Children

The project seeks to root the right of the child to a non-violent upbringing firmly in public discourse, in law and policy measures and in parental practice. Depending on the state of the debate and the legal and political progress made in each of the project countries, *Respect Works Out!* is organising a number of national events targeted at parents, policy makers, experts, media representatives and the general public. In the UK and Poland, a lot of effort is focusing on the introduction of a legal ban on corporal punishment. In Germany, the project is supporting the call for children's rights to be explicitly enshrined in the German Constitution to strengthen child protection amongst other things.

For the different national activities, we are benefitting from the exchange of experience between the three project partners that the project facilitates. (…)

Joining Forces – working together across national boundaries

Only in partnership, by joining forces, exchanging and pooling skills and know-how, can our vision of a Europe free from smacking, hitting, spanking and of all other forms of violence against children, become a reality.

This website (<www.respectworks.eu>) is seeking to make a contribution to building and strengthening informal and formal European networks. Programmes, projects, organisations and initiatives have the opportunity to represent themselves in our European link list *What works* and to find others they might want to get in contact or involved with.

TASK/TEXT 4.24: EFFECTIVE DISCIPLINE FOR CHILDREN – THE REPORT ON PHYSICAL PUNISHMENT IN THE UNITED STATES

<www.phoenixchildrens.com/about/community-outreach-education/effective-discipline.html#The_Report_on_Physical_Punishment>, accessed 16 April 2009

Children don't come with training manuals. And disciplining children is one of the most important – and hardest – jobs parents have. It's not something we are taught, so most parents "learn on the job" or repeat what their parents did, which may not be effective. Phoenix Children's Hospital endorses effective discipline for children which does not involve physical punishment, and is proud to make available a leading report on physical punishment of children in the US.

The *Report on Physical Punishment in the United States: What Research Tells Us About Its Effects on Children*, authored by Elizabeth T. Gershoff, PhD, synthesizes one hundred years of social science research and many hundreds of published studies on physical punishment conducted by professionals in the fields of psychology, medicine, education, social work, and sociology, among other fields.

The research supports several conclusions:

- There is little research evidence that physical punishment improves children's behavior in the long term.
- There is substantial research evidence that physical punishment makes it more, not less, likely that children will be defiant and aggressive in the future.
- There is clear research evidence that physical punishment puts children at risk for negative outcomes, including increased mental health problems.
- There is consistent evidence that children who are physically punished are at greater risk of serious injury and physical abuse.

TASK/TEXT 4.25: UNITED KINGDOM – JUDGE RULES SLAPPING AND KICKING CHILD IS NOT 'SIGNIFICANT HARM'

Crinmail 1097 – 6 August 2009, <www.crin.org>, <www.walesonline.co.uk>

Judges in the UK have ruled in the case of a young girl repeatedly kicked and slapped by her parent, defining the point at which disciplining children becomes "physical abuse." Law lords sitting at London's Civil Appeal Court said there was a difference between "harm" and "significant harm," adding: "Reasonable physical chastisement of children by parents is not yet unlawful in this country."

The ruling, which means the girl will now return home, was described by children's charities last night as "beyond belief" and will have major implications for parents, children and local authorities' child protection services across the UK.

The parents, who cannot be identified, came to the attention of social services in Swansea when it was discovered they had subjected a young girl – who was in their care but not one of their own three children – to what a judge described as "shocking treatment." That included regular beatings and threats a dog would be set upon her if she didn't behave herself. The girl was taken into care last year and the situation between the parents and their own children was closely scrutinised.

Following revelations from their natural daughter – known only as M – that she had been kicked and slapped by both her parents, the couple's natural children were placed with foster parents and care proceedings were instigated by

Swansea council. However, in a judgement delivered at the family division of the High Court in Cardiff earlier this year, Mr Justice Roderick Wood dismissed the proceedings, despite having found that the allegations relating to the kicks and slaps were borne out.

Line not crossed

The judge found that the statutory threshold for making a care order in relation to the children had not been crossed, as in his view they had not suffered "significant harm." The children's court-appointed guardian yesterday challenged that finding at the Civil Appeal Court, where solicitor advocate Graham Jones argued it was "irrational" of Mr Justice Wood not to order that all the children be taken into care. But the court yesterday upheld the family court decision. The ruling means the children, who were kept away from their parents pending the ruling, will now return home.

Delivering the judgement, Lord Justice Ward, said: "This is, as I understand it, the first time this court has had to consider where the dividing line between harm and significant harm is established. "I understand that the words of the judgement [from the family court] record a catalogue of findings capable of causing any social services department concern. "On an unspecified occasion, or occasions, M was slapped on her hand by her parents, she was slapped on her face by her mother, kicked by her father, kicked by her mother, hit on the side of her face by her father, hit to the right-hand side of her face, kicked and pushed by her father. "It sounds terrible. It could speak of a persistent campaign of abuse causing real suffering. "But it could equally amount, in fact, to no more than a handful of isolated minor acts of chastisement forgotten as soon as administered. "Yes, it amounts to ill treatment and therefore to harm. "Yet, despite intensive outside intervention in this family's life, no-one ever saw a mark on that little girl and the stark fact is that she appeared to be well nourished, well cared for and with close attachments to her parents. "So was the harm significant? That was for the judge to decide. "The harm must, in my judgement, be significant enough to justify the intervention of the state and disturb the autonomy of the parents to bring up their children by themselves in the way they choose.

"The judge heard this case for six days. He is highly experienced in this class of case. The nuances would set his antennae reverberating. "In my judgement he was fully entitled to come to the conclusion that he did. I am inclined to think that I may well have come to the same conclusion myself."

Lady Justice Hallett agreed with Lord Justice Ward's assessment, saying: "Reasonable physical chastisement of children by parents is not yet unlawful in this country. "Slaps and even kicks vary enormously in their seriousness. "A kick sounds particularly unpleasant, yet many a parent may have nudged their child's nappied bottom with their foot in gentle play without committing an assault. "Many a parent will have slapped a child on the hand to make the point that running out into a busy road is a dangerous thing to do. What M alleged therefore was not necessarily indicative of abuse. It will all depend on circumstances."

The hearing related to the two parents, trapped in what was described as a loveless marriage, who had conceived three natural children – all still very young. The couple were said to have only had sex on a single occasion and the other children were the result of artificial insemination.

The father, described as wealthy and well-educated, and his wife said their marriage was merely "a product of cultural and family expectations".

Children's charities in Wales reacted strongly to the ruling last night.

'Major implications'

Catriona Williams, chief executive of the charity Children in Wales, said: "It is beyond belief that in a civilised society a case like this leads to a debate about how much significance can be attached to the harm inflicted by adults kicking or slapping children. "This would be a case of assault if inflicted by one adult on another. "Adults, of course, are much stronger and bigger than the children they kick or slap. "We know from paediatricians that some parents regard injuries they have inflicted on their children as a case of reasonable chastisement. "The fact that the notion of significant harm is subjective makes it a very worrying concept. "Clearly, rulings such as this have major implications for the welfare of other children."

Greta Thomas, director of NSPCC Cymru/Wales, said: "Currently the law in the UK on hitting is confusing and leaves children of all ages vulnerable to abuse. "It is a national embarrassment that the UK is one of only five remaining EU countries which have not given children equal protection under the law on assault or committed to doing so.

"There is a danger that the use of physical punishment by parents and carers can escalate and may result in serious harm to a child. "Changing the law to make physical punishment of children illegal would provide a clear basis for child protection and the promotion of alternative forms of discipline." (...)

TASK/TEXT 4.26:

TASK/TEXT 4.26.1: TEN REASONS NOT TO HIT YOUR CHILD (DR. WILLIAM AND MARTHA SEARS[37])

<www.askdrsears.com> (<www.askdrsears.com/html/6/T062100.asp>), accessed 18 August 2009

[37] Their eight children are called James, Robert, Peter, Hayden, Erin, Matthew, Stephen and Lauren.

1. HITTING MODELS HITTING

There is a classic story about the mother who believed in spanking as a necessary part of discipline until one day she observed her three-year-old daughter hitting her one-year-old son. When confronted, her daughter said, "I'm just playing mommy." This mother never spanked another child. Children love to imitate, especially people whom they love and respect. They perceive that it's okay for them to do whatever you do. Parents, remember, you are bringing up someone else's mother or father, and wife or husband. The same discipline techniques you employ with your children are the ones they are most likely to carry on in their own parenting. The family is a training camp for teaching children how to handle conflicts. Studies show that children from spanking families are more likely to use aggression to handle conflicts when they become adults.

Spanking demonstrates that it's all right for people to hit people, and especially for big people to hit little people, and stronger people to hit weaker people. Children learn that when you have a problem you solve it with a good swat. A child whose behavior is controlled by spanking is likely to carry on this mode of interaction into other relationships with siblings and peers, and eventually a spouse and offspring.

But, you say, "I don't spank my child that often or that hard. Most of the time I show him lots of love and gentleness. An occasional swat on the bottom won't bother him." This rationalization holds true for some children, but other children remember spanking messages more than nurturing ones. You may have a hug-hit ratio of 100:1 in your home, but you run the risk of your child remembering and being influenced more by the one hit than the 100 hugs, especially if that hit was delivered in anger or unjustly, which happens all too often.

Physical punishment shows that it's all right to vent your anger or right a wrong by hitting other people. This is why the parent's attitude during the spanking leaves as great an impression as the swat itself. How to control one's angry impulses (swat control) is one of the things you are trying to teach your children. Spanking sabotages this teaching. Spanking guidelines usually give the warning to never spank in anger. If this guideline were to be faithfully observed 99 percent of spanking wouldn't occur, because once the parent has calmed down he or she can come up with a more appropriate method of correction.

Verbal and emotional "hitting"

Physical hitting is not the only way to cross the line into abuse. Everything we say about physical punishment pertains to emotional/verbal punishment as well. Tongue-lashing and name-calling tirades can actually harm a child more psychologically. Emotional abuse can be very subtle and even self-righteous. Threats to coerce a child to cooperate can touch on his worst fear – abandonment. ("I'm leaving if you don't behave.") Often threats of abandonment are implied giving the child the message that you can't stand being with her or a smack of emotional abandonment (by letting her know you are withdrawing your love, refusing to speak to her or saying you don't like her if she continues to displease you). Scars on the mind may last longer than scars on the body.

2. HITTING DEVALUES THE CHILD

The child's self-image begins with how he perceives that others – especially his parents – perceive him. Even in the most loving homes, spanking gives a confusing message, especially to a child too young to understand the reason for the whack. Parents spend a lot of time building up their baby or child's sense of being valued, helping the child feel "good." Then the child breaks a glass, you spank, and he feels, "I must be bad."

Even a guilt-relieving hug from a parent after a spank doesn't remove the sting. The child is likely to feel the hit, inside and out, long after the hug. Most children put in this situation will hug to ask for mercy. "If I hug him, daddy will stop hitting me." When spanking is repeated over and over, one message is driven home to the child, "You are weak and defenseless."

Joan, a loving mother, sincerely believed that spanking was a parental right and obligation needed to turn out an obedient child. She felt spanking was "for the child's own good." After several months of spank-controlled discipline, her toddler became withdrawn. She would notice him playing alone in the corner, not interested in playmates, and avoiding eye contact with her. He had lost his previous sparkle. Outwardly he was a "good boy." Inwardly, Spencer thought he was a bad boy. He didn't feel right and he didn't act right. Spanking made him feel smaller and weaker, overpowered by people bigger than him.

Slapping hands

How tempting it is to slap those daring little hands! Many parents do it without thinking, but consider the consequences. Maria Montessori, one of the earliest opponents of slapping children's hands, believed that children's hands are tools for exploring, an extension of the child's natural curiosity. Slapping them sends a powerful negative message. Sensitive parents we have interviewed all agree that the hands should be off-limits for physical punishment. Research supports this idea. Psychologists studied a group of sixteen fourteen-month-olds playing with their mothers. When one group of toddlers tried to grab a forbidden object, they received a slap on the hand; the other group of toddlers did not receive physical punishment. In follow-up studies of these children seven months later, the punished babies were found to be less skilled at exploring their environment. Better to separate the child from the object or supervise his exploration and leave little hands unhurt.

3. HITTING DEVALUES THE PARENT

Parents who spank-control or otherwise abusively punish their children often feel devalued themselves because deep down they don't feel right about their way of discipline. Often they spank (or yell) in desperation because they don't know what else to do, but afterward feel more powerless when they find it doesn't work. As one mother who dropped spanking from her correction list put it, "I won the battle, but lost the war. My child now fears me, and I feel I've lost something precious."

Spanking also devalues the role of a parent. Being an authority figure means you are trusted and respected, but not feared. Lasting authority cannot be based on fear. Parents or other caregivers who repeatedly use spanking to control children enter into a lose-lose situation. Not only does the child lose respect for the parent, but the parents also lose out because they develop a spanking mindset and have fewer alternatives to spanking. The parent has fewer preplanned, experience-tested strategies to divert potential behavior, so the child misbehaves more, which calls for more spanking. This child is not being taught to develop inner control.

Hitting devalues the parent-child relationship. Corporal punishment puts a distance between the spanker and the spankee. This distance is especially troubling in home situations where the parent-child relationship may already be strained, such as single-parent homes or blended families. While some children are forgivingly resilient and bounce back without a negative impression on mind or body, for others it's hard to love the hand that hits them.

4. HITTING MAY LEAD TO ABUSE

Punishment escalates. Once you begin punishing a child "a little bit," where do you stop? A toddler reaches for a forbidden glass. You tap the hand as a reminder not to touch. He reaches again, you swat the hand. After withdrawing his hand briefly, he once again grabs grandmother's valuable vase. You hit the hand harder. You've begun a game no one can win. The issue then becomes who's stronger – your child's will or your hand – not the problem of touching the vase. What do you do now? Hit harder and harder until the child's hand is so sore he can't possibly continue to "disobey?" The danger of beginning corporal punishment in the first place is that you may feel you have to bring out bigger guns: your hand becomes a fist, the switch becomes a belt, the folded newspaper becomes a wooden spoon, and now what began as seemingly innocent escalates into child abuse. Punishment sets the stage for child abuse. Parents who are programmed to punish set themselves up for punishing harder, mainly because they have not learned alternatives and click immediately into the punishment mode when their child misbehaves.

5. HITTING DOES NOT IMPROVE BEHAVIOR

Many times we have heard parents say, "The more we spank the more he misbehaves." Spanking makes a child's behavior worse, not better. Here's why. Remember the basis for promoting desirable behavior: The child who feels right acts right. Spanking undermines this principle. A child who is hit feels wrong inside and this shows up in his behavior. The more he misbehaves, the more he gets spanked and the worse he feels. The cycle continues. We want the child to know that he did wrong, and to feel remorse, but to still believe that he is a person who has value.

The Cycle of Misbehavior:
Misbehavior > Worse behavior > Spanking > Decreased self-esteem, anger.

One of the goals of disciplinary action is to stop the misbehavior immediately, and spanking may do that. It is more important to create the conviction within the child that he doesn't want to repeat the misbehavior (i.e., internal rather than external control). One of the reasons for the ineffectiveness of spanking in creating internal controls is that during and immediately after the spanking, the child is so preoccupied with the perceived injustice of the physical punishment (or maybe the degree of it he's getting) that he "forgets" the reason for which he was spanked. Sitting down with him and talking after the spanking to be sure he's aware of what he did can be done just as well (if not better) without the spanking part. Alternatives to spanking can be much more thought-and-conscience-provoking for a child, but they may take more time and energy from the parent. This brings up a main reason why some parents lean toward spanking – it's easier.

6. HITTING IS ACTUALLY NOT BIBLICAL

Don't use the Bible as an excuse to spank. There is confusion in the ranks of people of Judeo-Christian heritage who, seeking help from the Bible in their effort to raise godly children, believe that God commands them to spank. They take "spare the rod and spoil the child" seriously and fear that if they don't spank, they will commit the sin of losing control of their child. In our counseling experience, we find that these people are devoted parents who love God and love their children, but they misunderstand the concept of the rod.

Rod verses – what they really mean
The following are the biblical verses which have caused the greatest confusion:

"Folly is bound up in the heart of a child, but the rod of discipline will drive it far from him." (Prov. 22:15)

"He who spares the rod hates his son, but he who loves him is careful to discipline him." (Prov. 13:24)

"Do not withhold discipline from a child; if you punish him with the rod, he will not die. Punish him with the rod and save his soul from death." (Prov. 23:13–14)

"The rod of correction imparts wisdom, but a child left to itself disgraces his mother." (Prov. 29:15)

At first glance these verses may sound pro-spanking. But you might consider a different interpretation of these teachings. "Rod" (shebet) means different things in different parts of the Bible. The Hebrew dictionary gives this word various meanings: a stick (for punishment, writing, fighting, ruling, walking, etc.). While the rod could be used for hitting, it was more frequently used for guiding wandering sheep. Shepherds didn't use the rod to beat their sheep – and children are certainly more valuable than sheep. As shepherd-author Philip Keller teaches so well in A Shepherd Looks At Psalm 23, the shepherd's rod was used to fight off prey and the staff was used to gently guide sheep along the right path. ("Your rod and your staff, they comfort me." – Psalm 23:4).

Jewish families we've interviewed, who carefully follow dietary and lifestyle guidelines in the Scripture, do not practice "rod correction" with their children because they do not follow that interpretation of the text.

The book of Proverbs is one of poetry. It is logical that the writer would have used a well-known tool to form an image of authority. We believe that this is the point that God makes about the rod in the Bible – parents take charge of your children. When you re-read the "rod verses," use the concept of parental authority when you come to the word "rod," rather than the concept of beating or spanking. It rings true in every instance.

While Christians and Jews believe that the Old Testament is the inspired word of God, it is also a historical text that has been interpreted in many ways over the centuries, sometimes incorrectly in order to support the beliefs of the times. These "rod" verses have been burdened with interpretations about corporal punishment that support human ideas. Other parts of the Bible, especially the New Testament, suggest that respect, authority, and tenderness should be the prevailing attitudes toward children among people of faith.

In the New Testament, Christ modified the traditional eye-for-an-eye system of justice with His turn-the-other-cheek approach. Christ preached gentleness, love, and understanding, and seemed against any harsh use of the rod, as stated by Paul in 1 Cor. 4:21: "Shall I come to you with the whip (rod), or in love and with a gentle spirit?" Paul went on to teach fathers about the importance of not provoking anger in their children (which is what spanking usually does):

"Fathers, do not exasperate your children" (Eph. 6:4), and "Fathers, do not embitter your children, or they will be discouraged" (Col. 3:21).

In our opinion, nowhere in the Bible does it say you must spank your child to be a godly parent.

SPARE THE ROD! There are parents who should not spank and children who should not be spanked. Are there factors in your history, your temperament, or your relationship with your child that put you at risk for abusing your child? Are there characteristics in your child that make spanking unwise?

- Were you abused as a child?
- Do you lose control of yourself easily?
- Are you spanking more, with fewer results?
- Are you spanking harder?
- Is spanking not working?
- Do you have a high-need child? A strong-willed child?
- Is your child ultra-sensitive?
- Is your relationship with your child already distant?
- Are there present situations that are making you angry, such as financial or marital difficulties or a recent job loss? Are there factors that are lowering your own self-confidence?

If the answer to any of these queries is yes, you would be wise to develop a no-spanking mindset in your home and do your best to come up with non-corporal alternatives. If you find you are unable to do this on your own, talk with someone who can help you.

7. HITTING PROMOTES ANGER – IN CHILDREN AND IN PARENTS

Children often perceive punishment as unfair. They are more likely to rebel against corporal punishment than against other disciplinary techniques. Children do not think rationally like adults, but they do have an innate sense of fairness – though their standards are not the same as adults. This can prevent punishment from working as you hoped it would and can contribute to an angry child. Oftentimes, the sense of unfairness escalates to a feeling of humiliation. When punishment humiliates children they either rebel or withdraw. While spanking may appear to make the child afraid to repeat the misbehavior, it is more likely to make the child fear the spanker.

In our experience, and that of many who have thoroughly researched corporal punishment, children whose behaviors are spank-controlled throughout infancy and childhood may appear outwardly compliant, but inside they are seething with anger. They feel that their personhood has been violated, and they detach themselves from a world they perceive has been unfair to them. They find it difficult to trust, becoming insensitive to a world that has been insensitive to them.

Parents who examine their feelings after spanking often realize that all they have accomplished is to relieve themselves of anger. This impulsive release of anger often becomes addicting – perpetuating a cycle of ineffective discipline. We have found that the best way to prevent ourselves from acting on the impulse to spank is to instill in ourselves two convictions: (1.) That we will not spank our children. (2.) That we will discipline them. Since we have decided that spanking is not an option, we must seek out better alternatives.

8. HITTING BRINGS BACK BAD MEMORIES

A child's memories of being spanked can scar otherwise joyful scenes of growing up. People are more likely to recall traumatic events than pleasant ones. I grew up in a very nurturing home, but I was occasionally and "deservedly" spanked. I vividly remember the willow branch scenes. After my wrongdoing my grandfather would send me to my room and tell me I was going to receive a spanking. I remember looking out the window, seeing him walk across the lawn and take a willow branch from the tree and come back to my room and spank me across the back of my thighs with the branch. The willow branch seemed to be an effective spanking tool because it stung and made an impression upon me – physically and mentally. Although I remember growing up in a loving home, I don't remember specific happy scenes with nearly as much detail as I remember the spanking scenes. I have always thought that one of our goals as parents is to fill our children's memory bank with hundreds, perhaps thousands, of pleasant scenes. It's amazing how the unpleasant memories of spankings can block out those positive memories.

9. ABUSIVE HITTING HAS BAD LONG-TERM EFFECTS

Research has shown that spanking may leave scars deeper and more lasting than a fleeting redness of the bottom. Here is a summary of the research on the long-term effects of corporal punishment:

- In a prospective study spanning nineteen years, researchers found that children who were raised in homes with a lot of corporal punishment, turned out to be more anti-social and egocentric, and that physical violence became the accepted norm for these children when they became teenagers and adults.
- College students showed more psychological disturbances if they grew up in a home with less praise, more scolding, more corporal punishment, and more verbal abuse.

- A survey of 679 college students showed that those who recall being spanked as children accepted spanking as a way of discipline and intended to spank their own children. Students who were not spanked as children were significantly less accepting of the practice than those who were spanked. The spanked students also reported remembering that their parents were angry during the spanking; they remembered both the spanking and the attitude with which it was administered.
- Spanking seems to have the most negative long-term effects when it replaces positive communication with the child. Spanking had less damaging long-term effects if given in a loving home and nurturing environment.
- A study of the effects of physical punishment on children's later aggressive behavior showed that the more frequently a child was given physical punishment, the more likely it was that he would behave aggressively toward other family members and peers. Spanking caused less aggression if it was done in an overall nurturing environment and the child was always given a rational explanation of why the spanking occurred.
- A study to determine whether hand slapping had any long-term effects showed that toddlers who were punished with a light slap on the hand showed delayed exploratory development seven months later.
- Adults who received a lot of physical punishment as teenagers had a rate of spouse-beating that was four times greater than those whose parents did not hit them.
- Husbands who grew up in severely violent homes are six times more likely to beat their wives than men raised in non-violent homes.
- More than 1 out of 4 parents who had grown up in a violent home were violent enough to risk seriously injuring their child.
- Studies of prison populations show that most violent criminals grew up in a violent home environment.
- The life history of notorious, violent criminals, murderers, muggers, rapists, etc., are likely to show a history of excessive physical discipline in childhood.

The evidence against spanking is overwhelming. Hundreds of studies all come to the same conclusions:

1. The more physical punishment a child receives, the more aggressive he or she will become.
2. The more children are spanked, the more likely they will be abusive toward their own children.
3. Spanking plants seeds for later violent behavior.
4. Spanking doesn't work.

10. SPANKING DOESN'T WORK

Many studies show the futility of spanking as a disciplinary technique, but none show its usefulness. In the past thirty years in pediatric practice, we have observed thousands of families who have tried spanking and found it doesn't work. Our general impression is that parents spank less as their experience increases. Spanking doesn't work for the child, for the parents, or for society. Spanking does not promote good behavior, it creates a distance between parent and child, and it contributes to a violent society. Parents who rely on punishment as their primary mode of discipline don't grow in their knowledge of their child. It keeps them from creating better alternatives, which would help them to know their child and build a better relationship. In the process of raising our own eight children, we have also concluded that spanking doesn't work. We found ourselves spanking less and less as our experience and the number of children increased. In our home, we have programmed ourselves against spanking and are committed to creating an attitude within our children, and an atmosphere within our home, that renders spanking unnecessary. Since spanking is not an option, we have been forced to come up with better alternatives. This has not only made us better parents, but in the long run we believe it has created more sensitive and well-behaved children.

EIGHT ADMONITIONS TO PARENTS WHO CHOOSE TO SPANK

By now you should realize that our position on spanking is simple: don't. But we are also experienced enough to realize that some loving, nurturing, committed parents believe in spanking as part of their overall discipline package. As a pediatrician with thirty years in practice, I am also quite aware that regardless of our advice against spanking, some parents are going to spank their children. For these parents, the best we can hope for is to help them spank in a way that is less likely to become abusive. Consider these suggestions.

1. Examine your overall parenting style

If you are generally a nurturing parent practicing the attachment style of parenting, an occasional spanking is unlikely to damage your child or relationship – but it's unlikely to help it either. If, on the other hand, you are practicing a more restrained style of parenting, spanking will be another obstacle that prevents you from knowing your child.

2. Examine your relationship with your child

Do you generally feel connected to your child? Do you feel that you have a handle on why your child behaves the way he or she does and can anticipate the undesirable behaviors before they begin? Do you know what triggers undesirable behaviors and what fosters desirable ones? Do you see signs that your child feels close to you: eye contact, approaching you, putting his arms around you, wanting to be picked up, enjoying being with you, and being able to communicate with you? If this is true, then an occasional spanking is unlikely to harm your relationship. If, however, you have a distant relationship and don't feel connected to your child, physical punishment is likely to increase the distance between you.

Here is a story from a mother of two of my patients. She is an intuitive, loving parent with a strong connection to her children, and she has a huge repertoire of alternatives to spanking.

"There have been a few times when we have had to spank our kids, and it was when they were between three and five years old. It was three or four times for our daughter, maybe once or twice for our son. I don't like to see tantruming children flailing out of control. They need something to help them get control back. So on the few occasions that they were literally out of control we've used spanking. I can remember when one of them was throwing a tantrum, my husband said, 'I have to swat your bottom to help you stop.' It shocked him and he was able to regain his control."

Other parents would handle this differently and would not respond this way to tantrums. Yet these parents know their children and know their own tolerances for "out of control" behavior. One comment I do have is that the reason the swat worked is that it had shock value, meaning it was the first (and rare) occurrence. It got the child's attention because these parents saved it for the one situation they personally could not tolerate.

3. Determine where spanking fits in your overall discipline package

Do you raise your hand in the swatting position or grab the wooden spoon as a knee-jerk response the moment your child misbehaves? One way to tell if you are a reflex hitter is if your child flinches anytime you move your hand suddenly upward in his vicinity. Reflex spanking is rarely helpful for several reasons: It's done out of anger, you may spank harder than intended, and you don't allow yourself time to try alternatives. If you resolve to put spanking way down on the list of correction techniques, you will have to try alternatives first rather than immediately click into "hit mode."

4. Don't spank in anger

If you are an angry person given to impulsive hitting, realize you are at risk for spanking abusively and dangerously. Some children have a way of pushing "hot buttons" in adults, and some adults have very sensitive buttons. Examine your feelings during and after spanking. Do you spank to punish your child, or to vent your anger? Who's the spanking for, you or your child?

Says Martha: Martha's Comments: "Previously, when I did spank our children, I never felt right about it. I didn't spank because the behavior was so bad, but because I had been inconvenienced, and I was taking it out on the child. I used to slap our first two children in anger, and as I slapped I could see in my mind's eye how I had been slapped by angry adults as a child. It was those flashbacks that made me realize how wrong I was for me to hit our child."

When you are angry, you are likely to spank too hard because you are out of control. (Seeing you out of control traumatizes them as much as the spanking.) Spanking in anger leaves the wrong impression on children's minds. They may be so bothered by the anger in your eyes and face that they don't realize the reason or the justification for the spanking. As a result, the punishment has no teaching value. A proper disciplinary action should improve the relationship with your child by creating a feeling that the parents are fair and consistent boundary setters; the child can depend on them to be in charge when he himself is out of control. Spanking, especially in anger, disturbs the trust between caregiver and child. In our family, we have found the best way to avoid spanking in anger is to mentally program ourselves against spanking. We have resolved never to spank. This preprogramming against spanking will override the reflex to smack a child, and give us time to think about what type of correction is best in this situation. Programming against spanking is a sort of safety valve that keeps you from possibly hurting your child.

5. Do not violate your child

Removing underwear in order to spank bare skin is a humiliating invasion of personal and private space and sexually threatening and confusing to the child. So firmly resist the traditional image of the bare-bottomed child stretched across your lap.

Should you use your open hand, paddle, or a switch to spank? Use of any one of the above will not cause permanent physical harm if you avoid too much force. The one tool we definitely advise against is a wooden spoon because we have seen bodily injury result from this club-like instrument. Any spanking that leaves black and blue marks (bruising) is wrong whether you use an object or your hand. Keep your hand open and flat – a fisted hand will be too forceful and damaging. A child old enough to spank (see number 6) will also understand that your loving hand is holding the spanking tool. The hand-versus-object debate is meaningless to him.

6. Explain the spank

Spanking without an explanation contributes little to discipline. In fact, studies have shown that calm spanking preceded by a rational explanation does less harm and more good than spanking without such reasoning. Explaining the punishment can be therapeutic for both the spanker and the spankee. It helps you decide whether or not your action is appropriate. It makes it less likely that the child will repeat the misbehavior, gives your child a chance to make a judgment about the fairness of the action, and preserves the self-image of the child by treating him as a rational person. The child will feel angry and humiliated about the spanking if he feels that there is no reason for it.

Getting the child to understand why he is being spanked helps to clear the air of angry feelings and contributes to his gaining self-control. If during your explanation you either begin to realize that you have the facts wrong or your heart is telling you there is a better way to deal with the situation, by all means switch to another corrective action and make a mental note to give this whole thing more thought.

A child under three will not be able to fully understand your explanation; he'll just know he's being hit and it has something to do with his being bad. He's probably also too young to separate his person from his action, so he'll think he's bad even though you are telling him "that was a bad thing to do."

7. Ask yourself, "Is spanking working?"

Evaluate your discipline techniques every month or two, especially physical punishment. Which ones are working? Is your child misbehaving less? Is your relationship with your child getting better? Is your child's self-worth increasing? If the answers to all the questions are "yes" then you are on the right track. If any disciplinary action is not working, drop it. If you are spanking harder and more often, this technique is obviously not working and you need to consider alternatives. You need to consider other modes of discipline if you find your child is misbehaving more. Change what you're doing if the distance between you and your child is increasing.

8. Examine the time you spend with your child

Is much of your quality time with your child spent punishing? If this is so, you are likely to have an angry child and a weak parent-child relationship. The joys of parenting and the stages of growing up are too precious to waste on such negative interaction. Consider changing your approach; spend a lot of time with your child just having fun. Let your child help you work around the house or run errands. Tell him you enjoy his companionship. As your child realizes how much fun it is to be with you, he will translate this into behaving well – which can be fun, too.

CORPORAL REDIRECTION VERSUS CORPORAL PUNISHMENT

Here is an example of an alternative to spanking that physically corrects misbehavior without inflicting pain. Lauren is our family monkey; she is always climbing on things. One day Martha walked into the kitchen to see then twenty-two-month-old Lauren standing on the countertop sorting through the spice rack. (Rarely had she gotten to this level in her adventures without someone intervening.) In a rapid reflexive move, Martha swung one hand under Lauren's bottom and the other arm around her middle as she swooped her off the countertop with a firmness and swiftness that surprised them both, while saying something like "Not safe! You stay down!" Lauren happened to be bare-bottomed, so the swift, firm hand made a slightly stinging sensation on her bare skin. This registered with Lauren. She looked closely at Martha to detect anger or intent to hurt in her mother's body language. Finding none, she interpreted her removal as protection and correction rather than punishment, and she cut short her howl of protest. Martha's physical action inflicted direction, not pain. The sureness and swiftness of the movement certainly left its mark on Lauren's mind. Lauren learned, once again, that Martha is the parent and she is the child. To Lauren, Martha's bigness is not a threat but a security ("Mom can rescue me because she is big"), even though the rescues are limits to freedom that are often frustrating to Lauren. It is very important for children to get the clear message that their parents are in charge. With young children most of this impression will need to be made physically. Words alone won't work.

SIGNS YOU NEED PROFESSIONAL HELP ABOUT DISCIPLINE

Most discipline problems can be handled by just taking the time to assess the strength of your parent-child connection, using common-sense techniques, and trying one approach after another until you find what works. Yet there are times when you need outside help. Consider two different types of counselors. Consult experienced, happy parents whose advice you value. They can offer practical tips to make living with your child easier. You may need to dig more deeply into disciplining yourself in order to discipline your child. You may require the help of a therapist. Here are some red flags that mean you are at risk for disciplining unwisely.

- **Yelling.** Do you go into frequent rages that are out of control, calling your child names ("Brat," "Damn kid") and causing your child to recoil and retreat? This means that you are letting your child punch your anger buttons too easily, that you may not have control of your anger buttons, or that there are simply too many anger buttons.
- **Mirroring unhappiness.** Do you walk around all day reflecting to your child that you are unhappy as a person and as a parent? Kids take this personally. If they bring you no joy, they must be no good. Life is a "downer."

- **Parentifying.** Are your children taking care of you instead of vice versa? Are you crying and complaining a lot and showing immature overreactions to accidents or misbehaviors? This scares children. You're supposed to be the parent, the one in control protecting them.
- **Blame shifting.** Do you unload your mistakes on your kids or your spouse? If so, children learn that the way you deal with problems is to avoid taking personal responsibility for them, and that somehow these problems are just too big for you to manage or that you don't know how to ask for help.
- **Modeling perfection.** Are you intolerant of even trivial mistakes made by yourself or your child? The child gets the message that mistakes are horrible to make. This is particularly difficult for the "sponge child," the one who soaks up your attitudes and becomes too hard on himself.
- **Spanking more.** Are slaps and straps showing up in your corrections? Are most of your interactions with your child on a negative note?
- **A fearing family.** Is your child afraid of you? Does she cringe when you raise your voice and keep a "safe" distance from you? Is your child becoming emotionally flat, fearing the consequences of expressing her emotions?

While even the most healthy parent may experience one of these red flags occasionally, if you find they are becoming a routine way of life, for the sake of yourself and your child, ***get professional help***.

TASK/TEXT 4.26.2: TWELVE WAYS TO HELP YOUR CHILD BUILD SELF-CONFIDENCE (DR. WILLIAM AND MARTHA SEARS[38])

<www.askdrsears.com> (<www.askdrsears.com/html/6/T061500.asp>), accessed 18 August 2009

Self-esteem is your child's passport to lifetime mental health and social happiness

It's the foundation of a child's well-being and the key to success as an adult. At all ages, how you feel about yourself affects how you act. Think about a time when you were feeling really good about yourself. You probably found it much easier to get along with others and feel good about them.

[38] Their eight children are called James, Robert, Peter, Hayden, Erin, Matthew, Stephen and Lauren.

Self-image is how one perceives oneself
The child looks in the mirror and likes the person he sees. He looks inside himself and is comfortable with the person he sees. He must think of this self as being someone who can make things happen and who is worthy of love. ***Parents are the main source of a child's sense of self-worth.***

Lack of a good self-image very often leads to behavior problems
Most of the behavioral problems that I see for counseling come from poor self-worth in parents as well as children. ***Why is one person a delight to be with, while another always seems to drag you down?*** How people value themselves, get along with others, perform at school, achieve at work, and relate in marriage, all stem from strength of their self-image.

Healthy self-worth doesn't mean being narcissistic or arrogant
It means having a realistic understanding of one's strengths and weaknesses, enjoying the strengths and working on the problem areas. Because there is such a strong parallel between how a person feels about himself and how a person acts, helping your child build self-confidence is vital to discipline.

Throughout life your child will be exposed to positive influences builders and negative influences breakers. Parents can expose their child to more builders and help him work through the breakers.

1. PRACTICE ATTACHMENT PARENTING
Put yourself in the place of a baby who spends many hours a day in a caregiver's arms, is worn in a sling, breastfed on cue, and her cries are sensitively responded to. How do you imagine this baby feels? This baby feels loved; this baby feels valuable. Ever had a special day when you got lots of strokes and showered with praise? You probably felt like queen for a day and hopefully you behaved accordingly. The infant on the receiving end of this high-touch style of parenting develops self-worth. She likes what she feels.

Responsiveness is the key to infant self-value. Baby gives a cue, for example, crying to be fed or comforted. A caregiver responds promptly and consistently. As this cue-response pattern is repeated many hundreds, perhaps thousands, of times during the first year baby learns that her cues have meaning: "Someone listens to me, therefore, I am worthwhile." A stronger self emerges.

Of course, you can't always respond promptly or consistently. It's the predominant pattern that counts. You will have days when you are short on patience. Babies pick out the prevailing parenting style and form impressions. As baby gets older it becomes important for him to learn how to deal with healthy frustration, as this will teach him to adjust to change. The important thing is that you are there for him; that's the message on which baby builds his sense of self.

The confidence-building aspects that result from attachment-parenting pay off especially with high-need babies. Because of these infants' more intense demands, they are at higher risk of receiving negative responses. When attachment parenting produces mutual sensitivity between connected parents and high-need babies, they learn to see themselves in a good light.

Because of responsive nurturing, the connected baby knows what to expect. On the other hand, the disconnected child is confused. If his needs are not met and his cues unanswered, he feels that signals are not worth giving. This leads to the conclusion that "I'm not worthwhile. I'm at the mercy of others, and there's nothing I can do to reach them."

We emphasize the importance of early nurturing because during the first two years the baby's brain is growing very fast. This is the period when a baby develops patterns of associations – ***mental models of the way things work***. The developing infant's mind is like a file drawer. In each file is a mental picture of a cue she gives along with the response she expects. After a certain interaction, the baby stores a mental image of what happened. For example, baby raises her arms and a parent responds by picking her up. Repetition deepens these patterns in the infant's mind, and eventually emotions, positive or negative, become associated with them. A file drawer full of mostly positive feelings and images leads to a feeling of "rightness." Her sense of "well-being" becomes part of baby's self.

Infants who get used to the feeling of well-being they get from attachment parenting spend the rest of their lives striving to keep this feeling. Because they have so much practice at feeling good, they can regain this right feeling after temporary interruptions. These ***secure infants cope better with life's setbacks*** because they are motivated to repair their sense of well-being, which has become integrated into their sense of self. They may fall down a lot, but they are likely to wind up back on their feet. This concept is especially true for a child who is handicapped or seems to come into this world relatively short-changed in natural talents. Children who do not have this early sense of well-being struggle to find it, but they are unsure of what they are looking for because they don't know how it feels. This explains why some babies who get attachment parenting in the early years manage well despite an unsettled childhood because of family problems. Consider the famous case of ***Baby Jessica***, the two-year-old who because of a legal quirk was taken from the familiar and nurturing home of her adoptive parents whom she had known since birth, and given to her biological parents who were strangers to her. She is likely to thrive because she entered a strange situation with a strong sense of well-being created by early nurturing. She will spend the rest of her life maintaining that feeling despite the trauma she endured.

Playing catch-up

But what if I didn't practice all those attachment styles of parenting, you may wonder? Don't be too hard on yourself. Babies are resilient [reparation of insecure attachment may be possible, JW] and, of course, it's never too late to start building up your child's self-image. Getting to know your child and seeing things from his point of view will help you help him learn to trust himself. This kind of nurturing cements together the blocks of self-worth, and can also repair them. Still, the earlier the cement is applied, the smoother it goes on and the stronger it sticks.

2. IMPROVE YOUR OWN SELF-CONFIDENCE

Parenting is therapeutic. In caring for your child you often heal yourself. A mother with a high-need baby in our practice once declared, "My baby brings out the best and the worst in me." If there are problems in your past that affect your present parenting, confront them. Get psychological help if they are interfering with your ability to remain calm and parent effectively.

Heal your past

A child's self-esteem is acquired, not inherited. Certain parenting traits and certain character traits, such as anger and fearfulness, are learned in each generation. Having a baby gives you the chance to become the parent you wish you had. If you suffer from low self-confidence, especially if you feel it's a result of how you were parented, take steps to heal yourself and ***break the family pattern***. Try this exercise (therapists call this "passing on the best, and discarding the rest"):

- List the specific things your parents did to build your self-image.
- List the specific things your parents did to weaken your self-image.
- Now resolve to emulate the good things your parents did and avoid the rest. If you find it difficult to follow through with this exercise on your own, ***get help from a professional***. Both you and your child will benefit.

Don't be too hard on your parents

They probably did the best they could given their circumstances and the prevailing advice of the times. I remember once hearing a grandmother say to a mother, "I was a good mother to you. I followed exactly the schedule the doctor gave me." This new mother felt that some of her present problems stemmed from the rigid scheduling that she endured when she was a baby. She was determined to learn to read her baby's cues. I reminded her not to blame her own mother because the prevailing parenting practice at the time was to follow the "expert's" advice on childrearing. The mother of [since?] the [19]90's, however, is more comfortable becoming the expert on her own child.

Polish your mirror

No one can put on a happy face all the time, but a parent's unhappiness can transfer to a child. Your child looks to you as a mirror for his own feelings. If you are worried, you can't reflect good feelings. In the early years, a child's concept of self is so intimately tied up with the mother's concept of herself that a sort of mutual self-worth building goes on. What image do you reflect to your child? She will see through a false facade to the troubled person beneath. Matthew, on a fill-in-the-blanks tribute to his mother, wrote: "I like being with my mother most when she's happy." Children translate your unhappiness with yourself to mean unhappiness with them. Even [especially?] infants know they are supposed to please their parents [that's why they look so cute; to please is to survive, JW]. As they get older, they may even come to feel responsible for their parents' happiness [parentification, JW]. If you are not content, [they feel] they must not be good (or good enough). If you are experiencing serious problems with depression or anxiety, ***seek help*** so that you can resolve these feelings before they affect your child.

Martha notes: Tip of the day

> "Shortly after the birth of our eighth child, I was overwhelmed with two babies in diapers and the needs of four older children at home. My stress was reflected in my face; I was often not a happy person. Fortunately, I recognized what I was showing of myself to my children. I did not want my children growing up believing that mothering is no fun or that they caused me to be unhappy. I sought help, fixed my inner feelings and polished my mirror so that my children could see a better image of themselves."

3. BE A POSITIVE MIRROR

Much of a child's self-image comes not only from what the child perceives about herself, but from how she thinks others perceive her. This is especially true of preschoolers who learn about themselves from their parents' reactions. Do you reflect positive or negative images to your child? Do you give her the idea that she's fun to be with? That her opinions and desires matter to you? That her behavior pleases you?

When you give your child positive reflections, he learns to think well of himself. He will also willingly rely on you to tell him when his behavior is not pleasing. This becomes a discipline tool. "All I have to do is look at her a certain way, and she stops misbehaving," said one mother. She had saturated her child's self awareness with positive feelings, and the youngster was used to the way he felt being on the receiving end of these strokes. When mother flashed a negative reflection, the child didn't like the feeling it produced. He changed his behavior quickly to regain his sense of well-being.

Be realistic

You can't be up and smiling all the time and still be human. Your child should know that parents have down days, too. Children can see through fake cheerfulness. Your sensitivity toward him will increase his sensitivity toward you, and someday he may be the one lifting your self-confidence.

Putting Humpty-Dumpty Back Together Again

You spend the early years building your child's self-confidence. You spend the later years protecting it. Many thin-skinned children need protection from situations they find overwhelming. I was examining five-year-old Thomas for his school-entry physical. Thomas was a sensitive child whose mother had spent years helping him build a strong sense of self-worth. We were engaged in a philosophical discussion of the long-term benefits of attachment parenting and Thomas was understandably bored. He began hanging on my scale – an expensive scale that is built into the top of the examining table. My first thought was the safety of my table. To me it was more at risk than Thomas, so I firmly asked, "Thomas, would you please stop hanging on the scale?" Just as Thomas was about to crumble from my unintended put-down, his mother interjected a saving, "… because you're so strong." She knows how to get behind the eyes of her child.

4. PLAY WITH YOUR CHILD

You will learn a lot about your child – and yourself – during play. Playtime gives your child the message "You are worth my time. You are a valuable person." It is well known that children learn through play. It improves a child's behavior by giving him feelings of importance and accomplishment. Instead of viewing playtime as a chore, use it to make an investment in your child's behavior.

Let your child initiate the play

A valuable learning principle that parents should keep in mind is this: an activity initiated by the child holds the child's attention longer than one suggested by the adult playmate. More learning takes place when the child chooses what to do. Child-initiated play also increases self-worth: "Dad likes to do the things I do!" of course, you may be thinking, "oh no, not the block game again!" or "We've read that story twenty times!" That's the ordeal of parenting. You'll get bored with The Cat in the Hat long before your child. If you want to bring something new to the same old play activity, add your own new twists as the play continues. Stop to talk about the book: "What would you do if the Cat in the Hat came to our door?" "Let's turn this block tower into a parking garage."

Make your child feel special

During play, focus your attention on the child. If your body is with your child but your mind is at work, your child will sense that you have tuned out, and neither one of you benefits from the time together. Your child loses the value of your being with her, concluding that she is not important. You lose the opportunity to learn about and enjoy your child – and to relearn how to play. I remember the fun six-month-old Matthew and I had in our "play circle." I sat him facing in front of me with a few favorite toys (mine and his) making a circle around him with my legs. This space contained him and provided support in case he, as a beginning sitter, started to topple sideways. Matthew had my undivided attention. He felt special and so did I. Making all those goofy baby noises is fun.

Parents need play

As a busy person, I had a hard time getting down to a baby's level enjoying unstructured, seemingly unproductive play. After all, I had so many "more important" things on my agenda. Once I realized how much we both could benefit, this special time became meaningful. Play became therapeutic for me. I needed time away from some of those other things to focus on this important little person who was, without realizing it, teaching me to relax. Play helped me to get to know Matthew's temperament and his capabilities at each stage of development. The child reveals himself to the parent – and vice versa – during play; the whole relationship benefits greatly. Playtime puts us on our child's level, helping parents get behind the eyes and into the mind of their child. Take time to enjoy the simple pleasures of play.

Play is an investment

Consider playtime one of your best investments. You may feel that you are "wasting time" stacking blocks when you could be "doing something" instead. Some adults panic at the thought and really have to struggle to be able to let go of their grown-up agenda. Of course, you don't have to play all day long, nor will your child want you to (unless he senses your resistance!). What may seem like a meaningless activity to you, means a lot to your baby. The more interest you show in doing things with your baby early on, the more interest your child will have in doing things with you when he's older. As your child grows, you can involve him in your play and your work, since being with you is the best reward.

Think of it this way – you are doing the most important job in the world – raising a human being.

5. ADDRESS YOUR CHILD BY NAME

What's in a name? The person, the self – little or big. I can still remember my grandfather impressing on me the value of using and remembering peoples' names. This lesson has proved profitable. One year I was a pre-med student competing with a bunch of marketing majors for a summer sales job. After I landed the job I inquired why I, though less qualified, had been hired. "Because you remembered and used the names of all of your interviewers." Addressing your child by name, especially when accompanied by eye contact and touch, exudes a "you're special" message. Beginning an interaction by using the other person's name opens doors, breaks barriers, and even softens corrective discipline.

Children learn to associate how you use their name with the message you have and the behavior you expect. Parents often use a child's nickname or first name only in casual dialogue, "Jimmy, I like what you are doing." They beef up the message by using the full name to make a deeper impression, "James Michael Sears, stop that!" One child we've heard about refers to his whole name as his "mad name" because that's what he hears when his parents are angry at him. We have noticed that children with self-confidence more frequently address their peers and adults by name or title. Their own self-worth allows them to be more direct in their communication with others. Our two-year-old Lauren dashes by my desk chirping: "Hi, Dad!" The addition of "Dad" impressed me more than an impersonal "Hi!" A school-age child who is comfortable addressing adults by name will be better able to ask for help when needed.

6. PRACTICE THE CARRY-OVER PRINCIPLE

As your child gets older, encourage her talents. She can do well at something, whether as a two-year-old who packs exceptional pretend picnics or a ten-year-old who loves ballet. Over the years, we've noticed a phenomenon we call the carry-over principle: enjoying one activity boosts a child's self-image, and this carries over into other endeavors. One of our sons is a natural athlete, but he wasn't interested in academics. Operating on the carry-over principle, we encouraged his enjoyment of athletics while supporting him as he worked on the academics. The schoolwork improved as his overall self-confidence increased. Recognize your child's special talents, and help her build on them, then watch the whole person blossom.

7. SET YOUR CHILD UP TO SUCCEED

Helping your child develop talents and acquire skills is part of discipline. If you recognize an ability in your child that he doesn't, encourage him. Strike a balance between pushing and protecting. Both are necessary. If you don't encourage your child to try, his skills don't improve, and you've lost a valuable confidence builder. If you don't protect your child from unrealistic expectations, his sense of competence is threatened.

Beware of value-by-comparisons

Children measure their own value by how they perceive others value them. And in our measuring-and-testing society, children's skills – and therefore their value – are measured relative to others. Your child may bat an exceptional.400 on the softball team, but she will feel inadequate if her teammates are batting.500. Be sure your child believes you value her because of who she is, not how she performs. Do this by giving her plenty of eye contact, touching, and focused attention. In other words, give of yourself regardless of how the game or the achievement test turns out.

Don't expect your child to excel in sports or music or academics just because you did. The one thing your child can excel in is being herself. She must know that your love for her does not depend on your approval of her performance. That's a tough assignment for a parent who may have been raised to perform for love and acceptance.

Wall of fame

In our Sears' family gallery of accomplishments, our walls display Hayden's cheerleading trophies, Erin's horse ribbons, Matthew's Little League pictures, etc. Every child is good at something. Discover it, encourage it, frame it, and display it. If your home is missing this wall, your child is missing his moment of fame. If you have a child who is not athletic, try scouting. With Boy Scouts and Girl Scouts everyone wins and everyone gets lots of badges. As children walk by their showcase, they can see at a glance five to ten years of achievement. This gives them a lift, especially during times when their self-worth is faltering.

8. HELP YOUR CHILD BE HOME-WISE BEFORE STREET-SMARTS

Sometime during your parenting career you may run into the idea that a young child should be exposed to children with different values so that he can choose for himself. This may sound good, or at least politically correct, but it just plain doesn't work. It's like sending a ship to sea without a rudder or a captain. Only by chance will that ship reach a desirable destination. Children are too valuable to be left to chance.

Screen your child's friends

The child's values and self-concept are affected by persons of significance in his life – relatives, coaches, teachers, religious leaders, scout leaders, and friends. It's up to the parents to screen out those who pull down the child's character and encourage those that build it. Keep a watchful eye on your child's friendships. First, let your child choose his own friends and monitor the relationships. At the end of a play experience examine your child's feelings. Is he at peace or upset? Are the children compatible? Coupling a passive person with a strong personality is all right if the stronger child pulls your child up rather than knocking him down.

While some children will wisely seek out complimentary playmates on their own, sometimes it is helpful to set up your child by purposely exposing him to appropriate peers. Some groups of children just naturally seem to get along well. If your child's group does not seem to have the right chemistry, it would be wise to intervene. By being a monitoring mom, Martha was able to come to the rescue of one of our children who was being intimidated and blackmailed into stealing money from us. This junior racketeer in the neighborhood was busted because Martha became suspicious of certain phone calls and listened in one day. Our frightened seven-year-old was in way over his head and was greatly relieved when we intervened.

Keep a kid-friendly home

Make your home inviting to your child's friends. Yes, you will have more messes to clean up, but it's worth it. Hosting the neighborhood helps you monitor your child; it gives you the opportunity to observe your child's social style and generally learn more about your child's personality – which social behaviors are appropriate and which need improving. You'll be able to make on-the-spot disciplinary interventions, either with your child in a private lesson or in group therapy if the whole pack needs some redirecting.

The roots of a young child's self-concept come from home and nurturing caregivers. After six years of age, peer influence becomes increasingly important. The deeper the roots of home-grown self-confidence, the better equipped kids are to interact with peers in a way that builds up self-worth rather than tearing it down. They know how to handle peers who are fun to play with and those that give them problems. When children are attachment parented, they are well equipped to manage different environments (home, grandparents, preschool, Sunday school) with different rules very well. For healthy social development, a child first must be comfortable with himself before he can be comfortable with others.

Clinging to homebase

In normal development a child moves out from the known into the unknown. She tries out new experiences in much the same way that an attached infant learns to separate from mother. It is quite normal for a child to retreat periodically into the comfort of the known (her home and family) as she progressively ventures into the jungle of the unknown. It is important for the child to have a strong attachment base. Being shy does not mean that a child has a poor self-image. She needs an extra dose of confidence so that she can follow her own inner timetable in adjusting to new situations and relationships. Parents often wonder what degree of clinging to homebase is normal. Look at the problem over the course of an entire year. If you see no change in the child's willingness to venture out, that may be unhealthy. But if you see some gradual moving out, then your child is simply a cautious social developer, which is characteristic of sensitive children, who may form a few meaningful and deep relationships, rather than numerous superficial ones.

9. LOSE LABELS

"I'm asthmatic," seven-year-old Greg proudly said to me when I inquired why he came to my office. Indeed, Greg did have asthma, but the physical problem was much easier to treat than the emotional side effects of his label. A few puffs of a bronchial dilator and his wheezing cleared, but his label persisted. I mentioned privately to Greg's mother that there are two issues to address in any child with a chronic illness: the problem itself, and the child's and family's reactions to the problem.

Every child searches for an identity and, when found, clings to it like a trademark. "Asthmatic" had become Greg's label, and he wore it often. His whole day revolved around his ailment, and his family focused on this part of Greg instead of on the whole person. Instead of feeling compassion, Greg's brothers and sisters had become tired of planning their lives around Greg's asthma. They couldn't go on certain trips because Greg might get too tired. It became a family illness, and all, except Greg, were put into roles they didn't like.

To take away Greg's label would be to take away Greg's self-esteem. So, we made a deal. I would treat Greg's asthma; the family would enjoy Greg, and we all worked at giving "the asthmatic" a healthier label to wear.

10. MONITOR SCHOOL INFLUENCES ON YOUR CHILD

Schools can be hazardous to a child's emotional health. School choice (if you have one) needs to be carefully considered. The connected child who enters the school arena with peers from various upbringings and degrees of attachment will have a set of expectations that he may not find at school. Children meet the challenges of a new social group with different behaviors. If a child is securely attached to his caregivers and armed with a strong self-image, he may not be disturbed by these different behaviors. He may stick cheerfully to his own style of play. Or, he may be frustrated, creating stress on his emerging personality. If his self-confidence is shaky, a child may view aggressiveness or bullying as normal and make these behaviors part of himself or allow himself to be victimized.

Around age six, when your child begins elementary school, other adults become influential in her life. These are people who are around your child enough to influence her behavior and model values. Once upon a time persons of significance in a child's life came primarily from within the extended family, but in today's mobile society a child is likely to have a wider variety of peers and persons of significance. This means that today's parents need to be vigilant as to who is modeling what behavior to their children. Here is where there is confusion in the ranks of parents as disciplinarians. There are two extremes. On the one side are the parents who feel it's healthy for children to experience a lot of different value systems while growing up so that they will be more open-minded as adults. On the other side are parents who want to protect their child from all outside influences and any ideas that may differ from their own beliefs. This child grows up in a bubble-like atmosphere.

Somewhere between these two extremes is the right answer for your child. Throwing a child into the melting pot of diverse values at too young an age, before she has any of her own values, may produce a child who is so confused that she develops no conscience and no standing value system. Parents who overprotect may end up with a child who cannot think for herself, leaving her vulnerable to challenges or so judgmental that she condemns anyone with different beliefs. Somewhere in the middle is the parent who grounds the child in a firm value system and guides her as she encounters other value systems. The child, because she has a strong value system to begin with, is better able to weigh her parents' value system against alternatives and develop her own firm code of values. It may be different from the parents' [code]. It may include many of the parents' values with a sprinkling of alternatives learned from peers or teachers. But the important thing is that the child has a value system from which to operate. He is not a leaf hurried downstream in the river that takes the path of least resistance, overflows its bounds, and eventually drains into a large sea of uncertainty. Many children flounder, sometimes for the rest of their lives, searching for values that should have been formed in infancy and early childhood.

Parents, don't be misled by the complacent term "latent" applied to middle childhood. This is not the time to sleep and get careless. This is the age in which your children build consciences and learn your value system. In fact, it's the only time in their entire life when they unquestionably, at least early in that stage, accept their parents' value system. Slowly they form their own standards through interaction with peers, other families, and teachers, and through neighborhood relationships and church/synagogue[/mosque] friendships. They discover a larger world with a variety of beliefs and behaviors. As they talk (endlessly) and observe and experiment in a variety of situations, they learn about how they will choose to act and react. Trying belatedly to impose your values on a teenager whose main developmental task at this stage is to identify his own values is difficult. The best way to get your values across is to "walk your talk" by living your values.

11. GIVE YOUR CHILD RESPONSIBILITIES

Children need jobs. One of the main ways children develop self-confidence and internalize values is through helping maintain the family living area, inside and out. Giving children household duties helps them feel more valuable, besides channeling their energy into desirable behavior and teaching skills. Try these tips:

Enter the work force early

Beginning around age two, children can do small jobs around the house. To hold a child's interest, choose tasks the child has already shown an interest in. Our two-year-old, Lauren, had a thing about napkins, so we gave her the dinner-time job of putting napkins at each place. A mother in our practice told us: "I couldn't keep our three-year-old away from the vacuum cleaner. So I gave him the job of vacuuming the family room. He kept busy and I got some work out of him." ***Starting between ages two and four, a child can learn the concept of responsibility*** to self and to parents and for his personal belongings. Once he learns a sense of responsibility for these things, a sense of responsibility to society will come naturally in the next stage of development.

By three years of age, a child can be taught to clean sinks and tubs (using a sponge and a small can of cleanser). Young children love to scrub. Three's and Four's love to sort laundry into darks and lights. At five, the child can be doing dishes every night. Teach him exactly how you want them handled (for example, excess food in the garbage, dishes rinsed, and then put in the dishwasher). Be sure to use unbreakable cups and plates and put messy pans in the oven to be cleaned later by an adult.

By seven, a child can be cooking at least one meal a week from start to finish. Teach him how to fix his favorite meal and let him learn how to pick out the ingredients at the market. Encourage school-age children to make their own lunch. Besides giving them a sense of responsibility for their own nutrition, they are more likely to eat what they make. Once taught, the child can be left alone in the kitchen – no hovering mother. Relax and talk to your mate.

Give special jobs

Call a job "special" and it's more likely to get done. Whatever magical ring the word "special" has, it sure gets results. Perhaps a child infers that "I must be special because I get a special job." A four-to-five-year-old can have pre-assigned chores, with reminders, of course. To put some order in our busy house we announce: "It's tidy time." Try assigning one room for each child to tidy up. Children at all ages suffer a bit of work inertia, especially as tasks wear on and lose their fun appeal. But sometimes children need to learn that work comes before play. To get them started, work with them.

Create job charts

Make this a creative activity for a family meeting. List the jobs to be done, and let each child choose and rotate if they want. We divide jobs into paying, extra-credit jobs they can earn money for, and non-paying or those that are naturally expected of the children for the privilege of living in our home. Expect to pay a higher price on the most unwanted jobs. Best is to pay immediately after the work is responsibly done, since children are immediate-reward oriented. In the next stage of development, from five to ten years, children can make the connection that with increasing privileges come responsibilities. When we decided to get a family cottage, the deal was that Saturday mornings would be family fix-up time at the cottage, and only after the work was completed would the recreation begin.

Plant a family garden

Planting a garden teaches children that they reap what they sow. During our family garden phase, when our children were younger, we tied in caring for a garden and caring for them: Water the plants and they grow nicely, keep the weeds away and the flowers bloom better.

Other jobs boys and girls love and do well when first taught alongside a parent include: washing the car, sweeping outdoor living areas and sidewalks, gardening, vacuuming, dusting, and baby tending. By seven or eight they can put in a load of laundry, and by ten they can be doing their own laundry. When children have jobs in the home, not only are parents relieved of some of the busywork, but children feel they are contributing to a cause. ***They feel useful and needed.*** And the energy they spend on the home becomes an investment they are making into the value system of that home.

12. ENCOURAGE CHILDREN TO EXPRESS, NOT STUFF, THEIR FEELINGS

Expressing feelings comfortably does not mean the child is free to explode at every emotional twinge, but rather develops a comfortable balance between expressing and controlling feelings. She should eventually be able to keep a lid on her emotions when needed, but not so tightly that she can't remove the lid in a "safe" setting, such as exercising (i.e., run like mad to blow off steam), or with a trustworthy friend. All babies freely express their feelings. Maturity develops through years of learning how to stay calm in difficult situations. A child with unbridled emotions becomes a brat. A person who never expresses emotions becomes too reserved. Too much control or too much emoting will both produce problems in adult life.

Stuffing feelings doesn't do any good for the child, the parents, or the relationship. It tells the child that you are threatened by her feelings or she gets the message that you don't care to understand her feelings. The child picks up on your attitude and learns that expressing or even having feelings is not okay. The child decides that the feelings that accompany the ups and downs of her daily life are not worthwhile. In a child's logic, if her feelings are not worthwhile, she is not worthwhile. If this unfeeling pattern repeats itself over and over, the child quickly learns both to suppress the feelings and especially to hide them from her parents.

Even more devastating than being uncaring is responding to a child's feelings with anger messages, "I don't want to hear any more bellowing about that stupid fish!" The fear of parents' reactions to her feelings turns a child into a feeling stuffer.

On the positive side, picture what happens when a child feels free to express herself and a parent accepts her feelings. Consider this example: "Daddy, the necklace Grandma gave me for my birthday broke." Dad stops what he is doing and focuses on his child, looking into her eyes and placing his hand around her shoulder. He says, "I'm sorry. That was such a special necklace." Both his verbal and his body language convey: "I am available to you; your feelings are important to me. You are important to me." His reaction frees the child to tell him more about her feelings and to work through them by talking to him. Instead of retreating into her shell or erupting into a tantrum, she has been given a way to express her sorrow. And he has boosted her self-worth by accepting her feelings, which are a reflection of herself.

Do you owe your child self-esteem?

Parents may misunderstand the meaning of self-esteem and feel that this is just one more thing they are required to give their child along with regular meals and a warm winter jacket. They guard against anything that may undercut self-esteem – to the point where it becomes ridiculous. ("Oh, Billy, you don't really sing flat. You're just tonally challenged.") They measure self-esteem daily, as one might take a temperature. ("Julie's self-esteem is low today. Her big brother beat her at checkers last night.")

Every infant whose needs are met has self-esteem built in. Like an arborist caring for a tree, your job is to nurture what's there, do what you can to structure your child's environment so that she grows strong and straight, and avoid whittling away at the tender branches. You can't build your child's self-esteem compliment by compliment, activity by activity. Parents are already overloaded with guilt because they may not be doing enough to foster their child's self-worth. You don't need a degree in psychology to raise a confident child. Much of parenting is easy and fun. Hold your baby a lot, respond sensitively to her needs, enjoy your baby. Then sit back and enjoy the person whose self-esteem is developing naturally.

TASK/TEXT 4.27: CORPORAL PUNISHMENT – SUMMARY BY VICE-CHAIR OF THE COMMITTEE ON THE RIGHTS OF THE CHILD

Editorial by Mr Jean Zermatten, IDE Director and Vice-Chair of the Committee on the Rights of the Child, 1 September 2009, <www.childsrights.org/html/site_en/index.php?c=>

In a world striving to curb violence, it is quite surprising that corporal punishment is still largely admitted and practiced in numerous countries, not only in the family circle, but also in institutions and sometimes in the criminal justice system. And yet, ever since it started its activities, the Committee on the Rights of the Child has addressed this form of child abuse.

The Committee defines very clearly corporal punishment as "any punishment in which physical force is used and intended to cause some degree of pain or discomfort, however light." Examples given by the Committee are "smacking", "slapping", "spanking" with the hand or with an implement – a whip, stick, belt, shoe, wooden spoon, etc. Other forms illustrate the phenomenon, like "kicking, shaking or throwing children, scratching, pinching, biting, pulling hair or boxing ears, forcing children to stay in uncomfortable positions, burning, scalding or forced ingestion." **In the view of the Committee, corporal punishment is invariably degrading.** In addition, there are other ***non-physical*** forms of punishment that are also cruel and degrading and thus incompatible with the Convention. These include, for example, punishment which belittles, humiliates, denigrates, scapegoats, threatens, scares or ridicules the child.[39]

---

[39] General Comment no 8: The right of the child to protection from corporal punishment or other cruel or degrading forms of punishment (arts. 19; 28, para. 2; and 37, inter alia), CRC/C/GC/8, par 11.

CRC provisions are very clear as well: **article 19** pledges State parties to take *"all appropriate legislative, administrative, social and educational measures to protect the child from all forms of physical or mental violence, injury or abuse."* **Article 37 litt. a** sets forth the very clear principle of elimination of all forms of degrading treatment, pledging the States to ensure that *"no child shall be subjected to torture or other cruel, inhuman or degrading treatment or punishment,"* and as far as education is concerned, **article 28, para 2 CRC** (school discipline) demands from States to *"take all appropriate measures to ensure that school discipline is administered in a manner consistent with the child's human dignity and in conformity with the present Convention."*

Moreover, in 2006, the Committee has issued General Comment no 8: "The right of the child to protection from corporal punishment and other cruel or degrading forms of punishment (arts. 19; 28, para 2; and 37, inter alia)."

The General Comment aims to highlight the obligation of all States parties to **move quickly to prohibit and eliminate all corporal punishment and all other cruel or degrading forms of punishment of children** and to outline the legislative and other **awareness-raising and educational measures that States must take.** And even more, to **address the widespread acceptance or tolerance of corporal punishment of children** [with a view to] eliminating it, in the family, schools and other settings. The basic idea is that this ban is not only an obligation of State parties, but also a **key strategy for reducing and preventing all forms of violence in societies.**

In its latest session[40], the Committee has reviewed 6 States under the Convention and issued recommendations to each of them, **except Sweden**, ground-breaker in the matter since it has banned by law any resort to corporal punishment, as early as **1979**. To take the example of France, the Committee clearly recommended to *"explicitly prohibit corporal punishment in all settings, including in the family, in schools, in institutions and other childcare settings, increase awareness-raising in this respect and promote the value of education without violence according to article 28, para 2 of the Convention."*

The Committee also evoked a few issues **like the notions of correction or discipline**: in the Committee's view, rating acceptable for corporal punishment of a "*reasonable*" or "*moderate*" degree to be inflicted in the best interests of the child, is met by an unequivocal answer in the General Comment no 8 and in the constant practice of the Committee: the obligation under the Convention to take the **best interests of the child as major consideration** in any decision affecting children (para 1 of article 3) **cannot possibly be invoked to justify the use of corporal punishment** or to disguise it as "discipline."

---

40 51st session from May 25th to June 12th, 2009.

Let the police in?

Another frequently evoked issue is: possible and numerous police intervention in families, as soon as corporal punishment comes under a law text. The Committee has a clear stand on the issue, too: "The principle of equal protection of children and adults from assault, including within the family, does not mean that all cases of corporal punishment of children by their parents that come to light should lead to prosecution of parents. The ***de minimis* principle** – that the law does not concern itself with trivial matters – ensures that minor assaults between adults only come to court in very exceptional circumstances; the same will be true of minor assaults on children."[41] In this respect, the example of New Zealand is eloquent: The country amended its legislation in 2007, making corporal punishment a crime (Crimes Amendment Act, art. 59), but this has not given way to a significant increase in the police workload, and even less so of the Courts.[42]

Equity between adults and children / However, children's vulnerability demands the need for more protection

For the Committee, inflicting corporal punishment directly conflicts with the equal and inalienable rights of children to respect for their human dignity and physical integrity. A child cannot be subjected to harsher treatment than an adult is: what is judged intolerable and a ground for prosecution among adults, must be judged so at least to the same extent when inflicted to a child.

Moreover, children's singularity, **physical and affective dependence, and their situation of developing person** (notion of **evolving capacities**, art. 5 CRC), as well as their vulnerability are as many arguments pleading in favour of particular protection for children, and for a clear cut legal status of victim. Children must be protected against any form of violence.

In Conclusion, the Committee thinks that States have a very clear responsibility in this field, and an obligation ensuing ratification of the Convention: not to permit the use of force towards children under educational, curative or disciplinary pretence. States must promote other forms of intervention based on respect. Banning corporal punishment also means preventing violence globally, any form of violence!

---

41 GC no 8, par 40.

42 Source: <www.stuff.co.nz/national/769094>.

TASK/TEXT 4.28:

TASK/TEXT 4.28.1: SPANKING DETRIMENTAL TO CHILDREN, STUDY SAYS

Elizabeth Landau, <www.cnn.com/2009/HEALTH/09/16/spanking.children.parenting/index.html>, CNN, 16 September 2009

Story highlights
- Study: Spanking at age 1 predicts aggressive behavior problems at age 2.
- Spanking also linked to lower scores on a mental development test at age 3.
- Experts say parents should explore other methods of disciplining children.
- Spanking reinforces negative memories in the child's mind.

Think a little spanking won't do much harm to kids? New research says the effects can be long-lasting.

Experts say "popping" kids can do more harm than good. A new study of more than 2,500 toddlers from low-income families found that spanking may have detrimental effects on behavior and mental development.

"We're talking about infants and toddlers, and I think that just, cognitively, they just don't understand enough about right or wrong or punishment to benefit from being spanked," said Lisa Berlin, the study's lead author and research scientist at the Center for Child and Family Policy at Duke University.

Berlin and colleagues found that children who were spanked as 1-year-olds tended to behave more aggressively at age 2, and did not perform as well as other children on a test measuring thinking skills at age 3. The study is published in the journal *Child Development*.

Although these effects were somewhat small, the study is just the latest of many supporting psychologists' advice against spanking. Still, some experts say spanking has a time and place.

The new study focused on children from low-income families because prior research suggested that spanking is more common among them, Berlin said. This may be because of the added stresses of parenting in a low-income situation, or because of a "cultural contagion" of behaviors among people. For example, in some families this study examined, a grandmother would spank a child, or neighbors would encourage physical discipline, she said.

Her study found that about one-third of the 1-year-olds, and about half of the 2- and 3-year-olds, had been spanked in the previous week, according to mothers' self-reporting to the researchers. At all three ages, African-American children were spanked significantly more frequently than those from white and Mexican-

American families, and verbally punished more than the other children at ages 2 and 3, the study said.

Previous research had also found that parents who spank are more likely to be younger, less educated, single, and/or depressed and stressed, Berlin's study said. Spanking is most commonly used among parents who were spanked themselves, who live in the South, and/or who identify themselves as conservative Christians. These parents also tend to believe in the effectiveness of spanking or believe the child is at fault in a given situation, the study said.

The new research refutes the idea that more aggressive children are more likely to be spanked, Berlin said. On the other hand, the study did find that children who were fussier at age 1 were more likely to be spanked and verbally punished, she said.

Verbal punishment did not appear to have the same detrimental effects as spanking in this study, Berlin said.

Some remain unconvinced that parents should never spank their children. Robert Larzelere, associate professor of human development and family science at Oklahoma State University, conducted a meta-analysis of 26 studies on the subject, and found that, overall, spanking seemed more effective than 10 of 13 alternative disciplinary methods for getting a child to behave or do as asked.

Much of the research on the subject does not clearly demonstrate a causal link, Larzelere said. For example, in comparing studies, children who are spanked and children who are taken to psychologists both are more likely to have aggressive behavior later, he said.

The best use of spanking, Larzelere said, is in children between the ages of 2 and 6 when milder discipline tactics, such as time out, fail.

"That's why psychologists trained parents to use spanking that way for 25 years [from the] late '60s to mid-'90s," he said. Now, the trend of advice is away from spanking, but there's not much hard evidence to support it, he said.

Berlin's study focused on particularly early ages, Larzelere noted; much of the spanking literature focuses on ages 2 and older. Twelve months is probably too early to spank children, but there's no established point between ages 1 and 2 at which it is appropriate, he said.

Others say parents should not resort to spanking at any age. Susan Newman, social psychologist and author of *Little Things Long Remembered: Making Your Children Feel Special Every Day*, said parents should discourage bad behaviors by taking away privileges such as dessert, or setting an earlier bedtime. They should also reinforce good behaviors verbally, saying how nice it is when their children share, for example.

The study corroborates what clinical psychologist Laura Markham, who was not involved in the study, has observed about the negative effects of spanking.

Many mothers describe their children as fussy, resistant and demanding at age 1, which is a critical junction in the parent-child relationship, she said in an e-mail.

"If the mother sees this fussiness as willful misbehavior and begins verbally punishing or spanking, rather than empathizing with the child, the child's behavior deteriorates into more tantrums and other frustrating behavior," said Markham, who also offers advice at <AhaParenting.com>.

Newman also noted that children are too young to understand when parenting behavior is wrong, even at the level of abuse. Physical violence gets passed down in families because the only parenting skills people know are the behaviors that they saw at home, she said.

Spanking, moreover, reinforces negative memories in the child's mind, Newman said. Parents should aim instead to build "prominent, happy memories" of childhood for their kids, she said.

Regardless of income level, all parents can benefit from training classes, Newman said.

For future research, Berlin is looking at programs that work with low-income or high-risk families and try to promote supportive parenting behaviors.

In the spanking study, some mothers said they were receiving parenting services in which they were counseled not to spank their children.

"This is definitively the direction in which services are going and in which, in general, American culture is going," Berlin said.

TASK/TEXT 4.28.2: EARLY SPANKINGS MAKE FOR AGGRESSIVE TODDLERS, STUDY SHOWS

Kids spanked at age 1 also had worse performance on cognitive tests at age 3
Jennifer Thomas, *HealthDay News*, <www.healthday.com/Article.asp?AID=630929>, 15 September 2009

Children who are spanked as 1-year-olds are more likely to behave aggressively and perform worse on cognitive tests as toddlers than children who are spared the punishment, new research shows.

Though the negative effects of spanking were "modest," the study adds to a growing body of literature that's finding spanking isn't good for children.

"Age 1 is a key time for establishing the quality of the parenting and the relationship between parent and the child," said study author Lisa J. Berlin, a research scientist at the Center for Child and Family Policy at Duke University. "Spanking at age 1 reflects a negative dynamic, and increases children's aggression at age 2."

The study is published in the September/October issue of *Child Development*.

Berlin and her colleagues looked at data on 2,500 white, Mexican American and black children from low-income families. The data included parents' reports about their children's behavior, their use of spanking, as well as home visits by trained observers to document parent-child interactions at ages 1, 2 and 3.

About one-third of mothers of 1-year-olds reported they or someone in their household had spanked their child in the last week, while about half of the mothers of 2- and 3-year-olds reported that their child had been spanked. The average number of spankings for 1-year-olds was 2.6 per week, while the average for 2-year-olds was nearly three.

The study found that children who were spanked at age 1 had more aggressive behaviors at age 2 and performed worse on measures of thinking abilities at age 3.

Being spanked at age 2, however, did not predict more aggressive behaviors at age 3, possibly because the spanking had begun at age 1 and by age 2 the kids were already more aggressive, Berlin said.

Researchers also looked at the effects of verbal punishment, defined as yelling, scolding or making derogatory comments. Verbal punishment was not associated with negative effects if the mother was otherwise attentive, loving and supportive.

Researchers controlled for family characteristics such as race, ethnicity, mother's age, education, family income and the child's gender. Previous research has shown spanking is more common among low-income households than high-income households.

Researchers chose a sample of low-income families because some child behavior experts have argued that when spanking is "cultural normative" – that is, it's expected for parents to use physical discipline – the detrimental effects of spanking may be lessened. "We did not find that," Berlin said. "Even in a sample of low-income people where presumably it's more normative to spank your kids, we found negative effects."

The study also found that mothers who said their children were "fussy" babies were more likely to spank them at ages 1, 2 and 3. But children who were more aggressive at 2 were not more likely to get spanked.

"The implication or the suggestion in past arguments is that some kids who are more aggressive or difficult to control might elicit more spanking, but that's not what we found," Berlin said.

Researchers found that black children were spanked and verbally punished the most, possibly because of cultural beliefs about the importance of respecting elders and in the value of physical discipline, or because parents feel they have to prepare their children for a racist and potentially dangerous world.

Of all the debates over child-rearing, spanking "definitely touches a nerve," Berlin said.

"It's a parenting practice that has been around for a long time, and that's also in transition," Berlin said. "In general, the use of spanking is going down. But there is also a contingent of people who really believe in it, who say that's how they were raised and it's a tradition they want to continue."

Elizabeth T. Gershoff, an associate professor in the department of human development and family sciences at University of Texas at Austin, said the study adds to a growing body of research showing negative effects of spanking.

"Almost all the studies point to negative effects of spanking," Gershoff said. "It makes kids more aggressive, more likely to be delinquent and to have mental health problems. The more kids are spanked, the more they are likely to be physically abused by their parents. This does not mean everyone who spanks physically abuses, but that risk is there."

Because children tend to mimic parental behaviors, it's possible spanking "creates a model for using aggression," Gershoff said. "Spanking is just hitting."

Less is known why spanking could inhibit cognitive development. One possibility is that parents who spank are less likely to use reasoning with their children, something that's good for development, Gershoff said.

TASK/TEXT 4.29: CAN I BE A GOOD MUSLIM/ CHRISTIAN/JEW IN A COUNTRY THAT FORBIDS PHYSICAL PUNISHMENT?

<www.endcorporalpunishment.org> (<www.endcorporalpunishment.org/pages/frame.html>, <www.endcorporalpunishment.org/pages/pdfs/NeverViolenceSweden2009.pdf>), accessed 23 November 2009

Save the Children Sweden and the Swedish Ministry of Health and Social Affairs have published a review of the law in Sweden, the first country to achieve prohibition of all corporal punishment of children, including in the home – in 1979. The report, *Never Violence – Thirty Years on from Sweden's Abolition of Corporal Punishment* [2009; available at <http://shop.rb.se>], describes the process of enacting the prohibiting legislation and the impact that it has had on the prevalence of, and attitudes towards, corporal punishment and responses to parents who use it. [On the last page, the question is raised:]

Can I be a good Muslim/Christian/Jew in a country that forbids physical punishment?

– Of course. Our Prophet Mohammed is our role model and he never hit anyone, neither child nor adult. The Prophet Mohammed taught us that for seven years

we shall play with our children. For seven years we shall teach them. And for seven years we shall be their friend and companion.
(Abdallah Salah, Chairman of the Islamic Association in Stockholm.)

– To exercise violence against a child is unthinkable for a Christian. Jesus gives a very sharp warning to anyone who harms a child and also says about the children: "Whoever welcomes one such child in my name, welcomes me."
(Sven-Bernhard Fast, General Secretary of the Christian Council of Sweden.)

– No law of the Jewish Religion decrees physical punishment of children. It stands to reason that modern Jews repudiate all degrading treatment of children.
(Morton Narrowe, Chief Rabbi Emeritus.)

5. SAFETY AND DEVELOPMENT – AFFECTION, SECURE ATTACHMENT, BRAIN DEVELOPMENT, EARLY CHILDHOOD

TASK/TEXT 5.1:

TASK/TEXT 5.1.1: SECURE ATTACHMENT

Encyclopedia on Early Childhood Development, Centre of Excellence for Early Childhood Development – *Synthesis on attachment* (published online 26 November 2006), <www.child-encyclopedia.com/pages/PDF/synthesis-attachment.pdf>

How important is it?

All infants require attention, comfort and a sense of security. Infants who feel threatened will turn to their caregiver for protection and comfort; over time, the caregiver's response helps mold the relationship into a pattern of interaction.

Bowlby's attachment theory describes the importance of the early relationship that develops between the infant and the primary caregiver. This affective bond, called attachment, provides the foundation for the child's later social, emotional and even cognitive development. In addition, attachment relationships continue to influence thoughts, feelings, motives and close relationships throughout life.

Research shows that secure attachment is a protective factor that leads to more optimal developmental outcomes, while children with insecure attachment are more prone to social and maladjustment problems and children with disorganized attachment are at highest risk for psychopathology and poor outcomes.

What do we know?

To assess the quality of attachment in infancy, researchers often use a standardized separation-reunion method called the **Strange Situation Procedure**, in which infants' reactions to being reunited with their caregiver after a brief separation are used to assess how much trust the children have in the accessibility of their attachment figure.

There are four patterns of infant-caregiver attachment. Infants who actively seek proximity to their caregivers on reunion, communicate their feelings of stress and distress openly and then readily return to exploration are classified as ***secure*** [B: Best]. This type of attachment is believed to develop when the caregiver **consistently responds to the child's distress in a sensitive manner**. Infants who ignore or avoid the caregiver after being reunited are classified as ***insecure-avoidant*** [A: Avoidant]. This is believed to develop when the caregiver **consistently responds to the child's distress in ways that are rejecting.**

Infants who combine strong contact maintenance with contact resistance, or who remain inconsolable without being able to return to explore the environment, are classified as ***insecure-ambivalent*** [C: Clinging]. This develops when the caregiver responds **in ways that are inconsistent and unpredictable.** Finally, some infants do not seem able to resort to a single, organized attachment pattern. This is called ***disorganized*** attachment [D: Disorganized], and is believed to develop when the caregiver displays **unusual and ultimately frightening behaviours in the presence of the child.**

For a normative population, it is reported that **about 62% of infants are classified as secure**, 15% as insecure-avoidant, 8% as insecure-ambivalent and 15% as disorganized [**<2/3 secure; >1/3 insecure**].

Secure attachment is considered a **protective factor** as it has been associated with better developmental outcomes in areas such as self-reliance, self-efficacy, empathy and social competence in toddlerhood, school-age and adolescence. Infants with insecure attachment have been shown to be **at risk** for later adaptation problems such as conduct disorder, aggression, depression and anti-social behaviour.

Children with disorganized attachment are at the highest risk for **psychopathology**. There is a high percentage of attachment disorganization among children who have been **victims of maltreatment**. An array of parental behaviours has been linked to infant disorganization. These include affective communication errors (such as contradictory responses to infant signals), parental withdrawal, negative-intrusive responses, role-confused responses, disoriented responses and frightened or frightening behaviours.

Negative life events (such as **divorce**) can compromise attachment security, but differences in attachment security result primarily from the children's interactions with their social environment during **the first few years of life. Parenting therefore plays a crucial role. For this reason, preventive interventions in early childhood have enormous potential to alter behavioural and developmental trajectories**, especially in high-risk families.

What can be done?
To improve long-term developmental outcomes of infants and children, prevention and intervention programs should focus on **promoting secure parent-infant attachment**. Attachment-based interventions often target specific issues, such as parental sensitivity, behaviours and state of mind. However, exclusive focus on behavioural training for parent sensitivity rather than a focus on sensitivity plus support, or a focus on sensitivity plus support plus internal representations (e.g., individual therapy), the use of video feedback and brief (5- to 16-session) interventions focusing on parental sensitivity seem the most effective in improving attachment security, and also have yielded positive results with adoptive parents. In addition, the intervention site (home versus office) and the presence of multiple risk factors did not affect efficacy, but interventions conducted with clinically referred patients/clients and those that included fathers were more effective than interventions without such characteristics.

A few sensitivity-focused interventions have had some impact on disorganized attachment as well. However, it is believed that interventions focusing on atypical parental behaviours (e.g., failing to keep a child safe, failing to comfort a distressed child, laughing while the child is distressed, asking for affection and reassurance from the child, or threatening to harm) are most likely to reduce disorganized attachment. (…)

Attachment-based intervention programs should be incorporated into existing home visitation and parent education programs, while policies should identify means by which families can access consistent parenting and psychological support throughout their child's life. Economic analyses now clearly indicate the cost-effectiveness, both in dollars and in human suffering, of providing services to families with infants, before psychopathology develops.

TASK/TEXT 5.1.2: INTRODUCTION TO ATTACHMENT THEORY AND RESEARCH

<http://cehd.umn.edu/icd/EarlyExp/docs/Stovall-McClough, C.pdf>

Chase Stovall-McClough, Ph.D.,Weill Medical College of Cornell University, Network Trainee 2002–2003; readings and references not included

Bowlby and Attachment Theory
John Bowlby was a British psychoanalyst trained in part by Melanie Klein whose theory of infant development emphasized the role of infant drives and "phantasy" life as played-out in the mother-infant relationship. Bowlby, breaking away from Kleinian theory, emphasized what he believed was the central role of the actual

behavioral exchanges between mother and infant in the development of the infant. Bowlby was inspired to consider the role of maternal care in infant development from his observations of children that had been orphaned during WWII. Along with his colleagues (James Robinson, Anna Freud, Rene Spitz) Bowlby recorded the development of children being raised in orphanages by hospital staff and began documenting the significant delays in cognitive and interpersonal development that emerged from such caregiving deprivation.

Bowlby, integrating his experiences with severely deprived children and his study of evolutionary theory and primate anthropology, was the first to propose that there is a biological constraint to attach to a primary caregiver. In his 1958 Paper, "The Nature of the Child's Tie to His Mother" he introduced the idea that the strong bond between a child and a parent is explained best as a biologically based affectionate tie that has evolved in a Darwinian sense to promote the survival of the species. He argued that this in-born predisposition served the primary purpose of ensuring protection of the offspring.

Bowbly proposed that during the time in which humans were evolving, infants who were biologically predisposed to seek out their caregiver when frightened or distressed and to stay close to their parents under conditions of threat were less likely to be killed by predators, go hungry, or die from neglect. His arguments flew in the face of popular psychoanalytic thought at the time that placed infant libidinal and aggressive drives at the heart of personality development.

According the Bowlby, repeated interactions with primary caregivers under conditions of infant distress lay the **templates** for "internal working models." Internal (i.e. unconscious) working (i.e. always under construction) models are analogous to mental representations of the child's interpersonal world. In the simplest terms, a child whose caregiver responds sensitively and consistently to the infant's signals of distress (attachment behaviors) will develop an internal working model of himself as lovable and effective and of the "other" as loving, reliable, and responsive. Bowlby suggested that a child's attachment system moves from a behavioral system in infancy – where security of attachment initially hinges on the actual physical availability and contact between parent and child – to a representational system – where security of attachment can be represented in the mind and expressed in language. Bowlby, breaking away from his Kleinian training, suggested a model in which early real experiences between parent and child form the child's first sense of himself in relation to others and that early attachment experience lay the ground work for internal working models. (…)

What are the functions of infant attachment?
(...) [T]he attachment system serves a homeostatic function. Sroufe highlights the importance of understanding differences in attachment quality as differences not in the type or quantity of attachment behaviors, but rather how they are organized in relationship to the goal of obtaining "felt security." Sroufe goes on to argue that a critical function of this attachment system is its basis in the learning of affect regulation. He argues that the caregiver's behavior acts as an external regulator of the baby's distress and the baby relies on this external source of regulation until it begins to self-regulate. Hofer goes further to show evidence, mostly through studies of rats, that the mother serves as an external regulator of the general neurochemical development of the infant brain including the regulation of temperature, hormone regulation, and circadian rhythms. (...)

How is infant attachment measured?
Mary Ainsworth working as a postdoctoral with Bowlby operationalized Bowlby's concepts of attachment. She began her studies observing women and their children in Uganda. She noted a remarkably predictable pattern of interactions between mother and child under conditions of stress. When these infants were distressed, they would invariably seek proximity and/or contact from the mother until soothed and then return to play. When Mary Ainsworth returned to the United States she continued her observations with moms by devising a laboratory procedure designed to induce small amounts of stress in the infant while in the presence of the mother. Ainsworth's Strange Situation laboratory procedure involves a series of 8 increasingly stressful 3-minute episodes where infants are introduced to an unfamiliar environment and an unfamiliar person and undergo two brief separations and reunions with their primary caregivers. The procedure allows for an examination of infants' reliance on caregivers when the infants are distressed. Ainsworth found, unlike the Uganda infants, that there were striking individual differences in the behavior of distressed infants when in the presence of the mother. Based on her careful categorization of differences in infant behavior during the reunion episodes of the Strange Situation, Mary Ainsworth developed a scoring system for the classification of **Secure (B), Avoidant (A), and Resistant (C) [Ambivalent] Attachments.**

Infants classified as securely attached (B) looked the most similar to the Uganda infants. These infants actively seek proximity and contact during the reunion episodes of the Strange Situation. They maintain proximity and/or contact with the caregiver until they are soothed and can return to play. A great deal of exploratory behavior is seen in episodes where the infant is alone with the caregiver before separation. These dyads have struck the most optimal balance between proximity and exploration.

Avoidantly attached infants (A) are characterized by active avoidance of the caregiver upon reunion, often turning away from the caregiver or ignoring her. These babies, despite looking as if they are not distressed during the separation episodes, show elevations in heart rate similar to that of secure babies (…) and show greater pre-to-post Strange Situation rises in cortisol than secure babies (…). In these dyads, the infant's attachment strategy favors distance over proximity, even when the infant is distressed.

Infants with resistant attachments (C) to caregivers tend not to explore the environment before separation in the Strange Situation, or if they do explore, they do so very anxiously. When the caregiver leaves the room, these infants tend to respond with extreme distress. Upon reunion, these infants tend to seek out their caregiver but then show displays of anger. These infants are very difficult to soothe and often alternate between periods of distress and calm. Their play is usually poor because they are more preoccupied with their caregiver. Resistant strategies involve a heightened level of proximity monitoring, at the expense of exploration.

Disorganized / Disoriented Attachment (D): A fourth category of attachment was developed in the late 80's and early 90's in response to difficulties using the traditional categorization system, particularly in high risk samples. According to Mary Main and Judith Solomon's formulation, the disorganized/disoriented attachment behavior of infants does not reflect an organized strategy of attachment as do the A, B, and C categories. Rather, the disorganized/disoriented category is meant to capture momentary disorganized behavioral responses to the stress of the Strange Situation. These infants display conflicting, odd, and/or bizarre behaviors during the reunion episodes of the Strange Situation that are thought to reflect the paradox of having to seek proximity with a caretaker who is also a source of danger (…). As a result, an infant will display disorganized behaviors that can include incomplete movements or expressions, confusion or disorientation, freezing, unusual posturing and/or movements, and vivid expressions of fear. (…)

What is *adult* attachment organization and how is it measured?

In adulthood, attachment representations or attachment *states of mind*, are measured by administering a standardized interview called the **Adult Attachment Interview** (AAI) developed by Carol George and Mary Main at the University of California at Berkely in 1985. The AAI was designed to tap into adults "internal working models of attachment," also called attachment "states of mind." According to Main and others, attachment states of mind reflect the way in which adults process and organize attachment related thoughts, feelings, and memories. The AAI requires the subject to describe their early relationships with their parents, to provide specific memories including memories of traumatic experiences, and to comment on how childhood experiences in their family have shaped their personality.

A subject can receive one of four attachment state of mind classifications: Autonomous (also known as Secure or **Free** to Evaluate), **Dismissing**, Preoccupied/**Enmeshed**, and **Unresolved** with regard to loss or trauma. Importantly, classifications are NOT based on the nature of the actual experiences during childhood, but rather they are based on the extent to which a subject organizes a coherent narrative of their experiences and the effects of these experiences on their personality.

Adults described as autonomous (**F**) are the best at this task. They are collaborative, provide a balanced description of their childhood experiences, do not avoid or become overwhelmed by negative emotion, their memories and descriptions are believable, and there is some awareness and thoughtfulness displayed about the influence of these experiences on their current personality.

Subjects who are classified as dismissing (**D**) have an overall strategy for organizing these early memories and thoughts that keep them at a distance. In these subjects you may see **idealization of parents**, strong absence of memory, a claim that negative experiences have had no effect on them or have even benefited them. They tend to emphasize their own strength, their normal childhoods, and value being independent ["survivors" not victims, JW].

Subjects who are classified as preoccupied/enmeshed (E) employ an overall strategy that is the opposite of dismissing. That is, they display a hyperactivation of attachment. Individuals in this category share an **inability to move beyond** an excessive preoccupation or sense of involvement in past and present attachment relationships ["Eternal" victims, JW]. The conversational turns can be very long as the subject discusses negative experiences. This entangled verbal style during the AAI reflects the fact that the emotions triggered by the interview questions overwhelm subjects' ability to engage in a collaborative exchange. In general these subjects have difficulty stepping away from specific memories to provide a coherent "big picture" of their experiences.

Finally, subjects can be classified as unresolved with regard to loss or trauma (U).

The unresolved scale deals exclusively with subjects' discussions of loss and other potentially frightening and/or traumatic experiences. An unresolved classification is assigned when a subject shows a marked disorganization in their speech around topics of trauma or loss. Specifically, these subjects show momentary lapses in their monitoring of speech/discourse and/or a lapse in their monitoring of reasoning. (...)

(...) Does adult attachment organization predict infant attachment via maternal sensitivity, or is it a matter of shared biological characteristics (temperament)?

(...) According to attachment theory, infants organize their behavior around the pattern of caregiver responses to the infant's distress. Again, Bowlby and Ainsworth were convinced that the real behaviors exchanged between parent and child formed the basis of differences in quality of attachment. Based on repeated behavioral exchanges, babies pattern their behavior directed to the mother in a way that maximizes the experience of "felt security" within the relationship (...). With the development of the AAI, attachment theory goes further to argue that the quality of the parent's internal working model of attachment is critical to the way in which a parent will behave when in the presence of a distressed baby, thus directing the quality of attachment formed with an infant.

So, for example, a parent who is autonomous is thought to be "free to evaluate" attachment related experiences including the needs of his or her child. These parents tend to be more consistently **responsive and sensitive** to their children compared to parents with other attachment states of mind. In turn, babies of autonomous parents behave in ways that suggest they have developed a confident expectation that they can securely rely on their parent when they need them.

Parents with dismissing states of mind are thought to be under-responsive and/or actively rejecting of their child's attachment needs. The child in turn develops a strategy that involves actually ignoring or avoiding their caregiver when they are need. It is thought that this strategy maximizes caregiver availability by minimizing rejection.

Parents with preoccupied states of mind are thought to be inconsistent in responding to their children because they are caught up and overwhelmed by attachment related stimuli (including the distress of a baby). Inconsistency in responsivity leaves the child anxious or insecure about the availability of the parent. The child, in turn, is likely to develop a resistant attachment that maximizes caregiver availability by heightening the parent's focus of attention to his or her distress.

Currently, much attention is being paid to the link between unresolved adult attachment and disorganized infant attachment. Indeed recent efforts have demonstrated that parents with unresolved trauma on the AAI display odd behaviors that are thought to be frightening to the child. These include mild dissociative episodes, disorganized behaviors and overtly threatening behaviors.

There is an enormous literature on the association between attachment and temperament which is discussed nicely by Vaughn and Bost (1999). Their conclusion after reviewing this vast literature is that parental report of infant temperament does not consistently predict attachment quality. However, there is some data suggesting that maternal reports of very early levels of irritability predict security of attachment.

Interestingly, these effects have been found to be mediated by the quality of the mothers' social support. Also, when temperament and attachment security are both measured using maternal report, the correlations are higher (shared variance?).

It does remain the case, however, that among biologically intact mother-infant dyads, the strongest predictor of infant attachment found thus far is the caregiver's state of mind with regard to attachment (van IJzendoorn, 1995). In meta analysis of 18 samples, parental state of mind was found to be best predictor of infant attachment (75% concordance). In addition, in our study of predictors of attachment in the context of foster care (involving exclusively non-biological dyads) concordance between parental AAI classifications and infant SS classifications was 72% (…).

TASK/TEXT 5.2: THE EFFECTS OF MALTREATMENT ON THE DEVELOPING BRAIN

The Link **– The Official Newsletter of the International Society for Prevention of Child Abuse and Neglect (ISPCAN)**
Vol. 16; No. 2, Northern Summer/Southern Winter 2007

This paper describes the effects of maltreatment on the child's developing brain. Much more is now understood about brain development, including the fact that while the first three years of life are of great importance to the child's later development, continuing and new experiences in childhood and adolescence also influence brain development. There is, therefore, potential for change even after significant early disadvantage which should encourage us to intervene to protect the child from further harm. While this paper is concerned with maltreatment which occurs from birth onwards, it is important to remember that brain development is also strongly influenced by prenatal factors, including maternal alcohol and drug abuse, and significant maternal stress. There is no legal mandate currently available for protecting the vulnerable fetal brain from adverse circumstances [***quod non:*** **prenatal child protection, JW**]. While the focus in this chapter is on the relationship between the primary caregiver(s) and the young child, this relationship is obviously nested within the family which is, in turn, significantly influenced by the social environment within which the family is located.

In light of our understanding of brain development, there are three different ways in which maltreatment can exert its harmful effects:
• Extreme deprivation; • Distorted experiences; • Stress.

Brain development

By birth, most of the brain's 100 billion neurons (nerve cells) are in their permanent position in the brain. Each neuron has branches or processes carrying signals to and from the nerve cell body. The branches from different neurons connect with each other at junctions called synapses. The signal is transmitted from one neuron to another across the synaptic gap by chemical neurotransmitters. Most post-natal brain growth occurs in the first 4 years, with the rate being highest in the first year. This post-natal growth is accounted for by a massive, sequential (over)production of new branches and synapses (synaptogenesis) in the brain. During early childhood, the number of synapses reaches nearly double the number ultimately found in adulthood. This new synapse growth requires structural support provided by proliferation of glial cells and nourishment by new blood capillaries. All this accounts for the growth in brain size.

The rate and timing of synaptogenesis varies between brain regions, which have different functions. Not all the synaptic connections survive, as many are subsequently 'pruned' due to lack of use. The overproduction of synapses is found especially in brain regions which have been genetically programmed to anticipate and respond to experiences which are part of the expected environment of the infant. These experiences include basic sensory input, the handling of young infants, responsive gaze by the parent, talking to the infant and responding sensitively to the infant's attachment needs. The absence of these inputs and interactions with the infant would be unusual for the majority of infants. This aspect of brain development is called *experience-expectant*. For some children, absence or insufficient input at the appropriate time will lead to failure of development of particular functions.

When a neuronal pathway is activated by a stimulus, the synapses that have become engaged will store a chemical signal, and repetition of the same or similar stimuli will stabilise the neuronal connection, establishing a pattern which will become less susceptible to subsequent change. The stimuli which trigger the signals between neurons come largely from the baby and child's environment. They include sensory input (light, touch, smell, sound) and interactions between the primary carers and the baby. The nature of the day to day experiences, including interactions with the primary caregivers, determine which brain circuits are reinforced and retained in the baby's brain. This aspect of brain maturation has been termed *experience-dependent*. Although learning (e.g. emotional development, acquisition of languages) proceeds much more easily at the appropriate developmental stage early in life, it is clear that experience-dependent development continues into adulthood although its rate is greatest in early life. Experience-dependent processes can generate new synapses in response to new experiences.

The brain's ability to change its own structure in response to the environment and experience is termed plasticity. While neural plasticity enables change to continue to occur, it also implies that the child remains vulnerable to the effects of harmful experiences in shaping brain development. Learning continues throughout the lifespan, although the rate of acquisition slows with increasing maturity. Since brain maturation is an orderly process, learning is initially a sequential process which relies on the development of prior skills for the acquisition of new ones. Moreover, the *nature* of what has previously been learnt will either shape or interfere with subsequent learning.

Implications of the process of brain development for child maltreatment

The importance of experiences in infancy and early childhood is clear but the mechanisms are complex. We need to consider both the effects of lack of provision of experiences (neglect), and the effects of particular undesirable, stressful or traumatic and neglectful experiences.

Extreme neglect

Neglect and failure of environmental stimulation during sensitive periods of brain development may lead to permanent deficits in certain functions. In the domain of interpersonal development, there is now evidence from work with adoptees from very neglectful orphanages that some of these children will not develop stranger wariness and selective attachments. Rather, these children will remain socially disinhibited, expressed by a lack of differentiation between adults, a lack of checking back with the (adoptive) parent in anxiety-provoking situations, and a clear indication that the child would go off with a stranger. These effects may be a result of extreme emotional neglect due to parental drug and alcohol abuse. Some of these children will also have great difficulty in regulating their emotional arousal and respond angrily or excitedly in an uncontrolled way to apparently minor triggers.

Undesirable, insensitive and stressful – distorted experiences

Early harmful experiences can have significant long-term negative effects on the developing brain. Negative experiences, for instance, significant exposure to angry faces or to violence, lead to amplification of synapses and neuronal networks associated with negative affect and the under-use and pruning of those involved in positive affect and approach behaviour. Enduring changes have been found in [the] behaviour and emotional state [of abused children].

In comparison to non-abused children, children who have been abused in early life have been found to have a more intense response recorded on an electro-encephalogram (EEG) when focusing on angry, rather than happy faces. Moreover, they have also been found to interpret facial expressions, which are ambiguously sad/angry or frightened/angry, as angry. In practice, it has been repeatedly found that both boys and girls who had been physically abused before the age of five years have been found to be aggressive and have difficulty with externalising behaviour and peer relationships in later childhood and into adolescence, even when the abuse had ceased. The implication is that a negative and angry affect carries a different meaning for maltreated children and elicits a physiologically measurable different response. For a child in danger, it is adaptive for their survival to construe possible signals of danger as such. This predisposition becomes maladaptive when used indiscriminately and outside of abusive situations.

The stress response

The body's response to stress is a physiological coping response necessary for survival, and involves several body systems. They include the hypothalamic-pituitary-adrenal axis (HPA), the autonomic nervous system, the neurotransmitter system and the immune system. There are individual variations in the threshold above which an individual perceives an experience to be stressful. These individual differences in stress responsiveness are partly innate (genetically determined) and partly based on prior experience. There are costs to the stress response and individual children who are innately more reactive to stress are therefore more vulnerable to its consequences.

The end result of the HPA axis response to stress is the increased secretion of cortisol and other hormones in this system, and this response commences in early infancy. Serum cortisol acts in a number of different ways and on most tissues and organs. Its actions include suppressing the immune response, increasing the level of circulating glucose and dampening of fear responses to the stressor, as well as adverse effects on the hippocampus, which is particularly involved in the processing of memory for events. Children with raised levels of cortisol during normal days at nursery, have greater difficulty in focusing and sustaining attention.

The response of the sympathetic nervous system to stress results in secretion of adrenaline and noradrenaline (norepinephrine). The effects of these hormones include raising heart rate and blood pressure, sweating and activation of the fight or flight response. There is also an increase in neurotransmitter secretion in the brain in response to stress which includes noradrenaline and dopamine and serotonin. Significantly raised levels of these neurotransmitters in the prefrontal cortex interfere with such functions as the planning and organising of actions using 'working memory' and the inhibiting of inappropriate responses and attention to distractions ('executive functions'), disturbance not unlike Attention Deficit Hyperactivity Disorder (ADHD).

What are the specific effects on the developing child of early stressful events and activation of the stress response? Early stress caused by neglect, abuse or exposure to inter-parental violence is often the beginning of an enduring pattern. Predictability and a sense of control modulate the stress response to potentially threatening experiences. Both predictability and the sense of control are compromised in the face of abuse and neglect. Children who have been abused and neglected have been found to show dysregulated cortisol responses as well as other evidence of neurobiological changes. One study, has found some decrease in brain volume in children who had been abused and who suffered from post traumatic stress disorder, thought to be an effect of prolonged and heightened stress response.

Overactivation of the stress response early in life with overstimulation of the noradrenergic system may lead to a long lasting reactive repression of noradrenaline. 'Normal' children learn to avoid responses which have negative consequences such as excessive anger, which is mediated by noradrenaline in the brain. Children who have been abused continue to respond more angrily to a perceived threat. This is postulated to be related to a diminished noradrenergic behavioural inhibition system, leading to continued arousal.

Young children who are securely attached to their mothers have been found to show a less intense stress response when faced with threat than children whose attachment was insecure. Insecure, particularly disorganised attachment is commonly found in children who have been physically and psychologically abused and neglected. They may therefore lack the protective effect which a secure attachment confers in the face of stress.

Conclusions

Young children who lack appropriate interactions during particular stages of development, such as the opportunity for forming an attachment before the age of three, may not develop the normal aspects of these functions. Harm also follows stressful, inappropriate early experiences which are incorporated into the neural networks at the time of synapse formation, as part of experience dependent brain maturation and the effects of the stress response on the developing brain. Although later experience will be incorporated and added on to past neuronal connections, the new experiences cannot undo established patterns, only modify them over time. In younger children, it is the changes in the interactions with the child and their parents and with other significant persons in their immediate environment. The primary focus for early intervention, therefore, needs to be with the primary carers and the carer-child relationship. Later direct therapeutic work with the child who is in a more optimal environment will also be required. **The most effective intervention is undoubtedly the prevention, or very early recognition of inappropriate parent-child interactions when effects on the young child may not yet be apparent.**

Danya Glaser (England), Consultant Child & Adolescent Psychiatrist, ISPCAN President

References:
Glaser, D. (2000), Child abuse and neglect and the brain – a review, *Journal of Child Psychology & Psychiatry*, 41, 97–116.
Glaser, D. (2003), Early Experience, Attachment and the Brain in: Corrigall, J. & Wilkinson, H. (eds.), *Revolutionary Connections: Psychotherapy & Neuroscience*, London: Karnac, pp. 117–133.

TASK/TEXT 5.3:

TASK/TEXT 5.3.1: INTERVIEW WITH BRUCE PERRY (CHILD TRAUMA ACADEMY)

Excerpts from an interview by Lou Bank, <www.childtrauma.org/ctamaterials/loubank.asp>

Maltreatment of a child will always result in some loss of that child's potential and often can result in such impaired development that the child will develop severe problems such as pervasive anxiety, depression, substance abuse and dependence, school failure, vulnerability to future abuse, violent sociopathy, or criminality. Abused children absorb the pain and either pass it on to others in a destructive way (*e.g.*, violence) or keep it and let it eat at themselves like a cancer. These 'social ills' rob the individual and, in the end, rob our society of the benefits these individuals could have made to us. Without understanding how maltreatment of children is related to the health and capacity of a society, we will never truly meet our potential – as individuals, as families, as communities, and as a culture. If we can make these connections, change the ways we treat women and children, and provide enriched, predictable, nurturing environments for our growing children, we can experience, as a species, transformation of amazing proportions. The human species 20,000 years ago had the same potential as today, yet there were few 'manifestations' of our true potential – we were brutal, cruel, and devoid of complex abstract art or culture. The elements of 'humanity' – those things that we have created – are not really genetic. They are creations of thousands of generations of experience. And during this time we have slowly moved to a more 'humane' set of values – we are trying to rid ourselves of racism, sexism, random predatory violence. Yet each generation, we have to re-create for our children an environment which can nurture those 'humane' qualities – and all too often we are failing to do so. We are raising children in an 'incubator of terror,' and creating impulsive, aggressive, anxious, and fearful children who fall far short of their potential.

By [elements of] humanity, I mean those elements of our existence which we have 'created' – the by-products of culture – our language, religious beliefs, political structures, arts and sciences. We are at great risk of losing these things, cultural devolution can take place in a generation. This is seen in what happened to the Native Americans, it is seen in what [happened] in Bosnia, it is seen in certain parts of our inner cities – the loss of cultural 'DNA': beliefs, language, child-rearing practices, elements of humanity. As Andrew [Andrew Vachss, see <www.vachss.com>, and see Vachss' statement below] says: each generation of children is 'Another Chance to Get It Right' – but that depends on what we provide for our children, what structure, what education, what beliefs, what love, what pain.

All experiences change the brain in some fashion. During childhood, however, it is clear that the brain is being shaped, literally formed by experience. Since the brain determines what we are as individuals, if we can understand how the brain is shaped and changed by childhood experiences, we can begin to answer some important questions about maltreatment of children. We are trying to understand how it is that one child can be beaten and humiliated and end up being a caring and productive (but depressed) person and how another with apparently similar childhood trauma can end up being a remorseless predator. To answer some of these questions, we need to know how nerve cells change and how the brain grows in the face of traumatic experience. Our research ranges from very basic molecular neuroscience, such as looking at how nerve cells connect to each other and develop, to very clinically oriented work with children.

The pervasive nature of the neglect, abuse, and traumatization of children is hard to truly communicate. Conservative estimates indicate that over 4 million American children each year are exposed to some severe form of abuse or neglect. This means that by the time a child reaches age 20, over 20 percent of our population has experienced severe traumatic stress, often in a chronic way. This means that 16 to 20 million children and adolescents currently are at risk for developing trauma-related problems (such as post-traumatic stress disorder). To put this in perspective, during the entire ten-year Vietnam era, 3.14 million American soldiers served in a combat setting. Of these, over 1 million developed emotional, behavioral, and physical problems related to their one year exposure to traumatic stress. These soldiers rotated out of combat. These children can't. They stay on the front – day in and day out – for years. And they carry their wounds into adolescence and adulthood, all too often without the benefit of any medical, social, or political support for these wounds.

One of the most important facts about the development of the brain is that early in life – say the first three years – experiences organize the brain and determine how that individual will function, in large part, for the rest of [his or her] live. Many capacities, while not completely lost, are tremendously difficult to grow after this window of opportunity is lost. One of the most important of these capacities is the ability to be attached to – and to 'love' – others. The part of the brain that allows us to feel pleasure and positive emotional connection to others is dependent upon consistent, nurturing experiences during the first few years of life. The child left alone, inconsistently touched or smiled at, infrequently 'cuddled,' will have a brain with an undeveloped area. This is a biological, physical phenomenon. These parts of the brain grow just like a muscle. And without 'exercise' the muscle atrophies. So it is with these parts of the brain. Without 'love' at these critical times, that part of the brain atrophies. And, as stated before, it appears that this atrophy can be permanent and almost impossible to reverse. This leads to clear implications for public policy and for how we should target our intervention dollars. Currently, we are missing the windows of opportunity. There is a tremendous mismatch between where we spend most of our intervention dollars (adults) and when the brain is most easily changed (early childhood).

It is important to keep in mind the difference between neglect and a traumatic experience. The absence of a set of critical experiences in childhood – love, touch, education – can lead to permanent absences of capabilities. And this is reflected by the lack of growth of parts of the brain. While a traumatic experience is not an absence of experience, it is the abnormal and persisting presence of a response which, in turn, alters an existing part of the brain. It is so much easier to treat and change a part of the brain that has been influenced by a trauma, than it is to try to 'grow' a part of the brain after the critical periods in childhood are over.

If we cannot structure our schools, our communities, and our social agencies in a manner that will identify, protect, and, at a minimum, provide hope to our children, we will be swept away by the inevitable decay of socio-cultural devolution. Similar deterioration of pre-existing cultural achievements was seen after the fall of the Roman Empire – the Dark Ages – where, for centuries, no new literature or significant art was produced. Abstract cognition disappeared in western Europe. The planet was populated by generation after generation of superstitious, brutal, racist, misogynist, and non-creative people. We are not as far from that as we like to think. Repression, oppression, superstition, racism, sexism, and reactionary and simplistic views of the world persist – and, without smart and aggressive research and training, these anti-humane qualities may prevail. If we provide enriched, nurturing, predictable, and safe environments for our children, they will create an enriched, safe, and humane society. If we keep raising our children with ignorance, unpredictability, and fear, we will have a rigid and reactionary society. It is our choice – our responsibility – our opportunity.

TASK/TEXT 5.3.2: NOBODY'S CHILDREN

Interview with Bruce Perry (by Liz Else), *New Scientist*, 10 February 2007, pp. 42–43, <www.newscientist.com>

Can we avoid violence by reinventing the way people live together and raise children? Bruce Perry thinks so.

Bruce Perry received his medical degree at Northwestern University in Illinois and completed a residency in general psychiatry at Yale University School of Medicine. He is now senior fellow at the ChildTrauma Academy, a not-for-profit organisation that studies childhood trauma (<www. childtrauma.org>). He is co-author of *The Boy Who Was Raised As A Dog* (…).

When psychiatrist Bruce Perry was called in by staff at a paediatric hospital in Houston, Texas, the first thing he heard was an eerie, animal-like shriek. Turning around, he saw a bony six-year-old boy in an iron crib with plywood wired to the top, throwing faeces, then whimpering a primitive lullaby as he rocked back and forth, soaked in urine. Unable to cope with the child's violent outbursts, staff at the hospital had built a sort of cage to restrain him. So who was the boy, and how had he ended up like this? In a new book, Perry tells the story of 'Justin' and other traumatised children whose lives, he believes, hold important lessons as we try to integrate psychiatry with the cutting edge of neurology. Liz Else caught up with him.

How did Justin end up crouching in a cage?

He'd been brought in for an evaluation with a developmental paediatric clinic and was found to have pneumonia. So they put him on a normal hospital floor, where he was completely overwhelmed, terrified and out of control. In turn, he terrified the staff so they decided to cage him. I called the book *The Boy who was Raised as a Dog* because he seemed more like a dog than a child at that time.

How did you try to make contact?

I approached him very gradually and cautiously, trying not to establish eye contact or use any of the non-verbal signals that I knew were associated with power and authority. I was very non-threatening and talked very slowly. I offered him a bit of food that I nibbled to show him it was safe.

How on earth had he got like this?
His mother was a 15-year-old who had left the two-month-old Justin with her mother. This grandmother had cared very well for him for the first 11 months, then she died, leaving him with her boyfriend Arthur, a man in his late sixties who knew nothing about children but a lot about dogs. Arthur asked the child protection services for help but they evidently felt the child was safe enough where he was. So Arthur started to raise him in the only way he knew how – as a dog. He put Justin in a dog cage, fed and watered him, changed him, but rarely spoke to him or played with him. Justin's only real companions were dogs. Arthur wasn't cruel, just ignorant and possibly a bit retarded.

Did you make any progress at all?
Other doctors had told Arthur that Justin was brain-damaged – by the age of five, he still couldn't walk or talk. These doctors hadn't known how he was being brought up, however. The first thing I did was decrease the chaos in Justin's life by moving him to a private room, minimising his interactions, and bringing in physical, occupational and speech therapists. The improvement was remarkable. As Justin started to feel safer, he smiled. He even showed signs of a sense of humour: he knew how much everyone hated having faeces thrown at them, so when someone gave him a chocolate bar he let it melt in his hand and pretended he was going to throw it. Over the next few weeks he took his first steps and was taught the basics of self-care.

Surely all the textbooks say that a child like Justin who has missed developmental milestones can never be helped later?
That had generally been our experience. But Justin had received some pretty solid nurturing from his grandmother in the first few months of his life. We think these early basic human interactions laid down some of the neurological structures in his brain necessary for further development.

Does that challenge conventional wisdom about developmental corridors in areas such as speech?
The thing people forget is that the most malleable part of the brain, and the last to develop, is the cortex, where speech and language are centred. Conversely, the most difficult parts of the brain to change are those that develop earlier, in the midbrain and brain stem. When children have been deprived in their early years, it's a lot easier to build up their cognitive capabilities than it is to develop their ability to relate to others.

What happened next?
After some more weeks of amazing progress he went to live with a foster family, where he continued to make what I think was the most rapid recovery from such severe neglect I've ever seen. It challenged my thinking about the potential for recovery. We still get reports on him and he's doing pretty well in school, he's passing his classes, he has friends and has learnt to speak properly.

How many children like Justin do you believe there are?
In the US alone, we know that every year there are at least half a million new cases of children found to have suffered from severe trauma or neglect. So at any one time, there are going to be between 8 and 10 million children [**well over 10%**, JW] with some kind of profound trauma or neglect-related dysfunction. That's a huge burden on any society. If you look at a society or culture that's been badly affected by famine or war, then those numbers climb still higher. You can imagine the experiences of children in some parts of Africa. These things have a significant impact on the way a culture develops.

In your book, you also draw some strong political conclusions from your work.
If you have an ill-educated and half-starved population, the chances are they will rear children who will suffer some kind of trauma. Some of these children then grow up to become leaders, but their ability to be creative is compromised by their early trauma's. These concepts are fundamental to truly understanding and developing policy. I believe that if you understand how the brain works, how people function under stress and the way that this can carry across generations, then you realise that some of the attempts of the west to bring peace to the Middle East are neurologically doomed to fail.

Why?
Because the people are traumatised to the point where they literally can't hear what you say and take it in.

Have you ever tried to explain any of this to the people attempting to negotiate peace?
Increasingly at our unit we are being asked to communicate these ideas to state legislators, governors and other people in policy-making positions. I am part of a group that's doing this on a small scale through a **UK-based charity called Worldwide Alternatives to Violence** [<www.wavetrust.org>, JW]. The charity is trying to help people understand that there really is a relationship between childhood trauma's such as exposure to violence, and criminality. There is a way to divert people from risky and unhealthy futures by paying attention to the way they are treated when they are young.

You're against drug therapies aren't you?
We need to learn how to use psychotropic drugs in a way that is responsible and is a true adjunct to treatment, as opposed to a cop-out. There are physicians in the US who will see 35 children in a day, each one for only 15 minutes. And every one of these children are put on medication. It's stunning but it happens all over the country.

What kind of therapies would you prefer to see?
Everything from speech, physical, play and art therapies to massage, to desensitising techniques, to cognitive behaviour therapy. We're thinking a lot about how we can reinvent the way human beings can live together and raise children.

TASK/TEXT 5.3.3: ALL THEY NEED IS LOVE

The Scotsman, Tuesday 13 March 2007 – Jim Gilchrist

The child in the hospital's paediatric unit was six. He was filthy, painfully thin and giving out alarming, animal-like shrieks. His crib had iron bars, and a plywood panel on top to prevent him throwing faeces at the staff. He was called Justin and had been looked after since the age of 11 months by a man of subnormal intelligence who only knew about dogs. He had raised the child accordingly.

Then there was Sandy, a four-year-old who was terrified of milk. A year earlier she had witnessed the rape and murder of her mother in their home and had her own throat slit, twice, by the perpetrator, who left her for dead. Alone with her mother's body for 11 hours, she had gone to the fridge and tried to drink milk – which dribbled through her throat wounds – and then attempted to give it to her dead mother, "but she wasn't thirsty."

Or Laura, another four-year-old, who simply stopped growing, quite literally through being starved of affection …

Dr Bruce Perry's casebook can make depressing, sometimes harrowing reading, detailing as it does the scarcely imaginable physical or sexual abuse, or sheer neglect, that can blight a child's life – and quite possibly the lives of their future offspring. But as he recounts in his new book, *The Boy Who Was Raised as a Dog*, some deeply traumatised children can still respond to innovative and insightful treatment.

The book, co-written with New York science journalist Maia Szalavitz, may highlight some of Perry's most memorable cases, but his concerns range much wider: he calls for urgent rethinking on what he sees as the decline of the extended family, our devaluing of the importance of human relationships and, ultimately, the effect of this on society at large. "We're at a transitional point in history where people are recognising that modern societies have abandoned many of the fundamental elements required for optimal human mental health," he declares in the book.

When Perry opines to me that "we need to recapture the strength of the clan," he isn't being sentimental – even though his grandfather was a Scots Gaelic speaker who emigrated to Canada, then North Dakota, where the 52-year-old psychiatrist grew up. "I don't want to seem over-dramatic," he says, speaking from the ChildTrauma Academy, a nonprofit organisation he co-founded in Houston, Texas, which promotes innovative research and education in child maltreatment. "But I really do think that, because of the tremendous changes in technology, transportation and social demographics, there is a potential inflection point where, if we don't begin to develop biologically respectful policies and practices in communities, and recapture some of the strength of the clan, we will end up with multiple generations that are more selfish, more self-absorbed and less concerned about the core issues of humane values and social justice."

As a psychiatrist specialising in traumatised children, consultant to the FBI and former chief of psychiatry at Texas Children's Hospital, Perry is frequently called in to advise on the heartbreaking aftermath of incidents such as the Branch Davidian siege at Waco, the Columbine school shootings and the Katrina and Rita hurricane disasters. His book, subtitled *What Traumatised Children Can Teach Us About Loss, Love and Healing*, is an unsettling revelation into the ways in which emotional and physical neglect can damage children, but it also highlights the way in which **neuroscience** has affected our understanding of **child development**. "These different disciplines have kind of evolved in parallel and it's only just been within the past 15 years or so that there's been cross-talk between neurobiology and clinical psychiatry, in a way that really allows people to take the principles we were learning in the laboratory by studying the brain and use them in the clinic."

Take Laura, who at the age of four weighed only 26lb, despite the best high-calorie efforts of the hospital. Eventually, Perry elicited that her mother had been abandoned at birth by her own drug-addicted parent, then had been short-changed by an inadequate state foster-care system and later, when she became pregnant, by the healthcare system. While she did her best to look after her baby, she was emotionally disconnected and rarely held the child, rocked her or sang to her in the bonding [attachment, JW] processes we take for granted.

Perry explains that all mammals need these physical and emotional signals to stimulate growth, so her daughter "failed to thrive," to use the clinical term. The condition has been known for centuries, he adds, particularly in orphanages and other institutions where personal care is lacking. One study in the 1940s suggests that more than a third of children institutionally raised without individual attention died by the age of two.

Absence of essential physical contact prompted her body to respond with "a hormonal dysregulation that impeded normal growth, despite receiving more than adequate nutrition." Yet, when she was given a course of what amounted to tender loving care, she made remarkable progress.

And Justin was almost certainly saved by the fact that, for the first 11 months of his life, his grandmother had nurtured him lovingly, before dying, leaving him to her extremely limited boyfriend who, while ensuring the boy was well fed and changed, kept him in a dog cage.

Within a fortnight of Perry finding him in hospital and patiently establishing contact with the terrified child, Justin was with foster parents and made what the psychiatrist describes as the most rapid recovery from severe neglect he'd seen, significantly changing the psychiatrist's views on recovery potential. "I think [that first 11 months] was enough to help the brain build up the skeletal elements of normal functioning." Justin is now at primary school: "He still has some problems but, considering where he was, he's made remarkable progress."

Some neglected children, however, remain beyond help, sometimes with tragic results. Thus Perry finds himself in a maximum-security prison, interviewing Leon, who at 16 had murdered two girls in their early teens, then sexually violated them. When Perry asks him whether, in hindsight, there was anything he'd have done differently with his life, he thinks for a minute, then replies: "I don't know. Maybe throw away those boots." It was the boots, bloodstained after he had stabbed the girls to death, which led to his arrest.

Through interviewing the young murderer's uncomprehending parents, Perry established a chain of events, mundane then critical, which saw the couple, who already had one child, having to move hundreds of miles away from the mother's extensive family as her husband sought employment. When Leon was born, his mother, who was slightly mentally impaired and cut off from any family or neighbourly support, had found the new arrival so demanding that, after feeding him, she and the older toddler would leave him alone in their dark apartment while they went for lengthy outings.

The previously fractious baby ceased to cry any more, she told Perry. Then, as Leon grew up, his parents wondered why he never responded to them. He never displayed any emotion (he'd learned from infancy that crying brought no attention) and his behaviour became increasingly troubling and disruptive. He grew into what Perry describes as "a classic sociopath … and one, I think, who was almost entirely a product of his environment, not his genes."

All down the line, he stresses, "trauma and our responses to it cannot be understood outside the context of human relationships." And what maltreated and traumatised children most need, he adds, "is a healthy community to buffer the pain, distress and loss." Sadly, he acknowledges that those children most vulnerable to trauma tend to be the least likely to have a healthy, supportive family or community. When I express astonishment that Justin, in his dog pen, had so dramatically plummeted through the social welfare safety net, he is dismissive: "We have a very sick child-protection system in the US."

He is also critical of many of the counselling and other services offered by state systems: "I think, in the US certainly, a lot of the limited resources in the child mental health system are focused on reactive intervention, but we don't put any money into prevention and other kinds of therapeutic activities known to be helpful. I suspect it's probably similar in the UK."

As educationalists, healthcare specialists and others talk in terms of a **mental health epidemic** among children (an estimated 250 million worldwide are on prescription drugs such as Ritalin), Perry has strong views on what he regards, in the US at least, as "a fractured community and our unrelenting focus on competition," the most extreme results of which he identifies as incidents such as school shootings. "What I've found time and again in these cases is a winner-takes-all school culture, where **bullying** is pervasive and accepted and where the 'losers' are not considered people who need understanding and support, but utterly deserving of their alienation and exclusion."

He attacks supposedly "caring" childcare practices, such as the Californian preschool centre that no longer permits its staff to touch the children, even in situations where a hug might be in order. He cites school curricula so intensively structured that students no longer have time to build relationships with each other: "This is insane."

Basically, he argues, we need to build a healthier society: "Human beings are designed for living in relatively close-knit, multi-family, intergenerational groups. With the increasing compartmentalisation of the family in the West, the impact of television and the vertical models we use for education: it all leads to significant relational poverty."

Perry is involved with an English-based WAVE Trust (Worldwide Alternatives to ViolencE), concerned with reducing child abuse and interpersonal violence through understanding its root causes. Also in the UK, he commends more holistic initiatives such as the One Nottingham strategic partnership, for its emphasis on creating a safe overall social environment. The knock-on effect of child trauma takes on a geopolitical dimension if one considers areas subject to **endemic violence, famine or other disasters**, which may produce leaders whose policies may reflect that trauma. "Part of what we're learning," says Perry, "is that there is this **trans-generational impact of abuse and violence**, which increases the number of children who grow up to be more impulsive, more reactive in their thinking, and more easily influenced by **hateful beliefs**. We've seen examples of that throughout history."

He acknowledges that getting his message across can be an uphill struggle: "One of the reasons we thought writing this book would be helpful is that these concepts should be in the public mind whenever we have debates about **childcare policy**, about **foreign policy**, about all kinds of things where we, as a collective society, are making decisions about the way we live."

There may be those who still regard child development as either a specialist study or simply a domestic incidental: Perry is arguing that it might just be the most important thing in the world.

TASK/TEXT 5.3.4: RESILIENT CHILDREN ARE MADE, NOT BORN

Bruce D. Perry & Maia Szalavitz, *The boy who was raised as a dog, and other stories from a child psychiatrist's notebook; What traumatized children can teach us about loss, love and healing*, New York: Basic Books, 2006, pp. 38–39

Unfortunately, the prevailing view of children and trauma (…) – one that persists to a large degree to this day – is that "children are resilient." (…) If anything, children are more vulnerable to trauma than adults (…). Resilient children are made, not born. The developing brain is most malleable and most sensitive to experience – both good and bad – early in life. (This is why we so easily and rapidly learn language, social nuance, motor skills and dozens of other things in childhood, and why we speak of "formative" experiences.) Children become resilient as a result of the patterns of stress and of nurturing that they experience early on in life (…). Consequently, we are also rapidly and easily transformed by trauma when we are young. Though its effects may not always be visible to the untrained eye, when you know what trauma can do to children, sadly, you begin to see its aftermath everywhere.

TASK/TEXT 5.3.5: ANIMAL ASSISTED THERAPIES (TRANSLATIONAL NEUROSCIENCE)

The ChildTrauma Academy Newsletter September 2009 (e-list 23 September 2009)

A recent study (Topal *et al.*, *Science*, 325:1269–71, 2009) demonstrated another fascinating aspect of the unique human-dog relationship. Dogs, even puppies, are able to understand subtle adult human social-cognitive cues in the same fashion as a human infant. No other species, wolf or great ape, can do this. The unique connection between dog and human is likely due to the domestication and co-evolution of our species. Dogs, with their sensitive hearing and smell, helped keep our clans safe. In turn, we fed and nurtured dogs. In a very real way, dogs became an extension of the human stress-response system. The underlying neurobiology suggests a "mirroring neuron" relationship between human and dog similar to that between human and human. An calm parent can calm an anxious child. A calm dog can calm a nervous child in the hospital. Studies show that some of the most effect elements of AAT (with dogs primarily) include the capacity to calm, sooth, and "engage and relate." This unique capacity of dogs make them perfect for helping children with social impairments learn more normal social interactive capabilities; and to sooth anxious overwhelmed humans. AAT is an emerging area; there are some but few quality studies examining the impact of these supplemental services in traditional therapy. Yet meta analysis and quality studies do demonstrate a very promising role for AAT in work with maltreated children. And, the mechanisms, very likely, will turn out to be related to the unique neurobiological connection between dog and human.

TASK/TEXT 5.4: ANDREW VACHSS – LAWYER, AUTHOR, JUVENILE JUSTICE AND CHILD ABUSE CONSULTANT

Andrew Vachss' Statement, taken from <www.childtrauma.org/links/andrew.asp> (see also <www.vachss.com>)

Every year, millions of children in the United States are victimized by severe abuse. This maltreatment takes many forms, but all have this in common: they rob children of some percentage of their potential, some vital human piece of themselves. And by such robbery, all America is looted. The problem has been documented to the point of nausea. The media dutifully reports the body counts, but the one-sided war rages on. Domestic violence, sexual exploitation, rape, sociopathic plundering, homicide … we are under siege even as our 'protective' institutions rot from within.

We know the root cause of our societal ills and evil – the transgenerational maltreatment of children. We know today's victim can be tomorrow's predator. We know that while many heroic survivors refuse to imitate the oppressor, the chains remain unbroken as abused children turn the trauma inward and lose their souls to self-inflicted wounds … from drug and alcohol abuse to depression and suicide. Their lives are never what they could have, should have been.

We know the enemy, but where is the counter-attack? More social engineering? More pious whining? More networking? More conferences? More unfocused, blundering incompetence? There is a Rosetta Stone[44] to societal decay. Child abuse, simply, modifies development of the brain. It alters 'processing,' so that the abused child (of whatever age) assimilates and responds to stimuli in distinctly aberrant ways. Most of those ways are self-destructive. Some destroy others. All destroy us as a country.

TASK/TEXT 5.5:

TASK/TEXT 5.5.1: ALICE MILLER – *THE ROOTS OF VIOLENCE*

Availabe at <www.alice-miller.com/sujet/framen.htm>, flyers

For some years now, there has been proof that the devastating effects of the traumatization of children take their inevitable toll on society (...). This knowledge concerns every single one of us and – if disseminated widely enough – should lead to fundamental changes in society, above all to a halt in the blind escalation of violence. The following points are intended to amplify my meaning:

1. All children are born to grow, to develop, to live, to love, and to articulate their needs and feelings for their self-protection.
2. For their development, children need the respect and protection of adults who take them seriously, love them, and honestly help them to become oriented in the world.
3. When these vital needs are frustrated and children are, instead, abused for the sake of adults' needs by being exploited, beaten, punished, taken advantage of, manipulated, neglected, or deceived without the intervention of any witness, then their integrity will be lastingly impaired.
4. The normal reactions to such injury should be anger and pain. Since children in this hurtful kind of environment are forbidden to express their anger, however, and since it would be unbearable to experience their pain all alone, they are compelled to suppress their feelings, repress all memory of the trauma, and idealize those guilty of the abuse. Later they will have no memory of what was done to them.

44 After many years of studying the Rosetta Stone and other examples of ancient Egyptian writing, Jean-François Champollion deciphered hieroglyphs in 1822 (<www.ancientegypt.co.uk/writing/rosetta.html>).

5. Disassociated from the original cause, their feelings of anger, helplessness, despair, longing, anxiety, and pain will find expression in destructive acts against others ([from] criminal behavior [to] mass murder) or against themselves (drug addiction, alcoholism, prostitution, psychic disorders, suicide).
6. If these people become parents, they will then often direct acts of revenge for their mistreatment in childhood against their own children, whom they use as scapegoats. Child abuse is still sanctioned (…) in our society as long as it is defined as child rearing. It is a tragic fact that parents beat their children in order to escape the emotions stemming from how they were treated by their own parents.
7. If mistreated children are not to become criminals or mentally ill, it is essential that at least once in their life they come in contact with a person who knows without any doubt that the environment, not the helpless, battered child, is at fault. In this regard, knowledge or ignorance on the part of society can be instrumental in either saving or destroying a life. Here lies the great opportunity for relatives, social workers, therapists, teachers, doctors, psychiatrists, officials, and nurses to support the child and to believe her or him.
8. Till now, society has protected the adult and blamed the victim. It has been abetted in its blindness by theories, still in keeping with the pedagogical principles of our great-grandparents, according to which children are viewed as crafty creatures, dominated by wicked drives, who invent stories and attack their innocent parents or desire them sexually. In reality, children tend to blame themselves for their parents' cruelty and to absolve the parents, whom they invariably love, of all responsibility.
9. For some years now, it has been possible to prove, through new therapeutic methods, that repressed traumatic experiences of childhood are stored up in the body and, though unconscious, exert an influence even in adulthood. In addition, electronic testing of the fetus has revealed a fact previously unknown to most adults, that a child responds to and learns both tenderness and cruelty from the very beginning.
10. In the light of this new knowledge, even the most absurd behavior reveals its formerly hidden logic once the traumatic experiences of childhood need no longer remain shrouded in darkness.
11. Our sensitization to the cruelty with which children are treated, until now commonly denied, and to the consequences of such treatment will as a matter of course bring to an end the perpetuation of violence from generation to generation.
12. People whose integrity has not been damaged in childhood, who were protected, respected, and treated with honesty by their parents, will be –

both in their youth and in adulthood – intelligent, responsive, empathic, and highly sensitive. They will take pleasure in life and will not feel any need to kill or even hurt others or themselves. They will use their power to defend themselves, not to attack others. They will not be able to do otherwise than respect and protect those weaker than themselves, including their children, because this is what they have learned from their own experience, and because it is this knowledge (and not the experience of cruelty) that has been stored up inside them from the beginning. It will be inconceivable to such people that earlier generations had to build up a gigantic war industry in order to feel comfortable and safe in this world. Since it will not be their unconscious drive in life to ward off intimidation experienced at a very early age, they will be able to deal with attempts at intimidation in their adult life more rationally and more creatively.

TASK/TEXT 5.5.2: ALICE MILLER – *THE CHILDHOOD TRAUMA*

Excerpts taken from <www.vachss.com/guest_dispatches/alice_miller2.html>

We all know – or, today, we *should* all know – that physical punishment only produces *obedient* children but cannot prevent them from becoming violent or sick adults precisely *because* of this treatment. This knowledge is now scientifically proven and was finally officially accepted by the American Academy of Pediatrics in 1998. Contrary to common opinion prevalent as recently as fifteen years ago, the human brain at birth is far from being fully developed. It is use-dependent, needing loving stimulation for the child from [his or] her first day on. The abilities a person's brain can develop, depend on experiences in the first three years of life.

Studies on abandoned and severely maltreated Romanian children, as an example, revealed striking lesions in certain areas of the brain. The repeated traumatization has led to an increased release of stress hormones which have attacked the sensitive tissue of the brain and destroyed the new, already built-up neurons. The areas of their brains responsible for the 'management' of their emotions are twenty to thirty percent smaller than in other children of the same age. Obviously, all children (not only Romanian) who suffer such abandonment and maltreatment will be damaged in this way.

The neurobiological research makes it easier for us to understand the way Nazi's like Eichmann, Himmler, Hoss and others functioned. The rigorous obedience training they underwent in earliest infancy stunted the development of such human capacities as compassion and pity for the sufferings of others.

Their total emotional atrophy enabled the perpetrators of the most heinous crimes imaginable to function 'normally' and to continue without the slightest remorse to impress their environment with their efficiency in the years after the war. Dr. Mengele could make the most cruel experiments with Jewish children in Auschwitz and then live for thirty years like a 'normal,' well adjusted man.

Those turn-of-the-century [around 1900] children who were (...) systematically subjected to obedience drilling were not only exposed to corporal correction but also to severe emotional deprivation. The upbringing manuals of the day described physical demonstrations of affection such as stroking, cuddling and kissing as indications of a doting, mollycoddling attitude. Parents were warned of the disastrous effects of spoiling their children, a form of indulgence entirely incompatible with the prevalent ideal of rigor and severity. As a result, infants suffered from the absence of direct loving contact with the parents, which also caused certain areas of the brain to remain underdeveloped.

Working toward a better future cannot be done without legislation that clearly forbids corporal punishment toward children and makes society aware of the fact that children are people too. The whole society and its legal system can then play the role of a reliable, enlightened and protecting witness for children at risk, children of adolescent, drug addicted criminals who may themselves become predators without such assistance. The only reason why a parent might smack his children is the parent's own history. All other so-called reasons, such as poverty and unemployment, are pure mystification. There are unemployed parents who don't spank their children and there are many wealthy parents who maltreat their children in the most cruel way and teach them to minimize the terror by calling it the right education. With a law prohibiting corporal punishment towards children, people of the next generation will not have recorded the highly misleading information in their brain, an almost irreversible damage. They will be able to have empathy with a child and understand what has been done to children over millennia. It is a realistic hope to think that then (and only then) the human mind and behavior *will* change. With a law that forbids spanking every citizen becomes an enlightened witness.

TASK/TEXT 5.6: ECEC (EARLY CHILDHOOD EDUCATION AND CARE) – A RIGHT TO EDUCATION … FROM BIRTH

Martin Woodhead, Professor of Childhood Studies, The Open University, United Kingdom, in: Martin Woodhead & Peter Moss (eds.), *Early Childhood and Primary Education*, Early Childhood in Focus No. 2, The Open University Child and Youth Studies Group, Milton Keynes, UK (with the support of Bernard van

Leer Foundation (The Hague), <www.bernardvanleer.org>), 2007, p. 2; <www.bernardvanleer.org/publication_store/publication_store_publications/early_childhood_and_primary_education_transitions_in_the_lives_of_young_children/file>

A major transformation has been taking place in the lives of the world's youngest children, especially in relation to schooling. Where education was once the privilege of a minority, it is now recognised as a universal entitlement, with every child's right to education reaffirmed by the UN Convention on the Rights of the Child, CRC (United Nations, 1989). This principle was translated into the *World Declaration on Education for All* (UNESCO, 1990) and in the targets set out in the *Dakar Framework for Action* (UNESCO, 2000). These targets include ensuring that by 2015 all children have access to good-quality primary education, with particular attention to girls, ethnic minorities and children in difficult circumstances. The targets also include expanding and improving comprehensive ECEC [**Early Childhood Education and Care, i.e. all kinds of early childhood services for children and families, JW**], especially for the most vulnerable and disadvantaged children.

Global enrolment in primary education increased from 83 to 86 per cent between 1999 and 2004, with an estimated 682 million children enrolled in 2004. Even so, primary education provision is still marked by inequalities and there are serious shortages in resources available for buildings, teachers and materials. These inequalities are widespread within countries, as well as between countries. As a general rule, the poorest and most vulnerable children and families are least likely to have access to quality education (UNESCO, 2006).

The CRC asserts the right of every child to education, without discrimination, and places particular emphasis on making primary education compulsory and available free to all (Article 28). The Committee on the Rights of the Child has gone a step further in General Comment 7 (2005), interpreting **every child's right to education as beginning at birth and closely tied to the right to development (as set out in Article 6.2 of the CRC)**. The Committee goes beyond a narrow interpretation of 'education' as 'schooling.' Instead, General Comment 7 offers a vision for comprehensive, community services throughout early and middle childhood, both for children and for parents as their educators and caregivers. This vision acknowledges that family and home settings offer the foundation (and for most children the underlying continuity) on which progression through early childhood and primary education is constructed.

– Every child's entitlement to education is now widely recognised, and affirmed by the Convention on the Rights of the Child (1989).

– Primary education provision is still marked by inequalities in enrolment levels, and serious shortages in resources.
– The Committee on the Rights of the Child interprets every child's right to education as beginning at birth and closely tied to the right to maximum development.

TASK/TEXT 5.7:

TASK/TEXT 5.7.1: UNICEF INNOCENTI RESEARCH CENTRE ON EARLY CHILDHOOD DEVELOPMENT

UNICEF Innocenti Research Centre, Report Card No. 8 on Early Childhood Development, <www.unicef-irc.org>, visited 17 March 2008

A considerable body of evidence points to the importance of the early years as a window of opportunity to make a difference in the lives of children and to break the intergenerational cycle of poverty [both socio-economic and socio-emotional, i.e., transism, JW]. Recognizing this evidence, many countries of the Organisation for Economic Co-operation and Development (OECD) have national strategies for enhancing the experiences of young children.

Report Card No. 8 will analyse these countries' response to families and young children, notably in the area of early childhood care and education [ECEC]. OECD governments invest public resources in early childhood services. However, from the point of view of the best interests of the child, the situation in many OECD countries leaves room for improvement and requires a doubling of resources. The report aims to present, in an internationally comparable manner, a set of indicators of coverage, quality and impact of national policies and investment in early childhood services, so as to encourage closer monitoring and more focused debate among political leaders, the media and the public.

See The child care transition; A league table of early childhood education and care in economically advanced countries, UNICEF Innocenti Research Centre, Report Card No. 8, available at <www.unicef-irc.org/publications/pdf/rc8_eng.pdf>.

TASK/TEXT 5.7.2: THE CHILD CARE TRANSITION – A LEAGUE TABLE OF EARLY CHILDHOOD EDUCATION AND CARE IN ECONOMICALLY ADVANCED COUNTRIES

Crinmail 1041 – 11 December 2008, <www.crin.org>

In the past decade, two developments have occurred that have the potential to greatly benefit and greatly harm children.

According to UNICEF Innocenti Research Centre's Report Card 8, *The Child Care Transition*, today, a majority of the rising generation in economically advanced societies is spending a significant part of childhood in out-of-home childcare. In the countries of the Organisation for Economic Co-operation and Development [OECD], almost 80 per cent of three- to six-year-olds are in some form of early childhood education and care. For under-threes, the proportion is 25 per cent, rising to more than 50 per cent in individual countries. In the last decade many countries have also begun to see sharp increases in the numbers of the children **under the age of one year being cared for outside the home**.

At the same time, progress in the scientific understanding of **early brain development** is confirming that the **quality of care and interaction in the earliest months and years of a child's life are critical for almost all aspects of a child's development**. The early years provide a key window of opportunity to make a difference in the lives of children and to **break the intergenerational cycle of** [material, mental and emotional –JW] **poverty**.

But poor quality child care may result in **weak foundations and shaky scaffolding for future learning, as well as psychological and emotional development**. Some OECD countries, says the report, have engaged closely with the childcare issue, pursuing policies designed to realise the potential benefits. In others, out-of-home child care is proceeding in an ad hoc way with less assurance of quality.

Drawing on academic and governmental expertise, Report Card 8 proposes **ten benchmarks** by which progress in early childhood education and care might be monitored and compared across the countries of the OECD. These benchmarks can pave the way for the establishment of **minimum standards for early childhood services** in OECD countries and beyond.

See The child care transition; A league table of early childhood education and care in economically advanced countries, UNICEF Innocenti Research Centre, Report Card No. 8, available at <www.unicef-irc.org/publications/pdf/rc8_eng.pdf>.

TASK/TEXT 5.7.3: THE CHILD CARE TRANSITION – IGNORE QUALITY AT YOUR PERIL

Eurochild Press Release on "The child care transition"; Brussels, 12 December 2008 [email]

A report out yesterday from *UNICEF* calls for much closer monitoring of the quality of early childhood services, as **out-of-home care becomes the norm** for pre-school children across economically developed countries.

Some 80% of children aged 3–6 are in some form of education and care in the OECD [Organisation for Economic Co-operation and Development, Paris 1960] countries. For the under-3s, it's approximately 25% of children, but this ranges from over 70% in Denmark to under 10% in Germany, Hungary, Austria and Italy. There is no comparable data available for the under-1s.

But according to Jana Hainsworth, Secretary General of Eurochild, "What is so important about this report is that it puts **children's best interest at the heart of the child care debate**. In the EU, we tend only to think of early childhood services in the context of the Barcelona childcare targets – basically providing enough places to 'park' children so their parents can work. This report re-dresses that balance and puts emphasis on quality not quantity."

The report is the eighth in a series of Innocenti Report Cards designed to monitor and encourage progress by **OECD countries in advancing the rights of the child**. It offers a comparative analysis of the early childhood care and education services in 25 OECD countries across 4 dimensions presented in a league table of 10 benchmarks: policy framework, access to services and their quality, and supporting economic and social context.

Eurochild's member in Ireland, the *Children's Rights Alliance*, urged their government to take note. "Having met only one of the study's ten minimum standard benchmarks and having one of the lowest spends on pre-school education in developed countries, less than 0.2% of GDP compared to the EU average of 0.5%, the Irish Government must now act to ensure this trend is overturned," says Chief Executive, Jillian Van Turnhout.

The report raises crucial questions about how rising child care needs are being met. A key concern for Eurochild, is how **early years services can contribute to breaking poverty cycles** and improving outcomes for children. There is evidence that children from low-income families, or from a migrant background can benefit from starting day-care early, as they are more socialized and better equipped for school. But worrying the prevailing pattern among OECD countries is that child care actually accentuates existing social inequalities, as children from disadvantaged backgrounds receive lower quality early childhood education and care.

Governments have a responsibility to deliver high quality, universally available early childhood services, which concentrate resources, staff and skills on the most disadvantaged. Only this way, can the transition to out-of-home care achieve its full potential in helping to reduce poverty and inequality.

TASK/TEXT 5.8: SUPPORTING HEALTHY RELATIONSHIPS BETWEEN YOUNG CHILDREN AND THEIR PARENTS

<www.childandfamilypolicy.duke.edu/eca/Attachment/index.htm>, visited January 7, 2008

Karen Appleyard, Ph.D.; Lisa J. Berlin, Ph.D. –
LESSONS FROM ATTACHMENT THEORY AND RESEARCH

At a child care center, 18-month-old Hannah is clinging to her mother and crying as they enter. Her mother pulls Hannah's hands from her arm, saying, "Don't be such a crybaby and go play." In a pediatrician's waiting room, two-year-old Carlos climbs dangerously high on the furniture. He throws a toy at his mother when she calls his name. His mother laughs nervously and says quietly, "I don't know what to do with him." In a family's kitchen, one-year-old Keisha yanks on a locked kitchen cabinet while her father is cooking. Her father kneels next to Keisha and says, "Oh – I see you are trying to get into this cabinet, but these glass pans are for me. Let's make a drawer with some plastic kitchen things for you. You can use them while Daddy cooks."

These examples illustrate how much child-parent interactions can differ from each other. Many people would see Keisha's interactions with her father as the most harmonious and developmentally appropriate example. What may be less apparent is why these types of interactions matter, and what can be done to support healthy relationships between young children and their parents.

One theory about child development – attachment theory – is particularly useful for understanding early child-parent relationships and how to support them. According to attachment theory and research, early child-parent relationships lay the foundation for children's later social, emotional, and school functioning. Attachment theory and research also point to specific strategies for supporting relationships between young children and their families.

What are Attachments?

Attachments are unique, lasting emotional ties between infants and their parents. All infants will develop attachments to their parents, even if the parent is harsh or abusive. The only exception to this rule is children reared without parents or specific primary caregivers (such as children in some orphanages). Thus, rather than describing a child as being attached or not, attachment theory and research focus on the quality of the relationship between the child and parent. An attachment usually takes the first year of life to develop, through repeated interactions between the child and parent.

Attachment differs from bonding. Bonding refers to the parent's tie to the infant which develops in the first few hours of life. Infants are capable of developing multiple attachments (e.g., to mothers, fathers, grandparents). Usually, however, they have one parent who is their "primary attachment figure."

Attachment "Quality"

There are two basic patterns of attachment: "secure" and "insecure." The key factor in promoting a secure attachment is parenting behavior. Many research studies have shown that sensitive, responsive parenting promotes secure attachment. Insensitive, rejecting, or inconsistent parenting has been linked to insecure attachment.

A **secure attachment** is characterized by the child's ability to use his or her parent as a source of comfort and a "secure base" from which to explore. A key principle of attachment theory is that dependence leads to independence. In other words, it is only when a child feels confident in his parent's availability that he can fully explore and play on his own.

Parental behaviors typically associated with secure attachment include:

- Sensitive and responsive care.
- Clear, consistent, developmentally appropriate expectations and supervision.
- Warm, positive, and responsive verbal interaction.
- Seeing the child as a unique individual, having insight into the child (i.e., why he does what he does).
- "Holding the child in mind" (i.e., awareness of and ability to reflect on the parent's own feelings and responses to the child).

Infant and early childhood behaviors associated with secure attachment include:

- Comfort exploring in presence of an attachment figure.
- When hurt, going to an attachment figure for comfort (i.e., not a stranger).
- Seeking help when needed.
- Willingness to comply with requests with minimal conflict.
- No pattern of controlling or directing the behavior of caregivers (no role-reversal).

An **insecure attachment** is characterized by the child's inability to use his or her parent for comfort or as a secure base. There are three basic types of insecure attachment.

1. Some children are overly dependent, expressing difficulty with separation and with independent play. This pattern is called **insecure-resistant** attachment.
2. Some children are under-dependent, seeming disengaged from the parent and barely noticing them upon separation. This is called **insecure-avoidant** attachment. Such "independence" in an infant or toddler, although sometimes praised, is usually developmentally inappropriate.
3. **Disorganized/disoriented** attachment refers to children who seem frightened or disorganized in the presence of their parents.

Parental behaviors typically associated with insecure attachment include:

- Interfering with the child's attempts at exploration (i.e., intrusive, overly controlling).
- Unclear, inconsistent, developmentally inappropriate expectations and supervision.
- Ignoring the child's needs and cues.
- Inconsistent, unreliable responsiveness.
- Hostile, threatening, and frightening behaviors.
- Prioritizing the parent's needs over the child's (i.e., self-absorbed).
- Behaving like a child or treating the child as though he/she is in charge (i.e., role-reversal).
- Marked withdrawal, fright, hesitance or timidity around the child.
- Sexualized or overly intimate behaviors.

Infant and early childhood behaviors associated with insecure attachment include:

- Excessive dependence.
- Marked shyness, withdrawal, or unfriendliness.
- Failure to seek contact, comfort when needed.
- Indiscriminate friendliness or contact seeking.
- Punitive, bossy behaviors.
- Over-concern with the parent's well-being (i.e., role reversal).
- Disoriented or frightened in presence of the parent, such as approaching while looking away, stilling, freezing, or rocking.
- Promiscuous, sexualized behavior.

The Importance of Early Attachments for Later Development

Early attachments lay the foundation for social and academic skills. A number of studies that have followed children from infancy to adolescence or adulthood have illustrated that attachment quality is one of the strongest predictors of later development.

Secure attachment forecasts healthy social, emotional, cognitive, and motivational development. For example, a child who had a secure attachment with her parent as an infant is more likely in childhood to be independent and self-confident, to have appropriate interactions with peers and teachers, to manage her emotions, to be focused, curious and motivated in school, and to have strong problem-solving skills.

Insecure attachment forecasts developmental and adjustment problems. For example, a child who was insecurely attached in infancy is more likely in childhood to have poor social skills (e.g., withdrawal or aggression), to act out and be disobedient, to have poor communication skills, to be impulsive and easily distracted, and to lack curiosity and motivation in school.

It is important to note that an insecure attachment does not fate a child to failure. Change certainly can occur. The longer a child is on a specific path, however, the harder it is to alter the course.

Lessons from Attachment Theory and Research for Supporting Healthy Relationships between Young Children and Their Parents

Attachment theory and research suggest several guidelines that practitioners may follow to support early child-parent relationships in a variety of contexts (e.g., home visiting, child care, mental health). These guidelines, in turn, may help practitioners prevent or intervene to address child behavioral, emotional, and academic problems. We begin this section with an overview of these guidelines. Specific strategies for following the guidelines will vary based on the contexts in which they are used and the nature and age of the child. (…)

Guidelines for Supporting Healthy Relationships between Young Children and Their Parents

First and foremost, attachment theory and research suggest that establishing a supportive and trusting relationship between the parent and practitioner is key to the practitioner's work with the child-parent relationship. The parent-practitioner relationship also serves as a model for the child's relationship with the parent. A healthy parent-practitioner relationship is especially important in working with parents who themselves received harsh or inconsistent care as children.

Within the framework of a supportive relationship between the parent and the practitioner, we offer the following guidelines based on attachment theory and research:

1. *Help parents understand that two of their principal responsibilities as a parent are to comfort their child and to facilitate their child's exploration of the world.* Moreover, knowing how to tailor the responsibility to the situation and according to the needs of the child is central to supportive parenting. For example:

An in-home practitioner could provide praise, positive reinforcement, or modeling during playtimes with the parent and child. She could encourage the parent to respond to the child's requests for comfort and to follow the child's lead in play. (…)

2. *Help parents understand typical child development.* Providing parents with verbal and written information about developmental milestones and typical child development can help parents be more in tune with their children. For example:

- Many parents are frustrated by infants' frequent crying. A practitioner in a pediatric clinic might offer information about normal crying and how some babies cry more than others. She also could explain that a parent cannot spoil a crying baby by picking her up. Rather, parents who respond to their babies typically have children who become more self-sufficient.
- Parents of two-year-olds may experience difficulties balancing their children's intense need to explore with the need to set boundaries and limits. In the example at the beginning of the brief, a home visitor working with Carlos's mother might talk about Carlos's need to explore and to do everything "by myself." The home visitor also could discuss how to set firm but gentle limits in order to establish the mother's authority and keep Carlos safe.
- Many parents have difficulty with children's sadness or clinginess. Child care providers might use "teachable moments" during drop off and pick up times to "wonder" with parents about strategies that might help their child transition more smoothly.

3. *Help parents reflect on their own parenting strengths and challenges.* Some parents have more difficulty comforting; others letting go. Every parent brings a history of their own relationships (with parents, caregivers, loved ones) that "filter" how they interpret their child's actions. For example:

- A father whose mother mocked him when he cried as a child may find himself scolding his own infant when she cries.

- A mother whose parent was anxious and overprotective may struggle when her toddler explores the world.
- A parent who was mistreated by her mother may know that she does not want to be the same kind of mother as she had.

Talking with parents about these issues may help parents see themselves and their children in new and different ways. For example, a practitioner could ask, "Who does Joey remind you of? What is the hardest/easiest part of being his mom/dad? What experiences that you had growing up do you want for him? What would you like to be different?" With carefully structured self-examination and guided practice, parents may learn how to interact differently with their children.

4. *Use the parent-child relationship as an "engine of change."* Practitioners working with young children who show behavior problems may find it useful to consider children's challenging behaviors through the lens of attachment. Many behavior problems are rooted in relationship difficulties with the parent. Helping a parent to see their child's acting out as a cry for attention, or as a need for parental limit-setting, may engage the parent in working with the child. It may: (a) help the parent see how important they are to their child, (b) increase the parent's empathy for their child, and (c) suggest specific, perhaps new, parenting strategies such as daily "special playtimes" when the child has the parent to himself. In short, practitioners can use the child-parent relationship to help drive healthier child functioning.

The strategies outlined above may work better for some families than others. Certainly parenting does not occur in a vacuum. Many factors can promote or impede supportive parenting, such as financial stability, mental health, marital quality, social support, and neighborhood safety and cohesion. Promoting healthy child-parent relationships cannot be viewed as a cure-all, but, rather, as one component of good practice.

(…)

Conclusion

Attachment theory and research illuminate key dimensions of early relationships between young children and their parents. Attachment theory and research also have informed a number of strategies and programs for supporting early child-parent relationships. A growing body of research illustrates the promise of these strategies for promoting the health and development of young children. Drawing upon these lessons from attachment theory and research, practitioners can support parents to raise secure, well-adjusted children. (…)

– **The Name of the Game is Delight**: Babies are "hard-wired" to experience joy with their caregivers in the early months of life. Researchers are finding that mutual joy is the basis for increased brain growth. A baby feels more secure knowing that "Life is good, because my parent enjoys life when s/he is with me."

– **Every Baby Needs a Holding Environment:** Babies soak up affection and love through their skin. Gentle touch shares the tenderness that every infant requires. Playful touch encourages joy. Holding your baby not only provides pleasure and reassurance, it is essential in helping to soothe and organize difficult feelings.

– **"The Eyes Have It":** Gaze into your baby's eyes from the first day of life, and pay close attention to when your child wants to look back. At about six weeks, your child will regularly focus in on your eyes and read what they are "saying." Lots of pleasurable eye contact will translate into a feeling of reassurance and connection for your baby.

– **Whenever Possible, Follow Your Child's Lead:** Security of attachment requires a caregiver who is sensitive and responsive to her/his child's needs. Your willingness to answer subtle requests for attention, comfort, holding, exploration, and discovery (with you nearby) will provide an increased sense of security for your child.

– **You Can't Spoil a Baby:** Contrary to those who may be saying that you will harm you child if you are "too responsive" to her/his needs, it isn't possible to spoil a baby in the first 9–10 months of life. Researchers are finding that the most responsive parents actually have children who are less demanding and more self-reliant as they grow older.

– **Stay With Your Child During Difficult Feelings:** Young children often have upset feelings (anger, hurt, sadness, fear) that are too difficult to manage on their own. When your child has an intense feeling, stay with her/him until the feeling has been worked through. Your child will be learning basic trust: "Someone is here with me when I am in difficulty and pain," and "I can count on a good outcome to follow a difficult experience."

– **Talk Out Loud About Feelings:** From your child's earliest days, talking out loud about feelings (your child's and your own) will begin to help your child to eventually label feelings and realize that they can be shared. As your child gets older, s/he will realize that intense feelings can be named (mad, sad, glad, and afraid) and discussed with another, thus ending a need to act them out.

– **"Mistakes Happen (You Only Need To Be 'Good Enough')":** Perfection is impossible in parenting. In fact, it isn't even recommended. A child who knows that everyone in the family makes mistakes, and that they will eventually be worked out, will feel more secure than a child who thinks everything has to be right the first time.

– **Be Bigger, Stronger, Wiser, and Kind:** At the heart of secure attachment is a child's recognition that s/he has a parent who can be counted on to lovingly provide tenderness, comfort, firm guidance and protection during the inevitable difficulties of life. If the truth be told, all of us have this need some of the time, no matter what our age.

TASK/TEXT 5.9: WORKING GROUP ON THE QUALITY OF CHILDHOOD WITHIN THE EUROPEAN PARLIAMENT

[Email 3 January 2008 by Michiel Matthes, Secretary-General Alliance for Childhood European Network Group; subject: European Parliament, session on 'Attachment, what it is, why it is important and what we can do about it to help young children acquire a secure attachment?' with Sir Richard Bowlby]

Seventh session: '**Attachment, what it is, why it is important and what we can do about it to help young children acquire a secure attachment?** with Sir Richard Bowlby from the UK.

Sir Richard Bowlby
Sir Richard Bowlby is the son of the famous Dr. John Bowlby, who was the first in 1958 to publish the theory of attachment. This theory was based on his work with young children during the war in London in 1940, when he observed how distressed babies and toddlers became, when their primary attachment figure, normally the mother, was separated from them. Sir Richard Bowlby was born in 1941 and became a scientific photographer. Alongside this he furthered the work of his father and the subject of children's attachment and in that way he became one of the key-note speakers on attachment both in Britain and internationally.

What is a secure attachment?
Secure attachments are thought to occur when children have consistent, emotionally attuned, contingent communication with their parent or other primary caregiver. Relationships that provide contingency, especially at times of

emotional need, offer children repeated experiences of feeling connected, understood, and protected.

One way to understand how attachment is created through communication is by looking at what we call the ABC's of the attachment process: attunement, balance, and coherence.

When a parent's initial response is to be attuned to his child, the child feels understood and connected to the parent. Attuned communications give the child the ability to achieve an internal sense of balance and supports her in regulating her bodily states and later her emotions and states of mind with flexibility and equilibrium. These experiences of attuned connections and the balance they facilitate enable the child to achieve a sense of coherence within her own mind (the text of this invitation is partly taken from D.J. Siegel and M. Hartzell, Parenting from the Inside Out, pages 103 and following).

What happens when children do not have a secure attachment?

- The child can become avoidantly attached, meaning that the child adapts by avoiding closeness and emotional connection to the parent;
- The child may become ambivalently attached when the child cannot rely upon the parent for attunement and connection;
- The child will internalize in the brain these types of relationships and it may **become the model for relationships the child will develop with other persons** later in life.
- Insecure attachment is acknowledged as a **risk factor** that often contributes to mental health problems of children and adults.

Insecure attachment is found in approximately 40% of toddlers in the UK and USA.

What are the advantages of a secure attachment?
Attachment is an inborn system of the brain that evolved to keep the child safe. It enables the child to:

- Seek proximity to the parent;
- Go to the parent at times of distress for comforting as a source of a safe haven;
- Internalize the relationship with the parent as an internal model of a secure base. This sense of security is built upon repeated experiences of being contingently connected with the attachment figure.

The impact of these experiences is to provide children with an internal sense of well-being that enables them to go out into the world to explore and make new connections with others.

What can we, as society, do about it to help babies, toddlers and young children acquire a secure attachment?

In the first place it is important to know as society, that a secure attachment is important for a young child, and for the adult that it will become. As society we can take steps to enable parents and care-givers to have sufficient time with their child and to ensure that the contact between the parent / care giver and the child is of sufficient quality. We can explain to parents what is secure attachment and how children can acquire it. If a parent is not securely attached himself or herself, then we can in many cases help the parent to overcome this. It has been shown that also the child will then often acquire secure attachment, even if it is already older than one.

Conclusion: there should be a pedagogical infrastructure in each EU member state, that is, made responsible for the quality of attachment of young children in its geographical area in the same way as medical authorities are now responsible for the health in their area.

Working Group on the Quality of Childhood

Personally I have been involved for some time in the activities in this area and I am deeply concerned about the quality of childhood in the member states of the European Union. For this reason I have taken the initiative to set up the Working Group on the Quality of Childhood within the European Parliament. Together with the Alliance for Childhood European Network Group we hold a number of sessions, the seventh of which will take place on 8 January 2008.

Objectives of these meetings:

- To gain a better understanding of the Quality of Childhood in the EU member states; this time we will focus on the theme 'attachment.'
- To think about the role that the European Parliament could play to improve the situation
- To get to grips with the principles and approaches that could lead to a betterment for children
- To form an effective working group and to get a sense of how to move on.

I take pleasure in inviting you for the seventh session on 8 January 2008. I believe that we as members of the European Parliament working together with likeminded NGOs and committed individuals can and should play an important role in this area.

Yours sincerely, Karin Resetarits, Member of the European Parliament

TASK/TEXT 5.10:

TASK/TEXT 5.10.1: ATTACHMENTS NEEDS AT DIFFERENT AGES

Sue Palmer, *Detoxing Childhood; What parents need to know to raise happy, successful children*, London: Orion Books, 2007, p. 70

0–6/9 months
For secure attachment a baby needs a constant and consistent 'mother-figure.'[45]

Others can help, but the less the baby is separated from the mother-figure, the better.

Care should be home-based. Institutional care at this age should be avoided.

6/9 months–2 years
A child who is securely attached should be now be happy to spend a couple of hours a day away from the mother-figure. But too many changes of carer can still be damaging, and home-based care is preferable to institutional care.

2–3 years
Securely attached children should by now enjoy spending time with other children and will probably thrive in a nursery for several hours a day. But they still need the security of plenty of time spent with the mother-figure, in a familiar domestic environment.

TASK/TEXT 5.10.2: THE IMPORTANCE OF ATTACHMENT

Sue Palmer, *Detoxing Childhood; What parents need to know to raise happy, successful children*, London: Orion Books, 2007, pp. 69/70

---

45 The 'mother-figure' options are: – Mum, Dad or another family member (...); – a nanny (...); – a childminder (...); – a named key-worker in a day nursery providing care in a home-like environment.

The mother-figure is a child's first and most important attachment figure. Over the first six to nine months, s/he should be a constant, consistent loving presence in the child's life.

Children who are secure in this first relationship easily form attachments to other people – family members, nursery workers, and so on.

In later life, they'll continue to find it easy to form strong relationships.

Even so, in the first couple of years, there shouldn't be too many people involved. Small infants don't cope well with change, so too many new faces are unsettling.

TASK/TEXT 5.11: SPEAKING ON BEHALF OF BABIES

Zero to Three Alert, email 25 June 2008, <www.zerotothree.org>

ZERO TO THREE Statement Regarding NBC's Reality Series "Baby Borrowers"

"It's not TV, it's birth control" is how NBC promotes its new reality series "Baby Borrowers." On June 25th, the show will be launched on national television as an "intriguing new social experiment that asks five diverse teenage couples to fast-track to adulthood by setting up a home, getting a job and becoming caring parents." Unfortunately, the NBC series exploits very young children in the pursuit of entertainment.

The babies and toddlers participating in this series will be separated from their parents and caregivers for three days. Unfamiliar teenagers will take care of them during this time. This setup can be very harmful for the babies and toddlers involved. **For the past 80 years, many studies have shown unequivocally** that babies and toddlers suffer when they are exposed to this kind of prolonged separation from family and left with people that they do not know or love. As all parents know, babies and toddlers are very distressed by separation. They cry, cling, and search for their parents. The longer the separation, the more upset they become. Some children are unable to sleep and refuse to eat. The responses routinely last long past the child's reunion with the parent. Prolonged separations heighten young children's separation anxiety and damage their trust that their parents will be available to protect and care for them. Children can become angry and rejecting of their parents after being reunited with them, damaging the fabric of the child-parent relationship.

These findings have become the basis for a new science of early childhood. A robust body of **early childhood development and brain research** clearly confirms the critical nature of early development. It is a time when young children form attachments with parents and caregivers, develop security and a sense of self, and learn what to expect from the world around them. Studies show that babies and toddlers need to feel safe and secure in order to form a positive sense of self, to form healthy relationships, and to feel confident to explore their world. This sense of security is dependent on the availability and stability of their trusted primary caregivers. Being separated for a three-day period from a parent or trusted, familiar adult, and being thrust into the care of a total stranger who has no experience with the child – how he or she is comforted, likes to be fed, held, etc. – and who has no experience caring for young children at all, can be very stressful for the child.

As a "safeguard," NBC has hired a nanny to be nearby in case there are concerns. However, the nanny is no more familiar to that child than the two strangers who will be caring for him for three days. The nanny does not know him or what his signals mean – such as what he needs when he cries out in the middle of the night, or how he shows he is hungry, tired, or is overwhelmed and needs a break from play. Moreover, even though the parents of these young children are watching via closed-circuit television, the babies are not aware of that and have no way of knowing how long the parents will be gone.

Legitimate social experiments are not conducted on national television or on reality shows. "Baby Borrowers" may have a catchy theme, but it exploits young children with potential harmful consequences. This is no social experiment. It is an extremely misguided endeavor that puts at risk our most vulnerable citizens, young children who need our love and protection.

TASK/TEXT 5.12:

TASK/TEXT 5.12.1: TOBACCO AND PREGNANCY

Encyclopedia on Early Childhood Development, Centre of Excellence for Early Childhood Development – *Synthesis on tobacco and pregnancy* (published online 21 September 2004), <www.child-encyclopedia.com/pages/PDF/synthesis-tobacco.pdf>

How important is it?
In Canada, the 1990s have been marked by a rise in public awareness regarding the harmful effects of tobacco on health, and by the emergence of studies and laws about the use and price of cigarettes.

The *Report on Smoking in Canada* reveals that, from 1985 to 2001, the prevalence of daily smokers declined significantly among both sexes and in all age groups: the population of smokers 15 years and older decreased from 35.1% of the total population to 21.7%.

Nonetheless, smokers are still predominantly young, in their early reproductive years. This fact is far from trivial since chronic exposure to cigarette smoke during the fetal period significantly increases the risk of **physical and mental health problems**.

Indeed, while the devastating effects of tobacco on the health of adults are well known, its effects on children are proving to be troubling, especially when exposure to tobacco smoke starts during the fetal period.

Results from the *National Longitudinal Study on Children and Youth (NLSCY)* indicate that 23.3% of Canadian women smoke during pregnancy. Of these women, 84% smoke throughout pregnancy. Rates of daily tobacco use among pregnant women break down as follows: 65% smoke between 1 and 10 cigarettes a day; 34% smoke between 11 and 25 cigarettes; 1% smoke more than 25 cigarettes.

A CEECD poll on the perceptions of tobacco use among pregnant women shows that the Canadian population is not aware of the number of pregnant women who smoke. Although there is some public awareness around the negative effects of smoking on the birthweight of babies, most people still appear to discount the long-term ravages of fetal exposure to tobacco smoke on the physical and mental health of children.

What do we know?

Prenatal exposure to tobacco is recognized as a serious and preventable child health challenge. National surveys conducted over the past decade in North America found that between 1 and 4, and 1 in 5 pregnant women smoked cigarettes during pregnancy. The number of children exposed prenatally to tobacco smoke via maternal smoking has extensive repercussions.

The psychosocial outcomes for children associated with prenatal maternal smoking can be numerous, including:

- Reduced auditory orientation and responsiveness;
- Increased tremors and startles in newborns;
- Lower scores on tests of general cognitive performance in the preschool years;
- Behavioural and psychological problems before school entry;
- Reduced scores in the verbal domain during the school years;
- Increased activity, inattention, and impulsivity in school;
- Behavioural problems in school;
- Conduct disorder and substance abuse during adolescence.

There is consistent evidence to suggest that increased exposure to nicotine in utero is associated with increased rates of **conduct problems and hyperactivity** during childhood and adolescence as well as increased rates of **juvenile and adult crime**. However, prenatal exposure to tobacco does not seem to be associated with an increased risk in children for emotional problems, such as depression. Gender also seems to moderate the long-term effects of smoking in pregnancy, as **boys tend to manifest conduct disorders and girls tend to turn to substance abuse**.

Moreover, research with animals suggests that smoking is linked to both **structural and functional changes to the fetal brain**. Animal studies show that nicotine and carbon monoxide can limit oxygen transmission to the fetus, resulting in problems with learning and memory. In humans, there is evidence of **neurological, emotional, and behavioural changes**.

The challenge of studying the effects of tobacco use during pregnancy lies in the fact that women who smoke during pregnancy tend to differ significantly from non-smokers in terms of their **socio-economic status, mental health, personality characteristics, parenting styles, and exposure to stress**. All of these factors contribute to confounding findings and make **causal connections** more difficult to establish. Animal studies are therefore very important in understanding separate biological mechanisms. However, cross-sectional and longitudinal studies conducted with clinical and community samples show strong associations between smoking in pregnancy and long-term problems with children's psychosocial development after controlling for a wide variety of individual, family and social factors.

What can be done?

There is already compelling evidence to motivate all smokers to give up smoking. But pregnant smokers should be especially motivated, given the risks their smoking poses for their pregnancies and children. We know that during the parenting stage of life, parents (and, more specifically, pregnant women) are increasingly receptive to smoking cessation interventions due to their increased contact with health care systems and other facilities where smoking cessation can be encouraged. These are therefore the obvious sites for promoting awareness around tobacco use and fetal/child development.

While the literature on tobacco treatment supports widespread **screening and treatment for smoking**, pregnant women may need specific interventions along with self-help materials focusing on pregnancy issues. Research shows that quitting during the first trimester seems to provide the greatest benefits, but the positive effects of quitting at any time during pregnancy are also undeniable.

Therefore, we should not only help pregnant women stay smoke-free from the time they make their first prenatal visit, but also throughout their pregnancy.

A variety of intervention designs have been used to increase parents' motivation to quit smoking both during and after pregnancy:

- Practical counselling (including problem solving/skills training recalling past experiences at quitting, anticipating triggers, challenges to quitting)
- The Five-Step counselling approach
- Printed self-help materials
- Telephone counselling
- Social support outside of treatment, supporting a partner's efforts to quit, and receiving support from other family members, friends and co-workers
- Nicotine delivery systems that give intermittent rather than continuous exposure.

The abiding problem of investigation in this area remains how to identify smokers, especially pregnant smokers. Social pressure to not smoke during pregnancy can inhibit pregnant women from revealing their smoking status. Studies show high rates of deception (between 28% and 35%) when women are asked to self-report tobacco use and then are biochemically tested.

In fact, among the sizeable proportion of women who quit smoking for the duration of their pregnancy, rates of postpartum relapse are disappointingly high. Often the **reasons for relapse can be found at home**. Indeed, the presence of other smokers (i.e., an intimate partner or other family member) in the household has been shown to significantly increase the likelihood that smokers smoke during pregnancy and after giving birth.

Fortunately, there is ample evidence to support the effectiveness of treatment programs for pregnant and parenting smokers. Approximately 35% of pregnant women who quit smoking remain smoke free, improving their health as well as that of their children and other family members.

TASK/TEXT 5.12.2: ALCOHOL USE DURING PREGNANCY – A DANGEROUS "COCKTAIL"

Encyclopedia on Early Childhood Development, Centre of Excellence for Early Childhood Development – *Key messages*, <www.child-encyclopedia.com/en-ca/key-messages-list.html>, *Alcohol use during pregnancy, A dangerous "cocktail"* (published online 3 February 2009), <www.child-encyclopedia.com/pages/PDF/FASD_ANGmcP.pdf>

What do we know?

- The many negative effects of alcohol consumption during pregnancy are increasingly well known and affect about one in 100 children in Canada.
- Frequent consumption of alcohol during pregnancy can lead to complex health and developmental problems in children including physical malformations, delayed growth, as well as severe intellectual and behavioural problems.
- Consuming large amounts of alcohol by day (approximately 5 or more drinks) during pregnancy, even only occasionally, can have serious negative effects on the growth of children, and their visual and brain development.
- These children may have difficulty paying attention or planning a task and they may have special difficulty with subjects such as arithmetic.
- These children may also have difficulty managing their emotions and developing good social skills.

Paying attention to ...
... alcohol consumption during pregnancy, which can harm a child's development.

... the reality that it can be demanding to parent a child suffering from the negative effects of alcohol.

What can be done?

- Avoid alcohol completely during pregnancy.
- Consult a health professional if you have consumed alcohol while pregnant.
- Ask for help from a professional if you find it hard to stop drinking.
- Accept help provided by the healthcare system to support you.
- See a professional if you are worried about your child's development in order to get the appropriate care and services for his/her optimal development.

TASK/TEXT 5.13:

TASK/TEXT 5.13.1: PARENTING EDUCATION FOR ALL PARENTS, ALWAYS, EVERYWHERE (1)

UNICEF, *The State of the World's Children 2000*, A vision for the 21st century – Within a single generation: (...) Early childhood care (pp. 5, 45–46); <www.unicef.org>, Publications (retrieved 11 August 2008):

Science now tells us that optimal neural development in a child, which affects physical, mental and cognitive development, depends on the good nutrition and loving stimulation the child receives during the first months and years of life. Research also clearly illustrates the powerfully positive effects of the bonding [i.e., secure attachment] and interaction between infants and young children and their parents and caregivers on all aspects of the child's survival, growth and development. On the negative side, it demonstrates that poor nutrition may trigger a downward spiral for the child as malnourished infants, lacking energy, appetite and curiosity, may be less able than healthy babies to elicit their caregiver's attention and affection.

The long-term benefits of good prenatal care and breastfeeding, and especially the rich effects of talking and playing with infants from their earliest days, are commonly acknowledged. Communities and governments are increasingly committed to the idea that the best way to care for children is to ensure their access to integrated health and social services based in the community, in which the child and family are the focus.

These ideas are catching fire in communities around the world. In many of these settings, parents and local health, nutrition and education workers have embraced a broad perspective on children's well-being. Much of this work takes place without fanfare, but, every day, significant changes in consciousness and practice are occurring somewhere.

In the Lao People's Democratic Republic, the Lao Women's Union on the Early Childhood and Family Development Project is a village-based community initiative in which traditional caregivers are taught about health, nutrition and the value of play and child-to-child activities. This vital training, provided both in centres and in the home, is a core feature of many other programmes in countries that include Jamaica, Nepal, Sri Lanka and Turkey.

The Community Childcare Project in Malawi is another pioneering effort integrating early childhood care with play in 216 community-based centres. Families attend the centres where they receive training in nutrition and learn about opportunities for generating income. In addition, they receive play and teaching materials and tools for community gardens. There has also been a focus on broader issues of childcare sparked by widespread concerns about the situation of children orphaned by HIV/AIDS in the country.

Communities such as these are demonstrating that early, low-cost interventions can both help secure children's rights and save millions of dollars in later costs to society.

TASK/TEXT 5.13.2: PARENTING EDUCATION FOR ALL PARENTS, ALWAYS, EVERYWHERE (2)

<www.ipetitions.com/petition/effectiveparentingusa/index.html> (<www.effectiveparenting.org>), accessed 23 July 2008

Effective Parenting Petition (USA)

"Every child deserves to be raised sensitively and effectively by loving and skillful parents.

"When children are so raised, they are on a path to reach their full potential as human beings. They are best prepared to become healthy, peaceful and productive adults.

"Parents and others who assume the awesome responsibility of raising children deserve the best possible parenting education, guidance and support.

"Love is not enough. The dangers of childhood and the pressures of modern family life require parents to be especially knowledgeable and skillful.

"It is in the best interests of our children and our nation for all parents to be educated and supported as fully as possible."

In signing this petition, I am affirming the importance of advocating, celebrating and promoting effective parenting and parenting education.

This petition will be used to show the nation how important effective parenting is.

It will also be emailed to the President, Members of Congress and other elected representatives to encourage them to take the practical steps that are needed to make effective parenting and parenting education national, state and local priorities.

TASK/TEXT 5.13.3: PARENTING EDUCATION FOR ALL PARENTS, ALWAYS, EVERYWHERE (3)

What norms are we trying to change?

<www.zerotothree.org/site/DocServer/Communications_PP_2.pdf?docID=5063>, Zero To Three Policy Summit – June 5, 2007, slide 5 (accessed 23 July 2008)

Parenting is a private issue	> Health and safety of children is everybody's responsibility
I was parented so I know how to parent	> Parenting skills are learned – every parent can use classes
Not much is going on with an infant until they walk and talk	> An infant's brain is developing at an incredible rate
If I ask for help my children may be taken away	> It is okay to 'ask for' and 'receive' help
I can not make a difference	> Everyone has a role to play

TASK/TEXT 5.14:

TASK/TEXT 5.14.1: GLOBAL STRATEGY FOR INFANT AND YOUNG CHILD FEEDING

World Health Organization, <www.who.int/nutrition/topics/global_strategy/en/index.html>, retrieved 22 August 2008

Infant and young child feeding are a cornerstone of care for childhood development. World-wide about 30% of children under five are stunted as a consequence of poor feeding and repeated infections. Even in resource poor settings, improved feeding practices can lead to improved intakes of energy and nutrients, leading to better nutritional status.

Over the past decades, the evidence of biological requirements for appropriate nutrition, recommended feeding practices and factors impeding appropriate feeding has grown steadily. Moreover, much has been learned about interventions that are effective in promoting improved feeding. For example, recent studies in Bangladesh, Brazil and Mexico have demonstrated the impact of counselling, in communities and health services, to improve feeding practices, food intake and growth.

The **Global Strategy for Infant and Young Child Feeding** aims to revitalize efforts to promote, protect and support appropriate infant and young child feeding. It builds upon past initiatives, in particular the **Innocenti Declaration** and the **Baby-friendly Hospital initiative** and addresses the needs of all children including those living in difficult circumstances, such as infants of mothers living with HIV, low-birth-weight infants and infants in emergency situations.

The strategy calls for action in the following areas:

- All governments should develop and implement a comprehensive policy on infant and young child feeding, in the context of national policies for nutrition, child and reproductive health, and poverty reduction.
- All mothers should have access to skilled support to initiate and sustain **exclusive breastfeeding for 6 months** and ensure the timely introduction of adequate and safe complementary foods **with continued breastfeeding up to two years or beyond.**
- Health workers should be empowered to provide effective feeding counselling, and their services be extended in the community by trained lay or peer counsellors.
- Governments should review progress in national implementation of the **International Code of Marketing of Breast milk Substitutes**, and consider new legislation or additional measures as needed to protect families from adverse commercial influences.
- Governments should enact imaginative legislation protecting the **breastfeeding rights of working women** and establishing means for its enforcement in accordance with international labour standards.

The strategy specifies not only responsibilities of governments, but also of international organisations, non-governmental organisations and other concerned parties. It engages all relevant stakeholders and provides a framework for accelerated action, linking relevant intervention areas and using resources available in a variety of sectors.

TASK/TEXT 5.14.2: EXCLUSIVE BREASTFEEDING

World Health Organization, <www.who.int/nutrition/topics/exclusive_breastfeeding/en/index.html>, retrieved 22 August 2008

Breastfeeding is an unequalled way of providing ideal food for the healthy growth and development of infants; it is also an integral part of the reproductive process with important implications for the health of mothers. A recent review of evidence has shown that, on a population basis, **exclusive breastfeeding for 6 months** is the optimal way of feeding infants. Thereafter infants should receive complementary foods **with continued breastfeeding up to 2 years of age or beyond.**

To enable mothers to establish and sustain exclusive breastfeeding for 6 months, WHO and UNICEF recommend:

- Initiation of breastfeeding within the first hour of life.
- Exclusive breastfeeding – that is the infant only receives breastmilk without any additional food or drink, not even water.
- Breastfeeding on demand – that is as often as the child wants, day and night.
- No use of bottles, teats or pacifiers.

Breastmilk is the natural first food for babies, it provides all the energy and nutrients that the infant needs for the first months of life, and it continues to provide up to half or more of a child's nutritional needs during the second half of the first year, and up to one-third during the second year of life.

Breastmilk promotes sensory and cognitive development, and protects the infant against infectious and chronic diseases. Exclusive breastfeeding reduces infant mortality due to common childhood illnesses such as diarrhoea or pneumonia, and helps for a quicker recovery during illness. These effects can be measured in resource-poor and affluent societies (…).

Breastfeeding contributes to the health and well-being of mothers, it helps to space children, reduces the risk of ovarian cancer and breast cancer, increases family and national resources, is a secure way of feeding and is safe for the environment.

While breastfeeding is a natural act, it is also a learned behaviour. An extensive body of research has demonstrated that mothers and other caregivers require active support for establishing and sustaining appropriate breastfeeding practices. WHO and UNICEF launched the **Baby-friendly Hospital Initiative** in 1992, to strengthen maternity practices to support breastfeeding. The foundation for the BFHI are the **Ten Steps to Successful Breastfeeding** described in Protecting, Promoting and Supporting Breastfeeding: a Joint WHO/UNICEF Statement. The evidence for the effectiveness of the Ten Steps has been summarized in a scientific review document.

The BFHI has been implemented in about 16.000 hospitals in 171 countries and it has contributed to improving the establishment of exclusive breastfeeding world-wide. While improved maternity services help to increase the initiation of exclusive breastfeeding, support throughout the health system is required to help mothers sustain exclusive breastfeeding.

WHO and UNICEF developed the 40-hour Breastfeeding Counselling: A training course to train a cadre of health workers that can provide skilled support to breastfeeding mothers and help them overcome problems. Basic breastfeeding support skills are also part of the 11-day Integrated Management of Childhood Illness training course for first-level health workers, which combines skills for adequate case management with preventive care. Evaluation of breastfeeding counselling delivered by trained health professionals as well as community workers has shown that this is an effective intervention to improve exclusive breastfeeding rates (…). The Global Strategy for Infant and Young Child Feeding describes the essential interventions to promote, protect and support exclusive breastfeeding.

TASK/TEXT 5.14.3: WORLD BREASTFEEDING WEEK

Crinmail 904 – 7 August 2007, <www.crin.org>

A weak formula for legislation – how loopholes in the law are putting babies at risk

7 August 2007 – A coalition of charities is demanding baby milk be treated like tobacco and subjected to a total advertising ban in the United Kingdom.

The call mirrors campaigns in other parts of the world aimed at curbing formula milk advertising.

The National Childbirth Trust, Save The Children and UNICEF blame adverts for many mothers abandoning breast feeding before the recommended six months.

In a new report, they have asked the government to extend a ban on infant milk adverts to include "follow-on" milks for older babies.

England's policy on the promotion of formula milk is currently being reviewed by the Food Standards Agency.

At present, companies are not allowed to advertise formula milk for babies under six months. But they are allowed to promote so-called follow-on milks, a range for children aged between six months and two years. The charities accuse baby milk companies of using their follow-on milks to promote their products for younger infants by giving them the same name and logo so as to make them "virtually indistinguishable" to parents.

"In similar ways to how tobacco companies found their way through loopholes in legislation restricting the advertising of cigarette promotion, formula milk companies are finding ways to exploit ambiguity in the law and to continue aggressively marketing their products to parents," says Belinda Phipps of the NCT.

'Sense of guilt'

Breastfeeding is recommended for the first six months of a baby's life and the charities note that those children who are breastfed are better protected from infections and potentially from even more serious conditions later on in life.

At present, some 76 per cent of UK mothers start out breastfeeding – up 7 per cent from 2000. However most move on to formula within weeks, and fewer than half still breastfeed by the time their child is six weeks old. By six months, only 25 per cent of mothers are breastfeeding at all.

But Dr Ellie Lee of the University of Kent who has researched women's experiences of infant feeding said the impact of advertising on the decision to switch from breast to bottle was "negligible." In a study of mothers commissioned by The Infant and Dietetic Foods Association (IDFA), Dr Lee found that the decision to bottle feed was a "pragmatic decision based on personal circumstances."

"Some do it because of the pain of feeding or so they can feed their child at more regular intervals, some so they can share responsibility for feeding the baby, others because they are thinking of going back to work.

"Many mothers feel an immense sense of guilt and failure when they move on to the bottle, and this latest debate about advertising is likely to make them feel even worse."

EU recommendations

It has also been suggested that the increasing reluctance of health professionals to discuss formula milk as an option may mean some parents are not aware of the thorough sterilisation of feeding equipment that is needed to limit the risk of infection.

The Food Standards Agency is currently working on new regulations for the promotion of formula milk which would take into account the latest EU **directive**.

The charities involved in the report want the FSA to agree to a ban, noting that the new European recommendations in particular stress that information on formula "should not counter the promotion of breast feeding."

It is unclear whether a ban is likely, but it is thought that companies will no longer be able to make claims about similarity to breast milk on their packets under new restrictions.

A number of companies have slogans such as "even closer to breast milk," "the closest to breast milk" on their packaging, pointing to the fatty acids and probiotic bacteria found in breast milk that are included in the ingredients.

UN call for World Breastfeeding Week

Two United Nations agencies kicked off World Breastfeeding Week, which began on 1 August, with a call for enabling new mothers to nurse their babies immediately after birth to prevent a significant number of neonatal deaths in developing countries.

"More than one third of child deaths occur during the first fragile month of life," said Ann M. Veneman, Executive Director of the UN Children's Fund

(UNICEF). "Early breastfeeding provides critical nutrients, protects infants against deadly diseases and fosters growth and development."

UNICEF estimates that exclusive breastfeeding to the age of six months can prevent the deaths of 1.3 million children under the age of five each year.

The issue is particularly relevant in sub-Saharan Africa, which has the highest infant mortality rate in the world. Some 10 per cent of all babies there die before the age of one and most neonatal deaths occur at home.

Though the rate of exclusive breastfeeding until the age of six months has more than doubled in the region since 1990 – to 30 per cent – this still leaves hundreds of thousands of children vulnerable to disease and death.

The UN World Health Organization (WHO) too recommends that all children be exclusively breastfed for six months, and believes colostrum – the sticky, yellowish substance that is rich in antibodies and produced by the mother soon after birth – is the perfect food for every newborn.

Mother's "first milk" not only nourishes, but it also protects and is "just what the baby needs during its first few days," according to WHO.

"In a world where more than 10 million children die before their fifth birthday due to preventable causes, and where malnutrition is still rampant and associated with over half of all childhood deaths, there is simply no time to waste," stated WHO Director-General Dr. Margaret Chan, stressing that breastfeeding needs to start in the first hour of life.

However, due to a widespread lack of awareness of its qualities and its key role in contributing to the health and growth of newborns, colostrum is frequently discarded. Feeding water or other liquids deprives babies of a good start in life, notes the agency.

TASK/TEXT 5.14.4: KYRGYZSTAN – DRAFT LAW TO CURB FORMULA MILK SALES, BOOST BREASTFEEDING

Crinmail 1009 – 21 August 2008, <www.crin.org> [Source: IRIN, <www.irinnews.org>; UN-OCHA]

BISHKEK, 19 August 2008 – A draft law on promoting breastfeeding as a means of tackling health and nutrition problems among infants is being discussed in Kyrgyzstan.

"Today many mothers in Kyrgyzstan do not go in for exclusive breastfeeding of babies under six months old. Besides their breast milk, they give cow's milk, tea with milk, 'kefir' [fermented cow's milk] or food from the family table to their babies," Tursun Mamyrbaeva, a child nutrition specialist at the Science Centre for Maternity and Childhood Protection, told IRIN in the Kyrgyz capital, Bishkek.

Health experts say newborns need to be exclusively breastfed at least until they are six months old. Breast milk contains all the microelements and nutrients that children need during the first months of their lives. These nutrients are extremely important also for further their development, they say.

"Medics are concerned by the proliferation of various artificial baby milk formula products, and breastfeeding is being displaced," said Mamyrbaeva.

The prevalence of anaemia among pregnant women, lactating mothers and children is a major health issue, especially in Talas Province, northwestern Kyrgyzstan, where 71 per cent of pregnant women and nursing mothers, and 50 percent of children, are anaemic, according to the Kyrgyz Health Ministry.

The ministry also said 25 per cent of stunting among children in the province was caused by insufficient nutrition.

After studying the situation in Talas, UNICEF discovered that the children with iron-deficiency anaemia had been bottle-fed babies or babies that were not breastfed.

Public hearings in Talas

In early August representatives of the Health Ministry, Kyrgyz lawmakers, experts and UNICEF representatives held public hearings in Talas at which they discussed the draft law on breastfeeding and possible curbs on the marketing of children's food.

Deputy governor of Talas Province Baktygul Saparbaeva said: "We are grateful to parliamentarians, UNICEF and doctors for raising this issue and for the drafting of a bill that will help our women and children."

Lawmaker Dinara Moldosheva said the problem was topical. "There is a demographic crisis in the country, birth rates are not increasing, and we need to adopt this law. It is the first time we have discussed the bill with the civil sector and donors. I think its adoption could help improve the situation."

If passed, the bill will help regulate the sale of artificial baby products, believe those advocating it.

"Breast milk substitutes are being imported into Kyrgyzstan from 15 countries," said Yulia Aleshkina from the Healthcare Drevelopment Centre.

Violations

Recently, the Centre conducted studies of the sales, marketing and advertising of several companies' baby nutrient formulas, including those of Nestlé and Nutricia.

According to Aleshkina, a number of violations were revealed. For instance, some formula food packaging did not include the warning that the product could not replace breastfeeding, merely supplement it.

Aynura Eralieva, aged 23 and from Talas Province, said she breastfeeds her son, giving him nothing else. "But I know that many mothers give [baby] formula to their children because there is a general opinion that it is healthy. Even [some] doctors say that."

"Formula milk manufacturers are interested in quick sales and even work with medical organisations," Aleshkina said.

"Doctors are given various gifts and the logos of famous milk formula companies are to be seen on paramedics' premises. This is a violation of the rules," said Aleshkina.

UNICEF representative in Kyrgyzstan Timothy Shaffter said: "It is very important that the authorities and civil society members are actively involved in the solution of this problem. This gives hope that the situation will change for the better."

TASK/TEXT 5.14.5: BREASTFEEDING – MORE THAN LOVING CONTACT

<www.child-encyclopedia.com/pages/PDF/BreastfeedingANGmcP.pdf>
(CEECD: What's new? 12 December 2008)

What do we know?

- The World Health Organization (WHO) recommends that babies be nourished through breastfeeding only, with no other liquids or foods, during the first six months of life.
- The WHO also recommends that mothers continue to breastfeed their children while also giving them other appropriate foods, until the age of two, if both mother and child are comfortable with it.
- Many studies have confirmed the benefits of breastfeeding for the child's nutrition, growth and development, as well as for the mother's health.
- Mother's milk contains substances that nourish and protect the baby from infections.
- Mother's milk also contains fatty acids that are essential to the development of the baby's brain and nervous system.
- Breastfeeding promotes the young child's intellectual development.
- Breastfeeding makes babies more resistant to infections such as diarrhea, otitis (ear infections) and pneumonia.

- In suckling, babies learn to control their appetite as they stop drinking when they are no longer hungry. This learning helps prevent them from gaining excess weight.
- The warm contact provided by breastfeeding strengthens the relationship of emotional security between mother and child.
- Researchers have observed that breastfeeding mothers have more self-confidence, less stress, and fewer bad moods.

TASK/TEXT 5.14.6: LONGER NURSING MAY AID KIDS' MENTAL HEALTH; BREASTFEEDING FOR 6 MONTHS OR MORE MAY REDUCE ISSUES, STUDY SUGGESTS

Reuters, <www.msnbc.msn.com/id/34826200/ns/health-kids_and_parenting>, accessed 15 January 2010

Children who are breastfed for longer than six months could be at lower risk of mental health problems later in life, new research from Australia suggests. "Breastfeeding for a longer duration appears to have significant benefits for the onward mental health of the child into adolescence," Dr. Wendy H. Oddy of the Telethon Institute for Child Health Research in West Perth and her colleagues report in *The Journal of Pediatrics*. Breastfeeding could help babies cope better with stress, the researchers note, and may also signal a stronger mother-child attachment and these benefits may last.

Oddy and her colleagues studied 2,366 children born to women enrolled the Western Australia Pregnancy Cohort (Raine) Study. Each of the children underwent a mental health assessment when they were 2, 5, 8, 10, and 14 years old. Eleven percent were never breastfed, 38 percent were breastfed for less than six months, and just over half were breastfed for six months or longer.

The mothers who breastfed for less than six months were younger, less educated, poorer, and more stressed, and were also more likely to be smokers, than the moms who breastfed for longer. They were also more likely to suffer from postpartum depression, and their babies were more likely to have growth problems.

At each of the assessments, the researchers found, children who were breastfed for shorter periods of time had worse behavior. Differences were seen for internalizing behavior, in which negativity is directed inwards, for example depression; and in externalizing behaviors, such as aggression.

For each additional month a child was breastfed, behavior improved.

Breastfeeding for six months or longer remained positively associated with the mental health and well-being of children and adolescents after the investigators adjusted for social, economic and psychological factors as well as early life events. They conclude: "Interventions aimed at increasing breastfeeding duration could be of long-term benefit for child and adolescent mental health."

TASK/TEXT 5.15: DEMOGRAPHIC RENEWAL

Eurochild's Key Messages on the Demographic Renewal, <www.eurochild.org>, 1 December 2008, Press release[46]

Last week's European Demographic Forum focused on "*Better societies for families and older people.*" The focus on family policies is welcome. Against a background of demographic slowdown in Europe and economic insecurity, well-formulated family policies may give people more confidence to have the number of children they desire. They should certainly contribute to achieving greater gender equality both in the home and the work place, and better reconciliation of family and working life. More employment opportunities and support for working parents may help lift some children out of poverty.

But despite this emphasis on family policies, children's rights and analysis of the impact of policies on the *quality* of childhood was notably absent from this Forum's agenda.

Across the EU, 19% of children are at risk of poverty. Some 15% of children leave school without achieving a secondary education [Eurostat, 2005 data (<http://ec.europa.eu/employment_social/emplweb/news/news_en.cfm?id=207>]. There are pockets of communities where joblessness is the norm, and may span several generations. We live in a society where the socio-economic status into which a child is born is still probably the most important determinant of their future health, education and employment outcomes.

Breaking the cycle of poverty takes on a new urgency when we consider the demographic reality, notably the population ageing. The children of today are the ones who will be supporting the growing number of pensioners in the coming years. Intergenerational solidarity is a key issue. The policy discussions – such as those that took place during the Forum – are neither far-reaching nor ambitious enough to support the most vulnerable and disadvantaged groups of children and young people.

Eurochild believes that it is absolutely crucial that policy makers take a child-centred approach based on the principles enshrined in the UN [Convention on the Rights of the Child]. Such an approach ensures that children's well-being is

---

46 Eurochild is funded by the European Commission DG Employment, Social Affairs and Equal Opportunities. The views expressed in this Press Release do not necessarily reflect the opinion of the European Commission.

addressed in a holistic way and that their needs are seen from their perspective. It also requires a fundamental shift in our way of viewing children. They are not passive recipients of support or protection, but rather active citizens in their own right and, as they develop, have increasing control over their lives and influence over the policies and decisions that affect them. Support for families should be approached in such a way that it recognizes children as having rights independently of adults or their parents and acknowledges them as social actors who must be supported in the gradual transition to adulthood.

– **We need urgently to invest more in early year's services.** And it is not only about ensuring more child care places, as assumed by the Barcelona targets. To secure the child's best interest, Member States must look holistically at parental leave, labour market policies, family and early years' services, the quality, availability and affordability of early childhood services are critical. We also need to ensure inclusion of children most at risk of exclusion from an earliest age such as children with disabilities, ethnic minorities and immigrant children.

– **We need to review and reform education systems.** Important progress has been made at the EU level to support the vital importance of the quality of education in child's development. [In its Communication "Improving Competences for the 21st Century: An Agenda for European Cooperation on Schools," presented on 3 July 2008, the DG Education and Culture of the European Commission has proposed an agenda for cooperation among the Member States in order to make school systems more relevant to the knowledge-based Europe of the future.] Schools are not only there to transmit knowledge and learning; they have a key role in supporting the psychological, emotional and social nurturing of children, empowering them to exercise their own rights, transferring responsibility to the child, in line with the child's evolving capacities. This is critical not just for the growth and well-being of children today, but also for the best interest of our society tomorrow.

– Above all, **we need to ensure family policy is developed in such a way that it enables children and parents to spend quality time together.**

Investing in children is not only a moral obligation but also an economic priority. Investment in children and families is probably the most effective route towards sustainable social, economic and political progress in Europe. We call on the EU and Member States to reinforce efforts to put children's rights at the heart of policy making. The future of Europe depends on it.

About Eurochild:
Eurochild (<www.eurochild.org>) is an international network of organisations and individuals working in and across Europe to improve the quality of life of children and young people. Its work is underpinned by the principles enshrined in the United Nations Convention on the Rights of the Child.

TASK/TEXT 5.16: OBAMA PLEDGE STIRS HOPE IN EARLY EDUCATION

New York Times 17 December 2008, frontpage <www.nytimes.com/2008/12/17/us/politics/17early.html?_r=4&hp> (A version of this article appeared in print on December 17, 2008, on page A1 of the New York edition)

CHICAGO – It was the morning after the presidential election, and Matthew Melmed, executive director of Zero to Three, a national organization devoted to early childhood education, could barely contain his exultation.

Mr. Melmed fired off an e-mail message to his board and staff, reminding them of President-elect Barack Obama's interest in the care and education of the very young and congratulating Mr. Obama for campaigning on a "comprehensive platform for early childhood."

Mr. Melmed was not alone in his excitement. After years of what they call backhanded treatment by the Bush administration, whose focus has been on the testing of older children, many advocates are atremble with anticipation over Mr. Obama's espousal of early childhood education.

In the presidential debates, he twice described it as among his highest priorities, and his choice for secretary of education, Arne Duncan, the Chicago schools superintendent, is a strong advocate for it.

And the $10 billion Mr. Obama has pledged for early childhood education would amount to the largest new federal initiative for young children since Head Start began in 1965. Now, Head Start is a $7 billion federal program serving about 900,000 preschoolers.

"People are absolutely ecstatic," said Cornelia Grumman, executive director of the First Five Years Fund, an advocacy group. "Some people seem to think the Great Society is upon us again."

Despite the recession, Mr. Obama has emphasized his interest in making strategic investments in early childhood education. Asked if the financial troubles might force him to scale back, Jen Psaki, a spokeswoman for the transition, said, "We simply cannot afford to sideline key priorities like education."

It is not as though Mr. Obama is running against the wind. Major philanthropists including Bill Gates; Warren Buffett's children; and George B. Kaiser, an Oklahoma oil billionaire, are financing education efforts for the very young. And the chairman of the Federal Reserve and many governors have said that expanding early childhood education should be a national priority.

Driving the movement is research by a Nobel Prize-winning economist, James J. Heckman, and others showing that each dollar devoted to the nurturing of young children can eliminate the need for far greater government spending on remedial education, teenage pregnancy and prisons.

Now that new initiatives seem likely, experts are debating how best to improve America's early childhood system, which they call fantastically fragmented, unconscionably underfinanced and bureaucratically bewildering. Some hesitate to use the word "system" at all.

"It's a patchwork quilt, a tossed salad, a nonsystem," said Libby Doggett, executive director of Pre-K Now, a group that presses for universal, publicly financed prekindergarten.

There are federal and state, public and private, for-profit and nonprofit programs. Some unfold in public school classrooms, others in storefront day care centers, churches or Y.M.C.A.'s, and still others in tiny centers run out of private homes.

"California has 22 different funding streams for child care and preschool, and that mirrors the crazy labyrinth of funding sources coming out of Washington," said Bruce Fuller, an education professor at the University of California, Berkeley, who is the author of "Standardized Childhood: The Political and Cultural Struggle Over Early Education."

Debates cut many ways. Some advocates want the nation to start by expanding services to all 4-year-olds. Others say improving care for infants and toddlers cannot wait. Some insist that middle-class and wealthy children must have access to public preschool. Others say the priority should remain with the poor.

Mr. Obama's platform, which Mr. Duncan helped write, emphasizes extending care to infants and toddlers as well, and it makes helping poor children a priority. It would also provide new federal financing for states rolling out programs to serve young children of all incomes.

Outright opponents are fewer, and certainly less influential than they once were. In 1971, President Richard M. Nixon vetoed a bill that would have underwritten child care for everyone, arguing that the bill "would commit the vast moral authority of the national government to the side of communal approaches to child rearing over against the family-centered approach."

For years after that, conservatives blocked many early childhood initiatives, but resistance has diminished in recent years.

The last major federal initiative came in 1994, when the Clinton administration worked with Congress to create Early Head Start, which serves pregnant women and children from birth to age 3. Since then, states have largely carried the ball.

In 1995, Georgia became the first state to commit to making prekindergarten classes available to every 4-year-old. New York and Oklahoma followed with similar plans in 1997 and 1998. But in New York, at least, the effort is far from complete.

During the Bush administration, federal financing for early learning programs has fallen. At the same time, many states have made substantial new investments in publicly financed classes for disadvantaged 4-year-olds, according to Pre-K Now.

In 2007, total spending by state governments for preschool education reached $3.7 billion. Six entities have outlined plans to offer classes to all preschoolers, regardless of income: Florida; Illinois; Iowa; Louisiana; Washington, D.C.; and West Virginia.

"Expectations and investments are soaring now as never before in the nation's history," Sharon Kagan, a professor of early childhood policy at Teachers College at Columbia University, said in a paper she wrote last year and presented at a conference last month.

In Illinois, Mr. Obama supported efforts to expand child care and education. His interest traces, at least in part, to Barbara T. Bowman, the mother of Valerie Jarrett, a senior adviser. Ms. Bowman leads early childhood education for the Chicago Public Schools. "I talked with him a lot about these issues, but he understood it from the beginning," she said. "He was always on board. I don't think I was the person who convinced him."

That person may have been Irving B. Harris, a Chicago philanthropist who helped finance Mr. Obama's campaigns for the Illinois Senate, said Harriet Meyer, president of the Ounce of Prevention Fund [<www.ounceofprevention.org>], a nonprofit devoted to child development issues founded by Mr. Harris.

"Irving could mesmerize you," Ms. Meyer said, "and Barack met with Irving many times."

Ms. Meyer recalled a 2001 reception her group hosted in Springfield to discuss prekindergarten issues. She said only one lawmaker showed up: Mr. Obama, at the time a state senator.

In his presidential campaign platform, Mr. Obama pledged to establish a Presidential Early Learning Council to coordinate federal, state and local policies; to quadruple financing for Early Head Start; to provide federal challenge grants for states to use for early care and education programs; and to expand home visiting programs for low-income mothers. The platform emphasizes improving quality, not just reaching more children.

One program that embodies many of these features is Educare, a national consortium of early childhood centers financed by taxes and several family foundations. The first Educare Center, built in 2000 on the South Side of Chicago, offers all-day care and education to about 150 children from 6 weeks to 5 years.

Marquia Fields, who works at a Target store, leaves her 2-year-old son, Winter, and his infant sister, Summer, at the Chicago Educare Center from 8 a.m. to 4:30 p.m. each workday. On a typical morning, Winter scoots down the hall to his classroom, where he joins seven other children and three teachers, since a high teacher-child ratio is a requisite for quality toddler care.

After breakfast, the children sit on a rug while teachers read a story, then practice recognizing the letters of their name. At midmorning, Winter romps in a gymnasium, and after lunch, he naps before arts and crafts.

"It's learning through play," Ms. Fields said. "They learn routines. They learn boundaries. They learn to share, to express emotions instead of lashing out."

Educare costs about $18,000 a child, roughly the annual tuition of an elite Manhattan nursery school. By contrast, spending per child in state prekindergarten programs ranges from $10,494 in New Jersey to $2,335 in Florida.

Whether the top figures sound outrageous or like sound investments depends on how much one believes the research that shows large paybacks for the careful nurturing of poor children.

One much-cited study is of a preschool program that offered high-quality services to a few dozen black children in Ypsilanti, Mich., in the early 1960s at a two-year cost per child of about $15,000. The study found that the investment, 40 years later, had rendered economic returns to society of some $244,000 per child, much of that in savings from reduced criminal activity. Critics have challenged the findings, in part because of the small number of children involved.

Mr. Obama's platform accepts the broad logic of the Ypsilanti study. "For every one dollar invested in high-quality, comprehensive programs supporting children and families from birth," the platform says, "there is a $7-$10 return to society in decreased need for special education services, higher graduation and employment rates, less crime, less use of the public welfare system and better health."

TASK/TEXT 5.17: CHILDHOOD EXPERIENCE AND THE EXPRESSION OF GENETIC POTENTIAL – WHAT CHILDHOOD NEGLECT TELLS US ABOUT NATURE AND NURTURE

<www.feralchildren.com/en/pager.php?df=perry2002> (News from The ChildTrauma Academy, email 31 December 2008), references not included.

Dr Bruce D Perry, The ChildTrauma Academy

More than 200,000 years ago, the first homo sapiens, our genetic ancestors, began to spread across the planet. For 99 percent of the time our species has been on this planet, we lived in small hunter-gatherer clans. Humans lived with few material possessions, no written language, no complex world economy, advanced technologies or systems of governance. The major predator of humans was (and remains) other humans – usually from competing clans or bands. The lifespan was short, infant mortality high and the overall population of [humans] on the planet only slowly increased over tens of thousands of years. How different our Earth is today! Only one of thousands of mammals on the planet, humankind – slow, naked and weak creatures, biologically suited to few of the Earth's many climates and ecosystems – ultimately came to dominate the planet. Humankind is now capable of living in all of the planet's climates and harsh environments. No longer bound by cold, absence of natural grains or migrating herds, the natural boundaries of sea and sky, we humans – unlike any other of the planet's species – have created our own world. We have learned to cultivate natural grains and fruits – and now alter their genome; to domesticate and now, create, other animal species; from our own genetic capacity to make complex associations, symbolic representations and 40 basic sounds we have created 10,000 languages, and invented writing; we have invented belief systems, styles of governance, housing, economies – we have invented ourselves. We have made our own world with its own rules. In good ways and in bad, we stand out from all other species. So much so that we often forget that we are ultimately accountable to the laws of nature. Yet we *are* biological creatures, bound by the laws of nature to a time-limited existence. We are conceived and born, live our lives and then we die. From conception to death, our biological matrix organizes in remarkably complex ways to create multiple organ systems – bone and muscle, heart and liver, senses and brain. These biological systems allow each of us to move through space and time in a host of natural and, now, man-made, environments, interacting in complex ways with a diversity of biological creatures and environments. Within that single lifetime the range and variety in how we live is stunning. Genetically-comparable humans can live as Inuit in the tundra of

Nunavut, a banker on Wall Street, a hunter-gatherer in the rainforest in Brazil. At times, a life is lived with grace and beauty, sharing with and caring for others, creating ideas, objects and concepts never before known on this planet. And at other times humans are cruel, ruthless and destructive – both random and systematic in the ways we destroy, hate and kill. How is this possible in the same species?

This question has been at the heart of centuries of debate on the "nature" of humankind. Are we born evil – natural born killers or the most creative and compassionate of all animals? Are we both? Does our best and our worst come from our genes or from our learning? Nature or nurture? These questions have tainted political, sociocultural and scientific processes for thousands of years. Its simplicity – suggesting that the essence of a person is the inevitable product of one or the other – genes or learning – is seductive. The human mind tends to prefer simple linear explanations rather than complex ambiguity. Unfortunately, simple categorical explanations of humankind feed destructive belief systems and deflect from a healthy process of inquiry about our true complexity. We now know more about our genes and more about the influence of experience on shaping biological systems than ever before. What do these advances tell us about the nature or nurture debate? Simply, they tell us that this is a foolish argument. Humans are the product of nature *and* nurture. Genes and experience are interdependent. Genes are merely chemicals and without "experience" – with no context, no microenviromental signals to guide their activation or deactivation – create nothing. And "experiences" without a genomic matrix cannot create, regulate or replicate life of any form. The complex process of creating a human being – and humanity – requires both. The amazing malleability and adaptability of humankind is allowed by our genetically-mediated capacity to perceive and respond to myriad environmental cues including the complex social-emotional milieu created when humans live together; and the organ most sensitive and responsive to the environment is the human brain.

The Human Brain

Humankind's transient but magnificent rebellion against nature is allowed by the brain. In ways not yet understood, activation of neural networks – chains of neurons – allow us to think, feel and act. It is our brain which allows us to laugh, cry, hope and act in humane ways. It is the brain that mediates our humanity – or not. Yet the brain's prime mandate is survival of the species. The human nervous system senses, processes, stores and acts on information from the inside and outside environments to promote survival of the species. Three key brain-mediated capabilities must be present for our species to survive: individual survival, procreation and the protection and nurturing of dependents. Failure in any of these three areas would lead to extinction of our species. The brain, therefore, has crucial neural systems dedicated to (1) the stress response and responding to threats – from internal and external sources; (2) the process of mate selection and reproduction and (3) protecting and nurturing dependents, primarily the young. The primary strategy we use to meet these objectives is to create relationships. Relationships which allow us to attach, affiliate, communicate and interact to promote survival, procreation and the protection of dependents. It is the brain that allows humans to form the relationships which connect us – one to another –creating the myriad groups – that have been the key to our success on this planet. It is not as independent and solitary individuals that we succeed; it [is] through our interdependent relationships – our families, clans, communities and societies – that we survive and thrive. We need each other. Therefore, some of the most powerful and complex neural systems in the human are dedicated to social affiliation and communication.

Yet even these essential neural systems do not develop without necessary experiences. The neural systems which allow us to create relationships – and think, feel and act – are the product of the interactive, dynamic processes taking place during the history of each individual. These neural systems, then, are created, organize and change in response to experience throughout the life-cycle. The time in life, however, when the brain is most sensitive to experience – and therefore most easy to influence in positive and negative ways is in infancy and childhood. It is during these times in life when social, emotional, cognitive and physical experiences will shape neural systems in ways that influence functioning for a lifetime. This is a time of great opportunity – and great vulnerability – for expressing the genetic potentials in a child.

Neurodevelopment

The mature human brain is comprised of 100 billion neurons and ten times as many glial cells – connected by trillions of synapses (…). A complex dynamic of continuous activity, it is the product of neurodevelopment – a long process orchestrating billions upon billions of complex chemical transactions. In a few short years, one single cell – the fertilized egg – becomes a walking, talking, learning, loving, and thinking being. In each of the billions of cells in the body, a single set of genes has been expressed in millions of different combinations with precise timing. Development is a breathtaking orchestration of precision micro-construction that results in a human being. The most complex of all the organs in the human body is the human brain. In order to create the brain, a small set of pre-cursor cells must divide, move, specialize, connect and create specialized neural networks that form functional units. This requires nature and nurture. The key role of genetics and environment are outlined for eight of the key neurodevelopmental processes involved in creating a mature, functional human brain.

Major Processes of Neurodevelopment

1. Neurogenesis: The brain develops from cells present in the embryo in the first weeks following conception. From these few undifferentiated cells come billions of nerve cells and trillions of glia. The vast majority of neurogenesis, the "birth" of neurons, takes place in utero during the second and third trimester. At birth, the vast majority of neurons used for the remainder of life are present. Few neurons are born after birth, although researchers have demonstrated recently that neurogenesis does take place in the mature brain (…). Neurogenesis in the mature brain may be one of the important physiological mechanisms responsible for the brain's plasticity (i.e., capacity to restore function) following injury. Despite being present at birth, most neurons have yet to organize into completely functional systems. The billions of neurons present at birth need to further specialize and connect with other neurons in order to create the functional neural networks of the mature brain.

2. Migration: As neurons are born and the brain grows, neurons move. Often guided by glial cells and a variety of chemical markers (…), neurons cluster, sort, move and settle into a location in the brain that will be their final "resting" place. It is the fate of some neurons to settle in the brainstem, others in the cortex, for example. (…) It is clear that both genetic and environmental factors play important roles in determining a neuron's final location. Migration takes place primarily during the intrauterine and immediate perinatal period but continues throughout childhood and, possibly, to some degree into adult life. A host of intrauterine and perinatal insults – experiences such as infection, lack of oxygen, exposure to alcohol and various psychotropic drugs can alter migration of neurons and have profound impact on the expression of genetic potentials for a host of functions (…).

3. Differentiation: Neurons specialize during development. Each of the 100 billion neurons in the brain has the same set of genes, yet each neuron is expressing a unique combination of those genes to create a unique neurochemistry, neuroarchitecture and functional capability. Some neurons are large, with long axons; others short. Neurons can mature to use any of a hundred different neurotransmitters such as norepinephrine, dopamine, serotonin (…). Neurons can have dense dendritic fields receiving input from hundreds of other neurons, while other neurons can have a single linear input from one other neuron. Each of these thousands of differentiating "choices" are the product of the pattern, intensity and timing of various microenvironmental cues, i.e., experience, which tell the neuron to turn on some genes and turn off others. Each neuron undergoes a series of "decisions" to determine their final location and specialization. These decisions, again, are a combination of genetic and microenvironmental cues. Neurons are specialized to change in response to chemical signals. Therefore, any experience or event that alters neurochemical or micro-environmental signals during development can change the ways in which certain neurons differentiate, thereby altering the functional capacity of the neural networks in which these neurons reside (...).

4. *Apoptosis*: During development, redundant or under-activated neurons die. In many areas of the brain, there are more neurons born than are required to make a functional system. Many of these neurons are redundant and when unable to adequately "connect" into an active neural network will die (...). Research in this area suggests that these neurons may play a role in the remarkable flexibility present in the human brain at birth. Depending upon the challenges of the environment and the potential needs of the individual, some neurons will survive while others will not. Again, this process appears to have genetic *and* environmental determinants. Neurons that make synaptic connections with others and have an adequate level of activation will survive; neurons with little activity resorb. This is one example of a general principle of activity-dependence ("use it or lose it") that appears to be important in many neural processes related to learning, memory and development (...).

5. *Arborization*: As neurons differentiate, they send out one form of fiber-like processes called dendrites. Dendrites become the receptive area where other neurons connect. Dozens to hundreds of other neurons are able to connect to one neuron via this dendritic tree. The density of these dendritic branches is related to the frequency and intensity of incoming signals. When there is high activity, the dendritic network extends. This arborization allows the neuron to receive, process and integrate complex patterns of input that, in turn, influence its activity – including the activity and specificity of gene transcription. In turn, the neural signals coming into any given neuron are often dependent upon the complexity and activity of the sensory experiences of the animal (...). Dendritic density appears to be one of the most experience-sensitive physical features of a neuron.

6. *Synaptogenesis*: The most experience-sensitive feature of a neuron is, however, the synapse. Developing neurons also send out fiber-like processes which become axons and synapses. The major mechanism for neuron-to-neuron communication is 'receptor-mediated' neurotransmission that takes place at specialized connections between neurons called synapses. At the synapse, the distance between two neurons is very short. A chemical (classified as a neurotransmitter, neuromodulator or neurohormone) is released from the 'presynaptic' neuron into the extra-cellular space (called the synaptic cleft). The neurotransmitter crosses the synaptic cleft and binds to a specialized receptor protein in the membrane of the 'postsynaptic' neuron. By occupying the binding site, the neurotransmitter helps change the shape of this receptor which results in a cascade of catalyzed chemical reactions mediated by "second messengers" such as cyclic AMP, inositol phosphate and calcium. In turn, these chemicals

shift the intracellular chemical milieu which will influence the activity of specific genes. This cascade of intracellular chemical responses allows communication from one neuron to another.

A continuous dynamic of synaptic neurotransmission regulates the activity and functional properties of the chains of neurons that allow the brain to do all of its remarkable activities. These neural connections are not random. They are guided by important genetic and environmental cues. In order for our brain to function properly, neurons, during development, need to find and connect with the "right" neurons. During the differentiation process, neurons send fiber-like projections (growth cones) out to make physical contact with other neurons. This process appears to be regulated and guided by certain growth factors and cellular adhesion molecules that attract or repel a specific growth cone to appropriate target neurons. Depending upon a given neuron's specialization, these growth cones will grow (becoming axons) and connect to the dendrites of other cells and create a synapse. During the first eight months of life there is an eight-fold increase in synaptic density while the developing neurons in the brain are "seeking" their appropriate connections (…). This explosion of synaptogenesis allows the brain to have the flexibility to organize and function with a wide range of potential. It is over the next few years, in response to patterned repetitive experiences that these neural connections will be refined and sculpted.

7. Synaptic sculpting: The synapse is a dynamic structure. With continuous, but episodic release of neurotransmitter, occupation of receptors, release of growth factors, shifts of ions in and out of cells, laying down of new microtubules and other structural molecules, the synapse is continually changing. A key determinant in this synaptic sculpting process is the level of pre-synaptic activity. When there is a consistent active process of neurotransmitter release, synaptic connections will be strengthened with actual physical changes that make the pre- and postsynaptic neurons grow closer together, making neurotransmission between these two neurons more efficient.

When there is little activity, the synaptic connection will literally dissolve. The specific axonal branch to a given neuron will go away. While somewhat simplistic, it appears that synaptic sculpting is a "use it or lose it" process (…). This powerful activity-dependent process appears to be the molecular basis of learning, memory and, therefore, at the core of neurodevelopment.

8. Myelination: Specialized glial cells wrap around axons and, thereby, create more efficient electrochemical transduction down the neuron. This allows a neural network to function more rapidly and efficiently, thereby allowing more complex functioning (e.g., walking depends upon the myelination of neurons in the spinal cord for efficient, smooth regulation of neuromotor functioning). The process of myelination begins in the first year of life but continues in many key areas throughout childhood with a final burst of myelination in key cortical areas taking place in adolescence.

The eight key neurodevelopmental processes described above are dependent upon the genome and environmentally-determined microenvironmental cues (e.g., neurotransmitters, neuromodulators, neurohormones, ions, growth factors, cellular adhesion molecules and other morphogens). Disruption of the pattern, timing or intensity of these cues can lead to abnormal neurodevelopment and profound dysfunction. The *specific* dysfunction will depend upon the timing of the insult (e.g., was the insult *in utero* during the development of the brainstem or at age two during the active development of the cortex), the nature of the insult (e.g., is there a lack of sensory stimulation from neglect or an abnormal persisting activation of the stress response from trauma?), the pattern of the insult (i.e., is this a discreet single event, a chronic experience with a chaotic pattern or an episodic event with a regular pattern?) (…).

Several key principles emerge from the research on these neurodevelopmental processes. These principles, as outlined below, further suggest that while the structural organization and functional capabilities of the mature brain can change throughout life, the majority of the key stages of neurodevelopment take place in childhood.

Core Principles of Neurodevelopment

1. Genetic and environmental influences: Genes are designed to work in an environment. Genes are expressed by microenvironmental cues, which, in turn, are influenced by the experiences of the individual. How an individual functions within an environment, then, is dependent upon the expression of a unique combination of genes available to the human species. We don't have the genes to make wings. (…) [W]hat we become depends upon how experiences shape the expression – or not – of specific genes we *do* have. For thousands of years, the genetic potential to use "joysticks" was not expressed – nor that for written language or reading. Yet when experiences are provided in a structured, patterned and appropriately timed way, that potential can be expressed and neural systems which mediate all of those functions will develop.

The influence of gene-driven processes, however, shifts during development. In the just fertilized ovum, all of the chemical processes that are driving development are very dependent upon a genetically-determined sequence of molecular events. By birth, however, the brain has developed to the point where environmental cues mediated by the senses play a major role in determining how neurons will differentiate, sprout dendrites, form and maintain synaptic connections and create the final neural networks that convey functionality. By adolescence, the majority of the changes that are taking place in the brain of that child are determined by experience, not genetics. The languages, beliefs, cultural practices, and complex cognitive and emotional functioning (e.g., self esteem) by this age are primarily experience-based.

2. *Sequential developmental*: The brain develops in a sequential and hierarchical fashion; organizing itself from least (brainstem) to most complex (limbic, cortical areas). These different areas develop, organize and become fully functional at different times during childhood. At birth, for example, the brainstem areas responsible for regulating cardiovascular and respiratory function must be intact for the infant to survive, and any malfunction is immediately observable. In contrast, the cortical areas responsible for abstract cognition have years before they will be 'needed' or fully functional.

This means that each brain area will have its own timetable for development. The neurodevelopmental processes described above will be most active in different brain areas at different times and will, therefore, either require (critical periods) or be sensitive to (sensitive periods) organizing experiences (and the neurotrophic cues related to these experiences). The neurons for the brainstem have to migrate, differentiate and connect, for example, before the neurons for the cortex. The implications of this are profound. In the development of socio-emotional functioning, early life nurturing appears to be critical. If this is absent for the first three years of life and then a child is adopted and begins to receive attention, love and nurturing, these positive experiences may not be sufficient to overcome the malorganization of the neural systems mediating socio-emotional functioning. Disruptions of experience-dependent neurochemical signals during early life may lead to major abnormalities or deficits in neurodevelopment. Disruption of critical neurodevelopmental cues can result from (1) lack of sensory experience during sensitive periods (e.g., neglect) or (2) atypical or abnormal patterns of necessary cues due to extremes of experience (e.g., traumatic stress (…)).

3. *Activity-dependent neurodevelopment*: The brain organizes in a use-dependent fashion. As described above, many of the key processes in neurodevelopment are activity dependent. In the developing brain, undifferentiated neural systems are critically dependent upon sets of environmental and micro-environmental cues (e.g., neurotransmitters, cellular adhesion molecules, neurohormones, amino acids, ions) in order for them to appropriately organize from their undifferentiated, immature forms (…). Lack, or disruption, of these critical cues can alter the neurodevelopmental processes of neurogenesis, migration, differentiation, synaptogenesis – all of which can contribute to malorganization and diminished functional capabilities in the specific neural system where development has been disrupted. This is the core of a neuroarcheological perspective on dysfunction related adverse childhood events (…). These molecular cues that guide development are dependent upon

the experiences of the developing child. The quantity, pattern of activity and nature of these neurochemical and neurotrophic factors depends upon the presence and the nature of the total sensory experience of the child. When the child has adverse experiences – loss, threat, neglect, and injury – there can be disruptions of neurodevelopment that will result in neural organization that can lead to compromised functioning throughout life (…).

4. *Windows of opportunity/windows of vulnerability*: The sequential development of the brain and the activity-dependence of many key aspects of neurodevelopment suggest that there must be times during development when a given developing neural system is more sensitive to experience than others. In healthy development, that sensitivity allows the brain to rapidly and efficiently organize in response to the unique demands of a given environment to express from its broad genetic potential those characteristics which best fit that child's world. If the child speaks Japanese as opposed to English, for example, or if this child will live in the plains of Africa or the tundra of the Yukon, different genes can be expressed, different neural networks can be organized from that child's potential to best fit that family, culture and environment. We all are aware of how rapidly young children can learn language, develop new behaviors and master new tasks. The very same neurodevelopmental sensitivity that allows amazing developmental advances in response to predictable, nurturing, repetitive and enriching experiences make the developing child vulnerable to adverse experiences.

Sensitive periods are different for each brain area and neural system, and therefore, for different functions. The sequential development of the brain and the sequential unfolding of the genetic map for development mean that the sensitive periods for neural system (and the functions they mediate) will be when that system is in the developmental 'hot zone' – when that area is most actively organizing. The brainstem must organize key systems by birth; therefore, the sensitive period for those brainstem-mediated functions is during the prenatal period. The neocortex, in contrast, has systems and functions organizing throughout childhood and into adult life. The sensitive periods for these cortically mediated functions are likely to be very long.

The simple and unavoidable conclusion of these neurodevelopmental principles is that the organizing, sensitive brain of an infant or young child is more malleable to experience than a mature brain. While experience may alter the behavior of an adult, experience literally provides the organizing framework for an infant and child. Because the brain is most plastic (receptive to environmental input) in early childhood, the child is most vulnerable to variance of experience during this time. Two forms of "neglect" will be considered below: extreme multi-sensory neglect in childhood and a more subtle, insidious decrease in our opportunities to elaborate our socio-emotional potential caused by the sociocultural changes in how we choose to live. The sensory deprivation neglect results in obvious alterations in neurobiology and function while the second form has an almost invisible toxic impact on the developing child – and ultimately, society.

The Neurodevelopmental Impact of Neglect in Childhood

Neglect is the absence of critical organizing experiences at key times during development. Despite its obvious importance in understanding child maltreatment, neglect has been understudied. Indeed, deprivation of critical experiences during development may be the most destructive yet the least understood area of child maltreatment. There are several reasons for this. The most obvious is that neglect is difficult to "see." Unlike a broken bone, maldevelopment of neural systems mediating empathy, for example, resulting from emotional neglect during infancy is not readily observable.

Another important, yet poorly appreciated, aspect of neglect is the issue of timing. The needs of the child shift during development; therefore, what may be neglectful at one age is not at another. The very same experience that is essential for life at one stage of life may be of little significance or even inappropriate at another age. We would all question the mother who held, rocked and breastfed her pubescent child. Touch, for example, is essential during infancy. The untouched newborn may literally die; in Spitz' landmark studies, the mortality rates in the institutionalized infants was near thirty percent (…). If one doesn't touch an adolescent for weeks, however, no significant adverse effects will result. Creating standardized protocols, procedures and "measures" of neglect, therefore, are significantly confounded by the shifting developmental needs and demands of childhood. Finally, neglect is understudied because it is very difficult to find large populations of humans where specific and controlled neglectful experiences have been well documented. In some cases, these cruel experiments of humanity have provided unique and promising insights (…). In general, however, there will never be – and there never should be – the opportunity to study neglect in humans with the rigor that can be applied in animal models.

With these limitations, however, what we do know about neglect during early childhood supports a neuroarcheological view of adverse childhood experience. The earlier and more pervasive the neglect is, the more devastating the developmental problems for the child. Indeed, chaotic, inattentive and ignorant caregiving can produce pervasive developmental delay (…) in a young child (…). Yet the very same inattention for the same duration if the child is ten will have very different and less severe impact than inattention during the first years of life.

There are two main sources of insight to childhood neglect. The first is the indirect but more rigorous animal studies and the second is a growing number of descriptive reports with severely neglected children.

Environmental Manipulation and Neurodevelopment: Animal Studies

Some of the most important studies in developmental neurosciences in the last century have been focusing on various aspects of experience and extreme sensory experience models. Indeed, the Nobel Prize was awarded to Hubel and Wiesel for their landmark studies on development of the visual system using sensory deprivation techniques (...). In hundreds of other studies, extremes of sensory deprivation (...) or sensory enrichment (...) have been studied. These include disruptions of visual stimuli (...), environmental enrichment (...), touch (...), and other factors that alter the typical experiences of development (...). These findings generally demonstrate that the brains of animals reared in enriched environments are larger, more complex and functional more flexible than those raised under deprivation conditions. Diamond's work, for example, examining the relationships between experience and brain cytoarchitecture have demonstrated a relationship between density of dendritic branching and the complexity of an environment (...). Others have shown that rats raised in environmentally enriched environments have higher density of various neuronal and glial microstructures, including a 30% higher synaptic density in cortex compared to rats raised in an environmentally deprived setting (...). Animals raised in the wild have from 15 to 30% larger brain mass than their offspring who are domestically reared (...).

Animal studies suggest that critical periods exist during which specific sensory experience was required for optimal organization and development of the part of the brain mediating a specific function (e.g., visual input during the development of the visual cortex). While these phenomena have been examined in great detail for the primary sensory modalities in animals, few studies have examined the issues of critical or sensitive periods in humans. What evidence there is would suggest that humans tend to have longer periods of sensitivity and that the concept of critical period may not be useful in humans. It is plausible, however, that abnormal microenvironmental cues and atypical patterns of neural activity during sensitive periods in humans could result in malorganization and compromised function in a host of brain-mediated functions. Indeed, altered emotional, behavioral, cognitive, social and physical functioning has been demonstrated in humans following specific types of neglect. The majority of this information comes from the clinical rather than the experimental disciplines.

The Impact of Neglect in Early Childhood: Clinical Findings

Over the last sixty years, many case reports, case series and descriptive studies have been conducted with children neglected in early childhood. The majority of these studies have focused on institutionalized children. As early as 1833, with the famous Kaspar Hauser, feral children had been described (...). Hauser was abandoned as a young child and raised from early childhood (likely around age two) until seventeen in a dungeon, experiencing relative sensory, emotional and cognitive neglect. His emotional, behavioral and cognitive functioning was, as one might expect, very primitive and delayed. In the early forties, Spitz described the impact of neglectful caregiving on children in foundling homes (orphanages). Most significant, he was able to demonstrate that children raised in fostered placements with more attentive and nurturing caregiving had superior physical, emotional and cognitive outcomes (...). Some of the most powerful clinical examples of this phenomenon are related to profound neglect experiences early in life.

In a landmark report of children raised in a Lebanese orphanage, the Creche, Dennis (...) described a series of findings supporting a neuroarcheological model of maltreatment. These children were raised in an institutional environment devoid of individual attention, cognitive stimulation, emotional affection or other enrichment. Prior to 1956 all of these children remained at the orphanage until age six, at which time they were transferred to another institution. Evaluation of these children at age 16 demonstrated a mean IQ of approximately 50. When adoption became common, children adopted prior to age 2 had a mean IQ of 100 by adolescence while children adopted between ages 2 and 6 had IQ values of approximately 80 (...). This graded recovery reflected the neuroarcheological impact of neglect. A number of similar studies of children adopted from neglectful settings demonstrate this general principle. The older a child was at time of adoption (i.e., the longer the child spent in the neglectful environment), the more pervasive and resistant to recovery were the deficits.

Money and Annecillo (...) reported the impact of change in placement on children with psychosocial dwarfism (failure to thrive). In this preliminary study, 12 of 16 children removed from neglectful homes recorded remarkable increases in IQ and other aspects of emotional and behavioral functioning. Furthermore, they reported that the longer the child was out of the abusive home the higher the increase in IQ. In some cases IQ increased by 55 points (...).

A more recent report on a group of 111 Romanian orphans (...) adopted prior to age two from very emotionally and physically depriving institutional settings demonstrate similar findings. Approximately one half of the children were adopted prior to age six months and the other half between six months and 2 years old. At the time of adoption, these children had significant delays. Four years after being placed in stable and enriching environments, these children were re-evaluated. While both groups improved, the group adopted at a younger age had a significantly greater improvement in all domains. As a group, these children were at much greater risk for meeting diagnostic criterion for autism spectrum disorder, a finding that sheds light on the evolving relationships between early life trauma, neglect and subsequent development of severe neuropsychiatric problems including psychotic disorders and schizophrenia (…). These observations are consistent with the clinical experiences of the ChildTrauma Academy working with maltreated children for the last fifteen years. During this time we have worked with more than 1000 children neglected in some fashion. We have recorded increases in IQ of over 40 points in more than 60 children following removal from neglectful environments and placed in consistent, predictable, nurturing, safe and enriching placements (…). In addition, in a study of more than 200 children under the age of 6 removed from parental care following abuse and neglect we demonstrated significant developmental delays in more than 85% of the children. The severity of these developmental problems increased with age, suggesting, again, that the longer the child was in the adverse environment – the earlier and more pervasive the neglect – the more indelible and pervasive the deficits.

Neglect in Early Childhood: Neurobiological Findings

All of these reported developmental problems – language, fine and large motor delays, impulsivity, disorganized attachment, dysphoria, attention and hyperactivity, and a host of others described in these neglected children – are caused by abnormalities in the brain. Despite this obvious statement, very few studies have examined directly any aspect of neurobiology in neglected children. Yet clues exist. On autopsy, the brain of Kaspar Hauser was notable for small cortical size and few, non-distinct cortical gyri – all consistent with cortical atrophy (…). Our group has examined various aspects of neurodevelopment in neglected children (…). Neglect was considered global neglect when a history of relative sensory deprivation in more than one domain was obtained (e.g., minimal exposure to language, touch and social interactions). Chaotic neglect is far more common and was considered present if history was obtained that was consistent with physical, emotional, social or cognitive neglect. History was obtained from multiple sources (e.g., investigating CPS workers, family, and police). The neglected children (n = 122) were divided into four groups: Global Neglect (GN; n = 40); Global Neglect with Prenatal Drug Exposure (GN+PND; n = 18); Chaotic Neglect (CN; n = 36); Chaotic Neglect with Prenatal Drug Exposure (CN+PND; n = 28). Measures of growth were compared across group and compared to standard norms developed and used in all major pediatric settings. Dramatic differences from the norm were observed in FOC (the frontal-occipital circumference, a measure of head size and in young children a reasonable measure of brain size). In the globally neglected children the lower FOC values suggested abnormal brain growth. For these globally neglected children the group mean was below the 5th percentile. In contrast, the chaotically neglected children did not demonstrate this marked group difference in FOC. Furthermore in cases where MRI or CT scans were available, neuroradiologists interpreted 11 of 17 scans as abnormal from the children with global neglect (64.7%) and only 3 of 26 scans abnormal from the children with chaotic neglect (11.5%). The majority of the readings were "enlarged ventricles" or "cortical atrophy" (see Figure 1). In following these globally-neglected children over time we observed some recovery of function and relative brain-size when these children were removed from the neglectful environment and placed in foster care (...). The degree of recovery over a year period however was inversely proportional to age in which the child was removed from the neglecting caregivers. The earlier in life and the less time in the sensory-depriving environment, the more robust the recovery.

These findings strongly suggest that when early life neglect is characterized by decreased sensory input (e.g., relative poverty of words, touch and social interactions) there will be a similar effect on human brain growth as in other mammalian species. The human cortex grows in size, develops complexity, makes synaptic connections and modifies as a function of the quality and quantity of sensory experience. Sensory-motor and cognitive deprivation leads to underdevelopment of the cortex in rats, non-human primates and humans.

Studies from other groups are beginning to report similar altered neurodevelopment in neglected children. In the study of Romanian orphans described above, the 38% had FOC values below the third percentile (greater than 2 SD from the norm) at the time of adoption. In the group adopted after six months, fewer than 3% and the group adopted after six months 13% had persistently low FOCs four years later (...). Strathearn (...) has followed extremely low birth weight infants and shown that when these infants end up in neglectful homes they have a significantly smaller head circumference at 2 and 4 years, but not at birth. This is despite having no significant difference in other growth parameters.

More recently advanced neuroimaging techniques have demonstrated altered brain development in neglected children. Chugani and colleagues have been pioneers in neuroimaging studies in maltreated children. Their most recent study using functional MRI in Romanian orphans has demonstrated decreased metabolic activity in the orbital frontal gyrus, the infralimbic prefrontal cortex, the amygdala and head of the hippocampus, the lateral temporal cortex and in the brainstem (...). Together these findings suggest a global set of abnormalities matched by the functional abnormalities in cognitive, emotional, behavioral and social functioning. (...)

Figure 1. Abnormal brain development following sensory neglect in early childhood. These images illustrate the negative impact of neglect on the developing brain. In the CT scan on the left is an image from a healthy three year old with an average head size (50th percentile). The image on the right is from a three year old child suffering from severe sensory-deprivation neglect. This child's brain is significantly smaller than average (3rd percentile) and has enlarged ventricles and cortical atrophy.

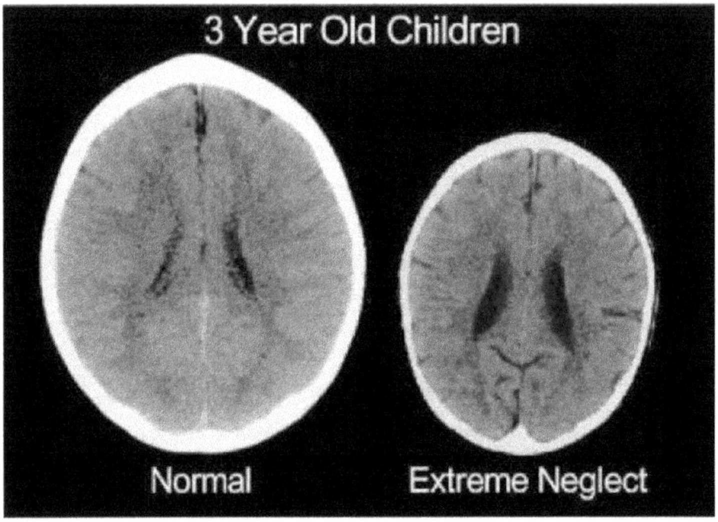

Emotional Neglect in Early Childhood: The Under-Expression of Socio-Emotional Potential

Clinical attention has been focused on extremes of neglect. The obvious clinical syndromes which result from pervasive neglect have facilitated research in this area. More recently, however, many researchers have observed and studied abnormalities in the capacity of children – and adults – to form healthy relationships. An emerging area of study is focusing on "attachment" – a special form of emotional bond. While usually not framed in context of developmental neglect, attachment problems in children often are the result of mistimed, abnormal or absent caregiving interactions and, therefore, may represent a special case of neglect. As with other brain-mediated capabilities, the capacity to form relationships results from the experience-based expression of an underlying genetic potential to create the neural systems mediating socio-emotional behaviors.

At birth an infant has yet to form a true relational bond with another person. In most instances, the infant will be cared for by an attentive, attuned and loving caregiver. When this happens, a caregiver will, again and again, come to the hungry or cold or scared infant. Warming, soothing, feeding, cleaning and calming the infant, the caregiver creates a set of specific sensory stimuli which are translated into specific neural activations in areas of the developing brain destined to become responsible for socio-emotional communication and bonding. The somatosensory bath – the smells, sights, sounds, tastes and touch – of the loving caregiver provides the repetitive sensory cues necessary to express the genetic potential in this infant to form and maintain healthy relationships. This first and most primary of all relationships is this attachment bond.

The attachment bond has several key elements: (1) an attachment bond is an enduring emotional relationship with a specific person; (2) the relationship brings safety, comfort, soothing and pleasure; (3) loss or threat of loss of the person evokes intense distress. This special form of relationship is best characterized by the maternal-child relationship. The maternal-child attachment provides the working framework for all subsequent relationships that the child will develop. A solid and healthy attachment with a primary caregiver appears to be associated with a high probability of healthy relationships with others while poor attachment with the mother or primary caregiver appears to be associated with a host of emotional and behavioral problems later in life. More than 85% of children removed from their parents for abuse or neglect have disturbed attachment capacity, for example (…). The relationships between disordered attachment and increased risk for violent and aggressive behaviors are well documented (…).

The Modern World and Neglect of Socio-Emotional Growth

Healthy attachment capacity is not enough to create healthy socio-emotional functioning. Attachment is only one form of the many kinds of relationships we form to create a healthy productive life. Certainly a securely attached child will have an easier time forming friendships, relationships with teachers, coaches, siblings and, over time, in the work place and larger community. As the brain organizes and develops in response to patterned, repetitive experience, the nature, timing, intensity and quality of an array of other relationships in the developing child's life will make a difference in the development of complex socio-emotional development. Yet without the opportunities to have friends, teachers, coaches, grandparents, neighbors, team mates and the many other kinds of relationships of childhood, these capabilities remain unexpressed. And if a child starts with attachment problems and has few opportunities to develop other relationships, they will have very poor or even pathological socio-emotional functioning.

Figure [2]. Decrease of number of persons living in a "household" in Western societies: From hunter-gatherer to the modern era. For more than 90 percent of human history we have lived in bands, clans or extended families of roughly 40 persons. In the West, by 1500 the average household had decreased to 20 persons; by 1850 to ten; in the United States to less than three persons in the average American household by 2000.

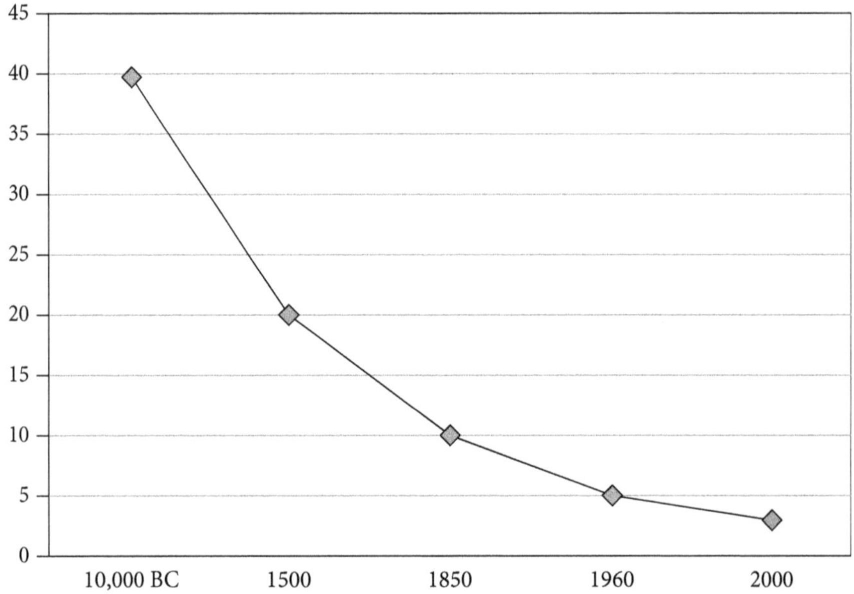

Our brain evolved over hundreds of thousands of generations in hominid and pre-hominid social groups. In these small hunter-gatherer bands a complex interactive dynamic socio-emotional environment provided the experiences for the developing child. At equilibrium in a group of fifty, there were three or more adult caregiving adults for every dependent child under age six. And there was little privacy. A dependent child grew up in the presence of the elderly, siblings, adults – related and not. There was a more continuous exposure and wider variety of socio-emotional interactions. The child in this situation had many opportunities to form relationships and, in a use-dependent way, develop the capacity to have a rich array of relationships. The genetic potential for healthy socio-emotional functioning – to be empathic, to share, to invest in the welfare of the community – is better expressed in children living in hunter-gatherer bands or extended families or close-knit communities in comparison with our compartmentalized modern world.

In this modern era, we separate from each other in many ways. The number of people we live with has shrunk (Figure [2]); fewer than three people live in the average American household. And in our own homes, we have our own rooms. We rarely eat family meals. We spend thirty percent of our available time watching television – certainly not allowing for any use-dependent expression of an underlying genetic capacity for socio-emotional functioning. Our children are segregated with same age children for hours a day. In healthy homes the time a parent spends with older children is counted in minutes. We think a healthy ratio of adult caregiver to dependent child in our child care settings is one adult for five children – $1/16^{th}$ the ratio in a hunter-gatherer clan. We have over-scheduled our children and they have little time for spontaneous social play with peers.

The inadvertent effect of our modern advancements in lifestyle, communications, technology and economies is that we are now raising children in environments that are very different from the rich social context for which our brains are most suited. The effects of television and other electronic activities have significantly exacerbated this. Taking huge portions of the available day away from socio-emotional or other "human" activities, television ensures that new – and non-social – neural systems are being activated in comparison with humans raised one hundred years ago. The implications of this have yet to be fully understood although some indications suggest that we are losing "social capital." One indicator of this is the percentage of individuals who volunteer and vote. From 1972 to 2000, the percentage of young adults (age 18–24) voting in the Presidential election fell from 47% in 1972 to 27% in 1996 to 23% in 2000!

Summary and Future Directions

The many functions of the human brain result from a complex interplay between genetic potential and appropriately timed experiences. The neural systems responsible for mediating our cognitive, emotional, social and physiological functioning develop in childhood and, therefore, childhood experiences play a major role in shaping the functional capacity of these systems. When the necessary experiences are not provided at the optimal times, these neural systems do not develop in optimal ways.

Healthy development of the neural systems which allow optimal social and emotional functioning depends upon attentive, nurturing caregiving in infancy *and* opportunities to form and maintain a diversity of relationships with other children and adults throughout childhood. In our modern world, we are more mobile, compartmentalized and socially-disconnected. The true costs of our lifestyle choices may be difficult to see; yet an understanding of neurodevelopment suggests that the modern world's socio-emotional milieu is not sufficient for most children to express their true potential for forming and maintaining healthy relationships.

As a society, we value cognitive development and, therefore, provide consistent, repetitive and enriching cognitive experiences in the home and through our educational systems. In an age where more people must share increasingly limited resources, however, it is imperative that our children develop the capacity to share, be empathic and understanding of others. We must provide an investment in socio-emotional development comparable to our investment in cognitive development. The world, natural and manmade, now more than ever, needs the best of humankind.

Acknowledgements

(...) Elements of this article were adapted from Perry, B.D., 2001: The euroarcheology of childhood maltreatment: the neurodevelopmental costs of adverse childhood events. In K. Franey, R. Geffner, and R. Falconer (eds.), *The Cost of Maltreatment: Who Pays? We All Do.* San Diego: Family Violence and Sexual Assault Institute, pp. 15–37. [Also see: Perry, B.D., 2002: Childhood experience and the expression of genetic potential: what childhood neglect tells us about nature and nurture, *Brain and Mind* 2002, pp. 79–100, available at <www.childtrauma.org/ctamaterials/MindBrain.pdf>.]

TASK/TEXT 5.18: WHY HEALTH AT CONCEPTION NEEDS TO BE IMMACULATE

<www.herald.ie/world-news/why-health-at-conception-needs-to-be-immaculate-1638901.html>, 13 February 2009

SURVEY: Women trying for a baby should eat like a pregnant woman well in advance

By Jeremy Laurence, Friday February 13 2009

The lives of future generations are being threatened because women trying for a baby are neglecting their health at the crucial moment of conception, doctors have warned.

The environment in which a foetus is conceived can be critical to the later physical and mental development of the child, affecting its IQ, risk of obesity and of a range of diseases throughout life. Advice about nutrition and lifestyle is widely followed in pregnancy, but few women pay attention to the recommendations when they are attempting to get pregnant.

A study of more than 12,000 women aged 20 to 34 who were followed for four years found those who became pregnant were only marginally more likely to have followed recommendations on smoking, alcohol consumption and folic acid intake than their non-pregnant peers.

Vulnerable

More than three-quarters of the 238 women who became pregnant had planned their pregnancy to some degree but there was little difference between their lifestyle and that of the women who had not planned to conceive.

Professor Hazel Inskip, an epidemiologist at the Medical Research Council Centre in the University of Southampton and lead author of the study published in the British Medical Journal, said: "The foetus is particularly vulnerable in the first few weeks. Early influences affect the risk of miscarriage, may contribute to the obesity epidemic, have an impact on IQ and all sorts of subtle long-term effects.

"How we protect the next generation is very important. Parents want the best for their children but people get more twitchy once their children are alive."

The National Institute for Clinical Excellence recommends that women trying to become pregnant should avoid tobacco and alcohol, take daily folic acid supplements to prevent birth defects, eat a healthy diet and take exercise, the scientists said, but few do so. The results showed that fewer than 3pc of the women who became pregnant complied fully with the guidance on alcohol and folic acid. But when they knew they were pregnant, they followed the advice more closely.

Professor Inskip said: "The difficulty is that few women know when they are going to get pregnant. If your lifestyle is to go out drinking with friends you might not want to tell them. No one wants to say they are trying for a baby because it is so difficult if they fail."

Specialists at the University of Southern Denmark said: "Pregnancy has been called a window of opportunity for health promotion because it is thought to be the time when women are most willing to give up unhealthy habits. Sadly, the window often opens too late."

TASK/TEXT 5.19:

TASK/TEXT 5.19.1: EDUCATE PEOPLE … ON FIRST EXPERIENCES

"If you are planning for a year,
sow rice; if you are planning for
a decade, plant trees; if you are
planning for a lifetime,
educate people."
– Chinese saying

<www.cyc-net.org/cyc-online/cyconline-february2009.html>, accesssed 28 February 2009
<www.cyc-net.org/cyc-online/cyconline-feb2009-perry.html>, accesssed 28 February 2009

First experiences
By Bruce Perry[47]

This is my first column for CYC-Net. First experiences are important; they provide the template for subsequent similar experiences. The power of first experiences to shape – for better or worse – future perceptions, interactions and behaviors is pervasive in our work with maltreated children. To better understand that power, one must know a little bit about how the brain develops and works. Which is the reason I am writing this column. I hope to add a tiny bit to your toolkit; I hope to share some new findings, thoughts, hopeful moments and failures, all through the lens of neurobiology, to help shift – even just a fraction – the frame of reference from which to do your work.

That shift in perspective has helped in our work. For the last twenty years, my colleagues and I have been living and working with maltreated and traumatized children. We have struggled to understand the impact of developmental trauma, neglect, chaos and a host of adverse experiences on the child and, when we could, help in the healing process. We are an interdisciplinary group; we have a variety of strengths and, Lord knows, limitations. Each of us started this long process with a frame of reference based upon our individual experiences and education. We quickly realized that each of our views was too narrow, limited and, while often useful for some specific problem in a given child, not capable of adequately explaining or dealing with the diverse range of problems related to developmental trauma and maltreatment. Over time we found that one of the most useful exercises clinically was to begin to think about what was actually happening in the brain of the child – during development, during the actual moment-to-moment interactions in the foster home, school or therapy. And as we folded a healthy dose of neurobiology and neurodevelopment into our clinical mix, we gained new insights about origins of symptoms, reasons that some clinical or educational efforts were inefficient and, most important, clarity about what

47 Bruce D. Perry, M.D., Ph.D. is the Senior Fellow of *The ChildTrauma Academy*, a not-for-profit organization based in Houston that promotes innovations in service, research and education in child maltreatment and childhood trauma (<www.ChildTrauma.org>). Dr. Perry is the author, with Maia Szalavitz, of *The Boy Who Was Raised As A Dog: What Traumatized Children Can Teach Us About Loss, Love and Healing*, a popular book based on his work with children, published by Basic Books. Over the last twenty years, Dr. Perry has been an active teacher, clinician and researcher in children's mental health and the neurosciences, holding a variety of academic positions.

would be more effective therapeutic activities. The results have been promising. But I digress, more of that in future columns.

Back to first experiences. To understand the power of first experiences we need to review a couple of simple but important neural principles. The first is that the brain has the capacity to "pair" or connect patterns of neural activity that co-occur. Two or more incoming sensory signals taking place at the same time with sufficient frequency or intensity become "associated" (e.g., the sight of mother's face, the sensation of sucking and the feeling of becoming satiated). This association – or connection – is created by making and then reinforcing new synaptic connections; essentially creating a new memory. For a newborn with an attentive, attuned and nurturing mother, a complex set of associations is created. This is the infant's first "memory" of the nature and quality of what a human being is. This first memory is unique. And, as the infant grows, this first memory acts as a template for all future human interactions.

Why? Well, simply because the human brain – despite all its complexies – is limited in the number of unique neural networks it can create. Even with the 100 billion neurons and multiple thousand times more synaptic connections, the brain can not possibly make a new neural network – a new memory – for every single aspect of every single moment of experience. The solution the brain uses is to make new associations, new synaptic connections, new memory only when the experience is sufficiently unique. If a given experience is similar to other experiences, the brain will essentially process the new interaction as a current version of something already experienced and essentially reinforce the existing memory template.

Let me give some examples; each day we get up, brush our teeth, get ready for work and, for most of us, do a set of activities all day long that are very similar to what we have done many times before. And, because of the familiarity, we really do not create a unique memory for every single aspect of every single day; we don't remember days. Some of us don't remember unique details of whole years! These routine day-to-day experiences are "categorized" as today's version of memory templates and just provide more repetitive stimulation of these existing neural networks.

By the time a child is four years old, the majority of these "template" memories have been created. We have experienced some version of most of the sensory, motor, emotional and even cognitive elements of life and, therefore, created the working templates for our life. The child's template for what a caregiver is; for how reliable and trustworthy people are; for whether the world is predictable or chaotic; for what touch "means" have all been created in those first years of life.

And sadly, maltreated children with early histories of overwhelmed, disorganized, absent or abusive caregivers have created a catalogue of templates about humans, relationships and the world that reflect their abusive backgrounds. And they carry that into their interactions with us; where we intend to give a reassuring hug, their template may categorize that as "seductive and sexualized"; where we mean to be firm and clear their templates may categorize that as "yelling"; where we mean to establish eye-contact for relational respect and intimacy their template may interpret "threat." It is a sad reality that the first experiences of these children distort future interactions and lead to behaviors and feelings that make sense to their brain – but are confusing, frustrating and very sad to those of us working to help them.

Their current style of interaction with a foster parent is based upon their history with caregivers and previous foster parents. Their views about therapists are shaped by their experiences with their first therapists; and on and on with teachers, peers, with the world.

It is our greatest battle with these children; to shift their worldview. To alter and replace the inaccurate, distorted and destructive memory templates created by a maltreated child's first experiences is our greatest challenge. Yet it can happen; you have seen it, we have seen it. But all too infrequently.

Yet there is hope. By better understanding how the brain works and how it changes we can become more efficient and effective in our therapeutic work. But that will have to wait for future columns.

TASK/TEXT 5.19.2: TRANSITIONS

Bruce Perry, <www.cyc-net.org/cyc-online/cyconline-mar2009-perry.html>, accessed 30 January 2010

Each week I have the opportunity to learn from my colleagues and their clients in our web-based clinical teaching series. Participants will present a child they are working with and we will, together, examine the developmental history and current clinical issues of the child through the lens of neurodevelopment. This approach, the Neurosequential Model of Therapeutics or NMT, has been useful in our efforts to understand the origins of a child's strengths and vulnerabilities, and often this approach can lead to useful therapeutic insights and provide direction for clinical, educational and caregiving work moving forward. In future columns I will share more about this approach but I wanted to provide the context for many of my learning opportunities; they come not only from direct clinical work with children and caregivers but also from these consultations with colleagues.

This week I heard about a 14 year old boy, lets call him T, living with a wonderful foster family for many years. Yet he continues to struggle. There were many contributing factors, genetic, epigenetic, intrauterine exposure to alcohol, a disengaged neglecting mother, active substance abuse and severe domestic violence all of which led to his removal from his mother in the first years of life. After removal he was placed in a shelter with his half-brother for almost three years (yeah, seriously, a shelter – a short-term, transient, last ditch temporary placement). One day a staff member came to get his brother for something, took his hand, walked him out of the room and T never saw him again. No explanation to T; no preparation for T; no therapeutic follow up for T – or I suspect for his brother. The family of his half-brother's father came to take his brother – but not T; T was not related to them. This precipitous, catastrophic and confusing loss of the one stable relationship in the life of a four-year old boy was an example of how often our systems replicate and add to the traumatic, chaotic, neglectful experiences of these children.

This poorly handled transition reminded me of another in my earlier work. A boy in foster care had been struggling in his placement. The foster family told CPS (Child Protective Services) that they could no longer handle the child. The caseworker arranged for placement at a residential treatment center where I consulted. One day the caseworker came to the foster home, told the boy to collect his clothes and put them in a plastic garbage bag. "Why?" "We are going to go do laundry." "Why should I put all my clothes in? Most of them are clean." "My friend has a special washing machine." They drove to the residential center; "OK, go up and ring the bell. I'm going to go park the car." A residential staff member, expecting this child, answered the door. The boy was standing alone at the door with all of his earthly possessions in a garbage bag. She let him in. "I'm here to do my laundry." "What?" And the boy told the story his caseworker had told him. Again, no preparation, no opportunity to say goodbye to foster siblings or foster parents; we lie to these children all too often. When later confronted the caseworker claimed his insensitive and destructive behavior was to prevent the boy from melting down. Yet all he was doing was setting this boy up to be even more suspicious, guarded and even more likely to meltdown in the future. The caseworker's avoidance of a little personal distress on his part led to much more distress for the child and for anyone working with him in the future.

Transitions permeate our lives. The capacity to successfully transition from one place to another, one activity to another, one internal state to another is fundamentally related to the capacity to self-regulate. And this, of course, is one of the main areas of difficulty with children and youth who have been exposed to developmental chaos, threat and trauma. And, as you might expect me to say, self-regulation is a brain-mediated function. Further, the reason maltreated children often struggle with this capacity is that the stress response systems in their brain are 'sensitized.' This basically means that they are overly sensitive to any experiences or cues that in ANY way activate the stress response networks in the brain. So any function related to these stress-response networks will predictably be altered in traumatized children; attention, impulse control, sleep, fine motor control, regulation of lungs, heart, gut, skin, and a host of other functions.

Let's back up a little. The brain's stress response systems exist to keep us alive. These systems are continually getting input from the outside world (e.g., visual, auditory, tactile) through our senses and from the internal world (e.g., oxygen, glucose levels) from various sensory apparatus in the body. These incoming signals are matched against previously experienced and stored patterns of neural activity. The first and most categorical of 'processing' steps takes place in the lowest areas of the brain (brainstem and diencephalon): is this information similar to patterns of safe and familiar or unsafe or unfamiliar? If safe and familiar, the stress response networks will stay at their current level of activity. If the cue is similar to previous threatening or traumatic experience, the brain will activate the stress response systems. **And in most of us there is activation proportional to the level of novelty, challenge or threat. But not so with maltreated children**; earlier in their lives they had to activate these systems in extreme ways and in chaotic patterns. The result is a poorly regulated and overly reactive stress network. Now when their brain receives input related to even minor challenges such as a test in school, a new child in the foster home or the need to stop playing at recess and go back to class, their stress response networks activate as if they are under threat! The extreme stress response in these children changes the way they think and perceive, the way they feel and the way they act. They will distort or miss verbal input, they will feel anxious and angry; they will be inattentive, impulsive and aggressive.

So. Back to transitions; each transition – in large or small ways – will change the pattern of neural activity coming into the brain. And in each of us this shift in incoming input makes our stress response systems – even if for a few seconds – turn on. Waking, dressing, travel to work, community meetings, public presentation, child's soccer game, home and sleep. Hundreds of little transitions, dozens of moderate transitions; all require our stress response to activate, proportionally-respond, re-set.

So now, think of the children and youth we serve. How challenging, how exhausting, how sad these children become as their brain works so hard to negotiate these hundreds of little transitions and dozens of moderate transitions in any day. And how much easier this would be for these children if we had, earlier in their lives, worked harder to help them negotiate their major transitions; to have more gradual and more predictable transitions with opportunities for regulating their dysregulated neural systems with healthy touch, positive relational engagement and honest, clear cognitive explanations.

There are ways to help these children begin to master transitions and build in healthy self-regulation capacity; but first we must regulate ourselves. How could the caseworker help that child with a healthy transition if he couldn't regulate his own fear and distress about a potential 'meltdown?' And how much of that caseworker's self-regulation issues were [compromized] because he was in a system where he was experiencing precipitous decisions, changes in job responsibility, punitive supervision and indifferent administration? Ah... so much to say, so little space.

TASK/TEXT 5.19.3: HOW WE REMEMBER

Bruce Perry, <www.cyc-net.org/cyc-online/cyconline-apr2009-perry.html>, accessed 30 January 2010

An attorney representing the mother of a five year old girl who was removed from her care at age two following severe sexual abuse by mother's boyfriend, neglect and an assortment of other traumatic experiences all at the hands, or in the presence of, the mother asked me, "Why would you suggest that reunification could be an overwhelming experience for this child? I can understand it if the abuse occurs with an older child who remembers the abuse but with an infant? How can an infant possibly remember a traumatic event?"

After, biting my tongue and counting to ten, I tried to explain. And, **in all fairness to this attorney, her ignorance about the nature of traumatic memory and development is shared by far too many responsible, well-educated and caring people.** It is a common misperception that very young children are 'so resilient' and often 'unaware' of the nature of the traumatic experiences that they [are] more capable of coping with trauma than adults. This is just not so. And in my role as a willing teacher to this misinformed attorney I attempted to explain this. A fair, but edited, version of my responses to this person's questions about the impact of maltreatment on the infant follows.

How can an infant possibly recall a specific abusive event?

The key word in this question is 'recall.' Most people think of memory as limited to the storage and recall of cognitive, narrative memory. With this understanding, a pre-verbal infant would not be capable of 'remembering' and 'recalling' any event. And, of course, we are all familiar with the developmental amnesia that occurs at approximately age three. At about this age it is normal for the brain to essentially reorganize cognitive and memory functions such that narrative memory for events prior to age three or four are difficult to access later in life. These two points have led to **the pervasive, inaccurate and destructive view that**

infants do not recall traumatic experience, including sexual abuse. Nothing could be further from the truth.

The human brain has multiple ways to 'recall' experience. Indeed, the brain is designed to store and recall experience in multiple ways; we have motor, vestibular, emotional, social and cognitive memories. When you walk, play the piano, feel your heart race in an empty parking lot at night, feel calmed by the touch of a loved one or create a 'first impression' after meeting someone for [the] first time, you are using memory. All incoming sensory information creates neuronal patterns of activity that are compared against previously experienced and stored patterns. New patterns can create new memories. Yet the majority of these stored memory templates are based upon experiences that took place in early childhood (…) – the time in life when these patterns of neuronal activity were first experienced and stored. And the majority of our 'memories' are non-cognitive and pre-verbal. **It is the experiences of early childhood that create the foundational organization of neural systems that will be used for a lifetime.**

This is why, contrary to popular perception, infants and young children are more vulnerable to traumatic stress – including sexual abuse. If the original experiences of the infant with primary caregiving adults involve fear, unpredictability, pain and abnormal genital sensations, neural organization in many key areas will be altered. For example, abnormal associations may be created between genital touch and fear, thereby laying the foundation for future problems in psychosexual development. Depending upon the specific nature of the abuse, the duration, the frequency and the time during development, a host of problems can result. In many ways, the long-term adverse effects of sexual abuse in infancy are the result of memories – **physiological state memories, motor-vestibular memories and emotional memories**, which in later years can be triggered by a host of cues that are pervasive.

Incestuous abuse in infancy is most destructive in this regard. It will result in **the association of fear, pain and unpredictability into the very core of future human functioning – the primary relational templates**. If these original 'templates' for all future relationships are corrupted by sexual exploitation and abuse, the child will have a lifetime of difficulties with intimacy, trust, touch and bonding – indeed **the core elements of healthy development** and **functioning throughout the lifecycle** will be altered.

Furthermore, if the child is sexually abused during early childhood, they may not have any cognitive 'memory' and be completely unaware that the source of their fears, difficulties with intimacy and relationships has its roots in this betrayal in infancy. This can lead to problems with self-esteem and, will make any therapeutic efforts more difficult.

So abuse during infancy can impact cognitive, emotional or behavioral development?
Yes. The abuse of an infant is often accompanied by extreme disruptions of normal caregiving behaviors and by extreme and prolonged stress responses. Altered caregiving and a prolonged stress response will alter the development of the infant's brain, which is, of course, the organ responsible for emotional, cognitive, social and physiological functioning. Furthermore, the primary caregivers are the source of the majority of emotional, cognitive and social experiences and therefore, the learning opportunities of the child during infancy. Development in all domains can be disrupted if these primary relationships are compromised. If the primary caregivers are abusive it is almost inevitable that emotional, behavioral and cognitive development will be arrested by early traumatic experience.

Are you saying that abuse in infancy impacts attachment?
Again, yes. **The development of attachment and healthy socio-emotional functioning depends upon the presence of consistent, responsive, attuned and nurturing caregivers.** One of the central tasks of these relationships is to keep the child safe. If these caregivers are unable to protect, or worse, if they participate in the abuse of the child, the core of all future relational interactions is corrupted. **The distortions in attachment that result from abuse in infancy can be toxic to all future relationships.** Again, the cascade of problems that result from impaired socio-emotional functioning due to early life sexual abuse can impact all domains of functioning and be a source of ongoing confusion and pain to anyone experiencing abuse in infancy.

Does abuse change the brain of the infant?
The brain is designed to change in response to experience. Indeed, all experience changes the brain. With traumatic experiences, the changes are in those parts of the brain involved in the stress and fear responses. Many studies with adults and, now with children, have demonstrated a host of neurophysiologic changes that are related to traumatic stress. More controlled studies are needed but there is no doubt that the major neurophysiological networks and neuroendocrine systems in the brain and the rest of the body are altered by developmental trauma.

Do infants have problems similar to older children who are abused?
The adverse effects that result from abuse will vary as a function of several keys factors: what is the nature of the abuse, the duration, frequency, intensity, time during development and the presence of attenuating factors such as other caring, attentive caregivers in the child's life. In general, however, with all traumatic experiences, the earlier in life, the less 'specific' and more pervasive the resulting

problems appear to be. For example, when traumatized as an adult, there is a specific increase in sympathetic nervous system reactivity when exposed to cues associated with the traumatic event. With young children, following traumatic stress, there appears to be a generalized increase in autonomic nervous system reactivity in addition to the cue-specific reactivity. Due to the sequential and functionally interdependent nature of development, traumatic disruption of the organization and functioning of [the] neural system can result in a cascade of related disrupted development and dysfunction. Examples of this include the motor and language delays in traumatized children under age six. The 'causes' of these delays are likely due to the primary, trauma-induced alterations in other domains (e.g., the stress response systems, thereby influencing physiological reactivity, hypervigilence, concentration), which, in turn, impair the young child's willingness to explore, capacity to process new information and ability to focus long enough on new information to learn.

The bottom line – all jargon aside – trauma during infancy has a profound impact on the developing child; and sadly, most traumatized infants end up 'remembering' the trauma in one way or another for the rest of their lives.

TASK/TEXT 5.19.4: HOPE SPRINGS ETERNAL

Bruce Perry, <www.cyc-net.org/cyc-online/cyconline-may2009-perry.html>, accessed 30 January 2010

Hope springs eternal in the human breast;
Man never Is, but always To be blest:
The soul, uneasy and confin'd from home,
Rests and expatiates in a life to come.
– Alexander Pope, *An Essay on Man, Epistle I*, 1733

It is spring in the Northern Hemisphere. For centuries during this time of year, we hopeful humans have celebrated the return of life – the greening of the trees, the return of migrating birds. The long dark nights pass and cold winds calm. It is during these bitter cold months that hope sustains us. We tolerate and survive the winter because we know spring is coming; hard times will pass. How discouraged, demoralized and defeated we would be in winter if we did not know spring was coming. Hope is the powerful protective force that gets us through distressing, even traumatic experiences. And hope is the most wonderful gift we give the maltreated children we live and work with.

So what exactly is hope? Where does it come from? And what can give a child hope – or take it away? As you might expect, I believe that hope is a brain-mediated capability. **Hope is the internal representation of a better world**; essentially a belief that things can be better. It is, in essence, a memory. We have a memory of spring – and we use this memory to warm us during the cold; to give us the strength to keep on going because it always isn't going to be like this; things will get better. The internal representation of a better world – the spring – is memory created within our brain based upon an earlier experience with spring. Even transient exposure to the perfect crisp air, the warming sun, the symphony of birds and the pallet of wildflowers in the mountain meadows can create a strong sustaining memory of spring. Ahh, just wait until we can sit in that sun again … it's soon now. Not much more of this – hard times will pass.

The most powerful source of hope, then, comes from our own personal experience; we have seen better times and feel confident that they will come again. A maltreated child living in the pain and chaos of a displaced life with disengaged, overwhelmed or abusive caregivers passed from person to person, home to home, community to community is living in the deepest of winters. And all too often, despite opportunities to engage, to learn, to grow and to heal, these children quit. They are hopeless; they have had too few experiences with reliable, honest, fully present and nurturing adults in their short lives.

Yet all too often the systems intended to help these children merely replicate the chaos, unpredictability and disengaged caregiving that characterized their dysfunctional homes. This merely reinforces a sense of powerlessness – hopelessness. An important factor is how distressed the people in these systems feel. First, a little neurobiology – in our brain we have a very powerful and important network of neurons involved in forming and maintaining relationships. A central aspect of that network is the capacity to read and respond to the emotional and social cues that are being projected by the people you interact with. If they are distracted and distressed, you will feel dismissed; you essentially will feel the way they feel – distressed. An angry adult will make a child feel threatened; a bored adult will make the child feel insignificant; a happy adult can cheer a child up. And on and on. **We have the neurobiological capacity to absorb and be influenced by the emotions of those around us.**

So if we create systems that overwork, disrespect and generally do not care for the carers, they will have a difficult time healing these children. This can push a foster parent, child and youth care worker, and teacher to be more focused on the work than on the child. Fill out the forms, get them to their appointments, take the tests. These resource-depleted, overworked adults find little time to be quiet, present, positive and caring. And yet, when we can look past these inevitable elements of the work place and remember what is important, when we do focus on the child, amazing things can happen. When we take care of ourselves; keep ourselves healthy, manage our own distress, find ways to be present, calm, patient and nurturing we change this children. We make a difference. Hope springs eternal.

So where does hope for these children come from? It comes from you. In the moment to moment experiences you have each day you can **show the child that adults can be trusted, that people can be honest, caring and safe**. It is not the sophistication of your psychological interpretations of their behavior but the consistency of your kindness that changes the child. It is not the completed form but the smile and gentle pat on the back that creates hope. Each day in the smallest of interactions, with your attention, your calm and your patience you are creating memories for this child. Memories of spring.

This month is the Child and Youth care workers month. It is appropriate that this comes in the spring. You, my colleagues, are, in your caring interactions with these children, Spring. And in the depth of the bitter cold of this child's winter, you create hope; you build an internal representation of a better world – a world where people are decent and kind and good. And this child's hope will whisper to him in the long, dark night of winter: these hard times will pass.

TASK/TEXT 5.20: NEW EARLY LEARNING DEVELOPMENT STANDARDS HIGHLIGHT NEEDED REFORMS AND INVESTMENTS

<www.unicef.org/tfyrmacedonia/media_11493.html>, 16 April 2009

SKOPJE – Following a two year development process, today the Ministry of Labour and Social Policy together with UNICEF presented new early learning and development standards (ELDS) for children aged 0–6 years. The standards build on evidence that the first years of life are crucial years for children for the development of the cognitive, physical, social and emotional skills they need to reach their full potential and succeed in school and life. The standards will help parents and care givers ensure that they are on track in meeting their obligations to young children.

"The evidence is unambiguous. Setting ambitious early childhood development standards for learning and care, and investing state and community resources to ensure that these standards are met, has enormous potential to boost educational achievement, promote social inclusion and promote good citizenship," said UNICEF Representative Sheldon Yett. "It is one of the best investments a state can make."

"Investments in early childhood development, either through improving access to kindergartens or other cost-effective alternatives organized in the communities, will pay tremendous dividends down the road," he added.

Studies have shown that investments in early childhood education yield a return that far exceeds the return on most other public investments. For every dollar spent on early childhood care there is at least a seven dollar return through cost savings. This figure is derived from studies showing that children who participate in pre-school are less likely to suffer illnesses, repeat grades, drop out of school, or require remedial services later in life.

Unfortunately, kindergartens are the only form of organized early learning opportunities currently funded by the state and do not receive adequate budgetary resources. Moreover, due to limited infrastructure that is often available only in urban areas, and due to the fees which many parents cannot afford, only 11% of young children attend kindergarten – a far lower percentage than in most countries in the region. This means that almost nine in every ten children are enrolling in primary school at a disadvantage.

To address this, the Ministry of Labour and Social Policy together with UNICEF have been working on establishing other cost effective forms of ECD to increase access, such as outreach services by kindergartens, community-based centres and programmes for parent education.

In the broader context, ensuring ELDS are in place is important since they are the basis for ensuring minimum standards of provision and quality of services. During the process of validation of the ELDS it was revealed that young children are not given sufficient support in all areas of development. Focus is given on the physical well-being and motor development with insufficient stimulation of other domains such as cognitive and social and emotional development. The standards provide information on what children 0–6 years should know and be able to do. Equally important they also provide practical information to help stimulate development for parents, educators and other professionals working with young children.

While the ELDS will be used by parents and professionals working with young children, they present a basis for reforming services that support early childhood learning and development in the country and are being used to guide the development of the National Early Childhood Development Policy, currently being drafted by the Ministry of Labour and Social Policy. As part of this policy, it is expected that the existing pre-school education programme and teacher training programmes will be revised, new parent education programmes will be developed and monitoring system will be put in place.

The development and implementation of the ELDS are part of a broader Early Childhood Development (ECD) Programme supported by UNICEF. This programme includes support to build the capacity of kindergartens to increase access to quality pre-school services; support to community-based ECD centres in the most disadvantaged communities and support to develop a National ECD Policy.

TASK/TEXT 5.21: THE SCIENCE OF EARLY CHILDHOOD DEVELOPMENT

National Scientific Council on the Developing Child, Harvard University Center on the Developing Child, 2007, Executive summary, <www.developingchild.net> (accessed 16 July 2009)

The future of any society depends on its ability to foster the health and well-being of the next generation. Stated simply, today's children will become tomorrow's citizens, workers, and parents.

When we invest wisely in children and families, the next generation will pay that back through a lifetime of productivity and responsible citizenship.

When we fail to provide children with what they need to build a strong foundation for healthy and productive lives, we put our future prosperity and security at risk.

Two recent developments have stimulated growing public discussion about the right balance between individual and shared responsibility for that strong foundation. The first is **the explosion of research in neurobiology that clarifies the extent to which the interaction between genetics and early experience literally shapes brain architecture**. The second is the increasingly recognized need for a highly skilled workforce and healthy adult population to confront the growing challenges of global economic competition and the rising costs of Social Security, Medicare, and Medicaid for the aging baby boomers.

In an effort to identify those aspects of development that are accepted broadly by the scientific community, the National Scientific Council, based at the Center on the Developing Child at Harvard University, brought together several of the nation's leading neuroscientists, developmental psychologists, pediatricians, and economists. This document presents their critical review of the existing literatures in their fields and a consensus about what we now know about development in the early childhood years. The objective of the Council is to move beyond the public's fascination with "the latest study" and focus on **the cumulative knowledge of decades of research** that has been subjected to rigorous and continuous peer review. The goal of this document is to help the public and its policy makers understand the core principles of that body of work that are now sufficiently accepted across the scientific community to warrant public action.

It is our hope and belief that better public understanding of the rapidly growing science of **early childhood and early brain development** can provide a powerful impetus for the design and implementation of policies and programs that could make a significant difference in the lives of all children. Without that understanding, **investments that could generate significant returns for all of society** stand the risk of being rejected or undermined. Thus, there is a compelling need for scientists to share with the public and its representatives an objective basis for choosing wisely among competing demands on limited resources.

This paper is designed to provide a framework within which this complex challenge can be addressed most effectively. Its goal is to promote an understanding of the **basic science of early childhood development, including its underlying neurobiology**, to inform both public and private sector investment in young children and their families. To this end, the paper presents a set of core developmental concepts that have emerged from decades of rigorous research in **neurobiology, developmental psychology, and the economics of human capital formation**, and considers their implications for a range of issues in policy and practice.

Core Concepts of Development

- Child development is a foundation for community development and economic development, as capable children become the foundation of a prosperous and sustainable society.
- Brains are built over time.
- The interactive influences of genes and experience literally shape the architecture of the developing brain, and the active ingredient is the "serve and return" nature of children's engagement in relationships with their parents and other caregivers in their family or community.
- Both brain architecture and developing abilities are built "from the bottom up," with simple circuits and skills providing the scaffolding for more advanced circuits and skills over time.
- Toxic stress in early childhood is associated with persistent effects on the nervous system and stress hormone systems that can damage developing brain architecture and lead to lifelong problems in learning, behavior, and both physical and mental health.
- Creating the right conditions for early childhood development is likely to be more effective and less costly than addressing problems at a later age.

Implications for Policy and Practice

- Policy initiatives that promote supportive relationships and rich learning opportunities for young children create a strong foundation for higher school achievement followed by greater productivity in the workplace and solid citizenship in the community.
- Substantial progress toward this goal can be achieved by assuring growth-promoting experiences both at home and in community based settings, through a range of **parent education, family support, early care and education, preschool, and intervention services.**
- When parents, informal community programs, and professionally staffed early childhood services pay attention to **young children's emotional and social needs**, as well as to their mastery of literacy and cognitive skills, they have maximum impact on the development of sturdy brain architecture and preparation for success in school.
- When basic health and early childhood programs **monitor the development of all children**, problems that require attention can be identified in a timely fashion and intervention can be provided.
- The basic principles of neuroscience and the technology of human skill formation indicate that later remediation for highly vulnerable children will produce less favorable outcomes and cost more than appropriate intervention at a younger age.
- The essence of quality in early childhood services is embodied in the **expertise and skills of the staff** and in their capacity to build positive relationships with young children. The striking shortage of welltrained personnel in the field today indicates that substantial **investments in training, recruiting, compensating, and retaining a high quality workforce must be a top priority.**
- Responsible investments in services for young children and their families focus on benefits relative to cost. Inexpensive services that do not meet quality standards are a waste of money. Stated simply, **sound policies seek maximum value rather than minimal cost.**

[Conclusion]

The need to **address significant inequalities in opportunity, beginning in the earliest years of life**, is both a fundamental moral [and for states parties to the CRC: legal, JW] responsibility and a critical investment in our nation's social and economic future.

Thus, the time has come **to close the gap between what we know** (from systematic scientific inquiry across a broad range of disciplines) **and what we do** (through both public and private sector policies and practices) to **promote the**

healthy development of all young children. The science of early childhood development can provide a powerful framework for informing sound choices among alternative priorities and for building consensus around a shared plan of action. The well-being of our nation's children and the security of its future would be well-served by such wise choices and concerted commitment.

TASK/TEXT 5.22: EARLY CHILDHOOD PROGRAMMES AND THE ROLE OF THE FAMILY

An interview with James Heckman: "We have to understand more the relationship between early childhood programmes and the role of the family," *Early Childhood Matters* June 2009, pp. 24–29, Bernard van Leer Foundation, <www.bernardvanleer.org>

Professor **James Heckman**, of the University of Chicago, is a Nobel Laureate in economics and an adviser to President Obama on early childhood policy. He is regarded as the leading authority on the economic case for investing in early childhood programmes.

[Question:] *The theme of this edition of* Early Childhood Matters *is parental stress. You're an economist. So let's start with the grim economic outlook, which is surely adding to the stress that many parents already feel. It is also creating, however, a new enthusiasm for government-led stimulus programmes. Does this present an opportunity for advocates of greater public investment in early childhood?*

James Heckman: The recession is certainly exacerbating resource problems, but families were under stress long before the recession. An increasing percentage of children are growing up in families where the resources aren't there. From low-skilled immigrant families and others outside the mainstream, more and more children are emerging into society at age five or six as if from a cocoon, from family environments that are not conducive to launching them into the wider world.

Is the recession an opportunity? It should be. Keynes pointed out that you can stimulate economic activity merely by paying someone to dig holes and fill them in again, but this has a multiplier of one – in other words, it has zero longer-term effect. Unfortunately, a lot of things that are being proposed in stimulus packages now are little better. Things like repairing potholes on the streets of my city, Chicago, are fine, but the increments of return you get there are very marginal. In comparison, the returns on early childhood programmes are extremely high. Investing in young children gives you double benefits – stimulus from the extra spending now, and the increase in human capital in the years to come. So yes, there's an extremely good case for governments to include it in stimulus packages. It's a shame that most arguments about stimulus packages are about building bridges and roads, not building human skills and human capital.

You've advocated that instead of the state providing universal early childhood services itself, it should give parents vouchers to use in private programs. But when we're talking about children who are disadvantaged in early life by poor parenting, isn't it overly optimistic to assume that the parents of such children will have the capacity to use such vouchers wisely?

There are two things to say here. First, it's been well established by research done by people such as Justine Hastings and colleagues at Yale that when parents who are not well informed are first given school vouchers, the decisions they make are not that good. They send their kids to schools that are close by, or where their friends go. But when parents are given education about which schools are better, they make wiser choices.

So I completely agree that we need to educate parents to enable them to use vouchers wisely. But there's a second part of the answer. There are a number of reasons why it's preferable to bring in other providers instead of having universal services provided by governments. One reason is that you get more resources if you involve religious groups, social groups and communities. Another is that the early years are a very sensitive time, and people are very worried about the central government inculcating values in their children that they don't agree with.

Many times I've heard people who hold more conservative values – not just evangelical Christians, but Mormons, Orthodox Jews and Muslims – say they're really worried that early childhood provision is going to teach their children values that will undermine the ones they want to inculcate in their children. We need to bring in these parents, respect their cultural sensitivities, and give them an informed choice among diverse early childhood services.

How do you avoid the danger that early childhood services provided by religious groups might merely extend the cocoon phenomenon that you spoke about earlier?

There's no reason why you can't teach noncognitive skills but still keep it in a cultural tradition. It is essential that these programmes should have a core concept of promoting the development of certain human abilities, but I think this can be done within a religious framework. Of course there have to be minimum standards enforced, not just a core curriculum of noncognitive skills but also to guard against the possibility of rip-offs from poor quality providers.

There will be cases of a fundamental disconnect, where some religious groups will not want certain aspects of the core curriculum taught. But I think even those groups would welcome many parts of the core curriculum – for example, their children being helped to become more self-disciplined and selfconfident in their social interactions with others.

The majority of parents mean well for their children. There is a small percentage of parents who don't, and I'm very interested in knowing more about them – but for the majority who do, what I'm trying to do is make family supplementation programmes 'incentive-compatible.' It's essential that parents are informed and involved, and that early childhood provision doesn't come to resemble a government bureaucracy. I have an abiding image from a trip to Amsterdam a few years ago of a centre in which schoolmarms were handing down Dutch values to North African preschool children. The children's parents were offended, quite understandably.

Early childhood organisations typically use two complementary, but very different, arguments to advocate for greater attention to disadvantaged children: the child rights argument and the case from cost-benefit analysis, which you've done so much to establish.

My most important contribution has been to show that there is no contradiction between the economic case and the equity [child rights] case, because the economic benefits are greatest with the children who are most disadvantaged.

Former US President Harry Truman used to joke that he wanted to meet a one-handed economist, because every economist he worked with would say "on the one hand, on the other hand." Early childhood policy is a rare example of a one-handed economist argument. The case for social justice coincides perfectly with the lessons of cost-benefit analysis.

Within the community of early childhood advocates, there is frustration that the economic argument for investing in early childhood is seen as firmly established but is not more widely accepted and acted on by decision makers. Do you share this frustration?

Well, there's less agreement than you might think. Broadly, yes, the economic argument is accepted. But the details are very fuzzy. Take a collection of proposed programmes – say, nurses visiting pregnant mothers, a focus on the 1–3 year age group, or the 4–5 year age group. Proponents of [each of] these programmes won't publicly attack each other, but a smart guy is going to lay all the programmes out on a coffee table and say, "hang on, there's no agreement here on what works best."

I have great respect for advocates for early childhood, but they have a tendency to think their case is 100 percent solid when it's not. Often, I think legislators are smart enough to know there's more disagreement than the advocates say, and their stridency alienates them. Early childhood advocates need to be more willing to admit weaknesses in the evidence and to be less prone to saying to each other, "we know this is important, why doesn't everyone else get it?" They should also push for more and better evidence.

How should the early childhood community go about strengthening the details of the economic case for investing in early childhood?

Experimentation and evaluation. There are many experiments going on in the education of older children right now – some of them are nuts, some are interesting, but all are of potential value.

In early childhood programmes, we're also groping; experimentation is used, but much more is needed. We still have a long way to go.

The need for more experimentation is another argument for vouchers, by the way, for private sector diversity and choice. I worry that if Obama, or anybody else, commits too much time and investment into any one programme at this stage, we'll lose the opportunity to go forward and learn more. The best programme is almost certainly one that hasn't been tried yet.

I get the impression that early childhood advocates feel the need to put forward an appearance of unanimity, which in reality is an illusion. We need programmes openly competing with each other. One of my current projects is a book, with Craig and Sharon Ramey, looking at the hundreds of programmes that have been tried so far. The problem is that many current programmes haven't been adequately evaluated. European countries in particular are only recently starting to document properly. After all these years, the strongest data on early childhood programmes still comes from the old American longitudinal surveys, like the Perry pre-school programme.

You advised Barack Obama on his early childhood education policy. The president's first budget included extra funding for early education, the Nurse-Family Partnership programme and Head Start. How optimistic are you that Obama's early childhood policy will be pursued with sufficient political will to effect significant change for American children?

Obama is serious – it's more than rhetoric. And it's not just him, but also the people around him. My paper, *Schools, skills and synapses*, was widely circulated at the Democratic convention. Arne Duncan, the Secretary of Education, is also from Chicago, which by the way has been an innovative place for early childhood programmes – intellectually aggressive, a hotbed of research.

The problem is that Obama is launching this [during] an economic tempest. There are competing priorities, like healthcare, and the early childhood advocacy lobby is less well-funded and well-organised than other interest groups. I think he'll get the funds he's asking for, but against all the competing demands, I'm not sure what that will convert into – Head Start for example is usually underfunded per child, and arguably not that successful as a consequence. The danger is adding more children to programmes at a low level of quality instead of raising quality.

Are you aware of countries where investment in young children is actually happening in the way you would like, which could be held up as an example to others?

Until a few years ago I would have said that France, with its so-called crèche programme, was a nice example. Then I saw research by the child development psychologist Richard Tremblay that compared children of similar backgrounds growing up in Paris and Montreal, where there were no such programmes, and found essentially no difference. The French crèche programme looked good, but it turns out that it didn't achieve much.

Although we need more evaluation of different programmes, what is clear is that you need to invest significant amounts to get positive results – we're talking $5000–8000 per child per year in the US, comparable to the costs of high school. Typically politicians are talking the talk but investing far less, maybe one or two thousand. They get the good headlines that say they're doing something, but without the long-term results. Some haven't realised that this is about more than childcare, or that bad childcare can be worse than none at all.

Also, although I haven't studied them in depth, it seems to me that family-friendly policies in the Scandinavian countries – policies like family supplements and parental leave – may have a greater positive effect on young children than many programmes that are considered to be early childhood development in the more traditional sense.

Apart from the economic case and the equity [child rights] case, what arguments are important to persuade political decision-makers to take a greater interest in early childhood programmes?

We need to be honest in pointing out how failed families are failing children. It's a sensitive argument, as the danger is that if you make the argument you're accused of blaming the victims. But we have to recognise that divisions are becoming more entrenched. Children who had good parenting are becoming even better parents. Children who had poor parenting are becoming worse parents – and having more children than the better parents, too. Society is becoming more unequal – the extremes are polarising. At one end of the spectrum, the percentage of children graduating college is growing. At the other end, the percentage dropping out of high school is also growing.

It's interesting to note that many of the US states where early childhood programmes are most enthusiastically embraced are those with strong rightwing religious values, the people who are most concerned about the negative effects of breakdown of family structures. I'm not saying I'm endorsing the family values agenda. I am saying that we have to talk more about failed families. Here in Chicago, four in five African American children are born out of marriage. Something like 15–20 percent of all American children are growing up without ever having a second parent around. We have to talk more openly about family failure, and understand more the relationship between early childhood programmes and the role of the family.

At the same time, we have to get people to realise the value of noncognitive skills. The Perry programme had no effect on IQ; it was the lasting effect of the noncognitive skills that made the difference. But people forget that. Go to any website that talks up the benefits of early childhood programmes, and you'll likely find that they are far too hung up on IQ, on improving academic test scores, on 'smarts.'

Evaluations of early childhood programmes need to be more rigorous and more sophisticated in evaluating their impact on noncognitive skills, because they have a huge impact on the ability to learn and succeed in life – skills like curiosity and engagement with the world, the ability to delay pleasure, the ability to relate to other people and to tolerate criticism. We need to get that into the public consciousness.

One problem is that 'noncognitive' is hardly a catchy word or one that's immediately understandable to the general public.

It's a terrible word, as it's defined as a negative. It's better to talk about words like motivation, drive, ambition, personality, sociability, dignity, self-respect, and ability to co-operate and integrate. An old-fashioned word that I think is appropriate is 'character.'

Do you have any further thoughts to share with readers of Early Childhood Matters *on what the early childhood advocacy community should be doing to advocate more effectively?*

I'm often struck that a lot of child advocates haven't noticed that the discussion has moved on. They are stuck on repeatedly asserting that the early years are important. Yes. We know that.

The question now is what is the best way to develop children's noncognitive skills, the best way to improve parenting. Early childhood advocates need to recognise there's nothing to fear from open competition between different ways of doing things – that's what makes the case more airtight.

I also think the early childhood community can tend to be too parochial. You hear people talking about neurons being pruned at age three, as if that's the whole story of what's coming out of neuroscience – which it's not (neuronal changes happen all through life). Early childhood advocates need to reach out more to advocates for other life stages to develop a combined approach that advocates for ways of building skills and developing human potential over the whole life cycle.

TASK/TEXT 5.23:

TASK/TEXT 5.23.1: BABIES OF LESS EDUCATED PARENTS HAVE MORE DIFFICULT TEMPERAMENT

Erasmus Medical Center Press Release, Rotterdam 7 December 2009, <www.erasmusmc.nl/perskamer/2009/2247885/?lang=en>

Babies from low income families and with a lower education level have a more difficult temperament than babies of highly educated parents. According to the PhD research carried out by Pauline Jansen at Erasmus MC [Medical Center], the difference can be perceived just six months after birth. A difficult temperament could predict behavioral problems later in life. The doctoral student therefore pleas for early detection and action.

Babies with a more difficult temperament are prone to developing stress symptoms from normal daily activities. They cry very loudly when having a bath, for example, or when being dressed or having their diapers changed. They also have more difficulty falling asleep, are more easily distracted and react more intensely to changes. "Although all babies experience these things to some extent, children with more difficult temperaments experience these problems more intensely," according to Jansen.

There appear to be several reasons for the fact that babies from families with a lower socioeconomic position have a more difficult temperament. The parents or guardians, for example, are more prone to stress and the mother suffers from psychological problems more often. In addition, they are more often families with single mothers.

The doctoral student hopes that her dissertation will contribute to a reduction in behavioral problems. "We know that children with a more difficult temperament get more behavioral problems later in life. They are more susceptible to anxiety disorders, ADHD and problems at school. They have difficulty fitting into society. As my research has shown that a difficult temperament can already be determined in babies of only six months of age, efforts to deal with behavioural problems should be started early in life."

Jansen also studied the influence of social inequality on pregnancies. She showed, among other, that women with a lower level of education have an increased risk of premature births and low birth weight deliveries. There are several reasons for this. These pregnant women smoke more often and are more prone to stress. With regard to work, Jansen did not see the social inequality in pregnancy results: the chance that women without paid jobs have pregnancy complications is the same as that for women with paid jobs. It does, however, appear that women who work full-time during pregnancy get smaller babies than women who work part-time. "This may be due to the fact that full-time working mothers are physically more tired and more prone to psychological stress. But further research is necessary to determine whether this is really the case," according to Jansen.

The doctoral student used data from the Generation R study. This is research into the growth, development and health of 10,000 children in Rotterdam. The children are followed from early pregnancy until they are young adults.

TASK/TEXT 5.23.2: TEMPERAMENT CAUSED BY NURTURE RATHER THAN NATURE

Pauline W. Jansen, *Social inequalities in pregnancy outcomes and early childhood behaviour*, Dissertation Erasmus University Rotterdam 2009, Summary

The social position of individuals in a society is associated with health and disease, with socially disadvantaged persons being worst off. The prevention of these health inequalities is a major public health goal. As inequalities in health between socially advantaged and disadvantaged persons are already present early in life and persevere throughout the whole life span, attempts to tackle this gradient should start by reducing socio-economic and ethnic inequalities in fetal life and infancy.

However, the indicators of social disadvantage, such as low socio-economic status and ethnic minority status, are not easily amendable. Therefore, it is important to unravel the pathways through which social disadvantage leads to health and disease, because these so-called mediating factors might provide opportunities for prevention and intervention programs.

The objective of this thesis was to extend the existing knowledge on the relation of social disadvantage with pregnancy outcomes and behaviour early in life. Since the exact pathways how social disadvantage 'gets under the skin' and causes pregnancy complications and behavioural problems are partly unknown, we aimed to identify the mechanisms underlying these associations. The specific aims of this thesis were:

1a. To study the association between social disadvantage and pregnancy outcomes, of which preterm birth and birth weight were the main focus.

1b. To examine explanatory mechanisms in educational and employment-related inequalities in adverse pregnancy outcomes.

2a. To study the association of social disadvantage with child behaviour and parental harsh discipline in early childhood.

2b. To examine explanatory mechanisms in socioeconomic and ethnic inequalities in child behaviour and parental harsh discipline.

The studies described in this thesis were embedded in The Generation R Study, which is a prospective population-based cohort study from fetal life onwards in Rotterdam, the Netherlands.

In chapter 2 of this thesis, we studied the association between social disadvantage and different pregnancy outcomes. Chapter 2.1 described that low maternal educational level, as an indicator of low SES, was associated with slower fetal growth resulting in differences in fetal weight. The adverse effect of low education was largest for growth of the fetal head, followed by growth of the fetal femur and abdomen. The educational inequalities in fetal growth characteristics were largely due to determinants of fetal growth, such as maternal smoking during pregnancy and maternal height. The inequalities in fetal head circumference, however, remained partly unexplained.

In chapter 2.2, we showed that pregnant women with a low educational level had a nearly two-fold higher risk of preterm birth as compared to women with a high educational level. A combination of several risk factors for preterm birth among women with a low education, namely pre-eclampsia, intrauterine growth retardation, mothers' young age, short stature and high body mass index, smoking habits, financial concerns, and indicators of poor psychosocial functioning, explained this elevated risk. Moreover, low educated women were more likely to abstain from drinking alcohol during pregnancy, which also contributed to their increased risk of preterm birth. We hypothesized that low to moderate alcohol consumption during pregnancy may be genuinely beneficial in preventing preterm birth, but the effects may also be explained by the 'healthy drinker effect.' This phenomenon implies that women with a poor obstetric history are more likely to abstain from drinking during pregnancy.

Chapter 2.3 indicated that offspring's birth weight was on average 176 grams lower among the lowest educated women as compared to high educated women. A substantial part of this lower birth weight was the result of a shortened gestational period among women with a low educational level. The remaining birth weight difference of 126 grams between low and high education was partially due to an accumulation of risk factors for low birth weight among low educated women, namely: parental height and birth weight, hypertension, maternal age, parity, single motherhood, unplanned pregnancy, financial difficulties, number of people living in the household, weight gain, and most importantly maternal smoking during pregnancy. Despite the contribution of these mediating variables, part of the relationship between educational level and birth weight remained unexplained.

Next to this, we also showed that, besides a relatively high prevalence of certain risk factors for low birth weight, lower educated women also have a relatively high prevalence of certain factors that have a suppressive effect on low birth weight. The suppressing variables were body mass index and weekly working hours.

Another indicator of social disadvantage included in this thesis was employment status. In chapter 2.4, we showed that unemployment among pregnant women, as compared to being employed, was associated with a higher risk of several adverse pregnancy outcomes, specifically preterm ruptured membranes, preterm birth, meconium stained amniotic fluid and small-for-gestational-age. These risks were entirely attributable to the less optimal socio-economic circumstances and poorer mental health of unemployed women. In contrast, unemployed women had a lower risk of a complicated delivery, i.e. poor progress of delivery and non-vaginal delivery, than employed women. The reason for this was that the unemployed women in our study were more often multiparous than employed women. In-depth analysis of the unemployed group revealed that women receiving disability benefit had the highest risk of several pregnancy complications. Among those with paid employment, we observed that **long weekly working hours during pregnancy were significantly associated with a lower birth weight in the offspring**. Weekly working hours were not associated with other pregnancy outcomes under study.

The second part of this thesis provides information on the association of social disadvantage with child behaviour and parental harsh discipline early in life. In chapter 3.1 we showed that several indicators of **low SES, such as low parental educational level, low family income and low maternal occupational level, were associated with a more difficult temperament in six months old infants as compared to indicators of high SES**. Only the direction of the association between SES and Sadness was reversed. The effect of SES on the temperamental scales Distress to Limitations, Recovery from Distress, and Duration of Orienting was largely attributable to a young maternal age, single motherhood, family stress and poor maternal psychological well being. These covariates could not explicate the higher levels of Activity and Fear nor the lower Sadness scores of infants from low SES groups.

Chapter 3.2 described higher levels of parent-reported behavioural problems in toddlers from various backgrounds as compared to native Dutch children. This association was partly mediated by maternal psychopathology and indicators of SES. Besides this, we showed that the reported behavioural problems of non-Dutch children were more pronounced among those with unfavourable immigration characteristics of the mothers, such as being first generation immigrant, older than 15 years at immigration, having poor Dutch language skills and lack of feelings of acceptance by Dutch natives.

Finally, in chapter 3.3, we aimed to identify determinants of harsh discipline used by mothers and fathers of 3-year old toddlers. We demonstrated that **psychosocial characteristics of parents, such as psychopathology and stress, were risk factors for use of harsh discipline by both mothers and fathers. Moreover, sociodemographic characteristics like young parental age and being first generation non-Western immigrant consistently predicted maternal and paternal harsh discipline.**

Indicators of socioeconomic status, however, were clearly associated with maternal harsh discipline, but hardly with paternal harsh discipline. A substantial part of the association between educational level and maternal harsh discipline was due to other sociodemographic characteristics such as ethnicity, family income, and young maternal age.

In chapter 4 we considered our main findings regarding the mechanisms underlying the association of social disadvantage gradient with pregnancy complications and behaviour early in life. Next, we hypothesized about which factors might mediate the remaining social inequalities in pregnancy outcomes and child behaviour that could not be explained by the mediators we studied. We also discussed relevant methodological issues that possibly have influenced our findings. The last part of this chapter outlined some implications for public health policies.

6. BEST INTERESTS OF THE CHILD – POSITIVE PARENTING, PUBLIC POLICY

TASK/TEXT 6.1: DEMANDS ON THE FAMILY

Mary Daly (ed.), *Parenting in contemporary Europe: A positive approach*, Strasbourg: Council of Europe Publishing, 2007, p. 7

We have reached a dramatic point in the history of parenting and the family. As the decades roll by, the fabric of family life seems ever more affected by rapid and profound social change. The drama lies mainly in the fact that the demands on the family are growing almost exponentially, whether from the media, employers, the public authorities or family members themselves. Moreover, the task of parenting nowadays is historically unique: because of profound changes in norms and laws, adults are compelled not just to reinvent the meaning of partnership but to forge a new path of leadership in relation to children and young people (…). Hence, those involved in parenting today need specific information, support and skills to enable them to fashion and realise their hopes for their own and their children's development. For this and other reasons, public policy and public debate cannot afford to lie idle on the matter of parenthood.

TASK/TEXT 6.2:

TASK/TEXT 6.2.1: POLICY TO SUPPORT POSITIVE PARENTING

Recommendation Rec(2006)19 of the Committee of Ministers [of the Council of Europe] to member states on policy to support positive parenting *(Adopted by the Committee of Ministers on 13 December 2006 at the 983rd meeting of the Ministers' Deputies)*, <www.coe.int>, Committee of Ministers, Adopted texts, Recommendations (…)

The Committee of Ministers, under Article 15.*b* of the Statute of the Council of Europe,

Considering that the aim of the Council of Europe is to achieve a greater unity between its member states, *inter alia*, by promoting the adoption of common rules;

Referring to the work of the Council of Europe in the field of children and families and reaffirming in general the following legal instruments:

- the Convention on Human Rights and Fundamental Freedoms (ETS No. 5), which protects the rights of everyone, including children;
- the European Social Charter (ETS No. 35) and revised European Social Charter (ETS No. 163), stating that "the family as a fundamental unit of society has the right to appropriate social, legal and economic protection to ensure its full development" (Article 16);
- the European Convention on the Exercise of Children's Rights (ETS No. 160);
- the Convention on Contacts concerning children (ETS No. 192);
- the Recommendations of the Committee of Ministers to member states: No. R (84)4 on parental responsibilities; No. R (85)4 on violence in the family; No. R (87)6 on foster families; No. R (94)14 on coherent and integrated family policies; *No. R (96)5* on reconciling work and family life; No. R (97)4 on securing and promoting the health of single parent families; No. R (98)8 on children's participation in family and social life; Rec(2005)5 on the rights of children living in residential institutions and Rec(2006)5 on the Council of Europe Action Plan to promote the rights and full participation of people with disabilities in society: improving the quality of life of people with disabilities in Europe 2006–2015;

Bearing in mind the Revised Social Strategy for Social Cohesion for which families are the place where social cohesion is first experienced and learnt and that a social cohesion strategy, while fully respecting the autonomy of the private sphere and of civil society, must seek to be supportive of families;

Recalling the Parliamentary Assembly's Recommendations 751 (1975) on the position and responsibility of parents in the modern family and their support by society; 1074 (1988) on family policy; 1121 (1990) on the rights of children; 1443 (2000) on international adoption: respecting children's rights; 1501 (2001) on parents' and teachers' responsibilities in children's education; 1551 (2002) on building a 21st-century society with and for children: follow-up to the European strategy for children (Recommendation 1286 (1996)); 1639 (2003) on family mediation and equality of sexes; 1666 (2004) on a Europe-wide ban on corporal punishment of children; 1698 (2005) on the rights of children in institutions: follow-up to Recommendation 1601 (2003) of the Parliamentary Assembly;

Stressing the importance of the United Nations Convention on the Rights of the Child, to which all the member states of the Council of Europe are Parties, and the basic principles of which should always underlie the rearing of children;

Recalling the Third Summit of Heads of State and Government (Warsaw, Poland, May 2005) and the commitment made [there] to fully comply with the obligations of the United Nations Convention on the Rights of the Child, to effectively promote the rights of the child and to take specific action to eradicate all forms of violence against children, and the ensuing programme "**Building a Europe for and with children** [**<www.coe.int/children>**]," officially launched in Monaco, on 4 and 5 April 2006;

Referring to the Final Communiqué and Political Declaration of the European Ministers responsible for Family Affairs at their 28th session (Lisbon, Portugal, 16–17 May 2006), particularly:

- recognising that parenting, though linked to family intimacy, should be designated as a **domain of public policy** and **all the necessary measures** should be adopted for supporting parenting and creating the **conditions necessary for positive parenting**;
- recalling their commitment to promote and pursue a common European policy in the field of family affairs and the **rights of the child** within the framework of the Council of Europe;

Recognising the child as a person with rights, including the right to be protected and to participate, to express her/his views, to be heard and be heeded;

Recalling that public authorities have a vital role to play in supporting families in general and parents in particular, which is expressed through three core elements of family policy: public transfers and taxation, measures to balance work and family life, childcare provision and other services;

Considering that the family is a primary unit of society and that parenting plays a fundamental role in society and for its future;

Conscious of the many changes and challenges facing families today which require parenthood to be given greater prominence and better support, considering that such support is essential for children, parents and society as a whole;

Recognising that all levels of society have a role to play in supporting children, parents and families;

Considering that public authorities in conjunction with the economic and social sectors and civil society can, in taking action in support of parenting, help strive for a healthier and more prosperous future for society, as well as an improvement in the quality of family life;

Noting the need for a cross-sectoral and co-ordinated approach;

Keen to promote positive parenting as an essential part of the support provided for parenting, and as a means of ensuring respect for and implementation of children's rights,

Recommends that the governments of member states:

- **acknowledge the essential nature of families and of the parental role and create the necessary conditions for positive parenting in the best interests of the child;**
- **take all appropriate legislative, administrative, financial and other measures adhering to the principles set out in the appendix to this recommendation.**

Appendix to Recommendation Rec(2006)19

1. Definitions

For the purpose of this recommendation, the term:

"**Parents**": refers to persons with parental authority or responsibility;

"**Parenting**": refers to all the roles falling to parents in order to care for and bring up children. Parenting is centred on parent-children interaction and entails rights and duties for the child's development and self-fulfilment;

"**Positive parenting**": refers to parental behaviour based on the best interests of the child that is nurturing, empowering, non-violent and provides recognition and guidance which involves setting of boundaries to enable the full development of the child.

2. Fundamental principles of policies and measures

Policies and measures in the field of support for parenting should: [bold, JW]

i. adopt a rights-based approach: this means treating children and parents as holders of **rights and obligations**;
ii. be based on a voluntary choice by the individuals concerned, except when public authorities have to intervene to protect the child;
iii. acknowledge that parents have the prime **responsibility for their child, subject to the child's best interests**;
iv. consider parents and children as partners sharing, as appropriate, the setting up and implementation of the measures relating to them;

v. be based on the equal involvement of parents and respect for their complementarity;
vi. guarantee equal opportunities for children irrespective of their gender, status, abilities or family situation;
vii. take into account the importance of a **sufficient standard of living** to engage in positive parenting;
viii. be based on a clearly expressed concept of positive parenting;
ix. address parents and key players having childcare, health and educational and social responsibilities towards the child and who should also respect the principles of positive parenting;
x. recognise the diverse types of parenting and parental situations through adopting a pluralistic approach;
xi. adopt a positive approach to parents' potential, particularly through placing priority on incentives;
xii. be long-term in order to guarantee stability and continuity of policy;
xiii. ensure that the number of common rules of principle at national or federal level are kept to a minimum to promote equal standards at local level and that there is a **local network of services** providing parenting support measures;
xiv. ensure inter-ministerial co-operation, encouraging and co-ordinating the action(s) in this field of the different ministries, departments and agencies concerned in order to implement policy that is coherent and comprehensive;
xv. be co-ordinated at international level, through facilitating exchanges of knowledge, experience and good practice in the application of the guidelines on positive parenting.

3. Objectives

Governments should organise their policies and programmes on positive parenting with a view to achieving the following three types of objectives:

i. the creation of the conditions for positive parenting, by ensuring that **all those rearing children have access to an appropriate level and diversity of resources** (material, psychological, social and cultural) and that broad social attitudes and patterns of prevailing life are receptive to the needs of families with children and also those of parents;
ii. the removal of barriers to positive parenting, whatever their origin. Employment policy, in particular, should allow a better reconciliation of family and working life;

iii. the promotion of positive parenting by developing awareness of it and taking all the necessary measures to make it a reality. In order to have efficient policies to support parenting, public authorities should promote initiatives aiming to make people aware of the value and importance of positive parenting. Governments should take a pro-active approach to promoting awareness of parenting issues and to normalising participation in parenting programmes. Information should present different images of parenting in order to avoid stigmatising differences.

The goal of policy and measures should be the **harmonious development (in all its dimensions)** and proper treatment of children, with due regard for their fundamental rights and dignity.

As a priority, measures should be taken to **eliminate all child neglect and abuse and physical or psychological violence** (including humiliation, degrading treatment and corporal punishment).

It is also essential to implement and further develop a suitable policy to bring about a change in social attitudes and patterns of life in order to accommodate more effectively the needs of children, parents and families and in particular to promote family-friendly working environments and services.

4. Incorporating children's rights in public policies

Public policies on support for parenting should incorporate childhood-related issues, acknowledging the needs and interests of all children and paying attention to their varying needs depending on their age, capacity, and level of maturity. For this purpose, the principles enshrined in the United Nations Convention on the Rights of the Child should be respected by all, regardless of context, and particularly guide the activities of all bodies working in the field, both public and private, especially for the following rights and general principles:

i. the right to non-discrimination;
ii. the best interests of the child should be of primary consideration;
iii. the child's right to life and development;
iv. the child's right to participation, to express her/his views, to be heard and be heeded, to receive information and to join associations and other organisations;
v. the right to protection and care.

For this purpose, it is important for the child to grow up in a favourable family environment and in a positive atmosphere.

5. Considering parents' responsibilities, rights and obligations

In the best interests of the child, the rights of parents, such as entitlement to appropriate support from public authorities in fulfilling their parental functions, must also be given prominence. The exercise by parents of equal and shared responsibility for their children makes a major contribution to the harmonious development of the child's personality.

Particular attention should be paid to the important role of fathers in the care and rearing of their children, taking into account in particular the principle of gender equality, the impact on families of the reconciliation of work and family life and family breakdown, which can often result in fathers living apart from their children.

6. Core components of policies and measures

Policies to promote and encourage positive parenting will work best if they are based on consultation and dialogue with parents and on their voluntary involvement and participation, in order to reach a real partnership. In addition to the essential elements at point 4 and 5 of this recommendation, core components include the following:

6.1. Supporting parents

i. alongside the measures proposed by public authorities to afford and improve support for parents, support from other agencies (such as municipalities, social security and associations) should also be acknowledged and encouraged;

ii. policies should be geared to engendering support for parenting at the following three levels:
   - informal: creating and strengthening existing social bonds and encouraging new links between parents and their family, neighbours and friends;
   - semi-formal: empowering parents' and children's associations and NGOs and activating a range of self-help and other community-based groups and services;
   - formal: facilitating access to public services.

6.2. Promoting education in children's rights and positive parenting

i. parents should be encouraged to become more aware of the nature of their role (and how it is changing), children's rights, the responsibilities and obligations that derive from these and their own rights;
ii. governments should also arrange for comprehensive guidelines and specific programmes to assist them in challenging life situations, conflict resolution, anger management through non-violent approaches and mediation techniques;
iii. prevention programmes regarding the different forms of ill-treatment of children should be promoted and parents made aware of this serious problem and of its consequences on the child's development;
iv. children should also be taught about their rights and duties in order to make them aware of the concept of positive parenting and what this means for them.

6.3. Reconciling family and working life

i. public authorities should create the necessary conditions – and employers should be encouraged – to implement a better reconciliation of family and working life through legal and other provisions (such as flexible working arrangements, adjustment of working and school hours, leave policies, various types of good quality childcare services, provisions for looking after children with disabilities as well as sick children, etc.);
ii. the social partners should be encouraged to negotiate and develop tailor-made policies adapted to the specific needs of each company and of their employees;
iii. good practices make it clear to employers that a comprehensive work/life balance policy creates a win-win situation within companies.

6.4. Policies at local level

The action taken at local level is particularly important in providing a response tailored more closely to the needs and characteristics of the populations concerned. Co-operation and co-ordination at national or federal and local levels and between these levels are necessary in order to offer families better service and optimise available resources and the use made of them. Administrative procedures should allow for an appropriate level of flexibility in service provision, consistent with ensuring equitable treatment of all families.

7. Targeting of policies and measures

Particular attention should be paid to difficult social and economic circumstances and to crises within families, which require more specific support.

It is also essential to supplement general policies with a more targeted approach. Parenting in certain situations and at certain periods in the life cycle is by its nature more challenging. Despite the variations from country to country, the needs of the following groups should be especially attended to:

i. first-time parents;
ii. teenage parents;
iii. families with particular needs;
iv. families in difficult socio-economic circumstances.

In the case of separated parents, support policies should be aimed in particular at maintaining links between children and both their parents, unless this is contrary to the child's best interests. Access to professional counselling should be provided and attention should be paid to cases where the parents have different cultural backgrounds or are of different nationalities.

Public authorities should stimulate and facilitate the creation of networks of mutual assistance associations between families and make available places where parents could meet to discuss – with professionals, if necessary – on issues relating to parenting, and provide parents with adequate support services like free help lines and counselling services.

8. Parenting in situations of social exclusion

Parenting in situations of social exclusion or at risk of social exclusion can be particularly difficult and special attention should be paid to the needs of children and families in this situation, with reference in particular to the following:

i. providing long-term support, as appropriate, to help them achieve the same results as other children and families; this support should include reaching out to them in their homes or in the places they frequent, and take into consideration the possible fear of parents in a situation of social exclusion towards social services, particularly of having their children taken away;
ii. giving sufficient means to support parents and to allow them to **acquire the necessary competence to fulfil their responsibilities towards their children**;

iii. guaranteeing access to social rights (including the right to adequate income, health, education, housing and employment) and the same quality targeted services as those enjoyed by other families;
iv. ensuring that families and children suffering exclusion are considered in their social context (including the extended family, the community and their relational networks) and enjoy the same quality services, including local ones, as those enjoyed by other families, in accordance with their needs;
v. building a trustworthy relationship with the families and enabling parents to regain control of their own lives;
vi. organising training for professionals and parents together in order to achieve better mutual knowledge and understanding, to build a common project in the best interests of the child and enabling professionals to learn about what these families are experiencing and to better know their family project, with a view to focusing their practice on it;
vii. ensuring personal and collective support for professionals in order to raise their level of competence in working with people in very difficult situations and take the necessary steps to create new approaches;
viii. taking ad hoc measures to avoid the risk of marginalisation of migrant families;
ix. avoiding measures and administrative practice that stigmatise children and parents by treating them differently because their families are less well-off than others;
x. introducing measures to prevent dropout from school as an efficient means to counteract family distress.

9. Qualitative guidelines for professionals

In order for the above rights and principles to be applied, benchmarks and standards must be set. Guidelines on the focus of their services – such as the Council of Europe guidelines on positive parenting – should be given to professionals and practitioners (including those not directly involved with children but whose work could have an impact on their rights), with particular emphasis on:

i. the principle of equity and accessibility, which should underlie all action taken;
ii. the principle of becoming partners with and empowering parents. Partnership presupposes recognition of parents' own experience and their knowledge of their own children;

iii. application of the concept of partnership to co-operation and interdisciplinary co-ordination between agencies, specifying the particular areas of activity of each department, providing for a sharing of facilities and working in a cross-curricular network;
iv. ensuring that the application of comprehensive services is conceived in terms of support and assistance, encouraging family initiative without creating excessive dependency. Accordingly, strengths and resources of families should be supported. This also means that professionals should act as support for parents, in ways that are non-judgmental and non-stigmatising;
v. building up parents' self-confidence, enhancing their competencies and potential and motivating parents to be informed and trained;
vi. enabling children to communicate their feelings and needs, in particular very young children and children with communication impairments;
vii. the importance of service provision and professional practices by ensuring that the emphasis is placed on:
   - thorough training of the professionals concerned;
   - ongoing evaluation, both external and internal (self-evaluation);
   - continuity of action;
   - responses based on the understanding of the child and families in their context;
viii. devising methods to identify risk factors regarding failure to provide parental care to be disseminated among social services, health-care professionals, those dealing with young people, teachers and childcare staff to train them in identifying families with problems in this respect and offer support. A better co-ordination among the services working to support a family should constantly be sought;
ix. co-ordinating the implementation of measures to separate children from their parents, when this is necessary, with work with the family of origin (particularly in partnership with the parents) in order to enable them to prepare or better prepare for and accept this step as a means of ensuring the best interests of the child. The aim of any such measure should be the return, if possible, of the child in the family environment.

10. School and childcare environment

An integrated approach to the provision of assistance with schooling and support for parenting should be encouraged (especially where children lack stable roots or a permanent home – for example children with a Roma or Gypsy background, children of migrants); childcare and school integration as well as dialogue between these service providers and parents should be encouraged, with special attention to families in difficult situations and to those with particular needs.

11. Key messages for parents and all those having responsibilities for children and their rearing

Key messages on positive parenting should be issued to all parents and persons providing care and involved in the rearing of a child on a daily basis (such as childminders or school staff). These messages should make clear how the child is to be respected as a person and how his/her participation should be promoted, and that parents have rights as well as responsibilities. Key messages should be drawn up on the basis of consultation with all the stakeholders involved, especially parents, service providers and children, and be monitored to ensure that they are effective and are being adhered to.

12. International co-operation

Measures should be put in place to improve international co-operation and exchange of best practice in relation to parenting.

TASK/TEXT 6.2.2: EXPLANATORY REPORT [ON POLICY TO SUPPORT POSITIVE PARENTING]

***Ministers' Deputies* – CM Documents – CM(2006)194 add** 27 November 2006[48]
983 Meeting, 13 December 2006

European Committee for Social Cohesion (CDCS) – Draft recommendation Rec(2006) … of the Committee of Ministers to member states **on policy to support positive parenting – Explanatory Report** [Item to be prepared by the Rapporteur Group for Social and Health Questions (GR-SOC) at its meeting on 30 November 2006]

1. Aims and definitions

The aim of the Recommendation is to make states recognize the importance of parental responsibilities and the necessity of providing the parents with sufficient support in meeting their responsibilities in bringing up their children. The Recommendation aims to improving the quality and conditions of parenting in

[48] This document has been classified restricted at the date of issue. It was declassified at the 983rd meeting of the Ministers' Deputies (13 December 2006) (see CM/Del/Dec(2006)983/6.2).

European societies and must be seen in relation with the report "Parenting in Contemporary Europe: A positive approach,"[49] Keys for parents, Guidelines for professionals and Principles and Guidelines for providing support in parenting for families at risk of Social Exclusion.

In almost 50 years, since its first conference of Ministers responsible for Family Affairs held in Vienna in 1959, family policy has been on the agenda of the Council of Europe. The conferences have not only identified current matters of importance for families across Europe, but also addressed necessary actions to be taken.

The importance that the Council of Europe attaches to families is also reflected in the Organisation's legal instruments, (like the Convention for the Protection of Human Rights and Fundamental Freedoms, the European Social Charter and the Revised European Social Charter) and in the Revised Strategy for Social cohesion. While fully respecting the autonomy of the private sphere, the family is described as a fundamental unit in the society with the right to appropriate social, legal and economic protection to ensure its full development. The Council of Europe has been at the forefront in progressing knowledge and understanding of childhood and family life as well as in working for the improvement of the lives of vulnerable and excluded individuals.

Even though family policy is not a new topic, the content of positive parenting has not yet been put on the political agenda. There is a shift from parental authority to parental responsibility and children are nowadays seen as valuable members of society as children, not only as future adults. There is a more obvious recognition of the value of the childhood in itself. The role of the child within the family and the society is given increased attention. The Council of Europe recognises that the balance between children's rights and parental responsibility and resources needs to be further developed, and that the present situation calls for renewed attention.

Families in Europe are faced with numerous economic, social, cultural and political challenges, such as population decline and ageing, increased variety of family arrangements and the impact of new gender roles on family life and higher work participation of women. As most changes, these also carry with them positive as well as negative aspects. The present demographic trends can signify that values of duty and responsibility have been replaced by individualism and social instability, but new trends can also be seen as contributing to the democratisation of the relations between children and parents as well as between parents themselves.

[49] Council of Europe 2006. The report edited by Prof. Mary Daly [Mary Daly (ed.), *Parenting in contemporary Europe: A positive approach*, Strasbourg: Council of Europe Publishing, 2007] contains contributions from several European experts.

However, the rapid and profound social changes carry with them growing demands on the family, from the employers, the public authorities, the media as well as family members themselves. Many of these demands are historically new and those involved in parenting today need information, support and skills to enable them realise their children's and their own potential. For this and other reasons, public policy must take a pro active role in the matter of parenting and give parenthood greater prominence and better support.

Parenting is a stage of family life taking place within a precise family context with ties binding family members to each other. There is a strong 'social' component to parenting. While it is in many respects private, it is also shaped by society's understanding and expectations of appropriate parental behaviour and how the state and the public authorities frame and construct public policy. Parenting is a gendered activity in that the experiences and approaches of mothers and fathers often differ, as those of girls and boys.

Positive parenting can be described as promoting development of positive parent-child relationships and optimising the child's developmental potential.

The term 'parents' refers not only to biological parents but also to those who are involved in caring for and raising children

When dealing with the issues of supporting parents it is important to underline the complexity involved in parenting as well as in supporting parents. The United Nations Convention on the Rights of the Child as well as Council of Europe's legal instruments which have already been mentioned, give some guidance as to what should be emphasised in these important tasks. All levels of society have a role to play.

Public authorities can, in conjunction with the civil society and NGOs take action to support parents and children and improve the quality of family life, in cross-sectoral and co-ordinated approaches. It is also up to the public authorities to implement and adapt the provision of this Recommendation accordingly to the situation of their country and to deliver the message in the most appropriate – and varied – manner according to the target group.

2. Basic principles

Policies and measures in the field of support for parenting should adopt a rights-based approach, treating children and parents as holders of rights and obligations. It should be acknowledged that parents have the prime responsibility for their child, with the exception when the State has to intervene to protect the child. The diverse types of parenting and parental situations must be recognised through adopting a pluralistic approach, and the importance of an appropriate standard of living in order to ensure positive parenting must be taken into account. Parents and children should be considered as partners, and efforts should be made to ensure an equal involvement of parents. Children and young people should be guaranteed equal opportunities irrespective of their gender, status, abilities or family situation.

The policies and measures should also be long-term in order to guarantee stability and continuity of policy. Efforts should be made to avoid severe difference at local levels and to coordinate services at local and national level. Exchanges of knowledge and good practice in the field of parenting should be encouraged.

3. Core elements

Member states should consolidate and develop their support for families through the following core elements of family policy: (1) general policy measures, (2) positive parenting, (3) services to support parents, (4) services for parents at risk of social exclusion and (5) principles guiding the professionals. This support is highly important also for the implementation of positive parenting.

3.1 Policies to support families

Public authorities have a vital role to play in ensuring that all those bringing up children have access to an appropriate level and diversity of material, social, psychological and cultural resources. They should strive to remove barriers that hinder people from accessing these resources. Access to the five main social rights such as employment, housing, health, education and social protection are not dealt with in depth in this recommendation, but we must bear in mind their fundamental impact on family life. The following elements seem to be fairly common in the social policy landscape in addressing the situation of families and children directly:

- Public transfers and taxation are important to secure the living standards of families with children and enhance social security. Child benefits or family allowances are the primary form of such transfers. They exist in almost all countries, although they are universal in some countries and means-tested in others. In countries where the allowances are generous, they may contribute to considerably lower the child poverty rate. There has also been an increasing interest in exploring the experience of poverty seen from children's own perspectives. In their reports to the 28th Conference of European Ministers Responsible for Family Affairs, taking place in Lisbon in May 2006, several countries mentioned their special measures to reduce child poverty. Actions taken in order to improve the situation of single mothers are often seen as a part of fighting child poverty.

- Work-family balance is another common focus of family policy having a great impact on the quality of parenting. For this purpose, a number of measures are being put into practice, such as flexible working hours and part-time work, paid parental leaves and allowances and the right to take time off when children or other family members are ill. Some countries have also introduced a father's quota of leave – a period of family leave reserved solely for the father – in order to encourage fathers to participate more actively in the care of younger children.
- An infrastructure of child care provision is a third axis of family policy. High quality day-care is an increasing degree seen as a way of ensuring children's well-being. In its Recommendations [Rec(2002)8] on day-care, the Council of Europe describes good quality child day-care as an important contribution to social cohesion, insofar as it serves to foster the social, emotional, intellectual and physical development of all children and creates possibilities for children to make their opinions heard on matters concerning them.

Even though all countries describe ongoing activities in these areas, the gap is still wide between what governments can offer and what families and children need in order to organise their everyday life in an appropriate way.

Paid work is important from many perspectives, but there seems to be an increasing understanding of the fact that principles of care to inform policy are needed alongside principles of work. Care should not only be fitted in with the requirements of work but be seen as having value in itself. Societies need to address fundamental questions such as what people need in order to provide proper care and support for close kin and friends and for themselves.

3.2 The content of positive parenting

Today children are recognised as active, creative citizens and social actors. They are granted rights as individuals by the United Nations Convention on the Rights of the Child as well as by the legal instruments of the Council of Europe and of member states. Information about the content of positive parenting must therefore highlight children's rights. However, the rights of parents must also be given attention. Not least the entitlement to appropriate support from the state in fulfilling the parental functions. Efforts must also be made to involve fathers more in the care and upbringing of their children.

In short, 'parenting in the best interests of the child' means that parents must have the child's well-being and development as their main concern and bring up children in ways that enables them to achieve their best at home, in school, with friends and in community. Children do best when their parents are warm and supportive, spend generous amounts of time with them, understand their life and behaviour, expect them to follow rules, encourage open communication and react to misbehaviour by talking rather than with harsh punishment.

The CRC includes the child's right to protection (e.g. to be treated non-violently) and the child's right to participation (e.g. respect for the child's views). Further, parents should provide their children with:

- **Nurture – which means responding to the child's need for love, warmth and security.**
- **Structure and guidance – which implies providing the child with a sense of security and predictability, regularity and yet the necessary flexibility.**
- **Recognition – which refers to each child's need to be seen, heard and valued as a person.**
- **Empowerment – which aims to enhance the child's sense of competence and personal control.**

Corporal punishment breaches the human rights of the child, being an assault on their dignity and physical integrity. It should not be allowed in Europe according to the European Convention for the Protection of Human Rights and Fundamental Freedoms, the Revised European Social Charter (article 17) and to the CRC.

The negative effects of this punishment can be physically dangerous for the child (for instance slapping, shaken baby syndrome) and have consequences, particularly at a psychological level, which may last for life.

Promoting the use of non-violent upbringing, does not mean to encourage a permissive parenting style. Parents who are convinced that corporal punishment of children is both ineffective and humiliating for the child are finding other more efficient non-violent ways to resolve conflicts and ensure compliance with their standards of behaviour. The already mentioned report "Parenting in Contemporary Europe: a positive approach" and the Keys for parents (the latter are included in Appendix 1), provide further details about the alternatives that can be applied.

3.3 Services to support parents

While the family policy measures (described under 3.1) aim at providing the necessary material conditions for families, such as preventing poverty and reconciling work and family life, there is also a need to support the qualitative aspects of parenting and for that purpose provide parents with access to a set of services and programmes focusing on the content of the parental tasks.

Particular attention should be given to what kind of information and support parents need at the different stages of their children's lives, like first-time and teen-age parents, parents of young children and teen-agers. Families where the parents or the child are suffering from diseases, disabilities, drug addictions or other problems do also need special attention. Families in difficult socio-economic circumstances, a group where low-income, lone-parent and migrant families are over-represented, should receive measures addressing their situation.

Recent contributions provided by the member states, indicate that six main trends characterise the development of services for families and children:

- *Local centres and services* providing universal or preventive measures to inform parents about parenting and good marital practices and to offer counselling;
- *Help lines* which are another valuable way of reaching out to parents and children;
- *Educational and supporting programmes for parents,* for example during pregnancy or at different stages in the child's development;
- *Initiatives to support children's development and education,* which can be divided into three broad categories: (1) programmes directed towards children themselves to enhance their school performance and prevent school drop out, (2) programmes with parents as target group, aiming at enabling them to support their children's education, and (3) programmes focusing on the cooperation between schools and parents;
- *Services and programmes targeting populations at risk* such as health and educational services for migrant and Roma children, services for adults as well as children with disabilities, programmes for teen age parents or parents in difficult socio-economic circumstances;
- *Child protection services* which are becoming more wide-spread as well as institutions to safeguard and promote children's rights, such as *Children's Ombudsman.*

Even though these are general trends, the development of services aimed at supporting parents in their role as carers/educators of their children is a relatively recent phenomenon in many states and needs to be considerably improved. Governments and local authorities should also facilitate parents' opportunities to come together and discuss and support each other in promoting a positive and non-violent upbringing.

In the further development of services for parents two core principles should be taken into consideration: (1) the necessity of reducing the impact of risk factors and increasing the likelihood that protective factors will come into play and (2) the necessity of ensuring that parents and children are treated as agents in their own lives.

3.4 Services for parents in risk of social exclusion

The general principles outlined in this Recommendation are relevant to all parents, but supporting parents and children at risk of social exclusion is a challenging endeavour and may need some additional consideration. Sufficient means should be provided to support these parents and to allow them to acquire the necessary skills to fulfil their responsibilities (for instance through family workers, help at home, open environment educational activities, …).

A partnership between professionals and parents and their children is an essential way of working both at policy level as well as at grass-root level. Stigmatisation must be avoided so that parents and children do not feel different because they are from a family suffering from exclusion. They need to feel recognised, valued and enabled to participate fully in the activities which concern them. Material aspects such as economy, housing and medical needs must be given priority in order to enable them to parent adequately for their children, in addition to legal and psychological assistance, if needed. Professionals must reach out to adults in their homes or in the places they frequent, if necessary, and support them in accessing the appropriate services.

The contribution of informal resources, traditional networks and community solidarity to bringing up children must be encouraged. Projects which allow the involvement of parents and families in new relationship networks (family connections, supporting families, sponsorship…) must be considered as important, as well as to create places and networks that support parents to exchange opinions and experiences with other parents in similar situations.

If all children have access to high quality day-care and after school facilities, free access to education facilities as well as leisure activities, this is supportive also to children in families at risk and avoids stigmatising children with special needs. Further school curricula should be designed with a view of reducing social inequalities and school failure. Children, who do not receive enough support from their families concerning their education, should be provided with assistance.

In order to meet these needs and deal with parents and children in situation of social exclusion in a constructive way, professionals should be provided with education and training. The Principles and Guidelines for providing support in parenting for families at risk of Social Exclusion develop these aspects.

3.5 Guidelines for professionals

In order to strengthen parental skills, professionals are recommended to focus on understanding the developmental needs of the child, the responsibilities and capacities of their parents to respond to these needs, the relationships and interactions between family members and the needs of the family as a basic unit of society. The child should be the focus of their work and the child's rights and needs should be given priority.

Parents want to be treated with respect for their life experiences and to take on roles as subjects and contributors and not only as objects and recipients. For instances, schools should enhance a positive communication with children as well as parents and ensure that their views are taken into account.

Professionals should play a critical role in facilitating parents understanding of child development and assisting them to use this information to parent their children. This requires that each professional maintain their professional knowledge base so that they are able to assist parents.

Professionals further play a vital role in facilitating parents' access to services – informing parents about services is not sufficient. They should speak "with" parents not 'to' them. A range of programmes needs to be provided which are sufficiently broad and flexible to be applicable across the cultural spectrum in each community. Each programme should take efforts to be non-judgemental and non-stigmatising, to avoid creating dependency by parents on professionals and to develop these programmes from the bottom-up in order to positively address the parents' issues and the context in which they are parenting their children. Services should be multifocused and flexible in order to deal with the uniqueness of each family and the complexity of the problems that they face. It is further important that programmes are inclusive of ethnic and other minority ethnic groups and that procedures for evaluating its effectiveness are integrated into each programme.

In order to support professionals in this task it is important that each service provider operates on the principle that its staff will be partners with parents and empower them so that they are able to bring up their children successfully. Guidelines for professionals in Appendix 2 provide further details.

APPENDIX 1 – KEY MESSAGES FOR PARENTS: 'GROWING UP TOGETHER'

Today's children are living in a different world from the one in which their mothers and fathers grew up. This presents parents with some challenges both to reconsider and in some situations to relearn how to bring up their children. This leaflet is intended to provide parents with guidance in understanding their responsibilities as parents in the 21st century. It is based on a Council of Europe report 'Positive parenting in contemporary Europe' published in 2006.

Parenting is about learning to cooperate, through give and take between the child and the parent and about making sure parents respect their child's and their own integrity. We know that some parental behaviours are good for children. They, just like the adults, cooperate best with people who treat them with kindness, respect, understanding and recognition that they also are individuals.

View of the child and the role of parents

Today, children are seen as persons with their own rights, not as their parents' property. Children are competent and capable, but do also need protection and guidance in order to enjoy their childhood and become adults who can function well in society. It is considered as the most important that parents are able to provide their children with the following:

- *Basic care*
  Making sure that the child's physical needs are met, for example for food, warmth, shelter, hygiene, appropriate clothing and medical care;
- *Ensuring safety*
  Ensuring that the child is safe by protecting him or her from harm or danger both in the home and outside it;
- *Emotional warmth*
  Ensuring that the child receives emotional support and feels valued;
- *Stimulation*
  Stimulating the child's learning and intellectual development through talking with the child, encouraging and joining the child's play, and promoting his or her educational opportunities;
- *Guidance and boundaries*
  Providing guidance and boundaries and showing the child how to behave appropriately;
- *Stability*
  Consistently providing emotional warmth, responding to the child and ensuring he or she has contact with people who are important to him or her.

The UN Convention of the Rights of the Child (CRC) – a tool for children and parents

The Council of Europe is promoting the rights of the child (Convention for the Protection of Human Rights and Fundamental Freedoms and the European Social Charter and the revised European Social Charter) and do fully comply with the obligations of the United Nations Convention on the Rights of the Child (CRC), to which all its member States are parties.

The CRC:

- Sees the child as a subject of rights and sets standards for states i.e. countries, about the rights that they should assure to all children aged under 18 years.

Some obligations fall directly on states, while others are addressed to the child's parents or legal guardians;

- Allocates to parents or the child's legal guardian the primary responsibility for the upbringing and development of their child, and states that the best interests of the child should be their main concern. This means that in parenting parents need to have their child's well-being and development as their priority.
- Requires states to recognize the responsibilities of parents and to support parents bringing up their children.
- Requires states to intervene to protect the child if you neglect or abuse him or her.

The CRC and the vision of parenting
The CRC includes the child's right to protection (e.g. to be treated non-violently) and the child's right to participation (e.g. respect for the child's views). It also emphasises the importance of each child achieving his or her developmental potential, i.e. doing as well as he or she can, and recognises that children develop over time and have different needs at different stages in their life. The different aspects of the CRC mean that parents should provide their children with nurture, structure and recognise them as people in their own right and empower them to act as individuals.

Positive Parenting includes the following parental behaviours and values:

– *Nurturing behaviour* means responding to the child's need for love and security. The child needs acceptance, sensitivity, responsiveness, involvement and support. The parent can show the child affection and joy, comfort him or her when in distress, talk about what he or she is concerned with, maintain a positive emotional tone in the home as well as providing basic care and safety. This enables the child to explore the world and come back to the parents when he or she feels anxious or distressed.

– *Structure and guidance* provides the child with a sense of security and predictability. It helps the child to accept responsibility for his or her own behaviour, become aware of the needs of others and develop self-control. To achieve this, the parent needs to help the child to understand what the standards are, set reasonable and appropriate limits and take account of the child's views and reactions. The parent also needs to have an orderly (but not rigid) schedule to each day with regular times and patterns for family activities It is important to be flexible, and to talk and negotiate with your child as she or he grows older.

– *Recognition* refers to each child's need to be seen, heard and valued as a person. It requires the parents to show an interest in their child's daily experiences as well as listening to him or her, trying to understand his or her point of view and helping him or her to express feelings. It also means allowing the child to have a say and to play an active part in your family's life and decision-making.

– *Empowerment* refers to enhancing your child's sense of competence, of personal control and ability to affect the attitudes and behaviours of others. Parents can focus on the child's strengths and express belief in his or her potential. Further parents can create opportunities for him or her to learn, have new experiences and social relationships. All children have times when they are more grown up, and others when they go back to behaving as a younger child. During these times it is important for parents to support the child and help him or her to grow into the next stage of development.

In short, "parenting in the best interests of the child" means bringing up children in ways that mean they achieve their best at home, in school, with friends and in your community. We know that children do best when their mothers and fathers are warm and supportive, spend generous amounts of time with them, understand their life and behaviour, expect them to follow rules, encourage open communication and react to misbehaviour by talking rather than with harsh punishment.

Reasons for a non-violent upbringing of children

Corporal punishment breaches the human rights of the child victim, being an assault on their dignity and physical integrity. It is not allowed in Europe according the Convention for the Protection of Human Rights and Fundamental Freedoms and article 17 of the revised European Social Charter.

Still, some parents believe that corporal punishment (i.e. hitting children with the hand or an implement such as a stick or a belt) is an effective way of getting children to do what they are told. Although these children may do what you want them to at that moment in time, the negative effects of this punishment may last for life.

We know children who have experienced corporal punishment tend to have:

- poorer mental health (e.g. less self-confidence, more depression),
- poorer relationships with their parents (i.e. violence does not teach them to respect their parents but to fear them, and it pushes children towards resisting and retaliating towards their parents, and/or withdrawing from them)
- less developed self-control and weaker moral standards (i.e. violence does not teach children the reasons for or ways of behaving correctly.)

- increased aggression and anti-social behaviour (i.e. corporal punishment gives children the impression that aggression might be normal, acceptable and effective).

We also know that adults who experienced corporal punishment as children tend to have more mental health problems and higher levels of criminal and antisocial behaviour, including family violence than adults who did not experience corporal punishment as children.

Corporal punishment is, however, not the only behaviour having a severe impact on children's health. It is also important to avoid other degrading or humiliating behaviour towards children including ridiculing, making your child feel worthless, unloved or inadequate and causing the child to frequently feel frightened.

Practical guidelines for a non-violent upbringing

Bringing up children in a non-violent way is far from encouraging a permissive parenting style. Parents who are convinced that corporal punishment of children is both ineffective and humiliating for the child are finding other ways to resolve conflicts and ensure compliance with their standards of behaviour.

Non-violent ways of responding to your child's erroneous, hurtful, dangerous or antisocial behaviour can include:

- with younger children – using distraction; making jokes; calming your child down by finding alternative ways of doing something together; hugging and getting him or her to listen and point out what is wrong; taking a break from the situation and discussing it later when emotions have subsided; time-out;
- with older children – having a firm talk about behaviours parents do not want to see, having the child, eventually together with the parent, repair any damage she or he may have caused and make amends for any wrongdoing, or restricting privileges (e.g. watching TV, or meeting friends).

In these situations it is always important to avoid insulting the child's sense of self and his or her dignity – it is the undesirable behaviour that should be disapproved of, not the child. The parent should also think about the child's capacity to understand and follow the rules, the circumstances and the seriousness of the behaviour. When setting limits, the parent should consider what is right for the child in view of it's age and stage of development, and think about the reasons for setting them.

A lot of parents find they can avoid coercing their children if they have engaged in sensitive, mutually respectful and rewarding relationships with them from birth. The key to be effective in teaching children to regulate their own behaviours is establishing mutual respect and expecting cooperation from the child from a young age. Children respond to respect and positive expectations. This means that parents should expect good behaviour and focus on it rather than poor behaviour, and make sure the child understands what is expected of her/him and is capable of doing it.

In order to help children learn positive behaviours, parents can:

- Provide regular positive attention and communicate this to the child no matter what their age. As the child grows older this includes being aware of and interested in peer relationships and their school performance;
- Listen carefully to their children and help them express their feelings;
- Help them to understand the potential consequences of their choices;
- Encourage their emerging desirable behaviours by providing attention and praise, and ignoring minor undesirable behaviours;
- Behave as parents want their child to behave, communicate with him/her in a respectful manner, and demonstrate how to resolve conflicts (constructively).

Supporting desirable behaviours and reducing undesirable ones is best done by parents who are respected by their children. This requires that parents recognise and acknowledge that they also make mistakes, whilst taking responsibility for their parenting behaviour and the quality of the relationship with their child (rather than blaming the child).

Resources for parenting

All parents want to be a good mother or a good father to their child. This is sometimes difficult to achieve. Parenting, besides being a joyous and pleasurable experience, can also be a stressful one.

Many parents divide their time and energy between different commitments (e.g. employment, caring for children, caring for elderly family members). Time with children is very precious – it passes quickly and will not come back. Positive parenting does require time to enable parents and children to be together. Whilst this is especially important in the earliest years of the child's life, we should not forget that teenagers also need their parents to be available to them.

It is also vital that parents find time to take care of themselves as adults, to pay attention to their own needs for intimacy, companionship and recreation. In order to be able to parent effectively, to provide contact, support and guidance to children, parents need resources and support.

Parents can learn a great deal from discussing their experiences with other parents, friends and family. Parents can also use professional services that directly (e.g. parenting education) and indirectly (e.g. couple therapy) support them in their parenting role. Asking for help is a sign of responsibility, not of weakness.

REMEMBER THAT PARENTS ARE REALLY IMPORTANT TO THEIR CHILDREN, NO MATTER HOW YOUNG OR OLD THEY ARE! (...)

APPENDIX 2 – GUIDELINES FOR PROFESSIONALS

THE ROLES AND RESPONSIBILITIES OF PROFESSIONALS

1. Introduction

This document is intended for all professionals who are working with children and families, or with adults who have parenting responsibilities for children aged under 18 years. Its purpose is to provide professionals with guidelines on how to support positive parenting. Positive parenting is defined as parental behaviour and values, based on the best interests of the child, which involves setting boundaries using non-violent methods to enable each child to achieve their full developmental potential.

In order to strengthen parental skills, professionals are recommended to focus on understanding the developmental needs of the child, the responsibilities and capacities of their parents to respond to these needs, the relationships and interactions between family members and the needs of the family as a basic unit of society. The child should be the focus of interventions – the child's rights and needs as embodied in the United Nations Convention of the Rights of the Child (CRC) and in Council of Europe main legal instruments (like the Convention for the Protection of Human Rights and Fundamental Freedoms, European Social Charter and the revised European Social Charter).

Information about the developmental needs of the child and the responsibilities of parents is set out in section 2, whilst section 3 contains guidelines for professionals when working with parents. An interdisciplinary approach of the work of services is particularly important and their "compartmentilisation" should be avoided or broken.

In order to support professionals in this task it is important that each service provider operates on the principle that its staff will be partners with parents and empower them in exercising their parental responsibilities and capacities. This means service providers' policies on positive parenting should include the following four core components:

- Promotion of parental learning about how to parent their children in a positive way, to enhance that each child's developmental potential is reached

- Provision of support for parents to enable them to undertake their roles and responsibilities to the best of their capacities, and
- Where appropriate, facilitating and encouraging changes in parental behaviour, so that their behaviour enhances the developmental outcomes of their children.

Managers/administrators who consider the three core components of positive parenting set out above to be part of the professional roles and responsibilities of their employees will play an important role in enabling their staff to support mothers and fathers in bringing up their children.

2. Keys for parents: children's needs and parental responsibilities

I. The Child focus: the child as a subject of rights

The rights defined in the CRC include the right to protection and the right to participation. To this should be added the emphasis given to the child's development i.e. supporting the evolving capacities of the child. Good parenting in line with these basic CRC principles, together with established knowledge through research, includes:

Providing a safe environment and meeting the child's basic needs, including those for shelter, food, water and medical and dental care.

Nurturing behaviour that responds to the child's need for emotional nourishment, security, belonging and secure attachment. The parents should meet the child needs for warmth, acceptance, sensitivity, responsiveness, involvement and support.

Structure which refers to setting out and adhering to standards of appropriate and inappropriate behaviour and role models provided by parents. Each child's needs limits and guidance for his or her physical and psychological security, and the development of his or her own values and sense of personal and social responsibility.

Recognition which refers to the child's need to be acknowledged and have his/her personal experiences responded to and confirmed by his/her parents. Acknowledging and respecting the child's experience and views contributes to enhancing the child's personal development to its full potential.

Empowerment refers to combining a sense of personal control and self-discipline with the ability to affect the attitudes and behaviours of others. It implies a focus on enhancing existing strengths in a child, and reflects a belief that power can be generated and regenerated. Thus parents should respect the evolving capacity of a child by accommodating to their behaviour and ideas through involvement and discussion.

II. Parental responsibilities

The CRC emphasizes that parents should be supported in exercising their responsibilities towards their children. Parents should be able to:

- provide their children with basic care such as providing for their physical needs and appropriate medical and dental care, including nutrition, warmth, shelter and clothing;
- ensure their safety by protecting the child from harm in the home or elsewhere;
- ensure the child's emotional needs are met, the child has a positive sense of being specially valued and a positive sense of his or her own ethnic and cultural identity;
- stimulate the child by promoting learning and intellectual development through encouragement, cognitive stimulation and promoting social opportunities;
- provide guidance and boundaries, enabling the child to regulate their own emotions and behaviour using non-violent methods; and
- provide the child with a stable family environment which enables the child to maintain a secure attachment to their primary caregiver(s).

In terms of the resources needed for parenting, they can usefully be thought of in terms of three levels or sources:

- Internal to the parent – such as using their knowledge and skills (for example, of child development), and having good physical/mental health and problem solving skills;
- Internal to the family – models of good parenting, inter-personal household relationships;
- External to the household – support from wider family and friends, neighbourhood, community, economic resources, employment, welfare, child-care, education.

III. Parental capacities

Resources internal to the parent can be enhanced by empowering parental capacities, i.e. by educational measures. The following issues should be addressed:

- The child's uniqueness and changing developmental needs from early childhood to adolescence;
- The importance of attachment to a primary caregiver in the child's development;

- Parent's self confidence and skills in utilizing positive parent management strategies;
- Competence in enhancing children's pro-social skills;
- Limit setting techniques used in non-violent ways;
- Understanding the significance of the child's spirituality and moral development;
- The parent's self care as a prerequisite for managing the demands of life, interpersonal
  relationships and understanding the lives of each person within the family;
- The factors that impair parenting capacities, such as domestic violence, substance abuse and other mental health issues, disorganized lifestyles, emotional problems, critical attitudes and insensitivity towards children's needs.

IV. Interpersonal relationships

The quality of interpersonal relationships within the family is a basic resource for healthy parenting. The following aspects are of special significance:

- The significance of parental respect for the child, and sensitivity and responsiveness to his or her needs;
- Behaving with dignity, talking to and involving the child and providing adult leadership;
- The quality of relationships between adults who have parenting responsibilities, irrespective of the configuration of the family;
- The quality of the relationships between siblings and other children in the household;
- The importance of non-violent conflict solving and methods of discipline in the family.

V. The extended family and informal support systems

The extended family and informal social networks can be valuable resources for parents and children. Work with children and families should, wherever possible, seek to identify:

- The quality of relationships with members of the extended family or in the neighbourhood or community;
- The extent to which family, friends and the local community support both the parents and child;
- The significance and quality of relationships between the child and his or her peer group.

3. Guidelines for professionals

I. Principles underpinning professionals work with children and families

The role of professional should be underpinned by clear values, ethics, knowledge and skills. The following are significant when working to enhance and support positive parenting:

- Building trust based on empathy and respect for the human dignity of all members of the family and significant others;
- All interventions and their outcomes are child focused having addressed the rights, developmental needs and uniqueness of each child
- The language and approach used is user friendly and supportive;
- The principles of equity and accessibility underpin all interventions;
- Professionals and parents work together collaboratively so that parents are empowered to bring up their children.
- A comprehensive and interdisciplinary approach is taken when working with children and families
- The strengths of parents, actual and potential, are identified and built on when intervening in family life in order to maximise their capacities;
- Parents capacities are not judged on the basis of one harmful event, but in any case the safety of the child is the primary concern and should not be compromised;
- Professional advice is addressed to both mothers and father or other caregivers of both genders. The importance of the father's parenting role is recognized.
- The provision of services which are responsive to the diverse needs of parents from minority ethnic groups.

II. Facilitating access to services

In facilitating access to services, professionals assume an active role in identifying and providing parents with access to the types of support and services necessary to enhance their parental capacity to bring up their children, starting with the least interventionist type of service being offered first:

- informal support (i.e. strengthening parents' existing social bonds and encouraging new links with family, friends, neighbours, and other people based locally),
- semi-formal support (i.e. empowering parents' (including through the use of advocates) and children's NGOs and activating a range of self-help and other community-based groups and services), and then
- formal support (i.e. professional services)

It is further important that professionals:

- ensure that parents are in receipt of their "state" benefits, for example, finance, or other entitlements i.e. they have access to their social rights;
- where necessary, appoint an advocate for parent;
- give priority to services that have been evaluated with appropriate methods and demonstrated to be effective at achieving the goals of positive parenting.

III. Parental Programmes

Parental programmes can have different goals and characteristics. The range of programmes provided should be sufficiently broad and flexible to be applicable across the cultural spectrum in each community. Categories of parental programmes include those:

- designed to meet parents' needs and interest for general knowledge on the roles of parents and how to bring up children so that they achieve their developmental potential;
- addressing specific issues which parents may have to address with their children such as anti-social behaviour, preventing substance abuse and enhancing self confidence;
- focusing on targeted groups of parents or of children with special needs. These may include single parents, separated parents, socially excluded and vulnerable parents, parents or children with disabilities or age specific programmes.

IV. Recommended delivery of parenting programmes

When providing parental programmes to support positive parenting, professionals should aim to:

- Have a primary focus on the principle of the "best interests of the child" and on achieving the best developmental outcomes for each child;
- Be relevant to the needs of children, parents and families;
- Be non-judgmental and non-stigmatising;
- Avoid creating dependency by parents on professionals;
- Address the complexity of family life and be responsive to the needs of each child and family;
- Be sensitive to the local community context;
- Develop these programmes from the bottom-up in order to positively address the parents' issues and the context in which they are parenting their children;

- Recognise the importance of families sharing experiences with each other and the role of self-help groups;
- Be inclusive of ethnic and other minority groups;
- Integrate into each programme appropriate procedures for evaluating its effectiveness.

V. Providing information on and facilitating understanding of positive parenting

Professional knowledge and skills should be applied and developed in a dynamic manner, in particular in the following areas:

- Be able to help both parents understand children's development and support them in their parenting roles;
- Providing fathers and mothers with information on children's rights;
- Facilitating an understanding of the consequences of children's rights not being upheld.

VI. Professional knowledge

It is the responsibility of each professional to:

- know which organisation/agency has a responsibility to provide which types of services, and which has specific statutory duties;
- keep up to date with knowledge on child development and how to support positive parenting and use this knowledge in their work
- be skilled in working with both mothers and fathers as well as children and families;
- be knowledgeable about the CRC and the Council of Europe's respective parenting policies, and understand the implications for practice;
- create 'space' to be able to reflect on their work and its impact on children and parents, as well as on the developmental outcomes of children in receipt of their services;
- evaluate their own practice, including by the use of peer evaluation and feedback from children and parents.

TASK/TEXT 6.3: COUNCIL OF EUROPE CONFERENCE OF MINISTERS RESPONSIBLE FOR FAMILY AFFAIRS

<www.coe.int/t/dg3/youthfamily/MinisterialConf_June2009/default_en.asp> (accessed 4 August 2009), Conference 16–17 June 2009, Vienna (Austria), 29th Session, Final communiqué

1. The 29th Session of the Council of Europe Conference of Ministers responsible for Family Affairs was held in Vienna on 16 and 17 June 2009 on the invitation of the Austrian government.
2. The Conference was opened by Ms Maud de Boer-Buquicchio, Deputy Secretary General of the Council of Europe and Mr Heinz Fischer, Federal President of the Republic of Austria.
3. The Conference elected Ms Christine Marek, State Secretary of Family and Youth (Austria) as chair and Ms Lotte Grepp Knutsen, State Secretary for Children and Equality (Norway) as vice-chair of the Conference.
4. The Conference was attended by Ministers, or their representatives, of the Council of Europe member and observer states. Participants also included representatives of Council of Europe bodies and institutions (Committee of Ministers, Parliamentary Assembly, Congress of Local and Regional Authorities, Conference of INGOs and various committees), international organisations, NGOs and independent experts.
5. The theme of the Conference was "Public policies supporting the wish to have children: societal, economic and personal factors."
6. The Conference was divided into two sub-themes:
   a.) Why many Europeans have fewer children than they actually want: Societal and economic factors.
   b.) Family-friendly policies: measures for an optimal framework.
7. At the closure of the Conference, the Ministers and other participants expressed their gratitude to the Austrian authorities for the hospitality and excellent organisation of the event.
8. Following their discussions, the Ministers adopted the following conclusions:

We, the Ministers of the Council of Europe member states responsible for family affairs,

RECALLING

1. The Convention for the Protection of Human Rights and Fundamental Freedoms [ECHR], which guarantees the right to respect for private and family life;
2. The European Social Charter (revised), which states that the family as a fundamental unit of society has the right to appropriate social, legal and economic protection to ensure its full development;
3. The United Nations Convention on the Rights of the Child and in particular its preamble stating that the family, as the fundamental group of society and the natural environment for the growth and well-being of all its members,

should be afforded the necessary protection so that it can fully assume its responsibilities within the community;

4. The Warsaw Summit Action Plan, in which the Heads of State and Government of the Council of Europe renewed their commitment to social cohesion and children's rights;
5. The Political Declaration of the 28th Session of the Conference of European Ministers responsible for Family Affairs (Lisbon, 16–17 May 2006) and the undertakings therein;
6. The Final Declaration of the 1st Council of Europe Conference of Ministers responsible for Social Cohesion (Moscow, 26–27 February 2009), which underlined the important role of the family for building confidence in the future and developing viable life projects, while stressing the need to reconcile private and working life;

7. The various Council of Europe legal standards relevant to the domains of family policy, children's rights and family law and the importance of promoting their implementation.

RECOGNISING THAT

1. The wish for a child is often postponed or remains unfulfilled because of unfavourable social and economic circumstances, which should be targeted by a cross-cutting family policies approach;
2. All couples and individuals have the right to decide **freely and responsibly** on the number, spacing and timing of their children, to **have the information and means to do so** and to be free of discrimination;
3. The legitimate concern about low birth rates must not eclipse the fact that **children are holders of human rights and not objects of adults' wishes.** Thus all policies in this area must be informed of children's rights standards and fully integrate the principle of the best interest of the child;
4. Family today means a variety of living arrangements and children in Europe are growing up in different family forms. These may vary from one country to another and change during the child's life course;
5. Despite the progress achieved in promoting **balanced participation of women and men in work and family life**, women remain chiefly responsible for child rearing and caring for dependents. The current demographic challenges, however, cannot be properly addressed without integrating the dimension of **gender equality** in all measures adopted;
6. Many young women and men experience difficulties in establishing job security, reconciling work and family life and affording adequate housing,

which might constitute an obstacle for them when planning to form a family of their own;
7. Childlessness is not always voluntary and an unfulfilled wish for a child may be a painful situation that deserves attention by policy makers;
8. Adoption is sometimes seen as a way to fulfil one's wish for a child. However, **adoption is first and foremost a service for children** and **the rights and the best interest of the child, and not the wishes of adoptive parents, must be the paramount consideration** in all decisions relating to adoption;
9. Family policy today requires a coherent and integrated approach by member states that derives from co-ordinated policy measures developed by local, regional and national authorities, social partners and non-governmental organisations;
10. The Council of Europe has a unique place that allows it to bring together the various aspects of family policy and the potential to develop holistic policies in this field based on human rights, including **children's rights as well as gender equality**, and the promotion of **social cohesion**.

AGREE AND UNDERTAKE

To work together in supporting the wish to have children in accordance with the principles and policy measures set out below.

I. Family-friendly societies and children's rights
Ensure that respect for children's rights and the child's best interest inform all policies and decisions affecting children. In particular, **children's rights to family life and to grow up in a safe, supportive and non-violent environment** should be guaranteed, notably by:

1. Providing the appropriate **material, social, psychological and cultural resources that families with children need** to fulfil their functions, thereby paying particular attention to families in difficult social or economic circumstances, families with children with disabilities, families with many children, single parent families and families with underage parents;
2. Recognising the importance of parental responsibilities and providing parents with the necessary support in **practising positive parenting as a means of ensuring respect for children's rights**;
3. Encouraging family and child friendly living environments in local communities and respecting the needs of children in urban planning;
4. Ensuring that the child's best interest is the paramount consideration in all decisions relating to adoption. Member states are encouraged to ratify and implement the ***Council of Europe Convention on the Adoption of Children***

(revised) [2008] applicable to national adoption as well as the Hague Convention on Protection of Children and Co-operation in Respect of Intercountry Adoption.

II. Equality between women and men
Ensure gender equality as an integral part of human rights and as a prerequisite to sustainable family policy, in particular by:

1. Adopting measures aimed at promoting participation and combating discrimination of women and in particular women with children in the labour market;
2. Consider creating **equal possibilities for both parents to obtain parental leave** and encourage fathers to take up paternity / parental leave, for instance through the introduction of a period of **non-transferable parental leave for each parent**;
3. Encouraging the equal sharing of parental and other family responsibilities between women and men;
4. Integrating a gender equality perspective in all policies at all levels, including in the budgetary process, in order to take into account the needs and interests of both women and men.

III. Reconciliation of work and family life
Create favourable conditions for parents to reconcile work and family life, in particular by:

1. Creating conditions for accessible, affordable and **quality early childhood education and care services** and allowing for freedom of choice between different forms of childcare, based on the best interest of the child;
2. Adjusting, where existing, leave policies to care for children and other dependants to reflect as far as is possible the needs and wishes of families and children, and taking the employers' concerns into account;
3. Promoting with employers the need for, and benefits of, a family friendly work culture and policies that allow both women and men to reconcile professional and family life.

IV. Support for young women and men
Remove, where appropriate, social and economic obstacles for young people, who wish to start a family of their own, in particular by:

1. Providing advice and support to young people in their transition from education to the labour market and ensuring that they have equal access to work;
2. Consider the needs of young people for decent housing;
3. Creating the necessary conditions to enable young parents to pursue education and combine this with bringing up their children; for example, by facilitating access to childcare, while having policies to reduce teenage parenthood.

V. Family policy and the unfulfilled wish to have children

Be attentive to the painful situation of persons having an unfulfilled wish for a child, in particular by:

1. Providing social and psychological support to persons who are in distress due to involuntary childlessness;
2. Informing prospective adopters about the impact of adoption on their lives and providing the necessary regulations and procedures to secure that the paramount consideration in all adoption-related decisions is the best interest of the child.

VI. Coherent and integrated family policies

Regard family policies as a cross-cutting issue and promote mainstreaming of family and children's perspectives throughout national policies, in particular by:

1. Ensuring inter-sectoral and inter-ministerial co-ordination in all public policies that have an impact on families;
2. Fostering co-ordination and co-operation between the national, regional and local levels;
3. Actively promoting the participation of social partners, non-governmental organisations, parents and children in the policy making process.

RECOMMEND

To the Committee of Ministers of the Council of Europe to:

1. Continue to promote the implementation by member states of the Council of Europe standards related to family policies and family law, in particular in the fields of reconciliation of work and family life, rights of children without parental care, gender equality and adoption;
2. Continue giving a high priority to promoting children's rights and mainstreaming its children's rights approach in all family policies;

3. Consider the feasibility of setting standards related to the rights and legal status of children being brought up in various forms of family settings, taking national legislation into account;
4. Consider the feasibility of developing initiatives that promote a philosophy of family friendliness among enterprises and other workplaces;
5. Continue to promote among member states **policies to support positive parenting**, good childhood, as well as the **abolition of corporal punishment of children.**

TASK/TEXT 6.4: COMMISSION OF THE EUROPEAN COMMUNITIES – IMPROVING THE MENTAL HEALTH OF THE POPULATION

Excerpts from Commission of the European Communities, *Green Paper: Improving the mental health of the population. Towards a strategy on mental health for the European Union*, Brussels, 14 October 2005, COM(2005) 484 final (<europa.eu.int/comm/health/ph_determinants/life_ style/mental/green_paper/mental_gp_en.pdf>)

Mental ill health affects every fourth citizen and can lead to suicide, a cause of too many deaths. Mental ill health causes significant losses and burdens to the economic, social, educational as well as criminal and justice systems (…). There is no health without mental health. For *citizens*, mental health is a resource which enables them to realise their intellectual and emotional potential and to find and fulfil their roles in social, school and working life. For *societies*, good mental health of citizens contributes to prosperity, solidarity and social justice. In contrast, mental ill health imposes manifold costs, losses and burdens on citizens and societal systems.

Mental health, mental ill health and its determinants:
The WHO describes *mental health* as: 'a state of well-being in which the individual realizes his or her abilities, can cope with the normal stresses of life, can work productively and fruitfully, and is able to make a contribution to his or her community' (WHO, *Strengthening mental health promotion*, Geneva 2001 (Fact sheet no. 220).

Mental ill health includes mental health problems and strain, impaired functioning associated with distress, symptoms, and diagnosable mental disorders, such as schizophrenia and depression.

The mental condition of people is determined by a *multiplicity of factors* (...), including biological (*e.g.*, genetics, gender), individual (*e.g.*, personal experiences), family and social (*e.g.*, social support) and economic and environmental (*e.g.*, social status and living conditions).

The health dimension
More than 27% of adult Europeans are estimated to experience at least one form of mental ill health during any one year (...).

The most common forms of mental ill health in the EU are anxiety disorders and depression. By the year 2020, depression is expected to be the highest ranking cause of disease in the developed world. Currently, in the EU, some 58,000 citizens die from suicide every year (...), more than the annual deaths from road traffic accidents, homicide, or HIV/AIDS. (...)

The impact on prosperity, solidarity and social justice
The implications of mental ill health are manifold:

Mental ill health costs the EU an estimated 3%-4% of GDP, mainly through lost productivity. Mental disorders are a leading cause of early retirement and disability pensions.

Conduct and behavioural disorders in childhood incur costs for the social, educational as well as criminal and justice systems (...).

Further intangible costs concern how society treats mentally ill and disabled persons. Despite improved treatment options and positive developments in psychiatric care, people with mental ill health or disability still experience social exclusion, stigmatisation, discrimination or the non-respect of their fundamental rights and dignity. (...)

Promoting mental health and addressing mental ill health through preventive action
Promotion of mental health and prevention of mental ill health address individual, family, community and social determinants of mental health, by strengthening protective factors (*e.g.*, resilience) and reducing risk factors (...).

Risk factors: access to drugs and alcohol; displacement; isolation and alienation; lack of education, transport, housing; neighbourhood disorganisation; peer rejection; poor social circumstances; poor nutrition; poverty; racial injustice and discrimination; social disadvantage; urbanisation; violence and delinquency; war; work stress; unemployment.

Protective factors: empowerment; ethnic minorities integration; positive interpersonal interactions; social participation; social responsibility and tolerance; social services; social support and community networks.

(WHO: *Prevention of Mental Disorders. Effective Interventions and Policy Options, Summary Report*, Geneva 2004, 21.)

Building mental health in infants, children and adolescents
As mental health is strongly determined during the first years of life, promoting mental health in children and adolescents is an investment for the future. Teaching parenting skills can improve child development. A holistic school approach can increase social competencies, improve resilience, and reduce bullying, anxiety and depressive symptoms.

Some successful actions identified through EU-projects:
Babies and children: address postnatal depression in mothers; improve parenting skills; home visits of nurses to assist future and new parents; interventions of nurses at school.

Adolescents and young people: conducive school environment and ethos; resource packs on mental health for students, parents and teachers.

Targeting vulnerable groups in society
Low social and economic status increases vulnerability for mental ill health. Job loss and not being in employment can lower self-esteem and lead to depression. Migrants and other marginalised groups are at increased risk for mental ill health. Interventions for the unemployed to re-enter the labour market can be cost effective. Support to vulnerable groups can improve mental health, strengthen social cohesion, and avoid associated social and economic burdens.

Some successful actions identified through EU-projects:
Counselling for groups at risk; support to enter the labour market; supported employment for those with mental ill health or disability.

TASK/TEXT 6.5: THE ROLE OF PARENTS AND THE SUPPORT FROM THE GOVERNMENTS IN THE EU

Anna Buia (ed.), *Survey on the role of parents and the support from the Governments in the EU*, European Network of National Observatories on Childhood, Florence: ChildONEurope Secretariat, October 2007, <www.childoneurope.org/events/pdf/reportSurveyRoleParents.pdf>, pp. 11 *i.f.*-13, 17–21, 22–24, 34–35, 38, 42–44

Council of Europe
(…) [A] particularly important initiative of the [Council of Europe] that added new elements of discussion to the current debate on [the] issue of socio-pedagogical support to parents though parental education programmes and/or counselling is without doubt the [Council of Europe] Recommendation (2006)19 on positive parenting adopted by the Committee of Ministers on 13th December 2006. Recommendation (2006)19 defines "parenting" as "all the roles falling to parents in order to care for and bring up children" (…) [T]here is an evident shift in the definition, more focused on the relationship between parents and their children (…). This seems to suggest that parenting needs to be considered as the interaction between parents and children, promoting an approach that entails rights and duties for the child's development and selffulfilment. For the first time, Rec (2006)19 also provides the definition of "positive parenting," considered as the parental behaviour ensuring the fulfilment of the best interests of the child "that is nurturing, empowering, non-violent and provides recognition and guidance which involves setting of boundaries to enable the full development of the child."

This recommendation underlines the importance to children of growing up in a positive family environment and the State's responsibility to create the right conditions for positive parenting is also emphasised, whereas the family is considered as the primary unit of society and parenting has an essential role for the future of the society. It encourages an integrated (united) approach, in the process of creating the necessary conditions for positive parenting in the best interest of the child, including cooperative action between the public authorities, the economic and social sectors and civil society. As a consequence of the Final Communiqué and Political Declaration of the European Ministers responsible for the family adopted at their 28th session in Lisbon (Portugal) in 2006, the Recommendation (2006)19 considers the "creation of the right conditions" as the ensuring of access to appropriate **material, psychological, social and cultural resources**; taking steps to remove barriers to positive parenting, such as policies to promote a better reconciliation of family and working life; and importantly, raising awareness of the value of positive parenting, to parents, children and the state.

The national programmes and policies suggested need to be adopted with the intention to achieve three main objectives:

a) facilitate access to appropriate and variegated material, psychological, social and cultural resources for all of those rearing children;
b) remove all the existing obstacles to positive parenting;
c) promote positive parenting through awareness raising actions.

In particular for the third objective, the public authorities are invited to promote initiatives aiming to make people aware of the value and importance of positive parenting and take a pro-active approach to promoting awareness of parenting issues and to normalising participation in parenting programmes. It recommends the adoption of an empowerment approach – based on consultation and dialogue with parents and on their voluntary involvement and **participation** in the spirit of a working partnership. These should be geared towards providing support on three levels:

a) *informal*: creating and strengthening existing social bonds and encouraging new links; between parents and their family, neighbours and friends;
b) *semi-formal:* empowering parents' and children's associations and NGOs and activating a range of self-help and other community-based groups and services;
c) *formal:* facilitating access to public services.

Fulfilling the provisions and spirit of the CRC, the Recommendation promotes the development of positive parent-child relationships, based on the exercise of parental responsibility to optimise the child's potential development, rather than the exercise of parental authority. It recognises **both parents and children as holders of rights**, confirming the parents' role as **guardians of their children's rights**, whereas the **State is considered as a final guarantor** with the responsibility of supporting (...) the positive parenting exercise. Thus, the Recommendation invites States to adopt public policies on parenting support incorporating childhood related issues, acknowledging the needs and interests of all children depending on their age, capacity and level of maturity.

Moreover a combined activity of promoting **education in children's rights and positive parenting** need to be adopted in particular for parents, who need to become more aware of the nature of their role, children's rights, the responsibilities and obligations that derive from these and their own rights.

Always in relation to the education and counselling support for parents, the recommendation calls for the adoption of **preventive programmes** regarding the different forms of **ill-treatment of children**, making parents aware of the serious problem and of its consequences on the child's development. Governments are also invited to adopt comprehensive guidelines and specific programmes to assist parents in complicated life situations, conflict resolution, anger management through non-violent approaches and mediation techniques.

All this always needs to be achieved through intervention based on education and counselling activities [i.e., universal prevention, or Provision, linked to selective prevention, that is: Prevention = Provision-Prevention, JW] that with Recommendation (2006) 19 become one of the essential parts of the state support activity in favour of positive parenting, which the Recommendation suggests implementing through an empowerment approach, based on consultation and dialogue with parents in the spirit of working in partnership. (...)

CRC on parental guidance and the child's evolving capacities

Art. 5 *States Parties shall respect the responsibilities, rights and duties of parents or, where applicable, the members of the extended family or community as provided for by local custom, legal guardians or other persons legally responsible for the child, to provide, in a manner consistent with the evolving capacities of the child, appropriate direction and guidance in the exercise by the child of the rights recognized in the present Convention.*

Article 5 of the CRC provides a flexible definition of "family" and introduces two key concepts: parental "responsibilities" and the "evolving capacities" of the child. The article also clearly expresses a vision of the child as having active rights, emphasizing the exercise "by the child" of his or her rights.

The parents' primary responsibility in their children's upbringing is recognized also in other parts of the CRC that place strict limits on State intervention and any separation of children from their parents (articles 3(2), 7, 9, 10, 18) while one of the aims of education is the development of respect for the child's parents (article 29).

The first important aspect to note emerging from article 5 is that it provides a flexible understanding of the concept of family that reflects the wide variety of kinship and community arrangements within which children are brought up around the world. This concept has been better specified during the Committee General Discussion on "The role of the family in the promotion of the rights of the child" which stated that "When considering the family environment, the CRC reflects different family structures arising from various cultural patterns and emerging familial relationships. In this regard, the Convention refers to the extended family and the community and it applies to situations of nuclear family, separated parents, single-parent family, common-law family and adoptive family." In this respect consideration should also be given to General Recommendation 21 of the Committee on the Elimination of Discrimination against Women calling for the "prohibition of bigamy and polygamy and the protection of the rights of children."

Article 5 introduces the concept of "parental responsibilities" while article 18 requires States parties to "use their best endeavours" to ensure recognition of the principle that both parents have common responsibilities for the upbringing and development of the child. However the CRC does not provide a definition of "parental responsibilities," although it appears clearly from the whole CRC that such responsibilities must be exercised to support the enjoyment by the child of the rights recognised in the CRC.

In addition, the CRC Committee Guidelines for Periodic Reports ask for information on "the consideration given by law to parental responsibility, including the recognition of the common responsibilities of both parents in the upbringing and development of the child and that the best interests of the child will be their basic concern." States are also required to "indicate how the principles of non-discrimination, respect for the views of the child and the development of the child to the maximum extent, as provided for by the Convention, are taken into account."

The implication is that the concept of parental responsibilities should be reflected and defined in the law, using the framework of the CRC.

Article 5 further specifies that parental guidance must not be understood as being unlimited, rather it must be exercised "in a manner consistent with the evolving capacities of the child" and must be "appropriate." The concept of the "evolving capacities of the child" is a key concept in the CRC that aims to acknowledge that children's development towards independent adulthood [i.e. responsible – and thus also interdependent – adulthood, JW] must be respected and promoted throughout childhood. The use of this concept has also avoided the need for the CRC to set arbitrary age limits or definitions of maturity tied to particular issues.

Article 5 must also be read in conjunction with article 19 providing that in no circumstances must parental guidance be exercised using physical or mental violence and the Committee has consistently upheld the view that corporal punishment is not consistent with the CRC.

CRC on parents' joint responsibilities and assistance from the State

Art. 18. *1. States Parties shall use their best efforts to ensure recognition of the principle that both parents have common responsibilities for the upbringing and development of the child. Parents or, as the case may be, legal guardians have the primary responsibility for the upbringing and development of the child. The best interests of the child will be their basic concern.*

2. For the purpose of guaranteeing and promoting the rights set forth in the present Convention, States Parties shall render appropriate assistance to parents and legal guardians in the performance of their child-rearing responsibilities and shall ensure the development of institutions, facilities and services for the care of children.

3. States Parties shall take all appropriate measures to ensure that children of working parents have the right to benefit from child-care services and facilities for which they are eligible.

Article 18 regulates the balance of responsibilities between the child's parents and the State, and particularly addresses support for parents in the performance of their responsibilities. The article must be read **in conjunction with article 5 as well as articles 3(2) and 27** (the State's responsibility to assist parents in securing that children have adequate protection and care and an adequate standard of living).

These four articles of the CRC, taken together, make clear that parents have primary responsibility for securing the best interests of the child as their "basic concern," but that this responsibility is circumscribed by the child's rights under the CRC and may be shared with others such as members of the wider family. The State must take appropriate steps to assist parents in fulfilling their responsibilities. If parents cannot, the State must intervene to ensure that the child's rights and needs are met.

Protection of the family by the State had already been provided by the International Covenant on Economic, Social and Cultural Rights that in article 10 states "The widest possible protection and assistance should be accorded to the family, which is the natural and fundamental group unit of society, particularly for its establishment and while it is responsible for the care and education of dependent children."

Article 18 explicitly recognizes the common responsibilities of both parents for the upbringing and development of the child. This article clearly goes beyond financial responsibility, calling for both parents to play an active part in their child's upbringing.

The Committee has underlined the importance of this principle recognizing that most societies have only recently acknowledged that fathers, as well as mothers, can and should undertake the day-today care of their children, and that mothers, as well as fathers, have financial responsibilities and legal rights in relation to children.

This principle had already been recognised by the Convention on the Elimination of All Forms of Discrimination against Women (CEDAW) that in article 5 requires States to declare "… the common responsibility of men and women in the upbringing and development of their children, it being understood that the interest of the children is the primordial consideration in all cases."

For the Committee, the State shall use its best efforts to ensure recognition of the principle that both parents have common responsibilities for the upbringing and development of the child. The principle of common responsibilities applies also in the case of fathers of children born out of wedlock. The Committee has often expressed its concern at the large number of single-parent families – a concern that does not relate to the state of marriage but to the need of children to have both parents actively involved in their upbringing and to the greater likelihood of poverty for children in one-parent families.

Again the principle of common responsibilities should also apply when parents separate, as explicitly recognised in article 9 of the CRC stating "… the right of the child who is separated from one or both parents to maintain personal relations and direct contact with both parents on a regular basis, except if it is contrary to the child's best interests." This implies that unless it is proved to the contrary, the continued involvement of both parents in the child's life is [considerde to be] in his or her best interests.

Finally, the paragraph 2 of article 18 emphasizes the **State's responsibility to provide appropriate assistance to parents.**

For the purpose of guaranteeing and promoting the rights set forth in the CRC, the Committee underlines that States shall:

render appropriate assistance to parents and legal guardians in the performance of their child-rearing responsibilities;

ensure the development of institutions, facilities and services for the care of children;

take all appropriate measures to ensure that children of working parents have the right to benefit from child-care services and facilities for which they are eligible.

The Committee's [Concluding Observations] on articles 5 and 18

[In] the CRC Committee's [Concluding Observations], [f]irst of all the attention is focused on the most frequent positive achievements, [and then] on the most frequent Committee's concerns and recommendations on the specific issue of family support – as named by the Committee – taken into consideration by the Committee and followed by an explanation of the Committee's approach to the issue addressed.

One of the key points of the [present] survey remains the identification of the achievements reached by the 27 EU Member Countries and the obstacles and challenges, which remain to be addressed in the process of the implementation of the CRC in relation to the articles 5 and 18.

The Committee has devoted much attention to the subject of family support, in particular as regards the principle of parental guidance and the protection owed to families by the State (articles 5 and 18) on which [the Committee] has issued relevant [Concluding Observations] for 12 EU member Countries. The Committee has commented positively on a number of initiatives undertaken by the States in this field, first of all at a legislative level, such as laws and plans of action on family policy, on support to family with children and against poverty and social exclusion aiming at setting up a global policy on the family and/or at tackling the issue of child poverty or specific laws or legislative amendments on child benefits, parental leave and shared parental custody. The Committee has further appreciated the creation of specific centres to support families by providing counselling and parental education. Notwithstanding these positive achievements, the Committee has expressed its concern about the following issues:

- insufficiency of support by the State to families in terms of parental education and counselling;
- insufficiency of support by the State to families as regards economic support and furnishing of childcare services;
- inadequate respect for the principle that the child should maintain contact with both parents also in case of separation or divorce.

The first point has been addressed by the Committee in the [Concluding Observations] of 5 EU member Countries. The Committee has underlined the need to **prepare parents for their responsibilities** and in its Guidelines for Periodic Reports has asked for information on parental education programmes and on counselling for parents, and how knowledge about child development and the evolving capacities of the child are conveyed to parents and others responsible for children. The Guidelines also request information on any evaluation of the effectiveness of such educational measures.

The States have been invited to provide effective counselling and community-based programmes for families, to improve social assistance and support to families to help them with their child-rearing responsibilities, to support parental education programmes, to implement fully the programme of cooperation with UNICEF on enhancing family capacity, in particular for parents of disadvantaged children and also with a view to prevent abandonment and institutionalisation as well as to help families to provide appropriate direction and guidance in the exercise by the child of the rights recognized in the CRC in a manner consistent with his/her evolving capacities and by encouraging the perception of the child as an holder of rights.

The Committee has also focused on the importance of **improving the efficiency and the quality of professional support** and counselling for families through the availability of **qualified staff** and **resources**.

As regards the second point on the economic support and furnishing of child-care services, the Committee has addressed this issue in its [Concluding Observations] for 5 EU member Countries.

The Committee has indicated that the economic support from the State referred to in article 18 is obviously appropriate [*sic*, JW] when parents are unable to undertake their child-rearing responsibilities, whether or not this is their fault. For instance it has requested States to adopt a family policy that includes social security for the child and the family, housing and social services; that every effort be made to the maximum extent of the available resources to support families in their child-rearing responsibilities, to reduce the number of persons living in poverty and to ensure access for all children and parents to financial assistance.

However the Committee has made clear that the protection referred to in article 18 should not be interpreted according to a narrow definition, rather it should be understood as including the State's responsibility to assist all parents by "ensuring the development of institutions, facilities and services for the care of children." In addition, States are required to ensure "that children of working parents have the right to benefit from child-care services and facilities for which they are eligible." In relation to this last point the Committee has requested the provision of **maternity and paternity leave** as well as services for the conciliation of working and family life and child-care services.

Finally the Committee has recommended States to guarantee the principle that the child should maintain contact with both parents including in case of separation or divorce, and that disputes for the custody of children are resolved in appropriate time and in the best interest of the child.

What we mean by the concept of parenting support

As already specified, this survey focuses in particular on the socio-pedagogical support given to parents though parental education programmes and counselling. The survey does not take into consideration the other forms of parental support, such as economic support, child-care services, measures of conciliation of family and working life. The latter are undoubtedly key elements in supporting parenting, but the aim of this survey is to look specifically at the different forms of parental education and counselling that have been developing across the EU in recent years as they represent a new tool to help parents in their child-rearing responsibilities, that needs to be further analysed and developed.

As indicated in the introduction, this chapter is based on the information received from the ChildONEurope partners, as well as from the documents of the Council of Europe and the national reports to the UN CRC Committee. As a consequence the reference made in the text to specific projects carried out in the different EU countries does not claim to be exhaustive, but rather aims at presenting different kinds of experiences as a basis for reflection and knowledge-sharing on parenting programmes in the EU.

More specifically, the different forms of promotion of parenting competence that will be analysed include actions aimed at improving parents' knowledge of children's developmental needs and parents' educational strategies (family education), as well as actions aimed at helping parents to deal with ordinary as well as difficult situations in family life (family counselling). From a theoretical point of view, parenting support must be included in the framework of education sciences and included among the objects of a discipline called "family education" (...). Such a discipline deals with the study and the intervention on intrafamily (parent-child relationship) educational processes as well as extra-family interventions (services-to-parents relations).

In this framework parenting support programmes are primarily aimed at contributing to the preservation of family functions by strengthening family support services and the services do not substitute parents and their responsibilities.

Personal responsibility, justice and solidarity principles form the basis of family policy. The particular emphasis placed on gender equality is considered as one of the family policy principles and its consistent application is the prerequisite of identified priorities, especially in support of working and family life harmonization. The principle of balance and flexibility reflects the need for balanced assistance to families at every stage of the family cycle. Therefore assistance to families should consist of different types of support depending on the life situation of the family in question. Furthermore parenting programmes should support parents (fathers and mothers) irrespective of the legal form of the family, in order to prevent the preferential treatment of a certain form of a family to the detriment of another.

The main theoretical concepts that have emerged from research carried out on parenting programmes are the following:

- *Look for strengths and potential, not just problems,* namely look at the resources that even families in difficulties may have and build on those. Even

if this process may be longer and difficult, research has demonstrated that the results are more long-lasting and it is important to map the resources of the community involved before starting a project (...).
- *Support neighbourhood parenting,* namely strengthen the social support in particular from the neighbourhood. The social work action is said to be based on the so-called five "C": ***consulting, connecting, convening, constructing, coaching,*** that is to say working with a participative and shared programming logic and by promoting a "neighbourhood proximity" among families.

The prevailing logic seems to be not so much and not only to work to reduce risk-factors, but above all to strengthen opportunity factors (...).

Legislative framework and bodies involved in the realization of parenting programmes

Regarding the legislative framework, few States have enacted specific legislation on the issue of parenting programmes. References to this can be found in more general legislations, such as on parental support (for instance the Austrian *Family Burden Equalization Act,* §39c, 1 January 2000) or on children's rights and protection (for instance the Portuguese Law 147/99 on the Protection of Children and Young People at Risk refers in article 41 to parental education programmes).

An interesting Act is the Belgian (French Community) Plan of Action on parental support adopted in June 2006, which covers the different sectors involved: social, education, health, culture and sports. This Plan has three main aims: promoting existing initiatives and informing on best practices; promoting the training of practitioners involved; developing services able to respond to families needs.

In Germany in its resolution of 22/23.5.2003, the Conference of Ministers for Youth emphasized the need to consider the legal, financial and expertise requirements in order to specify the parenting education services and to ensure their provision at regional and local levels.

Also in the Netherlands the programme of the Ministry for children and families gives a high priority to parenting support.

In Italy a reference to parenting support can be found in Law No. 285 of 28 August 1997 that has represented one of the main instruments for implementing the rights of children and the adolescents. Law 285/97 states that the Fund may provide financing, among other programmes, for projects which pursue objectives such as providing preparatory and support services for parent-child relations to combat poverty and violence, and providing alternative measures to taking children into care in educational and help-oriented institutions, considering also foreign children. The objectives which recur most frequently in the projects realised thanks to this law include the following: promoting and strengthening forms of self-help for families, providing support in parenting for families by disseminating a culture for sharing experiences, placing emphasis on mutual help and the skills of parents perceived as partners and not merely receivers-users of the intervention. There are very few interventions with objectives towards creating "parenting schools" based on the assumption that parents can be taught pre-packed knowledge divulging precepts instead of solving problems. In addition, the strategies indicated for achieving the objectives focus highly on local realities: they range from teaching mothers in depressed areas in the south of Italy to read and write, to trial projects within companies as a support to single mothers for gaining access to the labour market, and developing the practice of home-visiting in the immediate post partum period, to providing pedagogical support to the parents of children who do not attend day-nursery, establishing family-oriented structures and selfmanaged day-nurseries and building neighbourhood networks etc.

In other countries as well, the legislative framework concerning parenting support is represented not by a specific law or specific provision, but is entrusted to governmental authorities that give expression to their policies through regulamentary acts or circulars. What frequently happens is that those activities directed to promote support for parents are not compulsory, even if recommended.

As regards the bodies involved in the provision of service, it is possible to distinguish between three different levels of intervention: there are bodies responsible for planning, bodies that finance the activities, and bodies that are entrusted with the task of realizing the different parenting programmes. The first two levels of intervention are generally carried out both by central authorities (e.g. competent Ministries) and by local governments, while the last one is normally entrusted to local agencies, local services and private organizations, such as NGOs, associations, foundations. Sometimes private agencies are also involved in the planning phase.

Therefore, generally the government itself does not run parenting programmes. Local authorities, schools and voluntary organisations run a wide range of parenting programmes, mostly using funding provided by the government. A general trend that can be identified is therefore that of the decentralization of the provision of parenting services and programmes, while at the same time it seems that in this field, the issue of public and private integration has found specific and innovative ways of expression.

In the Netherlands for instance there is no national programme or standard because the municipalities are responsible for offering parenting support programmes and services. However, as a result of Operation Young, a 3 year programme on the reform of the chain of children's and young people's services, the recommendation has been made that in each municipality a Centre for Children and Families should be created and this process is currently in place.

Some countries have also created specific bodies, for instance the United Kingdom has set up the National Advisory Group to strengthen parenting education in schools, the National Family and Parenting Institute and the National Academy for Parenting Practitioners, while France set up Networks for listening, support and counselling of parents (REAAP) (...). In Italy it is worth mentioning the setting up of the National Observatory on Family, in the framework of the activities of the Ministry of Labour and Social Policies, that includes among its institutional aims the monitoring of the projects for parenting support. In recent years the Observatory drafted various surveys in the field of parenting support and conciliation of family and working life giving to professionals of the field an important occasion for training and in-depth study.

(...)

Aims and contents of parenting services and programmes

Notwithstanding the great variety of parenting programmes introduced throughout the EU, it is possible to affirm that in many countries the parenting support programmes that we have analysed concern the area of primary prevention, namely of promotion [Provision, JW]. Usually projects focus on the empowerment of parents and families in the context of families-services partnerships and aiming at strengthening social networks as well.

Prevention activities vary also on the basis of the specific goals to be reached, various States for instance put emphasis on the prevention of child abandonment (e.g. Denmark, Ireland, Italy, Slovakia). In the Netherlands great attention is being paid to earlier recognition of problems in families in order to prevent unnecessary suffering for the child, difficulties for the parents and escalation of problems. For this aim an electronic child file has been created in order to make information available more quickly and on a larger scale. As of 1st January 2007 all newborn children in the Netherlands receive their own electronic files from the young persons' health services. In addition to the electronic files there will be a referral index / risk box where various sectors involved with young people can report risks and incidents. Together, the electronic child file and the referral index must ensure that risks for children can be better monitored and problems can be more easily prevented.

In the United Kingdom there has been particular interest in the contribution of parenting programmes to help families and children who may be drifting into antisocial behaviour. The youth justice system, locally administered, is increasingly investing in such programmes; it expects to spend more than £4 million on them in 2006–07. The government's "Respect" Action plan, published in January 2006, makes a general commitment to improve parenting provision nationally, ensuring that all parents, but particularly parents/carers of children at risk of negative outcomes, receive early, relevant multi-agency support.

Concerning the contents of parenting education and counselling, a special mention should be made of the issue of corporal punishment as such programmes normally include a part on alternative educational methods. In the EU, 11 countries also declare the prohibition of corporal punishment by law: Austria (1989), Bulgaria (2000), Cyprus (1994), Denmark (1997), Finland (1983), Germany (2000), Hungary (2004), Latvia (1998), Portugal (2007), Romania (2004), Sweden (1979), [The Netherlands (2007)]. In addition Italy's Supreme Court has declared that all corporal punishment, including that in the home, is unlawful, while in Greece a Network for the Prevention and Combat of Corporal Punishment, consisting of governmental and non-governmental agencies, is in the process of being formed. In Spain there has been a special emphasis for promoting a legal reform of the article[s] 154 and 238 of Spanish Civil Code which is waiting for the final approval of the Parliament before the end of 2007. The final objective of this legal reform proposal is to eliminate any misunderstanding about the legal ban of physical and psychological punishment to children in any setting in Spain.

The introduction of these provisions was not so much aimed at providing for sanctions or punishment but was rather aimed at serving the development of parental capabilities and **providing for a clear support framework**. These measures are intended to encourage parents to seek assistance if they encounter difficulties in bringing up their children as well as to encourage them to acquire alternative methods of disciplining their children. At the same time these provisions strive to reduce the use of corporal punishment in disciplining children, and to alter the public notion of corporal punishment in society and to make everyone more sensitive to issues concerning the human dignity of the child.

It is interesting to look at the effects which such legislation produced in particular in those countries that introduced it a long time ago. For instance, in Sweden research shows that the provision has had a great impact on the population. A study from 2000 where parents were asked about their experience of and attitudes towards corporal punishment showed that forceful corporal punishment of children, which potentially could cause severe injuries, has decreased substantially as well as parental attitudes to the use of corporal punishment as a means to raise their children. A study of children's experience from the same year shows that the absolute number of children subjected to corporal punishment has decreased and the children who are exposed to punishments experience this much less often than before.

Alongside the introduction of laws prohibiting corporal punishment, awareness raising campaigns have been organized in various States, e.g. Estonia held the campaigns: "Don't hit the child" and "The child is not a doll." Romania as well organized a campaign entitled "Violence breeds violence" by Save the Children Romania (…). The Spanish Ministry of Labour and Social Affairs and Save the Children Spain in collaboration with more than eighty other NGOs and institutions have been working since 1999 for promoting positive parenting and ending physical and humiliating treatment to children in the families. Two main campaigns have been developed: "Educate, do not punish" from 1999 to 2001 and "To teach is not to hit" from 2005 until now. The objectives of the campaigns have been:

- to raise awareness among parents and society about the negative consequences of physical punishment
- to promote positive and non violent parenting skills
- and to encourage children to know and defend their rights. (…)

Critical points in the provision of parenting programmes and services

A critical point in the provision of parenting programmes and services that has been indicated by several countries is their **limited availability** in terms of geographical distribution or the impossibility of reaching all interested families also due to the limitation of the parenting support programmes budget. Another general trend that can be identified is the provision of these programmes **only or mainly for families at risk and not also as a general instrument to support all parents** in their child-rearing responsibilities.

A further critical point is represented by the inclusion in these programmes of migrant families, for instance Denmark specifically pointed out this issue, but also Hungary by recognizing that the integrating role of social welfare services is to be strengthened by facilitating the access by the Roma population to social welfare services and Ireland that indicated the importance of family support for travellers. In Denmark attention to migrant families' needs has been greatly developed as well. In January 2003, the Government introduced a bill on education in Danish for adult immigrants that took effect from January 2004 meaning considerably improved education in cultural and social conditions in Denmark in the Danish language programmes. The difficulty in networking among the different bodies involved due to the privacy requirement was also underlined. Finally the specific needs of lone parents and families of people with disabilities should be better met. (...)

Conclusions

The present survey highlights that the issue of family support by the States was given a specific and increasing attention in the recent years both at international and at national level. Through the analysis of the international instruments it is evident that the issues of family support by the EU Member States represents an area of increasing attention and concern for several reasons, moving from the realisation of the strict connection existing between social and economic issues and the need for policy intervention in the areas affecting families and children, to the demographic challenges, the increasing child poverty and the changing of the family structure and of the gender roles.

The United Nations provide, through variegated instruments, a series of recommendations aimed at leading the States interventions, underlining their essential role as **guarantors, enablers and promoters** of all those actions directed at removing the obstacles that prevent parents from achieving the positive and complete exercise of their parental role. However, such documents only address the specific issue of parental education and counseling in the wider context of family support policies, based on the respect of the fundamental principles for children's rights as stated by the CRC. Whereas, the European Union even though has no common family policy as family policies remain the exclusive responsibility of the Member States, it gives great importance to it, as highlighted by its legislative activities in a number of areas: migration and free movement, equal opportunities, labour law and working conditions, and social protection. However the main concern in all these acts is still the issue of the conciliation between work and family life, without mentioning other forms of support dedicated in particular to the socio-educational dimension. As underlined in the recent Communication from the European Commission promoting solidarity between the generations (May 2007), the Lisbon Strategy is considered as a framework for the modernisation of family policies through the promotion of equal opportunities and in particular for a better reconciliation of work and private/family life which contributes to female labour force participation.

We can notice that there is no specific reference to socio-educational forms of support from State to family life in the activities of the EU and UN, thus at the international level it is possible to say that the work of the [Council of Europe] contributed to add new elements of discussion to the importance of socio-educational supplies for positive parenting by the States. The Recommendation (2006)19 underlines the importance for children of growing up in a positive family environment and the State's responsibility to create the right conditions for positive parenting and to provide parents with the knowledge for appropriate guidance and direction (in a non-violent manner) of their children, to have the opportunity to provide materially for the child and to enable the child to be heard. Moreover, it invites the public authorities to promote initiatives aiming to make people aware of the value and importance of positive parenting and take a pro-active approach to promoting awareness on parenting issues and to normalising participation in parenting programmes. It also recommends the adoption of an empowerment approach based on consultation and dialogue with parents and on their voluntary involvement and participation in the spirit of a working partnership.

It is important to remind also that the [CRC] Committee in its [Concluding Observations] on the EU member States reports on the implementation of the CRC, devoted much attention to the subject of family support, in particular as regards the principle of parental guidance and the protection owed to families by the State (articles 5 and 18). The Committee has commented positively on a number of initiatives undertaken by the States in this field, first of all at a legislative level, such as laws and plans of action on family policy, on support to family with children and against poverty and social exclusion aiming at setting up a global policy on the family and/or at tackling the issue of child poverty or specific laws or legislative amendments on child benefits, parental leave and shared parental custody. The Committee has further appreciated the creation of specific centres to support families by providing counselling and parental education.

Notwithstanding these positive achievements, the Committee has expressed its concern about the following issues:

- insufficiency of support by the State to families in terms of parental education and counselling;
- insufficiency of support by the State to families as regards economic support and furnishing of child-care services;
- inadequate respect for the principle that the child should maintain contact with both parents also in case of separation or divorce.

Concerning the national level, from the analysis undertaken of EU Member States policies, it clearly emerges that EU Member States are devoting an increasing attention to parenting support policies and programmes focusing specifically on a socio-educational dimension. There is a general acknowledgement of the importance of such programmes based on the recognition of the fact that the nature of parenting has deeply changed, due among others to the modified gender roles inside the family and in the society as well as to the new labour organization.

Certainly the extension and availability, as well as the characteristics, of such programmes vary greatly across the EU from those Countries that have since several years developed specific and comprehensive parenting programmes addressed to all parents, to those that have just started to set up programmes in this field that are mainly addressed to families at risk or to parents in difficulty. However there is general acknowledgement that the setting up or consolidation of parenting policies and programmes is needed in order to meet the new needs and exigencies expressed by the todayfamilies.

Concerning the ways to provide parental support, first of all it must be recognised that all EU Member States introduced a family support dimension in the provision of health services. Secondly among the most common forms of parental support we can find also parental education and counselling that can be provided through general courses, workshops or conferences addressed to all interested parents or through individual advice to parents upon request. The use of telephone help-lines, web-site[s] as well as awareness-raising campaigns is also increasingly used.

Other forms of parenting support provided in various EU Member States are: pre-marital counselling for young couples, often offered by church related services or associations, involvement of parents in relation with child-care services or the school, family mediation, specific programmes for families at risk or for families with children with special needs.

An important role is also played by parents associations that often provide networks that link families, community networks and parents self helping groups.

Parenting programmes are mostly provided by local bodies in accordance with the administrative decentralization taking place in EU Member States, while the central level usually maintains the function of planning the general policies and providing funds for the services.

Regarding the legislative framework, few States have enacted specific legislation on the issue of parenting programmes as references to this can be found in more general legislations, such as on parental support or on children's rights and protection.

Another common element in the provision of parenting support programmes is the public-private integration that in this field has proved to work rather well. Access to most of the parenting programmes and services is free of charge as they are supported by public funds; some require a low participation fee from the participants. Private institutions that are not funded by the government ask for a higher participation fee.

As regards the aims of parenting support services and programmes, usually projects focus on the empowerment of parents and families in the context of families-services partnerships and aiming at strengthening social networks as well. This aspect is very important because parental support should not be understood as a form of control of parental behaviour or as way to replace the parents, but as a way of empowering parents' competences and skills. It appears therefore necessary to realise programmes directed at supporting parents making emerge their personal resources as well as those of the family and social context. To this aim it appears fundamental not only to use empowerment techniques but also to know in-depth the territory in which to intervene.

Concerning the contents of parenting support programmes, many of them also promote alternative discipline methods to corporal punishment that in 11 EU Members States is forbidden by law.

From the survey it also emerges that States are increasingly paying attention to the issue of training and research as well as at the importance to identify replicable best practices. Some EU Member States, as well as international organizations like the Council of Europe, also developed guidelines for work with parents that point out a number of principles that should orient the work of professionals, among others the principle of becoming partners with and empowering parents, as well as the principle of equity and accessibility, which should underlie all action taken.

Finally the survey points out some critical aspects in the provision of parenting support services, namely the limited availability of such services having as a consequence the impossibility to reach all interested families, the provision of these programmes only or mainly for families at risk and not also as a general instrument to support all parents, the difficulty in including migrant families and the difficulty in networking among the different bodies.

According to studies of international organizations, such as the Council of Europe the limited availability of parenting programmes appears to be, even if with different degrees in the various EU Member States, one of the most serious shortcomings in this fields that leads the organization to affirm that "the process of ascertaining the needs of parents has just started and requires more political attention and priority."

The wish is that this survey may be helpful to provide more information on this subject, both by making a review of the most important international instruments on this issue and by identifying policies, programmes and interventions carried out by the EU Member States at national level as well as by sharing some of the most significant and innovative experiences in this field.

TASK/TEXT 6.6: PARENTS WITH INTELLECTUAL DISABILITIES (ID) OR BORDERLINE INTELLECTUAL FUNCTIONING (BIF)

Working Group on Parenting and Parenthood (in Dutch: Werkgezelschap Ouderschap en Kinderwens), 30 October 2007 (ZonMW), Carlo Schuengel (VU) *et al.*

Children of parents with intellectual disabilities (ID) or borderline intellectual functioning (BIF) are at significant risk for maladaptive parenting, including abuse and neglect. Children with a parent with ID or BIF are overrepresented in child protection cases. (…) The majority of Dutch parents with ID were judged by their professional caregivers as failing to provide 'good enough' parenting (…), and perhaps as a result, a disproportionate number of children of parents with ID are taken into foster or adoptive care (…). Van IJzendoorn *et al.* (2007) conclude from their national incidence study of child abuse [National Prevalence Study Child Abuse, Netherlands, <www.leidenattachmentresearchprogram.eu/NPM-2005-Van-IJzendoorn-abstract-EN.pdf>, JW] that children from parents at the lowest educational level face a seven-fold risk of child abuse and neglect, ranking as the strongest risk factor.

This grim picture of parenthood with ID has been challenged based on evidence from several studies that despite ID, parents do benefit from parenting support, and may be able to learn important skills to safeguard their children's safety, health, cognitive development, and wellbeing (…). However, while these skills are important, they may not necessarily protect children from emotional neglect and abuse. **Sensitive-responsive caregiving and gentle discipline require attentional and planning skills, and skills to balance signals and demands from the child against the other signals and demands that capture parents' interest. It is not evident that parents with learning difficulties may learn these complex skills as easily as parents of normal intelligence.** (…)

A conservative estimate is that 1.5% of the 120,000 people in the Netherlands known to care organizations for persons with ID have one or more children (…), a figure which may be growing due to societal changes with respect to inclusion and rights to self-determination [of persons with intellectual disabilities, whereas societal changes with respect to children's rights are lacking far behind, JW] (Pixa-Kettner & Sanders, 2006, reported a doubling between 1995 and 2005). (…) The group of parents with borderline intellectual functioning (BIF) is likely to be even larger. BIF is usually defined as having an IQ between 70 and 84, which would include an estimated 7 percent of the general population. In practice, many parents from this larger group are judged as functioning at a lower level on one or more areas (intellectual, emotional, daily living skills) (...). (...)

TASK/TEXT 6.7: MODERN LIFE LEADS TO MORE DEPRESSION AMONG CHILDREN

Letter to the *Daily Telegraph*, written by **Sue Palmer**[50] and child mental health specialist Richard House, and signed by more than a hundred influential academics, writers and others, <www.telegraph.co.uk/news/main.jhtml?xml=/news/2006/09/12/nosplit/njunk112.xml>

Modern life leads to more depression among children

As professionals and academics from a range of backgrounds, we are deeply concerned at the escalating incidence of childhood depression and children's behavioural and developmental conditions. We believe this is largely due to a lack of understanding, on the part of both politicians and the general public, of the realities and subtleties of child development.

Since children's brains are still developing, they cannot adjust – as full-grown adults can – to the effects of ever more rapid technological and cultural change. They still need what developing human beings have always needed, including real food (as opposed to processed "junk"), real play (as opposed to sedentary, screen-based entertainment), first-hand experience of the world they live in and regular interaction with the real-life significant adults in their lives.

They also need time. In a fast-moving hyper-competitive culture, today's children are expected to cope with an ever-earlier start to formal schoolwork and an overly academic test-driven primary curriculum. They are pushed by market forces to act and dress like mini-adults and exposed via the electronic media to material which would have been considered unsuitable for children even in the very recent past. Our society rightly takes great pains to protect children from physical harm, but seems to have lost sight of their emotional and social needs. However, it's now clear that the mental health of an unacceptable number of children is being unnecessarily compromised, and that this is almost certainly a key factor in the rise of substance abuse, violence and self-harm amongst our young people.

This is a complex socio-cultural problem to which there is no simple solution, but a sensible first step would be to encourage **parents and policy-makers** to start

50 Author of *Toxic Childhood; How the modern world is damaging our children and what we can do about it*, London: Orion Books, 2006 (<www.suepalmer.co.uk>).

talking about ways of improving children's well-being. We therefore propose as a matter of urgency that:

- public debate be initiated on child-rearing in the 21st century
- this issue should be central to public policy-making in coming decades.

TASK/TEXT 6.8: MENTAL HEALTH IMPROVEMENTS FOR NATIONS' DEVELOPMENT

The WHO MIND Project (<www.who.int/mental_health/policy/en>, accessed 19 December 2009)

Towards concrete changes in people's daily lives
Mental and neurological disorders such as depression, schizophrenia, epilepsy and substance abuse, among others, cause immense suffering for those affected, amplifies people's vulnerability and can lead individuals into a life of poverty. Despite the worldwide availability of cost-effective treatments the vast majority of people are left without access to the treatment they need. Instead of getting the help and support they require to lead productive lives, many people are subject to stigma, discrimination and human rights violations and are denied the basic life opportunities given to other citizens.

Mental health improvements are central to nations' development
By treating many of the debilitating mental disorders and by promoting mental health, people will experience major improvements in their lives. They will be able to work and rise out of poverty, provide their children with the right social and emotional environment to flourish, participate productively in community life, and contribute to the economy of their country. In order to achieve this countries need to put in place human rights oriented mental health policies, strategic plans and laws to ensure that effective treatment, prevention and promotion programs are made available to all people who need them.

TASK/TEXT 6.9: THE BEST INTERESTS OF THE CHILD – WHAT IT MEANS AND WHAT IT DEMANDS FROM ADULTS

Lecture by Thomas Hammarberg, Commissioner for Human Rights, Council of Europe, Warsaw, 30 May, 2008; Crinmail 995 – 1 July 2008 (<www.crin.org>)

It is a particular honour to be rewarded in this city – the home of such extraordinary personalities as Janusz Korczak and Irene Sendler who gave us ideals which we now should feel obliged to bring forward to coming generations.

This very institution, the Academy for Special Education, gives a significant contribution to the realisation of such endeavours. In my work as Commissioner for Human Rights I have often been reminded about the utmost importance of inclusive education – that every child, also those with a difficult background or disability, be given a genuine chance to meaningful learning on our schools. This in turn requires teachers of special; pedagogic skills.

Janusz Korczak once wrote: 'To reform the world means to reform the methods of bringing up children.' At the same time he stressed the fact that the child lives today and deserves respect today. The child's right to respect is one of the major themes in his writings.

'There appears to be two lives,' he pointed out. 'One serious and respectable, the other indulgently tolerated, less valuable. We say: a future person, a future worker, a future citizen. That children will be, that they will really begin to be serious only in the future.'

He not only exposed these attitudes, he saw them as the basis for the injustices against children – many of them abandoned, neglected, exploited and maltreated. He questioned the minimal resources allocated to the wellbeing of children. Referring to the emerging affluence he proposed a calculation of how much of the total resources belonged to children – if they had their fair share. This he wanted to be compared with the actual budget shares allocated for the needs of children.

What he requested was more respect for the interests of children, not as charity or a favour, but as a right.

The idea that society should respect the best interests of the child is seen as fundamental in all cultures. After all, children do symbolize the survival of the family, the group, the nation and even humanity itself. Going beyond rhetoric, however, we must ask – as Janusz Korczak did – whether this idea is respected in reality.

From the very first draft of the UN Convention on the Rights of the Child, put forward by the Polish Government in 1978, it was clear that the principle of the 'best interests' should be included and given a prominent position.

The 1959 Declaration of the Rights of the Child had in fact already evoked the principle, stating that 'the best interests of the child shall be the paramount consideration' in the enactment of laws relating to children, as well as 'the guiding principle of those responsible for (the child's) education and guidance.'

Several international conventions had also subsequently incorporated this provision. One of them was the 1979 Convention on the Elimination of All Forms of Discrimination against Women. At the national level, the best interests principle had long been included in the legal systems of a number of countries, although its scope was generally limited to family law matters on individual situations, mainly divorce, custody and adoption cases. Less frequently, the principle was also applied to school and childcare issues.

The Convention on the Rights of the Child extends the principle to cover all decisions affecting the child. This is a radical departure. The best interests of the child shall now be a primary consideration in all actions concerning children – not just actions taken by the state authorities, parliamentary assemblies and judicial bodies but also those taken by relevant private institutions.

The drafters of the Convention not only widened the scope of the principle, but they also made it one of the 'umbrella' provisions and thereby important for the overall framework of the Convention. The Committee on the Rights of the Child has taken the principle one step further, defining the best interests of the child as a 'general principle' guiding the interpretation of the entire Convention.

ARTICLE 3

The 'best interests of the child' is mentioned in several articles of the Convention: relating to the separation of the child from the family (Art. 9); parental responsibility (Art. 18); foster placement (Art. 20); adoption (Art. 21); deprivation of liberty (Art. 37); and juvenile justice (Art. 40). The key formulation, however, is found in the first paragraph of Article 3:

'In all actions concerning children, whether undertaken by public or private social welfare institutions, courts of law, administrative authorities or legislative bodies, the best interests of the child shall be a primary consideration.'

Article 3 can only be fully understood by studying its precise formulation. It refers to executive authorities, law-makers (parliaments) and judicial bodies. It applies to all actions by these authorities as well as by relevant private institutions. Importantly, it also concerns 'children' in the plural. The Committee on the Rights of the Child has interpreted this wording to mean that the article is applicable in both individual cases and in relation to groups of children or children in general – which makes it even more relevant political and policy terms.

The broad scope of Article 3 naturally had a price in the drafting process. There was considerable discussion on whether the formulation should be 'a' or 'the' primary consideration. In the end it was recognized that given the widened scope of Article 3, situations would arise when other legitimate and competing interests could not be ignored. The conclusion was to settle for the somewhat less decisive wording 'a primary consideration.'

Thus, the best interests of the child cannot normally be the only consideration, but should be among the first aspects to be considered and should be given considerable weight in all decisions affecting children.

On family issues such as parental visitation, foster placement and adoption, the interests of the child, however, will be the paramount consideration, as made clear in the substantive articles of the Convention as well as in earlier standards. The 1979 Convention on the Elimination of All Forms of Discrimination against Women, for instance, states in relation to family education that the best interests of the child should be 'the primordial consideration'(Art. 5.b); and in relation to guardianship, that the child's interests should be 'paramount'(Art. 16). The Convention on the Rights of the Child does not, of course, dilute those standards.

The recognition that there are other interests besides children's in decision-making processes has not, as might be assumed, weakened the force of Article 3. On the contrary, its broader scope makes Article 3 more politically relevant. The 'best interests' principle has accordingly been the starting point for discussions on a number of significant policy issues (some of which I will examine later). It is clear, however, that the principle's full policy potential has not yet been fully understood or utilized. Only a few governments have taken the 'best interests' principle seriously outside the area of family affairs, an omission that continues to be a major concern.

A guide

The Committee has often referred to Article 3 in its Concluding Observations on State Parties' reports. It has noted that the article, by virtue of its status as a general principle, can be seen as a guide to both the interpretation and the implementation of the Convention.

A guide to the interpretation of other articles. It is significant that in its Concluding Observations the Committee seldom refers only to one article. It has instead tended to see the Convention as a comprehensive set of interdependent rules with the best interests of the child as an overarching principle.

By being linked to the 'best interests' principle, the substantive articles gain in clarity and depth. The principle also provides guidance on problems and situations not specifically mentioned in the Convention. For instance, although the Convention requires States to establish a minimum age of criminal responsibility (Art. 40.3), it makes no mention of what exactly that age should be. When that decision is taken, the best interests of the child should be a primary consideration.

The principle also guides the interpretation of the Convention when articles might appear to contradict each other. In some unfortunate cases a conflict may arise between the right to have access to both parents and the right to be protected against abuse. In such situations, the best interests of the child must determine the course of action.

A guide to the overall implementation. The principle of the best interests of the child should influence lawmaking, administrative decisions and all other actions affecting the child. In addition, the principle can be a useful tool when laws or policies are to be evaluated. How is this principle reflected in the legislation? Are there policy documents reflecting the principle? Are there routine procedures ensuring that the best interests of the child are considered in decision-making?

Laws and policy documents are of course not sufficient to ensure the effective implementation of the Convention. The Committee also monitors the legal and practical application of the principle. One example was its discussion with a government delegation from Colombia. Though the report from that State emphasized an unusual constitutional provision giving the rights of the child precedence over the rights of other persons, the Committee found reason to be concerned about the gap between legislation and the reality of many children in the country.

WHAT IS MEANT BY THE 'BEST INTERESTS OF THE CHILD'?

Governments – or individual adults – have sometimes misused the 'best interests of the child' to justify actions that in reality have violated the rights of the child. Corporal punishment has been defended with the argument that it teaches children necessary limits and is therefore for their own good in the long run. Adopted children have been prevented from knowing their biological family 'in their own interests.' Children of indigenous peoples have been forcefully removed from their families and placed in boarding schools so that they could be introduced to 'civilization,' again in the name of their 'best interests.' I heard recently from a government representative a similar suggestion in a discussion about Roma children.

Such actions are based on extreme patronizing and not on any genuine concern for children's interests; they have no support in the Convention on the Rights of the Child. Excuses for violations of children's rights are clearly not what the principle of the best interests is about.

The definition of the child's best interests, however, is not always obvious, especially in a long-term perspective. Consequently, there have been heated debates about the interpretation of Article 3 and the best interests principle. The article has been criticized as being too vague and general. Furthermore, it has been argued that what is in the best interests of the child varies from one era to another and also depends on the resources, the developmental level and the culture of the country in which the child lives.

Child labour is one example of a controversial application of the best interests principle. In developing countries, families do in many cases depend for their survival on income earned by all productive family members, including children.

Attitudes towards education provide another example. Girls are deprived of schooling in some societies with the argument that, given their future needs, it is more important for them to learn how to manage a household than to receive an academic instruction. A more sophisticated international interpretation on these issues is gradually emerging, however. Work that is hazardous to a child can never be in his or her best interests. The right to education on the basis of equal opportunity is fundamental.

Thus, the Convention does not offer any definite statement of what is in the best interests of an individual child in a given situation. It does, however, provide a normative framework that defines these interests to some extent. Since Article 3 is one of the general principles and an 'umbrella' provision, it should always be linked to other articles in the Convention. The substantive articles of the Convention give clear directions and limits on how children should and should not be treated.

Though necessarily general and incomplete, a reasonable first building block towards the definition of what is in the best interests of the child is the sum total of the norms in the Convention. This means, for example, that it is in the best interests of the child to: receive education (Art. 28); have family relations (Art. 8); know and be cared for by his or her parents (Art. 7); be heard in matters concerning him or her (Art. 12), and to be respected and seen as an individual person (Art. 16). In the same way, the Convention states what is not in the best interests of the child: for instance, to be exposed to any form of violence (Art. 19); to be wrongly separated from his or her parents (Art. 9); to be subjected to any traditional practices prejudicial to the child's health (Art. 24); to perform any work that is hazardous or harmful (Art. 32), or to be otherwise exploited or abused (Arts. 33–36).

Such a definition has the advantage of providing a universal interpretation of what is in the best interests of the child. Differences will inevitably arise of course during actual practice, requiring the delicate balancing of competing interests or the child's interests over time.

A 'relativism' that suggests that the rights themselves should be compromised should not be accepted. There may, however, be cultural differences that justify different approaches and strategies to information and education about children's rights. In addition, different family structures, education levels and standards of living are factors that cannot be ignored. It is essential to consider these differences when an effective strategy for implementation of the Convention is planned. Naturally the Convention itself is universal. Indeed, one of its greatest strengths is that it defines rights that cut across cultural, religious and other frontiers.

The views of the child

There is another important aspect of the Convention that is relevant to this discussion: the emphasis on respecting the evolving capacities of the child. For the best interests of the child to be determined, it is important that the child himself or herself be heard. With increased age and maturity, the child should be able to influence and decide more. This obvious point is often forgotten. Adults tend to discuss what is best for children without seeking their opinions or even listening to them.

The interplay between Articles 3 and 12 is one of the most interesting aspects of the Convention. Article 12 states that the child who is capable of forming an opinion on matters affecting him or her has the right to express that opinion freely and that the child's opinion should be given due weight in accordance with his or her age and maturity.

This approach does not necessarily mean that the child can take complete responsibility for the decision. The spirit of Article 12 is rather to ensure consultation and growing participation than to relinquish all power to the child.

THE INTERESTS OF THE CHILD VERSUS THE INTERESTS OF OTHERS

The first step in this analysis was to seek an approach to defining the interests of the child. Two aspects were considered to be especially important: looking at the substantive articles of the Convention itself, and seeking the views of the child. The next step is to clarify what is meant by giving these interests 'a primary consideration.'

It is often necessary in the real world to balance various 'interests' against each other. When a child's interests compete with other children's or with adults' interests, how should one strike a fair balance? That is, of course, where the real difficulty lies.

The discussions within the Committee have highlighted three types of conflicts, either perceived or real, that can occur:

- (a) the interests of a child or a group of children stand against those of other children;
- (b) the interests of a child clashes with the wishes of one or both parents or guardians;
- (c) the interests of a child or a group of children contradict a broader societal interest (for instance, of an economic character).

How to balance the interests of one child against those of others?

Such dilemmas are common in schools, pre-schools or other community activities for children. One example is when a country does not have sufficient resources to build more schoolrooms for a growing number of children. Would it be better to adopt a two-shift system, which would cut down the school hours for some children, but provide education for all children? In other words, would it be better to educate all children for a half day or half the number of children for a full day?

A similar dilemma arise in the discussion about private schools. These could bring more creative approaches to learning but also exclude pupils without means to pay the fees. Faced with such choices, decision makers must balance various considerations, such as those expressed in the Convention that no child should be discriminated against and that the needs of disadvantaged children should be attended to and given special attention.

How to balance the interests of the child versus those of the parents?

First, it has to be recognized that there can be conflicts, hidden or open, between children's and parents' interests. It is sometimes argued that what is good for the family by definition is good for the child, and that only the parents can know what is good for the family. This position is contrary to the very spirit of the Convention, which is clearly family-supportive but ultimately stands on the side of the child, for instance in cases of parental abuse and neglect.

The Convention assumes that parental responsibility will be exercised in the best interests of the child (Art. 18). When the child's survival or development is threatened by her or his parents or guardians, however, it is obviously in the child's best interests to be separated from them (Art. 9). Such separations are often highly traumatic and require an approach that will not cause further damage, but that will instead create conditions for the healthy development of the child. A general lesson is the importance of early detection of problems and preventive action. This, in turn, requires a willingness to listen to the individual child, for instance, in schools and in health centres, and appropriate training for teachers and health care providers who work with children on a daily basis.

How to balance the interests of the child versus the whole society?

What is good for an individual child or for children in general may well clash with what is seen as important for other groups or for the community as a whole. Such contradictions or competing interests are often about resources. Given all other needs, the costs of responding to the very best interests of a child can be unacceptably high, especially in low-income countries. One example could be when a child needs advanced, and therefore expensive, hospital care. In such cases, it will sometimes be necessary, however painful this may be, to seek the fairest possible solution, within the given constraints, though still respecting the principle that the best interests of the child should be a primary consideration.

The Convention does give some guidance on the issue of resources. Article 4 asserts that States should allocate the maximum extent of their available resources for the implementation of the rights of the child. A serious decision maker would therefore have to determine what reasonably should be regarded as the 'maximum extent' possible.

Another, somewhat more indirect example can be cited from Sweden. The Swedish immigration authorities had at one stage decided to expel some child refugees in spite of there being strong humanitarian reasons for their staying. The argument was that generosity towards these children would undermine the overall asylum policy with its strict requirements. After public discussion, this decision was reversed. It was concluded, first, that each child had the right to have his or her individual case considered on its own merits; and, second, that it was more important to respect each child's best interests by allowing the child to remain in Sweden than it was to avoid misunderstandings of the general refugee policy.

The Convention does not give concrete answers on how conflicts of interest should be resolved, except for the most obvious cases. The weighing of legitimate but different interests is naturally delicate and difficult. Often it is a question of assessing and comparing degrees of benefit and damage. If the interests of a child or group of children would be less infringed by a certain proposed action, there would naturally be more room to accommodate the interests of others, and vice versa.

The important point is that the 'best interests' principle must remain present in such processes: that the interests of the child have to be an important consideration in all decision-making that has a significant impact on the child's well-being and the fulfilment of her or his rights.

THE PROCESS IS THE KEY

The Convention implicitly admits that other interests besides the child's must also be considered. Still, the principle of the best interests will, as intended, lead to changes. The challenge is to develop a policy that will give real substance to the phrase 'a primary consideration' in different situations.

Working with flexible norms is of course not the same as being unprincipled. But can human rights standards that are somewhat relative be of any use? This is a key question in relation to the Convention on the Rights of the Child, which to a large extent is built on principles whose application will have to depend on various considerations and actual circumstances.

There is of course a risk that empty rhetoric, so usual when it comes to children and their welfare, will prevail. The experience so far, however, seems to indicate that the complexity and the general nature of the basic principles of the Convention can be an important asset. These characteristics make the Convention more 'real' in political discussions, more flexible in changing circumstances, more interesting intellectually and thus a more effective instrument.

Crossing the line between empty rhetoric and genuine change depends largely on how decisions are taken. As indicated above, there are two major stages in the implementation of Article 3: to assess what is best for the child, and to balance her or his best interests against competing claims.

Regarding the first stage, the Convention as a whole gives pointers as to what is good for the child. It also requires that the child be heard and that his or her opinions be taken seriously. As for the second stage, it is important to remember that the basic idea is that priority should be given to the child, although the interests of others should also be considered as relevant. Impact analyses will facilitate the assessment and balancing of competing interests.

When considering decisions that are likely to affect a child or children considerably, decision makers should always systematically attempt to assess and evaluate the consequences of the proposed action. Again, in the second stage of the process as in the first, it is important that children be heard whenever possible, and that their opinions be sought before the final decision is taken.

The purpose, of course, is to encourage decision makers to give serious consideration to possible consequences for children before they proceed. They should not only undertake a child-impact assessment before taking a decision; they should also eventually be able to show that they have done so. In other words, they must be able to show that they have indeed considered how children would be affected. This means, in effect, that the burden of proof will be placed on those who move against children's interests. One outcome might be that a search for alternatives to the original proposal will be encouraged when it is made clear that the impact on children was – or is likely to be – unfavourable.

Such a serious process is what the Committee on the Rights of the Child has asked for. In its General Comment No. 5 (CRC/GC/2003/5 paras. 45–47) it states that the best interests principle 'requires active measures throughout Government, parliament and the judiciary.'

'Every legislative, administrative and judicial body or institution is required to apply the best interests principle by systematically considering how children's rights and interests are or will be affected by their decisions and actions – by, for example, a proposed or existing law or policy or administrative action or court decision, including those which are not directly concerned with children, but indirectly affect children.'

The Committee goes on to demand a continuous process of child impact assessments and child impact evaluations. The first is defined as predicting the impact of any proposed law, policy or budgetary allocation; the second as evaluating the actual impact of implementation. The Committee states that the process needs to built into government at all levels and as early as possible in the development of policy and affirms: 'Self-monitoring and evaluation is an obligation for Governments.'

Progress so far

The Convention's approach to the principle of the best interests of the child represents a major departure from most established routines in national and local politics and administration in all countries of the world. So far, such procedures have only been established in situations related to the previous, more limited, definition of the best interests principle, for instance, in regard to decisions about custody in divorce cases or sanctions on young law offenders. The broader scope of the principle has very rarely been implemented anywhere.

Some experiments have been made, however. In Norway, there have been attempts to assess the impact of the national budget on children, which could be the first step towards clarifying government accountability in this regard. The Swedish parliament adopted a National Strategy for the Implementation of the Convention on the Rights of the Child, which, inter alia, prescribes that child impact analyses should be included and documented in relevant decision-making. In both countries, efforts are being made to introduce the best interests principle into relevant legislation. The momentum gained has already brought about some changes – for instance, changes in the way the Swedish asylum law has been applied in specific cases.

In Belgium, the Flemish Parliament has passed legislation requiring that 'all proposed decrees when laid before the Flemish Parliament shall be accompanied by a report on their impact on children, to the extent that the proposed decision directly affects the rights of the child.' In Scotland a system for 'child-proofing' policy proposals and new legislation is being developed.

In local politics, the problems tend to be specific, which may make it easier to consider a child dimension. In the United Kingdom, many local Councils have adopted the Convention on the Rights of the Child to guide their activities. This is an interesting first step and would, if pursued, mean that a child-impact analysis would generally be undertaken before decisions are made on such matters as school policy, social security, local policing, city planning and environmental protection – not to mention the local budget itself.

The intention is not to introduce new bureaucratic elements into child-related decisions for the sake of form; rather it is to compensate for the fact that children have little political power, even indirectly through parents or other representatives. The new procedures may be seen as an unusual display of adult 'self-discipline' to force our decision-making systems to take steps to bridge that gap. The procedures clearly require discussions on methodology in order to be made 'real.' But if consciously used, they may one day contribute to what is really intended: a genuine attitudinal change leading to children being fully respected as human beings endowed with rights.

CONCLUSION

The Convention on the Rights of the Child has a progressive approach to the 'best interests' of the child. It deals with the concept as a general principle and an umbrella provision for the whole Convention. The definition of what is indeed in the best interests of the child is rooted in the substantive articles of the Convention itself.

However, the Convention does not give precise norms on how the best interests should be assessed – that would not have been possible. Instead the principle should be understood to define a procedural requirement: that decision-makers examine before decisions are taken which affect a child or a group of children whether the proposed solution is consistent with the best interests of the child or the children.

In any assessment of what is best for the child, it is essential that the child herself or himself be allowed to express an opinion and that that opinion is taken seriously. When interests clash, it is of course also necessary to consider other interests than those of the individual child or children as a group, as may be relevant. Such assessments and the balancing between the various interests will be facilitated by impact analyses. The consequences of proposed actions should be analysed and evaluated.

The intention of this process is to encourage decision makers to consider the child dimension seriously and routinely – before decisions are taken. They should not only undertake an assessment; they should also be able to demonstrate that they have done so. All this should be seen as an obligation dictated by the Convention.

The next step in this evolution of the 'best interests' approach is to develop models for how impact assessments and evaluations could be designed. When and how should they be carried out? What areas should be given first priority? How should these analyses be linked to ordinary political processes? What kinds of questions should be asked – and to whom? What training needs to be provided to decision makers and others in order to make all this meaningful?

These are urgent questions as children cannot wait too long. To quote Janusz Korczak once again:

'Children are not the people of tomorrow, but are people of today. They have a right to be taken seriously, and to be treated with tenderness and respect. They should be allowed to grow into whoever they were meant to be – the unknown person inside each of them is our hope for the future.'

TASK/TEXT 6.10: JOINT PARENTAL AUTHORITY (AND CONTACT) AFTER DIVORCE AND THE BEST INTERESTS OF THE CHILD

C.G. Jeppesen de Boer, *Joint Parental Authority; A comparative legal study on the continuation of joint parental authority after divorce and the breakup of a relationship in Dutch and Danish law and the CEFL principles*, PhD Utrecht University, Antwerpen: Intersentia, 2008, pp. 320 and 322–323

Not joint parental authority after divorce and contact wit both parents are *per se* in the best interest of the child but "the parenting potential of the resident parent and a lack of parental conflict."

Research does not prove that joint parenting, joint parental authority or even contact benefit children independently of the parents' ability and willingness to co-operate. The most important factors for children's well-being in the postdivorce family seem to be related to the parenting potential of the resident parent and a lack of parental conflict.

Dutch research has clearly shown that the changes pursuant to the 1998 reform, which provided for the automatic continuation of parental authority and soon developed into the strong legal norm, led to substantively increased conflict levels.

On the other hand, Danish research clearly indicates that the foundations for joint parenting after divorce and after the breakup of a relationship depend upon the parents' relationship with each other, with the understanding that the foundations for joint parenting are connected to circumstances which were already present at the child's birth.

Further Danish research provides the insight that a lack of ability or the potential to co-operate is often associated with other social vulnerability factors such as being connected to violence within the relationship and substance abuse, giving rise to the understanding that the parent-child relationship affected by conflicts after divorce is a vulnerable construction due to factors other than the divorce itself. (…)

It is a pertinent question whether the aim of promoting the amicable postdivorce family and the child's right or obligation to have two parents does not harm children in families where this aim is unattainable and where the concrete result is that the family become embroiled in legal procedures for many years to come. Furthermore, it is worth posing the question whether it is possible to compel parents to co-operate in pursuit of an ideal and to protect vulnerable family life at the same time.

In answering these questions the bottom-line should be that the choice of a certain form of regulation will determine the level of processes involving children in post-divorce families. The price for the present type of regulation is to be paid by children who come from families where the aim of promoting the amicable post-divorce family is unattainable. Research shows that this often encompasses children in families where there are other social vulnerability factors such as violence or substance abuse indicating that there is a special need for protection. Compelling parents to co-operate in these situations may prolong the procedures unnecessarily and may even prove to threaten the safety of certain family members. These circumstances are to be taken into account when considering the role of the State. Would it not be more appropriate for the State to adopt a protective role aiming to prevent distress through the requirement that joint parental authority is based upon the parents' request and a continued ability to hold parental authority jointly?

According to this author's view, a feasible approach which will limit the amount of processes is to base the allocation of joint parental authority after divorce and after the breakup of a relationship upon the parents' (continued) willingness to hold joint parental authority. This implies a return to the joint request procedure for married parents [for unmarried parents parental authority will continue unless a request for sole parental authority is made]. The advantage of this approach is that it provides an unambiguous legal regulation of the allocation of parental authority while being amenable to parents who can agree on joint parental authority. This approach strengthens the effective exercise of parental authority and reduces the need for a detailed regulation.

TASK/TEXT 6.11: GOOD HEALTH, STRONG FAMILIES, POSITIVE EARLY LEARNING EXPERIENCES – AN OVERVIEW OF THE POLICY AGENDA FOR INFANTS AND TODDLERS; BABY MATTERS

<www.zerotothree.org/site/PageServer?pagename=ter_pub_infanttodller>; <http://policy.db.zerotothree.org/policyp/home.aspx>, accessed 12 February 2009

How, and how well, we think, learn, communicate, concentrate and relate to others when we get to school and later in our lives depend on the experiences we have and the skills we develop during the earliest days, months and years of our lives. When experiences fail to support an infant's or toddler's biologically inherent desire to learn, grow, and succeed, "a child's motivation diminishes, shifts, or finds problematic outlets." Ensuring that babies have good health, strong families, and positive early learning experiences will lay the foundation for success throughout their lives.

Why focus on babies?

Research shows that experiences in the earliest years of life play a critical role in a child's ability to grow up healthy and ready to learn. Indeed, during the first three years of life, the brain undergoes its most dramatic development and children acquire the ability to think, speak, and reason. Our knowledge of the early years has been significantly enhanced by the incredible advances made by neuroscientists who have found that the way a baby reacts emotionally to how he or she is treated releases chemicals that affect his or her brain's structure and functioning.

How, and how well, we think, learn, communicate, concentrate and relate to others when we get to school and later in our lives depend on the experiences we have and the skills we develop during the earliest days, months and years of our lives. When experiences fail to support an infant's or toddler's biologically inherent desire to learn, grow, and succeed, "a child's motivation diminishes, shifts, or finds problematic outlets." Ensuring that babies have good health, strong families, and positive early learning experiences will lay the foundation for success throughout their lives.

The need to invest early

Leading economists such as Dr. James Heckman, Nobel Laureate and Professor of Economics at the University of Chicago, have done extensive research on the value of investing in early childhood programs and have found that dollars invested early in a child's life yield extraordinary public returns. In fact, research has shown that for every dollar invested in early childhood programs, savings of $3.78 to $17.07 can be expected. While many of these savings directly benefit individuals, the public reaps far more of the benefits in terms of reduced crime, abuse, neglect, and welfare dependency while increasing educational performance and job training, leading to higher incomes and a better quality and more productive workforce. By investing early, we can build upon skills and have a longer timeframe in which to recoup the benefits of our investment.

Informing public policy

While almost every social policy from welfare reform to education to substance abuse and mental health treatment affects infants and toddlers, the impact of these policies on very young children is seldom sufficiently addressed. We must translate what we know from science about the needs of infants and toddlers into effective, evidence-based policies and practices.

We need policies that support parents and other caregivers in providing young children with the foundations of early learning and healthy adjustment. The needs of infants and toddlers must be addressed in the context of their families, primarily by supporting parents in nurturing and teaching their children. School success begins not with learning ABC's as a preschooler, but with learning as an infant how to trust and feel secure, explore one's environment, and form close attachments. Research shows that it is these early experiences and warm, loving relationships that form "both the foundation and scaffold on which cognitive, linguistic, emotional, social, and moral development unfold."

Children learn and grow through their relationships with parents and other caregivers. Policies that build strong families starting even before a child is born are the best way to point children toward later success in school and in life. Such policies must recognize that very young children have physical and mental health needs. These needs must be considered when supporting positive early learning experiences for infants and toddlers, both in their homes and in other settings. As leaders work to strengthen comprehensive services for young children, science dictates they include systems that support social and emotional development in order to substantially improve the course of children's growth.

Intervention with at-risk children must begin early. Policies that wait until children are already behind are inadequate: children who start behind, stay behind. The early years represent an unparalleled window of opportunity to support children. Research shows that programs that serve infants and toddlers such as Early Head Start can positively impact success in school, family self-sufficiency, and parental support of child development. Devoting resources to programs to improve success in school for preschool-age and older children is important. But unfortunately, by the time they reach preschool, underprivileged children are often playing "catch up" with their more advantaged peers. Expanding funding for early interventions for these at-risk infants and toddlers will help them be fully prepared when they reach preschool. Developing such proactive policies today can reduce the need for more expensive reactive policies in the future, while helping to ensure that all children enter school healthy and ready to learn.

(…) **Baby Matters: A Gateway to State Policies and Initiatives** (…) is a searchable database that contains resource information on state policies and initiatives that impact infants, toddlers and their families. The policies and initiatives are searchable by category, state, or keyword. A detailed description of each policy or initiative is provided, as well as links to additional related resources. The policies and initiatives presented in *Baby Matters* are categorized by the elements of the ZERO TO THREE Policy Center's Infant & Toddler Policy Framework [see above]. Our framework focuses on key strategies across four main areas known to impact the healthy development of infants and toddlers:

Good Health

- Physical Health
- Social and Emotional Health
- Developmental Screening

Positive Early Learning Experiences

- Child Care
- Early Head Start
- Early Intervention

Strong Families

- Basic Needs
- Parent Education
- Home Visiting
- Child Welfare
- Family Leave

System

- Governance/Leadership
- Quality Improvement
- Accountability and Evaluation
- Financing
- Public engagement and Political will building
- Regulations and Standards
- Professional Development.

TASK/TEXT 6.12:

TASK/TEXT 6.12.1: PREVENTING MENTAL, EMOTIONAL, AND BEHAVIORAL DISORDERS AMONG YOUNG PEOPLE (1)

Mary Ellen O'Connell, Thomas Boat, and Kenneth E. Warner (eds.); Committee on the Prevention of Mental Disorders and Substance Abuse Among Children, Youth and Young Adults: Research Advances and Promising Interventions; Institute of Medicine; National Research Council, *Preventing Mental, Emotional, and Behavioral Disorders Among Young People: Progress and Possibilities*, Washington, DC: The National Academies Press, 2009; Executive Summary: <www.nap.edu/catalog/12480.html>, accessed 17 March 2009

A. AREAS OF PROGRESS

Several decades of research have shown that the promise and potential lifetime benefits of preventing mental, emotional, and behavioral (MEB) disorders are greatest by focusing on young people and that early interventions can be effective in delaying or preventing the onset of such disorders. National priorities that build on this evidence base should include (1) assurance that individuals who are at risk receive the best available evidence-based interventions prior to the onset of a disorder and (2) the **promotion of positive mental, emotional, and behavioral development for all children, youth, and young adults.** (...)

Key Areas of Progress since 1994

- Evidence that MEB disorders are common and begin early in life.
- Evidence that the greatest prevention opportunity is among young people.
- Evidence of multiyear effects of multiple preventive interventions on reducing substance abuse, conduct disorder, antisocial behavior, aggression, and child maltreatment.
- Evidence that the incidence of depression among pregnant women and adolescents can be reduced.
- Evidence that school-based violence prevention can reduce the base rate of aggressive problems in an average school by one-quarter to one-third.
- Promising evidence regarding potential indicated preventive interventions targeting schizophrenia.
- **Evidence that improving family functioning and positive parenting serves as a mediator of positive outcomes and can moderate poverty-related risk.**
- Emerging evidence that school-based preventive interventions aimed at improving social and emotional outcomes can also improve academic outcomes.
- **Evidence that interventions that target families dealing with such adversities as parental depression and divorce demonstrate efficacy in reducing risk for depression among children and increasing effective parenting.**
- Evidence from some preventive interventions that benefits exceed costs, with **the available evidence strongest for early childhood interventions.**
- Evidence of interactions between modifiable environmental factors and the expression of genes linked to behavior.
- Greater understanding of the biological processes that underlie both normal brain function and the pathophysiology of MEB disorders.
- Emerging opportunities for the integration of genetics and neuroscience research with prevention research.
- Advances in implementation science, including recognition of implementation complexity and the importance of relevance to the community.

B. TRUE PREVENTION

Preface (Kenneth E. Warner, *Chair;* Thomas Boat, *Vice Chair;* Committee on the Prevention of Mental Disorders and Substance Abuse Among Children, Youth and Young Adults), p. xiii.

This report calls on the nation – its leaders, its mental health research and service provision agencies, its schools, its primary care medical systems, its community-based organizations, its child welfare and criminal justice systems – to make **prevention of mental, emotional, and behavioral disorders** and the **promotion of mental health** of young people a very high priority. By all realistic measures, no such priority exists today.

The report therefore urges action at the highest levels to ensure that public health decision makers and the public understand the nature and magnitude of this problem; that research to prevent it is carefully coordinated and well funded; and that institutions and communities have the resources and the responsibility to promote the implementation of prevention interventions that can address shortfalls in the public response.

Mental, emotional, and behavioral disorders incur **high psychosocial and economic costs** for the young people who experience them, for their families, and for the society in which they live, study, and will work. Yet there is a significant imbalance in the nation's efforts to address such disorders.

People await their emergence and then attempt to treat them, to cure them if possible, or to limit the damage they cause if not. This happens with any number of expensive interventions, ranging **from psychiatric care to incarceration**. Myopically, we devote minimal attention to preventing future disorders or the environmental exposures that increase risk. (...) This report documents that an increasing number of mental, emotional, and behavioral problems in young people are in fact preventable. The proverbial **ounce of prevention will indeed be worth a pound of cure**: effectively applying the evidence-based prevention interventions at hand could potentially save billions of dollars in associated costs by avoiding or tempering these disorders in many individuals. Furthermore, devoting significantly greater resources to research on even more effective prevention and promotion efforts, and then reliably implementing the findings of such research, could substantially diminish the human and economic toll. This could be done, but as Hadorn has observed, **the basic tendency is to focus on "the rule of rescue ... the powerful human proclivity to rescue endangered life."** As a society, we suffer from a **collective health care myopia**: we have not yet figured out how to balance rescue – which is after-the-fact treatment – with the less dramatic but often far more cost-effective and socially desirable prevention of the onset of a problem (...) the disproportionate emphasis on treatment of existing conditions needs to be corrected. We propose a new emphasis on **true prevention**, which (...) we define as occurring prior to the onset of disorder, as well as mental health promotion (...). We do not disparage society's emphasis on treatment and indeed think that in the domain of mental health, far more resources should be devoted to the effort. Rather, we want to highlight the critical need for a more **proactive, preventive focus** on mental health.

The primary charge for this committee is prevention, but we add to our focus the emerging field of mental health promotion, an important and largely ignored approach toward building healthy development in all young people. Prevention emphasizes the avoidance of risk factors; promotion strives to **promote supportive family, school, and community environments** and to identify and imbue in young people protective factors, which are traits that enhance well-being and provide the tools to avoid adverse emotions and behaviors. While research on promotion is limited, emerging interest and involvement in it and the potential it holds for enhancing health warrant its inclusion in the consideration of how the nation can improve its collective well-being.

The committee's focus on young people and the stigma associated with the term "mental disorder" led us to adopt the term "mental, emotional, and behavioral disorders" to encompass both disorders diagnosable using *Diagnostic and Statistical Manual of Mental Disorders, 4th Edition* (DSM-IV) criteria and the problem behaviors associated with them, such as violence, aggression, and antisocial behavior. Many mental, emotional, and behavioral disorders of youth exist on a continuum and exert significant costs on the young people themselves, the people affected by them, and society at large. The term "mental, emotional, and behavioral disorders" encompasses mental illness and substance abuse, while including a somewhat broader range of concerns associated with problem behaviors and conditions in youth.

One factor lurks in the background of every discussion of the risks for mental, emotional, and behavioral disorders and antisocial behavior: **poverty**. Poverty in the United States often entails a range of material hardships, such as overcrowding, frequent moves (which often mean changes of school), poor schools, limited health care, unsafe and stressful environments, and sometimes lack of **adequate food**. All of these imperil cognitive, emotional and behavioral development. Although not the focus of this report, there is evidence that **changes in social policy that reduce exposure to these risks** are at least as important for preventing mental, emotional and behavioral disorders in young people as other preventive interventions. We are persuaded that the future mental health of the nation depends crucially on how, collectively, the costly legacy of poverty is dealt with. (...)

TASK/TEXT 6.12.2: PREVENTING MENTAL, EMOTIONAL, AND BEHAVIORAL DISORDERS AMONG YOUNG PEOPLE (2)

Report Brief for Policymakers, March 2009, <www.bocyf.org/prevention_policymakers_brief.pdf>

Mental, emotional, and behavioral (MEB) disorders – which include depression, conduct disorder, and substance abuse – affect large numbers of young people. Studies indicate that MEB disorders are a major health threat and are as commonplace today among young people as a fractured limb – not inevitable but not at all unusual. Almost **one in five young people have one or more MEB disorders at any given time**. Among adults, half of all MEB disorders were first diagnosed by age 14 and three-fourths by age 24.

Many disorders have life-long effects that include high psychosocial and economic costs, not only for the young people, but also for their families, schools, and communities. The financial costs in terms of treatment services and lost productivity are estimated at $247 billion annually. Beyond the financial costs, MEB disorders also interfere with young people's ability to accomplish developmental tasks, such as establishing healthy interpersonal relationships, succeeding in school, and making their way in the workforce.

Clear windows of opportunity are available to prevent MEB disorders and related problems before they occur. Risk factors are well established, preventive interventions are available, and the first symptoms typically precede a disorder by 2 to 4 years. And because mental health and physical health problems are interwoven, improvements in mental health will undoubtedly also improve physical health. Yet **the nation's approach to MEB disorders has largely been to wait to act until a disorder is well-established and has already done considerable harm**. All too often, opportunities are missed to use evidence-based approaches to prevent the occurrence of disorders, establish building blocks for healthy development in all young people, and limit the environmental exposures that increase risk – approaches likely to be far more cost-effective in addressing MEB disorders in the long run.

Interventions before a disorder manifests itself offer the best opportunity to protect young people. Such interventions can be integrated with routine health care and wellness promotion, as well as in schools, families, and communities. A range of policies and practices that target young people with specific risk factors; promote positive emotional development; and build on family, school, and community resources have proven to be effective at reducing and preventing MEB disorders. Making use of the evidence-based interventions already at hand could potentially save billions of dollars by preventing or mitigating disorders that would otherwise require expensive treatment.

Proven Approaches

A recent study by the National Research Council and the Institute of Medicine reviewed the research on the prevention of mental disorders and substance abuse among young people and recommended multiple strategies for enhancing the psychological and emotional well-being of young people. Research including meta-analyses and numerous randomized trials demonstrate the value of:

- *Strengthening families* by targeting problems such as substance use or aggressive behavior; **teaching effective parenting skills**; improving communication; and helping families deal with disruptions (such as divorce) or adversities (such as **parental mental illness or poverty**).
- *Strengthening individuals* by building resilience and skills and improving cognitive processes and behaviors.
- *Preventing specific disorders*, such as anxiety or depression, by screening individuals at risk and offering cognitive training or other preventive interventions.
- *Promoting mental health in schools* by offering support to children encountering serious stresses; modifying the school environment to **promote prosocial behavior**; developing students' skills at decision making, self-awareness, and conducting relationships; and targeting violence, aggressive behavior, and substance use.
- *Promoting mental health through health care and community programs* by promoting and supporting prosocial behavior, teaching coping skills, and targeting modifiable life-style factors that can affect behavior and emotional health, such as sleep, diet, activity and physical fitness, sunshine and light, and television viewing.

The key to most of these approaches is to identify risks – biological, psychological, and social factors – that may increase a child's risk of MEB disorders. Some of these risks reside in specific characteristics of the individual or family environment (such as parental mental illness or substance abuse or serious family disruptions), but they also include social stresses such as poverty, violence, lack of safe schools, and lack of access to health care. Most risk factors tend to come in clusters and are associated with more than one disorder. Currently, treatment interventions tend to isolate single problems, but there is growing evidence that well-designed prevention interventions reduce a range of problems and disorders and that these efforts are sustained over the long term. These programs often help children, families, and schools build strengths that support well-being. A focus on prevention and wellness can have multiple benefits that extend beyond a single disorder.

Policy Implications

Officials at the local, state, and federal levels all play a role in mental health promotion and the prevention of MEB disorders. Many providers and agencies are responsible for the care, protection, or support of young people: the child welfare, education, and juvenile justice systems, as well as medical and mental health care providers and community organizations. Yet resources within these agencies are scattered, not coordinated, and often do not effectively support prevention programs or policies. The result is a **patchwork that does not perform as an integrated system** and fails to serve the needs of many young people and their families.

National leadership is necessary to make systematic prevention efforts a high priority in the health care system as well as an integral aspect of the network of local, state, and federal programs and systems that serve young people and families. Leaders at the national, state, and local levels need to pursue specific strategies, such as:

- *A White House initiative to develop an inter-departmental strategy* that identifies specific prevention goals, directs multiple federal agency resources toward these goals, and provides guidance to state and local partners.
- *Development of state and local systems* involving partnerships among families, schools, courts, health care providers, and local programs to create coordinated approaches that support healthy development.
- *Investment in prevention and promotion,* including setting aside resources for evidence-based prevention in mental health service programs and investment in proven prevention approaches by school systems.
- *Workforce training,* including development of prevention training standards and training programs across disciplines including health, education, and social work.
- *Long-term tracking* of the prevalence and frequency of MEB disorders.
- *Implementation and evaluation of screening* with community involvement, parental support, valid tools, and interventions to address identified needs.
- *Continued research* on both the efficacy of new prevention models and real-world effectiveness of proven prevention and wellness promotion interventions.
- *Adaptation of research-based programs* to cultural, linguistic, and socioeconomic subgroups.
- *Public education,* with mass media and the internet offering the opportunity to greatly expand the reach of specific messages about risk factors and

available resources, to reduce stigma, and to deliver some kinds of interventions.

Implementing a systems focus will require innovative efforts to provide societal institutions that affect young people – families, schools, health care systems, and community programs – with the tools to **promote healthy development and prevent MEB disorders.** Policies are also needed to help ensure families' financial security, provide safe neighborhoods and schools, improve access to health care and other services, and **provide enriched early childhood environments.**

Tools to equip young people who are at risk with the skills and habits they need to live healthy, happy, and productive lives are available. **What is lacking are the will, social policies, and collaborative strategies to adequately support the healthy development of the nation's young people.**

TASK/TEXT 6.13: PERCEPTION OF CHILDREN ON PARENTING PRACTICES

Save the Children Sweden, Regional Office for South and Central Asia, 2008; <www.crin.org/docs/Perceptionpractices.pdf> (Crinmail 1067 – 17 March 2009)

The Convention on the Rights of the Child (CRC) states that the family has the key responsibility to ensure the fundamental rights of children as it is the primary setting within which children are cared for and parented and where first significant relationships develop and the foundations of their development take place. The CRC also recognizes that governments have the responsibility [obligation, JW] to provide support to parents and families as duty bearers [in accordance with national laws, to be put in place by the state, JW]. All countries in South Asia have ratified the CRC, which means that the government has accepted the responsibility [duty, JW] to fulfil its obligations.

Articles in the CRC that state the obligations of State Parties to support parents and families for ensuring children's rights include:

- **Article 3.2:** States Parties undertake to ensure the child such protection and care as is necessary for his or her well being, taking into account the rights and duties of his or her parents, legal guardians, or other individuals legally responsible for him or her, and, to this end, shall take all appropriate and administrative measures.

- **Article 4:** States Parties shall undertake all appropriate legislative, administrative and other measures for the implementation of the rights recognized in the present Convention.
- **Article 18.2:** For the purpose of guaranteeing and promoting the rights set forth in the present Convention, States Parties shall render appropriate assistance to parents and legal guardians in the performance of their child-rearing responsibilities and shall ensure the development of institutions, facilities and services for the care of children.

Parenting

Parenting may be defined as "purposive activities aimed at ensuring the survival and development of children. These actions may or may not be performed by the child's biological parent." The term "parent" in general denotes the biological relationship of a father or mother to a child, though it may be extended to adults without a biological relationship who are bringing up children. This report will mainly focus on the role of both biological and non-biological parents, though it will also look at the role of extended family members such as the grandparent, aunt, uncle or older sibling.

Save the Children Sweden Regional Office for South and Central Asia in collaboration with its partners in South Asia has carried out this qualitative study that focuses on the perception of girls and boys on parenting styles. The study was conducted in five countries of South Asia – Afghanistan, Bangladesh, India, Nepal and Pakistan – and focused on disadvantaged children in the 8–16 age range including children in poor rural homes, children with disability, indigenous children, trafficked children (trafficking survivors), homeless children (street children and children living in railway platforms), working children, children from brothels, children in conflict with the law, and children engaged in or affected by armed conflict. Parents living in rural households were also interviewed to draw information on their perceptions about parenting.

The study builds a general picture of children's views and experiences and the factors influencing their perception on parenting. It also focuses on the extent to which parenting behaviours may vary according to cultural and socio-economic circumstances. It further demonstrates how gaining children's perspectives greatly increases understanding of the various parenting practices, showing that what children and young people think is not necessarily what adults think they do.

The study explores children's perception on men's role as fathers, women's role as mothers and the factors that influence their thoughts. It also examines parenting styles that may affect children's emotional and social development and their capacity to express their opinions.

Key findings from the study

Role of fathers and mothers: Fathers are expected to be providers and protectors and take major decisions regarding children; whereas mothers are expected to comply more with the role of nurturing, caring and home maintenance. This view is based on how girls and boys were socialized to think of what is appropriate and improper for both genders.

Parental behaviour disliked by children: Girls and boys do not like to witness domestic violence, especially when the father beats his wife. They also do not like alcoholic or promiscuous parents. Nearly all the children in this study disliked physical and humiliating punishment by their parents and other caregivers.

Role of other family members: Grandparents show love, shower them with affection and are always willing to help and comfort their grandchildren. They also provide refuge and protection to children when they get into trouble. The other family members such as uncles, aunts or older siblings also play an important role in their lives.

Love and emotional support: All children in the study said that what they want most from parents is to be loved and cared for. However, parents usually do not express love for their adolescent children in outward displays of affection.

Communicating with children: Adolescent girls and boys felt that open communication with parents was very important to prevent children from not only making serious mistakes but also to prevent them from indulging in behaviours that threaten their health, safety and welfare. They said that it was the parents' responsibility to talk to their children about sexual and reproductive health, sexual exploitation, HIV and AIDS, drugs, trafficking and armed conflict and to caution them not to fall into the hands of recruiters for armed conflict and traffickers.

Consulting with children: Children generally do not get the opportunity to take part in most of the decisions that influence their lives. It is usually the parents and other adults who take decisions on their behalf. They said that parents should consult with them before they decide to withdraw them from school, send children to work, marry girls off at an early age, sell their children or make any important decisions that concern them.

Spending quality time with children: Children have fun with their parents during special occasions (…), depending on the religion and culture of the community. Both young and older children love to hear stories. Some children said that they like to eat together as a family.

Punishment and discipline: Most girls and boys do not like physical and psychological punishment. They hate it when they are punished for something they did not do. Most of the girls and boys said that they should be given a proper explanation of what they had done wrong, instead of unnecessarily being beaten. Physical and psychological punishments were found to be one of the prime reasons for some children to leave home, quit school and end up in prostitution, jails or in the streets. This revelation challenges **the myth that children end up in vulnerable situations only because of poverty.**

Discrimination: Girls and boys do not like any form of discrimination on the basis of gender, disability, religion, social class, ethnicity and social status of parents. Some children reported being discriminated against by their step-parents. In some cases parents have demonstrated a special preference for one of their children.

Work and play: Most of the children expressed their disliking for going to work. Almost all girls and boys said that they liked to play. Younger girls and boys get more opportunities to play. Adolescent girls are not allowed to play outside their homes. Both girls and boys said that they did not get much time to play as they had too much work.

The way forward

The knowledge gained from the current study will facilitate discussions on how to develop an **effective parenting education programme**. Parenting education may be defined, then, as the **set of programmes, resources or services whose goal is to increase parents' capacities to foster children's health, education, protection and participation in matters that affect them.**

Parenting education programmes can start with the development of a **parenting manual**. This manual can be developed with inputs from children, parents, child development experts and findings from this study. The parenting manual will not only recognize and build upon positive traditional practices but also identify and change practices that are harmful to girls and boys. Parenting education should take account of children's recommendations in the study and address gender roles, discrimination and the importance of father's role as nurturers.

Parenting education can be **cost effective** if it is integrated into ongoing programme activities of governments, Save the Children and partner organizations. The national governments, donors, UN agencies and I/NGOs in the region already have established programmes on primary healthcare, reproductive health, nutrition, education, gender, HIV/AIDS and child protection. Some of these programmes work directly with families and adolescents and therefore provide opportunities for these organizations to integrate parenting education.

Parenting education may be incorporated into the national education system, so that girls and boys are **prepared for their future responsibilities**. School programmes could change the sexrole stereotyping and combat discrimination based on gender, ability, ethnicity, religion and socio-economic status. The media can be an effective delivery vehicle for parenting information and advice for reducing violence against children, and promoting gender equality and child development.

TASK/TEXT 6.14:

TASK/TEXT 6.14.1: INVESTING IN CHILDREN MAKES ECONOMIC SENSE

Contribution to the Czech [EU] Presidency Conference Child Friendly-Europe
Messages to Child-Friendly Europe Conference in Prague (6–7 April 2009), email 6 April 2009

Eurochild[51] welcomes the initiative of the Czech EU Presidency to organise a high level event on children's rights and promoting children's best interest across EU and national policies. It is an opportune moment. The current economic crisis presents difficult choices. But upholding children's rights makes economic sense. For example, every euro spent in early high quality years' education and care services can be expected to give a return of over 7 euro – in terms of reduced social and health costs, better educational performance and employment opportunities, reduced criminality. The realisation and protection of children's

---

51 Eurochild is a network of organisations and individuals promoting the rights and welfare of children and young people in Europe. The network currently has 67 members in 27 European countries. Our work focuses particularly on the fight against child poverty in Europe. Members participate actively in thematic working groups, focussing i.a. on early years; family and parenting support; child participation and children without parental care. Eurochild is supported by the European Community Programme for Employment and Social Solidarity (2007–2013). This programme is managed by the Directorate-General for Employment, social affairs and equal opportunities of the European Commission. It was established to financially support the implementation of the objectives of the European Union in the employment and social affairs area, as set out in the Social Agenda, and thereby contribute to the achievement of the Lisbon Strategy goals in these fields. The seven-year Programme targets all stakeholders who can help shape the development of appropriate and effective employment and social legislation and policies, across the EU-27, EFTA-EEA and EU candidate and pre-candidate countries.
PROGRESS mission is to strengthen the EU contribution in support of Member States' commitments and efforts to create more and better jobs and to build a more cohesive society. To that effect, PROGRESS will be instrumental in:
- providing analysis and policy advice on PROGRESS policy areas;
- monitoring and reporting on the implementation of EU legislation and policies in PROGRESS policy areas;
- promoting policy transfer, learning and support among Member States on EU objectives and priorities; and
- relaying the views of the stakeholders and society at large.

For more information see: <http://ec.europa.eu/employment_social/progress/index_en.html>.

rights, as enshrined in the CRC, can be seen as a litmus test of social well-being. A child-friendly society benefits all of society. By respecting the best interest of the child in all decisions affecting them and ensuring children have the right to say what they think and have their opinions taken into account, we build the foundations for a society based on respect and civic responsibility. We hope these principles will light the way in the themes under discussion in Prague. But aspiration is not good enough. We need leadership at the highest political level to make children's rights a priority, accompanied by resources and policy reform that puts children's interest at the centre. In particular we call on delegates to conclude the event with a strategy for action, including:

A clear road map for adoption of an EU strategy on child rights

The 2006 Communication [COM(2006) 367 final, Towards an EU Strategy on the Rights of the Child] charged the European Commission with developing an '*EU strategy to effectively promote and safeguard the rights of the child in the European Union's internal and external policies and to support Member States' efforts in this field.*' It is vital the EU holds to its commitment and sets a clear road map for adopting an EU strategy on child rights in 2010, based on a widespread consultation that will take also account the views of children. A future strategy must pave the way for meaningful and safe children's participation in all decisions that affect them, in accordance with Article 12 of the CRC.

A commitment to end child poverty and social exclusion

Heads of States are agreed on the "*the need to fight poverty, especially child poverty*" [European Council Conclusions March 2007]. But few Member States have made any progress and the current economic crisis risks plunging many more families into debt, poverty and stress. Despite the fact that there is more understanding of what policies are needed to lift families out of poverty and support children in achieving their full potential, governments are slow to act. Eurochild calls on the EU to commit to clear quantified targets for ending child poverty, and adoption of an EU Recommendation on the issue in 2010 the European Year against Poverty and Social Exclusion.

Promote a child-centred approach to early years policy

High quality, accessible early year's education and care conceived with the child's best interest in mind have significant social value. They have proven social and educational benefits for children, especially those from deprived backgrounds, whilst also creating employment and increasing parents' availability for work. The Barcelona targets set an important goal in terms of provision. But they must be a part of a child-centred approach to early years' policy, which includes care and education services, parental and maternity leave, other reconciliation measures, labour market policies, family support, and the formal education system. Primary responsibility for the upbringing and development of the child of course remains with the parents – as stated by Article 18 of the CRC – and families must be given adequate support to ensure [that they] have the necessary resources and information to protect their child's interest. Eurochild embraces the Council of Europe definition of positive parenting: "*parental behaviour, based on the best interests of the child, that is nurturing, empowering, nonviolent, and provides recognition and guidance which involves setting of boundaries to enable the full development of the child*" (Recommendation 19, December 2006). States have at their disposal a range of measures that can foster the right conditions for positive parenting: from ensuring access to appropriate material, psychological, social and cultural resources, to actions that remove barriers to positive parenting, such as policies to promote improvements in the reconciliation of family and working lives and providing parenting education and training. We also need a coherent vision at EU level of early years' policy that puts children's best interest at the heart of debates on maternity leave, demographic change and economic recovery.

TASK/TEXT 6.14.2: CHILD DEVELOPMENT IS ECONOMIC DEVELOPMENT

A Conversation with Economist Art Rolnick, National Scientific Council on the Developing Child, <www.developingchild.net/pubs/persp/Child_Development_Is/Child_Development_Is.html> (accessed 27 June 2009; references omitted)

Abstract: The public dollars spent to stimulate economic development would be more wisely invested in child development programs, according to two different streams of research. Brain research shows the impact of experiences and environments on the developing brain architecture, with weaker architecture leading to increased vulnerability to later problems ranging from anxiety and depression to cardiovascular disease, diabetes, and stroke. Longitudinal [economic] studies show that high-quality early childhood programs reduce the number of low-income children who later need special education, public assistance, or incarceration, and increase the number who have well-paying jobs and high school degrees. These studies show a long-term rate of return of up to 16 percent for every dollar spent, making programs such as these a smart economic development strategy.

Council Member **Arthur J. Rolnick**, Ph.D., is senior vice president and director of research at the Federal Reserve Bank of Minneapolis. He also serves as an associate economist with the Federal Open Market Committee, and as an adjunct professor of economics in the MBA program of Lingnan College, Guangzhou, China, and at the University of Minnesota's Carlson School of Management. As a top official of the Federal Reserve Bank, he regularly attends meetings of the Federal Open Market Committee – the Federal Reserve's principal body responsible for establishing national money and credit policies. He is past president of the Minnesota Economic Association and he serves on several nonprofit boards, including the Minnesota Council on Economic Education, the Center for Economic Progress, the Citizen's League, and Ready 4 K, an advocacy organization for early childhood development. He is also on the Minneapolis Star and Tribune's Board of Economists, and is a member of Minnesota's Council of Economic Advisors.

The interviewer: **Richard Louv** is the author of six books, including *Last Child in the Woods: Saving Our Children From Nature-Deficit Disorder* (Algonquin) and *Childhood's Future* (Anchor). A longtime columnist at *The San Diego Union-Tribune*, he served on the editorial advisory board for *Parents magazine* and was one of the founders of Connect for Kids, the largest child advocacy site on the World Wide Web. He is a Visiting Scholar at The Heller School for Social Policy and Management at Brandeis University.

[Interview]
The best investment in economic development that government and the private sector can make is in the healthy development of children, says Art Rolnick, Ph.D, senior vice president and director of research at the Federal Reserve Bank of Minneapolis. Judging by where the money now goes, such thinking is unconventional. For decades, state and local governments have annually spent billions of public dollars to stimulate economic development. Their primary tool: subsidies, in the form of tax breaks, free land and other incentives to companies that locate or expand their businesses in hometown markets.

Has the traditional strategy paid off?
"No," says Rolnick, a contributing member of the National Scientific Council on the Developing Child. "I'm speaking for myself here, and not necessarily for the full Council. But our research shows that, nationally, the traditional approach creates no new jobs or businesses. The bidding war among communities to attract companies is, at best, a zero-sum game that distorts market outcomes and diverts public funds from more productive investments in economic development. Here in Minnesota, one suburb invested a huge amount of money luring a big-box store from another suburb." Rolnick questions the wisdom of that investment.

A New Approach for Long-Term Economic Growth

Whatever one thinks about traditional economic development strategies, focusing on child development could become a new and positive approach for long-term economic growth, says Rolnick. He and research associate Rob Grunewald, an economic and public policy analyst for the Federal Reserve Bank, propose that society adopt the perspective of **child-development-as-economic-development**, based on two independent streams of research.

One comes from the institutions that study brain development and the impact of experiences and environments on the developing architecture of the brain. This research shows that a large percentage of the brain is built by the time a child reaches age five, and that a child's home and community environment play a critical role in the formation of a strong or weak brain structure. If, for example, a child is raised in an environment of toxic stress, or suffers a psychological trauma, the architecture of his or her brain can be severely compromised; the body can release harmful chemicals in the brain, potentially impairing physical growth and making it more difficult for neurons to form connections with each other.

The weakening of the brain's architecture, in turn, weakens a child's ability to respond positively to future stresses, including normal life obstacles, and can increase a child's vulnerability to later problems, ranging from anxiety and depression to cardiovascular disease, diabetes and stroke. The child's ability to learn and interact positively with other children is therefore diminished. (For more information on stress and brain development, see "Stress and the Architecture of the Brain" [<www.developingchild.net/pubs/persp/Stress_Architecture/Stress_Architecture.html>].)

The second stream of research Rolnick cites in support of child development as economic development comes from a set of longitudinal studies of children from low-income families, including the Perry Preschool in Ypsilanti, Mich.; Abecedarian Project in North Carolina; Chicago Child-Parent Centers; and New York's Elmira Prenatal/Early Infancy Project. These studies illustrate the benefits to children who participate in high-quality early childhood development programs. Such children were less likely to be placed in a special-education program, more likely to graduate from high school, and, as adults, more likely to have well-paying jobs, and less likely to be on public assistance or commit crimes. Other studies showed similar results:

Economic investments keep kids on track. An evaluation of the 1995–96 class of the Michigan School Readiness Program for children showed that a sample of participants through grade four were less likely than non-participants to be held back a grade, and also had higher percentages of satisfactory ratings on standardized achievement tests in reading and mathematics.

Language scores improve. Assessments of kindergarten children in New Jersey's highest-poverty school districts showed the children displayed marked improvement in the 2003–04 school year, compared to previous years. Since 1999, these districts were mandated by the state's Supreme Court to provide preschool for three- and four-year-old children. Language scores were significantly higher in the 2003–04 school year, compared with scores four years earlier, and the percentage of children scoring "very strong" in early reading skills increased from 42 percent to 47 percent a year later.

Low-income kids get a better start. A recent study of children attending Oklahoma's Pre-K program (available to all four-year-old children statewide) showed particularly strong gains for low-income children, including a 31 percent increase in cognitive skills, and an 18 percent increase in language skills. Hispanic children demonstrated a 54 percent increase in test scores.

Center-based childcare shows benefits. The results of two studies of childcare, released in 2004, clearly indicate that enrollment in center-based childcare is associated with positive cognitive outcomes for young children, particularly when providers have high skill and education levels coupled with low child-teacher ratios.

As to the economics, such programs help society avoid the enormous costs associated with fixing – or not fixing – later social and economic problems. This approach offers "an extraordinary rate of return when compared with other public investments," says Rolnick. A cost-benefit analysis, based on the Perry Preschool study, shows "the real internal rates of return on these programs range from about 7 percent to more than 16 percent annually, inflation-adjusted," he says.

Moreover, this is an investment that keeps on giving. A recent 40-year summary report of the Perry Preschool Study – published after Rolnick and Grunewald did their initial analysis – shows that the total benefit to investment cost-ratio registered at the 27-year mark of the study is even higher than Rolnick's and Grunewald's original estimates, when measured over three decades.

"So, the two independent lines of research – brain studies and longitudinal economic analyses – lead us to conclude that the early years (of childhood) are critical to society's economic development," says Rolnick. "We recognize that public funding of childhood development programs will be difficult to sell politically, because the real returns from such programs are much less visible and less immediate than conventional economic development investments." But it shouldn't be. The numbers alone speak to the wisdom of the strategy. And then there's the fact that this "capacity building" is about maximizing the future of all our nation's children.

Questions remain regarding how to shape the best childhood-development programs. "But in our view," he adds, "**the economic case for why we should invest in early childhood development is closed.**"

For additional information on Rolnick and Grunewald's analysis of children and economic development, go to <www.minneapolisfed.org/research/studies/earlychild>.

TASK/TEXT 6.14.3: FEARS OVER REDUCED SPENDING ON CHILDREN IN INDUSTRIALISED NATIONS

Crinmail 1105 – 3 September 2009, <www.crin.org>

The United States allocates more public funds to its children than most other industrialised states but gets relatively less than its peers in return, the OECD said in a report on Tuesday. The United States spends 140,000 dollars (97,500 euros) per child compared with an average of just over 125,000 dollars in the 30-member Organisation for Economic Cooperation and Development, the report found. "But despite the higher spending, US children do less well in areas such as health and education than their peers in most other countries," the OECD said.

For children under the age of six, however, the United States spends 20,000 dollars per child, less than the OECD average of 30,000 dollars. Ireland, Japan, the Netherlands and New Zealand also "spend relatively little" on young children, according to the report, entitled *Doing Better for Children*.

The study compares public spending and policies targeting children according to such indicators as education, housing, family income and quality of school life. The OECD said countries which spend relatively more on children up to the age of six include Finland, France, Hungary, Iceland and Norway.

OECD Secretary General Angel Gurria acknowledged that the global financial downturn had squeezed public budgets around the world. "But any short-term savings on spending on children's education and health would have major long-term costs for society," he warned. "Governments should instead seize the opportunity to get better value from their investment in children. And **spending early, when the foundations for a child's future are laid, is key**, especially for disadvantaged children, and can help them break out of a cycle of poverty and social exclusion."

The report specifically recommended that policymakers consider financial incentives, such as cash payments for food vouchers, to high-risk pregnant women to encourage them to take advantage of pre-natal services. It cited

Hungary, where grants are available to expectant mothers who have at least four pre-natal health checks.

TASK/TEXT 6.15: US DEPARTMENT OF HEALTH AND HUMAN SERVICES, CENTERS FOR DISEASE CONTROL AND PREVENTION (CDC.GOV) – CHILD DEVELOPMENT

[The seven stages of parental responsibility – from preconception to adulthood – are:

1. **Preconception** ***(maybe the most important one!)***
2. **Pregnancy**
3. **Infants (0–1 year old)**
4. **Toddlers I (1–2 years old); Toddlers II (2–3 years old); Preschoolers (3–5 years old)**
5. **Middle Childhood I (6–8 years old); Middle Childhood II (9–11 years old)**
6. **Early Adolescence (12–14 years old)**
7. **Middle Adolescence (15–17 years old)]**

<www.cdc.gov/ncbddd/child>; <www.cdc.gov/ncbddd/child/infants.htm>, accessed 30 April 2009

The early years of a child's life are crucial for cognitive, social and emotional development. Therefore, it is important that we take every step necessary to ensure that children grow up in environments where their social, emotional and educational needs are met.

Cost to society of less than optimal development are enormous and far-reaching. Children who grow up in environments where their developmental needs are not met are at an increased risk for compromised health and safety, and learning and developmental delays. Failure to invest time and resources during children's early years may have long term effects on the foster care, health care, and education systems. Therefore, it is in the public's interest to ensure that children develop in safe, loving, and secure environments.

Positive Parenting Tips for Healthy Child Development – [3.] Infants (0–1 year old)

Developmental Milestones

Cognitive development for your baby means the learning process of memory, language, thinking and reasoning. Your baby is learning to recognize the sound of your voice. She is also learning to focus her vision from the periphery or the corner of her eyes to the center. Language development is more than uttering sounds ("babble"), or mama/dada. Listening, understanding, and knowing the names of people and things are all components of language development. During this stage, your baby is also developing bonds of love and trust with you. The way you cuddle, hold, and play with your baby will set the basis for how he will interact with you and others.

For more information on developmental milestones and warning signs of possible developmental delays, visit Learn the Signs, Act Early, <www.cdc.gov/ncbddd/autism/ActEarly>.

Positive Parenting

- Talk to your baby. It is soothing to hear your voice.
- When your baby makes sounds, answer him by repeating and adding words. This will help him learn to use language.
- Read to your baby. This helps her develop and understand language and sounds.
- Sing to your baby.
- Play music. This helps your baby develop a love for music and math.
- Praise your baby and give him lots of loving attention.
- Spend time cuddling and holding your baby. This helps her feel cared for and secure.
- The best time to play with your baby is when he's alert and relaxed. Watch your baby closely for signs of being tired or fussy so that you can take a break.
- Parenting can be hard work! Take care of yourself physically, mentally, and emotionally. It is easier to enjoy your new baby and be a positive, loving parent when you are feeling good yourself.

Child Safety First

Now that your newborn is at home, it is time to make sure that your home is a safe place. Look around your home for household items that might present a possible danger to your baby. As a parent, it is your responsibility to ensure that you create a safe environment for your baby. It is also important that you take the necessary steps to make sure that you are mentally and emotionally ready for your new baby. Here are a few tips to keep your baby safe during her first year of life.

- It is important that you **never shake your newborn baby**. Newborn babies have very weak neck muscles that are not yet able to support their heads. If you shake your baby you can damage his brain and delay normal development.
- To prevent SIDS (Sudden Infant Death Syndrome), it is recommended that you always put your baby to sleep on her back. For more information on SIDS, visit National Institute of Child Health and Human Development (<www.nichd.nih.gov/sids/sids.cfm>).
- Place your baby in a car safety seat every time he rides in the car. The safest place for his safety seat is in the back seat of the car. Children who are less than one year OR are less than 20 pounds should be placed in a rear-facing care seat.
- To prevent your baby from choking, cut her food into small bites. Don't allow your baby to play with anything that may cover her face or is easy for her to swallow.
- Never carry hot liquids or food near your baby or while holding him.
- Immunizations (shots) are important to protect your child's health and safety. Because children are susceptible to many potentially serious diseases, it is important that your child receive the proper immunizations. Please consult your local health care provider to ensure that your child is up-to-date on her childhood immunizations. You may visit the CDC immunization website (<www.cdc.gov/nip/recs/child-schedule.htm>) to obtain a copy of the recommended immunization schedule for US children.

TASK/TEXT 6.16: STRENGTHENING FAMILIES – FIVE PROTECTIVE FACTORS IN FAMILIES

<www.strengtheningfamilies.net>, accessed 5 May 2009

The **five Protective Factors** are the foundation of the Strengthening Families approach. Extensive research supports the common-sense notion that when these Protective Factors are present and robust in a family, the likelihood of child abuse and neglect diminish[es].

- Parental resilience: The ability to cope and bounce back from all types of challenges.

- Social connections: Friends, family members, neighbors, and other members of a community who provide emotional support and concrete assistance to parents.
- Knowledge of parenting and child development: Accurate information about raising young children and appropriate expectations for their behavior.
- Concrete support in times of need: Financial security to cover day-to-day expenses and unexpected costs that come up from time to time, access to formal supports like TANF [Temporary Assistance for Needy Families] and Medicaid, and informal support from social networks.
- Children's social and emotional development: A child's ability to interact positively with others and communicate his or her emotions effectively.

1. Parental Resilience

- Parental psychology plays an important role in both the causes and prevention of child abuse and neglect. Parents who are emotionally resilient are able to maintain a positive attitude, creatively solve problems, and effectively rise to challenges in their lives – and they are less likely to abuse or neglect their children.
- Parents who have experienced violence or abuse and neglect themselves or who have other risk factors for becoming abusers need caring relationships to help them develop and maintain positive relationships with their children.
- Parents who know and trust staff are more likely to reveal problems such as domestic violence or feelings of frustration and ask for assistance.

2. Social Connections

- Helping parents build constructive friendships and other positive connections can reduce their isolation, which is a consistent risk factor in child abuse and neglect. Isolation is a problem in particular for family members who are in crisis or need intensive help, such as victims of domestic violence.
- Social connections build parents' "social capital," their network of others in the community – family, friends, neighbors, churches, etc. – whom they can call on for help solving problems.
- Social connections also enable parents to develop and reinforce community norms about behavior. Norms against violence help reduce child abuse and neglect.
- Friendships lead to mutual assistance in obtaining resources that all families need from time to time, including transportation, respite child care, and other tangible assistance as well as emotional support.

3. Knowledge of Parenting and Child Development

- Parents who understand normal child development are less likely to be abusive and more likely to nurture their children's healthy development. Observing other children helps parents understand their own children in context.
- Parents often need timely help from someone they trust in order to address children's problem behaviors, such as biting or hitting, without resorting to harsh discipline techniques.
- People who model alternative discipline techniques, males who serve in nurturing roles, and programs with a norm of non-violence demonstrate alternatives for parents.
- Parents of children with developmental or behavior problems or special needs require support and coaching in their parenting roles to reduce their frustration and provide the help their children need.

4. Concrete Support in Times of Need

- Child neglect can be a consequence of family crisis, a parental condition such as substance abuse, or stresses associated with lack of resources.

5. Children's Social and Emotional Development

- Children with challenging behaviors are at greater risk for abuse. Identifying and working with children early to keep their development on track helps keep them safe.
- Programs' essential work of helping children develop socially and emotionally also has impact on the way parents and children interact. As children learn to verbalize their emotions rather than act them out, they are more able to tell parents how they feel, what they need, and how their parents' actions make them feel. Parents can then be more responsive to their children's needs and less likely to yell or hit.
- In particular, children who have experienced or witnessed violence need a safe environment, trained staff, and opportunities to develop normally.

TASK/TEXT 6.17: BACKING THE FUTURE – WHY INVESTING IN CHILDREN IS GOOD FOR US ALL

Action for Children (<http://actionforchildren.org.uk), *Backing the Future* (2009), Executive summary, <http://actionforchildren.org.uk/content.aspx?CategoryID=

561&ArticleID=616&fp=1> (Full report, <http://actionforchildren.org.uk/uploads/media/36/7857.pdf>)

Backing the Future provides the economic and social case for transforming the way we invest in the future of society through our children. The report makes clear the need for a comprehensive investment programme in preventative services for children and young people that would both save spending on dealing with the impact of problems later, and deliver wider benefits to society. To achieve lasting change, *Backing the Future* demonstrates why it is essential to address the impact of the structural factors affecting the circumstances of children's lives, such as poverty and inequality, together with psychological and social dimensions of their well-being. We show how this can be achieved and present an economic model for how the UK Government could fund **a transition to a more preventative system**, therefore turning aspiration into reality.

Given the current economic climate, you might ask is it wise for more public spending on children, particularly now? Government debt incurred from bailing out the banks coupled with deepening recession is likely to lead to a sharp squeeze on public services. Yet *Backing the Future* shows that the scale of our problems and what it will cost the UK in public spending to remedy them mean we can ill afford not to invest. The recommendations put forward will in fact help plant the seeds of future prosperity and insulate children today from the worst effects of the current recession.

Evidence of the need for decisive action by national governments is compelling. When compared with our European neighbours, the UK comes bottom of the pile on almost every preventable social problem – **crime, mental ill health, family breakdown, drug use, or obesity**. Our analysis shows that the UK has to spend a third more in addressing the consequences of its social problems than the next most troubled nation. But the costs are not only economic. The prevalence of these social problems has a direct impact on **how children experience their lives** and on the **cohesiveness of our communities**. This means that the UK has some of the lowest levels of child well-being when compared with countries of similar economic wealth, and across social and psychological dimensions. Our 16–24-year-olds, for example, record the lowest levels of **trust and belonging** in Europe.

Yet is it so hard to imagine a different future? A future where all children feel loved, are free from poverty, have supportive relationships with other children and adults, feel happy and safe, and are free to imagine and explore as they journey through their local neighbourhoods. A future where all children feel valued; where they give their ideas, time, passions, and their creativity to everyone they meet and to all that they do. A future where the UK no longer languishes at the bottom of international rankings of child well-being and indices of social dysfunction.

Action for Children, one of the largest providers of services to children, and NEF [the New Economics Foundation], one of the UK's leading independent think-and-do tanks, believe this future is both imaginable and within our grasp. But it requires governments across the UK to make it a priority to:

- Invest in targeted interventions that work for our most vulnerable children to improve outcomes and short-circuit the **[trans]generational cycle of deprivation.**
- Invest in high-quality **universal** childcare services and **paid parental leave** to build the foundations for a more equitable and well-functioning society over the medium and longer term.
- Re-shape the way targeted and universal services work so that they build on the assets and strengths of children, young people and their families as well as addressing their needs.

Our key findings

Our analysis looks first at the economic case for making this transition. We demonstrate that investing more in children is necessary, economically viable and a better use of public money in the long run.

- The cost to the UK economy of continuing to address current levels of social problems will amount to almost £4 trillion over a 20 year period. This includes addressing problems such as crime, mental ill health, family breakdown, drug abuse and obesity.
- Investing in a dual investment package, including targeted interventions and universal childcare and paid parental leave, could help address as much as £1.5 trillion worth of the cost of these social problems. This would leave the UK in a similar position to European nations such as Finland, Sweden and Denmark which have the best social outcomes.
- To make the investment, there is a strong case for raising the funds needed through a series of annual bond issues with 10-year maturities. Even after factoring in the transition costs from the system we have now to a move preventative approach returns to the UK economy would total £486 billion over 20 years. This is roughly five times the current annual budget of the whole of the NHS. These savings are calculated on the basis of an investment of £620 billion to fund the transition and £394 billion to implement the bond scheme. The bond scheme is suggested as it allows the investment to be front-loaded, while delaying payments until the savings have been realised, making it an affordable way to fund the transition in the current economic climate.

However it is only one possible option for raising the necessary investment. If other options are followed the potential savings could be between £486 billion and £880 billion, depending on the cost of implementing the chosen scheme.

Drawing on evidence from case studies of a range of children's services, the second stage of our analysis shows that the benefits of investing in children are not limited to economic returns alone. By ensuring investment is used effectively, we also demonstrate how local services can help promote the **psychological and social well-being of children**.

- Six key service pathways to child well-being. These pathways help create the conditions for improving children's psychological and social well-being, and influencing positive outcomes over the longer term. They were found to have applicability in universal and targeted service settings:
- Link up and link in – where services build relationships based on stability and trust and link children into their wider community and 'core economy.'
- Think family – where services help improve the well-being of those in closest contact with children, as well as children themselves, and provide guidance and support when it is needed most.
- Promote the positive – where the promotion of positive emotions and experiences is pursued to help ensure happy childhoods and drive longer term positive outcomes.
- Encourage action – where children and young people are viewed as providers of services and activities, as well as recipients, and are encouraged to use their strengths in a practical way.
- Factor in fun – where services provide opportunities for play, enjoyment and fun to help boost children's happiness and stimulate their creativity and potential for learning.
- Recognise children's wider world – where services are aware of the complex interplay between children's external circumstances, such as poverty, with their overall sense of well-being.
- Co-production offers a mechanism to help promote the service pathways to child well-being. We found services fostering reciprocal working between child and professional which move 'beyond voice' to incorporate an active and valued role for children in the design and delivery of projects are central to effective services, and also appear to help promote the pathways to child well-being.

The final stage of our analysis shows that by getting the type and timing of investment right, and by addressing the psycho-social dimensions of children's lives, economic and social benefits are generated for a range of stakeholders. We completed SROI analyses of three of Action for Children's services taking an early intervention and preventative approach.

Our findings reveal:

- For every £1 invested annually in Action for Children's targeted services designed to catch problems early and prevent problems from reoccurring, society benefits by between £7.60 and £9.20. This social value can be generated, for example, through improved family relationships.
- For every £1 invested in an Action for Children children's centre, a forecast social return to society of £4.60 is expected to be generated. Benefits are forecast to accrue to a range of stakeholders including children, parents, community, and the state.

Key recommendations: invest in children to bring benefits to all

To establish an environment in which children can live happy and fulfilled lives, and where we create the conditions for a better and fairer society for families and communities in the long run, the UK must invest differently and change the way services work. Our proposals for reform are grouped into three 'reform packages,' each a direct response to the evidence on what is needed and designed to tackle the barriers that currently stand in the way. To achieve a successful transition, these packages will need to be implemented alongside each other.

Reform 1: Buy the services that make a difference

Our recommendations under this package are designed to promote investment in high-quality, targeted interventions for our most vulnerable children to short-circuit [trans]generational cycles of disadvantage and to intervene early when additional support is required.

They also aim to address key barriers which stand in the way of progress in this area. These include inadequate policy tools – which restrict investment decisions being made beyond their narrow financial return – and poor measurement and evaluation frameworks which make it difficult to identify needs and gaps in services to make our investments count.

We recommend that all levels of government:

- Roll-out targeted interventions that have been evaluated and shown to work to provide **a continuum of support** to children and young people who need it most.
- Replace conventional cost-benefit analyses with techniques able to show the full public benefit of interventions, like SROI.
- Improve understanding of children and young people's needs as a basis to effective targeting of resources and commissioning, by introducing a '**children and young people's well-being assessment duty.**'

- Commission and de-commission children's services on the basis of value rather than cost, using innovative models and measurement techniques to ensure services deliver improvements in outcomes.

Reform 2: Invest in essential universal provisions

Our recommendations under this package are designed to help set all children on a pathway of positive social, psychological and material well-being from a young age, and to provide a basis for more equal outcomes over the longer term.

To facilitate a successful reform, our recommendations are designed to better recognise child and family policy as a public issue, to address the limitations of current measures of societal progress, and to tackle political barriers so that we are able to look beyond short-term policy-making cycles when it comes to making investment decisions.

We recommend that the UK Government, with support from the devolved administrations:

- Provides **universal childcare provision for all children aged 0–4 years**, so that the same high-quality and affordable childcare is accessible to every parent.
- Extends **paid parental leave**, including for fathers, to enable parents to spend more time developing **intimate relationships with children, which are essential to their happy and healthy development**.
- Achieves cross-party commitments to invest in essential universal provisions for children and families in the UK.
- Establishes new measures of societal progress as a mechanism to better value children and young people as 'public goods,' through the introduction of National Accounts of Child Well-being.

Reform 3: Improve the way services work

Our recommendations under this package are designed to get the 'how' of service reform right. Although a range of factors will influence children and young people's psychological and social well-being, the way in which services are provided at **both a universal and targeted level** plays a key role.

Our proposals are particularly designed to identify mechanisms to overcome conventional approaches to service delivery that tend to overlook the importance of relationships for children's well-being and fail to enhance the capacity of children and families to work alongside professionals in seeking solutions to problems.

We recommend that all levels of government:

- Promote the six service pathways to child well-being.
- Fund and evaluate a national pilot on co-production in children's services.

- Invest in workforce development and establish a 'Children's Services in the twenty-first century' learning network.
- Develop clear, evidence-based messages to better support families and communities to promote change for children.

The findings outlined in *Backing the Future* provide a compelling economic and social case for transforming the way in which we invest in the future of society through our children. We show that the way governments configure targeted and universal service provision for children has a direct impact on the way children experience their lives and a bearing on their longer term outcomes. We also show that investing now to promote child well-being is in the public interest, not just because it ensures more effective use of public resources but because it delivers improved social outcomes and ultimately, benefits us all.

TASK/TEXT 6.18: MENTAL HEALTH PROBLEMS THREATEN THE KNOWLEDGE ECONOMY

<www.innovations-report.de/html/berichte/studien/bericht-73267.html>, 2 November 2006

Developing countries should study possible pitfalls in the race for economic growth

In a knowledge economy, people work increasingly with their heads instead of their hands. This makes mental health a crucial component of economic growth. However, the knowledge economy leads to high levels of stress and mental health problems. By damaging its 'mental capital' [i.e., emotional capital, JW] the knowledge economy undermines the basis for its own success. These are some of the conclusions of the report 'Mental Capital' by Rifka Weehuizen, researcher at UNU-MERIT – a joint research and training centre of United Nations University, and Maastricht University in the Netherlands.

The study: *Mental Capital: a preliminary study into the psychological dimension of economic development*, was commissioned by the Dutch Council for Health Research.

Weehuizen notes that while this report deals with the situation in the Netherlands, the same is happening in all modern economies.

> "My research focuses on the Netherlands, but all modern knowledge economies are damaging their human capital to some extent. It is a result of the pressure to be ever more productive. In the industrial sector you can achieve that by putting in more and

better machines, but in the service economy the main way to achieve this is by making people work more and more intensely. By giving workers autonomy they have to effectively self-manage and self-regulate, which is much more efficient from the firm's perspective, but which adds substantially to the load and pressure of the worker."

In the modern knowledge economy – in which increasing numbers of people are working in the services sector – workers need to be autonomous, flexible, adaptive, and able to continuously deal with new circumstances, tasks and knowledge. The increased interaction with customers and colleagues that this requires means that workers need to regulate their emotions and feelings. Research shows that this is difficult for many workers, and it is leading to greater levels of stress and mental health problems.

Mental health is also a major problem in economic terms. In the Netherlands stress and work pressure are the cause of 29% of sick leave and of 30% of work disability. Thirty percent of the cost of health care in the Netherlands is directly or indirectly related to metal health problems like work related stress, burn out, depression and other ailments. According to the World Health Organisation (WHO) about 4% of gross national product (GNP) in countries such as the Netherlands is lost due to the direct and indirect costs of mental health problems.

This may help to explain why ever growing numbers of people in the leading economies appear to be less happy in spite of their increased wealth (the 'happiness paradox'). The study found that what drives economic growth is not necessarily good for the mental health of people. But mental health is essential for further growth, which leads to the question of what the net result will be of our attempts to grow even more. Even from an economic perspective this may not be the optimal strategy.

Policy measures – Governments should therefore invest more in the mental capital of their economies by putting more money into treatment of mental health related problems and, even more important, into prevention.

Weehuizen's research shows that even in a small country like the Netherlands this would result in savings of billions of euros.

> "Each euro spent on treatment of mental health related problems saves 20 to 30 Euros in future costs, that would occur without effective treatment. Prevention is even more cost effective. Research shows that currently 45 to 70% of people with mental health related problems in European countries do not receive effective treatment."

She outlines a long list of needed measures: **Parents and education should be teaching young people more coping skills.** Self-awareness and cognitive, social and emotional skills have to be increased to make workers better able to function in the knowledge economy. The human resource departments of companies should extend their policies to prevent mental health problems. Quite often they only react, after the problems have arisen. Mental resilience of workers is a critical success factor of an organisation.

Weehuizen also points out that this is not only an issue for rich countries such as the Netherlands. Many developing countries are facing poverty and conflict – major stress factors that are leading to mental health problems and a lack of self-efficacy.

> "People learn that they do not control their own fate, and this does not give them the optimal psychological profile for economic development which requires optimism, trust and taking risks. The mental capital of developing countries is something we should think more about."

> "More generally, if the development strategies adopted by rich countries have not resulted in healthy economic development, meaning maximally contributing to the well-being of people, then developing countries should be wise to find out why this is so, before blindly trying to follow the same path."

See also Rifka Weehuizen, *Mental capital: The economic significance of mental health*, PhD Maastricht University 2008; Dutch author interview: *Psy*, 14 July 2008, <http://psy.nl/nieuws/nieuwsbericht/article/economische-waarde-van-geestelijke-gezondheid-zwaar-onderschat>.

TASK/TEXT 6.19: MENTAL CAPITAL – THE ECONOMIC SIGNIFICANCE OF MENTAL HEALTH

Rifka Weehuizen, *Mental capital: The economic significance of mental health*, PhD Maastricht University, Universitaire Pers Maastricht, 2008, pp. 131–132, 137–144

Chapter 4. Mental Capital
(...)
4.2. Mental capital?

Capital is an important concept in economic theory. Though widely used, its use is not unproblematic, as we will see in section 4.3 when discussing the 'capital controversies.' First we look at the characteristics that currently are associated with capital and capital goods in economic theory. Capital is generally understood to refer to a means of production, which is produced (man-made) and is used to produce itself, which can be increased at a cost (investment), yielding benefits over time (returns).

In this section we will discuss to what extent agency, the productive correlate of mental health, has these characteristics, and thus to what extent we could speak of 'mental capital.' We will find the characteristics of agency match closely with those of capital, and that the concept of capital is analytically useful for organizing and integrating the empirical observations presented in chapters 2 and 3.

4.2.1. Mental capital as a durable produced means of production

The term 'capital' is generally used to refer to the existing stock of goods which are used in the production of other goods or services and which have themselves been produced by previous human activities. In other words capital refers to 'produced means of production.' In this section we will discuss to what extent our main variable, agency, can be seen as a means of production. (...)

4.2.2. The production of mental capital

In this section we discuss how and where is agency produced. The potential level of agency of a person is to some extent given by nature (genetic), but it needs to be actively developed, and is thus largely man-made. Important elements of agency such as mental resilience and self-efficacy are the product of formal and informal 'production processes,' which continue all through a person's life. Here we will discuss the most important 'production sites' of (elements of) agency: the family, school, work, and the mental health care sector. Agency is a composite factor which is generally investigated by studying its constituent elements such as self-efficacy and mental health. To get more insight into the production of agency, we will refer to research on the production of its main elements.

A major producer of elements of agency and of mental health (for better or worse) is the family.[52] Many studies look at the effect of family situation on mental health status. Empirical research shows that the proverbial 'bad childhood' is rightly associated with different kinds of mental health problems.[53] Empirical research has investigated a number of characteristics

---

52 The notion that the family is a major producer of health (e.g. Grossman, 2003) and of human capital (Becker 1989) has been around for some time. Some economists, such as Marshall (1959) thereby underlined the psychological component of this, stating that among the "cost of production of efficient men," the costs involved of families "to make their homes happy, to bring up their children vigorous in body and mind, truthful, cleanly, gentle and brave" should be included (p. 469).

53 Prospective longitudinal research has shown substantial continuity of youth depression into adulthood, with impaired functioning in work, social, and family life, and markedly elevated risk of adult suicide attempts and completed suicide (see, e.g., Costello *et al.* 2002; Weissman *et al.* 1999). Research for risk factors in the development of mental health problems at an early age has found a numerous risk factors, ranging from the presence of prenatal negative

of family life and their effects on the mental health of family members,[54] especially from parents to children,[55] including the effect of parental mental health problems[56] and abuse;[57] but also between siblings[58] and spouses – the effects of marital dissatisfaction,[59] divorce[60] and social

maternal life events (e.g. Gutteling *et al.*, 2000) to different types of parenting (e.g. Magaro and Weisz 2000). Retrospective studies using reports of depressed adult psychiatric patients and depressed nonpatients depict certain characteristics of family processes in the past and/ or present. Depressed adults recall, less affection and tolerance and greater rejection (Coyne and Downey, 1991), and parent's use of control techniques such as derision, negative evaluation, and love withdrawal (Crook and Raskin 1981; Mezulis *et al.* 2006). A review of the research literature on the relationship between childhood experiences and depression in adulthood can be found in Bemporad and Romano (1993); A review of the research on the relationship between early environment characteristics and anxiety in adulthood can be found in Chorpita and Barlow (1998).

54 E.g. Strazdins *et al.* (1997), reviewing literature on the psychological role of the family, point out that in family settings family members do emotional work, in order to create and maintain 'mental hygiene' which keeps family members emotionally healthy. Emotional work involves caring for, and understanding, other family members' emotional needs, as well as monitoring and maintaining the quality of interpersonal interactions within the family. In families, women often take primary responsibility for emotional support, nurturing, setting limits, establishing routines, and organizing their children, particularly when children are young. Mental hygiene is an important factor for helping to prevent mental health problems (Strazdin *et al.* 1997). Providing 'mental hygiene' is effortful, it is a clear example of 'production' of mental health by the family.

55 E.g. Serbin and Stack (1998), introducing a special journal issue on intergenerational social-psychological risks, find that there is an intergenerational continuity (of varying magnitudes) in terms of cognitive, social and emotional development (including mental health problems); parenting practices are found to be the main gateway for transfer of a variety of characteristics between generations.

56 For an overview of the research findings on the adverse effects of parental depression on child psychological functioning see Cummings, Davies and Campbell (2000).

57 E.g. Reckling and Buirski (1996) give an overview of the effects of abuse on children: difficulty identifying and acknowledging their affect; increased aggression and rage; increased dysthymia, depression and anxiety, lack of empathy, lower performance on cognitive tasks. Reckling and Buirski show that these effects can be understood more fully as derailments in self-development and the capacity to regulate affect.

58 E.g. Kramer and Bank (2005) in a special issue reviewing research on siblings find that research clearly shows that sibling relationships serve as important contexts for psychological development, social-emotional skills, behavioural regulation and relational functioning.

59 Research involving diverse methods and samples demonstrates that depressive symptoms co-vary reliably with marital dysfunction and that longitudinal links between these variables exist in both directions (Davila *et al.* 2003). Marital dissatisfaction is found to contribute to the onset of depression, and depression is found to contribute to marital dissatisfaction, through behaviors that interfere with interpersonal relationships or through the generation of increased stress (Davila *et al.* 1997). For a review of literature on this topic, see Beach (2001).

60 The rate of divorce has grown substantially in the past decades, currently divorce rates in developed countries are up to 50% (Hetherington *et al.* 1998). Marital dissolution is marked by depression and periods of disequilibrium and emotional numbness, the restabilization process usually takes from 2 to 5 years (Kaslow 2001). For children, parents' divorce can have long-term adverse mental health consequences in terms of emotion regulation and self-esteem, important correlates of agency (Hetherington *et al.* 1998).

support[61] – and between friends and colleagues.[62] Other studies directly look at the relationship between family characteristics and core elements of agency itself,[63] such as the important feature of emotion regulation.[64]

Next to family and friends, education is also an important producer of agency and its constituent elements such as mental health and self-efficacy. The level and quality of education is found to be positively related to mental health and self-efficacy.[65] To some extent this is a selection/screening effect, but to some extent agency proxies are also actually produced during education rather than merely signalled by education level.

In later life, one of the most important 'production sites' of mental health and agency is work.

In chapter 2 and 3 it was discussed how working conditions can erode or improve mental health and important elements of agency such as self-esteem and self-efficacy. Work provides the environment in which most adults spend most time in per day, so it is a major provider of (positive and negative) experiences. It was therefore argued in chapter 3 that work not only produces goods or services that it is intended to produce, but that it also produces mental health effects, as a side-product, for better or worse.[66] Gaining work experience, learning to deal

---

61 Research shows that the presence of a supportive marital relationship decreases vulnerability depression, whereas the absence increases vulnerability; the spouse is found to be perhaps the most important contemporary producer of an adult's mental health, for better or worse (DeLongis *et al.* 2004).

62 Social support in the form of family, friends and colleagues produces effects on mental health and self-esteem; and it has been found to act as a moderator or buffer of the stressor-strain relationship (Beehr 2003).

63 E.g. Sroufe (1991) finds that the operation of the family system is important in determining the ego-resiliency of adolescents. Ego-resiliency is an important correlate and building block of agency; it refers to the ability of a person to flexibly respond to the demands of internal need states and external environmental constraints. The ego-resilient person is characterized by resourcefulness, having an ability to maintain an integrated performance when under stress, being able to process two or more competing stimuli, and having the capacity to become less or more controlled under varying conditions (Sroufe 1991).

64 Emotional self-regulation refers to the ability to initiate behavioral and emotional changes during emotionally charged situations in order to meet goals and manage arousal and predicts current and later adjustment (Denham 1998). In early childhood, persistence during challenges, frustration tolerance, and compliance with caregiver demands are hallmarks of successful emotional self-regulation (Eisenberg *et al.* 2001). Parenting and sibling interaction is found to have crucial influence on developing agency in toddlerhood, the phase when a child develops more mobile, willful, and unsafe behavior, and at the same time lacks the skill to regulate emotions or to consider his or her own safety or the needs of others (e.g. Gardner *et al.* 2007).

65 E.g. Bear *et al.* (2003) observe that schools have an important role as one of the key mechanisms by which children come to perceive themselves as the cause, source, or agent of their own behavior, and act accordingly; e.g. Hoge *et al.* (1990) find that school experiences are causally related to mental health and self-esteem.

66 Adam Smith (1776) already observed that production processes produce also mental states, and given the working conditions of his time in factories, he was mainly concerned with the

with more complex tasks and with higher stress levels is a sign of increasing agency. Agency is thus the result of labour and increases the productivity of later labour.[67] In addition, the current HRM [Human Resource Management] practices are explicitly targeted at increasing agency of workers, for example through courses to increase personal effectiveness, and management and leadership training.

Another production facility is the mental health care sector. Mental health care is generally given to people who are lacking mental health, suggesting some sort of repair function rather than a production function. However, since a person enters the sector with a certain mental health status and in principle leaves it with a much higher mental health status, one can plausibly say that mental health and thereby agency has been produced.[68] Furthermore there is the 'self-help industry,' which has impressive growth rates, and is of increasing importance to people as a source of self-insight, self-efficacy and self-esteem – important elements of agency.[69]

Agency is being produced as a result of learning experiences of an individual, based on his experiences with the world[70] and what these experiences tell him about himself and his abilities. Especially in the beginning of life, the agency of a person is actively produced with the help of the agency of others, such as parents and teachers, shaping and guiding a child towards sufficient agency to become a stand-alone person (in other words, towards adulthood which should indicate a minimum level of agency). The basic production process of agency takes place inside the head of the person, through organizing information about the self, using information about successes and failures as feedback to further develop a

---

adverse mental effects associated with division of labour: "The man whose whole life is spent in performing a few simple operations [...] has no occasion to exert his understanding [...]. His nature loses therefore the habit of such exertion and generally becomes as stupid and ignorant as it is possible for a human creature to become [...] incapable of relishing or bearing a part in any rational conversation.[...] The uniformity of his stationary life naturally corrupts the courage of his mind" (p. 734–735).

67 As chapter 2 and 3 showed, work experiences can also diminish agency when it concerns negative experiences which reduce self-esteem and self-efficacy, leading to insecure, demotivated and depressed employees with a low level of agency.

68 There is a substantial body of empirical evidence showing that mental health care treatments often (but not always) improves mental health status and thus is 'producing' mental health (e.g. Westen and Morrison 2001). For example, treatments with demonstrated benefits in reducing symptoms and improving functioning have been developed for mental problems such as anxiety disorders (e.g. Beidel *et al.* 2000), attention deficit disorders (e.g. Jensen and Cooper, 2002), and depression (e.g. Clarke *et al.* 1999). The evidence on the effectiveness of treatment is mixed because different treatments are more or less effective for different disorders; the growing body of studies on effectiveness improve evidence-based therapy and thus the all-over effectiveness of mental health care.

69 See the discussion on the self-help industry in section 3.3.2.

70 For an overview of research on other aspects of society that appers to have an effect on agency formation and mental health (e.g. immigration, the new media), see Kaslow (2001).

sense of how to think, feel and act optimally, and practicing to self-regulated thoughts, feelings and behaviour. In this process of reflection (partly conscious, partly not), a person uses his existing agency to get more insight and control over himself; thus using agency to create more agency.[71] Like traditional capital goods, agency is used to produce itself, showing that the analogy with capital goods further helps to develop an economic perspective on mental health and agency.

Summarizing, agency, its constituting elements such self-esteem, self-efficacy and mental health, can be seen as 'produced goods,' and are used in their own 'production.' With this it fulfils yet another important characteristic of capital.

4.2.3. Investment in and returns of mental capital

Capital is income not consumed for the sake of (more) future income. This points to yet another important characteristic of capital. Capital is a stock of value, which can be increased (both quantitatively and qualitatively) at a cost, resulting in a stream of benefits (productive services) later in time. Future revenue gives current cost the character of an investment. Capital can be increased by means of investment, and this investment has returns over time in terms of additional revenues. In this section we look at these aspects more carefully, in order to further assess the appropriateness of the mental capital concept.

Agency can be increased, at a cost: for example, the costs of mental health care,[72] the (opportunity) costs of parental attention, or the costs of training and human resource management for employees.[73] Furthermore, increased agency has clear pay-offs,[74] both for the individual and for his environment (work,

71 Life reflection is a fundamental social-cognitive process of self-understanding that emerges during the first two decades of life and continues to occur throughout the remaining life span (e.g. Habermas and Bluck, 2000). Staudinger (2001) in a review of research on this topic shows that life reflection leads to the accumulation of self-insight and personality growth, needed for personality continuity in times of change; this is correlated with agency, self-insight being an important condition for self-efficacy.

72 There are many studies on the cost-effectiveness of mental health care, usually performed to compare the improvement on certain scales of mental illness of different types of therapy (e.g. see Barrett *et al.* 2005; Gold *et al.* 1996); the effectiveness of therapy can be used to estimate the costs and (wider) benefits (including productivity benefits) and thus to estimate ROI [return on investment].

73 E.g. Gist and Mitchell (1992) reviewing empirical studies find that self-efficacy can be enhanced by training in the areas of self-management and behavioral modelling, and that when self-efficacy is enhanced, performance improves.

74 For an overview of research on the relationship between constituent elements of agency (self-efficacy, self-esteem, mental health) and performance, see section 3.4. To have an idea of the size of pay-offs, see section 3.3 on costs related to lack of mental health, taking mental health as a proxy for agency. Let it be noted that given the definition of mental health in section 3.2, a person with low self-esteem has reduced mental health.

home);[75] it has been found to lead to better performance, higher productivity, better decision-making, higher income, less absenteeism, and less chance to be unemployed or work disabled.[76]

Research in psychology predominantly looks at the consequences of lack of mental health and the accompanying lack of agency. The costs of improving mental health problems can be seen as the investment, and the various costs resulting from mental health problems as a proxy for the return of this investment.[77]

Due to the feedback loops[78] and spillovers[79] of mental capital, loss of mental capital tends to trigger a cascading, downward spiral, while increase of mental capital tends to have a cascading upward spiralling effect. This makes mental capital an interesting object for investment.[80] In spite of the substantial pay-offs

---

75 Clearly, increasing agency and its correlate mental health has also an important consumption character, since mental health and the ability to know what you want and to do what you want are goods with high intrinsic utility. However, we focus here on the production effects of investment in agency and mental health. The fact that a factor such as mental health has both consumption and production value can make the questions of public vs. private funding more difficult, but it is in that respect in principle similar to education.

76 See chapters 2 and 3 for elaborate empirical evidence on this.

77 As illustration, a schematic example is given here. If a depressed individual unable to work receives mental health care worth 1200 euros, after which he is able to work again a year sooner than a depressed individual who receives no treatment, the benefits of this are the amount of a year's worth of his salary, or alternatively, a year of disability benefits if this person would have entered a work disability arrangement otherwise. If work disability benefits amount to 1000 euros a month, the cost of mental health care would have a return of 12,000 euros, thus a ROI of 1000%.

78 The main feedback loop referred to here is described in some detail in chapter 3: high levels of stress affect the fontal lobe systems and the HPA axis, which in turn affects the ability to deal with stress effectively, thereby further increasing stress levels, feeding a downward spiral. Conversely, increasing mental health and agency will trigger an upward spiral, making it an interesting object for investment.

79 Empirical evidence shows that stress, moods, mental health problems and other mental capital relevant variables spill over from one domain to the other and from one person to the other; the empirical evidence for these spill-over effects is discussed extensively in chapter 6.

80 The idea of mental health being an object of investment can increasingly be found in research. For example, Halpern (2005), who was president of the American Psychological Association (APA) in 2004, in her presidential address: "Reducing stress is a good business practice." (p. 406); "These findings convert 'soft' psychological data into return-on-investment dollars." (p. 407). Blount *et al.* (2007) observe that the more broadly we account for the impact of behavioural health services in primary care, the greater the identified savings are, but the more difficult it is to document these savings rigorously. Improved occupational functioning is one of the most immediate results of improvement from depression through treatment. Depression is associated with an average of 4 to 5 lost work days per month in addition to any days lost to accompanying medical conditions. Underfunctioning ('presenteeism') as a result of depression can equal the same loss in productivity as 2.3 days absent per month (Wang *et al.* 2004). The monthly cost to an employer of an employee with depression is over $550, substantially greater than the monthly cost of evidence-based treatment. Patients with severe depression who improved reduced their disability days by 36%, and patients with moderate depression who improved reduced their disability days by 72% (Korff *et al.* 1992). The

of spending on agency-enhancing factors such as mental health and self-efficacy, there appears to be significant under-investment, at the level of public spending, spending by firms, and spending by individuals.[81] Public expenditure on mental health in many European countries is disproportionately low compared to overall expenditure on health care, given high prevalence and high costs associated with mental health problems.[82]

Secondly, firms also tend to underinvest, though this seems to be getting less. Firms are increasingly spending more on better human resource management upgrading the psychological skills of employees and especially of managers, who have to optimize working conditions also from a psychological perspective. The increasing recognition of psychological factors as an item for investment in business can be illustrated by the increase of popular books with titles such as *Emotional capital: Maximizing the Intangible Assets and the Heart of Brand and Business Success* (2000),[83] *Emotional Capitalists: The New Leaders* (2005),[84]

---

estimated annual cost to employers in lost productive time of employees suffering from depression was estimated to be $44 billion per year in 2001–2002, 31 billion more than employees without depression (Stewart *et al.* 2003). For the purpose of illustration, assuming that treatment could reduce the depression-related lost productive time by 50%, this would result in a 'return on investment' of about 15 billion a year.

81 Research consistently finds significant under-investment in mental health and mental resilience. For example, the *World Health Report 2001* estimated that in European countries, 45–70% of people with mental health problems are not in treatment (...). An important reason is that there is significant market failure: mental health problems affect the rationality of people reducing their ability to act as rational consumers of products and services that would fulfil their need for mental health. This implies an important role for governments, similarly to the role the state has in other areas with market failure, such as requiring citizens to save for their pension and to have a health insurance.

82 E.g. Mental health problems account for nearly 20% of all health problems in Europe; however of 28 countries, only 4 countries allocating more than 10% of their health budgets to mental health (Frank and McGuire 1999).

83 Illustrative excerpt from *Emotional Capital*: "[P]eople assets can only be harnessed by managing both intellectual capital (your peoples' knowledge) and emotional capital (the feelings and beliefs that motivate people to take positive action). Knowledge management is moving up the agenda in many companies. Yet organizational knowledge is meaningless if your people are unmotivated, apprehensive or uncommitted. How many companies have paid the price of an alienated workforce with problems like poor customer service, labour disputes and low productivity – all hallmarks of low emotional capital? Emotional capital can be managed as a tangible asset and a direct contributor to the balance sheet." (Thomson, 2000; back cover).

84 From *Emotional Capitalists*: "[A]nyone who is genuinely motivated can develop their emotional intelligence and boost their stocks of emotional capital" (p. 16). "Emotional independence expressed as self-reliance and self-belief is indispensable to becoming an emotional capitalist and building emotional capital in your personal lief and business." (Newman 2005, p. 26).

Unleashing Intellectual Capital (2000),[85] and *Psychological Capital: Developing the Human Competitive Edge* (2006).[86]

In line with this, there is increasing early recognition of (work-related) mental health problems and increased early intervention to prevent downward spirals of employees, going from increased absenteeism towards work disability. In countries such as the Netherlands, the legal framework give[s] firms (...) strong incentives to pay more attention to the mental health of employees and to prevent work stress and work-related psychological problems. It is difficult and expensive to fire employees, and firms are legally obliged to pay at least 70% of the wages of sick employees for a period of two years; this inspires employees to work on prevention and early recognition and solution of problems.[87]

Thirdly, there is underinvestment at the level of the individual. If anyone, it is the individual himself who would profit from increasing his mental capital. It would help him to become more productive thus gaining a better position in the labour market, a higher income, less chance to lose a job. In addition, it will help him to enjoy the fruits of his work more, in terms of real 'experienced utility'

---

85 From *Unleashing Intellectual Capital*: "[O]rganizations in the Knowledge Age need a new management model for generating, capturing and leveraging intellectual assets in order to stay competitive" (p. 5). "Machines need to be monitored, controlled and maintained by external sources. [...] People and organizations, however, are living systems, not machines. Living systems have the innate capacity to self-assemble, self-sustain, change constantly, reproduce, learn and self-organize" (p. 7). "People are not simply a means of production, They are biological systems constantly seeking to fulfil their needs and aspirations. [...] Even from an economic perspective, people in companies are not assets, but investors, similar to shareholders. Shareholders invest their money in an institution, whereas members of a firm invest their time, energy and intellect" (p. 8). (...)

86 Excerpt from *Psychological Capital*: "How can organizations and individuals ready themselves to achieve distinct competitive advantages? [...] We call for the investment and development of psychological capital. [...] [M]ore important but to often slighted in this war, we would argue, is finding innovative ways of capitalizing on and developing human, social and especially the psychological capacities of human resources for sustained competitive advantage. [...] Simply concentrating and accumulating more of the traditional resources once considered vital for organizational success have proven insufficient for attaining sustainable sources of competitive advantage. [...] We propose that such advantage can be gained through investing, leveraging, developing and managing psychological capital" (p. 7). (...)

87 See for more details on the Dutch law in this area: <www.werkennaarvermogen.nl>. When mental health problems are the result of work stress, the practice of requiring the employer to carry the costs of employees with mental health problems is effective, since it is a way of endogenizing costs of production. However, mental health problems of employees can also originate in the non-work sphere, and the employer is nevertheless responsible. On the one hand, endogenizing mental health costs results in improvement of working conditions and psychological sustainability. On the other hand it leads to 'front-door selection' (Schaufeli and Kompier 2001); employees get screened more intensively psychologically before being hired, with the help of psychological tests and assessment centres. This latter strategy can lead to exclusion of people with less mental capital on the labour market, which is undesirable since exclusion can lead to further erosion of their mental capital.

(Kahneman 2000). After all, if a person is stressed or depressed (thus low on mental capital), his new car, house or gadget will make him much less happy, effectively meaning a loss of utility. Nevertheless, individuals do not always actively build up more mental health and more agency; even worse, they often let their mental capital slip away, in stressful jobs, worries, loss of self-esteem, burnout and depression.

One of the reasons for this under-investment is the occurrence of serious flaws in the market for mental health care and related markets such as the self-help industry. Frank and McGuire (1999) show that mental health economics is like health economics only more so: uncertainty and variations in treatments are greater; the assumption of patient self-interested behaviour is more dubious; there is more risk of moral hazard and adverse selection; market failures are more serious, and the social consequences and external costs of mental illness are 'formidable' (Frank and McGuire 1999).

Mental health problems lead to diminished rationality and reduced agency capacity of people; they are less capable to act on their own behalf and in their own best interest, and this leads to increased market failure. Mental illness reduces an individual's ability to function in a consumer role vis-à-vis for example mental health care services, and interferes with the maintenance and creation of social networks (family and friends), weakening the connection with others who might serve as caregivers or 'substitute decision-makers' by taking over the failing agency function of the person with mental health problems. This leads to a suboptimal amount of spending on improvement of mental health, and calls for an active role of the government. By increasing the supply of mental health care and services for strengthening the agency of a person such as psychotherapy or a 'life coach,' and making these services easily accessible and affordable, more people that need help would receive help, often in an earlier phase so that more serious problems can be prevented.

However, as always there is a scarcity of financial means and there are many other worthy destinations for public money, so the question of how much should be spent on dealing with mental health problems is important. This question is not easy to answer. The demand for mental health has a high price elasticity, making it difficult to identify the 'real' demand.[88] The result of increasing demand by increasing awareness of mental health problems and the possibilities for solution, in combination with offering more and more easily accessible supply can also be suboptimal; due to the high price elasticity and the important subjective dimension of mental health problems, part of mental health care would be used by people that may not really need it. It may not be possible to ever find out the optimal level of expenditure or construct an optimal meeting of

[88] Ringel *et al.* (2002) based on a review find price elasticity estimates for mental health care between 2.66 and 4 times those estimated for general ambulatory health care.

supply and demand. However, Frank and McGuire (1999) suggest that underconsumption may in the end be more costly than overconsumption. Early recognition and intervention is generally much more effective than later treatment, and saves the direct and indirect costs associated with more serious problems.

Introducing cost-sharing for example could result in an initial decrease of health care consumption, but a delayed, much higher increase in consumption and therefore costs later in time, because medical problems will be diagnosed in a later stage when is it harder and more expensive to treat them.[89]

In this section 4.2, we have explored to what extent the characteristics of agency correspond with the characteristics generally associated with capital and capital goods. We have found that there is a good match: agency is a produced means of production, which is durable, which is used in the production of (own or other people's) agency, which can be invested in with substantial returns over time. It herewith satisfies all the important characteristics of capital, justifying the term 'mental capital.' (...)

TASK/TEXT 6.20: MONEY OR MENTAL HEALTH

Christopher J. Boyce, Alex M. Wood, Money or mental health – the cost of alleviating psychological distress with monetary compensation versus psychological therapy, *Health Economics, Policy and Law,* published online by Cambridge University Press 18 November 2009 (references omitted)

Abstract: Money is the default way in which intangible losses, such as pain and suffering, are currently valued and compensated in law courts. Economists have suggested that subjective well-being regressions can be used to guide compensation payouts for psychological distress following traumatic life events. We bring together studies from law, economic, psychology and medical journals to show that **alleviating psychological distress through psychological therapy could be at least 32 times more cost effective than financial compensation.** This result is not only important for law courts but has important implications for public health. Mental health is deteriorating across the world – improvements to

89 Frank and McGuire (1999) show that investment in mental health eliminates costs associated with low levels of mental health. Mental disorders correlate substantially with other costly problems: unemployment, crime, violence and homelessness (also see chapter 2). Many of these problems have consequences for others as well as the person with the illness, which means that decentralized market-decision-making will tend to undervalue effective treatments for mental illnesses. For this reason government has historically taken a large role in provision and regulations of some forms of mental health care (Frank and McGuire 1999).

mental health care might be a more efficient way to increase the health and happiness of our nations than pure income growth.

Putting a price tag on 'pain and suffering' seems an impossible task but judges in law courts are regularly expected to make such decisions. Equating money with an intangible loss may seem peculiar but in tort law an individual who has suffered should, as nearly as possible, be restored to the same position had they not sustained some wrong (...). In law courts monetary compensation is the expected remedy and there are established monetary guidelines to compensate for the 'pain and suffering' of various injuries (...). In the UK, the Fatal Accidents Act 1976 provides a one off payment for the 'bereavement' of family members. Economists have developed a method to place monetary values on various life events (...). It has further been suggested that such monetary values could be offered as compensation to help overcome psychological distress after particularly traumatic life events (...). The economists' calculations would suggest that court settlements would need to be much higher than present to fully compensate an individual. The high monetary values reflect money's ineffectiveness at compensating someone for pain and suffering.

We assess the evidence across law, economic, psychology and medical journals and suggest psychological therapy as an alternative. Psychological therapy would be substantially more cost effective than financial compensation at alleviating psychological distress. We extend our argument beyond the law courts and suggest that moneys low importance in achieving mental health has important implications for public health. **National happiness levels have remained flat in developed countries in spite of large economic gains. Mental health, on the other hand, appears to have been deteriorating across the world for some time and is estimated to deteriorate still further** (...). The comprehensiveness and accessibility of mental health services, in particular the provision of psychological therapies in publicly funded services, have regularly been questioned. Increasing the investment in mental health and generally broadening access, therefore, might be a more efficient way to increase the health and happiness of our nations than pure income growth.

Money: a common metric for valuing life events and the movement towards compensation

Monetary values have been calculated across numerous areas of life including marriage (...), social relationships (...), the fear of crime (...), noise (...), health (...) and disabilities (...). The income equivalences attached to such events are typically large. For example, the value of a marriage is estimated to be equivalent to having an extra $100,000 (...) each year (...). Such values have been calculated using subjective well-being data and computation is relatively simple.

The average impact of some life event on an individual's well-being can be determined statistically across a large sample. This impact is then compared to the effect that income has on an individual's well-being. Typically, a one standard deviation rise in income would be expected to induce a rise in well-being of between 0.17 and 0.21 standard deviations (…). By comparing the two effects researchers can estimate how much extra income an individual would need on average to achieve an equivalent level of well-being as the life event.

Compensation for injustices is an important aspect of society. In tort cases, particularly those involving psychological distress, judges are commonly faced with the dilemma of awarding compensation to restore an individual to the position they were before any injustice took place. Such a decision is mostly subjective, arbitrary and normally takes the form of a one off monetary payment (…). Some researchers have suggested that the psychological impact of particularly traumatic life events can be evaluated in purely financial terms (…). With the aim of alleviating psychological distress recent studies have suggested that such figures could be useful in a court of law to guide compensation payouts for individuals who have lost family members (…) or become disabled (…).

Such events can devastate the lives of individuals and the sums suggested to help alleviate the psychological distress are large, much larger than those presently awarded by courts. For example, were an individual to lose a partner, then it is suggested that a compensation amount ranging from £114,000–£206,000 per annum would be needed to overcome psychological distress. For the loss of a child, individuals would require anything from £89,000–£140,000 to compensate (…). In the UK the Fatal Accidents Act 1976 recommends a substantially lower payout of just £10,000. If such a financial compensatory argument were extended to unemployment, which is well known to have deep psychological effects beyond the simple loss of income (…), the income equivalence of psychological distress alone would be in the region of £34,000–£59,000 per annum (…).

The clinical and cost effectiveness of psychological therapy

Researchers have assessed the clinical and cost effectiveness of various treatments for depressed patients (…). The effectiveness of general practitioner care with both cognitive-behaviour therapy (CBT) and nondirective counselling were all compared. Over 12 months all treatments reduced average depression levels by at least one and a half standard deviations. The average total cost, which even included indirect costs such as work-time lost, was less than £1,500. In fact, the improvement was achieved by both CBT and non-directive counselling within the first four months at a total cost of less than £800.

A cost effectiveness comparison between psychological therapy and direct financial compensation

Comparing the cost effectiveness of psychotherapy and direct financial compensation in alleviating individuals from severe psychological distress has not been carried out before. There are several ways in which the costs between psychological therapy and direct financial compensation can be compared using the studies already outlined. Oswald and Powdthavee (...) estimate that the average psychological impact of losing a partner is about one standard deviation.

They suggest that the individual would need to be compensated with at least £114,000. Pro-rata it would cost less than £600 to help the individual adjust to such a difficult life event using psychological therapy. Similarly for unemployment, which has deep psychological consequences, it would be more cost effective to provide individuals with psychological therapy (around £100–£200 pro-rata) to overcome their loss of purpose in life and help them back to work rather than solely offering financial compensation.

To compare the costs in another way, psychological therapy alleviates psychological distress by one and a half standard deviations at a cost of £800 over 4 months. To achieve a one and a half standard deviation reduction in psychological distress using money alone would require (...) somewhere in the region of £179,000–£292,000 of extra income every year. This illustrates that the alleviation of severe psychological distress could be worth at least £179,000 of extra income each year and suggests that financial compensation is an inefficient way of helping individuals overcome distress.

The wide disparity between the effects of psychological therapy and income arises out of the poor ability of income to improve mental health. However, income's effect on psychological distress in studies such as Oswald and Powdthavee (...) is likely to be underestimated. More realistic income effects can be obtained by allocating income randomly to individuals and observing the effects on individuals' lives. Such an experiment is not possible but researchers have analyzed longitudinally the effect of medium sized lottery wins on psychological distress. An average lottery or pool win of £4,300 is found to bring approximately a quarter of a standard deviation improvement to mental health two years after the win (...). This suggests that even when the best income-psychological distress estimates are considered (...), psychological therapy is still calculated to be at least 32 times more cost effective than financial compensation. This figure is large and places huge questions on the use of income as an effective compensation method.

Our argument is not without its limitations. There are of course inherent difficulties in making inferences across studies and just like the proponents of the use of monetary compensation it is necessary to draw some conclusions from one group of individuals to another. The evidence on the cost-effectiveness of psychological therapy is not based exclusively on individuals experiencing loss as a result of a devastating life event. Some psychological distress will undoubtedly follow from the loss of a loved one but one may question whether, what could be considered a fairly normal response, would benefit from psychological therapy. This perhaps calls into question the purpose of psychological treatment more generally. One view of psychological therapy is that mental health is a continuum and that everyone, no matter their level of psychological distress, can benefit from psychological therapy. Under this view any psychological distress would be viewed as mental disorder and therefore treatable. Another viewpoint is that mental disorder is dichotomous, in that individuals either have mental disorder or do not. This view suggests that mental disorder is the presence of distorted thought processes that can result in protracted psychological distress. In this latter view the psychological distress that arises as a normal reaction to loss might not be seen as directly treatable. However, it is likely that, without adequate support, some unnecessary mental disorder will arise from the loss. Therapy should aim to avert such mental disorder. Additionally, even if there were a substantial cost difference in helping individuals with loss and those with mental disorders, the cost-effectiveness comparison figure calculated earlier should be high enough to absorb any extra expense.

A further issue that requires some discussion is the process of adaptation.

People adapt to many of life's events (…) and some individuals will naturally return to their baseline level of psychological functioning given time. If individuals adapt anyway then an argument could be made against the use of psychological therapy. The same argument, however, could be made against the use of monetary compensation, the current default method of addressing loss. In any case individuals do not always fully adapt and even if they did resources should be used in the most efficient manner to relieve psychological distress in the interim. Oswald and Powdthavee (…) address the issue of adaptation and as such suggest that annual compensatory amounts should be reduced each year. Similarly, psychological therapy could be proportionally reduced to help with the lower levels of distress in later years after an event. However, it may turn out that psychological therapy, focusing directly on psychological distress, speeds up the process of adaptation and may even make therapy unnecessary in later years.

Practical implications of our argument: for judges

In tort law an individual who has suffered should, as nearly as possible, be restored to the same position they had not sustained some wrong. The loss of future earnings must undoubtedly be compensated financially. The evidence suggests that following a devastating life event an individual is likely to experience an adverse psychological reaction and our concern is with the efficiency of compensating such an intangible and fairly normal psychological reaction financially. Currently, monetary compensation seems to be unquestionably taken in law courts as the only way of helping an individual overcome psychological distress after a traumatic event. The values currently offered as compensation are arbitrary (...) and, according to economists' subjective well-being equations, should actually be much higher (...). Rather than giving individuals more income to cope with distress it seems sensible to consider other alternatives such as psychological therapy.

Can bestowing an individual with money really be expected to help an individual with psychological distress after a traumatic life event? As a compensatory device, money, like most things, can never truly fulfill such a role. The purpose of financial compensation, however, is to alleviate an individual's psychological distress by helping them to find enjoyment elsewhere.

Thus, if a tool is judged by its ability to alleviate an individual's psychological distress then the answer may be found in medical research. We have shown that psychological therapy could be much more cost effective than financial compensation. We are not claiming that psychological therapy will entirely prevent what could be considered as a normal adverse psychological reaction but therapy may provide some short-term relief. Moreover, such devastating life events if not adequately dealt with may lead to maladaptive thoughts and result in undue distress. It is unlikely that financial compensation will protect against such maladaptive thinking.

On punitive grounds we are not necessarily suggesting that large court payouts are not justified. However, we are suggesting that the sums currently offered may not be the best way to help the injured party overcome any psychological distress unless it is decreed, in the best interests of the injured party, that the money gets spent on some form of psychological therapy. There is currently no legal obligation for individuals to undertake steps to alleviate their psychological distress. However, there is some legal support in New Zealand for an increased use of psychological therapy to help individuals overcome psychological distress that occurs due to the actions of a third party. The Injury Prevention, Rehabilitation and Compensation Act of 2001 requires that the cost of psychological therapy be borne by the state.

Financial compensation may not even have the causal effect on a traumatized individual in the way that economists suggest. Additionally, individuals are likely to be unequally affected by financial compensation; for example, due to the diminishing marginal utility of income wealthier individuals may require even more income to replenish lost well-being. Financial compensation seems like a poor device for alleviating psychological distress. In contrast, psychological therapy does not attempt to act as compensation but instead focuses directly on helping individuals to overcome their loss. Psychological therapy acknowledges that trauma is person-dependent and is therefore effective, inexpensive and compassionate.

Practical implications of our argument: for policy makers and society

We believe our argument has important implications for public health. The high levels of financial compensation that economists suggest help to highlight how inefficient money is at alleviating psychological distress and generally improving individual well-being. Economists are puzzled as to why developed societies are becoming no happier in spite of large income gains (...). However, in 1999 unipolar major **depression was the fifth leading cause of the disease burden** and by 2020 major **depression is expected to rise to the second biggest burden** (...). These conflicting findings, along with the evidence presented here, indicate that although income growth may provide some benefit to well-being, **the greatest benefit to the health and happiness of our nations could come from improving access to mental health care.**

Our argument, although clearly comparing across studies and extending from the law courts to wider society, adds a new perspective to public health debate on mental health. Regarding the UK's National Health Service, Richard Layard (...) has suggested that the cost of helping individuals overcome mental health issues using psychological therapy more than outweighs the money saved from reducing the individuals on benefits who are incapacitated by their mental health. Our argument adds further support for increasing the availability of mental health resources by instead suggesting that mental health in its own right is something to be valued alongside economic progress. The importance of improving mental health for national well-being needs to be further recognized and policy makers must consider improving mental health care further. Individuals are also probably not fully aware of the powerful effects that good psychological therapy can have on their mental health and general well-being.

It needs to be understood that aspiring to good mental health can often be more important than aspiring to high income for well-being. Since individuals are unlikely to unilaterally invest in their own mental health there is a strong case for public provision.

(...)

TASK/TEXT 6.21: NEW HORIZONS – WORKING TOGETHER FOR BETTER MENTAL HEALTH

<www.newhorizons.dh.gov.uk>, accessed 17 December 2009

The New Horizons vision for 2020

Our mental health, like our physical health, will vary throughout our lives – whether we're young or old, working or not and wherever we live. It is important that we all understand what we need to do in order to build and maintain good mental health right from the start, from infancy into adulthood and older age, for individuals, families and communities.

By 2020, we hope that:

- everyone will understand why good mental health is important and know what to do to help their own mental health;
- children will be taught in school about how to protect their mental health;
- a person's physical health and their mental health will be equally important to health services;
- people with mental health problems and their families will be able to get all the high quality support they need;
- medicines will be better and have fewer side effects;
- people with mental health problems will not be treated differently just because of their problems;
- mental health services will make special plans that give people a bigger say in what their treatment is and how they get treatment;
- older people with mental health problems will be treated with the same respect as younger people;
- people from ethnic minorities with mental health problems will get the treatment they need, in a way that suits them;
- different services will work well together to give the best possible care;
- people who cannot work because of mental health problems will be able to do other things that help them to be part of their community;
- people with mental health problems will not have more health problems than other people, for example they will not be more likely to smoke, to be overweight or to have heart problems;
- we will understand why poor people are more likely to have mental health problems;
- other parts of government will think about the needs of people with mental health problems when planning things like: housing, education or transport.

Counting the cost

Mental health is important to us all. One in six people has a mental health problem at any one time. A mental health problem can be big or small but, without the right treatment or support, it can make it difficult for someone to live a normal life. Good mental health is also important because it means you are more likely to: have a happier life, be more healthy, live longer, be able to work and have good relationships. Everyone needs to care about their own mental health and everyone should try to make things better for people with mental health problems.

Impact on every part of society

Mental illness begins early; 10% of children have a diagnosable mental health condition. 71% of adults with depression first developed symtoms in adolescence. At any one time, just over 20% of working age women and 17% of working age men have depression or anxiety. Up to 50% of older people in residential care have severe depression. Many people need support from family and friends. Over 500,000 family members care for people with dementia alone.

Biggest single health condition

No other health condition matches mental ill health in the combined extent of prevalence, persistence and breadth of impact. The NHS [National Health Service] spends about 14% of its annual budget on mental health services. In 2003, the annual cost of mental health care in England provided by the NHS, local authorities, privately funded services, family and friends was estimated at £12.5 billion.

Economic consequences

The wider cost of mental health problems to the UK in 2006/7 was estimated at £110 billion. Costs to employers of mental ill health are around £26 billion per annum or £1035 for every employee in the UK workforce – of which nearly two thirds can be accounted for by lost productivity. Mental ill health is a leading reason for incapacity benefit payment; around 44% of the 2.6 million people currently on long-term health-related benefits have a mental health or behavioural disorder condition.

Strong link to other issues

In mental health services, studies indicate that **48% of female service users have been subjected to sexual abuse and 48% to physical abuse in childhood. Of male users, 28% report sexual abuse and 50% report physical abuse in childhood.** Personality disorders are also common among people in the criminal justice system, affecting 50 to 70% of prisoners.

A growing problem that New Horizons aims to tackle

At current rates, the cost of mental health problems will double in over next 20 years.

Better mental well-being

It is important that we all understand what we need to do to build and maintain good mental health right from the start, from infancy into adulthood and older age. We need to identify what may cause poor mental health and provide solutions to help prevent mental illness. People need a good start in life and we know that [a] child is more likely to have poor mental health if, for example, a parent has poor mental health or the child suffers abuse. Children also need a secure and safe environment in which to grow up.

We also know that physical and mental well-being are linked. For example, a person with two or more physical illnesses is more likely to develop a mental health problem, and an anxious person is more at risk of dying from coronary disease. Living a life that has a sense of purpose and meaning is also important for our mental well-being; whether it is achieved through work, family, volunteering, or through developing creativity and shared values.

New Horizons sets out a number of ways of improving the well-being of people in England and help prevent mental illness. These include:

- promoting good parenting skills to ensure children have a good start in life;
- improving the environment by doing things like having more green spaces in urban areas;
- treating physical and mental health together, for example if someone has a mental health problem, they should also be offered support to improve their diet and physical health;
- encouraging communities to work together to tackle the stigma that people with mental health problems often experience;
- providing more opportunities for people to participate in society, through activities like volunteering;
- the Government has also committed to make people more aware of the steps we can all take to protect our mental health, this includes socialising regularly, exercising, enjoying nature and learning new things.

Right help, right time

People with mental health problems can often lead their lives the way they want to, but they need to get the right treatment and support to help them live independently, stay healthy and recover quickly. Although mental health services have improved in recent years, we need to do more to intervene earlier when someone develops a problem and offer more personalised services. For example, we know that one in ten children and young people have a mental health problem but many do not receive the care they need soon enough. This can lead to emotional and behavioural problems and antisocial behaviour at great cost to the young person, their families and to society that may continue into adulthood. We also know that preventing and actively treating depression in young people will lessen the burden of mental illness in adult life.

When someone develops a mental health problem, evidence suggests that the more control someone has over his or her own recovery, the better that recovery will be. This is why we need to provide services that offer tailored care and support, which give more control to people with mental health problems. We also know that certain groups of people do not always get access to the care they require. By creating services tailored to people's needs, all individuals – whatever their age, background, income or need – will have access to care and services. This will allow groups that are often excluded from society – the homeless, BME [Black and Minority Ethnic] communities or those with learning difficulties – to access services and treatment.

New Horizons sets out a number of things we can do:

- we want to do more to target those people who are at high risk of developing a mental health problem – such as young offenders;
- ensure that people from marginalised groups have access to services that meet their particular needs;
- we want people to receive a personal care package that meets their individual needs and wishes – this means offering a greater range of treatment options and dealing with other issues such as employment, housing and physical health;
- enabling people to make their own decisions about their care, treatment and goals for recovery;
- encouraging people to take greater responsibility for monitoring their own condition;
- ensuring that people receive treatment as soon as possible after their need is recognised.

Tackling discrimination

Society does not view mental health problems in the same light as physical health problems. Mental illness is still surrounded by ignorance, fear and prejudice despite the fact that one in six people has a mental health problem. Stigma and discrimination has an impact. It can stop people from getting jobs, prevent people from seeking help, make people feel isolated and delay recovery from a mental health problem.

Discrimination against people with mental illness can occur in many situations: be it in the media, in the school playground, in the workplace or in the quality of services offered. Although it is already illegal to discriminate against people with mental health problems, more needs to be done. Both children and adults need to understand that mental illness can happen to anyone and know how to protect their own mental health.

The Government has already done a lot but New Horizons aims to tackle this issue in a number of ways. By 2020, we want to:

- see universal mental health promotion in schools, national campaigns like Time-to-Change will also help to improve adults' understanding;
- encourage more employers to give people with mental health problems the chance to work;
- work with schools to teach emotional and social skills to lessen bullying;
- influence the way that people with mental illness are depicted in scripted television;
- continue working with the media to challenge the language used;
- decrease the stigma that military personnel and veterans feel in accessing mental health services;
- do more to tackle the double discrimination that certain groups experience for example, older people.

7. DIRECTION AND GUIDANCE – POSITIVE DISCIPLINE, PARENT EDUCATION

TASK/TEXT 7.1: POSITIVE DISCIPLINE – WHAT IT IS AND HOW TO DO IT; AUTHOR INTERVIEW

Crinmail 914 – 11 September 2007, <www.crin.org>, <http://seap.savethechildren.se/South_East_Asia/Latest/Author-Interview-Positive-Discipline-What-it-is-and-how-to-do-it>

This new publication '**Positive Discipline: What it is and how to do it**' authored by Joan Durant, a child-clinical psychologist and an Associate Professor of Family Social Sciences of the University of Manitoba (Canada), provides concrete answers to parents who want to raise their children without corporal punishment, in a positive climate.

About the Author – Joan E. Durrant, Ph.D. is a Child-Clinical Psychologist and an Associate Professor of Family Social Sciences at the University of Manitoba in Winnipeg, Canada. She conducts research on the factors that lead parents to strike their children, as well as on the impact of laws that prohibit physical punishment. She was the principal researcher and co-author of the Canadian *Joint Statement on Physical Punishment of Children and Youth*; a member of the Research Advisory Committee of the United Nations Secretary-General's *Study on Violence against Children*; and a co-editor of *Eliminating Corporal Punishment: The Way Forward to Constructive Discipline* (UNESCO). She has written parenting materials for the Canadian government, and has given speeches and workshops in many countries on the topics of physical punishment and positive parenting.

What was your inspiration for writing this manual?

Joan: Increasingly, parents are being advised to use positive discipline. But parents often ask, 'What is positive discipline and how to do it?' People working for Save the Children and the Global Initiative to End all Corporal Punishment of Children suggested we should compile a guide explaining to parents and professionals the principles of positive discipline.

What exactly is positive discipline?

Joan: The word 'discipline' has often been associated with 'punishment.' So the idea of 'positive discipline' might seem odd to some. But the word 'discipline' actually means 'teaching.' Teaching is based on setting goals for learning, planning an effective approach, and finding solutions that work. Positive discipline is an *approach to teaching* that helps children succeed, gives them information, and supports their growth.

The major characteristics of positive discipline are that it:

- is non-violent and respectful of the child as a learner,
- is about finding long-term solutions that develop children's own self-discipline,
- involves clear communication of parents' expectations, rules and limits,
- builds a mutually respectful relationship between parent and child,
- teaches children child life-long skills,
- increases children's competence and confidence to handle challenging situations,
- teaches courtesy, non-violence, empathy, self-respect, human rights and respect for others.

The four principles of positive discipline are:

1) identifying your long-term parenting goals;
2) providing warmth (love, security) and structure (information, expectations, guidelines);
3) understanding how children think and feel; and
4) problem solving.

There are many parenting guides to choose from, what makes this one different from the others?

Joan: Simplicity. All of the research findings on positive discipline are boiled down to four basic principles that parents can use to guide their interactions with their children.

Another unique aspect of this guide is the opportunity it provides for practice. It can be very difficult to think rationally in situations of parent-child conflict. It takes effort and practice to shift from impulsive punitive responses to thought-out constructive responses in such situations. This guide gives parents practice in thinking through their responses so that they are better prepared when difficult situations arise.

A third unique feature of this manual is that it interweaves findings of academic research with children's rights principles. It will help readers understand the links among child development, effective parenting and children's rights.

The manual strongly discourages parents from using corporal punishment. Why is this important?

Joan: Corporal punishment has been repeatedly shown to interfere with parents' long-term goals for their children. Most parents want their children to grow into non-violent problem-solvers who have good relationships with their families and high self-esteem and who are happy people. Corporal punishment interferes with development in all of these areas. It predicts higher levels of aggression in children, poorer parent-child relationships, and poorer child mental health. It serves no useful purpose in teaching children what we want them to learn.

This manual begins with an introduction on children's rights. What are the links between children's rights and positive discipline?

Joan: Children's rights are based on knowledge of what children need to develop to their full potential. The necessities of life for a child include not only food, water and shelter, but also emotional security and physical safety. Children need positive relationships with, and strong attachments to, their caregivers. Almost all countries of the world have ratified the United Nations Convention on the Rights of the Child. This Convention sets out the fundamental rights of children based on their developmental needs. Three of these rights have particular relevance to discipline.

First, children have the right to freedom from all forms of violence. This means that we need to learn ways of responding to parent-child conflict without hitting.

Second, children have the right to be treated with respect for their dignity. This means that we need to learn ways of teaching children without humiliating them with put-downs, name-calling, or threats.

Third, children have the right to express themselves. This means that we need to learn not only how to talk *to* children, but how to listen and understand how they think and feel.

As a parent, can you share with us some real life situations when you used positive discipline at home?

Joan: Once, my 3-year-old son dropped his father's toothbrush into the toilet. I considered my options. I could spank him to teach him not to do that again, scold him, or take something away from him to punish him. But I realized that these responses wouldn't teach him anything about why he shouldn't drop toothbrushes in the toilet. I also realized that, at 3 years of age, he didn't understand anything about germs, money or plumbing. He didn't do this because he wanted to damage the toothbrush or the toilet. He didn't know that it was any different from dropping a toothbrush into the sink.

I thought about the situation from his point of view and considered what he needed to know in order not to do it again. I didn't scold him or hit him because I wanted him to listen to me and learn. I calmly explained that the toilet is not the place for things we put into our mouths and why. I explained that his father wouldn't be able to use that toothbrush again and this would mean that his father would have to go out and buy a new one. I told him that I understood that he had not intended to damage his Dad's toothbrush. I also explained that when we damage other people's belongings, even by mistake, we need to take responsibility and fix the situation. I asked him how he could fix this mistake. He suggested that he could buy his Dad a new toothbrush.

He got some of his own money and we went to the store. He picked out a toothbrush that he thought his Dad would like. When we went home, he went to his father and explained what had happened. He apologized and gave his Dad the new toothbrush. His Dad expressed his respect for how he had handled the situation, as well as appreciation for his honesty and for taking responsibility.

My son has never dropped anything else into the toilet or damaged anything, for that matter. From that experience, he obtained information that he used in other situations. He also saw himself as honest and capable of repairing his mistakes, which he continues to do. He felt respected by his father and respects him, in turn. He felt understood and supported by me, so he is not afraid to tell me when he has made a mistake. He trusts his parents to provide the structure that he needs, but in an atmosphere of warmth, rather than fear. This is the foundation of positive discipline.

The example you give works within Canada's culture. Will this method work in Southeast Asia and the Pacific and other parts of the world?

Joan: The manual was piloted in Asia, with a group of professionals who work with parents. What we found was that the fundamental principles applied across all of those countries, but some of the specific examples of parent-child conflict were more relevant to some countries than to others.

The principles of positive discipline are universal. Parents everywhere have long-term goals for their children. Children everywhere thrive on warmth and structure. And parent-child conflict can be resolved everywhere through considering each other's points of view and problem-solving. So the fundamental principles can be applied all over the world.

Where there can be differences is in the situations that lead to conflict. For example, in North America it is common for parents and children to sleep in separate rooms. This situation often results in conflict because children are afraid to be alone in the dark. In other cultures, it is common for parents and children to sleep together. This situation reduces conflict about going to bed. So, in North America, parents could use the positive discipline approach to resolve bedtime problems. In other cultures it might not be necessary to use positive discipline at bedtime, but it would be useful in other situations.

The positive discipline approach is based on principles that can be applied in all cultures across a wide range of situations. We have aimed to make the examples in the manual as universal as possible, but we have also provided space for parents to think about their own unique situations and work through the problem-solving process for those specific areas of conflict.

Your book mentions the importance of knowing how children think and feel, as well as providing children with warmth and structure … Why is that important?

Joan: In resolving any problem or conflict, it helps tremendously to see the situation from the other person's point of view. This is particularly true in the case of parents and children. We are often mistaken about children's motivations. When we think that they are intentionally defying us or trying to make us angry, we are likely to respond with anger and punishment. But, in most cases, children are not trying to make us angry or 'defy' us. They are simply trying to learn. They don't have all of the knowledge that we have, as adults, so they make mistakes. They need to feel safe when they make mistakes. They need to be able to trust us to respond in a respectful way that teaches them what we really want them to learn.

How in your opinion will this manual help parents, guardians, or future parents?

Joan: It will give parents, guardians and other caregivers a few simple principles to follow when they are feeling frustrated. Because it is difficult to think about principles in a moment of frustration, they will have opportunities to practice and prepare for situations that they find particularly challenging. If they follow the principles, they will feel less anger toward their children, they will build their relationships with their children, and they will help their children become respectful, confident and competent people.

Future parents can use the manual to learn about child development so that they are better prepared for typical parenting challenges. They also can learn the principles ahead of time and work through the exercises. This should help them to think more clearly when they are in actual situations of conflict with their children. Preparing for difficult situations can make a very big difference to our ability to manage them well.

Who else could benefit from using this manual?

Joan: This manual could be very useful to professionals who work with parents. It can be used with individual parents or with groups. It could also be useful to people working in advocacy organizations who don't necessarily work directly with parents, but who would like to have a better understanding of what positive discipline is.

The Positive Discipline Manual ***Positive Discipline: What it is and how to do it*** is available at <www.crin.org/docs/PositiveDisciplineManual_Final.pdf>; and at: <http://seap.savethechildren.se/South_East_Asia/Misc/Puffs/Positive-Discipline-What-it-is-and-how-to-do-it>.

TASK/TEXT 7.2: WORLDWIDE ALTERNATIVES TO VIOLENCE

<www.wavetrust.org>, About WAVE, Our Commitment:

WAVE believes that preventing child abuse is the key to reducing violence in society.

Although there are many causes of violence, WAVE has identified child abuse or neglect as a fundamental contributor to antisocial, aggressive or violent behaviour. This is because:

- Patterns of behaviour are adopted very early on in life. Many children who are abused or neglected learn that the world is cruel place and act accordingly.
- Antisocial behaviour is difficult to change – once adopted, this character trait is strong and often leads to adult violence.
- This pattern of violence is then repeated within the family as the antisocial/aggressive adult raises their own child.

WAVE's 4 Key Recommendations are:

- No child should leave school without receiving fundamental training in how to 'attune' with babies and to parent in a non-violent manner. An example of this type of programme is provided by Roots of Empathy, – <www.rootsofempathy.org>.
- During a first pregnancy, every mother- and father-to-be should receive supportive coaching on how to 'attune' with babies, how to ensure the child's successful emotional development and how to parent in a non-violent

manner. An example of this type of support is offered by PIPPIN – <www.pippin.org.uk>.

- Babies in 'at risk' families should be monitored during the first three years, with their parents receiving regular visits by specially trained Health Visitors who provide practical encouragement and support. An example of what could be provided can be seen via the Nurse Family Partnership – <www.nursefamilypartnership.org>.
- Post Traumatic Stress Disorder in violent individuals should be recognised, and steps taken to heal it in children and adults entering the legal and prison systems [*see* Extract from the *WAVE Report 2005*, <www.wavetrust.org>, WAVE Reports].

<www.wavetrust.org>, About WAVE, WAVE Trust:

Interpersonal violence is a major problem in many countries around the world. There is violence on the streets, in schools, hospitals and even in churches and doctors' surgeries. It is also rife in the family. Three or four children die per week in the UK at the hands of their parents. 10 per cent of elderly people in Britain are subject to abuse and neglect. In Canada, 3 women per week die at the hands of a partner or former partner.

Supported by leading international researchers, psychologists, psychiatrists and criminologists, WAVE has been studying the root causes of violent behaviour for 9 years. This study concluded that pathways to violence are often laid down by 2–3 years of age, creating aggressive personalities for life. Our understanding of how these pathways are laid down has expanded enormously in recent years, boosted by new discoveries about the workings of the brain. Key positive or negative building blocks include a mother's earliest handling of her baby, her subsequent style of interacting with her baby, and traumatic stress from abuse or neglect.

WAVE draws on the best know-how worldwide – for example, the Nurse-Family Partnership is a US based home visiting programme which uses highly educated nurses who make 33 visits to 'at risk' families, beginning in early pregnancy and continuing until the child is two. Key elements include support for emotional attunement and non-violent parenting. Nurse-Family Partnership is the most rigorously tested programme of its kind. Among its striking successes have been reductions in child abuse and neglect by 50%-75% in one study and reduced hospitalisations due to non-accidental injuries by 75% in another. In a 15 year follow-up study nurse visited children had 50% lower arrests, 80% fewer convictions, significantly lower drug, alcohol and tobacco abuse, and less promiscuous sexual activity than the control group. Economic evaluation of the programme shows a payback of four times its cost.

We now know there are effective means to reduce the root causes of violence, and these means are a sound financial investment because of the huge savings they offer in the costs of crime. They are also a sound moral investment through reduced human suffering. We ask for your support to help us spread this knowledge, and reduce that suffering.

TASK/TEXT 7.3: PARENTS AS TEACHERS

<www.parentsasteachers.org>, For parents:

In the first few years, children learn more and at a faster pace than at any other time in life. You help shape your child's future through the kinds of experiences you provide. Your baby was born to learn, and as a parent, *you* are your child's first and most important teacher. Parents as Teachers is here to help you! Parents as Teachers (PAT) is a parent education and family support program serving families throughout pregnancy until their child enters kindergarten, usually age 5.

Parents are supported by PAT-certified parent educators trained to translate scientific information on early brain development into specific *when*, *what*, *how* and *why* advice for families. By understanding what to expect during each stage of development, parents can easily capture the teachable moments in everyday life to enhance their child's language development, intellectual growth, social development and motor skills.

As a PAT family, you receive:

Personal visits – during which your parent educator will share age-appropriate child development and parenting information, help you learn to observe your child, and address your parenting concerns.

Parent group meetings – which are opportunities to share information about parenting issues and child development. Parents learn and support each other, observe their children with other children and practice parenting skills.

Screenings – to assess your child's overall development as well as health, hearing and vision.

Resource network – that links your family to other community services. (...)

Parents as Teachers is designed to foster strong, loving relationships between parents and their children. You and your baby deserve the support Parents as Teachers offers. Give your child the best possible start in life because your baby was born to learn!

<www.parentsasteachers.org>, About us:

Parents as Teachers is the overarching program philosophy of providing parents with child development knowledge and parenting support. (...)

Vision: All children will learn, grow and develop to realize their full potential.

Mission: To provide the information, support and encouragement parents need to help their children develop optimally during the crucial early years of life.

Program Goals:

- Increase parent knowledge of early childhood development and improve parenting practices.
- Provide early detection of developmental delays and health issues.
- Prevent child abuse and neglect.
- Increase children's school readiness and school success.

Core Values:

- The early years of a child's life are critical for optimal development and provide the foundation for success in school and in life.
- Parents are their children's first and most influential teachers.
- Established and emerging research should be the foundation of parent education and family support curricula, training, materials and services.
- All young children and their families deserve the same opportunities to succeed, regardless of any demographic, geographic or economic considerations.
- An understanding and appreciation of the history and traditions of diverse cultures is essential in serving families.

TASK/TEXT 7.4: PEACE-TEACHING PARENTING PLEDGE

Peace-teaching parenting for a peaceful society, <www.stophitting.com/disathome/parentSupport/PEACETeachingParentingPledge.php>

I PLEDGE to teach children how to be kind and caring in their interactions with others. I will notice and correct instances of unkindness including nasty name-calling, bigotry, hitting, and bullying. I will teach children to notice and correct unkindness among siblings or peers.

I PLEDGE to teach children to persistently search for peaceful ways to address problems. I recognize that these teachings begin with my own behavior. I will, therefore, find peaceful ways to address any behavioral or other problem that I may have with my child.

I PLEDGE never to resort to physically aggressive discipline, including all variations of hitting, spanking, smacking, whipping, or mouth-burning. I will never threaten my children with physical aggression. I will not call children nasty names such as "bad" or "stupid," as I recognize that words may also cause harm.

I PLEDGE that I will recognize the many other ways that I am teaching either peace or violence. In choosing to teach peace, I will not provide pretend weapons, violent music, war games, violent computer games, or violent media to children. When judging the merit of any particular item, I will simply ask: "Is this teaching peace or teaching violence?" or "Is this causing children to practice peacemaking or to practice violence?" I will not merely ask, "Is this really going to do that much harm?" We must do much more than "not cause much harm." We must proactively cause and create peace.

I PLEDGE to practice peace everyday and in every way I can. I understand that it is the moment-to-moment practice of peace that truly teaches the lesson of peace. I will remember to sit and breathe and smile together with my children as I look into their eyes and feel love.

……………… [Signature of Parent(s)]
……………… [At present, I do not directly care for children but I have signed this pledge in my role as a parent to society's children.]

Written by Cheryl Landy, Ph.D., Licensed Psychologist. Please join in helping to create a new societal standard for the practice of peace, and, a new societal standard for the treatment of children. Invite key persons of influence to parents, such as religious and educational leaders, as well as family practitioners and pediatricians, to post this Pledge and to advocate for peace-teaching parenting.

Contact DrLandy@bellsouth.net (…) for no-fee supportive educational papers. Contact <www.stophitting.com> and <www.epochnz.virtualave.net> for peaceful discipline alternatives. Contact <www.gandhiinstitute.org> for peace-teaching support.

TASK/TEXT 7.5: BULLYING PREVENTION

<member.preventchildabuse.org/site/News2?page=NewsArticle&id=5545&Jserv SessionIdr006=ow8eicgk91.app14a>, Friday, August 31, 2007 – By: PCA Florida

Support Your Child's Social Development

- Prevent bullying by talking with your child about what bullying is, why bullying is wrong and what they can do if they witness their peers being bullied.
- Continue having a safe and healthy atmosphere at home. Keeping the lines of communication open between family members will allow the child to know the difference between appropriate and inappropriate behavior.
- Teach your child what qualities to look for in a friend, such as someone that makes them feel comfortable when acting themselves.
- Encourage your child to get involved in pro-social activities. Such activities include organized school and community groups and team building activities and play. Parents' involvement in groups with their children will increase the likelihood of their children's willingness to participate.
- Help your child establish a positive self esteem by also encouraging participation in out of school activities. This will help them gain confidence while participating in a team activity with a different peer group and give them an opportunity to make additional friends outside of the school yard.
- Encourage them to make friends and play with others during times when bullying can occur. They are less likely to be the victim of bullying if they are not alone.
- Teach children not to participate in the teasing of others or hurting children by making them feel bad about themselves.
- Teach children that reporting bullying is different from tattling on someone. Bullying hurts someone and can be stopped. If they are scared to tell by themselves, they should seek help with a friend or even an older sibling.
- If they witness bullying occurring, encourage them to seek help from teachers or other adults that will be able to stop and further monitor the bullying.

Children react in many different ways from being bullied. Here are some signs and symptoms children may express if being bullied:

- Shy, insecure, suffers from low self esteem
- Torn articles of clothing or missing belongings
- Unexplainable bruises, cuts, or scrapes
- Fear of going to school or participating in organized activities

- Anxious or depressed when returning home from school
- Quiet or seems withdrawn
- Complains of illness such as stomachaches
- Changes in diet
- Has trouble sleeping or numerous bad dreams.

Here are some tips to help your child if he or she is being bullied:

- Listen to what your child says. Support your child by talking about problem-solving solutions. Avoid any blame to your child for provoking the situation; this can further make the child feel victimized and may close the lines of communication.
- Be supportive and ask specific questions about what, who, where, and how long the bullying has been happening.
- Reassure your child to continue being themselves. Changing their ways for others is not the right solution or reason to end bullying.
- Teach your child tips to withdraw from the situation instead of fighting back. This will help to diffuse the situation instead of escalating it.
- Contact the school, principal, or teacher immediately. They will have a better understanding of how the children interact together at school. They will also be alert to the situation and able to keep an eye on the children during such periods when the bullying can occur (lunch, recess, before and after school).

Children who bully other children may have some of the following characteristics:

- Easily frustrated
- Impulsive or dominant
- Has difficulty following rules
- Views violence in a positive way
- Shows no signs of empathy.

What should you do if your child is the bully? Finding out your child is a bully may come as a shock and as a parent you may feel disappointed or angry. Feelings of denial are also common. It is important to remember children act differently in different social settings. Guiding children and teaching them appropriate behavior is a responsibility parents must take. Here are some useful tips to help **STOP** your child from bullying.

- Tell them their behavior is inappropriate and will not be tolerated. Making clear expectations for your child helps them to recognize desired behavior. Tell them that it is unkind to make others feel unhappy.
- Praise children for kind acts offered to other children. This helps them to recognize appropriate social skills and learn the kind of behavior that is appreciated and accepted.
- Spend more time with your child and monitor his or her behavior. Surrounding your child with positive role models will help create a positive attitude.
- Teach your child there are other ways to make and have friends that doesn't involve bullying others.
- Seek help and other tips from school counselors for ways to add an extra layer of education for your child at school.

TASK/TEXT 7.6:

TASK/TEXT 7.6.1: SYNTHESIS ON OBESITY

Centre of Excellence for Early Childhood Development, Encyclopedia on Early Childhood Development, <www.child-encyclopedia.com/pages/PDF/synthesis-obesity.pdf>; published online 25 March 2008

How important is it?

Obesity has become a pandemic, with more than a billion people affected worldwide. Over the past 30 years, the frequency of overweight children, defined as those having a body mass index (BMI) greater than the 85th percentile for age and sex, has tripled. Data from the International Obesity Task Force indicate that 22 million of the world's children under 5 years of age are overweight or obese. Obesity has even replaced malnutrition as the major nutritional problem in some parts of Africa, with overweight/obesity being as much as four times more common than malnutrition.

The first years of life are a critical period for the development of food and flavour preferences, the ability to self-control food intake, the transmission of cultural and familial beliefs about food and eating, and the susceptibility to overweight and obesity later in life. Overweight in infancy tends to increase the risk for subsequent overweight in childhood and this risk appears to increase with age. Obesity by age 4 or 5 is a concern because it tends to persist.

As the incidence of childhood obesity has increased, more consequences of obesity in children have been identified, including obstructive sleep apnea (episodes of pauses in breathing during sleep due to obstruction of the airways), orthopaedic problems, type 2 diabetes, and cardiovascular disease. Psychological problems – for example, depression and reduced quality of life – are also serious correlates of obesity. Bias, prejudice, and discrimination are part of everyday life for overweight children. Moreover, the consequences of bias, such as isolation or social withdrawal, could contribute to the exacerbation of obesity through psychological vulnerabilities that increase the likelihood of over-eating and sedentary activity.

What do we know?

The development of overweight and obesity during the early years of life is influenced both by child characteristics and by factors related to the child's parents and home environment. Childhood obesity develops when the body's self-regulatory system fails to modulate environmental influences relative to the person's genetic background. Since it is not possible for the gene pool to change in less than a generation, it is likely that changes in nutrition and lifestyle are primarily responsible for the current epidemic of obesity.

Obesity develops when there is an imbalance between energy intake and energy expenditure: reduced physical activity and increased food intake (especially high-fat, energy-dense foods such as snacks, sugar-added beverages and fast-food products) are the primary causes. In young children, levels of physical activity lower than the recommended 60 minutes per day and excessive television viewing (more than two hours per day) are likely to have adverse effects on cardiovascular and bone health, and possibly on cognitive function and social and emotional development.

Prenatal factors that may lead to overweight in children from birth to five years include maternal smoking, maternal diabetes, and maternal overweight prior to and during pregnancy. Breastfeeding, however, may protect children from obesity. Possible mechanisms for this protective effect include metabolic programming and early-learned self-control of food intake. Another possible explanation is that breastfeeding may influence parental control of child consumption patterns. As well, breastfed babies experience a variety of flavours through the mother's diet, which may make them more accepting of typically rejected foods (such as vegetables) later on.

Introduction to complementary foods (cereal, fruit, vegetables or meat) before 16 weeks of age in combination with a short duration of breastfeeding (less than 20 weeks) has been associated with higher weight gains from birth to one year. Studies suggest that the late introduction of solids (waiting until at least 15 weeks of age) may have a beneficial effect on childhood obesity and reduce the risk for allergic reactions. Rapid weight gain in infancy and early childhood appears to be a risk factor for later obesity.

Parents have a major role to play in helping their children to develop healthy eating habits and an active lifestyle. Since children imitate what they see, it is not surprising that parents' own eating behaviours are associated with children's eating behaviours and weight status. Children naturally prefer sweet and salty tastes and do not need to learn to like these foods. However, when given the opportunity to taste new foods repeatedly, such as fruits and vegetables, children learn to like foods they once rejected. Studies have shown that it may take 5 to 16 exposures before a child accepts a new food.

While it is advisable for parents to limit their children's consumption of unhealthy snacks and encourage them to eat more fruits and vegetables, excessive restriction or pressure to eat may actually have negative impacts on child food intake and weight status by disrupting the child's ability to naturally control their food intake. Parental pressure to eat certain foods may decrease the children's preferences for those foods, while excessive restriction may encourage over-consumption of the restricted foods when they are readily available.

Finally, psychosocial factors that potentially increase the risk that a child will become obese include low socio-economic status, being an only child, and living with a single parent.

What can be done?

Prevention of obesity in children should be the first line of treatment. This requires a broad-based public health program.

Developments in health and education services are required to provide more effective surveillance of overweight and obesity in early childhood, better identification of overweight and obese children, and greater and more effective support for families to prevent and treat obesity.

Paediatricians are encouraged to become advocates for the prevention of obesity by identifying and targeting influential specialists (e.g., health care professionals, nutritionists, and child development specialists) for education on obesity. They should also encourage, support, and protect breastfeeding, promote healthy eating habits, promote physical activity, and recommend limitation of television viewing in their day-to-day practice. In addition, recommending a good night's sleep is of high importance given the emerging literature showing that short sleep duration is associated with overweight/obesity, particularly in children.

Interventions should target modifiable behaviours that might improve child health or development and should target behaviours that are important to the development and maintenance of a healthy weight (i.e., reduction in TV viewing, promotion of breastfeeding, reduction in soft drinks and sugar intake, increase in physical activity).

Parents and caregivers should be positive role models for children's eating and physical behaviours. They should model healthful eating behaviours and make healthful food available to their children in an effort to lower the risk of obesity for their children. In this respect, insufficient knowledge about healthy nutrition, unhealthy eating behaviours and physical inactivity among parents can lead to poor eating and physical activity behaviours in their children. Treatment is therefore more likely to be effective if the family is the focus (not just the obese child), if the family is motivated to make the necessary lifestyle changes, if the treatment is of significant duration and if it focuses on modifying sedentary behaviour as well as diet.

However, obesity prevention will likely fail if the child's environment is not addressed. For example, research suggests that reducing snack food advertising helps to prevent detrimental eating behaviour. The nutritional quality of foods and beverages served and sold in schools should also be improved. Children should be encouraged to reduce their consumption of soft drinks and other sugar-added beverages, to increase their level of physical activities, and to reduce their amount of television viewing. Macro-environmental changes that promote physical activity and play are urgently required if the paediatric obesity epidemic is to be addressed.

TASK/TEXT 7.6.2: CHILDHOOD OBESITY

Eurochild e-News Bulletin November 2007, <www.eurochild.org/fileadmin/user_upload/Enews_Bulletin/Eurochild_e-News_Bulletin_November_2007.pdf>

European 'School Fruit Scheme'

Childhood obesity in Europe is growing at an alarming rate. In 2005, 14 million children were categorised as overweight or obese with an estimated 400,000 children entering this category every year. In 2007, the number has risen to 22 million. Increased consumption of fruit and vegetables as part of a balanced diet and healthy eating habits has been identified to play an important role in combating this phenomenon. In several EU member states, school-based enticement schemes for children exist and show remarkable success. The European Council has asked the Commission to come forward with a proposal for a European 'School Fruit Scheme' based on an impact assessment of the benefits, practicability and administrative costs involved. Within the scope of this exercise, the Commission is undertaking an extensive consultation process. In order to provide up-to-date information on the progress of this policy initiative and to allow for active contributions by stakeholders and the interested public, a web page has been created at: <http://ec.europa.eu/agriculture/markets/fruitveg/sfs/index_en.htm>.

Tackling Childhood Obesity: European Day of Healthy Food and Cooking
On 8 November, EU Health Commissioner Markos Kyprianou launched the "European Day of Healthy Food and Cooking," which aims to encourage healthy eating amongst children, with a view to tackling the rising childhood obesity levels in Europe. Across 14 Member States, EU officials, top chefs and school children are coming together for demonstrations on how to cook healthy, tasty food and workshops to promote a balanced lifestyle. Commissioner Kyprianou attended interactive cooking lessons at a European school in Brussels in the morning, where 4 professional chefs explained the benefits of eating well to 60 children. EU Agriculture Commissioner Mariann Fischer-Boel also visited a school in Copenhagen with a leading Danish chef. With around 22 million overweight or obese children in the EU today, the aim is to instil an interest in children in the food that they eat and to make them aware of the basic principles of good nutrition. The European Healthy Food and Cooking Day was coorganised by the European Commission and the European Chefs' Association (Euro-toques).

For more information: <http://europa.eu/rapid/pressReleasesAction.do?reference=IP/07/1663&type=HTML&aged=0&language=EN&guiLanguage=en>.

MEPs back compulsory sport at school
The European Parliament agreed with the Commission that physical education is increasingly marginalised in today's school curricula and has called on member states to make three hours of sport compulsory for all primary and secondary schools to boost children's appetite for a more active lifestyle. Parliament's resolution, adopted by an overwhelming majority on 13 November, identifies a number of problems concerning physical education across the EU. It points to the ever-decreasing amount of time allocated to sport at school and the limited choice of sport options, and argues that sport in schools is often too competitive. Under-funded sports facilities and insufficient coordination between sport inside and outside of school are also identified as problems to be solved in order to get children to exercise more.

For more information: <www.euractiv.com/en/sports/meps-backcompulsory-sport-school/article-168331>; <www.europarl.europa.eu/news/expert/infopress_page/041-12898-316-11-46-906-20071109IPR12779-12-11-2007-2007-false/default_en.htm>.

TASK/TEXT 7.7:

TASK/TEXT 7.7.1: EIGHT ESSENTIAL PARENTAL RESPONSIBILITIES

<www.familyresource.com/parenting/parent-education/8-essential-parental-responsibilities> (visited 28 March 2008)

By Chris Theisen[90]

Introduction

Nobody ever said that children were easy to raise. They don't come with guidelines or instructions, and they certainly don't come with a *pause* button (...). What they do come with is a crucial set of physical and emotional needs that must be met. Failure of the parents to meet these specific needs can have wide-ranging and long-lasting negative effects.

The following outline provides eight essential responsibilities that parents must adhere to in order to foster their child's physical and/or emotional well-being:

1. Provide an environment that is SAFE

- Keep your child free from physical, sexual, and emotional abuse.
- Keep unsafe objects locked up or out of reach of your child.
- Get to know your child's caregivers (get references or background checks).
- Correct any potential dangers around the house.
- Take safety precautions: Use smoke and carbon monoxide detectors, lock doors at night, always wear seatbelts, etc.

2. Provide your child with BASIC NEEDS

- Water
- Plenty of nutritious foods
- Shelter
- A warm bed with sheets, blankets, and a pillow

[90] Chris Theisen is a Mental Health Specialist who earned his degree from the University of Northern Colorado in 1994. Since then he has spent over 10 years working directly with children who have been diagnosed with such problems as: ADHD, bipolar disorder, conduct disorder, oppositional-defiant disorder, PTSD, and autism. He is the author of the Parent Coach plan (<www.parentcoachplan.com>). The Parent Coach plan was developed through a combination of Chris' experience with these children, and the effects that he has seen by using behavior management programs in various facilities where he's worked.

- Medical care as needed/Medicine when ill
- Clothing that is appropriate for the weather conditions
- Space (a place where he or she can go to be alone)

3. Provide your child with SELF-ESTEEM NEEDS

- Accept your child's uniqueness and respect his or her individuality.
- Encourage (don't push) your child to participate in a club, activity, or sport.
- Notice and acknowledge your child's achievements and pro-social behavior.
- Encourage proper hygiene (to look good is to feel good …).
- Set expectations for your child that are realistic and age-appropriate.
- Use your child's misbehavior as a time to teach, not to criticize or ridicule.

4. Teach your child MORALS and VALUES

- Honesty
- Respect
- Responsibility
- Compassion
- Patience
- Forgiveness
- Generosity

5. Develop MUTUAL RESPECT with your child

- Use respectful language
- Respect his or her feelings
- Respect his or her opinions
- Respect his or her privacy
- Respect his or her individuality

6. Provide DISCIPLINE which is effective and appropriate

- Structured
- Consistent
- Predictable
- Fair

7. Involve yourself in your child's EDUCATION

- Communicate regularly with your child's teacher(s).
- Make sure that your child is completing his or her homework each night.

- Assist your child with his or her homework, but don't DO the homework.
- Talk to your child each day about school (what is being studied, any interesting events etc.).
- Recognize and acknowledge your child's academic achievements.

8. Get to KNOW YOUR CHILD

- Spend quality time together.
- Be approachable to your child.
- Ask questions.
- Communicate. Communicate. Communicate.

Eight responsibilities parents do NOT have

Now that we've looked at the responsibilities parents HAVE, let's look at what responsibilities parents do NOT have. The following is a list of responsibilities that no parent should be expected to meet.

1. Supplying your child with the most expensive designer clothes or shoes available.
2. Picking up after your child/Cleaning your child's room.
3. Dropping everything you're doing to give your child a ride somewhere.
4. Providing your child with a telephone, television, computer, or game system.
5. Bailing your child out of trouble every time he or she does something wrong.
6. Maintaining an unlimited supply of treats, chips, sodas, or junk foods for your child's unlimited consumption.
7. Replacing toys or other items that your child has lost or misplaced.
8. Welcoming any or all of your child's friends into your home for social or other activities.

TASK/TEXT 7.7.2: TEN PARENTAL RESPONSIBILITIES & TEN PARENTAL RIGHTS

From: Dr. Maggie Mamen (psychologist), The pampered child syndrome – and how to avoid it ..., <www.rccdsb.edu.on.ca/jbosco/Dr. Maggie Mamen Presentation.pdf> (visited 28 March 2008)

Ten parental responsibilities

1. To nurture children
2. To keep them safe
3. To provide for their basic needs
4. To build trust, credibility and respect
5. To socialize children
6. To teach moral values
7. To encourage a sense of self
8. To foster a sense of community
9. To be a positive role model
10. To prepare them for real life.

Ten parental rights

1. To be the architects of the family
2. To constitute the management team
3. To set policy and procedures
4. To have a weighted vote
5. To not be verbally, physically or otherwise battered
6. To make choices
7. To make decisions
8. To think before deciding *("If you want an answer now, it's no")*
9. To enjoy our home and family
10. To have adult time.

TASK/TEXT 7.8: ISRAEL – REALITY SHOW "EXPLOITS CHILDREN"

<www.crin.org/resources/infoDetail.asp?ID=16917>, The Jerusalem Post – 10 April 2008

Top Israeli life coach Alon Gal was in the Knesset (Israeli parliament) this week to defend his new television series Heroes of Life against charges that it – and other reality-based shows – unfairly exploit minors. The hearing, which was sponsored by the Committee for Children's Rights, was called during the Knesset recess after MK Arye Eldad (NU/NRP) submitted a letter two weeks ago demanding the immediate removal of popular television program **Super Nanny**, arguing then that "the use of helpless children, in the goal of educating their parents and giving advice to the viewers, as wise at it may be, is extremely unethical and possibly even illegal."

In the letter, Eldad called on MK Nadia Hilou (Labor), the chairwoman of the Knesset Committee on Children's Rights, to hold a discussion on the subject. And Eldad was apparently not alone – after Hilou announced that such a discussion would be held, around 70 different people representing television interests and children's and parents' groups submitted requests to be allowed to weigh in on the discussion.

"In my eyes, more of these discussions should occur," said Gal, addressing the committee. "But we must be careful not to throw out the baby with the bathwater." Gal said that the use of educational programs that ride on the wave of the "reality TV" trend should continue, but only when done by professionals with the intent to really help their young subjects – and not just to search for ratings.

"If we wanted to do this for just ratings, we would do auditions for the show and hundreds of thousands of youth would volunteer for it," Gal explained, adding that "all of the scenes that could bring the highest ratings and the most drama remained on the editing floor out of concern for the subjects."

In his programme, which received sponsorship from the Israel 60th Anniversary Committee, Gal served as a life coach for 11 troubled teens who attend a boarding school. The treatment lasted for a full year, Gal said, with the oversight of the teaching faculty at the school, and helped the teens realise their goals and overcome their individual difficulties.

"Television in Israel is one of the strongest tools to talk to our youth – whoever doesn't understand that is living in the 19th century together with Fred Flintstone," he argued. He said that teenager recognized him on street, but rather than requesting his autograph, turn to him for advice on how to increase their self-esteem.

But many in the room were less than convinced by Gal's arguments. Dr. Yitzhak Kadman, the chairman of the National Council for the Child. said that he had been receiving complaints for years about the unfair use of children on reality shows.

"We must look at the implications of the day after the show is aired," he said. "The use of children in this way does an injustice to them. It can harm them on the 'day after' and it doesn't just affect the child who was portrayed, but other children as well."

Kedman compared the arguments made by Gal and the television franchise owners airing Super Nanny to a situation in which children are "treated" for problems successfully – but using harmful methods. "Some say that electrical shock therapy is also very effective for teaching children, but we still don't use that," he said, calling for the establishment of "red lines" to prevent children from being degraded on the screen. "I propose that each of us ask himself or herself if they would want to be shown on television in such an embarrassing situation," he said.

Ultimately, although the discussion ended without concrete conclusions, almost all of the speakers – both those opposing the popular shows as well as those supporting their content as "educational" – agreed with the proposal to tighten the language of consent forms signed by parents before their children appear on such shows.

TASK/TEXT 7.9: DISCIPLINE – HOW MUCH IS ENOUGH?

Centre of Excellence for Early Childhood Development (<www.excellence-earlychildhood.ca>), 29 May 2008 (<www.child-encyclopedia.com/pages/PDF/DisciplineANGmcP.pdf>)

What do we know?

- A loving attitude, clear rules and applying the consequences that were stated will encourage the development of positive behaviours in children.
- When the parent behaves in this way, the child is encouraged to explore his environment while respecting certain limits.
- An enthusiastic parent who gives his child the opportunity to do fun things and be successful will give him confidence and will encourage him to explore his environment.
- Respecting each child's personality, parents should apply discipline that is not too authoritarian and not too permissive, so that the child will obey instructions.
- Children who are too tightly controlled will have trouble making decisions and expressing their needs.
- On the other hand, children who are allowed to do anything they want will have trouble knowing what is acceptable and what isn't.
- Good discipline leads to success in school and the ability to make friends.
- If parents aren't able to build respect for rules in their child in the early years (0 to 5), he may develop different types of behaviour problems.
- If parents don't provide enough supervision (aren't involved in the child's activities, aren't encouraging), and react with punishments, temper outbursts or rigidity, there is greater risk that the child will have behaviour problems.
- Discipline that helps the child understand what is acceptable and what isn't helps him develop social skills, empathy, self-control and the ability to pay attention and plan ahead.

Paying attention to behaviours in the child that should be discouraged: What can be done?

- Establish clear rules.
- State the consequences that will follow if the rules are not respected.
- Apply the consequences that were stated.
- Ignore the child if his behaviours are not aggressive or disrespectful.

- Apply the technique of withdrawal (short and repeated). For example, take away an object that is a source of conflict between 2 children or ask the child to withdraw to a quiet place where he can calm down.

Paying attention to behaviours in the child that should be encouraged: What can be done?

- Say what the child does well.
- Congratulate the child using both words and actions. For example, express your pride, give hugs, smiles, winks, etc.
- Help the child to see the connections between what he does and the successful outcome.
- Encourage the child to continue.

Paying attention to situations that might lead the child to lose control: What can be done?

- Support the child by offering enjoyable ways to calm down. For example, change activities, breathe calmly, distract or redirect the child attention, etc.

TASK/TEXT 7.10: NEARLY ONE-THIRD OF US PARENTS DON'T KNOW WHAT TO EXPECT OF INFANTS

<www.urmc.rochester.edu/pr/news/story.cfm?id=1976>, May 05, 2008

Almost one-third of US parents have a surprisingly low-level knowledge of typical infant development and unrealistic expectations for their child's physical, social and emotional growth, according to new research from the University of Rochester. The findings, which suggest that such false parenting assumptions can not only impair parent-child interactions, but also rob kids of much-needed cognitive stimulation, will be presented Sunday, May 4, at the Pediatric Academic Society meeting in Honolulu, Hawaii.

"There are numerous parenting books telling people what to expect when they're pregnant," said Heather Paradis, M.D., a pediatric fellow at the University of Rochester Medical Center. "But once a baby is born, an astonishing number of parents are not only unsure of what to anticipate as their child develops, but are also uncertain of when, how or how much they are to help their babies reach various milestones, such as talking, grabbing, discerning right from wrong, or even potty-training."

Moms and dads often misinterpret behaviors – some parents expect too much of babies too soon and grow frustrated; others underestimate their child's abilities, preventing them from learning on their own.

Using data from the Early Childhood Longitudinal Study's Birth Cohort (ECLS-B), Paradis and her colleagues analyzed the average parenting knowledge of a nationally-representative sample of parents of more than 10,000 9-month-old babies born in 2001. These parents first answered an 11-point survey designed to distinguish informed parents from less-informed parents (asking questions such as "Should a 1-year-old child be able to tell between right from wrong?" and "Should a 1-year-old child be ready to begin toilet-training?"). Those who scored 4 or fewer correct answers were considered to have low-level knowledge of typical infant development.

Paradis and colleagues then compared these knowledge scores to both scores from (1) a 73-point videotape analysis of the same families' parent-child interactions while teaching a new task, and (2) from these parents' self-reports of how often they engaged their child in enrichment activities (e.g. reading books, telling stories, or singing songs).

The analysis revealed that 31.2 percent of parents of infants had low-level knowledge of infant development, and that this low-level knowledge correlated with lower parental education level and income. Still, even when controlling for maternal age, education, income and mental state (e.g., depression), low-level knowledge of infant development still significantly and independently predicted parents being both less likely to enjoy healthy interactions with their infants during learning tasks and less likely to engage their children in regular enrichment activities.

"This is a wake-up call for pediatricians," Paradis said. "At office visits, we have a prime opportunity to intervene and help realign parents' expectations for their infants, and in turn, promote healthy physical, social, and emotional development for these children. On the other hand, we still have more work cut out for us – additional research is needed to explore how these unrealistic expectations form in the first place."

TASK/TEXT 7.11: SIX TIPS FOR BETTER FAMILY COMMUNICATION

Prevent Child Abuse, Creating a Supportive Family (email 30 January 2009)

We know that family communication is important in creating a positive home environment for children and youth to develop, but how do we do that and how else can we create a nurturing and supportive family?

Healthy communication, providing a stable home and environment, creating healthy outlets of expression, and showing affection to other family members as well as our children, are some of the tools we can use to build a supportive structure for families and communities.

The Search Institute reports while 47% of sixth graders report positive family communication, only 22% of high school seniors do. No matter the age of your children, family communication is an ongoing challenge.

<http://member.preventchildabuse.org/site/News2?page=NewsArticle&id=5775>
29 January 2009, from <www.lifescript.com>; By: Stephanie Tallman Smith

1. Create opportunities for talking

It's no secret that Americans are overworked, overcommitted and overscheduled. Parents rush home from work to take children to soccer practice, piano lessons and Girl Scout meetings, all before hitting the drive-through window to pick up fast food for dinner. Mix in kids who'd rather text their friends than chat with Mom or Dad and we have a family communication crisis.

So what can you do? Make time for talking by reducing the number of activities your family is involved in each week – the time it frees up for communication will be invaluable. And if you do find yourself in the car running from place to place, make a point to turn off the radio, the cell phones and the personal game players, and use that opportunity to catch up on the day's activities.

2. Insist on family meals

In addition to bringing everyone together for a wrap-up of the day's activities, insisting on a few standing family meals creates ritual and routine that kids come to expect and look forward to. Use the family dinner table as opportunity to share what's going on in family members' lives.

3. Go on individual dates with your children

Spending time with each of your children lets them know that they matter and aren't getting lost in the hubbub of a busy day or large family. Older teens might enjoy going out for a hamburger or a latte at their favorite coffee place. Younger children often enjoy going to the supermarket, especially when you let them select their favorite cereal or special dessert. Don't forget your spouse or the older family members who live near you. Regular date nights for couples and lunches with aging parents keeps those relationships healthy, as well.

4. Remember the 80/20 rule
When trying to improve any relationship, listening is far more important than talking, so when it comes to family communication, listen four times longer than you speak. Likewise, think twice about what you say *before* you say it. Sometimes a parent's first reaction is to rant and scream, especially to negative news. Do your best to avoid this, and if you do verbally explode before your child is finished, apologize quickly and assure him or her that you're now ready to listen.

5. Use technology to your advantage
If the family computer's been relegated to homework duties or surfing the Web, why not put it to work by creating a family newsletter that you publish monthly, just for your immediate family? Ask everyone in the family to contribute "articles" and information about themselves, then print out a copy for each person and hand deliver it. Or maybe you could create a family website or blog. This would be especially helpful to families that find keeping in touch more difficult as the kids grow up and move away. Or put your texting abilities to work to let your loved ones know you're thinking about them. If your son is facing a big test one afternoon, for instance, send him a text message at lunch letting him know you're behind him.

6. Create family traditions
Tucking the kids into bed at night, setting up a family movie night, attending religious services or creating special holiday treats are all examples of family traditions. Family members come to expect and appreciate these traditions, seeing them as opportunities to come together as a unit. If your family is short on traditions, there's no reason you can't start some now. Why not set up a bowling night once a month? Or grow a family garden? Or visit the same spot every year for summer vacation?

Maintaining positive family communications benefits your family in so many ways. Children feel comfortable sharing their problems with parents, reducing the risk of peers having an undue influence on their lives. Parents remain connected and intimate with each other and their children, strengthening the family bonds. And all family members develop effective communication styles that can improve the quality of their relationships beyond the family home. Why not start talking today?

TASK/TEXT 7.12: THE FIVE CRITICAL EMOTIONAL NEEDS OF CHILDREN

Center for the Improvement of Child Caring (<www.ciccparenting.org>), e-list 8 October 2009

Emotional health provides a foundation for success in school, work, marriage and life in general. Failure to recognize and satisfy these five needs jeopardizes our children's future and that of succeeding generations. The five critical needs as a family value contribute to a healthy family environment and strengthen us as a nation.

(1) Need to Feel Respected
Children need to feel respected. For that to happen, they need to be treated in a courteous, thoughtful, attentive and civil manner. One of the best ways for children to learn about respect is to feel what it's like to be treated respectfully and to observe their parents and other adults treating one another the same way.

If we want children to grow up feeling respected and treating others with respect, we need to avoid sarcasm, belittling, yelling; we need to keep anger and impatience to a minimum; we need to avoid lying; we need to listen more and talk less; we need to command less and suggest and request more; we need to learn how to say "please," "thank you," "excuse me", "I'm sorry"– yes, even to children. We need to become conscious of our mistakes, willing to admit them and ready to make corrections. This will help us cultivate these values in our children.

(2) Need to Feel Important
Feeling important refers to a child's need to feel: "I have value. I am useful. I have power. I am somebody." This need is evident at a very early age. Pressing a button in an elevator – me, me. Children want to do things for themselves, and so often we get in their way.

Parents need to avoid being all powerful, solving all family problems, making all decisions, doing all the work, controlling everything that happens. Involve your children – ask their opinions; give them things to do; share decision-making and power; give them status and recognition, and have patience with mistakes when it takes a little longer or is not done as well as you could have done yourself.

If children do not feel important, if they don't develop a sense of value in constructive ways, they may seek negative ways to get attention, to feel "I am somebody."

(3) Need to Feel Accepted
Children have a need to feel accepted as individuals in their own right, with their own uniqueness, and not treated as mere reflections of their parents, as objects to be shaped in the image of what parents believe their ideal child should look like. This means that children have a right to their own feelings, opinions, ideas, concerns, wants and needs. Trivializing, ignoring or ridiculing a child's feelings or opinions is a rejection which weakens the relationship. Paying attention to and discussing them, even when you do not like or disagree with some, strengthens the relationship.

(4) Need to Feel Included
Children need to feel included. They need to be brought in, to be made to feel a part of things, to feel connected to other people, to have a sense of community. It happens when people engage with others in activities and projects, when they experience things together in a meaningful way. It is important for the family to create these opportunities. People who do things together feel closer to one another. Family activities offer a way to become closer and also to have fun, learn, and contribute to others.

(5) Need to Feel Secure
Children need to feel secure. Security means creating a positive environment where people care for each other and show it, where people express themselves and others listen, where differences are accepted and conflicts are resolved constructively, where enough structure exists for children to feel safe and protected, and where children have opportunities to actively participate in their own and family evolution through family planning and decision making, problem solving and feedback activities.

TASK/TEXT 7.13:

TASK/TEXT 7.13.1: ATTACHMENT PARENTING

<www.attachmentparenting.org>, Eight Principles (accessed 13 February 2009)

The long-range vision of Attachment Parenting is to raise children who will become adults with a highly developed capacity for empathy and connection. It eliminates violence as a means for raising children, and ultimately helps to prevent violence in society as a whole.

The essence of Attachment Parenting is about forming and nurturing strong connections between parents and their children. Attachment Parenting challenges us as parents to treat our children with kindness, respect and dignity, and to model in our interactions with them the way we'd like them to interact with others.

Attachment Parenting isn't new. In many ways, it is a return to the instinctual behaviors of our ancestors. In the last sixty years, the behaviors of attachment have been studied extensively by psychology and child development researchers, and more recently, by researchers studying the brain. This body of knowledge offers strong support for areas that are key to the optimal development of children, summarized below in **API's *Eight Principles of Parenting.*** (...)

Introduction

The mission of Attachment Parenting International (API) is to promote parenting practices that create strong, healthy emotional bonds between children and their parents. API believes that Attachment Parenting (AP) practices fulfill a child's need for trust, empathy, and affection and will provide a foundation for a lifetime of healthy relationships.

Rooted in attachment theory, Attachment Parenting has been studied extensively for over 60 years by psychology and child development researchers, and more recently, by researchers studying the brain. These studies revealed that infants are born "hardwired" with strong needs to be nurtured and to remain physically close to the primary caregiver, usually the mother, during the first few years of life. The child's emotional, physical, and neurological development is greatly enhanced when these basic needs are met consistently and appropriately. These needs can be summarized as *proximity, protection, and predictability.*

The baby's crying, clinging, and sucking are early techniques to keep her mother nearby. As the child grows and feels more secure in her relationship with her mother, she is better able to explore the world around her and to develop strong, healthy bonds with other important people in her life.

To help guide parents along their journey, API created *The Eight Principles of Parenting.* These guidelines are founded on sound research and are known to be effective in helping children develop secure attachments.

API acknowledges that every family has unique circumstances with distinct needs and resources. *The Eight Principles* are intended to help parents better understand normal child development, to help parents identify their children's needs, and to aid parents in responding to their children with respect and empathy. By educating themselves about children's health and development, parents will become more conscious of and attuned to their children's needs when making decisions.

Developed to promote optimal attachment, these principles are developmentally appropriate and comprehensive enough to apply to a broad spectrum of family situations. These principles may be applied through the practices outlined in this document. *The Eight Principles* addresses attachment – promoting behaviors that can be started during pregnancy and extend through a child's seventh or eighth year. Although the terms "mother," "father," and "caregiver" are used throughout *The Eight Principles*, API embraces the diversity of family structures and values all people in a child's life who actively foster a strong attachment relationship with the children in their care.

In 2008, API will publish a companion document addressing the preservation of attachments with older children.

Attachment Parenting is not a one-size-fits-all recipe for raising children, therefore API recommends parents use their own judgment and intuition to create a parenting style that fosters attachment and works for their family. Some practices listed in *The Eight Principles* are inherently more attachment-promoting than others. The most ideal practices are listed first. Many API support groups start each meeting by saying "Take what works for your family and leave the rest." This sentiment also applies to *The Eight Principles*.

[Principle I:] Prepare for Pregnancy, Birth, and Parenting

The remarkable journey of new life is a positive, transformative experience. Pregnancy offers expectant parents an opportunity to prepare physically, mentally, and emotionally for parenthood. Making informed decisions about childbirth, newborn care, and parenting practices is a critical investment in the attachment relationship between parent and child. **Education is a key component of preparation** for the difficult decisions required of parents and is an ongoing process as each stage of growth and development brings new joys and challenges.

When preparing for the birth of a child, it is easy to get caught up in the material things associated with pregnancy, childbirth, and newborn care. Tiny infant clothing, the latest maternity fashions, and baby gear can all be part of preparing for a baby, but the lasting investment of preparation involves becoming informed so that you can create a peaceful, loving environment in which to grow, birth, and care for a new life.

Preparing for Pregnancy & Birth

- Reflect on childhood experiences and current beliefs about parenting
- Explore parenting philosophies
- Work through negative emotions surrounding the pregnancy
- Prepare physically for pregnancy; eat nutritious foods, exercise regularly, avoid stress when possible
- Explore different types of healthcare providers and birthing options. Consider reading "Ten Questions to Ask" and "Ten Steps" by the Coalition for

Improving Maternity Services [<www.motherfriendly.org>], and visiting the Baby Friendly Initiative website by UNICEF [<www.babyfriendly.org>].
- Recommit to a strong, healthy relationship between expectant parents
- Educate yourself about breastfeeding
- Be alert and physically active during childbirth
- Research all aspects of "routine" newborn care, such as bathing, circumcision [*sic*, JW], eye drops, blood samples, collecting cord blood, etc. Document your preferences and share them with health care providers.
- Prepare to have extra help in the first few weeks after birth
- Consider a birth and/or postpartum doula [<www.dona.org>]
- Be prepared with questions to ask should unexpected birth or newborn situations arise:
  - What are the benefits of this intervention, and what are your instincts telling you?
  - What are the risks and possible outcomes if I choose to do this or if I choose not to?
  - What are the other options?
  - How long do I have to make the decision?

Preparation for Becoming a Parent

- Continuously educate yourself about developmental stages
- Set realistic expectations for both parents and children
- Discuss concerns before they become crises
- Remain flexible!
- Become educated about educational options
- Come to terms with your own childhood, seeking professional help if it involved abuse or neglect.

[Principle II:] Feed with Love and Respect

Feeding a child involves more than providing nutrients; it is an act of love. Whether providing for the very intense hunger needs of a newborn, or serving meals at the family dinner table, parents can use feeding time as an opportunity to strengthen their bonds with their children.

The newborn's rooting, sucking, and crying reflexes evolved to ensure the close proximity of a mother or other caregiver that the baby can depend on to meet her intense needs. The more parents learn to identify and meet their baby's needs, the more securely attached the parent-child bond becomes. Although older children are better able to feed themselves and to communicate their needs, parents should continue to respect the child's hunger cues, offer healthy foods, model healthy eating habits, and make mealtimes a time for love and connection.

Breastfeeding and Attachment

- Breastfeeding satisfies an infant's nutritional and emotional needs better than any other method of infant feeding
- Feed on cue, before the stage of crying
- Breastfeeding continues to be normal and important nutritionally, immunologically, and emotionally beyond one year
- Breastfeeding has many benefits for both mother and baby
- Nursing is a valuable mothering tool to naturally comfort a baby
- "Comfort Nursing" meets a baby's sucking needs.

"Bottle Nursing"

- Feeding is one of the primary ways a mother can initiate a secure attachment relationship with her baby.
- Familiarize yourself with breastfeeding behaviors, and model them when bottle feeding:
    - Hold the baby when bottle feeding, positioning the bottle alongside the breast
    - Maintain eye contact, talk softly and lovingly
    - Switch positions from one side to another
    - Feed on cue and avoid schedules
    - Consider reserving feeding for the mother only
    - Pacifiers satisfy a baby's sucking need. Hold the baby or child in the feeding position when he uses the pacifier
    - Associate the bottle and pacifier with being held and having undivided attention, so that it doesn't become a transitional object
    - Wean from the bottle as one would wean from the breast.

Nurturing Through Feeding

- Parents can nurture themselves when feeding a baby
- Mothers flourish when nurtured by their partners
- Fathers can develop a relationship with the baby in many other ways than feeding.

Introducing Solids

- Introduce solids at signs of readiness, not based upon age
- Start slowly with foods that are not likely to cause allergens
- Offer breast or bottle first, followed by solids

- Follow the baby's cue on what and how much to eat; let him develop his tastes naturally
- Breast milk and/or artificial milk will be the primary nutrition source until about 1 year of age.

Nurturing a Taste for Nutritious Food

- Model healthy eating habits
- Try to make at least one meal a day a time for connection and community
- Toddlers need to eat small meals during the day and should not be expected to sit at a dinner table for long periods of time
- Encourage a child to follow his bodily cues for hunger and thirst, to eat when he is hungry and stop when he is full
- Forcing a child to eat, or to eat a certain food, is counterproductive and can lead to unhealthy eating habits and potentially eating disorders
- Avoid the use of food as a reward or punishment, or of making food (or dessert) contingent on behavior
- Rather than restricting access to certain foods, consider having only healthy options available in the home and allowing the child to choose.

Gentle Weaning

- Weaning begins the moment solid foods are introduced
- Food gradually takes the place of milk in terms of caloric need, but nursing continues to meet many other needs such as comfort and nurturing
- If a mother needs to wean before the child has displayed readiness, proceed gently.

[Principle III:] Respond with Sensitivity

You can build the foundation of trust and empathy by understanding and responding appropriately to your infant's needs. Babies communicate their needs in many ways including body movements, facial expressions, and crying. They learn to trust when their needs are consistently responded to with sensitivity. Building a strong attachment with a baby involves not only responding consistently to his physical needs, but spending enjoyable time interacting with him and thus meeting his emotional needs as well.

There are many societal challenges that can interfere with parents' ability to develop a responsive relationship with their babies. For example, parents may encounter myths about spoiling a baby or unsolicited advice from well-meaning family, friends and media. Advice that conflicts with science, facts about normal development, or a parent's own intuitive feelings can cause stress for the parent who must decide how to respond.

In the course of normal child development, babies form primary attachments with the person or people who spend the majority of time nurturing and caring for them – usually the mother and/or father. Frequent holding and interactions with baby increase bonding and promote secure attachment. In the first six months or so your baby may seem happy being held by or interacting with other people. Then at eight to nine months of age, many babies will suddenly begin to show fear and anxiety about being separated from their mother. This, too, is a normal phase.

Babies and children require empathy and respect for their feelings to help them learn to feel safe and secure. Intense fears of separation will naturally subside as the child matures. It may take considerably longer for more sensitive children to be comfortable in the care of non-parental adults. Follow the child's cues and do not force children to accept strangers or expect them to overcome stranger/separation anxiety before they're ready.

Needs and the Benefits of Responding with Sensitivity

- Babies' brains are immature and significantly underdeveloped at birth, and they are unable to soothe themselves
- Through the consistent, repeated responsiveness of a compassionate adult, children learn to soothe themselves
- Some babies and children appear more sensitive to the environment and stimulation
- Understand your child's natural inner rhythms, and try to schedule around them
- It is perfectly normal for babies to want constant physical contact
- High levels of stress, such as during prolonged crying, cause a baby to experience an unbalanced chemical state in the brain and can place him at risk for physical and emotional problems later in life
- Symptoms of burnout or inability to cope with baby's needs are signals that extra support and/or professional help are necessary.

Responding to Tantrums and Strong Emotions

- Tantrums represent real emotions and as such should be taken seriously
- Some emotions are too powerful for a young child's underdeveloped brain to manage in a more socially acceptable manner
- A parent's role in tantrums is to comfort the child, not to get angry or punish her.

Responding to the Older Child

- Continue to nurture a close connection by respecting the child's feelings and trying to understand the needs underlying his outward behaviors
- Support explorations by providing a safe environment for discovery and remaining close by
- Show interest in the child's activities and participate enthusiastically in child-directed play
- Some children enjoy preschool or other programs where parents are not included, but they [are] not necessary for child development. Consider the child's readiness to separate and the amount and type of support provided by adults.

[Principle IV:] Use Nurturing Touch

Babies are born with urgent and intense needs and depend completely on others to meet them. Nurturing touch helps meet a baby's need for physical contact, affection, security, stimulation and movement. Parents who choose a nurturing approach to physical interactions with their children promote development of healthy attachments. Even as children get older their need to stay connected through touch remains strong.

Needs and the Benefits of Nurturing Touch

- For the child, nurturing touch stimulates growth-promoting hormones, improves intellectual and motor development, and helps regulate babies' temperature, heart rate, and sleep/wake patterns
- Babies who receive nurturing touch gain weight faster, nurse better, cry less, are calmer, and have better intellectual and motor development
- Cultures high in physical affection, touch, holding or carrying, rate low in adult physical violence.

How to Provide Nurturing Touch

- Skin-to-skin contact is especially effective
- Breastfeeding and joint baths offer opportunities to snuggle skin-to-skin
- Massage can soothe babies with colic, help a child unwind before bedtime, and provides opportunity for playful interactions
- Carrying, or babywearing using a soft carrier, meets a baby's need for physical contact, comfort, security, stimulation and movement, all of which encourage neurological development
- Be conscious to avoid the overuse of devices designed to hold a baby independently, such as swings, jumpers, plastic carriers, and strollers.

Nurturing Touch and the Older Child

- Frequent hugs, snuggling, back rubs and massage all meet the older child's need for touch, as do more physical play such as wrestling and tickling
- Wrestling and tickling should follow the lead of the child and should not be forced
- Use playfulness and games to encourage physical closeness
- If you find your child is too heavy to hold comfortably, provide the closeness that carrying provides by providing attention or comfort in your lap
- All humans (**including adults**) thrive on touch and the reconnection it provides.

[Principle V:] Ensure Safe Sleep, Physically and Emotionally

"Is your baby sleeping through the night yet?" is often the first question people ask a new parent. The truth is that most babies do not sleep through the night, yet it is a myth that is perpetuated from generation to generation. Babies have needs at night just as they do during the day; from hunger, loneliness, and fear, to feeling too cold or too hot. They need the reassurance of a loving parent to feel secure during the night. Many babies do go through a phase where they sleep for longer periods of time only to begin waking at night during different developmental stages. They may wake occasionally during nightmares, teething, illness, growth spurts, or during times of transition in their lives. Babies are very sensitive to their parents' stress, which can affect their sleep patterns.

Parents can help their children learn that bedtime or naptime is a peaceful time; a time of quiet connection and snuggles. Even though young children may outgrow needing to eat during the night, they might still require comfort and reassurance.

Parents who are frustrated with frequent waking or who are sleep deprived may be tempted to try sleep training techniques that recommend letting a baby cry in an effort to "teach" him to "self-soothe." New research suggests that these techniques can have detrimental physiological effects on the baby by increasing the stress hormone cortisol in the brain, with potential long term effects to emotional regulation, sleep patterns and behavior. An infant is not neurologically or developmentally capable of calming or soothing himself to sleep in a way that is healthy. The part of the brain that helps with self-soothing isn't well developed until the child is two and a half to three years of age. Until that time, a child depends on his parents to help him calm down and learn to regulate his intense feelings.

The Case Against Solitary Sleep

It's important to note that infant solitary sleep is a relatively new practice that has evolved in the western world only within the last 100 years. Recently, there have been efforts by various medical and professional organizations to discourage parents from sleeping with their children for fear that it contributes to an increase in Sudden Infant Death Syndrome (SIDS). However, new research demonstrates that co-sleeping, when practiced by informed parents, can be safe and beneficial. In fact, many cultures where parents routinely sleep with their children report some of the lowest SIDS rates. In some of these cultures SIDS is non-existent.

API encourages parents to respond to their children's needs at night just as they do during the day. Parents are also encouraged to explore the variety of different sleeping arrangements, and to choose the approach that best allows them to be responsive at night. Individual babies' sleep patterns and needs vary a great deal. Remain flexible and understand that it is developmentally appropriate and normal for babies to wake up during the night to feed and seek contact.

What is Co-Sleeping?

Many terms related to infant sleep are used interchangeably, which can create confusion. API uses the following definitions:

- *Co-sleeping* refers to sleeping in "close proximity," which means the child is on a separate sleep surface in the same room as the parents. This includes the use of a bassinet, co-sleeper, or "sidecar," which is a crib-like bed with only three walls, with the fourth side remaining open and pushed up against the parents' bed. For the older child, this can include sleeping in a separate bed in the same room as the parents, or two or more older siblings sleeping together in a separate room.
- *Bed-sharing*, also called the "family bed," describes a sleep arrangement where the family members sleep on the same sleep surface. This practice is recommended for only for breastfeeding families using API's Safe Sleep Guidelines.

Nighttime Routines

- Regardless of sleeping arrangements, nighttime routines often help everyone unwind from a busy day and help establish healthier sleep habits
- Experiment to find the routine that works best for the child and remember that any bedtime routine may take 30 minutes or an hour or more
- Keep in mind that sleep routines change as the child grows and matures. Keep your sense of humor and remain flexible

- Help your child learn to trust her body when she is tired by recognizing the signs of tiredness, and not forcing her to sleep when she is not tired, or keeping her awake when she is tired, just for the sake of a routine
- When the time comes for a child to transition to her own bed, make sure that the transition is gentle and that parents respond to any feelings of fear or upset experienced by the child
- Young children who have their own bed often go to sleep more willingly when parents lie down with them in their bed until they are very drowsy or until they go to sleep. Children outgrow this need when they are developmentally ready and will happily go to sleep on their own
- Older children may still enjoy a brief snuggle time with parents before bed
- Neither parenthood nor co-sleeping needs to put a damper on intimacy; a little creativity, including timing and location, can ensure that intimacy is not unduly disrupted by a new baby.

[Principle VI:] Provide Consistent and Loving Care

Babies and young children have an intense need for the physical presence of a consistent, loving, responsive caregiver: ideally a parent. Daily care and playful, loving interactions build strong bonds. By providing consistent, loving care from early infancy, parents strengthen their relationship with their child and build a healthy attachment. If neither parent can be a full-time caregiver, then a child needs someone who is not only consistent and loving, but has formed a bond with them and consciously provides care in a way that strengthens the attachment relationship.

Create Schedules with Baby in Mind

- Instead of trying to fit baby into the existing pre-baby schedule, come up with creative ways to design new routines that include the baby
- Consider taking a sleeping baby along on date night, getting exercise by taking walks with baby in a sling, taking a trusted caregiver along for long evenings or special events, and working with employers to create a schedule that maximizes both parents' time with their child.

Practical Tips for Short Separations

- Use a trusted caregiver to whom the child is attached and who supports *API's Eight Principles of Attachment Parenting*
- Respect the child's feelings and follow his lead about his readiness to separate, using creativity to avoid unnecessary anxious experiences
- Accept that even older children have occasional difficulties with separation

- Avoid using shame, fear, threats or intimidation to force the separation, or to attempt to prevent children from crying about it
- It is critically important that parents who are separated from their children spend very focused and intentional time reconnecting with their child after separation
- Different children are ready for separation at different ages, but research shows separations of longer than two nights can be very difficult for children under the age of three
- Daycare situations that exceed twenty hours a week can be extremely stressful and detrimental to the long-term health of children under the age of thirty months. In-home care, either by a trusted caregiver or parent, is preferable.

Working and Alternate Caregivers

- Explore a variety of economic and work arrangement options to permit your child to be cared for by one or both parents at all times
- It is extremely important to have continuity of care with a consistent, loving, caregiver
- Parents should expect and encourage their child to form an attachment to the caregiver
- Frequent turnover of caregivers can be very damaging to the attachment process
- Make the transition to a caregiver well in advance of any separation so that it is a gradual process and is comfortable for the child
- Minimizing the number of hours in non-parental care as much as possible provides the best opportunity for a child to build secure attachments with parents
- Holding and cuddling helps parents and babies reconnect after being apart. Include the child in day-to-day tasks, and spend non-work time with family.

[Principle VII:] Practice Positive Discipline

Attachment Parenting incorporates the "golden rule" of parenting: parents should treat their children the way they would want to be treated. Positive discipline is an overarching philosophy that helps a child develop a conscience guided by his own internal discipline and compassion for others. Positive discipline is rooted in a secure, trusting, connected relationship between parent and child. Discipline that is empathetic, loving and respectful strengthens that the connection between parent and child, while harsh or overly-punitive discipline weakens the connection. Remember that the ultimate goal of discipline is to help children develop self-control and self-discipline.

The Dangers of Traditional Discipline

- Instilling fear in children serves no purpose and creates feelings of shame and humiliation. Fear has been shown to lead to an increased risk of future antisocial behavior including crime and substance abuse
- Studies show that spanking and other physical discipline techniques can create ongoing behavioral and emotional problems
- Harsh, physical discipline teaches children that violence is the only way to solve problems
- Controlling or manipulative discipline compromises the trust between parent and child, and harms the attachment bond
- It is a sign of strength and personal growth for a parent to examine his or her own childhood experiences and how they may negatively impact their parenting, and to seek help if they are unable to practice positive discipline.

A Gentler Approach to Discipline

- Positive discipline begins at birth. The bonds of attachment and trust that are formed when parents consistently and compassionately respond to an infant's needs become the foundation of discipline
- Positive Discipline involves using such techniques as prevention, distraction, and substitution to gently guide children away from harm
- Help your child explore safely, seeing the world through his eyes and empathizing as he experiences the natural consequences of his actions
- Try to understand what need a child's behavior is communicating. Children often communicate their feelings through their behavior
- Resolve problems together in a way that leaves everyone's dignity intact
- Understand developmentally appropriate behavior, and tailor loving guidance to the needs and temperaments of your child
- Children learn by example so it's important to strive to model positive actions and relationships within a family and in interactions with others
- When parents react in a way that creates tension, anger or hurt feelings, they can repair any damage to the parent-child relationship by taking time to reconnect and apologize later.

Tools for Positive Discipline
This list is not all-inclusive, and some techniques described may not be suitable for children of a particular age or temperament. (…)

- Maintain a positive relationship
- Use empathy and respect

- Research positive discipline
- Understand the unmet need
- Work out a solution together
- Be proactive
- Understand the child's developmental abilities
- Create a "yes" environment
- Discipline through play
- Change things up
- State facts rather than making demands
- Avoid labeling
- Make requests in the affirmative
- Allow natural consequences
- Use care when offering praise
- Use time-in rather than time-out
- Use time-in as a parent, too
- Talk to a child before intervening
- Don't force apologies
- Comfort the hurt child first
- Offer choices
- Be sensitive to strong emotions
- Consider carefully before imposing the parent's will
- Use logical consequences sparingly and with compassion
- Use incentives creatively with older children.

Learning to use positive discipline may not come easily for many parents especially if they were raised in a more traditional, authoritarian environment. That's why it's so important to attend API support groups, talk with other parents, or seek professional help.

[Principle VIII:] Strive for Balance in Your Personal and Family Life
Striving for Balance involves ensuring that everyone's needs – not just the child's – are recognized, validated, and met to the greatest extent possible. In an ideal world, every family member's needs are met all the time, everyone is happy and healthy, and the family is perfectly in balance. In the real world, nobody's family life is perfectly balanced all the time. It is not unusual for parents to feel out of balance at times. Parents who practice AP continuously look for creative ways to find balance in their personal and family life.

Balance is the Foundation Upon Which Attachment Grows

- When in balance, family members are more able to be emotionally responsive
- The best defense for feeling isolated is to look outward to create a support network in the local community
- The child's needs must be a priority, and the younger the child, the more intense and immediate his needs. Even so, he is one piece of the complete family picture that also includes the needs of the parents as individuals and as a couple, siblings, plus the family as a whole.

Practical Tips for Maintaining Balance

- Enjoy today, and accept that having a child changes things
- Set realistic goals
- Put people before things
- Don't be afraid to say "no"
- Turn "unpleasant" parental duties into enjoyable ones
- Be creative in finding ways to spend couple time
- Take time for yourself
- Use a "mother's helper"
- Eat healthy foods
- Exercise regularly
- Take naps
- Take care of yourself
- Avoid over-scheduling
- Look for ways to make routine tasks easier
- Get out of the house
- Follow your heart and listen to your baby.

Tips for Supporting New Mothers
A new mother can become so involved in the care of her infant that she doesn't recognize her own needs until she is in emotional or physical trouble.

- Be patient and sensitive
- Say something appreciative about each other every day
- Be grateful
- Be an empathetic listener.

Tips for Balance and the Older Child

- Bring a friend or mother's helper to activities
- Avoid over-scheduling
- Spend time just being together
- Develop family traditions
- Have parent-child "dates"
- Create family nights
- Rekindle hobbies and interests.

Tips for Dealing with Parent "Burn-Out"
Recognize the symptoms of burn-out. Burn-out is a physical, emotional, and mental response to high levels of stress. Parents may feel relentlessly fatigued, strained, and physically, emotionally, and mentally exhausted. They may also feel overworked, under-appreciated, angry, resentful, powerless, hopeless, drained, frustrated, detached, anti-social, unsatisfied, resentful, like a failure, indifferent, and lacking motivation. Parents who feel their emotions are taking over should get help immediately!

- Make regaining balance a priority TODAY
- Cultivate friendships with other AP parents
- Simplify and let go of unnecessary things
- Take frequent deep breaths
- Use yoga, meditation, or visualization
- Consider professional counseling
- Remember that "this too shall pass."

TASK/TEXT 7.13.2: DOES ATTACHMENT PARENTING ENSURE SECURE ATTACHMENT?

<http://mainstreamparenting.com>, accessed 29 April 2009, <http://mainstreamparenting.wordpress.com/2008/01/02/does-ap-ensure-secure-attachment>, posted on January 2, 2008 by estherar

While parenting practices such as "natural" birth, breastfeeding, babywearing, "gentle discipline" and bedsharing might make some western women feel all warm and fuzzy inside, are these the things which really promote secure attachment of their babies to them? In other words, is there any correlation between the parenting practices of different human societies and the number of children who are securely attached to their main caregiver?

The term "secure attachment" relates to an infant's behavior in a test designed by Mary Ainsworth, an Attachment Theory researcher, given to children from about 1 year of age. The test goes as follows:

1. Parent and infant are introduced to the experimental room.
2. Parent and infant are alone. Parent does not participate while infant explores.
3. Stranger enters, converses with parent, then approaches infant. Parent leaves inconspicuously.
4. First separation episode: Stranger's behavior is geared to that of infant.
5. First reunion episode: Parent greets and comforts infant, then leaves again.
6. Second separation episode: Infant is alone.
7. Continuation of second separation episode: Stranger enters and gears behavior to that of infant.
8. Second reunion episode: Parent enters, greets infant, and picks up infant; stranger leaves inconspicuously.

The infant's behavior upon the parent's return is the basis for classifying the infant into one of three attachment categories. Securely attached infants are distressed when the mother leaves the room, but easily comforted by her when she returns. This is considered the most healthy sort of attachment, and is predictive of the child's future social and psychological wellbeing.

According to a meta-analysis of various attachment studies utilizing the **Strange Situation test** in different countries, about 65% of American babies tested were considered securely attached. Yep, those bottle feeding, CIO-ing Americans ["crying it out," that is, not picking up a crying baby; on which see, e.g., <www.phdinparenting.com/2008/07/05/no-cry-it-out>: Cry it out (CIO): 10 reasons why it is not for us, by phdinparenting] had secure attachment rates comparable to the cosleeping Japanese (67%) or the homebirthing Dutch (67%). And they fared *way* better than the one-baby having, toddler-nursing Chinese (50%), for example.

(…) Let's have a look at the secure attachment rates among the Gusii of Kenya. The Gusii mothers babywear, breastfeed into toddlerhood, and are known to respond quickly to a crying infant. The secure attachment rate among the Gusii? 61% (…). And which human society, you might ask, has the highest proportion of securely attached infants? I hope you're sitting down. It's the stiff-upper-lip, bottlefeeding…British. (75%).

"But but but …" you might say. Yes, all the Strange Situation tests were done on relatively small populations; yes, different societies within the same country show markedly different results; yes again, we don't even know if this test is applicable to non-white people in non-western societies. All very valid concerns.

(...) While I see no reason why they would hinder secure attachment, following the tenets of Attachment Parenting has, as yet, not been shown to either guarantee or enhance the secure attachment of infants as compared to mainstream parenting.

There's probably a good reason why the prominent International Attachment Network [<www.attachmentnetwork.org>] (a psychological organization devoted to attachment theory) has the following non-endorsement of Attachment Parenting on its website:

Question: **What is attachment parenting?**

Answer: Information about "Attachment Parenting" can be found at other websites. Some adherents of the "Attachment Parenting" movement have very strong beliefs about how parenting should be done, for example, they think that skin-to-skin contact is essential for good attachment relationships to form, or that parents should behave in particular ways towards their children or that day care is bad for children. While IAN [the International Attachment Network] accepts that responsive and sensitive parenting is important for healthy social and emotional development, we shy away from advocating hard-and-fast general principles because we recognise that relationships between parents and children depend on the unique characteristics (temperament, lifestyle, social situation, support systems, quality of adult relationships, family size, culture, etc.) of individual relationships.

TASK/TEXT 7.14:

TASK/TEXT 7.14.1: NATIONAL EFFECTIVE PARENTING PLAN

National Effective Parenting Initiative [<www.ciccparenting.org>, <www.effectiveparentingusa.org>, <ciccparenting@sbcglobal.net>], Tuesday, July 28, 2009

The founder of the National Effective Parenting Initiative [NEPI[91]], psychologist Dr. Kerby T. Alvy, announced today the National Effective Parenting Initiative's four-part plan to make the United States of America the premiere nation for educating parents to be as effective and successful as possible in raising children.

91 The National Effective Parenting Initiative (NEPI) is about working together to make it the birthright of every child in the United States to be raised effectively and humanely by loving and skillful parents who receive the best possible parenting education and support (<https://effectiveparentingusa.org/What_s_It_About_.html>).

Working with the Obama Administration

The plan includes working with President Obama and his administration to become champions of effective parenting and parenting education, and to support actions and policies that will make it possible for every parent in the United States to receive the best parenting education and support.

The plan includes …

(1) Issuing Parents' Day Proclamations that honor parents for enrolling in and completing parenting classes,
(2) Issuing Presidential Certificates of Appreciation for doing so,
(3) Conducting White House Conferences on Effective Parenting and Parenting Education, and
(4) Creating a Department or Office of Effective Parenting with appropriate research, training and clearinghouse capabilities.

Research Based

"The plan is based on decades of research that has shown that certain ways of raising children are more productive than others in preparing children for life success in a democratic society," says Dr. Alvy, "and that there now exists an excellent array of educational programs from which parents of all backgrounds can learn to be maximally effective and successful in carrying out their awesome societal responsibilities."

Dr. Alvy further indicates that "by making sure that all parents have the opportunity to benefit from these programs, and are motivated to do so, a nation increases its overall chances of success and continuation. This is so because when more parents are effective, more children enter school ready and capable of learning and more children eventually reach their full potential as caring and educated human beings."

"In addition," Alvy asserts, "children raised effectively and non-abusively are less likely to become school dropouts, welfare recipients, delinquents, drug abusers, gang bangers and criminals, thereby saving the nation billions of dollars in tax monies that are used to manage and control these preventable social, health and psychological problems."

Parents' Day Proclamations

The first steps in actualizing this plan have already been taken by urging President Obama to include in his Parents' Day Proclamation for 2009 the acknowledgement of parents who are already enrolling in and completing parenting programs. Attached is a copy of the letter to President Obama and suggested proclamations [<https://effectiveparentingusa.org/uploads/Revised_070709_-_White_House_Parents__Day_Proclamation_Ltr.pdf>].

TASK/TEXT 7.14.2: EFFECTIVE PARENTING PETITION

<www.ipetitions.com/petition/effectiveparentingusa/index.html>, accessed 29 July 2009

[1.] Every child deserves to be raised sensitively and effectively by loving and skillful parents.

[2.] When children are so raised, they are on a path to reach their full potential as human beings. They are best prepared to become healthy, peaceful and productive adults.

[3.] Parents and others who assume the awesome responsibility of raising children deserve the best possible parenting education, guidance and support.

[4.] Love is not enough. The dangers of childhood and the pressures of modern family life require parents to be especially knowledgeable and skillful.

[5.] It is in the best interests of our children and our nation for all parents to be educated and supported as fully as possible.

[6.] In signing this petition, I am affirming the importance of advocating, celebrating and promoting effective parenting and parenting education.

[7.] This petition will be used to show the nation how important effective parenting is.

[8.] It will also be emailed to the President, Members of Congress and other elected representatives to encourage them to take the practical steps that are needed to make effective parenting and parenting education national, state and local priorities.

TASK/TEXT 7.14.3: AN EFFECTIVE PARENTING INITIATIVE

Kerby T. Alvy, An Effective Parenting Initiative to Make the United States of America a Model Child and Family-Friendly Nation, Center for the Improvement of Child Caring (<www.ciccparenting.org>, accessed 3 August 2009), <www.ciccparenting.org/pdf/NPI.pdf>, pp. 3–18, 23–24 (references omitted)

INTRODUCTION AND SUMMARY

This proposal is being made directly to the elected leadership of the United States of America to ask them to become the champions of a broad-based initiative to **make the effective parenting of the children of the United States a national priority**. It also requests that equal prioritization be given to the most direct approach for helping more parents to be as effective as possible in raising the nation's children, **and that approach is parenting education**.

The proposed Effective Parenting Initiative involves and benefits all segments of American society, because effective parenting benefits us all. The proposal begins by bringing attention to these comprehensive societal benefits and to the research that helps to define what is effective parenting. This section also draws attention to the costs of having to deal with problems that emanate from **ineffective parenting, such as child abuse, juvenile delinquency, drug abuse, gangs and school failure**.

Turning to the matter of **how parents learn to be parents**, the proposal highlights the informal ways that parents have learned to raise children. Then it details how **formal parenting education** programs are a more modern approach which has proven highly successful with those who have been fortunate enough to participate in modern parenting skill-building programs. It also shows how these programs are excellent vehicles for helping parents to instill in children a wide range of cherished family values.

The proposal then describes the numerous public and private institutions of American society that are already involved in using and promoting this modern approach to improve the quality of parenting in our society. All of the actions of these numerous and diverse groups reflect that an Effective Parenting Movement is actually occurring in our society. But the Movement has yet to reap its full harvest because of its unevenness and because it has yet to be championed and supported by leaders who are in a position to assure its full effectiveness and impact.

The President and members of Congress are leaders who have the necessary clout.

A National Effective Parenting Initiative is then presented. It involves the creation of new structures within our federal government, led through the creation of a Department of Effective Parenting or a White House Office on Effective Parenting, which would be supported by a prestigious National Council on Effective Parenting composed of leaders from all segments of American society. Additional new structures are also proposed to carry out the Initiative. These include a National Clearinghouse on Effective Parenting, a National Parenting Instructor Training Center, and a new research and evaluation agency, a National Institute on Effective Parenting. The functions of each new agency are described and shown how they are all directed at achieving the prioritization of effective parenting and parenting education in American society. The description of the National Institute on Effective Parenting contains an example of the type of research study that shows how billions of dollars can be saved through the types of programs this initiative will bring to every community in the nation.

A variety of ways of financing this Effective Parenting Initiative are recommended, including the reallocation of existing federal tax dollars and the use of private sector corporate and philanthropic dollars, as well as through the financial support of parents themselves.

With the President and the members of Congress championing and embracing the Effective Parenting Initiative, our nation is likely to become the world model of a child and family-friendly society.

THE SOCIETAL BENEFITS OF EFFECTIVE PARENTING

Research study after research study confirms that communities benefit greatly when children are raised effectively.

The societal benefits are evident very early, as effectively parented preschool children are more likely to enter school eager and ready to learn. They are also much more likely to achieve at high levels and to be well liked by their peers and teachers. The research also shows that as teenagers, these effectively parented young people make positive contributions to community life and are of service to others. And as adults they are more likely to have productive careers, healthy and stable marriages, and to become effective parents themselves.

Studies on Effective Parenting

Many of the scientific studies that have captured these benefits have been supported by federal government research grants. A good early example is the study underwritten by the National Institute of Mental Health in the 1960s that explored the family situations of young people who valued themselves as individuals, who were personally effective, poised, competent and capable of independent and creative action, and whose high self-esteem was verified by their teachers.

As was shown in the **1967** book that reported on the results of this classic study, *The Antecedents of Self Esteem* by Dr. Stanley Coopersmith, parents of the high self-esteem children were themselves high in selfworth.

They approached their children with a great deal of **warmth and acceptance**. They also set very **clear limits** on the child's behavior and were vigilant about enforcing family rules, thereby establishing the authority of parents and providing standards by which the child could judge his or her competence and progress. They demonstrated a great deal of regard for the personal **rights of the child**, seeking out the **child's views**, respecting their opinions and granting concessions where warranted. Because these finding held true regardless of the socio-economic background of the parents, Coopersmith concluded that the **quality of home life and parenting** was the most influential in children developing a strong sense of personal worthiness.

Numerous other studies presented in the prestigious *Review of Child Development Research* (...), studies of both a laboratory and field nature, also pointed in the direction of **parents having a great shaping influence on their children's development**, as did another extensive review by Doctors Eleanor F. Maccoby and John A. Martin of Stanford University which appeared in the *Handbook of Child Psychology* (... 1983).

The pattern of parenting that was emerging from the hundreds of studies in these reviews as being the most effective gained even greater coherence and support in the work of developmental psychologist, Dr. Diana Baumrind of the University of California. In the late 1980s and early 1990s, Dr. Baumrind's research uncovered what she referred to as the **"authoritative pattern" of parenting**, a pattern that **combines a great deal of warmth with fair and firm family leadership**, just like what was seen in the families of high self-esteem children described above (...). It is this pattern that has consistently been associated with positive child outcomes. The enduring importance of this pattern continues to be reflected in the latest reviews of research on parent-child relations (...).

Additional individual studies and reviews of the latest research in the United States and in other countries continue to demonstrate the **power of positive parenting** to help produce healthy and competent young people. (...) So there is an enormous body of knowledge that helps define what is effective in raising children. And there are very talented people who can continue to conduct research that further defines the contours of what is best in raising today's children.

All of this scientifically-based knowledge, and all of the work of these talented individuals, tells us over and over again that the benefits of effective parenting are numerous, ranging from enhancing the development and futures of the children who are effectively parented, to stabilizing and enhancing family life.

The Costs of Ineffective Parenting

These and other studies also show us the costs of **ineffective, abusive and neglectful** parenting.

In the classic study by Coopersmith on self-esteem, the children who felt the least worthy and who performed the poorest at school were from homes where their parents provided little warmth and few and poorly defined limits. These parents used harsh and autocratic control measures. They were dictatorial, rejecting and uncompromising in their family leadership.

These parents had much in common with those from Diana Baumrind's studies who she characterized as **authoritarian.** Parents who approached their children in this manner, or in an **extremely permissive** manner, were the least likely to have self-confident, achieving and **emotionally healthy** children.

Authoritarian and extremely permissive parents are among those who are most likely to be reported for **abusing, exploiting or neglecting** their children. We have as many as three million children from these types of families who are reported each year for being maltreated in these ways (...).

Abused and neglected children often have **learning disabilities** and **mental health problems**, as well as **extreme difficulties in getting along with others.** They are much more likely to become school drop-outs, to become gang members and delinquents, to be drug abusers and criminals, and to repeat a **cycle of abuse when they become parents themselves.**

To help these unfortunate children avoid such negative life outcomes, a wide range of remedial, legal, and foster care services need to be provided. Because of the large numbers of such children, the cost to tax-payers is enormous. Direct costs (judicial, law enforcement and health system responses to child maltreatment) are estimated at $24 billion each year. The indirect costs (long-term economic consequences of child maltreatment) exceed an estimated $69 billion annually.

Thus, there are as numerous negative consequences of ineffective parenting as there are positive benefits of effective parenting.

Now, let's look at how people learn to be parents, whether effective or ineffective.

EDUCATION FOR PARENTING

Parenting is learned behavior, and all parents learn how to be parents through a variety of means.

Informal Means

These means include the informal ways that all parents have learned historically; that is, through what they were exposed to in their homes and communities and what they choose to repeat or reject.

Informally, all parents learn from how they were raised by either their biological parents or by whomever else, like adoptive, foster or grandparents, played parental roles throughout their childhood and adolescence. They learn from how they were treated and regarded, and how their siblings were treated and regarded. They learn from the models of human relations and the models of conflict resolution that were available in their homes.

All parents have historically and informally also learned from other family members like aunts and uncles, as well as from how their friends and neighbors raise their children. If they are religious, they learn from what is emphasized at their places of worship.

All parents have also learned their parenting through observing the fictional models of parenting and family life that are depicted on television, in films and through other mass media.

Formal Means

Some parents also learn how to be the best parents they can through formal parent education vehicles that have been carefully designed to help them become as knowledgeable and as effective as possible.

Formal parenting education is usually sponsored and made available through such community institutions as the schools and the government and community agencies that are responsible for preventing and treating the social and health problems mentioned earlier. In addition, some corporations through their work and family programs also make some type of parenting education available, as do some places of worship as part of their services and supports for families.

Indeed, in the United States, some type of formal parenting education has been made available since the 1800s when the first mothers' groups were formed in a few cities (...).

In the 1960s, a new and much more effective approach to parenting education emerged and began to be used in selected communities, an approach where parents were not only educated about the various facets of child development which are needed to understand children but where they received training in the skills and strategies of effective parenting, i.e., how to praise and encourage positive behaviors, how to effectively resolve conflicts without resorting to violence, and how to conduct family decision-making meetings, etc.

This new how-to-do-it approach is based on research on what is effective in relating to children, and is called the Parenting Skill-Building Approach (see *Parent Training Today: A Social Necessity*, Alvy, 1994). Since the 1960s, a wide range of such evidenced-based parenting skill-building programs have been created for different populations of parents, most of which were created and tested through research and demonstration grants from federal government agencies. These programs are usually taught in the form of parent effectiveness classes which are led by instructors who have received training in how best to teach such classes. The research on the impact of these classes on the families, parents and children who have been fortunate enough to be in communities where there are instructors who are qualified to deliver them, has consistently show[n] that **these classes significantly improve and enhance family togetherness and cohesion, promote positive parenting practices and reduce negative, abusive parenting, as well as significantly reducing child behavior problems and increasing child competencies** [emphasis Alvy].

As ha[s] been implied, not all communities in the United States have local institutions that sponsor and conduct parenting education, let alone institutions with staff that are qualified to teach the parenting skillbuilding programs. Also in those communities that do have local institutions that provide parenting education, very few of these schools, government departments and community service agencies provide the full range of excellent parenting programs and materials that now exist. Many of these groups are simply unaware of what is available for them to use in helping educate more parents to be effective, and certainly not aware of the full range of evidenced-based skill-building programs that now exist.

Effective Parenting Newsletter and Effective Parenting Programs

This unevenness of knowledge and use of parenting education resources was the main reason why one of the our nation's foremost parenting education groups, the 33 year old, nonprofit Center for the Improvement of Child Caring (CICC), began publishing an online *Effective Parenting* newsletter in 2004. This *Effective Parenting* newsletter provides a wealth of information on the latest research on effective parenting and where to find this foundational information. At the same time, it provides descriptions of the parenting skill-building programs that teach the concepts, values, skills and strategies of the **authoritative parenting** pattern that the research has consistently shown to be instrumental in raising healthy and competent young people. These include skill-building programs for different populations of parents, i.e., for parents of infants, toddlers, school age and teenage children; for parents from different cultural backgrounds; and for parents with children with disabilities and other special needs.

The *Effective Parenting* newsletter also orients its readers to how they can bring these programs to their communities, such as where they can obtain the instructional kits and materials, and where they can receive training and certification to qualify them to deliver these important parenting and family life education programs. The readership of this online publication increases daily as more individuals and groups visit CICC's website to subscribe (<www.ciccparenting.org>). Its readership passed 40,000 in mid-2006 and will grow to be greater than 100,000 as more school districts, child and family serving institutions and their staffs, and all health, social service and educational professionals learn of its existence.

The types of parenting skill-building programs that are featured in the editions of the *Effective Parenting* newsletter include the nation's and world's most influential and successful programs, including the most honored and revered of such programs, Dr. Thomas Gordon's Parent Effectiveness Training (PET) Program (…).

Dr. Gordon created PET in the early 1960s and it has been in use ever since. PET has introduced millions of parents in the United States and in numerous other countries to *actively listen* to their children to better understand and appreciate their needs and viewpoints. It has taught, and still teaches, how to deliver *"I"-Messages* so that children gain a clear understanding of the impact of their own behavior on others. And it continues to provide parents with a *No-Lose* problem-solving approach which brings children into the family decision-making process and generates greater cooperation. The careful use of these PET skills has helped millions of parents worldwide to bring a greater sense of harmony into their relationships with their children and into their families. It is no wonder, then, that Dr. Gordon was nominated for a Nobel Peace Prize. (…)

Today's parents are also able to learn the skills and concepts of effective contemporary parenting over the Internet, as America's parenting program creators learn how to provide their classes over this amazing communication vehicle. (…) Modern technology has also made it possible for parents to observe and learn the skills of effective contemporary parenting through such excellent issue-focused video programs like *Spanking, Shaking and Hitting: What To Do Instead*, and *Yelling, Threatening and Putting Down: What To Do Instead.* (…)

Excellent guidebooks that distil and simplify the research on effective parenting are now available that parents can use to determine whether their current functioning is consistent with what is known to be effective, thereby reinforcing and rewarding parents for doing the right things. These succinct guides, like *The Power of Positive Parenting* (Alvy, 2004), also alert parents to what they may be doing to harm their children and what they should be doing instead. *The Power of Positive Parenting* guide has, for example, been termed by parents who have read it a "mini-bible for parents" and the "manual that should come with every child."

Popular television shows, like Dr. Phil and the Supernanny shows, also provide discussions and examples of effective parenting. Dr. Phil draws upon his personal and professional experiences as a practicing psychologist, and the Supernannies employ the behavior management skills and strategies that are taught in many of the parenting skill-building programs mentioned already.

So there now exists an extraordinary array of parenting skill-building programs that research indicates are highly effective in teaching and reinforcing the authoritative approach to parenting. There are television shows that discuss, exemplify and encourage the use of this approach. There are numerous websites that convey helpful child development information, and a few that even teach effective parenting skills. There are also excellent videos and CDs that convey and reinforce effective parenting, and there are guides and other books that inform parents about what is effective and what is not.

These vehicles for training and educating are unevenly available in communities across our nation, and this is especially true of the most powerful vehicles, the parenting skill-building programs. Even so, America clearly possesses the widest array of programs, materials and outlets through which every parent could potentially be trained and educated to be as effective as possible.

Parenting Education and Family Values

For at least the last two decades, the issue of family values has often taken center stage in debates about what is wrong with American society. Problems such as crime, violence, drug abuse, divorce, teen pregnancy, and welfare dependence have all been discussed as consequences of a diminished respect for family values.

A broad consensus has emerged from one end of the political spectrum to the other, that family values must be upheld and supported if we are to solve these seemingly intractable problems. While a consensus exists that this needs to be done, no one has come up with a vehicle for how it can be done.

Well, such a vehicle does exist. The key ingredient is effective parenting: parenting that instills in children the values that are needed for them to become responsible, healthy and productive adults.

And, as we have just seen, there now exists a wide range formal parenting education programs and resources for helping parents to instill our cherished values. For example, the parenting skill-building programs that we have just reviewed teach parents the skills of effective contemporary parenting: positive reinforcement, nurturing, communication, disciplining and non-violent conflict resolution skills. In so doing, they provide parents with the tools to instill in their children the important values of mutual respect, empathy, compassion, hard work, responsibility, self-discipline, and non-violence.

With the widespread use of such family life enhancing programs, more families will have the tools for instilling, promoting and reinforcing these values.

Let's see what is currently being done with these family values instilling programs.

THE EFFECTIVE PARENTING MOVEMENT

The availability of all of these wonderful educational vehicles for helping more parents to be as effective as possible, and especially the availability of the parenting skill-building programs, has formed the intervention foundation of what has been termed the **Effective Parenting Movement in the United States** (...). This growing movement has been taking place in specific spheres of American life and through the various fields and disciplines that address the social and health problems that plague our communities and institutions. All recognize that parental effectiveness is pivotal to the success of our institutions and to the prevention and treatment of social and health problems.

Schools as Part of the Movement

Our schools now recognize more than ever that their success is greatly determined by the quality and quantity of parents' involvement in their children's formal education (...). Parental involvement activities sponsored by schools and community agencies now include school readiness and family literacy programs, all of which teach basic parenting skills as part of their programmatic thrust.

The current federal government, through its No Child Left Behind school reform initiative, stresses the importance of parental involvement, as do all state, county and city school districts, though very few of them currently use the full spectrum of parent education programs and materials that are now available.

The National PTA [National Parent Teacher Association, <www.pta.org>] recently became a major part of the education-based arm of this movement with its new emphasis on parenting education. It too, however, does not yet use all of the resources that are now available to help more parents to be effective.

Because America's children bring with them to school all of the problems that exist in their homes and communities, such as drug abuse, violence, gangs and child abuse, many schools now see it as their responsibility to provide programs and services to deal with these problems. And because all of these problems are influenced or caused by how children are parented, some schools now provide parenting skillbuilding programs to combat child abuse, drug abuse and delinquency. Many also see parenting training as being pivotal in diminishing the drop out rate of students, and provide parenting programs for these critical purposes.

Child Welfare Movement Involvement

In the child welfare field itself, the public social service and child and family service departments in our states, counties and cities, now provide or contract for the provision of parenting skill-building programs.

These institutions face the horror and tragedy of child abuse and neglect on an hourly basis and have the official responsibility for treating and preventing these extraordinarily costly problems that impact as many as three million of America's children each year. Here too these often overwhelmed institutions do not use and are not aware of all the excellent programs and materials that are now available to assist them with their life saving, family preservation and family unification efforts.

Delinquency Prevention Involvement

Our youth and delinquency prevention institutions are also part of this movement through their use of parenting skill-building programs and materials. Here again this massive undertaking through probation and youth services departments, does not yet utilize all of the available resources.

Mental Health Movement Involvement

The mental health field, its state and county departments, its psychiatric and child guidance clinics and its community mental health centers, all know that the disorders of childhood they treat can be better managed and their negative effects diminished by parents being trained in how best to cope with childhood disorders.

These include autism spectrum disorders, hyperactivity, obsessive compulsive and antisocial disorders.

Indeed, many of these disorders may be the direct result of ineffective parenting, and parenting training is the first service that is needed (...). Many of the parenting skill-building programs that are now being used in numerous schools and community agencies nationwide were originally developed as part of treatment efforts for families with behavior problem and disordered children.

However, just because many of these programs were created as treatment interventions within the mental health field, it does not mean that all of our country's mental health agencies and clinics provide the full spectrum of such programs. They too are uneven in their use and knowledge of the full range.

Substance Abuse Movement Participation

Our substance abuse treatment and prevention agencies and institutions are also part of the effective parenting movement, as they recognize that children and youth often turn to alcohol and other drugs when their relations with their parents are strained or abusive, and when their needs are not being met at home. When the Reagan administration started a War on Drugs and created the Office of Substance Abuse Prevention, (now the Center for Substance Abuse Prevention), it established a Parent Training Is Prevention Project, (1991, Department of Health and Human Services), which utilized the program and research expertise of organizations like CICC, Active Parenting, the Family Development Resources group that created the Nurturing Programs, and experts like Dr. Alvy and Dr. Gordon. This project led to nearly all states incorporating parent and family life education into their overall substance abuse prevention plans. Many states like Illinois, Kansas and Washington began utilizing several of the parenting skill building programs through having local agency personnel trained to deliver the programs. Again, state and county substance abuse prevention departments now make very uneven use of these interventions.

Those in the drug abuse treatment field, such as the institutions that treat drug abusing adults like cocaine addicted mothers, have begun to use a few of these parenting skill-building programs as part of their overall treatment interventions. They too have become part of this effective parenting movement.

The federal government currently brings widespread attention to the fact that parents are pivotal players in the fight against youth drug abuse through its multi-million dollar Parents: The Anti-Drug program as part of its overall National Youth Anti-Drug Media Campaign.

Health System Involvement

Health departments and agencies that are responsible for the treatment and prevention of developmental disabilities are also uneven users of parenting education programs. They are part of the movement as they recognize that the health of every child is greatly influenced by their parents' general effectiveness and by their knowledge of health matters. They recognize that families with developmentally disabled or special needs children are especially in need of parenting and family life education to manage the very difficult and challenging behaviors of these vulnerable children and youth.

Health Maintenance Organizations (HMOs) and health care insurance plans are increasingly more aware that if they provide services and programs to prevent health problems they can reduce the escalating costs of health care.

Parent training is a service that can reduce the health care costs of both children and adults. The parenting skill-building programs that have been mentioned are known to reduce one of the most powerful stressors on adults, the stress that comes from conflicts and problems in raising children. Stress is one of the known major contributors to a wide range of health problems, including cardiovascular and depression problems. With more parents receiving and benefiting from this type of stress-reducing service, it is likely that fewer parents will develop stress-related health problems.

This same parent training service also can reduce the need for some health services for children, as some physical and emotional problems of childhood are the direct result of ineffective parenting and/or are maintained because of ineffective parenting. In addition, there are now parent training programs that are specifically designed to prevent specific child health problems, such as programs that teach nutritional practices to prevent childhood obesity.

The Child Care System and the Movement

Our country's current focus on child care and early childhood education, which is fueled by the fact that now more than 60 percent of young children are in some form of out-of-home care while their parents work or continue their educations, provides other major venues through which more parents can learn the ideas and skills of effective parenting. Our nation's early childhood care and education systems, with their public and privately supported child care centers, their privately operated family child care homes, and the federallysponsored Head Start programs, are excellent venues through which parents can learn about effective parenting. Indeed, many such systems are using or beginning to use some of the latest parenting education materials and programs. (…)

Faith-Based Movement Participation

Some faith-based institutions, which have such strong and historic commitments to strengthening family life and helping the poor and disadvantaged, are also members of this important movement. (…)

Corporate and Employer Participation

Forward-thinking corporations who have wellness and work and family programs to help their employees often have lunch-and-learn parenting seminars, and some have sponsored parenting skill-building classes for their employees. Also, some school district and government departments have started parenting education efforts to support the family lives of their employees.

As was mentioned above in the section on health care system involvement, these types of services also have the potential to reduce employers' health benefit costs because they reduce a source of major stress on employees, the stress of parenting.

Other major benefits to employers for providing parenting services are that they increase employee loyalty because they demonstrate that employers care about their families, and because they reduce the time that parent employees spend discussing problems with their children rather than attending to job tasks. Both of these benefits speak to increased productivity on the part of America's labor force as a result of participation in this movement.

Philanthropy Community Participation

Numerous private, corporate, family and community foundations have been involved in funding the delivery of parenting education programs and services, and some have even funded the development of parenting programs. They usually do this under broader categories of funding priorities like child and family, child welfare, and child services headings. A few foundations currently list parenting education as a specific area of funding.

There are also a few foundations that support research efforts, which could include research to explore the various benefits of effective parenting and parenting education. So this broad spectrum of private sector funding sources is already involved in the movement but not in any focused, systematic or organized way.

Court and Custody Participation

Many courts that deal with divorces and child custody matters are now aligned with and supportive of programs that teach divorcing parents how to be as effective as possible during these traumatic times, and how to keep their hurt feelings from spilling over into destructive relations with their children that undermines the future growth and happiness of such children. Parenting programs for divorcing parents, like so many other parenting programs mentioned previously, have often been developed through federal government research and demonstration grants.

National Organizations and the Movement

Several nationwide organizations have already and/or are primed to play important roles in this movement. Here are brief descriptions of some of these organizations.

- The Center for the Improvement of Child Caring, with its national model parenting skill-building programs, its *Effective Parenting Newsletter*, and its parenting instructor training workshops through which more than 6,000 parenting instructors nationwide have already been trained, is an acknowledged leadership group.
- The National PTA and its new emphasis on parenting education reach into every school in our country.

- The National Coalition for Parent Involvement in Education includes many national organizations that promote this type of parental effectiveness.
- The United Way of America now has Success by Six programs in all states which help parents of young children to be more effective. The United Way also funds numerous local agencies, many of which provide parenting services themselves.
- The National Association for the Education of Young Children, which is the professional organization for the personnel who teach and run our nation's early childhood education and care centers and homes, is in an excellent position (as has been suggested) to play an even greater roll in the movement as it now relates to the majority of American families at the earliest and most influential times in the lives of children.
- The American Psychological Association (APA), which is the world's largest association for psychologists, has a membership that not only includes the majority of the creative individuals who have developed and evaluated our nation's extraordinary array of parenting skill-building programs. The APA also includes nearly all of the nation's top researchers on parenting and child-parent relations, the people who help us to know what is and is not effective in raising children.
- The National Council of Family Relations has been promoting family life education for decades and has a Family Life Educators credentialing process.
- The Prevent Child Abuse USA organization, with its chapters in every state and its Healthy Families America program, has been a movement participant for over thirty years.
- The Family Support America organization with its emphasis on all communities having viable family resource centers available, which are operated in accordance with principles and policies that respect diversity and which can provide parenting education services, also has a long history of movement participation.
- The Parents as Teachers National Center provides home visiting services through its Born to Learn, Professional Development, Meld and Advocacy work.
- The American Pediatric Society helps to set important standards of health care for children and families, publish authoritative books and pamphlets for parents, and provide extensive parenting advice over its website.
- The American Academy of Child and Adolescent Psychiatry is the leading national professional medical association dedicated to treating and improving the quality of life for children and adolescents and families who are affected by mental, behavioral and developmental disorders. It participates in the movement through many means, such as through providing fact sheets for

parents and other caregivers regarding these disorders and taking positions on such matters as the use of corporal punishment.
- The Child Welfare League of America has created its own parenting curriculum and is currently running a nationwide parenting enhancement project, as well as being the organization that supports all public and private child welfare groups in our country.
- Parents Action for Children (formerly the I Am Your Child Foundation) emerged under the leadership of child advocate, director and actor Rod Reiner in 1997, and has become a movement participant with its parenting videos and booklets, educational website, and forums for parents to speak directly to elected officials about their and their children's needs.

Several other highly creative groups that have already been mentioned because of their roles in developing parenting skill-building programs are also major movement participants, such as Active Parenting Publishers, American Guidance Services (the STEP Programs), Family Development Resources (the Nurturing Programs), Gordon Training International (the original PET program and its latest version, Family Effectiveness Training), and Hummingbird Coaching Services with its About My Kids online parenting services.

[But how about national and/or international **Human rights, Women's rights and – especially – Children's rights organizations and the Movement**? –JW]

Mass Media Movement Involvement

Various sectors of the mass media have been involved in the Effective Parenting Movement for years through developing and broadcasting programs that have highlighted the role of parents in such matters as preparing their children for school and for keeping their children off drugs. Some television networks have had national campaigns about everyone working to enhance the development of children, with clear implications about the important roles that parents play.

Programs and tips about "how to parent" are sometimes broadcast as part of local and network news shows. The value of this sort of parenting programming to these media outlets is reflected in the fact that they often schedule these types of shows during the periods when their shows are rated ("the sweeps"). What they charge for advertising time is a function of these ratings. Thus, being seen as a source for helping parents seems to enhance the revenues that support these broadcasts.

The Advertising Council of America, through some of its pro bono campaigns, has been an indirect movement participant through creating campaigns that address such problems as child abuse.

As has already been mentioned, the Internet has become a major participant through the numerous websites that are devoted to providing parents with valuable information and products about children and child rearing.

The Federal Government and the Movement

As has also been mentioned several times, the federal government itself has been a major part of this Effective Parenting Movement, both historically and contemporaneously. In addition to the programs already mentioned that federal government grants helped to create, evaluate, and conduct, the federal government, through its Health and Human Services Department, previously sponsored an Education for Parenthood Program to train youth how to be effective parents. That federal government program no longer exists, but community groups like the Prepare Tomorrow's Parents organization has continued to advocate for this type of education for our youngsters, and there are now several locally developed programs for training our youth for effective parenting, like the Parents Under Construction Program in Houston.

The federal government, through the Department of Agriculture's decades old Cooperative Extension efforts, has been sponsoring a wide range of parenting education services nationwide through local cooperative extension offices. It has also, through the Department of Health and Human Services' Children's Bureau, been sponsoring parenting involvement and education services as part of the nationwide Head Start program, including its own Exploring Parenting curriculum.

Various federal government departments, beginning with Health and Human Services' previously mentioned Parent Training Is Prevention Project, have begun identifying and acknowledging those parenting and family life enhancement programs that have the strongest research to support their effectiveness. In addition to HHS [Health and Human Services], through its current National Registry of Evidence-based Programs and Practices (NREPP), the Departments of Education and Justice have also been promoting the use of evidenced-based parenting and family life enhancement programs.

The George W. Bush administration has initiated several parenting education and parenting enhancement projects during its tenure. These include the already mentioned parent involvement emphasis in its No Child Left Behind school reform initiative. Also included is its related parent educating initiative to help parents learn to read regularly to their children. A Promoting Responsible Fatherhood program is also a Bush Administration undertaking to promote more parents being effective, as is its initiative to encourage Healthy Marriages, because the research shows that children who are raised within healthy marriages are more effectively parented.

Another federal government undertaking that speaks to its participation in the Effective Parenting Movement is the fact that in 1994 a National Parent's Day law was passed that established the fourth Sunday of every July as a recurring, perennial day of commemoration. The law indicates that "all private citizens, organizations, and government and legislative bodies at the local, State and Federal level are encouraged to recognize Parents' Day through proclamations, activities and educational efforts in furtherance of recognizing, uplifting and supporting the role of parents in the rearing of their children."

Summary and Status of the Movement

So our country has a movement with participants from nearly all segments of American life, and its purpose is to better prepare parents to carry out the awesome responsibilities of guiding the development of the next generation of adults, workers, parents and leaders. We also have a national holiday to celebrate the work of America's parents.

But the movement is not an organized and officially acknowledged undertaking. The holiday that could bring it visibility is only sporadically celebrated and basically unknown to the average person.

In addition, **the movement in its current state is itself far from being as effective as it could be, as is reflected in the millions of children who continue to be abused by parents, who drop out of school, who become drug abusers, join gangs, and become criminals and abusers of their own children**.

While some groups and individuals from nearly all segments of society are involved and committed to this movement, only a fraction of American families have benefited from those elements of the movement that are known to create significant improvements in the quality of parenting that America's children receive. For example, it is estimated that less than 10 percent of parents have ever enrolled in a parenting skill-building program.

What this important movement needs – what America needs – are champions to bring its benefits to the attention of everyone in our society, and to strengthen the movement so that every parent can receive the best possible education, training and support.

Only persons with high status and stature in our country can be effective in such a championing role.

The best person for this championing role is the person who has the overall responsibility in our nation for insuring life, liberty and the pursuit of happiness, the President of the United States. Other excellent candidates to be champions are the members of Congress from every state.

Therefore, it is herein proposed that the President and the members of Congress become the champions of **The Effective Parenting Movement in the**

United States, with the goal of making effective parenting and parenting education viable and visible national priorities.

A plan for such high level championing follows – a plan that involves organizing the participation of every sector of our society with leadership from our highest elected officials.

NATIONAL EFFECTIVE PARENTING INITIATIVE

Because of the many benefits that effective parenting brings to communities, and because of the costly and tragic problems that effective parenting helps to prevent, it is herein proposed that the President of the United States and members of Congress become the champions of an Effective Parenting Initiative.

The four interrelated purposes of the Effective Parenting Initiative will be to:

1. Acknowledge and celebrate the importance of effective parenting and parenting education,
2. Increase the awareness and use of effective parenting programs and resources,
3. Increase the availability of the full spectrum of effective parenting programs and resources, and
4. Increase the effectiveness of current programs and resources, as well as develop new programs and resources as needed.

These objectives are to be achieved through the creation of new federal government entities that would work closely with both the current federal government departments that are involved in the effective parenting movement and with all of the previously mentioned private sector institutions that compose this unorganized but critically important movement. As has been indicated, these societal institutions include faith-based, education, mass media, philanthropic, business, health, mental health, social service, child care, legal, and child welfare institutions, as well as the organizations that create and disseminate effective parenting programs and resources, and the professions and groups who conduct the research on parent effectiveness and on the effectiveness of parenting programs.

All of these government and private sector institutions would be systematically brought together to work on achieving the four major objectives through a new Department of Effective Parenting with cabinet level status and with a Secretary of Effective Parenting. If this highest level structure is not possible to create right now for political and other considerations, a White House Office of Effective Parenting could be created with a presidential appointee heading it up. (...)

Department of Effective Parenting/White House Office of Effective Parenting (...)
National Clearinghouse on Effective Parenting (...)
National Parenting Instructor Training Center (...)
National Institute on Effective Parenting (...)

Financing the National Effective Parenting Initiative

Creating new federal government agencies like the Effective Parenting Clearinghouse, Instructor Training Center and the National Institute will require an expenditure of tax dollars. However, the funds needed to run these agencies do not have to be all new tax dollars. Some of the funding can be through re-allocating existing federal funding. (...)

Even if new tax dollars are needed they should be monies well worth expending, given that it seems likely that any such funds allocated today will be offset by monetary savings tomorrow, to say nothing of the human suffering that is likely to be avoided and the immediate benefits of healthier and more achieving children that are likely to be observed. (...)

And every parent in America could support and fund this Initiative by budgeting each year to pay for its own parenting education. Indeed, if every parent who could afford $200 a year for paying the enrollment fee for a parenting skill-building class set aside that minimal amount, free market forces would be set in motion that would help fund the delivery of parenting skill-building programs. For example, more professionals and more local organizations are likely to pay themselves for their becoming certified to deliver parenting skill-building programs if they knew that the programs can be offered on a fee-for-service basis and that numerous parents are prepared to enroll and pay the enrollment cost. In a situation like that, an abundance of a variety of programs and classes are likely to be made available.

So, one of the many things that the President and members of Congress could do to lead this Initiative is to orient America's parents to take more responsibility for funding their own education for parenting. For, indeed, if a person chooses to be a parent, it is that person's responsibility to be the best parent he or she can be. And part of being the best possible parent involves seeking out and paying for one's own parenting education.

CONCLUSION

Embracing and actualizing the proposed Effective Parenting Initiative has the potential to make America the model of the world in terms of being a child and family-friendly nation. At a juncture in history when the United States of America is seen as being a particularly aggressive nation, it would be timely to offset that view with strong evidence of compassion and competence in carrying out the most basic responsibility of any society, the raising of its young.

Championing the proposed Effective Parenting Initiative would be totally consistent with the current President's own words in a proclamation on Parents' Day: "Parents are role models for their children. With patience, sacrifice, and love, they teach their children life lessons and prepare them for the future. We honor parents for their dedication to providing our Nation's children with the love and support they need." Actualizing a National Effective Parenting Initiative would be honoring parents for becoming as effective and as humane as possible in loving and supporting the children of America.

TASK/TEXT 7.15:

TASK/TEXT 7.15.1: DO WE KNOW WHAT COMPETENT PARENTING IS? [1994]

Dave Riley, Some principles for designing effective parenting education/support programs, in: *Can Government Promote Competent Parenting?* Wisconsin Family Impact Seminars Briefing Report 3, University of Wisconsin-Madison/Extension (Center for Excellence in Family Studies, School of Human Ecology) 1994 (<www.familyimpactseminars.org/s_wifis03report.pdf>), pp. 7–14; Policy Institute for Family Impact Seminars (<www.familyimpactseminars.org>, accessed 3 August 2009), <www.familyimpactseminars.org/s_wifis03c02.pdf>, pp. 8–9 (references omitted)

Do we know what competent parenting is?

Parenting seems like such a personal matter, and children are all so different from each other, that we might wonder if there can be any agreement on what "competent parenting" is. To a surprising extent, researchers can agree. The greatest agreement is in the infancy period, where the characteristics of competent parenting are most strongly influenced by biology, and least by culture.

With increasing age, competent parenting is increasingly defined by the cultural context; a society that depends upon hunter/gatherers raises its children to have different skills and attitudes than does a society based on agriculture. Similarly, a democracy must raise a different kind of citizen than an authoritarian regime.

And cultures also differ in values that are not related to their economies or politics; for example, a talkative child (and adult) is more highly valued in the dominant American culture than it is in Chippewa society, and therefore "competent" parenting must be defined differently within these two cultures.

Thinking just of US culture in this era, researchers can give a surprisingly coherent picture of competent parenting across the years of childhood. The picture will have some variations depending upon the gender of the child and the subculture, social class, and (...) structure of the family. The picture is complex, and will not be summarized here.

Researchers are also quick to admit that their knowledge is incomplete. But it is fair to summarize that, to a surprisingly great extent, researchers can observe normal interactions of parents and their children at home, and from these observations can predict quite a bit about children's later compliance with adults, cooperativeness with peers, empathy with the distress of others, aggressiveness across their childhood years and into adulthood, school failure or success, and many other outcomes of interest to most parents.

Much of the complex picture of parenting that is painted by research findings can be summarized in terms of (1) the development of a **secure attachment** between the child and one or more parents in **infancy**, and (2) the use of **authoritative parenting** in the years of **childhood and adolescence**.

Secure attachments derive from parenting that is sensitively responsive and reliably available to the infant.

Authoritative parenting is a style that combines high demandingness (high expectations for the child, a willingness by the parent to exert authority, set rules, act consistently), and high responsiveness (expression of warmth with the child, a willingness to listen to the child's point of view, to engage in verbal give-andtake with the child, a willingness to explain the reasons for the parent's rules).

Hundreds of research studies document that children who experience secure attachment relationships and authoritative parenting are much more likely than other children to "do better" in almost any way that you might ask about. They are less resistant with their parents as two-year olds; they are more cooperative with peers as preschoolers; they get better grades and get drunk less as teenagers. Research also documents that we know ways to help parents establish secure attachments and become more authoritative in their parenting.

TASK/TEXT 7.15.2: DO WE KNOW WHAT GOOD PARENTING IS? AND CAN PUBLIC POLICY PROMOTE IT? [1999]

Dave Riley and Karen Bogenschneider, Do we know what good parenting is? And can public policy promote it? In: *Raising the Next Generation: Public and*

Private Parenting Initiatives, Wisconsin Family Impact Seminars Briefing Report 13, University of Wisconsin-Madison/Extension (Center for Excellence in Family Studies, School of Human Ecology) 1999 (<www.familyimpactseminars.org/s_wifis13report.pdf>), pp. 1–17; Policy Institute for Family Impact Seminars (<www.familyimpactseminars.org>, accessed 9 August 2009), <www.familyimpactseminars.org/s_wifis13c01.pdf>, pp. 2–3, 8–13 (references omitted)

Does parenting matter?

Almost every year, best-selling books gain momentary fame with proclamations that parents matter little to children's development, usually suggesting that children grow according to a fixed genetic script, or sometimes that peers and other influences matter more. Some books even argue that children have a bigger impact on parents than parents have on kids (a view we can sympathize with when our toddler is crying at midnight or our teenager is rebelling).

Researchers familiar with the hundreds of studies on parenting are virtually unanimous in agreeing that genes and social influences, in addition to parents, are crucial to understanding why children grow into one kind of person or another. But these same scholars quickly add that **child rearing by the family is still the first and foremost influence on most child development outcomes** (…).

The best evidence for the importance of parenting comes from two kinds of studies. The first is of children who are deprived of any or most parental influence, typically children raised in orphanages. The recent case of Rumanian children who spent many years in orphanages with no parent-like figure, for example, re-confirms what earlier studies have shown: most children in such situations sustain lifelong effects and many never leave institutionalized care. Parents matter.

The second form of data comes from experiments where parents are trained to change their child rearing behaviors, and the effects on children's development can be charted. Experiments of this sort solidly prove a cause-and-effect relationship, with changes in parenting behaviors having the power to raise children's intelligence or reduce their juvenile delinquency, for example.

In the apt words of Urie Bronfenbrenner, **the family is the "most powerful, the most humane, and by far the most economical system known for building competence and character"** (1986 …) **in children and adults alike**. As the only institution based primarily on love and caring, families teach connectedness and a commitment so strong that we would give our life for each other (…). More than any other institution, families perform the magic feat of "making and keeping human beings human" (Bronfenbrenner, 1986 …).

Do we know what competent parenting is?

Parenting is such a personal matter, and children are all so different from each other, that we might wonder if there can be any agreement on what "competent parenting" is. To a surprising extent, researchers can agree (...). The greatest consensus surrounds the infancy period, when the characteristics of competent parenting are most strongly influenced by biology and least affected by culture.

By just examining US culture in this era, researchers can give a surprisingly coherent picture of competent parenting across the years of childhood. The picture will have some variations depending upon the gender of the child and the ethnic subculture, social class, and family structure. The picture is complex, and researchers are quick to admit that their knowledge is incomplete. But it is fair to summarize that, to a surprisingly great extent, researchers can observe normal interactions of parents with their children at home, and from these observations can predict quite a bit about children's later compliance with adults, cooperativeness with peers, empathy with the distress of others, school failure or success, aggressiveness across their childhood years and into adulthood, and many other outcomes.

Much of the complex picture of parenting that is painted by research findings can be summarized in terms of (1) parent-child attachment in infancy, and (2) authoritative parenting in childhood and adolescence. A secure attachment bond in infancy is the result of parenting that is sensitively responsive and reliably available to the infant. Beginning in the preschool years, authoritative parenting combines high demandingness (high expectations for the child, a willingness by the parent to exert authority, set rules, and act consistently), and high responsiveness (expressing warmth to the child, listening to the child's point of view, engaging in verbal give-and-take with the child, and explaining the reasons for the parent's rules).

Hundreds of research studies document that **children who experience secure attachment relationships and authoritative parenting are much more likely than other children to "do better" in almost any measurable way**. They are less resistant with their parents as 2-year olds; more cooperative with peers as preschoolers; and get better grades and get drunk less as teenagers (...). (...)

Can we mount effective programs to improve parenting?

The short answer is "yes." This may surprise many parents who believe that effective child rearing is: ... either common sense *(Everybody knows what good parents do, just ask my grandmother)*, instinctive *(Some people are naturally good parents; either you are or you aren't and it can't be taught)* or relative *(Who's to say what a good parent is, anyway? ...)*.

But studies of actual parenting education and support programs verify that the specific knowledge and skills of effective parenting can be promoted in parents, ultimately benefitting children's development. Effective programs are of many types, and one convenient way to categorize them is in terms of the level of needs of the parents they target. At one extreme we have **primary prevention** programs, which are provided to every family in a community. **Secondary prevention** programs are provided to only those families who are "at risk" of parenting difficulties. And **tertiary prevention** programs are really "treatment" programs for families that have shown serious difficulties, such as child abuse. They are "prevention" programs in the sense that, if successful, they prevent a re-occurrence of the problem. (...)

Parent Training

The efficacy of parent training can be discussed using the example of juvenile crime. In longitudinal studies, **the strongest predictor of juvenile delinquency is ineffective parenting** (...). More specifically, researchers have learned that 30 to 40 percent of **antisocial behavior** of early offenders, who are those most likely to become violent and chronic offenders later, can be tied to **harsh, inconsistent parenting during the preschool years** (...). Parents of these early offenders **threaten, nag, and scold but seldom follow through** (...). This teaches children to resolve conflict through coercion – specifically **whining, yelling, temper tantrums, or physical attacks** (...). This aggressive behavior leads to **rejection by prosocial peers, trouble with teachers, and poor school performance** (...). Negative consequences snowball, and these youngsters, who are poorly monitored by their parents, drift into **deviant peer groups** (...) and increase their use of illegal substances (...). Over time, they fail to develop the skills for stable work or marriages that might enable them to drop out of crime as an adult (...).

Based on this evidence of family and peer influence, it is not surprising that programs focusing disproportionately on individual youth have seldom demonstrated lasting success (...). (...)

Is parenting a proper issue for public policy? Or is it strictly a personal matter?

This question concerns values and judgment [and principles and provisions of the CRC, to which the US is not (yet) a party, JW], not research findings. Nonetheless, let us suggest that for most people, the best answer is that parenting is both inherently private, and inevitably affected by public policy.

On one hand, our American tradition, born in reaction to the unbridled power of monarchy, has been to protect **the private sphere from government intrusion**. This view has moderated over time, for example by acceptance of public intrusion into the families of child abusing parents (originally through the use of farmers' **animal cruelty laws** [which were in existence before child protection laws, JW]). But most Americans would still agree that raising the child is the family's responsibility, not the government's.

On the other hand, families don't exist in a vacuum. Families do better when supported by close friendships, good schools, and caring communities. Some communities make it easy to raise children well, while others make it hard. For example, moving families out of Chicago's public housing projects and into working class neighborhoods leads to much more effective parenting in those families and far better outcomes for the children (...). These parents don't need more knowledge or better attitudes nearly as much as they need a supportive community for their efforts.

Can government policies promote good parenting?

The answer is both yes and no. Public policies, of course, play a strong role in creating the conditions for parents to do their best. Parents themselves voice a desire for government help in the private matter of childrearing. In recent [1998] public opinion polls, only 6 percent of parents said government *was doing a great deal* to help them. Yet 47 percent said government *could be doing a great deal* to help them, and 37 percent said government *could do something* to help them (...).

Government could help families with some of the stresses that parents say make parenting harder today than it used to be – excessive work demands, social isolation, economic pressures, and unsafe streets and neighborhoods (...). Policies that support parents deal with such issues as schools, libraries, parks, public health, child care, workplace law, employment programs, family resource centers, and training for foster parents. For example, zoning laws could make it easier to allow child care programs inside residential neighborhoods, encouraging the formation of parenting social networks and a sense of community.

It takes only a moment of reflection to realize that most legislative bills have some impact on family life, just as they often have an economic and an environmental impact. Policymakers do not have a choice about whether to affect family life or not: they already do.

Yet, just because government can do something to help parents, doesn't mean it can do everything. Some of the changes we need to promote good parenting must come from parents themselves.

What can parents do to promote good parenting?

In a recent book on the New York Times best seller list, a renowned social scientist said "The widespread disengagement of parents from the business of childrearing is a public health problem that warrants urgent national attention" (...). Parents may find it difficult to be engaged in childrearing, according to the President of the National Council on Family Relations, because they find themselves competing for time with their children in an **over-busy, over-scheduled, over-commercialized society** (...). For example, active marketing of clothing to preteens has preempted parent influence on the clothing choices of children as young as 7 and 8. Most educational, economic, recreational, and religious activities are aimed at individuals, thereby pulling families apart, rather than bringing them together (...).

Because it is difficult to mandate parents to spend more time with children and to legislate cultural changes such as **a greater valuing of parenting** or **less emphasis on materialism**, some activists argue that instead of looking to government or professionals, **parents must take action themselves** (...). One thing that is needed to promote competent parenting is a nonpartisan, **grass roots movement generated and sustained by parents themselves** to make family life a priority and to support parents' attempts to create a better balance between time for relationships inside the family and activities outside the family (...).

In summary, raising children is clearly the parents' responsibility, yet it may fall to policymakers to help create the conditions under which parents can do their best.

Government policies to promote good parenting may work best when enacted in a cultural climate that values children and cherishes parents.

What policy options and personal actions can promote good parenting?
Because good parenting depends on both the public and private realms, this section identifies both government policies and personal actions that can promote competent parenting. While this list is not intended to be exhaustive, hopefully it will stimulate creative thinking and constructive dialogue about how society as a whole and we as individuals can take steps to promote the type of parenting that produces the responsible citizens and productive workers upon which the future of our nation rests.

Policy options at the government level
Examples of policy options for promoting more competent parenting come from both conservative and liberal sources. They include:

- Community-based family support and parent education programs can provide parents with the knowledge, skills, and social support they need to do their best in raising their children (...).
- Home visiting programs can help parents get off to a good start in raising their children (...).
- Employment policies can provide paid family leave, part-time or job sharing opportunities, and other family-friendly work policies that allow time away from work for family responsibilities (...). Because some employers are not required to participate, the right to family leave and other family-friendly workplace policies could be made more widely available to employees (...).

- Marriage education and enrichment programs have proven to reduce rates of separation and divorce, leading to a more stable environment in which children thrive (...). Married parenthood can be encouraged through supportive tax policies, benefits, and marriage rules. Yet when marriages fail, systems need to be in place that ensure reliable child support payments (...). Also, mandated programs on how to co-parent after divorce have been shown to reduce by half future re-litigation rates over custody and child support (...).
- Foster parents can benefit from parent training and support. A foster parent education program (...) increases the willingness of foster parents to provide care, prevents multiple foster home placements, and is more effective than group care in preventing repeat crimes among chronic juvenile offenders (...).
- Policies that lead to decent incomes, reliable child care, safe neighborhoods, quality schools, and affordable health care give parents the peace of mind that allows them to focus on the important work of raising the next generation (...).

In addition to taking steps to enact these specific family policies, policymakers can promote a **family perspective in any legislation** by the following actions:

- Policymakers can raise questions about how legislation would affect family well-being, just as the economic or **environmental impacts of legislation** are routinely considered in policy debate. Specifically, policymakers can ask in what ways families contribute to a problem, how they are affected by it, and whether they should be involved in the solution (...).
- Policymakers can require parent or family criteria in any evaluations of programs or policies that affect families.

Actions at the personal level

- Family coalitions can be organized to develop and actively pursue policies that would strengthen families and support their decision to make family time a priority (...).
- Just as parents used to receive support at barn raisings, church meetings, and other community gatherings, communities could provide opportunities for parents to get to know each other and to become familiar with community rules and standards for childrearing (e.g, curfews, age of dating, rules regarding teen alcohol use ...).
- A broad menu of parent education opportunities could be offered through businesses, civic clubs, religious institutions, and schools (...).

- Volunteers can establish parents' groups, organize neighborhood activities, and lend clothes, books, computers, and toys to neighbors with children (...).

In summary, government and personal options can be quite distinct from each other, but they also can overlap. For example, government can provide seed money to jump-start the formation of family coalitions or public forums at the community level. These family coalitions, in turn, could develop a range of strategies to make family time a priority, which could include advocating for specific family-friendly government policies. (...)

Conclusion

In their importance to both policymakers and the public, child and family issues are now at their strongest point in recent decades. However, as one scholar recently lamented, there is often little connection between what is funded and the specific programs known to be effective or most promising (...). While the knowledge created by the research community grows at a slow pace and seldom seems to provide the facts needed by policymakers today, we at least have knowledge of some flagship programs, and perhaps enough knowledge to help us avoid jumping on the latest bandwagon. We know enough, at least, to increase the odds that parenting education programs will deliver on their promise. Fulfilling this promise may depend on a dual-pronged focus of moving forward on both a government and a personal front.

TASK/TEXT 7.15.3: ACTIVATING A GRASS-ROOTS PARENTS' MOVEMENT [1999]

William J. Doherty with Harry Boyte, Family life 1st: activating a grass-roots parents' movement, in: *Raising the Next Generation: Public and Private Parenting Initiatives*, Wisconsin Family Impact Seminars Briefing Report 13, University of Wisconsin-Madison/Extension (Center for Excellence in Family Studies, School of Human Ecology) 1999 (<www.familyimpactseminars.org/s_wifis13report.pdf>), pp. 27–30; Policy Institute for Family Impact Seminars (<www.familyimpactseminars.org>, accessed 15 August 2009), <www.familyimpactseminars.org/s_wifis13c03.pdf>, pp. 27–29 (references omitted)

Increasingly, parents find themselves competing for time with their owe children in an over-busy, over-commercialized society. Most educational, economic, and recreational activities are aimed at individuals, thereby pulling families apart rather than bringing them together.

Doherty contends that the principal momentum for competent parenting must come from diverse parents working together in powerful, non-partisan ways. What is needed is not a top-down state or federal initiative, but a public, grass-roots movement generated and sustained by parents themselves.

State and federal governments can serve as a catalyst for a national movement to make family life a priority.

Recent federal policy initiatives for parents have focused on helping parents have more time at home with their children after a birth and when a child is ill, and on encouraging voluntary television and movie rating systems.

While these policies are helpful and needed, they do not seriously tackle the underlying erosion of parents' ability to steer the development of their children in a world increasingly dominated by the consumer culture, the media, and over-scheduled family hyperactivity. In homes across the country, parents are fighting – and often losing – the battle for influence over their children against powerful forces far stronger than most individual parents.

How Has Consumerism Eroded the Influence of Parents?

A case in point for how the culture has undermined family life is the declining influence of parents on the clothing decisions of young children. It's not that pre-teen children are becoming more truly independent in choosing what to wear. Instead, their tastes for increasingly sexier and more expensive clothes are driven by clothing marketers.

According to the Wall Street Journal, children's clothing manufacturers have concluded that parents now have little influence over their pre-teen daughters' clothing choices. Brands are now marketing and selling sexualized names and styles (...). Advertising is going around the parents and directly to the children who are the decision-makers, if not yet the purchasers.

It is difficult for most parents to compete with a multi-billion dollar industry marketing directly to young children with well-researched and captivating images of pseudo-mature teen sexuality.

What Other Forces Have Invaded Family Life?

The exaggerated emphasis on athletics is another argument for social change. One mother in a Minnesota public discussion on putting families first reported that she feels "terrorized" by coaches who insist on practicing on Mother's Day and Thanksgiving Day. Another participant was told by the soccer coach that her family could take vacation only during a two-week period in August.

In fact, most social, educational, and religious programs in America today are aimed at individuals who are pulled out of their families. In one town, the coaches and clergy met in a "summit meeting" to divide up families' times so as to avoid competition between church and sports.

Ironically, despite the over-abundance of community activities currently available on the consumer menu (in one community, there are 14 organized activities for three-year-olds), there are few chances for whole families to participate in common, intergenerational activities, and even fewer opportunities for families to engage in citizenship activities that build the commonwealth. We are increasingly a hyper-individualistic, consumer-oriented society that values family life as a political icon and marketing target, but not as a place for nurturing active, productive citizens.

What is Needed to Counter These Attacks on Family Life?

We need a movement of families to take back our kids and make family life the first priority. "Family Life 1st" is a group of citizens in suburban Minneapolis who are committed to building a community in which family life has first priority in an over-scheduled world. The group is committed to reversing the deleterious effects of the consumer culture of childhood, in which parents see themselves as competitive providers of services to children, and children are overscheduled in a frantic pursuit of experiences and opportunities for personal enrichment and advantage over peers.

Family Life 1st was created out of a town meeting in Wayzata, Minnesota, attended by parents and community leaders concerned with this nameless social problem. It consists of parents, community activists, clergy, teachers, and other professionals.

The democratic theory underlying this effort is that the family can only be a seedbed for current and future citizens if it achieves a balance between internal bonds and external activities. This balance has become gravely out of whack for families of all social classes. What is sorely needed to retrieve family life is a public, grass roots movement generated and sustained by families themselves.

What Can a Parents' Movement Accomplish?

Thus far, Family Life 1st has generated a vision of a desired future for families in our community, and begun a series of stakeholder interviews to better understand the problem and solicit allies. We want to inspire a broad community discussion, and we are committed to a "no villains" approach that does not blame parents, coaches, clergy or any other group. A specific task will be to develop, along with community activity groups, youth, and families, a set of working policies that acknowledge, support, and respect families' decisions to make family time a priority.

What Can the State and Federal Governments Do to Help?

Clearly, top-down state or federal initiatives will not be successful or well-received. In fact, beginning with government programs or policies – without widespread citizen deliberation and input – contradicts the basic democratic theory underlying families' civic work. The principal momentum must come from diverse families working together in powerful but non-partisan ways.

Government, however, can serve an important role as a catalyst for such a national movement. Here is a proposal for state or federal action:

- Create and fund a national network of community circles, family coalitions, or public discussion forums, consisting of demographically representative groups of parents and grandparents. (Grandparents are very worried, and have a big stake in this discussion about the welfare of their grandchildren.)
- Give this national initiative a striking name. One possibility: Taking Back Our Kids and Making Family Life 1st.
- These groups will explore and define, via their own experience, reading, and the testimony of experts on childhood and family life, the central challenges that parents face in raising children in today's culture.
- The groups will make recommendations for action in four areas: what individual families can do, what families collectively can do in their local communities and nationally, what private organizations such as faith communities and non-profits can do, and what government at different levels can do.
- Publicize widely the activities and conclusions of these family forums.
- Call a White House Conference to address the findings and recommendations from the forums.
- Catalyze a national, non-partisan movement of families that would take on civic projects to strengthen families and promote a sense of common purpose among families. After being launched, this movement would operate autonomously and without further direct federal or state support.

Summary

We aim to stimulate a national movement of families taking back their lives through democratic public work. We are committed to reversing the encroachment of the consumer culture on what has been called the world's smallest democracy – the family.

Today's "triple threat" to children and families – consumerism, media saturation, and family hyperactivity – calls for national leadership to create a civic space for families to join in common purpose to recapture their influence over the development of the next generation of citizens and, in the process, to rebuild the commonwealth.

8. EVOLVING CAPACITIES – PARTICIPATION, IDENTITY, YOUTH VIOLENCE, YOUTH RIGHTS

TASK/TEXT 8.1: ADDRESS BY SEVERN SUZUKI (12 YEARS)

Address to the Plenary Session of the UN Conference on Environment and Development (The Earth Summit)
Rio de Janeiro, 3–14 June 1992 (<www.un.org/geninfo/bp/enviro.html>)

Video: <www.youtube.com/watch?v=5g8cmWZOX8Q>
Text: <www.slothclub.org/pages/activity/japan/sevtour/sevspeech1992.htm>:

Hello, I'm Severn Suzuki speaking for ECO – The Environmental Children's Organization. We are a group of twelve and thirteen-year-olds from Canada trying to make a difference: Vanessa Suttie, Morgan Geisler, Michelle Quigg and me.

We raised all the money ourselves to come six thousand miles to tell you adults you must change your ways. Coming here today, I have no hidden agenda. I am fighting for my future. Losing my future is not like losing an election or a few points on the stock market. I am here to speak for all generations to come.

I am here to speak on behalf of the starving children around the world whose cries go unheard. I am here to speak for the countless animals dying across this planet because they have nowhere left to go. We cannot afford to be not heard.

I am afraid to go out in the sun now because of the holes in the ozone. I am afraid to breathe the air because I don't know what chemicals are in it.

I used to go fishing in Vancouver with my dad until just a few years ago we found the fish full of cancers. And now we hear about animals and plants going extinct every day – vanishing forever.

In my life, I have dreamt of seeing the great herds of wild animals, jungles and rainforests full of birds and butterflies, but now I wonder if they will even exist for my children to see.

Did you have to worry about these little things when you were my age? All this is happening before our eyes and yet we act as if we have all the time we want and all the solutions.

I'm only a child and I don't have all the solutions, but I want you to realize, neither do you!

You don't know how to fix the holes in our ozone layer.

You don't know how to bring salmon back up a dead stream.

You don't know how to bring back an animal now extinct.

And you can't bring back forests that once grew where there is now desert.

If you don't know how to fix it, please stop breaking it!

Here, you may be delegates of your governments, business people, organizers, reporters or politicians – but really you are mothers and fathers, brothers and sister, aunts and uncles – and all of you are somebody's child.

I'm only a child yet I know we are all part of a family, five billion strong, in fact, 30 million species strong and we all share the same air, water and soil – borders and governments will never change that.

I'm only a child yet I know we are all in this together and should act as one single world towards one single goal. In my anger, I am not blind, and in my fear, I am not afraid to tell the world how I feel.

In my country, we make so much waste, we buy and throw away, buy and throw away, and yet Northern countries will not share with the needy. Even when we have more than enough, we are afraid to lose some of our wealth, afraid to share.

In Canada, we live the privileged life, with plenty of food, water and shelter – we have watches, bicycles, computers and television sets.

Two days ago here in Brazil, we were shocked when we spent some time with some children living on the streets. And this is what one child told us: "I wish I was rich and if I were, I would give all the street children food, clothes, medicine, shelter and love and affection."

If a child on the street who has nothing, is willing to share, why are we who have everything still so greedy?

I can't stop thinking that these children are my age, that it makes a tremendous difference where you are born, that I could be one of those children living in the Favellas of Rio; I could be a child starving in Somalia; a victim of war in the Middle East or a beggar in India.

I'm only a child yet I know if all the money spent on war was spent on ending poverty and finding environmental answers, what a wonderful place this earth would be!

At school, even in kindergarten, you teach us to behave in the world. You teach us:

not to fight with others,

to work things out,

to respect others,

to clean up our mess,

not to hurt other creatures,
to share – not be greedy.
Then why do you go out and do the things you tell us not to do?

Do not forget why you're attending these conferences, who you're doing this for – we are your own children.

You are deciding what kind of world we will grow up in. Parents should be able to comfort their children by saying "everything's going to be alright"; "we're doing the best we can"; and "it's not the end of the world."

But I don't think you can say that to us anymore. Are we even on your list of priorities?

My father always says: "You are what you do, not what you say." Well, what you do makes me cry at night.

You grown up's say you love us. I challenge you, please make your actions reflect your words.

Thank you for listening.

TASK/TEXT 8.2:

TASK/TEXT 8.2.1: NORWAY – CHILDREN'S OMBUDSMAN CALLS TO LOWER VOTING AGE

Crinmail 910 – 28 August 2007, <www.crin.org>

The Children's Ombudsmen for Norway, Reidar Hjermann, is calling on all candidates for the municipal and county council elections to support lowering the age of voting to 16.

As young people are major consumers of municipal and county services, Hjermann says that they are also local experts with knowledge and competencies that adults lack. "As a politician, you will need their expert advice if you want to influence and build well-functioning municipalities," he says.

He explains that lowering the voting age would boost the development of district and rural municipalities. As such, enhanced participation in local democracies will not only benefit children and young people's well-being, but will also make the municipality more attractive for young families. An active children and youth policy will ensure dynamic local communities.

Today, the average first-time voter in municipal and county council elections in Norway is 20 years old. As a result of having elections every four years, and because many young people move away from the municipality for educational purposes, many first-time voters will have moved from their local environments at the time of election.

At this point, many no longer have first hand experiences with fledgling school buildings, the lack of proper bicycle paths, closing of youth clubs and a poor bus services. "If we give 16 year olds a vote, this will stimulate politicians to listen and improve communications with this age group, they will have no choice. Further, citizenship learning in schools will be all the more relevant, and the election campaigns will be brought into the schoolyard more so than before. One can also expect an earlier political and democratic wake-up call when youngsters see what they can achieve in their own environment," [he] explains.

Even though the government department responsible for elections has turned down the suggestion of lowering the age of voting for the upcoming elections, Hjermann argues that they should start now to work with young people, society at large and politicians to prepare everyone for the elections in 2011.

Many of those against this proposal assert that lowering the voting age to 16 means tampering with the age of majority; but Hjermann argues that there are already different age limits that suggest different degrees of maturity. "We are all potential tax-payers from 16 to 67. Today 15 year olds are sent to prison, 16 year olds are authoritative in medical terms, and they pay adult tickets on buses."

"We have ten years of compulsory school. It is the school system that will set us up to participate actively in our society. If the school does not prepare young people to elect politicians, it is not the young that have failed, but the school. Voting at 16 will coincide with the last year of compulsory school. The last year in school is indeed a fitting time to participate in the elections and forming of our society.

Lowering the voting age requires us to change the constitution. Testing it in the next Municipal and County Council elections does not. We have everything to gain and nothing to loose in this experiment," Hjermann concluded.

See also 'United States: Top ten reasons to lower the voting age' at <www.crin.org/resources/infoDetail.asp?ID=10143&flag=news>.

TASK/TEXT 8.2.2: AUSTRIA – CHILDREN ALLOWED TO VOTE

Crinmail 1020 – 30 September 2008, <www.crin.org> [Source: Herald Tribune]

Austria made history in the European Union on Sunday by becoming the first member of the 27-nation bloc to give 16-year-olds a voice in national elections.

And Stanke, one of up to 200,000 eligible Austrian teenagers, was not about to pass up this opportunity. "Yes, I'm going to vote," Stanke, who turned 16 last week, said on a recent afternoon as she chatted with friends outside her school in central Vienna. Stanke has a slew of choices.

Following the collapse in July of the governing coalition between the center-left Social Democrats and the center-right People's Party, 10 parties said they want to govern the Alpine republic. But only about half had a realistic chance of making it into Parliament, where 183 seats were up for grabs. With a tight race at the top, the two main parties were flirting with first-time voters and – to some extent – making an effort to cater to a younger crowd. For the Social Democrats, 27-year-old Laura Rudas, who is ranked fourth on the party's list of candidates, was doing most of the reaching out.

Vote could make the difference

"During this election, it could be decisive," she said. "Every vote counts." Rudas, who has held a seat in Parliament since January 2007, said she considers it her role to show young people that "politics can change the world." With her leather jacket and tight jeans, Rudas does not quite fit the picture of a politician. Neither does her counterpart at the People's Party, Silvia Fuhrmann, who is also 27. She said that how young people vote "won't be decisive, but is still important."

Lowering the voting age came about as a political compromise between the Social Democrats and the People's Party, which wanted to give citizens living in the country the option to vote by absentee ballot. In the end, both became law.

Austrian 16-year-olds have already been able to vote in some local elections. The same is true in other places, including neighbouring Germany. Other places that allow voting at 16 include Brazil, Cuba, Nicaragua and the Isle of Man, a British dependency in the Irish Sea.

Peter Filzmaier, one of Austria's most respected political commentators, said the Greens would likely benefit most from the young, first-time voters. Walter Holub, director of a high school in Vienna, said interest in politics varies among the teenagers he oversees. "A large majority still appears to be rather indifferent," Holub said.

TASK/TEXT 8.2.3: MOTION FOR A RESOLUTION PRESENTED TO THE COUNCIL OF EUROPE'S PARLIAMENTARY ASSEMBLY: "EXPANSION OF DEMOCRACY BY LOWERING THE VOTING AGE TO 16"

Intergenerational Justice Review 2009/4, pp. 155–156, <www.crin.org/docs/IGJR_4_2009.pdf>

In May 2009, a motion in favour of lowering the voting age to 16 in all countries of the Council of Europe was presented to the Parliamentary Assembly (not to be confused with the European Parliament):

1. Twelve years have passed since the Assembly adopted Recommendation 1315 (1997), recommending to "rapidly harmonise the age for the right to vote and stand for election at 18 years in all countries and for all elections." Since then, we have witnessed a significant development in issues concerning the minimum age for voting. It is therefore time to re-evaluate the Assembly's position on this very important topic.

2. The trend of lowering the voting age has spread throughout Europe: In Austria the voting age has been lowered to 16 years for all elections. In Germany and Switzerland, 16–17 year olds can vote at local elections in some of the constituent states. Current knowledge on the experiences from elections in these countries is very promising in terms of 16–17-year olds level of participation.

3. In Great Britain, Finland, Norway and the Czech Republic the possibility of lowering of the voting age to 16 is currently being evaluated by the governments. The primary reason hereof has been a deep concern over young people's reluctance to participate in democracy. Despite a widespread interest in political issues amongst the 16–17 year olds, they apparently do not show up at the ballot boxes or register as voters. According to IDEA, International Institute for Democracy and Electoral Assistance, voter turn-out amongst young people in the age from 18–29 years in Western Europe is systematically lower than the average level of turnout in the population (see Voter turnout since 1945, a global report – IDEA, 2002).

4. Furthermore, there is a fear that the demographic development in many European countries will worsen the problem. According to EUROSTAT statistics, we will for instance see a 44,5 percentage increase in the 65–79 year olds and a 24,3 percent decline in the 15–24 year olds by year 2050. There is a real risk that young people will be marginalised in the political process, both on a specific level as they will be numerically out-numbered, but also because the political agenda risks becoming dominated by issues that are primarily interesting for older people. This is particularly problematic in a time when societies more than ever will need the commitment and work efforts of young people in order to keep up economical growth, social security systems and social cohesion.

5. Needless to say, this development is dangerous for the future stability of European democracy. We need to find means to make young people engaged in democracy. Lowering of the voting age could be a part of that solution.

6. Recalling Recommendation 1019 (1985) on the participation of young people in political and institutional life, the Assembly said that it was "convinced – if democracy is to survive and develop – of the importance of the active and effective awareness, understanding, participation and commitment of young people in political and institutional life at local, national and European levels."

7. Recalling Resolution 1630 (2008) on Refreshing the youth agenda of the Council of Europe that underlines that in the youth policy of the Council of

Europe: "A key element has been encouragement of the active participation of young people in civil and institutional life."

8. The Assembly recommends an investigation on the advantages and drawbacks of engaging and securing young people's participation in democracy by lowering of the voting age to 16 in all member countries of the Council of Europe. (...)

TASK/TEXT 8.3:

TASK/TEXT 8.3.1: CAMPAIGN FOR A CRC COMPLAINTS MECHANISM

Crinmail 948 – 15 January 2008; <www.crin.org/law/CRC_complaints>

A group of agencies are campaigning for the United Nations to establish a complaints mechanism to the Convention on the Rights of the Child (CRC). Such a procedure would provide a mechanism that would ensure the availability of legal remedies for children at the international level.

What is it?

A complaints or communications procedure allows individuals, groups or their representatives who claim that their rights have been violated by a State that is a party to a convention or covenant to bring a complaint before the relevant committee, provided that the State has recognised the competence of the committee to receive such complaints.

Why such a mechanism?

The Convention on the Rights of the Child is the only international human rights treaty with a mandatory reporting procedure which does not have, in addition, an existing or draft communications procedure. This is a serious matter of discrimination against children. While children and their representatives can use the mechanisms established under other international instruments to pursue many of their rights, those instruments do not cover, separately or together, the full range and detail of rights in the CRC. Furthermore, communications or complaints made on behalf of children to the other bodies will not be considered by a Committee with special expertise on children's rights. Similar persuasive arguments were made for the adoption of the communications' mechanisms under CEDAW and under the new Convention on the Rights of Persons with Disabilities.

How would this be done?
The most likely method to establish a complaints mechanism would be through the development of a new Optional Protocol (OP) to the CRC. This would require:

- Building momentum for the Human Rights Council (HRC) to establish a UN Working Group with the mandate to consider elaborating such an instrument.
- Lobbying the working group to influence the drafting procedure.
- Lobbying members of the General Assembly to ratify the protocol to bring it into force.
- Undertaking more campaigning to bring about widespread ratification.

What is happening at the moment?
Representatives of the group met with the Committee on the Rights of the Child in September 2007 to seek its support for the drafting and adoption of an Optional Protocol. There was an enthusiastic response from many members and it was agreed that a more detailed paper would be prepared for the Committee's next session in January 2008, setting out possible provisions for the Protocol, answering in more detail the challenges to ensuring a mechanism that is child-sensitive and effective and analysing the experiences of the other treaty bodies and regional mechanisms.

African Initiative underway
A group of organisations in Kenya, chaired by The Cradle, recently set up the Complaints Procedure Working Group to campaign for a complaints procedure for the CRC. Find out more here: <www.crin.org/resources/infoDetail.asp?ID=15331>.

Challenges and objections: Questions and Answers – Answering arguments put forward against a complaints procedure for the CRC

"It would duplicate existing mechanisms":
Given the universality and interdependence of human rights there is of course overlap among the various instruments. However the CRC provides distinctive and in some cases additional rights for children and its Committee has special expertise on children. None of the other relevant mechanisms have been designed with the special status of children in mind. Provisions in the Protocol would avoid duplication.

"It would be preferable to establish a joint procedure for considering communications/complaints under all the major international instruments"
This proposal, made in the context of proposals for a single standing treaty body, has never had the support of the Committee nor of the wider children's rights community because of the dangerous risk of a loss of focus on children's rights. It would undermine the purpose and power for children of the CRC. And if there is, in time, some centralising of response to communications, children's position will be relatively weak if there is no procedure linked to the CRC.

"It would not be effective, its decisions would be non-binding"
This is a defeatist argument against all the other established procedures. While some States have not complied with some decisions on individual communications (just as some States ignore Concluding Observations), there are very positive examples of changes in law and practice following decisions. Communications procedures are complementary to the reporting process; they reinforce each other.

"It is better for the Committee to focus on persuading States to improve national remedies for breaches of children's rights"
This is not an alternative; of course States need to develop effective remedies for breaches of all children's rights. Children and their representatives also need to be able to appeal beyond the State when rights are breached and national remedies do not exist; having international remedies available in fact encourages the development of national remedies.

"The CRC covers economic, social and cultural rights, which are not justiciable like civil and political rights"
In its *General Comment No. 5* on general measures of implementation, the Committee emphasises, echoing other Treaty Bodies, "that economic, social and cultural rights, as well as civil and political rights, must be regarded as justiciable." Regional complaints mechanisms already consider economic, social and cultural rights and an OP to the International Covenant on Economic, Social and Cultural Rights is currently being drafted.

"The Committee does not have the capacity to deal with communications on top of its very demanding reporting process"
The Committee and the Secretariat have risen to the challenge of the massive workload of reporting under the CRC and the two existing Optional Protocols, removing the backlog through the temporary two-chamber system, supported by additional resources. Similarly, with appropriate specialisation and additional resources, it could – like other Committees – process communications.

"The Committee would be swamped with complaints, undermining its credibility"
Other procedures have not been swamped. All have reasonable gate-keeping devices which could be incorporated.

Who is supporting the campaign?
A core group of agencies is supporting the establishment of a communications procedure for the CRC, including: World Vision International, Save the Children UK, Save the Children Sweden, Save the Children Norway, the Global Initiative to End All Corporal Punishment of Children, CRIN, Kindernothilfe, the World Organization Against Torture (OMCT), SOS-Kinderdorf International and the European Network of Ombudspersons for Children (ENOC). (…)

Existing complaint/communication procedures for international Instruments
Four of the human rights treaty bodies can, under certain circumstances, consider individual complaints or communications from individuals:

- Human Rights Committee, under the International Covenant on Civil and Political Rights (ICCPR): states must have ratified the First Optional Protocol to the ICCPR.
- Committee to Eliminate Racial Discrimination, under the Convention on the Elimination of All Forms of Racial Discrimination: states must have made the necessary declaration under article 14 of the Convention.
- Committee against Torture, under the Convention against Torture and Other Cruel, Inhuman or Degrading Treatment or Punishment: states must have made the necessary declaration under article 22 of the Convention.
- Committee to End Discrimination against Women, under the Convention on the Elimination of all Forms of Discrimination against Women: states must have ratified the Optional Protocol to the Convention.

Detailed information on these procedures, which states have accepted them and on how to use them is available at: <www.ohchr.org/english/bodies/complaints.htm>.

Three newer Conventions include individual complaints/communications procedures which will come into force once they have been accepted by a sufficient number of states:

- The International Convention on the Protection of the Rights of All Migrant Workers and Members of Their Families;
- Convention on the Rights of Persons with Disabilities (…);
- International Convention for the Protection of All Persons from Enforced Disappearance: not yet in force (…).

In addition, (…) an Optional Protocol to provide a communications procedure for the International Covenant on Economic, Social and Cultural Rights [has been adopted].

TASK/TEXT 8.3.2: ACHIEVING A COMMUNICATIONS PROCEDURE FOR THE CONVENTION ON THE RIGHTS OF THE CHILD – COMMENTARY ON A DRAFT OPTIONAL PROTOCOL

Crinmail 959 – 21 February 2008, <www.crin.org>

Introduction

There is a strong and growing international campaign for the drafting and adoption of an Optional Protocol to the CRC to provide a communications procedure, supported by NGOs, human rights institutions and other bodies from all regions (see <www.crin.org/petitions/petition.asp?petID=1007>).

This paper is intended to move the process on. It includes a draft text of an Optional Protocol to the CRC, with a commentary. The commentary indicates that many of the provisions are drawn from, or adapted from, the instruments establishing existing communications procedures. The text has been developed from various detailed papers prepared over the last few years. We emphasise that we are circulating this draft as a basis for discussion, not as a finalised proposal.

The Convention on the Rights of the Child (CRC) is the only international human rights treaty with a mandatory reporting procedure which does not have, in addition, an existing or draft communications procedure. This is a serious matter of discrimination against children and weakens effective implementation of the CRC.

While children and their representatives can use the mechanisms established under other international instruments to pursue some of their rights, those instruments do not cover, separately or together, the full range and detail of rights for children in the CRC. The Convention guarantees many unique and important rights (see list in Annex 2, below). Furthermore, communications made on behalf of children to the other bodies are not considered by a Committee with special expertise on children's rights. Similar persuasive arguments were made for the development and adoption of the communications' mechanisms under CEDAW and under the new Convention on the Rights of Persons with Disabilities.

The CRC is the most universally ratified of the core human rights instruments, by 193 States. Its two existing Optional Protocols, on Sale of Children, Child Prostitution and Child Pornography and on the Involvement of Children in Armed Conflict, have each achieved more than 100 ratifications. A number of States parties to the CRC are already supportive of the proposal for an Optional Protocol to provide a communications procedure.

There is widespread recognition that the Convention has achieved a new visibility for the rights of children and that it has led to advances on many issues in many regions. But there is also ample evidence, for instance from the reporting process under the Convention and from UN agencies and NGOs, that the rights of millions of children are not adequately respected and that States' legal obligations are in many cases not being fulfilled.

The Committee has highlighted that for rights to have meaning, effective remedies must be available to redress violations. It has also emphasised: "Children's special and dependent status creates real difficulties for them in pursuing remedies for breaches of their rights." (General Comment No. 5.) The drafting and adoption of an Optional Protocol would deter States from breaching children's rights, encourage them to develop appropriate remedies for breaches of children's rights at national level, and provide an external mechanism for children to appeal to when national remedies do not exist or are ineffective.

The reporting system established by the Convention is acknowledged to be one of the most effective in the UN system. A communications procedure would complement States' reporting obligations, enabling individuals and groups to take up non-compliance of rights directly with the Committee, where any existing and effective domestic remedies have been exhausted. Furthermore, as with provisions in the Convention against Torture and in Optional Protocols to CEDAW and to the new Convention on the Rights of Persons with Disabilities, the OP to the CRC could enable the Committee to establish urgent inquiries when it is informed of grave or systematic violations of rights.

The World Conference on Human Rights in its 1993 Vienna Declaration and Programme of Action reiterates the principle of "First Call for Children" and states that "the rights of the child should be a priority in the United Nations system-wide action on human rights."

Children have waited too long for this essential mechanism to reinforce full implementation of their Convention. There should be no further delay. Many standard elements of an Optional Protocol to provide a communications procedure are already established in the Protocols linked to other instruments. Drafting should not be a long drawn out process: States could aim to have the OP open for signature by the 20th anniversary of adoption of the Convention.

Contents

Text of Draft Optional Protocol to provide a communications procedure for the Convention on the Rights of the Child, with commentary. [Not included here.]

Annexes:

- Other communications procedures for international and regional human rights instruments.
- Unique rights for children in the Convention on the Rights of the Child.

ANNEX 1
Existing communications procedures

Communications procedures exist for the following core international instruments, established either through an Optional Protocol or through provisions within the instrument, in order of adoption (some also establish systems for inter-state complaints and for inquiries into reports of grave or systematic violations of rights) (…):

- **International Covenant on Civil and Political Rights**: Optional Protocol adopted and opened for signature, ratification and accession, 16 December 1966; entered into force 23 March 1976 – same dates as adoption and entry into force of ICCPR
- **Convention against Torture and Other Cruel, Inhuman or Degrading Treatment or Punishment**: under article 22; communications procedure entered into force following declarations from 5 States accepting the competence of the Committee, (Convention came into force 26 June 1987)
- **International Convention on the Elimination of All Forms of Racial Discrimination**: under article 14; communications procedure entered into force in 1982, following declarations from 10 States accepting the competence of the Committee (Convention came into force 4 January 1969)
- **Convention on the Elimination of Discrimination against Women**: Optional Protocol adopted and opened for signature, ratification and accession 10 December 1999; entered into force 22 December 2000 (CEDAW entered into force 3 September 1981)
- **International Convention on the Protection of the Rights of All Migrant Workers and Members of Their Families**: Convention entered into force 1 July 2003. under article 77; communications procedure under article 77 will enter into force following declarations from 10 States accepting the competence of the Committee to consider communications
- **Convention on the Rights of Persons with Disabilities** (adopted 13 December 2006, not yet in force – January 2008): Optional Protocol adopted

13 December 2006, not yet in force, subject to entry into force of the Convention, the Protocol will come into force after 10 States have ratified or acceded to it.
- **International Convention for the Protection of All Persons from Enforced Disappearance** (adopted 20 December 2006, not yet in force – January 2008): under article 31, States can declare that they recognise competence of the Committee to consider communications.
- An ad hoc Working Group of the Commission on Human Rights, now the Human Rights Council, has developed an advanced draft of an Optional Protocol establishing a communications procedure to the **International Covenant on Economic, Social and Cultural Rights** [Adopted 10 December 2008].

Regional procedures and mechanisms:

- **African Commission on Human and People's Rights**: An individual, group or organisation can submit a complaint to the African Commission, under article 56 of the African Charter on Human and Peoples' Rights; for details see <www.achpr.org>. A Protocol to the Charter has established the African Court on Human and Peoples' Rights, not yet in operation; the Protocol allows the Court to apply any international or regional instrument in force in the particular State, thus making it a Court which can apply the CRC.
- **African Committee of Experts on the Rights and Welfare of the Child**: Under article 44 of the African Charter on the Rights and Welfare of Children, the Committee of Experts may receive communications from any individual, group or recognised organisation and investigate.
- **Inter-American Commission and Court of Human Rights**: Individuals, groups or organizations can submit complaints to the Inter-American Commission on Human Rights (article 44, American Convention on Human Rights). If the complaint meets certain requirements, and the state has accepted the procedure, the Commission will refer it to the Court; otherwise, the Commission may respond itself (for more information, see <www.cidh.org>).
- **European Court of Human Rights**: individuals may lodge an application with the Court if they consider that they have personally and directly been the victim of a violation of the rights and guarantees set out in the Convention or its Protocols (for details see <www.echr.coe.int/echr>).
- **European Committee of Social Rights**: under a Protocol which came into force in 1998, "collective" complaints of violations of the European Social Charter and Revised Social Charter may be lodged with the European Committee of Social Rights by certain organizations, including NGOs

holding participative status with the Council of Europe and approved for the purpose.

ANNEX 2
Unique rights for children in the CRC

The CRC is a uniquely broad instrument, covering children's civil, political and economic, social and cultural rights. Many of the rights safeguarded by it are not covered by provisions in the International Covenants or other international instruments. Children and their representatives need a communications procedure which enables them to pursue remedies about breaches of the full range of rights, when national remedies are not-existent or ineffective.

Some articles in the CRC mirror guarantees established for "everyone" in the International Covenants or other instruments, underlining that these rights apply equally to children. But many other provisions in the Convention, including the following, provide unique rights for children:

- Right to protection from all forms of discrimination or punishment on the basis of status, activities, expressed opinions or beliefs of the child's parents, guardians or family members; also added disability and ethnic origin to specifically prohibited grounds for discrimination against children (article 2)
- Best interests of the child to be a primary consideration in all actions concerning children (article 3(1))
- States to ensure the child protection and care necessary for his/her welfare, taking account of rights and duties of parents, etc. (article 3(2))
- Institutions, services and facilities for care and protection of children to conform to established standards (article 3(3))
- State respect for appropriate guidance by parents and others in the child's exercise of their rights, respecting the child's evolving capacities (article 5)
- Obligation to ensure maximum survival and development of the child (article 6)
- Right of the child to know and be cared for by parents (article 7)
- Preservation of the child's identity (article 8)
- Right not to be separated from parents unless in best interests with judicial review; right of all interested parties to participate in hearings; right to retain relations and contact with both parents unless contrary to best interests (article 9)
- States obligations in relation to children and parents entering or leaving a state for purposes of family reunification, etc., (article 10)
- Obligations to prevent abduction and non-return of children abroad (article 11)

- Obligation to give due weight to children's expressed views in all matters affecting the child; also to provide opportunity for child to be heard in any judicial or administrative proceedings affecting the child (article 12)
- Child's right to freedom of religion, with respect for parents' rights to provide direction to the child in the exercise of this right, consistent with the child's evolving capacities (article 14)
- Obligation to ensure the child's access to information and material from a diversity of national and international sources (article 17)
- Obligations to support parents in their child-rearing responsibilities, by provision of child care services; also child's best interests to be parents basic concern (article 18)
- Right to protection from "all forms of physical or mental violence while in the care of parents or others (article 19)
- Special protection rights for children deprived of family environment (article 20)
- Specific obligations and safeguards relating to adoption (article 21)
- Special protection for refugee children and those seeking refugee status (article 22)
- Disabled children's right to special care facilitating child's active participation (article23)
- Right of access for child to health-care services and obligations to take specific measures for health; protection from traditional practices prejudicial to health (article 24)
- Right of child cared for outside family to periodic review of care, protection or treatment (article 25)
- Obligation to recover maintenance from those having financial responsibility for the child (article 27)
- School discipline consistent with the child's human dignity, etc (article 28 (2))
- Detailed aims defined for the education of the child (article 29)
- Protection of the right of indigenous child to enjoy their culture, religion and language (article 30)
- Right to rest, leisure and play (article 31)
- Specific protection from economic exploitation and hazardous/harmful work (article 32)
- Obligations to protect children from illicit use of, and involvement in production and trafficking of, drugs (article 33)
- Specific protection from sexual exploitation and abuse including child pornography (article 34)
- Specific obligations to prevent abduction, sale and trafficking of children (article 35)

- Prohibition of life imprisonment of children without possibility of release; arrest, detention, imprisonment of the child only as a last resort and for shortest appropriate period (article 37)
- Specific limitations on recruitment and involvement of children in armed conflict (article 38)
- Rights of child victims to measures for recovery and social reintegration (article 39)
- Distinct aims for juvenile justice systems and rights of children involved (article 40)
- Obligations to make principles and provisions of Convention widely known to adults and children alike (article 42).

The Optional Protocols to the CRC – on the sale of children, child prostitution and child pornography and on the involvement of children in armed conflict – add further unique rights and safeguards.

TASK/TEXT 8.3.3: COMMUNICATIONS PROCEDURE – GO-AHEAD FOR ICESCR SIGNALS GREEN LIGHT FOR CRC

Crinmail 992 – 19 June 2008, <www.crin.org>

GENEVA – The Human Rights Council has adopted an Optional Protocal for a communications procedure to strengthen the protection of economic, social and cultural rights. The Protocol will allow persons to petition an international human rights body about violations of rights guaranteed in the International Covenant on Economic, Social and Cultural Rights (ICESCR).

The move clears the road for work on a parallel instrument for the Convention on the Rights of the Child (CRC). Participants at a recent meeting hinted that States may be unwilling to begin work on a communications procedure to the CRC until the parallel ICESCR instrument had been agreed upon.

NGOs have been campaigning for the establishment of such an instrument, arguing it would allow children and their advocates to appeal when domestic or regional remedies fail or simply do not exist. This would put new pressure on States Parties to fulfil their obligations and also encourage them to provide effective remedies at national level.

More than 400 international and national organisations have signed the petition: "An international call to strengthen the enforcement of the UN Convention on the Rights of the Child by the drafting of an Optional Protocol to provide a communications procedure."

New procedure welcomed

Louise Arbour, UN High Commissioner for Human Rights, welcomed the news. "This is a highly significant achievement," she said. "The Protocol will provide an important platform to expose abuses that are often linked to poverty, discrimination and neglect, and that victims frequently endure in silence and helplessness. It will provide a way for individuals, who may otherwise be isolated and powerless, to make the international community aware of their situation."

Adopted by the Human Rights Council on 18 June, the Protocol is expected to get the final approval by the United Nations General Assembly later this year. Thereafter, the Protocol will enter into force once it has been ratified by ten States.

"Since the adoption of the two core international human rights covenants in 1966, the lack of a complaint procedure for economic, social and cultural rights has been a missing piece in the international human rights protection system," Arbour said.

TASK/TEXT 8.3.4: OPEN-ENDED WORKING GROUP ON AN OPTIONAL PROTOCOL TO THE [CRC] TO PROVIDE A COMMUNICATIONS PROCEDURE

Human Rights Council – 11th session 29 June 2009 (advance unedited version); Resolution 11/1

The Human Rights Council,

Recalling the Principles proclaimed in the Charter of the United Nations and that recognition of the inherent dignity and the equal and inalienable rights of all members of the human family is the foundation of freedom, justice and peace in the world,

Recalling that, in the Vienna Declaration and Programme of Action adopted in June 1993 by the World Conference on Human Rights (A/CONF.157/23), the World Conference reiterated the principle of "First Call for Children" and emphasized that the rights of the child should be a priority in the United Nations system-wide action on human rights,

Welcoming the almost universal ratification of the Convention on the Rights of the Child and the ratification by more than 120 States of each of the two Optional Protocols to the Convention,

Taking note of Council resolution 10/14 of 26 March 2009, in which the Council celebrated the twentieth anniversary of the Convention on the Rights of the Child, and called for effective implementation of the Convention by all States parties to ensure that all children may fully enjoy all their human rights and fundamental freedoms,

Noting with interest general comment No. 5 (2003) of the Committee on the Rights of the Child, in which the Committee emphasized that children's special and dependent status creates real difficulties for them in pursuing remedies for breaches of their rights,

Noting that procedures allowing for individual communications have been established for other core international human rights treaties, namely, the International Covenants on Civil and Political Rights and on Economic, Social and Cultural Rights, and for the International Convention on the Elimination of All Forms of Racial Discrimination, the Convention on the Elimination of All Forms of Discrimination against Women, the Convention against Torture and Other Cruel, Inhuman or Degrading Treatment or Punishment, the International Convention on the Protection of the Rights of All Migrant Workers and Members of Their Families, the International Convention for the Protection of All Persons from Enforced Disappearance and the Convention on the Rights of Persons with Disabilities,

Noting also that children and their representatives lack a communications procedure under the Convention on the Rights of the Child by which communications concerning the effective implementation of the rights set out in the Convention can be considered by an appropriate committee of independent experts,

Recalling the view of the Committee on the Rights of the Child, expressed by its Chairperson in her oral report to the General Assembly at its sixty-third session, that the development of a communications procedure for the Convention on the Rights of the Child would significantly contribute to the overall protection of children's rights,

1. *Decides* to establish an Open-ended Working Group of the Human Rights Council to explore the possibility of elaborating an optional protocol to the Convention on the Rights of the Child to provide a communications procedure complementary to the reporting procedure under the Convention; (...)

TASK/TEXT 8.4: COUNCIL OF EUROPE – LISTEN SERIOUSLY TO THE VIEWS OF CHILDREN

Crinmail 935 – 22 November 2007, <www.crin.org>, <www.coe.int/t/commissioner/Viewpoints/Default_en.asp>

The viewpoint below by Thomas Hammarberg, Commissioner for Human Rights at the Council of Europe, was published on the 18th anniversary of the UN Convention on the Rights of the Child [20 November 2007].

The UN Convention on the Rights of the Child has been a remarkable success. It has not only been ratified by all countries of the world except the United States and Somalia, it has also acted as a catalyst for a series of concrete actions for real implementation of the agreed norms. However, much more needs to be done in several fields to grant children their full rights. One right which has not been ensured in reality is the right of children to have their views taken into account.

The importance of respecting children and their opinions was the main message of the Polish writer, doctor and educationalist, Janusz Korczak, whose teaching came to inspire the drafting of the UN Convention.

In an orphanage in the Warsaw Ghetto during World War II, he, his colleagues and some 190 children practiced the rights of the child for real. In the midst of the horrible brutality outside, they developed a small democracy. They all formed an assembly for important decisions. They agreed upon rules of behaviour and a court was established to deal with offenders (in most cases the "sentence" was to apologize). There was a bill board for messages and a newspaper for news and discussion.

This experiment of child democracy came to a terrible end on 6 August 1942 when the German Nazi soldiers marched them all, staff and children, to a train which would bring them to the gas chamber in Treblinka.

Korczak's example and writings have however not been forgotten. His books are still reprinted in different languages and are still influencing many. However, some of his ideas are still seen as either unrealistic or something for the future.

This seems to apply also the provision in the UN Convention about the views of children:

'States Parties shall assure to the child who is capable of forming his or her own views the right to express those views freely in all matters affecting the child, the views of the child being given due weight in accordance with the age and maturity of the child.'

This provision is probably the least implemented aspect of the Convention. It seems not to be fully understood that this Article 12 places an obligation on governments to ensure that children's views are sought and considered on all matters that affect their lives.

It is time to confront this challenge more concretely. Obviously, there is no clear vision of the content and implication of a child's right to be heard and to participate in decision-making. Therefore, as a first step, goals and standards for the realization of this right need to be spelled out in more concrete and substantive terms.

Implementing this right requires long and short-term objectives and strategies to address social attitudes and behaviours, and to develop viable models for children and adolescents to participate in political and societal decision-making. Mechanisms need to be developed within political bodies that ensure systematic consultation with children and serious consideration of their views.

The objective should be to create a culture of greater receptivity to and respect for children's views. Unfortunately many adults seem to consider this prospect a threat. The issue of children's influence is seen as a 'zero-sum gain' – that is, a situation in which one side wins only if the other side loses. In other words, if children get more power, adults believe they will lose some of theirs and be less able to control the family, or uphold discipline in the classroom.

In some countries, adults have aggressively opposed children's participation in the name of parents' rights or religious principles. To change such entrenched patriarchal attitudes towards children may take some time.

How can this issue be raised in a meaningful way? How can it be shown that there is no contradiction between giving children the possibility of influencing their lives and society, on the one hand, and safeguarding the role of adults to care for, guide and protect children, on the other? How can it be made obvious that this is not a win-lose game, but that all sides stand to gain if adults learn to support children in the exercise of their rights?

Here are some suggested first steps:

1. Children's primary arena is the home. Raising awareness among parents and caretakers about children's right to be heard, and helping them cope with their parenting roles in this respect, must be a priority.
2. The other key arena is the school and kindergarten. Interactive learning, relevant curricula and democratic attitudes and procedures are essential contributions. Such measures should focus on strengthening children's ability to express themselves, to handle democratic processes and to understand society and its problems better. A huge task ahead is capacity-building among teachers and school staff on how to listen to children, enhance dialogue and promote conflict resolution in a democratic manner.
3. Children's organizations advocating for the realization of children's rights could be promoted, and other NGOs working with or for children, such as sports clubs or charity groups, could be encouraged to listen to children and respect their views.
4. Political parties should be encouraged to develop their capacity to consider children's views and enhance children's influence in political affairs.
5. Television, radio and the press should have 'child-friendly' news presentations and make sure that children's views are presented on matters of special concern to them. More child-focused correspondents and young journalists should be welcomed.

6. Steps should be taken to make the justice system child-friendly. The court procedures must be adjusted the meet the needs of children, be they perpetrators, victims or witnesses. Children should have an influence on administrative or judicial decisions relating to themselves, for instance on custody care and adoption.
7. Governments should define issues which have great impact on children's lives and on which they should therefore ought to have a say, for instance family policies, the planning of community facilities, school policies, children's health care and recreation services. They should identify meaningful ways to take children's views into account and ensure that they are representative and relevant. Channels of expression should be explored which are adequate to different age groups, including young children – such as dialogues with pre-schoolers, school councils, opinion polls, representatives and other models. Special measures should be taken to enhance the voice of groups of children with disabilities or other disadvantaged groups and explore how to overcome possible constraints.

These steps would be in line with the vision of Janusz Korczak. Enabling children to express themselves and have their views heard and respected in the home, in the school and in the community from an early age will enhance their sense of belonging – and readiness to take responsibility.

TASK/TEXT 8.5:

TASK/TEXT 8.5.1: BIOLOGICAL ORIGINS OF IVF CHILDREN

Crinmail 903 – 2 August 2007, <www.crin.org> [Source: The Guardian, <www.guardian.co.uk>]

United Kingdom: A right to know – biological origins of IVF children to be stated on birth certificates

LONDON, 1 August 2007 – Children born from donated sperm or eggs will have the information marked on their birth certificates under sweeping changes to fertility laws proposed by an influential group of ministers and peers in the United Kingdom. The move, designed to bolster **childrens' right to know their origins**, is among a raft of far-reaching recommendations the government will consider ahead of its planned reforms of legislation which has been overtaken by science.

The proposals amount to a parliamentary demand for the government to tear up its draft fertility bill, published in May, in favour of a more permissive approach that would see substantial changes in ethically contentious areas, such as the creation of 'saviour siblings,' the use of surplus embryos in research and the need for children conceived through IVF treatment to have a legal father figure.

The joint Commons and Lords panel was set up to scrutinise the draft human tissue bill. Over the past two months the committee has taken evidence from 46 witnesses and received more than 100 written submissions. The report from the 18-member panel, published yesterday, said there must be significant changes when the bill is included in the Queen's Speech in November.

Under existing law, parents are not required to inform children if they are born from donated eggs and sperm. The committee concluded that while a law obliging parents to do so was unenforceable, children should be able to find out the information for themselves from their birth certificates.

Responsibility of State – "If parents want to deceive their children that's their decision, but it is our view that the state should not be complicit in that," said Phil Willis, chair of the committee.

Informing children about their biological origins would ensure they had proper access to donor registers that would allow them to find the identity of their genetic parent, he added.

Among other proposals, the panel urged government to extend the legal limit for storing IVF embryos from five to 10 years, bringing it into line with rules for freezing sperm and eggs.

Further proposals seek to relax laws on the creation of 'saviour siblings,' where children are conceived to save the life of a sick brother or sister. The selection of embryos to be donors of potentially life-saving tissues is currently only permitted if the sick child has a potentially fatal illness, but would be broadened to treat children with any 'serious medical condition,' possibly including autism if a cure was found in future.

See Article 7 of the UN Convention on the Rights of the Child.

TASK/TEXT 8.5.2: RIGHT TO INFORMATION

Crinmail 948 – 15 January 2008, <www.crin.org> [Source: Independent on Sunday]

Twins' marriage sparks debate over rights of adoptees

LONDON, 13 January 2008 – Twins separated at birth and adopted into different families in the United Kingdom married each other without realising that they were related, Lord Alton has revealed. The pair, whose identity has been kept secret, met as adults and married after feeling what the peer described as "an irresistible attraction."

When the couple discovered the truth about their incestuous relationship, they were granted an annulment by the courts, which ruled that their marriage had never actually existed. Their plight sparked widespread debate over the rights of children to know the identity of their birth parents.

Lord Alton, who learnt of the disturbing case from a judge involved in the case, referred to it during a House of Lords discussion on the Human Embryology and Tissues Bill. The Bill, which if passed will relax the rules governing fertility treatment, will be voted on in the Lords on Tuesday.

Lord Alton used the twins' case to support his argument that birth certificates should be changed to include information on both the genetic parents, as well as whether or not the child was conceived by a sperm donor. He insisted: "The state is colluding in a deception. We are opening the door to more cases like this one. The issue here is about human rights."

A German man recently served a two-year prison sentence after fathering four children with his sister, from whom he was separated at birth. The couple are now campaigning for the right to continue their relationship in violation of the country's ban on incest.

TASK/TEXT 8.6: APA ON YOUTH VIOLENCE (AMERICAN PSYCHOLOGICAL ASSOCIATION)

<www.apa.org/ppo/issues/pbviolence.html> – Published by APA in 1996

Some Kids Resilient; Some Kids At Risk

Are some children just prone to violence?

There is no gene for violence. Violence is a learned behavior, and it is often learned in the home or the community from parents, family members, or friends.

Children are more aggressive and grow up more likely to become involved in violence – either as a victimizer or as a victim – if they witness violent acts.

The home is the most fertile breeding place for this situation. A major example: A child who sees a parent or other family member abused is more likely to see violence as a way to solve problems and subsequently be more likely to abuse others.

However, studies do suggest there is a connection between violent behavior and some inherited traits. Research has shown that impulsivity, learning difficulties, low IQ, or fearlessness can make someone prone to violence.

Additionally, rates of violence vary in all groups, but are highest among males.

What do we know about preventing violence in children who seem most vulnerable?

Psychological research has not only demonstrated that violence is learned. It has also identified the factors that put children at the greatest risk of perpetrating or being victimized by violence, along with the prevention and intervention programs that work.

Aggression is often learned at an early age. In fact, according to *Reason to Hope*, the 1994 report by the APA Commission on Violence and Youth, it is possible to predict from an eight-year-old's aggressive behavior in school how aggressive that child will be in adolescence and adulthood – including whether he or she will exhibit criminal and antisocial behavior. **This is why prevention programs that start early in childhood and continue throughout adolescence have the best chance for success.**

(Ideally, the prevention program should even begin before birth; proper pre- and postnatal care can reduce the risk of birth defects that could cause learning difficulties, one reason a child may be susceptible to violent behavior.)

The prevention plan must encompass myriad components of the child's environment, including family members, teachers, peer groups, and media. Effective violence prevention and intervention programs also share three primary characteristics:

- The programs zero in on developmental and sociocultural risk factors that often lead to violence.
- The programs use theory-based intervention strategies with proven track records.

  (These measures are generally less costly and far more effective than building more jails.)
- The programs sustain their preventive approach over time.

There are methods that can achieve enduring effects:

- The High/Scope Perry Preschool Program [<www.highscope.org>], designed to help 3–4 year-olds at risk for failing school, included a 2-year classroom program and weekly teacher home visits. At age 19, fewer youth who had participated in the program had come to the attention of juvenile authorities

or had been arrested. Participants also showed greater literacy, higher employment levels, and greater attendance at college or vocational school.
- Providing young parents help in dealing with stress has shown promise in preventing later aggressive and antisocial behaviors by their children. In one study, the children of a group of parents who received help for 2 1/2 years – including assistance with finances and housing expenses, day care, and pediatric exams for their kids – attended school more, required fewer special services, and were rated more positively by their teachers. The children of the parent group that didn't receive assistance were more likely to stay out all night without their mother's knowledge, were cruel to animals, and exhibited aggressive behavior toward their siblings and parents.

What keeps some children who have been raised in violent circumstances themselves from becoming violent?
Some children demonstrate a resiliency, almost from birth, that protects them from becoming violent or that makes them less vulnerable to the effects of violence. Psychological research suggests that resilience can also come from early experiences that counter the negative effects of violence. These experiences include:

- Positive role models; exposure to a greater number of positive than negative behaviors.
- Development of self-esteem and self-efficacy.
- Supportive relationships, including those with teachers and friends.
- Sense of hope about the future.
- Belief in oneself.
- Strong social skills.
- Good peer relationships.
- A close, trusting bond with a nurturing adult outside the family.
- Great empathy and support from the mother or mother figure.
- The ability to find refuge and a sense of self-esteem in hobbies and creative pursuits, useful work, and assigned chores.
- The sense that one is in control of one's life and can cope with whatever happens. (...)

Where do we go from here?
The process by which violence is taught is circular: It begins in the family, expanding through the culture of the larger society in which a child grows and matures and then again is reinforced or discouraged in the family.

The search for ways to help children learn more appropriate behaviors (i.e., nonviolent responses to life stressors) requires a close look at institutional practices, public policies, and media programming that perpetuate violent attitudes, images, and behaviors.

When parents demean and strike each other or their children, when children are encouraged to be bullies or fight back on the playground, and when they have easy access to real or toy guns and other weapons, violence is being taught.

When stereotypes and prejudice frame interactions with people who are different from ourselves, the scene is being set for violence. Glorifying war and relishing violence in competitive sports may reinforce violent behavior.

When violence and sexual aggression are combined in the media, in song lyrics, in multimedia computer games, and in the vernacular, the message of violence (including sexual assault) is reinforced.

(…) Resources spent on positive learning and social opportunities in the lives of young children add up to dollars that we don't have to spend, sooner or later, on public safety and punishment programs. Public policy makers should be guided by this information.

Rather than waiting until violence has been learned and practiced and then devoting increased resources to hiring policemen, building more prisons, and sentencing three-time offenders to life imprisonment, it would be more effective to redirect the resources to early violence prevention programs, particularly for young children and preadolescents.
– APA Commission on Violence and Youth

See also Resolution on Violence in Video Games and Interactive Media, APA, 17 August 2005, <www.apa.org/releases/resolutiononvideoviolence.pdf>.

TASK/TEXT 8.7: UNITED KINGDOM – CHILD AGGRESSION WARNING TO PARENTS

Crinmail 924 – 16 October 2007, <www.crin.org>

16 October 2007 – Parents who fail to stop toddlers lashing out at other children risk creating the next generation of violent criminals, new research warns. Scientists also found mothers who smoke during pregnancy and parents on low incomes are more likely to find their children become aggressive.

Efforts to prevent child violence should focus on improving parenting, as well as the behaviour of children, according to Richard Tremblay, Professor of Paediatrics at the University of Montreal, Canada.

Speaking ahead of a conference at the Royal Society in London, Professor Tremblay said: "Physical aggression in children is a major public problem. It is not only an indicator of aggression in adulthood but it also leads to other serious behavioural problems such as alcohol and drug abuse, violent crimes and continues the cycle of abusive parenting. Identifying the factors which stop children becoming well socialised adults should help us design preventative measures which are employed at the right time in a child's development. These should put an appropriate emphasis on the behaviour of the parents, as well as that of the child."

Professor Tremblay continued: "Developmental studies show that infants aged three to four years old are more physically aggressive than adults. Learning how not to be violent, which mostly takes place during the pre-school years, is dependent on both genetic and environmental factors. These range from the type of parental care a child receives to whether its mother smoked when pregnant. Research has shown, for example, that nicotine affects the development of areas of a baby's brain which are responsible for emotional control."

TASK/TEXT 8.8: KINDER HABEN RECHTE!

Germany – Bundesministerium der Justiz, Publikationen: ***Meine Erziehung – da rede ich mit!*** und ***Ich habe Rechte***, <www.bmj.de/publikationen>, 20 September 2007

Quelle: Referat Presse- und Öffentlichkeitsarbeit des Bundesministeriums der Justiz

BERLIN, 20 September 2007 – Deutschland feiert heute den Weltkindertag. Unter dem Motto "Kinder haben Rechte" finden in über 400 deutschen Städten und Gemeinden Kinder- und Familienfeste statt. Die Rechte der Kinder und der Schutz der Kinder vor Gewalt und sexueller Ausbeutung müssen unser aller Anliegen sein.

"Auch juristisch machen wir uns für die Rechte von Kinder und Jugendlichen stark. Wir haben den strafrechtlichen Schutz von Kindern vor sexuellen Missbrauch verbessert und im Juli dieses Jahres einen Gesetzentwurf zur Erleichterung familiengerichtlicher Maßnahmen bei Gefährdung des Kindeswohls auf den Weg gebracht. Besonders wichtig ist mir das Recht auf eine gewaltfreie Erziehung," sagte Bundesjustizministerin Brigitte Zypries.

Solche Gesetze sind wichtig, doch nicht nur neue Gesetze helfen, die Situation von Kindern und Jugendlichen zu verbessern. "Wir müssen Kinder und Jugendliche auch über ihre Rechte informieren und ihnen Mut machen, bei gravierenden Problemen in der Familie Beratung und Hilfe von Dritten in Anspruch zu nehmen. Das Bundesjustizministerium hat deshalb die **Broschüre *Meine Erziehung – da rede ich mit!*** erstellt," sagte Zypries.

Nach der **Broschüre *Ich habe Rechte*** ist dies die zweite Publikation des Bundesjustizministeriums zum Thema Kinderrechte. Der neue Ratgeber gibt nicht nur Auskunft darüber, ob Jugendliche den Abwasch machen oder den Müll runterbringen müssen, er erklärt auch, wo junge Menschen im Notfall Hilfe bekommen können.

TASK/TEXT 8.9: A HOME REMEDY FOR JUVENILE OFFENDERS

New York Times – Published: February 20, 2008
<www.nytimes.com/2008/02/20/nyregion/20juvenile.html?ex=1204261200&en=835043d8d89cf8f6&ei=5070&emc=eta1>

When Jacob Rivera, 15, was resentenced in May on an assault conviction, he felt he had received a "blessing." Only months earlier he had been sentenced to a year in state custody, and he had already spent weeks bouncing between a juvenile detention center in the Bronx and a residential treatment campus upstate. Two of his older siblings had spent time in those facilities and, he said, had "come out a mess." He could see his future.

But the court gave him a second chance because his case had not been properly reviewed for inclusion in a new alternative sentencing program, which the city started in February 2007. The program, called the Juvenile Justice Initiative, sends medium-risk offenders back to their families and provides intensive therapy.

The city says that in just a year, it has seen significant success for the juveniles enrolled, as well as cost savings from the reduced use of residential treatment centers.

Under the program, Jacob went back home on probation, and he and his family were assigned a counselor, Eddy Lee, who visited the two-bedroom Bronx apartment that the teenager shares with his mother, Michelle Rivera, her husband, a younger brother and other relatives.

Within weeks, the situation improved as Mr. Lee provided intensive counseling to the family, with the aim of defusing what had become an increasingly angry relationship between Jacob and his mother. Instead of screaming at Jacob when he refused to comply with her curfew, Ms. Rivera called Mr. Lee. Over time, Mr. Lee persuaded her to agree to be less strict if her son would agree to be more forthcoming about his whereabouts, and more responsible.

Soon Jacob started meeting curfew and began passing his court-ordered drug tests and staying in school. If he continues on this course, he will end his probation in July, Mr. Lee said.

By the standards of juvenile justice, Jacob is a resounding success. And he is not alone. The city said that in the year since the program began, fewer than 35 percent of the 275 youths who have been through it have been rearrested or violated probation.

State studies found that more than 80 percent of male juvenile offenders who had served time in correctional facilities were rearrested within three years of their release, usually on more serious charges.

While in-home services mean that hundreds of teenagers with criminal records are returned to their communities, city officials say it is a trade they are willing to make. "It's an uphill battle," says Ronald E. Richter, the city's family services coordinator. "These young people and their families present complex challenges."

But whether the children go to residential correctional facilities or not, they come back to the community eventually anyway, Mr. Richter said, and the program "helps parents learn how to supervise and manage their adolescents so that they act responsibly instead of engaging in dangerous behaviors."

Every year, hundreds of children in the city under 16 are found guilty of crimes ranging from graffiti to assault. They are tried and sentenced in the family courts; more serious crimes like murder are usually sent to the criminal courts.

Until the Juvenile Justice Initiative, family court judges had few options for dealing with youngsters convicted of less-serious crimes. They could place them on probation and hope for the best, or send them to upstate residential centers. The decision would typically depend as much on the gravity of the crime as on the stability of the child's family. Judges are more likely to send a child into state custody if the home situation is complicated or unsafe.

"We were locking up way too many children, " said Leslie Abbey, who runs the program for the city's *Administration for Children's Services*. "It was relied on too heavily, and it wasn't working."

The problem with incarceration, as juvenile justice reformers saw it, was that it could make behavior worse by introducing teenagers to even more hardened youths.

Some states and other counties in New York, including Westchester, have been experimenting for years with intensive in-home and in-community therapy for children who have significant criminal records but are **not psychopathic**.

The basic idea is to reach and help **borderline** youths at a moment of crisis, and turn them away from a more serious criminal path. By treating them in the context of their families and environments rather than in isolation, officials found that recidivism was usually less than half that of residential correction programs. The city says that it hopes its program will be as successful, but that it will take many years before it can be sure. Still, at roughly $17,000 per child, such in-home therapy programs cost a fraction of the annual expense of keeping a child in secure detention, which can be $140,000 to $200,000.

In fact, the financial incentive is such that both the city and state are rapidly moving away from residential detention. Gladys Carrión, the commissioner of the state's Office of Children and Family Services, recently announced that she would close six nonsecure facilities, a cut that will save the state $16 million a year.

The elimination of detention beds puts more pressure on the city to succeed.

It is a tough order, but Qadriyyah Razzaaq, for one, is a believer.

Ms. Razzaaq has been caring for John Whittington, 15, the son of a cousin, since he was 5. But last year, Ms. Razzaaq, a home health aide with her own children to care for and a job that often requires her to work 12 hours a day, was ready to give up on John, who was getting into ever more serious trouble.

First, on a dare, he set a fire in a school toilet, she said. Then he began running with gangs, and his graffiti appeared in hallways in his apartment building. Finally, she said, he robbed someone of an iPod.

When he was arrested for the iPod theft, she didn't even go to detention to get him. "I was so angry," she recalled. "I thought, 'I am going to leave him there and teach him a lesson'."

When Ms. Razzaaq heard about the Juvenile Justice Initiative, she was not optimistic. "He had already been in counseling," she said, "I didn't believe it would help."

But to her amazement, the therapy at home made a difference. The counselors told her that John had been keeping secrets from her because he was afraid she would abandon him, the way his mother had. She spent more time with him alone, something he seemed to crave.

His behavior improved. John will still fail the seventh grade for a third time at the end of the school year, but so far he has not violated probation.

At home, Ms. Razzaaq has a new level of trust. "We have little problems, but we speak about it first," she said. "He doesn't wait to be caught.

"I know his future is so much better than it would have been if he had gone upstate."

TASK/TEXT 8.10:

TASK/TEXT 8.10.1: SEXUAL (YOUTH) RIGHTS – CHOICE FOR YOUTH

<www.choiceforyouth.org> (visited 22 June 2008)

CHOICE for youth and sexuality foundation is a youth organisation based in the Netherlands that promotes **sexual and reproductive health and rights** [SRHR] for young people, both on national and international level.

Sexual and reproductive rights are specifically important for young people, because they are the most vulnerable group and the choices they make can influence their whole future. Young people around the world often do not have the information they need and are not protected against harmful practices. Young people around the world and especially in developing countries have the highest risk of contracting HIV/Aids and for girls aged 15–19 pregnancy is the first cause of death. Therefore, CHOICE is aiming at the realisation of **sexual and reproductive rights** for all young people around the world.

What are SRHR?
SRHR is a term for a very broad range of topics that basically encompasses freedom within human's sexuality and having children. That freedom is rooted in having access to information and services to make decisions that are based on individual choice, not last resort or ignorance. Examples include receiving accurate HIV/AIDS and STI information as well as being informed about contraceptive options. Moreover, it includes having no fear of stigma for one's sexual orientation and identity. No person should be coerced or forced into sexual actions against their will. All people should remain autonomous over their bodies and sexuality. These rights extend so far as they do not impede the rights of another person.

In the International Conference on Population and Development in Cairo 1994, the following definition of reproductive health was drafted [**Platform of Action, ICPD, 1999**]:

7.2. *Reproductive health is a state of complete physical, mental and social well-being and not merely the absence of disease or infirmity, in all matters relating to the reproductive system and to its functions and processes. Reproductive health therefore implies that people are able to have a satisfying and safe sex life and that they have the capability to reproduce and the freedom to decide if, when and how often to do so. Implicit in this last condition are the right of men and women to be informed and to have access to safe, effective, affordable and acceptable methods of family planning of their choice, as well as other methods of their choice for regulation of fertility which are not against the law, and the right of access to appropriate health-care services that will enable women to go safely through pregnancy and childbirth and provide couples with* ***the best chance of having a healthy infant****.*

In line with the above definition of reproductive health, reproductive health care is defined as the constellation of methods, techniques and services that contribute to reproductive health and well-being by preventing and solving reproductive health problems. It also includes sexual health, the purpose of which is the enhancement of life and personal relations, and not merely counselling and care related to reproduction and sexually transmitted diseases.

This definition includes the notion that reproductive health cannot be had without sexual health and rights.

The WHO [World Health Organization] refers to the below definitions on their official website:

> "A state of physical, emotional, mental and social well-being related to sexuality …
> Not merely the absence of disease, dysfunction or infirmity.
> … Requires a positive and respectful approach to sexuality and sexual relationships, as well as the possibility of having pleasurable and safe sexual experiences, free of coercion, discrimination and violence.
> For sexual health to be attained and maintained, the sexual rights of all persons must be respected, protected and fulfilled."

The definition of Sexual Rights referred to by the WHO is the following:
"Sexual rights embrace human rights that are already recognized in national laws, international human rights documents and other consensus statements. They include the right of all persons, free of coercion, discrimination and violence, to:

- *the highest attainable standard of sexual health, including access to sexual and reproductive health care services;*
- *seek, receive and impart information related to sexuality;*
- *sexuality education;*
- *respect for bodily integrity;*
- *choose their partner;*
- *decide to be sexually active or not;*
- *consensual sexual relations;*
- *consensual marriage;*
- *decide whether or not, and when, to have children; and*
- *pursue a satisfying, safe and pleasurable sexual life.*

The responsible exercise of human rights requires that all persons respect the rights of others."

Charter

CHOICE for youth and sexuality foundation promotes the sexual and reproductive health and rights of young people worldwide. Sexual and reproductive rights are universal human rights, which means that everyone has the right to decide freely about his or her own sexual life and the number and spacing of children. These rights are essential for health and well-being, for a life free of illness and disease related to the sexual and reproductive system. Sexual and reproductive rights apply to everyone without discrimination or stigma based on gender, religion, cultural and traditional values, sexual orientation, nationality, socio-economic status, ethnicity, health status or age. Therefore, they apply to young people [**above 18? See *and discuss* Article 5 CRC, JW**] as much as they apply to adults.

Right to express and enjoy one's sexuality

Young people have the right to express and enjoy their sexuality, free from stigma, discrimination and judgement. Young people are free to decide and express themselves about their sexual and reproductive lives, including the free choice of a partner and sexual orientation. These choices must involve mutual respect, full consent and equality between the partners.

Right to health care

All young people have the right to sexual and reproductive health services that are available, safe, affordable, accessible, qualified and youth-friendly. These services include access to a variety of contraceptives and access to safe abortion. Health care can only be youth-friendly if young people meet no difficulties and barriers (social, legal, regulatory) to receive medical attention and counselling. Sexual and reproductive health care also includes information on the full range of contraceptive methods, STI and HIV/AIDS, prevention and treatment, safe motherhood and planned parenthood. Sexual and reproductive health services must be confidential and guarantee young people's privacy.

Right to be free from sexual violence

Every person has the right to live a life free from violence, including sexual violence. Sexual violence, coercion and harmful practices, such as Female Genital Mutilation, must be abandoned. Sex education and youth friendly services must be implemented to assure the highest degree of safety for young people's sexual and reproductive rights. Sex education and services for girls and boys must include mutual respect and gender equity in sexual relationships.

Right to information
Young people have the right to access to accurate and correct information about sexuality and reproduction, in order to make informed choices about one's sexual and reproductive life. Sex education should include the issues of sexual development, reproduction, contraception and relationships. It should also have a gender component that explains the differences between boys and girls and guarantees mutual respect of both. Sex education must reach youth at school as well as outside of school. It must be gender sensitive and should start early, before young people reach puberty and before they have developed established patterns of behaviour. Peer education can serve as an effective means to inform young people in a youth-friendly way and to bridge the gap between age differences and differences in cultural values.

Youth participation
Young people are important actors within the subject of sexual and reproductive health and rights. Society has the responsibility to provide young people with the means to behave in a responsible way. Young people should be respected and given the possibility to shape and express their own opinions in this field and live thereafter. Therefore, young people should be actively involved in the fulfilment of these rights. Youth participation in the design, decision-making, implementation and evaluation of policies, programmes and services for young people are crucial for their success.

TASK/TEXT 8.10.2: INTERNATIONAL PLANNED PARENTHOOD FEDERATION – COMPREHENSIVE SEXUALITY EDUCATION

<www.ippf.org>, Resources, Guides and toolkits, Framework for Comprehensive Sexuality Education (<www.ippf.org/NR/rdonlyres/CE7711F7-C0F0-4AF5-A2D5-1E1876C24928/0/Sexuality.pdf>), accessed 17 July 2009

A Definition of Comprehensive Sexuality Education

A rights-based approach to Comprehensive Sexuality Education seeks to equip young people with the **knowledge, skills, attitudes and values** they need to determine and enjoy their sexuality – physically and emotionally, individually and in relationships. It views 'sexuality' holistically and within the context of emotional and social development. It recognizes that information alone is not enough. Young people need to be given the opportunity to acquire essential life skills and develop positive attitudes and values.

Comprehensive Sexuality Education must help young people to:

- Acquire accurate information: On sexual and reproductive rights; information to dispel myths; references to resources and services.
- Develop life skills: Such as critical thinking, communication and negotiation skills, self-development skills, decision making skills; sense of self; confidence; assertiveness; ability to take responsibility; ability to ask questions and seek help; empathy.
- Nurture positive attitudes and values: Open-mindedness; respect for self and others; positive selfworth/esteem; comfort; nonjudgmental attitude; sense of responsibility; positive attitude toward their sexual and reproductive health.

Comprehensive Sexuality Education covers a broad range of issues relating to both the physical and biological aspects of sexuality, and the emotional and social aspects. It recognizes and accepts *all* people as sexual beings and is concerned with more than just the prevention of disease or pregnancy. (…)

Seven Essential Components of Comprehensive Sexuality Education

1. **Gender** – exploring gender roles and attributes; understanding perceptions of masculinity and femininity within the family and across the life cycle; society's changing norms and values; manifestations and consequences of gender bias, stereotypes and inequality.

2. **Sexual and reproductive health** – understanding STIs and HIV, what they are and how to prevent them; pregnancy options and information; sexual response; living with HIV; how to use condoms; anatomy; sexuality and the life cycle (i.e., puberty, menopause, sexual problems).

3. **Sexual citizenship** – knowledge of international human rights and national policies, laws and structures; understanding that culture is dynamic; available services and resources and how to access them; participation; practices and norms; advocacy; choice; protection; consent and the right to have sex only when you are ready.

4. **Pleasure** – understanding that sex should be enjoyable and not forced; that it is much more than intercourse; sexuality as part of everybody's life; the biology and emotions behind the human sexual response; gender and pleasure; masturbation; love, lust and relationships; interpersonal communication; the diversity of sexuality; the first sexual experience; consent; alcohol and drugs and the implications of their use.

5. **Violence** – exploring the various types of violence towards men and women, and how they manifest; rights and laws; support options available and seeking help; community norms (power, gender) and myths; prevention, including personal safety plans; self-defence techniques; understanding the dynamics of victims and abusers; appropriate referral mechanisms for survivors.

6. **Diversity** – recognizing and understanding the range of diversity in our lives (e.g., faith, culture, ethnicity, socio-economic status, ability/disability, HIV status and sexual orientation); a positive view of diversity; recognizing discrimination, its damaging effects and being able to deal with it; developing a belief in equality; supporting young people to move beyond just tolerance (see 'Olsson's Stairs of Tolerance' below).

Olsson's adapted 'Stairs of Tolerance'

Tolerance ↑↑:

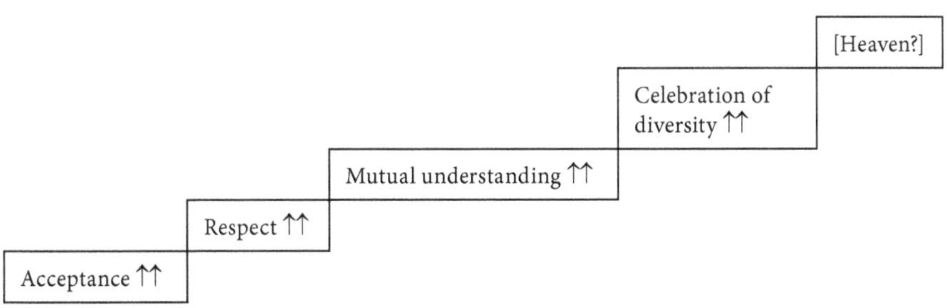

Tolerance ↓↓:

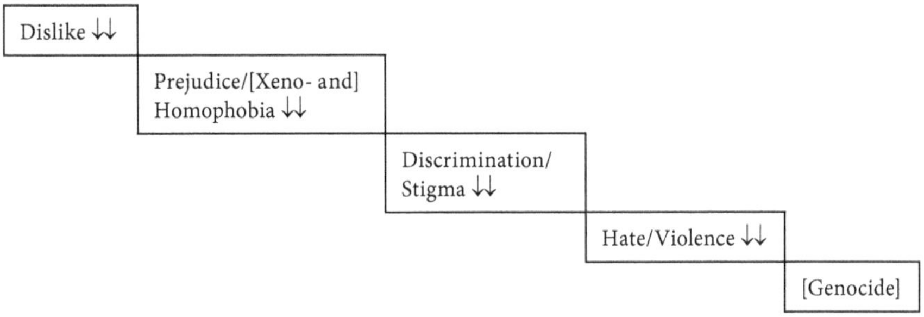

7. **Relationships** – different types of relationships (e.g., family, friends, sexual, romantic, etc.), emotions, intimacy (emotional and physical), rights and responsibilities, power dynamics, and recognizing healthy and unhealthy or coercive relationships.

TASK/TEXT 8.11: BRAVERY AND CHILDREN'S RIGHTS

<www.childsrights.org/html/site_en/index.php?c=>, 19 January 2009

"She is coping bravely." That is title given by the daily newspaper *Le Temps* to its (written and spoken) press review on Ramona. And indeed Ramona played her role smilingly in front of photographs, appearing in three complete pages in (German language) *Blick* and *Schweizer Illustrierte*, and in (French language) l'*Illustré* [<www.illustre.ch/index.cfm?id=3136>].

Who is Ramona? "The country's youngest mum," age 13, from Solothurn, Switzerland. Unaware of being pregnant, she gave birth last December to her son, the fruit of a youth romance. This January, media outlets rushed in to get the scoop, but Ramona's family was vigilant: access to Ramona and her baby was limited to one press conference.

Such an optimistic and supportive family atmosphere certainly spared Ramona a stigmatizing and miserabilist media coverage, such as our country experienced in a former case. This is positive. And yet …

Who can imagine the middle term effects of such a show on the life of two children (three with the father), endowed as it is with the right to be protected against arbitrary interference with their privacy, by virtue of article 16 of the CRC? Will Ramona and Nico be able to shield themselves from the further curiosity of media? Is there any reflection at all on child protection, sexual health, and the role models we want to provide our youth with?

Focused on anecdote, sensation, and cuteness, the media coverage *(Blick)* however takes on a vaguely academic tone when explaining that under the Criminal Code, the two parents face no persecution for their sexual encounter, due to their age proximity.

Embarking on psycho-social notions, that same newspaper, echoed by others, points out that its reporter has taken up "the role of communication coach" for Ramona. "Some of the questions, too personal, were thus given no answer." The rooster perched on the roof of the henhouse …

The investigative report of the very serious *Tages Anzeiger* to make out whether a pregnancy can really go unnoticed until coming to its end, makes it really clear that children's rights are far from being a priority for some Swiss media. (…)

TASK/TEXT 8.12: CANADA – SUPREME COURT TO HEAR CHILD RIGHTS AND RELIGIOUS BELIEFS CASE

Crinmail 984 – 20 May 2008, <www.crin.org> [Source: Globe and Mail, Canada]

20 May 2008 – By the age of 14, a Winnipeg girl known as A.C. felt that she had the right to prevent doctors from running roughshod over her religious beliefs and forcing a blood transfusion on her.

"I will not violate Jehovah God's command to abstain from blood," she said at the time. "I have dedicated my life to Him. Turning my back on God, who made my life possible, is not a compromise I am willing to make."

Her plea fell on deaf ears. A.C. was forcibly given a transfusion to replace blood she had lost through Crohn's disease – on Easter Sunday of 2006, no less.

The medical contretemps reaches the Supreme Court of Canada today, obliging the court to delve into the issue of when a mature minor can refuse medical treatment based on religious views.

The case of A.C. v. Director of Child and Family Services focuses specifically on older minors who are forced to accept treatment, even though they have the mental capacity to make treatment decisions.

On the day the drama began, A.C. had admitted herself to a Winnipeg hospital to receive treatment for Crohn's, a chronic inflammation of the gastrointestinal tract that can cause bleeding from the bowel. Doctors quickly obtained a treatment order from a judge.

In a brief to the Supreme Court, her lawyers – Allan Ludkiewicz and David C. Day – quote the child describing the experience as "painful spiritually, mentally, emotionally and even physically. Having someone else's blood pumped through my veins, stressing my body, caused me to reflect on how my rights over my body could be taken away by a judge who did not care enough to talk with me. … That day, my tears flowed non-stop."

The legal brief argues that a provision in the Manitoba Child and Family Services Act that authorises involuntary medical intervention is out of step with generations of judge-made law and with Charter of Rights guarantees to equality, freedom of religion and life, liberty and security of the person.

In an opposing brief, Manitoba Crown counsel Deborah Carlson and Nathaniel Carnegie maintain that any Charter violation that might exist would be more than justified by the importance of protecting children.

"Age as a prerequisite for the ability to make important decisions is a pervasive feature of the law throughout Canada," they said. "Legislation regulating marriage, voting, driving, drinking, contracting, will-making and many other areas establish minimum ages which, in turn, deny privileges or impose disabilities on those persons younger than a certain age."

The Crown lawyers said a child's capacity to make a treatment choice can also fluctuate, depending on the nature of the illness and the medication he or she might be taking.

"Moreover, there may be significant differences in the way adolescents make decisions, which may give rise to legitimate concerns about the outcome of these decisions," they said.

Lawyers Cheryl Milne and Mary Birdsell – arguing for a legal intervenor, Justice for Children and Youth, a Toronto legal aid clinic serving low-income youth – maintain that international law puts emphasis on allowing children to make choices. "By placing too much weight on children as future citizens, the danger is that we ignore the present assaults on their dignity premised on a paternalistic, 'it's for your own good' approach," they say in a brief to the court.

TASK/TEXT 8.13: EDUCATION FOR SUCCESSFUL PARENTING (ESP)

<www.eduparents.org/about.html>, visited 13 July 2009

Mission

The mission of Education for Successful Parenting (ESP) is to improve children's wellbeing by **preparing youth for parenting – before they conceive the next generation of children.**

We offer instructional materials, onsite classes, and consulting to youth and programs.

Vision

We envision a world in which …

- All parents are prepared, knowledgeable, competent and confident in handling their responsibilities.
- All children are safe and loved.

Our Philosophy

We believe "successful parents" are those who …

- Fulfill their responsibility to provide for, protect, and nurture their children
- Navigate the challenges and enjoy the journey of parenting
- Raise children who can realize their unique potential and dreams.

Our Goals
[1.] Improve the overall health and capabilities of children

- Improve preconception health awareness among youth
  - Reduce prenatal exposure to alcohol, drugs, and tobacco
  - Increase use of folic acid and prenatal care
- Prevent child maltreatment
- Increase child safety and wellbeing

[2.] Improve social and economic environments for families

- Encourage personal life-planning and goal-setting for family formation
- Reduce teen pregnancy
- Increase fatherhood involvement.

TASK/TEXT 8.14: PROTECTION AND PARTICIPATION IN THE NEW INFORMATION AND COMMUNICATIONS ENVIRONMENT

Recommendation CM/Rec(2009)5 of the Committee of Ministers [of the Council of Europe] to member states on measures to protect children against harmful content and behaviour and to promote their active participation in the new information and communications environment *(Adopted by the Committee of Ministers on 8 July 2009 at the 1063rd meeting of the Ministers' Deputies)*, <www.coe.int>, Committee of Ministers, Adopted texts, Recommendations (…)

1. Protecting freedom of expression and human dignity in the information and communications environment by ensuring a coherent level of protection for minors against harmful content and developing children's media literacy skills is a priority for the Council of Europe.

2. The risk of harm may arise from content and behaviour, such as online pornography, the degrading and stereotyped portrayal of women, the portrayal and glorification of violence and self-harm, demeaning, discriminatory or racist expressions or apologia for such conduct, solicitation (grooming), the recruitment of child victims of trafficking in human beings, bullying, stalking and other forms of harassment, which are capable of adversely affecting the physical, emotional and psychological well-being of children.

3. Attention should be drawn to the normative texts adopted by the Committee of Ministers designed to assist member states in dealing with these risks and, as a corollary, in securing everyone's human rights and fundamental

freedoms. These texts include Recommendation CM/Rec(2008)6 on measures to promote the respect for freedom of expression and information with regard to Internet filters; the 2008 Declaration on protecting the dignity, security and privacy of children on the Internet; Recommendation CM/Rec(2007)11 on promoting freedom of expression and information in the new information and communications environment; Recommendation Rec(2006)12 on empowering children in the new information and communications environment; and Recommendation Rec(2001)8 of the Committee of Ministers on self-regulation concerning cyber content (self-regulation and user protection against illegal or harmful content on new communications and information services).

4. **There is a need to provide children with the knowledge, skills, understanding, attitudes, human rights values and behaviour necessary to participate actively in social and public life, and to act responsibly while respecting the rights of others.**

5. There is also the need to encourage trust and promote confidence on the Internet, in particular by neutral labelling of content to enable both children and adults to make their own value judgments regarding Internet content.

6. The Committee of Ministers recommends that member states, in co-operation with private sector actors and civil society, develop and promote coherent strategies to protect children against content and behaviour carrying a risk of harm while advocating their active participation in and best possible use of the new information and communications environment, in particular by:

- encouraging the development and use of safe spaces (walled gardens), as well as other tools facilitating access to websites and Internet content appropriate for children;
- promoting the further development and voluntary use of labels and trustmarks allowing parents and children to easily distinguish non-harmful content from content carrying a risk of harm;
- promoting the development of skills among children, parents and educators to understand better and deal with content and behaviour that carries a risk of harm;
- bringing this recommendation and its appended guidelines to the attention of all relevant private and public sector stakeholders.

Appendix to Recommendation CM/Rec(2009)5

Guidelines

I. Providing safe and secure spaces for children on the Internet

7. The development of new communication technologies and the evolution of the Internet have led to a vacuum in appropriate measures to protect children against

content carrying a risk of harm. While the protection against content in the offline [real, JW] world is, in most cases, much easier to guarantee, it has become significantly more difficult to do so in the online world, especially considering that every action to restrict access to content is potentially in conflict with the right to freedom of expression and information as enshrined in Article 10 of the European Convention on Human Rights (...). It should be recalled that this fundamental right and freedom is a primary objective of the Council of Europe and its member states; at the same time states also have a legitimate right, and even **an obligation, to protect children from content which is unsuitable or inappropriate.**

8. While parental responsibility and media education are of primary importance in effectively protecting children, there are also tools and methods which can assist parents and educators in their efforts to inform and guide children about the Internet and Information and Communication Technologies (ICTs). The provision of safe and secure spaces (walled gardens) for children on the Internet and the Council of Europe's online game "Through the Wild Web Woods" are notable examples of such tools and methods.

9. On this basis, member states, in co-operation with the private sector, the media and civil society, are encouraged to develop safe and secure spaces on the Internet for children safely to explore and participate actively in the information society, in particular by:

- creating safe and secure websites for children, for example by developing age-appropriate online portals;
- developing professional standards for the maintenance of such Internet websites and portals, particularly with regard to links and references to other sites;
- raising awareness of these safe and secure Internet websites for children, in particular among parents, educators, content developers and their respective associations;
- considering the integration of the benefits of these safe and secure Internet websites in school curricula, and in educational materials such as "The Internet literacy handbook," a Council of Europe publication.

II. Encouraging the development of a pan-European trustmark and labelling systems

10. There is an increasing demand for systems which help to protect children from content carrying a risk of harm. The development of Internet content filters has provided one form of protection which subsequently led to the adoption of Recommendation CM/Rec(2008)6 of the Committee of Ministers on measures

to promote the respect for freedom of expression and information with regard to Internet filters.

11. Apart from automated content rating and filtering, there are initiatives which exist to label online content on a voluntary basis and labelling which is performed by the content creator. Among them, the Internet Content Rating Association (part of the Family Online Safety Institute (FOSI)) and PEGI Online (part of the Pan-European Game Information (PEGI) plus system), both of which have led to the development of systems which promote descriptions of online content.

12. The labelling of online content contributes to the development of safe and secure spaces for children on the Internet. However, the effectiveness and trustworthiness of labelling systems greatly depend on the accountability of those responsible for these systems and their interoperability. The development of a pan-European trustmark for responsible labelling systems – prepared in full compliance with the right to freedom of expression and information in accordance with Article 10 of the European Convention on Human Rights – would enhance these systems and initiatives, facilitate the provision of safe and secure spaces for children on the Internet and avoid and/or mitigate their exposure to content and behaviour carrying a risk of harm.

13. Online content which is not labelled should not however be considered dangerous or less valuable for children, parents and educators. Labelling has limited scope and should be seen as one possibility, among others, to promote the democratic participation and protection of children on the Internet in countering content and behaviour that carry a risk of harm.

14. On this basis, member states, in co-operation with the private sector, the media and civil society, are encouraged to develop and promote the responsible use of labelling systems for online content, in particular in:

- creating a pan-European trustmark for labelling systems of online content. Criteria for this trustmark would include:
  - adherence to human rights principles and standards, including the right to provide for effective means of recourse and remedy, for example the possibility to re-assess labelling when users and/or creators/authors of online content claim that content has been incorrectly labelled;
  - labelling systems are provided and used on a voluntary basis, both by creators/authors and users;
  - the inadmissibility of any form of censorship of content;
  - respect for the editorial independence of media and media-like online content services;
  - regular review of the labelled content, for example by introducing a maximum length of time of the validity of the label;

- promoting initiatives for the interoperability of labelling systems, including the creation of a unique pan-European logo which signals the suitability of content for different age groups;
- developing principles for the age-appropriate rating of content, taking into account the different traditions of member states;
- promoting research and development, in particular as regards the possibility to label content through metadata;
- raising awareness among parents and educators about the advantages of labelling content in order to facilitate access to safe and secure spaces for children on the Internet;
- assessing and evaluating labelling systems and their effectiveness, in particular with regard to their compliance with Article 10 of the European Convention on Human Rights and the accessibility and affordability of the services emanating from these systems for the general public.

III. Promoting Internet skills and literacy for children, parents and educators

15. Safe and secure spaces on the Internet and the labelling of online content can contribute to making the use of the Internet an enjoyable and confidence-building experience for children. It should, however, be accepted that it is not possible to eliminate entirely the danger of children being exposed to content or behaviour carrying a risk of harm, and that consequently media (information) literacy for children, parents and educators remains a key element in providing coherent protection for children against such risks.

16. On this basis, member **states, in co-operation with the private sector, associations of parents, teachers and educators, the media and civil society**, are encouraged to promote **media (information) literacy for children, young people, parents and educators**, in order to prepare them for possible encounters with content and behaviours carrying a risk of harm, in particular by:

- raising awareness and developing critical attitudes about both the benefits and risks for children freely using the Internet and ICTs;
- **adapting school curricula to include practical learning about how best to use the Internet and ICTs, and encouraging teachers to analyse and counter sexism in online content which shapes children's attitudes**;
- informing children, parents and educators about safe and secure spaces on the Internet and trustworthy labels for online content;
- fostering knowledge and practical understanding of the human rights dimensions of labelling systems and filtering mechanisms, and their potential risks to freedom of expression and information, *inter alia* by drawing the attention of all relevant stakeholders to the Council of Europe's standard-setting instruments and tools in this field.

TASK/TEXT 8.15: INDIA – CHILD RIGHTS ELECTION MANIFESTO LAUNCHED

Crinmail 1077 – 21 April 2009, <www.crin.org>

With the first round passed in India's marathon five-phase general election, **CRY (Child Rights and You)** has revealed that it sent a child rights manifesto to all political parties demanding children's rights take centre stage. The Child Rights Manifesto (...) lists the issues that are affecting children's lives in India, but are conspicuously absent from the pre-election agenda of political parties.

"Like in the last Elections in 2004, we have been watching the political arena closely to see if children's issues are reflected in the agenda of candidates," said education activist and CRY Director Ila Hukku. "We find that despite the large number of children's organizations pointing out this noticeable gap, political parties continue to ignore the children of India and their issues. So we are now going directly to the parties, knocking on doors to remind candidates that the ultimate winners should be children." CRY representatives will also be speaking to candidates directly in face to face meetings.

"As the nation goes to vote, we are reminding voters that one fourth of the country – as many as 400 million citizens – will not vote because they are children. As voters and candidates, we are charged with the responsibility to see to it that their interests do not slip off the political radar," said Dipankar Mazumdar, Director, Youth & Development Support.

Without the right to choose their political leaders, children cannot directly ensure that:

- 70 of every 1000 children born do not die each year.
- Every 2nd child under 5 is not malnourished.
- **All children are in school and complete formal schooling**: the 52% children who are out of school are enrolled and ensured complete formal schooling.
- **All children have access to adequate nutrition and equal opportunities.**
- **Children are protected from child labour, abuse and trafficking.**

Child rights can only become central to a country's political agenda if its people choose to make it priority by ensuring government accountability to actualise the rights of children. Children must be looked on as equal citizens, entitled to equal rights. CRY is calling on voters to voice the rights of children – thinking of the promises made to them in the Constitution to live a life of dignity that must include food, health, shelter, education, protection and play.

TASK/TEXT 8.16: UNITED STATES – LEGAL REPRESENTATION FOR ABUSED AND NEGLECTED CHILDREN

Crinmail 1118 – 20 October 2009, <www.crin.org>

A new study released this week, co-authored by First Star, a nonprofit advocacy group for neglected and abused children, and the Children's Advocacy Institute at the University of San Diego Law School, has concluded that states across the US are inadequately representing the legal rights of abused and neglected children in dependency hearings.

The study, entitled "A Child's Right to Counsel: A National Report Card on Legal Representation for Abused and Neglected Children," has given each state a grade based on a 100 point scale that evaluated six criteria in the states' legislation. States that received the poorest grades do not have any laws on the books mandating that lawyers be appointed to represent children in court. Even in states where lawyers are appointed, legislation does not require lawyers to be trained in domestic violence issues or to treat the child in the same way they would another client. Instead lawyers are often allowed (or even encouraged) to act in what they perceive to be the child's best interest, without taking into account the child's wishes.

Based on their findings, First Star and Children's Advocacy Institute have ranked 29 out of the 50 states with failing scores of C's, D's and F's. The organisations hope their work will inspire legislation reform at all levels of government.

The issue is especially relevant in 2009. "In every economic downturn, the children are the first to suffer," explains Amy Harfeld, First Star Executive Director. In our current economic recession, child abuse rates have quickly skyrocketed 30 percent over the past year, while state and federal funding for abused children has decreased at a similar rate.

Harfeld cautions Americans to "make sure that just because children don't vote, don't have lobbyists, that they're not getting shortchanged by the government." Right now, there's no continuity in legislation around the country. Harfeld asserts all children should have equal rights, whether they live in Massachusetts (which received an outstanding score of 104) or across the border in Maine (which received a pitiful 52).

Harfeld outlined the three avenues for significant reform:

- The American Bar Association is considering adopting a Model Act, co-written by First Star, that would require lawyers to be appointed to represent children in all dependency hearings and would give children the right to receive "client directed" representation. If successfully put into place, the ABA Model Act could put pressure on state and federal legislators to follow suit.

- On the state level, First Star encourages advocates to continue to pressure state legislators for reform. Unless you live in Connecticut or Massachusetts, your state's legal protections of neglected and abused children could be improved.
- The Child Abuse Prevention and Treatment Act is slated to be reauthorised in Congress in the coming year. Without a significant outpouring of attention surrounding this issue, this opportunity will pass by and no legal reform will be included in the bill.

TASK/TEXT 8.17: EVOLVING CAPACITIES EXPLAINED

Gerison Lansdown, *Evolving capacities* explained, in: Measuring Maturity; Understanding children's evolving capacities, CRIN Review 23, October 2009, pp. 7–9 (references omitted), <www.crin.org/docs/CRIN_review_23_final.pdf>

We all continue to develop knowledge and skills throughout our lives. But all societies acknowledge that the pace of growth is most accentuated in children, who acquire new capacities at an extraordinary rate. In most countries, an adult – at whatever age adulthood is determined in any given society – is legally presumed to be capable of taking responsibility for their actions. During childhood, the reverse applies: children are presumed to lack the competence to take responsibility for themselves and are therefore understood to need social and legal protection in accordance with their perceived immaturity and vulnerability.

The Convention on the Rights of the Child (CRC) provides a framework that recognises the right of every child to such protection. Article 5 states that parents or legal guardians "shall (…) provide, *in a manner consistent with the evolving capacities of the child*, appropriate direction and guidance in the exercise by the child of the rights recognized in the present Convention."

This requires that guidance provided by parents or legal guardians must be directed towards promoting respect for the rights of the child, and must respect the extent to which the child is capable of exercising their rights on his or her own behalf. For example, every child has a right to a name from birth. Clearly, a newborn baby lacks the capacity to determine their own name, so this right is exercised on their behalf by their parents. However, if the divorced mother of a 14-year-old child wishes to remarry, the child will have the competence, and therefore the right, to decide for themselves if they want to adopt the name of the prospective stepfather.

However, children's rights are not contingent on the ability to exercise their rights on their own behalf, or on legal age limits. All the rights embodied in the CRC extend to all children. The question is whether children themselves can exercise those rights or whether this responsibility is undertaken on their behalf by parents or other carers, and how decisions are made in a manner consistent with the child's best interests.

Three ways of understanding evolving capacities

The concept of children's evolving capacities can be understood through three conceptual frameworks: [a developmental, an emancipatory and a protective concept].

A developmental concept

The CRC can be seen as a tool for promoting children's development, competence and emerging personal autonomy. **Article 6** is the platform for other developmental principles throughout the Convention. It asserts that States parties shall "ensure to the maximum extent possible the survival and development of the child." In imposing these obligations, it clearly extends the mandate to the (...) [child's **holistic**, that is, **physical, emotional, social, moral and intellectual**] development. This [holistic] breadth is affirmed in the following articles:

- **Article 23 [para 3]** stresses the right to opportunities conducive to the [mentally or physically disabled] child's "achieving the fullest possible social integration and individual development including his or her **cultural and spiritual** development."
- **Article 27** explicitly recognises the importance of an adequate standard of living for children's "physical, mental [emotional and intellectual], spiritual, moral and social development."
- **Articles 28 and 29** spell out the role of [school] education in developing the "child's personality, talents and mental [emotional, social, moral and intellectual] and physical abilities to their fullest potential."
- **Article 31** acknowledges the importance of the right to play in children's [holistic] development.

These articles place obligations on States parties and other actors with responsibility for children to **fulfill** children's right to development of their optimum evolving capacities.

An emancipatory concept

The CRC includes a number of articles that acknowledge the child as an agent in the exercise of rights [with the connected right to parental direction and guidance in article 5, JW]:

- **Article 12** guarantees the right to express views [inclusion and participation, JW].
- **Articles 13 to 17** address rights to freedom of expression, religion, association, privacy and access to information.

Children have the right to respect for their capacities and to exercise their rights in accordance with their levels of competence. States have obligations to **respect** these rights [(that is, not to unnecessarily interfere with a parent's responsibility to provide direction and guidance); to **protect** these rights (that is, protect a child against a parent's lack of responsibility to provide *appropriate* direction and guidance); and to **fulfill** these rights (that is, educate and empower parents to provide direction and guidance *in a manner consistent with the evolving capacities of the child*)].

In reality, however, our knowledge of children's capacities for informed and rational decision-making remains limited. While research has been undertaken to identify pre-determined physiological or psychological factors linking age with the acquisition of competencies, this has largely been conducted in North America and Europe in laboratory conditions far removed from children's day-to-day lives. Even within these strict parameters, findings have varied widely. There is also inadequate comparative data to examine the contrasting competencies of children in different social, economic and cultural environments. Indeed, a growing body of recent research suggests the need for extreme caution in drawing conclusions on age-related competencies, arguing instead that a wide range of other factors influence how children function. Clearly, there is a need for much more research before definitive conclusions can be drawn. Nevertheless, neither legal frameworks nor policy and practice in most countries give sufficient consideration to the importance of recognising and respecting the capacities of children in the exercise of their rights.

A protective concept

Children have the right to protection from participation in or exposure to activities likely to cause them harm. For example, the CRC includes rights to protection from violence, economic exploitation and sexual abuse. States have [positive] obligations to [**fulfill**] these [child protective] rights.

[Positive, that is active and pro-active r]espect for children's evolving capacities to take responsibility for their own decisionmaking needs to be balanced against their relative lack of experience [that is, emotional immaturity, JW]. But it is also important not to undermine children's own capacities for contributing to their own protection [that is, parents should not be over-protective, JW].

The extent to which children are likely to be at risk of harm from potential threats is significantly mediated by a number of factors:

- the child's own personality and strengths;
- the level of support [affection-based direction and guidance, JW] afforded by key adults in the child's life;
- the degree of agency [or emotional maturity] experienced by the child in coping with the situation;
- the degree of social and cultural acceptance of the behaviour.

Traditionally, protection has been viewed as a one-way process, with adults as agents and children as recipients. The reality is more complex: legislation, strategies, policies and programmes designed to protect children need to recognise children's capacities to contribute towards their own protection and allow them to build on those strengths.

Encouraging children's capacities

The issue of evolving capacities highlights the necessary balance between, on the one hand, children's right to recognition of their increasing levels of responsibility in the exercise of their rights as they acquire the capacity to do so; and on the other, the need for protection in accordance with their relative youth and immaturity.

The CRC provides a mechanism for ensuring appropriate respect for children's rights without exposing them prematurely to the full responsibilities normally associated with adulthood. It requires primary consideration to be given to the rights of the child while taking into account their views and capacity for independent decision-making.

Of course, cultural considerations must be factored into the equation. Behaviours considered dangerous in one society are taken as the norm in another. Assumptions of responsibility deemed beyond a small child's capacities in one culture are part of their daily experience in another. Some limitations imposed on children are considered to be socially acceptable while others deny them opportunities to develop, and prevent adults from seeing what children are capable of achieving.

Support and encouragement can enable children to achieve skills and competencies far greater than would be possible through threats and punishment. Promoting children's best interests requires recognition of the importance of their evolving capacities. But it also necessitates a better understanding of how to provide protection in environments that respect and advance children's capacities. This poses challenges in almost every sphere of children's rights, including freedom of religion and association, access to information and the media, ages of criminal responsibility and sexual consent, the right to education, and the role of work.

There is an urgent need for better understanding of how to promote the cultural change necessary to ensure that children are protected in accordance with their evolving capacities, and that they are respected, whatever the level of those capacities.

9. AIMS OF EDUCATION – PSYCHOLOGICAL, HUMAN RIGHTS/ CITIZENSHIP AND CHILD RIGHTS EDUCATION

TASK/TEXT 9.1: UK – PUPILS TO GET LESSONS IN SOCIAL AND EMOTIONAL SKILLS

Crinmail 896 – 10 July 2007 (<www.crin.org>)

New Children's Secretary Ed Balls [UK] wants pupils in all primary and secondary schools to have lessons in social and emotional skills by 2011. A programme already running in 60 per cent of primary schools, which helps children deal with anger, anxiety and conflicts, is being rolled out across the nation. It has had a major impact on behaviour and attainment, the government says. The programme focuses on encouraging pupils to understand themselves, manage their feelings and promotes social skills and the understanding of others.

Benefits

The Department for Children, Schools and Families said such skills aided employability and social mobility by ensuring all children, regardless of background, had confidence in their abilities and understood how to interact with others in a positive way. The programme is also aimed at promoting positive behaviour and regular school attendance which will have an impact on learning and emotional health. (…)

Improved behaviour

(…) Mr Balls said many of the schools that had implemented the programme had seen a marked improvement in the way their pupils interacted with each other both inside and outside the classroom.

"The programme will make sure that all children understand the importance of being confident and interacting with other children in a respectful and positive manner," he added.

Research suggests the programme works best when it is embedded across the curriculum – rather than being confined to one lesson. For example sports lessons are seen as a good opportunity to teach pupils how to be good losers and gracious winners, and English literature offers a chance to examine characters who have overcome difficulties.

[New behaviour powers]
But Mr Balls was keen to stress that emotional intelligence lessons come hand in hand with the tough new behaviour powers which came into force in April this year. They aimed to remove any ambiguity over a teacher's right to confiscate items, such as mobile phones, give detentions and physically remove violent pupils from the classroom. "These initiatives give teachers some powerful tools to make sure good behaviour and an atmosphere of respect are the norm in all schools," Mr Balls added.

TASK/TEXT 9.2: AN EXAMPLE OF PSYCHOLOGICAL EDUCATION FOR STUDENTS, PARTNERS, PARENTS – BY APA (AMERICAN PSYCHOLOGICAL ASSOCIATION)

APA on Controlling Anger – Before It Controls You
<www.apa.org/topics/controlanger.html>

We all know what anger is, and we've all felt it: whether as a fleeting annoyance or as full-fledged rage. Anger is a completely normal, usually healthy, human emotion. But when it gets out of control and turns destructive, it can lead to problems – problems at work, in your personal relationships, and in the overall quality of your life. And it can make you feel as though you're at the mercy of an unpredictable and powerful emotion. This brochure is meant to help you understand and control anger.

WHAT IS ANGER?

The Nature of Anger
Anger is "an emotional state that varies in intensity from mild irritation to intense fury and rage," according to Charles Spielberger, PhD, a psychologist who specializes in the study of anger. Like other emotions, it is accompanied by physiological and biological changes; when you get angry, your heart rate and blood pressure go up, as do the levels of your energy hormones, adrenaline, and noradrenaline.

Anger can be caused by both external and internal events. You could be angry at a specific person (Such as a coworker or supervisor) or event (a traffic jam, a canceled flight), or your anger could be caused by worrying or brooding about your personal problems. Memories of traumatic or enraging events can also trigger angry feelings.

Expressing Anger

The instinctive, natural way to express anger is to respond aggressively. Anger is a natural, adaptive response to threats; it inspires powerful, often aggressive, feelings and behaviors, which allow us to fight and to defend ourselves when we are attacked. A certain amount of anger, therefore, is necessary to our survival. On the other hand, we can't physically lash out at every person or object that irritates or annoys us; laws, social norms, and common sense place limits on how far our anger can take us.

People use a variety of both conscious and unconscious processes to deal with their angry feelings. The three main approaches are expressing, suppressing, and calming. Expressing your angry feelings in an assertive – not aggressive – manner is the healthiest way to express anger. To do this, you have to learn how to make clear what your needs are, and how to get them met, without hurting others. Being assertive doesn't mean being pushy or demanding; it means being respectful of yourself and others.

Anger can be suppressed, and then converted or redirected. This happens when you hold in your anger, stop thinking about it, and focus on something positive. The aim is to inhibit or suppress your anger and convert it into more constructive behavior. The danger in this type of response is that if it isn't allowed outward expression, your anger can turn inward – on yourself. Anger turned inward may cause hypertension, high blood pressure, or depression.

Unexpressed anger can create other problems. It can lead to pathological expressions of anger, such as passive-aggressive behavior (getting back at people indirectly, without telling them why, rather than confronting them head-on) or a personality that seems perpetually cynical and hostile. People who are constantly putting others down, criticizing everything, and making cynical comments haven't learned how to constructively express their anger. Not surprisingly, they aren't likely to have many successful relationships.

Finally, you can calm down inside. This means not just controlling your outward behavior, but also controlling your internal responses, taking steps to lower your heart rate, calm yourself down, and let the feelings subside.

As Dr. Spielberger notes, "when none of these three techniques work, that's when someone – or something – is going to get hurt."

Anger Management

The goal of anger management is to reduce both your emotional feelings and the physiological arousal that anger causes. You can't get rid of, or avoid, the things or the people that enrage you, nor can you change them, but you can learn to control your reactions.

Are You too Angry?

There are psychological tests that measure the intensity of angry feelings, how prone to anger you are, and how well you handle it. But chances are good that if you do have a problem with anger, you already know it. If you find yourself acting in ways that seem out of control and frightening, you might need help finding better ways to deal with this emotion.

Why Are Some People More Angry Than Others?

According to Jerry Deffenbacher, PhD, a psychologist who specializes in anger management, some people really are more "hotheaded" than others are; they get angry more easily and more intensely than the average person does. There are also those who don't show their anger in loud spectacular ways but are chronically irritable and grumpy. Easily angered people don't always curse and throw things; sometimes they withdraw socially, sulk, or get physically ill.

People who are easily angered generally have what some psychologists call a low tolerance for frustration, meaning simply that they feel that they should not have to be subjected to frustration, inconvenience, or annoyance. They can't take things in stride, and they're particularly infuriated if the situation seems somehow unjust: for example, being corrected for a minor mistake.

What makes these people this way? A number of things. One cause may be genetic or physiological: There is evidence that some children are born irritable, touchy, and easily angered, and that these signs are present from a very early age. Another may be sociocultural. Anger is often regarded as negative; we're taught that it's all right to express anxiety, depression, or other emotions but not to express anger. As a result, we don't learn how to handle it or channel it constructively.

Research has also found that family background plays a role. Typically, people who are easily angered come from families that are disruptive, chaotic, and not skilled at emotional communications.

Is it Good to "Let it All Hang Out?"

Psychologists now say that this is a dangerous myth. Some people use this theory as a license to hurt others. Research has found that "letting it rip" with anger actually escalates anger and aggression and does nothing to help you (or the person you're angry with) resolve the situation.

It's best to find out what it is that triggers your anger, and then to develop strategies to keep those triggers from tipping you over the edge.

STRATEGIES TO KEEP ANGER AT BAY

Relaxation

Simple relaxation tools, such as deep breathing and relaxing imagery, can help calm down angry feelings. There are books and courses that can teach you relaxation techniques, and once you learn the techniques, you can call upon them in any situation. If you are involved in a relationship where both partners are hot-tempered, it might be a good idea for both of you to learn these techniques.

Some simple steps you can try:

- Breathe deeply, from your diaphragm; breathing from your chest won't relax you. Picture your breath coming up from your "gut."
- Slowly repeat a calm word or phrase such as "relax," "take it easy." Repeat it to yourself while breathing deeply.
- Use imagery; visualize a relaxing experience, from either your memory or your imagination.
- Nonstrenuous, slow yoga-like exercises can relax your muscles and make you feel much calmer.

Practice these techniques daily. Learn to use them automatically when you're in a tense situation.

Cognitive Restructuring

Simply put, this means changing the way you think. Angry people tend to curse, swear, or speak in highly colorful terms that reflect their inner thoughts. When you're angry, your thinking can get very exaggerated and overly dramatic. Try replacing these thoughts with more rational ones. For instance, instead of telling yourself, "oh, it's awful, it's terrible, everything's ruined," tell yourself, "it's frustrating, and it's understandable that I'm upset about it, but it's not the end of the world and getting angry is not going to fix it anyhow."

Be careful of words like "never" or "always" when talking about yourself or someone else. "This!&*%@ machine never works," or "you're always forgetting things" are not just inaccurate, they also serve to make you feel that your anger is justified and that there's no way to solve the problem. They also alienate and humiliate people who might otherwise be willing to work with you on a solution.

Remind yourself that getting angry is not going to fix anything, that it won't make you feel better (and may actually make you feel worse).

Logic defeats anger, because anger, even when it's justified, can quickly become irrational. So use cold hard logic on yourself. Remind yourself that the world is "not out to get you," you're just experiencing some of the rough spots of daily life. Do this each time you feel anger getting the best of you, and it'll help you get a more balanced perspective. Angry people tend to demand things: fairness, appreciation, agreement, willingness to do things their way. Everyone wants these things, and we are all hurt and disappointed when we don't get them, but angry people demand them, and when their demands aren't met, their disappointment becomes anger. As part of their cognitive restructuring, angry people need to become aware of their demanding nature and translate their expectations into desires. In other words, saying, "I would like" something is healthier than saying, "I demand" or "I must have" something. When you're unable to get what you want, you will experience the normal reactions – frustration, disappointment, hurt – but not anger. Some angry people use this anger as a way to avoid feeling hurt, but that doesn't mean the hurt goes away.

Problem Solving

Sometimes, our anger and frustration are caused by very real and inescapable problems in our lives. Not all anger is misplaced, and often it's a healthy, natural response to these difficulties. There is also a cultural belief that every problem has a solution, and it adds to our frustration to find out that this isn't always the case. The best attitude to bring to such a situation, then, is not to focus on finding the solution, but rather on how you handle and face the problem.

Make a plan, and check your progress along the way. Resolve to give it your best, but also not to punish yourself if an answer doesn't come right away. If you can approach it with your best intentions and efforts and make a serious attempt to face it head-on, you will be less likely to lose patience and fall into all-or-nothing thinking, even if the problem does not get solved right away.

Better Communication

Angry people tend to jump to – and act on – conclusions, and some of those conclusions can be very inaccurate. The first thing to do if you're in a heated discussion is slow down and think through your responses. Don't say the first thing that comes into your head, but slow down and think carefully about what you want to say. At the same time, listen carefully to what the other person is saying and take your time before answering. Listen, too, to what is underlying the anger. For instance, you like a certain amount of freedom and personal space, and your "significant other" wants more connection and closeness. If he or she starts complaining about your activities, don't retaliate by painting your partner as a jailer, a warden, or an albatross around your neck.

It's natural to get defensive when you're criticized, but don't fight back. Instead, listen to what's underlying the words: the message that this person might feel neglected and unloved. It may take a lot of patient questioning on your part, and it may require some breathing space, but don't let your anger – or a partner's – let a discussion spin out of control. Keeping your cool can keep the situation from becoming a disastrous one.

Using Humor

"Silly humor" can help defuse rage in a number of ways. For one thing, it can help you get a more balanced perspective. When you get angry and call someone a name or refer to them in some imaginative phrase, stop and picture what that word would literally look like. If you're at work and you think of a coworker as a "dirtbag" or a "single-cell life form," for example, picture a large bag full of dirt (or an amoeba) sitting at your colleague's desk, talking on the phone, going to meetings. Do this whenever a name comes into your head about another person. If you can, draw a picture of what the actual thing might look like. This will take a lot of the edge off your fury; and humor can always be relied on to help unknot a tense situation.

The underlying message of highly angry people, Dr. Deffenbacher says, is "things oughta go my way!" Angry people tend to feel that they are morally right, that any blocking or changing of their plans is an unbearable indignity and that they should NOT have to suffer this way. Maybe other people do, but not them!

When you feel that urge, he suggests, picture yourself as a god or goddess, a supreme ruler, who owns the streets and stores and office space, striding alone and having your way in all situations while others defer to you. The more detail you can get into your imaginary scenes, the more chances you have to realize that maybe you are being unreasonable; you'll also realize how unimportant the things you're angry about really are. There are two cautions in using humor. First, don't try to just "laugh off" your problems; rather, use humor to help yourself face them more constructively. Second, don't give in to harsh, sarcastic humor; that's just another form of unhealthy anger expression.

What these techniques have in common is a refusal to take yourself too seriously. Anger is a serious emotion, but it's often accompanied by ideas that, if examined, can make you laugh.

Changing Your Environment

Sometimes it's our immediate surroundings that give us cause for irritation and fury. Problems and responsibilities can weigh on you and make you feel angry at the "trap" you seem to have fallen into and all the people and things that form that trap.

Give yourself a break. Make sure you have some "personal time" scheduled for times of the day that you know are particularly stressful. One example is the working mother who has a standing rule that when she comes home from work, for the first 15 minutes "nobody talks to Mom unless the house is on fire." After this brief quiet time, she feels better prepared to handle demands from her kids without blowing up at them.

Some Other Tips for Easing Up on Yourself

Timing: If you and your spouse tend to fight when you discuss things at night – perhaps you're tired, or distracted, or maybe it's just habit – try changing the times when you talk about important matters so these talks don't turn into arguments.

Avoidance: If your child's chaotic room makes you furious every time you walk by it, shut the door. Don't make yourself look at what infuriates you. Don't say, "well, my child should clean up the room so I won't have to be angry!" That's not the point. The point is to keep yourself calm.

Finding alternatives: If your daily commute through traffic leaves you in a state of rage and frustration, give yourself a project – learn or map out a different route, one that's less congested or more scenic. Or find another alternative, such as a bus or commuter train.

Do You Need Counseling?

If you feel that your anger is really out of control, if it is having an impact on your relationships and on important parts of your life, you might consider counseling to learn how to handle it better. A psychologist or other licensed mental health professional can work with you in developing a range of techniques for changing your thinking and your behavior.

When you talk to a prospective therapist, tell her or him that you have problems with anger that you want to work on, and ask about his or her approach to anger management. Make sure this isn't only a course of action designed to "put you in touch with your feelings and express them" – that may be precisely what your problem is. With counseling, psychologists say, a highly angry person can move closer to a middle range of anger in about 8 to 10 weeks, depending on the circumstances and the techniques used.

What About Assertiveness Training?

It's true that angry people need to learn to become assertive (rather than aggressive), but most books and courses on developing assertiveness are aimed at people who don't feel enough anger. These people are more passive and acquiescent than the average person; they tend to let others walk all over them. That isn't something that most angry people do. Still, these books can contain some useful tactics to use in frustrating situations.

Remember, you can't eliminate anger – and it wouldn't be a good idea if you could. In spite of all your efforts, things will happen that will cause you anger; and sometimes it will be justifiable anger. Life will be filled with frustration, pain, loss, and the unpredictable actions of others. You can't change that; but you can change the way you let such events affect you. Controlling your angry responses can keep them from making you even more unhappy in the long run.

TASK/TEXT 9.3: EDUCATION FOR DEMOCRATIC CITIZENSHIP AND HUMAN RIGHTS

Global Human Rights Education list, email 7 November 2007 (Press contact in the Council of Europe: Ulvi Akhundlu, Press officer)

STRASBOURG, 6 November 2007 – Committed, vigorous and concerted national action is essential to ensure proper integration and implementation of human rights education in the school system, participants in a two-day Regional European meeting in Strasbourg concluded today.

"The development of **education for democratic citizenship and human rights** should be seen as a priority in the best interest of all nations. It contributes positively to the effectiveness of the national education system as a whole, which in turn plays a fundamental role in economic, social and political development," said Ibrahim Wani, Chief of the Research and Right to Development Branch of OHCHR.

The event was organised jointly by the Council of Europe, the Office of the UN High Commissioner for Human Rights (OHCHR), the United Nations Educational, Scientific and Cultural Organization (UNESCO) and the OSCE Office for Democratic Institutions and Human Rights (OSCE/ODIHR). Over 200 experts from governments of the Council of Europe and OSCE member states, NGOs and other bodies attended the meeting.

"The protection of Human Rights, democracy and the rule of law are the overall aims of our organisation," said Ólöf Ólafsdóttir, Head of Department of School and Out-of-School Education of the Council of Europe. "Since our mandate is to promote these common values, it is clearly necessary to ensure that these values are properly understood and embraced – through education."

Linda King, Chief of Section for the Promotion of Rights and Values in Education of UNESCO said that many avenues were open for strengthening responsible and coordinated partnerships: "Today, there is a strong call to build enhanced partnerships where each and everyone participates to bring a unique contribution to the cause of human rights education."

The meeting participants also noted significance of promotion of human rights education for ensuring peace and security. "Human rights education is an area widely recognised and accepted by governments and civil society as being instrumental to establishing and maintaining peaceful and democratic societies built on principles of respect for human rights," said Kirsten Mlačak, Head of Human Rights Department of the OSCE/ODIHR.

The co-organisers of this meeting have invited education practitioners to make submissions for a Compendium of good practices in human rights education in the school system, including citizenship education and education for mutual respect and understanding. The aim of this resource, currently under development, is to facilitate exchange of experiences and networking among relevant actors.

Follow up to the Regional European Meeting will be given at the UNESCO International Conference on Human Rights Education in October 2008, which is organised in the framework of the commemoration of the 60th anniversary of the Universal Declaration of Human Rights.

The Council of Europe also plans to host an inter-institutional meeting on teacher training in citizenship and human rights education in 2008.

TASK/TEXT 9.4: INDIA – CHILD RIGHTS TO BE TAUGHT IN SCHOOL

Crinmail 929 – 1 November 2007, <www.crin.org> [Source: Daily News and Analysis India; <www.dnaindia.com>]

NEW DELHI, 1 November 2007 – The National Commission for Protection of Child Rights (NCPCR) in India has written to district collectors to ask that articles from the United Nations Convention on the Rights of the Child are read out in every class, and morning assemblies, at least twice a week.

Children will now be educated about their rights and the laws protecting them in their classrooms.

Since children are least likely to be aware of their rights and the laws meant to protect them, the NCPCR wants the move to begin from 14 November, [national] Children's Day, to make the day meaningful for them.

Besides schools, the NCPCR wants hostels, orphanages, juvenile observation homes, children's homes and shelter homes etcetera also to take up this activity.

"Despite having certain rights and laws, children never complain against the atrocities or the humiliation they face. They are simply not aware about what to do and where to go in such situations. Hence, it is important [to] let them know of articles, laws and issues related to their rights so that they can stand up and speak against atrocities," said a member of NCPCR.

Accordingly, children will be told about their rights in schools and at home. They will be informed that they have the right to be protected from being hurt and mistreated in body or mind.

TASK/TEXT 9.5: EDUCATION – FEARS OVER CHILD RIGHTS EDUCATION MISPLACED

Crinmail 959 – 21 February 2008, <www.crin.org>

Fears that human rights education for children will undermine parents and families have been quashed by strong evidence that it has the opposite effect, according to Canadian researchers.

"Children who learn their human rights under the Convention on the Rights of the Child also learn their responsibility to respect the rights of others, including their parents," said Dr Katherine Covell from Cape Breton University.

Dr Covell and Dr Brian Howe have been monitoring the impact of children's rights education in Canada and the UK. They are in New Zealand to study a national project aimed at supporting the development of New Zealand early childhood education centres and schools as "communities that know, promote and live human rights and responsibilities."

"Far from reducing respect for parents and teachers, this approach to education results in improved child-adult relationships, along with better classroom behaviour and academic results," said Ced Simpson, director of New Zealand's initiative.

Mr Simpson was commenting on fears expressed by the Maxim Institute that human rights-based education may undermine the role of parents and act against the interests of children.

"Experience in Canada and the UK shows that such fears are groundless, and often based on ignorance of the Convention on the Rights of the Child," Mr Simpson said.

"The Convention on the Rights of the Child clearly reinforces the role of parents and families, emphasises that action should be in the 'best interests of the child,' and ties children's exercise of their human rights to their 'evolving capacities'."

"Responsibilities are clearly addressed by the international human rights framework, including the Convention on the Rights of the Child, and greater respect and more socially responsible behaviour is one of the most striking outcomes of human rights-based education."

New Zealand ratified the UN Convention on the Rights of the Child in 1993. All but two UN member states have ratified the Convention, making it the most widely ratified international human rights treaty in history. Article 42 of the Convention creates an obligation under international law to teach children their rights.

Although studies have shown little compliance with this requirement, the New Zealand Curriculum launched last November after extensive public consultation, requires that "respect for themselves, others and human rights" be "evident in the school's philosophy, structures, curriculum, classrooms, and relationships."

TASK/TEXT 9.6: ENGLAND – HUMAN RIGHTS ADDED TO CITIZENSHIP CURRICULUM

Association of Teachers and Lecturers (<www.atl.org.uk>), ATL Education News, 2 July 2008 (Global Human Rights Education list, email 3 July 2008)

Secondary schools in England are to have a brand new addition to the citizenship curriculum. Human rights will soon form part of the subject's syllabus, following the launch of a teacher resource pack for the new programme at an east London school yesterday.

A collaboration between Amnesty International UK, the Ministry of Justice, the British Institute of Human Rights and the Department for Children, Schools and Families resulted in the development of *Right Here, Right Now: Teaching citizenship through human rights.*

Lessons about identity and diversity will be taught as part of the addition to the curriculum.

Justice minister Michael Wills stated: "Ensuring everyone within a school understands their rights and responsibilities brings home the importance of respecting the rights of others."

And it is hoped that the programme will help stimulate debate and action among pupils, following the first annual citizenship week to occur in England that took place last month.

"I firmly believe it will help citizenship education become more inspiring, motivating and inclusive for young people," said Amnesty International director Kate Allen.

TASK/TEXT 9.7: KEEP THE COOL IN SCHOOL – PROMOTING NON-VIOLENT BEHAVIOR IN CHILDREN

By Bruce Duncan Perry, M.D., Ph.D.[92]
<http://teacher.scholastic.com/professional/bruceperry/cool.htm>, retrieved 29 August 2008

As you watch children cross the classroom threshold at the start of a new school year, you can't help but wonder: Will they connect with me? Will they get along with one another? Today, as children enter the "world" of school, you must consider another factor-how can I ensure the safety of all the children in my group?

School shootings and the graphic violence we all see in the media change the way adults and children view the world – from a world bright and full of promise to a dark and potentially dangerous place. Even at the tender age of 2, children may experience a bully's threat. A toddler may imitate his favorite cartoon character and suddenly tackle a friend on the playground. Exposure to violence can change the way children feel, act, and behave – and not in positive ways.

Children are born with a remarkable range of potential. They are not born violent, nor are they naturally immune to the effects of violence. Yet some

---

[92] Dr. Bruce D. Perry, M.D., Ph.D., is an internationally recognized authority on brain development and children in crisis. Dr. Perry leads the Child Trauma Academy, a pioneering center providing service, research and training in the area of child maltreatment (<www. ChildTrauma.org>). In addition he is the Medical Director for Provincial Programs in Children's Mental Health for Alberta, Canada. Dr. Perry served as consultant on many high-profile incidents involving traumatized children, including the Columbine High School shootings in Littleton, Colorado; the Oklahoma City Bombing; and the Branch Davidian siege. His clinical research and practice focuses on traumatized children – examining the long-term effects of trauma in children, adolescents and adults. Dr. Perry's work has been instrumental in describing how traumatic events in childhood change the biology of the brain. The author of more than 200 journal articles, book chapters, and scientific proceedings and is the recipient of a variety of professional awards.

The ChildTrauma Academy (<http://childtraumaacademy.org>) is a unique collaborative of individuals and organizations working to improve the lives of high-risk children through direct service, research and education.

We recognize the crucial importance of childhood experience in shaping the health of the individual, and, ultimately, society. By creating biologically-informed, child and family respectful practice, programs and policy The Child Trauma Academy seeks to help maltreated and traumatized children.

A major activity of the CTA is to translate emerging findings about the human brain and child development into practical implications for the ways we nurture, protect, enrich, educate and heal children. The "translational neuroscience" work of the CTA has resulted in a range of innovative programs in therapeutic, child protection and educational systems.

Our impact: Changing People, Changing Practice, Changing Programs, Changing Policy …

children are more resistant than others and a rare few are unaffected. During these early years, you can increase children's ability to be responsible, caring, and creative. You might say it's the chance of a lifetime!

A Vaccine Against Violence

Bruce D. Perry, M.D., Ph.D, a leading expert on brain development and children in crisis, has identified six core strengths that children need to be humane. A child who can form and maintain healthy emotional relationships, self-regulate, join and contribute to a group, and be aware, tolerant, and respectful of himself and others will be more resourceful, more successful in social situations, and more resilient. Studies show that when a child is violent, one or more of these core strengths did not develop normally. The child without these strengths will be in greater danger of becoming violent and also less able to cope with bullies and other verbal or physical abuse. A child who does not develop these core strengths is a vulnerable child. Significantly, though, children with these core strengths rarely become violent and, in fact, recover more quickly when exposed to violence.

To help children develop these crucial strengths, Scholastic has launched Keep the Cool in School, a company-wide campaign against violence and verbal abuse. With this campaign, we hope to offer teachers, parents, and children the tools to identify, develop, and enhance these core strengths. Promoting a child's emotional health is the most successful approach available to fighting violence. And the payback is unparalleled: with your help, more children will grow up to be kind, thoughtful, and productive. The following article by Dr. Perry offers an explanation of these six strengths. Over the year, *Early Childhood Today* will present six additional features, each focusing on one of the core strengths [see I-VI below].

THE SIX CORE STRENGTHS

by Bruce D. Perry, MD, Ph.D.

Violence infects our children. This infection is virulent in some and barely noticeable in others. Why do some children re-enact the violence they see on television while others do not? Why do some chronically teased children cope by developing a sense of humor, while others become self-loathing and yet others plot to shoot their taunting peers? Why do some children who make these murderous plans actually act on them?

It's almost impossible to answer these questions. We rarely know what makes a given child violent. But we do know that children with core strengths rarely become violent. Healthy development is an antidote to the violence they're exposed to.

These core strengths build upon each other to contribute to a child's emotional development. Together, they provide a strong foundation for future health, happiness, and productivity. Attachment, self-regulation, affiliation, awareness, tolerance, and respect will each be explored in depth in later issues of *Early Childhood Today*. Here is an overview of the six core strengths and why each is essential to healthy development.

1. ATTACHMENT: Being a Friend

Attachment is the capacity to form and maintain healthy emotional bonds with another person. It is first acquired in infancy, as a child interacts with loving, responsive, and attentive parents and caregivers.

Why it's important: This core strength is the cornerstone of all the others. An infant's interactions with a parent or primary caregiver create his or her first relationship. Healthy attachments allow a child to love, to become a good friend, and to have a positive and useful model for future relationships. As a child grows, other consistent and nurturing adults such as teachers, family friends, and relatives will shape his ability to develop attachments. The attached child will be a better friend, student, and classmate – which promotes all forms of learning.

Signs of struggle: A child who has difficulty with this strength has a hard time making friends and trusting adults. She may show little empathy for others and act in what seems to be a remorseless way. Children unable to attach lack the emotional anchors needed to buffer the violence they see. They may isolate themselves, act out, reject a peer's friendly overtures, or withdraw socially. With few friends, and apparently disconnected from her peers, this child is also at greater risk when exposed to violence.

2. SELF-REGULATION: Thinking Before You Act

Developing and maintaining the ability to notice and control primary urges such as hunger and sleep – as well as feelings of frustration, anger, and fear – is a lifelong process. Its roots begin with the external regulation provided by parents or significant caregivers, and its healthy growth depends on a child's experience and the maturation of the brain.

Why it's important: Pausing a moment between an impulse and an action is a life-tool. Developing this strength helps a child physiologically and emotionally. But it is a strength that must be learned – we are not born with it. As children grow, our expectations for them must be age-appropriate. For instance, it is unreasonable to expect a 2-year-old to have complete bladder and bowel control before his body has matured. In social situations, the age-appropriate strength to self-regulate may spell a child's success and build his self-confidence.

Signs of struggle: When a child doesn't develop the capacity to self-regulate, he will have problems sustaining friendships, learning, and controlling his behavior. He may blurt out a thoughtless and hurtful remark and express hurt or anger with a shove or by damaging another child's work. Just seeing a violent act may set him off or deeply upset him. Children who struggle with self-regulation are more reactive, immature, and impressionable, and more easily overwhelmed by threats and violence.

3. AFFILLIATION: Joining In

The capacity to join others and contribute to a group springs from our ability to form attachments. Affiliation is the glue for healthy human functioning: It allows us to form and maintain relationships with others – and to create something stronger, more adaptive, and more creative than the individual.

Why it's important: Human beings are social creatures. We are biologically designed to live, play, grow, and work in groups. A family is a child's first and most important group, glued together by the strong emotional bonds of attachment. But most other groups that children join – such as a pre-school class, kids in the neighborhood, friends made while traveling – are based on circumstance or common interests. It's in these groups that children will have thousands of brief emotional, social, and cognitive experiences that can help shape their development. And it is in these situations that children make stronger connections with peers – their first friendships.

Signs of struggle: A child who is afraid or otherwise unable to affiliate may suffer a self-fulfilling prophecy: she is more likely to be excluded and may feel socially isolated. Healthy development of the core strengths of attachment and self-regulation make affiliation much easier. But a distant, disengaged or impulsive child won't be easily welcomed into a group. And in fact, she may act in ways that lead others to tease or actively avoid her. The excluded child can take this pain and turn it on herself, becoming sad or self-loathing. Or she can direct the pain outward, becoming aggressive and even violent. Later in life, without intervention, these children are more likely to seek out other marginalized children and affiliate with them. Unfortunately, the glue that holds these groups together can be beliefs and values that are self-destructive or hateful to those who have excluded them.

4. AWARENESS: Thinking of Others

Awareness is the ability to recognize the needs, interests, strengths, and values of others. Infants begin life self-absorbed and slowly develop awareness – the ability to see beyond themselves and to sense and categorize the other people in their world. At first this process is simplistic: "I am a boy and she is a girl. Her skin is brown and mine is white." As children grow, their awareness of differences and similarities becomes more complex.

Why it's important: The ability to be attuned, to read and respond to the needs of others, is an essential element of human communication. An aware child learns about the needs and complexities of others by watching, listening, and forming relationships with a variety of children. He becomes part of a group (which the core strength of affiliation allows him to do) and sees ways in which we are all alike and different. With experience, a child can learn to reject labels used to categorize people, such as skin color or the language they speak. The aware child will also be much less likely to exclude others from a group, to tease, and to act in a violent way.

Signs of struggle: A child who lacks the ability to be aware of others' needs and values is at risk for developing prejudicial attitudes. Having formed ideas about others without knowing them, she may continue to make categorical, destructive, and stereotypical judgments: "She speaks English with an accent, so she must be stupid"; or "He's fat, so he must be lazy." This immature kind of thinking feeds the hateful beliefs underlying many forms of verbal and physical violence.

5. TOLERANCE: Accepting Differences

Tolerance is the capacity to understand and accept how others are different from you. This core strength builds upon another – awareness (once aware, what do you do with the differences you observe?).

Why it's important: It's natural and human to be afraid of what's new and different. To become tolerant, a child must first face the fear of differences. This can be a challenge because children tend to affiliate [on the basis of] similarities – in age, interests, families, or cultures. But they also learn to reach out and be more sensitive to others by watching how the adults in their lives relate to one another. With positive modeling, you can insure and build on children's tolerance. The tolerant child is more flexible and adaptive in many ways. Most important, when a child learns to accept difference in others, he becomes able to value the things that make each of us special and unique.

Signs of struggle: An intolerant child is likelier to lash out at others, tease, bully, and, if capable, will act out his intolerance in violent ways. Children who struggle with this strength help create an atmosphere of exclusion and intimidation for those people and groups they fear. This atmosphere promotes and facilitates violence.

6. RESPECT: Respecting yourself and others

Appreciating your own self-worth and the value of others grows from the foundation of the preceding five strengths. An aware, tolerant child with good affiliation, attachment, and self-regulation strengths gains respect naturally. The development of respect is a lifelong process, yet its roots are in early childhood, as children learn these core strengths and integrate them into their behaviors and their worldview.

Why it's important: Children will belong to many groups, meet many kinds of people, and will need to be able to listen, negotiate, compromise, and cooperate. Having respect enables a child to accept others and to see the value in diversity. He can see that every group needs many styles and many strengths to succeed and he can value each person in the group for her talents. When children respect – and even celebrate – diversity, they find the world to be a more interesting, complex, and safer place. Just as understanding replaces ignorance, respect replaces fear.

Signs of struggle: A child who can't respect others is incapable of self-respect. She will be quick to find fault with others, but she can also be her own harshest critic. Too often the trait a child ridicules in others reflects something she hates in herself. The core of all violence is a lack of respect, for oneself and for others. When respect is missing, children will likely become violent – because they value nothing.

These core strengths provide a child with the framework for a life rich in family, friends, and personal growth. Our world changes daily and becomes increasingly diverse – and how much more complex that world will be when our children become parents! Teaching children these core strengths gives them a gift they will use throughout their lifetimes. They will learn to live and prosper together with people of all kinds – each bringing different strengths to create a greater whole.

I. ATTACHMENT – THE FIRST CORE STRENGTH

The ability to form attachments is the first of six core strengths that are an essential part of healthy emotional development. These core strengths are the foundation of Scholastic's company-wide program, Keep the Cool in School: A Scholastic Campaign Against Violence and Verbal Abuse. In this article, Bruce D. Perry, M.D., Ph.D., explores attachment and how it contributes to preventing aggression and anti-social behaviors in children.

"My teacher!" – the 5-year-old child blurted out in the grocery as she ran, smiling, to hug her kindergarten teacher. It made both their days.

Throughout life, each of us will form thousands of relationships. These bonds take many forms. Some are enduring and intimate – our dearest friend – while others are transient and superficial – the chatty store clerk. Together, relationships in all forms create the glue of a family, community, and society. This capacity to form and maintain relationships is the most important trait of humankind, for without it none of us would survive, learn, work, or procreate.

The first and most important of all relationships are attachment bonds. Initially, these are created through interactions with our primary caregivers, usually parents. First relationships help define our capacity for attachment and set the tone for all of our future relationships.

What is Attachment?

Attachment is the capacity to form and maintain healthy emotional relationships. An attachment bond has unique properties. The capacity to create these special relationships begins in early childhood.

Unique features of an attachment bond:

- Enduring form of a bond with a "special" person.
- Involves soothing, comfort, and pleasure.
- Loss or threat of loss of the special person evokes intense distress.
- There is security and safety in context of this relationship.

At birth, a baby is essentially emotionally "unattached." Despite the obvious physical connection of the umbilical cord, the newborn does not yet have strong connections to another human. During infancy and early childhood, one form of attachment – socio-emotional – begins to replace the original physical attachment of the cord. As dependent as ever, a baby requires constant attention and care from another human being in order to survive. Calories and a "bath" of physical sensations – sight, sounds, smells, touch, and taste – help the infant survive and grow to meet her potential. This "somatosensory" bath from a loving caregiver – the rocking, hugs, coos, and smiles – is transformed by the infant's sensory systems into patterned neuronal activity that influences the development of the brain in positive ways. It is in this dependent relationship between the primary caregivers and the infant that the new form of attachment grows. This attachment – the emotional relationship – is not as easy to see or document, yet it is nonetheless as important for human development as the umbilical cord is *in utero.*

It is these experiences of infancy and early childhood that create the roots of attachment – the capacity to form and maintain healthy emotional relationships. Except in the most extreme cases we are all born with the genetic capability to form and maintain healthy emotional relationships. When the infant has attentive, responsive, and loving caregiving, this genetic potential is expressed. And as this infant becomes a toddler and more people – family, friends, peers – enter his life, he will continue to develop this capacity to have healthy and strong emotional relationships.

Attachment and Pleasure

Our brain is designed to promote relationships. Specific parts of the human brain respond to emotional cues (such as facial expressions, touch, scent) and, more important, allow us to get pleasure from positive human interactions. The systems in the brain that mediate pleasure appear to be closely connected to the systems that mediate emotional relationships. Indeed this inter-relationship – the capacity to get pleasure from other people – creates a major positive learning tool of infancy and childhood. Young children want to please their teachers. They model adults and children they admire.

When attachment capacity develops normally, the child gets pleasure from interacting with other people. The degree of pleasure is related to the degree of attachment – pleasing a parent brings more pleasure than pleasing a stranger. It is this very property that helps parents and teachers shape pro-social and social behaviors in a child. In the process of teaching children emotional, social, and cognitive tasks, the strongest rewards for a child are the attention, approval, and recognition of success that the parent or teacher can give. Conversely, when a child feels he has displeased a parent or teacher, he can be devastated.

Attachment Capacity Matures

In order to be capable of forming the wide array of healthy relationships required throughout life, a young child's attachment capacities must mature. While the roots of attachment are related to the primary caregiving experiences in early childhood, full expression of attachment potential requires social and emotional interactions with non-caregivers. As children become older, they spend less time with parents and more time with peers and other adults. This time with peers and other adults provides many opportunities for continued emotional growth. In early childhood, the relationships with peers start as acquaintanships. With more time together, however, young children create friendships and the opportunity for strong emotional bonds can develop. In a similar fashion, a young child may form a strong connection with an attentive and nurturing teacher. The acquaintance, the friend, and the teacher all provide different and complementing social and emotional opportunities that help a child's attachment capabilities mature.

When Attachment Goes Wrong

If a child has few positive relationships in early childhood or has had a bad start due to problems with the primary-caregiving experiences of infancy, this child is at risk for a host of problems. In a very real sense, the glue of normal human interactions is gone. A child with poor attachment capacity is much harder to "shape" and teach. This child will feel little pleasure from the teacher's smile or approving words. And he does not feel bad disappointing, angering, or upsetting a parent or teacher. Without the capacity to use human interactions to "reward" and "punish," the teacher and parent often are confused and frustrated in their attempts to promote appropriate social behavior. In extreme cases, the child with poor attachment capacity demonstrates no remorse when harming others and risks developing further anti-social or even aggressive and violent behaviors. This child needs help. Research and clinical experience show that attachment capacity is easiest to shape if early identification and intervention takes place.

What you can do to promote the development of healthy attachment:

- Smile and look children in the eyes as you greet them
- Spend time with the child. Quantity matters. During this time, get on the floor, listen and establish eye contact.
- Use touch to comfort – even as a pre-school teacher, it is appropriate to hug, gently touch a shoulder, or hold hands.
- Help children learn appropriate social-emotional language (how close to stand, how to use eye contact, when to touch, how to touch).
- Remember that there are many styles of forming and maintaining relationships – a shy child is not an unattached child. If you sense a child is having a hard time engaging others, help facilitate this by actively including her or pairing her with another child who has a matching temperament.

II. SELF-REGULATION – THE SECOND CORE STRENGTH

The ability to self-regulate is the second of six core strengths that are an essential part of healthy emotional development. These core strengths are the foundation of Scholastic's company-wide program, Keep the Cool in School: A Scholastic Campaign Against Violence and Verbal Abuse. In this article, Bruce D. Perry, M.D., Ph.D., explores self-regulation and how it contributes to preventing aggression and anti-social behaviors in children.

"Mine! Mine!" – the 4-year-old yelled, stamped his feet, grabbed at the toy, pushed his classmate, and finally collapsed to the floor sobbing and inconsolable. This was his third "tantrum" in the last two days.

A just-fed newborn, rocking in the arms of her loving parent, is warm, full, calm, and safe. Her needs are met – for now. But soon, her body will use all of the food, her mother will put her down, and a loud bang will startle her. When this happens, her body tells her *I'm hungry, alone, and in danger.* She feels distress and also feels unable to regulate herself. So dependent, her only response is to cry out, hoping that a responsive adult will come to protect and feed her. Again and again, attentive teachers respond to the needs of the dependent child. When infants and children are incapable of meeting their own needs, they depend upon the external regulation that comes from attentive, caring adults. It is in the context of this loving attention that a special bond grows between the dependent child and the teacher – attachment bonds. A responsive teacher provides the stimulation that helps the child's brain develop the capacity for creating and maintaining healthy emotional relationships. At the same time, in these same interactions, other crucial areas of the infant's brain are being shaped – the stress-response systems.

Responding to Stress

The brain is continually sensing and responding to the needs of the body. Specialized "thermostats" monitor our internal (for instance, levels of oxygen and sugar in the blood) and external worlds. When they sense something is wrong (that the body is "stressed"), they activate the brain's alarm systems. These stress-response systems then act to help the body get what it needs.

Much of this regulation takes place automatically – beyond our awareness. But as we mature, our brain requires that we actively participate in our own regulation. When the internal world needs food or water or the external world is overwhelming, or threatening, our body "tells" us. If we thirst, we seek water; when afraid, we prepare to fight or flee. In short, we "self-regulate." We act in response to the sensations and feelings that arise from our brain's alarm systems.

When these systems develop normally, we are able to deal with complex and challenging situations with age-appropriate solutions. By adulthood, these should be thoughtful and creative. When a child's capacity for self-regulation does not develop normally, he will be at risk for many problems – from persistent tantrums to impulsive behaviors to difficulty regulating sleep and diet.

What helps the stress-response systems develop in an optimal way is repetitive exposure to controllable "challenges." Every time a child is introduced to something new, a low-level alarm response is activated. But with repetition comes mastery, and what the brain once interpreted as a potential threat is now familiar and tolerable. It is not bad for the child to experience low levels of "anxiety" or distress when he is in a safe and responsive setting. Indeed, when the child gets a little hungry, there is no need to cry because he now knows that that feeling will go away soon ("We have snack time after free play"). Moderate, predictable stress in this responsive, controllable environment leads to resilience. Children become capable of tolerating significant distress. In turn, unpredictable or severe stress can lead to a hyper-reactive stress-response system and a host of problems. Central to the process of healthy development of stress-response capability is that children learn to read their bodies' signals.

Understanding Body Signals

Many of the sensations we feel when we are "out of regulation" are clear – thirst, for example. But the body tends to use a common set of "alarm" sensations for many different kinds of potential threats. The alarm response and the resulting feelings caused by frustration are very similar to those caused by fear. A fearful child may act sullen and "angry," unaware that they are actually anxious about starting in a new classroom. A hungry child may act distracted, irritable, and noncompliant, again unaware that the internal distress they feel is hunger. We all have had times when we have mislabeled these feelings. Sleep deprivation, illness, physical exhaustion, and family distress are among the things that can activate the alarm response and result in a set of behaviors that are misunderstood by teachers and by the children themselves. Sometimes, we just can't get what we need right away. We must endure the discomfort related to exhaustion, hunger, thirst, or fear. Learning to tolerate this distress, to correctly label the uncomfortable sensations, and to develop appropriate, mature ways to respond to these signals is central to healthy development. (When you are hungry or tired, you really aren't mad at someone – so you need not act mad. Just remember to eat something between lunch and a late dinner.)

How Self-Regulation Matures

The capacity for self-regulation matures as we grow. Infants are born with an undeveloped capacity to self-regulate. The dehydrated infant can not use words to ask for water nor can he get water. The infant feels thirst, distress and then cries, dependent upon an attuned adult to meet her needs. The transition from external regulation to self-regulation is one of the most important tasks of growing up. Healthy self-regulation is related to the capacity to tolerate the sensations of distress that accompany an unmet need. The first time the infant felt hunger, she felt discomfort, then distress and then she cried. An attuned adult responded. And after thousands of cycles of hunger, discomfort, distress, response, and satisfaction, the child has learned that this feeling of discomfort, even distress, will soon pass. An adult will come. The attuned, responsive teacher helps the child build in the capacity to put a moment between the impulse and the action.

As young children learn to read and respond appropriately to these inner cues, they become much more capable of tolerating the early signs of discomfort and distress that are related to stress, hunger, fatigue, and frustration. When a child learns to tolerate some anxiety, he will be much less reactive and impulsive. This allows the child to feel more comfortable and act more "mature" when faced with the inevitable emotional, social, and cognitive challenges of development. With the capacity to put a moment between a feeling and an action, the child can take time to think, plan, and usually come up with an appropriate response to the current challenge. For example, if you want another turn, wait in line and learn to tolerate the frustration of not getting exactly *what* you want exactly *when* you want it.

When to Worry

Many children have difficulty with self-regulation. Their stress-response systems are poorly organized and hyper-reactive. This could be related to many factors, including genetic predisposition, developmental insults (such as lack of oxygen *in utero*), or exposure to chaos, threats, and violence. (...) Children with poor self-regulation disrupt an entire classroom. They are often impulsive, hypersensitive to transitions, and tend to overreact to minor challenges or stressors. They may be inattentive or physically hyperactive. These children benefit from the structure, predictability, and enrichment that schools provide. Unfortunately this may not be enough. The degree of attention and nurturing that these children need is often beyond the capacity of a pre-school or kindergarten setting. If these problems are extreme and persistent, or if the behaviors disrupt the class, the child should be referred for further evaluation.

Helping Children Self-Regulate

- Model self-control and self-regulation in your words and actions when you are frustrated with a classroom situation.
- Provide structure and predictability. Children with self-regulation problems are internally "unstructured." The more freedom and flexibility they have, the more likely they are to demonstrate uncontrolled behaviors.
- Anticipate transitions and announce changes in classroom schedules.
- Reward children with good self-regulation capabilities with freedom and flexibility that will offer them opportunities for spontaneous, creative play and learning.

- Try to identify the most "reactive" and impulsive children and keep them apart from each other. Pairing children who face these challenges can escalate the problem.
- Remember that impulsive and aggressive children can create an atmosphere of chaos and fear that inhibit the capacity of other children to learn. Don't be afraid to immediately re-direct inappropriate words and actions. Your actions will make the rest of the children feel safer.
- Seek help. Don't be afraid to point out a child's self-regulation problems with parents or other school personnel. Early identification and intervention can save the child and family years of failure and pain.

III. AFFILIATION – THE THIRD CORE STRENGTH

Belonging to the Group: Help students feel included, connected and valued

Human beings are born dependent. In order for a baby to survive and thrive, it needs the constant support of other humans. Yet, as we grow, we do not gradually become independent of others; rather, we become interdependent. In the course of our lives we form many give-and-take relationships, building a healthy interdependence with family, community, and culture. Humans are so adept at this because we are biologically designed to live, play, grow, and work in groups. We are, at our cores, social creatures. Affiliation is the strength that allows us to join with others to create something stronger, more adaptive, and more creative than any individual: the group.

It Starts With the Family

A family is a child's first and most important group, held together by strong emotional bonds. Yet infants are indirectly connected to other groups; they are born as a part of a larger culture and community. As they grow, children will encounter and take part in many groups outside the immediate family – during school, at a neighbor's house, on a sports team, and so on. As a part of these groups, a child will have thousands of brief emotional, social, and cognitive encounters that help define his or her development. The capacity to join in, contribute to, and benefit from these various groups is essential to healthy development.

However inclined they are to group activities and behavior, humans must learn how to interact successfully within a group. We must learn how to communicate, listen, negotiate, compromise, and share with many diverse people in many situations. These social skills are not always easy to master.

The Rules of Play

From the primary relationships with adults – parents and caregivers – the child learns basic rules of social interaction. Group relationships, however, are more complex and dynamic than one-on-one relationships. For one, the first social rules a child learns are influenced by the child's dependence on the adult, and the adult's inherent size, strength, and power. None of these factors are present when a young child first starts to interact with other young children. In fact, young children are often more adept at affiliating with adults than with peers.

As children play together, they begin to learn and formulate their own social rules. Children with siblings have a head start in this process, as do children who have been involved in day-care or play-groups before beginning school. Children learn to join in with other children gradually. First, they observe what other children are doing. They often play in parallel, working side by side with others. Children then begin to explore dyadic, or one-on-one, interactions. They play together, pooling their strengths to build a tower out of blocks, for instance, or share imaginary characters and stories. Finally, children negotiate the transition to more complex, multipeer groups.

Best Friends and Enemies

Learning and mastering the rules of groups are very important yet difficult processes for many children. "Best friends" emerge. Temporary alliances form and may exclude one child and then later incorporate him or her. Being "in" or "out" can shift from hour to hour and day to day.

Some children manage this process well. Others do not; these tend to be children with immature attachment or self-regulation skills. A child's acceptance into a group depends heavily on his or her capacity to regulate anxiety, impulsive behavior, and frustration. Without these prerequisite strengths, a child will have difficulty forming and regulating the relationships with others that are necessary to develop affiliation skills. Group members will likely reject a child who is impulsive or disengaged. Unfortunately, this creates a negative cycle – having fewer opportunities to socialize leads to slower social learning. These children become more isolated from their peers. They perform poorly in group interactions and avoid opportunities to be with others.

Over time, the excluded child can take this pain and turn it inward, becoming sad or self-loathing. Or the pain can be directed outward, leading to aggression or even violence. Later, without intervention, these individuals are more likely to seek out other marginalized individuals and affiliate with them. Unfortunately, the glue that holds these groups together can be self-destructive or hateful beliefs.

Teachers Can Help

Teachers can intervene to stop this cycle from progressing. Structured and regulated group interactions, such as those found in school, give children essential practice in experiences that they might avoid if left to their own devices. Picking a partner for paired-reading sessions, playing a two-person computer game, or creating a group-science project provide opportunities to wait, share, take turns, cooperate, and communicate with others. The games and tasks can increase in complexity as the child grows and builds skills.

A teacher can help a socially isolated child by building on the prerequisite skills he or she will need to succeed in a group. (See … below.) First, observe the child to discover if he or she seems to do better in smaller groups or in one-on-one situations. If the child seems to have trouble being part of a group, try initially pairing the child with a reliable peer in a safe setting to build self-confidence and trust. Once the child has experienced success in a one-on-one setting, he or she will be more inclined toward group interaction – especially if the supportive peer is still by his or her side. The teacher can work to introduce the child into increasingly larger groups, making sure to give the child a group role in which he or she can prevail. For example, if a child is particularly good at math, make the child the "banker" in a group project to raise money for school supplies; if a child has artistic talent, give him or her opportunities to share and display artwork. Once other children observe the strengths this child can offer a group, they might be more likely to seek out him or her.

Of course, there is only so much an adult can do to promote friendships among children. Urging the class to make friends with a reticent child may backfire, making the child you are trying to help feel singled out. It's better to simply provide frequent opportunities for the child to work with other children without drawing attention to your goals. One thing you can do, however, is to step in immediately to prevent bullying, exclusionary behavior, and cruelty. If you work to provide all your students with a safe environment, they will be more likely to thrive in group settings.

Cooperative play

- *Affiliation skills develop in a sequential fashion.* Once a child has mastered parallel play, he or she is ready for interactive play with a peer. Once pairs have proved an ability to share, introduce games for three children.
- *Partner, partner, partner!* Children develop skills through lots of one-on-one practice.
- *Stop and redirect any exclusionary behaviors you see.* Often, children exclude others because too many participants in a group overwhelms their social skills. Remind the child that it's unacceptable to say "You can't play with us."

Instead, teach the child to say, "Why don't you ask Tommy to play? You can sit here next to us."

- *Use tasks that require two or three children to accomplish.* These activities will help children see the value in cooperating and team building.

IV. AWARENESS – THE FOURTH CORE STRENGTH

We're all Different (We're all the Same) – Teach children to embrace diversity, and give them a gift they can use throughout their lives

"I am a boy and she is a girl. She has brown skin and I have white skin. We both like to swing on the tire." – A four-year-old tells his teacher about his new friend.

From the moment we are born, we are swept into a never-ending stream of sensory information: sights, sounds, scents, and more. The brain is constantly processing, sorting, categorizing, and storing these incoming signals, allowing us to find order in the world. The most complex sensory signals come from those we are surrounded by in daily life – other human beings. As the young boy demonstrates by the quote above, children make sense of these complex signals by categorizing people in simple terms that they can understand. On a very basic level, the boy is aware that differences and similarities exist between himself and his new friend. The information that he gleans from this relationship will affect his future interactions, as he builds experience with each new relationship.

The ability to be attuned to others is an essential element of human communication and of successful school interactions. As a child grows, his or her understanding of the differences between genders, races, and cultures grows. The child forms friendships, participates in groups, and interacts with a variety of diverse human beings, consequently developing a sophisticated awareness of the ways in which he or she is like others and ways in which he or she is unique. Such ideal awareness builds the knowledge that a child needs to survive and thrive.

The Brain Stores Experiences

In this process of negotiating our infinitely complex variety of human relationships, the brain uses a set of rules. These rules of association and generalization are allowed by the brain's amazing capacity to store experience and create memories. As an example: if you take a ticking wristwatch and put it next to an infant's ear, his or her memory will store an association between the watch and the ticking. If you then show the infant a picture of a wristwatch, the infant will put his ear to the photograph – automatically listening for the sound associated with a wristwatch. This child's brain has "generalized," applying one experience to another. With a little experience, however, he or she will be able to distinguish between the actual watch and the image of the watch. The important point here is that it takes experience to transform a simple association into a more complex, complete, and accurate impression.

And so it is with people. If a child has limited experience with someone of another ethnicity, body type, skin color, religion, or culture, he or she can be much more vulnerable to forming categorical, simplistic, and inaccurate impressions. Invite diverse groups of people with different cultures, languages, and religions to visit your classroom and talk about their professions. Even if your school lacks obvious racial diversity, differences can still abound in the way children act, dress, and think; in the rituals they observe with their families; and in their personal experiences. Seek to highlight each child's unique personality by capitalizing on strengths, encouraging personal memoirs that are shared whenever appropriate, and pairing children who have different learning styles and behavior. Remind students that there are many types of diversity. Everyone is unique, and everyone has his or her own particular way of seeing the world. At the same time, we all share joys and fears, strengths and weaknesses – we are all human. Children can learn that just as they are similar to and different from their peers in many ways, so are they similar to and different from students elsewhere.

If you're geographically isolated, there are other ways to promote awareness of diversity without leaving your neighborhood. Research pen-pal programs with a foreign school, or participate in an initiative such as Students' Art for Peace (…). In your teaching, seek to avoid stereotypical aspects of a culture. Go beyond surface learning. For example, if studying Native Americans, avoid merely making construction-paper headdresses in arts and crafts; rather, commit to an in-depth study of tribal customs, languages, religions, and history. Invite a Native American speaker to your class to speak about his or her culture and profession. Ideally, every child should have the opportunity to learn about and interact with others who are different: in ethnicity, religion, language, learning styles, family background, and more. The more you do to build an awareness of diversity, the more solid a foundation a child will have as he or she grows into a mature, accepting individual – one who shares his or her strengths with the world and values the strengths others have to offer.

Struggling With Awareness

Occasionally, a child will struggle with awareness issues. Here are some warning signs to watch out for. When a child is struggling with awareness, he or she may:

- Tease other children about a very sensitive issue such as their weight, ethnicity, religion, or handicap. Some teasing is expected and normal in

young children – it is one form of verbal play – but it is important to listen and make sure it does not cross certain boundaries.
- Tend to see things as absolute: e.g., "Fat people are lazy."
- Form negative ideas about others based on stereotypes.
- Encourage peers to adopt their negative stereotypical views about others.
- Have a tendency to attack others who threaten their own insecurities (e.g., if a boy's parents are fighting a lot, he may tease another boy in the class who has no father in his life).

V. TOLERANCE – THE FIFTH CORE STRENGTH

The ability to tolerate differences is the fifth of six core strengths that are an essential part of healthy emotional development. These six core strengths are the foundation of Scholastic's company-wide program, Keep the Cool in School: A Scholastic Campaign Against Violence and Verbal Abuse. In this article, Bruce D. Perry, M.D., Ph.D., explores tolerance and how it contributes to preventing aggression and anti-social behaviors.

"At first no one would play with him because he was scary. But now we know he's nice. His face just got burned." – A 5-year-old boy telling his mother about a classmate with severe facial burns.

In this ever-changing world, our children will face more change, see more places, learn more things, and be exposed to more people and cultures than any other generation in history. Advances in communication, transportation, technology, and economics will provide more opportunities – and more challenges – for our children. To succeed in this complex and diverse world, they will need to develop the fifth core strength – tolerance.

Tolerance is the capacity to accept differences in others. Tolerance emerges when a child has the security arising from the healthy development of the four previous strengths (attachment, self-regulation, affiliation, and awareness). The attached child can form and maintain healthy intimate relationships and feels secure in them. Self-regulating children can better control their reactivity, anxiety, and fear when exposed to new people and situations. The affiliated child feels connected and secure in her peer groups. The aware child can see the strengths, needs, and interests of others. When these four strengths emerge, the child feels safe, special, and secure. Tolerance can follow.

Security: The Root of Tolerance

There are two components to this unique kind of safety. The first is the powerful and empowering feeling that comes when a young child feels special, valued, and accepted. This belief and feeling grows in a child when the important adults in his life tell him, and show him repeatedly, how important and loved he is. When the child feels this unqualified acceptance, it is so much easier for him to accept others.

The second key element of this security is related to how easily a child feels threatened by someone or something new. Our brain has dozens of neural systems involved in reading and responding to potential threats and will categorize new experiences as negative and potentially threatening until proven otherwise. New situations or novel stimuli, good or bad, activate the stress-regulating neural systems in the brain. A child who feels safe and is introduced to a new culture and new ideas will be stimulated and excited. But a child who feels anxious will perceive these new experiences as threatening.

All Children Can Learn

The development of tolerance requires active learning. We have a neurobiological tendency to form small groups with people who are similar to us and a tendency to be wary of, and even hostile to, people who are different. Becoming tolerant is not a passive product of development: it requires active modeling by adults and repeated exposure of children to different ways of living in our world. Fortunately, children can learn to accept and understand different views, cultures, and values. Once a child learns that differences make other people interesting, stimulating, and capable, she becomes more comfortable with the world. If a child is fearful of new things, including the diversity of people, she will be left behind. The more tolerant our children become, the easier it will be for them to enjoy all that the world has to offer.

Struggling With Tolerance

An intolerant child will be judgmental of others. She may tease, berate, and attack others who are different. Sometimes this can be overtly hostile and aggressive. Children who struggle with this strength help create an atmosphere of exclusion and intimidation for those people and groups they fear. This atmosphere promotes and facilitates violence and can be the first step in bullying. The intolerant child is, essentially, insecure – insecure about her status, skills, beliefs, and values.

What You Can Do

- Make children feel special and safe through words of praise and encouragement. Valued children learn to value others.
- Model tolerance. Children will learn to reach out and be sensitive to others by watching how comfortable you are as you discuss and relate to other people.

- Create opportunities for children to learn about new places, people, and cultures. Children feel safe with you, so explore new ideas and cultures together.
- Introduce new cultures and "different ways" by cooking ethnic dishes together.
- Have class celebrations for Cinco de Mayo, Chinese New Year, Carnivale, and other days and events that honor the traditions of different cultures.
- Invite children's families (and others from the community) to come to class and share the dress, language, traditions, and customs of their ancestors. Children can talk with your guest about how different things were "in the old days" and how different families still keep certain traditions.
- Intervene immediately when you hear or see intolerant behaviors or words in children. Don't be punitive. Try to understand and help children learn healthier ways of interacting with others.

VI. RESPECT – THE SIXTH CORE STRENGTH

The ability to respect oneself and others is the last of the six core strengths that are an essential part of healthy emotional development. These six core strengths are the foundation of Scholastic's company-wide program, Keep the Cool in School: A Scholastic Campaign Against Violence and Verbal Abuse. In this article, Bruce D. Perry, M.D., Ph.D., explores respect and how it contributes to preventing aggression and anti-social behaviors.

"My gramma is so old she knows everything." – A 5-year-old whispering in awe to her teacher.

Respect – the ability to see and celebrate the value in ourselves and others – is the sixth core strength. This is the most complex of the core strengths. It requires the emotional, social, and cognitive maturity that comes from developing the five previous strengths (attachment, self-regulation, affiliation, awareness, and tolerance).

Developing the capacity for respect is a lifelong challenge. Our sense of self tends to be fragile. It rises and falls as we face life's challenges with varying degrees of success. The development of self-respect, or, in essence, self-esteem, is guided by how we see ourselves. The people in our lives act as a mirror in this process. When people who are important to us give us attention and encouragement, we see positive images of ourselves. At other times, our interactions with others may make us feel unattractive, incompetent, or even invisible. As with adults, young children build their sense of self-respect from their interactions with others. When they are made to feel special and valued, children grow to respect themselves. A positive sense of one's self allows the maturing child to respect others.

Self-respect is at the heart of respecting others. When you can identify and appreciate your strengths and accept your vulnerabilities, it's easier to truly respect the value in others.

Valuing Others

We respect people who have traits we admire. Young children begin to respect things they see in the adults who are present in their lives – both good and bad. What a child respects, in other words, is determined in large part by what the child is exposed to. Young children raised in anti-social homes may actually respect and admire anti-social acts. They aspire to be just like Mom or Dad! Young children who watch hours of television and have few adult role models may begin to value persons in the media – with all of their distorted values and unrealistic traits. This becomes a trap for young children. They will never be able to be as athletic, beautiful, powerful, and popular as the false images they see on television. And, unable to meet these ideals, they will feel inadequate and unattractive.

Hopefully, through many quality experiences with attentive adults, the child begins to see more realistic qualities to admire. Consistency, predictability, grace under pressure, humor, and kindness are among the qualities that caring and competent adults model for young children. In the classroom, children see how respected adults – their teachers – solve problems and cope with challenges. If their teachers handle conflicts by listening, thinking, staying calm, and reaching thoughtful solutions, the child comes to respect these behaviors.

Struggling With Respect

There are two ways in which children struggle with respect. One is overt non-compliance and defiance. In this case, there is a lack of respect for classmates and for you and your authority as a teacher. This is almost always associated with a poor sense of self, despite the fact that these children will often brag and distort their strengths and capabilities. This bragging is merely a protective shell over a very fragile sense of self. Often these children have not had much attention or structure when they are away from school.

The other way in which a child struggles with respect is when he begins to say, "I'm bad," "I can't do that," "I'm stupid," "He's better than I am." Children with this type of poor sense of self start to limit their opportunities. They don't try as hard, and as a result, they may end up creating self-fulfilling prophecies. Because they don't try new things, they don't learn as fast. They fall behind. This negative cycle can be very destructive for young children.

What You Can Do

Children will come to respect the traits and values of the adults in their lives. Let children see how you show respect for all people, including the elderly, authority figures such as police officers, and people who are different from you in terms of ethnicity or religion.

- Strive to live what you teach. Be patient, consistent, caring, honest, and attentive.
- When a child is struggling, give him opportunities to succeed. Match his social and learning challenges with his stage of development. Slowly help him master new, but not overwhelming, challenges.
- Use positive comments and rewards to shape and reinforce behaviors. Remember the intense power of negative comments. Intervene and stop negative comments that are being used by any of the children against other children.

TASK/TEXT 9.8: UN DECLARATION ON HUMAN RIGHTS EDUCATION AND TRAINING

Global Human Rights Education listserv (HREA, <www.hrea.org>)

On 26 August 2008, Frank Elbers (Deputy Director HREA) wrote:

I would like to update you regarding the development of a draft UN Declaration on Human Rights Education and Training. A Drafting Group of the UN Human Rights Council Advisory Committee met with NGOs in Geneva on Friday, 7 August 2008 for a prelimary discussion about the Declaration. The meeting was facilitated by Kazunari Fujii, Chairperson of the NGO Working Group on Human Rights Education and Learning. For this meeting HREA submitted a memo that highlighted the rationale for, and possible elements of, such a Declaration on Human Rights Education and Training.

I would like to share the main arguments with you in the hope that it will spark debate and that at a later point we, as civil society organisations, can provide more input into the drafting process.

A UN Declaration on Human Rights Education and Training would:

1. Enhance commitment to human rights education and training

The value added of a Declaration on Human Rights Education and Training would be to establish a higher level of commitment among [UN] Member States.

It would send a message that human rights education is a crucial tool to prevent human rights violations and to realise a global culture of human rights.

2. Codify human rights education as a human right

Currently, the right to human rights education does not exist. A Declaration would contribute to the codification of human rights education as itself being part of human rights in order to ensure respect, protection and implementation of human rights worldwide.

3. Definitions and practice

The Declaration should incorporate a clear definition of human rights education and related terms (e.g., culture of human rights), and its relationship to the right to education, which should be drawn from good practices. It could also provide specific actions to be taken to replace the often general formulations in existing mechanisms while at the same time recognising the variations in context and practice in different country, target groups and methodologies. The Declaration could cover all contexts in which human rights education, learning and training are relevant: formal, non-formal and informal education, and lifelong learning. It would be an opportunity to update the existing definitions and incorporate the latest theory and practice, drawn particularly from the advances in the implementation of human rights education since the UNESCO Recommendation Concerning Education for International Understanding, Co-operation and Peace and Education Relating to Human Rights and Fundamental Freedoms (1974), the Vienna Declaration and Programme of Action (1993), the UN Decade for Human Rights Education (1995–2004) and World Programme for Human Rights Education (2005-ongoing).

4. Education and training of both duty-bearers and rights-holders

To date much emphasis has been placed on human rights education in formal education, especially primary and secondary education, both in practice and theory (partly flowing out of States' obligations to provide for the right to education). Fewer efforts have been undertaken in the training of professional groups (for example, members of the judiciary), continuing education (health professionals), non-formal education or informal education (e.g., communities, general public). At the same time human rights education has historically particularly addressed rights-holders with the aim of educating them about their rights in order to empower them. Duty-bearers, those individuals or institutions who have to guarantee or protect human rights – for example law enforcement officials and public officials –, have often not been part of human rights education programmes. The Declaration should also include references to various and international obligations that States have to train government personnel adequately in human rights, including the most recent human rights treaties and the protection of the most vulnerable groups. A human rights-based framework should be part of all human rights education, schooling, learning and training.

5. Monitoring

In order to be an effective instrument the Declaration will need to [be linked to] monitoring mechanisms. The purpose is to provide an incentive and encouragement to States to implement the obligations they have undertaken, giving them support and expert help where needed, for example through National Plans of Action for Human Rights Education. It would also allow NGOs, associations of professional groups, and other civil society organisations to be involved in the monitoring process (e.g., through consultations, shadow reports, etc.). The Declaration could include an article that stipulates that States Parties need to report on the status of human rights education when reporting to the monitoring bodies of the main human rights treaties. It is also worth considering to include human rights education in the Special Procedures by either expanding the mandate of the Special Rapporteur on the Right to Education or by establishing a Special Rapporteur on (the Right to) Human Rights Education.

6. Standard-setting

A Declaration would provide an opportunity to set and develop standards and practices in human rights education around the world by including benchmarks and indicators. This could go hand-in-hand with making more resources available for research and evaluation in order to measure progress.

7. Recognition and support for civil society organisations and other stakeholders

An instrument such as the Declaration that recognises the importance of human rights education and training would be a clear boost in morale of educational agencies, NGOs, professional associations and others working in this field. A Declaration could serve as a powerful tool for lobbying and advocacy, and a means of attracting financial resources from private sources as well as by governments. In Member States that have not ratified or signed the main human rights treaties, a soft-law instrument like a Declaration could provide legitimacy to civil society organisations involved in human rights education and training.

The Drafting Group is expected to meet again in January [2009] during the next session of the Human Rights Council Advisory Committee. I will share more information with you about the draft process as soon as it becomes available.

TASK/TEXT 9.9: CASEL – COLLABORATIVE FOR ACADEMIC, SOCIAL AND EMOTIONAL LEARNING

<www.casel.org>, accessed 29 September 2008

What is Social and Emotional Learning (SEL)?

SEL is a process for helping children and even adults develop the fundamental skills for life effectiveness. SEL teaches the skills we all need to handle ourselves, our relationships, and our work, effectively and ethically.

These skills include recognizing and managing our emotions, developing caring and concern for others, establishing positive relationships, making responsible decisions, and handling challenging situations constructively and ethically. They are the skills that allow children to calm themselves when angry, make friends, resolve conflicts respectfully, and make ethical and safe choices. (...)

Many of the programs that teach SEL skills have now been rigorously evaluated and found to have positive impacts. According to reliable research, schools are a highly effective setting for teaching SEL skills. (...)

SEL is also a framework for school improvement. Teaching SEL skills helps create and maintain safe, caring learning environments. The most beneficial SEL programs provide sequential and developmentally appropriate instruction in SEL skills. They are implemented in a coordinated manner, schoolwide, from preschool through high school. Lessons are reinforced in the classroom, during out-of-school activities, and at home. Educators receive ongoing professional development in SEL. And families and schools work together to promote children's social, emotional, and academic success.

CASEL: Vision

To promote children's success in school and life.

We envision a world where families, schools, and communities work together to promote children's success in school and life and to support the healthy development of all children.

In this vision, children and adults are engaged life-long learners who are self-aware, caring and connected to others, and responsible in their decision-making. Children and adults achieve to their fullest potential, and participate constructively in a democratic society.

Core Beliefs

1. We have a responsibility to help children to become knowledgeable, responsible, healthy, caring, and contributing members of society.

2. Rigorous science provides an essential foundation for effective educational policies and practices; a core aspect of rigorous science is to ground development and testing in real-life settings and conditions.
3. Effective, integrated SEL programming is the most promising educational reform to promote the academic success, engaged citizenship, healthy actions, and well-being of children.
4. Cross-disciplinary collaboration produces the richest insights, biggest impacts, and best outcomes in work on behalf of children.
5. We strive for excellence in all our work. We have high expectations for ourselves, and we encourage and expect the best from others.
6. CASEL leadership, staff, and collaborators must model social and emotional competence and ethical behavior.

Mission
To establish social and emotional learning as an essential part of education.

TASK/TEXT 9.10: HUMAN RIGHTS EDUCATION IS A PRIORITY – MORE CONCRETE ACTION IS NEEDED

Viewpoint of the Council of Europe Commissioner for Human Rights, Thomas Hammarberg, 6 October 2008, <www.commissioner.coe.int>

Human rights can only be realised if people are informed about their rights and know how to use them. Education about human rights is therefore central to the effective implementation of the agreed standards. While this was emphasised 60 years ago when the Universal Declaration of Human Rights was adopted, we are still far from ensuring that people know their rights and understand how to claim them.

The good news is that human rights education is receiving much needed attention at the European or international level. Resolutions have been adopted, conferences held and action plans issued by the United Nations agencies, not least UNESCO. The Council of Europe is particularly active in this field. Non-governmental organisations have also initiated valuable programmes.

The current challenge remains one of translating these recommendations into concrete action at the *national* level. Human rights education needs to be more than a simple repetition of the various legal conventions with little explanation as to their relevance to ordinary people in their daily lives.

My experience is that a number of governments have not given sufficient priority to human rights education in schools. The allocated time is limited and the pedagogic methods unsuitable. The emphasis has been on preparing the pupils for the labour market rather than developing life skills which would incorporate human rights values.

More worryingly, it seems that some governments fear that a human rights approach in the schools could breed unwanted criticism and even undermine government policies. This is an undemocratic and short-sighted attitude. Educating citizens in their human rights creates an informed society which in turn strengthens democracy. For the Council of Europe, therefore, human rights education is crucially important.

International actors should focus efforts on assisting countries to develop their own programmes, with education materials tailored to the particular needs of individual countries. The UN World Programme for Human Rights Education, which started in 2005, aims to give guidance on how such national efforts can be planned and enforced. **Education for Democratic Citizenship and Human Rights**, one of the projects currently being run by the Council of Europe, builds on the experience of a network of national coordinators.

A European resource centre on education for intercultural understanding, human rights and democratic citizenship (the European Wergeland Centre) will open in the autumn in Oslo. The centre will carry out and support research, provide in-service training for teachers and disseminate information and serve as platform and meeting place for relevant actors. Countries can indeed learn from one another.

The school system will certainly remain at the root of making young generations aware of their rights and how to use them. Not only should the school provide the key facts about human rights norms and the mechanisms for their protection, it also has a vital role to play in fostering values such as respect for others, non-discrimination, gender equality and democratic participation.

Inter-cultural understanding and respect have to be stressed in such learning. When the **Convention on the Rights of the Child** lists values to be promoted, it makes special mention of respect for 'the national values of the country in which the child is living, the country from which he or she may originate, and for civilizations different from his or her own' [Article 29]. Human right education should therefore be committed to an inclusive approach to societal diversity (…).

School curricula, education materials, pedagogic methods and the training of teachers have to be in conformity with such ambitions. At the same time, it is crucial that life in schools benefits from a human rights atmosphere. There should be both 'human rights *through* education' and 'human rights *in* education.'

The school itself must demonstrate that it takes human rights seriously. Pupils should be welcome to express their views and to participate in the running of the school as much as possible. The atmosphere in school should be characterised by mutual understanding, respect and responsibility between all actors. I have seen such schools and noticed that they tend to function much better than those run on an authoritarian model. Pupils learn social and other life skills, not only facts.

Teachers and principals have a key role for developing such schools. In addition, they need the support of local and central authorities and not least the Ministry of Education. Educational policies should promote a rights-based approach. Teacher training for all teachers, regardless of their specialisation, should be conceived along this model. Pedagogic methods should be promoted which are democratic and participatory and the textbooks and other education material should be consistent with human rights values.

The fact that many children now spend more time with screens than with teachers (or with their parents) also affects human rights learning. While the technology is value-neutral, the messages picked up or sent may not be. Efforts by the school in the field of human rights may be undermined by impressions on the screen, often dictated by purely commercial interests.

The school has to relate to the supply on the net and be prepared to take the necessary discussions. However, as important is that human rights thinking and discussion is provided *through* the new media – which certainly is a major challenge in the light of the commercial and private nature of the media landscape.

Extra efforts are also required in order to ensure that minorities and disadvantaged groups are reached in human rights education programmes. This requires that basic materials are produced in relevant languages, teachers are recruited from within these communities and that the pedagogic methods are culturally adapted.

Respecting human rights, disseminating information on the existing standards and making people aware about their rights are commitments which states have willingly entered into. These words should be put into deeds.

TASK/TEXT 9.11: HUMAN RIGHTS EDUCATION AND TRAINING – QUESTIONNAIRE TO GOVERNMENTS

Crinmail 1039 – 4 December 2008, <www.crin.org>

Questionnaire addressed to Governments as part of the consultations with all relevant stakeholders undertaken by the Human Rights Council Advisory Committee, at the request of the Human Rights Council pursuant to Human Rights Council resolution 6/10 of 28 September 2007, on the possible elements for a draft declaration on human rights education and training.

1. Is the right to human rights education and training considered as such in your national system?

2. If yes, which is the legal basis? International law, Constitution, National legislation, Administrative practice, Other.

[If answer to question 1 is positive]
3a. Which practical modalities have been set in place in terms of implementing the right to human rights education and training?

[If answer to question 1 is negative]
3b. In the absence of an explicit recognition of the right to human rights education and training, what is done in the area of human rights education and training?

4. In the framework of human rights education and training, what are the:
a) Priorities? b) Challenges? c) Good practices? d) Prospects for the future?

5. Comments and suggestions on possible new elements for a future declaration on human rights education and training.

To be returned by 31 December 2008 to: <hrcadvisorycommittee@ohchr.org> or Secretariat of the Human Rights Council Advisory Committee, c/o Ms. Elena Kountouri Tapiero, Office of the United Nations High Commissioner for Human Rights, Palais Wilson, Room 4–072, United Nations Office at Geneva, CH-1211, Geneva 10, Switzerland.

TASK/TEXT 9.12: PARENTHOOD EDUCATION – GUIDANCE FOR SCHOOLS

<www.parentinguk.org/files/downloads/guidanceforschools.pdf>, accessed 31 January 2009

Why deliver parenthood education?
Schools are required to prepare students for adult life and the government is now asking schools to consider parenthood education as an important element in this preparation. What weight is given to parenthood will be up to schools to decide, but there are obvious and relevant links to both the Citizenship and PSHE [personal, social and health education, JW] curriculum that mean schools can

integrate parenthood education effectively. Our adult experiences are many, varied and complex. We grow up to become citizens, employees, colleagues, partners, friends, parents and step-parents. We experience many challenges in life – such as the birth of a new family member; the death or illness of a loved one; choosing a partner for life; getting married; facing divorce or separation; poverty; poor mental or physical health; or caring for an elderly relative. We have to negotiate our way through numerous bureaucracies: legal, financial, educational and medical, amongst others.

In addition most children will become parents, though some will not be able to and some will choose not to. The task of bringing up children to be contented, confident and contributing human beings will be an adult's greatest responsibility, and often their greatest personal and social achievement. Yet young people often leave school without having thought through whether they will have children and if so, when. They will not have planned how they will cope with being a parent – as a mother or a father – and will often not realise who they can turn to for help. A few young people become parents whilst at school or soon after they leave full time education, and embark on this major change without considering the impact on their lives. The Social Exclusion Unit's report on teenage pregnancy emphasised the importance of ensuring that teenagers are aware of the real responsibilities of being a parent.

Twenty-first Century Parenting

Being a parent has always been hard work but it is particularly difficult in today's complex world. The agenda for the 21st century is different and demanding. Giving all children access to parenthood education in schools will help to prepare them for the challenges that lie ahead. Of course the new technologies and greater understandings of family relationships mean that parents are also enjoying parenthood more and education for parenthood needs to encompass the joys and fulfilment that parenthood can bring.

Britain is experiencing rapid social and economic change which creates both opportunity and insecurity. Many people marry and become parents but there is now more variety about partnerships and family form. Many bring up children alone, by choice or otherwise, and same-sex couples may choose to become parents. More mothers are working; gender roles are still changing; the working day is getting longer and jobs are rarely for life. Recent patterns of living and working may offer little guidance to tomorrow's young adults who need the space to think through the options that face them.

At the same time as parents need more help, many find themselves more isolated as the traditional sources of support become less available. For example, families tend to disperse and no longer live close by or, if they do, they have their own work commitments; and local networks are, in general, less evident and robust. Some fathers have a greater opportunity to be involved in their families and are learning new skills as a result. Britain is multicultural. Families can struggle as parents hold on to customs and values while children expect change. Many parents will have no extended family in the UK, and if, in addition, their partner is of a different cultural background, there may be different expectations about which customs are upheld.

Family poverty creates additional problems for families and children, affecting housing, jobs, health and self-esteem, all of which affect our sense of competence and ability to cope. The concept of resilience has an important part to play in parenting support whatever the family's circumstances. Self-esteem, self-confidence, a belief in one's own self-efficacy and an ability to deal with change and adaptation will all positively affect family life.

Within all families, relationships can be more highly charged as expectations for fulfilment between parents and partners grow and as children spend more time at home safe from the perceived dangers of public places.

What are the broad aims of parenthood education?

A key aim of the Parenting Education & Support Forum is to raise awareness of the importance of parenting and its impact on the personal, emotional, mental, social, intellectual and physical development of children. Parenthood education in schools offers the valuable chance to help children think about the role before they actually become parents. Parenthood education should not tell children what to think or how they should lead their lives when they become parents. It can, however, enable children and young people to:

- learn the skills that are necessary for successful family relationships, including marriage; continuing to develop relationships; social and communication skills; stress, conflict and time management skills; and how to nurture self-esteem in both children and parents, through acknowledgement and thanks
- acquire knowledge about child development including the role of play and conversation, how children best learn, and children's social, emotional, physical and intellectual needs
- develop their understanding of some of the reasons for good and bad behaviour and how the parent-child relationship changes
- stimulate reflection and discussion of, for example, what the phrase 'good enough parenting' is trying to convey, what it might mean in practice, and where it might shade into 'not good enough' or even abusive parenting.

What can parenthood education achieve?
Young people who:

- grow up with an understanding of the importance of the parenting role
- have acquired knowledge about the effects of positive parenting
- have the skills and personal resources to meet a child's need for love, safety and security
- have thought through some of the choices, responsibilities and issues involved in parenting

are likely to make more effective parents in the future.

Children flourish when they have a good relationship with at least one parent and if their family life gives them structure and security as a framework for managing change and difficulty.

Such children are less likely to take drugs, fail at school, engage in criminal activity, be derailed by divorce and separation and have difficulty sustaining their own relationships with friends and family both in childhood and as adults.

Families that talk and debate together will reinforce the active citizenship and political literacy being introduced through the new Citizenship Guidance. The family has been called 'The Smallest Democracy.'

PSHE and citizenship work that addresses parenthood issues directly, especially within a positive school culture and ethos, will:

- Contribute to the raising of educational attainment
In the short-term, parenthood education in PSHE and citizenship work that addresses children's lives in a direct and relevant way can help to make school seem more approachable and thus in turn may reduce disaffection and truanting. Parenthood education as part of a PSHE programme can also contribute to improved motivation, confidence and attitude to work, especially when academically less able students are able to contribute on equal terms. Students may feel more committed to school and will develop their basic learning skills such as reflective skills, communication skills and planning. These can then be applied to National Curriculum subjects.

- Improve the mental health of all young people and create healthy schools
If future parents are better informed of young children's emotional needs and then set out to meet these when and if they do become parents, children will start out with a better chance of fulfilling their potential. This fits well with the aims set out in the National Healthy School Standard Guidance.

– Act as a direct stimulus to schools to involve parents more directly
Parenthood education is an opportunity to present the education of children as a collaborative process and show respect for the work that parents do.

– Reduce family conflict
Parenthood education will promote the importance of effective listening and empathy within families and will also help future families resolve conflicts. These skills are useful for the future role that young people may play in their own families but may also help them to avoid some of the difficulties they experience in their current circumstances.

– Help reduce teenage pregnancy
A clear understanding of the importance of the parenting role may encourage young people to think through the consequences of unprotected sexual activity and understand the reasons for delaying pregnancy. Parenthood education will also support their skills in making choices and acting responsibly to keep themselves and their future families safe and happy.

– Help to reduce criminal behaviour
A willingness to live within a structured, rule-bound framework is inculcated early and within the home. The fundamentals of morality are established by learning that certain behaviours are not acceptable; by realising that actions have consequences for which individuals, even children, must take responsibility; and by being given responsibilities alongside rights and independence. This territory overlaps naturally with citizenship issues, and demonstrates the important role that parents play.

Do schools have to promote a particular approach to parenthood?
Families come in all shapes and sizes, with different cultural, social and religious traditions. Whatever type of family children belong to, including children in public care, the role of mothers, fathers and primary carers and the quality of their relationships is crucial.

Stable relationships underpin family life and good parenting and it is important that young people have an understanding of their value. The present government believes that for many, marriage can provide a strong foundation for stable relationships. Children should learn the significance of family and stable relationships as key building blocks of community and society. Teaching in this area needs to be sensitive so as not to stigmatise children on the basis of their home circumstances.

Successful parenting is underpinned by certain fundamental values that are widely accepted. These are:

- Every child is unique and should be valued. Every child has fundamental rights that should be universally respected. These include the rights set out in the UN Convention on the Rights of the Child, ratified by the UK government in 1991, to express views freely, to freedom of thought, protection of privacy and access to information and to protection from all forms of physical and mental violence.
- Every child deserves individual and continuous love and security.
- Every parent has responsibilities towards their children.
- Parenting is an interactive process concerned with the development of the whole person.
- Grandparents, step-parents and members of the extended family play significant roles in the care and development of children.
- Cultural diversity and the different needs of men and women must be respected.

What is the place of Parenthood Education in the whole school curriculum?
Parenthood education can be delivered both explicitly and implicitly within the whole school curriculum. The 'implicit' curriculum attends to the fundamental, or necessary, skills that must be in place to enable people to fulfil their parenting role effectively. (...). For example, work on building a sense of self and self-efficacy, moves to developing reflective, creative, social and decision-making skills. Not being exclusive to parenting, these skills do not require an overt 'parenting' identity (...). The emotional environment of the school is also an important consideration. For example schools can explicitly and implicitly fulfil a critical role in modelling listening skills and highlighting the importance of empathy, such as in the bullying policy.

The 'explicit' parenthood curriculum will cover information, skills and situations particular to parenting. As parenthood education becomes more explicit, young people will be invited to reflect on their future role as parents. This change of focus, from the reality of the present to speculation about the future, from 'what is' to 'what will be,' from experiential to more cognitive learning, is paralleled in other disciplines.

Explicit parenthood education at secondary level requires its own clearly identified syllabus within a time-specific module as part of a coherent PSHE programme. It also requires schools to attend to the place of parenting issues in:

- the whole school ethos and how it is followed through in practice
- pastoral arrangements
- quality partnership with and support for parents and carers.

The National Healthy School Standard is a vehicle by which schools can improve their standards. It enables schools to build the right ethos through developing the values, policies, structures and relationships at school and with the wider community. Parenthood education can form part of that development. (…)

What are the key elements of a parenthood curriculum?
Schools may wish to develop their own parenthood curriculum. Here is a sixpart summary of a curriculum that has been successfully developed by the Children's Society.

Growing up in a family
What is a family?
How family life has changed
Influences on the decision to have a child

What parents and children need
Support and appreciation
How important is money?
Emotional security

What it means to be a parent/carer
What changes?
Who is parenting?
Patterns of parenting
Aspects of 'good enough' parenting

Parent-child relationships
Emotional bonds and commitment
Getting along together – having fun
Motherhood, fatherhood, the importance of partnerships and marriage
Separation and divorce

Rights and responsibilities of parents and children
Parental responsibility
Children's rights / child protection
Baby-sitting for older children
Young carers

Health and development
Child development stages and the corresponding parental responses
Discussions about sex and relationships between parents and children
The importance of play and suitability of toys
Happy, safe and healthy children.

TASK/TEXT 9.13: ADULT ATTACHMENT REPRESENTATIONS

<www.ocfi.ca>, Select Articles by Dr. Sue Johnson; accessed 7 February 2009
Ottawa Couple and Family Institute (OCFI; <www.ocfi.ca>) and the International Centre for Excellence in Emotionally Focused Therapy (ICE-EFT; <www.eft.ca>)

Four articles by Dr. Sue Johnson, author of *Hold Me Tight* [2008]

A. TEN TIPS FOR A STRONG VIBRANT RELATIONSHIP

So love is illogical, random and mysterious, yes? Not any more. We have cracked the code. In the last few years social scientists and therapists who practice emotionally focused therapy (or EFT) have made a breakthrough. Now, at the beginning of the 21st century, we have a map to this passion, this fever that has baffled poets and lovers all through human history.

Here is some of what we know:

1. We are born to need each other. The human brain is wired for close connection with a few irreplaceable others [from infant to adult attachment, JW]. Accepting your need for this special kind of emotional connection is not a sign of weakness, but maturity and strength.

So don't feel ashamed of this need for a safe loving bond.

2. In love relationships emotional hurt is a mixture of anger, sadness but most of all, fear [adult attachment representations, that is, adult representations of early attachment, JW]. Fear of being abandoned, and rejected. This hurt registers in the same part of our brain as physical hurt. It is too hard to push these feelings aside or ignore them. The first step to dealing with injuries in love is to pinpoint the feeling and then to send clear messages about this hurt to the one you love.

So don't just "ignore hurts" with the idea that they will [(…)] up and go away.

3. The strongest among us are those who can reach for others. Love is the best survival strategy of all. We all long for a safe haven love relationship. Self-sufficiency is just another word for loneliness.

So risk reaching out and fighting for this safe haven. It is the best investment you'll ever make.

4. Relationships can survive partners being very different. Even if you think you are from different planets it's okay. The one thing love can't survive is constant emotional disconnection. Conflict is often less dangerous for your love than distance.

So after a fight, put it right. Repair it, heal the rift between you.

5. There is no perfect lover. That is only in the movies. We shut down when we think we have failed as lovers, when we have disappointed. But our lover doesn't want perfect performance. In the end he or she needs our emotional presence.

So it's okay to say "I don't know what to do or say." Just stay open and present.

6. The fights that matter are never about sex, money or the kids. That is just the ripple on the surface of the sea. They are about someone protesting, often in an indirect way that is hard to understand, the loss of safe emotional connection.

The most terrible trap in a love relationship is when one person really wants to say, "Where are you? Do I matter to you?" but instead becomes critical and demanding and the other person feels hopeless and inadequate and moves away. The lovers then get caught in emotional starvation, stalemate and more and more disconnection.

So do try to tell each other when you feel lonely and like you are failing at being the perfect partner, especially if you are having lots of fights about tasks. Look beneath the surface.

7. We only have two ways to deal with the vulnerability of love when we can't connect. Get mad and move in fast to break down the other's walls or try not to care so much, and build a wall to protect yourself. Which one do you do? You probably learned it very young.

So do try to listen to your longings and risk reaching to connect. These other two options are traps that drive your lover away from you.

8. A loving relationship is the best recipe for a long and happy life that exists. Holding your lover tight is the ultimate antidote to stress. Cuddle hormones turn off stress hormones!

So do take time to hold and canoodle. It's better than taking your vitamins.

9. Lasting passion is entirely possible in love. Infatuation is just the prelude. An attuned loving bond is the symphony. This kind of bond creates what I call synchrony sex. Sex becomes a safe adventure.

So don't give up when sex goes into a temporary slump. Talk about it. Making love without candid conversation is like landing a 747 without help from the control tower!

10. The key moments in love are when partners open up and ask for what they need and the other partner responds. This demands courage but this is the moment of magic and transformation.

So take a deep breath and listen into your emotions. Let them tell you what you need. Then tell your partner that they are so special to you that you want to take a risk and tell them what you need from them most. Keep it simple and honest.

When you have a blueprint for love you can build it. In EFT studies seven out of ten couples repair their relationship. Love doesn't have to be a mystery anymore.

B. THE THREE KINDS OF SEX

Sex often draws us into a relationship and then helps keep it alive. But what is "good" sex?

If you look at the images that bombard us every day from magazines and movies, good sex is instantaneous, totally mutual, cataclysmic, and is best at the very beginning of a relationship.

In fact, surveys tell us that in real life, folks in long term relationships who can talk openly about their sex life have more and better sex than new or more reticent couples. What really determines what kind of sex you are going to have isn't the novel positions you find in the sex manual or the new tips in the latest magazine. It's how **safely attached** you are to your partner. Emotional presence and trust are the biggest aphrodisiacs of all.

The **new science of attachment** [adult attachment representations, JW] tells us that there are really 3 kinds of sex.

Sealed-Off Sex

This is all about reducing sexual tension, achieving the big O and feeling good about your sexual prowess. The name of the game is sensation, the more the better and performance, or the "God I am hot" quotient. The relationship with the other person is secondary. For a one night stand this is maybe okay. In a long term relationship this is bad news. Men seem to be more able to practice this kind of sex. They are wired to move quickly from arousal to orgasm. Women take longer to become aroused and need more co-ordination happening with a partner to really enjoy sex.

Sealed-off Sex works fine for one night stands. It is one-dimensional so continual novelty is mandatory. This kind of sex can be mutually satisfying occasionally in long term relationships, but if it is the norm, the relationship is in trouble. This kind of impersonal sex has the effect of making a partner feel used and emotionally alone.

Regular physical contact actually tunes the brain into the need to feel emotionally close. When this is missing, partners are swamped with a sense of isolation and deprivation. "When we make love, I feel like I could be anyone," Kerrie tells me. "It just reinforces for me the sense that I don't really matter to him." Bill, her partner, tells her, "Well, we haven't been getting along, so I try to get close by coming onto you. But I guess I don't feel sure enough, safe enough to slow down and really get into it. So I just go with the sensation. In the end, I don't really enjoy it that much either." Lack of emotional connection shuts off real eroticism.

When this sex is the norm in a relationship, it's time to pay attention to the lack of safe emotional connection outside the bedroom.

Solace Sex

This occurs when we are not quite sure that our partner is really there for us, when we need lots of reassurance. If we are anxious about whether we can depend on our partner, we get caught up in pleasing our lover to win his or her approval. We concentrate on cuddling and affection rather than abandoning ourselves in love-making. Comforting tender touch is part of good sex, but when we get preoccupied with gaining reassurance, eroticism suffers.

With Solace Sex, we are highly sensitive to signs of rejection. So when our lover says, "I just don't feel like it tonight," we can't manage to respond, "Oh, that is disappointing. I was looking forward to making love. But we can make it another time or just chat for a while." Instead, we free fall into catastrophic thinking, doubting that we are really loved. As a result, we often wind up pressuring our partner to have sex or getting into arguments about exactly why they are not feeling sexy.

When this kind of sex is the norm, it's time to talk to your partner about your anxieties. The safer you feel the more you will be able to let go and enjoy your sexuality.

Synchrony Sex

This is when emotional openness and responsiveness, tender touch and erotic exploration all come together. This is the sex that fulfills, satisfies and connects. The key prerequisite here is not wild sexual techniques but a safe emotional bond. The safer we feel emotionally, the more we can communicate, express our needs, play and explore our responses and relax into sexual feelings. We can literally tune into each other and co-ordinate our sexual dance, sensing each others inner state and responding to how arousal shifts and peaks. Emotional safety shapes physical synchrony and physical synchrony shapes emotional safety.

Synchrony Sex that deepens our bond with our lover, feeds our own sense of ourselves as attractive desirable sexual beings, and makes lovemaking a reliable source of eroticism and joy. Research tells us that those who can count on their partner to be there for them emotionally, who say that they have a secure bond, have sex more often and enjoy sex more.

When people feel safe with each other they can also deal with the sexual differences and problems that inevitably come up in a long term love relationship. What I tell the couples who come to see me to improve their relationship is that "Practice and emotional presence make perfect in the bedroom." The thrill in this kind of sex is like the 'safe adventure' of dancing tango with a trusted partner. You are totally engaged in the dance and let the emotional and physical music take you over. The dance is then constant improvisation and play. Emotional presence and trust is the biggest aphrodisiac of all and the thrill can last a lifetime.

When you can have this kind of sex, rejoice and hold your lover tight. This is the way sex was supposed to be.

C. WHAT YOU NEED TO KNOW ABOUT LOVE

I am sitting in a restaurant shamelessly eavesdropping on a conversation at the next table. "People who expect all this woo woo stuff – love and closeness in marriage – are out of their minds," declares an elegantly dressed woman to her friend. "If you're lucky in love, you get a reasonable roommate and even that is just the luck of the draw. No-one will ever figure love out." I can't help myself. I lean across the space between us and whisper, "No – that's not true. We really *do* know about the woo woo stuff. We have cracked the code of love and you don't need luck! We know how to do it!"

The new science of love and loving [that is, of adult attachment representations or adult representations of early attachment, JW] has been evolving for over a decade. Now, as we begin the 21st century, we finally know what love is about and how it works. Here's what we've learned:

- The need we have as children to be able to call to a special one and know that this person will respond with reassurance and comfort never goes away. To know that we are loved is the safe haven we all long for. The longing for this is wired into our brains from the cradle to the grave.
- The strongest among us are not those who can take or leave other people, but who can risk and reach out to them. These individuals know how to send clear emotional signals that pull others close. And close connection makes us stronger. Many months after 9/11, survivors who were comfortable turning to loved ones seemed to recover well, while those who turned away or were scared about relying on others still struggled with the ghosts of that day.
  Our brains are wired to see emotional isolation as dangerous and send a panic signal when we cannot get a loved one to respond. If we can't reconnect, we either shut down or get demanding. Both of these strategies can backfire and push our lover away.
- When we have that special closeness to a loved one, while making love or just holding each other, we are flooded with a cuddle hormone, called oxytocin, found only in animals that are monogamous when they mate. Oxytocin gives us a sense of calm joy, while also tamping down our stress hormones.

Conflicts about the kids, sex or money don't make or break a relationship. What really matters is emotional connection. Underneath the discord, the real issue is that partners are questioning the security of their bond: "Are you there for me?" "Can I count on you to respond to me – to put me first?" When couples understand the fundamental issue, they can help each other reconnect. Then problems about the kids, sex or money are just differences, not relationship bombs.

Can this emerging knowledge help you come to a better understanding of your love relationship and build a closer, stronger and more trusting connection with your partner? Yes! You can learn to send clear emotional signals to your partner in a series of focused conversations that you can have with your partner. These conversations are the central element of emotionally focused couple therapy or EFT. This therapy doesn't give couples tips to tone down conflict or manuals on how to be nicer to each other. It teaches partners how to express our most basic needs and fears and how to engage in conversations that foster a secure, enduring and loving bond.

Twenty-five years of research tells us that after EFT, 7 out of 10 unhappy couples are able to repair their relationship. They are able to:

- Step out of what I call the Demon Dialogues where partners get stuck in spirals of negative emotions and wind up shutting down and shutting their partner out, or in becoming so demanding in an effort to counter the lack of connection that they push their partner away. When you understand the emotions that you and your partner feel, you can see these spirals of disconnection as they are happening. Dealing with emotional disconnection in a positive way is a huge part of making your love relationship strong.
- Forgive the injuries and hurts that poison love relationships and learn to trust again. If we understand the exquisite logic of love, we can understand how to heal the wounds love inflicts. The key moment in this forgiveness is when injured partners look into the eyes of their partner and see that their pain is shared. They are not alone.
- But most important of all, these couples can then create Hold Me Tight conversations. These positive exchanges of loving responsiveness cultivate the close connection we all long for. I recall one couple. "I get so freaked out when I hear that disappointment or frustration in your voice," Tim finally confided to Amy. "I guess I just run. I talk about tasks or concrete issues to get away from the feelings. I don't know how to tell you that I go all hopeless. A voice in my head says that I will never make it with you. At these times, I need to know that you are my lady, even if I am just blundering along and make all these mistakes." When Tim is open like this, he gives Amy what she has always wanted. She tells him, "I don't need a perfect Tim. I just need you to be with me, to share with me like this."

This kind of conversation creates the kind of safe connection that we all need and is the formula, at last we have one, for a lifetime of love.

D. WHERE DOES LOVE GO WRONG? OR THE THREE DEMON DIALOGUES THAT CAN WRECK YOUR RELATIONSHIP

Unhappy couples always tell me that they fight over money, the kids, or sex. They tell me that they cannot communicate and the solution is that their partner has to change. "If Mary would just not get so emotional and listen to my arguments about our [finances] and the kids, we would get somewhere," Brian tells me. "Well, if Brian would talk more and not just walk away, we wouldn't fight. I think we are just growing apart here," says Mary.

After 25 years of doing couple therapy and couple research studies, I know that both Mary and Tim are just seeing the tip of the iceberg. Submerged below is the massive real issue: both partners feel emotionally disconnected.

They are watching their backs, feeling criticized, shut-out and alone. Underneath all the loud arguments and long silences, partners are asking each other the key questions in the drama of love: "Are you there for me? Do I and my feelings matter to you? Will you respond to me when I need you?" The answers to these questions – questions that are so hard to ask and so hard to hear in the heat of a fight – make the difference between emotional safety and emotional peril and starvation.

We know from all the hundreds of studies on love that have emerged during the past decade that emotional responsiveness is what makes or breaks love relationships. Happy stable couples can quarrel and fight, but they also know how to tune into each other and restore emotional connection after a clash. In our studies we find that seven out of ten couples who receive Emotionally Focused Therapy or EFT can repair their relationship. They do this by finding a way out of emotional disconnection and back into the safe loving contact that builds trust. But why can't we all do this, even without a therapist? What gets in our way? The new science of love [adult attachment representations, JW] tells us.

Our loved one is our shelter in life. When this person is unavailable and unresponsive we are assailed by a tsunami of emotions – sadness, anger, hurt and above all, fear. This fear is wired in. Being able to rely on a loved one, to know that he or she will answer our call is our innate survival code. Research is clear, when we sense that a primary love relationship is threatened, we go into a primal panic.

There are only three ways to deal with our sense of impending loss and isolation. If we are in a happy basically secure union, we accept the need for emotional connection and speak those needs directly in a way that helps their partner respond lovingly. If however we are in a wobbly relationship and are not sure how to voice our need, we either angrily demand and try to push our partner into responding, or we shut down and move away to protect ourselves. No matter the exact words we use, what we are really saying is, "Notice me. Be with me. I need you." Or, "I won't let you hurt me. I will chill out, try to stay in control."

If these strategies become front and center in a relationship, then we are liable to get stuck in what I call the Demon Dialogues. These dialogues can take over your relationship. They create more and more resentment, caution and distance until we reach a point where we feel the only solution is to give up and bail out.

There are 3 main Demon Dialogues that trap couples in no-solution emotional starvation and insecurity:

Find the Bad Guy. This dead-end pattern of mutual blame keeps a couple miles apart. Fights look like a "who gets to define who" contest. As Pam says, "I am waiting for his put down. I have my gun ready. Maybe I pull the trigger when he isn't even coming for me." Both partners define the other as uncaring or somehow defective. Everybody loses. But this attack-attack pattern is hard to keep up. It is usually the opening measure to the most common and ensnaring dance of all – the Protest Polka.

The Protest Polka. Psychologists knew for years that this demand-withdraw dance leads to divorce, but they weren't able to figure out why is it so widespread and so deadly. We now understand that potent emotions and compelling needs keep this pattern going: the wired in need for emotional connection and the fear of rejection and abandonment. Even if our brains know that we are somehow making things worse by criticizing or shutting our partner out, we cannot just switch off this longing and fear. "The more he refuses to talk to me or dismisses my feelings, the angrier I get and the more I poke him," says Mia. "Anything to get a response from him." Her partner Jim picks up, "And the more I hear that angry tone in her voice, the more I just hear that I can never please her. I just get hopeless and more silent." It is this spiral that is the enemy, not the other partner, though neither partner recognizes this. Mia is protesting Jim's distance, Jim is frantically trying to avoid her disapproval. They talk this way because they sense an alarming answer to **the attachment question**, "Are you there for me?" In the Protest Polka, each person, in an attempt to deal with their sense of emotional disconnection unwittingly confirms the other's worst fears and keeps this spiral going. In the end, the demanding protesting partner begins to give up the struggle for connection, grieve the relationship and also move away. This leads into the last dance of all.

Freeze and Flee. In this dance both partner feel helpless. No-one is reaching for anyone here. No-one is taking any risks. Everyone has run for cover. In other relationships this might be fine for a while, but with the people we love, this "no response" dance is excruciating. Indeed, the partner's here aren't really dancing at all. They are sitting out. We are not wired to tolerate this kind of isolation. If nothing changes, the relationship is in free fall.

When folks caught in Demon Dialogues come in and ask, "Is there any hope for us?" I tell them, "Sure there is. When we understand what the drama of love is all about, what our needs and fears are, we can help each other step out of these negative dialogues into positive loving conversations that bring us in to each other's arms and safely home."

TASK/TEXT 9.14: EARLY RELATIONSHIPS INFLUENCE TEEN PAIN AND DEPRESSION

<www.nouvelles.umontreal.ca/udem-news/news-digest/early-relationships-influence-teen-pain-and-depression.html>, accessed 15 January 2010

Angst could be more than a rite of passage for insecure teenagers, according to a study published in *The Journal of Pain*. Researchers from the Université de Montréal, Sainte-Justine University Hospital Center and McGill University have discovered that insecure adolescents experience more intense pain in the form of frequent headaches, abdominal pain and joint pain. These teens are also more likely to be depressed than peers with secure attachments.

Dr. Isabelle Tremblay, a researcher at the Université de Montréal and its affiliated Sainte-Justine University Hospital Center, and Dr. Michael Sullivan, a psychology professor at McGill University, launched this study to build on previous findings that childhood experiences play a major role in the relationships people develop in later life. Simply put: insecure infants grow up to be insecure adolescents, and later, insecure adults.

"Although previous studies in adults found that an individual's security level was influenced by painful experiences, it was not clear why relationship security should be related to pain," says Dr. Tremblay. "We found that adolescents with insecure relationships tend to be more 'alarmist' about their pain symptoms; they have a tendency to amplify the degree of threat or severity of their pain. This amplification leads to more intense pain and more severe depressive symptoms."

Some 382 students, from Grades 8 through 12, were recruited for the study from a francophone high school in Montreal, Canada. Participants were asked to fill questionnaires on the frequency and intensity of their emotional and physical pain.

"It is possible that individuals who have insecure relationships may perceive the world as more threatening or more stressful and that manifests in physical symptoms," says Dr. Sullivan. "Alternately, it is possible that individuals who feel insecure might 'express' more intense distress as a means of eliciting support from others in their social environment."

Interpersonal factors must be considered when managing adolescent experiences of pain and depression, according to the researchers. "Adolescents have different health and mental health needs than adults. Although interpersonal factors have not been considered integral component of the treatment of pain and depression in adults, these factors might need to be considered in the treatment of adolescents," stresses Dr. Sullivan.

About the study: The study, "Attachment and Pain Outcomes in Adolescents: The Mediating Role of Pain Catastrophizing and Anxiety," published in *The Journal of Pain*, was authored by Isabelle Tremblay of the Université de Montréal / Sainte-Justine University Hospital Center and Michael J. L. Sullivan of McGill University.

10. VARIOUS ITEMS AND ISSUES – LEGAL, OTHER

TASK/TEXT 10.1: HUMAN RIGHTS EDUCATION ASSOCIATES – CHILDREN'S RIGHTS

<http://hrea.org/learn/guides/children.html>

Governments have taken the following types of measures to implement the Convention on the Rights of the Child at national level:

- Developed comprehensive national agenda;
- Developed permanent bodies or mechanisms for promote coordination of all sectors of government, monitoring and evaluation;
- Taken steps to ensure that all legislation is fully compatible with the CRC by incorporating it into domestic law or ensuring that its principles take precedence in cases of conflict with national legislation;
- Carried out child impact assessments to ensure children are taking into account in planning and policy decisions;
- Analysed government spending to determine the portion of public funds spent on children and to ensure that these resources are being used effectively;
- Carried out data collection;
- Raised awareness and disseminated information about the CRC;
- Involved civil society including children in the process of implementing and raising awareness of child rights;
- Set up independent statutory offices – ombudspersons, commissions or other institutions – to promote and protect children's rights.

TASK/TEXT 10.2: EUROPEAN SOCIAL CHARTER (REVISED) (1996)

Council of Europe, <http://conventions.coe.int/Treaty/en/Treaties/Html/163.htm>

Article 17 – The right of children and young persons to social, legal and economic protection

With a view to ensuring the effective exercise of **the right of children and young persons** to grow up in an environment which encourages the **full development of their personality** and of their physical and mental capacities, the Parties undertake, either directly or in co-operation with public and private organisations, to take **all appropriate and necessary** measures designed:

1. a. to **ensure** that children and young persons, taking account of **the rights and duties of their parents**, have **the care, the assistance, the education and the training** they need, in particular by providing for the establishment or maintenance of institutions and services **sufficient and adequate** for this purpose;
   b. to protect children and young persons against **negligence, violence or exploitation**;
   c. to provide protection and special aid from the state for children and young persons temporarily or definitively deprived of their family's support;
2. to provide to children and young persons a free primary and secondary education as well as to encourage regular attendance at schools.

TASK/TEXT 10.3: EUROPEAN FORUM ON THE RIGHTS OF THE CHILD

European Union, <http://europa.eu>; Euronet, <www.europeanchildrensnetwork.org>

BRUSSELS, 4 June 2007 – The European Commission, today, is launching, in cooperation with the German Presidency of the European Union, a Forum on the Rights of the Child. This Forum, the first of its kind, will involve children and bring together stakeholders to exchange information and practice and take positive action for children and young people. Towards and EU strategy on the rights of the child, adopted by the Commission on 4 July 2006, was the first step in the Commission's work on Children's rights. Today's Forum, in Berlin, is a further step.

Vice-President Franco Frattini, Commissioner responsible for Justice, Freedom and Security, said:

"I welcome today's Forum. Children and the future are interlinked. Children make us face up to the future and tackle the issues facing our society from demographic challenges to crime and climate change. This first forum will focus on child pornography and paedophilia. These require urgent attention. The number of internet sites with child sexual abuse material, increased 1500 percent from 1997–2005. New technology brings new challenges including how we guide and protect our children when they often are more knowledgeable, certainly IT literate, than parents."

The Forum brings together key players – Member States, the German Presidency, the UN, the European Parliament, the Council of Europe, Interpol, Unicef, national observatories on childhood, Ombudspersons for children, civil society and other stakeholders. How to ensure children's effective participation, as they will come to future forums, will be discussed.

Placing children at the heart of decision making and the positive opportunities this brings, for example, in education, integration and external relations will be a key theme. **Children make up a third of the population in Europe** – this is a lot of voices to exclude. This Forum aims to develop and implement strategies to promote the rights of children at national and international levels. Especially for the effective implementation of the United Nations Convention on the Rights of the Child, and the **European Union Strategy on the Rights of the Child**.

The Forum will include an opening address and Declaration from Vice President Frattini, research by the German Presidency on violent video games, and the high level discussion on child pornography and paedophilia. This will include tracing credit cards used to access pornographic material, something discussed at the recent G8 of Justice and Interior Ministers in Munich.

TASK/TEXT 10.4: STATE OF THE WORLD'S MOTHERS 2007 – THE BEST AND WORST COUNTRIES TO BE A MOTHER

Crinmail 878 – 8 May 2007 (<www.crin.org>), <www.savethechildren.org/publications/mothers/2007/SOWM-2007-final.pdf>

WESTPORT, 8 May 2007 – Save the Children USA global humanitarian organization, today released its eighth annual Mothers' Index that ranks the best – and worst – places to be a mother and a child and compares the well-being of mothers and children in 140 countries, more than in any previous year.

Sweden, Iceland and Norway top the rankings this year. Niger ranks last among countries surveyed. The top 10 countries, in general, attain very high scores for mothers' and children's health, educational and economic status. The 10 bottom-ranked countries – nine from sub-Saharan Africa – are a reverse image of the top 10, performing poorly on all indicators. The United States places 26th this year, tied with Hungary.

Conditions for mothers and their children in countries at the bottom of the Index are grim. On average, one in 13 mothers will die in her lifetime from pregnancy-related causes. Nearly one in five children dies before his or her fifth birthday, and more than one in three children suffers from malnutrition. About 50 per cent of the population lacks access to safe water, and only three girls for every four boys are enrolled in primary school.

The worst ten:	The best ten:	Below top ten:	Below top ten (ctd):
131. Djibouti	1. Sweden	11. Netherlands	21. Portugal
132. Burkina Faso	2. Iceland	12. UK	22. Ireland
133. Ethiopia	3. Norway	13. France	23. Greece
134. Eritrea	4. New Zealand	14. Switzerland	24. Czech Republic
135. Angola	5. Australia	15. Canada	25. Latvia
136. Guinea-Bissau	6. Denmark	16. Slovenia	26a. Hungary
137. Chad	7. Finland	17a. Austria	26b. US
138. Yemen	8. Belgium	17b. Estonia	28. Slovakia
139. Sierra Leone	9. Spain	19. Italy	29. Japan
140. Niger	10. Germany	20. Lithuania	30. Belarus

"If 75 years of field experience have taught us anything, it is that the quality of children's lives depends on the health, security and well-being of their mothers," said Charles MacCormack, president and CEO of Save the Children. "By providing mothers access to education, economic opportunities, and maternal and child health care, we ensure that mothers and their children will have the best chance to survive and thrive," he said.

The gap in availability of maternal and child health services is especially striking when comparing Sweden, at the top of the list, and Niger, at the bottom. Skilled health personnel are present at virtually every birth in Sweden, while only 16 per cent of births are attended in Niger. A typical Swedish woman has almost 17 years of formal education and will live to be 83. Meanwhile, 72 per cent of Swedish women use some modern method of contraception, and only one in 150 will lose a child before he or she has a fifth birthday. In Niger, a typical woman has less than three years of education and the life expectancy of a girl born today is only 45. Only four per cent of women use modern contraception, and one child in four never sees a fifth birthday. At this rate, every mother is likely to suffer the loss of two children.

Zeroing in on the children's well-being portion of the *Mothers' Index*, Italy finishes first and Afghanistan ties with Niger for last. While nearly every Italian child – girls and boys alike – enjoys good health and education, children in Afghanistan face a one in four risk of dying before age five. In Afghanistan and Niger, 40 per cent of children are malnourished. In Niger, less than 50 per cent of children are enrolled in primary school, and only one Afghan girl for every two boys is in school. More than half of all children in both countries lack access to safe water.

"Investing in the health of mothers everywhere is not just the right thing to do – it is the smart thing to do," urged MacCormack. "When we take care of mothers by ensuring that they have the basic tools they need to improve the quality of life for themselves and their children, we also improve prospects for generations to come. When mothers thrive, their children grow up healthy and, ultimately, all of society benefits," he added.

TASK/TEXT 10.5: CHILD RIGHTS COULD PROMPT SMOKING BAN IN HOMES

Crinmail 917 – 20 September 2007 (<www.crin.org>), <http://icwales.icnetwork.co.uk>, 17 September 2007 (Smoking ban at home could come in future)

Child law experts in the United Kingdom say parents could be banned from smoking in their homes to protect their children's health, following the success of the smoking ban in public places.

But such a ban may not happen for many years, because society is not yet ready for such a draconian step, they admit. One legal option would rest on the human rights of children, whose health is damaged more by passive smoking than adults. However, human rights rulings usually balance the rights of two sets of people, and one legal expert said judges would currently come down in favour of an adult's right to smoke in their home rather than the child's right to breathe clean air.

The ban on smoking in public places across Britain appears to have improved health already.

It emerged this week that heart-attack admissions to Scottish hospitals had dropped 17 per cent in the first year of Scotland's smoking ban. Researchers also said a national evaluation found a 39 per cent reduction in secondhand smoke exposure in 11-year-olds and in adult non-smokers. There was no evidence yet of smoking shifting from public places into homes.

Threat to children

But the British Medical Association says five million children in the UK are exposed to secondhand smoke in their homes. Those children are at higher risk of:

- Cot death;
- Asthma attacks;
- Respiratory symptoms;
- Impaired breathing, as children and adults;
- Middle-ear disease, which can be fatal.

They may also be at greater risk than other children of becoming asthmatic in the first place and of developing childhood cancer. Scottish research shows that even education is impaired, since children who live with smokers are 44 per cent to 77 per cent more likely to miss school than other children.

Prof Nigel Lowe, deputy head of Cardiff Law School, said smoking in homes could be addressed through smaller steps, such as smoke-free homes being a condition of fostering and adoption.

"The big leap will have to wait until the little leaps have been made," said Prof Lowe, an expert in child law. Who would have predicted 20 or 30 years ago that we couldn't smoke on trains or planes or in public places? The next logical step would be to protect the children, but I think we're quite a long way from that. I could see that it could happen. No current judge, I would predict, in England or Wales would be prepared to make that huge jump yet. But I wouldn't rule it out forever. The thing about human rights which always gets us into problem areas is that you've always got to balance it against other people's rights."

Competing rights?

While some might argue that a child's rights were infringed by smoking in the home, others would argue that adults have the right to respect for their private family lives. The ban on smoking in public places was premised on workers' rights to a smoke-free workplace. Workers can choose their workplace, while children do not choose their parents or homes. But Prof Lowe said, "There's a material difference between what you do in your own house and what you do outside."

Wendy Hopkins, a specialist family lawyer in South Wales, said it was premature for family law to proscribe smoking in the home. "Those are areas in which family law could go. There's no doubt that children living in a household where there's a heavy smoker are much more at risk."

"If one parent smoked, the family courts might take that into account when deciding on who had custody of children," she added.

Dr Tony Calland, who chairs the BMA's Welsh council, said the arguments against smoking in children's homes were as strong as those against smoking in workplaces, but he did not believe further legislation should be passed. "It's the principle that's the important thing – that you shouldn't poison anyone, including your own children. What will happen in time, and I think is already happening, is that smoking is becoming socially unacceptable. That will become the driver. It's a social evolution process, rather than being told by the Government or police or BMA that you mustn't smoke."

TASK/TEXT 10.6: NIGERIA – GOVERNMENT SUES TOBACCO FIRMS FOR DAMAGE TO CHILDREN

Crinmail 931 – 8 November 2007 (<www.crin.org>) [Source: Daily Trust, Abuja; <www.dailytrust.com>]

7 November 2007 – The Federal Government in Nigeria has filed a N5.3 trillion suit against British-American Tobacco [Public limited company] (BAT), Phillip Morris International and International Tobacco Limited over what it claims to be the damage done to children by the companies' products.

The government launched the case in the Federal High Court in Abuja. Also sued were two affiliates of BAT, British American Tobacco [Nigeria] Limited and British-American Tobacco [Investment] Limited. In the suit, filed by the Attorney General of the Federation and Minister of Justice Michael Kaase Aondoakaa, the government demanded the defendants pay N136.3 billion as special damages for selling their products to under aged persons, another N4.8 trillion as damages for future expenses incurred by the government for the damage caused to public health, and N130 billion more as punitive damages. Government's counsel Mrs. Maryam Uwais said her client wanted a court order restraining the companies from advertising and selling their tobacco-related products to under-aged Nigerians.

Not for sale around children

The government also asked the court to outlaw the sale and distribution of tobacco products in children's shopping areas, child care centres and other public areas where minors are predominantly located. They are also seeking a court injunction compelling the companies and their agents to cease marketing, promoting, distributing and selling the products. The plaintiff also asked for a court order restraining the defendants from representing or portraying to persons under the age of 18 years any alluring and misleading image regarding tobacco-related products.

They want to prohibit the sale and distribution of tobacco products within a kilometre radius from schools, hospitals, cinemas and playgrounds. The plaintiff wants all the defendants to look for a procedure by which a person's age could be verified at the selling point before their products are sold.

The government sought an order compelling the defendants to publicize tar and nicotine contents, addictiveness, relevant age limit, and other mandatory health warnings prescribed by the Federal Ministry of Health. It also asked the court to compel the companies to sponsor public awareness campaigns on smoking and its health effects. (…)

TASK/TEXT 10.7: DON'T FORGET ABOUT CHILD POVERTY NOW!

<www.Eurochild.org>, Press Releases, Brussels, 14 March 2008

On the occasion of the Spring Summit of EU leaders on 13–14 March, Eurochild urges EU heads of state & government to keep fighting child poverty beyond the 'light year' on the OMC

Successive Council Conclusions have called on EU member states to fight child poverty [the European Council in March 2006 concluded that EU member states should "take necessary measures to rapidly and significantly reduce child poverty"; the Council Conclusions of March 2007, stressed "the need to fight poverty, especially child poverty"]. As a consequence, this issue was chosen as the thematic focus for the 2007 'light year' within the EU's Open Method of Coordination (OMC) on social inclusion and social protection. This process raised hopes for Eurochild and other concerned actors in Europe, that the ambition to "***rapidly and significantly reduce child poverty***" will stay on the agenda and become a key focus of the renewed Lisbon Strategy.

"However, the conclusions of the Spring Council 2008 do not seem to have responded to the strong messages from previous Council conclusions," said Catriona Williams, President of Eurochild. Therefore **Eurochild and its member organisations call on EU heads of state and government to endorse the commitments made in previous Council conclusions and to demonstrate that the EU and member states continue to work together to fight child poverty** in the framework of the OMC. Eurochild expects the fight against child poverty to be a high priority in the renewed Social Agenda, especially regarding the conclusions of the Employment Council of 29 February, which explicitly talk about '*efforts to reduce child poverty*' as being an integral part of the interaction between the OMC and the Lisbon Strategy.

The OMC process, which has enabled a number of actions at EU level designed to make possible an in-depth analysis of child poverty and facilitate exchange of policy and practice between member states, should not lose momentum beyond the thematic focus of 2007. Despite increased economic growth, the numbers [78 million people are experiencing poverty in the EU] of people still experiencing poverty in the EU, of which many are children [across the EU, families with children under 16 are more likely to be at risk of poverty than the overall population (19% compared to 16%), one child in five lives under the poverty threshold], have for the most part remained stable, or have even increased in recent years.

The fight against child poverty should not only be seen in the framework of 'growth and jobs,' but rather in the context of children's rights and well-being – as enshrined in the Convention on the Rights on the Child (CRC). Eurochild welcomes the work done by the task force on child wellbeing indicators of the Social Protection Committee (SPC) in 2007, whose report was published in February ["Child Poverty and Well-Being in the EU – Current status and way forward," report on Child Poverty and Well-Being adopted by the Social Protection Committee on 17 January 2008: <http://ec.europa.eu/employment_social/spsi/docs/social_inclusion/ 2008/child_poverty_en.pdf>].

Member states should base their national strategy reports on social protection and social inclusion 2008–2010 on this important document, as suggested in the Guidance Note [Guidance Note for preparing National Strategy Reports on Social Protection and Social Inclusion 2008–2010: <http://ec.europa.eu/employment_social/spsi/ docs/social_inclusion/2008/080207_guidance_note_nsrs_cln_en.pdf> (see page 5)].

Eurochild, together with its member organisations, will continue to closely monitor those strategy reports from the point of view of child poverty and children's rights.

TASK/TEXT 10.8:

TASK/TEXT 10.8.1: KINDERRECHTE IM GRUNDGESETZ

Bundesministerium der Justiz [The German Federal Ministry of Justice]

Berlin, 19. Oktober 2007 – <www.bmj.bund.de>

<www.bmj.bund.de/enid/6e5a9a5d4b6f437a7bc28dd909123edb,4f9d45706d635f6964092d0934383739093a095f7472636964092d0933303334/Pressestelle/Pressemitteilungen_58.html>

Zypries für konkrete Maßnahmen zum besseren Schutz von Kindern
In den vergangenen Monaten sind vermehrt Fälle bekannt geworden, in denen Kinder von ihren Eltern misshandelt oder vernachlässigt wurden. Vertreter der Bundesregierung und die Ministerpräsidenten der Länder beraten heute über Maßnahmen zum besseren Schutz von Kindern. Bundesjustizministerin Zypries

hat konkrete Vorschläge unterbreitet, um gefährdete Kinder effektiv zu schützen.

"Die tragischen Fälle in den letzten Monaten haben erhebliche Defizite beim Schutz besonders gefährdeter Kinder offengelegt. Schätzungen zu Folge werden etwa 5 bis 10% aller Kinder unter 6 Jahren vernachlässigt. Immer häufiger sterben Kinder an den Folgen von Vernachlässigung und Misshandlung. Viele Risikofamilien können mit den herkömmlichen Angeboten der Jugendämter, der Erziehungsberatung oder der Familienbildung nicht im erforderlichen Umfang erreicht werden. Es ist deshalb dringend notwendig, den Schutzauftrag unserer staatlichen Gemeinschaft zu stärken. Ich habe konkrete Vorschläge unterbreitet, wie ein effektiver Schutz von Kindern erreicht werden kann," erklärte Bundesjustizministerin Zypries heute in Berlin. Zypries setzt sich insbesondere für die folgenden Maßnahmen ein:

- Verbindliches Einladungswesen für Vorsorgeuntersuchungen

Einige Länder sehen bereits ein verbindliches Einladewesen für Früherkennungsuntersuchungen von Kindern vor. Bundesjustizministerin Zypries unterstützt dieses System. Sie schlägt eine Ergänzung des §8a des Achten Buches Sozialgesetzbuch – Kinder und Jugendhilfe – um folgenden Absatz (1a) vor:

"Nehmen die Personensorgeberechtigten trotz wiederholter Aufforderung nicht an einer Früherkennungsuntersuchung für ihr Kind teil, prüft das Jugendamt, ob Anhaltspunkte für eine Gefährdung des Kindeswohls bestehen. Ergeben sich dabei aufgrund zusätzlicher Umstände Anhaltspunkte für eine Kindeswohlgefährdung, ist ein Hausbesuch durchzuführen. Die Stellen, die nach Landesrecht für die Überprüfung der Teilnahme an Früherkennungsuntersuchungen zuständig sind, teilen dem Jugendamt mit, wenn Personensorgeberechtigte trotz wiederholter Aufforderung nicht an einer Früherkennungsuntersuchung teilgenommen haben."

Die ärztlichen Früherkennungsuntersuchungen bieten die Möglichkeit, frühzeitig auf Vernachlässigung und Misshandlung von Kindern aufmerksam zu werden und eine Schädigung des Kindes abzuwenden. Die ganz überwiegende Mehrzahl der Eltern kümmert sich verantwortungsvoll und gut um ihre Kinder. Wir wollen daher die Eltern nicht gesetzlich zu Vorsorgeuntersuchungen zwingen. Allerdings kann die Versäumung einer Früherkennungsuntersuchung in Verbindung mit anderen Faktoren Anzeichen für eine Gefährdung des Kindes sein. So können etwa Hinweise aus dem Umfeld der Familie auf eine Vernachlässigung, Verwahrlosung oder Misshandlung schließen lassen.

Deshalb sollen die Jugendämter verpflichtet werden zu prüfen, ob Anhaltspunkte für eine Kindeswohlgefährdung vorliegen, wenn die Eltern trotz wiederholter Aufforderung nicht an einer Früherkennungsuntersuchung für ihr

Kind teilnehmen. Sprechen darüber hinaus weitere Umstände für eine Vernachlässigung des Kindes, muss ein Hausbesuch erfolgen. Auf diese Weise kann Risikofamilien besser geholfen und Kinder effektiver geschützt werden.

– Erleichterung familiengerichtlicher Maßnahmen bei einer Gefährdung des Kindeswohls

Bereits im Juli 2007 hat Bundesjustizministerin Zypries einen Gesetzesentwurf zur Erleichterung familiengerichtlicher Maßnahmen bei Gefährdung des Kindeswohls vorgestellt. Er wird derzeit im Deutschen Bundestag beraten. Der Gesetzesvorschlag setzt auf Prävention. Familiengerichte sollen früh tätig werden, bevor das Kind zu Schaden kommt bzw. ein Entzug des Sorgerechts notwendig wird. Deshalb werden den Gerichten konkrete Handlungsalternativen an die Hand gegeben, die sie schon frühzeitig anordnen können. Sie können die Familien z. B. zu einem Anti-Gewalt-Trainining verpflichten, eine Erziehungsberatung oder Maßnahmen der Gesundheitsfürsorge anordnen. Außerdem müssen familiengerichtliche Verfahren bei einer Gefährdung des Kindeswohls künftig vorrangig behandelt werden. Ein erster Gerichtstermin muss schon binnen eines Monats stattfinden. Darüber hinaus soll die Gefährdung des Kindes schon im Vorfeld und unabhängig von einem gerichtlichen Einschreiten erörtert werden. Dabei soll den Eltern der Ernst der Lage vor Augen geführt und darauf hingewirkt werden, dass sie notwendige Erziehungshilfen des Jugendamtes besser in Anspruch nehmen.

– Zusammenarbeit zwischen Gerichten und Jugendämtern verbessern

Bundesjustizministerin Zypries will eine reibungslose Kooperation der Familien- und Jugendgerichte mit den Jugendämtern zum Wohle gefährdeter Kinder und Jugendlicher sicherstellen. Staatliches Handeln gegenüber Eltern und Kindern in schwierigen Lebenssituationen sollte stets aufeinander abgestimmt und widerspruchsfrei sein.

– Kinderrechte im Grundgesetz

Nach Artikel 6 Abs. 1 des Grundgesetzes steht die Familie unter dem besonderen Schutz der staatlichen Ordnung. Das Recht der Eltern wird in Artikel 6 Abs. 2 des Grundgesetzes gewährleistet. Danach sind die Pflege und Erziehung der Kinder das natürliche Recht der Eltern. Freilich müssen sie ihr Elternrecht zum Wohl des Kindes ausüben. Zwar ist die Bedeutung des Kindeswohls seit langem auch in der verfassungsgerichtlichen Rechtsprechung anerkannt, das Kindeswohl selbst wird im Grundgesetz jedoch nicht ausdrücklich erwähnt. Bundesjustizministerin Zypries will die Rechte der Kinder in der Verfassung stärker zum Ausdruck bringen und als **eigenes subjektives Recht** formulieren.

Sie schlägt in Übereinstimmung mit dem Präsidium der SPD die Einfügung eines neuen Satzes 2 in Artikel 6 Abs. 1 des Grundgesetzes vor:

"Jedes Kind hat ein Recht auf Entwicklung und Entfaltung seiner Persönlichkeit, auf gewaltfreie Erziehung und auf den besonderen Schutz vor Gewalt, Vernachlässigung und Ausbeutung. Die staatliche Gemeinschaft achtet, schützt und fördert die Rechte des Kindes und trägt Sorge für kindgerechte Lebensbedingungen."

Diese Ergänzung des Grundgesetzes enthält eine objektive Handlungsanweisung an alle staatlichen Organe. Sie müssen das Recht des Kindes auf Entwicklung und Entfaltung seiner Persönlichkeit beachten. Die ausdrückliche Festschreibung der Kinderrechte wird bewirken, dass die Belange der Kinder im Rahmen staatlicher Entscheidungen bei der Abwägung der betroffenen Interessen größeres Gewicht erlangen. So werden der Gesetzgeber und die öffentliche Verwaltung z. B. bei der Finanzierung, dem Bau oder der Ausstattung von Kindergärten, Spielplätzen oder sonstigen öffentlichen Einrichtungen das Wohl des Kindes besonders in den Blick nehmen. Auch für die Gerichte wird damit ausdrücklich normiert, dass sie ihre Entscheidungen am Kindeswohl auszurichten haben.

Kinder können sich zudem selbst auf dieses subjektive Recht berufen und im Einzelfall z. B. mit einer Verfassungsbeschwerde durchsetzen. Im Gegensatz zu einer Staatszielbestimmung hat diese Grundgesetzänderung also nicht nur Appellfunktion.

TASK/TEXT 10.8.2: ECUADOR – NEW CONSTITUTION STRENGTHENS CHILDREN'S RIGHTS

Crinmail 1022 – 7 October 2008, <www.crin.org>

On 28 September, Ecuador voted in favour of a new constitution. The Constitution of Montecristi is the first to recognise children's rights throughout the text, including on issues of political participation, enforcement mechanisms and education rights.

According to Cecilia Lazo, consultant at the Instituto Nacional del Niño y la Familia (National Institute for Children and Families), "the new text maintains and enshrines those child rights which have already been recognised, but goes further by making them visible throughout the text in a way that has never been done before."

Her only comment was on education for which the State assumes total responsibility but which, in her opinion, is a responsibility of society as a whole, including of families and communities.

President of the Children and Adolescents' Forum, Patricio Cajas, highlighted the most relevant triumphs for child rights in the new Constitution as: the right to vote at 16 (article 62), the progressive eradication of child labour, free education up to secondary level and mechanisms for children's participation in decision-making in State bodies.

In response to arguments that 16 and 17 year olds will be manipulated by adults and lack experience in standing for elections, Cajas responded that "we must not be afraid," adding that these mechanisms will encourage political participation.

Assembly member Amanda Arboleda commented that one of the reasons that young people should have the right to vote is that politicians do not demonstrate interest in their problems and do not listen to them because they are unable to vote.

Arboleda also defended young people's right to stand for election from 18 and emphasised that the moral standing of a person was more important than university degrees or experience.

Another new provision in the Constitution is children's right to judicial protection, recognised in article 175, which states that "children and adolescents will be subject to specialised legislation and administration of justice, which will include suitably trained staff."

Article 186 establishes that "every canton, will have at least one judge who specialises in family, children and adolescents and one judge who specialises in young offenders."

TASK/TEXT 10.9: THE NEW DISABILITY CONVENTION AND THE PROTECTION OF CHILDREN

by Gerison Lansdown, Save the Children, December 2006, <http://crin.org/resources/infoDetail.asp?ID=11797&flag=report>

[In December 2006] the United Nations General Assembly [has] adopt[ed] a new Convention to protect the rights of the persons with disabilities round the world. This Convention will be the first major human rights Treaty of the 21st century, and addresses civil, political, social, economic and cultural rights (…). It will enter into force when ratified by 20 countries [April 2008]. (…) Countries that ratify the Treaty agree to enact laws and other measures to improve disability rights, and also to abolish legislation, customs and practices that discriminate against persons with disabilities. Currently only some 45 countries have legislation that deal with persons with disabilities [Cf. Articles 137c-f Dutch Criminal Code]. (...) So what does this mean for children with disabilities?

1. A paradigm shift

Throughout the drafting process of the Convention, the Chair of the Ad Hoc Committee in charge of the Convention stressed that what was needed was a 'paradigm shift' in the attitudes and treatment of people with disabilities – from seeing persons with disabilities as objects of charity to considering them as individuals with human rights.

This necessitates recognition that people with physical, **psycho-social**, intellectual or sensory impairments face many barriers that prevent them from full and effective participation in society on an equal basis with others. Those physical, linguistic, social and cultural barriers must be removed. The focus should no longer be on addressing the 'special needs' of children – the approach embodied in Article 23 of the Convention on the Rights of the Child. Rather, it should be on the realisation of their rights. The Convention recognises that a change of attitude in society is necessary if persons with disabilities are to achieve equal status, and includes a specific Article on awareness-raising to promote respect for the rights and dignity of people with disabilities. However, the Convention in its entirety is dedicated to achieving that change. The Convention will finally ensure that countries will no longer be allowed to relegate children with disabilities to the margins of society. Governments that ratify it will be legally bound to treat them as subjects of the law with clearly defined rights.

2. New obligations to protect the rights of children with disabilities

Children with disabilities, have the same human rights as all other children. Human rights are universal. But, in practice those rights are violated or neglected in almost all areas of their lives – they experience discrimination, for example, in relation to family life, education, health, participation and personal freedoms. The new Convention seeks to introduce new obligations on governments **and other duty bearers** to take all the measures necessary to ensure that all their rights are fulfilled, protected and respected.

All the provisions in the new Convention apply to children with disabilities as well as adults, but there are also additional measures included to address the specific situation of children. For example:

- The preamble recognises that children with disabilities should have full enjoyment of all human rights on an equal basis with others.

- The general principles include respect for the evolving capacities of children and their right to preserve their identities.
- The general obligation requires that children with disabilities must be consulted when States Parties are developing and implementing legislation and policies.
- A dedicated article (Artcile 7) on children with disabilities introduces obligations to ensure the enjoyment of all human rights and fundamental freedoms on an equal basis with other children, to ensure that the best interests of the child is a primary consideration, and to provide disability and age appropriate assistance to ensure that children with disabilities are able to realise the right to their express views on all matters of concern to them and have them taken seriously in accordance with age and maturity.
- Age appropriate measures must be introduced to ensure that children with disabilities have access to justice.
- Measures must be taken to provide age sensitive assistance to prevent exploitation, violence and abuse; age, gender and disability sensitive protection and rehabilitation services; and child focused legislation to ensure that exploitation, violence and abuse is identified and investigated.
- Measures must be taken to ensure that children with disabilities are registered immediately after birth.
- Children with disabilities are entitled to retain their fertility, thereby prohibiting [**forced?**] sterilisation.
- Children with disabilities have equal rights with respect to family life and States Parties have an obligation to provide services and support to families to prevent abandonment, concealment and segregation. In addition, children with disabilities must not be separated from parents unless this is in their best interests and never on the basis of disability. Where **parents are unable to care for children**, efforts must be made to provide alternative care within the wider family or within the community **in a family setting**.
- Education at all levels must be inclusive and children with disabilities have an equal entitlement to general education. Inclusive education requires provision of all necessary support and technical aids, including respect for linguistic identity, and facilitating the learning of Braille, orientation and mobility skills, and training of teachers.
- Children with disabilities must be provided with equal access to participation in play, recreation, and leisure and sporting activities, including in schools.

3. Recognising the importance of the process as well as the outcome – the participation of NGOs, disabled people and children (…)

4. Moving forward

The Convention represents a monumental step forward. However, of itself, it is only a paper document. It will take sustained commitment to translate its obligation into meaningful action at the country level.

- **Ratification** – organisations working in both the disability and children's field need to press their governments to ratify the Convention without reservations as soon as possible.
- **Implementation** – positive action is needed to encourage governments to take the necessary measures to implement the Convention. This will involve undertaking analyses of the current degree of compliance with the obligations in the Convention and identify the changes in law, policy and practice required. (...)
- **Awareness raising** – there is a major piece of work to be done in ensuring that people with disabilities, including children, are aware of the Convention in order to use it to claim their rights.
- **Committee on the Rights of Persons with Disabilities** – the Convention includes provisions to set up a treaty body similar to the Committee on the Rights of the Child. Initially it will have 12 members, but will increase to 18 once there are 60 ratifications. When electing members, States Parties are required to give explicit consideration to geographical distribution, gender representation and participation of experts with disabilities. There is a role for NGOs to identify potential members of the Committee and to encourage governments to give consideration to nominating experts on children with disabilities.
- **Reporting to the Committee** – States Parties are required to report to the Committee, initially after two years and subsequently every four years. It will be important to use the experience drawn from the work of the Committee on the Rights of the Child and encourage the greatest possible involvement of NGOs in the reporting process. It will also be essential to bring together civil society organisations to produce shadow reports. Organisations working with children with disabilities must be included in that process.
- **Individual petitions** – the Convention includes an Optional Protocol which will be adopted simultaneously, which allows individuals and groups to petition the Committee on the Rights of Persons with Disabilities once all national recourse procedures have been exhausted. This means that where State Parties fail to protect the rights of people with disabilities, including children, it will be possible to seek a remedy from the Committee.

TASK/TEXT 10.10:

TASK/TEXT 10.10.1: US RATIFICATION OF THE CRC

Crinmail 989 – 10 June 2008, Interview, <www.crin.org>

Tom Kennedy, 60, is the Chair of the Campaign for US Ratification of the Convention of the Rights of the Child (CRC). Along with Somalia, the US is one of only two countries in the world which have failed to ratify. The Campaign is a volunteer-driven network of individuals and organisations which was established in 2002 in the wake of the UN Special Session on Children. It became apparent at the session that the US government was trying to marginalise the CRC and limit references to it in the outcome document. A number of individuals felt that, in addition to implications for the US, encouraging ratification might be a good way to address the child rights issue internationally. Tom is also a Senior Vice President of Covenant House, which provides shelter and other services to homeless youth.

Our members are finding that even people who have conservative views have been expressing an openness towards ratification and the importance of the CRC. We have organised everything from grassroots events to a summit in 2006 which was attended by about 350 people. We have also organised about ten briefings in cities around the county, and regularly organise visits to senators.

I don't know the exact reasons for the opposition to ratification, but there is a an anti-UN group who oppose treaties in general. There is also this concern that children's rights will viscerate the rights of parents. But the more we talk to people, the more it seems that it is mostly just a lack of knowledge of what the CRC means. There is a history of taking a long time to ratify treaties in the US, for example the genocide treaty took 30 years. The CRC is the most swiftly ratified treaty of them all.

We feel there is a really good opportunity in the next two or three years. A new president will take some time to address the issue whoever it is. We will run a main event at some point in the first one hundred days of the presidency. It is likely that the Convention would be ratified with reservations.

There is a history of the US being less connected to the international community than, for example, Europe. There tends to be a hesitancy about any interdependence. There is a tradition of closely examining anything that will affect our internal laws. The treaty would have to be incorporated into law, but it as much an aspirational treaty which sets standards for everyone to follow. It has tremendous ramifications in this regard, for example for support services for children, or in juvenile justice.

The CRC is referred to already in the courts and that's encouraging. It was cited during the lead-up to the elimination of the death penalty in the US for children.

The US joining the CRC will help the international community to embrace the Convention and better implement it. The fact that there are only two countries left to ratify, and if one of those countries did so, would help enforcement and draw more attention to child rights.

Whoever next becomes President, we are confident that they will pass the issue to the Senate over the two or three years. Then the battle will begin with the Senate. We have shied away from getting it into the agenda [during the selection of presidential nominees] because we don't want the issue to get misrepresented, for example with people saying it is taking rights away from parents.

Some people can be very aggressive about the issue, but in general it is not at the forefront of people's agendas at the moments so lots of people are neutral.

I'm continually concerned about the abuse of children, but I think the area of education is critical, and undervalued as a right. In fact, in the US education is not a right. Considering some of these issues in terms of rights is very important.

One of the strengths of our group so far is that we have always been transparent, and open to ideas and participation. Although I am the chair, and there is a core group of three people who make the final decision, no one person dominates. I think this is part of the reason we have managed to stay alive with so little funding. We have also built in stages, and not tried to do too much in one go.

Implementation is a particular problem around the world, whether states have ratified or not. A movement towards ratification in the US would support implementation in the rest of the world.

Implementation is not just about governments but about people themselves, and about children being aware of their rights.

Child rights is about the idea that children are first and foremost human beings, as soon as they come into the world. About 100 years ago in the US, there was a case when some parents sued after their child was killed in an accident. They failed because the court said the child had no value because child labour had no value. In another case in the 1970s, parents in a similar situation were awarded $1 million for emotional loss. But the CRC says that children have value in themselves, and not in relation to other people because of the role they play.

Religious groups were originally opposed to the CRC, but as they became more involved and understood the Convention more, many have realised that this idea ties in with the concept of a child of God, deserving of these rights.

The best thing about my job is working with all these passionate individuals who give up their time for the Campaign. The worst is that the campaign has had to go on for so long.

TASK/TEXT 10.10.2: UNITED STATES – PARENTAL RIGHTS V. CHILD RIGHTS? FIRST SHOTS FIRED IN PHONEY WAR

Crinmail 1075 – 14 April 2009, <www.crin.org>

The bid to secure ratification of the Convention on the Rights of the Child in the United States has prompted a vigorous attempt from "parental rights" advocates to block the move. According to *Politico*, Republican congressman Pete Hoekstra last week introduced a bill in the House to amend the US Constitution to permanently "enshrine" in American society an inviolable set of parents' rights. The bill had 70 co-sponsors, all Republicans.

The bill follows moves from some corners of the Democratic party to initiate the ratification process. During the presidential campaign, then-Sen. Barack Obama replied to a question about the treaty by saying he found it "embarrassing" that the United States stood with Somalia – the only other UN member that has not ratified the treaty – and promised to review it as president.

In the confirmation hearing for Ambassador Susan Rice, Sen. Barbara Boxer (D-Calif.) asked: "[H]ow can we be proud of our country when we haven't ratified? … This is America … What is happening? What has happened?" Rice replied that it was a "shame" that the United States is one of only two countries that have failed to ratify, adding that "there can be no doubt that the president-elect and Secretary Clinton and I share a commitment to the objectives of this treaty and will take it up as an early question."

A false dichotomy

At first glance, the clash is a no-brainer. Why would you oppose something that promotes the protection, participation, health and best interests of children? The motives become more apparent when light is shed on the politics obscured by "moral" arguments. Campaigners hope to establish a false division between the rights of parents and the rights of children in order to cultivate irrational fears about a treaty that has been endorsed in every corner of the world for its commitment to the well being of children.

Pro-parental control groups worry that parents will lose power over their children, that ratification represents bigger government and less personal sovereignty, and that children's rights reflect liberal rather than conservative values. Furthermore, as Julian Zelizer, professor of history and public affairs at

Princeton University, notes: "Opposing the UN has been a rallying cry of the right for decades."

Unfortunately, politics is not only clouding the issue, it also resulting in the widespread distribution of false information that reflects personal beliefs rather [than] the actual provisions contained in the Convention. And it is the well being of children that is at stake.

Michael Farris – a conservative Christian and founder of the Home School Legal Defense Association – said on his website *parentalrights.org* that under the UN treaty [CRC], a "child's 'right to be heard' would allow him (or her) to seek governmental review of every parental decision with which the child disagreed." Farris, who helped draft Hoekstra's bill, said the treaty is "really about government empowerment" and "has nothing to do ultimately with the rights of children."

Parents centre stage

Firstly, the CRC is not about implementing children's rights *instead of* parents' rights. The treaty places parents centre-stage in children's development, and introduces the concept of parental responsibility for their children. It recognises the family "as the fundamental group of society and the natural environment for the growth and well-being of all its members and particularly children ...," and acknowledges "that the child, for the full and harmonious development of his or her personality, should grow up in a family environment, in an atmosphere of happiness, love, and understanding" (Preamble).

Secondly, the UN treaty [CRC] protects a child's right to be heard, but it is false and misleading to suggest this would mean children could "seek the review [of] every parental decision with which he or she disagreed." It is about the right to be heard, not the right to make decisions or take cases against parents – this is clear from the language of the CRC.

Lastly, the treaty is not about "government empowerment." In fact, ratification of the CRC means that the government will be held to account for their obligations under the Convention by the [CRC's] Committee on the Rights of the Child.

There are a number of other myths put forward by those opposing the US ratification of the CRC, all of them without merit, and most of them based on either ignorance or inaccurate propaganda. The Campaign for US Ratification of the Convention on the Rights of the Child lists more of such myths, and counters them [on the website of *The Campaign for US Ratification of the Convention on the Rights of the Child (CRC)*, <http://childrightscampaign.org>, go to <http://childrightscampaign.org/crcindex.php?sNav=getinformed_snav.php&sDat=faqs_dat.php>].

More than 190 countries have promised to abide by the Convention without the devastating consequences opponents argue are lurking around the corner. Furthermore, the treaty is supported by groups ranging from the Girl Scouts to the Christian Children's Fund in the United States; and opponents both overestimate and misunderstand the treaty's purpose and likely impact.

"The Committee on the Rights of the Child has been unfairly characterised as a kind of Big Brother apparatus ... but that was not the intent of it," says Meg Gardinier, chairwoman of the Campaign for US Ratification of the Convention on the Rights of the Child.

Ultimately, the losers of any successful political bid to block ratification will be children themselves.

TASK/TEXT 10.11: THE AFRICAN COMMITTEE OF EXPERTS ON THE RIGHTS AND WELFARE OF THE CHILD

<www.crin.org/RM/acrwc.asp>, see also <www.africa-union.org/child/home.htm>

What is the Committee of Experts on the Rights and Welfare of the Child?

The *African Committee of Experts on the Rights and Welfare of the Child*, which was established in July 2001, monitors the implementation of the African Charter on the Rights and Welfare of the Child. The Committee draws its mandate from Articles 32–46 of the Charter. The Committee reports to the Assembly of Heads of State and the *African Union* (AU) every two years. It must also consider any communications it has received about violations of children's rights under Article 44 of the Charter to the AU.

What is the African Charter on the Rights and Welfare of the Child?

The African Charter on the Rights and Welfare of the Child spells out the rights that African States must ensure for children living in their jurisdiction. It is the main instrument of the African human rights system for promoting and protecting child rights.

The Charter, which was adopted by the Organisation of African Unity (now the African Union) in July 1990, entered into force in November 1999. The Charter was the first regional treaty to address child rights.

The Charter is divided into two parts of four chapters. Part one deals with the rights, freedoms and duties of the child and has 31 articles. Part two deals with States' obligations to adopt legislative and other measures to implement the provisions of the Charter and has 18 articles.

The African Charter was created partly to complement the *UN Convention on the Rights of the Child* (CRC), but also because African countries were under-represented in the drafting process of the CRC, and many felt another treaty was needed to address the specific realities of children in Africa.

What is the difference between the UN Convention on the Rights of the Child and the African Charter on the Rights and Welfare of the Child?

The two treaties make many similar provisions and have the same over-arching principles of non-discrimination, participation, the best interests of the child, survival and development, evolving capacities.

Some of the other issues that African States wanted the Charter to include were: children living under apartheid, harmful practices against the girl child, such as female genital mutilation (FGM), internal conflicts and displacement, the definition of a child, the rights of children of imprisoned mothers, poor and unsanitary living conditions, the African conception of communities' responsibilities and duties, weak enforcement and monitoring mechanisms, role of the family in adoption and fostering, and the duties and responsibilities of the child towards the family and community. (…)

What are its powers and functions?

The role of the African Committee of Experts on the Rights and Welfare of the Child is to promote and protect the rights spelled out in the African Charter of the Rights and Welfare of the Child.

Its main functions are to:

- collect information
- interpret provisions of the Charter; monitor the implementation of the Charter
- give recommendations to governments for working with child rights organisations
- consider individual complaints about violations of children's rights; and,
- investigate measures adopted by States to implement the Charter by carrying out missions, collecting information, and questioning States (see Article 45 of the Charter).

The Committee also chooses the theme of the Days of the African Child which are held every year on 16 June to commemorate those killed in the Soweto uprisings in South Africa. (…)

When does the Committee meet?
The Committee meets twice a year in ordinary sessions of no more than two weeks. It held its first session in July 2001. The chairperson can also convene extraordinary sessions at the request of the Committee or of a State Party to the Charter. Sessions generally take place at the Headquarters of the African Union in Addis Ababa, Ethiopia, but can be held elsewhere at the Committee's request.

Who are the experts?
The Committee is formed of 11 experts, who serve in an individual capacity and are elected for a term of five years by the Executive Council. They are appointed by the Assembly of Heads of States and Government of the African Union. In contrast to the African Commission on Human and People's Rights, Committee Experts may not be re-elected. (…)

What types of investigations can the Committee undertake?
The Committee has not yet undertaken any investigations, but it is empowered to undertake two types of investigations under *Article 45* of the Charter:

1. on issues arising from the Charter based on allegations of violations of child rights
2. on measures taken by States Parties to implement the Charter.

Who would carry out the investigations?
The Committee could set up sub-committees or working groups to carry out the investigation. The Committee can designate a Special Rapporteur among its members or independent experts to accompany sub-committees, working groups and Special Rapporteurs on their missions.

The Committee will prepare a preliminary mission report on the situation of child rights in the country, and a final report in which it will make recommendations to the State Party concerned. The recommendations will also be sent to other public and private institutions responsible for monitoring and implementing child rights.

Will these investigations be followed up?
The Committee invites a State to submit a written reply with information on measures taken to follow up recommendations made by the Committee after the mission. It could also request additional information on measures taken by the State Party from other institutions and civil society organisations. It could also ask the State to include information about measures it has taken to follow-up recommendations in its next report to the Committee.

How does the State reporting process work?
States were due to submit their initial reports about the measures they have adopted to implement the provisions of the African Charter two years after they have ratified the Charter, and every three years thereafter. However, the Committee began its work in 2001 and as of December 2006, only the following countries had submitted their initial reports: **Egypt, Mauritius, Rwanda** and **Nigeria.** The Committee began examining State Party reports in May 2008. (…)

How can civil society organisations participate?
The parameters of civil society's participation have not yet been formally established. Some draft criteria for granting NGOs and other associations observer status to allow them to participate in the Committee's activities were agreed upon (…).

Some of the ways NGOs and associations will be allowed to participate include:

- attending opening and closing ceremonies of the Committee sessions,
- participating in the Committee's meetings
- accessing documents that are not confidential and do not deal with issues concerning the observers
- being invited to participate in closed sessions dealing with issues that concern them
- making statements on issues that concern them, provided the statement has been sent to the Committee in advance
- responding to questions they may be asked in meetings.

Does the Committee examine individual complaints?
Article 44 of the Charter empowers the Committee to consider individual communications alleging a violation of any of the rights enshrined in the Charter. However, States can make reservations on the extent of the Committee's powers; for example, Egypt does not consider itself bound by this article. Any individual, group or non-governmental organisation recognised by the African Union, by a Member State, the UN, or **children themselves** may bring such a complaint.

The Committee's guidelines state that "where a child is capable of expressing his or her opinions, they should be heard by a Committee member." Children may bring complaints under universal human rights treaties if their State is not a party to the African Charter. However, a communication may be presented on behalf of a victim without his consent if the author is able to prove that the complaint has been brought in the supreme interest of the child.

Communications are sent to all Committee members three months prior to each ordinary session. The Committee may set up a working group to meet before its sessions to consider whether a communication will be accepted. The working group then appoints a rapporteur. The Committee, working group or rapporteur brings the communication to the attention of the State concerned and requests an explanation or written statement within six months. The Committee may also request the presence of the person or group submitting the communication and the State party concerned for more information, clarification or observations.

Provisional measures
While the Committee is considering a communication, it can ask the State concerned to take certain measures to prevent any harm to the child mentioned in the communication, or other children who could be victims of similar violations. No such requests for provisional measures have yet been made (...).

TASK/TEXT 10.12: 60TH ANNIVERSARY OF THE UNIVERSAL DECLARATION OF HUMAN RIGHTS

Crinmail 1041 – 11 December 2008, <www.crin.org>

What is the Declaration?
The United Nations Charter was the first instrument to give formal recognition to the universal human rights movement, which began at the end of the Second World War.

However, the Charter stopped shy of incorporating a bill of rights – this was left to the Universal Declaration of Human Rights (UDHR), which was adopted by the UN General Assembly in 1948. Out of 56 Member States at the time, 48 voted in favour and eight abstained (including Saudi Arabia, South Africa and the Soviet Union).

The plan was to use the Universal Declaration as a springboard for the development of treaties – and two treaties on civil and political rights (ICCPR), and economic, social and cultural rights (ICESCR), duly followed. The UDHR, ICCPR and ICESCR are sometimes collectively called the International Bill of [Human] Rights. It was not until 1989 that the Convention on the Rights of the Child (CRC) was adopted, however.

Progress?
Terre des Hommes notes that since the declaration, there has been undoubted progress in the fields of health, education and the recognition that each child is a person with inherent rights and a vital socio-economic role. However child [abuse, neglect and] exploitation is still a very major issue and numbers seem to

be growing. Children also continue to suffer from inequalities at all stages in their development.

Of the 9.7 million child deaths in 2006, almost half were in Sub-Saharan Africa and almost one third in South Asia. About 57 per cent of the children of primary school age who are not in school are girls. "All in all, there is still a long way to go," says Eylah Hamouda, the TDHIF Coordinator. "We see, for example, that in times of economic crisis the progress for children, which has been so difficult to achieve, can easily be reversed."

Plan International is using the 60th anniversary of the Universal Declaration of Human Rights to highlight the fact that around 50 million children are born without birth certificates every year, which makes abolishing crimes like child sex trafficking more difficult.

"The registration piece of paper is a child's absolute first right and in many developing countries it never happens," said Australian Chief Executive Ian Wishart. "More than 50 million people go unregistered and what this has in terms of consequences for children is quite dramatic. Say in Bangladesh, where Plan has helped register another 5.9 million people, many children are forced into early marriages.

"Without a birth certificate they can't stand up and say 'I don't want to take part in this marriage,' and they can't prove their age very easily. It's the same thing for child trafficking.

"Places like Cambodia where children can be trafficked to places like Thailand – once they're in Thailand it's very hard for them to prove who they are, where they came from and the fact that they're just a child."

Why is the Declaration important?

As a declaration voted for in the General Assembly, the UDHR lacked the formal authority of a treaty that binds parties under international law (like the CRC). Nonetheless, it remains in some sense the constitution of the entire movement, as well as the single most cited human rights instrument. Some also say that it has become binding because it is now considered part of 'customary international law,' since it has been quoted and invoked in respect of human rights violations on so many occasions. Not all governments have become parties to all human rights treaties, but all countries have accepted the UDHR. "The Universal Declaration of Human Rights is a landmark [instrument] that has shaped our social history since its inception," said Raffaele Salinari, Chairman of Terre des Hommes International Federation. "It is also the common ground which unites mankind in reflecting the general aspirations of all human beings no matter what their culture."

What does it mean in practice?

Over the years, the commitments have been translated into law, whether in the form of treaties, customary international law, general principles, regional agreements or domestic law. The UDHR is the most translated document in the world.

As well as prompting the development of a raft of other international human rights treaties, which are binding on governments (such as the CRC), the UDHR has been deployed directly in domestic and international law cases where violations of human rights have occurred.

As with all human rights instruments its value is not confined to the legal sphere. Many grassroots organisations, human rights advocates, and individuals use the UDHR as an **advocacy tool to persuade, educate and shame**. For those with limited domestic protection, the UDHR, along with other human rights treaties, is a means of showing governments and oppressors that they have the backing of the international community, and that there are people committed to ensuring their demands for justice do not go unheeded.

The UDHR is also a powerful tool which policy makers and programmers may use, along with other human rights instruments, to ensure that policy and programmes which affect people's lives address the spectrum of exclusions and challenges people face in their daily lives around the world.

As the first international bill of rights, the impact of the UDHR has been profound and far-reaching.

What is its relation to the Convention on the Rights of the Child?

As discussed above, the UDHR was the precursor, sometimes referred to as the 'human rights constitution,' which spawned the proliferation of other binding international human rights treaties – of which the Convention on the Rights of the Child is of course a crucial member.

Since the CRC is binding, it means that [States parties] are obliged to implement its articles. How the CRC is incorporated into national systems depends on the domestic legal framework. In 'monist' systems, if a country ratifies the Convention, it automatically becomes part of national law. This is the case in The Netherlands and the US for example. In 'dualist' systems, the government has to enact extra legislation to incorporate the Convention into national law, for example in the United Kingdom. [Both monist and dualist States are accountable under international law, however. Monism and dualism are only a matter of national law. –JW]

Why rights? Why children?

The concept of rights goes much further than charity. It is not limited to the satisfaction of specific needs, it has to do with how needs are met. It is not about the state doing favours for children. It is about them meeting legal obligations to respect children's rights.

Children face particular exclusions and discrimination [worldwide "transism," that is transgenerational discrimination, JW] for which they [and their carers, JW] need special provision.

The fact that children are not adults means they may receive unfair treatment, or be left out of decision-making. Children cannot vote, for example, and most countries allow parents to hit their children, even though they would be prosecuted for assault if they hit another adult.

There are therefore a number of rights in the Convention on the Rights of the Child (CRC) which apply especially to children. These include, for example, the obligation to consider their views, and limitations on the use of children in armed conflict.

The CRC is important because it emphasises that children are the subjects of rights, as having agency (i.e., they can exert their own power and influence), and as having a voice that must be listened to and given due weight. It establishes a direct relationship between a child and the State [not only via parents, other carers or professionals, such as doctors or teachers, JW.]

The use and abuse of rights

Unfortunately, children's rights, and human rights, are often misunderstood. For example, those waging war have argued they are defending human rights, despite breaching numerous rights in the process. And some who say they want to enforce children's rights are in reality only worried about certain rights – these are usually the most horrifying, like sexual abuse.

Human rights education is often lacking, and reports, for example in the media, may create a misleading view of their nature. For example, reactionary newspapers often carry stories about 'demon' children escaping justice because of their 'human rights' claims. And for police men and women who do not receive appropriate training, human rights can simply represent the possibility of evading justice. Other groups and sections of society object to human rights because they challenge something about their beliefs, or because they find the concept of 'entitlement' threatening.

But across all professions, in all media, in each country and in most governments, there are pockets of human rights advocates who are striving to further the human rights of all people. They talk of rights because they believe people should not have to 'deserve' something to which they are entitled, and because they believe **rights are the best means with which to challenge power, exploitation and exclusion**. Sixty years may have passed since the adoption of the Declaration, and violations may still be the norm rather than the exception, but the global clamour for social justice through the language of human rights means the anniversary should be a day of hope not resignation.

TASK/TEXT 10.13: SARAH BLAFFER HRDY, MOTHERS AND OTHERS

<http://findarticles.com/p/articles/mi_m1134/is_4_110/ai_74693746/pg_1?tag=content;col1>, Sarah Blaffer Hrdy[93], *Natural History* May 2001; accessed 7 February 2009 (interview in Dutch: "Eerst was er het gevoel," *NRC Handelsblad*, Wetenschap, 7/8 February 2009, pp. 4–5)

From queen bees to elephant matriarchs, many animal mothers are assisted by others in rearing offspring. Anthropologist Sarah Blaffer Hrdy maintains that our human ancestors, too, were "cooperative breeders" – a mode of life that enabled them to thrive in many new environments. Today, argues Hrdy, our continued ability to raise emotionally healthy children may well depend on how well we understand the cooperative aspect of our evolutionary heritage.

Mother apes – chimpanzees, gorillas, orangutans, humans – dote on their babies. And why not? They give birth to an infant after a long gestation and, in most cases, suckle it for years. With humans, however, the job of providing for a juvenile goes on and on. Unlike all other ape babies, ours mature slowly and reach independence late. A mother in a foraging society may give birth every four years or so, and her first few children remain dependent long after each new baby arrives; among nomadic foragers, grown-ups may provide food to children for eighteen or more years. To come up with the 10–13 million calories that anthropologists such as Hillard Kaplan calculate are needed to rear a young human to independence, a mother needs help.

So how did our prehuman and early human ancestresses living in the Pleistocene Epoch (from 1.6 million until roughly 10,000 years ago) manage to get those calories? And under what conditions would natural selection allow a female ape to produce babies so large and slow to develop that they are beyond her means to rear on her own?

The old answer was that fathers helped out by hunting. And so they do. But hunting is a risky occupation, and fathers may die or defect or take up with other females. And when they do, what then? New evidence from surviving traditional cultures suggests that mothers in the Pleistocene may have had a significant

93 An anthropologist with a long-standing interest in the natural relationships among males, females, and their offspring, Sarah Blaffer Hrdy (...) began her research in the 1970s with a nine-year study of Hanuman langurs, a species that Indians regard as sacred. Her evolutionary perspective on families has resulted in two previous major essays for Natural History: "Daughters or Sons" (April 1988) and "Natural-Born Mothers" (December 1995). Hrdy (...) is professor emerita of anthropology at the University of California, Davis, and the author of four books, including, most recently, *Mother Nature: A History of Mothers, Infants, and Natural Selection* (Pantheon Books, 1999).

degree of help – from men who thought they just might have been the fathers, from grandmothers and great-aunts, from older children.

These helpers other than the mother, called **allomothers** by sociobiologists, do not just protect and provision youngsters. In groups such as the Efe and Aka Pygmies of central Africa, allomothers actually hold children and carry them about. In these tight-knit communities of communal foragers – within which men, women, and children still hunt with nets, much as humans are thought to have done tens of thousands of years ago – siblings, aunts, uncles, fathers, and grandmothers hold newborns on the first day of life. When University of New Mexico anthropologist Paula Ivey asked an Efe woman, "Who cares for babies?" the immediate answer was, "We all do!" By three weeks of age, the babies are in contact with allomothers 40 percent of the time. By eighteen weeks, infants actually spend more time with allomothers than with their gestational mothers. On average, Efe babies have fourteen different caretakers, most of whom are close kin. According to Washington State University anthropologist Barry Hewlett, Aka babies are within arm's reach of their fathers for more than half of every day.

Accustomed to celebrating the antiquity and naturalness of mother-centered models of child care, as well as the nuclear family in which the mother nurtures while the father provides, we Westerners tend to regard the practices of the Efe and the Aka as exotic. But to sociobiologists, whose stock in trade is comparisons across species, all this helping has a familiar ring. It's called **cooperative breeding**. During the past quarter century, as anthropologists and sociobiologists started to compare notes, one of the spectacular surprises has been how much allomaternal care goes on, not just within various human societies but among animals generally. Evidently, diverse organisms have converged on cooperative breeding for the best of evolutionary reasons.

A broad look at the most recent evidence has convinced me that cooperative breeding was the strategy that permitted our own ancestors to produce costly, slow-maturing infants at shorter intervals, to take advantage of new kinds of resources in habitats other than the mixed savanna-woodland of tropical Africa, and to spread more widely and swiftly than any primate had before. We already know that animal mothers who delegate some of the costs of infant care to others are thereby freed to produce more or larger young or to breed more frequently. Consider the case of silver-backed jackals. Patricia Moehlman, of the World Conservation Union, has shown that for every extra helper bringing back food, jackal parents rear one extra pup per litter. Cooperative breeding also helps various species expand into habitats in which they would normally not be able to rear any young at all. Florida scrub-jays, for example, breed in an exposed landscape where unrelenting predation from hawks and snakes usually precludes the fledging of young; survival in this habitat is possible only because older siblings help guard and feed the young. Such cooperative arrangements permit animals as different as naked mole rats (the social insects of the mammal world) and wolves to move into new habitats and sometimes to spread over vast areas.

What does it take to become a cooperative breeder? Obviously, this lifestyle is an option only for creatures capable of living in groups. It is facilitated when young but fully mature individuals (such as young Florida scrub-jays) do not or cannot immediately leave their natal group to breed on their own and instead remain among kin in their natal location. As with delayed maturation, delayed dispersal of young means that teenagers, "spinster" aunts, real and honorary uncles will be on hand to help their kin rear young. Flexibility is another criterion for cooperative breeders. Helpers must be ready to shift to breeding mode should the opportunity arise. In marmosets and tamarins – the little South American monkeys that are, besides us, the only full-fledged cooperative breeders among primates – a female has to be ready to be a helper this year and a mother the next. She may have one mate or several. In canids such as wolves or wild dogs, usually only the dominant, or alpha, male and female in a pack reproduce, but younger group members hunt with the mother and return to the den to regurgitate predigested meat into the mouths of her pups. In a fascinating instance of physiological flexibility, a subordinate female may actually undergo hormonal transformations similar to those of a real pregnancy: her belly swells, and she begins to manufacture milk and may help nurse the pups of the alpha pair. Vestiges of cooperative breeding crop up as well in domestic dogs, the distant descendants of wolves. After undergoing a pseudopregnancy, my neighbors' Jack Russell terrier chased away the family's cat and adopted and suckled her kittens. To suckle the young of another species is hardly what Darwinians call an adaptive trait (because it does not contribute to the surrogate's own survival). But in the environment in which the dog family evolved, a female's tendency to respond when infants signaled their need – combined with her capacity for pseudopregnancy – would have increased the survival chances for large litters born to the dominant female.

According to the late W.D. Hamilton, evolutionary logic predicts that an animal with poor prospects of reproducing on his or her own should be predisposed to assist kin with better prospects so that at least some of their shared genes will be perpetuated. Among wolves, for example, both male and female helpers in the pack are likely to be genetically related to the alpha litter and to have good reasons for not trying to reproduce on their own: in a number of cooperatively breeding species (wild dogs, wolves, hyenas, dingoes, dwarf mongooses, marmosets), the helpers do try, but the dominant female is likely to bite their babies to death. The threat of coercion makes postponing ovulation the better part of valor, the least-bad option for females who must wait to breed until their circumstances improve, either through the death of a higher-ranking female or by finding a mate with an unoccupied territory.

One primate strategy is to line up extra fathers. Among common marmosets and several species of tamarins, females mate with several males, all of which help rear her young. As primatologist Charles T. Snowdon points out, in three of the four genera of Callitrichidae (Callithrix, Saguinus, and Leontopithecus), the more adult males the group has available to help, the more young survive. Among many of these species, females ovulate just after giving birth, perhaps encouraging males to stick around until after babies are born. (In cotton-top tamarins, males also undergo hormonal changes that prepare them to care for infants at the time of birth.) Among cooperative breeders of certain other species, such as wolves and jackals, pups born in the same litter can be sired by different fathers.

Human mothers, by contrast, don't ovulate again right after birth, nor do they produce offspring with more than one genetic father at a time. Ever inventive, though, humans solve the problem of enlisting help from several adult males by other means. In some cultures, mothers rely on a peculiar belief that anthropologists call partible paternity – the notion that a fetus is built up by contributions of semen from all the men with whom women have had sex in the ten months or so prior to giving birth. Among the Canela, a matrilineal tribe in Brazil studied for many years by William Crocker of the Smithsonian Institution, publicly sanctioned intercourse between women and men other than their husbands – sometimes many men – takes place during villagewide ceremonies. What might lead to marital disaster elsewhere works among the Canela because the men believe in partible paternity. Across a broad swath of South America – from Paraguay up into Brazil, westward to Peru, and northward to Venezuela – mothers rely on this convenient folk wisdom to line up multiple honorary fathers to help them provision both themselves and their children. Over hundreds of generations, this belief has helped children thrive in a part of the world where food sources are unpredictable and where husbands are as likely as not to return from the hunt empty-handed.

The Bari people of Venezuela are among those who believe in shared paternity, and according to anthropologist Stephen Beckerman, Bari children with more than one father do especially well. In Beckerman's study of 822 children, 80 percent of those who had both a "primary" father (the man married to their mother) and a "secondary" father survived to age fifteen, compared with 64 percent survival for those with a primary father alone. Not surprisingly, as soon as a Bari woman suspects she is pregnant, she accepts sexual advances from the more successful fishermen or hunters in her group. Belief that fatherhood can be shared draws more men into the web of possible paternity, which effectively translates into more food and more protection.

But for human mothers, extra mates aren't the only source of effective help. Older children, too, play a significant role in family survival. University of Nebraska anthropologists Patricia Draper and Raymond Hames have just shown that among!Kung hunters and gatherers living in the Kalahari Desert, there is a significant correlation between how many children a parent successfully raises and how many older siblings were on hand to help during that person's own childhood.

Older matrilineal kin may be the most valuable helpers of all. University of Utah anthropologists Kristen Hawkes and James O'Connell and their UCLA colleague Nicholas Blurton Jones, who have demonstrated the important food-gathering role of older women among Hazda hunter-gatherers in Tanzania, delight in explaining that since human life spans may extend for a few decades after menopause, older women become available to care for – and to provide vital food for – children born to younger kin. Hawkes, O'Connell, and Blurton Jones further believe that dating from the earliest days of Homo erectus, the survival of weaned children during food shortages may have depended on tubers dug up by older kin.

At various times in human history, people have also relied on a range of customs, as well as on coercion, to line up allomaternal assistance – for example, by using slaves or hiring poor women as wet nurses. But all the helpers in the world are of no use if they're not motivated to protect, carry, or provision babies. For both humans and nonhumans, this motivation arises in three main ways: through the manipulation of information about kinship; through appealing signals coming from the babies themselves; and, at the heart of it all, from the endocrinological and neural processes that induce individuals to respond to infants' signals. Indeed, all primates and many other mammals eventually respond to infants in a nurturing way if exposed long enough to their signals. Trouble is, "long enough" can mean very different things in males and females, with their very different response thresholds.

For decades, animal behaviorists have been aware of the phenomenon known as priming. A mouse or rat encountering a strange pup is likely to respond by either ignoring the pup or eating it. But presented with pup after pup, rodents of either sex eventually become sensitized to the baby and start caring for it. Even a male may gather pups into a nest and lick or huddle over them. Although nurturing is not a routine part of a male's repertoire, when sufficiently primed he behaves as a mother would. Hormonal change is an obvious candidate for explaining this transformation. Consider the case of the cooperatively breeding Florida scrub-jays studied by Stephan Schoech, of the University of Memphis. Prolactin, a protein hormone that initiates the secretion of milk in female mammals, is also present in male mammals and in birds of Both sexes. Schoech showed that levels of prolactin go up in a male and female jay as they build their nest and incubate eggs and that these levels reach a peak when they feed their young. Moreover, prolactin levels rise in the jays' nonbreeding helpers and are also at their highest when they assist in feeding nestlings.

As it happens, male, as well as immature and nonbreeding female, primates can respond to infants' signals, although quite different levels of exposure and stimulation are required to get them going. Twenty years ago, when elevated prolactin levels were first reported in common marmoset males (by Alan Dixson, for Callithrix jacchus), many scientists refused to believe it. Later, when the finding was confirmed, scientists assumed this effect would be found only in fathers. But based on work by Scott Nunes, Jeffrey Fite, Jeffrey French, Charles Snowdon, Lucille Roberts, and many others – work that deals with a variety of species of marmosets and tamarins – we now know that all sorts of hormonal changes are associated with increased nurturing in males. For example, in the tuftedeared marmosets studied by French and colleagues, testosterone levels in males went down as they engaged in caretaking after the birth of an infant. Testosterone levels tended to be lowest in those with the most paternal experience.

The biggest surprise, however, has been that something similar goes on in males of our own species. Anne Storey and colleagues in Canada have reported that prolactin levels in men who were living with pregnant women went up toward the end of the pregnancy. But the most significant finding was a 30 percent drop in testosterone in men right after the birth. (Some endocrinologically literate wags have proposed that this drop in testosterone levels is due to sleep deprivation, but this would probably not explain the parallel testosterone drop in marmoset males housed with parturient females.) Hormonal changes during pregnancy and lactation are, of course, indisputably more pronounced in mothers than in the men consorting with them, and no one is suggesting that male consorts are equivalent to mothers. But both sexes are surprisingly susceptible to infant signals – **explaining why fathers, adoptive parents, wet nurses, and day-care workers can become deeply involved with the infants they care for.**

Genetic relatedness alone, in fact, is a surprisingly unreliable predictor of love. What matters are cues from infants and how these cues are processed emotionally. The capacity for becoming emotionally hooked – or primed – also explains how a fully engaged father who is in frequent contact with his infant can become more committed to the infant's well-being than a detached mother will.

But we can't forget the real protagonist of this story: the baby. From birth, newborns are powerfully motivated to stay close, to root – even to creep – in quest of nipples, which they instinctively suck on. These are the first innate behaviors that any of us engage in. But maintaining contact is harder for little humans to do than it is for other primates. One problem is that human mothers are not very hairy, so a human mother not only has to position the baby on her breast but also has to keep him there. She must be motivated to pick up her baby even before her milk comes in, bringing with it a host of hormonal transformations.

Within minutes of birth, human babies can cry and vocalize just as other primates do, but human newborns can also read facial expressions and make a few of their own. Even with blurry vision, they engage in eye-to-eye contact with the people around them. Newborn babies, when alert, can see about eighteen inches away. When people put their faces within range, babies may reward this attention by looking back or even imitating facial expressions. Orang and chimp babies, too, are strongly attached to and interested in their mothers' faces. But unlike humans, other ape mothers and infants do not get absorbed in gazing deeply into each other's eyes.

To the extent that psychiatrists and pediatricians have thought about this difference between us and the other apes, they tend to attribute it to human mental agility and our ability to use language. Interactions between mother and baby, including vocal play and babbling, have been interpreted as protoconversations: revving up the baby to learn to talk. Yet even babies who lack face-to-face stimulation – babies born blind, say – learn to talk. Furthermore, humans are not the only primates to engage in the continuous rhythmic streams of vocalization known as babbling. Interestingly, marmoset and tamarin babies also babble. It may be that the infants of cooperative breeders are specially equipped to communicate with caretakers. This is not to say that babbling is not an important part of learning to talk, only to question which came first – babbling so as to develop into a talker, or a predisposition to evolve into a talker because among cooperative breeders, babies that babble are better tended and more likely to survive.

If humans evolved as cooperative breeders, the degree of a human mother's commitment to her infant should be linked to how much social support she herself can expect. Mothers in cooperatively breeding primate species can afford to bear and rear such costly offspring as they do only if they have help on hand. Maternal abandonment and abuse are very rarely observed among primates in the wild. In fact, the only primate species in which mothers are anywhere near as likely to abandon infants at birth as mothers in our own species are the other cooperative breeders. A study of cotton-top tamarins at the New England Regional Primate Research Center showed a 12 percent chance of abandonment if mothers had older siblings on hand to help them rear twins, but a 57 percent chance when no help was available. Overburdened mothers abandoned infants within seventy-two hours of birth.

This new way of thinking about our species' history, with its implications for children, has **made me concerned about the future**. So far, most Western researchers studying infant development have presumed that living in a nuclear family with a fixed division of labor (mom nurturing, dad providing) is the normal human adaptation. Most contemporary research on children's psychosocial development is derived from John Bowlby's theories of attachment and has focused on such variables as how available and responsive the mother is, whether the father is present or absent, and whether the child is in the mother's care or in day care. Sure enough, studies done with this model in mind always show that children with less responsive mothers are at greater risk.

It is the baby, first and foremost, who senses how available and how committed its mother is. But I know of no studies that take into account the possibility that humans evolved as cooperative breeders and that **a mother's responsiveness also happens to be a good indicator of her social supports**. In terms of developmental outcomes, the most relevant factor might not be how securely or insecurely attached to the mother the baby is – the variable that developmental psychologists are trained to measure – but rather **how secure the baby is in relation to all the people caring for him or her**. Measuring attachment this way might help explain why even children whose relations with their mother suggest they are at extreme risk manage to do fine because of the interventions of a committed father, an older sibling, or a there-when-you-need-her grandmother.

The most comprehensive study ever done on how nonmaternal care affects kids is compatible with both the hypothesis that humans evolved as cooperative breeders and the conventional hypothesis that human babies are adapted to be reared exclusively by mothers. Undertaken by the National Institute of Child Health and Human Development (NICHD) in 1991, the seven-year study included 1,364 children and their families (from diverse ethnic and economic backgrounds) and was conducted in ten different US locations. This extraordinarily ambitious study was launched because statistics showed that 62 percent of US mothers with children under age six were working outside the home and that the majority of them (willingly or unwillingly) were back at work within three to five months of giving birth. Because this was an entirely new social phenomenon, no one really knew what the NICHD's research would reveal.

The study's main finding was that both maternal and hired caretakers' sensitivity to infant needs was a better predictor of a child's subsequent development and behavior (such traits as social "compliance," respect for others, and self-control were measured) than was actual time spent apart from the mother. In other words, the critical variable was not the continuous presence of the mother herself but rather **how secure infants felt when cared for by someone**

else. People who had been convinced that babies need full-time care from mothers to develop normally were stunned by these results, while advocates of day care felt vindicated. But do these and other, similar findings mean that day care is not something we need to worry about anymore?

Not at all. **We should keep worrying.** The NICHD study showed only that day care was better than mother care if the mother was neglectful or abusive. But excluding such worst-case scenarios, the study showed no detectable ill effects from day care only when infants had a secure relationship with parents to begin with (which I take to mean that **babies felt wanted**) and only when the **day care was of high quality**. And in this study's context, "high quality" meant that the facility had a high ratio of caretakers to babies, that it had the same caretakers all the time, and that the caretakers were sensitive to infants' needs – in other words, that the day care staff acted like committed kin.

Bluntly put, this kind of day care is almost impossible to find. Where it exists at all, it's expensive. Waiting lists are long, even for cheap or inadequate care. The average rate of staff turnover in day care centers is 30 percent per year, primarily because these workers are paid barely the minimum wage (usually less, in fact, than parking-lot attendants). Furthermore, day care tends to be age-graded, so even at centers where staff members stay put, kids move annually to new teachers. This kind of day care is unlikely to foster trusting relationships.

What conclusion can we draw from all this? Instead of arguing over "mother care" versus "other care," **we need to make day care better**. And this is where I think today's evolution-minded researchers have something to say. Impressed by just how variable child-rearing conditions can be in human societies, several anthropologists and psychologists (including Michael Lamb, Patricia Draper, Henry Harpending, and James Chisholm) have suggested that babies are up to more than just maintaining the relationship with their mothers. These researchers propose that babies actually monitor mothers to gain information about the world they have been born into. **Babies ask, in effect, Is this world filled with people who are going to provide for me and help me survive?** Can I count on them to care about me? If the answer to those questions is yes, they begin to sense that **developing a conscience and a capacity for compassion** would be a great idea. If the answer is no, they may then be asking, Can I not afford to count on others? Would I be better off just grabbing what I need, however I can? In this case, empathy, or thinking about others' needs, would be more of a hindrance than a help.

For a developing baby and child, the most practical way to behave might vary drastically, depending on whether the mother has kin who help, whether the father is around, whether foster parents are well-meaning or exploitative. These factors, however unconsciously perceived by the child, affect important developmental decisions. **Being extremely self-centered or selfish, being**

oblivious to others or lacking in conscience – traits that psychologists and child-development theorists may view as pathological – are probably quite adaptive traits for an individual who is short on support from other group members.

If I am right that humans evolved as cooperative breeders, Pleistocene babies whose mothers lacked social support and were less than fully committed to infant care would have been unlikely to survive. But once people started to settle down – 10,000 or 20,000 or perhaps 30,000 years ago – the picture changed. Ironically, survival chances for neglected children increased. As people lingered longer in one place, eliminated predators, built walled houses, stored food – not to mention inventing things such as rubber nipples and pasteurized milk – infant survival became decoupled from continuous contact with a caregiver.

Since the end of the Pleistocene, whether in preindustrial or industrialized environments, some children have been surviving levels of social neglect that previously would have meant certain death. Some children get very little attention, even in the most benign of contemporary homes. In the industrialized world, children routinely survive caretaking practices that an Efe or a!Kung mother would find appallingly negligent. In traditional societies, no decent mother leaves her baby alone at any time, and traditional mothers are shocked to learn that Western mothers leave infants unattended in a crib all night.

Without passing judgment, one may point out that only in the recent history of humankind could infants deprived of supportive human contact survive to reproduce themselves. Certainly there are a lot of humanitarian reasons to worry about this situation: **one wants each baby, each child, to be lovingly cared for.** From my evolutionary perspective, though, even more is at stake.

Even if we manage to survive what most people are worrying about – global warming, emergent diseases, rogue viruses, meteorites crashing into earth – **will we still be human thousands of years down the line?** By that I mean human in the way we currently define ourselves. The reason our species has managed to survive and proliferate to the extent that 6 billion people currently occupy the planet has to do with how readily we can learn to cooperate when we want to. And our capacity for empathy is one of the things that made us good at doing that.

At a rudimentary level, of course, all sorts of creatures are good at reading intentions and movements and anticipating what other animals are going to do. Predators from gopher snakes to lions have to be able to anticipate where their quarry will dart. Chimps and gorillas can figure out what another individual is likely to know or not know. But compared with that of humans, this capacity to entertain the psychological perspective of other individuals is crude.

The capacity for empathy is uniquely well developed in our species, so much so that many people (including me) believe that along with language and

symbolic thought, it is what makes us human. We are capable of compassion, of understanding other people's "fears and motives, their longings and griefs and vanities," as novelist Edmund White puts it. We spend time and energy worrying about people we have never even met, about babies left in dumpsters, about the existence of more than 12 million AIDS orphans in Africa.

Psychologists know that there is a heritable component to emotional capacity and that this affects the development of compassion among individuals. By fourteen months of age, identical twins (who share all genes) are more alike in how they react to an experimenter who pretends to painfully pinch her finger on a clipboard than are fraternal twins (who share only half their genes). But empathy also has a learned component, which has more to do with analytical skills. **During the first years of life, within the context of early relationships with mothers and other committed caretakers, each individual learns to look at the world from someone else's perspective.**

And this is why I get so worried. Just because humans have evolved to be smart enough to chronicle our species' histories, to speculate about its origins, and to figure out that we have about 30,000 genes in our genome is no reason to assume that evolution has come to a standstill. As gene frequencies change, natural selection acts on the outcome, the expression of those genes. No one doubts, for instance, that fish benefit from being able to see. Yet species reared in total darkness – as are the small, cave-dwelling characin of Mexico – fail to develop their visual capacity. Through evolutionary time, traits that are unexpressed are eventually lost. If populations of these fish are isolated in caves long enough, youngsters descended from those original populations will no longer be able to develop eyesight at all, even if reared in sunlight.

If human compassion develops only under particular rearing conditions, and if an increasing proportion of the species survives to breeding age without developing compassion, it won't make any difference how useful this trait was among our ancestors. It will become like sight in cave-dwelling fish.

No doubt our descendants thousands of years from now (should our species survive) will still be bipedal, symbol-generating apes. Most likely they will be adept at using sophisticated technologies. But will they still be human in the way we, shaped by a long heritage of cooperative breeding, currently define ourselves?

This article was adapted from "Cooperation, Empathy, and the Needs of Human Infants," a Tanner Lecture delivered at the University of Utah. It is used with the permission of the Tanner Lectures on Human Values, a Corporation, University of Utah, Salt Lake City.

TASK/TEXT 10.14: CONCLUDING OBSERVATIONS OF THE COMMITTEE ON THE RIGHTS OF THE CHILD – THE KINGDOM OF THE NETHERLANDS

Concluding Observations of the Committee on the Rights of the Child: The Kingdom of the Netherlands, 30 January 2009 (unedited version), par. 23, 37–40, 48, 60, 62
<www2.ohchr.org/english/bodies/crc/docs/co/CRC-C-NLD-CO3.pdf>

23. In line with its previous recommendations, the Committee recommends that the State party continue and further strengthen its efforts to ensure that all of the provisions of the Convention are widely known and understood by adults and children alike. In this regard, the Committee encourages the State party to undertake a **systematic education and training programme on the principles and provisions of the Convention for children, parents and all professional groups working for and with children**, including judges, lawyers, law enforcement officials, teachers, health-care personnel, social workers and media personnel.

37. The Committee recommends that the State party prohibit corporal punishment by law and **enforce the prohibition in all settings, including in the family**, the schools and out of home placements. It also recommends that the State party conduct **awareness-raising campaigns and parenting education programmes to ensure that alternative forms of discipline are used**, in a manner consistent with the child's human dignity and in conformity with the Convention, especially article 28, paragraph 2, while taking due account of the General Comment No. 8 (2006) on the right of the child to protection from corporal punishment and other cruel or degrading forms of punishment (CRC/C/GC/8).

38. With reference to the United Nations Study on violence against children (A/61/299), the Committee recommends that the State party:

a) Take all necessary measures for the implementation of the recommendations contained in the report of the independent expert for the United Nations study on violence against children while taking into account the outcome and recommendations of the regional consultation for Europe and Central Asia, held in Ljubljana, Slovenia, from 5 to 7 July 2005. In particular, the Committee recommends that the State party pay particular attention to the following recommendations:

(i) To prohibit all violence against children;
(ii) To **promote non-violent values and awareness-raising**;
(iii) To **provide recovery and social reintegration services**; and
(iv) To develop and implement **systematic national data collection and research**;

b) Use these recommendations as a tool for action, in partnership with civil society and in particular with the involvement of children, to ensure that every child is protected from all forms of physical, sexual and psychological violence and to gain momentum for concrete and, where appropriate, time-bound actions to prevent and respond to such violence and abuse.

39. While the Committee acknowledges that services for families and children are widely available, it notes that there are many children on waiting lists to obtain appropriate services. The Committee is concerned about the lack of sufficient family based services to ensure prevention and early intervention at the local level, which leaves children and young persons without adequate help.

40. The Committee recommends that the State party conduct **comprehensive research on the reasons behind the long waiting lists**, and take steps to **involve the families in preventing and solving their problems**. The Committee also recommends that the State party implement community based programmes with a view to assisting the extended family in taking an active role, e.g. conference models, and **provide parenting education in a culturally sensitive manner**.

48. The Committee urges the State party to:

a) establish mechanisms for **monitoring the number of cases and the extent of violence, sexual abuse, neglect, maltreatment or exploitation considered by article 19, including within the family**, in institutional or other care;
b) ensure that **professionals working with children** (including teachers, social workers, medical professionals, members of the police and the judiciary) **receive training on their obligation to report and take appropriate action in suspected cases of domestic violence affecting children**;
c) strengthen **support for victims of violence, abuse, neglect and maltreatment in order to ensure that they are not victimized once again during legal proceedings**; and
d) provide access to **adequate services for recovery, counselling and other forms of reintegration** in all parts of the Kingdom.

60. The Committee recommends that the State party enhance its efforts to promote **exclusive breastfeeding practices** and comply with the International Code of Marketing of Breast-milk Substitutes.

62. The Committee recommends that the State party:

a) strengthen efforts to overcome the **de facto ethnic segregation of school attendance** by providing support for ethnically diverse schools and networks of cooperation among schools;
b) ensure the right to education of all children by facilitating enrolment of children with missing or incomplete documents;
c) improve the safety situation at schools experiencing difficulties in this regard so that all children have access to **safe schools** and can learn without fear of violence and maltreatment; and
d) make sure that **human rights and child rights education is included in school curricula at all levels.**

TASK/TEXT 10.15: PETITION FOR RATIFICATION OF AMENDMENT VI OF THE CONSTITUTION OF THE UNITED STATES OF AMERICA

<www.childabuse.com/getinv.htm>, accessed 13 February 2009

In this world of equal opportunity and equal rights, it seems there are those of us left on the wayside. We are a majority amongst you, and yet our needs are quietly hushed and swept under the rug. We are not a single race or religious preference, nor are we confined to the limitations of just one sex or social stature. Our stories are told openly, more today than ever before. For some the scars are deeper than others, but our pain and suffering is a part of our daily lives that we cannot escape. We are most commonly treated as a burden on the very society that has promised over and over again to protect and shelter us from harm.

We are your abused children.

We appeal to you now with this petition to bring forth the ratification of Amendment VI of The Constitution of the United States of America, which reads as follows:

In all criminal prosecutions, the accused shall enjoy the right to a speedy and public trial, by an impartial jury of the state and district wherein the crime shall have been committed, which district shall have been previously ascertained by law, and to be informed of the nature and cause of the accusation; to be confronted with the witnesses against him; to have compulsory process for obtaining witnesses in his favor, and to have the assistance of counsel for his defense.

We do not argue this amendment, although we are joining together today to express our desire to extend this amendment to include the victims of crime. This in no way is a suggestion to allow cases which stem from civil matters to be included, as crimes are defined as a serious violation of the law; while civil cases are defined as relating to or being a lawsuit.

The victims of crime deserve the right to have adequate counsel and representation also appointed when they have reasonable documentation or other information regarding the said crime, regardless of their income or social stature. In guaranteeing the criminals rights, while not the victims, we have created a judicial system that leaves the victims behind in their defense. Equal rights should include the right to due process especially for the victims of crime.

TASK/TEXT 10.16: MANY CRIMES AGAINST CHILDREN CONTINUE TO GO UNPUNISHED

Global Human Rights Education listserv (HREA, <www.hrea.org>), 12 March 2009 (Human Rights Council – Day on the Rights of the Child)

11 March 2009 – A landmark treaty adopted 20 years ago has transformed the way the world views children but greater efforts are needed to ensure that their rights are protected and advanced, the United Nations human rights chief said today.

"Children are no longer regarded as the property of parents or the passive recipients of charity or goodwill, but as rights-holders," UN High Commissioner for Human Rights Navi Pillay told a meeting of the Human Rights Council focusing on the Convention on the Rights of the Child.

"This conceptual shift also underscored States' accountability in fulfilling their obligations towards children's rights," she added. "The Convention anchors these obligations to the principles of non-discrimination, the best interests of the child, children's right to life, survival and development, and respect for the children's right to express their views."

She noted that over the past two decades, national mechanisms and practices have furthered children's rights, which are now a feature of many school curricula, and awareness of children's rights has never been higher. (…)

In her speech to the Council, Ms. Pillay also said that despite the many positive developments, there was cause for concern in a number of areas, adding that many crimes against children continue to go unpunished.

According to the UN Children's Fund (UNICEF), each year nearly 10 million children die from preventable causes before their fifth birthday.

The UN Study on Violence against Children reported that some 80 to 98 per cent of children suffer physical punishment in their homes, with a third or more experiencing severe physical punishment inflicted with implements.

The World Health Organization (WHO) estimated in 2002 that 150 million girls and 73 million boys under 18 experienced forced sexual intercourse or other forms of sexual violence. Also, the latest data available shows that some 1.2 million children are trafficked worldwide every year.

In addition, as noted by the Special Representative of the Secretary-General for Children and Armed Conflict, young people pay a heavy price in situations of conflict, where they are victims of attacks against schools, and are abducted and forced to serve as combatants, sex slaves or servants. More than 250,000 children are estimated to have been recruited as soldiers.

The current global financial crisis is also taking a toll on children, undermining their survival, access to housing, health and education. "When crises strike, social spending in programmes protecting children is to be counted among the first casualties of budget adjustments," said Ms. Pillay.

"It is also true that in times of hardship, absent specific and targeted programs to support their education, children may be forced to abandon school and join the workforce. In this situation they may become more vulnerable to exploitation and trafficking," she noted.

"We must remain vigilant in order to confront emerging challenges and ensure that the spirit and letter of the Convention shape the responses and remedial measures of the international community," she said, adding that the Geneva-based Council can play an important role in advocating and advancing measures for the protection of the rights of the child.

"We need to translate our commitment, engagement, and work on children's rights into a tangible reality for each and every one of them," Ms. Pillay stated, pledging through her personal advocacy and the work of her staff to continue to draw attention to the rights of children and help States to fulfil their relevant responsibilities.

TASK/TEXT 10.17: GERMANY – NEO-NAZI YOUTH GROUP BANNED FOR TRYING TO INDOCTRINATE CHILDREN

CRIN Children and Armed Conflict 129 – 3 April 2009

31 March 2009 – A neo-Nazi youth organisation that ran military-style camps to teach children as young as six that Jews are a threat to the nation has been outlawed by the German Government.

Amid growing fears that the far-Right is gaining ground in Germany, the Interior Ministry announced an immediate ban on *Heimattreue Deutsche Jugend*, or German Youth Faithful to the Homeland, for attempting to indoctrinate children with racial ideology. Police carried out dawn raids on HDJ leaders' homes in four states to seize the organisation's assets and extremist materials.

Wolfgang Schäuble, the Interior Minister, said: "With today's ban, we are putting an end to the revolting activities of the HDJ. We will do everything in our power to protect our children and youth from these Pied Pipers."

HDJ claimed to be a "youth group for environment, community and homeland" but its supposedly harmless camps featured tents with names such as "the Führer's bunker." There, children of primary school age and upwards would take part in military drills and be taught about elements of Nazi ideology, including the importance of pure blood and the continuation of the German race.

The Interior Ministry said today that the group's ultimate aim was the creation of a Neo-Nazi elite.

Security services have been monitoring the HDJ for several years, but the prohibition of the group stemmed from raids last year that starkly demonstrated the true nature of its activities. In one raid last August, police searched a HDJ camp in a remote area of northeastern Germany and sent home 39 black-uniformed children aged 8 to 14.

"There was a regimented camp routine complete with flag-hoisting, in which behaviour and living conditions were exercised as in the time of National Socialism," a police report on the raid said.

Far-right literature was seized, along with tea towels and song sheets emblazoned with swastikas and old maps showing prewar names and boundaries. In October, police searched the homes of several HDJ activists and found further evidence that the group was opposed to Germany's democratic constitution and worshipped the Nazis.

It is illegal in Germany to display Nazi symbols or recite slogans from the Third Reich, although far-right groups have often found ways to circumvent the regulations. HDJ, whose name and initials evoke the Nazis' Hitler Youth (HJ) movement, was founded in 1990 and is thought to have about 400 members, although more children have passed through its camps. It has links to the far-right National Democratic Party (NPD), and is believed to be the successor to the Wiking-Jugend (Viking Youth) oganisation that was banned in 1994. As such, its small official membership belies its significant influence on the German neo-Nazi scene. The homes of its leaders in Berlin, Brandenburg, Lower Saxony and Saxony were searched this morning in raids timed to coincide with the ban.

Mr Schäuble said that today's ban was an example of "decisiveness" in the fight against far-right extremism, but Gabriele Fograscher, a member of parliament for the centre-left Social Democratic Party, said that the move should have come sooner after last year's raids.

"A faster analysis of the material confiscated and a quicker ban of the HDJ would have been a clearer signal against far-right groups," she said. "The HDJ had a paramilitary and unconstitutional character and there were close ties and staff links with the National Democratic Party and the neo-Nazi scene."

Parents and teachers needed to become more alert to the dangers of children drifting towards the far-Right, she said.

Concern has been growing in recent months that the German far-right scene is becoming more popular – and more dangerous – despite the financial crisis and political in-fighting that has rocked the National Democratic Party:

Crimes by the far-Right rose by 28 per cent to just under 14,000 in 2008. The number of violent crimes, including arson and assault, rose by 14.5 per cent compared with 2007.

A survey this month indicated that almost one in 20 boys aged 15 were members of a right-wing group or *kameradschaft*. In parts of the former communist east, that figure was up to one in eight, while almost 30 per cent of young people nationwide agreed with the statement "there are too many foreigners in Germany."

More than 6,000 neo-Nazis marched in Dresden in February to mark the 64th anniversary of the city's firebombing during World War Two – one of the biggest such demonstrations since German reunification.

TASK/TEXT 10.18: REALISING CHILDREN'S RIGHTS REQUIRES MORE THAN RHETORIC – SYSTEMATIC AND CONCRETE ACTIONS ARE NOW NEEDED

Viewpoint of the Council of Europe Commissioner for Human Rights, Thomas Hammarberg, 16 November 2009 (<www.commissioner.coe.int>)

The Convention on the Rights of the Child has become one of the most well-known and broadly supported international human rights treaties. Practically all the states in the world have ratified it and thereby legally bound themselves to implement its provisions. As a result, the situation of children has been put higher on the political agenda. Yet, the actual implementation of the Convention has been less effective than we anticipated. The main reason is the **absence of a systematic, comprehensive approach to children's rights as a political priority**.

Although children make up a large section of the population and constitute the future of society (in more ways than one), their concerns are seldom given top priority in politics. **Ministers responsible for children's affairs tend to be junior and stand outside the inner circle of power**. When political issues are divided into "soft" and "hard," those relating to children are dealt with as "soft-soft." Often these issues are seen as non-political and sometimes simply trivial. The image of politicians on the campaign trail kissing babies has become symbolic of this trivialisation.

Gestures are not enough to meet the requirements of the Convention – what is needed is serious **political discussion and real change**. Improvement in the status of and conditions for children is of course the very purpose of the Convention. With ratification, a state has committed itself to respect the principles and provisions of the Convention and to transform them into reality for all children.

One possible reason for the delay in implementing the Convention could be the decision-makers' lack of understanding or acceptance of the obligations arising from it. They may not always have made the **distinction between charity and a rights-based approach**. Children in need, just like persons with disabilities, have long been the favourite "objects" of charity. They have been given support, not as a matter of right, but because people have felt pity for them. This is one of the attitudes that the Convention challenges.

The Convention sees the child as a subject. He or she has the right to schooling, health care and an adequate standard of living as well as to be heard and have his or her views respected. This goes as much for the cute toddler as for the problematic teenager. The very **notion that children have rights is a radical one**, totally alien to the old-fashioned belief that children are only entitled to rights on their 18th birthday and that their parents hold these rights until that date.

That **children and their interests should be given priority is another important message in the Convention.** It states as an overarching principle that "the best interests of the child shall be a primary consideration" in all actions concerning them whether taken by local or national authorities, Parliaments, courts, or social welfare institutions, including those run on a private basis (Article 3).

The Convention also requires concrete steps to be taken to guarantee genuine implementation. It prescribes that governments must take legal, administrative and other measures and use "**the maximum extent of their available resources**" to ensure that children can enjoy their rights (Article 4).

Many of us who took part in the drafting of the Convention were aware of the risk that the final text would be seen by some as an idealistic wish list rather than as a definition of the human rights of children. The challenge was to give clear substance to the *obligations* which would follow from the rights approach. The Committee on the Rights of the Child, the elected [expert] body to monitor the application of the Convention, has attached a great deal of importance to the methods and means used for its implementation. Based on that experience and suggestions from UNICEF, non-governmental organisations and some governments, one could define key measures in a **checklist on systematic measures** that serious governments ought to take. These include the need to:

[1] develop a comprehensive national agenda for children;
[2] ensure that all legislation is fully compatible with children's rights which requires incorporating the Convention into domestic law and practice as well as ensuring that its principles and provisions take precedence in cases of conflict with national legislation;
[3] make children visible in the process of policy development throughout the government by introducing child impact assessments;
[4] carry out adequate budget analysis to determine the proportion spent on children and to ensure the effective use of resources;
[5] establish permanent bodies or mechanisms to promote co-ordination, monitoring and evaluation of activities throughout all sectors of government, including the local authorities;
[6] ensure that sufficient data are collected and used to improve the state of all children in each jurisdiction;
[7] raise awareness and disseminate information on children's rights and what they mean in reality, including through training for all those in government whose work relates to children or who work with children;
[8] involve children themselves as well as civil society in the process of implementation and awareness-raising;

[9] develop independent statutory offices for children – a children's ombudsman, commissioner or other similar institutions – to promote children's rights, and:
[10] give children's rights priority in all forms of international co-operation, including in programs for technical assistance.

These ten recommendations are mutually reinforcing and have several characteristics in common. Each relies on public debate and transparent procedures. Each advocates a "First Call" for children while recognising the need for co-ordinated efforts to ensure that children's rights are incorporated into the existing administrative structures. They require children themselves to take part in the procedures. The basic idea is that children's issues be moved from the exclusive realm of charity onto the political agenda – and placed high thereon.

Several European governments have taken action on these recommendations, for instance, through adopting a national strategy, improving their internal co-ordination on children's issues, developing the data collection system and appointing an ombudsman for children – within the office of the general ombudsman or separately. Yet, there are glaring gaps which appear to indicate that the governments have not been sufficiently serious. This is also reflected in the continued lack of child protection.

Too little is being done to give children with disabilities an opportunity for schooling. Children within minorities, not least the Roma, are disadvantaged in most spheres of life. Children in conflict with the law are too often detained. Children among the irregular migrants are vulnerable and suffer exploitation. Refugee children are not well treated. Corporal punishment is retained in about half of the countries in Europe and some children also face violence in school. Justice, schools and cities are not yet child-friendly.

One reason why powerful politicians tend to be rhetorical rather than concrete on children's issues is probably because many of them lead a life which isolates them from a child's everyday reality. The opinions of children themselves are not taken seriously and their parents or guardians have, in many cases, little time or opportunity to present their views.

In fact, the seriousness of the political commitment is now being tested in the ongoing budget discussions. In the wake of the current recession, there have already been budget cuts in several countries which have affected children – either directly in the state budget or via reduced support to local authorities. Funds for education, health care and social benefits for vulnerable groups have been significantly reduced in some countries. And this is before governments start paying back the debts incurred when state money was used to meet the financial crisis and rescue the banking system.

This has provoked a discussion on the concrete meaning of "the maximum extent" of the available resources to go to children. Inevitably, children's interests will also suffer when the whole society is forced to tighten its belt. However, what is clearly against the very spirit of the Convention are decisions which would penalise those who are already vulnerable and thereby increase the existing inequalities.

It is now particularly important that the short- and long-term impact on children are analysed before the next budgets are approved. Also in Europe we now already have a serious problem of child poverty – appallingly widespread in some countries. Here, a large number of children are disadvantaged from the very start. This has to be addressed, the current crisis is no argument for not doing so – on the contrary. Resource limitations cannot be seen as an excuse for ignoring obligations to protect child rights and for delaying the implementation of measures. The greater the difficulties, the more reason to act with a clear political will in order to address the problems in a systematic fashion. Indeed, it is particularly in times of crisis that the state has to reaffirm its commitment and to fully respect the rights of children – all children.

TASK/TEXT 10.19: TWENTY YEARS ON: THE CLINICAL IMPORTANCE OF CHILDREN'S RIGHTS

The Lancet 2009, p. 1723, 21 November 2009, <www.thelancet.com/journals/lancet/article/PIIS0140-6736(09)62006-7/fulltext>

During the past week, the Australian Government apologised for the mistreatment of UK children who were resettled in Australia between 1930 and 1970 as part of the child migrants programme; a similar apology from the UK Government is expected. This forced resettlement of 500.000 children is a reminder of their vulnerability. The 20th anniversary on November 20 of the Convention on the Rights of the Child (CRC) gives an opportunity to reflect on children's rights today – and the responsibility of health professionals to respect and defend those rights in all settings, including the clinic.

The Convention grew out of the non-binding 1959 Declaration of the Rights of the Child, which concentrated on needs, such as protection from maltreatment and provision of nutrition. The CRC was a quantum leap forward. First, the 54 interconnected Articles are based on rights, so that the foundation is justice, rather than charity. Second, it incorporates participation, recognising that people under the age of 18 years are individuals rather than objects. Third, it has the force of international law, having been ratified by all member states of the UN except Somalia and USA.

Despite the Convention's brevity, its availability in all six UN languages, and the obligation on ratifying states to conform to and publicise it, many health workers remain unaware of their responsibilities under the CRC. The implications of the Convention are profound and entail a fundamental change to the structure of consultations involving children. Put simply, anyone dealing with children or attending a person whose family includes children, has a duty to make the child's best interest paramount.

In daily clinical practice this means access, irrespective of circumstances or disabilities, to the highest attainable standard of physical and mental health. The goal of best practice is not an academic nicety, but a non-negotiable right of the Convention. Other Articles call for participation by the child in decisions affecting him or her, and the guarantee of information in an age-appropriate manner to enable such decisions. Good paediatricians demonstrate just such behaviours, which, under the Convention, should be practised by all who care for children. Engaging with children at this level poses a challenge to systems-centred, or worse, doctor-centred care. To build the necessary relationship for mutual understanding and effective child-centred care takes time, respect for the autonomy of children, and a broad appreciation of external factors that influence health.

The CRC recognises the central role of parents to nurture children. As a result, treatment decisions for family members, particularly mothers, have implications for children. Obstetricians, midwives, and public health authorities therefore have a responsibility to provide high standards of peripartum care for the safety of mothers, the continuity of the family, and to ensure the best start in life for neonates. In this context, widening the provision of antenatal care and skilled birth attendants where they are scarce is important, since improving maternal health is a critical driver for better child health. An example is tetanus vaccination at antenatal clinics in Ethiopia to prevent neonatal death from the disease.

A child-rights approach empowers health-care professionals to become actors for change by giving them a mechanism to confront causes of poor health in children. Whether the cause is inadequate vaccination programmes in developing countries or inappropriate advertisements for calorie-dense food in developed countries, the CRC provides a template for a multidisciplinary approach to address threats to health. For instance, in the USA, agencies concerned with child welfare have been united by medical-legal child health partnerships.

For researchers, the CRC is a lens to focus on questions that are in the child's best interest, rather than the competing interests of funders or scientists. For example, prioritising research in developing countries on neonatal deaths, pneumonia, diarrhoea, malaria, measles, and HIV/AIDS, which are major obstacles to achieving Millennium Development Goal 4.

The Convention on the Rights of the Child is not an end in itself but an instrument of justice for the world's most vulnerable and least regarded population. The potential strength of the Convention to realise better clinical (and social) outcomes for children is enormous. But unless health workers have an intimate knowledge of the CRC and apply it in their clinical work, they will let children down and the potential of both the Convention and of children will remain unrealised.

TASK/TEXT 10.20: CAIRO DECLARATION ON THE CRC AND SHARIAH LAW

Cairo Declaration on the Convention (CRC) and Islamic Jurisprudence Cairo, 23–24 November 2009, <www.crin.org/docs/Cairodec.pdf>

Under the patronage and in the presence of Her Excellency the First Lady of Egypt, **Mrs. Suzanne Mubarak**, the Cairo Conference was held to commemorate the 20th anniversary of the Convention on the Rights of the Child (CRC), which coincides with the 20th anniversary of Egypt's National Council on Childhood and Motherhood [NCCM], the national body mandated to coordinate and monitor the realization of the rights of the child in Egypt. The Conference was organised by the Ministry of State for Family and Population of Egypt and co-sponsored by the Organisation of the Islamic Conference (OIC) and UNICEF, with the valuable contribution of a wide range of partners who contributed to the success of the Conference. The representatives from most OIC Member States, as well as international organisations, national human rights institutions, NGOs and children from ten OIC countries participated in the Conference. Participants expressed their deep appreciation to the Ministry of State for Family and Population of Egypt for its excellent organization of the Conference.

All participants highly appreciated the presence of Mrs. Mubarak for her visionary and exemplary leadership in the promotion of the rights of the child and the consideration of children as a priority in the political agenda. Participants appreciated as well the child rights based approach adopted by the NCCM and the progress achieved in the realisation of the rights of the child. The Conference recognised that the 20th anniversary of the CRC provides an opportunity to acknowledge progress building upon two decades of experience, and to renew the commitment of OIC Member States to continue to strengthen action towards the effective implementation of the CRC and to address prevailing challenges related to the realisation of the rights of the child, with special emphasis on the contribution of principles of Islamic Shariah in fostering the purposes and objectives of this Convention.

The present Declaration reflects the deliberations during the Conference and identifies recommendations for action to enhance the full implementation of the Convention.

Member States and civil society organizations from OIC countries (hereinafter participants) gathered in Cairo to commemorate the 20th anniversary of the adoption of the Convention on the Rights of the Child, to renew their commitment to the rights of the child for all children without discrimination, including on the basis of gender, to be guided by the best interests of the child, to ensure children's survival and development and to involve children meaningfully in decision-making processes.

Review of reservations

Participants acknowledged that some OIC Member States formulated reservations upon ratification as a precautionary measure. They also noted that the national experience in the realisation of the rights of the child by OIC member-states has enriched the process of implementation of the Convention and helped to advance it further. Participants stressed that the experience gained over the two decades of implementation of the Convention has shown the **compatibility and convergence of the Convention with the principles of Islamic Shariah** and the opportunity to review reservations and consider their withdrawal. Participants welcome the increasing trend to review and withdraw reservations to the CRC which reflects the **dynamic nature of Islamic Shariah**, and the enriching exchange of national experiences amongst member states, particularly those who have withdrawn or are in the process of withdrawing the reservations. Participants welcome in particular the unanimous view expressed during the Conference that reservations, including those of a general nature, create an inaccurate perception of incompatibility between **the CRC and Shariah law** should be revisited with a view to withdraw them.

OIC Permanent Independent Expert Human Rights Commission

Participants welcome the decision to establish a permanent independent expert human rights commission as a principal organ of the OIC and call upon all OIC Member States to expedite this process which will enhance the promotion of children's rights among all human rights and foster the positive contribution of **Islamic law and tradition** in the process of implementation of the CRC.

The Optional Protocols to the CRC

Participants encourage OIC Member States that have ratified the Optional Protocol on the Sale of Children, Child Prostitution, and Child Pornography; and the Optional Protocol on the Involvement of Children in Armed Conflicts to continue to strengthen their implementation in accordance with the recommendations of the Committee on the Rights of the Child. Participants urge all other OIC Member States to ratify the optional protocols without delay. These two protocols are: 1. Optional Protocol to the Convention on the Rights of the Child on the sale of children, child prostitution and child pornography; 2. Optional Protocol to the Convention on the Rights of the Child on the involvement of children in armed conflict.

Proposal for a third Optional Protocol

Participants welcome the expressions of support from numerous OIC Member States to strengthen the mandate of the Open-Ended Working Group of the Human Rights Council to proceed with the drafting of a new Optional Protocol to the CRC to provide a communications procedure [and] encourage States and civil society to be actively involved. This should build upon positive experiences within OIC Member States in providing children with effective representation and remedies at the national level.

Enhanced Compliance with the Convention

Participants recommend that the OIC Member States make the implementation of the rights of children a matter of high priority on their political agenda and, building upon OIC positive national experiences, establish a national body with a clear and strong mandate and with the necessary financial and human resources to ensure the coordination of the implementation of the CRC and the regular evaluation of progress. Participants recommend that the OIC Member States develop and implement laws and programs on children's rights in close consultation with parliamentarians, traditional, religious and other national or local leaders. Participants recommend that OIC Member States encourage a cooperative and productive partnership with civil society, in particular NGOs, and support their active involvement in developing, implementing and assessing the impact of child related legislation, policies and programs.

- **Adequate resources for children** – Participants urge OIC Member States to provide necessary human and financial resources for the implementation of the CRC, including the enforcement of laws and policies. Furthermore, it is recommended that OIC Member States make expenditure on the rights of the child visible in their annual national budget.
- **Data Collection, analysis and dissemination** – Participants urge OIC Member States to establish effective tools for systematic collection, analysis and dissemination of data on the implementation of the CRC, disaggregated by age, gender, urban/rural and other relevant factors; and to use this data for the development, implementation and regular review of their laws, policies

and programs and to identify child vulnerabilities, to prevent discrimination and overcome disparities.

- **Child social inclusion and eradication of poverty** – Participants expressed deep concern at poverty and its negative impact on the realisation of the rights of the child and urge OIC Member States to target the elimination of child poverty and to ensure children's universal access to basic social services of quality and to invest in children as a high priority in their poverty reduction strategies, particularly in the context of the current economic and financial crisis, and in order to achieve the Millennium Development Goals for poverty reduction by 2015.
- **International Cooperation** – Participants recommend to States that are in a position to do so, to provide technical and financial assistance to other States in their implementation of the CRC, in the framework of bi-lateral or multi-lateral agreements, while taking into account country specific concluding observations made by the Committee on the Rights of the Child. Participants call upon Member States of the UN to provide additional financial and human resources to allow the Committee on the Rights of the Child and other treaty bodies to fulfil their mandates and call on the OIC, both Secretariat and Member States, to enhance their cooperation with OHCHR in this respect.

Specific recommendations [on] child participation – 40 children from 10 countries held a meeting for children on 21–22 November and participated equally in every session of the conference on 23–24 November. Participants underscore the importance of promoting and supporting the participation of children in decision making. They express their special appreciation for the contributions made by children during the Conference and for the recommendations they have put forward, which were prepared during their two day preparatory meeting. Participants strongly recommend to all OIC Member States to provide children with meaningful opportunities to express their views and to take part in the process of developing and implementing laws, policies and programmes that affect children's lives; OIC Member States who have not yet done so, should also consider the establishment of Children's Parliaments and ensure appropriate follow-up to their recommendations. Participants also recommend that OIC Member States promote and support active participation in the family, in schools and in institutions for children, taking into account the Committee on the Rights of the Child's General Comment on article 12 of the CRC, and the recommendation of their discussions.

Child protection from discrimination

Participants renew their commitment to ensure the realisation of the rights of all children without discrimination of any kind. Participants commit to giving special attention to the realisation of the rights of girls, including to achieve their right to education and to eliminate child marriage and other harmful traditional practices. Participants urge OIC Member States to take legislative, administrative and social measures to support without discrimination the rights of children born out of wedlock. These measures should include facilities for ensuring that **both parents support the child and the mother benefits from relevant financial support to ensure the upbringing of the child**. Children's inheritance rights should also be safeguarded. Measures should also be taken to establish the legal responsibility of the father to contribute financially in the upbringing of the child and to allow the mother to take the necessary legal actions to establish through courts the fatherhood of the biological child. Participants recognised that children with disabilities have a right to special attention and empowerment. The entry into force of the Convention on the Rights of Persons with Disabilities provides an opportunity for renewed commitment to the realisation of the rights of children with disabilities and for joint action between the two treaty bodies established by these treaties. Participants also recognised the particular vulnerability of children deprived of parental care, belonging to minorities, living and working on the streets and children victims of economic exploitation and reiterated their commitment to enhance their protection.

Child protection from all forms of violence

Participants valued the presence and contribution of the newly appointed Special Representative of the [Secretary-General] on Violence against Children, Dr. Marta Santos Pais, and expressed their commitment to develop productive cooperation with the Special Representative and to provide her with necessary technical and financial support. In light of the child's equal right to respect his or her human dignity and physical integrity, participants to the Conference recommend to the OIC member States to take all appropriate legislative, social and other measures for an effective follow-up to the recommendations made in the UN Study on Violence Against Children. Participants call upon the OIC Member States to urgently review and reform their legislation to ensure **the prohibition of all forms of violence against children and to link law reform with promotion of positive, non-violent forms of discipline**.

Building upon the promising experiences of OIC Member States, particular attention should be given to the prevention and combat against harmful practices, including FGM, child marriage, crimes committed in the name of honour, the use of children as camel jockeys, child trafficking, child domestic service and other forms of child labour.

Building upon positive national experiences from OIC Member States, participants to the Conference recommend that each State establish a high level focal point to coordinate all actions to prevent and combat all forms of violence against children, and promote the development of a well resourced national strategy on violence against children, engaging with civil society, including children and young people.

Participants requested: 1. That efforts should be exerted to provide protection for children under occupation, and in times of war. They demanded that those who violate the CRC by killing children or subjecting them to imprisonment, corporal and/or psychological torture, should be made accountable and brought to court.

2. That poverty alleviation should be targeted, as poverty is considered a primary cause for children's main problems which lead to their deprivation of enjoying a normal life.

Participants encourage the OIC and its Member States to facilitate the establishment of a children's forum to promote the contribution of children to the process of follow-up to the UN Study on Violence against Children and to keep children informed about developments in this area.

- **Child marriage** – Participants call upon all OIC Member States to raise the age of marriage to 18, ensuring full consent and registration of marriage.
- **FGM** – Participants to the Conference recommend the OIC member States to prohibit by law all forms of FGM and undertake awareness raising and informative campaigns, and promote social mobilisation in close consultation and cooperation with the traditional and religious leadership, NGOs, as well as with parliamentarians, to support the enforcement of the prohibition and the promotion of abandonment of this practice, and to provide people who are involved in this practice with alternative employment.
- **Corporal Punishment** – Participants to the Conference recommend that OIC Member States prohibit all corporal punishment and other cruel or degrading forms of punishment or treatment of children, in all settings including within schools and within the family, **linking law reform with the promotion of positive, non-violent forms of discipline.**
- **Juvenile justice** – Participants call on OIC Member States to complete the development of an effective and efficient juvenile justice system which ensures the full implementation of the CRC in particular articles 37 and 40, and other relevant international standards and taking into account the Committee on the Rights of the Child's General Comment No. 10. In that regard, special attention should be paid to the establishment and progressive raising of the minimum age for criminal responsibility.

Participants call on OIC Member States to take necessary measures to respond to children in conflict with the law without resorting to judicial proceedings providing that human rights and legal safeguards are fully respected, including community service, restorative justice, (taking into account the 2009 Lima Declaration on Restorative Juvenile Justice). Participants call on OIC Member States to take measures to ensure that all children in conflict with the law are provided with free legal or other appropriate assistance and that deprivation of liberty, including pre-trial detention, is only used as a measure of last resort and for the shortest possible period of time, by fully implementing recommendations of the CRC Committee made in General Comment No. 10 regarding the use of pre-trial detention and by introducing and effectively using suspended sentencing and early release.

Participants call on OIC Member States to take legislative measures to abolish the imposition of capital punishment on persons who committed a crime when under the age of 18, and suspend the execution of any pending capital punishment. Furthermore, it is recommended to abolish all forms of life imprisonment for crimes committed before the age of 18.

Participants call on OIC Member States to take legislative measures to ensure that children deprived of their liberty have access to education, adequate health care and to sports and other leisure opportunities, can maintain regular contact with their parents and other family members and are fully protected against all forms of violence, including inhuman and degrading treatment or punishment.

Participants call on OIC Member States to safeguard the rights of child victims and witnesses involved with judicial proceedings and take into consideration relevant UN standards and guidelines.

The participants express their profound thanks and appreciation to the Arab Republic of Egypt, represented by the Ministry of State for Family and Population, for the kind hospitality extended to them. Due recognition is also extended to the Organization of the Islamic Conference and UNICEF, and all entities that supported the successful outcome of this conference.

TASK/TEXT 10.21: SOCIETY HAS AN OBLIGATION TO SUPPORT ABANDONED CHILDREN AND OFFER THEM A POSITIVE HOME ENVIRONMENT – ALSO WHEN BUDGET RESOURCES ARE LIMITED

Viewpoint of the Council of Europe Commissioner for Human Rights, Thomas Hammarberg, 28 December 2009 (<www.commissioner.coe.int>)

The notorious large-scale institutions for orphans and children with disabilities are being phased out, including in the former Communist countries of Central and Eastern Europe. This process of de-institutionalisation must continue, but it has to be pursued with care in the best interests of the child. Suitable alternatives must be developed and supported by the authorities – also in a period of economic crisis.

An extreme example of a distorted attitude towards children was exposed after the fall of the Ceausescu dictatorship in Romania some twenty years ago. Steps had been taken there to prevent people from using contraceptives and as a result unwanted children were born. Parents who could not care for their children were asked to hand them over to state institutions.

These collectives functioned badly. Contacts between the parents and the children were actively discouraged or even prevented. The staff were too few to cope with the many children. They were untrained for their task and badly paid, which gave their job a low status. I visited some of these homes at the time and was struck by the difficult material conditions and the depressed atmosphere.

Some of the institutions, especially those for children with disabilities, were hidden far away from population centres and were hardly given the bare minimum of staff and material resources. No efforts were made to encourage the development of these children – no schooling, no organised play, no love. Some of the children were kept tied to their beds, day and night.

The situation in Romania was extreme but large, inhumane institutions also existed in countries such as Bulgaria, Estonia, Hungary, Latvia, Lithuania, Moldova, Poland and Russia. It became a major task for the new rulers to start the process of de-institutionalisation. Progress has been made during the past two decades, though major problems remain and require further efforts.

It has become widely recognised that a family environment is generally much better for children than institutional care. The adoption of the 1989 Convention of the Rights of the Child – and the discussion about its consequences – strengthened this understanding. Recommendations from Council of Europe bodies have contributed further to a child-friendly approach which could be summarised as follows:

- Placement of children in institutions should as far as possible be avoided. In particular the old-style, large institutions have a negative effect on children and their development. They tend to neglect children's need for affection and to be recognised as individuals. In such institutions cases of abuse tend to be common – both by adults and by other children.
- **A first line of defence would be to give a strong, sustained support to parents so that the rights of the child can be protected in the home environment.**

- **Unfortunately, there are situations in which it is in the best interests of the child to move somewhere else. The aim then should be to seek a good family environment – foster care might be the best option.**
- For each child in this situation there should be an individual plan based on his or her needs and the family circumstances. The principle of the best interests of the child should guide all decisions and the children themselves should be able to influence.
- **If an institutional placement is necessary, it should be as family-like as possible. Staff should be well-trained and professional.**
- The spirit in such child centres should be clearly child-friendly and education seen as a right for everyone. There should be clear and effective complaints procedures.
- If at all possible, the child should be able to communicate and see the parents – reintegration into the family should be an aim.
- Monitoring of the situation of each child is of key importance. All forms of alternative care should be regularly reviewed. There should also be a serious follow-up review of the situation after the period of alternative care.

The fact that these principles have been recognised does not mean that they are automatically applied. Some of the old-style institutions are still there and suitable alternatives have not been sufficiently developed. Also, **too little is being done to strengthen families and thereby prevent the risk that children become abandoned.**

It is of paramount importance that the current economic crisis does not undermine the process to support children at risk. Unfortunately, budget cuts have already been made which will inevitably damage the best interests of children.

There is an obvious risk that the number of abandoned children will increase as the social support for troubled families is reduced. Families break down under the pressure of poverty and unemployment. **Too many children are forced to grow up in families where alcoholism and other drug abuse is part of daily life. These factors are root causes which place children at risk.**

Most of the children in the orphanages have at least one parent alive. In her Korczak lecture, the Russian social policy expert Marina Gordeeva called them "**social orphans**" and explained some of the background:

"Traditional family ties between generations are disrupted, the number of divorces is growing, the level of material support of families with children is lowering, many parents lead an asocial life and avoid their parental duties."

She argued for a policy which would combine determined efforts to support vulnerable families, step-by-step closure of the old residential care institutions and creation of support services to substitute guardians, such as foster families. She stressed that the main aim is not to close down the residential institutions but to achieve a successful family placement of each child in need.

These steps would require strong political backing and sufficient budget resources. In addition, local authorities must take their share of responsibility for the efforts to provide support services for children. I have noticed that there are shortcomings in this regard in several countries, including in Russia and Bulgaria. Coordination between ministries also tends to be insufficient in family policy matters. Marina Gordeeva spoke about "a gap in managerial decision-making."

The financial and managerial gaps cannot be closed only through the work of civil society groups. **Non-governmental initiatives should in general be welcomed, but unpredictable charity is not the solution, this task is primarily a government obligation.**

We know now what to do to protect children in need. The programs are not controversial and they are backed by all available expertise. What is needed is the political will to turn them into reality.

TASK/TEXT 10.22: GUIDELINES FOR THE ALTERNATIVE CARE OF CHILDREN

Human Rights Council Resolution 11/7 (11th session, advance unedited version, 19 June 2009), <www2.ohchr.org/english/bodies/hrcouncil/docs/11session/L-11.doc> (adopted by the General Assembly on 20 November 2009)

The Human Rights Council,

Reaffirming the Universal Declaration of Human Rights and the Convention on the Rights of the Child, and celebrating the twentieth anniversary of the Convention in 2009,

Reaffirming also all previous resolutions on the rights of the child of the Council, the Commission on Human Rights and the General Assembly, the most recent being Council resolutions 7/29 of 28 March 2008, 9/13 of 24 September 2008 and 10/8 of 26 March 2009 and Assembly resolution 63/241 of 23 December 2008,

Considering that the Guidelines for the Alternative Care of Children, the text of which is annexed to the present resolution, set out desirable orientations for policy and practice with the intention of enhancing the implementation of the Convention on the Rights of the Child, and of relevant provisions of other international instruments regarding the protection and well-being of children deprived of parental care or who are at risk of being so,

1. *Welcomes* the accomplishment of the Guidelines for the Alternative Care of Children;

2. *Decides* to submit the Guidelines to the General Assembly for consideration with a view to their adoption on the twentieth anniversary of the Convention on the Rights of the Child.

Annex – GUIDELINES FOR THE ALTERNATIVE CARE OF CHILDREN

I. PURPOSE

1. The present Guidelines are intended to enhance the implementation of the Convention on the Rights of the Child and of relevant provisions of other international instruments regarding the protection and well-being of children who are deprived of parental care or who are at risk of being so.

2. Against the background of these international instruments and **taking account of the developing body of knowledge and experience** in this sphere, the Guidelines set out desirable orientations for policy and practice. They are designed for wide dissemination among all sectors directly or indirectly concerned with issues relating to alternative care, and seek in particular to:

(a) Support efforts to keep children in, or return them to, the care of their family or, failing this, to find another appropriate and permanent solution, including adoption and *kafala* of Islamic law;
(b) Ensure that, while such permanent solutions are being sought, or in cases where they are not possible or are not in the best interests of the child, the most suitable forms of alternative care are identified and provided, under conditions that promote the **child's full and harmonious development**;
(c) Assist and encourage governments to better implement their responsibilities and obligations in these respects, bearing in mind the economic, social and cultural conditions prevailing in each State; and
(d) Guide policies, decisions and activities of all concerned with social protection and child welfare in both the public and private sectors, including civil society.

II. GENERAL PRINCIPLES AND PERSPECTIVES

A. The child and the family

3. The family being the fundamental group of society and the natural environment for the growth, well-being and protection of children, efforts should

primarily be directed to enabling the child to remain in or return to the care of his/her parents, or when appropriate, other close family members. **The State should ensure that families have access to forms of support in the care-giving role.**

4. **Every child and young person should live in a supportive, protective and caring environment that promotes his/her full potential.** Children with inadequate or no parental care are at special risk of being denied such a nurturing environment.

5. Where the child's own family is unable, even with appropriate support, to provide adequate care for the child, or abandons or relinquishes the child, **the State is responsible for protecting the rights of the child** and ensuring appropriate alternative care, with or through competent local authorities and duly authorized civil society organizations. It is the role of the State, through its competent authorities, to **ensure the supervision of the safety, well-being and development of any child** placed in alternative care and the regular review of the appropriateness of the care arrangement provided.

6. All decisions, initiatives and approaches falling within the scope of the present Guidelines should be made on a case-by-case basis, with a view notably to ensuring **the child's safety and security**, and must be grounded in **the best interests and rights** of the child concerned, in conformity with the principle of non-discrimination and taking due account of the gender perspective. They should respect fully the **child's right to be consulted and to have his/her views duly taken into account in accordance with his/her evolving capacities**, and on the basis of his/her access to all necessary information. Every effort should be made to enable such consultation and information provision to be carried out in the child's preferred language.

6.bis In applying the present Guidelines, **determination of the best interests of the child** shall be designed to identify courses of action for children deprived of parental care, or at risk of being so, that are best suited to satisfying their needs and rights, **taking into account the full and personal development of their rights in their family**, social and cultural environment and their status as subjects of rights, both at the time of the determination and in the longer term. The determination process should take account of, inter alia, the right of the child to be heard and to have his/her views taken into account in accordance with his/her age and maturity.

7. States should develop and implement comprehensive child welfare and protection policies within the framework of their overall social and human development policy, with attention to the improvement of existing alternative care provision, reflecting the principles contained in the present Guidelines.

8. As part of efforts to prevent separation of children from their parents, States should seek to ensure appropriate and **culturally sensitive** measures:

(a) To support family care-giving environments whose capacities are limited by factors such as [physical, **emotional and mental**, JW] disabilities; drug and alcohol misuse; discrimination against families with indigenous or minority backgrounds; and those living in armed conflict regions or under foreign occupation;
(b) To provide appropriate care and protection for vulnerable children, such as **child victims of abuse and exploitation**; abandoned children; children living on the street; children born out of wedlock; unaccompanied and separated children; internally displaced and refugee children; children of migrant workers; children of asylum-seekers; or children living with or affected by HIV/AIDS and other serious illnesses.

9. Special efforts should be made to tackle discrimination on the basis of any status of the child or parents, including poverty, ethnicity, religion, sex, **[emotional,] mental and physical disability**, HIV/AIDS status or other serious **illnesses, whether physical or mental**, birth out of wedlock, and socio-economic stigma, and all other statuses and circumstances that can give rise to relinquishment, abandonment and/or removal of a child.

B. Alternative care

10. All decisions concerning alternative care should take full account of the desirability, in principle, of maintaining the child as close as possible to his/her habitual place of residence, in order to facilitate contact and potential reintegration with his/her family and to minimize disruption of his/her educational, cultural and social life.

11. Decisions regarding children in alternative care, including those in informal care, should have due regard for the importance of ensuring children a stable home and of meeting their basic need for **safe and continuous attachment to their caregivers**, with **permanency generally being a key goal**.

12. Children must be treated with dignity and respect at all times and must benefit from effective protection from abuse, neglect and all forms of exploitation, whether on the part of care providers, peers or third parties, in whatever care setting they may find themselves.

13. Removal of a child from the care of the family should be seen as a measure of last resort and should be, whenever possible, temporary and for the shortest possible duration. Removal decisions should be regularly reviewed and the child's return to parental care, once the original causes of removal have been resolved or have disappeared, should be in the child's best interests, in keeping with the assessment foreseen in paragraph 48 below.

14. **Financial and material poverty**, or conditions directly and uniquely imputable to such poverty, should never be the only justification for the removal of a child from parental care, for receiving a child into alternative care, or for

preventing his/her reintegration, but should be seen as a signal for the need to **provide appropriate support to the family.**

15. Attention must be paid to promoting and safeguarding all other rights of special pertinence to the situation of children without parental care, including, but not limited to, access to education, health and other basic services, the right to identity, freedom of religion or belief, language and protection of property and inheritance rights.

16. Siblings with existing bonds should in principle not be separated by placements in alternative care unless there is a clear risk of abuse or other justification in the best interests of the child. In any case, every effort should be made to enable siblings to maintain contact with each other, unless this is against their wishes or interests.

17. Recognizing that, in most countries, the majority of children without parental care are looked after informally by relatives or others, States should seek to devise appropriate means, consistent with the present Guidelines, to ensure their welfare and protection while in such informal care arrangements, with due respect for cultural, economic, gender and religious differences and practices that do not conflict with the rights and best interests of the child.

18. No child should be without the support and protection of a legal guardian or other recognized responsible adult or competent public body at any time.

19. The provision of alternative care should never be undertaken with a prime purpose of furthering the political, religious or economic goals of the providers.

20. Use of residential care should be limited to cases where such a setting is specifically appropriate, necessary and constructive for the individual child concerned and in his/her best interests.

21. **In accordance with the predominant opinion of experts, alternative care for young children, especially those under the age of 3 years, should be provided in family-based settings.** Exceptions to this principle may be warranted in order to prevent the separation of siblings and in cases where the placement is of an emergency nature or is for a predetermined and very limited duration, with planned family reintegration or other appropriate long-term care solution as its outcome.

22. While recognizing that residential care facilities and family-based care complement each other in meeting the needs of children, where large residential care facilities (institutions) remain, alternatives should be developed in the context of an overall deinstitutionalization strategy, with precise goals and objectives, which will allow for their progressive elimination. To this end, States should establish care standards to ensure the quality and conditions that are conducive to the child's development, such as individualized and small-group care, and should evaluate existing facilities against these standards. Decisions regarding the establishment of, or permission to establish, new residential care

facilities, whether public or private, should take full account of this deinstitutionalization objective and strategy.

C. Measures to promote application

23. States should, to the maximum extent of their available resources and, where appropriate, in the framework of development cooperation, allocate human and financial resources to ensure the optimal and progressive implementation of the present Guidelines throughout their respective territories in a timely manner. States should facilitate active cooperation among all relevant authorities and the **mainstreaming of child and family welfare issues within all ministries** directly or indirectly concerned.

24. States are responsible for **determining any need for, and requesting, international cooperation** in implementing the present Guidelines. Such requests should be given due consideration and should receive a favourable response wherever possible and appropriate. The enhanced implementation of the present Guidelines should figure in development cooperation programmes. When providing assistance to a State, foreign entities should abstain from any initiative inconsistent with the Guidelines.

25. Nothing in the present Guidelines should be interpreted as encouraging or condoning lower standards than those that may exist in given States, including in their legislation. Similarly, competent authorities, professional organizations and others are encouraged to develop national or professionally-specific guidelines that build upon the letter and spirit of the present Guidelines.

III. SCOPE OF THE GUIDELINES

26. The present Guidelines apply to the appropriate use and conditions of alternative formal care for all persons under the age of 18 years, unless under the law applicable to the child majority is attained earlier. Only where indicated do the Guidelines also apply to informal care settings, having due regard for both the important role played by the extended family and community and the obligations of States for all children not in the care of their parents or legal and customary caregivers, as set out in the Convention on the Rights of the Child.

27. Principles in the present Guidelines are also applicable, as appropriate, to young persons already in alternative care and who need continuing care or support for a **transitional period after reaching the age of majority** under applicable law.

28. For the purposes of the present Guidelines, and subject notably to the exceptions listed in paragraph 29 below, the following definitions shall apply:

(a) *Children without parental care:* all children not in the overnight care of at least one of their parents, for whatever reason and under whatever circumstances.

Children without parental care who are outside their country of habitual residence or victims of emergency situations may be designated as:

(i) *"Unaccompanied"* if they are not cared for by another relative or an adult who by law or custom is responsible for doing so; or
(ii) *"Separated"* if they are separated from a previous legal or customary primary caregiver, but who may nevertheless be accompanied by another relative.

(b) Alternative care may take the form of:
(i) *Informal care:* any private arrangement provided in a family environment, whereby the child is looked after on an ongoing or indefinite basis by relatives or friends *(informal kinship care)* or by others in their individual capacity, at the initiative of the child, his/her parents or other person without this arrangement having been ordered by an administrative or judicial authority or a duly accredited body;
(ii) *Formal care:* all care provided in a family environment which has been ordered by a competent administrative body or judicial authority, and all care provided in a residential environment, including in private facilities, whether or not as a result of administrative or judicial measures.

(c) With respect to the environment where it is provided, alternative care may be:
(i) *Kinship care:* family-based care within the child's extended family or with close friends of the family known to the child, whether formal or informal in nature;
(ii) *Foster care:* situations where children are placed by a competent authority for the purpose of alternative care in the domestic environment of a family other than the children's own family, that has been selected, qualified, approved and supervised for providing such care;
(iii) *Other forms of family-based or family-like care placements*;
(iv) *Residential care:* care provided in any non-family-based group setting, such as places of safety for emergency care, transit centres in emergency situations, and all other short and long-term residential care facilities including group homes;
(v) *Supervised independent living arrangements* for children.

(d) With respect to those responsible for alternative care:
(i) *Agencies* are the public or private bodies and services that organize alternative care for children;
(ii) *Facilities* are the individual public or private establishments that provide residential care for children.

29. The scope of alternative care as foreseen in the present Guidelines does not extend, however, to:

(a) Persons under the age of 18 years who are deprived of their liberty by decision of a judicial or administrative authority as a result of being alleged as, accused of or recognized as having infringed the law, and whose situation is covered by the United Nations Standard Minimum Rules for the Administration of Juvenile Justice and the United Nations Rules for the Protection of Juveniles Deprived of their Liberty;
(b) Care by adoptive parents from the moment the child concerned is effectively placed in their custody pursuant to a final adoption order, as of which moment, for the purposes of the present Guidelines, the child is considered to be in parental care. The Guidelines are, however, applicable to pre-adoption or probationary placement of a child with the prospective adoptive parents, as far as they are compatible with requirements governing such placements as stipulated in other relevant international instruments;
(c) Informal arrangements whereby a child voluntarily stays with relatives or friends for recreational purposes and reasons not connected with the parents' general inability or unwillingness to provide adequate care.

30. Competent authorities and others concerned are also encouraged to make use of the present Guidelines, as applicable, at boarding schools, hospitals, centres for children with mental and physical disabilities or other special needs, camps, the workplace and other places which may be responsible for the care of children.

IV. PREVENTING THE NEED FOR ALTERNATIVE CARE

A. Promoting parental care

31. States should pursue policies that **ensure support for families in meeting their responsibilities towards the child and promote the right of the child to have a relationship with both parents**. These policies should address the root causes of child abandonment, relinquishment and separation of the child from his/her family by ensuring, inter alia, the right to birth registration, access to adequate housing and to basic health, education and social welfare services, as well as by promoting measures to combat poverty, discrimination, marginalization, stigmatization, violence, **child maltreatment** and sexual abuse, and substance abuse.

32. States should develop and implement consistent and mutually reinforcing family-oriented policies designed to **promote and strengthen parents' ability to care for their children**.

33. States should implement effective measures to prevent child abandonment, relinquishment and separation of the child from his/her family. Social policies and programmes should, inter alia, **empower families with attitudes, skills, capacities and tools** to enable them to provide adequately for the protection, care and development of their children. The complementary capacities of the State and civil society, including non-governmental and community-based organizations, religious leaders and the media should be engaged to this end. These social protection measures should include:

(a) Family strengthening services, such as **parenting courses and sessions**, the promotion of positive parent-child relationships, **conflict resolution skills**, opportunities for employment, income-generation and, where required, social assistance;
(b) Supportive social services, such as **day care, mediation and conciliation services, substance abuse treatment, financial assistance**, and services for parents and children with disabilities. Such services, preferably of an integrated and non-intrusive nature, should be directly accessible at community level and should **actively involve the participation of families as partners**, combining their resources with those of the community and the carer;
(c) Youth policies aiming at **empowering youth** to face positively the challenges of everyday life, including when they decide to leave the parental home, and **preparing future parents** to make informed decisions regarding their sexual and reproductive health and to fulfil their responsibilities in this respect.

34. Various complementary methods and techniques should be used for family support, varying throughout the process of support, such as **home visits, group meetings with other families, case conferences** and securing commitments by the family concerned. They should be directed towards both **facilitating intrafamilial relationships** and **promoting the family's integration within its community**.

35. Special attention should be paid, in accordance with local laws, to the provision and promotion of support and care services for **single and adolescent parents and their children**, whether or not born out of wedlock. States should ensure that adolescent parents retain all rights inherent to their **status both as parents and as children**, including access to all appropriate services for their own development, allowances to which parents are entitled, and their inheritance rights. Measures should be adopted **to ensure the protection of pregnant adolescents and to guarantee that they do not interrupt their studies**. Efforts should also be made to reduce stigma attached to single and adolescent parenthood.

36. Support and services should be available to siblings who have lost their parents or caregivers and choose to remain together in their household, to the extent that the eldest sibling is both willing and deemed capable of acting as the household head. States should ensure, including through the appointment of a legal guardian, a recognized responsible adult or, where appropriate, a public body legally mandated to act as guardian, as stipulated in paragraph 18 above, that such households benefit from **mandatory protection from all forms of exploitation and abuse, and supervision and support** on the part of the local community and its competent services, such as social workers, with particular concern for the children's health, housing, education and inheritance rights. Special attention should be given to ensuring the head of such a household retains all rights inherent to his/her child status, including access to education and leisure, in addition to his/her rights as a household head.

37. States should ensure opportunities for day care, including all-day schooling, and respite care which would enable parents better to cope with their overall responsibilities towards the family, including additional responsibilities inherent in caring for children with special needs.

B. Preventing family separation

38. Proper criteria based on sound professional principles should be developed and consistently applied for **assessing the child's and family's situation**, including the family's actual and potential capacity to care for the child, in cases where the competent authority or agency has **reasonable grounds to believe that the well-being of the child is at risk**.

39. Decisions regarding removal or reintegration should be based on this assessment and made by **suitably qualified and trained professionals**, on behalf of or authorized by a competent authority, in full consultation with all concerned and bearing in mind the need to plan for the child's future.

40. States are encouraged to adopt measures for the **integral protection and guarantee of rights during pregnancy, birth and the breastfeeding period**, in order to ensure conditions of dignity and equality for the adequate development of the pregnancy and care of the child. Therefore, **support programmes should be provided to future mothers and fathers**, particularly adolescent parents, who have difficulties in exercising their parental responsibilities. Such programmes should aim at **empowering mothers and fathers** to exercise their parental responsibilities in conditions of dignity, and at avoiding their being induced to surrender their child because of their vulnerability.

41. When a child is relinquished or abandoned, States should ensure that this may take place in **conditions of confidentiality and safety for the child**, respecting his/her right to **access information on his/her origins** where appropriate and possible under the law of the State.

42. States should formulate clear policies to address situations where a child has been abandoned anonymously, which indicate whether and how family tracing should be undertaken and reunification or placement within the extended family pursued. Policies should also allow for timely decision-making on the child's eligibility for permanent family placement and for arranging such placements expeditiously.

43. When a public or private agency or facility is approached by a parent or legal guardian wishing to relinquish a child permanently, **the State should ensure that the family receives counselling and social support to encourage and enable them to continue to care for the child. If this fails, a social work or other appropriate professional assessment should be undertaken to determine whether there are other family members who wish to take permanent responsibility for the child, and whether such arrangements would be in the child's best interests. Where such arrangements are not possible or in the child's best interests, efforts should be made to find a permanent family placement within a reasonable period.**

44. When a public or private agency or facility is approached by a parent or caregiver wishing to place a child in care for a short or indefinite period, the State should ensure the availability of counselling and social support to encourage and enable them to continue to care for the child. A child should be admitted to alternative care only when such efforts have been exhausted and acceptable and justified reasons for entry into care exist.

45. **Specific training should be provided to teachers and others working with children, in order to help them to identify situations of abuse, neglect, exploitation or risk of abandonment and to refer such situations to competent bodies.**

46. Any decision to remove a child against the will of his/her parents must be made by competent authorities, in accordance with applicable law and procedures and subject to judicial review, the parents being assured the right of appeal and access to appropriate legal representation.

47. When the child's sole or main carer may be the subject of deprivation of liberty as a result of preventive detention or sentencing decisions, non-custodial remand measures and sentences should be taken in appropriate cases wherever possible, the best interests of the child being given due consideration. States should take into account the best interests of the child when deciding whether to remove children born in prison and children living in prison with a parent. The removal of such children should be treated in the same way as other instances where separation is considered. Best efforts should be made to ensure that children remaining in custody with their parent benefit from adequate care and protection, while guaranteeing their own status as free individuals and access to activities in the community.

C. Promoting family reintegration

48. In order to prepare and support the child and the family for his/her possible return to the family, his/her situation should be assessed by a duly designated individual or team with access to multidisciplinary advice, in consultation with the different actors involved (the child, the family, the alternative caregiver), so as to decide whether the reintegration of the child in the family is possible and in the best interests of the child, which steps this would involve and under whose supervision.

49. The aims of the reintegration and the family's and alternative caregiver's principal tasks in this respect should be set out in writing and agreed on by all concerned.

50. Regular and appropriate contact between the child and his/her family specifically for the purpose of reintegration should be developed, supported and monitored by the competent body.

51. Once decided, reintegration of the child in his/her family should be designed as a gradual and supervised process, accompanied by follow-up and support measures that take account of the child's age, needs and evolving capacities, as well as the cause of the separation.

V. FRAMEWORK OF CARE PROVISION

52. In order to meet the specific **psycho-emotional, social and other needs** of each child without parental care, States should take all necessary measures to ensure that the legislative, policy and financial conditions exist to provide for adequate alternative care options, with priority to family- and community-based solutions.

53. States should ensure the availability of a range of alternative care options, consistent with the general principles of the present Guidelines, for emergency, short-term and long-term care.

54. States should ensure that all entities and individuals engaged in the provision of alternative care for children receive due authorization to do so from a competent authority and be subject to the latter's regular monitoring and review in keeping with the present Guidelines. To this end, these authorities should develop appropriate criteria for assessing the professional and ethical fitness of care providers and for their accreditation, monitoring and supervision.

55. With regard to informal care arrangements for the child, whether within the extended family, with friends or with other parties, States should, where appropriate, encourage such carers to notify the competent authorities accordingly so that they and the child may receive any necessary financial and other support that would promote the child's welfare and protection. Where possible and appropriate, States should encourage and enable informal caregivers, with the consent of the child and parents concerned, to formalize the care

arrangement after a suitable lapse of time, to the extent that the arrangement has proved to be in the child's best interests to date and is expected to continue in the foreseeable future.

VI. DETERMINATION OF THE MOST APPROPRIATE FORM OF CARE

56. Decision-making on alternative care in the best interests of the child should take place through a judicial, administrative or other adequate and recognized procedure, with legal safeguards, including, where appropriate, legal representation on behalf of children in any legal proceedings. It should be based on rigorous assessment, planning and review, through established structures and mechanisms, and carried out on a case-by-case basis, by suitably qualified professionals in a multidisciplinary team, wherever possible. It should involve full consultation at all stages with the child, according to his/her evolving capacities, and with his/her parents or legal guardians. To this end, all concerned should be provided with the necessary information on which to base their opinion. States should make every effort to provide adequate resources and channels for the training and recognition of the professionals responsible for determining the best form of care so as to facilitate compliance with these provisions.

57. Assessment should be carried out expeditiously, thoroughly and carefully. It should take into account the child's immediate safety and well-being, as well as his/her longer term care and development, and should cover the child's personal and developmental characteristics, ethnic, cultural, linguistic and religious background, family and social environment, medical history and any special needs.

58. The resulting initial and review reports should be used as essential tools for planning decisions from the time of their acceptance by the competent authorities onwards, with a view to, inter alia, avoiding undue disruption and contradictory decisions.

59. Frequent changes in care setting are detrimental to the **child's development and ability to form attachments**, and should be avoided. Short-term placements should aim at enabling an appropriate permanent solution to be arranged. Permanency for the child should be secured without undue delay through reintegration in his/her nuclear or extended family or, if this is not possible, in an alternative stable family setting or, where paragraph 20 above applies, in stable and appropriate residential care.

60. Planning for care provision and permanency should be carried out from the earliest possible time, ideally before the child enters care, taking into account the immediate and longer term advantages and disadvantages of each option considered, and should comprise short- and long-term propositions.

61. Planning for care provision and permanency should be based on, notably, **the nature and quality of the child's attachment to his/her family; the family's capacity to safeguard the child's well-being and harmonious development; the child's need or desire to feel part of a family**; the desirability of the child remaining within his/her community and country; his/her cultural, linguistic and religious background; and relationships with siblings, with a view to avoiding their separation.

62. The plan should clearly state, inter alia, the goals of the placement and the measures to achieve them.

63. The child and his/her parents or legal guardians should be fully informed about the alternative care options available, the implications of each option and their rights and obligations in the matter.

64. The preparation, enforcement and evaluation of a protective measure for a child should be carried out, to the greatest extent possible, with the participation of his/her parents or legal guardians and potential foster carers and caregivers, with respect to his/her particular needs, convictions and special wishes. At the request of the child, parents or legal guardians, other important persons in the child's life may also be consulted in any decision-making process, at the discretion of the competent authority.

65. States should ensure that any child who has been placed in alternative care by a properly constituted court, tribunal or administrative or other competent body, as well as his/her parents or others with parental responsibility, are given the opportunity to make representations on the placement decision before a court, are informed of their rights to make such representations and are assisted in doing so.

66. States should ensure the right of any child who has been placed in temporary care to regular and thorough review – preferably at least every three months – of the appropriateness of his/her care and treatment, taking into account notably his/her personal development and any changing needs, developments in his/her family environment, and the adequacy and necessity of the current placement in these lights. The review should be carried out by duly qualified and authorized persons, and fully involve the child and all relevant persons in the child's life.

67. The child should be prepared for all changes of care settings resulting from the planning and review processes.

VII. PROVISION OF ALTERNATIVE CARE

A. Policies

68. It is a responsibility of the State or appropriate level of government to ensure the development and implementation of coordinated policies regarding formal

and informal care for all children who are without parental care. Such policies should be based on sound information and statistical data. They should define a process for determining who has responsibility for a child, taking into account the role of the child's parents or principal caregivers in his/her protection, care and development. Presumptive responsibility, unless shown to be otherwise, is with the child's parents or principal caregivers.

69. All State entities involved in the referral of, and assistance to, children without parental care, in cooperation with civil society, should adopt policies and procedures which favour information-sharing and networking between agencies and individuals in order to ensure effective care, aftercare and protection for these children. The location and/or design of the agency responsible for the oversight of alternative care should be established so as to maximize its accessibility to those who require the services provided.

70. Special attention should be paid to the quality of alternative care provision, both in residential and family-based care, in particular with regard to the professional skills, selection, training and supervision of carers. Their role and functions should be clearly defined and clarified with respect to those of the child's parents or legal guardians.

71. **In each country, the competent authorities should draw up a document setting out the rights of children** in alternative care in keeping with the present Guidelines. Children in alternative care should be enabled to understand fully the rules, regulations and objectives of the care setting and their rights and obligations therein.

72. All alternative care provision should be based on a written statement of the provider's aims and objectives in providing the service and the nature of their responsibilities to the child that reflects the standards set by the Convention on the Rights of the Child, the present Guidelines and applicable law. All providers should be appropriately qualified or approved in accordance with legal requirements to provide alternative care services.

73. A regulatory framework should be established to ensure a standard process for the referral or admission of a child to an alternative care setting.

74. Cultural and religious practices regarding provision of alternative care, including those related to gender perspectives, should be respected and promoted to the extent that they can be shown to be consistent with the children's rights and best interests. The process of considering whether such practices should be promoted should be carried out in a broadly participatory way, involving the cultural and religious leaders concerned, professionals and those caring for children without parental care, parents and other relevant stakeholders, as well as the children themselves.

1. Informal care

75. With a view to ensuring that appropriate conditions of care are met in informal care provided by individuals or families, States should recognize the role played by this type of care and take adequate measures to support its optimal provision on the basis of an **assessment of which particular settings may require special assistance or oversight**.

76. Competent authorities should, where appropriate, encourage informal carers to notify the care arrangement and should seek to ensure their access to all available services and benefits likely to assist them in discharging their duty to care for and protect the child.

77. The State should recognize the *de facto* responsibility of informal carers for the child.

78. States should devise special and appropriate measures designed to protect children in informal care from abuse, neglect, child labour and all other forms of exploitation, with particular attention to informal care provided by non-relatives, by relatives previously unknown to the child or far from the child's habitual place of residence.

2. General conditions applying to all forms of formal alternative care arrangements

79. The transfer of a child into alternative care should be carried out with the utmost sensitivity and in a child-friendly manner, in particular involving specially trained and, in principle, non-uniformed personnel.

80. When a child is placed in alternative care, contact with his/her family, as well as with other persons close to him or her, such as friends, neighbours and previous carers, should be encouraged and facilitated, in keeping with the child's protection and best interests. The child should have access to information on the situation of his/her family members in the absence of contact with them.

81. States should pay special attention to ensuring that children in alternative care because of parental imprisonment or prolonged hospitalization have the opportunity to maintain contact with their parents and receive any necessary counselling and support in that regard.

82. **Carers should ensure that children receive adequate amounts of wholesome and nutritious food** in accordance with local dietary habits and relevant dietary standards, as well as with the child's religious beliefs. Appropriate nutritional supplementation should also be provided when necessary.

83. Carers should promote the health of the children for whom they are responsible and make arrangements to ensure that **medical care, counselling and support** are made available as required.

84. Children should have access to formal, non-formal and vocational education in accordance with their rights, to the maximum extent possible in educational facilities in the local community.

85. Carers should ensure that the right of every child, including children with disabilities, living with or affected by HIV/AIDS or having any other special needs, to develop through **play and leisure** activities is respected and that opportunities for such activities are created within and outside the care setting. Contacts with the children and others in the local community should be encouraged and facilitated.

86. The **specific safety, health, nutritional, developmental and other needs of babies and young children**, including those with special needs, should be catered for in all care settings, including **ensuring their ongoing attachment to a specific carer**.

87. Children should be allowed to satisfy the needs of their religious and spiritual life, including by receiving visits from a qualified representative of their religion, and to **freely decide to participate or not in religious services, religious education or counselling**. The child's own religious background should be respected, and no child should be encouraged or persuaded to change his/her religion or belief during a care placement.

88. All adults responsible for children should respect and promote the right to privacy, including appropriate facilities for hygiene and sanitary needs, respecting gender differences and interaction, and adequate, secure and accessible storage space for personal possessions.

89. Carers should understand the importance of their role in developing positive, safe and nurturing relationships with children, and be able to do so.

90. Accommodation in all alternative care settings should meet the requirements of health and safety.

91. States must ensure through their competent authorities that accommodation provided to children in alternative care, and their supervision in such placements, enable them to be effectively protected against abuse. Particular attention needs to be paid to the age, maturity and degree of vulnerability of each child in determining his/her living arrangements. Measures aimed at protecting children in care should be in conformity with the law and not involve unreasonable constraints on their liberty and conduct in comparison with children of similar age in their community.

92. All alternative care settings should provide adequate protection to children from abduction, trafficking, sale and all other forms of exploitation. Any consequent constraints on their liberty and conduct should be no more than are strictly necessary to ensure their effective protection from such acts.

93. All carers should promote and encourage children and young people to develop and exercise informed choices, taking account of acceptable risks and the child's age, and according to his/her evolving capacities.

94. States, agencies and facilities, schools and other community services should take appropriate measures to ensure that children in alternative care are not stigmatized during or after their placement. This should include efforts to minimize the identification of the child as being looked after in an alternative care setting.

95. All **disciplinary measures and behaviour management** constituting torture, cruel, inhuman or degrading treatment, including closed or solitary confinement or any other forms of physical or psychological violence that are likely to compromise the physical or mental health of the child, must be **strictly prohibited in conformity with international human rights law**. States must take all necessary measures to prevent such practices and ensure that they are **punishable by law**. Restriction of contact with members of the child's family and other persons of special importance to the child should never be used as a sanction.

96. Use of force and restraints of whatever nature should not be authorized unless strictly necessary for safeguarding the child's or others' **physical or psychological integrity**, in conformity with the law and in a reasonable and proportionate manner and with respect for the fundamental rights of the child. Restraint by means of drugs and medication should be based on therapeutic needs and should never be employed without evaluation and prescription by a specialist.

97. Children in care should be offered access to a person of trust in whom they may confide in total confidentiality. This person should be designated by the competent authority with the agreement of the child concerned. The child should be informed that legal or ethical standards may require breaching confidentiality under certain circumstances.

98. Children in care should have access to a known, effective and impartial mechanism whereby they can notify complaints or concerns regarding their treatment or conditions of placement. Such mechanisms should include initial consultation, feedback, implementation and further consultation. **Young people with previous care experience should be involved in this process**, due weight being given to their opinions. This process should be conducted by competent persons trained to work with children and young people.

99. To promote the child's sense of self-identity, a life story book comprising appropriate information, pictures, personal objects and mementoes regarding each step of the child's life should be maintained with the child's participation and made available to the child throughout his/her life.

B. Legal responsibility for the child

100. In situations where the child's parents are absent or are incapable of making day-to-day decisions in the best interests of the child, and the child's placement in alternative care has been ordered or authorized by a competent administrative body or judicial authority, a designated individual or competent entity should be vested with the legal right and responsibility to make such decisions in the place of parents, in full consultation with the child. States should ensure that a mechanism is in place for designating such an individual or entity.

101. Such legal responsibility should be attributed by the competent authorities and be supervised directly by them or through formally accredited entities, including non-governmental organizations. Accountability for the actions of the individual or entity concerned should lie with the designating body.

102. Persons exercising such legal responsibility should be **reputable individuals with relevant knowledge** of children's issues, an ability to work directly with children, and an understanding of any special and cultural needs of the children to be entrusted to them. They should receive **appropriate training and professional support** in this regard. They should be in a position to make independent and impartial decisions that are in the best interests of the children concerned and that promote and safeguard each child's welfare.

103. The role and specific responsibilities of the designated person or entity should include:

(a) Ensuring that the rights of the child are protected and that, in particular, the child has appropriate care, accommodation, health-care provision, developmental opportunities, psychosocial support, education and language support;
(b) Ensuring that the child has access to legal and other representation where necessary, consulting with the child so that the child's views are taken into account by decision-making authorities, and advising and keeping the child informed of his/her rights;
(c) Contributing to the identification of a stable solution in the child's best interests;
(d) Providing a link between the child and various organizations that may provide services to the child;
(e) Assisting the child in family tracing;
(f) Ensuring that, if repatriation or family reunification is carried out, it is done in the best interests of the child;
(g) Helping the child to keep in touch with his/her family, when appropriate.

1. Agencies and facilities responsible for formal care

104. Legislation should stipulate that all agencies and facilities must be registered and authorized to operate by social welfare services or another competent authority, and that failure to comply with such legislation constitutes an offence punishable by law. Authorization should be granted and regularly reviewed by the competent authorities on the basis of standard criteria covering, at a minimum, the agency's or facility's objectives, functioning, staff recruitment and qualifications, conditions of care and financial resources and management.

105. **All agencies and facilities should have written policy and practice statements consistent with the present Guidelines**, setting out clearly their aims, policies, methods and the standards applied for the recruitment, monitoring, supervision and evaluation of qualified and suitable carers to ensure that those aims are met.

106. All agencies and facilities should develop a staff code of conduct, consistent with the present Guidelines, that defines the role of each professional and of the carers in particular and includes clear reporting procedures on allegations of misconduct by any team member.

107. The forms of financing care provision should never be such as to encourage a child's unnecessary placement or prolonged stay in care arrangements organized or provided by an agency or facility.

108. Comprehensive and up-to-date records should be maintained regarding the administration of alternative care services, including detailed files on all children in their care, staff employed and financial transactions.

109. The records on children in care should be complete, up to date, confidential and secure, and include information on their admission and departure and the form, content and details of the care placement of each child, together with any appropriate identity documents and other personal information. Information on the child's family should be included in the child's file as well as in the reports based on regular evaluations. This record should follow the child throughout the alternative care period and be consulted by duly authorized professionals responsible for his/her current care.

110. The above-mentioned records could be made available to the child, as well as to the parents or guardians, within the limits of the child's right to privacy and confidentiality, as appropriate. Appropriate counselling should be provided before, during and after consultation of the record.

111. All alternative care services should have a clear policy on maintaining the confidentiality of information pertaining to each child, which all carers are aware of and adhere to.

112. As a matter of good practice, all agencies and facilities should systematically ensure that, prior to employment, carers and other staff in direct

contact with children undergo an appropriate and comprehensive **assessment of their suitability to work with children.**

113. Conditions of work, including remuneration, for carers employed by agencies and facilities should be such as to **maximize motivation, job satisfaction and continuity**, and hence their disposition to fulfil their role in the most appropriate and effective manner.

114. Training should be provided to all carers on the rights of children without parental care and on the specific vulnerability of children, in particularly difficult situations, such as emergency placements or placements outside their area of habitual residence. Cultural, social, gender and religious sensitization should also be assured. States should also provide adequate resources and channels for the recognition of these professionals in order to favour the implementation of these provisions.

115. **Training in dealing appropriately with challenging behaviour, including conflict resolution techniques and means to prevent acts of harm or self-harm, should be provided to all care staff employed by agencies and facilities.**

116. Agencies and facilities should ensure that, wherever appropriate, carers are prepared to respond to children with special needs, notably those living with HIV/AIDS or other chronic physical or mental illnesses, and children with physical or mental disabilities.

2. Foster care

117. The competent authority or agency should devise a system, and should train concerned staff accordingly, to assess and match the needs of the child with the abilities and resources of potential foster carers and to prepare all concerned for the placement.

118. A pool of accredited foster carers should be identified in each locality, who can provide children with care and protection while maintaining ties to family, community and cultural group.

119. Special preparation, support and counselling services for foster carers should be developed and made available to carers at regular intervals, before, during and after the placement.

120. Carers should have, within fostering agencies and other systems involved with children without parental care, the opportunity to make their voice heard and to influence policy.

121. Encouragement should be given to the establishment of associations of foster carers that can provide important mutual support and contribute to practice and policy development.

C. Residential care

122. Facilities providing residential care should be small and organized around the rights and needs of the child, in a setting as close as possible to a family or small group situation. Their objective should generally be to provide temporary care and to contribute actively to the child's family reintegration or, if this is not possible, to secure his/her stable care in an **alternative family setting, including through adoption** or *kafala* of Islamic law, where appropriate.

123. Measures should be taken so that, where necessary and appropriate, a child solely in need of protection and alternative care may be accommodated **separately from children who are subject to the criminal justice system**.

124. The competent national or local authority should establish **rigorous screening procedures** to ensure that only appropriate admissions to such facilities are made.

125. States should ensure that there are sufficient carers in residential care settings to allow individualized attention and to give the child, where appropriate, the opportunity to bond with a specific carer. Carers should also be deployed within the care setting in such a way as to implement effectively its aims and objectives and ensure child protection.

126. Laws, policies and regulations should prohibit the recruitment and solicitation of children for placement in residential care by agencies, facilities or individuals.

D. Inspection and monitoring

127. Agencies, facilities and professionals involved in care provision should be accountable to a specific public authority, which should ensure, inter alia, frequent **inspections comprising both scheduled and unannounced visits**, involving discussion with and observation of the staff and the children.

128. To the extent possible and appropriate, inspection functions should include a component of training and capacity-building for care providers.

129. States should be encouraged to ensure that an independent monitoring mechanism is in place, with due consideration for the Principles relating to the Status of National Institutions for the Promotion and Protection of Human Rights (Paris Principles). The monitoring mechanism should be easily accessible to children, parents and those responsible for children without parental care. The functions of the monitoring mechanism should include:

(a) Consulting in conditions of privacy with children in all forms of alternative care, visiting the care settings in which they live and undertaking investigations into any alleged situation of violation of children's rights in those settings, on complaint or on its own initiative;

(b) Recommending relevant policies to appropriate authorities with the aim of improving the treatment of children deprived of parental care and ensuring that it is in keeping with the **preponderance of research findings on child protection, health, development and care**;
(c) Submitting proposals and observations concerning draft legislation;
(d) Contributing independently to the reporting process under the Convention on the Rights of the Child, including to periodic State party reports to the **Committee on the Rights of the Child** with regard to the implementation of the present Guidelines.

E. Support for aftercare

130. Agencies and facilities should have a clear policy and carry out agreed procedures relating to the planned and unplanned conclusion of their work with children to ensure appropriate aftercare and/or follow-up. Throughout the period of care, they should systematically aim at preparing the child to assume self-reliance and to integrate fully in the community, notably through the acquisition of social and life skills, which are fostered by participation in the life of the local community.

131. The process of transition from care to aftercare should take into consideration the child's gender, age, maturity and particular circumstances and include counselling and support, notably to avoid exploitation. Children leaving care should be encouraged to take part in the planning of aftercare life. Children with special needs, such as disabilities, should benefit from an appropriate support system, ensuring, inter alia, avoidance of unnecessary institutionalization. Both the public and private sectors should be encouraged, including through incentives, to employ children from different care services, particularly children with special needs.

132. Special efforts should be made to allocate to each child, whenever possible, a specialized person who can facilitate his/her independence when leaving care.

133. Aftercare should be prepared as early as possible in the placement and, in any case, well before the child leaves the care setting.

134. Ongoing educational and vocational training opportunities should be imparted as part of life skill education to young people leaving care in order to help them to become financially independent and generate their own income.

135. Access to social, legal and health services, together with appropriate financial support, should also be provided to young people leaving care and during aftercare.

VIII. CARE PROVISION FOR CHILDREN OUTSIDE THEIR COUNTRY OF HABITUAL RESIDENCE

A. Placement of a child for care abroad

136. The present Guidelines should apply to all public and private entities and all persons involved in arrangements for a child to be sent for care to a country other than his/her country of habitual residence, whether for medical treatment, temporary hosting, respite care or any other reason.

137. States concerned should ensure that a designated body has responsibility for determining specific standards to be met regarding, in particular, the criteria for selecting carers in the host country and the quality of care and follow-up, as well as for supervising and monitoring the operation of such schemes.

138. To ensure appropriate international cooperation and child protection in such situations, States are encouraged to ratify or accede to the Hague Convention of 19 October 1996 on Jurisdiction, Applicable Law, Recognition, Enforcement and Cooperation in Respect of Parental Responsibility and Measures for the Protection of Children.

B. Provision of care for a child already abroad

139. The present Guidelines, as well as other relevant international provisions, should apply to all public and private entities and all persons involved in arrangements for a child needing care while in a country other than his/her country of habitual residence, for whatever reason.

140. Unaccompanied or separated children already abroad should in principle enjoy the same level of protection and care as national children in the country concerned.

141. In determining appropriate care provision, the diversity and disparity of unaccompanied or separated children (such as ethnic and migratory background or cultural and religious diversity) should be taken into consideration on a case-by-case basis.

142. Unaccompanied or separated children, including those who arrive irregularly in a country, should not be, in principle, deprived of their liberty solely for having breached any law governing access to and stay within the territory.

143. Child victims of trafficking should neither be detained in police custody nor subjected to penalties for their involvement under compulsion in unlawful activities.

144. As soon as an unaccompanied child is identified, States are strongly encouraged to appoint a guardian or, where necessary, representation by an organization responsible for his/her care and well-being to accompany the child throughout the status determination and decision-making process.

145. As soon as an unaccompanied or separated child is taken into care, all reasonable efforts should be made to trace his/her family and re-establish family ties, when this is in the best interests of the child and would not endanger those involved.

146. In order to assist in planning the future of an unaccompanied or separated child in a manner that best protects his/her rights, relevant State and social service authorities should make all reasonable efforts to procure documentation and information in order to conduct an assessment of the child's risk and social and family conditions in his/her country of habitual residence.

147. Unaccompanied or separated children must not be returned to their country of habitual residence:

(a) If, following the risk and security assessment, there are reasons to believe that the child's safety and security are in danger;
(b) Unless, prior to the return, a suitable caregiver, such as a parent, other relative, other adult caretaker, a Government agency or an authorized agency or facility in the country of origin, has agreed and is able to take responsibility for the child and provide him/her with appropriate care and protection;
(c) If, for other reasons, it is not in their best interests, according to the assessment of the competent authorities.

148. With the above aims in mind, cooperation among States, regions, local authorities and civil society associations should be promoted, strengthened and enhanced.

149. The effective involvement of consular services or, failing that, legal representatives of the country of origin should be foreseen, when this is in the best interests of the child and would not endanger the child or his/her family.

150. Those responsible for the welfare of an unaccompanied or separated child should facilitate regular communication between the child and his/her family, except where this is against the child's wishes or is demonstrably not in his/her best interests.

151. Placement with a view to adoption or *kafala* of Islamic law should not be considered a suitable initial option for an unaccompanied or separated child. States are encouraged to consider this option only after efforts to determine the location of his/her parents, extended family or habitual carers have been exhausted.

IX. CARE IN EMERGENCY SITUATIONS

A. Application of the Guidelines

152. The present Guidelines should continue to apply in situations of emergency arising from natural and man-made disasters, including international and non-

international armed conflicts, as well as foreign occupation. Individuals and organizations wishing to work on behalf of children without parental care in emergency situations are strongly encouraged to operate in accordance with the Guidelines.

153. In such circumstances, the State or *de facto* authorities in the region concerned, the international community and all local, national, foreign and international agencies providing or intending to provide child-focused services should pay special attention:

(a) To ensure that all entities and persons involved in responding to unaccompanied or separated children are sufficiently experienced, trained, resourceful and equipped to do so in an appropriate manner;
(b) To develop, as necessary, temporary and long-term family-based care;
(c) To use residential care only as a temporary measure until family-based care can be developed;
(d) To prohibit the establishment of new residential facilities structured to provide simultaneous care to large groups of children on a permanent or long-term basis;
(e) To prevent the cross-border displacement of children, except under the circumstances described in paragraph 159 below;
(f) To make cooperation with family tracing and reintegration efforts mandatory.

B. Preventing separation

154. Organizations and authorities should make every effort to prevent the separation of children from their parents or primary caregivers, unless the best interests of the child so require, and ensure that their actions do not inadvertently encourage family separation by providing services and benefits to children alone rather than to families.

155. Separations initiated by the child's parents or other primary caregivers should be prevented by:

(a) Ensuring that all households have access to basic food and medical supplies and other services, including education;
(b) Limiting the development of residential care options and restricting their use to those situations where it is absolutely necessary.

C. Care arrangements

156. Communities should be supported to play an active role in monitoring and responding to care and protection issues facing children in their local context.

157. Care within a child's own community, including fostering, should be encouraged, as it provides **continuity in socialization and development.**

158. As unaccompanied or separated children may be at heightened risk of abuse and exploitation, **monitoring and specific support to carers** should be foreseen to ensure their protection.

159. Children in emergency situations should not be moved to a country other than that of their habitual residence for alternative care except temporarily for compelling health, medical or safety reasons. In that case, this should be as close as possible to their home, they should be accompanied by a parent or caregiver known to the child, and a clear return plan should be established.

160. Should family reintegration prove impossible within an appropriate period or be deemed contrary to the child's best interests, stable and definitive solutions, such as *kafala* of Islamic law or adoption, should be envisaged; failing this, other long-term options should be considered, such as foster care or appropriate residential care, including group homes and other supervised living arrangements.

D. Tracing and family reintegration

161. Identifying, registering and documenting unaccompanied or separated children are priorities in any emergency and should be carried out as quickly as possible.

162. Registration activities should be conducted by or under the direct supervision of State authorities and explicitly mandated entities with responsibility for and experience in this task.

163. The confidential nature of the information collected should be respected and systems put in place for safe forwarding and storage of information. Information should only be shared among duly mandated agencies for the purpose of tracing, family reintegration and care.

164. All those engaged in tracing family members or primary legal or customary caregivers should operate within a coordinated system, using standardized forms and mutually compatible procedures, wherever possible. They should ensure that the child and others concerned would not be endangered by their actions.

165. The validity of relationships and the confirmation of the willingness of the child and family members to be reunited must be verified for every child. No action should be taken that may hinder eventual family reintegration, such as adoption, change of name, or movement to places far from the family's likely location, until all tracing efforts have been exhausted.

166. Appropriate records of any placement of a child should be made and kept in a safe and secure manner so that reunification can be facilitated in the future.

APPENDIX: CONVENTION ON THE RIGHTS OF THE CHILD

Adopted and opened for signature, ratification and accession by General Assembly resolution 44/25 of 20 November 1989, entry into force 2 September 1990; 193 States Parties (The Netherlands as of 8 March 1995), 2 States non-Parties (2009): Somalia and USA [190 States and 3 'semi'-States parties]

PREAMBLE

The States Parties to the present Convention,

[1.] Considering that, in accordance with the principles proclaimed in the Charter of the United Nations, recognition of the inherent dignity and of the equal and inalienable rights of all members of the human family is the foundation of freedom, justice and peace in the world,

[2.] Bearing in mind that the peoples of the United Nations have, in the Charter, reaffirmed their faith in fundamental human rights and in the dignity and worth of the human person, and have determined to promote social progress and better standards of life in larger freedom,

[3.] Recognising that the United Nations has, in the Universal Declaration of Human Rights and in the International Covenants on Human Rights, proclaimed and agreed that everyone is entitled to all the rights and freedoms set forth therein, without distinction of any kind, such as race, colour, sex, language, religion, political or other opinion, national or social origin, property, birth or other status,

[4.] Recalling that, in the Universal Declaration of Human Rights, the United Nations has proclaimed that childhood is entitled to special care and assistance,

[5.] Convinced that the family, as the fundamental group of society and the natural environment for the growth and well-being of all its members and particularly children, should be afforded the necessary protection and assistance so that it can fully assume its responsibilities within the community,

[6.] Recognising that the child, for the full and harmonious development of his or her personality, should grow up in a family environment, in an atmosphere of happiness, love and understanding,

[7.] Considering that the child should be fully prepared to live an individual life in society, and brought up in the spirit of the ideals proclaimed in the Charter of the United Nations, and in particular in the spirit of peace, dignity, tolerance, freedom, equality and solidarity,

[8.] Bearing in mind that the need to extend particular care to the child has been stated in the Geneva Declaration of the Rights of the Child of 1924 and in the Declaration of the Rights of the Child adopted by the General Assembly on 20 November 1959 and recognised in the Universal Declaration of Human Rights, in the International Covenant on Civil and Political Rights (in particular in Articles 23 and 24), in the International Covenant on Economic, Social and Cultural Rights (in particular in Article 10) and in the statutes and relevant instruments of specialised agencies and international organisations concerned with the welfare of children,

[9.] Bearing in mind that, as indicated in the Declaration of the Rights of the Child, 'the child, by reason of his physical and mental immaturity, needs special safeguards and care, including appropriate legal protection, before as well as after birth,'

[10.] Recalling the provisions of the Declaration on Social and Legal Principles relating to the Protection and Welfare of Children, with Special Reference to Foster Placement and Adoption Nationally and Internationally; the United Nations Standard Minimum Rules for the Administration of Juvenile Justice (The Beijing Rules); and the Declaration on the Protection of Women and Children in Emergency and Armed Conflict,

[11.] Recognising that, in all countries in the world, there are children living in exceptionally difficult conditions, and that such children need special consideration,

[12.] Taking due account of the importance of the traditions and cultural values of each people for the protection and harmonious development of the child,

[13.] Recognising the importance of international co-operation for improving the living conditions of children in every country, in particular in the developing countries,

Have agreed as follows:

PART I [MATERIAL PART: RIGHTS / STATE OBLIGATIONS VIS-À-VIS CHILDREN AND/OR PARENTS/CAREGIVERS]

Article 1

For the purposes of the present Convention, a child means every human being below the age of eighteen years unless under the law applicable to the child, majority is attained earlier.

Article 2

1. States Parties shall respect and ensure the rights set forth in the present Convention to each child within their jurisdiction without discrimination of any kind, irrespective of the child's or his or her parent's or legal guardian's race, colour, sex, language, religion, political or other opinion, national, ethnic or social origin, property, disability, birth or other status.

2. States Parties shall take all appropriate measures to ensure that the child is protected against all forms of discrimination or punishment on the basis of the status, activities, expressed opinions, or beliefs of the child's parents, legal guardians, or family members.

Article 3

1. In all actions concerning children, whether undertaken by public or private social welfare institutions, courts of law, administrative authorities or legislative bodies, the best interests of the child shall be a primary consideration.

2. States Parties undertake to ensure the child such protection and care as is necessary for his or her well-being, taking into account the rights and duties of his or her parents, legal guardians, or other individuals legally responsible for him or her, and, to this end, shall take all appropriate legislative and administrative measures.

3. States Parties shall ensure that the institutions, services and facilities responsible for the care or protection of children shall conform with the standards established by competent authorities, particularly in the areas of safety, health, in the number and suitability of their staff, as well as competent supervision.

Article 4

States Parties shall undertake all appropriate legislative, administrative, and other measures for the implementation of the rights recognised in the present Convention. With regard to economic, social and cultural rights, States Parties shall undertake such measures to the maximum extent of their available resources and, where needed, within the framework of international co-operation.

Article 5

States Parties shall respect the responsibilities, rights and duties of parents or, where applicable, the members of the extended family or community as provided for by local custom, legal guardians or other persons legally responsible for the child, to provide, in a manner consistent with the evolving capacities of the child, appropriate direction and guidance in the exercise by the child of the rights recognised in the present Convention.

Article 6

1. States Parties recognise that every child has the inherent right to life.

2. States Parties shall ensure to the maximum extent possible the survival and development of the child.

Article 7

1. The child shall be registered immediately after birth and shall have the right from birth to a name, the right to acquire a nationality and, as far as possible, the right to know and be cared for by his or her parents.

2. States Parties shall ensure the implementation of these rights in accordance with their national law and their obligations under the relevant international instruments in this field, in particular where the child would otherwise be stateless.

Article 8

1. States Parties undertake to respect the right of the child to preserve his or her identity, including nationality, name and family relations as recognised by law without unlawful interference.

2. Where a child is illegally deprived of some or all of the elements of his or her identity, States Parties shall provide appropriate assistance and protection, with a view to re-establishing speedily his or her identity.

Article 9

1. States Parties shall ensure that a child shall not be separated from his or her parents against their will, except when competent authorities subject to judicial review determine, in accordance with applicable law and procedures, that such separation is necessary for the best interests of the child. Such determination may be necessary in a particular case such as one involving abuse or neglect of the child by the parents, or one where the parents are living separately and a decision must be made as to the child's place of residence.

2. In any proceedings pursuant to paragraph 1 of the present Article, all interested parties shall be given an opportunity to participate in the proceedings and make their views known.

3. States Parties shall respect the right of the child who is separated from one or both parents to maintain personal relations and direct contact with both parents on a regular basis, except if it is contrary to the child's best interests.

4. Where such separation results from any action initiated by a State Party, such as the detention, imprisonment, exile, deportation or death (including death arising from any cause while the person is in the custody of the State) of one or both parents or of the child, that State Party shall, upon request, provide the parents, the child or, if appropriate, another member of the family with the essential information concerning the whereabouts of the absent member(s) of the family unless the provision of the information would be detrimental to the well-being of the child. States Parties shall further ensure that the submission of such a request shall of itself entail no adverse consequences for the person(s) concerned.

Article 10

1. In accordance with the obligation of States Parties under Article 9, paragraph 1, applications by a child or his or her parents to enter or leave a State Party for the purpose of family reunification shall be dealt with by States Parties in a positive, humane and expeditious manner. States Parties shall further ensure that the submission of such a

request shall entail no adverse consequences for the applicants and for the members of their family.

2. A child whose parents reside in different States shall have the right to maintain on a regular basis, save in exceptional circumstances, personal relations and direct contacts with both parents. Towards that end and in accordance with the obligation of States Parties under Article 9, paragraph 1, States Parties shall respect the right of the child and his or her parents to leave any country, including their own, and to enter their own country. The right to leave any country shall be subject only to such restrictions as are prescribed by law and which are necessary to protect the national security, public order *(ordre public)*, public health or morals or the rights and freedoms of others and are consistent with the other rights recognised in the present Convention.

Article 11

1. States Parties shall take measures to combat the illicit transfer and non-return of children abroad.

2. To this end, States Parties shall promote the conclusion of bilateral or multilateral agreements or accession to existing agreements.

Article 12 [*See* General Comment 12]

1. States Parties shall assure to the child who is capable of forming his or her own views the right to express those views freely in all matters affecting the child, the views of the child being given due weight in accordance with the age and maturity of the child.

2. For this purpose, the child shall in particular be provided the opportunity to be heard in any judicial and administrative proceedings affecting the child, either directly, or through a representative or an appropriate body, in a manner consistent with the procedural rules of national law.

Article 13

1. The child shall have the right to freedom of expression; this right shall include freedom to seek, receive and impart information and ideas of all kinds, regardless of frontiers, either orally, in writing or in print, in the form of art, or through any other media of the child's choice.

2. The exercise of this right may be subject to certain restrictions, but these shall only be such as are provided by law and are necessary:

(a) For respect of the rights or reputations of others; or

(b) For the protection of national security or of public order *(ordre public)*, or of public health or morals.

Article 14

1. States Parties shall respect the right of the child to freedom of thought, conscience and religion.

2. States Parties shall respect the rights and duties of the parents and, when applicable, legal guardians, to provide direction to the child in the exercise of his or her right in a manner consistent with the evolving capacities of the child.

3. Freedom to manifest one's religion or beliefs may be subject only to such limitations as are prescribed by law and are necessary to protect public safety, order, health or morals, or the fundamental rights and freedoms of others.

Article 15

1. States Parties recognise the rights of the child to freedom of association and to freedom of peaceful assembly.

2. No restrictions may be placed on the exercise of these rights other than those imposed in conformity with the law and which are necessary in a democratic society in the interests of national security or public safety, public order *(ordre public)*, the protection of public health or morals or the protection of the rights and freedoms of others.

Article 16

1. No child shall be subjected to arbitrary or unlawful interference with his or her privacy, family, home or correspondence, nor to unlawful attacks on his or her honour and reputation.

2. The child has the right to the protection of the law against such interference or attacks.

Article 17

States Parties recognise the important function performed by the mass media and shall ensure that the child has access to information and material from a diversity of national and international sources, especially those aimed at the promotion of his or her social, spiritual and moral well-being and physical and mental health. To this end, States Parties shall:

(a) Encourage the mass media to disseminate information and material of social and cultural benefit to the child and in accordance with the spirit of Article 29;
(b) Encourage international co-operation in the production, exchange and dissemination of such information and material from a diversity of cultural, national and international sources;
(c) Encourage the production and dissemination of children's books;
(d) Encourage the mass media to have particular regard to the linguistic needs of the child who belongs to a minority group or who is indigenous;
(e) Encourage the development of appropriate guidelines for the protection of the child from information and material injurious to his or her well-being, bearing in mind the provisions of Articles 13 and 18.

Article 18

1. States Parties shall use their best efforts to ensure recognition of the principle that both parents have common responsibilities for the upbringing and development of the child. Parents or, as the case may be, legal guardians, have the primary responsibility for the upbringing and development of the child. The best interests of the child will be their basic concern.

2. For the purpose of guaranteeing and promoting the rights set forth in the present Convention, States Parties shall render appropriate assistance to parents and legal guardians in the performance of their child-rearing responsibilities and shall ensure the development of institutions, facilities and services for the care of children.

3. States Parties shall take all appropriate measures to ensure that children of working parents have the right to benefit from child-care services and facilities for which they are eligible.

Article 19

1. States Parties shall take all appropriate legislative, administrative, social and educational measures to protect the child from all forms of physical or mental violence, injury or abuse, neglect or negligent treatment, maltreatment or exploitation, including sexual abuse, while in the care of parent(s), legal guardian(s) or any other person who has the care of the child.

2. Such protective measures should, as appropriate, include effective procedures for the establishment of social programmes to provide necessary support for the child and for those who have the care of the child, as well as for other forms of prevention and for identification, reporting, referral, investigation, treatment and follow-up of instances of child maltreatment described heretofore, and, as appropriate, for judicial involvement.

Article 20

1. A child temporarily or permanently deprived of his or her family environment, or in whose own best interests cannot be allowed to remain in that environment, shall be entitled to special protection and assistance provided by the State.

2. States Parties shall in accordance with their national laws ensure alternative care for such a child.

3. Such care could include, *inter alia*, foster placement, *kafalah* of Islamic law, adoption or, if necessary, placement in suitable institutions for the care of children. When considering solutions, due regard shall be paid to the desirability of continuity in a child's upbringing and to the child's ethnic, religious, cultural and linguistic background.

Article 21

States Parties which recognise and/or permit the system of adoption shall ensure that the best interests of the child shall be the paramount consideration and they shall:

(a) Ensure that the adoption of a child is authorised only by competent authorities who determine, in accordance with applicable law and procedures and on the basis of all pertinent and reliable information, that the adoption is permissible in view of the child's status concerning parents, relatives and legal guardians and that, if required, the persons concerned have given their informed consent to the adoption on the basis of such counselling as may be necessary;

(b) Recognise that inter-country adoption may be considered as an alternative means of child's care, if the child cannot be placed in a foster or an adoptive family or cannot in any suitable manner be cared for in the child's country of origin;

(c) Ensure that the child concerned by inter-country adoption enjoys safeguards and standards equivalent to those existing in the case of national adoption;
(d) Take all appropriate measures to ensure that, in inter-country adoption, the placement does not result in improper financial gain for those involved in it;
(e) Promote, where appropriate, the objectives of the present Article by concluding bilateral or multilateral arrangements or agreements, and endeavour, within this framework, to ensure that the placement of the child in another country is carried out by competent authorities or organs.

Article 22

1. States Parties shall take appropriate measures to ensure that a child who is seeking refugee status or who is considered a refugee in accordance with applicable international or domestic law and procedures shall, whether unaccompanied or accompanied by his or her parents or by any other person, receive appropriate protection and humanitarian assistance in the enjoyment of applicable rights set forth in the present Convention and in other international human rights or humanitarian instruments to which the said States are Parties.

2. For this purpose, States Parties shall provide, as they consider appropriate, co-operation in any efforts by the United Nations and other competent intergovernmental organisations or non-governmental organisations co-operating with the United Nations to protect and assist such a child and to trace the parents or other members of the family of any refugee child in order to obtain information necessary for reunification with his or her family. In cases where no parents or other members of the family can be found, the child shall be accorded the same protection as any other child permanently or temporarily deprived of his or her family environment for any reason, as set forth in the present Convention.

Article 23

1. States Parties recognise that a mentally or physically disabled child should enjoy a full and decent life, in conditions which ensure dignity, promote self-reliance and facilitate the child's active participation in the community.

2. States Parties recognise the right of the disabled child to special care and shall encourage and ensure the extension, subject to available resources, to the eligible child and those responsible for his or her care, of assistance for which application is made and which is appropriate to the child's condition and to the circumstances of the parents or others caring for the child.

3. Recognising the special needs of a disabled child, assistance extended in accordance with paragraph 2 of the present Article shall be provided free of charge, whenever possible, taking into account the financial resources of the parents or others caring for the child, and shall be designed to ensure that the disabled child has effective access to and receives education, training, health care services, rehabilitation services, preparation for employment and recreation opportunities in a manner conducive to the child's achieving the fullest possible social integration and individual development, including his or her cultural and spiritual development.

4. States Parties shall promote, in the spirit of international co-operation, the exchange of appropriate information in the field of preventive health care and of medical, psychological and functional treatment of disabled children, including dissemination of and access to information concerning methods of rehabilitation, education and vocational services, with the aim of enabling States Parties to improve their capabilities and skills and to widen their experience in these areas. In this regard, particular account shall be taken of the needs of developing countries.

Article 24

1. States Parties recognise the right of the child to the enjoyment of the highest attainable standard of health and to facilities for the treatment of illness and rehabilitation of health. States Parties shall strive to ensure that no child is deprived of his or her right of access to such health care services.

2. States Parties shall pursue full implementation of this right and, in particular, shall take appropriate measures:

(a) To diminish infant and child mortality;
(b) To ensure the provision of necessary medical assistance and health care to all children with emphasis on the development of primary health care;
(c) To combat disease and malnutrition, including within the framework of primary health care, through, *inter alia*, the application of readily available technology and through the provision of adequate nutritious foods and clean drinking-water, taking into consideration the dangers and risks of environmental pollution;
(d) To ensure appropriate pre-natal and post-natal health care for mothers;
(e) To ensure that all segments of society, in particular parents and children, are informed, have access to education and are supported in the use of basic knowledge of child health and nutrition, the advantages of breastfeeding, hygiene and environmental sanitation and the prevention of accidents;
(f) To develop preventive health care, guidance for parents and family planning education and services.

3. States Parties shall take all effective and appropriate measures with a view to abolishing traditional practices prejudicial to the health of children.

4. States Parties undertake to promote and encourage international co-operation with a view to achieving progressively the full realisation of the right recognised in the present Article. In this regard, particular account shall be taken of the needs of developing countries.

Article 25

States Parties recognise the right of a child who has been placed by the competent authorities for the purposes of care, protection or treatment of his or her physical or mental health, to a periodic review of the treatment provided to the child and all other circumstances relevant to his or her placement.

Article 26

1. States Parties shall recognise for every child the right to benefit from social security, including social insurance, and shall take the necessary measures to achieve the full realisation of this right in accordance with their national law.

2. The benefits should, where appropriate, be granted, taking into account the resources and the circumstances of the child and persons having responsibility for the maintenance of the child, as well as any other consideration relevant to an application for benefits made by or on behalf of the child.

Article 27

1. States Parties recognise the right of every child to a standard of living adequate for the child's physical, mental, spiritual, moral and social development.

2. The parent(s) or others responsible for the child have the primary responsibility to secure, within their abilities and financial capacities, the conditions of living necessary for the child's development.

3. States Parties, in accordance with national conditions and within their means, shall take appropriate measures to assist parents and others responsible for the child to implement this right and shall in case of need provide material assistance and support programmes, particularly with regard to nutrition, clothing and housing.

4. States Parties shall take all appropriate measures to secure the recovery of maintenance for the child from the parents or other persons having financial responsibility for the child, both within the State Party and from abroad. In particular, where the person having financial responsibility for the child lives in a State different from that of the child, States Parties shall promote the accession to international agreements or the conclusion of such agreements, as well as the making of other appropriate arrangements.

Article 28

1. States Parties recognise the right of the child to education, and with a view to achieving this right progressively and on the basis of equal opportunity, they shall, in particular:

(a) Make primary education compulsory and available free to all;
(b) Encourage the development of different forms of secondary education, including general and vocational education, make them available and accessible to every child, and take appropriate measures such as the introduction of free education and offering financial assistance in case of need;
(c) Make higher education accessible to all on the basis of capacity by every appropriate means;
(d) Make educational and vocational information and guidance available and accessible to all children;
(e) Take measures to encourage regular attendance at schools and the reduction of drop-out rates.

2. States Parties shall take all appropriate measures to ensure that school discipline is administered in a manner consistent with the child's human dignity and in conformity with the present Convention.

3. States Parties shall promote and encourage international co-operation in matters relating to education, in particular with a view to contributing to the elimination of ignorance and illiteracy throughout the world and facilitating access to scientific and technical knowledge and modern teaching methods. In this regard, particular account shall be taken of the needs of developing countries.

Article 29 [*See* General Comment 1]

1. States Parties agree that the education of the child shall be directed to:

(a) The development of the child's personality, talents and mental and physical abilities to their fullest potential;
(b) The development of respect for human rights and fundamental freedoms, and for the principles enshrined in the Charter of the United Nations;
(c) The development of respect for the child's parents, his or her own cultural identity, language and values, for the national values of the country in which the child is living, the country from which he or she may originate, and for civilisations different from his or her own;
(d) The preparation of the child for responsible life in a free society, in the spirit of understanding, peace, tolerance, equality of sexes, and friendship among all peoples, ethnic, national and religious groups and persons of indigenous origin;
(e) The development of respect for the natural environment.

2. No part of the present Article or Article 28 shall be construed so as to interfere with the liberty of individuals and bodies to establish and direct educational institutions, subject always to the observance of the principles set forth in paragraph 1 of the present Article and to the requirements that the education given in such institutions shall conform to such minimum standards as may be laid down by the State.

Article 30

In those States in which ethnic, religious or linguistic minorities or persons of indigenous origin exist, a child belonging to such a minority or who is indigenous shall not be denied the right, in community with other members of his or her group, to enjoy his or her own culture, to profess and practise his or her own religion, or to use his or her own language.

Article 31

1. States Parties recognise the right of the child to rest and leisure, to engage in play and recreational activities appropriate to the age of the child and to participate freely in cultural life and the arts.

2. States Parties shall respect and promote the right of the child to participate fully in cultural and artistic life and shall encourage the provision of appropriate and equal opportunities for cultural, artistic, recreational and leisure activity.

Article 32

1. States Parties recognise the right of the child to be protected from economic exploitation and from performing any work that is likely to be hazardous or to interfere with the child's education, or to be harmful to the child's health or physical, mental, spiritual, moral or social development.

2. States Parties shall take legislative, administrative, social and educational measures to ensure the implementation of the present Article. To this end, and having regard to the relevant provisions of other international instruments, States Parties shall in particular:

(a) Provide for a minimum age or minimum ages for admission to employment;
(b) Provide for appropriate regulation of the hours and conditions of employment;
(c) Provide for appropriate penalties or other sanctions to ensure the effective enforcement of the present Article.

Article 33

States Parties shall take all appropriate measures, including legislative, administrative, social and educational measures, to protect children from the illicit use of narcotic drugs and psychotropic substances as defined in the relevant international treaties, and to prevent the use of children in the illicit production and trafficking of such substances.

Article 34 [*See* Optional Protocols]

States Parties undertake to protect the child from all forms of sexual exploitation and sexual abuse. For these purposes, States Parties shall in particular take all appropriate national, bilateral and multilateral measures to prevent:

(a) The inducement or coercion of a child to engage in any unlawful sexual activity;
(b) The exploitative use of children in prostitution or other unlawful sexual practices;
(c) The exploitative use of children in pornographic performances and materials.

Article 35

States Parties shall take all appropriate national, bilateral and multilateral measures to prevent the abduction of, the sale of or traffic in children for any purpose or in any form.

Article 36

States Parties shall protect the child against all other forms of exploitation prejudicial to any aspects of the child's welfare.

Article 37

States Parties shall ensure that:

(a) No child shall be subjected to torture or other cruel, inhuman or degrading treatment or punishment. Neither capital punishment nor life imprisonment without possibility of release shall be imposed for offences committed by persons below eighteen years of age;

(b) No child shall be deprived of his or her liberty unlawfully or arbitrarily. The arrest, detention or imprisonment of a child shall be in conformity with the law and shall be used only as a measure of last resort and for the shortest appropriate period of time;

(c) Every child deprived of liberty shall be treated with humanity and respect for the inherent dignity of the human person, and in a manner which takes into account the needs of persons of his or her age. In particular, every child deprived of liberty shall be separated from adults unless it is considered in the child's best interest not to do so and shall have the right to maintain contact with his or her family through correspondence and visits, save in exceptional circumstances;

(d) Every child deprived of his or her liberty shall have the right to prompt access to legal and other appropriate assistance, as well as the right to challenge the legality of the deprivation of his or her liberty before a court or other competent, independent and impartial authority, and to a prompt decision on any such action.

Article 38 [*See* Optional Protocols]

1. States Parties undertake to respect and to ensure respect for rules of international humanitarian law applicable to them in armed conflicts which are relevant to the child.

2. States Parties shall take all feasible measures to ensure that persons who have not attained the age of fifteen years do not take a direct part in hostilities.

3. States Parties shall refrain from recruiting any person who has not attained the age of fifteen years into their armed forces. In recruiting among those persons who have attained the age of fifteen years but who have not attained the age of eighteen years, States Parties shall endeavour to give priority to those who are oldest.

4. In accordance with their obligations under international humanitarian law to protect the civilian population in armed conflicts, States Parties shall take all feasible measures to ensure protection and care of children who are affected by an armed conflict.

Article 39

States Parties shall take all appropriate measures to promote physical and psychological recovery and social reintegration of a child victim of: any form of neglect, exploitation, or abuse; torture or any other form of cruel, inhuman or degrading treatment or punishment; or armed conflicts. Such recovery and reintegration shall take place in an environment which fosters the health, self-respect and dignity of the child.

Article 40

1. States Parties recognise the right of every child alleged as, accused of, or recognised as having infringed the penal law to be treated in a manner consistent with the promotion of the child's sense of dignity and worth, which reinforces the child's respect for the human rights and fundamental freedoms of others and which takes into account the child's age and the desirability of promoting the child's reintegration and the child's assuming a constructive role in society.

2. To this end, and having regard to the relevant provisions of international instruments, States Parties shall, in particular, ensure that:

(a) No child shall be alleged as, be accused of, or recognised as having infringed the penal law by reason of acts or omissions that were not prohibited by national or international law at the time they were committed;
(b) Every child alleged as or accused of having infringed the penal law has at least the following guarantees:
  (i) To be presumed innocent until proven guilty according to law;
  (ii) To be informed promptly and directly of the charges against him or her, and, if appropriate, through his or her parents or legal guardians, and to have legal or other appropriate assistance in the preparation and presentation of his or her defence;
  (iii) To have the matter determined without delay by a competent, independent and impartial authority or judicial body in a fair hearing according to law, in the presence of legal or other appropriate assistance and, unless it is considered not to be in the best interest of the child, in particular, taking into account his or her age or situation, his or her parents or legal guardians;
  (iv) Not to be compelled to give testimony or to confess guilt; to examine or have examined adverse witnesses and to obtain the participation and examination of witnesses on his or her behalf under conditions of equality;
  (v) If considered to have infringed the penal law, to have this decision and any measures imposed in consequence thereof reviewed by a higher competent, independent and impartial authority or judicial body according to law;
  (vi) To have the free assistance of an interpreter if the child cannot understand or speak the language used;
  (vii) To have his or her privacy fully respected at all stages of the proceedings.

3. States Parties shall seek to promote the establishment of laws, procedures, authorities and institutions specifically applicable to children alleged as, accused of, or recognised as having infringed the penal law, and, in particular:

(a) The establishment of a minimum age below which children shall be presumed not to have the capacity to infringe the penal law;
(b) Whenever appropriate and desirable, measures for dealing with such children without resorting to judicial proceedings, providing that human rights and legal safeguards are fully respected.

4. A variety of dispositions, such as care, guidance and supervision orders; counselling; probation; foster care; education and vocational training programmes and other alternatives to institutional care shall be available to ensure that children are dealt with in a manner appropriate to their well-being and proportionate both to their circumstances and the offence.

Article 41
Nothing in the present Convention shall affect any provisions which are more conducive to the realisation of the rights of the child and which may be contained in:

(a) The law of a State party; or
(b) International law in force for that State.

PART II

Article 42
States Parties undertake to make the principles and provisions of the Convention widely known, by appropriate and active means, to adults and children alike.

[FORMAL PART 1: MONITORING BY TREATY BODY]

Article 43
1. For the purpose of examining the progress made by States Parties in achieving the realisation of the obligations undertaken in the present Convention, there shall be established a Committee on the Rights of the Child, which shall carry out the functions hereinafter provided.

2. The Committee shall consist of eighteen experts of high moral standing and recognised competence in the field covered by this Convention. The members of the Committee shall be elected by States Parties from among their nationals and shall serve in their personal capacity, consideration being given to equitable geographical distribution, as well as to the principal legal systems.

3. The members of the Committee shall be elected by secret ballot from a list of persons nominated by States Parties. Each State Party may nominate one person from among its own nationals.

4. The initial election to the Committee shall be held no later than six months after the date of the entry into force of the present Convention and thereafter every second year. At least four months before the date of each election, the Secretary-General of the United Nations shall address a letter to States Parties inviting them to submit their nominations within two months. The Secretary-General shall subsequently prepare a list in alphabetical order of all persons thus nominated, indicating States Parties which have nominated them, and shall submit it to the States Parties to the present Convention.

5. The elections shall be held at meetings of States Parties convened by the Secretary-General at United Nations Headquarters. At those meetings, for which two thirds of States Parties shall constitute a quorum, the persons elected to the Committee shall be those who obtain the largest number of votes and an absolute majority of the votes of the representatives of States Parties present and voting.

6. The members of the Committee shall be elected for a term of four years. They shall be eligible for re-election if renominated. The term of five of the members elected at the first election shall expire at the end of two years; immediately after the first election, the names of these five members shall be chosen by lot by the Chairman of the meeting.

7. If a member of the Committee dies or resigns or declares that for any other cause he or she can no longer perform the duties of the Committee, the State Party which nominated the member shall appoint another expert from among its nationals to serve for the remainder of the term, subject to the approval of the Committee.

8. The Committee shall establish its own rules of procedure.

9. The Committee shall elect its officers for a period of two years.

10. The meetings of the Committee shall normally be held at United Nations Headquarters or at any other convenient place as determined by the Committee. The Committee shall normally meet annually. The duration of the meetings of the Committee shall be determined, and reviewed, if necessary, by a meeting of the States Parties to the present Convention, subject to the approval of the General Assembly.

11. The Secretary-General of the United Nations shall provide the necessary staff and facilities for the effective performance of the functions of the Committee under the present Convention.

12. With the approval of the General Assembly, the members of the Committee established under the present Convention shall receive emoluments from United Nations resources on such terms and conditions as the Assembly may decide.

Article 44

1. States Parties undertake to submit to the Committee, through the Secretary-General of the United Nations, reports on the measures they have adopted which give effect to the rights recognised herein and on the progress made on the enjoyment of those rights:

(a) Within two years of the entry into force of the Convention for the State Party concerned;
(b) Thereafter every five years.

2. Reports made under the present Article shall indicate factors and difficulties, if any, affecting the degree of fulfilment of the obligations under the present Convention. Reports shall also contain sufficient information to provide the Committee with a comprehensive understanding of the implementation of the Convention in the country concerned.

3. A State Party which has submitted a comprehensive initial report to the Committee need not, in its subsequent reports submitted in accordance with paragraph 1(b) of the present Article, repeat basic information previously provided.

4. The Committee may request from States Parties further information relevant to the implementation of the Convention.

5. The Committee shall submit to the General Assembly, through the Economic and Social Council, every two years, reports on its activities.

6. States Parties shall make their reports widely available to the public in their own countries.

Article 45

In order to foster the effective implementation of the Convention and to encourage international co-operation in the field covered by the Convention:

(a) The specialised agencies, the United Nations Children's Fund, and other United Nations organs shall be entitled to be represented at the consideration of the implementation of such provisions of the present Convention as fall within the scope of their mandate. The Committee may invite the specialised agencies, the

United Nations Children's Fund and other competent bodies as it may consider appropriate to provide expert advice on the implementation of the Convention in areas falling within the scope of their respective mandates. The Committee may invite the specialised agencies, the United Nations Children's Fund, and other United Nations organs to submit reports on the implementation of the Convention in areas falling within the scope of their activities;

(b) The Committee shall transmit, as it may consider appropriate, to the specialised agencies, the United Nations Children's Fund and other competent bodies, any reports from States Parties that contain a request, or indicate a need, for technical advice or assistance, along with the Committee's observations and suggestions, if any, on these requests or indications;

(c) The Committee may recommend to the General Assembly to request the Secretary-General to undertake on its behalf studies on specific issues relating to the rights of the child;

(d) The Committee may make suggestions and general recommendations based on information received pursuant to Articles 44 and 45 of the present Convention. Such suggestions and general recommendations shall be transmitted to any State Party concerned and reported to the General Assembly, together with comments, if any, from States Parties.

PART III

[FORMAL PART 2: FORMAL TREATY LAW]

Article 46
The present Convention shall be open for signature by all States.

Article 47
The present Convention is subject to ratification. Instruments of ratification shall be deposited with the Secretary-General of the United Nations.

Article 48
The present Convention shall remain open for accession by any State. The instruments of accession shall be deposited with the Secretary-General of the United Nations.

Article 49
1. The present Convention shall enter into force on the thirtieth day following the date of deposit with the Secretary-General of the United Nations of the twentieth instrument of ratification or accession.

2. For each State ratifying or acceding to the Convention after the deposit of the twentieth instrument of ratification or accession, the Convention shall enter into force on the thirtieth day after the deposit by such State of its instrument of ratification or accession.

Article 50

1. Any State Party may propose an amendment and file it with the Secretary-General of the United Nations. The Secretary-General shall thereupon communicate the proposed amendment to States Parties, with a request that they indicate whether they favour a conference of States Parties for the purpose of considering and voting upon the proposals. In the event that, within four months from the date of such communication, at least one third of the States Parties favour such a conference, the Secretary-General shall convene the conference under the auspices of the United Nations. Any amendment adopted by a majority of States Parties present and voting at the conference shall be submitted to the General Assembly for approval.

2. An amendment adopted in accordance with paragraph 1 of the present Article shall enter into force when it has been approved by the General Assembly of the United Nations and accepted by a two-thirds majority of States Parties.

3. When an amendment enters into force, it shall be binding on those States Parties which have accepted it, other States Parties still being bound by the provisions of the present Convention and any earlier amendments which they have accepted.

Article 51

1. The Secretary-General of the United Nations shall receive and circulate to all States the text of reservations made by States at the time of ratification or accession.

2. A reservation incompatible with the object and purpose of the present Convention shall not be permitted.

3. Reservations may be withdrawn at any time by notification to that effect addressed to the Secretary-General of the United Nations, who shall then inform all States. Such notification shall take effect on the date on which it is received by the Secretary-General.

Article 52

A State Party may denounce the present Convention by written notification to the Secretary-General of the United Nations. Denunciation becomes effective one year after the date of receipt of the notification by the Secretary-General.

Article 53

The Secretary-General of the United Nations is designated as the depositary of the present Convention.

Article 54

The original of the present Convention, of which the Arabic, Chinese, English, French, Russian and Spanish texts are equally authentic, shall be deposited with the Secretary-General of the United Nations.

In witness thereof the undersigned plenipotentiaries, being duly authorised thereto by their respective governments, have signed the present Convention.

MAASTRICHT SERIES IN HUMAN RIGHTS

The *Maastricht Centre for Human Rights* supervises research in the field of human rights conducted at Maastricht University's Faculty of Law. This research is interdisciplinary, with a particular focus on public international law, criminal law and social sciences. The titles in the Series contribute to a better understanding of different aspects of human rights *sensu lato*.

Published titles within the Series:

1. Ineke Boerefijn, Fons Coomans, Jenny Goldschmidt, Rikki Holtmaat and Ria Wolleswinkel (eds.), *Temporary Special Measures. Accelerating de facto Equality of Women under Article 4(1) UN Convention on the Elimination of All Forms of Discrimination against Women* (2003)
   ISBN 90-5095-359-X
2. Fons Coomans and Menno T. Kamminga (eds.), *Extraterritorial Application of Human Rights Treaties* (2004)
   ISBN 90-5095-394-8
3. Koen De Feyter and Felipe Gómez Isa (eds.), *Privatisation and Human Rights in the Age of Globalisation* (2005)
   ISBN 90-5095-422-7
4. Ingrid Westendorp and Ria Wolleswinkel (eds.), *Violence in the domestic sphere* (2005)
   ISBN 90-5095-526-6
5. Fons Coomans (ed.), *Justiciability of Economic and Social Rights* (2006)
   ISBN 978-90-5095-582-9
6. Jan C.M. Willems (ed.), *Developmental and Autonomy Rights of Children: Empowering Children, Caregivers and Communities. 2nd revised edition* (2007)
   ISBN 978-90-5095-726-7
7. Alette Smeulers and Roelof Haveman (eds.), *Supranational Criminology: Towards a Criminology of International Crimes* (2008)
   ISBN 978-90-5095-791-5
8. Hans van Crombrugge, Wouter Vandenhole and Jan C.M. Willems (eds.), *Shared Pedagogical Responsibility* (2008)
   ISBN 978-90-5095-813-4
9. Hildegard Schneider and Peter Van den Bossche (eds.), *Protection of Cultural Diversity from a European and International Perspective* (2008)
   ISBN 978-90-5095-864-6

10. Fons Coomans, Fred Grünfeld and Menno T. Kamminga (eds.), *Methods of Human Rights Research* (2009)
ISBN 978-90-5095-879-0
11. Jan CM Willems (ed.), *Children's Rights and Human Development. A Multidisciplinary Reader* (2010)
ISBN 978-94-000-0032-2

www.ingramcontent.com/pod-product-compliance
Ingram Content Group UK Ltd.
Pitfield, Milton Keynes, MK11 3LW, UK
UKHW051924100926
8556IPUK00022B/1359